5,6	Krasnozems Euchrozems and related soils
9,10	Yellow Earths Grey Earths
11	Solonetzic Soils
20	Terra Rossa
21	Calcareous Coastal Sands
28	Salt Lakes (Salinas)
1	Skeletal Soils

AUSTRALIA
a geography

Koala Books of Canada Ltd.
Australian Book Sales
14327 - 95 A Ave.
Edmonton, Alta. T5N 0B6

AUSTRALIA
a geography

edited by D. N. JEANS

St. Martin's Press   **New York**

All rights reserved. For information, write:
St. Martin's Press, Inc., Fifth Avenue, New York, N.Y. 10010
Printed in Australia
Library of Congress Catalog Card Number 77–85122
ISBN 0–312–06116–1
First published in the United States of America in 1978

CONTENTS

CONTRIBUTORS

R. BUNKER, MA(Birmingham), PhD(Sydney), formerly of the University of Sydney

J. A. CARNAHAN, MSc, PhD(New Zealand), Department of Botany, Australian National University

P. P. COURTENAY, BA, PhD(London), James Cook University of North Queensland

J. L. DAVIES, MA(Wales), PhD(Birmingham), Macquarie University

I. DOUGLAS, BLitt, MA, PhD(Oxon.), University of New England

C. DUNCAN, MA(New Zealand), PhD(Ohio State), University of Waikato

FAY GALE, BA, PhD(Adelaide), University of Adelaide

J. GENTILLI, OMRI, DPolSci(Univ. Econ. Inst. Venice), FRMetSoc, University of Western Australia

R. L. HEATHCOTE, BA(London), MA(Nebraska), PhD(Australian National University), Flinders University of South Australia

J. H. HOLMES, MA, DipEd(Sydney), PhD(New England), University of Queensland

D. N. JEANS, BA, PhD(London), University of Sydney

J. N. JENNINGS, MA, PhD(Cantab.), Australian National University

G. J. R. LINGE, BSc(Econ.) (London), PhD(New Zealand), Australian National University

J. A. MABBUTT, MA(Cantab.), University of New South Wales and formerly of the CSIRO Division of Land Research

ANN MARSHALL, MSc(Melbourne), MA (California), formerly of the University of Adelaide

R. S. MATHIESON, BSc(Econ.) (London), MA(Washington), PhD(London), University of Sydney

D. C. MERCER, MA, DipEd(Cantab.), PhD(Monash), Monash University

C. D. OLLIER, DSc(Bristol), Australian National University

P. J. RIMMER, MA(Manchester), PhD(Canterbury), Australian National University

K. W. ROBINSON, MA(New Zealand), University of Newcastle

P. SCOTT, MSc(Econ.), PhD(London), FASSA, University of Tasmania

C. G. STEPHENS, MSc(Tasmania), DSc(Adelaide), formerly of the CSIRO Division of Soils

R. G. WARD, MA(New Zealand), PhD(London), Australian National University

R. F. WARNER, BA(Birmingham), PhD(New England), University of Sydney

PREFACE

Systematic surveys of the resources and spatial characteristics of countries or continents have sometimes been occasioned by conferences of geographers, but in this case the book originated in a fairly general feeling that a comprehensive geographical overview of Australia was about due. In planning the book it was clear that even a large volume could not be comprehensive, and in fact the original plan is not completely fulfilled. It is however good to know that most serious students of Australian geography will have to hand the *Atlas of Australian Resources* now in process of revision. As they are, these chapters report the situation and state of knowledge in mid-1975.

To participate in a book of this nature is to understand how many minds have contributed to its making. At the outset acknowledgement must be made to the whole geographical profession; its accumulated research efforts have supplied the fundamental sources of the knowledge creatively distilled by our contributors, whose willing co-operation has considerably lightened the burden of editing.

The contributors would wish to acknowledge the help of research assistants, cartographers and typists upon whom they each, personally, rely. Thanks must also go to Mr Malcolm Titt, Director of the Sydney University Press who encouraged the project from its conception, and to Mr David New and Miss Lesley Corey who had much to do with preparing the book for publication. Mr Alan Bartlett acted as chief cartographer to the project, adding final requirements for reproduction to many of the maps and diagrams. I am grateful to the staffs of the Australian National Library and the Australian Information Service who helped in selecting many of the illustrations.

Although as editor I must take final responsibility for the outcome, I should like to acknowledge gratefully the advice I received from Professor J. A. Mabbutt, Dr R. S. Mathieson, Professor K. W. Robinson, Mrs Deirdre Dragovich, Dr G. J. R. Linge, Dr R. F. Warner and Professor T. Langford-Smith.

It would be appreciated if reviewers and other readers would draw attention to any errors and omissions in the text, in care of our publishers, Sydney University Press, so that it will be possible to secure improvements in any subsequent edition.

We hope that those who read this book will find in it an increased understanding of the complex Australian continent, and receive a stimulus to further reading and research in geography.

University of Sydney   D. N. JEANS

INTRODUCTION

D. N. JEANS

The 'Geography' of a country is written in many ways. There have always been men, travellers, observers, naturalists, who have written about the landscape, about man's use of the land, about the physical environment, and these in the past often contributed as much as those who wrote formal 'Geographies'. Australia has been rich in such contributions: there were the explorers, many of them men of high ability in observing country, and there has been a succession of travellers who wrote about the strange land for people at 'home', while historians, notably W. C. Wentworth and J. D. Lang contributed good accounts of the known regions of the continent (Dury, 1968).

But the making of formal 'Geographies', the forerunners of this volume, were significant acts which reveal a number of insights. At one level, the works display the continent as it became known to civilized men who write down their geography. Australia was explored rather quickly, given its harsh terrain and climates. At another level we can learn about changing environment and landscapes, and about the spread of man's works over the country. Once again, occupation was a rapid process, spanning only a century while the occupation of the United States, a comparable area, took about three times as long. At yet another level is revealed the changing nature of geography itself, for men have wanted different things of it at different times; its methods, aims and audiences have changed. The past geographies of Australia have not stood in the mainstream of the conceptual development of the discipline, but there is something to be learned from them at all three levels.

Australia's first appearance in a formal geography was in Pinkerton's *Modern Geography* (1807). This was an attempt to comprehend the great maritime discoveries of the eighteenth century, in which Cook had almost completed the earlier Dutch work on the Australian coasts, and also to place English geography on a new footing derived from French models. Henceforth, wrote Pinkerton, geography was to be occupied 'in the description of the various regions of the globe, chiefly as being divided among various nations and improved by human art and industry'. This was to be a descriptive discipline in its own right, divorced from history to which it had become a mere handmaiden in English practice. In Pinkerton's conventional format for the description of a region, natural environment was relegated to last place. Nature, he wrote, was 'only subservient to the distribution and industry of mankind', and had been so changed by the hand of man that its present state gave only a fallacious view of the pre-settlement landscape. Pinkerton is modern in his insistence on observation in place of tradition as the only reliable source of information.

Little could be said of New Holland in 1807 when only the 'skirts and extremities' were known. Most of the coast was established, except in the south where the discoveries of Flinders and Baudin were still unpublished. Flinders languished a prisoner in Mauritius, but Pinkerton had already reached his major conclusion, that New Holland was a single continent and not divided by a strait into western and eastern parts. *Modern Geography*, for its account of the land, drew mainly on David Collins's book on coastal New South Wales then last published in 1804, and following the dictum that the human aspect formed the 'most interesting department of the Science' the greater part of the Australian section was devoted to the aboriginals. But there was hope for the European future of the colony despite the convict nature of the settlement; coal had been found, wheat and maize were seen to flourish, the climate was salubrious. Wool was not mentioned, being still only a hope in a few enterprising colonial minds.

Exploration by Hume and Hovell, Sturt and Cunningham had far penetrated the southeastern interior when S. H. Collins published his *Geographical Description of Australia* in 1830. Alarmed by the rapid spread of settlement pushed on by thriving sheep and cattle graziers, government was attempting to halt the unstoppable expansion in New South Wales. Despite eastern success, Collins' book is no more than a puffing description of the new (1829) Swan River settlement which even then was running into a disastrous period of collapse and stagnation following its ill-planned expedition to an unattractive site. The eastern, greater settlements were treated only so far as

1

their prospects could be made to seem inferior to those of Western Australia. Works of this kind are a frequent accompaniment to overseas settlement, written with a scant regard for the truth to attract colonists to particular places. Here is geography pressed into the service of propaganda, as it has been sometimes not only for private gain but in the national interests of countries, often under the guise of 'education for citizenship'.

T. L. Mitchell's *Australian Geography* (1850) also had a special purpose, the education of schoolchildren according to the pedagogical principles of the time, though the method chosen was already becoming out of date. Learning proceeded by question and answer, thus:

Q. Where are the sources of the largest rivers?
A. At the highest parts of the land.

Mitchell's book is true 'capes and bays' geography of a kind that brought the subject into disrepute. There is no sign in this book, except perhaps in the treatment of the Riverina towns and crossing places, that Mitchell in his work as Surveyor General and explorer displayed all the qualities of the good geographer in his eye for country, keen observation and real curiosity. Nor is it apparent that a period of phenomenal pastoral expansion was coming to an end, in which South Australia was joined to Australia Felix, New South Wales north of the Murray, and to what in nine years would be southern Queensland, in a single economy based on sheep and cattle. There is no suggestion that the pastoral industry had temporarily reached its arid margins and must undergo a technological transformation before it could advance once more. Bound by a rigid and limited educational concept, this geography conveys little more than some place names, chief products and a few simple ideas in physical geography. In only one way was it in advance of its time, for Mitchell's pupil would learn about Australia in its Pacific and Asian setting. James Bonwick's school geography of Australia, written in a more conventional style, was more successful than Mitchell's and sold 50,000 copies between 1845 and 1872 in numerous editions.

The next attempt, Alfred R. Wallace's *Australasia* (1879) belongs to the late-Victorian thirst for useful factual knowledge packed into a 'compendium' which in this case was a geography of the world based on a German text. Wallace had made a tour of Australia and written usefully on its environment and agriculture. By this time Australia was known in its interior, even in the western centre because of the marathon journeys of Giles and Forrest. There was now also the work of some natural scientists to draw upon, H. C. Russell on climate and Mueller on botany among others. Wallace was not sufficiently in touch with local thinking to display the climatic optimism

which was drawing wheat farmers in South Australia and pastoralists in New South Wales onward to their destruction in great periodic droughts. Instead, as a European, Wallace shows in occasional glimpses, the shock of a dweller in humid areas in his encounter with much of Australia. 'Essentially the land of wastes and steppes', the continent was covered with 'dreary scrubs' and was 'usually arid and monotonous'. This book is the first of our series to employ the topical categories which came to be conventional in accounts of geographical regions, ranging from areal extent, climate and physical features, through the vegetation to economy, urban places and government. Despite changes in geographical ways of thinking, these categories still supply the means by which geographers indicate their topical specialisms, and are reflected in the arrangement of this book.

Another compendium-type book is J. W. Gregory's *Australasia* (1907) in which volume one gives 'a concise account of the physical and economic geography' of Australia and New Zealand. More impersonal than Wallace's book, it goes further in considering environmental causation by isolation and climate, thus taking up the trend of *fin de siècle* geography abroad.

The appearance of the *Federal Handbook* published in connection with the eighty-fourth meeting of the British Association for the Advancement of Science in Melbourne during 1914 marked an important stage in the maturing of several sciences in Australia. W. Baldwin Spencer, writing on 'The Aboriginals of Australia' was able to call not only on pioneering work by A. W. Howitt and A. S. Kenyon, but also on the growing conceptual structure of anthropology as it had been developing overseas. Similarly, geology and palaeontology had matured as scientific disciplines and T. W. Edgeworth David and his co-authors were able to write a long and comprehensive account of Australian geology and earth structure. The sparkling description with which David celebrated Australian scenery was far removed from the brown monotony that Wallace saw. Scientific maturation is particularly evident when Griffith Taylor's chapter of 'The Physiography and General Geography of Australia' is compared with its predecessors.

Taylor provided a concise regional geography of Australia in thirty-five pages by the use of physiographic regions. He was then physiographer in the Commonwealth Bureau of Meteorology (no other niche could be found for a geographer), and his chapter displays the growth of genetic analysis of landforms and drainage in the last twenty years beginning with W. M. Davis and amply supplied with Davisian terminology. Taylor was not a single-handed worker in the field, for he was able to draw upon studies by E. C. Andrews and Edgeworth David, but he was the first to sketch in the physiographic structure of the whole continent. In this chapter the human use of the land is well integrated with landforms, soils and climate, but there is no outright expression of the environmental determinism that Taylor was to adopt elsewhere. Plainly marked as 'desert' however, is the land within the ten inch isohyet, a jarring note when other contributors played so hard upon the horn of optimism based on irrigation, dry-farming and artesian water.

Environmental determinism flowered in the Australian context when Griffith Taylor published his *Australia, a Study of Warm Environments and their Effect on British Settlement* (1940). Among the general body of geographers, environmental determinism had been given up (though not buried as an issue) since the rise of Possibilism in the 1920s, but Taylor persisted with it, not only here and in his Canadian study but also in world-wide studies of race and migration. This *Australia* was a book of far greater stature than those discussed so far, and cannot be displaced as a geographical classic by later work. Taylor worked from general principles and set up hypotheses for investigation; he had a much clearer grasp than his predecessors of the underlying spatial patterns of Australia, its simplicity of structure, its uniformity of culture, its division into 'Economic' and 'Empty' regions. Such a work of imaginative synthesis needs to be the product of one man, and cannot be duplicated by collaborators, whose work must be seen as having other merits.

The most detailed analysis dealt with climate, both as to common misconceptions of tropicality and aridity which influenced settlers and legislators and led to bitter controversy between Taylor and 'boosters' in earlier years, and to the demonstration of reality by the use of 'hythergraphs' (an innovation) which revealed the homoclimes of the Australian regions and left few excuses for misconception. The word 'controls' is found very frequently in the text, and Taylor concluded his work still convinced that 'Nature has largely determined the future of a country before man entered it'. Man is not a free agent, but must adjust his activities to limits laid down by nature: he can alter the pace of adjustment to environmental dictates, but no more. In Australian development Taylor found clear confirmation of environmental determinism.

Griffith Taylor was the last major exponent in geography of the environmental determinism which dominated the discipline in the nineteenth century within a general intellectual climate which favoured deterministic modes of thought such as Marxism and was much influenced by Darwinism. In geography this idea persisted into the twentieth century: Ellsworth Huntington is the best-known writer of this kind, but E. C. Semple perpetrated the most extreme views, writing of man and his economic activities as 'products' of particular natural environments (Semple, 1913). Such argument broke down under a whole range of contrary observations. Comparative views of similar environments provided little support for extreme deterministic views, crops were often seen to be grown elsewhere than in the best environments for them, and case studies demonstrated that natural environment can provide only necessary, never sufficient, conditions in explaining man's use of the land.

'There are no necessities, only possibilities' wrote Lucien Febvre in the translated *A Geographical Introduction to History* (1925). Forsaking strict determinism, geographers came to acknowledge the freedom of man to choose from a range of alternatives within a natural framework, a system that came to be known as Possibilism. This dealt with the problem of man using similar environments in different ways, but retained an ultimate determinism in that the range of choices available at any one place was restricted by the natural environment. In Possibilism, men with predetermined wants selected the relevant elements from a localized environment, or were repelled by the absence of particular resources, or fell back in their absence on whatever the local environment would permit. It was not until more sophisticated economic theory was adopted, however, that geographers ceased to place environmental and cultural factors side by side in rather uncomfortable explanations.

Clearly it was illogical to suppose that all possibilities offered the same rewards for an equal expenditure of labour, so that O. H. K. Spate suggested Probabilism as a *via media* with man, as an optimizer, being likely eventually to choose the most rewarding possibility (Spate, 1952). This is dangerously close to environmental determinism, and it has taken the recent adoption of the view of man as a satisficer rather than an optimizer to solve the logical problems of Possibilism which however was strongly supported by geographers.

Possibilism opened the way for a revision of the concept of resources as absolute values in favour of a view of resources as relative to the needs and technologies of particular groups of men. A particularly clear and early view of the relativity of resources was stated in E. W. Zimmerman's *World Resources and Industries* (1933). It was C. O. Sauer however who seized on the work of those American anthropologists who formulated a theory of culture able to clarify man-land relationships (Sauer, 1941). Instead of referring environmental choices to vaguely-defined human wants it was now possible to refer to utilities, technology and ideology which directed the group's evaluation of any given environmental complex. Utilities, technology and ideology were given coherent organization within the culture of a group so that environmental choice was a cultural option. The culture concept accepts a continual process of change and adaptation where the Possibilist was wary of admitting environmental effects; within the culture there may be reverberative change caused by adaptation to the environment but also autonomous cultural change which may influence man's view of his environment and his methods of dealing with it. 'Man' ceased to be a universal term for geographers, who instead came to study particular groups of men with different cultures. Already we can see that the geographer, from considering man as a relatively plastic creature in relation to his environment, came to adopt a number of models of man, depending on free will, on man as a cultural agent, economic man, and satisficing man.

Belief in nature's dominant influence on man was not allowed entirely to obscure the reverse effect of man upon his environment which was so strongly emphasized by Pinkerton. Even H. T. Buckle's deterministic *History of Civilization in England* (1857, 1861) took account of this reverse effect (it is worth noting that the most extreme environmental determinists have not been geographers) as did George Perkins Marsh in his well-known *Man and Nature: or physical geography as modified by human activities* (1864). The idea of an impact of man upon the landscape is embodied in twentieth-century analytical ideas of natural and cultural landscapes (Sauer, 1925). Identifying geography as 'the explanatory description of landscape' elevated man from a subordinate status into a causal agent logically equivalent to natural forces (Williams, 1974). It was this logic of the landscape view of geography that prompted the massive and co-operative *Man's Role in Changing the Face of the Earth* (1956) rather than any prescient knowledge of an environmental crisis, though this tradition leaves geography well-placed to engage in the current debate.

The idea of groups of men assessing the environment in the light of their wants, skills and past experience was present in cultural relativism and commonly used in particular by historical geographers. More recently there have been attempts to refine the analysis of the process of assessing environment, especially following W. Kirk who drew attention to the analytical construct 'behavioural environment', or the environment as it is imperfectly perceived by men (Kirk, 1963). All means of observing the environment are partial and suffer from inaccuracies: all methods of assessing observations are subjective, yet it is in relation to such partial and subjective information that men make their decisions.

The perceived environment will contain some, but not all of the relevant parts of the real environment, and may well contain elements imagined or mis-construed by man and not present in the real environment. The less congruent the real and perceived environments, the less likely it is that the group's activities will have a successful outcome. Men see the real environment through a cultural filter; by studying the filter and the choices made it is possible to reconstruct the perceived environment and so explain particular options and actions on the part of the group being studied. Scope for analysing man's subjective view of his environment has been greatly increased by recent importation of phenomenological viewpoints into geography (Mercer and Powell, 1972).

If we suspend belief in a single possible objective world of reality, a host of subjective worlds rises up about us, in the light of which man lives his life, orchestrates his world and remakes his landscape. Lowenthal drew our attention to this phenomenological world over a decade ago, and Yi-Fu Tuan has shown us how to incorporate it into geographical study, notably in his book *Topophilia* (1974). Once again this geographical shift reflects changes in the wider worlds of the intellect: in this case we follow philosophical proposals of the 1920s which have already found their way into sociology and anthropology, and accommodate ourselves to the change in consciousness which was called the 'counter-culture' in the 1960s.

While some geographers have thus recently reformulated the man and nature dichotomy in terms of processes of interaction, others have introduced a monistic approach in which men, plants, animals and other elements are brought within a single framework for the analysis of the interaction of these components. The concept of 'ecosystem' has been put forward by D. R. Stoddart as an alternative to previous formulations of the man-environment relationship (Stoddart, 1965).

The earth is seen as occupied by a number of sociological communities within which the components interact in ways that can often be measured. Man, like the other organisms, occupies defined ecological niches within the various communities and his role is explained in terms of interactions involving both dominant and subordinate relationships. This approach has attracted attention at a time when many other sciences are taking up a systems approach within the framework of General Systems Theory. The ecosystems approach is a solution to the methodological problems raised by the continuing debate over man-land relationships, since the system and man's place in it can be 'explained' in a functional way.

The study of man-land relationships, over which we see Pinkerton and Griffith Taylor taking up extremely opposed views, forms only one strand in the web of geographical study, and one that diminished in importance with the failure of environmental determinism. For an understanding of the variety of approaches in this book it is necessary to grasp other geographical preoccupations.

Quite as old as the environmental strand in geography is the area studies tradition which has produced regional geography, the study of complex arrangements of phenomena in place. This tradition can be traced back at least to Strabo (?63 BC–?AD 24) and his *Geography*. The method is synthesis and the information comprehended is vast and various, so that the whole is often grasped by intuitive processes and the success of the project depends much on literary skills. Some most evocative studies of regional character have emerged as classics, but the increasing desire to adopt the fully-fledged scientific method, and the less worthy aim of having geography achieve status as a scientific discipline, have led to a decline in the practice of regional geography in favour of systematic studies in which hypotheses can be precisely mounted and investigated. An early attempt to achieve scientific rigour was the designation of the visible forms of the landscape as the object of study, something more easily handled and quantified than the total content of area which had been the earlier object of study. The study of landscape, the assemblage of physical forms in place at the human scale, remains a major area of geographical research (Heathcote, 1975). On the whole geographers have come to reject more and more the aim of synthesis, though this is still expected of them by scholars in other disciplines, while there arises a new impetus for multidisciplinary area studies in which geographers can take part as topical specialists.

In the search for a scientific basis of geography a spatial tradition has come to be emphasized more and more, the attempt to find general laws of spatial configuration depending on distance, form, direction and position. There is an appeal to mapping and projections as a basic geographical activity, and early studies in this *genre* contented themselves with drawing distribution maps and setting out to explain them, still a useful approach. There is recently a more generalizing approach, an attempt to identify general configurations of spatial patterns which can be interpreted by reference to statistical or mathematical procedures, such as the gravity model which has been widely applied perhaps to the limits of its utility. The most developed areas of spatial analysis in geography are the study of central places and their arrangement in space, and the study of industrial location. The discovery of general configurations applicable to several kinds of phenomena goes a long way toward solving the methodological problem raised by the question—how far is position to be abstracted from the other attributes of complex phenomena and studied separately? Even so, geographers find themselves making distributional studies of a kind also made by specialists not in spatial arrangement but in particular phenomena. Thus a medical geographer and an epidemiologist have much in common.

While spatial analysis has been moving towards a greater reduction of reality by dealing in primitive terms, networks, nodes, hierarchies and surfaces, some geographers have paid more attention to the conscious creation of spatial structures and their perception by actors who behave in a way that maximizes returns or satisfies goals. There remains the problem of blending spatial analysis with behavioural studies which is taken up by Holmes in Chapter 19.

The fourth geographical tradition may be called the Earth Science tradition, the study of the earth, its waters and atmosphere. In a way this too falls within the area studies tradition so far as it deals with complex arrangements of physical phenomena in place—the description and explanation of complex climatic regions for example—and the idea of landscape studies finds expression in the study of landforms. Similarly, there are links with the spatial tradition when generalized techniques are found to be applicable to both human and physical phenomena, as for example the common use of network analysis to investigate branching road and river systems. But there are real difficulties in identifying the common aims of physical and human geographers, particularly when synthesis is tacitly given up as an end purpose of geographical activity, and those concerned primarily with physical features may be said to embody a distinctive and separate geographical tradition.

Faced with the varied red, brown and green visage of Australia, its swarming cities and almost empty plains, its multiplicity of governments and uniform culture, geographers have a strong armoury of approaches and tools to bring to the task of analysis. More than any of its predecessors, this book reflects the current state of the geographical discipline within a world-wide profession of geographers. Where earlier efforts represented the work of individuals, even as masterly as Griffith Taylor, Frank Craft and James Macdonald Holmes, there are now even hundreds of geographers working in Australia, in schools, government departments, in commerce and in eighteen university departments of geography. In 1945 there was but one university department, at Sydney. This seems an appropriate time for a statement of the geographer's view of Australia, a synthesis of the growing volume of research carried out in the last thirty years, a statement of problems, and a new beginning for the future.

ACKNOWLEDGEMENT I am grateful for the helpful comments of Professor O. H. K. Spate on a draft of this Introduction.

REFERENCES

Collins, S. H. (1830), *A Geographical Description of Australia*, Joseph Noble, Hull.

Dury, G. H. (1968), 'Geographical descriptions of Australia', *Aust. Geogr.*, 10, 441–52.

Febvre, L. (1925), *A Geographical Introduction to History*, Paul, London.

Gregory, J. W. (1907), *Australasia*, Vol. 1, *Australia and New Zealand*, 2nd edn, Edward Stanford, London.

Heathcote, R. L. (1975), *Australia*, Longman, London.

Kirk, W. (1963), 'Problems of geography', *Geography*, 48, 357–71.

Knibbs, G. H. (ed.) (1914), *Federal Handbook prepared in connection with the eighty-fourth meeting of the British Association for the Advancement of Science*, Government Printer, Melbourne.

Mercer, D. C. and Powell, J. M. (1972), *Phenomenology and Related Non-Positivistic Viewpoints in the Social Sciences*, Monash Publications in Geography No. 1, Clayton.

Mitchell, T. L. (1850), *Australian Geography with the Shores of the Pacific and those of the Indian Ocean designed for the use of schools in New South Wales*, J. Moore, Sydney.

Pinkerton, John (1807), *Modern Geography. A description of the Empires, Kingdoms, States and Colonies with the Oceans, Seas and Isles in all parts of the World: including the most recent discoveries and political alterations*, Vol. 2, T. Cadell and Davies: Longman, Hurst, Rees and Orme, London.

Sauer, C. O. (1925), 'The morphology of landscape', *Univ. of Calif. Publ. in Geogr.*, 2, 19–53.

——(1941), 'Foreword to historical geography', *Ann. Ass. Am. Geogr.*, 31, 1–24.

Semple, E. C. (1913), *Influences of Geographic Environment*, Constable, London.

Spate, O. H. K. (1952), 'Toynbee and Huntington: a study in determinism', *Geogr. J.*, 118, 149.

Stoddart, D. R. (1965), 'Geography and the ecological approach: the ecosystem as a geographic principle and method', *Geography*, 50, 242–51.

Taylor, Griffith (1940), *Australia, a Study of Warm Environments and their Effect on British Settlement*, Methuen, London.

Thomas, W. J. (ed.) (1956), *Man's Role in Changing the Face of the Earth*, Chicago University Press, Chicago.

Tuan, Yi-Fu (1974), *Topophilia*, Prentice-Hall, Englewood Cliffs, N. J.

Wallace, A. R. (1879), *Australasia*, Stanford, London.

Williams, M. (1974), *The Making of the South Australian Landscape*, Academic Press, London.

Zimmerman, E. W. (1933), *World Resources and Industries*, Harper, New York.

1 CLIMATE

J. GENTILLI

A great geographer once remarked that Australia's geographical position was the worst possible from the climatic point of view. This is of course quite true, and is a rather unfortunate result of the continental drift experienced so far, although it would have been even worse had Australia remained stuck to Antarctica. Australia's shape, size and position make it the landmass most completely affected by the great travelling anticyclones, with the resulting heat and dryness, as any climatic map shows (cf. Fig. 1.21, drawn according to Köppen's system, well known and internationally most widely accepted even if now rather outdated). There are advantages too: plentiful sunshine (and potential thermal energy) and absence of killing cold (and extravagant heating bills).

Climate may be seen in a number of ways. Climatography and its new and more sophisticated relative, climatonomy, examine the normal characteristics of the area at different times and places. The movements of the air and variations in its characteristics fall within the domain of dynamic climatology, though the patterns of air flow and other dynamic aspects interpreted through sequences of weather maps may be termed synoptic climatology. The geographer also engages in the classification of climates, assessing the main characteristics of air according to accepted criteria so as to allow the comparison of different parts of the world. Classification may be statistical using climatic data, or genetic if it uses dynamic and synoptic data. The climatologist in Australia will find data summarized in the volumes of *Results of Rainfall Observations* for the various States and their successors, the *Meteorological Summary (Climate Survey)* booklets for each meteorological district (Fig. 1.1).

Systematic (Gentilli, 1971) and regional (Gentilli, 1972) accounts of Australian climate have recently appeared, and should be used to supplement the brief outline of the main characteristics of Australian climates presented here.

ATMOSPHERIC CIRCULATION

Some climatological schools begin with the study of solar radiation and consider a radiation energy budget the end-all of climatological research. This is quite unrealistic in regional climatology because large amounts of heat are imported or exported by air streams and in coastal regions by currents and drifts. The logical sequence entails an assessment of air and water movements first, then an analysis of their effects, and as a final synthesis an examination of their integrated results in space and time.

The seasonal pattern of the main atmospheric flows affecting Australia is as follows:

A. June-August ('Winter', Fig. 1.2): The subtropical subsidence, which manifests itself at the surface in the great travelling anticyclones (cf. Fig. 1.7), dominates central and northern Australia. The air that descends is very dry, hence usually clear and very sensitive to temperature changes. On the equatorward side, this anticyclonic air spreads out anticlockwise, becoming the very persistent southeasterly trades. This is northern Australia's driest season.

At some 10,000 metres above the poleward side of the anticyclones flows the westerly subtropical jet stream. It is a variable current, a hundred or more kilometres wide, thousands of kilometres long and only around one or two kilometres (cf. Fig. 1.5) deep. Its speed may rise to 150, 200 or more knots where it bends cyclonically (i.e. clockwise) but it slows down to less than a hundred knots as it bends anticyclonically. The speed slowly decreases downwards, so that below a 150-knot wind at 10,000 metres there may be a 40-knot wind at the surface. Below an 80-knot jet in the anticyclonic curve the surface wind may be little more than a breeze. Furthermore, inside the accelerating cyclonic bend of the jet the air tends to rise and the weather becomes unsettled, while inside the decelerating anticyclonic bend the air tends to sink and the weather is fine. The main parts of the cyclonic depressions lie to the south of the mainland or even to the south of Tasmania, so the spells of rainy and stormy weather mostly last three or four days, while the fine spells last five or six. Already in Tasmania the proportion is reversed, and further south the fine spells soon become insignificant. By August it is already noticeable that wind and weather systems are slowly moving southwards; the rainy spells are very

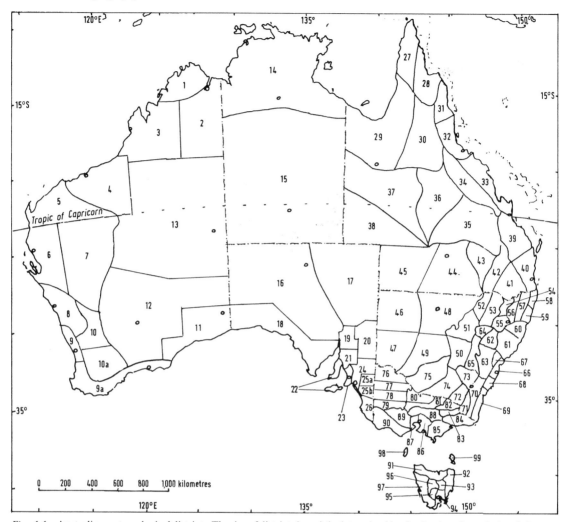

Fig. 1.1 Australian meteorological districts. The size of districts is mainly determined by the density of population, in inverse proportion (from Bureau of Meteorology).

short, and seldom stormy.

B. September-November ('Spring', Fig. 1.3): The trend begun in August continues. The anticyclones travel along more variable tracks and often a little further south; towards the end of the season the southeast trades occasionally fail to reach the northern shores, and moist northwesterly air may bring the first monsoon rains. Towards the south, the jet stream occasionally weakens, and anticyclonic spells become the normal weather type. Sunshine is received for longer periods, and the radiation is much stronger.

C. December-February ('Summer', Fig. 1.4): The travelling anticyclones travel along more southerly paths, and control the weather of the southern half of the mainland. To the western and most of the southern

shores they bring sunny hot weather only briefly interrupted by cool changes as each new anticyclone arrives. To the eastern shore, moist Pacific air brings those summer rains that so characterize the climate and are still not clearly understood. The dry anticyclonic air allows a greater proportion of the already much stronger radiation to reach the ground, and the fierce summer heat soon sets in. The subtropical jet stream is mostly quiescent, but intermittent westerlies still affect Tasmania. The anticyclones are now so far south that the southeast trades often fail to reach the northern shores, allowing a very shallow and inconsistent northwesterly monsoonal flow to penetrate inland. Occasionally the whole system is disrupted by a tropical cyclone; monsoon and cyclones are special

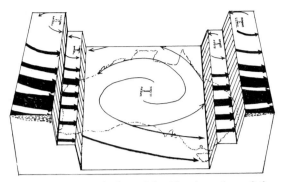

Fig. 1.2 Average air flow, July. The three tiers of the block diagram show the pattern of air flow at the surface, at the 500 millibar level and at the 250 millibar level, respectively. Notice the strong anticyclonic tendency at the surface, and the great increase in wind velocity with increasing height (the width of the arrows is proportional to the velocity, to a maximum of about 80 knots).

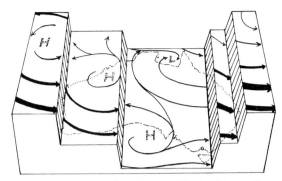

Fig. 1.4 Average air flow, January. The land is now hot, and the monsoonal low often appears over its northern margin. The cooler waters now favour some anticyclonic tendency. Upper winds are no longer of jet velocity.

phenomena which will be discussed in some detail later on.

D. March-May ('Autumn', Fig. 1.5): The gradual northward shift of the weather systems soon becomes apparent. Monsoonal air is far less frequent and only affects the northern coastal fringe. A broader belt is dominated by the southeast trades. In the south, the inter-anticyclonic troughs become slightly wider and admit cooler and more humid air. Later in the season, the subtropical jet awakens and occasionally conveys enormous masses of Indian Ocean air towards the tropical mainland. Frontal convergence and atmospheric uplift appear further south under the meanders of the jet, resulting in the first 'winter' depressions.

The time, duration and sequence of these complex atmospheric movements vary greatly within the general outline given above. The entire, immensely complex circulation over the southern hemisphere is reviewed by the contributors to Newton's (1972) volume, while the scale of the maps does not allow a detailed representation of the circulation affecting Australia in a most effective perspective. Other details are given by Gentilli (1971) and for the northern area by Wittwer (1973). Some aspects of the subtropical jet stream meanders ('troughs') have been examined by Healy (1972).

There is still much to be discovered and a great deal to be understood in this field. An important fact is that the monsoonal flow often dies out before reaching Australia; the Australian monsoon (Fig. 1.4) is shallower, more intermittent, and basically more 'chancy' than the Indian monsoon. Its penetration inland—when it occurs—is most variable. Its marginal position enhances the inherent instability of the oncoming air and favours very frequent thunderstorms.

The tropical easterlies (trade winds, cf. Figs 1.6 and

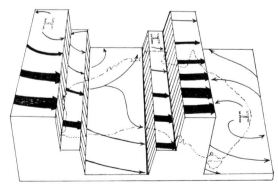

Fig. 1.3 Average air flow, October. The jet stream has weakened, and the mainland is no longer cold enough to generate strong anticyclonic tendencies.

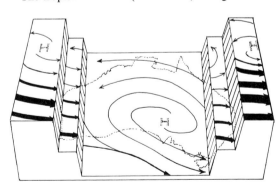

Fig. 1.5 Average air flow, April. The southern part of the mainland has cooled enough to give again rise to anticyclonic tendencies, which re-establish the trade winds over northern Australia. The anticyclone slopes northwards with increased altitude. The subtropical jet stream reappears with increasing frequency, heralding the coming winter flow (cf. Fig. 1.2.).

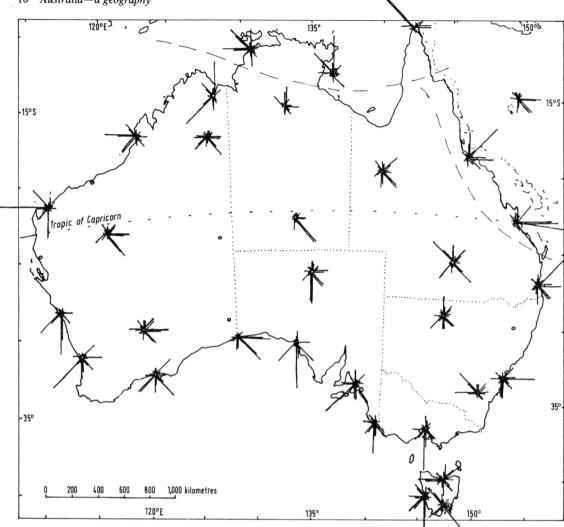

Fig. 1.6   Wind roses for January. The wind blows towards the centre; in each double arm shown, proceeding clockwise, the first line shows the 9 a.m. wind, the second line the 3 p.m. wind. The length of the arms is proportional to the frequency of wind from that direction. Notice the northern prevalently monsoonal area, and the very small eastern area where easterlies are dominant. Over most of Australia the wind varies daily with the transit of the anticyclones. Notice also the long single arms at coastal stations, showing the strong frequency of sea breezes.

1.7), coming from higher latitudes, are normally cool; only in eastern Queensland are they onshore, rain-bearing winds. The steep orographic rise releases heavy precipitation and the air is already much drier by the time it resumes its course. Everywhere else these winds are dry and readily over-heated as they travel over hot land. They play an important role in the transport of heat and in the evaporation and removal of moisture.

The subtropical subsidence, as it sections itself into anticyclonic cells (highs), gives origin to a five- or six-day weather cycle dominated mostly by gradual shifts in wind direction (Fig. 1.8). In times of strongly zonal circulation, the anticyclonic cells are regular in size and shape and follow one another regularly on their eastward journey at a rate of 500–600 km per day. When (as has been increasingly the case in recent years) the circulation is strongly meridional, the cells

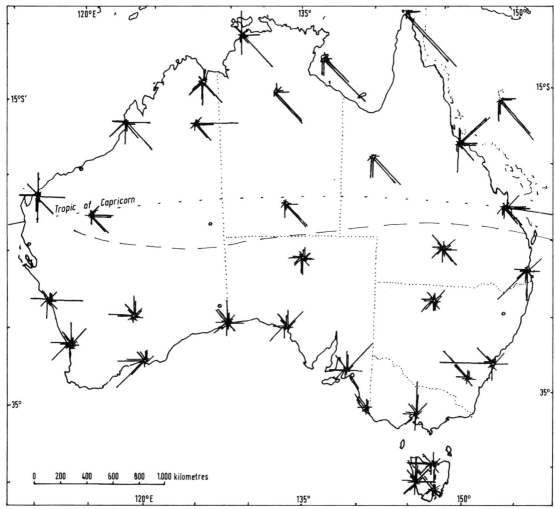

Fig. 1.7 Wind roses for July. The trade winds are now in almost full control of the flow over northern Australia. There is very little evidence of any predominant westerly flow in the south. Notice the long single arms showing the frequency of land breezes at coastal stations.

are divided by deep troughs as they cross the west coast and remain weaker during their Australian transit. Occasionally in winter the colder surface of eastern Australia or the Tasman Sea increases the density of the air, strengthening and delaying an anticyclone and blocking its progress for a day or two, seldom for longer.

The mid-latitude westerlies and their fronts, which

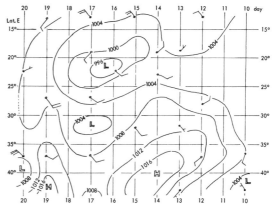

Fig. 1.8 Ten days of summer over eastern Australia. The time-latitude chart shows the progress of pressure patterns and air flow during ten days, across a line from Thursday Island to Hobart. The days follow from right to left; latitude is shown in the margin. Notice the duration of the weather patterns over many days.

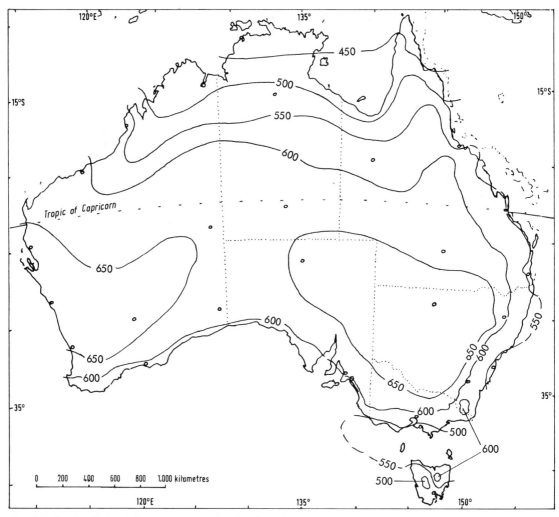

Fig. 1.9   Total radiation ly/day, January. Notice the effect of cloudiness caused by the monsoon in the northern regions, and of the banking up of clouds against western Tasmania. Notice also the very large areas of extremely intense radiation, associated with anticyclonic weather and diverging airflow (after Hounam, 1963).

so often control the weather of western Tasmania, are rare on the mainland (cf. Figs 1.6 and 1.7), where westerly winds (apart from sea breezes) are mostly the surface manifestation of the subtropical jet stream. In May and early June, with the awakening of the jet in its epitropical position, storms come with north-westerly blows. By mid-June and July the jet stream's meanders are fully developed with a three- or four-day transit length, and each storm begins with strong northwesterlies, followed by weaker westerlies with a cold front, and finally ending with southwesterlies. By August the circulation systems begin their seasonal poleward shift and only westerly-southwesterlies affect the mainland, mostly for a day or two at a time, while cold fronts travel further south.

ENERGY BUDGET

There being very few stations with direct measurements of solar radiation in Australia, Hounam (1963) derived two equations for its calculation from sunshine records:

$$Q/Q_o = 0.34 + 0.66 \, n/N$$

and

$$Q/Q_A = 0.26 + 0.50 \, n/N$$

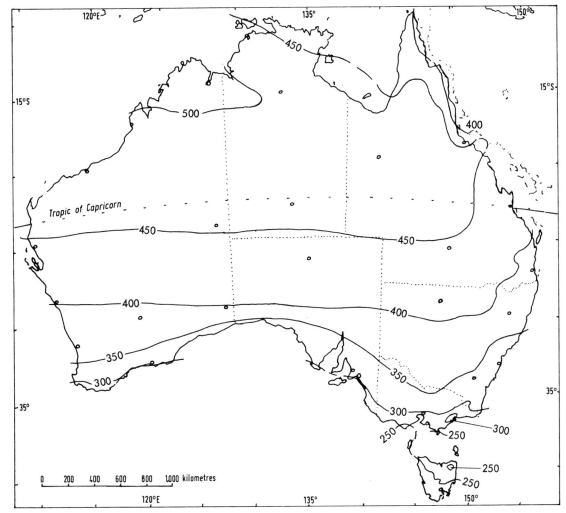

Fig. 1.10 Total radiation ly/day, April. Latitude is now the main control, except for a tendency to interception by clouds along the eastern coast (after Hounam, 1963).

where Q = total radiation actually received at the surface,

Q_o = total radiation received at the surface on a cloudless day,

Q_A = total radiation received at the top of the atmosphere,

n = actual duration of sunshine,

N = maximum possible duration of sunshine.

Radiation is expressed in langley (ly = cal/cm²) per day, and the duration of sunshine is given in hours.

From observations in very few perfectly clear days, it appears that Q_o varies between 0.7 and 0.8 Q_A with the lower values tending to occur in the wet season and in cities.

From Hounam's calculations, the highest radiation intensities in January, over 650 ly/day, occur from Carnarvon, W.A. to Perth and beyond Kalgoorlie, and from Oodnadatta, S.A. to Bourke, N.S.W., Mildura, Vic. and the western slopes of New South Wales (Fig. 1.9). To north and south, increasing water vapour and cloudiness reduce the insolation received to less than 450 ly/d near Darwin and just over 500 near Hobart. It hovers around 550 ly/d along a very narrow coastal belt in Victoria, New South Wales and east Queensland, and falls below 550 in the monsoonal belt, north of a line from Townsville to Broome.

In July (Fig. 1.11) the amount is over 450 ly/d only near Darwin; lower solar elevation and increasing moisture and cloudiness cause a gradual southward

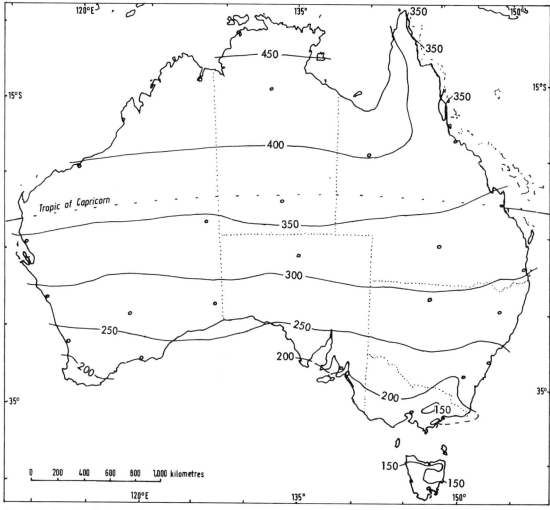

Fig. 1.11 Total radiation ly/day, July. Shorter days and lower angles of insolation reduce the intensity throughout. Latitude is the main factor, except for the onshore winds that bring cloudiness to the northeastern shore, and some effect of the southern highlands (after Hounam, 1963).

reduction, to under 200 ly/d in the far southwest and southeast, and under 150 over most of Tasmania. The October radiation (Fig. 1.12) is generally stronger than April's (Fig. 1.10).

Because of the scarcity of cloud and practical absence of snow in Australia, ground albedo is of the utmost importance. Recent direct measurements by Paltridge and Sargent (1970) and Paltridge (1971) gave values about 0.14 for eucalypt forest and 0.22 for dry grassland and semi-desert with a solar elevation of 40 degrees or more. These values, which increase considerably at lower solar angles, to a great extent confirm the estimates mapped by Gentilli (1971).

The radiation reflected by the surface according to these sixty estimates could amount to anything up to 200 ly/d off light-coloured arid land in summer or as little as 20 ly/d off close eucalypt forest in winter. Of the radiation that reaches the ground and is transformed in various ways, a good proportion is emitted directly. Hounam estimates at more than 150 ly/d the outgoing radiation from most of extratropical Australia in January, except for a very narrow coastal belt where humidity reduces the loss to about 100 ly/d. But north of the tropic the moisture brought by the monsoon, for all its limitations, reduces the outgoing radiation more and more, until it reaches less than 40 ly/d along the northern shore. The gradient is nearly − 10 ly/d for every 100 km.

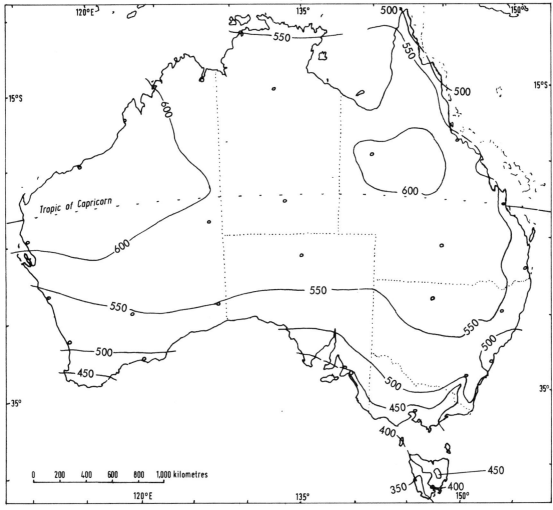

Fig. 1.12 Total radiation ly/day, October. The pattern differs significantly from that of April because of the preceding winter drought over tropical Australia (after Hounam, 1963).

In July the overall pattern is nearly reversed, with an enormous dry area north of about 30° S emitting over 150 ly/d (less in the coastal belts), rising to over 200 ly/d in the interior north of the tropic. In Tasmania, the seasonal range is very small, varying only between about 85–110 ly/d in July and 95–130 in January.

Hounam (1963) calculated the net radiation from the equation

$$Q_n = (1 - a) Q - Q_b$$

where Q_n = net radiation,
a = albedo (assumed at a uniform 0.23),
Q = total radiation received,
Q_b = outgoing radiation.
The albedo of forests being much less than 0.23, some

revision is needed. The net radiation in the eastern forests is likely to vary from an average of 380–400 ly/d in January to 60–80 ly/d in July, decreasing in Gippsland and increasing in New England. Further north it remains almost constant at 380–400 ly/d in January (less radiation is received because of moisture and cloudiness, but less is also lost because of the same causes), but it increases rapidly from 60–80 to 170 ly/d in July because of the clear winter skies. In the south-western forests it is the clear summer skies that favour outgoing radiation, so that net January radiation there is 30–40 ly/d less than in the southeastern forests, while there is no difference between the two regions in the winter.

Much of the energy received is spent in the

evaporation of water: at the vaporization rate of 540 cal/g, even the spare 250 mm of rain that falls at the desert's edge in the average year will use 13.5 kcal/cm² to evaporate, so that a square kilometre of land will be kept dry by 13.5×10^{10} kcal per year. This seems most impressive, but in fact it means only that at Alice Springs it would take the radiation of January or that of two winter months to evaporate the whole year's rainfall.

Budyko (1963) estimated Australia's overall radiation balance according to the common equation

$$R = LE + H$$

where R = radiation balance,
$\quad L$ = latent heat of vaporization,
$\quad E$ = actual evaporation, and
$\quad H$ = sensible heat flux from ground to air.
His estimate (in kly/year) was

$$70 = 22 + 48$$

with a Bowen ratio H/LE of 2.18, much higher than Africa's 1.61 or Asia's 1.14. In other words, in Australia more than twice as much heat is left to heat the air than is used in evaporation of the moisture available. In the arid and semi-arid parts of Australia, the Bowen ratio is far greater, as the sample calculation showed for Alice Springs.

Conversely, in the very narrow wetter rim of the mainland and most of Tasmania a little less solar energy is received, but proportionally far more is used in plant functions and the evaporation of rain water, with a Bowen ratio well below 1.

Australia is a great exporter of converted radiation. Not only is there a very large area with plentiful oncoming radiation and very little rainfall, which evaporates without any surplus to run off, but the winds that carry both the sensible heat which they have absorbed and the latent heat of the little locally raised vapour are mainly offshore. This is due to the subtropical divergence and to the shape of the continent.

A rapid survey shows that, during winter, offshore winds prevail along about two-thirds of the Australian coast, and mainly in the form of tropical easterlies they sweep over a far greater land area than their onshore counterparts. Most of the latent heat brought in by easterlies from the Pacific is almost immediately released when condensation and precipitation occur along the eastern escarpments. The runoff is very rapid; the air, warmer and much drier, continues its course, absorbing more heat from the ground and what little water vapour there is.

In summer the budget is reversed over northern Australia, which is repeatedly but erratically swept by a very moist warm northwesterly flow, i.e. air with immense amounts of latent heat. The trouble is that monsoonal spells alternate with spells of dry south-easterly winds which promptly re-export in latent form much of the heat that had just been brought in, plus, as sensible heat, some of the radiation energy received in the interior.

The important role played by air and water movements in the transport and distribution of heat over Australia may be inferred from a simple calculation. Taking the specific heat of dry air at 0.24 cal/g and its density at 1.1 g/l, it can be estimated that an air stream 1,000 m thick advancing over a front of 2,000 km at the speed of 1 knot and heated only 10° C above its initial temperature, conveys extra heat at the rate of 10^{13} kcal/h. Since the front of the easterlies is often longer (the longer diameter of a large anticyclone may reach 3,000 km), the wind velocity is often around 5 or 6 knots (Brookfield, 1970), and the easterly flow persists for days at a time, it can be estimated that the heat transported annually across the interior by the tropical easterlies exceeds 10^{16} kcal. As shown above, much of this heat is exported across the northern and western shores.

Along the west coast in winter there is a very slow southward drift of ocean water which takes Banda and Timor Sea water all the way past Cape Leeuwin. The difference in temperature is only some 3° C, but it means that a drift only 100 km wide and 100 m deep conveys 3×10^9 kcal. Some of this heat raises coastal temperatures, some contributes to the evaporation of water and increases precipitation.

ATMOSPHERIC DISTURBANCES

Superimposed on, or injected into, the general atmospheric circulation, are various types of disturbances: tropical cyclones, tornadoes, mid-latitude depressions, thunderstorms. There are also local cyclic phenomena, such as land and sea breezes, and local static situations, such as inversions. The latter went almost unnoticed until it was found that they impeded the dispersal of industrial or traffic emissions of gas and smoke or dust, and now they are an important aspect of urban climatology. Sea breezes, long praised and enjoyed because of the thermal relief they provide on hot days, are now further valued because of their dispersal of pollutants, and are studied with increased interest and accuracy (for Sydney, cf. McGrath, 1973 and Hawke, 1973). Unfortunately, by night time, the sea air can establish a new inversion that may have to be taken into account (Watson and Gentilli, 1974).

Tropical Cyclones

Tropical cyclones are by far the most spectacular and often disastrous of these atmospheric phenomena, as was shown by the almost total destruction of Darwin on Christmas Day 1974 (Plate 13.4). Cyclone Tracy had been first noticed as a tropical disturbance some distance to the north. The more normal path of cyclones formed north of Darwin takes them westwards and channels them around the Kimberleys, and in any case, the frequency of December cyclones near Darwin had been about one in twenty years. By an extraordinary set of circumstances, Cyclone Tracy rapidly intensified to produce winds of Australian record force, 260 km/h before the anemograph was wrecked, and swept exactly over the city, to continue southeastwards into western Queensland, where it brought short-lived floods. A comprehensive review of data on Australian tropical cyclones from 1909 to 1969 is given by Coleman (1972).

Tropical cyclones may begin almost anywhere on warm ocean waters ($> 27°$ C) such as prevail in the Coral and Timor Seas, especially if there is some atmospheric convergence at the surface. The initial phase, however, is very mild, and takes the form of a fairly large but very shallow and usually almost shapeless depression.

The movements of the initial tropical depression are slow and unpredictable, and may not lead to any further development. If the depression intensifies it becomes a disturbance, with stronger winds and an extensive cloud system. Further intensification causes the cyclone stage, with converging winds of hurricane force, spiral banding of clouds and torrential rain. Before Cyclone Tracy, the wind had reached records of 231 km/h at Onslow, W.A. in February 1963, and 202 km/h at Willis Island, off Queensland, in February 1957. More recently, in February 1975, a maximum gust of 259 km/h was recorded near Onslow. It may be that these high velocities occurred in earlier cyclones as well, but could only be recorded by modern instruments, or perhaps the intensity of cyclones has really increased in recent years. Their frequency has certainly increased from the 1940s onwards from around fifty to nearly a hundred per decade, and may increase even further for a few years if the global correlation detected by Milton (1974) continues to hold true. The damage caused by cyclones has increased immensely in the same period: in March 1960 damage to the town of Carnarvon and the nearby plantations amounted to $1 m; Cyclone Ada caused fourteen deaths and damage to the value of $12 million on Hayman Island and nearby Queensland holiday resorts in January, and Cyclone Ingrid damage costing $2 million in Western Australia in February 1970, also causing the death of 70,000 sheep and lambs from cold; Cyclone Althea caused damage of $50 million at Townsville on Christmas Eve 1971 (Hopley, 1974); Cyclone Tracy killed forty-nine people and caused $1,000 million damage to Darwin on Christmas Day 1974. The great increase in the size of settlements and in the value of their buildings makes an increase in damages unavoidable should a cyclone hit a city. The favourable trend

is in the decrease of casualties. In the early days, before the development of broadcast cyclone warning alerts, there were many victims when ships were surprised by a cyclone at sea: off Western Australia, 59 pearling crewmen died off Exmouth Gulf in 1875, 140 off Wallal in 1887, 40 between Onslow and Roebourne in 1894, 100 in two cyclones off Broome in 1908, 24 in 1909 and 40 in 1910. In 1912, the coastal steamer *Koombana* foundered off Port Hedland with the total loss of 150 crew and passengers. In 1935, Broome lost another 140 pearling fishermen.

Warm moist cyclonic winds sweeping over coastal land may bring colossal falls of rain: the absolute record is the 907 mm that fell at Crohamhurst, Q. on 3 February 1893, but the 869 mm brought to Mt Dangar, Q. by Cyclone Ada on 19 January 1970 comes a close second. The greatest rainfall intensity at Mt Dangar was over 140 mm per hour (the rain gauge overflowed). An important aspect of tropical cyclonic rainfall is that, according to the size of the cyclone, it is likely to continue for some days: the heavy rains from Cyclone Ada began on 1 January and reached a total 1,146 mm in three days (Bureau of Meteorology, 1973). It has been estimated that in five days of February 1964, Cyclone Dora brought 430 mm of rain to 50,000 km² of the Norman River basin and 230 mm to 106,000 km² of the Flinders River basin, plus smaller amounts to adjoining smaller basins east of the Gulf of Carpentaria, enough to cover 3,23 million hectares with one metre of water, something which would drain the entire Murray-Darling system over two whole years.

Tropical cyclones bring a valuable contribution of rain to arid and semi-arid regions, at times precipitating the equivalent of a normal year's rainfall in three or four days. In January 1964 Cyclone Audrey, after having brought heavy rains to much of Cape York Peninsula, recurved at $20°$S and proceeded southeastwards, crossing southwest Queensland diagonally and leaving on its right a trail of heavy rain which reached 296 mm in 24 hours at Metavale near Eulo (91 mm in three hours), causing major floods in normally dry rivers. The drowning of sheep and damage to fences probably outweighed the value of the new growth of pastures.

Very similar was the pattern of the two long-track cyclones that affected Western Australia in 1970: Glynis from 27 January to 7 February and Ingrid on 9–17 February. Glynis began on the land, somewhere east of Darwin, as a very weak depression on 26 January and moved to sea just north of Darwin. Its track continued all around the coast of Western Australia until it crossed overland in the far southwest on 6 February. It brought over 50 mm of rain to the south Kimberleys and to a large area between Port Hedland, Marble Bar and Carnarvon (mean annual rainfall around 250 mm).

Cyclone Ingrid (Table 1.1) began on the west Kimberley coast and moved out to sea, following a wide arc to cross the coast at Shark Bay, pass over Kalgoorlie and come out to sea again near Eucla. It brought over 25 mm of water to the south Kimberleys and to a wide strip of country west of a line from Carnarvon to Esperance, W.A. and over 100 mm to the pastoral lands north and east of Geraldton, W.A. with a maximum of 200 mm at Mt Gibson. The table shows that some 471,000 km² of arid to subhumid land received over 25 mm of water; at least 130,000 km² are pastoral lands where every drop of water is precious and over the 300,000 km² of agricultural land the replenishment of groundwater supplies and surface dam is most valuable. On the debit side go the 70,000 recently shorn sheep and lambs that died of exposure and the flood damage to local roads.

Examples of the geographical distribution of cyclonic rainfall in the late 1940s may be found in Gentilli (1971) and examples from 1964 onwards in the *Meteorological Summaries* of the Bureau of Meteorology. Some data are shown in Table 1.2 In several instances, falls of 200 or 250 mm have occurred in arid Western Australia (e.g. Cyclone Ingrid) or Queensland (e.g. Cyclone Audrey), both in infratropical and extratropical regions. It should be noted that the rainfall over the infratropical regions is entirely caused by the atmospheric uplift within the cyclone, and therefore affects a relatively small area very intensely. Outside the tropics subtropical air is drawn into the cyclone and a frontal or parafrontal trough situation develops, while the cyclone usually accelerates on its southeastward path. Most of this renewed heavy rainfall therefore appears to the west of the track and is scattered alongside it (cf. the cases of Audrey and Ingrid above). This subtropical rainfall from transformed tropical cyclones may be just as heavy as the earlier typical cyclonic rainfall. This is how there have been late summer or early autumn floods at Kalgoorlie, in the Nullarbor Plain, in western Queensland and central New South Wales.

Table 1.1   Rain brought by Cyclone Ingrid, 1970

Rainfall mm	Climatic region (south of Carnarvon, W.A.) Arid '000 km²	Semi-arid '000 km²	Subhumid '000 km²	Total '000 km²
25–50	31	48	12	91
50–75	27	30	16	73
75–100	22	181	32	235
100–125	—	62	—	62
> 125	—	10	—	10
Total	80	331	60	471

Table 1.2   Rain brought by Cyclones Rita and Sheila, 1971

Rainfall mm	Rita '000 km²	Sheila '000 km²	Total '000 km²
12.5–25	180	100	280
25–50	340	270	610
50–75	80	156	236
75–100	60	96	156
100–125	40	40	80
125–150	30	26	56
150–200	20	22	42
200–250	15	17	32
250–300	11	13	24
300–400	—	10	10
> 400	—	6	6
Total	776	756	1,532

Epitropical Storms

Australian regions more or less astride the tropic are affected by great rainstorms which do not fit into any known category. Their location is much more restricted in latitude than that of tropical cyclones and so close to the geographical tropic that the term epitropical (Gentilli and Milton, 1972) is the only apt one. They are more frequent in May (Fig. 1.13) and early June when ocean waters are already too cool for tropical cyclones to arise; in any case, the lack of strong winds distinguishes them from tropical cyclones.

An earlier example, complicated by a disturbance in the tropical easterlies, occurred early in May 1963, with a strong anticyclone west of Tasmania and in the middle and upper troposphere a cyclonic circulation which had developed to the north of Adelaide (Bureau of Meteorology, 1965). Heavy rains and floods were experienced on the south Queensland coast. The Bureau of Meteorology stated that it seemed likely that the most significant causative factor was the considerable vertical motion induced by the upper circulation which was itself probably the product of strongly divergent flow in the middle and upper troposphere.

Another example was the so-called Cyclone Lulu (Bureau of Meteorology, 1973) which

although it was classed as a tropical cyclone ... was not a tropical cyclone in the true sense. ... First, a strong cold front moved northward and affected the lower northwest coast on 29 and 30 April. ... During the second stage, a tropical disturbance in the upper air appeared to amalgamate with the cold front. ... By 4 May a closed low pressure system with a central pressure of 1002 mb could be identified on the surface, about 740 km northwest of North West Cape. During the next two days the centre moved east-southeast and deepened. On the morning of 6 May it was located

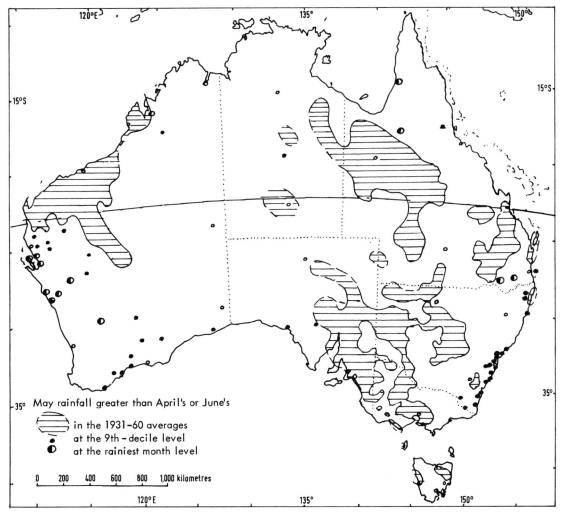

Fig. 1.13. The effect of May storms. Notice the predominantly epitropical and subtropical position of the areas where May rains are greater than April's or June's, and their general alignment, which may be linked with the strongest northwesterly flow of the subtropical jet stream at that time of the year.

about 195 km north-northwest of Roebourne and had reached maturity with central pressure of 996 mb. It then curved to the southeast and weakened. ... It brought widespread heavy rain to a large part of the northern half of Western Australia and many of the rivers and streams were flooded. All traffic between the north and south of the State was halted ... for over a week ... as roads became impassable and most airports in the Pilbara were either closed or partly closed.

Several stations received over 100 mm in 24 hours and 250 to 350 mm in a few days, and a large arid area was well watered. Onslow, W.A. received 345 mm of rain in nine days; its median annual rainfall is only 274 mm.

Various examples of these storms are quoted by Gentilli (1974). From all these examples it is clear that they are preceded by low-level anticyclones above which runs a strong subtropical jet. The autumn position of the newly awakened jet is in low latitude (epitropical or even infratropical) and its course generally straight. Then, above an anomalously warm surface such as normally occurs to the northwest or north of Australia (Gentilli, 1972b) the jet stream develops a sudden cyclonic inflexion, with consequent convergence at low level and the uplift of enormous masses of water vapour (Gentilli, 1974).

These large but infrequent storms are significant enough to affect the averages and extremes of rainfall

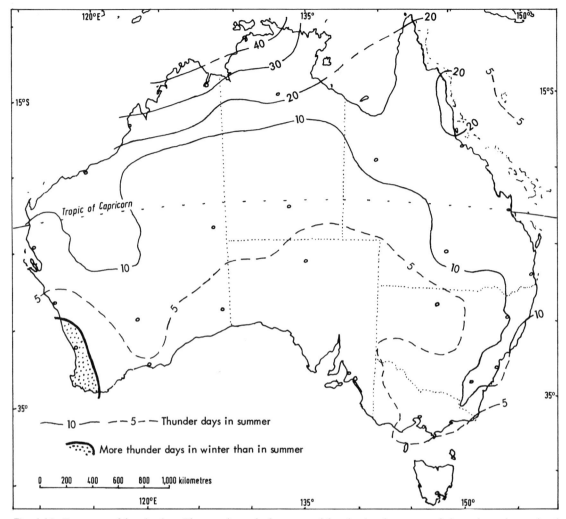

Fig. 1.14   Frequency of thunder days. The map shows the frequency of thunder days in summer; their maximum is associated with the inflow of moist unstable air when the monsoon is active. In the extreme southwest corner unstable humid air mainly comes in the late autumn and early winter.

over large areas (Fig. 1.13). In the southern hemisphere they are peculiar to Australia because the cooler ocean surface precludes their development off Chile and Namibia. Similar storms do however occur about November in the northern hemisphere in western Mexico and Mauritania; it is not known at this stage whether they are related to the *kona* storms of Hawaii. They differ in latitude, time of occurrence and above all in structure from the cutoff lows of the middle and higher latitudes. Because of their association with atmospheric fronts farther south they were confused with them; in fact much of the rain which falls in the epitropical regions from early May to early June (Fig. 1.13) is due to these storms.

Thunderstorms

Very little research has been done on thunderstorms in Australia. Statistics are based on the 'number of days in which thunder has been heard', and therefore give very incomplete information on a complex phenomenon.

Thunderstorms being localized, they contribute most unevenly to any station's rainfall. However, the statistics available show that there is a much greater frequency of thunder in the moist tropical regions (Fig. 1.14) where humid unstable air is very common ahead of the monsoonal flow, which itself may be most unstable.

Summer thunderstorms may occur anywhere in

Australia, although they are far more frequent where the humidity is high. Winter thunderstorms only occur where unstable air moves very fast over an obstacle, which may be a body of denser air, but more often is an orographic barrier. Thus in Perth about half of the year's thunderstorms come between May and August (Fig. 1.14), they are more common along the Darling Scarp, and produce small hailstones. The summer thunderstorms are distributed more at random, and produce bigger and often more irregularly shaped hailstones. A side effect is the squall wind: the strongest wind gust recorded in South Australia, 148 km/h, occurred during a thunderstorm at Leigh Creek in December 1953. Sydney may have thunderstorms and hail at any season, but the worst one was on 1 January 1947, where roof tiles were broken, cars dented and people injured. Some lumps of hail neared 2 kg in weight. Some of the worst weather experienced in Victoria was also caused by summer thunderstorms, with strong squalls, electrical discharges, and heavy hailstones. The widespread thunderstorm of 7 November 1954 caused wind and hail damage to much of the area between Horsham and Mildura, while the Melbourne storm of 17 January 1956 was most damaging because of its lightning, which interrupted all electrical supplies, telephones and radio broadcasts, and started many fires.

Thunderstorms, although uncommon, may occur in almost any month further south: Launceston had most damaging thunderstorms (with floods) in March 1915 and January 1937, much of western Tasmania had wind damage from thunderstorms in July 1918 and February 1922. Hobart has an average of four hailstorms a year, and five or six thunderstorms, not always on the same occasions. In general they are late spring and summer phenomena. Occasionally there are falls of hail during frontal storms in late winter or early spring, but the instability of the air is not sufficient to cause electrical phenomena.

TEMPERATURE

The solar radiation received and the energy budget outlined in a preceding section result in very high temperatures. With no very high mountains from which conspicuous katabatic warming may result, Australia has not reached the extreme heat of the record days in Death Valley, but in terms of duration and intensity of heat over large areas it is the hottest continent. Its situation predominantly under the subtropical subsidence, leading to clear air and great dryness, and its low altitude, make it a unique landmass in the southern hemisphere.

The distribution of heat is asymmetrical because of the tropical easterlies. The hottest locality, as far as mean annual temperatures go, is Wyndham, W.A., with a mean of 29.1° C; its hottest month is November, with 32.2° C. Night temperatures remain high: the mean daily minimum is 27° C in November, very little less in December. The mean daily range of 9.6° C for the hottest month is greater than would be expected at that latitude at the beginning of the rainy season; it is due to the long frequent spells of dry southeasterly winds.

Higher temperatures are recorded at other localities, especially where the tropical easterlies descend a slope. The locality with the highest monthly temperatures and the longest hot spells is Marble Bar, W.A.: its mean monthly temperature for December is 33.8° C. It had many sequences of hot days, including one of 160 days with a maximum above 37.8° C. Daytime temperatures are so high that the annual mean daily maximum is higher at Marble Bar than at Wyndham. It should be noted that the new mining centre of Pannawonica, some 240 km west of Marble Bar, has already recorded some very high temperatures and may be actually found to be hotter. The absolute maximum for Australia, 53.1° C, was recorded at Cloncurry, Q. on 16 January 1889, and was almost certainly due to several factors, including a katabatic effect.

As may be expected, although the outstanding heat records fall usually soon after midsummer, the average hottest month comes earlier, being November in the far north, December further south almost to the tropic, and January throughout most of the subtropical regions, except along the west and south coasts and in Tasmania, where February is hottest. In general, heat comes a little later in the highlands. The most significant lag, however, is caused by the ocean: along the east coast of Queensland January is hotter than December and within a very short distance from just west of the highland ridge to Cairns on the coast, the hottest time is delayed from November to January. On the west coast, thermal conditions are complicated by the reversal of ocean circulation: the northward drift of cooler waters delays the peak of heat until February all along the coast, while January is hottest only a few kilometres inland. The northwest coast records further complications because of some limited upwelling of cooler water during periods of easterly wind, and a later spread of warm surface water (Gentilli, 1972b) which gives March the hottest days in Port Hedland. A secondary peak of highest maxima in March or even April is also strictly coastal, being found from Port Hedland to Darwin and on Thursday Island. It should be noted also that at Bunbury, W.A., sheltered by the Naturaliste Peninsula from the northward coastal drift, it is January that is hotter than February, a unique case in some 2,500 km of coastline.

On the average, tropical Australia has at least nine months per year with mean daily maxima above

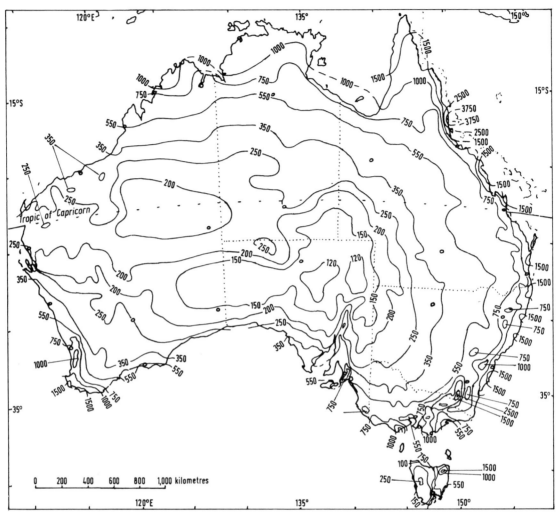

Fig. 1.15 Annual rainfall. The distribution is mostly affected by predominant onshore or offshore winds, topography, and distance downwind from the coast (Bureau of Meteorology).

27° C and six above 32°C. However, months with mean daily maxima above 38°C do not occur near the tropical coast, but only in the interior and up to a maximum of six annually (October-March) around Marble Bar, W.A. High temperatures are the main determinant of high water consumption in Australian cities (McMahon and Weeks, 1973).

Australia is too small and surrounded by too much ocean to show extremes of temperature except where heat transport intervenes; if the summers can be very hot, the winters are never cold, except in the south-eastern highlands. Often the cold clear nights are followed by warm days. Frosts are common in winter, especially in July, but are never extreme or prolonged.

They occasionally reach the higher ground beyond the tropic, especially in the Hamersley Ranges, W.A., around Alice Springs, and in southeast Queensland.

The Australian absolute minimum, − 22° C, was recorded on two occasions; the site, below Charlotte Pass near Mount Kosciusko, is a flat hollow which cools effectively because of night radiation while at the same time collecting the cold air that drains downslope. There are several mountains with nightly frosts from May to September and no thaw on many winter days; snow lasts long enough to support a short skiing season on the Snowy Mountains, Victorian Alps and Tasmanian highlands.

PRECIPITATION

Very nearly all precipitation comes as rainfall, other forms being negligible: traces of snow have been recorded at many points south of the tropic, and further north on the eastern highlands, but the only significant snowfalls have been in the southeastern corner. On the Australian Alps and in Tasmania snow falls every winter above 1,000 or 1,500 m, and may last over the summer in a few sheltered hollows. Hail, although locally disastrous at times, has an ephemeral duration in time; it falls only in the hot season in the northern regions and both with summer thunderstorms and winter fronts in the southern areas. Dew is common during clear nights in the rainy seasons and may be significant in environmental ecology, but would hardly affect any long-term climatic data.

Rainfall itself is far from plentiful: about half of Australia gets less than 350 mm of water per year and over a third gets less than 250 mm, which is the normal minimum to avoid aridity. In South Australia 83 per cent and in Western Australia 58 per cent of the land get less than 250 mm per year, and so do 20 per cent of New South Wales and 13 per cent of Queensland. On the other hand, 16 per cent of New South Wales, 23 per cent of Queensland, 27 per cent of Victoria and about three-quarters of Tasmania get more than 750 mm per year. The driest area is the low-lying Lake Eyre basin with less than 125 mm per year on the average, and occasionally much less (Fig. 1.15). It is in some ways more damaging when the expected rains fail and drought occurs in a normally rainy district: this happened over large parts of Australia in 1864–6, 1880–6, 1895–1903, 1914, 1918–20, 1939–45 (Foley, 1957), 1969 and 1970 (Fitzpatrick, 1970). Areas of normally wet climate may be subject to arid conditions long enough to kill plants and animals and to force the abandonment of agricultural or pastoral land.

There have been many studies of drought and it would be impossible to recapitulate them here. The very definition of drought varies from author to author. In recent years, after the general acceptance of the concept of 'effective' rainfall, the definition of drought has often been tied to that concept, but in some cases it has still been thought more practical to set a drought limit in some round figure, easily detected by inspection of the records. Other aspects of drought which have been studied, among others, are the waiting times for drought relief in Queensland (Verhagen and Hirst, 1961) which are greater for months following dry months than for months following wet months, i.e. a drought that has already begun is likely to last longer than one which has not started (and could in any case only be studied in retrospect). Fitzpatrick (1970) calculated the intensity and probability of droughts in the agricultural parts of Western Australia, setting the critical amount at the 15 percentile, and the indicator period at April-July.

Various statistical techniques have been used to assess the variability of the rainfall. They all agree that a most variable area occurs around Onslow, W.A., but the agreement ends there. Arithmetic measures of dispersal (mean and standard deviations) also agree on the second and bigger area of rainfall variability over the Simpson Desert where long dry sequences are interrupted by occasional deluges. Other measures emphasize Arnhem Land or Townsville instead, because in the latter regions there is a normally abundant rainfall which occasionally dips to very low amounts. Most measures agree that the most reliable rainfall (i.e. most consistent year after year) occurs in the far southwestern corner, followed by the similarly exposed southeastern South Australia and southwestern Victoria. Arnhem Land and Cape York Peninsula show good rainfall reliability only with the arithmetic tests.

For the short-term assessment of each year's (or each month's) rainfall, Gibbs and Maher (1967) used deciles, so that relative excesses or deficiencies are shown around the central median value. Amounts in the lowest two-decile range are taken as very deficient, irrespective of their absolute magnitude. This information is now currently given by the Bureau of Meteorology in its monthly climatic summaries.

Besides these irregular droughts, most of Australia is subject to periodical seasonal droughts. The dry semester is April-September along a diagonal belt which runs from Wyndham, W.A., to Bourke, N.S.W. The drought gradually lags away from this axis, following the monthly advance of the rainfall (Fig. 1.17), to occur in May-October as far as Townsville, Q. in the east and Derby, W.A., in the west. The trend continues farther west, with dry June-November from Broome to the western edge of the Nullarbor, dry July-December from Port Hedland to near Kalgoorlie, and so on, to end with dry November-April from Perth to Esperance, W.A. and beyond the Bight to Eyre Peninsula and most of the Murray Valley. This aridity or drought, be it occasional or persistent, or regularly or irregularly seasonal, is a most conspicuous feature of the Australian mainland environment.

The wetter parts of Australia are widely separated: much of the eastern seaboard with Tasmania, the extreme north, the extreme southwest. Of these, only the eastern seaboard has a relatively uniform rain, gradually changing from a pronounced summer maximum in the north to a subdued winter maximum in the south. The heaviest falls are usually registered on the steep seaward slopes of northeast Queensland, around Innisfail and Cairns. Several times annual totals have reached some 5 m; the yearly average at Innisfail is 3,912 mm. Only a short distance to the

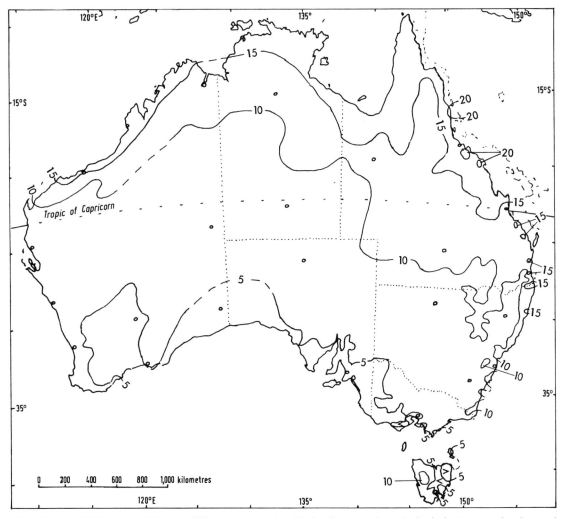

Fig. 1.16   Rainfall intensity. Units are millimetres per rain day. Notice the greater intensity in the hotter coastal regions and to a lesser extent against highland barriers (after Jennings, 1967).

south, the rainfall decreases very markedly, and the number of rainy days also drops from over 150 to less than 100 per year. At the southern end, in Tasmania, the heaviest falls are on the western slopes, the yearly average at Lake Margaret is 3,685 mm, falling in some 250 rainy days.

By comparison, both the northern rainy area from the Kimberleys to Arnhem Land and the south-western one which stretches from Geraldton to Albany are far less varied in their regimes, with rains between November and March in the former and between April and October in the latter (Fig. 1.17). There is a great difference in the intensity of the falls (Jennings, 1967): in the north, the mean fall is 15 mm per wet day, with a likely once-a-year maximum of 110 mm, whereas

in the southwest the mean fall varies around 5 or 6 mm per wet day (7–8 along the Darling Scarp), with a once-a-year maximum of 35 to 50 mm (Fig. 1.16).

Tropical cyclones mobilize such enormous quantities of water vapour that the derived precipitation may be extreme in total amount as well as intensity: it is not rare to record some 250 mm in 24 hours or totals of 700–800 mm in the three or four days that a cyclone takes to transit over a point. The greatest fall in one day was 907 mm, at Crohamhurst, Q.

The seasonal distribution of the rainfall has been studied mathematically by Fitzpatrick (1964) by means of the Fourier harmonic analysis. Six harmonics were separated but only the first (annual, Fig. 1.17) and second (semi-annual) are highly significant, in

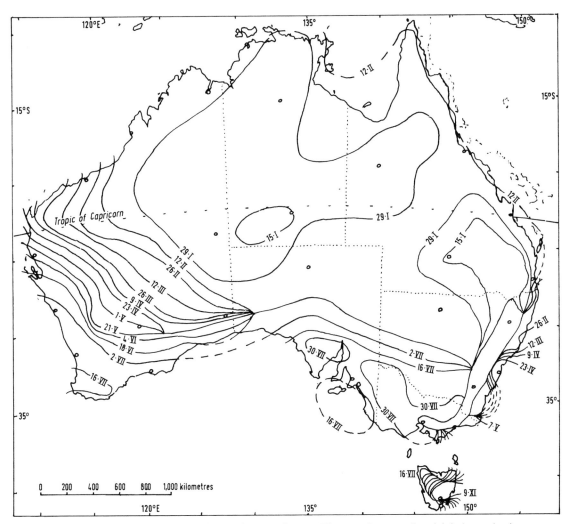

Fig. 1.17 Isochrones of maximum rainfall from the annual wave. The map shows, at fortnightly intervals, the progress of maximum rainfall with the advance of the seasons (from Fitzpatrick, 1964).

fact in the southwest of the mainland and in western Tasmania, the first harmonic accounts for 90 per cent of the variance of the monthly rainfall, and in most of tropical Australia for 75 per cent (Fig. 1.18). The major inadequacy of the first harmonic occurs in those dry areas where tropical cyclones are important late-summer rain-bearers and also in the winter-rain areas affected by the awakening of the subtropical jet stream. The second (semi-annual) harmonic fits the secondary peak of winter rains found in most of the areas dominated by summer rain (Fig. 1.19) and thus brings about a much better fit of the computed curve to the observed data.

More complex are the data used by McBoyle (1971), but more simplistic the outcome (Fig. 1.20). Twenty climatic variables were used, of which seven were quantities of rain or numbers of rainy days, and the most important composite Factor I detected explained 48.2 per cent of the total variance. Conspicuous in that factor were annual and July humidity, July precipitation, and annual and July numbers of rainy days, all variables which increase very rapidly in magnitude or frequency with increasing latitude south of the subtropical high pressure belt. Conversely, Factor II, which combined positively July mean and minimum temperatures, annual and January rainfall and humidity, and strongly negatively the yearly thermal amplitude, accounted for 32.3 per cent of the total variance. Obviously, these are the trends of variables increasingly associated with decreasing latitude and an

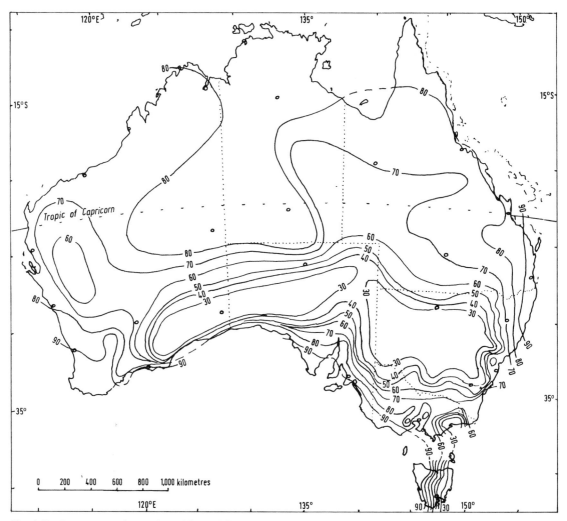

Fig. 1.18 Percentage variance of monthly rainfall due to the annual wave. The annual wave, or first harmonic in the analysis, accounts for up to 90 per cent of the monthly rhythm (from Fitzpatrick, 1964).

inflow of warm moist air. They recur in a subdued way in the southwestern corner of the mainland, where a warm coastal drift raises winter temperatures and reduces the yearly amplitude and yet one of the key variables, January rainfall, is minimal.

Factor III is dominated by the July/January rainfall ratio, and sharply separates the 'Mediterranean' climatic regions (boundary II in Fig. 1.20). One wonders what the computer's verdict would have been if the January/July ratio had been taken instead!

BIOCLIMATOLOGY

For many years, the climatic boundaries determined with Köppen's system (Fig. 1.21) were used as a first approximation of bioclimatic limits. A considerable

amount of agroclimatological research was carried out at the Waite Agricultural Research Institute at Adelaide; the relevant publications by J. Davidson, Prescott and Trumble are listed and reviewed by Gentilli (1970), while a thorough review with regard to the 'length of growing period' concept is given by Marshall (1973). Basically, the accepted principle is that plant growth is controlled by the availability of moisture, which results from the balance between water available from precipitation P and water loss through evaporation and transpiration E.

In earlier studies, the rainfall sufficient to begin plant growth was called 'influential', a term later replaced by 'effective'. The length of the growing season was taken as the period during which there is

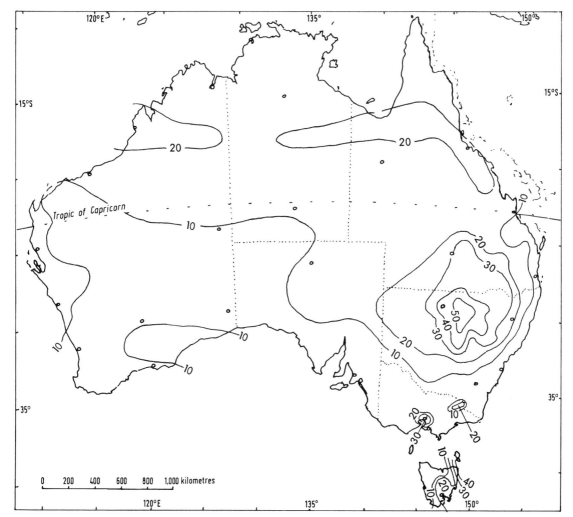

Fig. 1.19 Percentage variance of monthly rainfall due to the semestral wave. This, the second harmonic in the analysis, is much more localized, but very significant in northern New South Wales (from Fitzpatrick, 1964).

effective rainfall, i.e. rainfall above the minimum for growth. Also, favourable conditions must last sufficiently long to enable plants to complete a significant growth stage or function, hence the concept of length of climatic growing period.

A ratio P/E presupposed evaporation data for a sufficient number of stations, which was not at all the case, and for this reason a ratio $P/s.d.$ was proposed, *s.d.* being the saturation deficit of the air at the given temperature, expressed in height of a mercury column (obtainable from tables). Since saturation deficit is the main factor controlling evaporation, it is possible to calculate the conversion of one ratio into the other.

There is a great discrepancy in the values of P/E taken as critical or significant from the value of

1 proposed by Hettner, who was mainly concerned with hydrology and geomorphology, to the lower values determined by the Waite workers, 0.5 or 1/3 for the beginning of plant growth ('break of season'). Continued plant growth requires a higher ratio if the plants have a high rate of transpiration, and much less, perhaps 0.25 or less, if the plants are adapted to very low transpiration (cf. a review of such adaptations in Slatyer, 1964).

To allow for this varying response, Prescott (1946) suggested an exponential reduction of E, raising % to a power of 0.7. Thus the formula widely used now is $P/E^{0.7}$ and limiting values are set according to the adaptation of plants to drought.

A combined moisture and heat index (hydrothermal

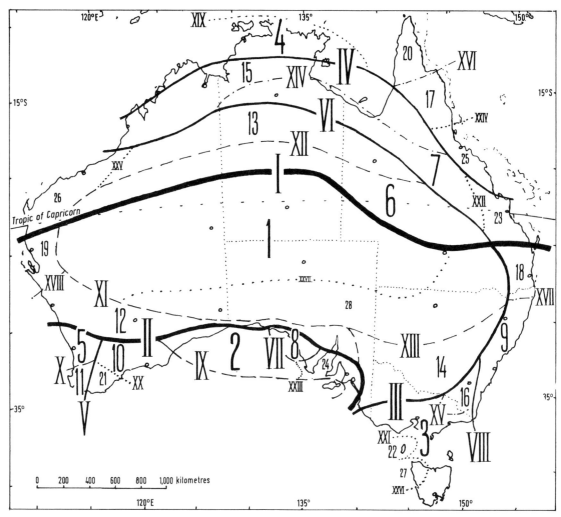

Fig. 1.20 Hierarchy of regional climatic differences. Lines and roman numerals show boundaries, and arab numerals regions. Thickness of lines and size of symbols are proportioned to climatological significance, assessed from the steepness of climatic gradients (after McBoyle, 1971).

index) was first devised by Livingston (1916) who used it to map the climatic zonation of the United States. The original expression was

$$I_{mt} = I_t \frac{I_p}{I_e}$$

where I_{mt} represents the moisture-temperature or hydrothermal index, I_t the index of temperature efficiency as expressed by a physiological index (Fig. 1.22) based on the rate of elongation of maize shoots at different temperatures, I_p and I_e the totals of precipitation and potential evaporation for the period concerned. Livingston's original paper is extensively quoted with all the necessary detail by Klages (1947)

in a publication which may be more readily available.

Livingston's work had been about half a century ahead of his time, partly because original evaporation data needed for the moisture index were far too scarce, and had subsequently been temporarily eclipsed by Thornthwaite's later and much more publicized work. The gradual evolution of the Waite studies provided a way of overcoming the difficulty. The ground was ready for the application of the principle to Australian conditions, and this was done independently by B. R. Davidson (1969), Fitzpatrick and Nix (1970) and Gentilli (1970). Davidson was mainly concerned with crops, Fitzpatrick and Nix with sown pastures, Gentilli with natural vegetation.

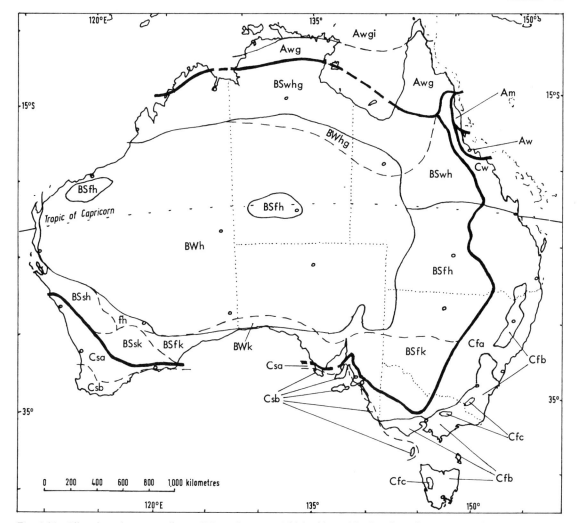

Fig. 1.21 Climatic regions according to Köppen's system. Thick, thin and broken lines show an approximate hierarchy of climatic boundaries. The letters are the standard Köppen symbols. Notice the concentric pattern, and the effect of highlands.

Davidson (1969) took as a moisture indicator one version of the Waite index, $P/s.d.^{0.75}$. He also assumed that the ground may store up to 5 inches (ab. 125 mm) of water. If any month's $P/s.d.^{0.75}$ exceeds the value of 12, the excess of P (up to 5 inches) is carried over into the next month, and added to its rainfall before the next month's $P/s.d.^{0.75}$ is calculated. Davidson took a value of 8 as the effective maximum moisture ratio used by plants on the assumption that field conditions are mostly well below full moisture capacity, and 4 the minimum below which growth is inhibited. To obtain it in percentage form, the moisture growth index was written

$$G_m = \frac{P/s.d.^{0.75} - 4}{8 - 4} \times \frac{100}{1}$$

and could well be rewritten here

$$G_m = \frac{100(P'/E^{0.75} - 0.4)}{0.4}$$

to stress the fact that P' is the actual month's rainfall plus any surplus from the previous month, and E to make it possible to use the existing estimates of evaporation.

Davidson (1969) also proposed a thermal growth index

$$G_T = \frac{R}{105} \times \frac{100}{1}$$

where R is Livingston's (1916) physiological index of

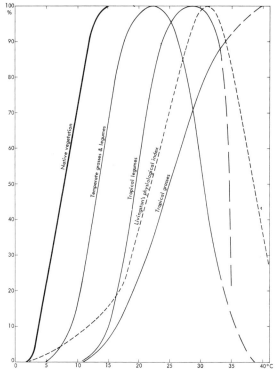

Fig. 1.22 Nomogram for the assessment of bioclimatic indices. Given the mean monthly temperature, the graph allows an approximate estimate of Livingston's physiological index of plant growth (as used by B. R. Davidson, short dashed line), of the thermal posture growth indices of Fitzpatrick and Nix (thin lines), and of Gentilli's coefficient of thermal inhibition for native vegetation (thick line).

plant growth, which had a significant maximum of 105 at a mean monthly temperature of 34°C, declining rapidly to 20 at 16° C at the cool end, and at 40° C at the hot end and zero at 2° C and at 48° C. The value of the index can easily be read from the graph (Fig. 1.22).

By combining the two indices, Davidson obtained a growth index, which could be rewritten here

$$G_{MT} = \frac{100\,R(P'/E^{0.75} - 0.4)}{42}$$

The number of months in which $P'/E^{0.75} > 0.4$ and also the mean monthly temperature $T > 36°$ F (for all practical purposes $T > 2°$ C) gives the length of the (agricultural) growing season. Davidson gives a map of the annual 'growth potential' of Australia for the peripheral belt where the growing season exceeds four months (Fig. 1.23). There is no provision for the yet important types of semi-desert and desert vegetation adapted to a shorter 'growing season', and to erratic falls of rain that fit into no 'season' at all.

B. R. Davidson's growth index has been severely criticized (Marshall, 1973) but it represented a revival of a fundamental concept and a synthesis worthy of further development. Among the points worthy of further study are the classification of monthly values and the evaluation of arid bioclimates.

Fitzpatrick and Nix (1970) went back to fundamental principles, computed weekly values of estimated solar radiation, maximum and minimum temperature, rainfall, relative humidity and estimated potential evaporation for a large number of stations. From the many observations of plant growth under experimentally controlled conditions they evolved a light index, a thermal index and a moisture index.

To assess the moisture index, they assumed that the potential evapotranspiration E_t equalled $0.8E$, the measured or estimated tank evaporation. They also allowed for a maximum ground storage of 4 inches (102 mm) of water, at any one time, from which plants can draw when the rainfall is not enough to counter E_t. The actual evapotranspiration E_a is thus calculated as part of the water budget. Perfect moisture conditions are achieved when $E_a/E_t = 1$.

From a comparison of summer and winter maps, it appears that only a very narrow coastal belt from Fraser Island, Q. to the eastern end of Gippsland and Tasmania has an index value higher than 0.8 throughout the year. This value reaches farther north to Cairns and across to Katherine, N.T. and the Kimberleys in the summer only and southwestwards past Portland, Vic. and along the South Australian coast in the winter only, with a large outlier from Geraldton to Esperance, W.A. However, the striking aspect is the extreme size of the area that remains below 0.4 or even below 0.2 throughout most of the year.

Evaluating the effects of heat on plant growth, Fitzpatrick and Nix recognized that distinct thermal responses separated three main groups of plants, namely tropical grasses, tropical legumes and temperate grasses and legumes, which achieve their optimal dry-matter production at mean daily temperatures around 40, 28 and 22° C respectively, and begin to decline at higher temperatures. This information gives a thermal index (Fig. 1.22) which can be calculated for any locality. In northern Australia, summer values are 0.70 to 0.80 for tropical grasses and 0.95 for tropical legumes; winter values drop to less than 0,50 for tropical grasses and 0.90 to 0.50 for tropical legumes, but rise to 0.80 or 0.90 for temperate grasses and legumes. In southeastern Australia values become insignificant for tropical plants, but reach summer values of 0.90 to 1.00 for temperate plants, to drop to 0.20 during the winter.

As to a light index, Fitzpatrick and Nix found summer values of 0.90 to 0.95 over most of Australia, with the exception of the rainiest coastal locations

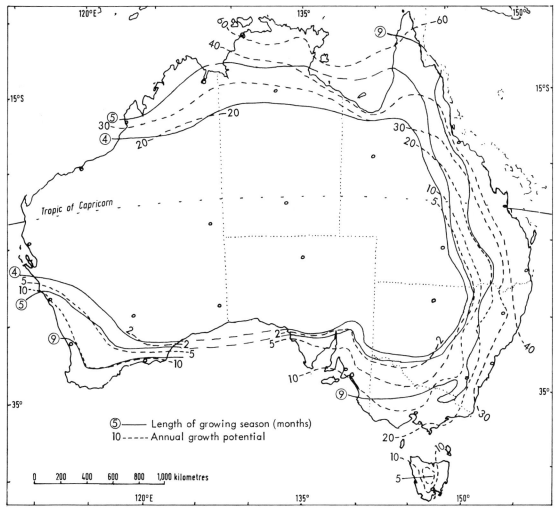

Fig. 1.23   Length of growing season and growth potential (after B. R. Davidson, 1969).

during monsoonal spells. The index fell to just below 0.90 during the dry tropical winter and to lower values further south, to reach a minimum of 0.50 in Tasmania.

From the three distinct indices was evolved a growth index equal to their product

$$G.I. = M.I. \times T.I. \times L.I.$$

which was calculated separately for each group of pastures. Conditions are moderately good for tropical grasses: areas > 0.6 are found only in the Kimberleys, W.A., north of Katherine, N.T. and from Georgetown to Mapoon, Q. Northern Australia is a better environment for tropical legumes: > 0.6 across from Broome, W.A. to Daly Waters, N.T. and west of Townsville, then south to taper out past Port Macquarie, N.S.W.; > 0.8 area only slightly less, to include Katherine,

N.T., Croydon, Q. and a very narrow belt from Cairns to Brisbane. Temperate pastures are limited by the phasing of the index values more than by their inadequacies: throughout the winter-rain area the peak of the moisture index corresponds to the trough of the thermal index and to some depression in the light index. In the summer-rain area, the summer heat is excessive while the moisture is plentiful, and when the heat moderates and becomes optimal there is no moisture at all. Only in the southeastern coastal and subcoastal belts are the three climatic indices favourable most of the time and with a combined peak in summer and a tendency to depression in winter, which becomes marked especially in the higher latitudes where heat and light become inadequate.

Fitzpatrick and Nix's work provides the foundation

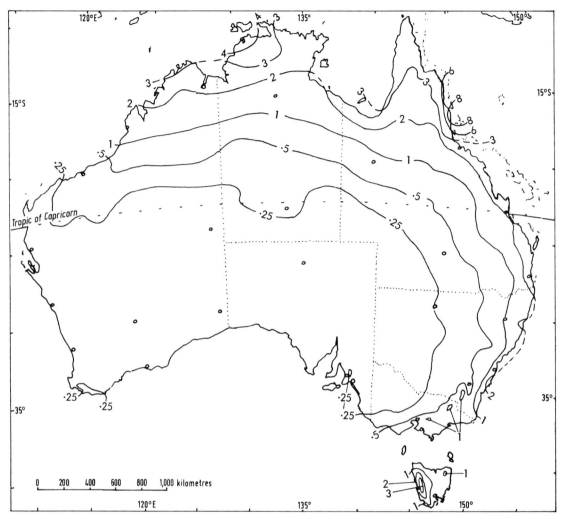

Fig. 1.24 Phytohydroxeric index, January. The index of moisture effectiveness at a time when there is no thermal inhibition on native plant growth.

for much further research. As it stands, it gives separate and not comparable thermal indices for tropical grasses, tropical legumes, and temperate grasses and legumes, so it still fails to provide a unified bioclimatic index. The subdivision into weekly instead of monthly periods allows a finer analysis, but calls for data not easily or readily available. It does not allow for a bioclimatic interpretation of the main vegetation regions, which are such a significant aspect of the Australian landscape.

A first approach towards an application of the moisture index to the natural environment involves the assessment of each month's moisture status (Figs 1.24 and 1.25). A general grading could be as follows (Gentilli, 1970):

Monthly moisture grading	Monthly $P/E^{0.7}$ ratio
perarid	< 0.12
arid	0.12 to 0.25
semi-arid	0.25 to 0.50
subhumid	0.50 to 1.25
humid	1.25 to 2.50
perhumid	> 2.50

Any amount in excess of 4 should be disregarded because the additional water will run off almost immediately, thus going beyond the reach of most plants.

In the southern half of Australia, winter is cold

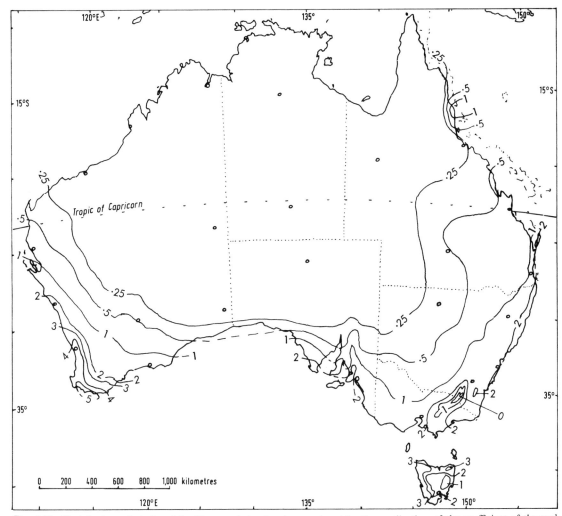

Fig. 1.25 Phytohydroxeric index, July. The raw index has been reduced by the application of the coefficient of thermal efficiency, hence the low values given for the southeastern highlands and Tasmania.

enough to retard or even prevent plant functions and it is necessary to take this thermal inhibition into account, but only to the extent that it is likely to affect native vegetation.

The basic relationship is approximately as follows:

Mean monthly temperature	Plant growth	Coefficient of thermal efficiency
⩽ 3C	absolutely none	0
> 3 to < 7C	almost none	0.1 to 0.3
7 to < 10C	minimal	0.4 to 0.6
10 to < 13C	moderate	0.7 to 0.9
⩾ 13C	active	1

The monthly moisture grading of the colder regions is thus reduced through multiplication by the *thermal efficiency* coefficient (Fig. 1.26). The final result (the monthly *phytohydroxeric* value) is an assessment of monthly bioclimatic effectiveness which may in turn show the length of the effective season in months' duration (Fig. 1.27).

This simple concept of effective season may exclude months which have less than the effective rainfall (although fractions of a month may be counted) and does not allow for the inclusion of different rates corresponding to different phases of plant growth. An alternative is to cumulate the twelve monthly values to arrive at an annual *phytohydroxeric index* (Gentilli, 1970) which is an indicator of vegetation potential (Fig. 1.28).

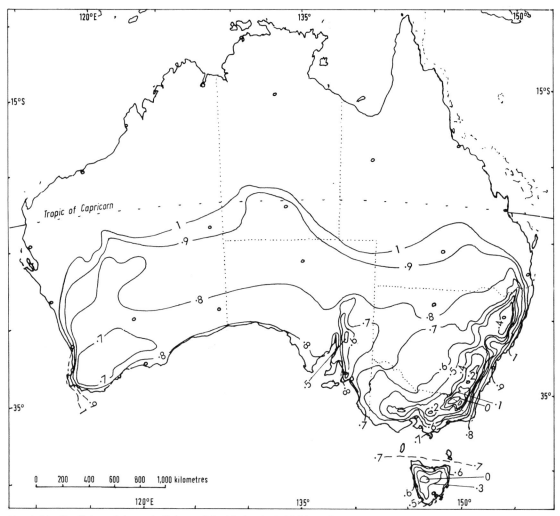

Fig. 1.26 Coefficient of thermal efficiency, July. Notice the inhibiting effect of altitude.

Annual phytohydroxeric index	Zonal vegetation
> 25	rainforest
10 to 25	forest
5 to 10	woodland or tree savanna
3 to 5	grassland or scler. woodlands
1 to 3	scler. grassland or arid scrub
0 to 1	sandy or stony desert

The lack of effective moisture conditions when potential transpiration reaches its maximum effects the vegetation, which responds with greater sclerophyl-

ly, hence the alternative vegetation types shown in the table.

The lists of climatic types found in Australia give the impression that there is a great variety of climates. This is only true up to a point, because long-day climates and very cold climates are obviously excluded by latitude. Also, several climates that occur in Australia do so only over very small areas, as our maps show all too clearly—and, most unfortunately, these are the wetter and the cooler climates. Perhaps, in order to savour more fully the significance of the chapters that follow, one might do the simple exercise that I recommend to my thinking students: draw Australia upside down, latitude for latitude, on a map of Euro-Africa on the same scale, and plot the position

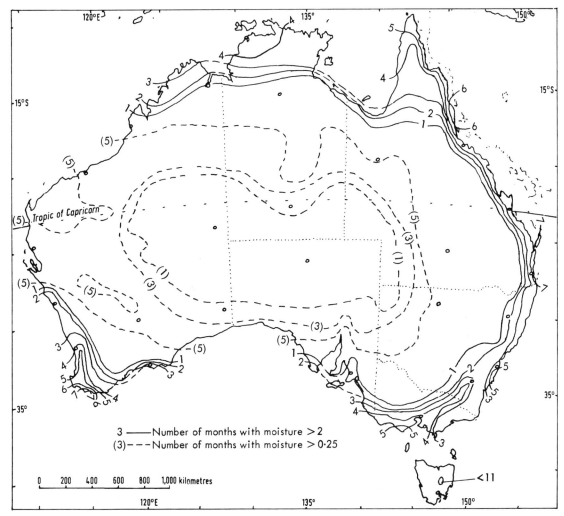

Fig. 1.27 Duration of the moisture growing season in months. This map complements Fig. 1.23, giving subdivisions of the arid regions, and showing how the moisture climate of the southeast may have a uniform rainfall regime but not necessarily plentiful moisture in most months.

of the main cities (Fig. 11.1). With much of Australia sprawling across the Sudan, Perth in Morocco and Tasmania in the latitude of Portugal, the developers of wide open spaces might gather some sobering thoughts.

REFERENCES

Brookfield, Muriel (1970), *Winds of Arid Australia*, CSIRO Div. Land Res. Tech. Pap. No. 30.

Budyko, M. I. (1956), *Teplovoi balans zemnoi poverkhnosti*, Gidrometeorologicheskoe Izdatel'stvo, Leningrad.

——(ed.) (1963), *Atlas teplovogo balansa*, Gidrometeorologicheskoe Izdatel'stvo, Leningrad.

Bureau of Meteorology (1964), 'Tropical cyclones in the northern Australian regions', *Met. Summ.* (annual).

Ceplecha, V. J. (1971), 'The distribution of the main components of the water balance in Australia', *Aust. Geogr.*, 11, 455–62.

Coleman, F. (1972), 'Frequencies, tracks and intensities of tropical cyclones in the Australian region 1909–1969', *Met. Summ.*, July 1972.

Davidson, B. R. (1969), *Australia Wet or Dry?* Melbourne University Press, Melbourne.

Fitzpatrick, E. A. (1964), 'Seasonal distribution of rainfall in Australia analysed by Fourier methods', *Archiv. Meteor. Geoph. Bioklim. B.*, 13, 270–86.

——(1970), 'The expectancy of deficient winter rainfall and the potential for severe drought in the southwest

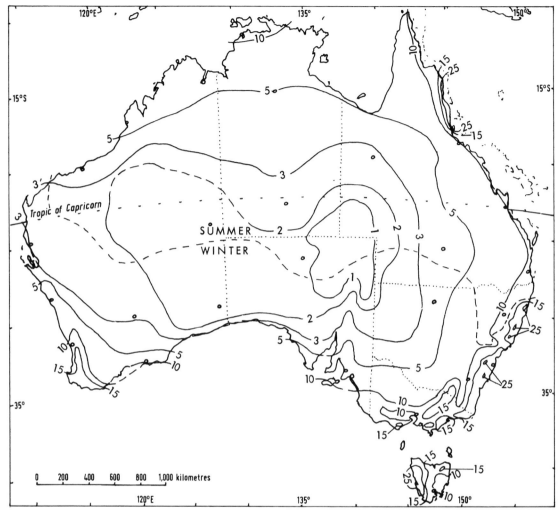

Fig. 1.28 Phytohydroxeric zones. The map shows the annual total of the twelve monthly net phytohydroxeric indices (i.e. allowing for excess overflow and thermal efficiency). Its merit is that it is strictly based on a single index. It provides climatic boundaries very close to the boundaries of the natural vegetation regions.

of Western Australia', Inst. Agric., *Univ. W. A., Agron. Dept., Misc. Publ.* 70/1.

Fitzpatrick, E. A. and Nix, H. A. (1970), 'The climatic factor in Australian grassland ecology' in R. M. Moore (ed.), *Australian Grasslands*, Australian National University Press, Canberra, pp. 3–26.

Foley, J. C. (1957), 'Droughts in Australia', *Bur. Met. Bull.* 32.

Gentilli, J. (1970), 'The evaluation of phytophydroxeric zones', *Colloquium Geographicum*, 12, 58–77.

——(ed.) (1971), *Climates of Australia and New Zealand* (Vol. 13 of *World Survey of Climatology*), Elsevier, Amsterdam.

——(1972a), *Australian Climate Patterns*, Nelson, Melbourne.

——(1972b), 'Thermal anomalies in the eastern Indian Ocean', *Nature Phys. Sci.*, 238, 93–5.

——(1974), 'Epitropical climatology of the subtropical jet stream', *Bonn Meteor. Abh.*, 17, 137–65.

Gentilli, J. and Milton, J. D. (1972), 'Zonal belt terminology', *Bull. Am. Met. Soc.*, 53, 26–7.

Gibbs, W. J. and Maher, J. V. (1967), 'Rainfall deciles as drought indicators', *Bur. Met. Bull.* 48.

Hawke, G. S. (1973), 'The "Botany Bay breeze"', *Weatherfront*, 1(2), 15–19.

Healy, T. R. (1972), 'Some climatological considerations of 200 mb troughs and associated jet streams over the Australian region', *Aust. Geogr. Stud.*, 10, 161–81.

Hopley, D. (1967), 'A statistical approach to the relationship between coastal erosion and changes in wind patterns at Byron Bay, N.S.W.', *Aust. Geogr.*, 10, 275–85.

——(1974), 'The cyclone Althea storm surge', *Aust. Geogr. Stud.*, 12, 90–106.

Hounam, C. E. (1961), 'Evaporation in Australia', *Bur. Met. Bull.* 44.

——(1963), 'Estimates of solar radiation over Australia,' *Aust. Met. Mag.*, 43, 1–14.

Jennings, J. N. (1967), 'Two maps of rainfall intensity in Australia', *Aust. Geogr.*, 10, 256–62.

Klages, K. H. W. (1947), *Ecological Crop Geography*, Macmillan, New York.

Livingston, B. E. (1916), 'A single index to represent both moisture and temperature conditions as related to plants', *Phys. Res.*, 1, 421–40.

McBoyle, G. R. (1971), 'Climatic classification of Australia by computer', *Aust. Geogr. Stud.*, 9, 1–14.

McGrath, C. A. (1973), 'Some characteristics of Sydney sea-breezes', *Weatherfront*, 1(2), 3–9.

McMahon, T. A. and Weeks, C. R. (1973), 'Climate and water use in Australian cities', *Aust. Geogr. Stud.*, 11, 99–108.

Marshall, Ann (1973), 'The use and misuse of the "length of growing period" concept', *Aust. Geogr.*, 12, 334–9.

Milton, D. (1974), 'Some observations of global trends in tropical cyclone frequencies', *Weather*, 29, 267–70.

Morse, R. N. and Read, W. R. W. (1967), 'The develop-ment of a solar still for Australian conditions', *Mech. Chem. Engineer. Trans. Inst. Engin. Aust.*, Vol. MC3 (1), 71–80.

Newton, C. W. (ed.) (1972), 'Meteorology of the southern hemisphere', *Met. Mogr.*, Vol. 13, No. 35.

Paltridge, G. W. and Sargent, S. L. (1970), 'Solar and thermal radiation measurements to 30 km altitude at low solar elevations', *J. Atmos. Sci.*, 28, 242–53.

Prescott, J. A. (1946), 'A climatic index', *Nature*, 157, 555.

Prescott, J. A. and Thomas, Joyce A. (1949), 'The length of the growing season', *Proc. R. Geogr. Soc. Aust.* (S. A.), 50, 42–6.

Slatyer, R. O. (1964), 'Efficiency of water utilization by arid zone vegetation', *Ann. Arid. Zone*, 3, 1–12.

Verhagen, A. M. W. and Hirst, F. (1961), *Waiting Times for Drought Relief in Queensland*, CSIRO Div. Math. Stat. Tech. Pap. No. 9.

——(1969), *First Occurrence Times of d Consecutive Dry Months in Queensland*, CSIRO Div. Math. Stat. Tech. Pap. No. 29.

Watson, I. and Gentilli, J. (1974), 'Thermal inversion by advection in a subtropical summer', *Aust. Geogr. Stud.*, 12, 119–25.

Wittwer, E. L. (1973), 'Seasonal changes in wind regimes of the north Australian and adjoining intertropical area', *Aust. Geogr.*, 12, 340–62.

2 PHYSIOGRAPHIC OUTLINES AND REGIONS

J. N. JENNINGS   J. A. MABBUTT

With its land area of 8.5 million km², Australia is the smallest of the continents, less than a fifth the size of Asia (Table 2.1). Even if brought to its true continental dimensions by including the continental shelf—and Australia has proportionately the largest continental shelf of all—it still remains less than Antarctica and surpasses only Europe, which is a continent in a cultural sense only.

If we were to take its continental shelf margin rather than today's resting point of the sea against the land, the Australian continent would be made more complete structurally and physiographically in that the Cenozoic folded mountain ranges of New Guinea would then be included. The meagre dimensions of Torres Strait, only 150 km wide and a mere 18 m in maximum sill depth, point to the almost accidental nature of this separation of Australia and the second largest island in the world.

It is this absence of lofty young fold ranges which renders Australia, in its narrower definition, the lowest of the continents, whether measured by the altitude of its highest point, Mt Kosciusko, or by mean continental altitude. The low mean altitude of 330 m is comparable only with that of Europe, but this matching conceals an important difference, for as Table 2.1 shows it is the *flatness* of Australia which must be stressed rather than the extent of lowland.

Australia is primarily a land of plateaux at low and medium altitudes, and only secondarily of low plains. Indeed there is a smaller proportion of coastal plain than in any other continent except South America. The monotony of the flat Australian landscapes is almost unparalleled: to travel hundreds of kilometres without significant change in landform is common-place.

The great extent of level surfaces is due partly to long episodes of subaerial planation in its geomorphic history and in part to the structural expression of subhorizontal platform strata which extensively overlie the granitic basement of the continent. Both types of

Table 2.1   Dimensions of Continents

	Australia	Europe	Asia (incl. Europe)	Africa	North America	South America	Antarctica
Area (km² × 10⁶)	8.5	10	54.2	29.8	24.2	18	13.1
Area incl. continental shelf	11	10.8	65	31	31	20	15
Mean altitude (m)	330	290	860	660	780	650	2,200
Highest point (m)	2,225	5,633	8,848	5,895	6,193	6,959	5,140
Lowlands below 200 m (%)	39	57	25	10	30	38	6
Plateaux, etc. above 1,000 m (%)	2	7	30	23	27	13	86

Sources: A. Cailleux (1968), *Anatomy of the Earth*, World University Library, London; H. Louis (1968), *Allgemeine Geomorphologie*, De Gruyter, Berlin; E. Kossinna, 'Die Erdöberflache' in B. Gutenberg (ed.) *Handbuch der Geophysik*, Vol. 2, pp. 854–69.

plateau surface reflect the tectonic stability of Australia, with an absence of important diastrophism since the Palaeozoic. Later earth movements have been mainly epeirogenic, in association with a marked broad upwarping of the continental margins. This has resulted in a pattern of peripheral higher ground, in which stepped erosion surfaces and incised valleys mark stages in uplift, and of vast lower-lying plateaux and plains in the interior.

Variety is brought into Australian relief more by the dissection of uplifted level surfaces than in any other way. 'Mountains of circumdenudation' carved out by the dissection of plateau margins are the commonest mountain type in this continent. Upland skylines are mainly subdued and the most impressive relief features are the deep V-shaped valleys and gorges cut below. The greatest relative relief in Australia, namely the great sweep of slope of 1,700 m from the Snowy Mountain summits to the Geehi River, is almost balanced in vertical range by the opposing valley side. The Pinnacle (1,582 m), isolated by erosion at the southwestern end of the Grey Mare Range, is not dwarfed by Mt Townsend (2,210 m), for the latter, like its neighbours including Mt Kosciusko, is but an erosional residual above the general surface of the upland. By causing this deep incision of plateau margins, Cenozoic epeirogenetic uplift has redeemed in some degree the lack of young orogenic movements in Australia. The marginal regions are well provided with deep gorges, from the Hamersley Plateaux to Tasmania. Wollombombi Falls, with a drop of 472 m the highest waterfall in Australia, are not grossly outmatched on a world scale, though relatively unimportant if the volume of water in the cascade is considered.

In a world view Australia is aseismic, although dislocation along the Meckering Fault in the earthquake of October 1968 was a sharp if minor reminder that no part of the continent, not even its ancient granitic shield nucleus, can be regarded as absolutely stable. It remains true however that the continent is lacking in major neotectonics, and we find here no landforms expressive of youthful rifting, faulting or folding on a large scale. Tectonic landforms such as the first-cycle anticlinal ridges of the Cape and Rough Ranges of Western Australia, the silcrete-capped domal structures of southwest Queensland, or the fault-block topography of the Mt Lofty Ranges are of modest relief only. The larger playa basins of arid Australia owe their origins to geologically young faulting and warping, but although extensive—Lake Eyre attains a magnificent 15,000 km² when it fills occasionally—they are nevertheless shallow and ephemeral and there are no equivalents here of deep tectonic basin lakes such as Lake Baikal or the Dead Sea.

A lack of earthquakes goes with a lack of active volcanoes, and Australia is the only continent to be without present vulcanicity. Nevertheless Mt Gambier erupted as little as 1,400 years ago, and in the Cenozoic volcanic provinces of east Queensland and western Victoria, the latter extending over the South Australian border to beyond Mt Gambier, the constructional piles of recent volcanoes add their special variety to the face of the land. But where these are steep and youthful they are only small, and where large they are denuded and consist mainly of gently sloping and unimpressive basaltic piles. The most striking volcanic forms have resulted from the exposure by deep erosion of the plugs of the older volcanoes which formed with the uplift of the Eastern Uplands. It suffices to refer to Mt Warning in northern New South Wales, the ominous finger of God seen and named by Cook on the first voyage of exploration of eastern mainland Australia by the white man.

Alpine crests and peaks attributable to glacial sharpening and hollowing of forms left by fluvial dissection are to be found in the Frankland Range and in Federation Peak in southwestern Tasmania. But only 0.5 per cent of Australia was high enough in relation to latitude to experience glaciation in the Pleistocene, and that almost entirely in Tasmania. No mountains remain sufficiently cold to retain glaciers today. A counterpart of glacial peaks and cirques, namely deep lake basins due to glacial valley erosion, is developed in Tasmania. The deepest, Lake St Clair (172 m), is of respectable depth by world standards for glacial piedmont lakes, for though the Tasmanian glaciers were small their budgets were dynamic. Nevertheless the Pleistocene ice masses of Tasmania remained modest and failed to reach the sea in sufficient mass to form true fjords.

What the continent lacks in cold wet climates it makes up in hot desert and semi-desert country. In such areas, through much exposure of bedrock and backwearing of the hillsides, even modest residuals and dissected plateaux can take on an impressive mountainous character. For instance the sinuous chains of sharp ridges and peaks of the Flinders Ranges in South Australia have resulted from the etching out under an arid climate of rugged relief from rocks which were anciently folded, later planed, and once more exposed to dissection by Cenozoic block-faulting. That well-known trio of central Australian inselbergs, Ayers Rock, the Olgas and Mt Connor, exemplify in their sharp piedmont angles and steep rocky slopes the impressive response of landforms of quite modest relief to geologic structure, under aridity.

However the most widespread physiographic legacy of aridity is in the lowlands of Australia, where lack of rainfall and gentle gradients have led to a general disorganization of river systems. In the absence of high ground sufficient to attract orographic rainfall, the Australian desert uplands generate only ephemeral rivers which flood briefly after episodic rainfalls. Over much of central and Western Australia the river systems die out on the desert plains without reaching base level. The only major integrated drainage system in arid Australia is that tributary to Lake Eyre. The many salt lakes that dot the map of arid Australia reflect this disintegration of surface drainage. A corollary of the failure of the river systems is the extent of aeolian sand surfaces, with almost 1 million km² of sandplain and an equal extent of sandridge desert. These aeolian sand surfaces are now mainly stabilized, indicating an extension during former episodes of greater aridity.

Given the prevailing flatness, the extent of the major river systems is not surprising. That of the Murray is the sixth largest in the world, and the length of its Murray-Darling arm is more than half that of the Nile. Some of the fragmented drainage systems of the drier parts of continent may have been of almost comparable extent. Despite their extent however, the discharges of these river systems are remarkably small in response to low average rainfall, and in its natural state even the Murray failed from time to time to reach the sea.

Even the main drainage divides share the general flatness of the continent: as in Africa they are broad upwarps of gentle relief rather than mountain ranges. This applies particularly to the misnamed 'Great Dividing Range' which separates drainage to the Tasman and Coral Seas from that to the continental interior. An aircraft leaving from Cooma airport starts at one side of the 'Great Dividing Range' and takes off on the other. Whatever the official decrees, no self-respecting physical geographer can employ such a misnomer.

PHYSIOGRAPHIC REGIONS OF AUSTRALIA

A physiographic region is a morphological unit with an internal coherence in its landform characteristics appropriate to the level of subdivision. It should be a discrete entity, although this requirement may be satisfied by a group of islands with intervening sea as well as by a continuous land area. Low-order regions should be entirely contained within the limits of regions of higher order. Uniformity of relief type may be a feasible criterion only for the smaller units; units at higher levels will be more complex and will normally comprise a variety of forms, although these should be systematically associated in a characteristic way which sets the region apart from its neighbours. Hierarchic systems of physiographic regions commonly progress from a basis of morphological unity at the lowest levels to landform associations in higher orders. In erosional landscapes these associations may be the

expression of geological structures at various scales, and in constructional landscapes of a common genesis or suite of depositional processes. Limitations of map scale may however enforce the grouping of adjoining contrasted relief types in compound regions.

Apart from its descriptive role, a map of physiographic regions provides a regional system of reference for geomorphological and related physical-geographical accounts. Through the groupings of physiographic regional characteristics at different levels, the action of underlying controls, for instance geologic or climatic, may be made apparent. Further, the map can provide a regional basis for an understanding of land characteristics that are dependent upon landforms, for example the distribution of soils or natural vegetation.

There have been few previous attempts to construct maps of physiographic regions of Australia. This is not surprising since a reasonable basis for mapping in the form of airphotos and topographic and geologic maps has only recently become available and even now remains incomplete. Improvement in this basic knowledge, particularly over the last two decades, has so far led chiefly to the mapping of landform types (Australian Water Resources Council, 1969; Mabbutt and Sullivan, 1970; Department of Minerals and Energy, 1973). The delineation of landform types has been a useful aid in mapping soils and vegetation, particularly by means of airphoto interpretation, and was basic to the land-system surveys employed in regional mapping by the CSIRO Division of Land Research.*

One of the few published maps of physiographic regions for the whole of Australia is that by Fairbridge and Gentilli (1951); this is an inset map at a scale of about 1:34 million accompanying a large physiographic diagram of the kind devised by Raisz (1931). Much fresh information has become available since that map was constructed and it is no criticism of it to embark on an improved version with that additional information, helped further by a somewhat larger publication scale. A similar limitation of scale also applied to a map by Dury (1968), in which in any case most of the regions were not completely defined by boundaries.

The map now presented (Fig. 2.1) was compiled on a scale of 1:12 million for reduction to the published scale of 1:21.5 million. Where physiographic division of parts of the continent on a broadly similar basis had previously been attempted, the earlier published maps have been drawn upon, though not followed in all respects. Notable sources of this kind were Jutson (1934) for Western Australia, Twidale (1968) for South Australia, Hills (1950) for Victoria and David

---

*Now the Division of Land Use Research

and Browne (1950) for New South Wales. The *Atlas of Tasmania* (Davies, 1965) and the *Landforms Map of New South Wales* (N.S.W. Department of Decentralization and Development, n.d.) were prime sources in a different manner for those States. For much of Queensland, Northern Territory and the north of Western Australia the CSIRO Land Research Series was indispensable. Maps of relief and landforms produced by the Geographic Branch, Department of National Development (1967, 1972) for the Fitzroy and Townsville-Burdekin regions of Queensland were also drawn upon, as was the *Geomorphic Map of the Riverine Plain* (Butler *et al.*, 1974). However these sources did not obviate the need to make reference to topographic maps, especially the 1 : 250,000 topographic series of the Division of National Mapping, and the many geologic maps of similar scale by Federal and State geological instrumentalities. To acknowledge sources in fuller detail would be invidious, both by way of unintentional omission of some sources and by commitment of all sources to the employment made of them here.

Though not compiled by a closely analogous procedure, the new map of Australian physiographic regions follows in large measure the well-known map by Fenneman of the United States (Fenneman, 1928), particularly in its threefold hierarchy of *major divisions*, *provinces* and *sections*. The problem of naming the units was at least as great as that of identifying and demarcating them, chiefly because the relatively short intercourse of literate man with the Australian environment has resulted in a dearth of regional names expressive of the popular recognition of natural land contrasts. Since the basis of mapping was landforms or associated surficial sediments it was decided to use only generic topographic descriptors of regions and to exclude terms deriving directly from bedrock structure or lithology. The descriptor has been used in the plural to indicate complexity or the recurrence of forms within the region (e.g. Cape River Plains) and in the singular to indicate more homogeneous landscapes. Compound regions have required two topographic descriptors (e.g. Townshend Ranges and Lowlands).

Although rules of topographic nomenclature are lax, there has been an attempt at a uniform use of terms. *Upland* has been preferred to mountains or highlands for areas of high ground of subdued crestal outlines and limited internal relief, such as characterize much of the Australian watersheds. At a more specific level, *plateau* is used of tabular relief with steep escarpments, commonly structural, and *tableland* for less regular and less sharply bounded upland surfaces, often of cyclic erosional origin. In this usage form and local relationships of levels may override absolute altitude or relief, and the same term is used of the Normanton Tableland,

which does not exceed 100 m, and of the Bathurst Tablelands reaching over 1,500 m. *Ranges* denotes a preponderance of linear crests, *ridges* is used of more closely dissected rugged terrain, and *hills* for isolated summits. *Lowlands* indicates a modest internal relief and a low altitude, locally relative to adjoining regions rather than to sea level; for example the Missionary Lowland within the Macdonnell Ranges has an altitude above 500 m. *Plain* has been used of flat landscapes irrespective of altitude, as in the Burt Plains at above 600 m in central Australia. Certain persistent Australian terms have been retained where they do not conflict with general usage, for example *slopes* for the gradual or stepped decline of the uplands towards the interior plains, and *fall* for the steeper and generally more dissected coastward descent. *Sandplain* is used of the extensive stabilized level aeolian sand surfaces characteristic of the shield landscapes of arid Australia.

Geographical names have been prefixed to the generic topographic terms to define the regions. For some regions more than one geographic prefix has been required to indicate extent (Springsure-Clermont Plateaux) or a compound character (Stirling and Barren Ranges). Names already existed for some regions, for example Wimmera and Mallee, and these have been supplemented by the topographic term; for others an existing name has been used in contracted form, as in Isa Ridges. In certain cases the combination of geographic and topographic terms corresponded with existing usage, e.g. Riverine Plain. For several others a possible conflict has arisen. Where confusion might arise, prior usage has been allowed to prevail, as in Barkly Tableland for which otherwise the topographic term 'plain' might have been preferred. In other names a compromise has been sought, e.g. in Darling Range Rim the last term is preferred as expressive of the dissected raised margin of the interior plateau, but the middle term is retained to identify the region with popular usage. For some names a departure from earlier terminology has appeared justified; in preferring Cumberland Lowland to Cumberland Plain, for example, the new generic topographic term is thought to describe more appropriately the proportion of low hills in the region. Retention of Australian Alps is perhaps justified more by vegetation than by landforms, although the modest intervention of past cold climatic processes gives some geomorphic rationale.

Pre-existing geographic terms employing cardinal directions within a state framework, for example the divisions of the slopes of the Eastern Uplands in New South Wales, have had to be revised so that the regional names could stand alone within the context of the whole continent. Some coinage of new names was inevitable here, as also for regions of higher order. In the case of the slopes of New South Wales the names

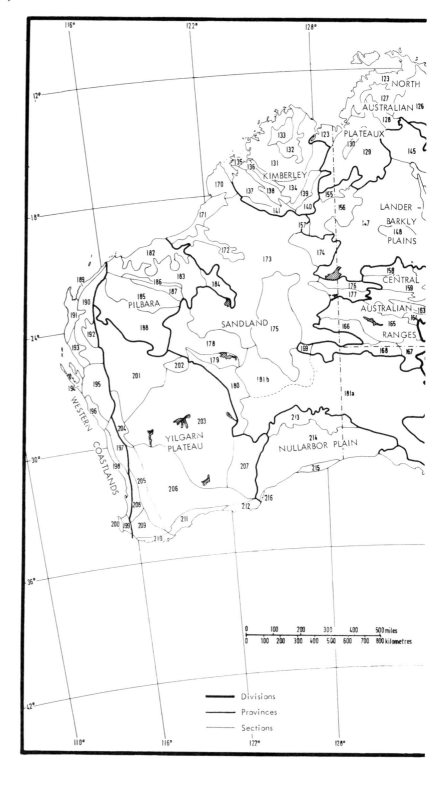

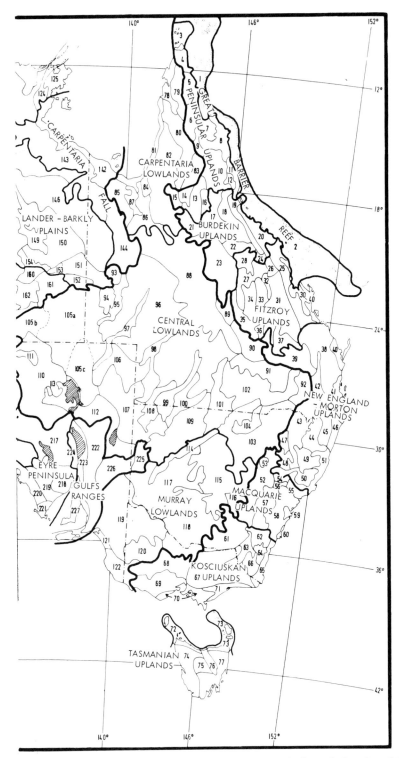

Fig. 2.1 The physiographic regions of Australia. Numbers indicate the location of the region in the following table which provides brief descriptions of each region.

of regional explorers have been used, namely Hume, Macquarie and Mitchell. Some of the newly coined names are bound to give rise to adverse reaction, as no doubt Jutson's Pilbaraland did originally.

The tripartite *major divisions* of this map, namely Eastern Uplands, Interior Lowlands and Western Plateau have long been recognized although not precisely under that nomenclature. They already appear for example as the 'geographical division' of Australia proposed by Gregory (1907). The outlines of many of the *provinces* also follow earlier maps, although many, in northern Australia especially, have been newly conceived. It is however at the *section* level that boundaries have had to be sought and new units named to the greatest extent. Two extensive and relatively uniform sections, the Great Victoria Desert Dunefield and the Simpson Desert Dunefield, have been subdivided at a lower level than the section. An arrangement which departs in some degree from the definition of region given above, namely one section totally surrounding another, occurs four times in the new map of Australian physiographic regions, but finds precedent in the corresponding map of the United States.

In Table 2.2, the breakdown into major divisions, provinces and sections is compared with that in Fenneman's map of the conterminous U.S.A. Some of the differences have a basis in reality. Australia has fewer major divisions because it is less diverse in its landforms as in its structural and geomorphic history. Perhaps this difference would be lessened if New Guinea were considered with Australia and if comparison were made with the whole continent of North America rather than with a political half. The fact that one major division in the U.S.A. map contains only one province and that with but one section highlights the artificiality of the political boundary.

Within Australia, degree of familiarity with the terrain may have influenced the detail of mapping, for

Table 2.2 Comparison of Maps of Physiographic Regions of U.S.A. and Australia

	U.S.A.	Australia
Number of major divisions	8	3
Number of provinces	25	22
Number of sections	85	197
Range in number of provinces within a major division	1–7	3–12
Range in number of sections within a province	1–10	3–29
Average area of a section	90,000 km²	39,000 km²

instance in the smaller areas of provinces and sections in the Eastern Uplands compared with those in the two other major divisions. However there can be no doubt that this contrast also reflects the greater physiographic complexity of the Eastern Uplands as a result of geologic structure. Variation in the numbers of sections within provinces is large. The 29 sections within the Central Lowlands Province in particular may seem suspect, but this province nevertheless has an overriding unity residing in its structure and reflected in its centripetal drainage and the approximately concentric arrangement of regional landscapes, and offers no apparent basis for further subdivision at the level of province.

Although the major features of Australia were roughed out in the Tertiary, whether by tectonism, vulcanism or by long-acting exogenetic processes, about a quarter of the sections owe their character to Quaternary landforms as the later expression of fluvial, aeolian or littoral processes. This is a significantly higher proportion than in the U.S.A. (about 15 per cent). Two factors are responsible for this. In the first case much of the bedrock foundation of Australia has been so reduced by prolonged exposure to erosion during Tertiary and earlier times that the Quaternary depositional processes have been much more effective in regional differentiation than would have been the case in areas of more contrasted underlying relief. Secondly, the aridity of much of the continent, and with it the disorganization of drainage on surfaces of low relief, has resulted in the masking by fluvial and aeolian deposition of bedrock physique which in a more humid climate might have been etched by fluvial attack into a more differentiated expression of structure.

The map now presented is thought to rest on firmer foundations than previous Australian ones of a similar kind, and to be more uniform in its systematics and nomenclature. Nevertheless, the long-continued deliberations that went into the ultimate fashioning of the Fenneman map of the U.S.A. may need to be paralleled here if the Australian map is to achieve the usefulness of its American counterpart. If this map of Australian physiographic regions sets in motion such a train of progressive improvement through consultation and the realization of errors through use its publication will have been justified.

ACKNOWLEDGEMENTS   The authors are grateful for comments on earlier versions of the map and its regional descriptions by H. F. Doutch and many of his colleagues in the Bureau of Mineral Resources, R. W. Galloway, E. Bettenay, M. Churchward, C. R. Twidale, R. F. Warner, J. Gentilli, A. Conacher, C. D. Ollier, D. Jeans and W. Hilder. At all stages in the mapping, naming and description of regions they were directly assisted by D. Johnson and K. Maynard of the School of Geography, University of New South Wales.

PHYSIOGRAPHIC REGIONS OF AUSTRALIA

EASTERN UPLANDS DIVISION

Great Barrier Reef Province
1. North Reefs —patch reefs with semi-continuous outer barrier
2. South Reefs —patch reefs with 'high' islands and discontinuous outer barrier

Peninsular Uplands Province
3. Torres 'High' Islands —islands and low coastal tableland of volcanic rocks and granite, with fringing reefs
4. Jardine Uplands —locally dissected rolling sandstone upland with transgressive coastal dunes along E lateritic cliffed margin
5. Wenlock Uplands —complex of tablelands and low plateaux with N-S lowlands; prominent scarp and outlying coastal hills on E
6. Coleman Plateau —rolling sandy granitic plateau with low ridges of metamorphic rocks; prominent E scarp
7. Laura Plain —soft-rock lowlands, alluvial plains of centripetal drainage, and littoral plain
8. Cooktown Ranges —deeply dissected sandstone plateaux with mountain ranges of granite and metamorphic rocks to E; small 'high' islands
9. Palmerville Hills —granitic hills and plateaux and sandstone mesas with intervening plains; steeper fall on E
10. Garnet Uplands —hilly uplands, with dissected greywackes and volcanics in N and undulating country on granite and metamorphic rocks in S
11. Cairns Ranges —high ranges forming E edge of interior upland; lowland corridor and coastal ranges and 'high' islands
12. Atherton Tableland —basaltic plateau
13. Newcastle Ranges —rugged hills on acid volcanics, granite and metamorphic rocks.
14. Gilbert Hills —rolling country on granite and ridges and valleys on metamorphic rocks
15. Gregory Range —dissected sandstone plateau and hilly country on acid volcanic rocks
16. Einasleigh Plains —undulating to irregular plains on granite and metamorphic rocks

Burdekin Uplands Province
17. Burdekin Plateaux —young basaltic plateaux with primary volcanic forms; N-S axial belt of rugged ranges, chiefly on granite and metamorphic rocks
18. Burdekin Hills and Lowlands —in E, hills and footslopes on volcanic and mixed sedimentary rocks with igneous intrusions; in W, dissected laterite-capped tablelands, largely sandstone
19. Hervey Tablelands —granitic uplands, rugged ranges on volcanic rocks and minor dissected laterite-capped plateaux forming steep E upland margin
20. Townsville Lowland —alluvial and deltaic plains with scattered high hills
21. Gilberton Plateau —partly-dissected sandstone plateau
22. Cape River Plains —plains with clay soils in E and sandier in W
23. Alice Tableland —perched sandy plain with interior drainage and higher lateritic rim
24. Bulgonunna Tableland —undulating tableland; higher centre and sloping margins on volcanic rocks with peripheral mantle of lateritic clayey sand

Fitzroy Uplands Province
25. Connors Ranges —rounded mountain ranges building dissected E margin of uplands
26. Carborough Ranges —sandstone and basalt plateaux and lower rolling country on sedimentary and volcanic rocks

27. Belyando Plains — clay plains and sandy plains; minor hills
28. Scartwater Hills — hills, ridges and vales on sandstone and minor metamorphic rocks
29. Townshend Ranges and Lowlands — mosaic of mountains, hills, lowlands and peninsulas; lowlands include alluvial plains, tidal flats and coastal dunes
30. Broad Sound Plains — plains, mainly alluvial, locally stony, with tidal flats
31. Mackenzie-Dawson Lowlands — floodplains, clay plains and sandy bedrock lowlands
32. Cotherstone Plateau — dissected sandstone plateau
33. Springsure-Clermont Plateaux — moderately dissected low plateaux, mainly basalt with minor sandstone
34. Drummond Uplands — ridges and vales on sandstone and minor metamorphic rocks; rolling country on granite
35. Nagoa Scarplands — sandstone strike ridges and clay vales
36. Buckland Plateau — dissected high plateau on basalt and sandstone
37. Expedition Scarplands — rugged plateaux and ridges on sandstone

New England-Moreton Uplands Province

38. Bunya-Burnett Ranges — mountain ranges, rugged and dissected on granitic and metamorphic rocks in E, broader uplands and upland basins, partly on sedimentary rocks, in W
39. Taroom Hills — sandstone ridges and shale lowlands
40. Maryborough Lowland — lowland on weak sedimentary rocks; partly dune-covered, including Fraser Island
41. Moreton Lowland — lowland on weak sedimentary rocks, with prominent volcanic plugs; includes dune islands
42. Toowoomba Plateau — basaltic plateau terminating SE in dissected volcanic pile
43. Cunningham Slopes — ridges and valleys in metamorphic rocks
44. Tenterfield Plateau — undulating granitic plateau with higher residuals including basalt cappings
45. Clarence Fall — dissected plateau margin on granite and metamorphics
46. Clarence Lowlands — coastal lowlands on weak sedimentary rocks, with littoral and alluvial plains
47. Nandewar Peaks — dissected volcanic pile
48. Gunnedah Lowland — alluvial plains, sandstone ridges and hills of basic intrusive rocks
49. Armidale Plateau — undulating granitic plateau, higher in S with residuals including basalts and metamorphic rocks
50. Liverpool-Barrington Plateaux — dissected basaltic plateaux
51. Macleay-Barrington Fall — plateau flank dissected into narrow strike ridges and valleys

Macquarie Uplands Province

52. Mitchell Slopes — tablelands stepping down W and breaking into detached hills
53. Warrumbungle Peaks — dissected volcanic pile with plugs
54. Merriwa Plateau — rolling basalt upland with sandstone cliffs
55. Hunter Valley — undulating to low hilly country on weak rocks, with alluvial and sandy littoral plains
56. Goulburn Corridor — broad valley floors on weaker rocks, overlooked by irregular dissected plateaux
57. Bathurst Tablelands — granitic and basaltic tablelands and minor lowlands; includes Canobolas dissected volcanic pile
58. Hawkesbury-Shoalhaven Plateaux — deeply dissected sandstone plateaux
59. Cumberland Lowland — undulating to low hilly country, mainly on shale
60. Illawarra Plain — narrow alluvial and deltaic plain, soft-rock lowlands and lagoon

Kosciuskan Uplands Province

61. Hume Slopes — tablelands stepping down westwards and breaking into detached hills

62. Werriwa Tablelands —upland plains with separating strike-aligned hills; closed lake basins

63. Australian Alps —dissected high upland, glaciated locally, but with more wide-spread periglacial features

64. Tinderry-Gourock Ranges —high hill chains of granite, sandstone and greywacke

65. Monaro Fall —deeply dissected, steeply sloping plateau margin in meta-morphics and granite

66. Monaro Tableland —undulating upland plains with tabular basalt relief and granite tors

67. East Victorian Uplands —dissected high plateaux on various resistant rocks

68. West Victorian Uplands —moderately high plateaux and strike ridges

69. West Victorian Plains —plains mainly on basalt lavas with many volcanic forms and lakes; partly on weak sedimentary rocks

70. South Victorian Uplands —low fault blocks, mainly of tilted and dissected sandstone; granite hills and islands

71. Gippsland Plain —terraced plains with sands and gravels

Tasmanian Uplands Province

72. Bass Plateaux —low coastal plateaux, trenched and partly basalt-capped; islands, partly dune-covered

73. Bass Plains —coastal plains and islands with much dune cover; low plateaux

74. Tasmanian Ridges —ridges of folded quartzite and conglomerate, commonly glaciated; parallel valleys on weaker rocks

75. Lakes Plateau —high dolerite plateau with many lakes; glaciated in W

76. Midlands Plain —fault-bounded lowland on weak rocks, with some dolerite hills

77. East Tasmanian Plateaux —fault-block mountains of dolerite and sandstone, with granite plateaux; ria coast

INTERIOR LOWLANDS DIVISION

Carpentaria Lowlands Province

78. Weipa Plateau —laterite-capped plateau on clayey sand and sandstone

79. Merluna Plain —undulating clay plains with lateritic rises

80. Holroyd Plains —slightly dissected sandy plains, partly lateritic

81. Karumba Plain —littoral plain

82. Clara-Mitchell Plains —sloping sandy plains with minor clay plains along distributary drainage

83. Bulimba Plateau —dissected low sandstone plateau

84. Normanton Tableland —stripped higher lateritic surface on siltstone and sandstone

85. Armraynald Plain —clay floodplain

86. Wondoola Plain —clay floodplain

87. Donors Tableland —stripped higher lateritic surface on siltstone and sandstone

Central Lowlands Province

88. Winton-Blackall Downs —undulating clay plains

89. Jericho Plain —sandplain

90. Maranoa Lowland —sandplain with low sandstone hills

91. Charleville Tableland —low sandy tableland of weathered sandstone and shale

92. Condamine Lowlands —undulating clay lowlands on siltstone and low sandstone hills; clay floodplains

93. Boulia Downs —undulating clay plains with minor stony limestone plains

94. Whelan Lowlands —undulating clay plains with silcrete-capped mesas in E floodplain

95. Eyre Creek Plain —stony plains with silcrete-capped mesas; minor alluvial and sandy tracts

96. Eromanga Lowlands

97. Diamantina Plain —floodplain

98. Cooper Plain	—floodplain
99. Bulloo Plain	—floodplain and terminal floodout with pans and calcreted flats
100. Paroo Plain	—sandplain with alluvial flats and claypans
101. Warrego Plains	—main and distributary floodplains; sandplains with minor alluvial flats and claypans
102. St George Plain	—sandplain
103. Upper Darling Plains	—floodplains of centripetal anastomosing rivers
104. Lightning Ridge Lowland	—stony plains with minor silcrete-capped mesas
105. Simpson Desert Dunefield	
a. Main Dunefield	—S-N longitudinal dunes
b. West Dunefield	—S-N longitudinal dunes and sandstone ridges
c. South Dunefield	—S-N longitudinal dunes and playas
106. Sturt Desert Plains	—stony plains with minor sand ridges
107. Strzelecki Desert Plains	—longitudinal dunes and stony plains; minor claypans and floodplains
108. Grey Range	—silcrete-capped tablelands
109. Warwick Lowland	—stony plains with silcrete-capped mesas
110. Oodnadatta Tablelands	—silcrete-capped low tablelands
111. Alberga Dunefield	—longitudinal dunes
112. Eyre-Frome Plains	—major salt lakes and adjacent alluvial plains; minor stony plains and longitudinal dunes
113. Denison Ranges	—bevelled low ridges of folded metamorphic rocks

Murray Lowlands Province

114. Lower Darling Plain	—floodplain and lunette lakes
115. Cobar Plains	—plains with remnants of silcrete and low sandstone ridges; sand cover in W, with W-E longitudinal dunes
116. Condobolin Plain	—plains of gravel and sandy alluvium
117. Ivanhoe Plains	—plains with low W-E stabilized longitudinal dunes and sandplain; small pans with lunettes, minor sandstone ridges, floodplains
118. Riverine Plain	—alluvial plain
119. Mallee Dunefield	—fixed W-E calcareous longitudinal dunes
120. Wimmera Plain	—aeolian and alluvial sandplain; minor low sandstone ridges
121. Coorong Plain	—coastal barrier, lagoons and limestone dunes
122. Millicent Plain	—parallel dune limestone ridges with intervening swamps; closed karst depressions and young volcanoes in SE

WESTERN PLATEAU DIVISION

North Australian Plateaux Province

123. Bonaparte-Diemen Lowlands	—dissected lateritic lowlands and minor islands; part alluvial, part estuarine coastal plains
124. Arnhem Ridges	—ranges of folded metamorphic rocks extending NE as islands
125. East Arnhem Plateau	—dissected plateau, mainly of sandstone
126. West Arnhem Plateau	—dissected sandstone plateau
127. Pine Creek Ridges	—rounded ridges of folded metamorphic rocks with minor quartzite plateaux
128. Daly Lowland	—lowlands of limestone and weak sedimentary rocks, including alluvial plains; minor laterite-capped plateaux and granite hills
129. Ord-Victoria Plateaux	—dissected plateaux, mainly basaltic but partly of sandstone and with local laterite cappings
130. Whirlwind Plain	—alluvial plain, mainly clay

Kimberley Province

| 131. Kimberley Plateau | —sandstone plateaux with tabular high summits; ria coast and islands to NW |

132. Drysdale Lowlands	—undulating to hilly lowlands, mainly on basalt
133. Couchman Uplands	—undulating to hilly lower plateaux, mainly on basalt
134. Leopold-Durack Ranges	—prominent ranges of dipping quartzites rimming the main plateau
135. Yampi Peninsula	—parallel ridges of quartzite and sandstone and narrow valleys of basalt; extending as a ria coast and islands
136. Richenda Foothills	—rounded hills and ridges and lowlands on a belt of granite and folded metamorphic rocks with minor basalt
137. Fitzroy Plains	—floodplains and broad estuarine plains
138. Napier Limestone Ranges	—limestone tableland and intricately dissected bevelled ridges; rocky karst surfaces with box valleys
139. Springvale Foothills	—granite hills and minor undulating plains
140. Halls Creek Ridges	—ranges and rounded hills on granite and metamorphic rocks
141. Fitzroy Ranges	—scattered sandstone tablelands and ranges; extensive sandplain and E-W longitudinal dunes

Carpentaria Fall Province

142. Manangoora Plains	—alluvial plains, minor lateritic lowlands and islands, and littoral plains
143. Borroloola Fall	—dissected coastal fall; tabular ridges giving place to sloping plains and low hills seawards
144. Isa Ridges	—rugged parallel ranges and narrow lowlands on folded metamorphic rocks and granites

Lander-Barkly Plains Province

145. Larrimah Plateau	—shallowly dissected plateau of lateritized sandstone with alluviated valleys
146. Barkly Tableland	—black clay plains, sandy rises of lateritized sandstone, and minor stony limestone plains; interior drainage with calcretes in depressions
147. Wiso Sandplain	—sandplain with minor longitudinal dunes in S; floodplains and floodouts on margins; stony rises in N
148. Lander Dunefield	—E-W longitudinal dunes
149. Ashburton-Davenport Ranges	—fold belt of bevelled sandstone ridges, with narrow lowlands on weaker rocks; central tract of lower hills and plains; extensive lateritic mantles
150. Frew-Sandover Sandplain	—sandplain with minor low sandstone tablelands and floodouts; sandy lateritic plains in S
151. Tobermory Plain	—slightly dissected limestone plain, part stony and part sandy
152. Toko Plateaux	—dissected sandstone plateaux
153. Jervois Ranges	—rounded ridges of folded metamorphics
154. Barrow-Dulcie Plateaux	—dissected sandstone plateaux
155. Birrundudu Plain	—low basaltic plain with clay soils; indeterminate drainage with large claypans
156. Tanami Sandplain and Ranges	—sandplain with scattered low ranges and tablelands and occasional granitic hills
157. Sturt Creek Floodout	—floodout with distributary channels and claypans

Central Australian Ranges Province

158. Doreen-Reynolds Ranges	—ranges and rounded summits, partly granitic and partly of quartzite and sandstone
159. Burt Plain	—granitic plains with laterite cappings; wash plains with sandplain, minor longitudinal dunes and calcrete-rimmed salt lakes in lowest parts
160. Alcoota Tablelands	—low tablelands of chalcedonic limestone, locally with clay plains; granitic plains with lateritic rises

161. Plenty River Plains
—sandplain with minor floodplains and irregular low dunes; stony granitic plains with low hills in NW
162. Macdonnell Ranges
—fold complex of prominent E-W ranges, mainly of quartzite; lowlands on limestone and shale with gravel terraces
163. Missionary Lowland
—stony lowland of calcareous conglomerate and other weak rocks, with extensive low dunes; anticlinal sandstone ridges
164. Henbury Ranges
—silcrete-capped plateaux and narrow ranges in stony and alluvial plains
165. Amadeus Lowland
—dunefields and sandplains with scattered sandstone ranges; salt lakes and calcrete plains along lowland axis
166. Rawlinson-Petermann Ranges
—dissected sandstone ranges with prominent escarpments
167. Kulgera Hills
—sandy granitic plains with prominent hills
168. Musgrave Ranges
—granitic ranges and rounded high hills
169. Warburton Ranges
—ranges and hills of basic volcanic rocks and granite

Sandland Province
170. Dampier Tablelands
—low sandstone tablelands, partially lateritized and with extensive sandplain cover
171. Eighty Mile Plain
—coastal dunes and estuarine plain
172. Anketell Hills
—low mesas, buttes and stony rises of lateritized sandstone and shale among E-W longitudinal dunes and sandy plains
173. Great Sandy Desert Dunefield
—E-W longitudinal dunes and minor salt lakes
174. Stansmore Dunefield and Ranges
—E-W longitudinal dunes locally broken by narrow sandstone ranges
175. Gibson Desert Plains
—sandy or stony lateritic plains
176. Redvers Dunefield
—E-W longitudinal dunes
177. Macdonald Sandplain
—mainly sandplain with dune-fringed salt lakes
178. Stanley Hills and Dunes
—isolated sandstone ridges among W-E longitudinal dunes and sandplain
179. Carnegie Hills
—sandstone tablelands, stony limestone plains, salt lakes and adjacent dunes
180. Leemans Sandplain
—sandplain with small salt lakes
181. Great Victoria Desert Dunefield
    a. Main Dunefield
—W-E longitudinal dunes
    b. Northwest Dunes and Hills
—W-E longitudinal dunes broken by low tablelands and ridges

Pilbara Province
182. De Grey Lowlands
—floodplains and deltaic plains; granitic and limestone lowlands; scattered ranges of metamorphic rocks in N
183. Nullagine Hills
—dissected flat-topped hills of granites and metamorphic rocks with partial lateritic cappings; narrow estuarine plain and islands
184. Rudall Tablelands
—dissected low sandstone tablelands
185. Hamersley Plateaux
—dissected bold plateaux and ranges of flat-lying or moderately folded sandstone and quartzite
186. Chichester Range
—narrow range of dipping quartzite and sandstone
187. Fortescue Valley
—mainly alluvial lowland, possibly a graben
188. Augustus Ranges
—parallel ranges and dissected plateaux with intervening sandy lowlands

Western Coastlands Province
189. Onslow Plain
—alluvial, deltaic and littoral plains; minor islands
190. Carnarvon Dunefield
—S-N longitudinal dunes
191. North West Cape Ridges
—low ridges and peninsula formed by folded sedimentary rocks and limestone dunes
192. Kennedy Range
—dissected sandstone plateau with partial laterite cappings, covered by longitudinal dunes

193. Carnarvon Plain
—alluvial plain

194. Shark Bay Peninsulas
—peninsulas and islands formed by indurated limestone dunes

195. Yaringa Sandplain
—sandplain with minor dunes

196. Greenough Hills
—dissected plateaux and hills of sandstone and shale, with extensive sand cover in lower parts

197. Dandaragan Tablelands
—dissected plateaux and hills of chalk and greensand, with minor laterite cappings and dry valleys; extensive sand cover in lower parts

198. Swan Plain
—dune ridges, mainly of limestone, and inner alluvial plain

199. Donnybrook Lowland
—lowland on down-faulted weak sedimentary rocks

200. Leeuwin Peninsula
—narrow granitic horst ridge with extensive cover of calcareous dune sands

Yilgarn Plateau Province

201. Murchison Plateau
—mainly granitic plains with out-going drainage, broken by ridges of metamorphic rocks

202. Glengarry Hills
—sandstone plateau sloping N to low hills of basic volcanic rocks

203. Salinaland Plateau
—sandplains and laterite breakaways; granitic and alluvial plains; ridges of metamorphic rocks and granitic hills and rises; calcretes, large salt lakes and dunes along valleys

204. Woodramung Hills
—low rounded ridges of folded metamorphics

205. Northam Plateau
—flat-floored valleys of moderately incised oceanward drainage; older laterite remnants with breakaways on divides in E; shallow younger laterites on valley sides in W

206. Narrogin-Ongerup Plateau
—sandplains and laterite cappings with breakaways on divides; stripped granitic plains on valley sides; small salt lakes and bordering dunes along shallow valley floors

207. Coonana-Ragged Plateau
—sandplain and stripped gneissic plains with low hills of granite and metamorphic rocks; calcretes and scattered small salt lakes along shallow valleys

208. Darling Range
—high plateau rim with steep western fall; remnant laterite cappings and deeply incised valleys of oceanward drainage

209. Collie-Kalgan Slopes
—gently sloping dissected edge of plateau on granite and gneiss with laterite cappings

210. Albany Headlands and Inlets
—granitic headlands and inlets with lagoons

211. Stirling and Bareen Hills
—hills and low ranges of granite and metamorphic rocks with intervening plains and moderately incised southerly valleys

212. Esperance Hills
—low granite hills and plains extending as headlands and inlets

Nullarbor Plain Province

213. Carlisle Plain
—sandstone plain with shallow closed depressions

214. Bunda Plateau
—covered karst plain of flat-lying limestone with closed depressions and caves; continuous cliff margin on S

215. Roe Plain
—coastal plain with extensive dunes

216. Israelite Plain
—narrow coastal plain with extensive dunes

Eyre Peninsula Province

217. Gairdner Plain
—alluvial plains and salt lakes with some dunes

218. Gawler-Cleve Ranges
—rounded ranges of acid volcanic rocks and hills of metamorphic rocks

219. Eyre Dunefield
—stable NW-SE longitudinal dunes, locally broken by granite hills and ridges of metamorphic rocks

220. Ceduna Dunefield
—low limestone dune ridges; small granitic islands with dunes

221. Lincoln Hills
—low rounded hills and minor islands of metamorphic rocks partly dune-covered

Gulfs Ranges Province

222. Flinders-Lofty Ranges — complex fold belt of prominent ranges in N, chiefly quartzite with vales on weaker rocks; stepped fault-blocks and islands in S, mainly of weathered metamorphic rocks with lateritic cappings

223. Torrens-Gulfs Plains — salt lake and bahadas in N; alluvial and littoral plains in S; NW-SE longitudinal dunes, mainly stabilized

224. Andamooka Tableland — dissected sandstone plateau with bold E escarpment

225. Barrier Ranges — ranges and undulating lowlands of granite and metamorphics

226. Olary Spur — low hill belt of folded crystalline and sedimentary rocks

227. Yorke Peninsula — undulating lowland of folded crystalline and metamorphic rocks; cover of calcrete and stabilized NW-SE longitudinal dunes

REFERENCES

Australian Water Resources Council (1969), *Land Form Map of Australia with Symbols for Rock Types of General Hydrologic Significance* (1 : 5 million).

Butler, B. E. *et al.* (1974), *A Geomorphic Map of the Riverine Plain of South-eastern Australia*, Australian National University Press, Canberra.

David, T. W. E. and Browne, W. R. (1950), *The Geology of the Commonwealth of Australia*, Arnold, London.

Davies, J. L. (ed.) (1965), *Atlas of Tasmania*, Lands and Surveys Department, Hobart.

Department of Minerals and Energy (1973), 'Landforms', *Atlas of Australian Resources*, Second Series, Canberra.

Department of National Development (1967), *Landforms, Fitzroy Region, Queensland*, Resources Series, Canberra.

——(1972), *Landforms, Burdekin-Townsville Region, Queensland*, Resources Series, Canberra.

Dury, G. H. (1968), 'An introduction to the geomorphology of Australia' in G. H. Dury and M. I. Logan (eds), *Studies in Australian Geography*, Heinemann, Melbourne, pp. 1–36.

Fenneman, N. M. (1928), 'Physiographic divisions of the United States', *Ann. Ass. Am. Geogr.*, 18, 261–353.

Gentilli, J. and Fairbridge, R. W. (1951), *The Physiographic Regions of Australia* to accompany a *Geomorphological Map of Australia* by J. Gentilli, University of Western Australia Press, Nedlands.

Gregory, J. W. (1907), *Australia and New Zealand. Stanford's Compendium of Geography and Travel*, Part i, London.

Hills, E. S. (1946), *The Physiography of Victoria*, Whitcombe and Tombs, Melbourne.

Jutson, J. T. (1934), 'The physiography (geomorphology) of Western Australia', *Geol. Surv. W. Aust. Bull.* 95.

Mabbutt, J. A. and Sullivan, M. E. (1970), 'Landforms and structure' in R. M. Moore (ed.), *Australian Grasslands*, Australian National University Press, Canberra, pp. 27–43.

Raisz, E. (1931), 'The physiographic method of representing scenery on maps', *Geogr. Rev.*, 21, 297–304.

Twidale, C. R. (1968), *Geomorphology*, Nelson, Melbourne.

3 HYDROLOGY

R. F. WARNER

Outside the polar regions, Australia is the driest continent. Though its size and latitudinal position allow for a great range of climates, it is generally characterized by a low mean precipitation of about 420 mm, a low mean runoff of 50 mm, and high water losses of about 370 mm. These compare with world average precipitation of 660 mm, runoff of 250 mm and internal losses (mainly evapotranspiration) of 410 mm. Average values are however of limited use in hydrology, particularly in Australia where marked fluctuations from year to year make this country one of climatic and hydrologic extremes, though the nature of the available data and the scale of this enquiry requires their use.

In hydrology, the drainage basin provides the fundamental unit for the calculation of the water budget, taking into account the inputs of precipitation, the throughputs of evapotranspiration, infiltration supplies to soil moisture, and percolation to groundwater levels, and outputs of stream discharge or net runoff. The discharge measured at a river gauge comprises rainfall less various losses:

$$RO = P - E - T \pm \Delta S + \Delta D \pm \Delta GW$$

where RO is runoff, P is precipitation, E is evaporation, T is transpiration, ΔS changes in soil moisture storage, ΔD changes in surface retention and ΔGW changes in groundwater storage.

Over 200 Australian drainage basins are listed in water resources publications, but it is necessary here to group these into the twelve drainage divisions defined by Federal agencies and which reflect fundamental differences in hydrology within the larger framework of Australia as a whole (Dept of National Development, 1967; Australian Water Research Council (AWRC), 1965, 1971a).

Seven divisions allow direct but highly variable runoff to the oceans from the mainland. Tasmania is the one island division, with direct runoff to the sea. The other four divisions include: the large internal basin of the Murray-Darling river system, with much runoff from the western flanks of the southeast highlands which reaches the sea only after crossing arid areas; a large interior basin which is served by a mainly

integrated drainage system flowing irregularly into the tectonically-depressed Lake Eyre; one disconnected division, the Bulloo-Bancannia lying between the Eyre and Murray-Darling divisions; and in the Western Plateaux is one vast disconnected network, again with no net outflow.

These drainage divisions, within which the contemporary precipitation is dispersed, have evolved geomorphologically over long periods of time. The divides between external and internal drainage are neither high nor spectacular, except perhaps in the southeast. Elsewhere it seems clear that high levels of aridity have had much to do with the disruption of what were formerly better integrated systems (Beard, 1973 and Sullivan, 1973). With increased aridity the potential evaporation is high enough to remove all precipitation.

When considering input and throughput stages such as precipitation and evaporation, climatic factors are clearly important. Vegetation and soil factors have to be added for any consideration of the losses through transpiration and evapotranspiration. Soil also affects infiltration and percolation to underlying bedrock storage. Lithological and structural factors in the geological platform do much to influence groundwater movement and storage, as well as shape basic elements of relief and catchment dimensions. Flow in rivers is derived from surface runoff, throughflow and baseflow and it is affected by the combined effects of all these factors. Therefore, it is not easy to avoid the implications of a black box treatment, i.e.

$$inputs - throughputs = outputs.$$

To obtain a net outflow of river discharge from a catchment or whole division, precipitation must be greater than the combined losses. Since this does not hold true for the major part of Australia, it is abundantly clear that precipitation is low and that losses are proportionately high. Thus, in this chapter, there is consideration of two basic hydrological systems: areas with net runoff and those with no runoff.

Hydrological data sources are numerous and only with the formation of the Federal Australian Water

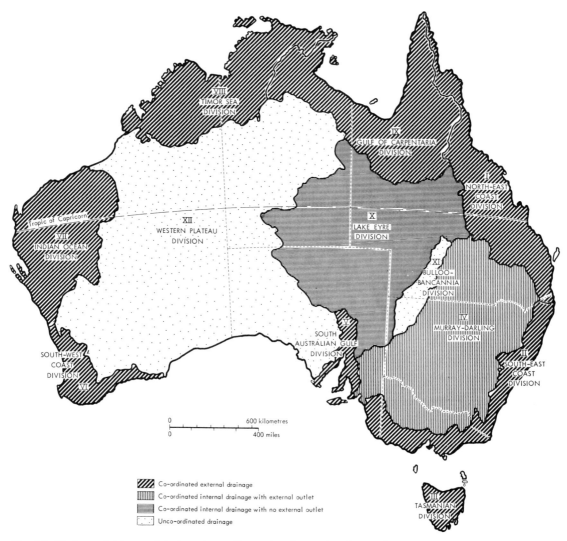

Fig. 3.1 Drainage divisions and drainage types. *Source*: based on *Atlas of Australian Resources*, 1967.

Resources Council (1962) has there been a real attempt to synthesize findings coming from Federal agencies like the Weather Bureaux and the CSIRO, State instrumentalities, such as water authorities, public works departments and geological surveys, and local bodies including flood mitigation authorities, research establishments and health authorities. This lead has been taken up in the International Hydrological Decade and has resulted in much more integrated work, important reviews, and the planning and sponsorship of important research programmes (Aust. Nat. Comm. UNESCO, 1974).

While the conceptual bases of hydrology are reasonably well known, the complex interactions of

water in the atmosphere, biosphere and lithosphere at the regional level in catchments are rather individual because of local variations in climate, geology, soils, landforms and vegetation, as well as the level of modification effected by human occupance. This is the best reason for the AWRC setting up about 100 representative basin studies as a kind of vigil network. Here local complexities through a wide range of catchment types can be studied more systematically (AWRC, 1969, 1974a). Their smooth plainlands programme will incorporate similar projects in arid areas (AWRC, 1972).

Most observations are but limited samples of water reality based on widely-spaced points. These include about 12,000 rain gauges, 3,500 stream gauges, a few hundred tank evaporimeters, a few lysimeters and evapotranspirimeters, a few soil moisture sites and hundreds of wells for groundwater. These data provide some knowledge of water quantities in various parts of the cycle, and are necessary for resource planning and for conservation. This is particularly true for surface water which may be held in dams or weirs for domestic water supplies, irrigation, industry and hydroelectric power generation. Observations on the quality of water first became necessary with the development of groundwater sources. These were found to vary in dissolved salts content and their use is conditioned by the level of concentration. Nowadays, water is contaminated by new sources, from the atmosphere, from fertilizers and from the disposal of human waste, creating a need for rapid data collection by those concerned for the environment. The erratic nature of inputs and outputs makes long-term observations necessary to have knowledge of the probability factors involved. Efficient storage of water in dams has to be based on often low and erratic inputs, as well as the safe and effective removal of occasional excessive flow.

The initial part of this chapter is concerned with precipitation. Then there is some treatment of the major atmospheric losses to the hydrological system, i.e. evaporation, transpiration and evapotranspiration. Other throughput losses, at least to surface runoff, are soil moisture and groundwater. These are considered not only as losses to the surface but also as supplies for vegetation and groundwater sources, some of which leave the system as the base flows of large rivers. Runoff as the output component is the final part of the system considered. The last section presents a summary review of modifications to parts of this system brought about consciously or unconsciously by man. Catchment surfaces have undergone great changes with the clearance of land, with the development of grazing and cropping enterprises and with the growth of urban communities, while channel systems and their flows have been modified by storage systems.

THE DRAINAGE DIVISIONS AND SOME OF THEIR BASIC CHARACTERISTICS

Since Australia is a dry continent with a long and varied coastline and a complex geomorphic history, and with a diversity of climatic regimes, numerous basin drainage types exist. Adding to this diversity is high infiltration over sandy terrains, vast sedimentary basins acting as groundwater reservoirs and flanked by ancient shields or denuded mountain ranges which often run close to the coast as divides. Over all this variety are the common factors of low, erratic and infrequent precipitation (Dept of National Development, 1970), high temperatures (Dept of Minerals and Energy, 1973a) and consequently high evaporation

from water bodies along with high potential evapotranspiration (Dept of Minerals and Energy, 1973b).

Therefore, some brief description of the major drainage divisions is required. Firstly, there is an important and relatively narrow peripheral discontinuous zone of Co-ordinated Exterior Drainage. This includes: I Northeast Coast (mainly the east coast of Queensland); II Southeast Coast (east of main divide in New South Wales, south of it in Victoria and part of southeast South Australia); III Tasmania (offshore island), V South Australian Gulf (South Australia not in II or arid); VI Southwest Australia (land draining into the area north and south of Perth); VII Indian Ocean (dry area of northwest); VIII Timor Sea (far northwestern Australia, wet summer tropics centred on Darwin); and IX Gulf of Carpentaria (all lands draining into this gulf). One division, IV Murray-Darling, is an integrated or co-ordinated internal drainage system with an external outlet for part of its total discharge. This has been referred to as a disconnected external drainage system or internal-external drainage (Dept of Minerals and Energy, 1973c; Sullivan, 1973). Another, X Lake Eyre, is essentially a co-ordinated internal system, with very low inputs being removed by high evaporation. The final two divisions are areas of uncoordinated or disconnected drainage and like Lake Eyre, they have no drainage into the ocean. These are the small XI Bulloo-Bancannia and large XII Western Plateau systems (Fig. 3.1).

Only those co-ordinated external and internal-external divisions have on average a positive water balance, with an excess of precipitation after all throughput losses and uses. This excess which runs off ranges from very low values for the Indian Ocean (12 mm) to very high for the Tasmanian (690 mm) divisions.

The interior and disconnected divisions are normally dry areas with only localized runoff following infrequent storms. On rare occasions, runoff may be high from large areas, such that Lake Eyre may be filled (Williams, 1969) or some of the disconnected drainage systems of the Western Plateaux become temporarily integrated again, but subsequent evaporation is high enough to prevent net runoff through any external outlets.

Some basic characteristics of these divisions are given in Table 3.1. Data there include the area of each division in km² and as percentages of external co-ordinated drainage, all external drainage and of the total landmass, the average total runoff volume and as percentages of the same areas, volumes of runoff per km², average runoff depth on each division, season of precipitation, and ranges of precipitation. Included also are tank evaporation and evapotranspiration data.

Table 3.1 General Characteristics of Runoff, Rainfall and Evaporation of the Drainage Divisions

Drainage division and type	Area (km²)	Percentage of			Average runoff (mill. m³)	Percentage of runoff			Runoff in m³/km²	Average runoff depth (mm)	Rainfall season	Precipitation range (mm)	Tank evaporation (mm)	Evapotranspiration (mm)
		a	b	c		a	b	c						
A. External Co-ordinated														
I Northeast Coast	454,000	16.8	12.1	5.9	82,867	26.0	24.3	24.0	183,000	183	VMS–MS	<500–>2,380	1,250– 1,800	<500–>1,000
IX Gulf of Carpentaria	640,800	23.7	17.1	8.3	63,146	19.8	18.5	18.3	98,500	99	VMS	300–1,600	<1,800–<2,800	>250–> 750
VIII Timor Sea	539,000	19.9	14.3	7.0	74,287	23.4	21.7	21.5	138.000	138	VMS	400–1,600	<2,300–<2,800	>250–>1,000
Summer Maximum Rainfall	1,633,800	60.4	43.5	21.2	220,300	69.2	64.5	63.8						
II Southeast Coast	268,000	9.9	7.1	3.5	36,400	11.6	10.7	10.5	136.000	136	SUW	<300–>2,380	< 750–<1,800	<250–> 750
III Tasmania	68,400	2.5	1.8	0.9	47,171	14.8	13.8	13.6	689.600	690	UW	<500–>2,380	< 500–> 750	<500–< 750
Mixed Seasonal Rainfall	366,400	12.4	8.9	4.4	83,571	26.4	24.5	24.1						
V South Aust. Gulf	75,370	2.8	2.0	1.0	532	0.2	0.2	0.1	7,060	7	AW	>100–> 610	<1,250–>2,800	<250– 750
VI Southwest Coast	140,000	5.2	3.7	1.8	7,223	2.3	1.2	2.1	51,590	51	VMW–MW	300– 1,200	1,000– 2,300	250–>1,000
Winter Maximum Rainfall	215,370	8.0	5.7	2.8	7,755	2.5	2.3	2.2						
VII Indian Ocean	520,000	19.2	13.8	6.8	6,160	1.9	1.8	1.8	11,800	12	A	200–300	<1,800–<2,800	<250–< 500
Arid External Rainfall	520,000	19.2	13.8	6.8	6,160	1.9	1.8	1.8						
All External Systems	2,705,570	100.0	71.9	35.2	317,786	100.0	93.1	91.9						
B. Internal/External														
IV Murray-Darling	1,057,000		28.1	13.8	23,663		6.9	6.9	22,400	22	ASUW	>200–>1,600	<750–>2,800	<250–> 750
	3,762,570		100.0	49.0	341,449		100.0	98.8						

Drainage division and type	Area (km²)	Percentage of runoff			Average runoff (mill. m³)	Percentage of runoff			Runoff in m³/km²	Average runoff depth (mm)	Rainfall season	Precipitation range (mm)	Tank evaporation (mm)	Evapotrans-piration (mm)
		a	b	c		a	b	c						
C. Internal Co-ordinated														
X Lake Eyre	1,144,000			14.9	3,906			1.1	3,414	3	AS	<100-> 400	1,800->3,000	<250-> 500
D. Internal Disconnected														
XI Bulloo-Bancannia	100,800			1.3	407			0.1	4,038	4	AS	<150-> 300	2,300- 2,800	<250-< 500
E. Uncoordinated Drainage														
XII Western Plateau	2,679,000			34.8	—			0	—	—	A	<150-< 400	>1,250->3,300	<250-< 500
All Internal Systems	3,923,800			51.0	4,303			1.2						
Total	7,686,370			100.0	345,762			100.0						

Sources: Atlas of Australian Resources; AWRC, 1965 and Munro, 1974.

a = external co-ordinated drainage
b = all external drainage, including internal-external
c = total landmass area

VMS	very marked summer precipitation	S	summer precipitation
VMW	very marked winter precipitation	U	uniform precipitation
MS	marked summer precipitation	W	winter precipitation
MW	marked winter precipitation	A	arid precipitation (very low erratic)

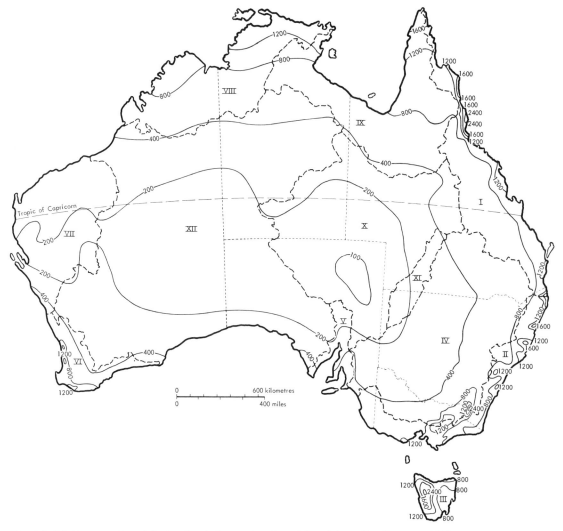

Fig. 3.2 Median annual precipitation (mm). *Source*: based on *Atlas of Australian Resources*, 1970.

Rainfall

The main input in Australia is rain. Primary concern is usually with the average or median amounts and also with the ranges and distributions, both in areal and temporal senses. Australia is located mainly between latitudes 15° and 35° S and as such is dominated by the subtropical high pressure cells, passing from west to east. These are normally associated with stable conditions, clear skies and low rainfall. Moisture-producing systems occur either between individual cells or to the north and south of them. So, in spite of being an island continent surrounded by seas, the latitudinal range and generally low relief make it one of the driest continents. Nevertheless, the range of median rainfall is high, from about 100 mm east of Lake Eyre to over 4,300 mm on parts of the north Queensland coast (AAR, 1970).

Four areal categories of rainfall may be defined. In the north and east, particularly on the coastal margins, most rain falls in summer. The thermal equator is then over the landmass and a semipermanent low pressure trough develops. With this are associated monsoonal rains drawn in from the north. Tropical cyclones from both northwest and northeast can supplement falls at irregular intervals over wide areas.

In the southwest, southeast coastal areas and Tasmania, much of the rain falls in winter. During this period, the high pressure cells are to the north over the mainland and cool polar maritime air is brought in around low pressure centres and their associated cold fronts. These move from west to east in constant succession.

Parts of the southeast are affected by both regimes and therefore get a fairly uniform precipitation. There is no distinct dry season as in the north or south.

Inland from these wetter perimeter zones and involving about two-thirds of the continent, average rainfall is low enough for the areas to be considered arid or semi-arid.

While this fourfold pattern is evident in median or average totals, great variations in input can and do occur annually, seasonally and even monthly. Such variations obviously affect other parts of the hydrological system. An extreme example shows the kind of variation possible in the far northwest. Port Hedland has a median annual rainfall of 273 mm but this has ranged from 32 to 1,019 mm (Dept of National Development, 1970).

Rain which falls is subject to interception, evaporation, infiltration, transpiration, percolation to depth or surface runoff. Some of these processes represent losses to part of the system or the whole, while others are increments to parts of the system. Therefore, in order to have some knowledge of on-going changes, it is necessary firstly to know what amounts are received. Important here are the amounts, nature of precipitation, durations of falls and intensities. In theory, such amounts are readily measured in simple standard rain gauges, located by convention so that nearby objects do not influence the catch. However, it is difficult to know what in fact is measured and how this compares with the local environment. Ground level or even canopy falls in a forest will be quite different to the catch in a gauge on the conventional short grass crop. Indeed, the fall on the grass may be 7 per cent more than in the gauge.

The surface area of the orifice is only about 127 cm^2 and represents a minute area sample. For instance there may be a gauge density of less than one per 100 km^2 in mountainous terrain where catches are highly variable. Most gauges are located where population densities are high and the density in arid and semi-arid areas is much lower. Thus, the detailed knowledge from the current 8,000 gauges (there were formerly up to 12,000) in nearly 8 million km^2 is spatially limited (Dept of National Development, 1970).

Rainfall is measured at 9 a.m. and credited to that day. Thus any rain between 9 a.m. on any day and 12 midnight is recorded for the following day. Five hundred gauges are read at 3 p.m. to give a six-hour fall value. From these observations, no indication is given for the time of fall, its duration and its intensity.

Such data are vital to subsequent hydrological processes. For instance, a ten minute downpour on steep impervious slopes already saturated will result in a high runoff. The same amount falling lightly over 24 hours will have very different effects, especially on flat and drier land. The standard rain gauge would show the same total in each case. For this reason, recording rain gauges or pluviometers are used. Currently about 1,200 are in use (Dept of National Development, 1970) and the knowledge gained in terms of intensities and duration is most valuable.

The Commonwealth Meteorological Bureau is charged with the responsibility of collecting rainfall data but anyone who wishes can record rainfalls. Farmers are keen collectors because management decisions around the property can be influenced by rainfall, particularly in preparing ground and sowing. Official gauges are located at airports where there may be meteorological officers, post offices and other locations.

Lengths of record are important for statistical analyses, particularly in deriving probability factors. The longest continuous records exist for Adelaide, where observations started in 1839. Thirty-four per cent of the 12,000 gauges have records for more than 50 years; 17 per cent for 30 to 50 years and 22 per cent are relatively new stations with less than 10 years of records (Dept of National Development, 1970).

What happens to rain in hydrological terms after it falls depends on its distribution, its seasonality and extreme values, and its frequency and intensity. These aspects are now considered together with brief comment on snow, storms, floods and, finally, droughts.

Rainfall Distribution

Precipitation and its distribution over the year, together with temperature, do much to characterize climates. In Australia, these range from the hot seasonally moist climates of the north and northeast to the more temperate always moist climates of the southeast and from the wet winters and hot dry summers of the 'Mediterranean' southwest to the hot dry climates of the centre. Median rainfall ranges from less than 255 mm in dry parts to well over 1,400 mm in wetter zones. General distributions are shown in Fig. 3.2 and Table 3.1. From these, it is apparent that most rain falls along a fairly narrow coastal perimeter and even this is discontinuous in the south and northwest. The following indicate just how dry large parts of the continent are:

0.8% of total area—less than 102 mm
51.4% of total area—less than 305 mm
62.5% of total area—less than 406 mm
3.9% of total area—more than 1,194 mm
0.6% of total area—more than 1,600 mm

(Dept of National Development, 1970)

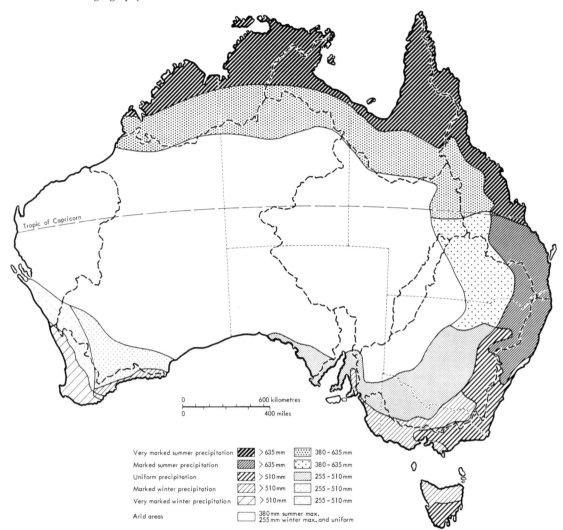

Fig. 3.3 Seasonal rainfall dominance. *Source*: adapted from *Atlas of Australian Resources*, 1973b.

The only areas away from the coast receiving moderate to heavy falls are in the Snowy Mountains and the western plateau of Tasmania. Elsewhere large coastal catchments drain from drier inland subcatchments towards wetter coastal ones. However, these areas near the divides are frequently the wettest parts of internal drainage systems because the greater part of these systems are in semi-arid or arid areas. Consequently, such upland tracts have profound effects on the general hydrology of these eastern divisions and also on water conservation potential, particularly in the Murray and Murrumbidgee.

SEASONS AND EXTREMES
Fig. 3.3 shows this distribution in terms of seasonal

dominance. Very marked summer rain (November-April to May-October ratio greater than 3:1) is limited to the three northern divisions (I, VIII and IX). This decreases from over 1,400 mm near the coast to about 380 mm at the arid margins. Marked summer precipitation (ratio greater than 1.3:1) is restricted to southern Queensland and northern New South Wales (Divisions I and II). Here the decrease is westwards from the coast 1,400 mm to 380 mm. Uniform rains (ratio less than 1.3:1) characterize southern New South Wales, eastern Victoria and southwest Tasmania (Divisions II and III). On the mainland, these fall to the west from 890 to 255 mm. The rest of the southeast has marked winter precipitation (greater than 1.3:1), with highest falls in western Tasmania and the Snowy

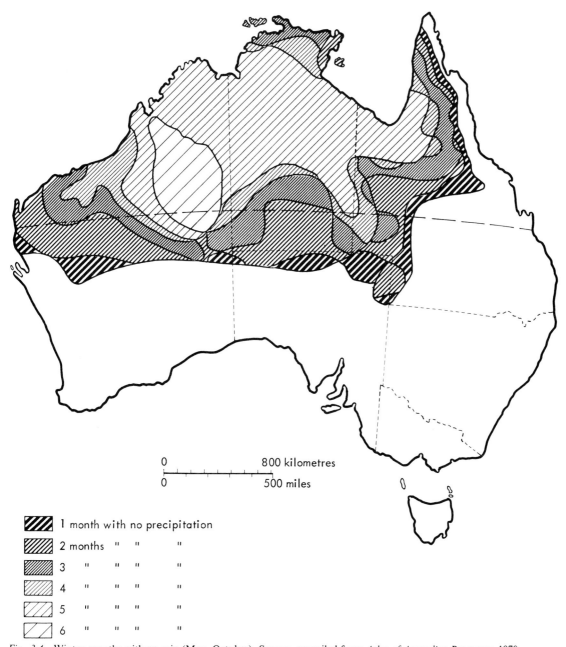

0   800 kilometres

0   500 miles

▨	1 month with no precipitation
▨	2 months " " "
▨	3 " " " "
▨	4 " " " "
▨	5 " " " "
▨	6 " " " "

Fig. 3.4 Winter months with no rain (May–October). *Source*: compiled from *Atlas of Australian Resources*, 1970.

Mountains (Divisions II, III, IV and V). Parts of the far southwest have a very marked winter rainfall (greater than 3:1) (Division VI) which falls from 890 mm at the coast to 255 mm near the arid margins. Much of the rest is arid with less than 255 mm in the south and east and less than 380 mm in the north.

This includes nearly all of Divisions VII, XII and XI and parts of IV and V (Dept of National Development, 1970).

Marked seasonal characteristics in inputs can place considerable stress on soil moisture through evaporation and transpiration in the dry season and also on

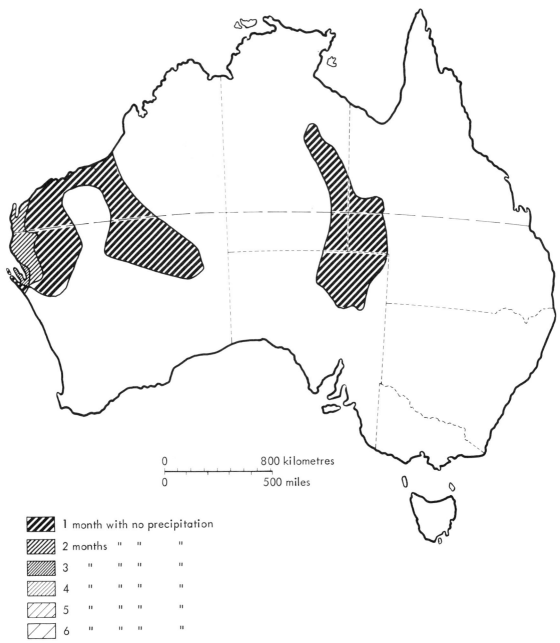

Fig. 3.5 Summer months with no rain (November–April). *Source*: compiled from *Atlas of Australian Resources*, 1970.

open water surfaces. Rivers often cease to flow and agricultural pursuits must be geared to seasonal conditions. Hydrological processes operate on a stop-go basis, as is evident from later parts of this chapter. Dry season characteristics prevail for most of the time in arid areas, with consequent adaptions by vegetation. However, processes can operate at higher rates following infrequent rather than seasonal inputs. Breaks in hydrological activities only become apparent in wetter areas during occasional droughts.

Variability of inputs is marked in most parts with water receipts being either very much above or below the fiftieth percentile. Munro (1974) mapped variability as the 'mean deviation of annual rainfalls from the

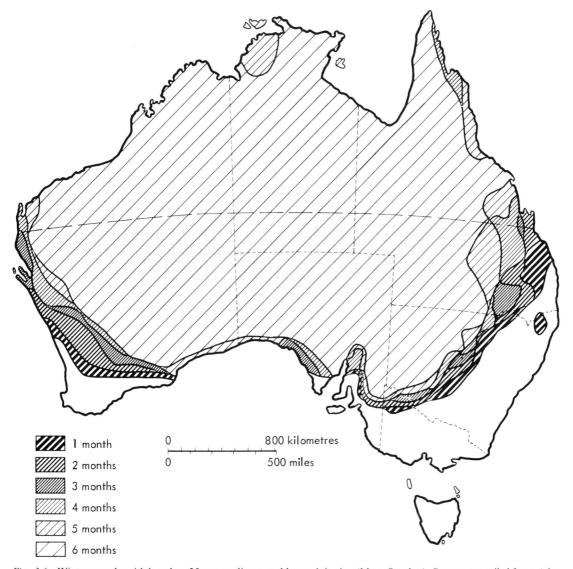

Legend:
- 1 month
- 2 months
- 3 months
- 4 months
- 5 months
- 6 months

0   800 kilometres

0   500 miles

Fig. 3.6 Winter months with less than 25 mm median monthly precipitation (May–October). *Source*: compiled from *Atlas of Australian Resources*, 1970.

long-term average' as a percentage. Lowest variability (and therefore the most reliable rain) of less than 15 per cent is in the far southwest (south of Perth) and far southeast coastal areas. In the area south of the line from the Eyre Peninsula to northern New South Wales it is less than 20 per cent, as it is around Darwin. Elsewhere around the arid centre, it is less than 30 per cent while most of the arid area has a variability of about 30 per cent. Much of the Indian Ocean division in the northwest has variabilities over 40 per cent. This can probably be attributed to the fact that, while for most of the time this area is very arid, there are occasional incursions of tropical cyclones bringing heavy downpours. Runoff from cyclonic rains may help to maintain a net outflow from this arid drainage division.

Examples of extremes are cited in the *Atlas of Australian Resources* (1970).

	Range	Median
Carnarvon, W.A.	68 – 644 mm	214 mm
Birdsville, Q.	34 – 542 mm	115 mm
Onslow, W.A.	14 – 997 mm	223 mm
Tully, Q.	2,666 – 7,897 mm	4,339 mm
Whim Creek, (1924)	4 mm – in one year	
Roebourne, W.A.	747 mm – in one day	324 mm

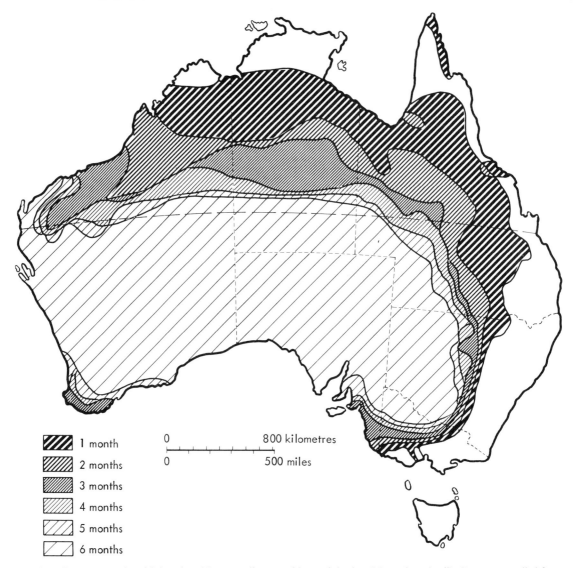

Fig. 3.7   Summer months with less than 25 mm median monthly precipitation (November–April). *Source*: compiled from *Atlas of Australian Resources*, 1970.

FREQUENCY AND INTENSITY

The frequency of rainfall, as well as quantity, is important hydrologically and in terms of vegetation growth. High frequency falls maintain a supply of water for soils, evaporation, transpiration, groundwater recharge and stream flow. Low frequency falls allow evaporation and transpiration to deplete soil moisture levels so that crops cannot be sown or will wilt and natural vegetation will eventually wilt; rivers dry up, as do surface waters in lakes and ponds; and water-tables fall. Such conditions obviously

characterize arid areas for most of the time but they also prevail in the north in winter and the south in summer and they affect uniform rainfall areas in time of drought.

Fig. 3.4 shows areas with no winter rain from one to six months. Much of the inland north has no rain for about five months. Fig. 3.5 indicates that the extent of no rain in summer months is much less and for much shorter periods. Fig. 3.6 shows the number of months with less than 25 mm using median values. All the arid core and most of the north have less than

Fig. 3.8 Twelve months with less than 25 mm median monthly precipitation. *Source*: compiled from *Atlas of Australian Resources*, 1970.

this for six months. Such low falls would not sustain much growth or maintain flow in rivers. Fig. 3.7 shows the same pattern for summer months. Here, most of the arid area and south has less than 25 mm per month for six months. Finally, Fig. 3.8 shows areas with less than this total for each of the twelve months. This area coincides with the central and southern deserts.

The average number of raindays can convey a crude measure of frequency as well as of intensity. However, a rainday is one where 0.25 mm is recorded and such low values have little hydrological significance. Measures of rainfall effectiveness such as those proposed by Prescott and Thomas (1949) are more relevant.

Number of raindays range from less than 20 (about once every 18 days if evenly spaced) for many parts of the arid core to over 240 in western Tasmania, two in every three days of the year. In the wetter parts of the north, there are from 80 to 120 raindays, mostly in summer, giving a high seasonal frequency. Most moister parts of the east coast have more than 120, while in the winter-rainfall areas of the south and southwest, there are more than 160 raindays. These would be much more frequent in winter than in summer.

Rainfall divided by raindays gives a measure of intensity. Jennings (1967) produced a map of such values based on the period 1911–40. Not unexpectedly the highest intensities (over 12.7 mm/day) were found in the north and values exceeded 20 mm on the wet coast of north Queensland. Even in arid areas, intensities are moderately high (5–12.7 mm), while in drier parts with winter rain, they drop below 5 mm. Even in wet Tasmania, only certain small areas show intensities above 10 mm.

Pluviograph data will replace the need for such computations and allow computation of probabilities of falls of certain magnitudes and duration with certain recurrence intervals. Such data are vital in runoff studies, especially where engineering design is necessary. Munro (1974) has given maximum rates for Sydney:

		Rate per hour
5 minutes	16.5 mm	198 mm
10 minutes	27.2 mm	163 mm
20 minutes	45.0 mm	135 mm
30 minutes	57. 9 mm	116 mm
1 hour	85.1 mm	85 mm

Data from the tropical north would probably show much higher falls as is indicated in the maximum daily falls for each State (Dept of National Development, 1970):

Cromanhurst, Q.	3.2.1893	907 mm
Whim Creek, W.A.	3.4.1898	747 mm
Dorrigo, N.S.W.	24.6.1950	636 mm
Roper Valley, N.T.	15.4.1963	545 mm
Ardrossan, S.A.	18.2.1946	460 mm
Mathinna, T.	5.4.1929	337 mm
Balook, V.	18.2.1951	275 mm

Jennings (1967), using engineering data, also produced a more effective rainfall intensity map, based on the maximum probable fall in 24 hours in a year. Ranges are from less than 25 mm for parts of the arid area to less than 64 mm for all the central core. However, local falls of this order would be quite significant in this type of environment as is shown later. In the north, the range is from 76 to over 114 mm and the upper level exceeds 178 mm around Cairns. The southeast coast is mainly over 64 mm, reaching 100 mm locally but dropping to 37 mm in western Victoria. In Tasmania, there is a wide range (less than 37 to over 114 mm) and elsewhere in the south, it is more limited (less than 37 to over 64 mm). Thus high intensity rains prevail in those areas of cyclonic, monsoonal and convectional rain, even into nearby arid areas. Lower intensities tend to characterize winter frontal rain areas of the south.

SNOW

Although snow falls infrequently over wide areas of the Eastern Highlands, it is only important as a hydrological input in the alpine areas of New South Wales and Victoria above 1,370 m and Tasmanian plateaux above 1,070 m. It is important because it represents a form of temporary surface storage in winter which then runs off in the spring melt. Falls and their survival are variable but there are no permanent snowfields.

STORMS AND FLOODS

Summer thunderstorms yielding high intensity rain or hail are more numerous in areas already described as having summer rain peaks. Around Darwin, there are over 80 per year, over 60 in the Kimberleys, over 50 in the Gulf country, 40–60 over the Eastern Highlands and only 10–30 elsewhere. Hail damage to crops can be high but it depends on the time of fall.

Prolonged high intensity rain is often associated with flooding but numerous circumstances can combine to promote flooding. Thus widespread flooding can occur almost everywhere at almost any time of the year, as can be shown where records are long. Obviously, there is a marked tendency for summer flooding from monsoonal and cyclonic rain in the north (Plate 12.1) but extratropical cyclones can give winter flooding in the summer rainfall maximum area of northern New South Wales. Coastal downpours have become common enough to make coastal valleys very flood prone, necessitating flood mitigation programmes. However, they are not uncommon west of the main divide where monsoonal soakings can affect large parts of the Eyre basin (Williams, 1969). Such inland floods are of long duration, moving slowly down the long rivers: they are also subject to high losses in evaporation and seepage, where influent conditions exist. In dry areas, flood rains may exceed median annual precipitation and the runoff resulting may be up to two and a half times the average annual runoff (Munro, 1974).

DROUGHTS

Low precipitation and high variability are common to most parts of Australia. Thus, it is inevitable in probability terms that there must be extended periods either without rain or with very little. This applies to the more arid areas particularly but also to the wide margins beyond.

Between 1855 and 1955, there were seven major droughts (AAR, 1970). These affected most of the continent; numerous others have affected smaller areas. Many definitions of drought exist but in terms of rainfall deciles, Gibbs and Maher (1967) have related drought years to the driest year in ten or the first decile, though this excludes some severe droughts of less than one year's duration. In hydrological terms, a drought represents the cessation of normal inputs. Consequently, evaporation and transpiration make great demands on available water in soils and shallow water-tables. Little excess water is available and rivers cease to flow. Crops and natural vegetation are eventually left without supplies and though drought-breaking rains often start processes again, they fall on unprotected surfaces and so create severe soil erosion and sedimentation in river channels.

It is apparent that rain and other inputs are important in hydrology but not just in terms of totals. Intensities, duration and extremes are all important in influencing subsequent levels of activity in this physical system which are examined in the following sections.

Atmospheric Losses
Australian inputs are subject to high rates of evaporation and transpiration. Evaporation occurs from moisture intercepted by vegetation and other objects, water surfaces, depression storages and soil moisture. Transpiration of water through plants removes water mainly from the soil but also from shallow groundwater reserves in low-lying areas. The combined loss is referred to as evapotranspiration. This is high, relative to other continents, because of high prevailing temperatures, high levels of radiation, low humidity and generally stable conditions with clear skies. Temporal variations occur with changes in availability of water, and also in the south with cooler more cloudy conditions in winter.

Two kinds of evapotranspiration have been defined (Thornthwaite, 1948; Penman, 1948): potential and actual. If there is never a shortage of moisture, whether natural or artificial, the potential rate dependent on atmospheric conditions and global position, will prevail and this will be the actual rate. Where water availability fluctuates with variable and often infrequent inputs, evapotranspiration proceeds at variable rates, sometimes at the potential rate but more often the actual rate is below the potential rate. Such losses are dependent not only on atmospheric conditions but also on soil and vegetal characteristics. Since rainfall is generally low in Australia and atmospheric losses potentially very high, it follows that residual water for other means of disposal such as runoff is quite limited. These unseen losses are significant (370 mm mean) but locally they are difficult to measure and to estimate. Evaporation from water bodies is virtually a continuous process, high by day and low by night, dependent on radiation, temperature, humidity, wind, length of day, percentage of direct sunlight and atmospheric pressure. It can be measured for small surface areas from tanks or evaporimeters as a water balance experiment.

$$E = P + I \pm \Delta S$$

with P being precipitation, I irrigation inputs and ΔS change in storage. However, no simple relationship exists between tank and nearby large surface water storage. Monthly tank coefficients can be derived with much observation and measurement and these can then be used to estimate real losses from storage (AWRC 1970a, 1971b and 1971c).

Fig. 3.9 shows losses from about 100 evaporimeters (cf. *c.* 8,000 rain gauges). They range from less than 500 mm for cool wet Tasmania to over 3,300 mm for the south central desert. Monthly and total values for two stations in most of the drainage divisions (AWRC, 1965) are given in Table 3.2. Only in five cases is precipitation greater than evaporation. In the other nineteen cases evaporation exceeds precipitation by up to 36.5 times.

In terms of area, losses from soils and vegetation are more important. These depend on water available in the soil which in turn is conditioned by prior inputs, soil type, depth, capillary suction, cover, depths of roots and textural variations. After extraction at the potential rate following rain or irrigation, it is the range of vegetation and soil types, as well as climatic factors, which condition the subsequent loss. A very complex and dynamic set of characteristics exists and these have been the subject of much research in recent times (Aust. Nat. Comm. UNESCO, 1974).

In very wet areas, there is either a balance between evapotranspiration and rainfall or an excess of precipitation which then runs off. Here evapotranspiration remains essentially at the potential rate. In dry areas, such conditions only prevail after infrequent inputs of rain. As pressure increases on soil moisture so evapotranspiration drops to a subpotential level and a soil moisture deficit builds up. This may or may not be remedied in subsequent rain events.

In Australia, there are three broad types of situation with fairly mobile geographic boundaries.

1. In the uniformly wet areas of the southeastern divisions and also the wettest part of Queensland, actual nearly equals potential evapotranspiration. Excess moisture either runs off or recharges groundwater sources.

2a. In the north and northeast divisions where summer rains are marked, actual equals potential evapotranspiration for most of the wet season and there is little stress except near southern margins. However, in the dry winters which are still warm, actual is less than potential evapotranspiration. Then soils dry out, shallow-rooted species die off, active vegetation is restricted to watercourses or swamp areas, where

Table 3.2 Median Monthly and Annual Precipitation, Average Monthly and Annual Tank Evaporation and Annual E:P Ratios for Selected Stations in Each Drainage Division (in mm)

Div. no.	Name	Median Precip. Aver. Evap.	J	F	M	A	M	J	J	A	S	O	N	D	Year	E:P ratio
I	Tully	P	787.4	726.4	744.2	436.9	322.6	200.7	170.2	109.2	116.8	86.4	147.3	160.0	4,476	
		E	127.0	101.6	101.6	101.6	88.9	76.2	76.2	101.6	127.0	152.4	152.4	152.4	1,346	0.3
	Emerald	P	86.4	83.8	68.6	20.3	20.3	22.9	22.9	12.7	10.2	35.6	48.3	76.2	607	
		E	215.9	190.5	177.8	139.7	114.3	76.2	76.2	114.3	139.7	203.2	215.9	254.0	1,905	3.1
II	Dorrigo	P	215.9	233.7	223.5	149.9	101.6	73.7	53.3	43.2	71.1	91.4	76.2	167.6	1,836	
		E	139.7	101.6	101.6	76.2	76.2	38.1	38.1	63.5	76.2	101.6	127.0	152.4	1,092	0.6
	Scone	P	61.0	55.9	40.6	33.0	22.9	33.0	33.0	33.0	33.0	43.2	45.7	61.6	612	
		E	152.4	114.3	114.3	76.2	50.8	38.1	38.1	50.8	76.2	101.6	152.4	152.4	1,117	1.8
III	Melrose	P	27.9	33.0	27.9	40.6	38.1	27.9	40.6	27.9	35.6	48.3	38.1	43.2	483	
		E	127.0	101.6	76.2	50.8	38.1	25.4	25.4	25.4	38.1	50.8	76.2	101.6	737	1.5
	Lake Margaret	P	236.2	190.5	223.5	320.0	330.2	322.6	365.8	365.8	353.1	330.2	322.6	226.1	3,597	
		E	101.6	76.2	76.5	50.8	38.1	25.4	25.4	25.4	38.1	38.1	76.2	101.6	686	0.2
IV	Nymagee	P	30.5	22.9	17.8	20.3	27.9	33.0	25.4	25.4	20.3	22.9	20.3	27.9	401	
		E	304.8	215.9	177.8	127.0	76.2	63.5	50.8	76.2	114.3	165.1	203.2	266.7	1,829	4.6
	Mt Buffalo	P	71.1	66.0	86.5	96.5	144.8	205.7	226.1	238.8	188.0	170.2	106.7	96.5	1,913	
		E	177.8	127.0	101.4	76.2	50.8	25.4	25.4	38.1	50.8	76.2	101.6	127.0	991	0.5
V	Adelaide	P	12.7	10.2	17.8	38.1	61.0	68.6	66.0	58.4	45.7	43.2	22.9	17.8	528	
		E	228.6	177.8	152.4	101.6	50.8	50.8	50.8	50.8	88.7	114.3	152.4	203.2	1,422	2.7
	Quorn	P	10.2	7.6	5.1	12.7	25.4	30.5	30.5	35.6	25.4	22.9	17.8	15.2	320	
		E	330.2	254.0	241.3	152.4	76.2	63.5	63.5	101.6	127.0	177.8	228.6	292.1	2,108	6.6
VI	Pingelly	P	2.5	2.5	7.6	25.4	55.9	76.2	81.3	63.5	40.6	22.9	7.6	7.6	445	
		E	279.4	203.2	190.5	127.0	76.2	50.8	50.8	50.8	76.2	127.0	177.8	228.6	1,626	3.7
	Pemberton	P	27.9	17.8	38.1	12.7	185.4	226.1	261.6	210.8	144.8	119.4	61.0	43.2	1,516	
		E	152.4	127.0	101.6	76.2	76.2	38.1	38.1	50.8	76.2	101.6	101.6	152.4	1,092	0.7
VII	Roebourne	P	12.7	27.9	17.8	0.0	10.2	15.2	2.5	0.0	0.0	0.0	0.0	7.6	279	
		E	304.8	203.2	203.2	203.2	165.1	101.6	127.0	139.7	177.8	228.6	279.4	304.8	2,438	8.7
	Murgoo	P	2.5	7.6	5.1	5.1	20.3	27.9	22.9	12.7	2.5	2.5	0.0	2.5	188	
		E	368.3	330.2	292.1	203.2	127.0	76.2	76.2	101.6	139.7	203.2	279.4	355.6	2,565	13.6

Div. no.	Name	Median Precip. Aver. Evap.	J	F	M	A	M	J	J	A	S	O	N	D	Year	E:P ratio
VIII	Darwin	P	383.5	304.8	248.9	68.6	0.0	0.0	0.0	0.0	2.5	38.1	109.2	213.4	1,524	1.5
		E	152.4	152.4	152.4	152.4	190.5	177.8	177.8	203.2	215.9	228.6	228.6	177.8	2,210	
	Halls Crk	P	104.1	86.4	40.6	2.5	0.0	0.0	0.0	0.0	0.0	5.1	22.9	53.3	447	6.0
		E	304.8	228.6	228.6	228.6	177.8	152.4	152.4	177.8	228.6	254.0	279.4	254.0	2,667	
IX	Burketown	P	170.2	154.9	83.8	5.1	0.0	0.0	0.0	0.0	0.0	0.0	27.9	73.7	693	3.3
		E	177.8	177.8	177.8	177.8	152.4	152.4	152.4	177.8	203.2	254.0	254.0	228.6	2,286	
	Cloncurry	P	88.9	86.4	38.1	5.1	2.5	2.5	0.0	0.0	0.0	5.1	25.4	43.2	434	6.3
		E	304.8	254.0	241.3	215.9	177.8	152.4	127.0	177.8	228.6	292.1	292.1	292.1	2,743	
X	Longreach	P	43.2	45.7	33.0	17.8	5.1	12.7	7.6	2.5	2.5	12.7	17.8	43.2	401	6.2
		E	292.1	228.6	228.6	190.5	139.7	101.6	101.6	139.7	203.2	266.7	292.1	304.8	2,489	
	Alice Springs	P	15.2	15.2	10.2	5.1	2.5	7.6	0.0	0.0	2.5	15.2	17.8	17.8	257	9.5
		E	330.2	279.4	241.3	177.8	127.0	88.9	88.9	127.0	177.8	241.3	266.7	292.1	2,438	
	Mulka	P	0.0	5.1	5.1	0.0	2.5	2.5	0.0	0.0	0.0	2.5	0.0	2.5	86	36.5
		E	406.4	368.3	355.6	228.6	152.4	114.3	101.6	152.4	215.9	304.8	368.3	381.0	3,150	
XI	Adavale	P	38.1	38.1	22.9	12.7	17.8	20.3	12.7	7.6	2.5	15.2	17.8	30.5	333	7.7
		E	330.2	254.0	254.0	190.5	139.7	88.9	101.6	127.0	190.5	254.0	304.8	317.5	2,565	
XII	Warburton Range	P	7.6	7.6	2.5	7.6	7.6	10.2	2.5	2.5	2.5	2.5	7.6	15.2	168	19.4
		E	406.4	368.3	355.6	254.0	177.8	127.0	114.3	165.1	215.9	317.5	368.3	368.3	3,251	
	Deakin	P	2.5	7.6	7.6	7.6	10.2	7.6	10.2	12.7	2.5	12.7	7.6	7.6	155	13.9
		E	304.8	254.0	228.6	152.4	114.3	88.9	76.2	114.3	152.4	190.5	215.9	279.4	2,159	

Source: based on AWRC, 1965.

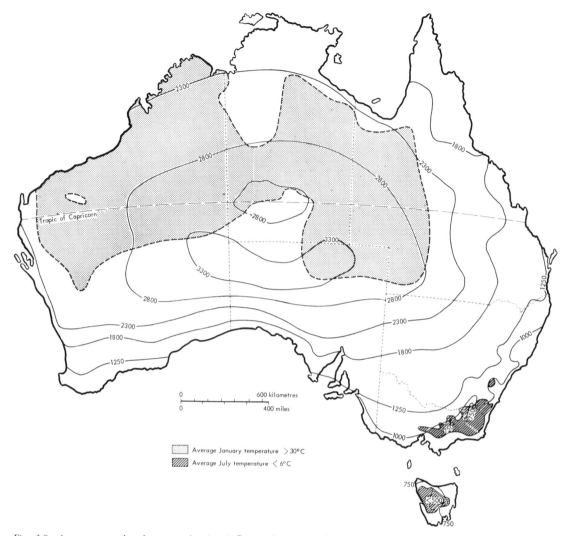

Fig. 3.9   Average annual tank evaporation (mm). *Source*: based on *Atlas of Australian Resources*, 1973b.

groundwater sources can be used. Water-tables fall in this period.

2b. In the southwest, the Gulf and parts of the other southeast divisions, winter rains predominate. Water surpluses occur in the cooler half of the year and actual equals potential evapotranspiration but rates are low. Although summers are not so dry as winters in the north, high temperatures and lower rainfall make actual much less than potential evapotranspiration. Then marked deficiencies occur.

3. Arid areas and broad marginal areas of lower rainfall always have actual less than potential evapotranspiration except for short periods after soaking rains. In such times plant growth is revitalized, soil

moisture replenished and there may even be localized runoff.

Evapotranspirimeters are used to measure potential losses in moist or irrigated areas and lysimeters to measure actual evapotranspiration (Rose *et al.*, 1966; McIlroy and Angus 1963), while Fitzpatrick (1963) has developed a technique for estimating potential losses from climatic data (.8 × Pan Estimates). This has been applied in numerous resource surveys (e.g. Fitzpatrick, 1967) for both evaporation and potential evapotranspiration. Other techniques have been reviewed (AWRC, 1970b).

Potential evaporation ranges from 500–3,300 mm (Fig. 3.9). In more than 75 per cent of the area it is

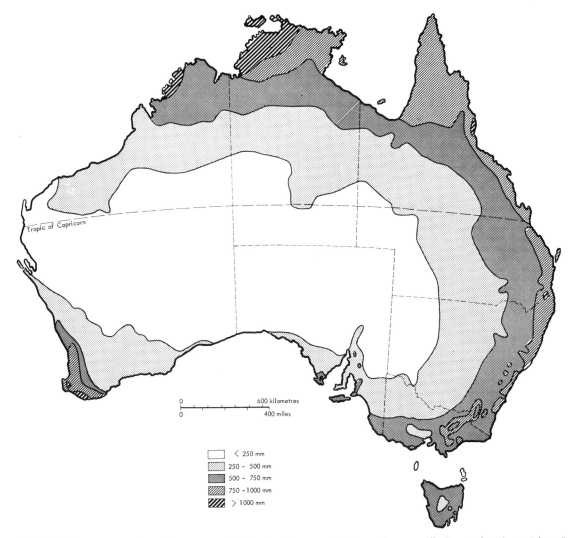

Fig. 3.10 Average annual actual evapotranspiration based on precipitation minus runoff. *Source*: based on *Atlas of Australian Resources*, 1973b.

over 2,000 mm but 78.2 per cent of the area gets less than 600 mm of rain. Thus evaporation opportunity is very limited in terms of area and duration. Also for any net runoff to occur in most dry areas, there must be large temporary surpluses. These waters drain to local low points in the interior and disconnected divisions where removal is completed by evaporation from salt lakes.

Actual evapotranspiration is obviously much lower than potential at most times and in most places because there is insufficient moisture for losses to proceed at the potential rate. Evaluation has been achieved by taking the difference between rainfall and runoff (Dept of National Development, 1967; Ceplecha, 1971). The range is from less than 250 mm to over 1,000 mm (Fig. 3.10).

In his work, Ceplecha (1971) defined three zones:

A. In the areas of no net runoff, in internal or disconnected drainage divisions, evapotranspiration equals rainfall. Actual evapotranspiration is determined by rainfall and losses from soil. In these dry areas, rain may very between about 100 and 625 mm but runoff approaches zero on average. In the north, maximum actual evapotranspiration is in summer when there is some moisture, but in the south, greatest losses probably occur in winter and spring, following small winter rains. In the hot summers there would be little moisture for actual evapotranspiration.

B. Actual evapotranspiration nearly equals potential evapotranspiration in all months in the wetter areas of uniform rainfall. Obviously actual evapotranspiration will decline in cooler months and most of the water lost is effected by heat availability. Surface runoff commonly occurs and larger streams are perennial, that is, they flow in nine years out of ten (Dept of National Development, 1967). These are the areas of greatest rainfall and runoff but actual losses may vary from less than 500 mm in cool Tasmania to over 1,250 mm on the hot coast of Queensland. Lower rates of evapotranspiration also occur in the highlands of the southeast. The higher rainfall and lower temperatures mean a much greater runoff.

C. Between A and B is a transition zone, the position and extent of which varies annually. For instance, at the rainfall probability expressed by the wettest year in ten, Zone B extends well into this zone. However, at the 90 per cent probability the reverse is true. In this zone, actual evapotranspiration equals potential only in some wet months, which occur during summer in the north and in winter in the south. For the rest of the year there are soil moisture deficits as reserves are lost by actual evapotranspiration. Consequently, runoff and groundwater recharge are either intermittent or seasonal and streams are either ephemeral or intermittent with cease-to-flow stages of variable durations in between rains or in dry seasons.

These represent largely average conditions. Annual variations in water balance which are very common are largely 'conditioned' by precipitation. In a wet year, both actual evapotranspiration and runoff can increase. Where actual equals potential evapotranspiration already, the potential rate will fall and the excess is all runoff. Elsewhere, runoff may get part of the excess, particularly after the rain event, but most may be stored to give higher actual evapotranspiration.

Ceplecha (1971) used the 10th, 50th and 90th percentiles to show variations in the three zones. With precipitation at the 90 per cent probability, the drier zone almost reaches the main divide in the east, whereas at the 10 per cent level, it shrinks to the west and centre. At the former level, Zone B only appears in the Eastern Highlands and east coast of Queensland. At the 10 per cent probability, it increases slightly as marginal areas attain equality of actual and potential evapotranspiration. Zone C at 90 per cent probability includes only coastal divisions but at 10 per cent both precipitation and runoff are greater. Then it extends well west of the divide, and it also takes in parts of the highly variable catchments like the Fitzroy, Burdekin and Darling.

Atmospheric losses cannot be ignored. They represent about 88 per cent of the precipitation. Over most of the landmass they are very much conditioned by the rain received and they would be much higher if more moisture were available. In other words, over most of the continent, rainfall is much lower than potential evapotranspiration. In dry areas, losses equal inputs but in wet areas, rains are sufficiently high to produce net runoff in hot areas. It cooler areas, losses are less considerable. Consequently, if they are wet, runoff is high. Ranges in evaporation and evapotranspiration are shown in Table 3.1.

Soil Moisture

Soil moisture is a complex hydrological subsystem: water in the soil is highly variable with depth, time, and in space. It is the bank of moisture essential for plant growth and as such is an important part of hydrology.

While it is possible to map many distributions of hydrological factors, this is not so easy with soil moisture. Moisture indices have been derived by Fitzpatrick and Nix (1970) and included in the *Atlas of Australian Resources* (Dept of Minerals and Energy, 1973b), but so many combinations of inputs, outputs and soil moisture conditions exist that to map average conditions it would be necessary to make many assumptions about soil and canopy. To determine the soil water balance at one point is difficult; to map it other than in any general term over a wide area would be extremely hazardous. Thus, a consideration of soil moisture conditions in Australia is restricted to some outline of the complex system and to some discussion of typical conditions which may exist.

Water reaching the soil surface may either infiltrate or run off. That which enters the soil does so by virtue of the physical characteristics of the soil and the level of moisture already there. Rainfall intensities and infiltration capacities, which decline with time in wetting, determine how much will enter the soil. Where two surfaces are adjacent and one is impervious, there may be run-on from that surface to the nearby pervious level. Water can thus enter the soils in two ways. Water can leave the soil in many ways: evaporation dependent on capillary suction; transpiration depending on the type of cover, depth of soil, type of root systems; throughflow or a lateral downslope movement on slopes; and percolation to lower depths and the water-table. Clearly, with such high evapotranspiration losses in Australia, most of the losses to the system are upwards through direct evaporation, which can concentrate salts in the upper layers of the profile where they are present in drier areas, or through transpiration where moisture is evacuated through the plants.

Where a water-table exists at depth, there may be an

intermediate subzone of varying thickness. Here water movements are mainly through the system from top to base. No roots are there to withdraw water and evaporation cannot take place. Above the water-table, the third subzone is the capillary fringe. Here water is held above the wholly saturated zone at depths dependent on textures. In finer materials this may be a metre or more in depth; in coarse materials it is shallow. Where the capillary fringe intersects the surface, direct evaporation can remove water from groundwater supplies.

The measurement of soil moisture and the various inputs and outputs helps to understand some of the complexities. Since plant growth is dependent on this source, it is necessary to know what is injected into the system with rain or run-on conditions. Knowledge of the response of vegetation to inputs and then to the rundown period as the water is removed can be vital in sustaining crops and vegetation.

Prediction of necessary changes may assist where water can be supplied by irrigation and where it cannot, in making appropriate production decisions.

It was considered necessary for the Representative Basins Committee 'to assist in assessing and verifying the predictive capability of sub-surface moisture phases of the (hydrologic) model, and the relationships between evaporation and potential evaporation in the derivation of rainfall excesses' (AWRC, 1969). In the past, undisturbed soil cores were extracted at various levels, and weighed before and after drying to find the water content. This is a slow destructive process. More often now, a neutron thermalization method is used. A neutron source and detector are used in a permanent access tube at various depths, usually from 30 cm up to 2 metres or more. Moisture levels are determined from the count of slow neutrons and a calibration curve for each level. This is a fast non-destructive method. For instance, it has been estimated that work taking 244 days under the old methods now can be completed in 36 (AWRC, 1974b).

Tensiometers have been used to measure water requirements for irrigation but many other developments have been made (AWRC, 1974b). Monitoring of soil moisture amounts and movement through time show the effects of inputs and their subsequent movements and losses. There is not such a demand for these data in wet environments but in drier areas the crop capabilities may be assessed.

The generally low precipitation over much of Australia and the seasonal characteristics of the north and south indicate the soil moisture deficits are more common than surpluses. Both the incidence and amount of rain, together with the subsequent high losses to evapotranspiration, do much to maintain low level of soil moisture. These create nearly permanent stress in arid areas and seasonal stress in the

northern winter and southern summer. These pressures are important in influencing types and patterns of native vegetation but their effects are often greater on introduced crops and grasses.

Thornwaite (1948) adopted an average figure of about 100 mm water in the soil profile of his evapotranspiration model as did Fitzpatrick and Nix (1970). Clearly some places in Australia would not receive that much in a year and in many places this might represent several months rain. Evapotranspiration rates are high enough to remove several times that amount. It has been estimated that, at the end of the dry summer in South Australia, the deficit is between 80 and 200 mm (AWRC, 1974b). Thus a large part of rain would seem to enter any soil receptive to infiltration, advance part way down the profile and then be used or lost, or survive at quite low levels. In heavier rains there is always the risk that intensity may overcome infiltration capacity. Then there would be localized runoff even in arid areas (Jackson, 1958; Williams, 1969).

In areas with uniform rain and lower temperatures, losses from the soil are less between rain events. Excess water runs off or percolates to water-tables. Such conditions prevail in northern summers, where there is sufficient rain in spite of high losses to maintain soil moisture, runoff and groundwater recharge. In the south, summer deficits are high. Winter surpluses are also high because of lower temperatures so that springs often have sufficient water, though this is depleted as rains become more infrequent with summer and temperatures rise.

Thus, in Australia, it is possible to distinguish in general terms, at least four broad types of soil moisture situations:

1. The almost permanently dry profiles of arid soils, where rain is so light and infrequent that field capacity throughout the profile is seldom reached. After rains, high evaporation from upper levels and transpiration from revitalized vegetation removes most of the moisture.

2. Shallow soil profiles or bare rock slopes may prevail in many areas of locally steep terrain. In these areas, runoff coefficients are high and in arid parts such locations provide important sources of run-on moisture. This can replenish adjacent more previous soils and also recharge local groundwater.

3. Seasonally wet and dry profiles typify monsoonal and convection areas of the north and frontal rain areas of the south. In the wet season water surpluses are common, decreasing naturally towards the arid margins, while in the dry season water resources are soon used up as inputs decline and higher evapotranspiration occurs.

4. In the high rainfall areas of the east coast and uniform rainfall areas of the southeast, soil moisture is

Table 3.3   Some Groundwater Characteristics for the Twelve Drainage Divisions

Division		Rainfall	Groundwater requirements	Geology		Unconsolidated[b]	Remarks
				Fractured	Sedimentary basins		
I	N.E. Coast	Wet summer	Low	Much in E. Highlands Low yields < 5m³/hr	Several incl. Bowen, part of Great Artesian Basin. Fig. 3.11	Coastal valleys A.D.C. locally important	Burdekin important. 46,000 hectares irrigated from bores (< 30m). Yields 45–450 m³/hr. Draft 320 mill. m³. Recharge 200 mill. m³ (Aust. Nat. Comm. UNESCO, 1974)
II	S.E. Coast	Fairly wet summer, winter or uniform	Low	Much in E. Highlands Low yields 1–3m³/hr	Clarence, Sydney, Otway, etc. Fig. 3.11	A Hunter C Tomago and Botany A_e Victoria	Tomago and Botany Sands yield 41.7 mill. m³/yr (Munro, 1974)
III	Tasmania	Wet winter and uniform	Low	80% of island	14%	C Flinders Island	Surface supplies more than adequate
IV	Murray-Darling	Dry but wet E. & S. perimeter S.U.W.A.[a]	High in parts: low settlement densities	Limited to E. & S. divides mainly	Great Artesian Basin (N.) Murray Basin (S.) Fig. 3.11	A large areas	Irrigation important in Namoi, Lachlan, St George areas from alluvial sources. Sub-alluvial sources important in Victoria. 1,140 N.S.W. bores in Great Artesian Basin (470 ceased to flow) yield 0.6 mill. m³/day
V	S. Aust. Gulf	Dry: winter rains in S.	High	Mt Lofty Ra. low yields but up to 50 m³/hr in permeable.	Pirrie, Torrens, Borossa, Vincent, etc.	A large areas	High yields from Vincent Basin but also high imports from River Murray
VI	S.W. Coast	Low: winter	High in some areas	Large areas but limited yields	Perth— W. of Darling Fault	C in several areas	Coastal sands water for Perth: also some water from Perth Basin
VII	Indian Ocean	V. low arid	High locally low population	Large areas no great potential	Carnarvon, part of Perth Basin	C wide areas A main valleys	Unconsolidated water sources used for Port Hedland, Onslow and Carnarvon. Confined water for stock from Perth Basin

Division	Rainfall	Groundwater requirements	Fractured	Geology — Sedimentary basins	Unconsolidated[b]	Remarks
VIII Timor	Wet summer dry winter	High in dry season	Large areas low yields	Fitzroy-Canning, Derby, etc. Fig. 3.11	C wide areas A locally	Good artesian water in Canning Basin. Sub-artesian conditions prevail at yields of < 70m³/hr from 300 m depth. Pine Creek dolomites give > 200m³/hr for Darwin. Water-tables fall up to 10 m in dry season
IX Gulf of Carpentaria	Wet summer	High in dry season	Large areas in N.T., smaller areas in Q.	N. part of Great Artesian Basin	C narrow in N.T. A veneer in Q. over basin sediments	Near coasts fairly good water available from unconsolidated sediments. Only limited development with very small population
X Lake Eyre	Dry	High locally	Limited areas in N.W.	Most of area dominated by Great Artesian Basin. Others see Fig. 3.11	A large areas of Channel Country A_s Simpson	Very thin population area. Surface and underground sources very important. Much stock water from artesian sources
XI Bulloo-Bancannia	Dry	High very locally	—	Mainly Great Artesian Basin	A large areas	Quality is often low from sediments and upper aquifer but useful from lower artesian levels. Very thinly populated
XII Western Plateau	Dry	High very locally	Vast areas, small yields for stock uses	Eucla, Fitzroy-Canning, etc. Fig. 3.11	A and A_s large areas	Very thinly populated area. Very poorly endowed with ground and surface water. Local details only are known with many areas not examined. Some water in ancient river channels (Beard, 1973).

Sources: mainly AWRC, 1965. Other sources noted in remarks.

[a] S Summer; U uniform; W winter; A arid

[b] A alluvial; D deltaic; C coastal; A_c aeolian coastal sands; A_s arid sands

high for most of the time. Either very heavy rains or frequent rain and lower losses mean that no great stresses are imposed on soil water.

Categories 1 and 2 are found mainly in the internal and disconnected drainage divisions and the inland parts of southwestern and western divisions. Northern and mainly southwestern divisions would be in the third category, while the wetter parts of the eastern and southeastern divisions would be in 4.

Precipitation is the major source of soil moisture and evapotranspiration the major sink. If $P - ET$ is positive there is an increase in storage. This can be nearly permanent, seasonal or intermittent. If negative, there is a decrease in storage. As extractable water approaches zero, plants will wilt and die. Where this is the norm or seasonal, there is adaptation but elsewhere this may not be the case and stress damage may be more permanent.

Groundwater

Below the ground surface vast quantities of water are held in voids and cavities in rocks and mantling unconsolidated materials. Most of this water exists below water-tables in what is often referred to as the zone of saturation. It has been estimated that 11 per cent of the world's fresh water is stored at depths of less than 800 m (Barry, 1969). Assuming that such water is beneath landmasses and is located in an average 5 per cent porosity, this represents about 40 m of water. Another 15 per cent of fresh water is held below 800 m and, with the same porosity, this is about 50 m of water. Assuming that 75 per cent of all fresh water is held in ice caps, the water on which hydrology focuses so intently represents less than 0.5 per cent of fresh water (i.e., atmosphere 0.035 per cent, rivers 0.03 per cent, lakes 0.03 per cent, and soil moisture 0.06 per cent (Barry, 1969).

Although there is much concern with groundwater in dry areas only minute quantities are involved with near-surface hydrology. For instance the annual yield from the Great Artesian Basin only averages 0.1 mm depth over the whole basin. That from the Adelaide Plains is only 3.2 mm. These are much less than average values for rain, runoff and losses from the soil which are 420,50 and 370 mm respectively.

In areas where potential evapotranspiration is many times the precipitation, clearly groundwater becomes important. It has advantages over surface storage in that it has low evaporation losses, and there are high capacities and low costs in development. These may be offset by slow responses in the aquifer and high costs of pumping (Aust. Nat. Comm. UNESCO, 1974). Water has to be found by exploration and drilling (Aust. Nat. Comm. UNESCO, 1974) but location of water may not satisfy any demand if concentrations of dissolved salts are too high.

The quality and quantity of groundwater is influenced very much by geology. The former depends on the time water has been underground and the characteristics of rocks it has passed through. The latter depends on the nature of rocks and unconsolidated material, as well as their structural arrangements. Because geology is so important groundwater classifications often utilize rock type and mineral concentration (AWRC, 1965 and Dept of National Development, 1953). Three rock type divisions are used:

1. unconsolidated rocks of alluvial, aeolian, coastal and lacustrine origins which occupy 1.825 million km² or 24 per cent of the total land area of Australia;

2. porous rocks, usually of the less deformed sedimentary basins, comprising 4.954 million km² or 64 per cent of the total area;

3. fractured rocks, including igneous, metamorphic and older more deformed sedimentary rocks, extending over 2.912 million km² or 38 per cent of the total area.

As the sum of these percentages suggests, unconsolidated rocks often mantle porous or fractured rocks. Water from these three sources has been sampled, unevenly in space and time, for flow rates and quality. Rates vary from less than 1 m³ hr to over 450 m³ hr but details of safe yields from all aquifers are not generally well known. Information too is often scattered but it has been brought together (Dept of National Development, 1953; AWRC, 1965; W.C. and I.C., 1971). Quality has also been mapped (AWRC, 1965 and Dept of National Development, 1953) and classified in terms of concentration of salts and dissolved solids:

less than 1,000 ppm	good quality for stock, domestic, irrigation and urban supplies if found in sufficient quantity;
1,000– 3,000 ppm	good quality for stock and irrigation of salt tolerant species;
3,000– 7,000 ppm	fair quality for most stock;
7,000–14,000 ppm	poor quality, suitable for sheep and cattle to about 10,000 ppm;
over 14,000 ppm	bad and unusable.

Since the suitable upper limit for people is only about 500 ppm, in most cases groundwater can only be used for stock and sometimes for irrigation (Munro, 1974).

Knowledge of safe yields is fairly limited but data are available for some important sources (Dept of National Development, 1953).

A. Great Artesian Basin. This vast basin of 1.735 million km² or 22.6 per cent of Australia yields 199 million m³ yr or a mean depth of 0.1 mm, rather less than the annual groundwater yield from the

Tropic of Capricorn

0 ___ 600 kilometres
0 ___ 400 miles

Fig. 3.11 Main sedimentary basins and drainage divisions. *Source*: based on AWRC, 1965.

Burdekin delta and about 10 per cent of the storage of the Warragamba Dam in the Sydney water supply system. If all the water were suitable the annual total would only be enough to supply Sydney for 114 days in 1963. Nevertheless its importance to Queensland cannot be underestimated because this water supports most of the sheep and a large part of the cattle population.

B. The Vincent Basin or Adelaide Plains yields 9.07 million m³ yr from about 2,850 km², a mean depth of about 3.2 mm. Although small in terms of runoff such water is protected from evaporation, which exceeds 2,300 mm in this area.

Groundwater supplies are important when rainfall is less than 750 mm: this includes about 80 per cent of the country. It is or was derived mainly from rainwater, which percolates to great depths in suitable lithologies, where hydrostatic conditions influence its movement. Because movement is very slow, particularly in confined artesian waters, water yields probably fell as rain in much earlier geological times.

Where groundwater supplies intersect the surface as in effluent rivers, springs, and temporary or permanent lakes, it is subject to evaporation losses. It is in this way that an internal dynamic balance is maintained in the large and small internal basins which occupy so much of interior Australia.

There is also some interdependence between groundwater and surface runoff. Run-on in dry areas, and then percolation and influent losses, where water-tables are below the stream bed, cause surface waters to recharge groundwater supplies. This is important around Alice Springs and some other areas investigated for local irrigation (Perry *et al.*, 1963). In wetter districts, excesses are returned to the surface in springs and marshes in depressions. This water forms base flow components for perennial and intermittent streams. Table 3.3 sets out details and examples of groundwater for the twelve drainage divisions (based on AWRC, 1965 and Munro, 1974) and Fig. 3.11 shows the distribution of the main sedimentary basins.

Thus although amounts of water change involved were small enough to have been ignored by Ceplecha (1971), they are nevertheless extremely important to the small and isolated communities of a large part of Australia. Much research has been continued in recent years and this has been reviewed (Aust. Nat. Comm. UNESCO, 1974).

Runoff

Water which enters channels from overland flow, interflow and base flow sources constitutes runoff or stream discharge. Overland flow occurs when rainfall overcomes local infiltration capacities and water moves down the slopes to join the hierarchical network of ephemeral, intermittent and perennial streams. Interflow or throughflow is the water which moves downslope just below the surface at much slower rates in the soil horizons. Base flow joins intermittent streams in the wet season or perennial streams from groundwater sources.

Normally, runoff is regarded as the final stage of the hydrological cycle, where excess water is returned to the oceans. However, water in a channel is still subject to evaporation and to bank and bed infiltration, particularly in hot dry regions. These factors become very important in Australia because many parts are so hot and dry and because so much of the drainage flows away from coastal divides into internal drainage systems. Thus for much of the continent water is lost not to the ocean but to evaporation and to infiltration. These losses occur both in the channel and in inland lakes.

Nearer the coasts, external systems characterized by generally short rivers behave in a more normal fashion. Here discharge increases in a downstream direction and water is discharged into adjacent oceans.

Runoff is highly variable throughout Australia and also through time in individual systems. It is nevertheless regarded as the most important water resource which can be harvested, manipulated and managed. It can be used directly if demands are low and flow constant or it can be stored in reservoirs and then be used for a variety of purposes. Water in a channel is

Table 3.4 Ranges of Maximum and Minimum Discharges as Percentages of Means

Division	Max. Q as percentage of $\bar{Q}$	Min. Q as percentage of $\bar{Q}$	
I	182–570	1.7–57.4	
II	141–640	3–59	
III	127–236	29–74	
IV	158–930	0–45	
V	260–400	4–22	
VI	136–432	9–51	
VII	—	—	
VIII	167–324	11–40	
IX	—	—	No data
X	—	—	No data
XI	—	—	No data
XII	—	—	No data

Source: AWRC, 1965.

that stage of the cycle which can be measured most efficiently through time to assess potential for irrigation, urban, and power generation uses.

The average runoff is only 50 mm. This, like rainfall, makes this the driest continent in terms of surface water resources when compared with S. America (480 mm), N. America (250 mm), Europe (230 mm), Asia (200 mm) and Africa (180 mm) (Munro, 1974). However, its distribution is very variable, ranging from over 3,500 mm per year in parts of coastal Queensland to less than 12.5 mm for more than two-thirds of the continent. Annual variations are also high, as would be expected with the variable nature of inputs (Table 3.4). Munro (1974) showed that the ratio of maximum twelve-monthly streamflow to minimum streamflow varies from 6 to over 11,000. Most rivers are in the range from 300–1,000, which is very high when compared with Europe (3–10) and United States of America (3–15). The range in the Darling is from 13,000 million m³ to 1.23 million m³ with a mean annual flow of 2,650 million m³.

With such ranges it is evident that much of the drainage is either ephemeral, short flashy flows following storms in small impervious basins, or intermittent, with flow only in wet seasons. Only in wet uniform rainfall areas and in very large basins with significant base flow components are the streams perennial. These are mainly limited to the southeast and far northeast (Dept of National Development, 1967). Thus the country is characterized by a great variety of channel types, with most of them fairly empty for much of the time. Floods however utilize their dimensions and adjacent floodplains at irregular intervals in a wide range of magnitude.

Measurement and establishment of records, vital

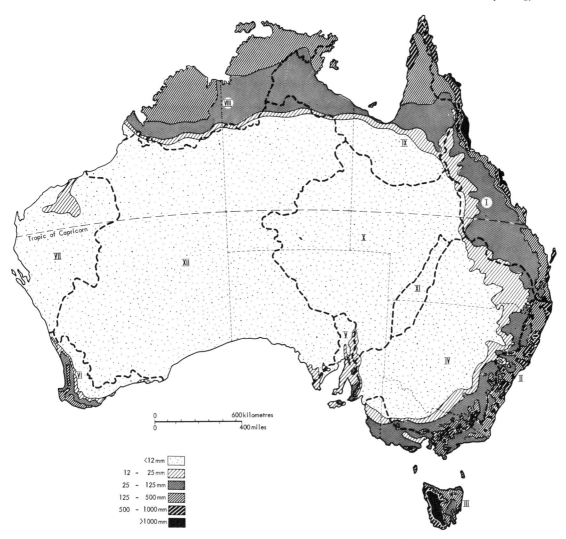

Fig. 3.12 Mean annual runoff. *Source*: adapted from *Atlas of Australian Resources*, 1967.

in determining safe yields where storage is contemplated, is normally a State responsibility.

Average runoff patterns for each division are given in Table 3.1. From this it is clear that runoff from summer rainfall divisions (I, IX and VIII) is by far the greatest. This area, 43.5 per cent of ocean-connected drainage or only 21.2 per cent of the total, yields an average 220,300 million m³ or 64.5 per cent of all the drainage into oceans. Other moist divisions with summer, uniform and winter rains (II and III) give a further 24.5 per cent of external runoff from only 4.4 per cent of the area. Thus these five divisions occupying about one-quarter of the area yield 89 per cent of all external runoff.

Divisions with winter rain only (V and VI) occupy a small area (2.8 per cent) and discharge a small volume (2.6 per cent). The arid division with a seaward outlet (VII) yields only 1.8 per cent of runoff from 6.8 per cent area, while the internal system with an ocean outlet (IV) takes up 13.8 per cent of the area and yields 6.9 per cent of the runoff. The internal system of Lake Eyre (X) covers a large area (14.9 per cent) but produces only 1.1 per cent of the runoff and wide ranges exist there.

Finally, the two disconnected systems (XI and XII) yield 0.1 per cent and 0 per cent of the flow from 1.3 and 34.8 per cent of the area respectively. The Western Plateaux, covering more than one-third of Australia, have no runoff yield but it should be noted that little of this area is gauged.

Summarizing then, those divisions with rivers flowing directly into the sea produce 91.9 per cent of runoff (317,768 million m³) from just over one-third of the land area. Nearly two-thirds of the landmass yields only 6.9 per cent of external drainage (23,666 mill m³) through the mouth of the Murray. Local runoff elsewhere is lost to evaporation.

Reasons for this generally low runoff include low precipitation, high temperatures, high evaporation, generally low intensity rains in the south, low frequency rains in many parts, high percentages of unconsolidated sediment areas, high percentage areas of sedimentary basins and generally low slopes (over half the land surface has slopes of less than 1 in 100—AWRC, 1972).

Although more than 3,500 river gauges have been used (AWRC, 1971a) only about 40 per cent of the total yield was actually measured; the rest is estimated (AAR, 1967). Most of the gauges are located in the east and southeast, generally where population densities are highest, or where major water developments are or have been planned. The distribution of runoff is generalized in Fig. 3.12 (Dept of National Development, 1967).

DEVELOPMENT OF WATER RESOURCES
The scarcity of water in most of Australia makes it a source of primary concern to man. The acquisition of knowledge in hydrology is chiefly geared to the development and management of water resources and the environments from which they are derived.

One of the first location decisions ever taken in Australia by European settlers was partly based on water. The First Fleet relocated its camp from Botany Bay to Sydney Cove partly to have access to the fresh water in the Tank Stream. The tanks dug in a small stream-bed were the first endeavour to impound water in what is now a subterranean stormwater channel.

The harshness and extremes of the Australian environment have made its people very conscious of weather and water. This is still particularly relevant in rural areas where land management and decisions are very dependent on weather and water availability. City dwellers are less concerned, except perhaps with driving hazards in the rain, with storms and cyclones, with urban floods, and with excess water rates from irrigating gardens or filling swimming pools. Local authorities or State bodies shoulder other water concerns, like provision and disposal of water.

Hydrological systems are subjected to all kinds of changes through the endeavours of man. The nature of modification in part reflects the level of development attained. Changes range from pumping some water from a river to the complete use of a catchment's supply, and from limited clearance and use of forested areas to greater clearance for farming or to complete modification for urban development. Impounding water behind a dam is only one obvious activity which changes the cycle. Many other changes have been introduced simply through occupance and development, deliberately or otherwise. These changes are often difficult to appraise in quantitative terms because no prior data are available.

Table 3.5 Total Yields, Estimated Uses in Mid-1960s, Authorized and Planned Commitments at that Time, Total Committed and as Percentages

Division	Potential yield annual in 000s m³	Mid-1960s use annual in 000s m³	Planned and authorized 000s m³	Total annual use 000s m³	Percentage of total potential
I	82,600	512	304	816	1.0
II	35,056	2,040	539	2,579	7.4
III	47,018	95	0	95	0.2
IV	24,852	11,101	4,973	16,074	64.7
V	530	107	26	133	25.1
VI	3,822 (fresh)	235	16	251	6.6
VII	4,978 (fresh)	0	0	0	0
VIII	74,046	140	2,286	2,426	3.3
IX	62,942	19	0	19	0.03
X	4,446	0	0	0	0
XI	406	0	0	0	0
XII	0	0	0	0	0
Total	340,696	14,249	8,144	22,393	6.6

Source: AWRC, 1965.

Modification of Hydrologic Systems

Impounding Surface Runoff

This most obvious form of modification ranges from local hillside farm dams to huge storages necessary for metropolitan water supplies, for extensive irrigation projects and for hydroelectric schemes. Data are usually readily available for most of the large projects because frequently there have been long histories of planning and political controversy (excellent summary in Munro, 1974, Ch. 5; Dept of National Development, 1967; AWRC, 1965).

Table 3.5 summarizes the development of water resources up to the mid-1960s and planned developments at that stage. Percentage developments seem small apart from those in the Murray-Darling Basin but there is often a false notion that all water can or should be 'developed'. The use of all water or a large part is often not desirable on ecological grounds and certainly not if it is returned to the system in a contaminated state. The current salting problems of the Murray-Murrumbidgee are increasing rapidly enough for the Pels plan to contemplate artificial freshwater channels adjacent to a river which in effect would then become a disposal channel. The high level of development in the South Australian Gulf reflects both the low inputs and high evaporation, together with the paucity of surface supplies. Interbasin transfers from the Murray already form a substantial part of water use. Eighty-five per cent of the South Australian population use water from this source (Munro, 1974) and the amount is growing each year. It does not help that State to be on the receiving end of problems from upstream or to be faced with political conflicts on the Chowilla project, to store some 6,200 million m^3 in South Australia for further regulating Murray waters.

The generally high variability of rainfall and runoff means that high storage levels have to be maintained for urban supplies. For instance, Sydney's storage of 932 m^3 per head represents one of the highest levels in the world (cf. 18 m^3 in London). Water use at 496 litres per head per day is only second to Perth with 509 litres. The total storage (1968) for Sydney was 2,603 million m^3 compared with 986 for Brisbane, 296 for Melbourne, 277 for Perth and 111 million m^3 for Adelaide and this was before the impact of new storages from the Shoalhaven Scheme (Munro, 1974).

Supplies for irrigation are also very large. The Snowy Mountain Scheme, although producing 5,000 kilowatt hours per annum peak load electric power, also delivers 1,300 million m^3 of water annually to the Murrumbidgee and 980 million m^3 of water to the Murray (Munro, 1974).

The following data extracted from Munro (1974) show the main storages and areas irrigated at about 1969.

Storage (million m^3)		Area (km^2)
N.S.W.	13,513	5,476
Vic.	8,696	5,268
S.A.	—	704
W.A.	6,033*	304
Q.	2,642	1,637

*Includes 5,670 for the Ord River.

Modification of Runoff Conditions in Catchments

In grazing and cropping communities forests and woodlands are cleared and the surface may be greatly modified in quite a short period. Change in the hydrology may be profound, with a decrease in transpiration levels, in interception of rainfall by vegetation and in infiltrated water, particularly with the loss of surface-protecting vegetation and litter. Consequently there is often an increase in runoff which may promote accelerated erosion in the form of sheet-wash, rilling and gullying, particularly in high intensity rainfall areas.

Such erosion not only depletes soil resources but causes siltation in river systems and State conservation authorities have been set up to investigate and deal with such problems. Here the aim is to slow down the rates of soil loss and to reverse the changed regime conditions. Numerous methods have been tried and proven, ranging from different cropping procedures to specific conservation structures, like contour banks. The basic aim is to slow down and reduce runoff and promote infiltration. Areas totally unsuited to cropping have in some places been incorporated in reafforestation programmes. The rising demand for forest products make such measures both important and useful. Much concern has been expressed about recent developments in forestry operations in clear felling for wood chip exports, where catchment stability is being threatened in several areas.

The incidence of flooding has increased in the last two decades and this has caused considerable hardships in eastern and southern coastal valleys. Some of these peak flows may reflect catchment modification, as well as a possible increased incidence of flood-producing storms, and vast sums have been expended in flood mitigation programmes. Town and farmland protection is accomplished in part by reinforcing levee banks and in part by the efficient drainage of water from inundated levee toes and flood basins, by a series of channels. Catchment conservation measures can also alleviate high runoff peaks. The scale and duration of flood events in inland rivers are quite different. Flood peaks move down these large systems very slowly and large areas can be inundated for lengthy periods. River towns have to be protected by artificial levee systems, but elsewhere low-lying country cannot be protected to the same level as near the coast. In this case there is often adequate warning for local civil defence authorities to take appropriate action to safeguard lives, stock and property. This is often not the case on the coast where warnings may be only a matter of hours in small torrential rivers and thus flood forecasting is important.

Use of Groundwater at the Surface

In the deep confined aquifers of artesian basins recharge of supplies is very slow. The pressure head in the Great Artesian Basin has fallen by an estimated 120 m since 1881 (Aust. Nat. Comm. UNESCO, 1974). Thus in a sense it is a supply where many bores have become subartesian. In the shallower unconsolidated deposits, over-use of water may lower the water-tables. Thus for sound management it is necessary to know what inputs are involved, as well as the amount used. In some cases artificial recharge may help maintain water levels below the ground surface. For instance, 320 million m³ are used in the Burdekin delta per year but the natural recharge is only 200 million m³ with the difference pumped for infiltration from the Burdekin River (Aust. Nat. Comm. UNESCO, 1974). In areas of high evaporation and shallow water-tables, there may be some concentration of salts near the surface. Additionally the fact that many underground supplies are already rich in dissolved minerals often makes them unsuitable for irrigation use. Such supplies are nevertheless extremely important in the provision of stock, some domestic and irrigation water in areas of low rainfall and potentially very high evaporation. The main modifications are essentially near-surface reactivation of water which is normally stored at depth and away from the more rapid interchanges of the hydrological cycle.

Urban Water Systems

Although small in total area, urban centres are where most Australian people live and work. Thus modifications to urban systems affect many people but people's awareness of effects is often quite limited. Great imports, often involving interbasin transfers are necessary to make potable water available for consumption. Thus vast areas are set aside as collecting grounds for urban water supply dams. Once used these waters have to be disposed of in systems which are overtaxed as a direct result of urbanization. The natural catchment in towns is much modified and most streams are ill-equipped to handle the increased runoff from the more impervious catchment surfaces. Disposal of water is often a health hazard, involving runoff from unsewered residential areas or overtaxing of sewage systems. Consequently pollution in urban areas and downstream from them is a real problem. Happily, in the short term, most of Australia's large cities are near the coast and often wastes can be discharged into the oceans. This however is not the long-term solution.

Thus cities often straddle catchments or subcatchments and in these there have been a succession of changes ranging from initial timber clearance, through farming to construction and completed urban structures. All of these have lowered infiltration levels and increased runoff coefficients. The increase in impervious conditions reflects the level of development. Little of the original soil surface and vegetation survives in downtown areas and densely settled suburbs, except for parks and open spaces. Consequently runoff is very high and rapid and sediment yields are lower than perhaps even in farming periods (Wolman, 1967). Water increases are not so marked in the less densely settled garden suburbs, where trees, lawns and gardens are retained on fairly large blocks. However the increased area of roofs and paving helps maintain a high runoff rate. Additionally the sediment load remains fairly high, as is indicated by the biennial practice, in Sydney at least, of top-dressing lawns with interbasin transfers of loam. Much soil is removed in the high intensity storms which are common in some areas.

Natural tributary channels cannot cope with the increased water and sediment and it is often necessary to make such outlets efficient by perimeter modification (i.e., concrete or iron) or making channels into open or closed stormwater systems. Only recently has a concern with urban hydrology become apparent and yet such areas are occupied by more than 80 per cent of the population (AWRC, 1973). In eastern and northern cities rainfall is high, and much water is derived from interbasin transfers for domestic and industrial use. Although much of this may be disposed of in sewers, it may flow into rivers, estuaries or coastal outfalls. However, large increments are added to natural runoff with garden irrigation. Up to 30 per cent of Sydney's water is used for this purpose and would represent a large part of urban drainage. Recent research by the CSIRO (Sharpe, 1974) has been directed towards conservation of urban rainfall and runoff with modified, more pervious structures. However, it seems that pervious roads and pavements will not replace existing structures but they could well be incorporated in new towns and subdivisions. It is fair to set alongside the large expenditure on urban water supply the fact that enough water for nearly four people, using nearly 500 litres a day, falls on a block 20 × 40 m with only 750 mm of annual rain. Of the capital cities only Adelaide has much less than this on average (523 mm).

The stormwater and city drainage systems carry a large pollution load from overcharged sewage systems, leaking sewers, overtaxed septic tanks and surface droppings of animals. These systems are natural sinks for other solid and liquid disposals, although the States now have legislation operating to combat these practices (Commonwealth of Australia, Senate, 1970). It is nevertheless true that the ever-increasing use of water means a greater disposal problem. This is costly if it is not to affect adversely resources, aquatic life and recreation facilities downstream, and on the coasts.

Future modification of hydrological systems will presumably go on in those sectors discussed above at increasing rates with larger populations and greater individual demands. However, with the present concern for both the environment and its ecology, it would be wrong to assume that the total water potential can or should be developed, because catchments can be over-regulated with disastrous consequences, particularly if the water used is returned in polluted states.

Rain-making experiments have only been partially successful (Aust. Nat. Comm. UNESCO, 1974) and even then the products are subject to the same high loss rates as in the natural system. It is probable that more purposeful and deliberate management of water on and under the ground offers the greatest scope. This may involve recycling in some places, desalination in others (AWRC, 1966), the reduction of evaporation (AUST. Nat. Comm. UNESCO, 1974) or just more prudent and effective use of present supplies elsewhere.

In the past there have been grand plans to water the desert or 'dead heart', like the Bradfield Scheme. The diverted waters of the Snowy River have already added to the problems of abundant regulation in the Murray and Murrumbidgee. Problems of salting and massive evaporation and transpiration have to be solved before such schemes will become feasible. Additionally there will have to be considerable population pressures before there will either be the desire or indeed the need to leave the damper coastal periphery. Even there river systems will become dead without safe disposal of wastes and effective utilization by basin management authorities.

REFERENCES

Australian National Committee for UNESCO (1974), *Progress in Australian Hydrology 1965–1974*, Australian Government Publishing Service, Canberra.

Australian Water Resources Council (AWRC) (1965), *Review of Australia's Water Resources. Streamflow and Underground Resources.* Department of National Development, Canberra.

——(1966), *A Survey of Water Desalination Methods and their Relevance to Australia*, Department of National Development, Hydrological Series No. 1, Canberra.

——(1969), *The Representative Basin Concept in Australia (a progress report)*, Department of National Development, Hydrological Series No. 2, Canberra.

——(1970a), *Evaporation from Water Storages*, Department of National Development, Hydrological Series No. 4, Canberra.

——(1970b), *Estimating Evapotranspiration: an Evaluation of Techniques*, Department of National Development, Hydrological Series No. 5, Canberra.

——(1971a), *Stream Gauging Information, Australia—December 1969*, Department of National Development, Canberra.

——(1971b), *Field Study of Evaporation: Installation, Operation and Maintenance of Equipment*, Department of Environment and Conservation, Technical Paper No. 1, Canberra.

——(1971c), *Field Study of Evaporation: Notes on the Extraction and Computation of Data*, Department of Environment and Conservation, Technical Paper No. 2, Canberra.

——(1972), *Hydrology of Smooth Plainlands of Arid Australia*, Department of National Development, Hydrological Series No. 6, Canberra.

——(1973), *Hydrologic Investigation and Design in Urban Areas.* Department of Environment and Conservation, Technical Paper No. 5, Canberra.

——(1974a), *Australian Representative Basins Programme—Progress 1973*, Department of Environment and Conservation, Hydrological Series No. 8, Canberra.

——(1974b), *Social Moisture Measurement and Assessment*, Department of Environment and Conservation, Hydrological Series No. 9, Canberra.

Barry, R. G. (1969), 'The world hydrological cycle' in R. J. Chorley (ed.), *Introduction to Physical Hydrology*, Methuen, London, pp. 18–26.

Beard, J. S. (1973), 'The elucidation of palaeodrainage patterns in Western Australia through vegetation mapping', *Veg. Surv. W.A. Occasional Paper* No. 1, Perth.

Ceplecha, V. J. (1971), 'The distribution of the main components of the water balance in Australia', *Aust. Geogr.*, 11, 455–62.

Commonwealth of Australia, Senate (1970), *Select Committee on Water Pollution, Water Pollution in Australia*, Australian Government Publishing Office, Canberra.

Department of National Development (1953) 'Underground Water', *Atlas of Australian Resources*, Canberra.

——(1967), 'Surface Water Resources', *Atlas of Australian Resources*, Canberra.

——(1970), 'Rainfall', *Atlas of Australian Resources*, Canberra.

Department of Minerals and Energy (1973a), 'Temperature', *Atlas of Australian Resources*, Second Series, Canberra.

——(1973b), 'Climate', *Atlas of Australian Resources*, Second Series, Canberra.

——(1973c), 'Landforms', *Atlas of Australian Resources*, Second Series, Canberra.

Fitzpatrick, E. A. (1963), 'Estimates of pan evaporation from mean maximum temperature and vapor pressure', *J. Appl. Met.*, 2, 780–92.

——(1967), *Climate in Lands of the Nogoa-Belyando Area, Queensland*, CSIRO Land Res. Ser. No. 18.

Fitzpatrick, E. A. and Nix, H. A. (1970), 'The climatic factor in Australian grassland ecology' in R. M. Moore (ed.), *Australian Grasslands*, Australian National University Press, Canberra, pp. 3–26.

Gibbs, W. J. and Maher, J. V. (1967), 'Rainfall deciles as drought indicators', *Commonw. Bur. Met. Bull.*, No. 48.

Jackson, E. A. (1958), *A Study of the Soils and Some Aspects of the Hydrology of Yudnapinna Station, South Australia*, CSIRO Soils and Land Use Ser. No. 24.

Jennings, J. N. (1967), 'Two maps of rainfall intensity in Australia', *Aust. Geogr.*, 10, 256–62.

McIlroy, I. C. and Angus, D. E. (1963), *The Aspendale Multiple Weighed Lysimeter Installation*, CSIRO Div. of Met. Phys., Tech. Pap. No. 14.

Munro, C. H. (1974), *Australian Water Resources and their Development*, Angus and Robertson, Sydney.

Penman, H. L. (1948), 'Natural evaporation from open water, bare soil and grass', *Proc. R. Soc. (Ser. A)*, 193, 120–45.

Prescott, J. A. and Thomas J. A. (1949), 'The length of the growing season in Australia as determined by the effectiveness of rainfall', *Proc. R. Geogr. Soc. Aust. (S.A.)*, 50, 42–6.

Perry, R. A., Quinlan, T., Jones, N. O. and Basinski, J. J. (1963), *Preliminary Assessment of Ground Water Suitable for Irrigation in the Alice Springs Area, and its Agricultural Significance*, CSIRO Div. of Land Res. and Reg. Surv. Tech. Pap. No. 21.

Rose, C. W., Byrne, G. F. and Begg, J. E. (1966), *An Accurate Hydraulic Lysimeter with Remote Weight Recording*, CSIRO Div. of Land Res., Tech. Pap. No. 27.

Sharpe, R. (1974), 'Planning water resource systems', Paper to Urban Water Resources Management Symposium, Water Research Foundation of Australia, Wollongong (unpublished).

Sullivan, M. E. (1973), 'Drainage disorganization of the Western Australian river-lakes', 45th ANZAAS Congress, Perth (unpublished).

Thornthwaite, C. W. (1948), 'An approach toward a rational classification of climate', *Geogr. Rev.*, 38, 55–94.

Water Conservation and Irrigation Commission of New South Wales (W.C. and I.C.) (1971), *Water Resources of New South Wales*, Government Printer, Sydney.

Williams, G. E. (1969), 'The Central Australian stream floods of February-March 1967', ANZAAS Arid Zone Symposium, Adelaide (unpublished).

Wolman, M. G. (1967), 'A cycle of sedimentation and erosion in urban river channels', *Geograf. Annlr.*, 49A, 385–95.

4 EARLY LANDFORM EVOLUTION

C. D. OLLIER

In contrast, for instance, to parts of Britain and the United States, where Quaternary glaciation provided a new starting point in landscape evolution, much of the land area of Australia dates back to Tertiary times and earlier. To find a fresh start comparable to the Quaternary glaciation of Europe we have to go back to the glaciation of Permian times (Fig. 4.1). This means that whereas some places affected by the last great Ice Age have a landscape history dominated by the effects of the last 25,000 years, Australian landscapes are affected by events of the past 250,000,000 years—a difference of four orders of magnitude. Many of our ideas on landscape evolution are coloured by the

work—and textbooks—of Europe and North America where pre-Quaternary landscapes are of minor importance: it is necessary to make a conscious effort to appreciate the vast time-scale appropriate to Australia.

On this extended time-scale we are not merely concerned with erosion and deposition in the creation of landforms, but also with continental drift, the creation of oceans and seas, and the collision of continental plates—events which not only affect landscapes but have enormous consequences for Australian biology.

CONTINENTAL DRIFT AND SEA FLOOR SPREADING

The continents of the southern hemisphere, and India, were once united in a super-continent, Gondwanaland. Gondwanaland cracked up and the various portions or 'plates' drifted apart as new sea floor was created between them. Various parts of the sea floor have been dated, and the date of splitting, the rate of movement of the continents, the rate of sea floor spreading and sometimes the cessation of drift have been determined for several areas around Australia.

Gondwanaland probably began to break up as recently as the Jurassic, and the severance of Australia from India and Africa occurred fairly early. The sedimentary basins of Western Australia are related to the split-up of Gondwanaland (Veevers, 1971). The pre-drift Bonaparte Gulf and Canning Basins have lain at the continental margin facing an open ocean for 600 million years, whereas the Perth Basin lay in the interior of Gondwanaland until it split apart in the Cretaceous. The Eucla Basin originated with the separation of Antarctica and Australia in the Eocene.

New Zealand was never actually adjacent to Australia, but with the creation of the Tasman Sea by sea floor spreading it drifted farther away between 80 and 60 million years ago. Australia and Antarctica, however, remained connected for a long time. Jurassic dolerites of Tasmania point to the probable development of a rift between the two continents at that time but actual separation occurred during the Tertiary. The main drifting between Australia and Antarctica took place between 55 and 10 million years ago.

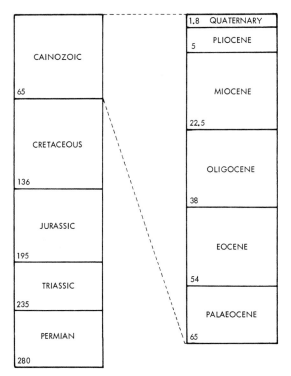

Fig. 4.1 Geological time-scale with ages in millions of years.

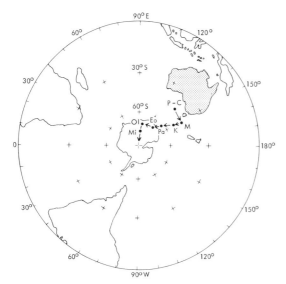

Fig. 4.2 Past positions of the South Pole relative to Australia. P-C, Permo-Carboniferous; M, Mesozoic (average); K, Cretaceous; Pa, Palaeocene; OL, Oligocene; Mi, Miocene.

The position of the South Pole relative to the Australian continent can be determined from the study of palaeomagnetism. In suitable rocks, such as basalts, the direction of magnetism at the time the basalt cooled is preserved in the rocks. Recent basalts have a direction that points to the present South Pole, but older rocks give quite different directions. Either the Pole has moved, or the continents, and the balance of evidence suggests that the continents have drifted. The apparent polar wander path for Australia from the Permian is shown in Fig. 4.2. It appears that the South Pole was fairly close to Tasmania in both Permian and Mesozoic times. From the end of the Cretaceous the palaeolatitude decreased gradually until about 20 million years ago; little change appears to have taken place since.

To the north we find that although the Papuan Shelf is structurally part of the Australian landmass, the Coral Sea opened like a wedge of new sea floor over a period of 11 million years in the late Eocene-early Oligocene. The collision zone between Australia and the Pacific plates is to be found in Papua New Guinea and Irian Jaya, and dates back to Eocene times. The area of Timor and the Timor Sea was deformed even later, in the Miocene and Pliocene, when Australia collided with this part of Southeast Asia. The great arc of Indonesia and Malaya marks the front of a plate moving into the gap left by the separation between Australia and India. It is as well to remember that all this area was created, and vertical movements produced mountains like the Himalaya,

during the time that Australia, the quiet continent, was experiencing relatively minor erosion and deposition in shallow marginal seas.

The Evidence of the Rocks—Stratigraphic History
We can disregard the older rocks which provided a basement for later sculpture and deformation, and look only at those periods which have left a direct mark on the landscape. This means we can ignore the Precambrian and almost all the Palaeozoic, and start with the Permian. In Permian times much of the continent was covered by a great ice sheet which moved from a southerly direction, and pebbles dropped by icebergs occur as far north as north Queensland. This gives us a fresh start for landform evolution, comparable to that afforded by the Quaternary glaciation of the northern hemisphere referred to above.

In Permian times a line of marine basins (the Tasman geosyncline) ran along the eastern side of the continent from Tasmania to Queensland (Fig. 4.3) These basins were filled first by glacial sediments and later by marine or terrestrial sediments, including important Permian coal deposits. Coal measures indicate a warmer climate than that of ice-cap times, but probably not very warm or tropical. There were many advances and retreats of the ice cap, and volcanic activity was located along the line of marine basins, as in an island arc.

In Triassic times Australia was almost entirely land with several basins where lake and river sediments accumulated. Many coal deposits were formed at this time. Only small areas of marine sedimentation existed and the volcanic belt in the east was more confined than in Permian times. Although Australia still occupied a high latitude the climate appears to have been generally warm.

Continental conditions continued into Jurassic times. In eastern Australia Jurassic deposits are almost exclusively non-marine, and while marine deposits are extensive in the west they are not deep water deposits. Volcanism was very restricted. The Great Artesian Basin became important at this time and extension and ponding of the basin during the Middle Jurassic permitted local coal accumulation. Tasmania was almost at the South Pole in Jurassic times but marine organisms and abundant plant fossils suggests that conditions were not very cold. The Permian and Triassic sediments of Tasmania were intruded by vast volumes of dolerite—thousands of cubic kilometres— in Jurassic times, probably associated with a major episode of crustal tension—perhaps the precursor to seperation of Australia and Antarctica.

A great Cretaceous marine flood that affected many parts of the world also occurred in Australia, and Lower Cretaceous deposits are especially widespread. Cretaceous rocks are present (sometimes buried under younger rocks) over one-third of the present landmass

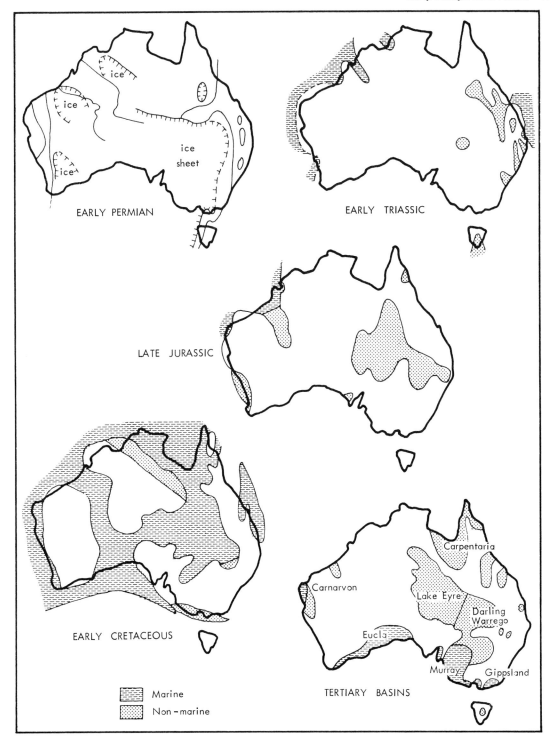

Fig. 4.3 Palaeogeography of Australia.

of Australia, and early Cretaceous seas divided the continent into three main landmasses. By the end of the early Cretaceous the sea had withdrawn from most of the continent, and an extensive river system developed in the region of the Great Artesian Basin. Elsewhere the drainage systems that would persist through Tertiary times and to the present day were initiated. Australia drifted away from the South Pole during Cretaceous times, and fossils imply a temperate or warm equable climate throughout. Acid volcanoes were active in Queensland during the Cretaceous and, as in the Jurassic, folding of any intensity was confined to the Maryborough Basin.

The series of palaeogeographic maps (Fig. 4.3) illustrate that by the start of the Tertiary a considerable part of Australia had a history as a land area going back to Mesozoic or even Triassic times. With long-continued erosion of these areas, together with widespread Cretaceous sedimentation, Australia was already a remarkably flat continent. This situation prevailed through much of Tertiary time, but broad epeirogenic movements gave rise to some regional variety.

Important clues to the evolution of land areas during the Tertiary are provided by sediments that accumulated in various depositional areas.

Apart from the Great Barrier Reef, which has a Tertiary base in part, marine Tertiary rocks are confined to a series of basins that encroached onto what is now the edge of the landmass along the south and west of Australia. A general pattern can be discerned in the sequence of events in all these basins, a pattern of alternating marine flooding and withdrawal that is of great importance for interpretation of Tertiary events.

1. At the base are littoral sandstones and shales of Palaeocene to Eocene age.

2. Marine conditions extended in the Upper Eocene.

3. The sea withdrew in the Oligocene.

4. The sea advanced even further in late Oligocene or early Miocene times.

5. In the late Miocene the sea withdrew.

6. After a brief and limited Pliocene transgression the sea again withdrew. Pliocene deposits are rare, and mainly estuarine or lagoonal sands.

In the Gippsland Basin there are extensive deposits of commercial brown coal which reach a total thickness of over 300 m overlain by deposits of the Oligocene and Miocene transgressions. In Pliocene times the basin was tilted and uplifted, but in the south deposition was continuous into the Pleistocene. The Gippsland Basin is the main source of oil in Australia.

In the Bass Basin Tertiary deposits are generally thin—less than 350 m in the Port Phillip area—while in the Otway Basin up to 1,500 m of Tertiary rocks are present. The Murray Basin has a maximum thickness of about 500 m in the west central part. The ridges of

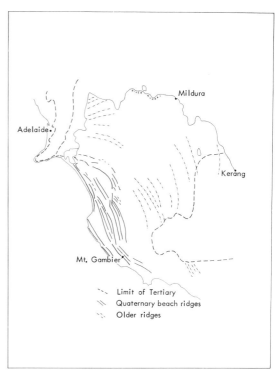

Fig. 4.4 Ridges associated with retreat of the sea from the Murray Basin, based on information from G. Blackburn and ERTS imagery.

the Murray Basin (Fig. 4.4) are probably barrier dunes laid down on the edge of a retreating sea during Pliocene and Pleistocene times. The St Vincent Basin situation is complicated by considerable uplift, faulting and monoclinal folding during the Tertiary, but the general sequence is as elsewhere.

At the head of the Great Australian Bight a veneer of Tertiary limestones, nowhere much over 300 m thick, covers a shelf area of about 110,000 km². Most extensive is the soft, chalky Wilson Bluff Limestone of late Eocene age, and unconformably above this is the harder Nullarbor Limestone of Miocene age. The sediments remain horizontal and the Nullarbor Plain is simply an old sea bed uplifted and modified by very limited erosion in a dry climate since then.

Extensive marine incursions occurred in the Carnarvon Basin, marked by large deposits of limestone and lesser sandstones and siltstones.

EROSION SURFACES

The long and stable history of Australia, punctuated by periods of uplift and changes of climate and associated geomorphic processes, has resulted in the widespread development of landscapes of plains and tablelands. Several erosion surfaces can be distinguished, which may sometimes be dated by overlying sediments or basalts on part of the surface, by relationship to other surfaces (the higher the surface the older) or by relationship to sedimentary basins. Periods of deep weathering, laterite formation, silcrete formation, and the stripping of weathered material may all be used with erosion surfaces to build up a local geomorphic history. Lester King (1962) described a sequence of erosion surfaces which was used as a basis by several later workers.

Several land surfaces can be recognized in the Northern Territory. The Ashburton is the highest and oldest, probably of Cretaceous age and preserved only on very resistant rocks such as Precambrian quartzites. Below this is the Tennant Creek surface with a well-developed lateritic profile. Below the Tennant Creek and stripping the laterite are one or more lower surfaces, and Miocene limestone (probably lacustrine) has been found on a surface well below the level of the Tennant Creek surface at Camfield near Wave Hill.

An account of erosion surfaces in the Daly Lowland given by Wright (1963) provides a detailed example of Northern Territory surfaces. Wright recognized three surfaces:

1. Bradshaw surface. This forms main divides, is of considerable perfection, and has a deep lateritic profile with a strongly silicified horizon forming the lower part of the pallid zone and extending into rocks immediately beneath. It is equivalent to the Tennant Creek surface.

2. The Maranboy surface. This forms secondary divides, with related rock-cut terraces. It was produced by stripping of the upper, less silicified parts of the Bradshaw pallid zone (therefore silicification was pre-Maranboy). The Maranboy surface is associated with a lateritic weathering profile less deep than the Bradshaw profile and mainly developed in the Bradshaw weathering mantle.

3. Tipperary surface. This advanced by removal of the Maranboy re-weathered layer, exposing the resistant Bradshaw silicified rock which commonly provides a structural base level for denudation. The Tipperary surface consists of broad plains and is relatively unweathered.

The erosion sequence in the Macdonnell Ranges (Mabbutt, 1966) includes crest bevels, which are remnants of a summit plain, and three terraces within the valleys:

1. High terrace, which grades to the summit surface and is lateritically weathered;
2. Middle terrace;
3. Low terrace with red soils.

Mabbutt suggests that this sequence results from a cyclic climatic variation superimposed on a general trend to aridity. Younger surfaces in central Australia are only superficially weathered, have closer texture of

dissection and a fuller expression of lithological contrasts, including stripping of regolith and exposure of weathering fronts. Laterite formation was halted by desiccation earlier in central Australia than farther north, where deep weathering extends on to relatively younger surfaces.

In all these Northern Territory studies it is made clear that successive erosion surfaces are not mere reflections of renewed erosion following base-level changes, but also involve climatic change and contrasting styles of landscape development, with some periods of dominant weathering and others of dominant erosion.

Pre-Tertiary land surfaces have been recognized in the Flinders Ranges (Twidale, 1968). The most ancient landscape elements (Mt Brown, Kanyaka surfaces) are remnants of a deeply weathered pre-Eocene land surface which has been warped but is in some places preserved under sediments of Upper Eocene age. By Middle Tertiary intermontane plains and broad valleys had developed (Proby surface), and renewed dissection of these resulted in the modern valley floors and piedmont plains.

Much of Western Australia consists of a plateau which is generally less than 600 m high and forms a vast undulating surface early known as the Great

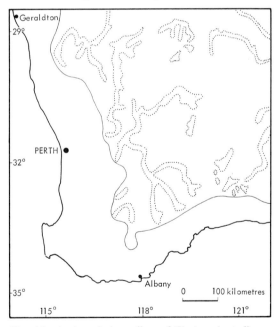

Fig. 4.5 Ancient drainage lines of Western Australia on an old, uplifted erosion surface bounded by the 'Meckering Line' to the west and the Southern Ocean watershed to the south. The headwaters of the broad drainage lines appear to have originated to the south before continental drift brought about the separation of Australia and Antarctica.

Plateau or Old Plateau. A few ranges rise above it, like the Hamersley Plateaux in the northwest and the Stirling Hills in the south. The plateau is deeply weathered and lateritized and is dissected by several generations of valleys.

Ancient broad valleys, partly filled with sediments and now containing chains of salt lakes, are remnants of a drainage system which apparently had its headwaters to the south of the present coastline (Fig. 4.5). The break-up of Australia and Antarctica therefore post-dates the drainage system. The break-up really became effective about 55 million years ago, but rifting probably started earlier perhaps as much as 70 million years ago, so there seems little doubt that the formation of the Great Plateau, the period of great weathering and the early drainage pattern belong to the Mesozoic.

A major divide separates drainage heading to the Indian Ocean from drainage towards the Nullarbor Plain. This is not a sharp divide but an undulating upland where deep weathering and extensive sand-plains are preserved. Laterite occurs as only small residuals on the minor divides, but occupies increasingly large areas on divides between main rivers and palaeo-drainage lines of the interior.

In the Eastern Uplands the plains of the Interior Lowlands generally rise gradually to the Great Divide, evidently due to tectonic uplift. Erosion has worked back from the coast to produce steep topography which meets the smooth landscapes of the old erosion surfaces with a remarkably abrupt break of slope. Remnants of the old surfaces may occasionally be preserved as isolated plateaux beyond the main front of this break of slopes, a feature especially obvious in the 'High Plains' of the East Victorian Uplands. These are areas of subdued relief at elevations of over 1,500 m surrounded by terrain of much greater relief and deeper dissection.

Neilson (1961) has provided the most detailed account of the High Plains. He states that the surface originated at no great height above sea level during the early Mesozoic, probably in the Triassic Period. Later in the Mesozoic it began to rise in the area which is now the Eastern Highlands, while subsidence further south formed the sedimentary basins of Gippsland. By Eocene times broad valleys had been cut in the up-warped surface, and lava flow remnants in such places as the Dargo High Plains (30 m.y.) and the Nunyong Plateau (42–38 m.y.) were valley fills at that time. Other basalts, such as that on the Bogong High Plains (36–30 m.y.), were erupted onto a little-dissected plain.

Lower surfaces below the Triassic plateau have been recognized by various workers—but in this region they are certainly discontinuous and difficult to reconstruct.

In Tasmania Davies recognized five major erosion surfaces, some of which coincide in part with resistant dolerite sheets or the sub-Permian plane of unconformity, both of which tend to preserve the surfaces. The oldest surface may be Cretaceous in age: the youngest surface is certainly later than early Miocene sediments which it truncates.

In New South Wales and Queensland many similar sequences of erosion surfaces have been described. These are warped, indicating a doming of the early surface, with steep descent to the coast, and rapid erosion on the coastal side. Fig. 4.6 shows some sections. The sequence in southern Queensland, described by Watkins (1967), may be taken as an example. The highest surface (equated with the Gondwana surface of King) is a dissected plateau at 1,000 to 1,200 m in the Stanthorpe area. The surface has been exhumed locally from below Cretaceous cover and cuts across early Mesozoic beds. What Watkins calls the Upper Erosion Surface (equated with the Australian surface of King) is the highest well-preserved plain. It has been deeply lateritized but frequently the lateritized mantle has been stripped leaving a sub-parallel plain with silcrete especially west of the divide. This is reminiscent of the Daly Lowland sequence (p. 89). This erosion surface has been warped along a north-south axis, and the axis tends to rise towards the south in the direction of New England. It is suggested that this surface was cut in Eocene-Oligocene times and warped in the Miocene. Younger Middle and Lower Erosion Surfaces are also recognized. Both of these are lateritized in the coastal area, and it appears that conditions suitable for lateritization continued in this area longer than in many parts of Australia.

Erosion surfaces are themselves part of the landscape, but more importantly their study enables us to decipher the landform evolution in many parts of Australia. The most significant point to stress is that Tertiary deposits often rest on the lowest erosion surfaces: this means that not only these low plains but also many of the plateaux, hills and ranges that rise above them—features like Ayers Rock and the Olgas—were already in existence in Tertiary times. Actual landscapes, not landscape remnants, date back to the Tertiary.

LATERITE AND SILCRETE

One of the most important features of the Australian Tertiary was the widespread development of laterite and silcrete. These have been used as climatic indicators and as stratigraphic markers, and their occurrence has a considerable effect on the form of succeeding landscapes. Both laterite and silcrete act as cap-rock, and lead to the formation of 'tent-hills' or mesas, and escarpments such as the Stuart Ranges at Coober Pedy.

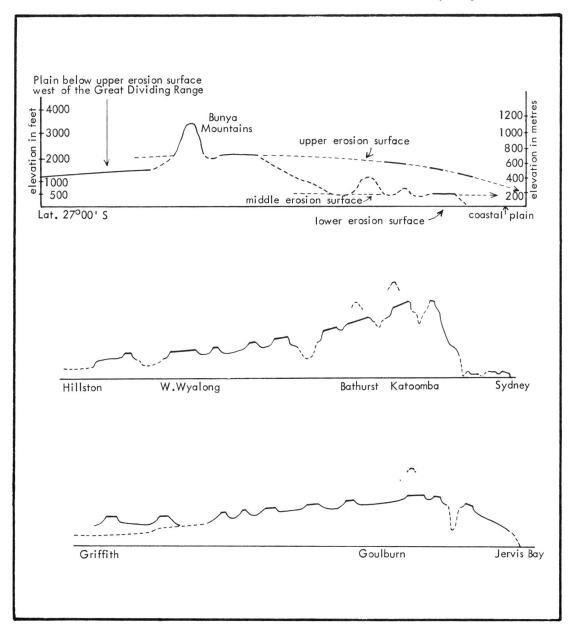

Fig. 4.6 Diagramatic cross-sections showing erosion surfaces in eastern Australia. Top section along lat. 27° S, after Watkins (1967). Centre and bottom sections across New South Wales, after King (1962).

The term laterite is much abused. It is seldom used in Australian literature in its original sense, that is a clay which on exposure to air hardens to brick-like consistency. In Australia it usually implies either (a) ferricrete—a hard layer of iron oxide at or near the ground surface, or (b) a kind of weathering profile which when fully developed includes a ferricrete or iron-rich but non-indurated horizon at the top, a mottled zone below, and a pallid zone at the bottom. Such profiles can be tens of metres thick. I shall use laterite in this latter sense.

Laterite formation requires a warm humid climate, probably with a dry season. It may be absent from areas that are too dry (e.g. Nullarbor Plain), or too

Plate 4.1   Ayers Rock, with Mount Olga in the background. Tertiary sediments are found on the lower erosion surface, so that it can be assumed that in Tertiary times these mountains appeared very much as they do now.

cold, and in areas with less-marked dry seasons laterites may be replaced by tropical red earths (with no duricrust) or bauxite (an aluminous duricrust) as in northern Queensland.

Overseas work on laterite, summarized by Maignien (1966), has shown that laterite may be formed over long periods of time with intervening periods of erosion, and is especially common on the lower slopes of broad valleys. Ferricrete is therefore not simply a residual deposit but results from the precipitation of iron carried in groundwater from up-slope and up-valley positions. In Australia, a general view, deriving from original work by Woolnough, is that laterite formation is restricted to surfaces of a very perfect planation and that there has only been one period of laterite formation. We now know that while it may be true that the Miocene was the main period of laterite formation, it has probably been formed at other times, and in some places with marked relief.

Basalts on Kangaroo Island, South Australia,

isotopically dated as Jurassic, overlie weathered material which may be the lower portion of an eroded laterite profile. Upper Eocene continental sediments near Coolgardie contain ironstone pebbles presumably eroded from laterite, indicating that laterite was formed there before the end of the Eocene. In western Victoria a thin lateritic profile has formed on basalts dated at about 4.5 million years. The earlier dates are somewhat dubious but it seems reasonable that the date of both the start and finish of laterite formation varies from place to place.

Laterite is absent from the Middle Miocene Colville Sandstone of the Nullarbor Plain, whereas lithologically similar Permian and Cretaceous rocks immediately to the north are strongly lateritized. This implies that lateritization here is probably pre-middle Miocene, and that the climate in the Eucla Basin has been too dry for lateritization since its emergence in the Middle Miocene.

Mabbutt (1966) has suggested that lateritization in

central Australia may have finished earlier than in more northern areas because of increasing aridity, although absolute dating is not possible. Upper Tertiary limestone overlies the duricrust. However, Wyatt and Webb suggest that even in northern Queensland lateritization may have finished in the early Miocene—at the same time as in the Nullarbor area. In the Roma-Amby area basalts overlying deeply weathered rocks have been dated at early Miocene (23 m.y.). Miocene sediments have been found on post-laterite surfaces in the Northern Territory.

Several generations of laterites are present in some areas. In southwestern Australia Mulcahy found that the oldest, most inland zone is associated with salt lakes and sandplains of the Narrogin-Ongerup Plateau containing lateritic profile debris. This zone is bounded to the west by the 'Meckering Line' and the dissected laterites and younger laterites of the Northern Plateau. Next is the zone of detrital laterite of the Darling Range terminating in the Darling scarp and overlooking the coastal Swan Plain. The youngest laterite here could be equivalent to the Lower Miocene of other areas.

A complication to the weathering story is brought in by silica-cemented materials—silcrete or grey billy. While lateritic weathering profiles may have ferricretes of either residual origin or formed by local iron enrichment, silcrete is formed only by addition of silica to a variety of pre-existing materials. It is not a residual deposit or a weathering profile, although it is often associated with these.

Silcrete deposition requires a source of silica and a suitable site for deposition. Some kind of impeded drainage is necessary or the silica will be carried away in throughflow. Impeded drainage may result from volcanic or tectonic damming, by aridity, or both.

Grey billy is very commonly associated with basalt and it has been supposed that it may be created by volcanic heat or by magmatic solutions rich in silica. It is much more likely that the silica is derived from the weathering of basalt, the silicate minerals of which weather to clay and iron oxides with release of considerable free silica. An extended period of time is required for sufficient weathering, and it is notable that the younger basalts of western Victoria and northern Queensland do not have associated grey billy. In some instances the association of grey billy and basalt may be fortuitous.

The most plausible explanation of the widespread silcretes of the centre is that of Stephens. He suggests that rivers draining towards the centre bring in silica, carrying it for over 1,000 km, and it is precipitated in the arid area of restricted drainage. It may be deposited in sediments or within old weathering profiles, either at the surface or at some depth dependent on the height of the water-table at the time.

As silcrete is deposited *within* pre-existing materials the laws of superposition do not apply, but various lines of evidence can be used to get some idea of its age. In the Roma-Amby area it has been found that abundant silcrete in the area has formed at various times during the Tertiary. In the Lake Eyre Basin Jessup and Norris found two stages of silcrete formation, one above and one below a sandstone of Oligocene age. In the Daly Lowland the silcrete was deposited in the pallid zone of a lateritic profile, so is of post-laterite age.

The massive silcretes of central Australia have a rather sharp top, probably coinciding with a former water-table. The upper metre or so is massive and columnar, and below this the silcrete is often nodular, forming a pseudo-conglomerate several metres thick. Some silica precipitated at various levels below the silcrete surface forms precious opal.

To summarize, although laterite and silcrete have been formed at several times over a very long period, it is possible that the most extensive laterites and silcretes correspond in age with the period of mid-Tertiary marine transgression and warm moist climates. Since the late Miocene regression the formation of laterite and silcrete has been very limited.

VOLCANIC ACTIVITY

Volcanic activity affected eastern Australia throughout Tertiary times and into historical times at a nearly constant rate. The distribution of volcanic products, shown in Fig. 4.7, is restricted almost entirely to the zone of uplift bordering the eastern coastline.

The work of Macdougall, Wellman and others has provided a wealth of data on the age of the volcanic rocks. Perhaps the most surprising result of their work is that many volcanics which had been commonly regarded as Miocene turned out to be Eocene.

The youngest volcanics are of Quaternary age and these preserve primary volcanic forms. The volcanics of the West Victoria Plains are known to be Quaternary: the basalts of northern Queensland have not yet been dated, but on physiographic grounds are almost certainly Quaternary. The Tertiary volcanics have often been extensively eroded. Some of the more massive cones such as Mt Warning remain roughly volcano-shaped, but others like the Warrumbungle Peaks have been eroded down to volcanic necks.

Some investigations of older basalts have revealed considerable changes in landscape between pre-basalts and post-basalt topography. Galloway, for instance, has shown that basalts of the Liverpool Range in central New South Wales were erupted onto a large drainage basin draining to the west, though the present River Hunter flows east.

The Great Lake basalts of Tasmania are dated as

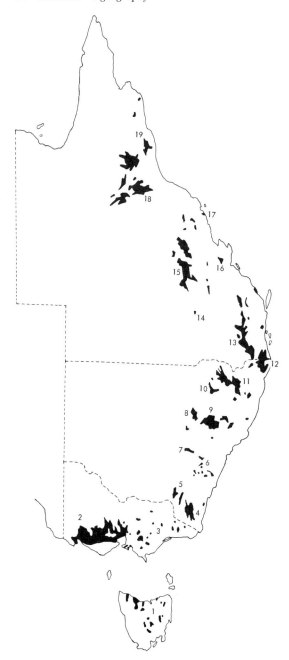

Fig. 4.7 Distribution of Cainozoic volcanicity in Australia.
1, Tasmania; 2, Newer Volcanics of Victoria; 3, Older
Volcanics of Victoria; 4, Monaro; 5, Snowy; 6, Abercrom-
bie; 7, Orange; 8, Warrumbungles; 9, Liverpool; 10,
Nandewar; 11, Inverell; 12, Tweed; 13, Toowoomba; 14,
Mitchell; 15, Springsure; 16, Rockhampton; 17, Cape
Hillsborough; 18, Nulla; 19, Mount Surprise.

latest Oligocene-earliest Miocene (23.6–21.8 m.y.)
showing that the related structural depression and
sub-basaltic drainage are relatively old features. They
also suggest that similar basaltic sequences elsewhere
down the Derwent drainage may be older than previously supposed, which leaves little young volcanism
in Tasmania.

In many places it is clear that lava was erupted onto a
subdued topography, but in others a considerable
degree of relief had been attained before the eruption.
In these areas it seems that uplift and erosion were
advanced before eruption, and sometimes this happened surprisingly early. In Victoria, for instance, it is
found that tectonically undisturbed Eocene basalts
differ in altitude by 700 m, so a relative relief of that
amount probably existed by Eocene times.

Wellman and McDougall divide the volcanics into
lava fields and central volcanoes and the latter provide
interesting distributional patterns. There is a strong
correlation between age of central volcanoes and
latitude, with an apparent migration of central type
volcanism in a southerly direction at a rate of about
65 m/1,000 yr.

The centres of eruption fall on two main lines, and a
migration of Australia over two magma sources
located in the upper mantle is an explanation of the
relationship based on plate tectonics. The rate of
movement corresponds quite well with the rate of
drift of Australia northwards from Antarctica, which is
somewhere between 50 and 74 m/1,000 yr.

There appears to be a longitudinal migration of
volcanicity, and volcanicity has moved westwards
from a position close to the crest of the highland. It is
interesting that the youngest (Quaternary) volcanicity
in Australia—in western Victoria and north Queensland—fits in with this trend.

The association of volcanicity with the zone of
uplift suggests that tensional stress in the lithosphere
permits passage of magma from the upper mantle,
and on a broader scale the volcanism and uplift are
both probably causally linked with the opening of the
Tasman Sea and the Southern Ocean.

TECTONIC MOVEMENTS

As we have seen in previous sections, the most
important Tertiary tectonic movement in Australia
was the uplift of the Eastern Uplands Until fairly
recently ideas of the tectonic evolution of eastern
Australia have been dominated by the concept of a
'Kosciusko uplift' of late Pliocene to early Pleistocene
age. It now seems that movement has taken place in
several stages over a much longer time-scale.

There are really two axes of uplift—one roughly
north-south paralleling the eastern edge of the continent, and another east-west through the Eastern
Uplands of Victoria with a culmination in the Kosci-

Plate 4.2 The Thredbo Valley, New South Wales, on the dissected plateau that makes the Australian Alps. On the right is the Ram's Head Range, which includes Mount Kosciusko, the highest point in Australia (2,234 m). The exceptionally straight valley follows a fault line. The area has perhaps the most rigorous climate in Australia, and snow covers the ground for several months in most years.

usko area where the two meet. There is evidence of differential uplift along, as well as across the Uplands. In the Oxley Basin-Hunter River area near the axis of the Eastern Uplands the Oligocene to Miocene lavas are still near present river level, indicating little erosion since outpouring. Similarly Middle Miocene lavas in the Nandewar and Warrumbungle areas at Dubbo and west of Orange are also near present river level, suggesting little erosion since Middle Miocene. But in many other areas there has been extensive erosion after volcanics erupted. The amount of post-volcanic erosion depends on time available, relative relief, post-volcanic earth movements and other factors, such as the resistance of the bedrock and the size of eroding rivers.

Wellmann has made estimates of tectonic uplift based on the assumption that basalts which erupted on to broad alluviated areas were originally close to sea level. Increasing knowledge of the ages of Tertiary volcanics has tended to push back the supposed age of uplift of much of the highlands, and what were once thought to be late Tertiary movements are now often known to be much older. Wellman suggests that uplift of the Eastern Uplands took place in several stages, starting in the Mesozoic. The last uplift is inferred to have begun some time after the Oligocene and to have resulted in less than 300 m of uplift in the central and southern parts of the highlands, and negligible uplift further north. In the Oligocene, Wellman thinks, the highlands had a relief of over 1,000 m and a drainage system similar to that of today.

The relationship between uplift and volcanicity may be more complex. In the Hunter area Galloway (1967) found that tectonic movements have affected the basalt, and with it the pre-basalt topography. Part of the post-basalt movements took the form of broad subsidence, possibly associated with the outpouring of lava and different from the simple uplift pattern sometimes assumed. In contrast, Wyatt and Webb suggest that in northern Queensland the divide was actively rising during eruptions.

In Victoria later tectonic movements seem to be more important than in much of the highlands. The fault block topography of south Gippsland, the tectonic framework of Port Phillip and Westernport Bay, and the tectonic outlines of the West Victorian Plains are all caused by Upper Tertiary tectonic movements.

Tasmania is perhaps more like New South Wales than Victoria, for there is little established evidence for significant late Cainozoic tectonic movement (Sutherland, 1971). Tasmania has a very well-marked tectonic structure, with horsts and grabens, but these were probably initiated in late Mesozoic or early Palaeocene times.

South Australia owes much of its relief and structure to tectonic movements, especially block faulting. These movements appear to have been continuous throughout Tertiary times. Faults outline the major structural and geomorphic units, and are responsible for the closing of the Lake Eyre Basin. Tectonic activity prevailed throughout the Tertiary, culminating in major uplift and faulting in late Pliocene to early Quaternary times.

In Western Australia the Darling Fault is of major importance, and bounds the Tertiary deposits of the coastal plain. Broad epeirogenic movements have also occurred. Near Norseman Upper Eocene marine sediments have been raised nearly 300 m, and although the uplift cannot be dated the amount of subsequent erosion suggests it is pre-Quaternary. Near North West Cape the Rough Range, Cape Range and Barrow Island provide examples of original fold topography where the uplands correspond to Tertiary anticlines. Some have been successfully drilled for oil.

CLIMATIC HISTORY

Throughout the Mesozoic the South Pole seems to have been almost stationary just south of Tasmaina, and yet the climate seems to have been generally temperate or warm. The Mesozoic warmth followed the Permian glaciation without a significant change of latitude. Gill has pointed out that the direction of latitude lines may have been different from the present, and that temperatures were lower in the southeast half of the continent where fossils of warmth-loving reptiles are rare. There are some suggestions that the Paleocene and Lower Eocene may have been relatively cool and humid in Victoria. The later Eocene saw a general warming up, with *Nothofagidites* spp. present. Humid tropical or subtropical conditions prevailed through the Oligocene and most of the Miocene.

Evidence for the higher temperatures comes from

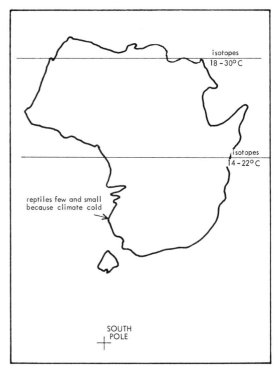

Fig. 4.8 Diagram (after Gill, 1968) showing how evidence of palaeotemperatures and the distribution of fossil reptiles, fits in with palaeolatitudes of the Mesozoic.

the evidence of fossils. In the Oligocene and Miocene of Victoria are large tropical foraminifera such as *Cycloclypeus* and *Lepidocyclina*, and a molluscan fauna reminiscent of northern Australian waters. In the Pliocene many of the tropical genera disappeared from Victorian waters, but temperatures higher than those of today are indicated by sharks, the echinoderm *Lovenia* (still common in northern Australia but not further south than Brisbane) and other warm-water species.

The widespread occurrence of lateritic soils of Tertiary age also indicates generally warm and wet conditions. Pedological indications of colder climates are not so easily recognized or preserved, so it should not be assumed from soil evidence alone that warm humid conditions were continuous.

In the early Tertiary climates appear to have been generally wet as well as warm, but from the Oligocene on there appears to have been a general trend towards aridity, spreading gradually out from southern central Australia.

The Australian Tertiary sequence can be compared usefully with that found in other parts of the world. Dated volcanic rocks erupted under ice indicate that polar ice began to accumulate in Antarctica at least 40 million years ago. Late Neogene (Miocene plus Pliocene) history shows a cooling trend which accelerated during the Pleistocene (but cannot be used to date it) and thick ice sheets were present in Antarctica throughout the Neogene. A great advance of shelf ice is related to late Miocene cooling, which had widespread eustatic effects on world sea levels. Low sea levels probably dropped to depths of 135 m and possibly as much as 200 m off Australia. Major rivers such as the Hunter deeply eroded their valleys, an effect of much consequence in later fluvial and coastal geomorphology. The late Miocene fall in sea level may relate also to the widespread presence of winnowed phosphate accumulation on a surface of Miocene marine regression, first noted by Bowler (1963) in the Geelong area, and later by Von der Borch on the continental slope. Shrinkage of the ice may relate to the Pliocene inundation which affected coastal areas of Australia and was particularly marked in the Murray Basin. In the northern hemisphere the initial Pliocene inundation of the Mediterranean Basin (earlier an extremely deep, dessicated lowland) may relate to this rise of sea level. Further cooling may be related to the regression of Pliocene times, associated with the beach ridges of the Murray Basin, and a precursor to the greater cooling of the Pleistocene. It should be noted that the northern hemisphere has a very different glacial history because floating ice first appeared there only 3 million years ago.

The lack of correlation between continental drift and climatic history indicates some cause or causes of major climatic fluctuations other than palaeolatitude. Changes in total incoming solar radiation may be one cause. Another is the change in continentality; climatic fluctuation may be due to different relationships of of land and sea. The great fall in sea level in late Miocene appears to be eustatic, brought about by the spread of Antarctic ice. We might reasonably expect the previous Miocene-Upper Oligocene period of marine transgression to be a warmer period, as is borne out by the palaeoclimatic evidence of fossils, and much lateritic weathering and silcrete formation date to this time.

It would be going beyond present evidence to attribute earlier transgressions and regressions to eustatic effects, but the possibility cannot be excluded. Eustatic-climatic controls are certainly important long before the Pleistocene, and their future elucidation is of great importance to stratigraphers and geomorphologists interested in the Tertiary.

AUSTRALIAN BIOLOGY: ISOLATION AND CONTACT

The unique flora and fauna of Australia results from its geographic isolation brought about by the geological history just recounted. In places the great time-scale brought about by tectonic stability has led to areas of leached and nutrient-depleted soils on which distinctive floras have evolved, such as the Western Australian Quonkan sandplain flora.

In pre-Tertiary times Australia shared much of its flora and fauna with other continents of Gondwanaland and in the Mesozoic had a population of dinosaurs comparable with that of the other continents. Surviving Gondwanaland relicts probably include the lung-fish, the side-necked tortoise, and the southern beech, *Nothofagus*. In Tertiary times the placental mammals became dominant animals in most of the world, but Australia was colonized by marsupials. The only terrestrial placental mammals to reach Australia before the Aborigines and their dogs were some bats, rats and seals. In Australia marsupials evolved to fill most of the available ecological niches and produced equivalents of the placental mammals of other continents. The evidence suggests that Australia was out of land contact with other continents at an early stage of mammalian evolution—before the placental mammals had appeared.

When Australia eventually collided with the Pacific plate a line of islands brought the Asian and Australian floras and faunas closer, though rather strangely no continuous land bridge was ever formed between the two continents. The Indonesian arc is of Tertiary age and the islands have been colonized from both ends by island-hopping of many species. There is a gradation of species between Asia and Australia, which for some is sharp enough to make a 'line' such as Wallace's Line (based mainly on birds) and Weber's Line (based mainly on mammals). The best botanical dividing line is Torres Strait, but even this is transgressed by many rainforest species of Indo-Malayan affinities occurring in Queensland and a few species of Australian type, such as eucalypts, occurring in New Guinea. It seems that plants have been able to invade almost to climatic limits, while animals (at least mammals, and surprisingly birds) have been restricted by marine barriers.

Some changes in species cannot be attributed to isolation. The fossils in Tertiary brown coals suggest that the flora consisted largely of conifers, Proteaceae, and southern beeches (*Nothofagus*), whereas the present flora is dominated by *Eucalyptus* and *Acacia* (wattle). In Victoria *Araucaria* and *Agathis* were present in the Tertiary, but these are now found only in the tropical and subtropical parts of Australia. These changes in flora appear to be consequences of the later Tertiary climatic drying and perhaps cooling.

Finally with the arrival of man there was a sudden breakdown in biotic isolation. The behaviour of naturalized as compared to native plants suggests that geomorphic history is important especially as it affects natural soil nutrient levels. However clearing, burning, hunting, agriculture, induced erosion, application of fertilizers and the introduction of exotic plants and animals have utterly altered the Australian scene, which has perhaps changed more in the last 200 years than in the previous 200 million.

Thus we see that the evolution of Australian scenery took hundreds of millions of years, and the time-scale of landform development is the same as the time-scales of biological evolution and continental drift. This background of quiet geological development, widespread climatic changes, and biological isolation explains much of Australian scenery and native life, and sets the stage for a quickening of events in the Quaternary, and the present.

REFERENCES

Berggren, W. A. (1972), 'A Cenozoic time scale—some implications for regional geology and palaeobiogeography', *Lethaia*, 5, 195–216.

Berggren, W. A. and van Couvering, J. A. (1974), 'The late Neogene: Biostratigraphy, geochronology and palaeoclimatology of the last 15 million years in marine and continental sequences', *Palaeogeogr. Palaeoclimatol. Palaeoecol.*, 16, 1–216.

Bowler, J. M. (1963), 'Tertiary stratigraphy and sedimentation in the Geelong-Maude area, Victoria', *Proc. R. Soc. Vic.*, 76, 69–136.

Brown, D. A., Campbell, K. S. W. and Crook, K. A. W. (1968), *The Geological Evolution of Australia and New Zealand*, Pergamon, Oxford.

Crowell, J. C. and Frakes, L. A. (1971), 'Late Palaeozoic glaciation of Australia', *J. geol. Soc. Aust.*, 17, 115–55.

Davies, J. L. (1962), 'Geomorphology and glaciation [of Tasmania]', *J. geol. Soc. Aust.*, 9, 243–8.

Embleton, B. J. J. (1972), 'The palaeolatitude of Australia through Phanerozoic time', *J. geol. Soc. Aust.*, 19, 475–82.

Exon, N. F., Langford-Smith, T. and McDougall, I. (1970), 'The age and geomorphic correlations of deep-weathering profiles, silcrete, and basalt in the Roma-Amby region, Queensland', *J. geol. Soc. Aust.*, 17, 21–30.

Galloway, R. W. (1967), 'Pre-basalt, sub-basalt and post-basalt surfaces of the Hunter Valley, New South Wales' in J. N. Jennings and J. A. Mabbutt (eds), *Landform Studies from Australia and New Guinea*, Australian National University Press, Canberra, pp. 293–314.

Gill, E. D. (1972), 'Palaeoclimatology and dinosaurs in south-east Australia', *Search*, 3, 11–12.

Hays, J. (1967), 'Land surfaces and laterites in the north of the Northern Territory in J. N. Jennings and J. A. Mabbutt (eds), *Landform Studies from Australia and New Guinea*, Australian National University Press, Canberra, pp. 182–210.

Jennings, J. N. and Mabbutt, J. A. (eds) (1967), *Landform Studies from Australia and New Guinea*, Australian National University Press, Canberra.

King, L. C. (1962), *Morphology of the Earth*, Oliver and Boyd, Edinburgh.

Mabbutt, J. A. (1967), Denudation chronology in Central Australia: structure, climate and landform inheritance in the Alice Springs area' in J. N. Jennings and J. A. Mabbutt (eds), *Landform Studies from Australia and New Guinea*, Australian National University Press, Canberra, pp. 144–81.

Morgan, W. R. (1968), 'The geology and petrology of Cainozoic basaltic rocks in the Cooktown area, North Queensland', *J. geol. Soc. Aust.*, 15, 65–78.

Mulcahy, M. J. and Bettenay, E. (1972), 'Soil and landscapes studies in Western Australia. (1) The major drainage divisions', *J. geol. Soc. Aust.*, 18, 349–57.

Neilson, J. L. (1961), 'Notes on the geology of the High Plains of Victoria', *Proc. R. Soc. Vic.*, 75, 277–84.

Stephens, C. G. (1971), 'Laterite and silcrete in Australia', *Geoderma*, 5, 5–52.

Sutherland, F. L., Green, D. C. and Wyatt, B. W. (1973), 'Age of the Great Lake Basalts, Tasmania, in relation to Australian Cainozoic volcanism', *J. geol. Soc. Aust.*, 20, 85–93.

Twidale, C. R. (1966), 'Chronology and denudation in the Southern Flinders Ranges, South Australia', *Trans. R. Soc. S. Aust.*, 90, 3–32.

Von der Borch, C. C. (1970), 'Phosphatic concretions and nodules from the upper continental slope, northern New South Wales', *J. geol. Soc. Aust.*, 16, 755–9.

Watkins, J. R. (1967), 'The relationship between climate and the development of landforms in the Cainozoic rocks of Queensland', *J. geol. Soc. Aust.*, 14, 153–68.

Wellman, P. and McDougall, I. (1974), 'Cainozoic igneous activity in eastern Australia', *Tectonophysics*, 23, 49–65.

Wellman, P., McElhinny, M. W. and McDougall, I. (1969), 'On the polar-wander path for Australia during the Cenozoic', *Geophys. J. R. astr. Soc.*, 18, 371–96.

Wright, R. L. (1963), 'Deep weathering and erosion surfaces in the Daly River basin, Northern Territory', *J. geol. Soc. Aust.*, 10, 151–63.

Wyatt, D. H. and Webb, A. W. (1970), 'Potassium-argon ages of some northern Queensland basalts and an interpretation of late Cainozoic history', *J. geol. Soc. Aust.*, 17, 39–51.

5 FLUVIAL LANDFORMS

I. DOUGLAS

In January 1974 vast sheets of water spilled across the arid interior of Australia, extending the boundaries of Lake Eyre and converting Coopers Creek into a major waterway several kilometres across. Such events are rare but significant in the evolution of Australian landforms. They are reminders of the role of fluvial processes throughout the whole of Australia, from the high snow melt discharges in the Australian Alps to the torrents on the Todd River at Heavitree Gap. Nevertheless, only the areas with sufficient rainfall to support a woodland or forest vegetation and to produce discharges in rivers and creeks several times a year at least, have landforms that are currently evolving under the dominant, if not exclusive influence of the work of running water. In these areas integrated drainage networks generally carry runoff to the sea, although a few endoreic drainage areas such as the Lake

Fig. 5.1 Humid Australia. Boundaries are based on classification of rainfall on seasonal maximum and annual amounts of median rainfall. S indicates a summer (November to April) maximum; U indicates uniform seasonal rainfall; and W a winter (May to October) maximum. The arid area has a median annual rainfall of less than 380 mm in the summer maximum districts or less than 255 mm in the winter maximum or uniform districts.

George catchment exist. In these integrated drainage networks present-day geomorphic change is largely a response to variations in hydrometeorological conditions, the alternation of flood and drought concomitant with the variability of precipitation in Australia.

Definition of the area of integrated drainage dominated by fluvial processes is difficult, but as an approximation, the areas outside arid Australia as defined by seasonal rainfall (Fig. 5.1) may be considered to represent humid Australia. The contrasts between summer and winter maximum rainfall reflect the relative significance of tropical or high latitude cyclonic disturbances. The arrival of heavy, widespread, persistent rain after a warm dry season in northern Australia may produce much runoff and erosion. In east coast catchments tropical cyclones may yield as much as 800 mm of rain in 24 hours. Winter rain, or snow at high altitudes, in southern Australia may not be as effective. However, even the uniform rainfall areas have marked periodicity of rainfall, for although heavy storms may occur in any month, dry spells of several months duration are also frequent. All Australian humid areas experience major flood events, such as the 'Burrinjuck Flood' of May 1925 which produced 380 mm of rain in 24 hours over the upper Shoalhaven catchment (Hounam, 1957). Such extreme events may cause landslips, erosion and deposition which produce minor landforms not significantly modified until the next major flood.

DENUDATION SYSTEMS

If the denudation process is taken to be an open system of continually varying interacting phenomena, tending to evolve into an energy balance or series of quasi-equilibrium states (Douglas, 1973), then the most severe ruptures of quasi-equilibrium in humid Australian denudation systems are caused by major flood events which provide large volumes of water to carry away dissolved and solid particles and high energy raindrop impact to detach soil particles. During day-to-day time-spans, the quasi-equilibrium changes gradually as the amounts of water and material flowing through the different segments of the denudation

99

system vary. Over the far longer geological time-span in which erosion surfaces are created, the components of the denudation system readjust as new rock structures are exposed and as available energy diminishes when gradients decline during the lowering of relief.

The great age of the broad structural features and the longevity of some features of the drainage network (Harrington, 1974, Ch. 4) of Australia make notions of the time-independence of landforms relative to quasi-equilibrium states of particular significance. If there has been relatively little topographic change in recent times, then Australian fluvial denudation systems may be approaching an equilibrium condition and it may be possible to follow the advice of Carson and Kirkby (1972) and regard the valleyside slopes as essentially sediment transport systems operating in graded time, while rivers are a water transport system operating in steady and graded time-spans. The crucial issue of the extent of these time-spans requires elucidation against the evidence of tectonic unity of humid eastern Australia and the supposed stability of Western Australia's humid southwest.

To analyse the characteristics of present-day geomorphic processes and the landforms on which they work and which they are creating, humid Australia will be divided into four sectors, three in the east and one in the west. The eastern area comprises the coastal valleys and plains including the whole of Tasmania; the tablelands, plateaux and mountains of the Eastern uplands; and the upper sectors of the western slopes and depositional plains of the inland flowing streams, including those draining to the Gulf of Carpentaria and those flowing northwards to the Murray in Victoria. The humid southwest will be treated as a unit, although in fact it contains a coastal plain, plateau and inland stream elements somewhat analogous to those in the east.

The present-day operation of fluvial denudation systems in Australia must be set against a long time-span of interaction between tectonics and denudation (Chapter 4). The landscape composed of ancient drainage lineaments, old land surfaces, reactivated faults, relatively young lava flows and recent drainage adjustments to changed climate and land use, responds in a number of ways to contemporary processes of denudation. Distinction must be made between landscape elements that are changing rapidly and those which are being modified much more slowly. To do this, emphasis must be placed on the operation of the denudation system and the significance of particular events and localities in present-day landscape evolution.

COASTAL STREAMS AND THEIR DRAINAGE SYSTEMS

The broad features of the east coast of Australia are a succession of relatively restricted coastal drainage basins, with streams descending steeply from the Great Divide, often over high waterfalls, and developing large deltas at the junction with the sea (Plate 5.1).

These deltaic flats and associated beach ridges are separated by rocky headlands. Not all streams end in deltas however. In the Sydney Basin, the drowned estuaries of the Hawkesbury, Parramatta and Port Hacking rivers contrast markedly with the deltas to the north and south. The contrast probably results in part from tectonic differences, but largely from differences in the rates of infilling of the estuaries, perhaps as a result of tidal flow being able to cope with the sediment supply from the rivers of the Sydney Basin (Jennings and Bird, 1957) and contrasts in coastal currents covering longshore drift of barrier beach material.

More significant perhaps is the contrast between the short streams, such as the Johnston, Tully, Mary, Tweed, Hastings and Manning Rivers and the major east coast rivers with catchments extending well inland such as the Burdekin, Fitzroy, Brisbane and Hunter. The westernmost headwaters of the latter group lie in subhumid areas where seasonal moisture deficits may be marked. For example, Dalkeith at the western extremity of the Hunter Valley has an estimated water deficit of 108 mm extending from October to April inclusive (Tweedie, 1963), while at Taroom on the Dawson River, the southern branch of the Fitzroy River, estimated mean potential evapotranspiration exceeds mean rainfall in every month of the year (Fitzpatrick, 1968). In their hydrometeorology many of the inland areas of the great east coast rivers are more akin to the western slopes of the main divide than to the coastal denudation systems. In the account of coastal stream denudation systems therefore only those parts of the major east coast catchments east of the general trend of the coastal escarpments are considered.

Between the escarpments and the sea, the coastal stream catchments exhibit a sequence of erosional and depositional landforms. Often the steep escarpments themselves have many bare rock outcrops from which rockfalls are not uncommon. On the southern side of the Hunter Valley, the northern outcrop of the Hawkesbury Sandstone forms massive sandstone cliffs from which rockfalls occur at frequent intervals. Below the almost vertical rock face (unit 4 of the 9-unit landsurface model of Dalrymple, Blong and Conacher, 1968) are less steep slopes, developed either from the slumping of weaker materials or from the debris supplies from above. Such slopes may be complex, consisting of a series of hillslope mantles of varied ages.

Near the lower Shoalhaven at Nowra, three massive accumulations of debris occur as hillslope mantles with associated accumulations forming terraces in tributary valleys. Walker (1962a, b) concluded that

Plate 5.1 The Burdekin delta, north Queensland. The Burdekin brings large quantities of sand to the coast during seasonal floods and has constructed a massive delta in late Quaternary times. *Photo*: David Hopley.

erosion and hillside mantle-movements were associated with more arid conditions whereas soil development was believed to have occurred during more humid climates (Butler, 1967). The floodplain stratigraphy of the Tea Tree Rivulet in the Buckland Basin of eastern Tasmania (Goede, 1965, 1972, 1973; Davies, 1967) reveals a similar set of erosion/deposition and soil formation conditions. Along larger rivers such alternating systems may have produced a series of terraces as the depositional correlates of the erosional activity further upstream. The Macleay River of northern New South Wales has a sequence of terraces with marked differences in soil characteristics (Walker, 1970) which are probably related to the same sets of climatic changes as the hillslope mantles at Nowra.

Hillslope Development in Coastal Catchments

The 'historical hangovers' from past phases of landform evolution represented by hillslope mantles, valley fills, terraces and deltaic deposits mean that the present-day system is not always operating on weather-

ing products being produced at the present time. The material now being carried into streams is often the product of weathering under a previous set of environmental conditions. If there is any area of humid Australia relatively free of such 'historical hangovers' it is probably the small area of humid tropical, Köppen Af, climate around Innisfail and Tully in north Queensland. The intensity of weathering and denudation under present conditions may well have removed many vestiges of past morphogenesis.

The granite hillsides of north Queensland rise steeply from narrow coastal alluvial plains. While a few bare patches of granite occur on the steepest hillsides, most of the slopes have latosols supporting a dense tropical rainforest. Under such conditions humidity is high and the decomposition of organic matter rapid. The high nutrient turnover and organic activity is part of a largely internal circulation of chemical elements in the rainforest ecosystem (Douglas, 1969), but the intensity of weathering is sufficient to break down minerals to iron and aluminium oxides, with high concentrations of silica being carried in soil water to streams. The rainforest vegetation protects the soil against much of the impact of raindrops, but some slopewash occurs between trees where the forest litter layer is thin. With storm rainfall intensities sometimes exceeding 100 mm/hr, surface wash of debris downslope between trees occurs. Tree roots are often exposed at the soil surface, leaf debris frequently accumulating on the upslope side of tree trunks and exposed roots. Subsurface water movement is also an important process of slope evolution. Water infiltrating down the soil profile may find lateral downslope paths, sometimes because the weathering profile becomes less permeable or because voids left by decayed plant roots offer paths of greater hydraulic efficiency than the spaces between mineral grains. This subsurface flow washes fine clay particles between the sand grains of the weathered granite, sometimes depositing the fine clay at a break of slope or channel edge. The sand grains themselves may be gradually lost by surface wash or removed by channel erosion, until core stones of unweathered granite are exposed at the ground surface. Removal of the weathered mantle in in this way allows core stones to slump into stream channels, producing the boulder strewn channels characteristic of low-order streams in steep granite country. Often the heads of such stream channels are beneath great boulder chokes of core stones which have slid or rolled into the stream head hollow. Subsurface water converging on the hollow emerges from beneath a boulder choke.

Minor mass movement associated with the slumping of individual core boulders is common. On exposed slopes frequent damage to forest trees by tropical cyclones can result in the collapse of small tracts of forest (Webb, 1958), the exposure of areas of soil to direct raindrop impact and landslips. Minor landslipping when soils become excessively wet is widespread in Queensland rainforest areas (Ellison and Coaldrake, 1954). Major landslipping is rare, but can produce major changes in slope form and even diversion of minor streams.

Mass movements may be major sources of sediment carried by rainforest streams. Although suspended sediment concentrations in steep coastal streams in north Queensland are usually less than 100 mg/l, occasional soil slips may cause dramatic increases in concentration. Behana Creek at Aloomba near Mt Belleden Ker carries the majority of its load in suspension, the ratio of dissolved to suspended load being 0.6:1, but as suspended load only exceeds dissolved load 2.2 per cent of the time, over 50 per cent of the sediment load is removed in less than seven days of the year (Douglas, 1973). Bed-load transport on such steep streams may be important, particularly in the lower reaches where an abundance of quartz sand

grains, the residual of granite weathering accumulates. Behana Creek at Aloomba carries at low flows as saltation load quartz particles which are thrown into suspension at higher discharges, overall bed load being equivalent to about 20 per cent of the measured suspended sediment load.

In their rapid descent from the boulder-chokes and rock bed channels of the steepest slopes, through the boulder stream foothill reaches and the sand bed channels of the coastal plains to the clay and silt channels of the mangrove swamps of the coastal deltas, these tropical stream channels exhibit a rapid downstream decrease in bed material grain size, probably due more to chemical decomposition of the material involved than to any mechanical abrasion.

In the more gentle slopes of the Rocksberg Basin at the head of the Caboolture River in southeastern Queensland, processes typical of much of the rolling hill country of subtropical coastal areas of southern Queensland and northern New South Wales differ in relative importance in various parts of the basin (Arnett and Conacher, 1973). In first-order basins, surface wash may be important following heavy rain but generally water moves as subsurface flow developing a seepage line rather than a permanent channel at the valley floor. Second-order slopes differ from first-order basin slopes by being more convex in form with creep and micro-rill action becoming more important. Greater variety of process is found on the more complex third-order slopes while on fourth-order slopes rapid forms of mass movement occur on steep lower slopes with slumping, earthflows and debris avalanches producing a complex surface form, thereby enabling rilling and gullying to further dissect the topography. Here the work of running water ranges from subsurface flow dominance to significant surface wash and from diffuse to concentrated flow phenomena. The propensity for rill or gully development on the convex unit 3 (in terms of the 9-unit landsurface model) or the mass-movement affected steeper unit 4 introduces linear dissection of the slope front.

Coastal Lowland Depositional Systems

While many coastal lowlands in eastern Australia have of old beach ridges and river terraces, many of them are contemporary depositional systems dominated by flood flows caused by cyclonic rains such as those from Cyclone Zoe in March 1974 which brought 660 mm in 24 hours to Woodburn on the lower Richmond River in northern New South Wales (Douglas and Hobbs, 1974). In these areas the floodplain may be inundated two or more times a year, overbank flow occurring far more frequently than in higher latitudes. In their natural state, these coastal lowland river channels would tend to have migrating meanders with large areas of backswamp, but man has built levees, dredged the channels and drained the backswamp in an attempt to stabilize floodplains and channels.

The great range of discharges found in rivers like the Brisbane and the Clarence means that stream channels are often wide but seldom fully covered with water. A short distance upstream of Grafton, for example, the Clarence River has a wide pebble-strewn bed with small islets supporting *Casuarina* trees in the middle of the channel. The banks of the channel are steep, but also stepped, giving the impression of a series of terraces. However, during major floods many of these steps in the banks will be inundated, some gauging stations experiencing changes in river level exceeding 20 metres. The grass or *Casuarina* covered islands are drowned by major floods, the bent trees on both islands and banks indicating the force of floodwaters. These fluvial systems operate in response to storm events when runoff from soaking rain fills gullies and causes all streams to rise rapidly. River bank undercutting and slumping during the floods are common, many sections of channels undergoing scour and fill.

In examining the denudation systems of the coastal streams of eastern Australia, the episodic nature of landscape change has to be considered. Even in the humid tropics of the Babinda-Tully area, where rain is frequent, most of the work of landscape change is done by the runoff from a few storms per year. The major events which trigger landslips, cause bank erosion, dislodge core boulders or produce channel changes, are the events which determine landform characteristics. Present-day changes are affected by human activity but much of the coastal zone, especially drier areas such as the Townsville-Bowen region and the Hunter Valley is naturally prone to serious soil erosion, bush fires and flooding (Galloway, 1963). Not all places erode or are subject to siltation at the same rate. Just as there are changes in intensity of geomorphic processes in time, so there are spatial variations. Zones of water accumulation, slope instability and channel weakness see rapid changes in short periods of time, while other parts of the coastal streams area change but slowly.

DENUDATION SYSTEMS OF THE EASTERN UPLANDS

The uplands of eastern Australia are the area of high erosion surfaces and residual hills west of the coastal escarpments. Most of the tableland areas are 600 to 1,000 metres above sea level, but they culminate in the peaks of the Australian Alps and the granite bosses of New England and north Queensland which are over 1,600 metres above sea level. The Great Divide runs through the uplands, often being barely distinguishable on the level surfaces characteristic of much of the area.

So indistinct is the divide in some localities that small areas of endoreic drainage occur on relatively humid areas, as at the Mother of Ducks Lagoon and the Llangothlin Lagoon near Guyra in nothern New South Wales (Fig. 5.2). Lake George, Lake Bathurst and The Morass near Canberra are similar fluctuating lakes which shrink or even disappear completely after a run of dry years. Evaporation from Lake George approximately balances inflow from the catchment (Galloway, 1965) and the lake level fluctuates from year to year. In the last 150 years it has been practically dry for half the time (Galloway, 1969). Around these lakes are extensive alluvial flats which may contain remnants of former lake shorelines dating from periods when evaporation was lower or inflow greater than at present.

Much of the geomorphology of the Eastern Uplands depends on the way in which the Tasman geosyncline evolved during the Palaeozoic. Uplift and faulting of the diverse and stratigraphically complex sediments of the geosyncline gave rise to rapid changes in surface lithology and created the many meridional fault structures, such as the Peel and Murrumbidgee faults, which remain prominent features of the landscape (Voisey, 1959; Evernden and Richards, 1962). Sedimentation in Carboniferous, Permian and Mesozoic basins eventually gave rise to the cuesta and tabular landscapes of the Clarence-Moreton and Sydney Basins. Volcanic eruptions, particularly prominent in the Tertiary, created the basalt flows characteristic of many tableland areas.

The majority of the tableland areas are characterized by the three major rock groups, Palaeozoic sediments, granites of various ages, and the Tertiary basalts. The lithological contrasts within the sediments may produce rapid variations in landform, as in the Nundle district of southern New England. However, characteristic granitic and basaltic landscapes occur throughout the tablelands from Queensland to Tasmania. Scoria cones and maars of the Newer Volcanics of Victoria (Ollier, 1967) have their counterparts on the Atherton Tableland of north Queensland. Granite domes, tors and corestones similarly extend from Tasmania to northern Queensland. Locally, these lithological contrasts affect the efficiency of geomorphic processes, quantities of solutes carried by streams varying more with lithology than with climate within an area like the Southern Tablelands (Douglas, 1968). However, over the whole of the Eastern Uplands variation in the rate of removal of material in solution and suspension by streams is more closely related to climate than to lithology (Douglas, 1973).

Granitic Landscapes of the Uplands

The granitic landscapes of the tablelands stem from the same type of weathering processes as those producing

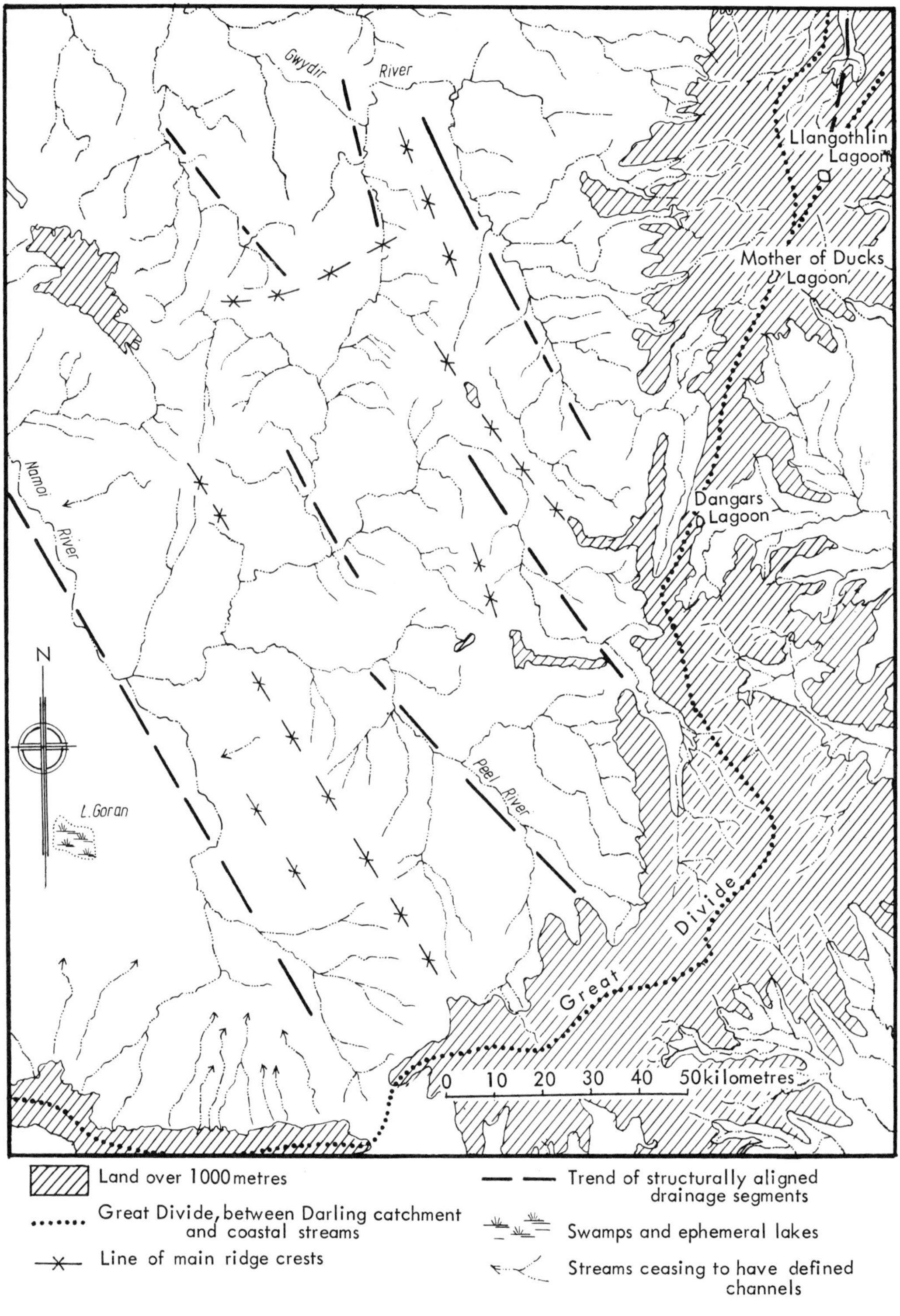

Gwydir River

Llangothlin
Lagoon

Mother of Ducks
Lagoon

Namoi River

Dangars
Lagoon

N

L. Goran

Peel River

Great Divide

0   10   20   30   40   50 kilometres

Land over 1000 metres

Great Divide, between Darling catchment
and coastal streams

Line of main ridge crests

Trend of structurally aligned
drainage segments

Swamps and ephemeral lakes

Streams ceasing to have defined
channels

Fig. 5.2 Adjustment of streams to structure on the western slopes of northern New South Wales. Lagoons on the Great Divide and strike-parallel streams are highlighted. Lake Goran is an ephemeral feature inundated in major floods.

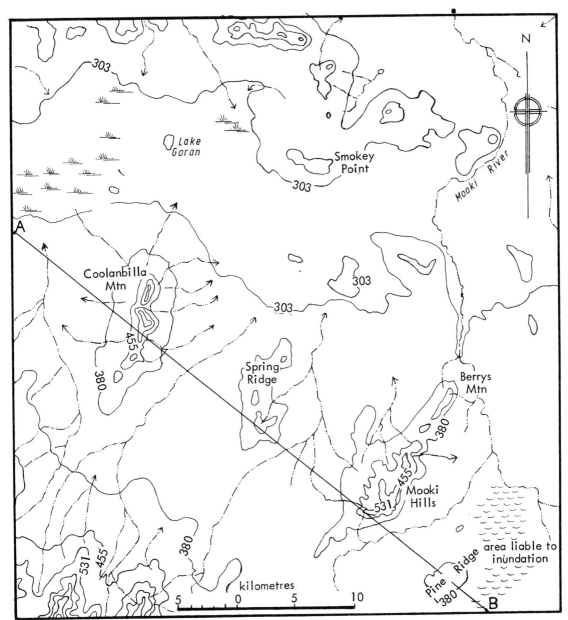

Fig. 5.3 Residual outlier hills and ill-drained depositional colluvial and alluvial flats in the Spring Ridge area of northwestern New South Wales. The cross-section AB is shown in Fig. 5.4. Contour internal approximately 75 m. Lake Goran and the southeastern floodable areas are in poorly drained depressions with only weak outlets to the Mooki River. Many streams cease to have defined channels once off the hillslopes.

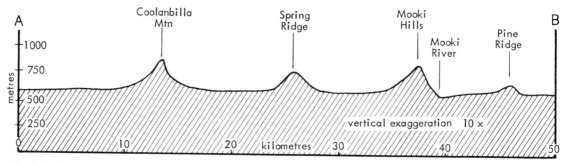

Fig. 5.4   Cross-section through residual hills in the Spring Ridge area of New South Wales.

granite core boulders in the coastal streams, but in the tablelands the residual forms, the domes and tors, probably attract most attention. Although an unambiguous distinction between tors and domes is difficult to make, characteristically, tors form groups of spheroidally weathered boulders rooted in the bedrock which may be exposed as a bare rock surface or concealed by a waste mantle. Constituent blocks may occasionally reach 8 m in diameter, but 1–3 m are common. On the other hand granitic domes typically rise as unbroken rock exposures sometimes exceeding 300 m in height.

Tors such as Cathedral Rocks on the Round Mountain Batholith in New England (Leigh, 1968, 1970) are bedrock residuals consisting of joint-bounded blocks, resting one upon the other, which have been isolated beneath the ground surface by differential chemical weathering along joints of varying intensity and openness and exposed by removal of the weathered material in subsequent denudation. Jointing, depth of weathering, extent of exposure from beneath the regolith and degree of subaerial decay all affect the size and shape of a tor. Once exposed, the rock surface may be subject to flaking, granular disintegration and spheroidal weathering. Flaking involves the lifting away of thin skins of relatively fresh rock (6–12 mm thick) from the surface. Granular disintegration is the decomposition of feldspars while the intact quartz falls away to leave a small talus surrounding the base of the tor. Spheroidal weathering probably results from the encroachment of chemical weathering upon cuboid joint blocks and gives rise to concentric rings of progressively decomposed rock passing into a structureless regolith (Thomas, 1974). The occurrence of tors in often associated with wide variations in the depth of weathering, which may be reflected also by differences in soil type, and thus their hydrologic behaviour (Bruce-Smith, 1972).

Between granite outcrops, weathering products accumulated as spreads of colluvium which coalesce in the centre along seepage lines or minor stream channels. The colluvial basins so formed act as sources

of streamflow, collecting the water which is shed from bare rock surfaces and, depending on the volume, intensity, and duration of precipitation, either being the place where concentrated linear flow begins, or being a seepage hollow from which runoff water drains by a subsurface percoline. In these basins, stream channel enlargement by bank erosion and slumping of the headwall of the channel at the point where the defined channel commences is common, making gullying likely if the rainfall:runoff relationship is altered by land use changes.

Streams draining these small colluvial basins flow from one basin to another over a series of rocky steps. First-order stream channels are usually dry, save after rain, when concentrated linear flow may sometimes commence upstream of the head of the defined channel. Below any given rocky step, water may seep into the channel from subsurface percolines. The development of these channels thus depends on the pattern of subsurface weathering, the presence of unweathered rock outcrops, the depth of colluvial fills and the frequency of storms producing concentrated runoff on the slopes above the channel heads.

Where major granitic residual hills stand several hundred metres above the surrounding country, large alluvial fans cover the footslopes of the hills. On the hillsides stream development is similar to the core boulder choked streams on coastal granitic mountain ranges, the channel often emerging from beneath the boulders as a grassed hollow clotted with other large blocks of unweathered rock. At the base of the slope the grassed hollow gives way to the surface of the alluvial fan. Within the fan however, percolines may have developed into pipes, or even subsurface tunnels, the collapse of whose roofs may lead to dissection of the fan by gullying. Such a situation prevails on alluvial fans around Mt Duval near Armidale, New South Wales, where pits formed by collapse of subsurface drainage lines are 1 to 2 metres deep and reveal tunnels of 25 to 40 cm in diameter carrying water beneath the surface of the fans.

The Basalt Tablelands

Large sections of the Eastern Uplands are characterized by the tabular landscapes of basalt flows, often occurring as a series of stepped plains separated by scarps which represent the consolidated fronts of lava flows (Twidale, 1956a, 1966). The scarps may attain 20 metres, but are more commonly of the order of 8 to 10 metres high. While in some areas, such as the Comboyne, Dorrigo, Darling Downs and Atherton Tablelands, the basalt is deeply weathered with some fairly level surfaces, in others, such as the Ben Lomond and McBride Plateaux, it is characterized by many stony ridges and rises with abundant boulders of unweathered basalt in the chocolate soils and black earths.

In discussing the basalt denudation systems of the tablelands distinction has to be made between the ages of the basalt flows, the soils and vegetation of the basalt surfaces and the climate of the areas involved. The basalts of the Eastern Uplands range from early Tertiary to late Quaternary in age. In some cases the volcanic cones are young enough to retain their characteristic forms, as do the Seven Sisters on the Atherton Tableland. Soils have had varying lengths of time to evolve on these basalt surfaces, and may have been subjected to changes in climate and vegetation. In the wetter areas, especially where rainforests exist under natural conditions, krasnozems occur, while chocolate soils are characteristic of the drier tableland basalts of the south, black earth developing in drier tropical tableland basalt areas such as the Einasleigh area of Queensland.

Patterns of weathering and erosion on the basalt tablelands from Victoria to north Queensland have many common characteristics, with radial drainage from ancient cones, amphitheatre-like valleys, and drainage diversions (Ollier, 1969). The basalts of the Atherton Tableland illustrate the unity of slope and channel processes. From a high vantage point, valley-side slopes appear rounded near the summit, but descend in an almost straight line to the floors of deep valleys. Closer inspection shows that the straight segments of these slopes meet the flat valley floor at an abrupt angle. In terms of the 9-unit landsurface model these basalt valleys lack units 4 and 6, there being a direct transition from unit 3, the creep zone of the slope to a transport slope (unit 5) and thence to the valley floor. The absence of the colluvial footslope (unit 6) is particularly noteworthy. These valleys represent a form of *Kehltal*, grooved-shaped, alluviated concave floored valley (Louis, 1968). They extend almost to the heads of first-order streams in basaltic areas.

Stream flow and erosion in the basalt tablelands is greatly affected by the permeability of the basalt terrain, the tendency for subsurface water to emerge at defined seepage points and the depth of the weathered regolith. The relatively high groundwater storage in basalt terrain tends to produce lower flood peaks and higher baseflows than in streams draining less permeable terrains.

The basalts of the Monaro Tableland of southern New South Wales are in a rain shadow area with a mean annual rainfall less than 600 mm. Here the chocolate soils are dominated by dry tussock grassland, with savanna woodland at the wetter margins. Only shallow-rooting plants exist because the subsoil is typically so closed and compact that inadequate aeration beyond the subsoil inhibits deep root development (Costin, 1954). Percolating water tends to leach the more soluble elements from these soils and carry them downslope, with chernozems and sierozems developing at the base of the slope. As evaporation usually exceeds precipitation in this environment, high concentrations of soluble salts develop and where water movement is impeded calcium carbonate and gypsum are precipitated. Such a trend towards salt accumulation is widespread in the drier tableland areas, not only on the basalt tablelands. However, as on the more humid basalt areas, translocation and loss of material in solution are the dominant erosion processes, as the structure of the chocolate soils provides a strong resistance to mechanical erosion.

The Sandstone Tablelands

The extensive, but deeply dissected, sandstone plateaux of the Sydney Basin (Hawkesbury-Shoalhaven Plateaux) provide rocky rugged landscapes, save where remnants of the original erosion surface persist. The broad features of hillslopes are determined by the structure of the sandstones, prominent cliffs coinciding with resistant beds (Galloway, 1963). In detail, minor sandstone landforms are determined by bedding planes, mineralogy and matrix composition, aspect and drainage. Chemical weathering is important, with organic acids playing a major role in well-vegetated areas (Johnson, 1974) where cavernous and honeycomb weathering and pitting of sandstones are common. Flat surfaces developed on bedding planes, on the other hand may remain relatively immune from weathering for long periods as the well-preserved aboriginal rock carvings on horizontal rock surfaces in the Ku-ring-gai Chase National Park indicate.

Sandstone uplands are characteristically dry, with extremely rapid runoff following heavy rain. Watercourses are slots cut in the nearly horizontally bedded rock, with abundant sand on the channel floor. Major rivers draining the escarpment rise rapidly, carrying large quantities of quartz sand derived from the disintegration of the Hawkesbury sandstone. In dry periods streams like the Wollombi Brook have but a small winding minor channel flowing through the sandbars of the major channel. Yet during storm runoff large changes in bed form, bank erosion and overbank flow occur. The rivers of the sandstone country exhibit extreme variability of discharge and intensity of sediment removal.

The bedding of the sandstones provides a major control of the character of the landforms of arenaceous terrain, tabular landforms with residual buttes, such as the Three Sisters at Katoomba being characteristic of the centre of the Sydney Basin. At the outer margins escarpment and cuesta landscapes occur, often with rockfalls and talus cones covering the lower parts of the slopes. Above, the free face shows fresh, unweathered scars where rock has fallen recently and the darker surfaces where chemical and biological processes have modified the outer layers of the rock. On the plateau surfaces, soils are usually thin and permeable, but remnants of Tertiary duricrusts are widespread. In hollows and valley floors detritus washed from higher areas has accumulated, often providing marshy conditions and supporting a more varied flora than the dry sandstone surfaces.

Elsewhere in the Eastern Uplands of Australia, sandstone mesas and tablelands occur, but seldom with such marked escarpments and such deeply incised streams as in the Hawkesbury-Shoalhaven Plateaux of the Sydney Basin. The relatively thin beds of late Mesozoic sandstones capping much of the Gilberton Plateau of north Queensland have been eroded into rugged topography with minor streams flowing through steep-sided rocky gorges and major rivers having sandy channels. Tertiary erosion surfaces cut across much of the north Queensland's sandstone outcrop, but a few mesas protrude above the general plateau level. Detailed surface weathering of some cross-bedded sandstones has produced striking weathered forms, termed 'beehives' by Twidale (1956b).

In this section contrasts in granitic, basaltic and sandstone landforms have been highlighted, but other rock types could be examined in a similar manner. Present-day processes are largely modifying an old landscape, cutting into remnants of erosion surfaces, changing stream channels, eroding back escarpments and dissecting the slope deposits of previous phases of landform evolution. On the local scale lithology and structure exert a major influence on landforms and the spatial variation in the efficiency of geomorphic processes.

DEPOSITIONAL SYSTEMS OF THE SLOPES AND PLAINS

Streams flowing inland from the Eastern Uplands drop with moderate declivity from the high-level erosion surfaces, sometimes through narrow gorges or gaps in the meridionally-orientated ridges of resistent Palaeozoic sediments, but often, as Andrews (1903) clearly described, following the prevailing north-south strike (Fig. 5.2). The Peel and Mooki tributaries of the Namoi, for example, flow from south to north in gradually widening valleys, before turning west through short defile sections to join the main Namoi River and eventually pass out on to the western plains.

At their western extremities, the hills on resistant Palaeozoic rocks of the Eastern uplands break up into isolated remnants, often fringed by steep, pediment-like slopes. The junction between the Eastern Uplands and the Interior Lowlands of the Gulf of Carpentaria, Lake Eyre, Bulloo and Murray-Darling drainage basins is characterized by landscapes with well-developed free-faces (unit 4 of the 9-unit landsurface model) and transportation slopes (unit 5 of the 9-unit landsurface model) on residual hills and ridges. Even these eastern fringes of the slopes and plains are properly described as depositional systems for the bulk of the landscape is made up of depositional colluvial and alluvial surfaces. Below the transportation slopes flanking the residual hills, colluvial foot-slopes (unit 6 of the 9-unit landsurface model) extend at gentle gradients towards valley floors (Fig. 5.3 and 5.4). Occasional stream lines cut these footslopes, but the drainage density is low and uncoordinated surface and subsurface runoff carries most of the water which enters the major streams. Much of the land surface is covered with a series of aeolian and fluvial Quaternary deposits which reveal the courses of prior and antecedent streams.

Today the depositional systems are dominated by the same episodic hydrologic events as the denudation systems of the tablelands. The same long duration widespread rain events which cause stream erosion in the tablelands produce flood flows in the westward-flowing streams which move gradually out onto the plains. As the flood wave proceeds downstream it spills over the minor channel benches into anabranches and is there either lost by evaporation, or infiltrates into subsurface storage or moves further out on to the alluvial plains. Major flows, however, overtop all the channel benches and spread across the plains, converting much of the landscape into a vast, slow-moving lake (Pigram, 1974).

While apparently superficially monotonously level, the riverine plains are full of landform diversity. Here the traces of past river and wind action are being altered by present-day deposition and local erosion. Within the diversity of stream patterns to the west of the uplands a great variety of depositional landforms are found. Both meandering and braiding channel patterns occur, streams on the Barwon system having meandering channels yet tending to overspill into braiding distributary systems. In north Queensland, extensive braided streams extend from the uplands to the coastal plains (Twidale, 1966), but individual meandering distributaries also occur. The braided condition arises in part from inherited conditions of large accumulations of sediment, possibly related to higher discharges in the past through which the present rivers flow. However, braiding is also the result of the dominance of the hydrologic regime by relatively infrequent flood flows which may not occur often enough to be the dominant channel-forming discharges. These infrequent flows thrust large quantities of silt down stream channels and develop overbank flows, but once the flood subsides, the streams braid through the sediments deposited by the flood. The extreme case of this process is exemplified by Cooper Creek which becomes a virtually continuous sheet of water tens of kilometres wide during such floods as those of early 1974, but which changes to a braided channel at low flows and a dry stream bed for most of the time (Plate 6.6).

As in other areas, detailed landform characteristics are often closely associated to the underlying structure and lithology. Bedrock outcrops in the alluvial plains have affected river courses in many ways. The deviation of the Murray River around the Cadell fault block is a well-known example, but in the Dirranbandi-Hebel area of southern Queensland, bedrock rises restricted drainage and formed shallow lakes in the late Cainozoic. The largest of these lakes, the 15 km² Lake Bokhara, is still marshy in wet seasons (Galloway, 1974).

The detailed topography of these depositional surfaces has the relicts of past fluvial and aeolian deposition as well as fluvial depositional forms associated with the present river systems. In the great inland deltas of the Barwon-Maranoa system, old and modern river channels, levees and backswamps may be recognized. Abandoned meanders and channels may have been modified by wind action or by recent water erosion through surface wash and rill erosion. The channels show an adjustment between erosion and siltation and many end in complex terminal areas with alluvial ridges or shallow ephemeral swamps. Recolonization of these flood basins by grasses and other ground flora facilitates the accumulation and retention of detrital material and the infilling of the terminal depression. The mass of floating vegetation in the Gwydir River downstream of Moree, termed 'The Raft', is another type of accumulation which modifies fluvial processes.

The Loddon River in Victoria illustrates the interplay of inherited features and present-day processes. At present the Loddon and its major distributary, Serpentine Creek, flow in incised channels at the side of the Quaternary fan. Downstream of the fan, both

streams spread into a complex pattern of anastomosing distributaries flowing over a clay surface. In many cases the distributaries spread out into a terminal or semi-terminal web-like system of fine distributaries, termed *playettes* by Macumber (1969). These fine distributary systems cause sheet flooding on the plains, reducing the flood flows carried northward along the main stem of the Loddon which reaches the Kerang as a smaller, meandering channel.

The development of playettes is a response to changes in gradient and sediment type. Minor distributaries, unable to incise channels into the plain, dissipate their energy by sheet flooding in which scouring of a multitude of minor courses replaces the more usual processes of channel widening or deepening. As the scour channels continue to subdivide until all energy is dissipated, on one minor distributary becomes dominant (Macumber, 1969).

The drainage of the areas between major streams is largely uncoordinated, sometimes with streams developing on the steeper slopes but losing any defined channel where their water spreads out over the clay plain. Soil water movement is a major factor in these areas of low relief, many areas developing deep cracking clay soils. Locally derived debris may interfinger with flood deposits in these back swamp areas.

The depositional systems of the westward-flowing streams are thus a fluvial landscape with much inheritance from wetter and drier periods in the past. The topography is complex in detail, revealing the impact of hydrologic events and sediment loads on extensive alluvial plains. The significance of a one-metre change in elevation is great, sometimes being the difference between inundation by flood and freedom from water.

DENUDATION SYSTEMS OF THE HUMID SOUTHWEST

Although a steep escarpment facing the coast and an area of high rainfall supporting a dense, wet sclerophyll jarrah forest vegetation give the Southwest of Western Australia considerable physiographic and hydrologic similarity to the east coast, Mulcahy (1967) claims that the landscape of the southwest is perhaps unique. Relative relief is much less than in the east and the transition from well-vegetated, permanent coastal streams to the ephemeral, depositional drainage systems of the interior takes only 200 km. Furthermore, long periods of relatively stable, humid and presumably warm climatic conditions have led to an abundance of iron- and aluminium-rich duricrusts on old land surfaces in the southwest. Today hydrologic regimes are dominated by winter rains associated with the seasonal northward shift of the circumpolar westerlies. Big seasonal contrasts in soil moisture dominate the processes on slopes. Soils in poorly drained sites on old plateau surfaces are waterlogged in winter but dry out to a depth of several metres in summer (Mulcahy, 1967). Although often lacking defined stream channels, the floors of many hollows carry concentrated surface runoff every winter. However, rainfall varies sufficiently from winter to winter for slumping and earthflows to be triggered by abnormally high rainfall over a period of three weeks to a month with particularly frequent heavy showers (Pilgrim and Conacher, 1974). Mass movement however is not so frequent as in the steeper and geologically more diverse terrain of the Eastern Uplands. In the southwest surface and subsurface runoff dominates the present-day denudation system.

The Darling Range possibly represents fragments of the Great Plateau of Western Australia which have been disturbed tectonically and have undergone differences in erosional history (Mulcahy, Churchward and Dimmock, 1972). The range thus carries not only relict duricrusts, but remnants of lunettes, swamps and slightly saline lakes analogous to those found in the now drier country to the east. Under the present-day hydrologic regime, water flowing over these residuals removes some of the soluble minerals and, particularly in the dry summer, carries high concentrations of chemical elements. Changes in the physical chemical environment often lead to secondary redeposition of iron and silica, particularly in stream channels where subsurface water has emerged a short distance upstream and chemical equilibria adjust to surface and open air conditions. There may be several layers of iron-rich duricrusts partly the product of several phases of dissection of the original ferruginous crust and secondary redeposition.

More far-reaching in its effects is the translocation of salt. Many soils in the southwest have marked texture-contrasts, with relatively impermeable B_2 horizons creating considerable lateral throughflow on slopes. Salt in the soil is carried by the throughflow to the lower parts of the landscapes where it accumulates seasonally on or below valley floors or in swamps or lakes. During the dry summer, salt concentrations rise as water is lost by evaporation and transportation from swamp and lacustrine plants. In winter, rapid surface runoff and throughflow tend to flush the systems clear of salt, the fresher water carrying the salt to the major rivers such as the Avon and thence out to sea. Under natural conditions, where forest vegetation consumes much of the available water, salt does not accumulate in sufficient proportions to alter vegetation and thus surface erosion. Removal of the forest however may lead to greater runoff and thus to salt accumulation.

The details of the landforms of the southwest are closely related to the degree of dissection and character of the old land surface. Steepness of slope and topographic condition affect geomorphic processes. Thus in the Avon drainage system, valley floor laterites may still be forming through secondary redeposition while on the old plateau, the laterites are reweathering to give well-drained yellow sandy soils (Mulcahy, 1967). Duricrusts form prominent scarps, or breakaways, but sandy materials from above the scarp occasionally spill out through gaps in the resistant layer, producing spillways (Mulcahy, 1960) through which relatively good quality water flows in winter to swamps or soaks downslope.

In much of the Avon valley, from Beverley north to York, Northam and Toodyay, duricrust mantles are absent and rocky granite hills reminiscent of the Eastern Uplands often dominate the landscape. Near York both skyline and valleyside tors occur, with extensive colluvial sandy aprons spreading downslope from them. Runoff and erosion processes are similar to those described earlier for the granitic landforms of the Eastern tablelands. Gullying on granite-derived colluvium is limited by the vegetation and spacing of rain events. However, bare rock surfaces may allow sufficient water to concentrate at the surface for concentrated linear flow to develop into a defined drainage line. The defined flow line may be lost further downslope as the gradient lessens and runoff changes to diffuse flow over and seeping into a colluvial fan.

In the humid southwest landforms demonstrate the influence of the past more markedly than elsewhere in humid Australia. The present-day processes are changing the details of the old landscapes, but even the patterns of gullying and the solute loads of streams are dependent on the relics of past landscape evolution.

THE IMPACT OF MAN ON AUSTRALIAN FLUVIAL LANDFORMS

Humid Australia is the home of the bulk of Australia's European population and almost certainly of the bulk of the pre-European Aboriginal population. As so often remarked, the landscape of humid Australia is now quite different from that the first European settlers saw. The same mountain ranges, gorges, plains and plateaux are there, but the forests have gone and consequently the hydrologic regimes of many streams have been altered. Gully erosion has increased the length and density of drainage networks. Stream channel cross-sections have altered to cope with changes in silt loads and flood flows, many tending to become wider, shallower and straighter with gravel or sand bars in their beds.

In rural areas, the most striking changes to denudation systems are associated with accelerated rates of erosion. Sheet wash from gentle slopes in the depositional systems of the inland rivers and gully erosion in the highlands have required widespread attention by state soil conservation agencies. The less obvious changes in geochemical processes have been equally important in terms of landform evolution and land use. From the Southern Tablelands of New South Wales (Van Dijk, 1969) to the wheatbelt of Western Australia (Conacher, 1974), salinity has become a land use problem. Relict salt in the texture-contrast soils of upland and tableland areas has been washed out by storm runoff from areas cleared of vegetation. In the Murray-Darling drainage system, streams were less saline before the country was settled by Europeans, but clearing, the trampling of ground by stock and the destruction of certain natural grasses have changed both the water and geochemical balances (Marker, 1959). In the basaltic plains, tree clearing has allowed salt to be brought to the surface by capillary action and thence to be washed off during rain. In the Avon drainage basin in Western Australia, salt is carried downslope by throughflow, coming to the surface on the valley floor where it may kill vegetation and create large areas of bare soil. Stream and rill erosion on the denuded flats soon turn a large part of the valley floor into a saline swamp. Elsewhere in the southwest of Western Australia, soil salinity is believed to be carried by a rise in the level of a saline water-table (Bettenay, Blackmore and Hingston, 1964).

In and around urban areas landforms are modified by construction, quarrying, gravel extraction, waste disposal and land filling. Many floodplains have been constricted by urban growth, with consequent flood hazards and levee bank construction. Urbanization has also led to profound modification of river regimes, not only by the building of dams for water supplies and power generation, but by stormwater drainage systems and the changes in landcover. Runoff from an urban area tends to be much more rapid and to carry more sediment than that from an adjacent rural area or the same area before urbanization. Flood peaks in urban areas are thus higher and come more quickly than in rural areas. River channels, unable to cope with these peak flows, erode banks and scour floodplains. Urban streams are thus out of phase with their altered catchments and tend to adjust their channels by erosion and deposition. River training and embankment works may counteract these natural tendencies, but may also induce problems further downstream.

In many parts of humid Australia, man has become the dominant factor in the denudation system, but extreme natural events such as the Australia Day floods of 1974 in southeastern Queensland, have much more widespread effects and their geomorphic activity is scarcely affected by man. Perhaps the proper way to envisage human activity is as a further modifier of the inherited Pleistocene and Tertiary landscapes which dominate so much of Australia.

REFERENCES

Andrews, E. C. (1903), 'An outline of the Tertiary history of New England', *Rec. Geol. Surv. N.S.W.*, 7, 140–216.

Arnett, R. R. and Conacher, A. J. (1973), 'Drainage basin expansion and the nine unit landsurface model', *Aust. Geogr.*, 12, 237–49.

Bettenay, E., Blackmore, A. V. and Hingston, F. J. (1964), 'Aspects of the hydrologic cycle and related salinity in the Belka valley, Western Australia', *Aust. J. Soil Res.* 2, 187–210.

Bruce-Smith, J. R. (1972), 'Soil formation, properties and distribution' in A. Lazenby and F. G. Swain (eds), *Intensive Pasture Production*, Angus and Robertson, Sydney, pp. 27–42.

Butler, B. E. (1967), 'Soil periodicity in relation to landform development in southeastern Australia' in J. N. Jennings and J. A. Mabbutt, (eds), *Landform Studies from Australia and New Guinea*, Australian National University Press, Canberra, pp. 231–55.

Carson, M. A. and Kirkby M. J. (1972), *Hillslope Form and Process*, Cambridge University Press.

Conacher, A. J. (1974), 'Salt scald: a W.A. case study in rehabilitation', *Aust. Sci. and Technol.* 11, 14–16.

Costin, A. B. (1954), *A study of the ecosystems of the Monaro region of New South Wales with special reference to soil erosion*, New South Wales Government Printer, Sydney.

Dalrymple, J. R., Blong R. J. and Conacher, A. J. (1968), 'A hypothetical nine unit landsurface model', *Z. f. Geomorph.*, 12, 60–76.

Davies, J. L. (1967), 'Tasmanian landforms and Quaternary climates' in J. N. Jennings and J. A. Mabbutt, (eds), *Landform Studies from Australia and New Guinea*, Australian National University Press, Canberra, pp. 1–25.

Douglas, I. (1968), 'The effects of precipitation chemistry and catchment area lithology on the quality of river water in selected catchments in eastern Australia', *Earth Sci. J.*, 2, 126–44.

——(1969), 'The efficiency of humid tropical denudation system', *Trans. Inst. Brit. Geogr.*, 46, 1–16.

——(1973), 'Rates of denudation in selected small catchments in eastern Australia', *University of Hull Occasional Papers in Geography*, 21.

Douglas, I. and Hobbs, J. E. (1974), 'Deluge in Australia', *Geogr. Mag.*, 46, 465–71.

Ellison, L. and Coaldrake, J. E. (1954), 'Soil mantle movement in relation to forest clearing in southeastern Queensland', *Ecology*, 35, 380–8.

Evernden, J. F. and Richards, J. R. (1962), 'Potassium-argon ages in eastern Australia', *J. Geol. Soc. Aust.*, 9, 1–49.

Fitzpatrick, E. A. (1968), *Climate of the Dawson-Fitzroy Area*, CSIRO Aust. Land Res. Ser. No. 21, 89–104.

Galloway, R. W. (1963), *Geomorphology of the Hunter Valley*, CSIRO Aust. Land Res. Ser. No. 8, 90–102.

——(1965), 'Late Quaternary climates in Australia', *J. Geol.*, 73, 603–18.

——(1969), *Geomorphology of the Queanbeyan-Shoalhaven Area*, CSIRO Aust. Land Res. Ser. No. 24, 76–91.

——(1974), *Geomorphology of the Balonne-Maranoa Area*,

CSIRO Aust. Land Res. Ser. No. 34, 134–47.

Goede, A. (1965), 'Geomorphology of the Buckland Basin, Tasmania', *Pap. Proc. R. Soc. Tasmania*, 99, 133–54.

——(1972), 'Discontinuous gullying of the Tea Tree Rivulet, Buckland, eastern Tasmania', *Pap. Proc. R. Soc. Tasmania*, 106, 5–16.

——(1973), 'Flood plain stratigraphy of the Tea Tree Rivulet, Buckland, eastern Tasmania', *Aust. Geogr. Stud.*, 11, 28–39.

Harrington, H. J. (1974), 'The Tasman Geosyncline in Australia' in *The Tasman Geosyncline—a symposium in honour of Professor Dorothy Hill*, Geological Soc. of Aust., Queensland Divn, Brisbane, pp. 384–93.

Hounam, C. E. (1957), 'Maximum possible rainfall over the Cotter River catchment', *Bur. Met. Melb. Met. Stud.*, 10.

Jennings, J. N. and Bird, E. C. F. (1967), 'Regional geomorphological characteristics of some Australian estuaries' in G. Lauff (ed.), *Estuaries*, Amer. Ass. Adv. Sci., pp. 121–8.

Johnson, A. R. M. (1974), 'Cavernous weathering at Berowra, N.S.W.', *Aust. Geogr.*, 12, 531–5.

Leigh, C. H. (1968), 'The form and evolution of Bald Rock, New South Wales', *Aust. Geogr.*, 10, 333–45.

——(1970), 'Tors of subsurface origin', *Aust. Geogr.*, 11, 288–90.

Louis, H. (1968), *Allgemeine Geomorphologie*, 3 Auflage, Walter de Gruyter, Berlin.

Macumber, P. G. (1969), 'Interrelationship between physiography, hydrology, sedimentation and salineization of the Loddon River Plains, Australia', *J. Hydrol.*, 7, 39–57.

Marker, M. (1959), 'Soil erosion in relation to the development of landforms in the Dundas area of western Victoria, Australia', *Proc. R. Soc. Vic.* 71, 125–36.

Mulcahy, M. J. (1960), 'Laterites and lateritic soils in southwestern Australia', *J. Soil Sci.*, 11, 206–26.

——(1967), 'Landscapes, laterites and soils in south western Australia' in J. N. Jennings and J. A. Mabbutt (eds), *Landform Studies from Australia and New Guinea*, Australian National University Press, Canberra, pp. 211–30.

Mulcahy, M. J., Churchward, H. M. and Dimmock, G. M. (1972), 'Landform and soils on an uplifted peneplain

in the Darling Range, Western Australia', *Aust. J. Soil Res.*, 10, 1–14.

Ollier, C. D. (1967), 'Landforms of the Newer Volcanic Province of Victoria' in J. N. Jennings and J. A. Mabbutt (eds), *Landform Studies from Australia and New Guinea*, Australian National University Press, Canberra, pp. 315–39.

——(1969), *Volcanoes*, Australian National University Press, Canberra.

Pigram, J. J. J. (1974), 'The Namoi Valley, New South Wales' in A. D. Tweedie, (ed.), *Man and the Valley*, Nelson, Sydney, pp. 108–50.

Pilgrim, A. T. and Conacher, A. J. (1974), 'Causes of earth flows on the Southern Chittering Valley, Western Australia', *Aust. Geogr. Stud.*, 12, 38–56.

Thomas, M. F. (1974), *Tropical Geomorphology*, Macmillan, London.

Tweedie, A. D. (1963), *Climate of the Hunter Valley*, CSIRO Aust. Land Res. Ser. No. 8, 62–80.

Twidale, C. R. (1956a), 'A physiographic reconnaissance of some volcanic provinces in north Queensland, Australia', *Bulletin volcanologique*, (2) 18, 3–23.

——(1956b), 'Der "Bienenkorb": eine neue morphologische Form aus North Queensland, North Australia', *Erdkunde*, 10, 239–40.

——(1966), *Geomorphology of the Leichardt-Gilbert Area of Northwest Queensland*, CSIRO Aust. Land Res. Ser. No. 16.

Van Dijk, D. C. (1969), 'Relict salt, a major cause of recent land damage in the Yass Valley, Southern Tablelands, N.S.W.', *Aust. Geogr.*, 11, 13–21.

Voisey, A. H. (1959), 'Australian geosynclines', *Aust. J. Sci.*, 22, 188–98.

Walker, P. H. (1962a), 'Soil layers on hillslopes at Nowra, N.S.W.', *J. Soil Sci.*, 13, 167–77.

Walker, P. H. (1962b), 'Terrace chronology and soil formation on the South Coast, N. S. W.', *J. Soil. Sci.*, 13, 178–86.

——(1970), 'Depositional and soil history along the lower Macleay River, New South Wales', *J. Geol. Soc. Aust.*, 16, 683–96.

Webb, L. J. (1958), 'Cyclones as an ecological factor in tropical lowland rain forest, north Queensland', *Aust. J. Bot.*, 6, 220–8.

6 DESERT LANDS

J. A. MABBUTT

In this treatment of the physical geography of the Australian deserts, *lands* is used to mean areas of distinctive natural character as determined by a complex of surface characteristics including landforms and geology, soils and the natural vegetation. Because of low rainfall, the main land use is likely to remain extensive pastoralism based on the grazing of the natural vegetation by domestic animals; consequently desert land types are distinctive in the opportunities they offer to development. This has been implicit in evaluations of Australian desert regions in terms of *pasture lands* (Perry, 1960).

Desert lands exhibit groupings of smaller landscape components. The definition of the *land system* of the CSIRO regional surveys, 'an area or group of areas, throughout which there is a recurring pattern of topography, soils and vegetation' (Christian and Stewart, 1953), also serves here, although the scale is broader. The descriptions that follow aim to show how this characteristic association of natural landscapes arises from a common geologic basis and from a shared climatic and geomorphologic history; however the association is also dynamic and functional, as is implicit in the term land system. A desert land type may accordingly be predicted to show an inherent and characteristic susceptibility to environmental stress and liability to degradation under use.

A land-system or landscape approach is suited to desert regions because component habitats tend to be clearly differentiated under aridity. Lithological contrasts are delicately reflected in differences of slope and soil which are critical to plants under moisture stress. Desert hydrologic and geochemical systems, discontinuous in time and space, tolerate the separateness of land components. An airphoto reveals these breaks with clarity because of sparse vegetation and thin debris mantles. Furthermore, the movement of water is critical in a general situation of moisture deficit, and the vital partition between areas of run-on and runoff points up the interdependence of adjacent components of the landscape.

Some general physical characteristics of the Australian arid zone will first be discussed, in the search for the broad controls that have determined the emergence of distinctive desert lands.

GENERAL FEATURES OF THE ARID ZONE

Climate

In its sense of desolate or uninhabited, *desert* expresses a climatic limitation on life, mainly through aridity. Accordingly, one first seeks an explanation of the character and regional differences of arid Australia through its climates.

Australia is often described as the driest of the continents, outside of the Polar Regions, either because of the relative extent of its arid zone (Fig. 6.1), which covers between 65 and 75 per cent of Australia, or the low mean continental precipitation and runoff, as shown in Table 6.1. Despite their great extent however, the Australian deserts are only moderately arid. No Australian climate station records a mean annual rainfall below 100 mm, a value taken as marking the northern limit of the Sahara proper! The moderate desert regime reflects the island setting of the Australian continent, the absence of relief barriers against the penetration of moist air, particularly from tropical sources, and the lack of a definite cool oceanic current inshore along the west coast (Gentilli, 1971).

This moderate aridity shows in many ways. For instance the vegetation forms a general mantle, unlike extreme deserts where it is confined to watercourses. On sloping ground there is everywhere evidence of the action of running water, in freshly scoured ephemeral stream channels or rilled surfaces subject to sheetflow, whilst the aeolian sand surfaces are now largely stabilized under a plant cover.

In consequence of the mitigated continentality, seasonal rainfall contrasts in arid Australia are less absolute than in most deserts. The southern part is commonly termed a winter rainfall area, but except in the west the summer rains are also significant and amount to between 30 and 50 per cent of the total. They are less reliable than the winter rains here and less effective in plant growth because they come with high temperatures and moisture loss, often in heavy falls; nevertheless they support important components of the natural pastures. Similarly, a winter rainfall increment of about 50 mm persists through the zone into the tropics, supplementing the summer rainfall of the northern deserts. Consequently, in the absence of inhibiting

Table 6.1 Precipitation, Evaporation and Runoff by Continents

Continent	Precipitation (cm yr^{-1})	Evaporation (cm yr^{-1})	P–E (cm yr^{-1})	Runoff (cm yr^{-1})
Europe	64	39	25	29
Asia	60	31	29	29
North America	66	32	34	26
South America	163	70	93	44
Africa	69	43	26	16
Australia	**47**	**42**	**5**	**5**
All land areas	73	42	31	25

Source: Budyko, 1974.

winter cold, there can be some expectation of pasture growth at all seasons throughout the Australian deserts, and prospects for year-round stocking.

Climatic gradients across the Australian arid zone are visible in its landscapes; for example the contrast between the fossil vegetated sand dunes of the desert borders and the more mobile forms in the drier heart. Changes in the seasonal incidence of rainfall explain a greater prominence of trees and perennial grasses in the north and an increasing importance of low shrubs southwards as summer rains give place to those of winter. Such changes tend to be gradual however, and to be encompassed within a low and vastly uniform relief. Noticeable changes in desert landscapes occur with contrasts in slope and surface materials, in consequent patterns of runoff and infiltration, and hence in vegetation response. Marked contrasts of this type are induced by geologic and associated geomorphic differences. Within the broader patterns of climatic stress therefore, a definition of desert lands must be sought in physiographic terms.

Physiography

The Australian deserts may be classed among the shield and platform deserts of the world. They owe their broad physiographic features to relative crustal stability over a long geologic history, expressed in ancient land surfaces and mainly horizontal cover rocks. Chief among these is a predominance of plains or low plateaux. Uplands are isolated within the broad plains (Plate 4.1) and generally of modest elevation; only small areas exceed 1,000 m and the highest point in arid Australia, Mt Zeil in the western Macdonnells, is a mere 1,520 m above sea level. Orographic rainfall is insignificant therefore, snow-

fields are absent, and all local river systems are ephemeral in regime. Streamfloods are mainly defeated by low gradients in the long plains sectors and most of the desert drainage patterns are disorganized to some degree. This has led in turn to widespread alluviation along lower stream courses and at terminal floodouts. Part of these depositional surfaces has later become subject to wind-working and extensive fields of dunes now occupy much of the lower plains.

These settings of slow landscape change are characterized by the survival of forms inherited from the past. Besides features left by Pleistocene climatic fluctuations, such as dunes and piedmont gravel spreads, arid Australia contains surfaces and soils developed in moister Tertiary periods. For instance granitic and related alluvial plains over much of central and northern arid Australia have acid soils leached to considerable depths and hence deficient in plant nutrients such as phosphorus. These deficiencies, expressed in features of desert vegetation, also impose limits on land use.

The major physiographic contrasts within the Australian deserts are those between areas of exposed granitic basement and those with cover rocks. The former will be treated collectively as *shield desert*, but the latter are much more varied. Uplifted old resistant rocks in sedimentary basins within the platform determine the main areas of *upland and piedmont desert*, whereas the lower-lying basins in which drainage has been obliterated and its deposits reworked by wind form the main areas of *sand desert*. In the interior lowlands to the east, the periphery of relatively weak rock forms *stony desert*, traversed by alluvial plains of still-integrated river systems which are mapped as *riverine desert*. Finally, the terminals of the interior

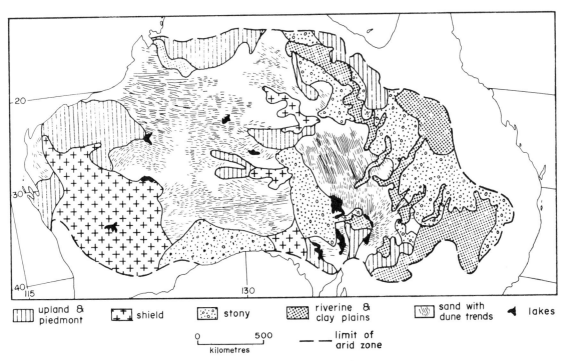

upland & piedmont shield stony riverine & clay plains sand with dune trends lakes

0   500
kilometres

limit of arid zone

Fig. 6.1 Physiographic desert types in Australia, showing trends of sand dunes.

drainage systems are everywhere distinguished as *desert lakes*. The distribution of these physiographic desert types is shown in Fig. 6.1 and their relative extent in Table 6.2.

Vegetation

The vegetation of the Australian deserts resembles that of other desert regions in its composition and structure. Apart from larger trees along watercourses,

Table 6.2 Extent of Physiographic Desert Types in Australia

Type	Area ('000 km²)	Percentage of arid zone
Upland and piedmont	818	16
Shield	697	14
Stony	894	18
Riverine and clay plains	650	13
Sand	1,916	38
Lakes	50	1
Total	5,025	100

forms tend to be low and the cover inadequate to protect the ground surface.

The plants shows features of adjustment to periodic moisture deficit. They include for instance *ephemeral or annual drought-evaders* which survive as seeds through dry periods. These comprise short grasses which respond to summer rains, and herbs, particularly composites. The young green growth is both palatable and nutritious and is grazed preferentially by stock. The *perennial drought-evaders* include particularly the tussock grasses such as the Mitchell grasses (*Astrebla* spp.) which die back in dry conditions and resume growth from tillers after rain. They are attractive as pasture when young and persist for some time into drought, but the dry mature plant has low nutritive value. The *perennial drought-resisters*, which suspend growth during drought and resist or tolerate a degree of water loss, include most desert trees and shrubs as well as the hummock grasses known collectively as spinifex (*Triodia* and *Plectrachne* spp.). Their adjustment commonly involves the development of a ligneous or sclerophyllous character which renders them unpalatable. Nevertheless the saltbushes and the evergreen acacias in this group yield valuable browse or topfeed through dry periods, and the perennials also provide important protection against erosion as well as shelter for smaller plants.

A visitor familiar with other deserts would note

Plate 6.1 Upland and piedmont desert in the Macdonnell Ranges, central Australia, showing characteristic structural control of landforms. In the foreground, tall shrubs are established on rock outcrop. *Photo*: CSIRO Division of Land Use Research.

distinctive features of the Australian vegetation attributable to the isolation of this continent during a long history of aridity, and to the infertile soils. Prominent among the trees and shrubs are the acacias, remarkable for the large number of needle-leaved species and a lack of thorns and spines so characteristic of the African deserts. The extensive sclerophyllous spinifex grasses are also unusual, as shrub-sized spiny evergreen hummocks or rings. Large succulents such as cacti are absent. More important, particularly in comparison with the Old World deserts, are differences arising from the absence of domestic grazing animals from the Australian arid zone until the last 100 years. There has been considerable selective degradation since that time but the natural vegetation survives extensively, notably the trees and shrubs, and still serves as an integrative expression of environmental controls.

The distribution of desert plants in Australia reflects climatic factors such as aridity and season of effective rainfall, but the distribution of the main structural types of vegetation, which determine the stability and productivity of desert lands, is closely linked with soil character and particularly with texture and other profile characteristics that determine the availability of moisture. *Tall acacia shrublands*, the most extensive

desert vegetation type, occur mainly on medium-textured red earth soils having a gradual increase in clay content with depth, and for this reason are characteristic of shield desert. Almost as extensive, the drought-tolerant *sclerophyllous hummock grasslands* dominated by spinifex correspond with the excessively drained soils of sand desert. *Xerophytic tussock grasslands* characterized by perennial grasses are associated with clay plains in stony and riverine desert, where they can respond to short periods of excess surface moisture during summer, followed by stress in these heavy soils. *Shrub steppe* in the southern areas of stony desert is a response to the salt-affected clay-loams of the area, with their sharp textural contrast between a light topsoil and a heavier subsoil, and to the intermingled lighter calcareous soils. Thus through the soil factor, desert lands defined on a physiographic basis are also meaningful for vegetation patterns within the arid zone.

UPLAND AND PIEDMONT DESERT
Only the larger uplands can be shown in Fig. 6.1, but their features are shared by many smaller relief islands. The steep rocky slopes are the sources of desert river systems, whilst the footslopes receive the streamfloods and their sediments. Accordingly, upland

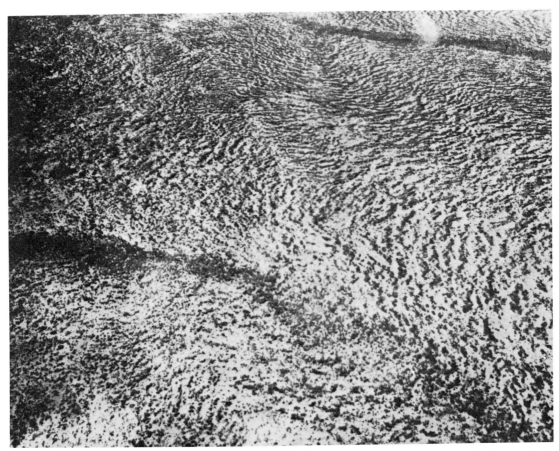

Plate 6.2 Wash plains on the lower slopes of shield desert in central Australia, with parallel groves of mulga woodland. *Photo*: CSIRO Division of Land Use Research.

and piedmont form a single desert land type.

Fig. 6.1 shows that the main upland deserts are in the arid portion of the Western Plateau, formed by the rigid Precambrian basement and its platform cover rocks. A variety of forms reflects structural differences. Forbidding plateaux, as the Kimberley Plateaux and the Hamersley Ranges, are found where older basin rocks have been uplifted with little deformation, and ridge-and-vale topography results where they have been folded, as in the Macdonnell and Flinders Ranges (Plate 6.1). Quartzites and sandstones are the main relief builders but limestones are prominent locally under the arid regime, as in the eastern Macdonnells. A more complex upland type occurs where basement rocks have been folded and uplifted, with a variety of upland forms expressive of the range of rock types, and usually a close grain of relief due to a prominence of gneisses, schists and slates. These forms are typified in the Isa Ridges.

Most desert hillslopes show an alternation of rock outcrop and coarse debris, expressive of the nature of desert weathering and its balance with slope erosion. The rock is commonly stained and crusted by chemical alteration, but only superficially because of the restricted penetration of moisture. Strong heating of bare surfaces and the disruptive expansion of surface layers due to crusting or salt weathering lead to spalling or to granular disintegration of the rock before decomposition is advanced, as shown by the relatively coarse, part-weathered debris. Pitted overhanging rock faces attest to the preferential weathering of moister hollows shaded from evaporation. Any plane of weakness in the rock tends to be exploited by these various forms of physico-chemical attack and any irregularity tends to be enlarged; the shaded cleft which traps water and rock waste is colonized by vegetation, and biological processes then reinforce the selective weathering.

In contrast to the slowness of rock breakdown, fine debris is moved fairly readily from sparsely-vegetated desert hillslopes, so that colluvial mantles tend to be thin and soils minimal. Dry, coarse and discontinuous slope layers offer little scope to overall smoothing processes such as creep, and harder rock bands are left in clear relief as ledges and faces on the slope.

Vegetation is sparse on the slopes, for they shed water, increasing the effective aridity. Nevertheless, trees and large shrubs may be prominent on the rockier sectors where runoff is trapped and where deep root systems can explore the fissures. Common upland trees include mulga (*Acacia aneura*), ghost gum (*Eucalyptus papuana*) and the cypress pine (*Callitris*) which is prominent in parts of the Macdonnell Ranges near Alice Springs and on sandstone ridges at Mootwingee, New South Wales. However a variety of species is characteristic because of the range of microhabitats and geochemical settings offered by the rocky slope. In contrast, the vegetation on debris-covered slopes tends to be sparser and more stunted and xerophytic, particularly on fine-textured rocks, and spinifex is very characteristic of such slopes in the Central Australian Ranges.

The desert piedmont characteristically joins the hill base abruptly. This may express a boundary between harder slope-building strata and softer rocks beneath the plain, but the sharp piedmont junction is favoured by differences in erosion and debris transport. The steep gravity-controlled hillslope of coarse debris contrasts with the low-angle footslope across which wash processes are facilitated by lack of vegetation. In a wide literature, various combinations of processes have been invoked to explain the maintenance of the piedmont junction, including mass movement, sheet-wash and stream swinging, and subaerial and sub-surface weathering, and these doubtless vary in importance between localities; however the calibre and abundance of surface debris play a vital part in maintaining the contrast in slope angles and the planar form of desert footslopes expressed in the term *pediment*. There is a common relationship between slope angle and the calibre of the larger slope debris, which in turn determines the roughness of the surface and its runoff response; and it is where the hillslope debris contrasts most strongly with that of the footslope that the piedmont junction is most angular. On the footslope itself, an abundance of finer transportable sediment tends to maintain runoff in a loaded state, prevent the selective incision of stream channels and so maintain a planate form.

Where little coarse debris is fed to the footslope an erosional surface or subaerial pediment may exist, but where hard rock yielding larger fragments is prominent in the hillslope there is commonly a spread of piedmont gravel, which may form a mantled pediment as below the Flinders Ranges (Twidale, 1967)

or a thicker terrace capping as in the more constricted vales of the western Macdonnells (Mabbutt, 1966). Gravel fans comparable with those of mountain-and-basin deserts in the western United States are almost lacking; they are restricted to a few active tectonic settings such as the western fault scarp of the Flinders Ranges (Williams, 1973).

The desert piedmont is sensitive to changes in the balance between runoff and sediment yield, since this in turn controls that between deposition and removal at the hill foot, or between planar and linear erosion. Changes in this balance, which result in dissected fans and terraces, are commonly attributed to fluctuations in effective rainfall.

The piedmont receives runoff from the backing upland but is itself a discharge slope, for gradients may approach 15 per cent near the head despite a deceptive smoothness of contour. The denser vegetation of trees and shrubs tends therefore to be concentrated near the hill foot or along the shallow sandy washes which traverse the piedmont, and intervening surfaces are commonly droughty, with coarse-textured, often shallow soils and a sparse xerophytic or ephemeral vegetation. This is particularly so where the piedmont has been dissected from the hillslope. For example the highest, bouldery terraces of the Macdonnells support only spinifex grassland, whereas the lower terraces, which still receive runoff from the hillslopes, have stony red earth soils and carry close mulga.

SHIELD DESERT

Granitic shield blocks within the platform give rise to interior plains, notably the extensive Yilgarn Block of the Yilgarn Plateau in the southwest of Western Australia and the Musgrave and Arunta Blocks in the Central Australian Ranges. The small relief and vast uniformity of these desert surfaces reflect the homogeneity of the granite and gneiss and attest to the tectonic stability of the blocks through a long subaerial history, as do the widespread relict land surfaces. Characteristic upland forms are granite domes and tors standing island-like in extensive erosional plains, with stable alluvial plains downslope. Descriptions of shield landscapes occur in two regional survey reports of the CSIRO Division of Land Use Research, namely Alice Springs (Perry *et al.*, 1962) and Wiluna-Meekatharra (Mabbutt *et al.*, 1963).

Dissected Lateritic Surfaces

Contrasts between the western and central Australian shield deserts (Fig. 6.2a, b) result from differences in the degree of past planation and in the related extent of deep weathering, a reflection of position in the evolving Australian continent during Mesozoic and early Tertiary time.

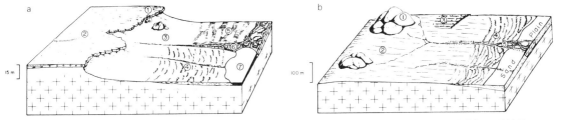

Fig. 6.2 Shield desert landscapes. (a) *Western Australia*: 1. Stripped laterite behind breakaway; 2. Sandplain on Old Plateau; 3. Pediment and tors on New Plateau; 4. Alluvial wash plain with mulga groves; 5. Wanderrie country; 6. Calcreted valley fill; 7. 'River lake'. (b) *Central Australia*: 1. Granite hills; 2. Pediment; 3. Laterite remnant; 4. Wash plain with mulga groves; 5. Calcreted valley fill.

The area of the Yilgarn Plateau of Western Australia was reduced to an undulating plain which was extensively lateritized. A zone of disaggregated rock between 10 and 30 m thick followed the contours of the plain, thinner over the rises and thicker in the valleys, from which the ironstone crust may have been lacking. No granite hills rose above this surface, which was broken only by low ridges formed by belts of schist. Landforms and soils in this area have evolved by the partial stripping of the saprolite and its ferruginous crust under conditions of low relative relief.

The lateritized surface has survived widely and has been identified by Jutson (1934) as the *Old Plateau*, in contradistinction to the little-weathered *New Plateau* below it. The ferruginous and hardened mottled zones of the weathered profile cap long low breakaways which separate the two levels. Various modes of etchplanation have been recognized in the formation of the New Plateau (Finkl and Churchward, 1973); on higher parts the profile has been stripped to the weathering front, exposing fresh granite, whereas along valleys only the upper horizons have been removed, leaving a weathered layer. The few granite hills that dot the New Plateau are small and have been excavated as cores of unweathered rock within the saprolite. The Old Plateau survives most extensively inland, notably in the Salinaland Plateau region of large river lakes (Jutson, 1934); in the west, for example on the Murchison Plateau, the laterite has been largely removed by more vigorous rivers.

Above the lateritic breakaways of the Salinaland Plateau, acid lateritic soils provide a relict environment, the refuge of a flora rich in the *Myrtaceae* and today characteristic of more humid environments to the southwest. But within a few hundred metres the ironstone and pisolitic gravels give place to the sandplain that blankets most of the Old Plateau. The sandplains could not be separated as sand desert at the scale of Fig. 6.1 and moreover form an integral part of the landscapes of the Yilgarn Plateau. The sand cover is generally thin over the divides, where it may result from the wind-working of residual lateritic sands, but thickens in the valleys where there are restricted short linear dunes. The sandplains of the Yilgarn Plateau differ from those of central Australia, which will be described under Sand Desert, perhaps due to the shallowness of the sands and the acid clay-rich subsoils as well as to climate; feathertop spinifex (*Plectrachne*) prevails over *Triodia*, shrubs and trees are widespread and locally dense, and there are perennial grasses such as *Danthonia*.

In central Australia on the other hand, at the continental watershed, granitic hills and uplands remained prominent above surrounding plains in which weathering appears to have been more selective, commonly being confined to valleys, although lateritic crusts encroached to the hill foot locally. Etchplanation has been less general here, and the later evolution of the landscape has been influenced by greater local relief and a more competent through-going drainage, giving a large-scale downslope sequence from erosional to depositional land surfaces. Remnants of laterite cap low rises on the piedmont plains or form platforms in etched valleys, for example in the Burt Plain and Kulgera Hills, but nowhere on the scale of Western Australia.

The change from moister climates to the arid regimes of the later Tertiary has led to disorganization of the long plains sectors of the drainage systems of the shield deserts. This also has taken different forms in the two settings. The main rivers of the Yilgarn Plateau occupied shallow valleys between featureless divides with sandy lateritic soils, and under the stress of drier climates they broke down along their length into aligned 'river lakes'. Cut off by alluvium or wind-blown sand, these now serve as separate terminals, though connections may be re-established by exceptional floods. In central Australia, river systems radiating from central watersheds first terminated in playas such as Lake Amadeus, but there has since been continued retraction of the effective channels, which now die out at intermediate points, leaving the playas isolated in dunefields.

Hills and Pediments

Larger granite hills and fringing pediments form

typical elements of shield desert in central Australia. The pediments maintain moderate slopes to the head and meet the steep hill faces in abrupt angles in a way characteristic of granitic landscapes. The slope contrast reflects an equivalent contrast in debris cover, itself a result of granite breakdown which proceeds directly from the joint blocks and boulders of the hillslope to the quartz grit and sand which strew the pediment. The piedmont angle also expresses a difference between the physical resistance of massive granite on a water-shedding hillslope and its vulnerability to chemical weathering beneath moisture-retaining mantles on the plain. Mantling, subsurface weathering and stripping may thus contribute to levelling at the hill foot. Preparatory weathering at the hill base may be inherited, as indicated by Tertiary laterite near the foot of some hills.

Valley Calcretes and Lake Limestones
In central and in Western Australia, there was extensive fluvial and lacustrine deposition in the lowlands during the Tertiary era. The upper parts of these deposits are limestones or are strongly calcreted, suggesting that calcareous pans existed during the final phase of aggradation. In the area of the Alcoota Tablelands northeast of Alice Springs, lacustrine silts and limestones which rest on the laterite have yielded fossils of Miocene or Lower Pliocene age, giving a date for the onset of aridity in the interior of Australia as evidenced by disorganization of drainage and the accumulation of calcareous alluvium.

The calcreted valley tracts of the Yilgarn Plateau and of the Burt Plains north of Alice Springs are remarkably similar. Islands of chalcedonic calcrete originating as pan crusts now form elongated platforms a metre or two above the interlacing modern floodways. In Salinaland the calcreted tracts may be several kilometres wide; they feed into the 'river lakes' and there open into delta plains a metre or so above the deflated salt pans. The platforms provide a calcareous environment for lime-loving acacias such as witchetty bush (*A. kempeana*) in central Australia and bowgada (*A. sclerosperma*) in the west, and their continuation beneath an alluvial cover may be marked by larger phreatophytes such as the river red gum (*Eucalyptus camaldulensis*), for the tracts are important lines of groundwater movement in amounts capable of supporting irrigation. Unfortunately the groundwater becomes salty towards the terminals, where the alluvial flats may also be saline as shown by the entry of bluebush (*Kochia* spp.) and other halophytes.

Northeast of Alice Springs particularly, the lacustrine limestones are now dissected in the Alcoota Tablelands. The stony scarps and rims are commonly covered with porcupine spinifex (*T. longiceps*) and mallee eucalypts, but on flat summits the fine-textured

deposits yield red clay soils in open plains with Mitchell grass.

Wash Plains
In central Australia the lowermost pediments and the alluvial plains downslope from them, as on the Burt Plains, are among the most featureless surfaces of the shield deserts. With gradients of less than 0.5 per cent over tens of kilometres, they are traversed by ill-defined wide floodways. The stability of these surfaces is reflected in deep red earth soils which, with their acid reactions, absence or great depth of lime pan, and illite-kaolinite clay fractions suggest pedogenesis under moister conditions and perhaps also the incorporation of pre-weathered sediments from lateritic land surfaces upslope.

The tracts of concentrated sheetflooding are belts of dense tall shrubland or low woodland dominated by mulga. In the intervening areas subject to more dispersed sheetwash, the mulga is arranged in bands or groves aligned along the contour for distances of a kilometre or more but extending only some tens of metres downslope (Plate 6.2). The groves are evenly arranged in series down the slope, separated by lightly timbered intergroves of comparable dimensions. The upslope margin of the groves is sharp and straight, with taller trees, whereas the lower edge is irregular, with salients of smaller trees reaching downslope. The slopes are slightly stepped, with the groves occupying the treads and overlapping slightly on the riser below, on which the intergrove is sited.

Groved patterns in acacia woodland are well known along the southern margins of the Sahara, in Somalia and in the *brousse tigrée* of the West African Sahel. There too it occurs on plains with modest slopes and with soils of medium texture, hence suited to sheetflow. It represents an adjustment of the vegetation to this form of runoff, whereby each grove intercepts the flow from the intergrove upslope.

In comparable settings on the Yilgarn Plateau the red earths are cemented in a siliceous hardpan which may extend to within a few centimetres of the surface and which drastically reduces the water-holding capacity of the soils and restricts the establishment of trees and shrubs. The hardpan is shallowest in medium-textured soils and the harsher environment is reflected in the grove patterns (Litchfield and Mabbutt, 1962). The groves are only a few metres across and are sharply demarcated, whilst the intergroves are several times larger and are almost bare. Root penetration and enhanced infiltration in the groves have depressed the hardpan locally, forming a deep trench, whereas elsewhere the pan lies close to the surface. Deterioration of the vegetation and of surface water relationships through overstocking has heightened these contrasts and the groves have locally been reduced to a single line of mulgas. The hardpan lies deeper on sandier soils and here the groves resemble those of central Australia.

On lower slopes of similar gradient on the granitic plains of the Murchison Plateau, drainage has moulded aeolian sand accumulations to form patterns of sandy banks and alluvial flats known as *wanderrie country* (Mabbutt, 1963) (Plate 6.3). The wanderrie banks are up to a metre high and may extend for a kilometre or so along the contour and a few hundred metres downslope, and the intervening flats are of similar size. Their outlines are adjusted to the relationship between the direction of sheetflooding and former WNW sand-moving winds; where these were directly opposed or coincident the banks are arranged in transverse series, whereas longitudinal or oblique patterns have arisen where flow was across or oblique to the wind. The contours of the siliceous hardpan here reflect soil texture and infiltration, being deeper beneath the sandy banks and shallow under the red earths of the flats. The name comes from the wanderrie grasses *Danthonia bipartita* and *Eragrostis lanipes*, which provide valuable perennial pasture on the banks; the shallow soils of the flats support only annual grasses with sparser trees and shrubs.

STONY DESERT

This is used of country with a widespread mantle of boulders or smaller gibbers, particularly those from a siliceous duricrust or *silcrete*. With this go other characteristics, for example tablelands and mesas capped by the duricrust and extensive lowlands of shale and other weak rocks left by its removal. Such landscapes, as shown in Fig. 6.1, are found on Cretaceous and Tertiary rocks of the Central Lowlands Province fringing the Simpson Desert and the Eyre-Frome Plains. However, stony desert also extends westwards on similar older rocks in the south of the Northern Territory and in northwestern New South Wales. To the north, for example, the stony limestone Tobermory Plain has also been mapped as stony desert.

The nature and origins of the silcrete have been discussed elsewhere as a feature of the oldest Australian landscapes, and we are concerned here mainly with surfaces arising from its partial destruction.

Upland Forms

The distribution and heights of the uplands have largely been determined by warping of the duricrust before dissection. Commonly they are ranged around the axes of domal uplifts, and tablelands may be replaced by narrow cuestas on steeply-dipping limbs. Relief rarely attains 100 m.

The tableland and mesa summits in the southern areas of stony desert, with their armour of boulders and bossy outcrops of red-brown silcrete, closely resemble the *hamadas* of the Old World deserts, with boulders and spalls of iron-stained rock lying loose or half-buried in the soil (Plate 6.4). Even moderate-sized shrubs are lacking. Sparse low saltbush (*Atriplex vesicaria*) is general, becoming denser in depressions, whilst spiny bassias, forbs and short annual grasses may grow between the stones after rain.

Locally the boulder pavement is patterned in circular *stony gilgai* up to several metres across. These consist of a slightly higher rim, stonier than average, in which the boulders show signs of upheaval, and an inner soil-covered flat with cracks and an occasional small depression near the centre. The gilgai are attributed to differential expansion on wetting and drying of subsoils rich in swelling clays and in sodium and calcium. Deep cracking of the drying subsoil leads to its rapid and unequal wetting in the next cycle and to compressional stresses which are relieved in the upward extrusion of blocks of soil. The soil just beneath the stony rim has all the features of a stripped subsoil, with its pedal structure, prominent red clayskins and calcareous nodules; in contrast such features occur at greater depth beneath the inner zone. Fine material washed from the rim down the central cracks enriches the subsoil further in clay and helps to maintain the process.

Excavation beneath the stone pavement into the underlying weakly solonetzic desert loam will in most cases reveal a surprising depth—perhaps a metre or so—of virtually stone-free subsoil (Mabbutt, 1965). Further down, stone from the underlying silcrete again predominates. It is claimed, as demonstrated experimentally, that stones have been moved upwards from a swelling wetted subsoil by extrusive compression similar to that forming stony gilgai; the only stones remaining are tiny fragments capable of falling back down soil cracks. In this way the stone pavement may have been concentrated from below, as well as by deflation from the surface. There remains however the problem of the deep fine-textured soil above the duricrust, and it is suggested that this may have been blown to the tableland from adjoining plains as a fine loess and trapped among the pavement stones, which may in turn have been displaced upwards as the aeolian layer grew in thickness.

Variations in upland character result from regional differences in lithology, the nature of the duricrust and the weathered profile, and from climate. In the northeast for instance, as in the Charleville Tableland, the breakaways are commonly formed by a massive red indurated layer up to 15 m thick beneath a negligible thickness of silcrete. Here the breakaways retreat by cavernous undermining and subsidence along large-scale fractures parallel with the margin. On the summits the indurated layer yields red earth

Plate 6.3 Wanderrie country in the Yilgarn shield desert of Western Australia. The relatively dense vegetation of the sandy banks, with its tree and shrub layers, contrasts with the low annual vegetation on medium-textured soils of the alluvial flats. *Photo*: CSIRO Division of Land Use Research.

soils with pisolitic gravel and supports close mulga woodland. In parts of the Eromanga Lowlands of West-Central Queensland where the silcrete has formed in Tertiary sandstone, the tablelands are sandy, with spinifex and shrubs, and pass into true sandplain locally. All rocky summits, including surfaces stripped of silcrete, carry shrubs, open mulga and locally spinifex.

With an upper breakaway of duricrust, a short straight debris slope of fallen blocks and a longer concave sector in which the protective silcrete boulders diminish in size downslope, upland margins in stony desert form classic faceted hillslopes. Many features point to processes on the slope involving interaction between the boulder cover and the soft-weathered rocks which characteristically underlie the duricrust. These include rotational slumps, debris flows flanked by boulder levees, and terracettes where fine material washed down the slope has become trapped behind lines of boulders. On the lower slopes are prominent stone-fronted steps with arcuate risers up to 30 cm high embanking flatter stone-free areas with cracks and depressions similar to those of stony gilgai. These forms are attributed to the distortion of gilgai processes through the effects of slope, whereby the stone rim develops only on the lower side. They have their equivalent in forms produced by freeze-thaw processes

in cold environments, just as stony gilgai have their counterparts in stone polygons. Due to the prevalence of swelling clays, the stony deserts rival the periglacial zones as areas of patterned ground.

The hillslope and its stony mantle passes smoothly into the adjacent stony plain. Accumulations of piedmont gravel as in upland desert are lacking because of the thinness of the duricrust, and the piedmont angle of shield desert is absent because of the complete size range of the silcrete gibbers. There is a continuity between pediment and hillslope matched in the size-grading of the gibber mantle, with which declivity is strongly linked. It appears that the coarser fragments limit regrading by running water through their determination of surface roughness, whilst the abundant fine debris chokes and defeats any tendency for runoff to concentrate and incise. But the downslope decrease in size of the largest stones is not matched by better sorting of the stones as a whole, and this, together with their arrangement in patterns, suggests that the stones are not now in transport. The downslope decrease in size may result from weathering *in situ*, and the finer stones of the lower pediment may reflect the greater age of that surface.

Lowland Forms

Stony desert lowlands comprise three regional variants

Plate 6.4 Stony desert tablelands in the south of the Northern Territory with a mantle of silcrete boulders. The stony surfaces carry sparse saltbush or low chenopods. *Photo*: CSIRO Division of Land Use Research.

reflecting differences of climate and bedrock. In the southwest and west, as in the lowlands of the Barrier Ranges, are flat to undulating plains with dense stone mantles above salt-affected desert loams and weakly solonetzic soils. Winter rainfall is effective here and the characteristic vegetation is halophytic shrub steppe, with saltbush on medium-textured soils and bluebush on calcareous soils. In the north-central and north-eastern stony deserts are gently to strongly undulating lowlands with red and brown clay soils formed from fine-textured Cretaceous rocks and bearing a patchy cover of silcrete fragments. These are summer rainfall areas and characteristically are open grasslands dominated by Mitchell grasses, as in the Eromanga Lowlands.

The lowlands of the southwest exhibit patterned ground on a remarkable scale. On moderate slopes the saltbush occurs in bands measuring only a few metres downslope but extending for up to 100 m along the contour. These are separated by stone-free bands with little perennial vegetation and adjoining bare strips of dense stone immediately above the next band of saltbush (Plate 6.5). The zones mark contrasts in microtopography and soils down the slope: the dense saltbush occupies the inner part of a flattish sector containing depressions a metre and more across and up to 30 cm deep, which are colonized by perennial grasses; the sparsely vegetated band occupies the other part of this tread, and the stone pavement constitutes a steep riser. The soil beneath the pavement is highly structured and compact and resists infiltration, whereas that in the saltbush band has a loose topsoil readily penetrated by water, and the third band has an intermediate character. The three zones correspond to the inner depression, level shelf and stony rim of a *gilgai*, although on a larger scale, and the processes of formation are probably similar, with domination by the riser on the downslope side. The patterns are particularly striking near the Barrier Range, where the white quartz stone of the pavements contrasts strongly with the dull green of the saltbush. The patterns reflect hydrologic systems in which the pavement sheds water and fine sediment to the vegetated flat below. The microrelief is thus perpetuated, resisting smoothing of the slope.

The stony plains of the Eromanga Lowlands to the northeast also have contour-orientated stony gilgai. The microrelief is marked in these strongly heaving soils, with prominent stony banks on the lower side enclosing deep depressions occupied by perennial grasses. However the scale is smaller than in the first type, generally only 10 or 20 m laterally, and neither the vegetation contrasts nor the brown silcrete stone show so clearly in the landscape.

Plate 6.5 Undulating lowlands in stony desert in the south of the arid zone, with contour-oriented bands of saltbush and intervening bare stony ground.

Throughout stony desert, the lowest parts are plains with an armour of close-packed small stones or *desert pavement* similar to the *regs* of the Sahara. The stone cover locally shows contour banding as well as polygonal arrangements on a smaller scale. This indication of cracking and heaving in swelling clay soils is corroborated by the presence of stony gilgai and by ubiquitous stone-free profiles beneath the pavement. The soils are moderate-textured desert loams and are subject to shallow erosion by wind, and the plains are dotted with small claypans. The plains are mainly treeless save along the watercourses, with perennial grasses in gilgai depressions and sparse small chenopods elsewhere, with ephemerals after rain.

Nullarbor Plain Province

Stony desert as mapped in Fig. 6.1 includes the Nullarbor Plain Province, particularly the limestone surface of the Bunda Plateau which is about 200,000 km² in extent, rising inland from between 40 and 90 m in the cliffs at the head of the Bight to between 200 and 240 m where it meets the dunefields of the Great Victoria Desert. In part the seaward slope expresses the dip of the tilted Nullarbor Limestone and in part a slow subaerial planation (Lowry and Jennings, 1974). This is a karst plain in which development has been restricted by aridity and it is the most even of the desert plains of Australia. Such relief as exists is solutional. The most extensive forms are linear rises and elongate depressions known as ridges-and-corridors, with a spacing of a kilometre or more and a relief amplitude generally below 5 m, although locally attaining 10 m. They locally form lattice-works. In flatter parts of the plain the corridors are replaced by aligned shallow circular solution depressions like the *dayas* of Algeria and Morocco. These rectilinear patterns contrast with the few winding relict river courses, mainly in the inland part of the plain. Also of restricted occurrence are collapse dolines, many with steep cliffs and rocky margins, commonly associated with caves.

The Bunda Plateau is a covered karst and rock outcrops are limited. There is a general cover of residual shallow calcareous soils, commonly above a calcrete horizon, lighter-textured on the rises and grading to loams or clays in depressions, where stony gilgai are common. As the name implies, the Nullarbor

Plate 6.6 Cooper Creek in flood stage, showing anastomosing channels typical of riverine desert in the Channel Country of southwest Queensland. Lighter-toned levees with gallery woodland stand above the flood waters. *Photo*: Australian Information Service.

is mainly a treeless shrub steppe, with a perennial cover of samphire in the lowest depressions, bluebush on stony rises and saltbush elsewhere. The better-watered coastal part and the dunes and flats of the narrow coastal plains below the cliffs support a tall shrubland with mallee eucalypts and acacias.

RIVERINE DESERT AND CLAY PLAINS

Only the largest floodplains and channels are shown in Fig. 6.1, but similar features are exhibited on a smaller scale within the bounds of other desert types. The main areas of riverine desert occupy the eastern slopes of the arid zone, convergent on Lake Eyre. All traverse areas of stony desert and tend to widen downvalley, but suddenly narrow and become unmappable where the channels enter the dunefields.

Several factors have contributed to extensive alluviation in this area. Most of the river systems rise on the better-watered eastern and northeastern upland rim of the desert and flood in more than half the summers; on the other hand, they are directed towards the driest part of Australia and undergo progressive loss of water downvalley through evaporation and from diversion of flow into lateral sumps by sand dunes and alluvial barriers. Further, they became tectonically reactivated during the Tertiary, leading to widespread erosion of soft rocks in upper sectors and to aggradation in areas of subsidence and back-tilting downstream.

Floodplains in deserts, as elsewhere, exhibit contrasts outwards from the channel as well as along their length. Accordingly, the desert floodplain will be typified at three points along its course, namely the upper plains sector of mainly coarse sediments, the lower plains sector of finer alluvium, and the terminal floodout.

Upper Plains Sector (Fig. 6.3a)

The channel is here adjusted to the transport of coarse bedload supplied from desert uplands under conditions of partial weathering, unrestricted slope wash and flash-flooding. Accordingly the banks and bed are predominantly sandy, the channel cross-section wide and shallow, and its course only slightly sinuous. A braiding habit is also characteristic where excessive widening has been accompanied by shoaling in mid-channel and where the bar has become stabilized by vegetation between flows. The channel is typically bordered by an inner floodplain of comparable width, consisting of longitudinal sand banks and intervening flood furrows formed during overbank flow.

The channel and the adjoining flood tract commonly bear a gallery woodland of large phreatophytes dependent on the underflow in the channel sands recharged from the ephemeral streamfloods. By far the commonest among the trees is the river red gum, although groves of casuarinas may occur along bouldery or rocky channels. Perennial grasses such as windmill grass (*Chloris* spp.) may occur in silt-floored depressions that hold water after floods, but the ground cover is commonly sparse.

The channel and its adjoining tract are subject to

frequent changes and remoulding by streamfloods, and this is reflected in a lack of soil development in the layered sandy alluvium of this zone. The more stable floodplain beyond is less frequently inundated and liable only to infrequent aggradation or shallow flood scour, and has layered alluvial soils with a thin sandy layer above a heavier subsoil, or weakly solonetzic soils with similar texture contrast between the A and B horizons. These are liable to stripping by wind or sheetfloods, and the process is aided where salinity weakens the soil structure. The eroded areas or *scalds* may develop into claypans by exposure and sealing of the subsoil. Airphotos show that this erosion is not random, but concentrated in bands across the fall of the plain, perhaps because of a rhythmic scour by sheetfloods, and records suggest that the process is a natural one, although accentuated by the overstocking to which river frontages are often subjected.

These flat surfaces with their sandy topsoils and impervious subsoils are droughty habitats, as reflected in a vegetation of scattered trees, such as the ironbark (*Acacia estrophiolata*) of central Australia, above a ground layer of short grasses and forbs, although a component of perennial grasses may have been diminished by heavy grazing. The floodplain may be diversified by distributary flood channels leading to small sump basins that are fed during floods. These areas of periodic inundation and heavier alluvial soils are generally flanked by coolibah (*Eucalyptus microtheca*), and the basins may be occupied by shrubs such as old man saltbush (*Atriplex nummularia*) or northern bluebush (*Chenopodium auriceum*).

In outermost parts of the floodplain, normally no longer subject to flooding, the older alluvia have commonly been reworked by wind. Small dunes, partially stabilized by vegetation, may occur locally. Continuing sand drift is shown by shallow blow-outs and by sand-mounding about shrubs. The open vegetation includes species adapted to deep sandy topsoils or to loose sands. There are scattered trees, including whitewood (*Atalaya hemiglauca*) in central Australia, and the shrubs, which tend to be more prominent here, include mulga and witchetty and various cassias and fuchsia bushes (*Eremophila* spp.). On loose sand are spinifex and the dune-colonizing cane grass (*Zygochloa paradoxa*).

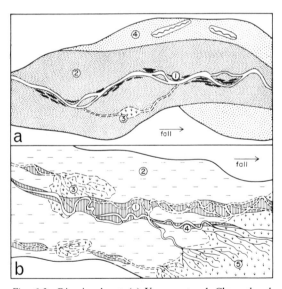

Fig. 6.3 Riverine desert. (a) *Upper sector*: 1. Channel and sand banks with gallery woodland; 2. Inner floodplain with short grasses and scattered trees; 3. Distributary and sump basin of heavier soils fringed by coolibah; 4. Sandy outer plain with dunes. (b) *Lower and terminal sectors*: 1. Anastomosing sinuous channel and levees; 2. Floodplain of fine-textured alluvium; 3. Sump basin with swamp shrubland or grassland; 4. Distributary channel; 5. Floodout and feeder channels.

Lower Plains Sector (Fig. 6.3b)

In contrast to floods in humid regions, desert streamfloods tend to diminish in volume beyond a certain distance into the plains. Losses due to infiltration or diversion are not compensated by the contributions of tributaries, nor by runoff from adjacent lowlands. The dimensions of the channel tend to decrease accordingly, with shoaling due to deposition of sands. This in turn leads to an increase in the percentage of silt and clay in the flood sediments of the lower plains and in the bed and banks of the channel, which now adjusts towards the requirements of suspended-load transport. This is seen in a greater depth in proportion to width and in a meandering habit.

The aggrading channel tends to build itself above the general level of the plain, developing prominent levees. These may be breached during floods, generating distributaries which tend to run parallel with the parent channel at the foot of the levee backslope before swinging sharply to rejoin, in a reticulate pattern of anastomosing channels with sharp angles of bifurcation and re-entry. A distributary that pursues a long independent course through the floodplain before rejoining the main stream is known as an *anabranch*. These features are well expressed in the riverine desert plains of southwest Queensland, for the prevalence of fine-textured rocks in the catchments has resulted in widespread clay plains, with the multiple channels that have given the name 'Channel Country' (Plate 6.6). At intervals, anastomosing arms may link in a deeply-scoured straight reach which is generally occupied by a long perennial waterhole.

This sector exhibits a fundamental contrast between the raised channel tract of reddish silt and fine sand and the lower backplain with dark cracking clay soils. The lighter soils of the channels and levees support trees and shrubs, with a gallery woodland of river red gums and collibahs along the banks, whereas the backplains are open grasslands with areas of perennial Mitchell grasses, supplemented seasonally by forbs and short grasses after flooding or heavy rains. In the Channel Country the belt of anastomosing channels may be a few kilometres wide, with meander scrolls and cutoffs as evidence of channel shifts. The silty loams of the levees are often prominently scalded.

The backplains form vast featureless surfaces relieved only by the silty rises of old tracts or by shrub-covered islands of red sand dunes aligned along prior sandy channels. Lines of trees mark small distributary channels which feed into sump basins near the outer margins. These may remain inundated for weeks after streamfloods and are areas of strongly cracking clay soils with extreme gilgai microrelief. The latter include networks of circular gilgai, orientated channel gilgai with deep elongate depressions, and reticulate gilgai with connected depressions across much of the basin floor. In these settings of heavy clay soils and periodic deep saturation and drying, heaving and microrelief are more marked than in stony desert, and the rise or 'puff' is stone-free. The flood basins are commonly ringed with coolibahs.

Terminal Floodouts (Fig. 6.3b)

In disorganized desert systems of interior drainage, the majority of streamfloods end in terminal basins where the flood becomes defeated and dispersed by its own alluvial barriers. These are inland deltas in which the channel adopts a distributary habit through the successive formation and breaching of levees along the aggrading terminals. The rivers of southwest Queensland such as the Cooper exhibit these features on a large scale where they traverse tectonic basins of subsidence, and the fan-shaped distributary systems have there been termed *deltoids* (Whitehouse, 1944). Commonly, terminal floodouts are located at topographic barriers, particularly sand dunes, for many streamfloods end near the boundary between riverine and sandy desert.

The channels feed into basins floored with clay and silt deposited from standing flood waters. Channels and basins resemble those in the lower floodplain sector, but the scale is larger. The perennial vegetation consists of close woodlands of coolibahs with bluebush, old man saltbush or cane grass (*Eragrostis australasica*) in the lowest tracts. A rank growth of annuals or short-lived perennials follows major flooding; for instance during 1974–5 the Finke floodout was transformed into a head-high thicket of shrubs. The maze of active and abandoned distributary channels, the strong microrelief and the obscuring vegetation render these areas difficult to traverse, but they are most important to the pastoralist.

Desert Clay Plains

Two areas of plainlands with largely residual clay soils occur in the northeast of the arid zone, namely in the Barkly Tableland of the Northern Territory and the Winton-Blackall Downs of central Queensland.

A little-altered Tertiary surface of low relief has been preserved on the Barkly Tableland, and the clay plains occupy its lower parts (Christian *et al.*, 1954) These poorly drained surfaces of Cambrian limestone and dolomite resisted the lateritization of adjoining higher levels and have extensive dark grey calcareous swelling clay soils, deeply cracking and with numerous gilgai in the lower tracts. They form open grasslands, with Mitchell grasses in the south giving place to bluegrass (*Dicanthium* spp.) or browntop (*Eulalia fulva*) northwards with increasing rainfall. Annual grasses with a sparse tree cover occur on stonier rises within the plains. Parts of these plains are alluvial and areas of Tertiary limestone mark former terminals of a sluggish interior drainage; they yield more calcareous 'fluffy' clay soils and support an open woodland of coolibah. The present interior drainage consists of anastomosing channels in floodplains of alluvial clay soils; these are grasslands broken by gallery woodlands of coolibah or lignum (*Bauhinia*) along the channels. They lead to seasonal swamps of very heavy clays with pronounced gilgai, occupied by shrublands of northern bluebush and areas of Mitchell grasses.

Plate 6.7   Sandplain in Western Australia with characteristic spinifex rings, a sparse shrub and tree cover, and much intervening bare ground. *Photo*: CSIRO Division of Land Use Research.

The Winton-Blackall Downs resemble the lowland element of the stony deserts to the southwest, and are formed on the same Cretaceous rocks. The dominant elements are undulating plains with red clay soils and Mitchell grass, traversed by floodplains of fine-textured alluvium and darker soils.

SAND DESERT

Sand desert comprises two main types of comparable extent, namely dunefields and sandplain. The dunefields consist of red sands that have originated mainly from sedimentary rocks, and sandplain of clayey sands derived from granitic rocks and their weathering products, or from lateritized surfaces. Although it accords most closely with the popular concept of a desert landscape, sand desert is not confined to the driest parts of arid Australia. As seen from Fig. 6.1 the main dunefields are found in lowland basins where sands originating as alluvium have been reworked by wind following the retraction of rivers under aridity. Similarly, sandplain occurs on the lower margins of shield desert or more broadly on lateritic surfaces of such low relief that river systems have completely disintegrated. Sand desert covers almost 2 million km² or nearly 40 per cent of the arid zone.

Sand desert mainly supports hummock grasslands of spiny evergreen spinifex, which is tolerant of infertile soils and which has an extensive root system suited to the excessively drained sands. Soft spinifex (*Triodia pungens*) dominates in the north, with more than 300 mm rainfall, and the larger tussocks and rings of hard spinifex (*Triodia basedowii*), south of 22° S, and there are also important areas of feathertop spinifex in an overlapping northern zone. The main contrasts lie in the upper storeys however, for these are rarely pure grasslands. In the north, scattered eucalypts including bloodwoods (*Eucalyptus terminalis*, *E. dichromophloia*) gradually increase to pass into woodland with an acacia shrub layer in the Pindan country on the northwestern desert margin. Tall shrubs, particularly mulga, become more prominent in the south, and in the southeastern sand deserts spinifex gives place to mixed low shrubland below open mulga, with cypress pine on deeper sands. In a large central zone the shrub and tree layers are sparser and vary with topography and the depth and character of the sands. Mulga occurs on heavier soils and in areas receiving run-on, as in dune swales and near the upslope margins of sandplain; mallee eucalypts and witchetty bushes indicate calcrete at shallow depth, and groves of desert oak (*Casuarina decaisnia*) occur with increased shallow ground moisture, as in the intermont dunefields of the Macdonnell Ranges. The bare sands between the spinifex may be occupied by herbs and

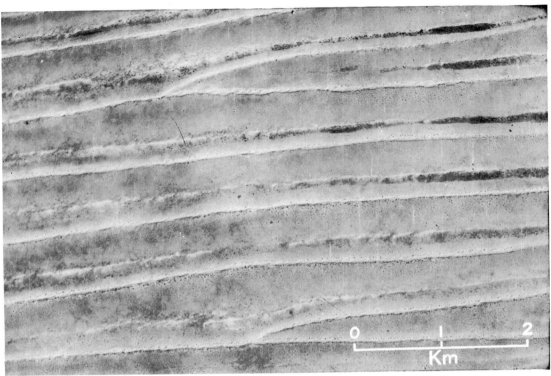

Plate 6.8 Regularly spaced parallel sand dunes in the Simpson Desert, with live sand crests, stable flanks, and flat swales with patches of mulga on heavier soils. The dunes run north-south and have extended northwards as indicated by occasional convergences. Offsetting of the dark swale vegetation reflects the asymmetry of the ridges, with the steeper face to the east. *Photo*: Division of National Mapping, Department of National Resources.

annual grasses after rains. Mature spinifex grassland is subject to fire, and burnt areas may be colonized extensively by ephemerals, but the spinifex resumes its former cover after a few years.

Sandplain

These monotonously uniform desert surfaces are mainly gently sloping (less than 0.5 per cent) or at most broadly undulating (Plate 6.7). Parts of the Frew-Sandover Sandplain in the Northern Territory are traversed by broad linear rises a metre or so high and about a kilometre apart, with the northwesterly trend of longitudinal dunes in the area. Sandplain soils are mainly clayey sands with about 10 per cent of clay at the surface increasing to 25 per cent at a metre or so. Sandy red earths occur along shallow drainage depressions near the upslope margins and red sands on low dunes and on rises marking prior channels. Below is a variety of substrates, including iron pisolithic horizons, gravels, and lime pans, and these variations are commonly expressed in the upper vegetation. In detail the surface is hummocky due to the accumulation of sand at the bases of spinifex hummocks and rings.

The restricted depth of wind mobilization of sandplain may be due to a higher original clay content in granite-derived sands and also to a component of coarse sand and grit which becomes concentrated in a stabilizing veneer. In many areas it reflects the thinness of sandy horizons in older lateritic soils. Sandplain near the upslope margins of dunefields also reflects the presence of coarser sand grades that have resisted wind-sorting, and possibly persistent fluvial action in such areas.

Dunefields

The most extensive dunes are parallel ridges. Commonly up to 15 m high, they continue for tens of kilometres, occasionally meeting in narrow junctions that almost invariably point in the direction of the formative wind. Spacing of crests in closed dune systems varies from 200 to 600 m, and in any area the spacing tends to be regular, as does the height, which is inversely related to spacing (Plate 6.8). On a continental scale the ridges extend in a huge arc of anti-clockwise extension, eastwards through the Great

Victoria Desert, northwards through the Simpson Desert and westwards in the Great Sandy Desert, to meet the ocean in the northwest near Derby (Jennings, 1968). Dune trend and growth lie close to the direction of the effective resultant of strong winds capable of moving sand (Brookfield, 1970).

The swales include narrow sandy hollows, firm flat floors with claypans, and stony plains. Generally, the greater the surface contrast between dune and swale the wider the spacing and the higher the dunes, indicating that the processes concentrating the sand into ridges were aided by the contrast.

Longitudinal dunes appear to be the most evolved dune type and occur in open plains in which the dominant winds have acted free from interference by relief or drainage in conditions of adequate but not excessive sand supply (Mabbutt, 1968). Other dune forms may be considered as subclimax forms, less advanced or arrested in their development. They include reticulate dunes in areas of conflicting wind systems, as in the Lake Amadeus lowlands west of the Simpson Desert, near the turn-around of the continental dune swirl; aligned short dunes in intermont basins; transverse source-bordering ridges at the downwind margins of playas and floodplains, from which longitudinal dunes may originate (Twidale, 1972); chains of short transverse dunes trending downwind, as along the Finke River bordering the Simpson Desert; and blow-out or parabolic dunes on desert margins where an anchoring vegetation has been partially and temporarily destroyed.

Over most of the arid zone the ridges are partly stabilized by vegetation and sand movement is now limited to the crests, which show a succession of changing forms. In the driest parts of the Simpson Desert the amount of mobile sand is markedly greater, but mobility may be an expression of sand supply rather than of regional aridity alone. For instance the dunes downwind from Lake Eyre are more mobile due to plentiful sand drift from the lake shores. Overall, the present status of the ridges indicates greater mobility of sand and hence a drier climate at the time of their formation, and a former greater extent of the arid zone.

Within the fields of partly-stabilized dunes, three contrasted habitats recur repeatedly. The loose sandy dune crests offer an unstable environment rendered more arid by rapid infiltration and exposure to drying winds, and the vegetation is patchy only. The most widespread colonizer of bare sand is the dune canegrass, which develops into a large hummock as it grows and traps sand but is subject to wind erosion and eventually dies, leaving the sand mound to be dispersed. Deeper-rooting small trees and tall shrubs may establish themselves in sheltered sites, as below slip faces. The most extensive dune habitat is that of the stable flanks, which generally support a hummock grassland of spinifex. In the north particularly, these also include scattered tall trees, notably bloodwoods, whitewood and the picturesque desert oak. In the drier south, acacias and various low myrtaceous shrubs such as *Thryptomene* become increasingly important above the spinifex. The third setting, that of the swales, is more variable. The narrowest swales are sandy hollows with spinifex, as on the adjoining dunes. Generally however, the swales support a larger vegetation indicative of more clay-rich soils and of a tendency for water to collect after rain, and typically there is a flat floor 50 to 100 m wide with patches of mulga and other acacias, low shrubs, and some perennial tussock grasses such as woollybutt (*Eragrostis eriopoda*). Where the dunes border stony desert, the swales may consist of broad stony corridors, and near riverine desert the dunes may be separated by alluvial flats.

In the semi-arid belts north and south of the arid zone the linear dunes are now completely stable, as indicated by their subdued rounded forms, complete vegetation cover, and degree of soil development. In the north of the Great Sandy Desert, where they carry open woodland, the upper sand horizons are brown rather than red, due to organic content, and the swales have loamy soils. In the southeast, as in western New South Wales, the age and stability of the dunes is shown in leaching of lime to a depth of more than a metre. South again are the more calcareous dunes of the Mallee, with their distinctive woodland of ground-branching eucalypts, in which partial leaching has produced solonized brown soils above a lime pan.

River Terminals

Many desert rivers end in the dunefields, diverted by dune barriers and absorbed by the sands, and there the swales are occupied by their channels and floodouts. In the north of the Simpson Desert the Hale, Todd and other rivers have been deflected along the swales for a hundred kilometres or more, and in the southwest the terminal floods of the Finke River back up between the dunes to the north. The Sturt Creek Floodout into the Great Sandy Desert is another example. Lines of coolibahs and tracts of floodplain vegetation mark these drainage lines. In addition there are more isolated desert lakes within the dunes, representing a further stage of obliteration of surface drainage. These are fed by local rains and are often salty. The Percival Lakes in the Great Sandy Desert mark a former winding river course several hundred kilometres long, and the many large claypans of the South Dunefield of the Simpson Desert are another manifestation of advanced disorganization of drainage.

DESERT LAKES

The large numbers of 'lakes' that dot maps of deserts

are an expression of the disorganization of drainage systems under aridity, with streamfloods terminating in basins inland or dying out at intermediate points on catchment slopes. Drainage is generally most disorganized on shields and structural platforms because of low gradients, and arid Australia is no exception. Patterns of disorganization, as reflected in the distribution and characteristics of the larger lake basins in Fig. 6.1, and of countless others too small to be mapped, have been influenced by structure and relief. In the shield desert of the Yilgarn Plateau of Western Australia, 'river lakes' mark the isolation of sectors along broad trunk valleys; in the basin lowlands of central Australia, Lake Amadeus and similar lakes have resulted from the more advanced retraction of former tributary river systems towards the upland rims; finally, the larger lake basins of the interior lowlands, such as Lake Eyre and Lake Torrens, occupy younger structural depressions in which centripetal drainage systems remain integrated to a large degree.

Many features of desert lakes are attributable to their water, sediment and salt budgets, which in turn reflect relationships with surface and groundwater systems. Lakes in the bottoms of structural basins commonly act as terminals for both surface and groundwater movements and constitute evaporative cells in linked hydrologic systems. Salts from groundwater concentrate on the floors to a relative degree dependent on frequency of flooding and the resulting supply of sediment. Lakes on intermediate slopes on the other hand may be bypassed by groundwater flow and so depend largely on surface inflow, and salts are likely to be less important than alluvial silts and clays on the floors. Salt lakes and claypans represent the two extremes, and many intermediate forms occur. A further classification is based on frequency of flooding. The term *playa*, used of lakes that are

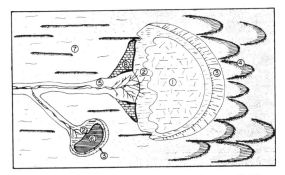

Fig. 6.4 Desert 'lake' landscapes: 1. Salt crust; 2. Playa margin with crusted gypseous sands and halophytes; 3. Lunette; 4. Sand dunes, including parabolics; 5. Feeder channels and floodplain; 6. Claypan; 7. Alluvial plain with sand dunes; 8. Calcrete platform.

flooded less than a quarter of the time, applies to most 'lakes' of arid Australia.

Playas at drainage terminals are areas of fluvial deposition, and adjoining alluvial flats, saline in part, are included in their landscapes (Fig. 6.4). Erosion and deposition by wind are also important in these open areas subject to flooding and drying, and bordering dunes are an integral part of the playa complex. Salinity and water levels exercise important controls on wind action. Salinity favours wind erosion of playas by preventing colonization by vegetation and by causing the pelletization of normally cohesive clays into transportable aggregates; deflation is of course prevented during flooding, and the groundwater table sets a limit to the lowering of the floor by deflation.

Most Australian playas have gently sloping margins, and variations in lake volume due to past climates have resulted in fluctuations in extent. Instead of flights of shore terraces as in intermontane playas, evidence of high-lake stages here takes the form of playa sediments and evaporites beyond present limits of flooding. On the other hand, fluctuating regimes with alternate filling and drying, have led to the periodic mobilization of playa sediments by wind and the building of crescentic source-bordering dunes or *lunettes*. Much of this evidence is now obscured by sand dunes which have encroached during subsequent drier phases of reduced flooding. Playas therefore can yield important evidence of changing desert climates.

Features of Playa Floors

Where saline groundwater is close to the surface, excess evaporation leads to a zonal concentration of salts in accordance with solubility. In the lowest part of such salt lakes or *salinas* a crust of sodium chloride will form during drying cycles, above a saturated mixture of mud and gypsum crystals; crusts of gypsum-cemented sediments may occur on higher parts of the floor, whilst calcium carbonate crusts are characteristic of upper margins and deltas. As the salt crust thickens it commonly cracks into polygonal plates up to a metre or more across. Further crystalization from rising solutions is concentrated towards the edges, forming raised rims and crack-fillings, and eventually the plates may overlap and buckle. Renewed flooding may smooth or destroy a salt crust by solution, but a crust that has developed over several cycles is characterized by greater thickness (up to 50 cm in parts of Lake Eyre) and unevenness, and with exposure the crust is discoloured reddish-brown through dust impregnation. The salt crusts are devoid of vegetation.

In claypans the playa floor is permanently above the water-table. If it lies within the capillary zone the silt-clay surface becomes blistery or flakey after drying, is commonly gypseous, and may be whitened by efflorescing sodium chloride. Dry playas, that is those unaffected by groundwater, generally have firm level surfaces of clay with fine polygonal cracks, and become increasingly calcareous in depth. Hard-setting claypan floors may resist colonization by plants, but many are at least partly vegetated, often with salt-tolerant species, for example canegrass in western New South Wales.

Features of Playa Margins

Most playa margins are smooth on the downwind side and irregular upwind, partly as a result of wave-trimming on exposed shores and partly in consequence of dune encroachment on the upwind shores. Apart from dunes, playa margins are flat surfaces of alluvial, littoral or aeolian sediments, partly crusted by gypsum and salt, extensively wind-eroded and locally gullied. Prominent sand mounds occur around shrubs. The vegetation is often zoned, with strongly salt-tolerant forms such as samphire in the lower parts and less halophytic shrubs, such as saltbushes and Frankenia, upslope. Tall shrubs such as tea-tree (*Melaleuca*) occur on higher sandy shores.

Groundwater playas, for example Lake Eyre, may have a seasonally moist seepage zone around the margins. The calcareous mound springs near Lake Eyre indicate former artesian outflows, possibly fault-aligned, which attained a few metres above the lake floor. They consist of lime-cemented sand and muds and are now inactive due to lowered groundwater levels. Calcreted deltaic flats and shoreline terraces above the playa floor, as around the river lakes of Western Australia, also attest to the subsequent effects of deflation and of lowered water-tables.

The dunes that commonly fringe these playas are of two main types, namely quartz sand dunes and those of gypseous clay or pure gypsum. The former include sand lunettes on downwind shores due to vegetation trapping sand blown from the beaches formed at full-lake stages as in coastal foredunes. Behind the lunette, parabolic dunes denote subsequent phases of sand mobilization and the development of blow-outs elongated downwind. Sand dunes often form islands within the larger playas. In general they offer the range of habitats described for sand desert, save for the presence of halophytic shrubs near the playa and the lesser importance of spinifex on the younger sands.

Clay dunes are formed of pellets of silty clay carried by wind from the brackish to salty floors of periodically drying playas and trapped by plants along the shore (Bowler, 1973). Clay lunettes differ from sand foredunes in having their steeper flank towards the playa and gentler slopes built up by seasonal accretion to leeward. They may attain 10 m in height and 100 metres or more across at their widest. Stabilization and weathering involve crusting, the complete leaching of chlorides and the removal of much gypsum and lime from the upper layer, which appears as a massive buff clay. Clay dunes support a specialized vegetation including salt-tolerant low shrubs. Locally one finds dunes of almost pure gypsum, generally where the playa is dependent on groundwater discharge, and in some Western Australian playas a younger gypsum dune occurs inside the clay dune, pointing to a diminishing importance of surface inflow and sediment supply in a shrinking playa. Lunettes occur on the lee sides of playas across the semi-arid belt in the south of the Australian desert zone and indicate more frequent flooding in the late Pleistocene. The playas became inactive and lunettes ceased to form in a subsequent drier period of dune extension between 12,000 and 16,000 years ago.

Aeolian forms may dominate the downwind sides of playas, but elsewhere the margins include features related to entering stream channels, such as alluvial flats and fan-deltas, and to former lake floors. These surfaces are often impregnated with gypsum and locally with sodium chloride and may exhibit polygonal cracking and related sorted stone patterns. Being saline and sparsely vegetated they are subject to erosion by wind armed with drifting sand. Old lacustrine silts on the north shore of Lake Eyre have been scoured by wind in the corridors between sand ridges, leaving the dunes perched at the level of a former lake floor. On the west of Lake Eyre North an extensive surface of gypsum-crusted lake and river deposits has been upfaulted and dissected into tablelands up to 30 m above the present floor of the lake.

REFERENCES

Bowler, J. M. (1973), 'Clay dunes: their occurrence, formation and environmental significance', *Earth Sci. Rev.,* 9, 315–38.

Brookfield, M. (1970), 'Dune trends and wind regime in central Australia', *Z. f. Geomorph..* 10, 121–53.

Budyko, M. I. (1974), *Climate and Life*, Academic Press, New York.

Christian, C. S. *et al.* (1954), *Survey of the Barkly Region, Northern Territory and Queensland, 1947–8*, CSIRO Aust. Land Res. Ser. No. 3.

Christian, C. S. and Stewart, G. A. (1953), *General Report on a Survey of the Katherine-Darwin Region, 1946*, CSIRO Aust. Land Res. Ser. No. 1.

Finkl, C. W. and Churchward, H. M. (1973), 'The etched landsurfaces of southwestern Australia', *J. Geol. Soc. Aust.*, 20, 295–307.

Gentilli, J. (1971), *Climates of Australia*, Elsevier, Amsterdam.

Jennings, J. N. (1968), 'A revised map of the desert dunes of Australia', *Aust. Geogr.*, 10, 408–9.

Jutson, J. T. (1934), 'The physiography (geomorphology) of Western Australia', 2nd edn, *Geol. Surv. W. Aust. Bull.* 95.

Litchfield, W. H. and Mabbutt, J. A. (1962), 'Hardpan in soils of semi-arid Western Australia', *J. Soil Sci.*, 13, 148–59.

Lowry, D. C. and Jennings, J. N. (1974), 'The Nullarbor karst, Australia', *Z. f. Geomorph.*, 18, 35–81.

Mabbutt, J. A. (1963), 'Wanderrie banks: micro-relief patterns in semiarid Western Australia', *Bull. Geol. Soc. Am.*, 74, 529–40.

——(1965), 'Stone distribution in a stony tableland soil', *Aust. J. Soil Res.*, 3, 131–42.

——(1966), 'Landforms of the western Macdonnell Ranges' in G. H. Dury (ed.), *Essays in Geomorphology*, Heinemann, London, pp. 83–120.

——(1968), 'Aeolian landforms in central Australia', *Aust. Geogr. Stud.*, 6, 139–50.

Mabbutt, J. A. *et al.* (1963), *Lands of the Wiluna-Meekatharra Area, Western Australia, 1958*, CSIRO Aust. Land Res. Ser. No. 7.

Perry, R. A. (1960), *Pasture Lands of the Northern Territory, Australia*, CSIRO Aust. Land Res. Ser. No. 5.

Perry, R. A. *et al.* (1962), *Lands of the Alice Springs Area, Northern Territory, 1956–57*, CSIRO Aust. Land Res. Ser. No. 6.

Twidale, C. R. (1967), 'Hillslopes and pediments in the Flinders Ranges, South Australia' in J. N. Jennings and J. A. Mabbutt (eds), *Landform Studies from Australia and New Guinea*, Australian National University Press, Canberra, pp. 95–117.

——(1972), 'Evolution of sand dunes in the Simpson Desert, central Australia', *Trans. Inst. Brit. Geogr.*, 56, 77–110.

Whitehouse, F. W. (1944), 'The natural drainage of some very flat monsoonal lands', *Aust. Geogr.*, 4, 183–96.

Williams, G. E. (1973), 'Late Quaternary piedmont sedimentation, soil formation and paleoclimates in arid South Australia', *Z. f. Geomorph.*, 17, 102–25.

7 THE COAST

J. L. DAVIES

Depending on how it is measured, the coastline of Australia is rather more than 20,000 km long and, in its great variety of form and process, it reflects the continental structures and climatic gradients which have been described earlier in this book. A first indication of this variety is given by the map in Fig. 7.1 which presents a broad categorization of coastal type in a necessarily generalized fashion. It envisages four main kinds of coast: *rock coasts*, more or less cliffed and usually with some sort of shore platform development, where beaches are distinctly secondary in terms of landscape impact and perhaps absent altogether; *mainland beach coasts*, where beaches are extensive and rocky sections become very limited in extent or are absent; *barrier beach coasts*, where extensive beaches are broken by occasional rocky promontories but are separated from the mainland coast by lagoons or estuaries variously infilled; and *tidal plain coasts*, where deposition, often of finer sediments, has taken place in conjunction normally with the development of salt marsh and mangrove.

Within the category of barrier beach coasts, a further distinction has been made between those where the sand barrier is massive relative to the tidal plains of the associated lagoons and those in lower energy environments where the tidal plains themselves tend to dominate and the barriers are relatively small features often forming as chenier ridges on or in the tidal plain sediments.

The five categories defined in this way form a series in which the coast becomes progressively more 'low-lying' and so Fig. 7.1 should reflect something of the likely visual appearance. The generalization necessary to produce a map at such a scale has naturally meant the obliteration of many local differences, but the broad patterns which emerge appear valid. The southern half of the east coast is strongly characterized by the bigger barrier systems. Cliffed coasts of a variety of lithologies are especially to be found on the west and south coasts and the northern coasts display a particularly extensive development of tidal plains, with or without smaller barriers.

STRUCTURAL INFLUENCES

The very broadest outlines of the Australian coast follow the edges of the continental shelves and so result from the geological evolution of the continent. The western and northwestern margins may have started to come into existence about 450×10^6 years ago with the breaking up of an earlier supercontinent, and the southern shelf edge and coast still show a remarkably close fit to the section of Antarctica from which Australia separated perhaps 100×10^6 years ago. In contrast, the outline of the east coast has been controlled by the intermittent addition of successive belts of land running roughly north to south as a result of large-scale sedimentation, folding and uplift between about 600 and 200×10^6 years ago.

Yet on only limited sections of the coast do the rocks of the old structures actually meet the sea. The old shield rocks of the western half of the continent come right to the shore in the Kimberley block and on the Albany-Esperance coast. Elsewhere they reach the shore in places, but more usually are fringed by recent sedimentary plains as in Arnhem Land or covered by Pleistocene dune rocks as on the Eyre Peninsula. Along the east coast, bedrock is very largely separated from the sea by long beaches and gives rise to occasional headlands rather than lines of cliffs. The big structural basins of the middle and west (Carpentaria, Bonaparte, Canning, Carnarvon, Perth, Eucla and Murray) provide coasts of subdued relief along which extensive Quaternary marine and fluvial deposition has occurred and which are now more or less lined with beaches or tidal plains. But this statement needs qualification, because in parts of the Carnarvon Basin near Cape Cuvier and the Murray Basin near Port Campbell, and above all on the Nullarbor coast of the Eucla Basin, Cainozoic limestones laid down in the subsiding basins lie above sea level today and have been truncated to form spectacular cliffs. Similarly in the east, although the rather smaller structural depressions which intersect the coast provide lowland embayments such as those of East Gippsland in Victoria or Princess Charlotte Bay in Queensland, the sandstones of the Sydney Basin form some of the most extensive cliffs.

PROCESS ENVIRONMENTS

The shoreline itself largely reflects contemporary or

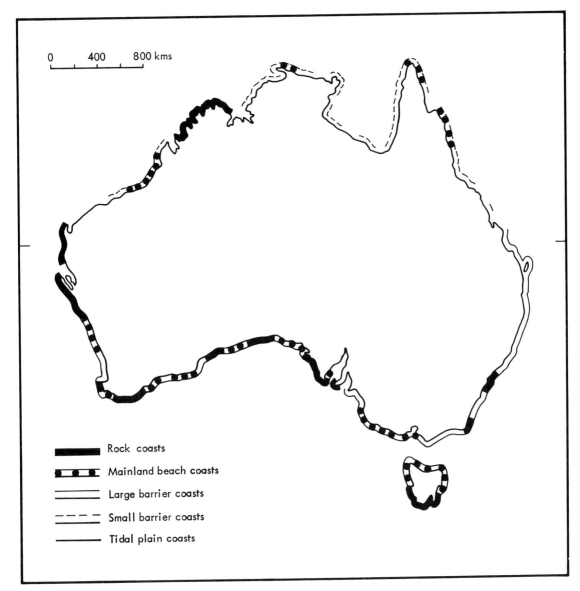

Fig. 7.1 Australian coastal types.

geologically recent morphologic processes which are only in a limited sense influenced by the legacy of the pre-Quaternary past. When interpreting wave and current regimes, the subaerial denudation systems and biological influences which have fashioned the details of the modern shore and control its dynamic evolution, it is necessary to look at climate in its widest sense as the fundamental arbiter of difference. In the terminology of a recent discussion of world shore process zones (Davies, 1972), Australia lies wholly within the low latitude zone, although the southern coasts are marginal to the mid-latitude zone. This chapter will serve to illustrate, among other things, how latitudinal variations in wave energy and longitudinal variations in precipitation are especially important in causing intrazonal differences.

The continent stretches north through 33 degrees towards the equator, but around the Tropic of Capricorn there is a sharp acceleration in latitudinal trends because of the way in which both east and west coasts bend to face equatorward. So an imaginary line joining North West Cape with the tip of Fraser Island divides

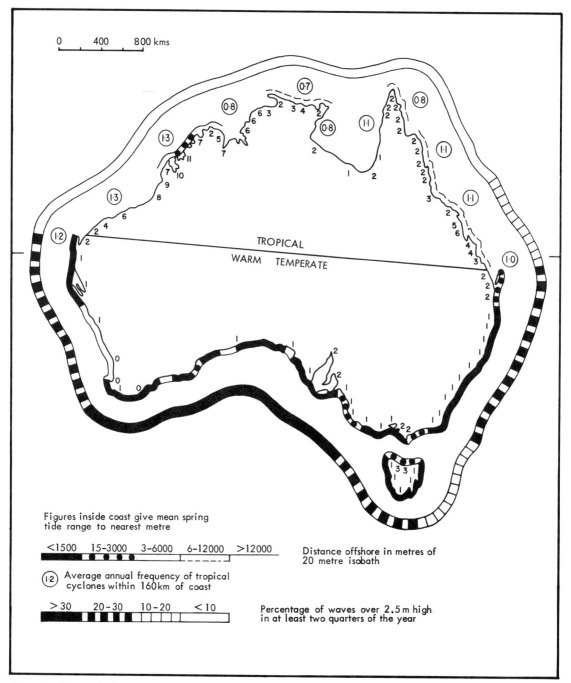

Fig. 7.2 The tropical and warm temperate coastal segments with some measures of deep water wave energy (after Meisburger, *US Army Engineer Research and Development Lab. Report* 1719–RR, 1962); tropical cyclone frequency (after Commonwealth Bureau of Meteorology, *Met. Summary*, 1972); spring tidal ranges (after Bird, *Aust. Marine Sci. Bull.* 39, 1972); and coastal ramp steepness (from chart data).

the littoral zone into two fundamental halves and, although the line is not strictly coincident with the Tropic, these two halves can be referred to for convenience as the tropical and warm temperate halves respectively.

The map in Fig. 7.2 illustrates some of these north-south differences. The most important variable is wave energy, although it is only possible to consider this in very general terms because of the paucity of quantitative data. In the southern warm temperate zone mean deep water wave energy levels are high. From North West Cape to the southern tip of Tasmania there is a basic genetic unity of regime resulting from the exposure of these coasts to local waves generated in offshore cyclonic depressions and to persistent swell coming from storm centres further to the south. The east coast of Tasmania is somewhat sheltered from these wave sources, but, further north in New South Wales, energy levels increase once more as the influence of onshore southeasterly air streams becomes greater and the occasional effect of northeasterly waves from tropical sources is felt. It is these easterly waves which are responsible for deep water wave energy decreasing only gradually northwards along the east coast in contrast to the west coast, where there is a very rapid drop in energy levels north of North West Cape. From North West Cape eastward through the tropical zone to northeast Queensland, mean wave energy is relatively low but the approach of tropical cyclones once or twice a year may introduce dramatic short period changes.

To obtain a better picture of wave energy levels on the shore itself it is necessary to take into account the gradient of the offshore sea floor. Where offshore sediments are mobile there is something of a feedback relationship with the wave regime, because, although initial shelf slope may have an overriding effect, higher energy tends to maintain steeper offshore ramps and steeper offshore ramps allow higher energy levels on the shore. The low offshore gradients of the tropical zone therefore are closely associated with low wave energy levels. Between North West Cape and Broome, around Joseph Bonaparte Gulf and in the Gulf of Carpentaria the 20 metre isobath lies more than 10 km from the shore and except for the Kimberley coast it is at least 6,000 m from the shore almost everywhere in the north. On the east coast north of the Tropic the extensive development of the Great Barrier Reefs significantly lowers wave energy on the mainland. Conversely the Kimberley coast has an offshore ramp abnormally steep for the tropics, but its intricate outline and numerous islands give rise to rapid local changes in exposure.

In the warm temperate zone, offshore gradients are considerably steeper and once again a particularly sharp change is evident at North West Cape. Along about 70 per cent of the coast from the Cape southward and eastward to Fraser Island the 20 metre isobath lies within 1,500 m of the shore. The only sections where it lies further than 3,000 m from shore are in parts of the west, notably between Geraldton and Bunbury, where submerged reefs derived from lithified Pleistocene beach and dune systems considerably reduce wave energy impact on the coast itself.

Related to the contrast in wave energy levels between north and south is the contrast in wind energy levels on the shore and particularly on the surface of beaches where they are important in the formation of coastal dunes. In attempting to explain the much reduced development of dunes on tropical shores compared with those in higher latitudes, Jennings (1965) analysed wind data for coastal stations in Australia by summing onshore vectors of the cubed velocity above 10 mph (4.4 m/sec) which he took as a general threshold speed for sand movement. He obtained a mean value of 794 outside the tropics and only 90 inside, which can be interpreted as an efficiency ratio of nearly 9 to 1.

The other major source of energy in the shore system is represented by the tides and here again Fig. 7.2 shows a general contrast between the tropical and warm temperate halves. In temperate Australia the spring tidal range exceeds 1.5 only around Fraser Island, in Bass Strait and in the South Australian Gulfs. Along the southwest facing coast from North West Cape to western Tasmania the range is less then 1 m. By contrast, in the northern half of the continent, spring tide ranges exceed 1.5 m almost everywhere and around Broad Sound in central Queensland and on the northwest coast from Port Hedland to Darwin they are greater than 3 m—rising in places to more than 6 m.

Tidal type tends to follow tidal range in that the higher ranges of the tropics and to some extent the New South Wales coast are associated with marked semidiurnal rhythms while from Tasmania to North West Cape the diurnal component becomes more prominent and tides are of a mixed type. On these southern coasts one high tide and one low tide in the tidal cycle is higher than the other. In the extreme southwest of the continent where the spring tidal range falls to about 0.4 m the tides become completely diurnal.

'Meteorological tides' produced by sharp changes in barometric pressure and by wind and wave set-up of water against the coast are of much greater absolute importance on tropical coasts where the biggest effects are associated with the passage of tropical cyclones. Such short-term sea-level changes superimposed on the normal astronomical tides and with a magnitude of over 3 m have been reported from many parts of the east Queensland coast and the north coast of Western Australia. The shallow Gulf of Carpentaria is particularly susceptible to changes

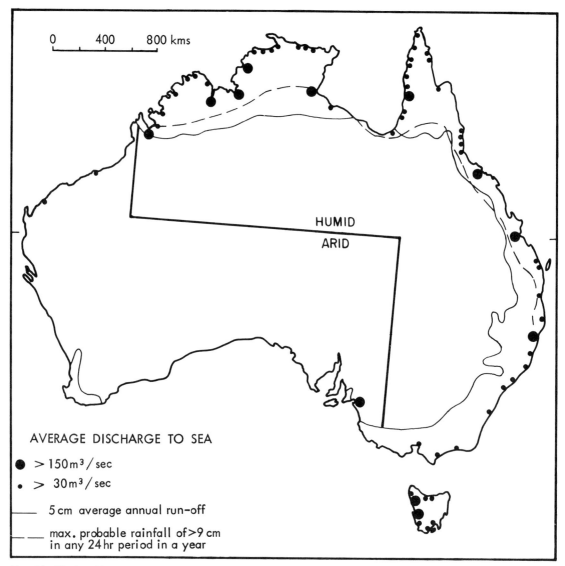

0   400   800 kms

HUMID

ARID

AVERAGE DISCHARGE TO SEA

● > 150 m³/ sec

· > 30 m³/ sec

——— 5 cm average annual run-off

— — max. probable rainfall of >9 cm
in any 24 hr period in a year

Fig. 7.3 The humid and arid coastal segments with some measures of rainfall intensity (after Jennings, *Aust. Geogr.*, 10, 1967), average runoff and discharge to the sea of the major rivers (after *Atlas of Australian Resources*).

in sea surface level not only as a result of cyclones but also of steady monsoonal winds; positive surges of up to 7 m and negative surges down to 1 m have been recorded. The low-lying nature of the Carpentaria coast makes such movements of special geomorphic importance.

In addition to these wave, wind and tide differences there are also of course expectable temperature differences of air and sea. The North West Cape-Fraser Island dividing line corresponds roughly to a mean daily minimum air temperature for the coldest month

of 12° C and maximum of 22° C and a cold month sea surface temperature of 20° C. North-south temperature differences are critical to the distribution of geomorphically important organisms such as corals, calcareous algae and mangroves and also to such phenomena as beach cementation. It is worth noting that the strong asymmetry in ocean temperatures between west and east coasts which is such a feature of the African and South American continents is much less evident in Australia.

Subsidiary to the fundamental latitudinal division

made on a basis of waves, winds, tides and temperatures is another division made on a basis of precipitation and surface runoff. For this we need an imaginary line running from near Broome in the northwest to near Portland in western Victoria. There are no convenient changes of coastal outline here as at North West Cape and Fraser Island so the divide is rather more blurred. There is also a small 'island' of higher precipitation and higher runoff in the extreme southwest. Even so the distinction between what may be called the humid and arid halves is a very important one. The map in Fig. 7.3 shows that the break corresponds roughly to an average annual runoff of 50 mm which approximates to an average annual precipitation of 500 mm. It also shows that almost all of Australia's large rivers reach the sea in the humid half and, allied with the overall runoff differences, this means that there is a strong asymmetry in the distribution of estuaries and deltas and in the extent of water and sediment discharge to the coast. In turn this is reflected in the nature of the shore sediments which are dominantly terrigenous and siliceous in the humid half but dominantly calcareous and marine in origin in the arid half. Other differences follow. The dominantly siliceous dunes of the humid coasts have been progressively podsolized through the late Quaternary and relatively readily destroyed by winds and waves. On the arid coasts, the predominantly calcareous dunes have been extensively lithified and subsequent erosion has produced coastal hills, seacliffs, islands and offshore reefs which are comparatively persistent and have played an important and continuing part in the evolution of the modern shore.

Superimposition of the north-south and east-west dichotomies gives the four basic coastal segments defined here in terms of process environments: warm temperate humid from Fraser Island to about Portland, warm temperate arid from about Portland to North West Cape, tropical arid from North West Cape to around Broome and tropical humid from there to Fraser Island. The four segments (demarcated in Figs 7.5 and 7.7) are unequal in length and are unequally known, but an attempt will be made to generalize about the salient characteristics of each and to point to internal homogenies of process, sediment system and evolution which may prove important, among other things, to our understanding of the problems of coastal evolution and coastal management.

Warm Temperate Humid Coasts

The warm temperate humid segment comprises the coasts of New South Wales, Victoria and Tasmania and a small part of the Queensland coast between Stradbroke and Fraser Islands, which is in many ways transitional to the tropical humid segment. In the light of the occurrence of calcareous beaches and of lithified Pleistocene dunes, the west coast of Victoria, a small part of northwestern Tasmania and the western coasts of King and Flinders Islands can also be considered transitional to the warm temperate arid segment from which much of the calcareous material may well have intruded. Away from this transitional area of western Bass Strait, beach sediments are strongly siliceous and dominantly terrigenous almost everywhere. However there appears to be relatively little supply from rivers today and most of the material is likely to have had a long history of transitory movement on the shelf, having been largely concentrated on the present coast by landward migration of the shoreline during the period of postglacial sea level rise which ended about 6,000 years ago. In some areas there was considerable further accession of sand between about 6,000 and 4,000 years ago and this too appears to have had its immediate origin on the shelf.

Superimposed on such transverse movements have been longshore translations of material, which have produced well-defined patterns of beach distribution. The proportion of the Tasmanian coast occupied by beaches increases from the southwestern corner to the northeastern corner. There is a similar increase from western Victoria east to Wilson's Promontory and most importantly along the New South Wales coast northward to Queensland, culminating in the great sand masses of Moreton, Stradbroke and Fraser Islands.

Through the region as a whole there is an overall trend from small pocket beaches in southwestern Tasmania to more continuous mainland beaches in northeastern Tasmania and western Victoria, smaller barrier beaches in southern New South Wales and bigger barrier beaches in northern New South Wales and southern Queensland. It is tempting to see this as the result of continual movement of sediment away from the southwest and towards the northeast under the influence of the strong southerly wave regime which must have controlled shoreline evolution at different sea levels right through Quaternary times. The biggest beach and dune systems on the Bass Strait coasts of Victoria and Tasmania face towards the west; those of western Tasmania and the whole east coast north to Fraser Island tend to face southward. All are more or less asymmetrical, displaying zetaforms with sharper curves at the end of the beach closer to the major wave source in the southwest. These general patterns are broken, but not contraverted, by the great re-entrant trap of Ninety Mile Beach in east Gippsland and similar, smaller traps in southeastern Tasmania.

However, the good adjustment of beach plans to wave approach, the sedimentological variation between and within beaches and the relative unimportance of littoral drift deflection in determining the location of coastal inlets all suggest that actual longshore trans-

Plate 7.1 Cliffed coast with mainland beach at Pirate's Bay, southeastern Tasmania. Cliffs with stripped structural marine platforms at their bases are cut in subhorizontally bedded sandstones. The beach is the low-energy southern end of a zetaform bay. *Photo*: Brian Curtis.

port of sand today is minimal, although it does appear to increase significantly in northern New South Wales and southern Queensland, where marked movement to the north is well established and the coast as a whole is more regular in plan and trends more obliquely to waves from southward. In line with this conclusion problems of beach maintenance in Tasmania, Victoria and New South Wales relate overwhelmingly to periodic movement of sand in and out from the beach and it is only in southern Queensland, notably on the resort beaches of the Gold Coast, that longshore movement becomes a major component.

Since the establishment of the present general sea level about 6,000 years ago, sand has been lost from the shore system by deflation inland in the form of dunes and by being washed into the mouths of different sorts of coastal inlets. The earliest dunes of this phase were frontal dunes built parallel to the back of the beach and, in areas where the coastal sand barrier subsequently prograded, this has usually been by the addition of successive lines of sand beach

ridges—low and closely parallel foredunes with an amplitude of about 1 to 5 m. Today these ridges are normally separated from the beach by at least one higher foredune, which can often be seen to be in retreat and rolling back over the ridge system behind. In northern New South Wales and southern Queensland natural dune form has often been obliterated by mining for economically valuable heavy minerals concentrated in old shorelines.

Near Smithton in northwest Tasmania, in the Gippsland Lakes area of Victoria and on the New South Wales coast north of Newcastle, older Pleistocene barriers occur inland from the modern barriers. The ridges of these older barriers are more subdued and in places more widely spaced than those of Holocene times and their sands are distinctly more podsolized, often displaying iron- and humus-rich hardpans which extend below present sea level (Thom, 1965). Northward from about Taree in central New South Wales, postglacial barriers seem to have been much more eroded than further south and in places, as

Plate 7.2 Large barrier beaches at Tweed Heads on the New South Wales-Queensland border. Massive sand barriers lie in front of the mainland coasts but are tied to islands of bedrock. The canalized Tweed River is impeding sand movement from the south. *Photo*: Douglas Baglin.

at Lake Cathie, Yamba and Evans Head, the Pleistocene sands are exposed at the shore.

The frontal dunes or beach ridges are replaced in many areas by transgressive dunes moving parallel to the direction of the strongest onshore winds and in most cases this has been a chronological replacement due to the erosion of the older systems. Often, as in the case of the Kurnell dunes south of Sydney, it can be shown to have occurred as a result of the destruction of vegetation by European man; in other instances it seems likely that the aboriginal occupation, so evidenced by shell middens and old hearths, has had at least some effect on dune evolution. But some transgressive dunes, such as those of the Tasmanian west coast, may be derived from even older transgressive complexes which originated before the sea reached its present level and are commonly Pleistocene in age. They are sometimes to be found stranded on cliff tops, having been divorced from their parent shore by removal of the sand ramp up which they once climbed. Such old cliff-top dunes are found at many places along the whole coast and underlie much of eastern Sydney.

The magnitude of dune masses depends mainly on onshore wind velocity and sand supply. Expectably big transgressive sheets occur on the west coasts of Tasmania and Victoria where onshore winds are strong. On the long stretch of east-facing coast they tend to have been generated towards the northern ends of sediment compartments where there has been accumulation of sand trapped from longshore transport. The climax to this trend comes in the south Queensland sand islands where enormous thicknesses of sand have accumulated by the progressive superimposition of dunes during Quaternary times (Coaldrake, 1962). On Moreton Island they reach heights of about 300 m and on Fraser Island support an extensive landscape of lakes and rainforest.

The overall gradient across the coast from the main continental divide to the edge of the shelf is much steeper in the warm temperate humid sector than in any other. The bigger rivers, essentially those indicated in Fig. 7.3, are bringing varying amounts of sediment to the present shore but, as has been already suggested, their contribution and that of the smaller rivers may have been greater in the past. Delta generation has been very limited and the most actively aggrading rivers such as the Clarence, Macleay and Shoalhaven have built fluvial plains behind sand barrier complexes (Hails, 1968). Many smaller rivers, such as the Wagonga at Narooma in southern New South Wales are still filling their estuaries which have often received more sediment from seaward than from landward. These estuaries, together with many coastal lagoons, commonly have a relatively deep residual 'hole' which separates a small inland river delta from a flood tide delta or inlet threshold formed by sand moved into the mouth of the inlet by wave and tide action. The two biggest rivers in the region—the Pieman and the Gordon in western Tasmania—also happen to have this type of estuary, apparently because they are having to fill exceptionally big 'holes'.

The degree to which river estuaries are blocked by barriers varies considerably from many smaller 'blind estuaries' where the river is blocked for much of the time to the fewer big estuaries which are never closed and where barriers are limited in extent (Jennings and Bird, 1967). Among the most open are the deeply drowned estuary of the Derwent in southern Tasmania which was soon discovered by the early navigators and settlers, and the equally deep Port Jackson on the central New South Wales coast which was the site of Australia's first British settlement. Elsewhere the strong barrier beach development throughout almost all of this coastal segment has led to the occurrence of a large number of coastal lagoons and some of the biggest are of major social and economic importance—Moreton Bay in Queensland, the Myall Lakes, Port Stephens, Lakes Macquarie, Tuggarah and Illawarra, and Botany Bay and Jervis Bay in New South Wales, the Gippsland Lakes and Corner Inlet in Victoria. Even Port Phillip Bay is basically of this nature, being largely formed behind old Pleistocene lithified barriers. Increasing competition for the use of these shallow, sheltered waters has created growing problems of management and planning (Bird, 1967). Because of the small tidal range, tidal plains are very limited in extent in almost all these estuarine and lagoonal inlets. They have evolved typically in conjunction with the establishment of *Salicornia-Arthrocnemum* salt marsh, especially on sandier substrates. The flora of muddy marshes appears reduced by comparison with some other parts of the world and the introduced *Spartina* has colonized formerly bare areas of the Tamar estuary in Tasmania and some inlets in southern Victoria. Except for Tasmania, mangroves occur throughout, but their geomorphological significance is very reduced south of Sydney, and the *Avicennia* mangroves of Victoria, which grow further from the equator than any other mangroves in the world, form shrubs of limited extent (Fig. 7.4).

The distribution of rocky coasts in the temperate humid segment is of course inverse to that of beaches.

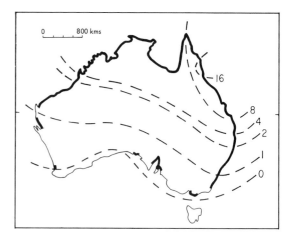

Fig. 7.4 Distribution of mangroves with isopleths showing number of species (from field data and various sources).

so that, with few exceptions such as the sandstone around Sydney and Jervis Bay, extensive lines of cliffs are to be found only in the south. Sub-horizontally lying sandstones, dolerites and limestones in Tasmania and western Victoria provide the best examples of walled cliffs, sometimes with concomitant stacks and arches. This coastal segment is *par excellence* the home of the high tide shore platform—an often remarkably horizontal feature wholly above mean swash level and terminating seaward in a low tide cliff. A large part of the literature on this landform and the water layer weathering processes which are believed to produce it has come from this part of the world. The New South Wales coast north to Newcastle, the Cape Otway coast of Victoria and the north and east coasts of Tasmania display particularly fine and extensively developed examples, normally in slightly dipping sandstones, siltstones and basalts. Rates of cliff retreat appear almost universally low and the supply of shore sediments from erosion of quartzose bedrock must be extremely small in relation to the total amount of coastal sand.

Warm Temperate Arid Coasts

The essential character of the coast between Victoria and North West Cape stems from the combination of relatively high levels of offshore wave energy with the relative aridity of the hinterland. So estuaries and coastal inlets generally are few but massive sand barrier systems have been built at different times through the Quaternary especially on those shores open to the southwest. Barrier sediments are largely marine in origin with a high proportion of biogenic carbonate and this, together with the favourable climatic conditions, has led to the extensive lithification of older Pleistocene barriers, so forming for instance the

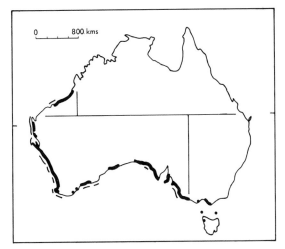

Fig. 7.5 Distribution of dune rocks and 'sandstone reefs' (from field data and various sources).

'coastal limestones' of Western Australia. However, the resulting material is often more truly described as a calcareous sandstone, being formed of cemented quartz and shell particles. Except that, along the west coast, beach rocks have been formed at many places by cementation within the beach berm, the postglacial beaches and dunes are not lithified and the modern dunes often climb over older dune rocks lying to landward.

Erosion of these old barrier dune rocks to form cliffs and their truncation or drowning to form offshore reefs (often called sandstone reefs) has given to this major coastal segment what are perhaps its most outstanding features (Fig. 7.5). Especially in exposed situations, where the old dunes piled up to considerable heights prior to lithification, extensive walled cliffs have been produced. Perhaps the best examples are near Robe, and on the west coast of the Eyre Peninsula in South Australia, and on the old barriers which partly close Shark Bay in the northwest. The cliffs on the outer edge of the lithified barrier of which Dirk Hartog Island is the drowned distal end are especially spectacular. Southward towards the mouth of the Murchison River the Zuytdrop Cliffs form a continuous wall about 130 km long and around 100 to 200 m in height, reaching 250 m at one point.

Offshore 'sandstone' reefs produced by the drowning or truncation at present sea level of old lithified barriers are particularly to be found between the Victorian border and Ceduna and along the whole west coast where, as Fairbridge (1950a) noted, they are better developed than anywhere else in the world. These reefs and also the shore platforms cut into similar material are often remarkably horizontal and lie a little above low water mark. They are usually considerably modified by growth of calcareous algae which build rim pools and terracettes and, north of Rottnest Island on the west coast, their outer edges become increasingly colonized by coral. The only true coral reefs appear to be in the Houtman Abrolhos Islands, but raised Pleistocene coral occurs here and there to form miniature cliffs along the mainland coast, for example near Dongara.

The dune rock reefs lie at varying distances from the coast as well as at varying depths. They may also be multiple and lie one inside another. They are particularly continuous in the extreme north between Cape Cuvier and North West Cape where for something like 300 km they form an almost continuous ribbon, broken here and there by narrow gaps and separated from the mainland by a lagoon up to about 5 km wide. Further south the reefs become more diffuse and diverse and where the shelf broadens and shallows, at it does in the Geraldton-Dongara area, they may lie further out. The big waves from the Indian Ocean lose energy as they move shoreward and the mainland beaches along much of the west coast are abnormally sheltered as a result. The same situation applies in South Australia around Streaky and Smoky Bays near Ceduna and also at the southern end of Encounter Bay near Kingston. All these beaches are commonly piled with the decaying strap-like leaves of sea-grasses, especially *Zostera* and *Posidonia*, which grow in the wave-protected waters behind the reefs and are torn away by occasional inshore storms. Through much of the temperate arid coastal segment, sea-grasses are particularly important in their effect on nearshore sedimentation.

Where the lithified Pleistocene barriers remain untruncated they provide more complete shelter to inshore waters and there are two outstanding examples on the west coast—Shark Bay in the north and the much smaller Cockburn Sound in the south. The peculiar sedimentological environment of Shark Bay, the inner more enclosed reaches of which become very shallow and hypersaline, has been described by B. W. Logan and his colleagues (1970). The deeper but still sheltered northern end is utilized by the small port of Carnarvon, located on the Gascoyne delta, an intermittent supplier of quartz which locally dilutes the ambient carbonate sediments. Cockburn Sound near Perth is sheltered in similar fashion. Rottnest Island, Garden Island and Point Peron represent emerged bits of an old drowned barrier system which, among other things, protects the mouth of the Swan River at Fremantle from the full force of the deep ocean waves (Fairbridge, 1950b).

In many places elsewhere, detached, eroded masses of dune rock have been tied tombolo fashion into the modern coastal outline and continue to influence shore evolution. The biggest examples are along the

Plate 7.3 Point Peron south of Perth, Western Australia. The promontory is formed of old lithified Pleistocene dunes which have been eroded to form offshore reefs and islets. Sea-grasses grow on the sea floor in the shelter of the reefs. *Photo*: A. Shepherd and A. S. Rundle.

west coast of the Eyre Peninsula and the coast around Port Lincoln is especially complex as a result. On a much smaller scale the west coast town of Geraldton lies on a tombolo tied to eroded barrier remnants.

The influence of the coastal limestones extends for great distances inland on many parts of the coast. In the southeastern corner of South Australia the 'ranges' of the Naracoorte district are lines of old lithified dunes formed at sea levels higher than the present. Similar lines of old stranded dunes occur along most of the west coast, and some of the more massive limestones have been quarried and used for building. Especially in the southern part of the west coast they are the site of extensive cave systems such as that at Yallingup.

The fact that the oldest and innermost of the stranded dune ridges are normally siliceous and unconsolidated has often aroused scientific interest. The explanation most generally advanced has been that this is a result of a long period of leaching which has removed the original carbonate; but it may also be that the older shore sediments were originally more siliceous because of their greater contiguity with the quartzose rocks of the shield hinterland. As successive lines of barriers

have been built the supply of quartz would have been much reduced on a coast where few rivers are supplying it in large enough quantities to dilute the carbonate sands coming from seaward. In this context it is notable that in Western Australia the most extensive deposits of heavy minerals, presumed to originate in the older rocks of the hinterland, have been discovered, as behind Dongara, in association with these oldest and innermost shorelines. Iron- and humus-rich hardpans reminiscent of the Pleistocene dunes of the east coast are also to be found here.

The south coast between Cape Leeuwin and the Recherche Archipelago differs from most of this coastal segment in that much more bedrock reaches the coast. Barriers are shorter and smaller and are interrupted by rounded granite headlands. Higher rainfall and higher runoff in the coastal streams has led to more small estuaries and more siliceous shore sediments. However lithified dunes still occur in places, sometimes perched on top of the granite, and drowned lithified barriers occur as reefs in several localities. Further east between Recherche Archipelago and the Head of the Bight, the coastal landscape is dominated

Plate 7.4 Small barrier beaches on the east coast of Joseph Bonaparte Gulf, Northern Territory. Ridges of sand capped by very small dunes lie on a substratum of finer sediments which form extensive tidal plains to seaward and also between the barriers and the mainland behind. *Photo*: L. D. Wright.

by the scarped edge of the almost horizontally bedded Tertiary Nullarbor limestones, the Baxter Cliffs and the Bunda Cliffs being actively attacked by the sea. The Israelite Plain and the Roe Plains lie seaward of similar, but stranded, cliffs and are extensively covered by calcareous dunes, some of which have been lithified (Lowry and Jennings, 1974).

Throughout the temperate arid coastal segment tidal plains are very limited, mainly because of the general lack of estuaries and other inlets and the low tidal range. Much the most extensive areas are in Shark Bay and at the upper ends of the drowned tectonic depressions of Spencer Gulf and Gulf St Vincent, where *Salicornia-Arthrocnemum* salt marsh occurs in association with *Avicennia* mangrove shrubland. Algal mats formed on especially saline surfaces occur as small patches in the southern gulfs but are especially extensive in Shark Bay.

The two South Australian gulfs each comprise an outer section in which there are beaches and small cliffs and an inner or northern section lined by tidal plains with mangroves. Tidal and minor storm surge effects become unusually high for the temperate arid segment. The sediments also become unusually siliceous and may be derived at least in part from the sea floor. Pronounced present-day transport to the north has been well documented at Adelaide.

In general terms it seems likely that the shore sediment system in this segment is at least as inactive as in the temperate humid segment. With few exceptions, such as the Gascoyne, the Murray and some small rivers in the Albany-Esperance area, negligible amounts of material seem to have been brought from landward. The carbonate sediments which make up so much of the shore sand are partly being derived today from biogenic sources but also from the erosion of old lithified carbonate sediments, so that much is being recycled.

Long-term net transport through the Quaternary seems to have been northward along the west coast, as evidenced by the great accumulations represented by the Shark Bay barriers which mirror Fraser Island on the east coast. On the south coast, Lowry and Jennings (1974) noted that there is an intrusion of quartz sand from the west along the limestone coast of the Nullarbor, the effect of which tapers off eastward. These overall directions of movement are what might be expected from a major wave source in the southwest.

It seems likely that low energy offshore areas, especially those lying within the shelter of the lithified Pleistocene barriers, are acting as traps for much of the sediment which is mobile today, although very little loss can result from the infilling of estuaries. Loss by deflation into dunes may also be smaller than on the temperate humid coasts. With some notable exceptions on the south coast, big transgressive dune sheets are less in evidence and this seems linked, at least in part, to the greater difficulty faced by the wind in reactivating older dunes where these have been lithified.

Tropical Arid Coasts

The tropical arid segment from North West Cape to around Broome is very short in comparison with the other three segments which have been defined. It shares many of the attributes of the temperate arid segment and most of its distinctive features stem from distinctly lower energy levels and bigger tidal ranges. Mean wave energy is low and the coast lies behind a very wide shallow shelf. West of Dampier there are many off-lying islands with coral and dune rock reefs which reduce wave effects still further. Mean wind velocities are also low and, all along the coast, dunes rarely exceed much more than 10 m in height. There is a very low overall gradient from hinterland to shelf edge—the antithesis of the situation in the temperate humid segment.

Since this condition has evidently prevailed also in the immediate geological past, the old lithified barrier features, which continue to be found along this coast, are distinctly lower and less bulky than on the temperate arid segment. Where, as around Port Hedland, they are integrated in the present coast, they form reefs or only very low cliffs. Sea cliffs are in fact very little in evidence along these shores.

The larger tidal range has also added to the general impression of flatness by producing wide low gradient beach fronts and extensive tidal plains. Russell and McIntire (1966) have described the nature of these wide beach fronts and the microfeatures associated with them. The tidal plains become progressively more extensive west from the De Grey delta to Exmouth Gulf. They incorporate large areas of bare saline sediments, with some shrubby salt marsh and low *Avicennia-Rhizophora* mangroves. Between the De Grey River and Dampier they lie mostly behind small beach barriers but in the west, as wave energies seem to decrease further in the shelter of the numerous offshore reefs, salt marsh and mangrove fringe extensive sections of the open coast.

East of the De Grey, the Great Sandy Desert meets the coast along the sweep of Eighty Mile Beach. Particularly when viewed from the air the low coastal dunes look astonishingly green and well vegetated. This is because of the presence of a coastal form of the desert grass *Triodia pungens* which is very characteristic of dunes through much of the tropical arid segment (Burbidge, 1944) and provides a further visual contrast with the west coast, where the pioneer dune grass *Spinifex longifolius* is replaced inland by shrubby vegetation (Sauer, 1965). As a general comment, it seems that coastal dunes throughout the more arid half of Australia are well vegetated and it is only in high energy sections of the south coast that extensive free sand masses are to be found. No part of these coasts is as dry as the driest sections of the Atacama and Namib but it may be too that Australian desert plants are peculiarly well adapted to colonize low rainfall dunes.

Biological effects are also well in evidence in the tidal and offshore zones of the tropical arid segment. Coral growth is more luxuriant than on coasts further south. There are numerous patch reefs, and large fringing reefs occur around offshore islands. On mainland shores the geomorphic effect of coral is principally to modify the form of truncated dune rock reefs as happens on the west coast. However the calcareous algae here assume their greatest role as platform builders and the most magnificent algal reefs (albeit on dune rock foundations) are to be found. The Port Hedland algal reef has been described by Russell (1968).

Massive beach rock occurs on sandy shores giving an armour-plated appearance to some stretches of beach. Here and there it has been broken by the big waves of infrequent tropical cyclones and piled into high boulder beaches. It may be that the major effect of cyclone waves is to cause periodic coastal retreat in ways such as this and there is certainly much evidence in the Port Hedland district to support this view. In general, however, the sediment regime appears to be a very inactive one. Inputs must mainly be from reef erosion and biological production, with very small quantities from the Ashburton, Fortescue and De Grey Rivers and there must be very little loss into dunes and inlets. The low mean wave energy and the high proportion of Quaternary sediment which is consolidated, both on the coast and on the sea bed, must also make for minimal transport.

Tropical Humid Coasts

The fourth and last segment to be defined is the longest of all and extends around the northern edge of the continent from Broome to Fraser Island. Its structural diversity gives rise to a great number of different sorts of coastal landscape and yet there are unities of process that distinguish the segment as a whole and cause certain basic associations of landforms to be repeated throughout. In the very broadest terms it is characterized by low to moderate mean wave energies with occasional tropical cyclones bringing very high

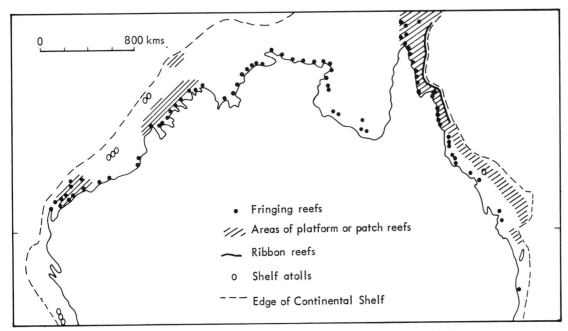

Fig. 7.6 Distribution of recent coral structures (from Fairbridge, 1950a, and various map and photo sources).

energy conditions and storm surges for brief periods; high to moderate tidal ranges; high aggregate and high intensity river discharges with higher sediment loads than elsewhere in Australia; a relative abundance of fine sediments; a varied and aggressive mangrove flora and a great richness of coral reef development.

Bedrock coasts rarely extend for very far, except in the Kimberleys where Precambrian rocks come to the coast almost everywhere and depositional shores are limited to the heads of deep re-entrants. The Kimberley coasts have been little studied but there are reports of well-developed shore platforms from several localities and descriptions of high steep cliffs, although commonly only the lower parts of these may be sheer. In the Darwin-Arnhem Land area and on the east coast of Queensland, rocky shores are intermittent and commonly take the form of sloping vegetated bluffs steepened only near the base by active marine erosion. In many lower-lying sections such as around the Gulf of Carpentaria and in the Darwin district, fossil cemented ironstone or bauxite soil horizons outcrop on the shore to provide miniature cliffs, platforms or reefs.

All these rocky promontories, and even some of the soil horizons, may be colonized by coral and this coastal segment incorporates some of the most prolific coral growth in the world (Fig. 7.6). Fringing reefs occur on parts of the mainland coast in east Queensland north of Cairns and at places along the Kimberley-Darwin-Arnhem Land coasts. They are much more frequent around islands throughout, but especially north of Townsville. The Great Barrier Reefs of Queensland (Maxwell, 1948) comprise a section of about 800 km north of Cairns, in which relatively continuous ribbon reefs near the shelf edge enclose an intensive complex of patch or platform reefs to landward; and a section of about 1,100 km south of Cairns, in which much less continuous and less aligned platform reefs lie further from the mainland coast. Numerous patch and platform reefs are also round off the Kimberley coast. The shallow but muddy Gulf of Carpentaria represents a major hiatus in the pattern of coral reef distribution and only some of the islands there carry fringing reefs.

Except on coral reefs, calcareous algae play a much smaller part in platform modification than they do on the arid coasts and this is linked with the greater rarity of other calcareous rocks along the shore. Beach rocks occur at widely spread localities throughout this coastal segment and are often quite massive, but dune rocks are limited to a few areas of exceptionally lime-rich sand.

The absence of the old lithified barriers which occur on arid coasts and the much greater quantities of sediment actively being supplied by rivers are probably the main reasons why a greater proportion of the coast of the tropical humid segment is of a depositional nature than any other. As Fig. 7.1 indicates, the open coast of the more sheltered gulfs may be formed by tidal plains, at least the outer edges of which are usually lined by mangroves. Much more extensively however, sand beach barriers of varying bulk actually form the shore (Valentin, 1961).

Something of a contrast exists between the northern and eastern coasts in the nature of the barrier and its relation to tidal plain sediments. On depositional shores between Broome and Cape York the rivers bring great quantities of fine material to the coast. Fig. 7.3 shows that about half of Australia's big rivers reach the sea here and that their catchments have high precipitation and high runoff aggregates. The runoff may be of high intensity (Fig. 7.3) and is concentrated in a relatively short wet season during the hotter part of the year, so that very big short-term flows are recorded regularly. At such times the rivers bring down large quantities of sediment, much of which is of clay size. The Ord River for instance has been recorded as carrying loads as high as 250 tonnes of mud per second while in flood. The fine material is deposited between tide-marks to form the extensive clay plains of the estuaries and other quiet water situations (Fig. 7.7) but is also transported in great quantity out on to the wide continental shelves of the Arafura Sea and the Gulf of Carpentaria.

Characteristically the tidal plains of the northern coasts display extensive surfaces of bare saline clay, only small sections of which carry a scanty salt marsh vegetation. Mangroves are confined to the seaward edge or along the banks of rivers and tidal channels. But, this picture is truer of the drier sections such as the southern coasts of the Gulf of Carpentaria and the Fitzroy estuary at King Sound than it is of the Darwin-

Arnhem Land coast and the northern part of Cape York; these, being wetter, have notably more extensive mangrove development. Nowhere in Australia however, not even on the wettest parts of the east Queensland coast, is there true 'high' mangrove such as occurs on some perennially wet equatorial shores.

All these northern coasts appear relatively deficient in quartz sand, so that beach and dune bodies are small. Often, as around much of the Gulf of Carpentaria, they are composed of shell or shell particles and, if dunes are present, they are very low and wooded. The beach and dune barriers are perched as chenier ridges on the bulky clay masses beneath and often form prograded systems in which a series of individual cheniers is interrupted by belts of tidal plain (Galloway, 1970). Some of the tidal plains are inundated relatively rarely at the highest tides but all tend to be extensively submerged during the wet season when, especially in the Gulf of Carpentaria, the coastlands from a peculiar amphibious landscape often accentuated by monsoon winds and cyclonic storm surges which back up the floodwaters coming from landward. The outermost chenier ridge commonly does not occur at the coast but is separated from the sea by a fringe of mangroves. Indeed the situation where mangroves grow seaward of the beach is a frequent one and has been commented on by Jennings and Coventry (1973), who, along with others, have remarked on the apparently paradoxical ability of the plants to survive occasional high wave energy conditions in such situations.

Some sections of the east Queensland coast such as Princess Charlotte Bay and Broad Sound closely resemble this general description of the north-facing coasts and the monograph of Broad Sound by Cook and Mayo (in press) is the most detailed description of this sort of environment. However, because of higher mean wave energies in many places, generally lower tidal ranges and above all greater sand supplies, the relative prominence of tidal plain deposits and barrier bodies is often different. Active sand supply to the coast by rivers draining relatively steep, quartz-rich catchments is probably greater along this coast than along any other in Australia. This is as true of the biggest rivers like the Fitzroy and Burdekin as it is of smaller rivers such as those listed by Bird and Hopley (1969) and Bird (1971). The Burdekin is the greatest sand supplier of all and has built a large delta containing a much greater proportion of coarse sediments than the estuarine deltas of big north coast rivers such as the Ord and Victoria (Hopley, 1970) (Plate 5.1).

The consequences of this greater prevalence of fluvially supplied sand are several. In the first place the mainland beaches of the Queensland east coast are strongly siliceous and contain much smaller quantities of carbonate than might be expected in view of the great abundance of biogenic carbonate on the offshore

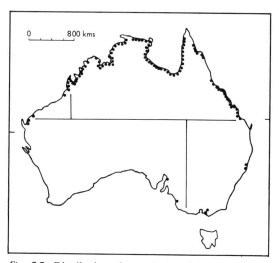

Fig. 7.7 Distribution of coastal clay plains (clayey soils of minimal development and plastic clay soils shown in K. H. Northcote (ed.), *Atlas of Australian Soils*, CSIRO Division of Soils, Melbourne 1960–8).

islands and reefs. One result of this seems to be that beach rocks occur more extensively on the islands than on the continental coast. The greater sand supply has encouraged the development of more massive barriers than further north and these sometimes comprise continuous beach ridge series like those of the south; yet chenier systems, such as occur in Broad Sound, are still frequent. In this respect these coasts are somewhat transitional towards the coasts of the temperate humid segment.

In places a local abundance of sand has led to development of coastal dunes which are unusually bulky for moist tropical coasts. Low wind velocities, limited sand supplies, high humidities and salt encrustation of the beach surface have been the major factors invoked to explain the absence or minimal development of dunes on hot, wet coasts throughout the world. In general the dunes of the Australian tropical humid coast accord well with this conception and take the form of low ridges or platforms, colonized initially by creeping *Ipomoea* and *Spinifex*. But on the east coast of the Cape York Peninsula around Cape Flattery and again around Cape Grenville are large areas of big transgressive dunes much more typical of southern shores and owing their existence, so it appears, to unusually large supplies of shore sand over long periods of time. In many respects they are miniatures of the Fraser Island complex further south.

As a corollary of all this, tidal plains are less extensive on the east coast than on north-facing coasts but more extensive than in the temperate south. Mangrove woodland (Fig. 7.4) occupies the edges and much of the surface, especially in the wettest areas around Cairns and Innisfail and in the most perennially wet areas around Rockhampton (MacNae, 1966). On the coast between and further north in Princess Charlotte Bay there is a greater proportion of bare, saline clay with very limited salt marsh, more closely resembling the southern shore of the Gulf of Carpentaria.

In summary it seems that the sediment system throughout the tropical humid segment differs from all the other three in that there is a much more active supply of sediment from landward, mainly by rivers. On the northern coasts there is a greater proportion of fine materials being supplied than on eastern coasts and on the shore itself this contrast must be exaggerated because the more extensive occurrence of low wave energy environments allows more of the fines to be retained between tide marks. Bedrock coasts are so limited that supplies from cliff erosion must approach zero; and the very small and local contribution made to shore sands by biogenic carbonate in east Queensland strongly suggests that offshore sources are also of very limited importance in the total budget picture. On the other side of the ledger, losses from the sediment system must also be small. Although there may be

some loss of fines to seaward in the rare, very high energy, cyclonic storms, the general effect on coarser material seems to be to move it further inland (for instance Jennings and Coventry, 1973). The small volume of dune sand and the high degree of filling which has been achieved in the estuaries are indications that little shore sediment is being lost by deflation or inlet filling.

There are few indications of extended unidirectional longshore transport in this segment, a situation which is consistent with the generally low mean wave energy and the generally irregular plan of the coast. Even on the east Queensland coast, where a general net movement from south to north can often be deduced, Bird (1971) has shown that many local reversals take place because of coastal configuration. On many shores through this segment, tidal currents are more important in sediment transport than wave-induced currents and beach drifting, and this applies especially of course to the big funnel-shaped re-entrants of the Kimberley region.

CLASSIFICATION AND MANAGEMENT

The broad categorization of the Australian coast into four major segments which has been proposed here and used as a basis for genetic description falls somewhere in scale between the global treatment of Davies (1972) and the provinces of Wright, Coleman and Thom (1973). The four segments are divisible into subsegments, sometimes clearly and sometimes not so clearly. The temperate arid segment for instance seems to subdivide fairly readily into a west coast section, a Cape Leeuwin-Recherche section, a Nullarbor section and a section east of the Bight. Of these four, the last is so similar to the first that they can be thought of as two parts of the same genetic unit. The tropical arid segment splits readily into two halves somewhere to the west of Port Hedland; but the tropical humid segment is more complex. The coasts of the Kimberley block, the Darwin-Arnhem Land coast, the Gulf of Carpentaria and the Pacific coast of Queensland appear to be natural units with much internal homogeneity. The first three differ more from the fourth than they do from each other and are separable on grounds of structure rather than process. Within the temperate humid segment there are well-known differences between the northern and southern sections of the New South Wales coast and something of the special nature of the western Bass Strait coasts has already been mentioned.

Below this level of generalization come the provinces which Wright, Coleman and Thom (1973) delimit between the East Kimberley and Darwin, while at a still lower level are such things as coastal sediment compartments (Davies, 1974). No attempt will be made here to subdivide on these smaller scales. If they are to be defined in a meaningful way, such smaller units need to be defined genetically and in terms of coastal processes and coastal systems. Even at the scale attempted in this chapter, it is obvious that our basic data are unequal and inadequate.

Genetically based schemes of categorization ought not simply to represent academic exercises but should be important to the proper understanding of differences in coastal evolution and therefore basic to management and planning. The temperate humid segment comes much the closest to European experience and historians have speculated on what would have happened in terms of human settlement if it, and not the tropical segments, had been most contiguous with Eurasia. Yet, just as the early land developers discovered that environmental similarities were often more apparent than real, so the understanding of coastal evolution in southeastern Australia has gained more from comparisons made with California than with western Europe. The remaining three coastal segments are even more 'foreign' to European and North American eyes and homologies have to be looked for in other little-researched parts of the world.

The temperate humid segment has more than half the total population of Australia strung out along its length. In management terms it is the most vulnerable and scientifically it has been the most studied (Thom, 1974). The other three segments are much emptier of human occupation and much less developed, but we also know less about them.

The broad generalizations attempted here need testing by further detailed work in representative environments, but fundamental differences in the nature of sediment systems and sediment budgets already appear evident. The tropical humid segment may be the only one in which there is a strong accession of new sediment to the coast and even here it may be only on the east Queensland coast that this sediment is sufficiently coarse to be of significance in beach replenishment. There is evidence in this segment for an excess of input over output and for barrier progradation continuing much longer into the late Holocene and in many cases down to the present day. By contrast in the temperate humid segment the phase of progradation which began with the initiation of the present shore about 6,000 years ago seems largely, if not entirely, to have come to an end. The shore sand resource is essentially a fossil one which on balance is probably being reduced, most obviously by deflation inland. In the temperate arid segment too, shore sediments must be regarded as essentially fossil, although in this case much is being recirculated after having been temporarily locked up in the form of beach and dune rocks. It is interesting to speculate that whereas on the humid coasts redistribution of older sands was comparatively rapid, on the arid

coasts there has been a distinct time-lag caused by the sea and the wind having to attack lithified materials. The result may have been that whereas barriers prograded rapidly in the east through recirculation of older Pleistocene material, similar progradation in the west has been spread more evenly through the late Holocene. In this respect it is notable that the systems of low, numerous, parallel sand beach ridges which are so characteristic of apparently rapid postglacial progradation east of the Murray are rare to the west, where more isolated and more massive frontal dunes are the rule.

In the tropical arid segment the long-term loss of sand to the shore system has been proportionately even greater with extensive lithification not only of beach and dune sands but also of sand on the shelf, where extensive submarine 'limestone pavements' are to be found (Jones, 1973). This, taken into consideration with the low mean energy levels, must have led to a very low rate of recycling of fossil sediments and compounded the apparently very inactive sediment system on these coasts.

ACKNOWLEDGEMENTS Joe Jennings, Roger MacLean, Bruce Thom and Don Wright took time to read a draft of this chapter and to suggest improvements. The author is grateful to them for this help but they must not be held responsible for the various generalizations made. These represent one person's view at the time of writing.

REFERENCES

Bird, E. C. F. (1967), 'Coastal lagoons of southeastern Australia' in J. N. Jennings and J. A. Mabbutt (eds), *Landform Studies from Australia and New Guinea*, Australian National University Press, Canberra, pp. 365–85.

——(1971), 'The origin of beach sediments on the North Queensland coast', *Earth Sci. J. (N. Z.)*, 5, 95–105.

Bird, E. C. F. and Hopley, D. (1969), 'Geomorphological features on a humid tropical sector of the Australian coast', *Aust. Geogr. Stud.*, 7, 89–108.

Burbridge, N. (1944), 'Ecological notes on the vegetation of the 80-mile Beach', *J. Proc. R. Soc. West Aust.*, 28, 157–64.

Coaldrake, J. E. (1962), 'The coastal dunes of southern Queensland', *Proc. R. Soc. Queensland*, 72, 101–16.

Cook, P. J. and Mayo, W. (in press), 'Sedimentology and Holocene history of a tropic estuary (Broad Sound, Queensland)', *Bur. Min. Res. Aust. Bull.*, 170.

Davies, J. L. (1972), *Geographical Variation in Coastal Development*, Oliver and Boyd, Edinburgh.

——(1974), 'The coastal sediment compartment', *Aust. Geogr. Stud.*, 12, 139–51.

Fairbridge, R. W. (1950a), 'Recent and Pleistocene coral reefs of Australia', *J. Geol.*, 58, 330–401.

——(1950b), 'The geology and geomorphology of Point Peron, Western Australia', *J. Proc. R. Soc. West. Aust.*, 34, 35–72.

Hails, J. R. (1968), 'The late Quaternary history of part of the mid-north coast, New South Wales, Australia', *Trans. Inst. Brit. Geogr.*, 44, 133–49.

Hopley, D. (1970), *The Geomorphology of the Burdekin Delta, North Queensland*, Dept Geogr. James Cook Univ., Monogr. Series No. 1.

Jennings, J. N. (1965), 'Further discussion on factors affecting coastal dune formation in the tropics', *Aust. J. Sci.*, 28, 166–7.

Jennings, J. N. and Bird, E. C. F. (1967), 'Regional geomorphological characteristics of some Australian estuaries' in G. H. Lauff (ed.), *Estuaries*, Amer. Ass. Adv. Sci., pp. 121–8.

Jennings, J. N. and Coventry, R. J. (1973), 'Structure and texture of a gravelly barrier island in the Fitzroy estuary Western Australia and the role of mangroves in the shore dynamics', *Marine Geol.*, 15, 145–68.

Jones, H. A. (1973), 'Marine geology of the Northwest Australian continental shelf', *Bur. Min. Res. Aust. Bull.*, 136.

Logan, B. W., Davies, G. R., Read, J. F. and Cebulski, D. E. (1970), 'Carbonate sedimentation and environments, Shark Bay, Western Australia', *Amer. Assoc. Petrol. Geol. Mem.*, No. 13.

Lowry, D. and Jennings, J. N. (1974), 'The Nullarbor karst, Australia', *Z. f. Geomorph.*, 18, 35–81.

MacNae, W. (1966), 'Mangroves in eastern and southern Australia', *Aust. J. Bot.*, 14, 67–104.

Maxwell, W. G. H. (1968), *Atlas of the Great Barrier Reef*, Elsevier, Amsterdam.

Russell, R. J. (1968), 'Algal flats of Port Hedland, Western Australia', *Coast. Stud. Bull.*, 2, 45–55.

Russell, R. J. and McIntire, W. G. (1966), 'Australian tidal flats', *Lousiana State Univ., Coastal Studies Series*, No. 13.

Sauer, J. D. (1965), 'Geographic reconnaissance of Western Australian seashore vegetation', *Aust. J. Bot.*, 13, 39–69.

Thom, B. G. (1965), 'Late Quaternary coastal morphology of the Port Stephens-Myall Lakes area, New South Wales', *J. Proc. R. Soc. N.S.W.*, 98, 23–6.

——(1974), 'Coastal erosion in eastern Australia', *Search*, 5, 198–209.

Valentin, H. (1961), 'The central west coast of Cape York peninsula', *Aust. Geogr.*, 8, 65–72.

Wright, L. D., Coleman, J. M. and Thom, B. G. (1973), 'Geomorphic coastal variability, northwestern Australia', *Coast. Stud. Bull.*, 7, 35–64.

8 SOILS

C. G. STEPHENS

The 1920s proved revolutionary in the study of soils in Australia and provided the impetus for subsequent field and laboratory investigations which have generated increasingly detailed information on the nature, classification and utilization of the soils of this continent. Before that time the limited interest in soils in Australia was almost entirely pragmatic: it was directed mainly towards the elementary classification of land into three categories termed first, second and third class, variably based on an assessment of the broad floristic composition and apparent vigour of the many different associations of the indigenous vegetation and on a rough appreciation of the texture and superficial drainage of the surface soil, with occasional consideration of the parent rock. Likewise Departments of Agriculture had already become interested in the amounts of the plant nutrients nitrogen, phosphorus, potassium and calcium present in the soils of arable areas, thus seeking a basis for specifying the fertilizer requirements of the various cultivated crops.

It is noteworthy that the first scientific publication on the soils of Australia, *The Soils of Australia in Relation to Vegetation and Climate*, by Prescott (1931) who introduced modern soil science to this country, provided both a link with the earlier preoccupation with the indigenous vegetation and a gateway to future progress based on an appraisal of a number of physical and chemical features of the full soil section, the soil profile, and the relationships of these morphological characteristics, individually and collectively, to the various environmental factors, particularly climate. This new emphasis on climate as a factor of soil formation, responsible in some large measure for the development of the morphological expression of the physical and chemical characteristics of the soil, as distinct from its role, through rainfall, as a provider of soil moisture required for plant growth, constituted the vital initial step which has developed into a systematic study of the soils of Australia in relation not only to climate but also to several other environmental factors.

This early emphasis on climate as the most important if not completely dominant factor followed essentially the same finding of a strong geographical zonal relationship between soil profile forms and their extent on the one hand and climatic features such as rainfall and temperature on the other, first made by Russian workers late in the nineteenth century, and confirmed elsewhere in the early twentieth century by other North American and European scientists. Although climatic zonality is extremely strongly expressed in European Russia, the existence of variably atypical soils within and overlapping the various zones was immediately recognized and these, according to their extent and degree of morphological variation from the zonal patterns, were termed intrazonal and azonal soils. This complex pattern of soil distribution has been recognized almost universally and in fact is usually more complicated than in the type area, nowhere more so than in Australia.

The recognition of intrazonal and azonal soils led inevitably to the realization that soils are the product of and necessarily relate to several environmental features, the factors of soil formation. Dokuchaiev, the pioneer Russian worker, recognized them as climate, organisms, substratum and age. In North America Jenny (1941) specified them as climate, organisms, relief, parent material and time, and treated them as independent variables. In Australia, Stephens (1947) added groundwater to this list and emphasized that, except for time, the factors are not independent of each other and that their interacting cumulative effects are integrated against time.

During the years which have passed since Prescott's first publication it has become increasingly apparent that Australian soils exhibit both a wide variation in the preciseness of their zonal distribution and a number of unusual morphological features, either not evident or only rarely seen in the soils of other continents.

The High Moor Peats, the Podzols and Podzolic Soils, the Red-brown Earths, the Desert Loams and the Desert Sandhills all occupy relatively precisely definable climatic zones ranging from alpine to desert areas (see map inside front cover). Somewhat less zonal distribution is exhibited by a range of typically shallow soils developed on limestones. These vary from a complex of Rendzinas, Terra Rossas and Brown

Forest Soils within the humid and subhumid zones to more clearly zonally defined soils in the semi-arid and desert regions, the Grey Calcareous Soils, and the Grey, Red and Brown Calcareous Desert Soils. Much less precise zonality is shown by the Krasnozems, the Black Earths, the Grey and Brown Soils of Heavy Texture, the Arid Red Earths, the Solonized Brown Soils and the Solonetz and related Solonized Soils. Even less zonality is displayed by the Lateritic Podzolic Soils, the Lateritic Red Earths and the Desert Sandplain Soils, all of which contain varying amounts of concretionary laterite and deeply weathered kaolinitic clay subsoils.

Equally remarkable are the atypical morphological features of some of these soils. The zonally distributed Podzols and Podzolic Soils, when compared to their readily recognizable counterparts in other continents, show an unusual paucity of both fresh and decomposed surface litter and a somewhat compensating greater depth of penetration of organic matter in the surface soil. Deeper in the profile of the Podzols the organic accumulation in the subsoil hardpan appears quite normal. The Stony Desert Tableland Soils of the central arid region appear to have no complete morphological counterpart in the arid regions of other lands, the one noticeable feature in common being the presence of a stony pavement of wind-polished pebbles and boulders which however in Australia are uniquely composed of one special rock type, silcrete. Additionally in the Australian arid region generally the Desert Sandhills exhibit almost universally an extreme redness of colour uncommon in other desert areas.

A unique but extensive Great Soil Group which occurs almost exclusively in the arid region of central Western Australia is the Red and Brown Hardpan Soil. This acid soil with a predominantly siliceous subsoil pan of extreme hardness appears to be completely out of climatic context. Its occurrence in any other part of Australia is practically unknown and no reference to similar soils in other continents has been encountered.

Another common feature of Australian soils, especially of those which are clay textured throughout the profile, but extending to some sharply differentiated soils with dense clay subsoils, such as Solodized Solonetz, is the widespread occurrence of sharply undulating to gentle surface microrelief known as gilgai. These microrelief surfaces are known in other lands but appear to be unduly common and to affect an unusually wide range of soils in Australia.

PROCESSES INVOLVED IN SOIL FORMATION

The factors of soil formation briefly dealt with above are involved in soil development by participation in a number of processes which not only change the parent material but continue to modify the soil profile as a slowly reacting dynamic body. It is useful to outline and interrelate these processes prior to discussing their involvement in developing and modifying the soils of Australia (Fig. 8.1).

Physical weathering, because it is a function of temperature gradient, is greatest on bare rock. The maximum and minimum temperatures involved in each effective temperature change may occur daily or seasonally and their effectiveness is increased if the gradient includes freezing and thawing. Physical weathering continues to operate at the soil-rock interface and on rock fragments within any accumulated mantle of soil but at a diminished rate according to warming temperature gradients with depth in the profile.

Chemical weathering increases more than proportionally with rise in temperature, but in most of its many varied forms it requires the presence of water and/or air. Consequently chemical weathering attains its greatest rate in wet tropical regions and in those parts of soil profiles which are well drained but remain moist for the longest periods. Certain forms of weathering such as laterization require alternating conditions of oxidation and reduction, most commonly generated by a seasonally fluctuating water-table. Rocks containing high proportions of feldspathic and ferromagnesian minerals are much more susceptible to rapid chemical weathering than those high in quartz. Limestones present a special case as they are very susceptible to removal by solution in water containing carbon dioxide, either rainfall or groundwater.

Leaching of the soil profile is mostly dependent on rainfall but the effectiveness of this is reduced by high temperatures and low relative humidities. These increase both direct evaporation from the soil surface and transpiration by plants. Thus the boundaries of zonal soils correlate better with functions of rainfall and evapotranspiration than with rainfall alone. Leaching of the profile is responsible for the translocation of both colloidal and ionic mobilized materials such as clay, organic matter, lime and soluble salts such as gypsum and sodium choloride. These may be taken to lower positions in the soil profile and deposited there or in the case of the ionic materials removed from the profile by drainage. Such losses by drainage are only possible where there is sufficient water to raise the whole profile to beyond its water-holding capacity and to provide for transpiration by plants. Such a condition may be virtually continuous in high rainfall areas or intermittent where rainfall is seasonal or irregular, but adequate to saturate the profile temporarily. In both cases the soil profile needs to be porous enough to allow percolation to lower levels, otherwise temporary or permanent water-tables will build up in the profile.

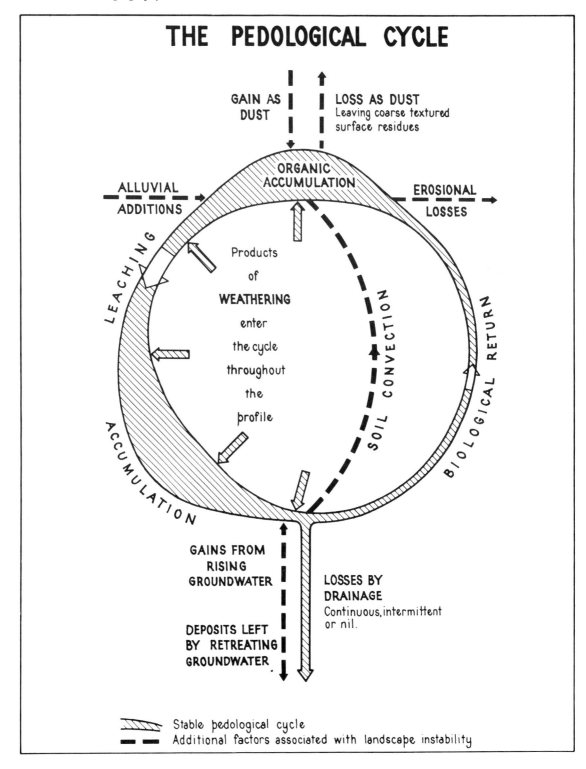

THE PEDOLOGICAL CYCLE

GAIN AS DUST

LOSS AS DUST
Leaving coarse textured surface residues

ALLUVIAL ADDITIONS

ORGANIC ACCUMULATION

EROSIONAL LOSSES

LEACHING

Products
of
WEATHERING
enter
the cycle
throughout
the
profile

SOIL CONVECTION

BIOLOGICAL RETURN

ACCUMULATION

GAINS FROM RISING GROUNDWATER

DEPOSITS LEFT BY RETREATING GROUNDWATER.

LOSSES BY DRAINAGE
Continuous, intermittent or nil.

Stable pedological cycle
Additional factors associated with landscape instability

Where water-tables occur in the soil, either perched within the profile or continuous with regional groundwater below, there is usually some seasonal movement of the phreatic surface. The resulting alternating conditions of oxidation and reduction due to the wetting and drying of the relevant part of the soil profile are mostly accompanied by the development of ferruginous, manganiferous or calcareous nodules and by sharply contrasting bright and dull mottling of the soil colour. Where such waterlogging is prolonged or permanent the mottling is replaced by a more general greyness and occasionally by a dull blue-green colour. These characteristics, together with peat accumulation where the soil is almost permanently wet throughout the profile, are characteristic features of the so-called hydromorphic soils.

Soils often receive additions of extraneous materials to their surfaces. These include cyclic salt in rain or atmospheric suspension, dust derived mainly from more or less distant arid areas, atmospheric nitrate from thunderstorms, and most commonly deposition of soil, gravel, sands and clays from superficial floodwaters resulting from erosional runoff from adjacent land. The dust and erosional deposits may be gradually incorporated in the soil by biological action, remain as a surface veneer, or completely bury the soil below and become the parent material of a new soil.

In contrast to both aeolian and fluviatile additions, soils also suffer corresponding losses, both normal and accelerated, from the surface. Deflation of dust from the immediate surface of the finer-textured arid soils is a normal phenomenon which is accelerated in times of drought and by the grazing of the associated vegetation. In periods of high wind speed and turbulence the dust is carried great distances and may be deposited on quite different soils elsewhere, often as muddy rain. The removal of finer material as dust naturally leaves a coarser fraction behind as a surface veneer of sand and gravel. Where surfaces are naturally sandy, or rendered sandy by deflation, local redistribution by wind action gives rise to a pattern of sand dunes. Surface losses by water erosion affect a wider range of soils extending from the humid zone to arid regions. Normal erosion consists of the very slow removal of small amounts of surface soil, more particularly on sloping sites and when the surface cover is depleted by drought. Such erosion is accelerated by grazing and cultivation and under these conditions may be accompanied by gully erosion which forms an extension and elaboration of the normal stream pattern.

The soil forms a substrate to much of the activity of the biosphere. Plants especially, but many animals and insects, use the soil in ways vital to their growth and survival. Thus the soil is involved in the biological cycle and is in turn affected by it. Most vegetative growth depends on the soil for water and nutrients which are extracted by the network of roots that often penetrate to considerable depths. The translocation of the nutrients to the aerial parts of the plants and their return to the soil, mainly by leaf fall and decomposition, supplemented by animal and insect consumption, make up part of an elaborate cycle vital to the development of organic matter in the soil profile, mostly in the surface soil. Soil-inhabiting insects and animals also take part in a wide variety of activities such as burrowing, mound building, root destruction etc., which all influence the development of some of the physical and chemical features of the profile and often give rise to sharply different soil conditions on a very local scale.

The common presence of microrelief features in the profiles of many Australian soils noted above is partly dependent on their plastic properties, especially of those with a high clay content. It is this rheological property of fine-textured soils that makes them subject to the degree of convection necessary for the disruption of the surface soil by the upwelling of the clay subsoil.

These soil-forming processes are summarized and integrated in a simplified manner in Fig. 8.1 which illustrates how they unite to constitute the pedological cycle. Only some of the immediate soil components of the largely extraneous biological cycle are included. The diagram exemplifies the dynamic nature of the soil as a natural body within an environment which may

---

Fig. 8.1 This cyclic diagram illustrates both the normal processes associated with soil profile development under a relatively stable environment and the additional processes imposed on the soil profile where the environment is less stable due either to natural occurrences or to activities associated with land use.

The 'normal' processes found under stable conditions, leaching, accumulation of clay and other materials, weathering throughout the profile, losses by drainage from the system, organic accumulation in the surface and the upward movement of plant nutrients and actual soil materials, is shown in the hachured part of the diagram. The processes associated with less stable conditions, alluvial and aeolian additions and losses, soil convection giving rise to surface microrelief, and groundwater alternations due to natural or artificial causes, are illustrated by heavy broken lines. Alluvial and aeolian activity and groundwater alterations can be radically accelerated by man's activities but there is no substantial evidence of this affecting soil convection, although altered surface configuration of the soil and distortion of the soil profile can be caused by excessive depletion of groundwater. Unstable soil conditions associated with steep slopes, involving downhill creep of the soil mantle, which takes many forms and is accelerated by excessive moisture, also occur but cannot be illustrated in the diagram in its present form.

impose changes from without on a differentiated soil mass within which soil-forming processes are still operating.

DEVELOPMENTS IN SOIL CLASSIFICATION

One of the features of the Australian revolution in soil science in the 1920s was the introduction of new concepts in soil classification together with a new terminology for the taxonomic classes involved and the adoption of names, some already established overseas, for broad largely zonal groups of soils which became widely known as Great Soil Groups. Predominantly following North American developments, both broader and more detailed classes were established as part of the taxonomic framework, the latter as Soil Series, Types and Phases being used extensively in detailed soil surveys related mainly to agricultural, pastoral and sylvicultural land-use developments and the problems thereof. A convention of describing the soil profile in terms of *A* (eluvial), *B* (illuvial), and *C* (weathering) horizons, together with other ancillary symbols, was also established early and has persisted with but minor modifications until the present time.

The development of greatest geographical significance has been the increased precision in the definition of the Great Soil Groups, these now numbering over forty compared to the original ten Major Soil Groups mapped by Prescott. This has resulted from some changes in the basis of definition and a searching for a greater degree of coherence of the characteristics of the soils included within each group, that is, a greater concentration on morphology and its range of variation and less attention to presumed or inferred genesis. Successive soil maps of Australia have reflected these changes by exhibiting much greater detail both in geographical distribution and in the legend, but the former has also been accentuated by greater accuracy in the mapping of boundaries made possible by the increasing use of aerial photographs and base maps derived therefrom.

In several countries in recent years a number of attempts have been made to develop new systems of soil classification, avoiding in varying degree the interpretative genetic aspects of the morphological approach. So far these new systems have reached little or no common ground; but that developed by Northcote (1965) in Australia, based purely on the physical and physico-chemical properties of the different parts of the profile, has been used as a basis for the compilation of an *Atlas of Australian Soils* (1960 et seq.) and has shown considerable utility in agronomic and other land-use investigation. *A Handbook of Australian Soils* (Stace *et al.*, 1968) deals in detail with the features and relationships of both systems as they have been used in Australia. Forty-three Great Soil Groups are listed in the handbook, with detailed

descriptions of their morphology and colour photographs of typical profiles. Any information about a soil is of very limited value without knowledge of the distribution of that soil. The basic method of conveying such information is to present it in relation to an appropriate unit of a classification and to show the distribution of that unit on a soil map. The units most commonly used in Australia have been the broadly defined Great Soil Groups on small-scale continental or regional maps and Series, Types and Phases either individually or as soil associations on larger-scale detailed district maps.

Soil boundaries, which are basic to mapping at any scale, vary from completely diffuse to sharply evident. Where changes are diffuse, any boundary line separating two classes of soil is arbitrary, but gains in realism and accuracy with increasing soil inflection. The sharpest boundaries are usually those associated with changes in parent material, and become increasingly diffuse with changes in relief, groundwater and climate. Although vegetation distribution has a marked correlation with soil occurrence it is often influenced by other factors such as aspect and ecotone transitions which can greatly alter such a relationship.

The strong interrelationship of soils, parent material and relief facilitates regional and continental mapping at the Great Soil Group level. Individual geomorphic units on a given parent material in an area of relatively uniform climate carry a consistent pattern of soils. These may be mapped either as an association or the dominant soils selected for presentation on a map. In effect the different geomorphic and petrologic units determine most mapping boundaries.

MAJOR AUSTRALIAN SOILS: THEIR MORPHOLOGY, GENESIS, GEOMORPHIC SETTING AND UTILIZATION

In the following discussion the more closely related groups of soils are considered together so that the significance of common or similar morphological features of the different soils can be linked with the geomorphic and other genetic factors of the environment. Because of their varied nature, widespread but broken occurrence, and lack of significant morphological development, alluvial and skeletal soils are not dealt with, except incidentally, nor are a number of less important Great Soil Groups of limited occurrence.

The Soils of Alpine Areas

These consist of Moor Peats and Alpine Humus Soils. They occur with some variation due mainly to aspect at elevations greater than 900 metres in the mountains of southern New South Wales, and eastern Victoria, and 800 metres in Tasmania (Plate 8.1). On south-facing slopes, especially in narrow valleys, the limits are lower in each case. Rainfall which varies from about 750 mm to more than 2,500 mm is not greater than in other areas where Podzols, Podzolic Soils, and Krasnozems occur, but in the alpine areas there is regular winter snow accumulation and temperatures are generally low. At 1,500 metres on Mt Kosciusko in southern New South Wales the mean maximum and minimum temperatures for July, the coldest month, are 4° C and -4° C respectively, and the average precipitation including the snow equals 1,200 mm of rain per year.

The physical features of the alpine regions owe their present expression to Pleistocene glaciations followed by normal erosion in Recent times. The primary sculpturing effects of the glacial periods are much more evident in Tasmania than in Victoria and New South Wales. The Tasmanian mountains and plateaux exhibit numerous occurrences of moraines, cirques, glacial lakes and tarns, solifluction deposits and extensive boulder fields.

The Moor Peats occur on both concave and gently convex surfaces in the higher and wetter situations, and the Alpine Humus Soils together with large areas of bare rock and boulder scree make up the balance of the alpine soil landscape. Coarse mineral and rock fragments evident in the less organic parts of the soil profiles and the low amounts of inorganic material in solution in the water which drains from the alpine areas show that physical weathering is very important in these soils. However the extreme acidity of the soils indicates rapid cation losses in the drainage water, and thin ferruginous pans in the deeper parts of some Alpine Humus Soils formed on solifluction deposits in Tasmania indicate chemical activity sufficient to mobilize and redeposit iron. The accumulation of large amounts of organic matter in both soils is due to the low temperature of the environment restricting decomposition of the plant debris shed by the very varied alpine flora to a rate even less than its slow rate of production.

The high water-holding capacity and the porous nature of these soils is of critical importance in controlling the rate of release of water to the streams which drain the alpine regions. These are a source of a large proportion of the water used for irrigation outside the mountain regions themselves, and for hydroelectric power development. Without proper protection of these special soils from erosion, runoff would be extremely rapid from the steep slopes and areas of bare rock. The complete preservation of the soils is essential and to this end a steady reduction in the use of the alpine areas for seasonal grazing of cattle and sheep, with its ancillary burning, is now taking place. The alpine areas are also being used increasingly for recreation purposes.

The Leached Soils of the Humid Regions
These consist principally of Podzols, Podzolic and Solodic Soils, Krasnozems and Yellow Earths, with very limited areas of other soils such as Swamps, Fens, Euchrozems, Red Earths, etc.

The more humid areas of southern, eastern and southwestern Australia and a small portion of the wetter northern part of the Northern Territory are dominated by leached, strongly to weakly acid soils. These regions are characterized by forest formations which vary widely in composition and form, from tropical and temperate rainforest to sclerophyll forests and savannah woodlands. Topography is widely variable. Parent materials cover the complete range of texture and base saturation, with the more basic igneous rocks, such as basalt, exercising strong control on the development of special forms of soil morphology.

Peaty Podzols occur exclusively in Tasmania particularly in the perhumid and cold southwestern quarter. These soils have developed predominantly but not exclusively on quartzitic rocks and the detritus therefrom. There is also a very close association with a particular plant, Button-grass, the cyperaceous *Gymnoschoenus sphaerocephalus*, which is practically monospecific in many sites, especially on valley floors where the water-table is at or near the surface for the longest periods, and where the peaty surface horizon is deepest.

The non-peaty Podzols have a wider distribution and also occur generally but not exclusively on coarse-textured and siliceous parent materials. Where a water-table is also associated with these conditions, Groundwater Podzols with more organic, more ferruginous, and denser B horizons are formed. In both cases a common parent material is redistributed siliceous sand produced by the complete leaching of the calcium carbonate from the fragmented shell lime of the older calcareous coastal dunes and their intervening swales. These older dune materials frequently abut younger dunes still largely retaining the comminuted shell fragments which makes them highly calcareous, up to 80 per cent $CaCO_3$ and more.

The various Podzolic Soils, Grey-brown, Brown, Red and Yellow, and the Meadow or Gley Podzolic Soils, together with variable proportions of Solodic Soils, occur generally on somewhat finer-textured materials but embrace the coarser ones where rainfall is less and presumably unable to form Podzols. Where groundwater occurs, sometimes in winter rainfall areas even on steep slopes, Meadow Podzolic Soils prevail, generally in a pattern mixed with other more freely drained Podzolic Soils. The widespread presence of Solodic Soils almost throughout the Podzolic Soil zone, and extending into drier areas, indicates an earlier and possibly continuing influence of soluble salts in the formation of the soil pattern.

Krasnozems are found on basalts generally, and in

Plate 8.1   High moor plateau at about 1,250 metres above sea level on the Hartz Mountains in southern Tasmania. Characteristic are the rocky summits separated by extensive open areas of High Moor Peats with their dense and low vegetative cover.

tropical areas on a few other sufficiently ferruginous
and feldspathic rocks. The controlling factor giving
rise to Krasnozems and the closely related Red
Earths and Euchrozems, all three so strikingly different
from other leached soils, is clearly the capacity of the
parent material to provide sufficient free ferric oxide by
weathering to keep the soil mass in a flocculated state.
The resulting great porosity assists cation removal
but the flocculation resists the dispersion and eluviation
of clay.

In some areas Krasnozems have been affected by
groundwater, most often with a strong lateral component. This has caused the formation of horizons of
laterite and of lower mottled and pallid clays, all of
variable thickness.

The Yellow Earths which occur with increasing
frequency towards the subtropical and tropical areas
have characteristics intermediate between the Krasnozems on the one hand and the Podzolic Soils on the
other. They show some degree of profile differentiation

in the upper horizons but little in the middle and lower
parts. They are predominantly yellow in colour but
merge into Grey Earths. These two soils show evidence
of both eluviation and flocculation, but whether these
processes took place simultaneously or separately
has not been resolved.

Podzols and Podzolic Soils together with associated
areas of Solodic Soils have been used extensively in
southern Australia for sown pastures of annual or
perennial species, depending on the duration of the
season of available moisture. These soils are also used
for horticultural purposes, particularly for pome
fruits, and for forest plantations, especially of *Pinus
radiata*. In more northerly areas sugarcane is sometimes
grown on them, but their use is largely restricted to the
grazing of natural pastures by beef cattle. In all cases
the Podzolic Soils have proved superior to the Podzols
and the Solodic Soils. Although practically universal
responses to superphosphate and very frequent responses to one or more of the trace elements copper, zinc,

Plate 8.2 Sugar cane fields on Krasnozem Soils near Childers in Queensland. Soil conservation measures, evident in the photograph, and large quantities of artifical fertilizers are employed so as to obtain and hold maximum yields on these favourably structured soils.

molybdenum, and boron, and to sulphur, have been obtained on all three soils, particularly in the more intensively developed southern and western areas, the Podzolic Soils because of their more moisture retentive but moderately freely draining clay subsoils have always performed the most satisfactorily. The most extensive use of Podzols, Podzolic and Solodic Soils has been for pastures based on several varieties of subterranean clover, *Trifolium subterraneum*, usually top-dressed annually with superphosphate. This form of development has increased stock carrying capacity severalfold and built up soil fertility to the stage where increasing use is being made of arable crops, such as potatoes and cereals, to take advantage of the enhanced nitrogen status. After a protracted period of grazing all three soils exhibit an uneven farm and district incidence of potassium deficiency, but the correction of this is straightforward once it has been recognized.

The Krasnozems, red, deep, friable clay soils, usually of moderate acidity, are amongst the most fertile of the naturally well-drained soils of Australia. They were originally densely forested, but, with little proper utilization of their fine timber resources, these soils were rapidly cleared and converted to intense forms of agriculture ranging from perennial pastures and temperate fodder, vegetable and grain crops in southern areas to widespread sugar, maize and peanut production in tropical and subtropical localities (Plate 8.2). The initial fertility of these soils, which was high, declined quite rapidly and they have a restricted response to superphosphate due to a high rate of reversion of phosphorus to less available forms. They respond widely to potash fertilizers and, in limited areas where they are more acid, to molybdenum. Where steep slopes and marginal climatic conditions occur, as in some parts of New South Wales, Victoria and Tasmania, small areas of these soils, formerly used for agriculture, have been planted to forests of *Pinus radiata* and other species. However, despite their limitations, including a somewhat difficult fertilizer economy, these soils retain their position amongst the most productive in Australia.

Other very fertile soils of much lesser extent, occurring mostly within the humid regions, are many areas of Alluvial Soils, Acid Swamp Soils and Fen Peats. The Alluvial Soils vary widely in their morphological features but are generally porous and fertile. They are used for a wide range of crops, usually those demanding intense plant husbandry, such as hops, vegetables, tree fruits, and sugar cane. They are often irrigated and, because they occupy the lowest terraces adjacent to rivers, this is usually either by channel diversion of the river or low lift pumping therefrom. Their greatest disability is proneness to flooding at times of high river levels.

In numerous areas of occluded drainage swamps of very variable size occur. In the main they consist of acid peats over a variety of subsoils. The water-table, unless controlled by artificial drainage, is usually at or near the surface. In a proportion of cases Acid Swamp Soils contain such quantities of sulphides, such as marcasite, in the profile that artificial drainage with its consequent increase in oxidation in the lower part of the profile causes extreme acidity to develop, reaction in some cases falling as low as pH 2. The soils are thus rendered sterile.

In a restricted number of cases, more commonly near the coastline in northwestern Tasmania and southeastern South Australia, the basement of the areas of occluded drainage is calcareous and the telluric water alkaline. Under these conditions neutral to alkaline Fen Soils, most often peats, accumulate. They show some variation in the structural character of the peat according to their relationship to the height of the groundwater and the associated vegetation. Coarse fibrous peats occupy the most depressed wetter areas growing sedges and rushes, and granular peats are located on the slightly more elevated and better-drained situations carrying dense thickets of tea-trees (*Melaleuca* and *Leptospermum* spp.). Where fens have been reclaimed by drainage, clearing and cultivation, the fibrous types of peats alter quite rapidly to a granular structure and so obliterate the differences seen under virgin conditions.

Although there are other minor agricultural activities, the drained Acid Swamps and Fen Peats are used principally for the growing of high-class pastures of perennial species which are used for the grazing of dairy cows at very high carrying capacities, often over two beasts per hectare.

Lateritic Soils of Old Landscapes
These consist of Lateritic Podzolic Soils, Lateritic Red Earths, Desert Sandplain Soils and Calcareous Lateritic Soils.

The Lateritic Podzolic Soils and the Lateritic Red Earths, whose lower mottled and pallid zone horizons often exhibit a great depth of kaolinitic weathering, occur on a wide range of original parent materials over an extremely wide humid to semi-arid climatic range. Often capped by their lateritic horizon in a state of disintegration, they lie on residual landscape surfaces, are acid in reaction and very low in exchangeable cations. Both soils occur in northern and eastern areas but only Lateritic Podzolic Soils occur in the southern

and southwestern parts of the continent. They are clearly the product of an earlier more widespread humid climate, of shallower groundwater and of more subdued relief than prevails today. The bulk of the available evidence indicates that they were formed principally late in Tertiary times, mostly in the Pliocene, but much soil survey data has shown that smaller occurrences located on a later series of surfaces belong to the Pleistocene. This topographic complexity is in accord with the findings of Lake (1890) who, during a geological survey around the type locality at Angadipuram in southern India, showed that differences in nature, age, and physiographic association are a feature of laterite.

The Desert Sandplain Soils of the arid areas appear to have had a similar origin to the Lateritic Podzolic and Red Earth Soils. Now found exclusively in desertic environments they nevertheless show lateritic gravels overlying mottled and pallid kaolinitic zones. The surfaces of these formations have been modified very markedly by deflationary action, the residual coarse-textured material often being built into dune-like features of low relief, and the complementary stripped areas showing disintegrated laterite, often pisolitic gravel, as a widespread surface pavement. In some areas, notably in the Gibson Desert in central Western Australia, this surface gravel is so massive, abundant, and of such extent, that it has given rise to the term 'stony desert' for a large part of that region.

Almost throughout the regions where laterite occurs, but principally in the drier areas, a small but noticeable fraction of the lateritic profiles is found to contain moderately large amounts of lime. In these Calcareous Lateritic Soils the lime appears either as a coating on the nodules or as a filling in the cavities of the laterite horizon or more diffusely in the mottled and pallid zones below. These occurrences of lime are attributed to either the addition of aeolian calcareous material, or more probably the invasion of the profile by calcareous groundwater for which there is corroborative evidence in other soils and in abandoned spring deposits in parts of the arid regions.

In the moister areas of southern and southwestern Australia Lateritic Podzolic Soils are used most widely for sown pastures of both perennial and annual species of grasses and clovers for sheep and cattle grazing. Almost totally unproductive without fertilizers they respond dramatically to superphosphate and often to molybdenum. Frequently deficiencies of potassium, copper, zinc and manganese also occur. Where they extend in large measure into the seasonally humid zones, as in the southwest of Western Australia, they are used for wheat growing in a rotation with annual sown and volunteer pastures.

In northern Australia both Lateritic Podzolic and Red Earth Soils are used almost exclusively for the grazing of natural pasture by beef cattle. In restricted areas, favourably situated for marketing, as near Brisbane, small occurrences of Lateritic Red Earths are used intensively for fruit and vegetable production. Where irrigated and well fertilized these permeable soils of good tilth have proved very productive. There is no significant use of Calcareous Lateritic Soils distinct from the other associated Lateritic Soils.

Desert Sandplain Soils are amongst the least fertile and hence least used soils in Australia. Some incidental sparse beef cattle grazing occurs on them along with other more favoured soils in arid regions, but for the most part they are unused and in fact comprise the dominant element in the landscape of the very extensive unpopulated desert region which embraces the most arid portions of Western Australia, the Northern Territory and South Australia.

All of the lateritic soils have provided enormous quantities of the so-called ironstone gravel for road making purposes. A very high percentage of second-class unsealed roads throughout Australia is paved with this material. Where the laterite is highly aluminous, as in many of the areas of Lateritic Red Earths in north Australia, and to a lesser extent on Lateritic Podzolic Soils in Western Australia, where it is bauxite, it is being increasingly strip-mined as an ore for the production of aluminium.

Soils on Limestones and Calcareous Loess

Excluding the Fen Peats and the Calcareous Sands of the immediate coastline mentioned above, these soils consist of Brown Forest Soils, Terra Rossas, Rendzinas, Groundwater Rendzinas, Grey Calcareous Soils, Grey Brown and Red Calcareous Desert Soils and Solonized Brown Soils. These soils form a broad climosequence extending from the humid regions to the desert areas, modified in some cases by groundwater and salinity factors.

Brown Forest Soils, Terra Rossas, and Rendzinas are all shallow soils found in the more humid regions on thin residual mantles of mineral material weathered from limestones. These soils are not particularly common and the rarest, the shallow, loamy Brown Forest Soils, are restricted to rocks rather lower in calcium carbonate but retaining some of it in the shallow soil profile. The equally shallow red, sandy to loamy Terra Rossas, which are often slightly acid in the immediate surface horizon, occur on harder limestones and sometimes share a karst-type landscape with the shallow, black, clay-textured Rendzinas which are neutral to alkaline in reaction and tend to occur on the softer surface parts of the limestone. However both soils also occur quite separately in comparatively large areas. In the lower southeast of South Australia a highly calcareous and gently sloping basement, together with telluric water annually rising into the soil

mantle, creates a rather special set of conditions giving rise to extensive areas of Groundwater Rendzinas. The initial development of these soils for agricultural and pastoral purposes, commencing earlier this century and continuing to more recent times, has depended on the provision of an extensive drainage system which has proved very effective.

In the subhumid to semi-arid areas the Terra Rossa and Redzina soils give way to rather more calcareous and lighter-coloured, shallow Grey Calcareous Soils whose occurrence is sporadic except in the wheat growing areas north of Adelaide in South Australia where they occur on the calcareous members of the Precambrian Adelaide Series. In the arid regions proper these soils are replaced by the very extensive, highly calcareous, shallow Grey, Brown and Red Calcareous Desert Soils. These soils are particularly common in the southern arid regions and the redder kind almost completely dominate the vast area of the Nullarbor Plain. The powdery calcareous structure and fine mechanical composition of most of these soils makes them very susceptible to deflation, especially where grazing has depleted the naturally scanty vegetative cover. Under conditions of very high summer temperatures, high wind speeds and resulting considerable air turbulence frequent in Australian arid regions, dust storms of great height and extent are frequently generated on these soils.

The Solonized Brown Soils are almost as extensive as the Grey Brown and Red Calcareous Desert Soils and tend strongly to lie adjacent to them on their southern fringe. Their environment is thus semi-arid and they are associated characteristically with so-called mallee vegetation, a low stunted type of multi-stemmed, lignotuberous, small tree formation predominantly composed of a number of species of *Eucalyptus*. This vegetation clearly distinguishes these soils and their environment from the saltbush-bluebush shrub steppe and the mulga-myall desert woodland of the Calcareous Desert Soils.

The Solonized Brown Soils vary in texture from sand to loam in the surface horizons and rise in texture with depth. This differentiation of texture is often masked by a rapid increase in calcareousness which takes the form of nodules, massive concretionary boulders and fine material, the nodules and boulders being closest to the surface horizons. This *kunkar* underlies all the soils, but under the sandier types it is more deeply placed because of the obvious dune structure of the coarser-textured soils. The parallel distribution of the dunes and the frequent occurrence of kunkar at or near the surface of the soils in the intervening swales points clearly to an earlier aeolian erosional history which modified the original depositional landscape, almost certainly before the development of the rather dense mallee cover found under virgin conditions on these soils, or in a period in which this cover was greatly weakened by aridity.

The fact that the Solonized Brown Soils occur almost exclusively on a variably thick, highly calcareous, mantle of material overlying a great variety of older formations is clearly indicative of an aeolian origin of the parent material and that it has been derived from calcareous sources. However the sand content of these soils is not low and has been partially concentrated in the dune structures. Further, the clay subsoils whose texture and structure are masked by much fine lime are also high in the sodium and to some extent magnesium content of the ex-changeable cations, indicating a high degree of solonization, the morphological evidence of which is likewise masked by the abundant concretionary and fine lime. In many profiles there is frequent evidence in repeated soil and kunkar horizons of soil profiles superimposed on each other, indicating alternate land surface and soil formation.

Crocker (1946) postulated that the Solonized Brown Soils were formed on a calcareous loess derived by winnowing of coastal calcareous aeolian deposits associated with exposures of the continental shelf in periods of low sea-level in the Pleistocene. It is difficult to reconcile this hypothesis with the humid conditions and presumably close vegetative cover which would prevail during times of low sea-level and with the fact that even in the present relatively arid times there is no evidence of such winnowing of the existing coastal dune structures. Moreover, southerly winds necessary to give the present distribution of these soils are not associated with the prerequisite hot and dry conditions; in fact the contrary. Furthermore, evidence from an extensive series of stranded dunes in southeastern South Australia and western Victoria indicates that coastal dunes, even where very high in carbonate content, do not lose calcareous material by deflationary suspension in the air, but that the surface residue of siliceous sand, remaining after the carbonate has been concentrated by leaching and deposition in the depth of the dune, is locally redistributed.

Three other possible alternative but not mutually exclusive hypotheses, concerning the origin of the parent material of the Solonized Brown Soils, are worth consideration.

First, that the extensive Grey Brown and Red Calcareous Desert Soils of the Nullarbor Plain and other southern arid areas, with their particular susceptibility to dust storms, have been in periods of greater aridity, an even more potent source of hot calcareous loess. This was borne on the strong dry winds which still blow seasonally dust-laden towards the areas of Brown Solonized Soils. Further, the high carbonate content of the Solonized Brown Soils and its concretionary crust and nodular form are due to

concentration by leaching into the middle and lower parts of the profiles of the original soils before the progressive loss of the finer fraction by aeolian activity from the surface soil, thus concentrating lime and leaving residues of sand to be moulded into dunes.

Second, that the calcareous parent material and its high exchangeable sodium and magnesium is the result of fluvial accumulation under conditions of endoreic drainage on depositional surfaces which subsequently have been modified by leaching and wind sculpturing as noted above. Bands of alunite in sediments beneath some of these soils and the relief of some central occurrences in New South Wales and in County Victoria in South Australia suggest this. The sand fraction in these soils is also readily accounted for by such a fluvial process.

Third, in parts of Western Australia, the parent materials of these soils have clearly been derived by the action of westerly winds lifting calcareous and saline material out of numerous salinas and spreading a mantle of it over the adjacent lee-side landscape, so covering a variety of older soils. Salinas are however not sufficiently common in all areas of Solonized Brown Soils for this to be of general application in other parts of Australia.

The use of Brown Forest Soils is purely incidental to that of the more extensive surrounding soils. This also tends to the case with Terra Rossas and Rendzinas which, however, where more extensive, deeper and less stony than the average, have been adapted to specialized forms of land use. The most notable examples of this occur in the southeast of South Australia, first, where the long subcoastal swales occupied by Groundwater Rendzinas have been drained and sown to very productive pastures based on Strawberry Clover (*Trifolium fragiferum*) and perennial grasses, this following an earlier history of cereal growing, mostly barley and oats; and second, where a number of moderately extensive gentle rises of Terra Rossas have, in recent years, been increasingly planted to grape vines for wine production, pre-dominantly dry red wines. In the summer of some years these shallow soils decline in moisture content to below the wilting point, but as necessary the vineyards are given supplementary irrigation by pumping from groundwater in the limestone beneath but lying at depths too great to benefit the soil profile naturally.

The Grey Calcareous Soils of the wheat growing areas of South Australia occur as an important but not dominant member of a hill and valley landscape dominated by Red-brown Earths and subjected on average to a three-year rotation of wheat, sheep grazing and fallow. The Grey Calcareous Soils lie exclusively on hillslope positions, have shallow profiles and surface soils of fine sandy to silty loam texture, very prone under cultivation to structural decline.

They are thus more subject to water erosion than the Red-brown Earths and call for selective preferential treatment by soil conservation techniques.

The Solonized Brown Soils have, over the last sixty years, been increasingly used for wheat growing and sheep grazing on fairly wide but variable rotations, with barley growing an important feature of the inner southerly fringe of these soils where rainfall is more abundant. Over the middle and outer parts of this 'mallee' region productivity is extremely variable, but low on the average, and sensitivity to wind erosion is high. Considerable acreages of the lower placed soils have been stripped down to the kunkar, thus rendering them unfit for cultivation, and the sandy soils of the dune ridges rendered mobile with consequent stripping and piling of sand as new drifts and dunes, probably comparable with conditions during an earlier stage of formation before the development of the stabilizing mallee vegetation. Whilst the inner fringe of the mallee areas is relatively stable the middle and outer zones are highly susceptible to wind erosion. Conservation measures which have brought a measure of stability have been, first, the retraction of cereal growing from the outer zone and the aggregation of former farms there into large-scale grazing properties; second, the increasing exclusion of sand ridges from cultivation in the middle zone and their stabilization with cereal rye and other plants; and third, the steadily increasing use of a number of annual legumes as a basis of more productive pastures in longer rotation cycles.

Where the Solonized Brown Soils lie adjacent to the Murray and Murrumbidgee Rivers they are extensively irrigated for citrus, stone fruit and grape vine production. Under these conditions the solonized and saline character of these soils is of major consequence to the techniques of irrigation used in these areas. Because of the elevation and porosity of the sandy dune soils and the occurrence of clay subsoils which build up shallow water-tables, waterlogging and salinity tend to develop very readily in the lower placed soils, with consequent death of the trees and vines. Extensive drainage systems and strict control of water applications become necessary to reclaim the affected areas. Disposal of saline drainage waters remains a problem, discharge into deep sumps, surface pans, or the rivers all being undesirable in the long term.

The Grey Brown and Red Calcareous Desert Soils, being largely confined to southern arid areas, are used for sheep rather than for cattle grazing. Large tracts, such as the Nullarbor Plain, are not used at all except around the southern fringes and the eastern and western extremities. The shrub steppe vegetative cover of these soils is readily damaged by grazing even at the very low carrying capacities used, and the powdery surface soils readily give rise to dust storms under hot, dry, windy conditions.

Medium and Fine Textured Soils of the Seasonally Humid Regions

These consist of Red-brown Earths, Non-calcic Brown Soils, Prairie Soils and Black Earths.

Red-brown Earths occur both widely on Pleistocene alluvium and to a lesser degree as sedentary soils on a wide variety of rocks. They have their widest occurrence in the winter-rainfall regions of southern Australia but extend in a minor but significant way to the summer-rainfall areas of subcoastal Queensland where, however, the appropriate environment is dominated by Black Earths on fine-textured parent materials. The Red-brown Earths are characterized by light to medium textured surface soils, red-brown in colour, overlying clay-textured well-structured subsoils red in colour, and with lime appearing in the lower part of this horizon or in the deeper subsoil. In County Victoria and surrounding areas in South Australia the old alluvium and colluvium of merging fans and detrital aprons often show an array of buried profiles. Correspondingly on nearby slopes there is clear evidence of natural erosional truncation of sedentary Red-brown Earths and of similar but finer-textured soils being formed on the stumps of the original profiles. There are thus strong indications of periods of erosional instability of the landscape with, however, insufficient change in climate to cause different soils to develop during the stable periods. This is in marked contrast to the evidence derived by Butler (1959) for the more humid Australian Capital Territory where buried soils belong to different Great Soil Groups than those formed on the latest deposits. Presumably climatic fluctuations in that area have either been greater or more significant in soil differentiation. Proximity to the alpine region suggests the former.

The Non-calcic Brown Soils strongly resemble the Red-brown Earths in their textural and structural profiles but they vary more widely in colour and lack the presence of lime in the profile. They occur in widely scattered areas in the subcoastal regions of eastern Australia and are a feature of the slopes below the Lateritic Podzolic Soils of southwestern Western Australia where they extend into the seasonally humid region. In eastern Australia these soils have not been submitted to any detailed study so that their environmental relationships are still obscure. In Western Australia however they occur on a variety of parent materials exposed by dissection below the level of the lateritic soils. Here they lie above the soils of the terraces and floodplains of the streams and this, together with their lack of lime in the profile, inappropriate in this particular climatic environment, clearly indicates that they are paleosols, developed

Plate 8.3   Wheat production under a crop and fallow system on Red-brown Earths in the Canowie Belt District of the mid-north of South Australia. The extensive valley floors of this region are covered by Red-brown Earths and the intervening ranges of hills by a complex of Red-brown Earths, Grey Calcareous Soils and Skeletal Soils.

under conditions of leaching more potent than at the present time. That they have been preserved from removal by erosion, and subsequent rejuvenation by weathering of their parent material on the slopes on which they lie, is probably linked with the minimal rate of natural removal of soil material, controlled in turn by the slow retreat of the edges of the hard laterite cappings above.

Black Earths are generally deep, black, clay-textured soils with lighter coloured, calcareous subsoils. They are mostly coarsely structured, the size of the soil aggregates increasing with depth in the profile down to the calcareous horizon where the soil mass becomes more friable. Frequently the larger structural units show smooth polished 'slickenside' faces indicating pronounced movement of the aggregates between wetting and drying. Black Earths are restricted to the seasonally humid regions, the main occurrences being in the northern tropical and subtropical areas of summer rainfall in subcoastal Queensland and northern

New South Wales. They are also found in small areas on basic parent materials or fine-textured alluvium in winter-rainfall areas in Victoria, Tasmania and South Australia, where they are a minor component in the landscape in association with Red-brown Earths. In mostly small areas on the moister side of the range of occurrence of Black Earths, where the efficiency of the rainfall is greater and leaching of the profile often complete, calcium carbonate is removed and Prairie Soils developed. Like the Black Earths these are fine-textured soils, black in colour, and mostly deep. However they are generally more finely structured than the Black Earths and are non-calcareous in the subsoil. Their largest area of occurrence is in the south coastal area of New South Wales.

Together the Red-brown Earths and the Black Earths make up the greater part of the more productive wheat growing areas of Australia. Historically the steadily rising yields on the Red-brown Earths have resulted from the increasing use of superphosphate

Plate 8.4 A view over the extensive Grey Soils of Heavy Texture of the Victorian Wimmera District taken from Mt Arapiles, a northwestern outlier of the Grampian Mountains. The pattern of crop and cultivated fallow land reflects the intensive use of this area for cereal production.

fertilizer since the turn of the century and the sowing of a number of species of annual legumes which build up soil nitrogen during the pasture phase of the three-year rotation now commonly used on these soils (Plate 8.3). Sheep grazing on these pastures and on the stubbles and fallowed land is essentially ancillary to the main purpose of grain production. Considerable barley and some oats are grown as well as wheat. The main problem on the Red-brown Earths is soil conservation, for both sheet and gully erosion are easily initiated on most of these soils and in some areas reached a considerable magnitude prior to the development and application of the soil conserving techniques which came into being in the late 1930s and have been extended ever since. Rotations shorter than three years, and over-grazing by sheep, were the main factors which led to deterioration of soil structure and increased surface movement of water, with consequent sheet and gully erosion.

The Red-brown Earths of the eastern part of the Riverina region in New South Wales and of the middle Murray Valley in Victoria are extensively irrigated for a variety of crops. The most important are stone, pome and citrus fruits, vines for dried fruit and wine production, and pastures mainly of perennial species for sheep and cattle grazing, a proportion of the latter being for dairy products. Although not entirely free of infiltration, waterlogging, salinity and other problems the Red-brown Earths are much easier to manage under irrigation than either the Solonized Brown Soils or the Grey and Brown Soils of Heavy Texture with which they sometimes intermingle or lie in juxtaposition. Where irrigation farms have limited water rights the Red-brown Earths are usually irrigated in preference to other soils.

The Black Earths of northern New South Wales and southern Queensland are used extensively for wheat and sorghum production. Most of these soils in this region do not respond significantly to superphosphate, and yields are normally high. Because of the two major crops grown, rotations are generally shorter and more elastic than on the Red-brown Earths, the main purpose of the short fallow phase being to conserve the summer rain in the soil profile so that it can be used by the wheat crop during the following winter and spring. Sorghum crops are more directly dependent on the summer rain. As well as grain production there is considerable cattle and sheep production on these soils based on both native and sown species, principally grasses. In common with the Red-brown Earths erosion is the main problem of these soils. Basically the reasons for the onset of erosion are the same, likewise the techniques of control.

The Black Earths are irrigated in a much more limited way than the Red-brown Earths. Extending from the Hunter Valley in central subcoastal New South Wales to the southeast of Queensland these soils are irrigated for a limited range of crops including perennial pastures for dairying and beef cattle, and cotton growing. The latter crop, after a pioneering phase on non-irrigated Black Earths and other associated soils, has eventually become concentrated with much greater yields on irrigated areas composed mainly of Black Earths.

The Non-calcic Brown Soils of eastern Australia are generally used for grazing or cereal production along with the other associated soils of the landscape but in Western Australia they are somewhat more specifically used for wheat growing in a landscape in which other soils are co-dominant and have an important influence on the pattern of erosion which may develop, the Non-calcic Brown Soils, because of their sensitive position on the more sloping elements in the landscape, being the most susceptible.

The use of the usual small areas of Prairie Soils is rarely different from surrounding soils but an important exception is on the south coast of New South Wales where their extent makes them a very important factor in the dairying and cattle raising industries, the dairying being mostly on sown pastures of perennial grasses and legumes such as paspalum (*Paspalum dilitatum*) and white clover (*Trifolium repens*).

Fine-textured Soils of the Semi-arid Regions
These consist of the Grey and Brown (and Red) Soils of Heavy Texture. The grey version of these soils is the dominant one, the brown somewhat lesser in extent and the red version of only occasional occurrence.

On the drier side of their climatic range the Black Earths grade into the clay textured Grey and Brown Soils of Heavy Texture which are even more coarsely structured than the Black Earths. The Grey and Brown Soils dominate a huge crescent-shaped region in eastern Australia with minor occurrences in the west and northwest. They are mainly associated with open grassland and savannah woodland formations. Parent materials vary from a wide range of rocks which produce a high percentage of clay on weathering to extensive areas of fine-textured alluvium both on older terraces and more recent floodplains. Soils on the latter tend to follow the associated streams outside the normal climatic range of these soils both on the endoreic streams into more arid areas, and on exoreic

ones into the seasonally humid zone of southeastern Australia, the latter also embracing the basin-like areas of the Wimmera region of western Victoria where there is some evidence of local aeolian redistribution of the original alluvium. The almost featureless Barkly Tableland of the Northern Territory and the great western plains of Queensland are almost completely dominated by Grey and Brown Soils of Heavy Texture.

The profiles of these soils are usually deep and of clay texture throughout their depth. Surface horizons are normally coarsely structured but the structural units increase in size with depth until the deeper subsoil is characterized by large individual interlocking masses of clay frequently showing slickensiding surfaces separated by cracks. Calcareous material, both as fine lime and as small concretions, occurs normally in the subsoil and is often accompanied by variable amounts of gypsum. Deep and wide cracks are a feature of these soils in the dry season of the year. At the surface these cracks may be as much as 10 cm wide and extend more narrowly to a depth of 1 metre or more into the subsoil where their sides are defined by the slickensided surfaces of the structural units, indicating not only lateral separation on drying but also more general sliding movements while sufficiently moist and plastic to give characteristic streaked and polished surfaces.

With the onset of rain of sufficient quantity and duration the cracks first receive a certain amount of surface runoff, of immediate local origin, leading to marked differential wetting of the subsoil and the gradual closing of the cracks. The grey soils consistently occupy the lower elements and the brown soils the higher sites of their associated very gentle undulating landscape, with the result that under sufficiently heavy rain the grey soils, following closure of the cracks, become subject to extensive surface inundation, which the brown soils escape. Where the grey soils occur on present-day floodplains they are naturally subject to more frequent and deeper flooding of greater duration.

Both the Black Earths and the Grey and Brown Soils of Heavy Texture, especially the latter, are widely affected by manifestations of surface microrelief for which the Australian term 'gilgai', of aboriginal origin, has gained widespread, even international, acceptance. The terms 'crabholey', 'melonhole' and 'hogwallow' have also been used to describe this condition. On the more arid side both Stony Desert Tableland Soils and Desert Loams also exhibit this phenomenon and in moister regions Prairie Soils, Red-brown Earths and Solodic Soils are also affected, but to a much lesser extent and with a much lower amplitude to the surface undulations. Mostly the pattern of surface microrelief is continuous and irregularly reticulate over sizeable areas but in some cases, often on moderate slopes, the formation takes on a parallel pattern referred to as linear gilgai. The amplitude between crest and hollow is on average a matter of a few centimetres but in extreme cases may be as much as a metre or more. The distance between crests is likewise extremely variable and may be less than one metre or more than ten metres. The crests or 'puffs' as they are generally known usually show subsoil features such as finer texture, coarser structure, lime nodules and powdery carbonate, gypsum crystals, etc. In pits excavated transversely across crest and hollow these are seen to be an upwelling of subsoil materials bursting through the surface horizon. Until recently this presence of subsoil materials on the crests, their connection with the same materials in the subsoil below the hollow, and the large smooth slickensided clay structural units have been taken to indicate quite strongly that differential swelling and shrinking, consequent upon unequal wetting and drying of parts of the profile through fissuring cracks, usually penetrating into the subsoil, were the cause of this phenomenon. Recent investigations in south-eastern Queensland by Paton (1974) have indicated that, in some instances at least, gilgai structures may be piercement structures resulting from natural differential surface loading.

In northern Australia, including Queensland, the Grey and Brown Soils of Heavy Texture are used almost entirely for the grazing of natural pastures by beef cattle, with some sheep grazing in southern Queensland. There is extremely variable seasonal productivity because of the sharp contrast between unreliable summer rain and certain winter drought, with consequent great variation in grass production and length of the grazing season. However these soils, in terms of area and fertility, are the most valuable soils in northern semi-arid areas. In New South Wales, in the Riverina, and in northern Victoria, fairly considerable areas of these soils are irrigated, mainly for pasture production for sheep grazing, but with some cattle, and, in the Riverina, rice production. The low permeability and slow infiltration rates of these soils when the profile is continuously moist makes them ideal for rice production and yields are outstandingly high. However the same properties make it difficult to achieve anything but moderate productivity under sown pastures, with the result that there is a tendency to use these soils for annual winter-growing pasture species and to use irrigation water as a supplement and extension to the rainfall which is concentrated in the winter-spring months. The use of gypsum either directly on the surface or applied in solution in the irrigation water improves the permeability and initial infiltration rate but the economics of this treatment are at best marginal.

The most southerly occurrence of the Grey and Brown Soils of Heavy Texture is in the Wimmera district of western Victoria and the adjacent Tatiara district of South Australia (Plate 8.4). Here in a fairly reliable seasonal winter-spring rainfall area of comparative abundance these soils are used intensively for wheat and other cereal production. Additionally the surface soils are more finely structured and self-mulching than usual and are resistant to structural deterioration under intense cultivation. Consequently yields are high and reliable. Under the cultivation regime of these districts the gilgai soils gradually lose their microrelief because of the transfer of soil from the crests to the hollows, but if land is left out of cultivation for some years gilgai redevelopment again gradually becomes evident.

Saline and Solonized Soils (excluding Solonized Brown Soils)

These consist of Solonchaks, Solonetz, Solodized Solonetz, and Soloths or Solodic Soils. These soils form a natural sequence related to their declining salinity and the residual chemical and morphological effects of this in the different horizons of their profiles. Solonchaks are saline soils sufficiently high in soluble salts, usually mainly sodium chloride, to seriously affect plant growth or limit vegetation to halophytic species: profile form is variable and of no consequence unless reclamation is attempted. Solonetz are largely desalinized soils retaining a relatively high amount of exchangeable sodium in the B horizon which is also characterized by large domed columnar structures sharply separated from the A horizon above. Solodized Solonetz show much the same characteristics as the Solonetz but with the A horizon differentiated sharply into A1 and A2 horizons, the latter being quite bleached. Solods or Solodic Soils have lesser amounts of soluble salts and exchangeable sodium in the B horizon and the structure of this shows little or nothing of the doming and columnar character of the Solonetz, but is sharply separated from the bleached A2 horizon above.

This saline-sodic-morphologic sequence of soils is widely occurring and extends regionally in the order given, but with some considerable overlap between members, and mostly in the lower parts of the landscape, from the desert to the region of Podzolic Soils. Solonchaks have an extreme expression in the salinas of the arid and semi-arid regions but extend in various forms, including man-induced salinity on both irrigated and non-irrigated agricultural land, through to the seasonally humid areas. Solonetz features are shown by soils extending from the desert to the semi-arid regions. Solodized Solonetz occur widely in the semi-arid and seasonally humid areas. Solodic Soils are a notable feature of the general region of Podzolic Soils, and it is often difficult to distinguish between them without recourse to analytical data, particularly the percentage composition of the exchangeable cations in the clay-textured *B* horizons. Not infrequently Solodic Soils contain small amounts of calcareous material as small nodules or fine lime in the *BC* horizon: this makes a clear distinction from the Podzolic Soils except where the latter have developed on residues weathered from and resting on limestones or dolomites.

Because of the scarcity of chlorine-bearing primary minerals such as the scapolites in Australia, the widespread occurrence of Solonetz and related soils in much of Australia can only be linked with the high incidence of wind- and rain-borne oceanic salt. The redistribution and persistence of this in the soils is to be correlated with the feeble and endoreic nature of much of the natural drainage of the continent and the very low coastal discharge by Australian rivers which, by comparison with an equal area of comparable latitude is but one-twentieth of the outflow of the rivers of the United States of America excluding Alaska.

Naturally-occurring Solonchaks are too saline for most cultivated plants and so are avoided by agriculturalists. In the drier pastoral areas their salt-tolerant plant cover is grazed along with that of other adjacent soils. Solonetz Soils are likewise not now favoured for agricultural purposes but much wheat growing has been attempted on them on the fringe of pioneering agricultural expansion especially in Western Australia. They are subject to extensive grazing and in a limited way some areas of these soils have been developed by the use of sown pastures of annual species usually in association with better soils. Much more extensive and reliable use is made of Solodized Solonetz Soils for both cereal growing and sown pasture production. Solodic Soils are used without distinction from the Podzolic Soils for sown pasture production on an extensive scale and in a more limited way for horticultural purposes such as vine and stone fruit production. However in some respects the Solodic Soils are more difficult to manage than the Podzolic Soils. They are more subject to temporary waterlogging of the surface horizons, especially after heavy rain, particularly if this follows supplementary irrigation; they are very susceptible to poaching by stock when wet, and are more prone to sheet, gully, and tunnel erosion.

The nature and utilization of the Solonized Brown Soils which also belong to the Solonetz and related soils group was dealt with previously under the heading of soils on calcareous materials. Their dry land agricultural use and erosion problems were described there and their problems associated with waterlogging and salinity under irrigated conditions detailed.

The sensitivity of soluble salts in soils with a genetic history of salinization to movement by alterations in hydrology, often slight, is exemplified on a large and disastrous scale in the wheat growing lands of Western Australia, and to a lesser degree elsewhere, where the clearing and agricultural or pasture development of soils on the upper levels of the landscape has caused soluble salts in the soils of the valley bottoms and lower slopes to rise to concentrations toxic to crop and pasture plants. The replacement of perennial deep-rooted native plants by shallow-rooted annual crop and pasture plants unquestionably alters the moisture regime by allowing more seasonal moisture, especially under clean cultivated fallow conditions, to reach the deeper subsoil and so escape immediate return to the atmosphere by evapotranspiration. The relative importance of the increased underground lateral flow of the additional moisture bringing more soluble salts to lower levels and of the simple rise of saline groundwater nearer to valley floors has yet to be fully assessed.

Much basic information on the nature and extent of Australian soils with saline and sodic properties and of the problems associated with these properties has recently been compiled by Northcote and Skene (1972). The map accompanying that report shows how the Solonetz-Solodic Soils make up a large part of the soil landscape in eastern and southern Australia and how they extend from the seasonally humid to the semi-arid regions and penetrate to the arid areas especially through the medium of the Solonized Brown Soils, the Grey, Brown and Red Calcareous Desert Soils and the Stony Desert Tableland Soils.

Soils of the Arid Zone

These consist of Arid Red Earths, Stony Desert Tableland Soils, Red and Brown Hardpan Soils, Desert Loams, Desert Sandhills, Grey, Brown and Red Calcareous Desert Soils, and Desert Sandplain Soils. The Calcareous Desert Soils were described in the section on soils on calcareous parent materials and the Desert Sandplain Soils under the section on lateritic soils of old landscapes. The other soils fall fairly clearly into two broad classes, the Arid Red Earths, the Stony Desert Tableland Soils and the Red and Brown Hardpan Soils being associated with essentially residual landscapes, and the Desert Loams and Sandhills with desert detritus.

Arid Red Earths are generally bright red, deep soils of coarse to medium texture and massive but vesicular structure. Textures usually become finer with depth and the whole profile is porous. These soils are acid in reaction in the upper horizons and sometimes at depth, but most often slight alkalinity and lime are features of the deeper subsoil. However the members of the Yambah soil family described by Jackson (1962), and occurring rather extensively in the Alice Springs region, have a prismatic-structured clay subsoil over a more deeply placed calcareous horizon and a well-marked *C* horizon of decomposed rock. Investigations have shown that these lower horizon features are not, as suspected, part of buried soils, but with the vesicular surface horizons make up complete pedological unit profiles. Thus the Arid Red Earths as a group are not strictly uni-modal in profile morphology and may be considered to represent two or more Great Soil Groups. Further, the profiles with the structured *B* horizons and calcareous subsoils often appear quite similar over extensive areas, particularly in Western Australia, to Red-brown Earths from which however they can usually be distinguished by the strongly vesicular, porous, and much less plastic deeper *A* horizons. Because of their arid environment they also have much sparser water relationships than the Red-brown Earths. The Arid Red Earths occur generally in extensive areas right across the desert region and extend markedly into the semi-arid areas of central Queensland and New South Wales. They are found at intermediate to low levels in the landscape on both older transported and sedentary parent materials. They generally surround higher rugged land or silcrete-capped residuals of even older land surfaces from both of which detrital material has been derived to build up the plains and terraces of very subdued relief on which the non-sedentary members occur. They are essentially soils of pediments with both depositional and erosional components.

It is difficult to explain the acid reaction of these arid soils unless one invokes more intense leaching under an earlier wetter climate than prevails today, or a cumulative effect of sporadic but intense leaching by heavy but only occasional rains, perhaps made more effective by surface sheet flooding following runoff from the adjacent higher skeletal soils. This condition prevails during present times but its duration and intensity are limited by rapid flow down the pediment slopes and by the natural diversion of much of the water from above into the slightly incised ephemeral streams which traverse the pediments. Further, the occurrence of lime at depth in some of these acid soils poses a problem unlikely to be explained, as with the Solonized Brown Soils, by any hypothesis invoking calcareous loess. It is more likely to be associated with a high phase of calcareous groundwater or to be due to subsequent weathering of base-rich minerals remaining deep in the profile and therefore escaping to some extent the earlier weathering and leaching causing acidity in the upper horizons.

Because of their porous profiles and gentle relief the Arid Red Earths and the limited areas of associated Alluvial Soils offer the greatest prospects in the Australian arid zone for some kind of intense development in selected small areas. Owing to their association with the stony ranges with their high runoff, they not only have the best prospects of using water from surface catchments and diversions, but also offer the most readily useable areas associated with local shallow aquifers with water of acceptable quality which itself is derived by the cobble bed infiltration of water periodically carried by the ephemeral streams that arise in the stony ranges. What has been done with such a soil and hydrological situation at Alice Springs where lucerne, fruit trees and vegetables have been grown should be possible on a restricted scale in many localities in arid Australia. The use of surface catchment water and flood diversionary systems has yet to be attempted even on an experimental scale, but there must be almost numberless sites suitable for such purposes.

Stony Desert Tableland Soils have deep clay-textured profiles brown to reddish-brown in colour and with little differentiation in colour and texture with depth. They exhibit considerable gilgai microrelief often with a wavy surface pattern. They universally carry a surface pavement of wind-polished siliceous stones, almost invariably silcrete, which shows a notable degree of desert varnish, a lustrous reddish-brown coating most strongly developed on the upper more exposed surfaces of the abrasion-rounded pebbles. This pavement is usually one or two pebbles thick and is commonly disrupted and rendered discontinuous by the gilgai pattern. The lower parts of the normal profiles are variably calcareous, gypseous and saline and these features also characterize the puffs of the areas of gilgai development. Many profiles show strong evidence of layering of the parent material and often include rounded siliceous stones, but these are of minute occurrence compared with the stones of the surface pavement.

Stony Desert Tableland Soils dominate large parts of the central Australian depression centred on Lakes Eyre and Frome but spill over into the Darling valley of western New South Wales and southwestern Queensland and into the Northern Territory. They are not found to any significant extent in arid Western Australia although silcrete-capped mesas occur widely in that region, where however Red and Brown Hardpan Soils and other desert soils occupy the lower parts of the landscape.

The soil landscape is characterized by many closely to widely spaced low mesa-like residuals invariably capped by a thick and very hard silcrete horizon from which the stony pavement has obviously been derived by fracture, surface movement and abrasion, and from beneath which the deeply weathered pallid clay horizons have been locally redistributed as the parent material of the soil profile proper (Plate 8.5). Backcutting, concave dissection has been the universal means by which the silcrete carapace has been undermined, leading to its collapse as large blocks on the immediately adjacent pediment surface below. With

Plate 8.5 The wooded stream bed of the ephemeral Neales River, west of Oodnadatta in central Australia, passing through extensive areas of Stony Desert Tableland Soils with their surface pebble pavement, and close to the foot of two remnant levels of silcrete-capped hills from which the Stony Desert Tableland Soils have been derived by headward erosion.

increasing distance from the scarp the silcrete fragments become smaller, smoother and rounder, and more polished by desert varnish.

The silcrete residuals frequently show small but noticeable differences in elevation amongst themselves, sometimes when in close proximity. Older abraded silcrete is sometimes found incorporated in a matrix of younger silcrete as a variation from the normal inclusion of clastic more or less rounded quartz grains and siliceous pebbles within the harder cementing material. This clastic material is invariably in marked contrast to the finer-textured pallid and mottled clay materials found below the silcrete, indicating a surface fluvial agent being involved in the process of silcrete formation, and predicating a series of land surfaces from the breakdown of which the soils have been derived.

Some residuals adjacent to higher land, such as the

northern Flinders Ranges in South Australia and the southern edge of the Macdonnell Ranges in central Australia, show gently sloping surfaces. Gypsum often as distinct beds, and alunite is commonly found under the silcrete, sometimes immediately subjacent, sometimes deeper in the section. A marked degree of salinity is always present. The presence of these evaporites points to a genetic history in an environment characterized by high evaporation or evapotranspiration such as salinas or sluggish slow-flowing streams and distributaries being dissipated under arid conditions such as occur in these regions today.

These features make it apparent that the silcrete-capped mesas of the Australian arid zone are but the remnants of an ancient much more extensive land surface which owed its development to surface and subsurface water bringing into an area of high evaporative power not only abraded siliceous materials but

Plate 8.6   Red and Brown Hardpan Soils on an extensive plain between Meekatharra and Wiluna in the arid central region of Western Australia. The surface of the plain on which these soils occur is subject to sheet flooding and lies at a slightly lower elevation than the silcrete or laterite-capped residuals of an earlier very ancient surface.

also silica in solution together with other soluble salts, and that deposition of these by sedimentation and evaporation took place on an extensive series of fluviatile and lacustrine surfaces below which deep weathering of the subjacent materials also took place under the influence of the subsurface water.

It has been shown by Stephens (1971) that there is a complementary distribution of silcrete-capped mesas and their associated Stony Desert Tableland Soils on the one hand with the various Lateritic Soils on the other, thus pointing to the origin of the silica which has been derived from the breakdown of feldspathic and other silicate minerals during the formation of laterite and its associated kaolin, and then transported, either in exoreic drainage to be lost to the ocean, or in endoreic and terminal drainage streams to the arid areas where it has suffered deposition as a result of evaporation. In the latter case silcrete has formed a hard surface over more deeply weathered materials. This formation then awaited the tectonic development of the central Australian depression and other land surface movements to provide the rejuvenation and fracture of the original drainage system which was thus enabled progressively to destroy the distorted silcrete surfaces by characteristic backcutting headward erosion. The dendritic pattern of small eroding streams so formed was responsible for the placing of the parent materials of the Stony Tableland Soils which in effect are composed of finer material derived from the deep weathering part of the original profile covered by a pebble pavement derived from the surface silcrete, thus fortuitously preserving the relative vertical distribution of these materials.

Stony Desert Tableland Soils make up a large percentage of the central Australian arid zone and are used solely for pastoral purposes. Sheep grazing in the southern areas and cattle in the more northerly regions is based on the sparse low shrub steppe saltbush-bluebush dominated vegetation at very low carrying capacities.

Red and Brown Hardpan Soils occur almost uniquely in the central arid region of Western Australia. Small and insignificant areas have been encountered in the northern parts of South Australia. They are brightly coloured porous soils of very variable depth ranging up to about one metre. Their true depth may in fact be much greater than this but the invariable occurrence of an impenetrable hardpan, itself of generally unknown thickness, makes accuracy in this regard impossible. Although brown in colour in the mass, the pan is predominantly siliceous, is light coloured when fractured or cut, and has a somewhat laminated structure with small cavities. It is also ferruginous and manganiferous to some slight and variable extent. Although obviously a secondary siliceous material it is not silcrete for it lacks the density, hardness and conchoidal fracture of that material and, except where exposed by erosion, is not a surface formation. It also lacks the varied array of clasts characteristic of silcrete.

The upper soil profile of Red and Brown Hardpan Soils varies in texture from sand to clay loam and shows no abrupt change in texture with depth until the pan is met very sharply. Occasionally a little calcium carbonate is found in the crevices of the pan, but there is a dearth of information on what lies below except from prospecting holes which mostly suggest an abrupt change to country rock. The soil and the pan, except where lime is present, are distinctly acid in reaction. These unusual soils have excited considerable speculation as to their genesis. The most likely explanation connects them with the special features of the arid climate and the physiographic nature of the surface of the region in which they lie. The occurrence of these soils practically exclusively on the Old Plateau of Western Australia at elevations around 400 to 600 metres, but just below the level of the tops of occasional lateritic, siliceous-lateritic, or silcrete residuals of an even older dismembered land surface, points to a long pedological history (Plate 8.6). The very low relief of the surface on which the soils lie and their coarse texture and porosity provide the maximum opportunity for widespread shallow surface flooding and leaching during the relatively few but normally heavy rains which occur always associated with severe southeasterly-moving cyclonic disturbances principally in the hottest months of the year when soil temperatures are extremely high. This is considered to have led to the solution of silica from weathering silicate minerals and possibly from quartz in the soil and its deposition in amorphous form with some iron and manganese compounds as

cementing agents at depths initially controlled by the depth of wetting of the profile, and subsequently at progressively shallower depths by the cumulative build-up of the pan itself. The origin of such lime as is present is not known but the widespread acidity of the soils and their pans suggests a later phase of development in the profile in localities subject to invasion by calcareous groundwater of which there is some evidence in the form of small outcrops of highly calcareous materials suggesting deposition from springs associated with formerly higher groundwater. The soil above the pan also contains an interestingly high proportion of exchangeable potassium.

The Red and Brown Hardpan Soils are characterized mainly by mulga woodland but there is a variety of other plant associations and considerable ephemeral vegetation following heavy rain. Sheep and cattle grazing at low carrying capacities constitute the main use of these soils.

Desert Loams occur mainly on fine to medium textured alluvial and colluvial materials in arid areas, more particularly in the southern part of continent. With the recognition of other arid soils they are now known to be much less extensive than was originally thought. They display medium to fine textures in the surface soil and have a well-marked clay *B* horizon. Normally they are not well structured and often the lower *A* and the upper *B* horizons show signs of solonization. They are neutral to alkaline in the surface and alkaline below, and always contain lime and generally gypsum in the lower part of the *B* horizon where soluble salts as well as the gypsum also rise to appreciable values. Colours are red to red-brown in the surface soil and red in the *B* horizon. This and the other profile features noted above indicate a clear relationship to the Red-brown Earths into which they sharply grade and with which they make a distinct climosequence. They are found on flat to gently-sloping sites and usually on wide valley floors where they are subject to very occasional sheet flow and ponding of surface water.

Desert Loams are an important but not individually extensive feature of the southern shrub steppe regions where they have a wide-ranging association with the Calcareous Desert Soils and the hills and mountains with Skeletal Soils. Because they are usually deep and relatively fertile soils, often with the best moisture regime of the soils of a given area, they generally carry a denser stand of saltbush and bluebush, varying amounts of mulga desert woodland, and a wealth of ephemeral plants following rain. This makes them of more than average importance in the local pastoral industry. However, where agricultural production such as wheat growing has been attempted on them, failure due to inadequate moisture status and to wind and water erosion has resulted. Small areas which have been irrigated have also failed, but where diverted and controlled floodwaters have been used some success has resulted with lucerne stands.

The Desert Sandhill Soils are almost without exception vivid red in colour, so much so that they lie outside the usually accepted colour range of soils. They are coarse textured and deeper on the ridges than in the swales where they are shallower and a little more coherent, sometimes loamy sands. There is no texture differentiation in any of the profiles but a little lime may be found deep in the subsoil. For the greater part the dunes have an exaggerated seif or linear form, but on the edge of the dunefields the pattern of crests is usually more complex and may even be reticulate. In other localities junctions of dune crests are common. In still other places where rocky hills are surrounded by sandridges the dunes may persist over the lower obstacles, indicating a limited degree of movement longitudinally, and in other localities the dunes continue unbroken through gaps in the hills.

The physiographic setting of the desert dunes in areas of relatively low elevation and in association with the lower courses and distributary systems of a varied array of small to large arid region ephemeral streams, much subject to flash flooding, points clearly to their origin over a long period of time as coarse-textured alluvium which has been deflated and progressively moulded into dune structures. Many of the stream courses terminate at the edge of, or within the dunefields, but some of the larger ones such as the Finke and Diamentina Rivers and Cooper's Creek of central Australia traverse large distances through the dunes to terminate in the Lake Eyre salina. Examination of the dunes in the immediate vicinity of the stream banks, more particularly within their ox-bow formations, frequently shows that here the dunes are much less red in colour, are of more subdued relief, and less directional in pattern. With distance from the stream beds they assume more characteristic redness, seif form, and directional pattern. Thus, in contradistinction to the Desert Loams and Arid Red Earths which have formed on fine to medium textured arid alluvium which has not been modified significantly by aeolian action, the desert sand dunes are the result of wind sculpturing of coarse-textured alluvium under conditions of extreme aridity.

Naturally these sandy soils are very porous and wet deeply in the occasional heavy rains, although the average rainfall is very low, at between 10 and 25 cm per year, and summer maximum temperatures are frequently over 40° C for prolonged periods. Dune corridors and slopes are sparsely but permanently vegetated with a variety of small trees such as mulga, grasses such as spinifex (*Triodia*), and many shrubs. Following sufficient rain a wealth of ephemeral plants appears, temporarily colonizing even the crests of the dunes, which however are normally bare and unstable.

The desert sand dunes, together with the dunes of the Desert Sandplain Soils and the Solonized Brown Soils, make up a directional pattern over a great part of semi-arid and arid Australia consistent with the present-day directions of the strongest winds.

The sands of the ridges and corridors of the dune-fields of arid Australia are not used for any productive purpose except incidentally on their margins with other soils. In these situations some occasional grazing does occur, more particularly following heavy rain, when stock range over greater distances from permanent watering points. In fact the sandridge deserts such as the Simpson, Great Victoria and Great Sandy Deserts and the Desert Sandplain Soils, together with the stony version of the last named, such as the Gibson Desert in Western Australia, make up by far the greater part of the unpopulated region of the continent.

CO-ORDINATION OF AUSTRALIAN SOILS

From the account of the individual properties of the various Great Soil Groups given above it will be seen that there are both normal and unusual features about the Australian continental soil pattern. Some soils such as the Podzols, Pozolic Soils, Red-brown Earths and Black Earths have fairly clear counterparts in other continents; others such as the Arid Red Earths, Red and Brown Hardpan Soils and Stony Desert Tableland Soils appear on information presently available to be unique; the saline and Solonized Soils are unduly extensive; others such as Brown Forest Soils and Prairie Soils, commonly found elsewhere, are but poorly represented; and further the desert sand dunes show an extreme redness of colour although otherwise morphologically typical of desert dune formations.

The association of the various arid zone soils with sharply different geomorphic features etched most strikingly on the desert landscape is most apparent. The inevitable conclusion is that here pedogenic and hydrologic processes, such as the formation of siliceous and lateritic pans, the development of either very porous or very impermeable soil cover, and sparsely vegetated soils due to saline conditions, have been involved with and controlled to a degree the geomorphic processes responsible for the construction, preservation and dismembering of land surfaces. Additionally parent material composition, such as high calcareousness, and placement, such as coarse detritus in the most arid localities, are just as functional as is soil development itself in the arid zone where profile morphology is so distinct at Great Soil Group level.

In general the unusual features of the Australian

soil landscape can be attributed to, first, the great prevalence of very old and moderately aged land surfaces bearing ancient soils only partly modified by the passage of time; second, relatively ineffectual continental drainage leading to the prevalence of saline and solonized soils; and third, the prevalence of limestones and to a lesser degree basic igneous rocks as parent materials which impose limitations on the types of weathering that can take place during soil formation. However the whole soil pattern can be regarded as a normal geographical expression if soils are accepted as the product of the interaction of more than one of climate, parent material, topography, groundwater and vegetation over varying periods of time.

ACKNOWLEDGEMENTS The material included in this chapter on the soils of Australia is partly new and partly derived from a wide range of publications listed under References. The most-used sources have been CSIRO Soil Publication No. 18 and the commentary on the Soils Map from the *Atlas of Australian Resources*, Crown copyright reserved, material supplied by the Department of Minerals and Energy, Canberra, A.C.T., both of which are gratefully acknowledged.

REFERENCES

Butler, B. E. (1959), *Periodic Phenomena in Landscapes as a Basis for Soil Studies*, CSIRO Aust. Soil Publ. No. 14.

Crocker, R. L. (1946), *Post Miocene Climatic and Geologic History and its Significance to the Genesis of the Major Soil Types of South Australia*, CSIRO Aust. Bull. No. 193.

Department of National Development (1963), 'Soils', *Atlas of Australian Resources*, 2nd edn, Canberra.

Jackson, E. A. (1962), *Soil Studies in Central Australia. Alice Springs-Hermannsburg-Rodinga Areas*, CSIRO Aust. Soil Publ. No. 19.

Jenny, H. (1941), *Factors of Soil Formation*, McGraw-Hill, New York.

Lake, Phillip (1890), 'The geology of south Malabar between the Beypore and Ponnani Rivers', *Mem. Geol. Surv. India*, 24(3), 1–46.

Northcote, K. H. (ed.) (1960 et seq.), *Atlas of Australian Soils*, CSIRO Aust. Div. of Soils and Melbourne University Press, Melbourne.

——(1965), *A Factual Key for the Recognition of Australian Soils*, 2nd edn, CSIRO Aust. Div. of Soils, *Div. Report* 2/65.

Northcote, K. H. and Skene, J. K. M. (1972), *Australian Soils with Saline and Sodic Properties*, CSIRO Aust. Soil Publ. No. 27.

Paton, T. R. (1974), 'Origin and terminology for gilgai in Australia', *Geoderma*, 11, 221–42.

Prescott, J. A. (1931), *The Soils of Australia in Relation to Vegetation and Climate*, CSIRO Aust. Bull. No. 52.

Stace, H. C. *et al.* (1968), *A Handbook of Australian Soils*, Rellim Technical Publications, Adelaide.

Stephens, C. G. (1947), 'Functional synthesis in pedogenesis', *Trans. R. Soc. S. Aust.*, 71, 168–81.

——(1961), *The Soil Landscapes of Australia*, CSIRO Aust. Soil Publ. No. 18.

——(1971), 'Laterite and silcrete in Australia', *Geoderma*, 5, 5–52.

9 VEGETATION

J. A. CARNAHAN

The distinctive character of the natural vegetation of Australia is related to the distinctive nature of the native flora. Many of the native plants differ markedly from those of any other region. The most prominent and widespread of the essentially Australian elements are the eucalypts and the phyllode-bearing acacias; but there are many other significant groups, including the hummock grasses or 'spinifexes'.

After two centuries of European occupation, the vegetation has been modified in many places. However, the native elements continue to give a distinctively Australian character to most of the actual vegetation of the present day. The nature of the plant cover reflects the major environmental factors, and in particular the aridity and the infertility that are characteristic of much of the country. The overall pattern of distribution of the vegetation is related to gradients of effective precipitation, and notably to the general decline towards the interior of the continent; but this pattern is greatly complicated by soil factors. Elevation is of only limited significance, in a country of generally subdued relief.

Before European settlement, the plant cover of Australia could be regarded as an approximation to 'original natural' vegetation. Human influence was limited to the hunting and gathering activities of the sparse Aboriginal population. The Aborigines undoubtedly modified the vegetation to some extent by the use of fire (Jones, 1969), but fires caused by lightning are after all part of the natural environment of Australia (Mount, 1964). Whatever may have been the influence of Aboriginal man, it must in any case have been minor in comparison with later European disturbance.

EFFECTS OF SETTLEMENT

Settlement has involved various types of land use, each with its own effects on the natural vegetation (Marshall, 1966). These different types of land use have affected differing proportions of the total area of the country (Dept of National Resources, 1973). However, some activities that are confined to relatively small areas have by necessity or coincidence been concentrated on types of vegetation that also exhibit limited distributions.

Urban forms of land use naturally involve marked changes in the plant cover; but they directly affect only a fraction of one per cent of the land surface. Commercial forestry takes various forms, including selective extraction of native timbers, clear felling, and plantation forestry using exotic species; together, these currently affect less than 2 per cent of the total area of the country. Cropping and intensive animal production occupy less than 10 per cent of the total area. The establishment of these activities has involved the removal of the native vegetation, and the introduction and maintenance of exotic crop and pasture species under regimes of cultivation and intensive management.

These various types of land use occupy a large part of the better-watered sections of temperate Australia, and much more limited but increasing areas north of the Tropic. For the country as a whole, however, the most widespread form of land use is extensive livestock grazing, which affects nearly 60 per cent of the total area. The obvious effects of pastoralism are those of grazing, browsing, and trampling by sheep and cattle on a flora and vegetation that evolved in the absence of ungulates. However, these effects have been compounded by the removal of some woody plants; by new patterns of burning; and by the deliberate or accidental introduction of a range of exotic plant species and of certain animals, notably the rabbit. Detailed accounts of the effects of pastoralism are included in the publications edited by Barnard (1962) and Moore (1970).

The direct impact of the various agencies of European settlement upon the natural vegetation is reinforced through the changes that they bring about in the soil environment; and to these must be added the effects of agricultural chemicals. Changes in the soil environment include a special case of current interest, namely the possible residual effects of mining. Mining occupies only very limited areas, relative to other forms of land use; but some operations are impinging on relics of natural vegetation that have not previously been markedly affected by settlement.

For various reasons, the rest of the country is not

subjected to significant use by Europeans except for recreational activities in some localities. However, the vegetation of unused land is still affected indirectly, as by the spread of feral introduced animals from occupied land.

VEGETATION REGIONS

The map (inside back cover) shows the probable distribution of the major groupings of natural vegetation immediately before European settlement. This map has been very considerably generalized from a larger-scale compilation (Carnahan, 1976); fuller information on the natural vegetation may be obtained from the original map and from the commentary that accompanies it. The classification is based on a system devised by Specht (1970), which defines structural forms of vegetation in terms of the growth form and projective foliage cover of the tallest stratum. The use of foliage cover rather than canopy cover in classifying Australian vegetation takes account of the open nature of *Eucalyptus* crowns in particular (Küchler, 1973).

Specht (1970) recognizes twenty-five structural forms in Australian vegetation. These are defined as follows, in terms of seven growth forms and four classes of projective foliage cover (70–100 per cent; 30–70 per cent; 10–30 per cent; less than 10 per cent).

Trees above 30 m: tall closed-forest, tall open-forest, tall woodland, tall open-woodland.

Trees 10–30 m: closed-forest, open-forest, woodland, open-woodland.

Trees below 10 m: low closed-forest, low open-forest, low woodland, low open-woodland.

Shrubs above 2 m: closed-scrub, open-scrub, tall shrubland, tall open-shrubland. Tall shrubs are distinguished from low trees in being multi-stemmed from or from near the ground.

Shrubs below 2 m: closed-heath, open-heath, low shrubland, low open-shrubland.

Hummock grasses ('spinifex'): hummock grassland (cover 10–30 per cent), open-hummock grassland (cover less than 10 per cent). The distinctive hummock grass growth form is discussed in the section, 'Hummock Grasslands'.

Herbs: closed-herbland, herbland, open-herbland. Very open-herbland (cover less than 10 per cent) is recognized by some contributors to a later publication (Specht *et al.*, 1974). Specht subdivides these forms on the nature of the dominant herbs; most major herblands are dominated by tussock grasses, and a few by forbs (non-grassy herbs).

The systematic treatment of vegetation in this chapter is based on groups of these structural forms, namely: closed-forests; open-forests; woodlands; open-woodlands; scrubs and heaths; shrublands; open-shrublands; hummock grasslands; herblands.

Each of these major groups is described in terms of its general structural and floristic characteristics; its character and location are related to major factors of the natural environment; and the changes leading to the actual plant cover of the present day are outlined in terms of the effects of European settlement within the original limits of distribution of the group.

Insofar as this treatment constitutes a regional examination, it must be stressed that the regions are defined by the natural vegetation itself. They are not presented as environmental regions, although relationships between structural groups and major environmental variables are of course to be expected. In particular, there is no separate treatment of certain special environmental situations, such as littoral, wetland, and alpine habitats, that may be of ecological interest but occupy only very small proportions of the land surface. Appropriate reference is made to these habitats in the accounts of the structural groups that are represented in such situations.

A special comment however is necessary in respect of the variably spaced parallel or sub-parallel longitudinal sand dunes that occur over a large part of the more arid sections of the country. In such sections, the map shows the characteristic vegetation of the interdune areas and the stable lower slopes of the dunes, and this is indicated at appropriate points in the text. Many of the dune crests however carry a different type of vegetation which is often extremely sparse; this may consist largely of floristic elements from the neighbouring stable areas, or it may involve distinctive dune species.

PLANTS AND ENVIRONMENT

The principal environmental factors referred to in the accounts of the vegetation groups are generalized soil categories and mean annual rainfall. The latter is a convenient general parameter, but it has only limited meaning unless considered in relation to seasonal distribution and seasonal effectiveness, and also to the often large variation about annual means.

Seasonal effects are most marked in the case of the herbaceous native species. In the better-watered parts of the country, such species are predominantly perennials, but many of these exhibit reduction of foliage during the unfavourable seasons. As rainfall becomes lower and more erratic, this fluctuation in the foliage of the herbaceous perennials becomes more marked, and the proportion of annual or ephemeral species increases. The hummock grasses are evergreen perennials. Australian trees and shrubs are predominantly evergreen; further, they are in general sclerophyllous (having hard and tough leaves) rather than orthophyllous (having leaves of ordinary texture). The sclerophyllous group includes the large proportion of the Australian species of *Acacia* in which the 'leaves' are actually phyllodes.

Closed-forests

Closed-forests are defined as having an uppermost stratum of trees, with projective foliage cover in excess of 70 per cent. Most of the closed-forests of Australia are in the category loosely known as 'rainforests'. The canopy height of these forests often exceeds 30 m on favoured sites, but the general level is probably somewhat lower. Most of the trees are evergreen, although there is a deciduous element, and most of them are orthophyllous, although some are sclerophyllous.

The distribution of these forests cannot readily be represented on the map, since their total area is relatively small, and much of that is widely distributed in small patches. Fire is one of the factors explaining this patchy distribution. They are associated with mean annual rainfalls that range from less than 1,200 mm to more than 2,400 mm, and that vary markedly in seasonal distribution. They occur at all latitudes in eastern Australia, from Cape York to Tasmania, with small outliers near the northern coasts of the Northern Territory and Western Australia; and at altitudes ranging from sea level up to 1,200 m or more. Further, they occur on a considerable range of soils, although there is some tendency to favour krasnozems. Their environmental relationships are complex, and this is reflected in their classification (Webb, 1959, 1968).

In very general terms, the optimum development of these forests north of the Tropic may be regarded as of the type commonly known as 'tropical rainforest'; of those on the mainland south of the Tropic as 'subtropical rainforest', grading through to 'warm temperate rainforest'; and of those in Tasmania as 'cool temperate rainforest'. The last is also sparsely represented in southern Victoria. These types correspond respectively to Webb's 'mesophyll vine forest', 'notophyll vine forest', 'microphyll fern forest', and 'nanophyll moss forest'.

The mesophyll vine forests characteristically exhibit great floristic diversity and structural complexity, as do many of the notophyll vine forests; the smaller leaves of the latter may be the main distinguishing character. The uppermost tree stratum of any stand consists of many different species, representing a wide range of families. There is a reduction in complexity in the transition from notophyll vine forest to microphyll fern forest. The nanophyll moss forests may consist of little more than a tree stratum, and are often dominated by a single species, namely *Nothofagus cunninghamii* (myrtle beech).

There are many variations from this pattern, relative to such factors as seasonal drought, increasing altitude, and decreasing soil fertility. As conditions become less favourable, there is an overall tendency towards types that are of lower stature and are generally more depauperate. Such low closed-forests largely correspond to the various types of 'thicket' in the detailed classification of Webb (1959, 1968).

The classification of closed-forests is further complicated by the occurrence of emergents. In particular, there is a tendency for species of *Araucaria* to occur as emergents above some closed-forests in Queensland and northern New South Wales, and for species of *Eucalyptus* to do the same in Tasmania. As the emergents exceed 30 m in height, and as their projective foliage cover tends to be in the range 10–30 per cent, these vegetation types might be classed as tall woodlands with closed-forest under-storeys. However, they are grouped here with closed-forests, since they may be regarded as stages in long-term transitions, the uppermost stratum being the relict element.

Some areas of closed-forest have been preserved as managed forests, to provide a wide range of valuable timbers; one of the best-known timbers is that of *Toona australis* (red cedar), which is now much depleted. Some other areas have been preserved as timber reserves or in national parks. However, large areas have been cleared and given over to cropping, or to intensive animal production on sown exotic pastures. The crops include sugar and bananas in the tropical and subtropical regions, and potatoes in the more temperate regions. The principal animal industries are dairying and beef production. In the tropical and subtropical regions, the pastures are based on a wide range of grasses and legumes, including *Panicum maximum* (guinea grass), *Paspalum dilatatum*, *Centrosema pubescens* (centro), and *Glycine wightii*. In the more temperate regions, the characteristic species include *Lolium perenne* (perennial ryegrass) and *Trifolium repens* (white clover).

On many sites, the continued dominance of the introduced economic species depends on very intensive management. Under the high rainfalls, much cleared land is susceptible to soil erosion and to the loss of soil fertility. It is further subject to invasion by a wide range of exotic weeds, including *Lantana*, and there is a considerable trend towards the regeneration of the native vegetation, pioneered by such species as *Pteridium esculentum* (austral bracken) (Plate 9.1).

Many of the intertidal stands of mangroves may be defined structurally as low closed-forest, or even closed-forest, although in less favourable situations they may be attenuated as far as low open-shrubland. The total area of such stands is relatively very small, but they constitute a distinctive feature of many sheltered shores and estuaries along the coasts of the Australian mainland. They range in floristic composition from assemblages of up to thirty species, notably members of the Rhizophoraceae, in northern tropical areas to monospecific stands of *Avicennia marina* on the southern coasts.

Plate 9.1   Closed-forest cleared and sown to pasture. Native species now regenerating; *Pteridium esculentum* (austral bracken) is pioneer. Near Ravenshoe, Queensland.

Open-forests

Open-forests are defined as having an uppermost stratum of trees, with projective foliage cover in the range 30–70 per cent. In most of the open-forests of Australia, the uppermost tree stratum of any stand consists of very few species, and in many cases these are members of a single genus. The most prominent genus is *Eucalyptus*, which is followed by *Acacia* and *Callitris*; *Casuarina* and *Melaleuca* are of local importance. The trees are evergreen, and typically sclerophyllous. The leaves of *Callitris* are much reduced; in *Casuarina*, they are vestigial teeth, and slender branchlets function as leaves.

Eucalyptus open-forests vary greatly in height, in structural complexity, and in characteristic dominant species. The tallest and most complex are the tall open-forests that occur under mean annual rainfalls above about 1,000 mm in the southwestern corner of Western Australia and from Tasmania to southeastern Queensland. These forests largely correspond to what is often called 'wet sclerophyll forest'. They are distinguished not only by the height of the dominant trees, which is often well above 30 m, but also by the dense subordinate stratum of low trees and tall shrubs, many of them orthophyllous. The

dominant species include *E. diversicolor* (karri) in Western Australia, *E. saligna* (Sydney blue gum) on the east coast, and *E. regnans* (mountain ash) in Victoria and Tasmania. The last ranges up to 100 m in height.

In Tasmania and eastern Australia, these tall open-forests are replaced under lower annual rainfalls or on poorer soils by open-forests that are distinguished by the smaller stature of the dominants and by the lesser density and the sclerophyllous or reduced leaves of the low trees and tall shrubs (including species of *Acacia* and *Casuarina*). The dominant species include *Eucalyptus viminalis* (manna gum) in the cooler climates and *E. maculata* (spotted gum) in the warmer.

Under lower rainfalls again (down to about 600 mm), or on less fertile soils, *Eucalyptus* open-forests are often characterized by a dense subordinate stratum of low sclerophyllous shrubs. This type of forest corresponds to 'dry sclerophyll forest' in the original restricted sense. It occurs in southeastern Australia, where the dominants include *E. macrorhyncha* (red stringybark), and in the southwestern corner of Western Australia, where *E. marginata* (jarrah) is prominent.

Eucalyptus open-forests with an understorey of tussock grasses are prominent in eastern Queensland.

Plate 9.2 Eucalyptus diversicolor (karri) tall open-forest cleared and sown to pasture. Cleared land taken over by *Pteridium esculentum* (austral bracken). Near Pemberton, Western Australia.

The nature of the understorey may have been due initially to regular burning by Aborigines. The dominants include *E. drepanophylla* (grey ironbark); and *Themeda australis* (kangaroo grass) is a major component of the herbaceous stratum. In northern Queensland and the Northern Territory, under monsoonal rainfalls in excess of 1,000 mm, there is a distinctive type of open-forest that usually has a prominent grassy stratum, including annual and perennial species of *Sorghum*, but is also characterized by a woody understorey that includes deciduous orthophyllous elements. *Eucalyptus tetrodonta* (Darwin stringybark) is a notable dominant species.

Some areas of *Eucalyptus* open-forest are managed for timber extraction. This may involve either selective extraction of timber or clear felling followed by regeneration. Others have been preserved as timber reserves, or in national parks or Aboriginal reserves, or for catchment protection. Some have been cleared and replaced by planted forests; various native and exotic species have been established in such plantations, but by far the most prominent is the exotic *Pinus radiata*, a species of temperate climates.

However, considerable areas of these forests have been converted to other forms of land use. In the case of the tall open-forests, this has involved clearing the forests and establishing cropping or intensive animal production, along similar lines to those described for land formerly occupied by closed-forests, and with similar problems (Plate 9.2). The situation is rather different in the case of the main body of the *Eucalyptus* open-forests, which are in general associated with lower rainfalls, or more variable rainfalls, or poorer soils, than are the tall open-forests. Some of these forests are used as they stand, or with some degree of clearing, for extensive grazing by beef cattle, or by sheep in the drier parts of the temperate regions (Plate 9.3). Repeated burning, combined with grazing and browsing, tends to select against the woody species of the understorey, and in favour of the grasses, including members of such genera as *Danthonia* (wallaby grasses) in the temperate regions and *Heteropogon* (spear grasses) in the tropical and subtropical regions. Some graziers go considerably further, and replace the forests with sown

Plate .9.3   Eucalyptus macrorhyncha-E. rossii open-forest largely cleared to induce growth of native tussock grasses; these have been depleted under grazing and replaced by *Nassella trichotoma* (serrated tussock). Near Gundaroo, New South Wales.

pastures of exotic grasses and legumes. This practice is widespread in Tasmania and eastern Australia, and is fairly well mandatory in the southwestern part of Western Australia, where there are few useful native grasses. In the temperate regions, the typical sown pasture species of the higher-rainfall areas, such as *Lolium perenne* and *Trifolium repens*, give way under lower or less reliable rainfalls to other species, such as *Phalaris tuberosa* and *Trifolium subterraneum* (sub-terranean clover); and in the warmer regions, species such as *Paspalum dilatatum* give way to such others as *Chloris gayana* (Rhodes grass).

Acacia open-forests are generally of somewhat lower stature than *Eucalyptus* open-forests, and tend to occur under lower rainfalls. Thus, *Acacia harpo-phylla* (brigalow) is the principal dominant species of many areas of open-forest, with canopy heights up to about 15 m, in southeastern Queensland. These forests occur under mean annual rainfalls ranging down to about 500 mm; further inland, they are replaced by rather lower open-forests dominated by *A. aneura* (mulga) under rainfalls ranging down to about 400 mm. Again, *A. shirleyi* (lancewood) is the dominant species of low open-forests that occur under rainfalls of about 500 mm or more in central and northern

Queensland and in the Northern Territory.

The *Acacia harpophylla* open-forests occupy fertile heavy soils. *A. harpophylla* is associated with several other tree species, notably *Casuarina cristata* (belah), which on some soils may be the principal dominant. There is a wide range of subordinate low trees and tall shrubs, and a very sparse ground layer (Plate 9.4). The *A. aneura* open-forests are associated particularly with red earths. A few other tree species, notably *Eucalyptus populnea* (poplar box) may occur in the general canopy, or as emergents. Subordinate strata of grasses and low shrubs may be present, but these are typically very sparse. The *A. shirleyi* low open-forests are associated particularly with shallow gravelly soils; they usually consist of pure stands of the dominant species, with virtually no understorey, alternating with more open stands characterized by a grassy understorey and by an admixture of other tree species.

Some of the *Acacia* open-forests are used for extensive grazing by beef cattle, and also by sheep in the case of the southern forests. Clearing the timber induces a better growth of native grasses. However, even this induced growth is sparse in the lower-rainfall areas. In the case of *A. aneura*, the dominant itself is often used for browse. Further, the dominants tend to

Plate 9.4 Partially cleared open-forest dominated by *Acacia harpophylla* (brigalow), with subordinate stratum of *Eremophila mitchellii* (false sandalwood) and very sparse ground cover. Near Augathella, Queensland.

regenerate after clearing. In the case of the *A. harpophylla* forests, which are associated with fertile soils and better rainfalls, regeneration has been controlled in many places by the establishment of cropping or intensive animal production. Considerable areas have been sown to wheat or other crops, and the sown exotic pastures include such grasses and legumes as *Chloris gayana* and *Medicago sativa* (lucerne).

Callitris columellaris ('*C. glauca*' race; white cypress pine), sometimes associated with species of *Eucalyptus*, dominates considerable areas of open-forest in northern New South Wales and southern Queensland. These tend to occur towards the inland limit of forests, under mean annual rainfalls ranging down to about 500 mm or less. They are usually associated with sandy soils. The understorey may include woody species, or it may be limited to sparse grasses.

Some areas of *Callitris* open-forest have been retained as managed forests. Some are used for extensive grazing by sheep (in the south) or by beef cattle (in the north); clearing induces a better growth of native grasses, including species of *Aristida* (wire

grasses). Some of the southern forests have been cleared and the land has been cropped for wheat, or sown with exotic pasture species suited to lower rainfalls, including species of *Medicago* (medics).

Open-forests dominated by species of *Melaleuca* (paperbarks), usually with a grassy understorey, are of local importance in tropical Australia, mostly within the mapped limits of *Eucalyptus* open-forest.

Woodlands

Woodlands are defined as having an uppermost stratum of trees, with projective foliage cover in the range 10–30 per cent. They have considerable floristic affinities with the open-forests. In general terms, the woodlands may be regarded as the extension of these forests into regions of lower rainfall; however, in many instances the relative distribution of the two groups is also related to soil or other factors.

Woodlands exhibit a lesser range of height than do open-forests. The dominants do not often exceed 30 m, and where they do approach this stature they tend to be associated with special environments.

Plate 9.5   Eucalyptus alba (white gum) grassy woodland; *Heteropogon contortus* (bunch spear grass) has increased under grazing. Near Mingela, Queensland.

For example, relatively tall woodlands, dominated by such species as *Eucalyptus moluccana* (grey box), occur on the heavy soils of some low-lying areas within or near the climatic limits of open-forest. However, the main range of heights is from about 20 m to well under 10 m. There is a general tendency for stature to decline, and usually for cover to decrease, as rainfall or other factors become less favourable.

Woodlands dominated by species of *Eucalyptus* are widespread in northern Australia, under mean annual rainfalls ranging down to about 600 mm; in eastern Australia, under rainfalls down to less than 400 mm; and in the southwestern part of Western Australia, under rainfalls as low as 200 mm.

Eucalyptus woodlands characterized by an understorey of tussock grasses are very prominent in northern Australia and in the better-watered parts of eastern Australia. Among the woodland types, they tend to be associated with the heavier or more fertile soils. The wide distribution of this type is reflected in the wide range of dominant species, including *E. dichromophloia* (a bloodwood) in northern Australia, *E. populnea* in mid-eastern Australia, and *E. melliodora* (yellow box) in southeastern Australia. Some of the

grassy woodlands of monsoonal northern Australia are distinguished by the presence among the dominants of some of the few deciduous species of *Eucalyptus*, notably *E. alba* (white gum) (Plate 9.5). *E. camaldulensis* (river red gum) is prominent in riverine situations within the climatic limits of woodlands, and is also conspicuous as the dominant of a distinctive fringing grassy woodland, often only one tree wide, along many of the intermittent watercourses of arid Australia (Plate 9.6).

There is also a wide range of species of tussock grasses, representing many genera, including *Aristida* in the north and *Stipa* (corkscrew grasses) in the south. *Themeda australis* is widespread. Hummock grasses may also be present in some tropical areas.

Under lower rainfalls or on poorer soils, the *Eucalyptus* woodlands of eastern Australia tend to be characterized by an understorey of low trees or tall shrubs. Species of *Acacia*, *Casuarina*, and *Callitris* are often prominent in the understorey, which may be of considerable density. Typical dominant species include *Eucalyptus woollsiana* (inland grey box) in the south and *E. populnea* in the north. Similar types of vegetation also occur in some parts of northern Australia, where

Plate 9.6 Eucalyptus camaldulensis (river red gum) grassy woodland on intermittent watercourse. Wongawall Creek, Western Australia.

E. tetrodonta is a characteristic species, and of southwestern Western Australia, where *E. loxophleba* (York gum) is prominent.

Some areas of *Eucalyptus* woodland in southeastern and southwestern Australia have an understorey of low shrubs. Some of these may be regarded as lower-rainfall extensions of adjacent forests of similar structure, but others have distinctive features, notably the woodlands dominated by *E. salmonophloia* (salmon gum) that occur in Western Australia under rainfalls as low as 200 mm. The low shrubs of the subordinate stratum are generally sclerophyllous; but semi-succulent Chenopodiaceae, including species of *Atriplex* (saltbushes), are characteristic of the alkaline soils that are widespread in the lower-rainfall woodland areas of Western Australia.

Eucalyptus low woodlands with an understorey of low shrubs occur on poor sandy soils in various temperate coastal or near-coastal situations; there is a wide range of dominant species of *Eucalyptus*, and species of *Banksia* are often co-dominant. Low woodlands dominated by *Eucalyptus pauciflora* (snow gum), and with a wide range of low shrubby species, are prominent on mountain soils above about 1,500 m in southeastern mainland Australia.

Most of the *Eucalyptus* woodlands have been modified under settlement. The exceptions, mainly tropical, include some stands on rough terrain or in Aboriginal reserves. Because of the lesser density of the trees, and in many cases the well-developed grass stratum, the woodlands are better suited than the open-forests for extensive grazing, predominantly by sheep in the temperate regions and by beef cattle in the tropical regions.

Extensive grazing by beef cattle, usually on grasses that are fired annually, is still the principal form of land use in the tropical woodlands. In general, this form of land use does not appear to have resulted in marked structural changes in the vegetation, although there do appear to have been some floristic changes in the grass stratum, including a decline in *Themeda australis* and an increase in the less desirable *Heteropogon contortus* (bunch spear grass) (Plate 9.5). In many places, the exotic legume *Stylosanthes humilis* (Townsville stylo) has now been sown broadcast among the native grasses, and there has been some development of more intensive cattle grazing involving the use of other exotic species, such as *Cenchrus ciliaris* (buffel grass).

The situation is fairly similar in subtropical southeastern Queensland, although there has been more

Plate 9.7   Eucalyptus populnea (poplar box) woodland largely cleared to induce growth of native grasses, including species of *Bothriochloa*. Near Gayndah, Queensland.

emphasis on intensive production and therefore more modification of the natural vegetation (Plate 9.7). In the temperate regions of Australia, where sheep are usually predominant, extensive grazing has led to much greater changes. There has been much more widespread removal of timber, and the natural or induced native herbaceous stratum has been greatly modified. There is a general tendency for the tussock grasses to be reduced, and in many areas these have been virtually eliminated and replaced by volunteer exotic forbs and grasses, such as *Hordeum leporinum* (barley grass). In some places the depletion of the native grasses has been followed by an increase in native species detrimental to grazing, such as *Bassia birchii* (galvanized burr) and a range of unpalatable shrubs. There has often been a further modification, in that sown exotic pastures have been established, largely based on *Trifolium subterraneum*, or on species of *Medicago* in the lower-rainfall areas.

In addition to the changes brought about by extensive and intensive grazing, very large temperate areas that once carried *Eucalyptus* woodland are now cropped, mainly for wheat. There are also limited areas of crops in the better-watered tropical woodland areas.

Woodlands dominated by species of *Acacia* or *Casuarina* tend to occur under lower annual rainfalls than do those dominated by species of *Eucalyptus*, and they are generally of lower stature. There are scattered examples of these low woodlands through the southern half of Australia, but the principal area extends from south central Queensland through western New South Wales into South Australia. *Acacia aneura* is the principal dominant species in the north, and *Casuarina cristata* in the south. Both types have a grass stratum, that includes species of *Aristida* in the north and *Stipa* in the south. The *Casuarina* low woodland often has an understorey of low shrubs as well.

These low woodlands have largely been utilized for extensive grazing, mainly by sheep (Plate 9.8). In some places this has led to profound changes in the vegetation, including the destruction of much of the timber and the degradation of the herbaceous stratum to sparse native forbs, including species of *Bassia*.

The sandy plains around the head of the Gulf of Carpentaria are largely occupied by low woodlands dominated by species of *Melaleuca*. These generally have an understorey of tussock grasses, including species of *Aristida*; the hummock grass *Triodia pungens* (soft spinifex) is also present in some places.

Plate 9.8 *Acacia aneura* (mulga) low woodland under grazing. Near Eulo, Queensland.

In the southeast these woodlands grade into mixed low woodlands, of similar structure but with a wide range of dominants, including the deciduous *Bauhinia cunninghamii* (bean tree). These various woodlands are utilized for extensive grazing by beef cattle.

Small patches of grassy woodland dominated by species of *Callitris* occur in many parts of the country. They are generally utilized for extensive grazing.

Open-woodlands

Open-woodlands are defined as having an uppermost stratum of trees, with projective foliage cover less than 10 per cent. It may be argued that some of the vegetation types in this group would be better assigned to other groups, on the grounds that they are dominated by the understorey rather than by the uppermost stratum. It is true that the apparent significance of the uppermost stratum depends in part on the height and density of the understorey; however, the tree stratum is still quite conspicuous in many circumstances.

The principal tree genera are the same as those of the open-forests and woodlands. *Eucalyptus* and *Acacia* are particularly prominent, followed by *Casuarina*; *Melaleuca* and *Callitris*, together with some other genera, are of local importance. In general terms, the open-woodlands may be regarded as the extension of

the woodlands into habitats that are only marginally suitable for tree growth. Not only is the tree stratum sparse but it is generally less than 10 m in height, that is, most of the open-woodlands are low open-woodlands. Low or variable water supply is probably a major factor, in terms both of rainfall (with annual means down to less than 150 mm in the arid interior) and of the moisture-holding capacity of the soil; fire may also be involved in some situations.

It is convenient to classify the open-woodlands primarily in terms of structure, because of the relative significance of the understorey. Thus, one subgroup may be defined as having an understorey of tall shrubs, and may be regarded as occupying an intermediate position between woodlands and shrublands. The understoreys are of varying density, and species of *Acacia* are prominent.

The most distinctive example of this subgroup is the 'pindan' vegetation that occupies considerable areas of light soil in the southwestern part of the Kimberley region of Western Australia. Pindan vegetation is characterized by species of *Eucalyptus* (especially *E. dichromophloia*) in the tree stratum and of *Acacia* (especially *A. tumida*) in the shrub stratum. There is some evidence that the shrub stratum has become denser since the grassy ground layer has been utilized

Plate 9.9   Eucalyptus dichromophloia-E. brevifolia low open-woodland; ground cover of *Triodia wiseana* reduced by burning. Near Wittenoom, Western Australia.

for extensive grazing by beef cattle, and to some extent by sheep. More recently, some areas have been cleared and sown to pastures of such exotic species as *Cenchrus setigerus* (Birdwood grass). Two examples of the subgroup in South Australia are characterized by the presence in the tree stratum of *Casuarina cristata* and *Callitris columellaris* respectively. The former is unused, but the latter has been modified by extensive grazing with sheep.

Some open-woodlands have an understorey of low shrubs. This subgroup includes limited areas of the tropical *Eucalyptus* open-woodlands. However, the main examples occur in southern Australia, under mean annual rainfalls of less than 300 mm and especially on calcareous soils. The principal tree species are *Acacia sowdenii* (myall) and lesser *Myoporum platycarpum* (sugarwood), and most of the low shrubs are semi-succulent Chenopodiaceae, especially *Kochia sedifolia* (bluebush).* Where waters for stock are available, this type has been used for extensive grazing by sheep.

---

*The Australian species of *Kochia* (bluebushes) have recently been transferred to the genus *Maireana* and the latter name is beginning to appear in accounts of Australian vegetation.

It has proved to be fairly tolerant of this form of land use.

The open-woodlands that have an understorey of hummock grasses largely correspond to the 'tree steppe' of Beard (1967). The distinctive hummock grass growth form is discussed in the section 'Hummock Grasslands'. Although the hummock grass layer is usually very conspicuous, the plants are distinctly spaced and the overall cover of this layer is therefore usually relatively sparse. Open-woodlands with hummock grass understoreys are associated particularly with skeletal soils and with the sandy soils of sandplains and dunefields.

The most widespread example of this subgroup is dominated by species of *Eucalyptus* (Plate 9.9). This type of vegetation occurs across tropical Australia under mean annual rainfalls from about 600 mm to less than 300 mm. It also occurs under considerably lower rainfalls (to less than 150 mm) in the Great Victoria Desert area of South Australia and Western Australia. The characteristic trees include *E. dichromophloia* in the north and *E. gongylocarpa* (desert gum) in the south; the latter is often associated, or alternating, with very sparse tall shrubs. The hummock grasses include a wide range of species of *Triodia*, but *T. pun-*

Plate 9.10 Mallee species of *Eucalyptus* regenerating on land cleared and sown to *Trifolium subterraneum* (subterranean clover). Near Porongorups, Western Australia.

gens is particularly prominent in the north and *T. basedowii* (hard spinifex) in the south. *Plectrachne schinzii* (feathertop spinifex) is prominent in some of the northern sand country.

A considerable area of predominantly sandy country in central Australia carries an open-woodland association characterized by *Casuarina decaisneana* (desert oak) and *Triodia basedowii*. The *Acacia* open-woodlands of western Queensland mostly have an understorey of tussock grasses, but some examples on poorer soils have a ground layer dominated by several species of *Triodia*. Some other mapped examples of the subgroup have a range of genera in the tree layer.

Some areas of 'tree steppe' are not utilized, because of roughness of the terrain or other disabilities, and some are preserved in Aboriginal reserves or national parks. However, other areas are subject to extensive grazing by cattle or sheep, typically at low stocking rates. The vegetation is fired frequently, to induce more palatable young green growth on the hummock grasses, and there are usually some pickings from herbaceous species in the interspaces between the hummocks. Continued grazing tends to eliminate the herbaceous feed, and may change the balance among the hummock grasses in favour of the less palatable species.

The open-woodlands that have an understorey of tussock grasses largely correspond to the 'tree savanna' of Beard (1967). Some of these grassy open-woodlands occur under lower rainfalls than do the woodlands, and in such situations they appear to be associated largely with the heavier or more fertile soils. However, others occur within the apparent climatic limits of denser woodlands. Some of these occurrences may be on soils (especially heavy soils) that are not favourable to tree growth, while others may be associated with fire.

Some of the *Eucalyptus* grassy open-woodlands have much the same floristic composition as the adjacent woodlands. However, *E. microtheca* (coolibah) is the characteristic species of a distinctive open-woodland that occurs with a range of grasses on many areas of intermittently inundated country in northern and inland Australia. The *Acacia* grassy woodlands of southern Queensland and western New South Wales give way to the west, with decreasing rainfall, to open-woodlands. In the far west of Queensland, and in the southeastern part of the Northern Territory, there is a distinctive open-woodland dominated by *Acacia georginae* (Georgina gidyea), with a ground layer of ephemeral grasses and forbs. Other examples of grassy open-woodlands are dominated in southern Australia by species of *Casuarina* and in northern Australia by species of *Melaleuca* and of a range of other genera.

Many of the grassy open-woodlands have been used for extensive grazing, predominantly by beef cattle in the north and by sheep in the south. In some places, grazing has resulted in virtually complete destruction of the vegetation, leaving the ground bare and unproductive, and often eroded. Little can be done for much of this country, although exotic grasses, for example species of *Cenchrus*, have been successfully established in some parts of tropical Australia.

A further example of low open-woodland occurs in Arnhem Land, where the broken sandstone country supports a very sparse cover of small trees (mainly species of *Eucalyptus*), shrubs, and hummock grasses, fragmented by areas of bare rock.

Scrubs and Heaths

Scrubs are defined as having an uppermost stratum of tall shrubs (exceeding 2 m), with projective foliage cover in excess of 70 per cent (closed-scrub) or in the range 30–70 per cent (open-scrub). Examples of closed-scrub may be found in the field, but they are usually either very limited in area or else not readily separable from less dense forms. The principal examples of open-scrub are dominated by species of *Acacia*, *Casuarina*, and *Eucalyptus*. The shrubs are evergreen, and typically sclerophyllous. (The leaves of *Casuarina* are vestigial teeth, and slender branchlets function as leaves.)

Reference is made in the section 'Open-woodlands' to the 'pindan' vegetation of the Kimberley region of Western Australia. To the southwest, under lower rainfalls, the *Eucalyptus* tree layer loses significance, leaving the tall *Acacia* shrubs predominant. This latter vegetation type is therefore mapped as *Acacia* open-scrub. The ground layer is dominated by hummock grasses. This vegetation type is utilized to some extent for extensive grazing by beef cattle and sheep.

In the southwestern part of Western Australia, another form of open-scrub occurs under annual rainfalls from about 225 mm to more than 300 mm, and mainly on infertile sandy soils. The uppermost stratum is dominated by shrubby species of *Acacia* and *Casuarina*. The subordinate stratum consists of low sclerophyllous shrubs, many of them ericoid; these represent a wide range of families, including Myrtaceae and Proteaceae. This kind of vegetation is unsuitable for grazing, and it is largely unused. Marginal areas have been cleared for wheat cropping.

Reference is made in the section 'Shrublands' to the types of vegetation dominated by species of *Eucalyptus* of the 'mallee' form. In these types, the overall project-

ive foliage cover of the tallest stratum rarely exceeds 30 per cent. However there appears to be a tendency towards greater cover values at the southeastern margin of mallee vegetation in Victoria, and this denser type, which usually has a sparse grassy understorey, is therefore mapped as *Eucalyptus* open-scrub. Most of it has now been cleared for wheat cropping and intensive sheep grazing.

Heaths are defined as having an uppermost stratum of low shrubs (below 2 m), with projective foliage cover in excess of 70 per cent (closed-heath) or in the range 30–70 per cent (open-heath). The latter density is the more usual. The principal examples of heaths exhibit a very patchy distribution in coastal and near-coastal situations throughout eastern Australia and in the southwestern part of Western Australia. They are typically associated with very infertile soils.

Fire is also an important environmental factor; most heaths tend to develop into taller and more complex types of shrubby vegetation if they remain unburnt for more than a few years. Many of them are probably best regarded as successional stages towards 'scrub heath' or 'mallee-heath', which are discussed in the sections on 'Shrublands' and 'Open-shrublands' respectively. The floristic characteristics of the heaths are largely those of the understoreys of these more developed types. The earlier heath stages are likely to have a considerable component of grass-like monocotyledonous plants; species of *Xanthorrhoea* (yacca) are often prominent, and there may be a ground layer of Cyperaceae (sedges) and Restionaceae (jointed rushes).

Shrublands

Shrublands are defined as having an uppermost stratum of shrubs, with projective foliage cover in the range 10–30 per cent. They are divided according to the height of the dominants into tall shrublands (above 2 m) and low shrublands (below 2 m).

In the case of the tall shrublands, the principal shrub genera are *Acacia* and *Eucalyptus*; some other genera, including *Banksia* and *Grevillea*, are of local importance. The shrubs are evergreen, and typically sclerophyllous.

Tall shrublands dominated by species of *Acacia* are widespread in the arid zone of Australia, under mean annual rainfalls ranging from about 300 mm (400 mm in northern Australia) down to less than 150 mm. The predominant species is *Acacia aneura*. In the central and western parts of Australia the growth form of this species is generally that of a tall shrub rather than a low tree, although there is at least one example of *A. aneura* low woodland in the Warburton region of Western Australia. At the margins of the *Acacia* tall shrublands, *A. aneura* is replaced by such species as *A. linophylla* in the south and west and *A. stipuligera* in the north. The cover of the dominant shrubs is variable (including some groving), and this variation is compounded by the effects of periodic droughts.

The nature of the understorey tends to vary with soil type. Herbaceous understoreys are the most widely distributed; these usually include some perennial grasses such as species of *Eragrostis*, but there is also a large component of ephemeral grasses and forbs that fluctuates greatly under seasonal conditions. Shrublands with these understoreys are associated particularly with red earths, and with the interdune areas in some sandhill country. Other shrublands have a well-developed understorey of low shrubs, including species of *Eremophila*. This type is associated particularly with large areas of red and brown hard-pan soils in Western Australia. On alkaline soils there is a low shrub layer characterized by semi-succulent Chenopodiaceae, including species of *Atriplex* and *Kochia*. Understoreys of hummock grasses, notably *Triodia pungens* in the north and *T. basedowii* further south, are associated with the poorer soils, as on some sandplains and on the laterite plains of the Gibson Desert.

With the exception of the last type, the *Acacia* tall shrublands are largely used for extensive grazing by sheep or by beef cattle. In some places grazing has resulted in virtually complete destruction of the vegetation, leaving the ground bare and unproductive, and often eroded. Little can be done for much of this country.

Eucalyptus tall shrublands have a widespread distribution in southern Australia, mostly under mean annual rainfalls in the range 200–450 mm, and especially on solonized brown soils and solodized solonetz soils, and on some deep sands. They also occur on rocky soils in some mountainous areas. The species of *Eucalyptus* exhibit the 'mallee' form, in which several stems grow from a massive underground lignotuber to produce a distinctive multistemmed shrub habit (Plate 9.10). There are numerous dominant species, including *E. oleosa* and *E. socialis* (red mallees) and *E. incrassata*.

There is commonly a subordinate stratum of low shrubs. Under the higher rainfalls, this is usually dense, and the low shrubs are characteristically sclerophyllous. There is a very wide range of species, including species of *Acacia* and members of the Proteaceae and Myrtaceae. With decreasing rainfall, the understorey becomes more open, and there may be some sparse ground cover, including such tussock grasses as species of *Stipa*, or the hummock grass *Triodia irritans*. Towards the lower rainfall limit, the low shrub stratum tends to become dominated by semi-succulent Chenopodiaceae, including species of *Atriplex* and *Kochia*.

Some areas of mallee vegetation have been extensively grazed by sheep. Much more of the land under rainfalls in excess of about 280 mm has been cleared for cropping with wheat or for sown exotic pastures based on *Trifolium subterraneum* or on species of *Medicago* (Plate 9.10).

A distinctive kind of tall shrubland typically has a range of genera represented in the tallest stratum, including *Banksia*, *Grevillea*, and *Acacia*. There is a dense understorey of sclerophyllous low shrubs, many of them ericoid. This lower stratum contains a very large number of species; these represent a wide range of families, including Proteaceae and Myrtaceae. This type of vegetation largely corresponds to the 'scrub heath' of Beard (1969).

Scrub heath is prominent on various sandy soils in the southwestern part of Western Australia. However, examples of similar vegetation have a patchy distribution in coastal and near-coastal situations throughout eastern Australia. They are associated particularly with very infertile soils, such as deep sands and some podzols.

This kind of vegetation is generally unsuitable for grazing as it stands, and some areas have been left unused. Some other areas have been cleared and sown with exotic pasture species. The rainfall is usually suitable for the establishment of these, but it is necessary to overcome the gross infertility of the soil by massive applications of appropriate fertilizers, and by attention to deficiencies in trace elements.

The most widespread examples of low shrublands are those dominated by members of the family Chenopodiaceae. These shrublands occupy large areas of southern Australia, generally under rainfalls below 250 mm, except that the upper limit is nearer 350 mm in southern New South Wales. They occur on soils that exhibit a considerable range of profile and texture but are generally calcareous or saline.

The dominant low shrubs are evergreen, typically with semi-succulent or succulent leaves. The principal genera represented are *Atriplex* and *Kochia*. The various major species of these genera exhibit intricate patterns of distribution, but there are some trends towards dominance on a broad scale, as of *Atriplex vesicaria* (bladder saltbush) in southern New South Wales and of *Kochia sedifolia* on the Nullarbor Plain. There is usually a herbaceous ground layer. The heavier and lower-lying soils tend to support perennial grasses, including species of *Eragrostis*. The lighter and more elevated soils carry a cover of grasses and forbs that fluctuates greatly with seasonal conditions.

Many of these low shrublands are used for extensive grazing by sheep in the south and by beef cattle in the north. The dominants appear to be fairly tolerant of lenient grazing, at least in the higher-rainfall areas (Plate 9.11). However, they have been overgrazed in many places, often to the extent of the virtual

Plate 9.11   Atriplex vesicaria (bladder saltbush) low shrubland. Ungrazed in foreground, with ground layer of tussock grasses, including species of *Danthonia*; lightly grazed by sheep beyond fence. Near Deniliquin, New South Wales.

elimination of the dominants and the reduction of the herbaceous stratum to sparse native forbs, notably species of *Bassia*. Rabbits appear to have played a part in this process, and on the Nullarbor Plain, which is largely ungrazed because of the lack of stock waters, they appear to have been primarily responsible for removing the shrubs in many places, to leave the herbaceous species predominant.

There are other examples of Chenopodiaceous low shrublands. The most distinctive are the stands of succulent dwarf shrubs ('samphires') that are widely distributed on the highly saline soils (solonchaks) of low-lying areas both on the coast (including many intertidal areas) and in the arid interior. *Arthrocnemum* is a characteristic genus of these stands.

There are also some low shrublands dominated by sclerophyllous shrubs. The most distinctive of these occur in southeastern Australia above the treeline, which ranges from 1,200 m or lower in Tasmania to about 1,800 m in southern New South Wales. The limited areas above these altitudes are occupied by a mosaic of shrubby and herbaceous vegetation. Both components are rich in species and varied in composition. The shrubs include members of the Epacridaceae, and the herbaceous layer is characterized in particular

by tussock grasses of the genus *Poa* and by the forb *Celmisia longifolia* (snow daisy). Extensive grazing in the past has led to some degradation of this vegetation type. However, much of it is now preserved in national parks.

Open-shrublands
Open-shrublands are defined as having an uppermost stratum of shrubs, with projective foliage cover less than 10 per cent. As in the case of the open-woodlands, it may be argued that some of the vegetation types in this group would be better assigned to other groups, on the grounds that they are dominated by the understorey rather than by the uppermost stratum. However, the shrub stratum is still quite conspicuous in many circumstances.

Open-shrublands are divided according to the height of the shrubs into tall open-shrublands (above 2 m) and low open-shrublands (below 2 m). The principal shrub genera are *Eucalyptus* and *Acacia* in the former case and *Acacia* in the latter.

Mallee species of *Eucalyptus* comprise the uppermost stratum of 'mallee-heath'. This is a tall open-shrubland (though in some cases hardly exceeding 2 m) with a dense understorey of sclerophyllous

Plate 9.12 *Acacia aneura* (mulga) tall open-shrubland with ground layer of *Triodia basedowii* (hard spinifex). Near Carnegie Homestead, Western Australia.

low shrubs, that occurs on the south coast of Western Australia and in the 'Big Desert' region of south-eastern Australia, largely on sandy duplex soils. Characteristic species of *Eucalyptus* include *E. tetragona* in the west and *E. incrassata* in the east. The understorey consists of many species, representing a wide range of families, including Proteaceae and Myrtaceae.

Mallee-heath is generally unsuitable for grazing as it stands, and some areas have been left unused. However, some other areas have been cleared and sown with exotic pasture species, including *Trifolium subterraneum*. It is necessary to overcome the gross infertility of the soil by massive applications of appropriate fertilizers, and by attention to deficiencies in trace elements.

Other mallee open-shrublands, with an understorey of hummock grasses, occur throughout the southern interior of Western Australia. They are associated particularly with the earthy sands of sandplains and of some interdune areas. The characteristic mallee species of *Eucalyptus* include *E. kingsmillii*, and *Triodia basedowii* is the principal hummock grass. Some of these open-shrublands are grazed extensively by sheep or beef cattle, but others are unused.

Open-shrublands with hummock grass understoreys

largely correspond to the 'shrub steppe' of Beard (1967). Other writers have used the term 'shrub steppe' to describe an entirely different kind of vegetation, namely the Chenopodiaceous low shrublands. The most widespread example of this subgroup has the uppermost stratum dominated by species of *Acacia* (Plate 9.12). This type of vegetation occurs on various kinds of terrain, but is particularly characteristic of large areas of sandplain, especially in the Northern Territory, and of sandridge country on the interdune areas and the stable lower slopes of dunes, notably in the Simpson Desert and the Great Sandy Desert. It occurs under mean annual rainfalls ranging from more than 300 mm to less than 150 mm.

The tallest stratum consists of a fairly wide range of species. *Acacia* is usually sufficiently well represented to be regarded as the characteristic genus, but other genera are also prominent, including *Hakea*, which exhibits some local dominance. Typical species of *Acacia* include *A. aneura* in the southeast and *A. pachycarpa* in the western deserts. There is considerable variation in the height and density, and therefore in the apparent significance, of the shrub layer.

Although the hummock grass layer is conspicuous, the plants are distinctly spaced, and the overall cover of this layer is therefore usually relatively sparse. The principal species of *Triodia* are *T. pungens* and *T. basedowii*; the former is more prominent in the north, and the latter in the south. *Plectrachne schinzii* is a common associate of these species, except in the southeast.

Considerable areas of these open-shrublands are preserved in national parks or Aboriginal reserves. Most of the other areas are also unused; they are unattractive for pastoralism, in terms both of the environmental difficulties and of the feed available. However, some areas are used, especially where they border on better country. The hummock grasses, being evergreen perennials, can supply some grazing in unfavourable seasons. Grazing is predominantly by beef cattle, typically at low stocking rates. The effects of grazing are similar to those described for 'tree steppe' in the section 'Open-woodlands'.

Some open-shrublands have an understorey of tussock grasses and forbs. Some of these are characterized by *Acacia aneura*, and may be regarded as the extension of the corresponding low woodlands or tall shrublands into less favourable environments. Other open-shrublands of this type are dominated by other species of *Acacia*, or by other genera, such as *Hakea*. One distinctive example is the tall open-shrubland, dominated by a shrub form of *Acacia cambagei* (gidyea), that occurs on the clayey soils of the interdune areas in the southeastern part of the Simpson Desert. The ground layer includes perennial grasses, such as species of *Eragrostis*, but there is also a prominent component of annual and ephemeral forbs.

Some areas of these grassy open-shrublands are preserved in national parks or Aboriginal reserves. Others are used for extensive grazing by beef cattle or sheep, and in some cases this has led to the destruction of much of the vegetation and to soil erosion.

Hummock Grasslands

The distinctive hummock grass growth form usually has the appearance of a mound, ranging in height from about 0.3 m up to 1 m or more; this consists of a mass of repeatedly branched stems, bristling with long spine-like leaves. One common name for this form is the very appropriate 'porcupine grass', but the more popular common name is the botanically misleading 'spinifex' (Plate 9.12). Only two closely related genera, namely *Triodia* and *Plectrachne*, exhibit this form. They are evergreen perennials.

Although hummock grasses are a characteristic component of the vegetation over very large areas of Australia, they rarely occur without some sort of upper storey of trees or shrubs. The most widespread examples of such associations are 'tree steppe' and 'shrub steppe', which are discussed respectively in the sections on 'Open-woodlands' and 'Open-shrublands'.

However, there are some areas of virtually pure hummock grassland, the 'grass steppe' of Beard (1967). For example, there are areas where the shrub stratum is virtually absent within the great expanses of sandplain and sandridge country that are mapped as occupied by *Acacia* open-shrubland with hummock grasses. Likewise, there are examples of virtually pure hummock grassland on some steep and rocky mountainous areas in central and northwestern Australia. The plants of these various hummock grasslands are distinctly spaced, and the overall cover is therefore usually relatively sparse. In general, these hummock grasslands occur in inhospitable or inaccessible situations, and are not used.

Herblands

Most of the major examples of herbaceous vegetation are dominated by grasses or grass-like plants. However, in many cases there is a forb component, and some types of vegetation are dominated by forbs.

The grasses and grass-like plants may be characterized as 'tussocks', since they are predominantly of this form. Species of *Astrebla* (Mitchell grasses) and *Dichanthium* (blue grasses) are particularly prominent among the true grasses or Gramineae (Poaceae), but there are many other important genera. The sedges (Cyperaceae) are prominent among the families of grass-like plants.

Tussock grasslands dominated by species of *Astrebla* occupy large areas of cracking clay soils in northern and eastern Australia. They occur under mean annual rainfalls that are generally less than 600 mm and may be as low as 200 mm. The principal species of *Astrebla* are *A. lappacea* (curly Mitchell grass) and *A. pectinata* (barley Mitchell grass). The former is particularly prominent in the east and the latter in the north and in the lower-rainfall areas. A distinctive feature of the 'Mitchell grass downs' of Queensland is the presence of occasional patches of low open-forest or low woodland, dominated by such species as *Acacia cambagei*.

Some *Astrebla* grasslands may contain very few other grasses, but in others there is a considerable range of species. With increasing rainfall, there is a change in dominance on similar soils from species of *Astrebla* to species of *Dichanthium* (and other associated species).

The projective foliage cover of the *Astrebla* tussock grasslands is generally in the range 30–70 per cent. In southwestern Queensland, under rainfalls of 200 mm or less, and on some clay soils with stony or gravelly mantles, the cover of *A. pectinata* is typically much more sparse and fluctuating, and there is an admixture of Chenopodiaceous forbs, including species of *Bassia*. Areas of similar soils in South Australia carry similar but more mixed vegetation; *Astrebla pectinata* is still

Plate 9.13 *Astrebla pectinata* (barley Mitchell grass) tussock grassland, grazed by cattle during drought. Near Elliott, Northern Territory.

present, but other grasses, including species of *Eragrostis*, are also prominent. This last type occurs under rainfalls as low as 100 mm, and fluctuates greatly with seasonal conditions.

Astrebla tussock grasslands are grazed extensively by sheep in the southeastern part of their range and by beef cattle in the north and west. Most of the sheep that are grazed north of the Tropic in Australia are carried on these grasslands. *Astrebla* has been considerably reduced in some places, but in general the grasses of this genus have proved remarkably persistent under grazing (Plate 9.13). Apart from some areas that have been converted to agriculture in southeastern Queensland, the *Dichanthium* grasslands are generally grazed by beef cattle; the dominants tend to decrease under grazing.

In southeastern Australia, there are limited areas of a range of tussock grassland types, usually with projective foliage cover in the 30–70 per cent class. They occur on various soils, including cracking clay soils, basaltic soils, and skeletal or mountain soils. Numerous genera are involved, including *Stipa* under lower rainfalls and *Poa* under higher rainfalls.

Some of these southern grasslands have been used for extensive grazing, especially by sheep,

and there has been a general tendency towards reduction of the native tussock grasses and the entry of volunteer exotic grasses and forbs. However, much of the lower-rainfall country is now cropped, especially for wheat. Other areas are used for intensive animal production on sown exotic pastures. These are largely based on such species as *Trifolium subterraneum*, and, where rainfall permits, on perennial grasses such as *Lolium perenne*.

A distinctive kind of herbaceous vegetation occupies much of the 'Channels', the alluvial beds, up to 60 km wide, that carry the intermittent south-flowing drainage from the western interior of Queensland. The better-defined watercourses are marked by lines of low trees, and the moister depressions carry such species as the tall perennial *Eragrostis australasica* (cane grass), but the vegetation of the broad floodplains is predominantly herbaceous and ephemeral, being largely dependent on occasional floods. Summer floods result in the development of a grassland containing many species, notably *Echinochloa turneriana* (Channel sorghum), whereas the herbage resulting from winter floods is dominated by forbs, notably *Trigonella suavissima* (Cooper clover). In both cases the vegetation is dense while it lasts, which may be for several months, and provides valuable feed for beef cattle.

The off-channel areas carry quite different vegetation. Some of these areas carry vegetation types similar to those of the regions adjoining the Channel country. A distinctive type occurs particularly under mean annual rainfalls that range from about 200 mm to less than 100 mm, and is characteristic of duplex soils with dense mantles of stones ('gibbers'). This type is dominated by herbaceous species of the Chenopodiaceae. The projective foliage cover is typically less than 10 per cent, so that this is 'very open-herbfield'. Vegetative cover and composition fluctuate greatly with seasonal conditions. Typical dominants include annual species of *Atriplex*, notably *A. spongiosa* (pop saltbush), and numerous species of *Bassia*. The latter are usually regarded as perennials, and even as dwarf shrubs, but in these circumstances some of them probably function as annuals. This vegetation type provides some grazing for beef cattle.

Various coastal saline soils (including some in intertidal areas) support grasslands that tend to have projective foliage cover in excess of 70 per cent; these are 'closed-grasslands' in Specht's terminology. There is a wide range of tussocky or rhizomatous grasses; *Sporobolus virginicus* (salt-water couch) is a prominent component. These grasslands are widely distributed but are better developed on tropical coasts. They are attractive to stock, and are extensively grazed in some situations, sometimes to the point of denudation.

Several types of herbaceous vegetation are dominated by sedges, and strictly should be called 'sedgelands'. In the Top End of the Northern Territory, estuarine plains that are inundated during the wet season carry stands of tussocky and rhizomatous sedges and grasses with foliage cover in excess of 70 per cent. A wide range of species is involved; notable examples are species of *Eleocharis* (spike-rushes) among the sedges and *Oryza rufipogon* (wild rice) among the grasses.

Two other distinctive types of vegetation are dominated by large tussocky sedges. Projective foliage cover in these types is in the 30–70 per cent class. Some seasonally flooded soils in the southeastern part of South Australia are dominated by species of *Gahnia*, associated with some grasses. On the peaty podzols of western Tasmania, the dominant species is *Gymnoschoenus sphaerocephalus* (button-grass), which may occur in almost pure stands or with very small Epacridaceous shrubs.

Sedges are generally unpalatable to stock, and any grazing of sedgelands is largely confined to such grasses as are present. Some areas of the tropical sedgelands are extensively grazed by beef cattle at low stocking rates; in other areas numerous feral buffaloes (*Bubalus bubalis*) have caused considerable degradation by their grazing and trampling. The South Australian sedgelands have largely been drained and converted to exotic sown pasture, while those of Tasmania are generally unused.

THE PRESENT SITUATION

The present patterns of distribution of Australian vegetation are complex, but the major trends are readily recognizable in terms of the relationships between European settlement and the natural vegetation.

In some areas the natural vegetation has been cleared and replaced by exotic pastures, crops, or plantations, which are maintained under intensive management. Such changes are prominent in the better-watered parts of temperate Australia, and much less prominent, although increasing, in the tropical regions. Much larger areas of vegetation have been modified by pastoralism. The modifications have been brought about not only by the activities of the grazing animals themselves, but also by various management practices. These last include the broadcast sowing of exotic pasture species in the rather limited areas where climatic and other factors are favourable. Some indigenous forests are managed for timber production, and, for a variety of reasons, considerable areas of various types of vegetation are preserved, or left unused, in a relatively natural condition.

This outline is complicated by various factors. Some native species may regenerate on cleared land, even under relatively intensive management, and extensive grazing in some types of indigenous vegetation may lead to an increase in the proportion of useless or harmful species. Again, many exotic volunteer species have become established, and some of these are major impediments to plant or animal production. Examples of the wide range of such exotic weeds include *Chondrilla juncea* (skeleton weed) in some wheat crops, and *Nassella trichotoma* (serrated tussock) and species of *Xanthium* (burrs) in some grazed areas (Plate 9.3). Even intensively managed exotic pastures may contain weeds that are favoured by high soil fertility, such as some thistles, including species of *Cirsium*, *Carduus*, and *Onopordum*. Further, the effects of feral exotic animals, especially rabbits, both in settled and unsettled areas, must not be overlooked.

Many of these effects of settlement involve changes in dominance, either among the native species, or in terms of the replacement of the native species by exotic species, which may be sown or volunteer. However, there are other situations, especially in the lower-rainfall regions, in which settlement has led to the general depletion of the native plants and there are no suitable exotic species to replace them. This problem is well exemplified in the classical work of Ratcliffe (1936).

There is much yet to be learned about the complex of native and exotic species that constitutes the present vegetation of Australia. A most desirable prerequisite for further study would be an organized systematic survey of the plant cover of the whole country.

ACKNOWLEDGEMENT The generous assistance that I received from many people while I was compiling the map of natural vegetation is detailed and acknowledged in the commentary that accompanies the original map (Carnahan, 1976). I gratefully acknowledge that this assistance also produced much information on the effects of settlement on the natural vegetation.

REFERENCES

Barnard, A. (ed.) (1962), *The Simple Fleece, Studies in the Australian Wool Industry*, Melbourne University Press, Melbourne.

Beard, J. S. (1967), 'Some vegetation types of tropical Australia in relation to those of Africa and America', *J. Ecol.*, 55, 271–90.

——(1969), 'The vegetation of the Boorabbin and Lake Johnston areas, Western Australia', *Proc. Linn. Soc. N.S.W.*, 93, 239–69.

Department of National Resources (1973), 'Land Use', *Atlas of Australian Resources*, Second Series, Canberra.

——(Carnahan, J. A.) (1976), 'Natural Vegetation', *Atlas of Australian Resources*, Second Series, Canberra.

Jones, R. (1969), 'Fire-stick farming', *Aust. Nat. Hist.*, 16, 224–8.

Küchler, A. W. (1973), 'Problems in classifying and mapping vegetation for ecological regionalization', *Ecology*, 54, 512–23.

Marshall, A. J. (ed.) (1966), *The Great Extermination*, Heinemann, London.

Moore, R. M. (ed.) (1970), *Australian Grasslands*, Australian National University Press, Canberra.

Mount, A. B. (1964), 'The interdependence of the eucalypts and forest fires in southern Australia', *Aust. For.*, 28, 166–72.

Ratcliffe, F. N. (1936), *Soil Drift in the Arid Pastoral Areas of South Australia*, CSIR Aust., Pamphlet, 64.

Specht, R. L. (1970), 'Vegetation' in G. W. Leeper (ed.), *The Australian Environment*, 4th edn, CSIRO and Melbourne University Press, Melbourne.

Specht, R. L., Roe, Ethel M. and Boughton, Valerie H. (eds) (1974), 'Conservation of major plant communities in Australia and Papua New Guinea', *Aust. J. Bot.*, Supplementary Series No. 7.

Webb, L. J. (1959), 'A physiognomic classification of Australian rain forests', *J. Ecol.*, 47, 551–70.

——(1968), 'Environmental relationships of the structural types of Australian rain forest vegetation', *Ecology*, 49, 296–311.

10 RURAL LAND USE

PETER SCOTT

By world standards rural land use in Australia is characterized by highly specialized, large-scale, capital-intensive, owner-operated farming systems oriented mainly to markets overseas and subject to a complex pattern of government intervention. Of the total land surface amounting to 770 million ha, one-quarter remains unused while three-fifths is used for very sparse grazing and only one-twelfth for intensive farming. Yet the intensive farming systems generally incur large inputs of land relative to capital and particularly labour, so that by comparison with their counterparts in western Europe even these systems appear for the most part strikingly extensive. It is in the ratio of capital to labour that Australian agriculture, defined in this chapter as including both arable and livestock enterprises, is capital intensive. Only a few markedly localized and specialized cropping systems may be described by European standards of land use as intensive.

Specialization and scale together produce homogeneity of land use over large areas. Specialization derives from the low man-land ratio and the orientation of most agricultural production to export markets while the precise types of specialized farming represent a response both to areal variations in the physical environment and to changing relative cost-price relationships. The principal physical determinants are the availability of soil moisture and of water supply throughout the year; a shorter growing season and a lower yield per unit area tend to give a more extensive type of farming and an increase in its scale. Specialization, the changing relative cost-price relationships, and scale are therefore not only basic to the character of Australian agriculture but closely interrelated.

All three characteristics bear on the profitability of land use, a key feature of a highly commercialized, essentially export-oriented agriculture. In Australia not only does the scale of farming tend to vary inversely with the length of the growing season but the larger properties tend to have a higher output per property and a higher average net farm income than the smaller properties. Australia thus presents the seeming paradox that the profitability of agriculture tends to be highest

in areas of low and unreliable rainfall and lowest in areas of high, dependable rainfall. This characteristic highlights the limitations of employing in geographical analysis merely physical indices of crop and livestock yields per unit area, since many of the areas with the highest productivity of land are also the areas with the lowest profitability of farming.

Accordingly this chapter has four parts. First it examines the distinctive attributes of agricultural land use in Australia, notably specialization, scale, and market orientation but also other, partially related attributes. Secondly, within this setting it discusses the salient geographical features of each of the major agricultural systems and subsystems. Thirdly, there follows a spatial assessment of the input-output relationships in agricultural land use, involving an appraisal of the input and productivity of land, labour, and capital and culminating in broad comparisons of regional profitability. Finally, the chapter concludes with brief comments on other uses of rural land and on conflicts in land use.

AGRICULTURAL LAND-USE CHARACTERISTICS

Although specialization, scale, and market orientation are probably the basic characteristics that distinguish agricultural systems in Australia from their counterparts elsewhere, it is nevertheless possible to cite numerous other distinguishing attributes as well. In this section the selected characteristics are presented in a reasonably logical sequence but their relative importance may well assume a markedly different order.

Specialization

Some insight into the extent of farm specialization in Australia is furnished by the number of rural holdings classified by type of activity (Table 10.1). A rural holding is defined as a tract of agricultural land exceeding 0.4 ha in extent. If an owner or occupier of land possesses or works more than one holding, the Australian Bureau of Statistics (ABS) requires a separate return for each holding. An exception is allowed where the holdings are in close proximity and

Table 10.1 Number of Rural Holdings Classified by Type of Activity and by State and Territory, 1970–1

Type of activity	Q.	N.S.W.	Vic.	Tas.	S.A.	W.A.	N.T.	A.C.T.	Australia
Vineyards	84	649	1,987	..	1,447	197	..	..	4,364
Other fruit	2,016	3,748	1,815	869	1,720	846	3	1	11,018
Potatoes	384	215	655	100	131	76	..	1	1,562
Other vegetables	1,384	1,554	999	282	1,244	904	11	3	6,381
Tobacco	739	87	327	..	..	..	..	..	1,153
Sugar	6,923	544	..	..	..	..	..	..	7,467
Cereal grain	2,845	1,970	881	8	506	1,006	..	..	7,216
Sheep and cereals	465	12,007	5,850	89	7,234	6,575	..	1	32,221
Sheep	2,702	17,226	15,885	1,714	5,099	5,146	1	108	47,881
Meat cattle	8,967	6,619	4,908	444	726	1,560	206	10	23,440
Milk cattle	6,773	7,523	16,263	2,448	2,341	1,129	3	6	36,486
Pigs	933	816	620	150	396	164	5	..	3,084
Poultry	421	1,293	946	59	316	290	10	6	3,341
Other	774	519	331	89	113	122	15	4	1,967
Multipurpose	1,108	867	463	211	474	159	5	..	3,287
Total	36,518	55,637	51,930	6,463	21,747	18,174	259	140	190,868

Source: Bureau of Statistics (1974), *Rural Land Use, Improvements, Agricultural Machinery, and Labour, 1972–73*, Reference No. 10.59, Canberra, Table 6.

are worked as one, in which case one return only may be submitted covering the two or more holdings concerned. In some States separate returns are obtained for holdings wholly or partly share-farmed. In 1970–1 a rural holding was classified as commercial if its estimated gross receipts at the holding—that is, gross receipts less marketing costs—were $2,000 or more. Multipurpose holdings other than those designated sheep and cereal grain were defined as holdings where no enterprise contributed 50 per cent to gross receipts; even with so liberal a definition they amounted to less than 2 per cent of all classified holdings. Specialized holdings, each of which had one enterprise contributing more than 50 per cent to gross receipts but none of which met the criteria for holdings classified as sheep and cereal grain, totalled 155,360, or more than four-fifths. Thus even though rural holdings cannot be equated with and are certainly more numerous than farms, specialization clearly dominates Australian farming.

The only outstanding combination or mixed type of rural holding is that designated sheep and cereal grain. Although Australia ranks among the world's leading wheat exporters, wheat is grown typically in association with other cereal grains and sheep. Consequently the ABS employs special criteria to differentiate holdings with sheep and cereal grain from other combination or mixed holdings. On a holding with sheep and cereal grain the combined receipts from sheep and cereals must account for at least three-quarters of the gross return and neither enterprise

can furnish more than four times the contribution of the other. On this basis the 1970–1 census returned a total of 32,220 holdings with sheep and cereal grain. While this combination type is therefore nearly ten times as numerous as multipurpose holdings, it makes up only one-sixth of the classified holdings.

It should perhaps be noted that if the criteria used to define holdings with sheep and cereal grain were to be applied to all enterprise combinations the classification would contain numerous other combinations. Thus the writer has differentiated twenty combinations that are significant locally in Australia (Scott, 1975). But at the national level none ranks as a major type of rural activity, and even if several were to gain prominence, most Australian farms would remain by world standards remarkably specialized. In short, most Australian farms are highly specialized in that they have only one enterprise or at most two enterprises contributing substantially to farm income.

Pastoralism

Agriculture in Australia is not only specialized but focused on livestock rather than arable enterprises. In 1972–3, out of a gross value of agricultural production totalling $4,984 million, crops accounted for only $1,598 million, or just under one-third. The gross value is the value placed on recorded production at the wholesale prices realized in the principal markets, mainly the metropolitan markets in each State. Arable enterprises also contributed only 30 per cent to the net value of production, obtained by deducting

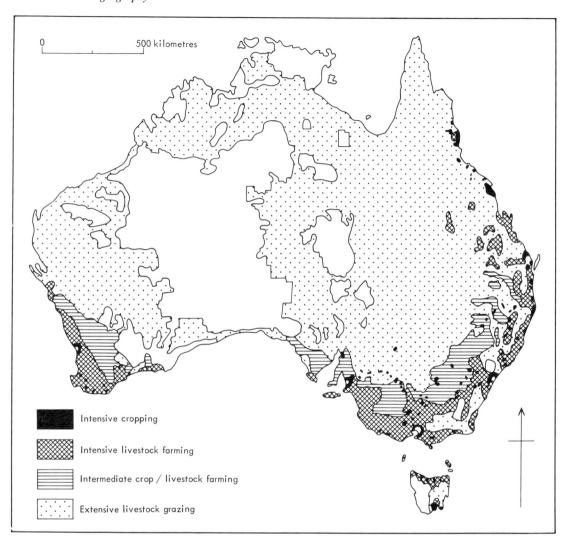

Fig. 10.1 Four basic types of rural land use in Australia. *Source*: Department of Minerals and Energy (1973), 'Land Use', *Atlas of Australian Resources*, Second Series, Canberra.

marketing costs and the value of materials used in production from the gross value. Beef cattle and particularly sheep enterprises together returned $2,070 million net value, or 55 per cent of the total, and dairying $446 million, or nearly 12 per cent. The balance derives from poultry and bee-farming.

Pastoral activities assume an even greater significance in respect of the relative areas used for crops and livestock. Thus in 1972–3 rural holdings occupied nearly 500 million ha, of which only fourteen million were used for crops and three million lay fallow. On the other hand, the area under sown pastures amounted to only twenty-six million ha, symptomatic of the

very extensive grazing that characterizes rural land use in Australia.

While the pastoral industries including dairying account for two-thirds of the value of agricultural production, holdings specializing in livestock enterprises number only three-fifths of the classified holdings (Table 10.1); the discrepancy stems primarily from the important group of holdings with sheep and cereal grain. Table 10.1 shows that dairying is the premier activity among holdings in Victoria and Tasmania, sheep in New South Wales and the Australian Capital Territory, sheep and cereal grain in South Australia and Western Australia, and beef cattle in Queensland and the Northern Territory. Although the classification of holdings is simply by enterprise structure and takes no account of the intensity with which the land is used, the sequence from dairying in Victoria to beef cattle in the north broadly reflects the spatial structure of Australian land use. It is necessary however to examine the pattern of land use not solely by enterprise structure but also by land-use intensity.

Four Basic Types

A simple model of Australian land use has been proposed by the writer elsewhere (Scott, 1968). Since the crop and livestock association would seem to be of paramount importance in classifying western commercial agriculture, a basic typology derived from this criterion would comprise, without specifying individual enterprises at this stage, crop farming, livestock farming, and a combination crop-and-livestock type in which each enterprise contributes roughly the same amount to farm income. A second major criterion is the intensity of application of labour and capital to land; this criterion yields a basic dichotomy of intensive and extensive land use. If these two criteria are combined, and given the tendency for crop farming to employ greater inputs of labour and/or capital per unit of land than livestock farming located in the same area, then the sequence of specialized land uses, for instance outward from a major metropolis, would, other things being equal, be intensive cropping, intensive livestock farming, extensive cropping, and extensive livestock farming. Within this sequence the position of a combination crop-and-livestock type would depend on its degree of intensity relative to the specialized types.

Of the five basic types thereby postulated, four dominate the Australian rural landscape (Fig. 10.1). Intensive cropping is highly localized within three types of setting: first, the peri-metropolitan areas dependent on the production of fresh vegetables and in some localities fruit for nearby markets; secondly, the locations favoured for the production of specialized crops, such as viticulture in the Barossa Valley of South Australia, or apple and pear growing in the Huon Valley of Tasmania, or sugar cane along the Queensland coast; and thirdly, the inland areas of government-sponsored irrigation agriculture, notably in the Murray-Darling basin. Intensive livestock farming, made up of dairying, beef-cattle fattening, and sheep for meat and/or wool, occupy the southwestern and the southeastern higher-rainfall coastal fringes and adjoining country. A combination of crops and livestock is exemplified largely by sheep-wheat farming, which occupies adjoining belts inland in the southwest and the southeast. Although sheep-wheat farming in the Australian context is essentially an intermediate type—that is, intermediate between intensive and extensive farming—it displays a fairly wide range of land-use intensities. Finally, extensive livestock grazing, consisting of sheep in southern and especially southwestern and southeastern Australia and of beef cattle in the north, the centre, and the northeast, is by far the most widespread system. The fifth basic type postulated by the model but unimportant in Australia is extensive cropping. It is represented by only some of the holdings specializing in cereal grain, a mere 4 per cent of holdings classified in 1970–1 (Table 10.1).

Scale

Since agriculture in areas of intensive land use is on a markedly smaller scale than in areas of extensive grazing, the pattern of average property size largely reverses that of the four basic types of agricultural land use (cf. Figs 10.2 and 10.1). Nevertheless, Fig. 10.2, which is based on sample survey data derived from reports of the Bureau of Agricultural Economics (BAE), brings out some pertinent features. Thus the average size of properties exceeds 50,000 ha, not only in the beef cattle regions of northern and central Australia, where they even average more than 500,000 ha in the Barkly Tableland and Victoria River regions of the Northern Territory, but also in the extensive sheep region of Western Australia. In other States regions of extensive sheep grazing have properties considerably smaller in average size comparable to the cattle properties of eastern Queensland. Properties averaging from 500 to 5,000 ha characterize the entire sheep-wheat belt together with intensive sheep farming in New South Wales, Tasmania, and Western Australia but not Victoria and South Australia where farms tend to be smaller. Dairy farms tend to be even smaller still, falling within the fourth size category in Fig. 10.2, but a feature not brought out by the map and of economic significance is that dairy farms in Western Australia average twice the area of those in the southeast. Finally, most regions of intensive cropping, particularly those of irrigated horticulture, have farms averaging less than 50 ha. But holdings are larger in the viticultural districts of the Swan Valley in Western Australia and the Barossa Valley, in the orcharding districts of Tasmania, northern Victoria, and Western Australia, in almost all districts specializing in the field production of vegetables, and markedly in most regions producing industrial crops such as peanuts, tobacco, and cotton.

A more general indicator of the business size of properties is the average gross return per property. In general, the pattern, as discernible from the findings of numerous BAE surveys, closely resembles that of average property size. Certainly by far the highest average gross return occurs in the pastoral regions of great production uncertainty in northern, central,

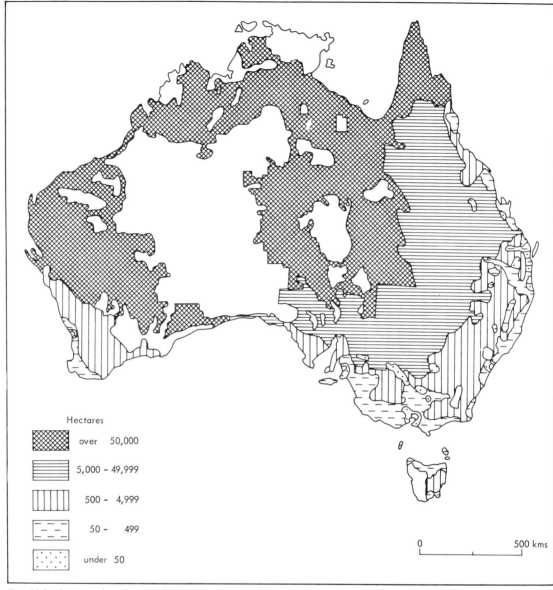

Fig. 10.2 Average size of properties.

Sources: Bureau of Agricultural Economics, Canberra:
1974, *Beef Research Reports*, Nos 12, 13, 14, 15
1973, *Beef Research Reports*, Nos 10, 11. 'The New South
    Wales beef cattle industry', *Q. Rev. Agric. Econ.*, 25,
    117–39
——*The Australian Dairyfarming Industry: Report of an
    Economic Survey*
——*The Australian Sheep Industry Survey: 1967–68 to
    1970–71*

——*The Australian Tobacco Growing Industry: Prelimi-
    nary Report on an Economic Survey: 1970–71 to
    1972–73*
——*The Australian Wheatgrowing Industry: An Economic
    Survey: 1969–70 to 1971–72*
——*The Australian Wine Grape Industry: An Economic
    Survey 1972, Apple and Pear Growing in Tasmania,
    Victoria and Western Australia: An Economic Survey:
    1965–66 to 1968–69*

Sources continued:
——*Pig Raising in Australia: An Economic Survey: 1967–68 to 1969–70*
——*Results of an Economic Survey of Western Australian Currant Producers: 1965–66 to 1967–68*
1971, *The Australian Deciduous Canning Fruitgrowing Industry: An Economic Survey: 1965–66 to 1968–69*
——*The Australian Dried Vine Fruit Industry: An Economic Survey: 1965–66 to 1967–68*

——*The Australian Ginger Growing Industry: A Continuous Farm Study: 1965–66 to 1967–68*
——*The Australian Peanut Growing Industry: An Economic Survey: 1965–66 to 1967–68*
——*The Australian Processing Tomato Growing Industry: A Continuous Farm Study: 1966–67 to 1968–69*
1970, *The Australian Cotton Growing Industry: An Economic Survey: 1964–65 to 1966–67*

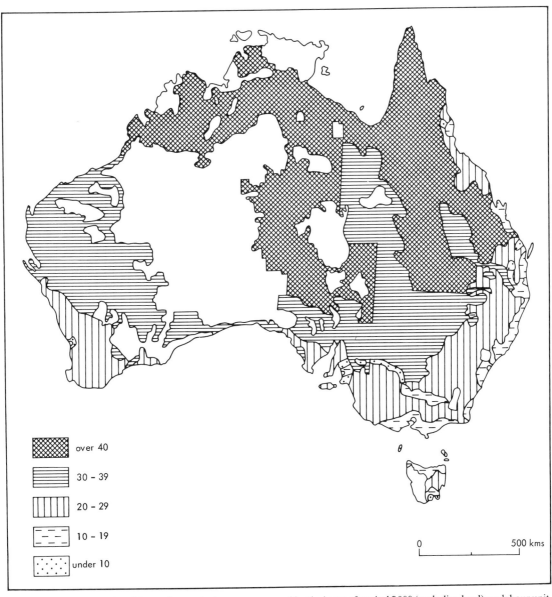

over 40

30 – 39

20 – 29

10 – 19

under 10

0   500 kms

Fig. 10.3 Capital intensity of Australian agriculture, as measured by the input of capital $000 (excluding land) per labour unit. *Sources*: as for Fig. 10.2.

and western Australia. But comparatively high returns also characterize many regions producing industrial crops, notably cotton and tobacco, and several sections of the sheep-wheat belt, the highest sheep-wheat returns being in the northern region of Western Australia which significantly also has the highest average area for sheep-wheat farms. By contrast, almost all Victoria together with a narrow eastern coastal strip from northern Tasmania to southeastern Queensland, has very low average returns, despite a favourable agro-climatic environment in most areas. The pattern is not unlike that of net property return which is discussed toward the close of this chapter (Fig. 10.14). It should be added that by comparison with manufacturing most farm businesses are small, the most prominent exceptions being the pastoral properties of the north and the centre.

Land Tenure

A highly distinctive feature of rural land use, closely related to the scale with which pastoral lands are used, is the proportion of agricultural land leased or licensed for grazing; Australia is probably unique among western countries, as Campbell pointed out, in that nearly nine-tenths of its land used for agriculture remains in public ownership (Williams, 1967). In this respect the States fall into two markedly different groups: those with a substantial ratio of agricultural land alienated in private possession—only Victoria has a predominance of alienated land—and those where the ratio is very small. Thus land owned or being purchased by the operator amounts to three-fifths of agricultural land in Victoria, two-fifths in Tasmania, and one-third in New South Wales, indicative again of relative land-use intensities. In the three remaining States it is only about 7 per cent while in the Northern Territory the ratio is negligible (Fig. 12.2).

Australia is outstanding not only for its ratio of agricultural land in public ownership but also, perhaps paradoxically, for its high proportion of owner-operated farms. Although the States exhibit a wide variety of government leases, most are for long periods, and in practice properties held under perpetual leases are virtually indistinguishable from alienated land. While sales or transfers require government approval, properties are sold as if freehold.

An indication of the pre-eminence of owner-operated farms may be gleaned from the 1970–1 Agricultural Census, which contained supplementary questions relating to the tenure of land comprising rural holdings. These questions were inserted at the request of the Food and Agriculture Organization of the United Nations for inclusion in the 1970 World Census of Agriculture. Data from the questions show that holdings owned or in owner-like possession, which includes land in the process of purchase and crown leases providing tenure for ten years or more, amounted to 88 per cent of all classified holdings (CBCS, 1973). Significantly there is little variation among the States and Territories, the range being from 94 in the Northern Territory to 86 in Queensland. Holdings rented from others, which includes crown leases providing tenure for less than ten years, made up 10 per cent of the classified holdings, the range being from 12 in Victoria to 4 per cent in the Northern Territory.

Owner operation together with the scale of farming has contributed to the emergence over the past two decades of family partnerships, which according to the annual *Taxation Statistics* have now replaced sole ownership as the most important form of farm business organization. Thus in 1970–1 the rural sector contained 125,000 partnerships, compared with 55,000 in 1953–4. Although they were mainly family partnerships, usually husband and wife, the number of partners relates fairly closely to the net income of the partnerships. Companies have also increased substantially in number from 1,700 in 1953–4 to 7,400 in 1970–1, the bulk being private family companies and fewer than 100 public companies. However, the 1970–1 Agricultural Census, which contained FAO questions on the legal status of operators, returned 128,000 sole owners, only 111,000 partnerships, and 8,800 companies. The data suggest that the percentage of holdings held by partnerships relates directly to the size of holdings and inversely to the intensity of land use. Yet despite these trends and spatial variations the most important type of farm business organization is still the family farm.

Low Labour Intensity

Owner operation together with the scale of farming also produces by world standards a remarkably low level of labour input per unit area. Agricultural census data are inadequate to permit assessment of the total physical input of labour in the production process. Although they furnish totals of various categories of workers employed on holdings at the end of March each year, in many enterprises the peaks for employing seasonal and casual workers occur at other times. To some extent this drawback is overcome by the data on wages and salaries paid during the preceding year; but the use of these somewhat unreliable totals to estimate the amount of the physical input of labour is made difficult by the inclusion of unknown amounts paid to contractors usually at rates considerably above those prevailing for temporary workers. In the circumstances the BAE industry surveys assume a special relevance, for they mostly convert the labour input of operator, family, hired workers, and contractors into adult male equivalents or readily convertible man weeks. By relating the labour units to the area of land used agriculturally one can arrive at a comparative assessment of labour use in land-use systems (Fig. 10.10).

On this basis the intensity of application of labour to land tends to decrease sharply through the four basic types of land use outlined above. An input of five or more labour units per 1,000 ha is confined to discontinuous coastal regions, irrigation districts, and pockets of intensive cropping. In these areas, as well as in many others of less land-use intensity, the prevalence of the family farm tends to limit expansion of farm business. Expansion mainly occurs through investment in technology, thereby permitting a more efficient use of family labour, or through the formation of family partnerships, or through sharefarming agreements. Most of the remaining regions of more intensive agriculture in southeastern Australia have an input of between five and two units, a range which is significantly absent from the larger-scale agricultural areas of southwestern Australia. In almost all regions of extensive grazing the input averages less than one unit per 1,000 ha, and over central and northern Australia, as well as in the regions of extensive sheep grazing in Western Australia and South Australia, the input is even less than one per 10,000.

On the other hand, the regions of very low input per unit area, given the scale of land use, are the very regions where the input per property is highest. Thus in the extensive sheep country of Western Australia, the cattle country of the centre, and the Gulf region of Queensland, labour input per property averages five or six units. But in the Kimberleys and the Darwin and Gulf region of the Northern Territory the input rises to nine or ten, while on the Barkly Tableland and in the Victoria River region the input averages about twenty-five. Regions with two or three units per property comprise the rest of the extensive pastoral country together with southeast Queensland, the sheep-wheat belts in southern New South Wales and Western Australia, the Tasmanian midlands, a few dairying localities, and most irrigation areas. Almost all other regions, embracing most of the country where the input exceeds two units per 1,000 ha, have less than two units per property, the operator's labour being supplemented with varying proportions of family, hired, and contract labour.

High Capital Intensity

A further distinctive feature resulting from the scale of farming and the prevalence of owner operation is the high level of capital input in farm business. Land use in Australia, by comparison with other western countries, is capital intensive, and whether measured by capital per labour unit or per unit of output, is considerably more intensive than manufacturing industry. Farmers tend to substitute capital for labour, particularly in times of rapidly rising wages, and to

expand their businesses through investment in technology. In addition, depreciating assets require gradual replacement and farming must keep pace with technological developments. Since farm capital is largely financed internally, the level of capital expenditure tends to vary with farm income, credit availability, and future prospects.

Some insight into the spatial pattern of total capital investment (other than land) relative to labour can be gleaned from sample BAE survey data. In Fig. 10.3 the data have been adjusted and expressed as an average annual value for the three-year period ending 1970–1. Since most surveys of intensive cropping relate to the mid-'sixties, the adjusted data for these activities are less reliable than for the other three basic types of land use. No data exist for the sugar industry and market gardening. It should also be noted that over the period in question wool prices were depressed relative to the prices of most other agricultural products. While too much emphasis cannot therefore be placed on specific detail, the data permit some tentative broad regional comparisons.

Capital intensity, as expressed in Fig. 10.3, tends to be lowest in areas of intensive cropping, as along the Murray (most crop farming is too localized to be shown), and highest in areas of extensive grazing. The pattern has in fact many features in common with that of average property size; it illustrates the tendency for the larger property to employ more capital relative to labour than the smaller farm. It also displays many other features of interest. Thus cotton growing, whether on the Ord or along the Namoi or elsewhere, tends to be more capital intensive than most other crop farming; it tends to be roughly comparable with most dairying, which in turn tends to be less capital intensive than other forms of livestock farming. However irrigation dairying in northeastern Victoria and extensive dairying in the far southwest are notable exceptions; they are similar in capital intensity to most regions of intensive livestock farming. The sheep-wheat belt, as on the map of average property size, mostly resembles the regions of intensive pastoralism. Within the extensive grazing zones the main contrast is between the south and west on the one hand and the centre, north, and northeast on the other. Although this broadly corresponds with the sheep and cattle zones respectively, sheep grazing is more capital intensive in Queensland than elsewhere and cattle grazing less capital intensive in western and southeastern Queensland than in other areas (cf. Figs 10.3 and 10.7).

Market Orientation

Annual variations in farm capital expenditure are but one facet of the response of farm businesses to changing cost-price relationships. Throughout the 'fifties and 'sixties the terms of trade generally moved against

Table 10.2   Number of Rural Holdings Classified by Type of Activity, 1959–60 to 1970–1

Type of activity	Number of rural holdings				% Average annual change			% Change
	1959–60	1965–6	1968–9	1970–1	1959–60 to 1965–6	1965–6 to 1968–9	1968–9 to 1970–1	1959–60 to 1970–1
Vineyards	4,483	4,715	4,342	4,364	0.86	−2.67	0.26	−2.65
Other fruit	13,304	11,977	11,180	11,018	−1.66	−2.22	−0.73	−17.18
Potatoes	2,274	2,367	2,630	1,562	0.68	3.70	−20.31	−31.31
Other vegetables	6,816	6,249	5,907	6,381	−1.39	−1.82	4.01	−6.38
Tobacco	976	992	1,080	1,153	0.27	2.96	3.38	18.14
Sugar	7,012	7,554	7,814	7,467	1.29	1.15	−2.22	6.49
Cereal grain	8,151	12,274	15,593	7,216	8.43	9.01	−26.86	−11.47
Sheep and cereals	32,606	31,832	33,049	32,221	−0.40	1.27	−1.26	−1.18
Sheep	52,026	43,671	37,108	47,881	−2.68	−5.01	14.52	−7.97
Meat cattle	11,267	16,339	19,768	23,440	7.50	7.00	9.28	108.04
Milk cattle	55,443	49,334	42,101	36,486	−1.83	4.89	−6.67	−34.18
Pigs	1,276	1,576	2,166	3,084	3.92	12.48	21.19	141.69
Poultry	5,116	4,194	3,558	3,341	−3.00	−5.05	−3.05	−34.70
Other	1,824	1,954	2,172	1,967	1.19	3.72	−4.72	7.84
Multipurpose	8,133	8,995	9,545	3,287	1.77	2.04	−32.78	−59.58
Total classified	210,697	204,023	198,013	190,868	−0.53	−0.98	−1.80	−9.41
Subcommercial	29,993	33,878	40,454	42,563	2.16	6.47	2.61	41.91
Unused	11,553	14,261	15,800	16,064	3.91	3.50	0.84	39.05
All holdings	252,243	252,162	254,267	249,495	−0.01	0.28	−0.84	−1.09

Source: Bureau of Census and Statistics (1963), *Classification of Rural Holdings by Size and Type of Activity, 1959–60*, Bulletin No. 7—Australia, Canberra; ibid. (1968), *1965–66*, Bulletin No. 7—Australia, Canberra; ibid. (1971), *1968–69*, Bulletin No. 7—Australia, Canberra; Bureau of Statistics (1974), *Rural Land Use, Improvements, Agricultural Machinery, and Labour, 1972–73*, Canberra.

Australian agriculture, which is heavily dependent on overseas markets. Farmers experienced a cost-price squeeze brought about by rising input prices and static or falling commodity prices. In the 'fifties the squeeze depressed average real farm income but in the 'sixties a high level of farm investment facilitated an increase in productivity and income recovered. Even so, farmers failed to share in the growth in gross national product per head, to which agricultural export earnings had made a significant contribution.

Within this context may be set changes in the number of rural holdings by type of activity (Table 10.2). Although no census of rural holdings was undertaken in the 'fifties, the first four censuses span the 'sixties. Over this period the total number of rural holdings underwent little change but the number classified as commercial fell by nearly one-tenth. However the minimum estimated gross receipts at the holding were regarded as $1,200 in 1959–60, $1,600 in 1965–6, and $2,000 in each of 1968–9 and 1970–1. While the criteria are not therefore strictly comparable, the data nevertheless suggest a substantial growth in the number of subcommercial and unused holdings,

particularly as the 1970–1 threshold of $2,000 appears to have been too low.

From 1959–60 to 1970–1 subcommercial and unused holdings together increased by three-fifths in Queensland, by two-fifths to one-half in each of New South Wales, Victoria, and South Australia, by one-eighth in Tasmania, and by one-tenth in Western Australia. This pattern suggests that holdings unclassified by type of activity are not simply peri-urban commuter properties, even though strong concentrations occur around the capital cities and the larger towns. In New South Wales for instance the Sydney region accounted for nearly one-quarter of the State's unused and subcommercial holdings in 1970–1 but the north coast also returned nearly one-fifth. Some of these north-coast holdings are week-end and holiday properties belonging to urban residents. But others include the dry runs which are operated by dairy-farmers in conjunction with main dairies but are located some distance away. Over the period the number of rural holdings unclassified by type of activity increased in almost all land-use regions whether coastal or far inland and whether peri-urban or remote from large centres. At the end of the period these unclassified holdings totalled more than one-sixth of all rural holdings but together accounted for only one per cent of all gross farm receipts.

Among the commercial holdings the principal types have shown different trends in response to changing relative cost-price relationships of specific farm enterprises. Although the classification of holdings by type of activity bears only limited relationship to the four basic types of Australian agriculture classified by crop-livestock association and land-use intensity, Table 10.2 nevertheless brings out some highly relevant features. Crop farming made up of the first eight categories and predominantly intensive land use showed an overall decline in number of holdings from 43,036 to 39,161, or 9 per cent. While holdings specializing in sugar and especially tobacco increased in number, all others declined, notably fruit and latterly potatoes. Among the major types of livestock farming the number of holdings with beef cattle dominant more than doubled, while those with dairy cattle declined by one-third and those with sheep by one-twelfth. Yet these overall changes mask significant short-term fluctuations and trends, as witness the high but declining rate of increase among beef cattle holdings, the fluctuating but generally downward movement in dairying, and the decline and then sharp recovery in sheep farming. Holdings with pigs consistently increased in number while those with poultry consistently declined. Yet perhaps the most striking feature of the entire table is the outstanding stability of holdings combining sheep with cereal grain.

Much might be said, if space permitted, concerning the underlying changes in cost-price relationships and the resultant movements from one enterprise to another within farming systems. Thus for example the rapid expansion in beef production was occasioned not only by the comparative buoyancy in the 'sixties of markets for beef but also by the depressed markets for dairy products and wool. Consequently many dairy-farmers, sheep farmers, and graziers switched either wholly or partly to beef cattle. But what is important geographically is that these movements tended to be most pronounced in areas marginal for the production of either dairy products relative to beef or wool relative to beef. In general, the areal distribution of a specific enterprise tends to contract in times of depression and to expand in times of boom. These tendencies are discussed later in relation to particular land-use systems or subsystems.

Yet notwithstanding the short-term fluctuations in the number of rural holdings specializing in particular enterprises the four basic types of Australian agriculture outlined earlier display a marked stability, at least in the short term. The classification of rural holdings highlights the stability of the sheep-wheat belt, though in times of boom the belt may expand outward on the drier margins and in times of depression contract toward the wetter margins. But most short-term land-use changes take the form of a switch from either one intensive livestock enterprise to another (for example, from dairying or fat lambs to beef) or one extensive livestock enterprise to another (for example, from beef to wool). Similar substitution occurs within intensive cropping systems, such as from potatoes to other vegetables or from one industrial crop to another. Latterly however, many farmers engaged in more extensive cropping systems have switched to livestock enterprises, notably from apple and pear production to dairying or beef and from cereal grain to sheep. In sum, the four basic land-use types provide an appropriate framework for examining the structure of Australian agriculture and more particularly the changing patterns of agricultural subsystems.

Government Intervention

Before considering specific agricultural subsystems it is necessary to note, however briefly, the intervention of government in Australian agriculture (Australia, 1974). Since agricultural production is fragmented among numerous producers, varies greatly from season to season, experiences wide fluctuations in market prices, contributes significantly to export earnings, and constitutes in other respects an important sector of the economy, government intervenes to reduce inequities and inefficiencies. Moreover the complex structure of the rural sector combined with the acute difficulties encountered from time to time by particular farming enterprises has led to a highly complex pattern of government intervention. As a consequence, the differential impact of intervention measures is basic to an understanding of the spatial organization of Australian rural land use.

Since the range of intervention measures is extensive, only the broadest indication of the nature of Federal government intervention is possible at this stage; some reference will be made later to intervention by State governments. The pattern of agricultural development has been directly affected by water resources development programmes, which have aimed primarily at increasing the productivity and production potential of selected areas through irrigation and flood mitigation projects (see Rutherford, 1968). Other examples of government investment in infrastructure includes beef roads in northern Australia (see Rimmer, Ch. 22) and brigalow land development in Queensland (see Courtenay, Ch. 13). Agricultural production has been influenced by such measures as input subsidies designed to encourage the use of more fertilizer but effectively reducing production costs, by expenditure on research and extension designed to improve farming efficiency, and by taxation conces-

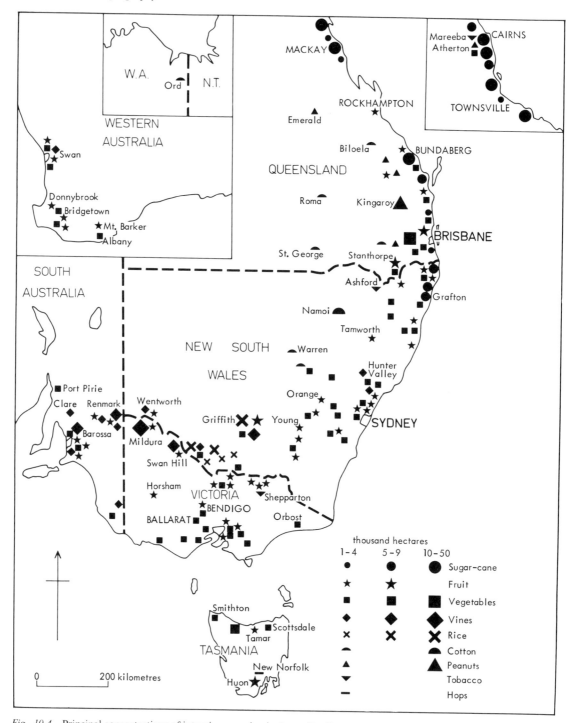

Fig. 10.4 Principal concentrations of intensive cropping in Australia. *Sources*: Bureau of Statistics, various reports.

sions that encourage capital investment. Marketing is assisted by the promotion overseas of such commodities as wool, dairy products, and canned fruit, by the financing of marketing boards and the Australian Wool Commission, and above all by price stabilization schemes, notably for wheat but also for dairy products, sugar, apples and pears, and dried vine fruits. Finally, structural change has been facilitated since 1971 by the Rural Reconstruction Scheme which seeks to promote necessary resource relocation and movement through the provision of loans and the amalgamation of production units. It should be added that the Industries Assistance Commission established in 1973 aims to ensure that in future intervention measures not only foster efficiency in resource allocation and facilitate any necessary adjustment to change but are integrated with national economic policy as a whole.

AGRICULTURAL LAND-USE SYSTEMS

While the four basic types of land use present a remarkably homogeneous landscape over wide areas, this apparent simplicity masks a variegated mosaic of subsystems, particularly of intensive agriculture, each distinctive in its enterprise structure and use of resources. This section focuses on the location and changing nature of these subsystems, drawing on numerous sources and especially the valuable BAE

Table 10.3 Intensive Crops by Area and Gross Value of Production, 1972–3

Crop	Area in hectares	Gross value of output	
		Total $ 000	Per hectare $
Nurseries and flowers	2,602	23,184	8,910
Tobacco	9,598	37,896	3,949
Hops	1,080	4,263	3,947
Fruit (excluding grapes)	115,502	223,524	1,935
Vegetables	110,947	182,678	1,647
Vines	68,502	64,871	947
Sugar cane	283,264	234,174	827
Cotton	93,616	32,625	748
Rice[a]	45,150	24,995	554
Peanuts	29,136	10,539	499
Totals and average	709,397	838,749	1,182

[a]Excluding the Northern Territory (not available).

Source: Bureau of Statistics (1974), *Crop Statistics, Season 1972–73*, and *Value of Primary Production 1972–73*, Canberra.

reports which relate to most industries. Space permits only passing reference to specific crop and livestock enterprises but maps showing their distribution supported by extended commentary are readily available in the *Yearbook of Australia* and the *Atlas of Australian Resources* (see also, *inter alia*, Alexander and Williams, 1973; Leeper, 1970; Wadham, Wilson and Wood, 1964; and Williams, 1967).

Intensive Cropping

Intensive cropping is confined largely to peri-metropolitan areas, the inland irrigation districts, and localized tracts favoured by soil, slope, and climate (Fig. 10.4). In 1972–3 the area under crops other than sown pastures amounted to 14.4 million ha, or less than 3 per cent of the total area of rural holdings. However only 0.7 million ha were under intensive crops, which had a combined gross output of $839 million compared with $749 million for all other crops (Table 10.3). Extensive crops comprised cereal grain other than rice, oilseeds, and fodder crops. It is a measure of relative land-use intensities that intensive crops furnished a gross output per ha of $1,182 and extensive crops only $55. Although intensive crops are normally grown in farming systems essentially specialized, small scale, and labour intensive, they are also incorporated in a heterogeneous range of farming systems. It is necessary to illustrate the diversity of land-use systems by a brief reference to each of the principal intensive crops.

Since most vegetables are grown close to the market, the distribution of cultivation by State broadly corresponds with that of population distribution. Nevertheless Queensland and South Australia have comparative climatic advantages for the marketing of vegetables 'out-of-season' in Sydney and Melbourne; each has about one-third more land under vegetables than population might suggest. Western Australia, normally isolated by transport costs from the eastern metropolitan markets, produces merely its fair share, though tomatoes are sometimes shipped from Geraldton to the eastern States in winter and spring. Tasmania has no less than twice its fair share, for soils, climate, farming systems, and accessibility to metropolitan markets facilitate the production of processing peas and potatoes. In Australia vegetables for processing are produced under a wide range of climatic conditions by companies anxious to hedge against the risk of regional crop losses. In 1973–4 vegetables occupied less than one-sixth of the land under intensive crops but returned more than one-fifth of the gross value of intensive crop production.

Within each State vegetable growing is not only strongly localized but displays a wide range of locations, production characteristics, and land-use intensities. In peri-metropolitan locations the most

Plate 10.1   Paradise Valley, an area of intensive orcharding and dairying, in the Mt Lofty Ranges, near Adelaide, South Australia.

labour-intensive properties tend to be enmeshed in the expanding metropolitan fringe; they comprise very small properties of a few hectares often worked by gardeners of southern European origin (Rutherford *et al.*, 1971; Smith, 1966, 1972). Away from the metropolis properties tend to increase in size and to become relatively more capital intensive, producing crops that are more amenable to mechanization. In coastal areas, as well as in favoured settings inland, vegetables may be a subsidiary or even dominant enterprise in association with livestock production: dairying in the coastlands of the southeast and southwest; and sheep on the tablelands of New South Wales and in the central highlands of Victoria. Some vegetables are also grown with tropical fruits, as in Queensland, or with citrus and pome fruits, as in Western Australia, the Murray and Murrumbidgee irrigation districts, and the Goulburn Valley of Victoria. In all, about three-fifths of the land growing vegetables is irrigated.

Fruit other than grapes occupied one-sixth of the intensive croplands but returned more than one-quarter of the gross value of intensive crop production. Significantly more than one-half of the output was made up of apples, oranges, and bananas, indicative of Australia's self-sufficiency in temperate, subtropical, and tropical fruits. In general, the distribution of fruit growing has much in common with that of vegetable production but regional specialization is more pronounced (Leeper, 1970, pp. 106–9). The Huon Valley in southern Tasmania for example is renowned for its apple orchards while the Murrumbidgee Irrigation Area and the Goulburn Valley are outstanding for their apricots, peaches, and pears grown for canning. In peri-metropolitan regions fruit growing tends to be farther from the city than market gardening, which requires frequent, speedy transport of its highly perishable products to market and smaller holdings, but the distinctive land requirements of each activity are paramount factors. Nevertheless, because a higher proportion of fruit than of vegetables is grown in the irrigation districts, the gross return per ha in 1972–3 averaged $1,935 for fruit other than grapes compared with $1,650 for vegetables. The return for vegetables is depressed largely by potatoes which accounted for one-third of the area under vegetables and averaged only $1,390 per ha.

Intensive irrigation horticulture may yield a higher return per unit of area than fruit growing using only limited spray irrigation or wholly dependent on rainfall but on other efficiency criteria its economic performance is probably inferior (cf. Davidson, 1969). The average size of fruit farms ranges typically from 25 to 75 ha, some tropical and berry-fruit farms being much smaller and many orcharding properties particularly in Western Australia much larger. But the larger the property the higher tends to be the ratio of land used for livestock enterprises and the greater the degree of diversification. On the small specialized farm characteristic of the fruit industry labour input by Australian standards is very high, even exceeding 10 units per 100 ha in the irrigation districts and averaging 3–5 units elsewhere. Yet the highest labour productivity is probably achieved outside the irrigation districts, and in the apple and pear industry, for example, labour productivity tends to vary directly with labour input and the scale of farming. However, fruit growing exhibits a relatively low input of capital, despite the long-term trend for the level of capital investment to increase with technological advance. Currently the export-oriented apple and pear industry requires structural reorganization but the employment of such specialized resources as trees, certain land types, and orchardist skills militates against rapid farm adjustment.

Of the four types of fruit and vegetable holdings classified in the census by type of activity, vineyards displayed between 1960 and 1971 the greatest stability in numbers (Table 10.2). Yet the area under grapes had latterly risen in response to the rapid growth in Australian wine consumption. In 1972–3 grape production was 598,300 tonnes, of which 55 per cent was used for winemaking, 42 per cent for drying, and 3 per cent for table and other purposes. In the previous season, when production had soared to a record 831,900 tonnes, the percentages used for winemaking and drying had been reversed (that is, 42 and 55 respectively). However the quantities used for winemaking in 1971–2 and 1972–3 were much the same (352,600 and 331,600 tonnes respectively), whereas the quantities used for drying fell sharply (from 455,700 to 247,900 tonnes). These figures illustrate not only the fluctuations in output attributable to the low and variable yields obtained in non-irrigated, major producing regions but also the practice of switching in years of low yield such dual-purpose varieties as sultanas from drying to winemaking. Wine is produced almost entirely for domestic consumption and dried fruit for export.

Most dried vine fruits—sun-dried currants, sultanas, raisins—are produced in the Murray irrigation areas, chiefly Sunraysia, while most wine grapes are produced in dryfarming regions, chiefly the Barossa Valley. Land use in the irrigation districts, which have very small properties (12–18 ha) and a very high labour input (10–20 labour units per 100 ha), contrasts sharply with that in the dryfarming regions, which have larger properties (averaging 50–100 ha) and a low labour input (2 units per 100 ha). Moreover the non-irrigated properties include a wide variety of land-use systems: winery vineyards, which concentrate on varieties highly prized for winemaking but not always readily obtainable from small growers; specialized vineyards, most of which have at least one subsidiary enterprise (apricots, prunes, vegetables, poultry, dairying, pigs, fat lambs, wool); combination or multipurpose farms, where viticulture is combined with other major enterprises either intensive (other fruit, vegetable, poultry, dairying) or fairly extensive (fat lambs, cereals, wool); and part-time vineyards (Smith, 1970).

Yet in economic performance the basic regional differences in viticulture appears to be between the dryfarming regions together with the mid-Murray irrigation areas, which generally perform poorly, and other irrigation districts, which perform significantly better. The poor performance of the mid-Murray region stems from low yields attributable to climatic conditions less suitable for dried vine fruits than in Sunraysia, and increasing soil salinity. Even so, land-use efficiency in all viticultural regions, whether measured by labour productivity or vineyard returns, is by the general standards of Australian agriculture almost everywhere low.

Five industrial crops accounted for more than one-half of the area but less than two-fifths of the gross output of intensive crops in 1972–3. Of these, sugar cane, a crop that has become markedly more capital intensive and less labour intensive in recent decades is discussed by Courtenay (Ch. 13). Tobacco and cotton are also discussed by Courtenay in relation to tropical Australia but require additional comment since one-half of the area under tobacco and more than four-fifths of the cotton area are located south of the Tropic. Peanuts and hops, the other two industrial crops, are of minor importance but contrast sharply in land-use intensities. Peanuts are grown under not very intensive conditions at Kingaroy and on the Atherton Tableland in Queensland, where properties average 230 and 70 ha respectively. At Kingaroy, which is by far the principal producing region, peanuts are an important enterprise in mixed-cropping systems or in association with dairying, while

Plate 10.2 The Murrumbidgee Irrigation Area, producing *inter alia* apricots, peaches, and pears grown for canning, in southwestern New South Wales.

on the Atherton Tableland peanuts are usually subsidiary to maize. Although the peanuts give a fairly high return per unit of area, production costs are high, so that both labour productivity and property returns are low, notably on the Atherton Tableland. By contrast, hops are a highly intensive crop, even by European standards of hop growing, and are largely confined to Tasmania, along the middle Derwent and in the northeast, and in Victoria.

Tobacco, like hops, is grown almost entirely under irrigation in various land-use systems. The most intensive are those of the Ovens, King, and other river valleys of northeastern Victoria, where subsidiary enterprises include hops, potatoes, and dairying, and the Queensland south coast, where tobacco is grown in association with sugar or occasionally with pineapple, bananas, and other tropical fruits or on specialist farms. In both regions properties average less than 50 ha, have a labour input of about 20 units per 100 ha, and return the highest productivity of

both labour and land of all the producing areas. The most extensive land-use systems are those along the Dumaresq River in northern New South Wales and southwestern Queensland, where properties average 900 ha, carry beef cattle and sheep, have a labour input of only one or two workers per 100 ha, and record low returns per worker and per unit area. Between these extremes are the 250 ha properties of the Mareeba-Dimbulah district of north Queensland which are essentially intermediate in both labour input and productivity. Yet all tobacco-growing regions have some important features in common: a labour input per property of 5–9 units, a below-average level of capital investment, a low productivity of labour, and high returns per property, markedly so in Victoria.

Since 1963, when cotton was a sideline on Queensland dairy farms, the crop has trebled in area under the stimulus of a Commonwealth government bounty that encouraged large-scale irrigated cultivation and the production of high-quality lint. Accordingly the focus of cotton growing shifted to the Namoi valley near Narrabri but some cotton is grown in the Murrumbidgee Irrigation Area, in Queensland, and the Ord River district in Western Australia. The bounty also prompted many Queensland farmers to irrigate cotton, so that cultivation in Queensland has shifted southward and almost all cotton grown in Australia is now irrigated. Properties average 800–900 ha in the Namoi valley and the MIA but only 300 ha along the Ord and 200–500 in Queensland. Along the Namoi and the Ord cotton farms are highly specialized, though in some years near Narrabri wheat, sheep, and cattle assume minor importance and recently the Ord has seen the development of sorghum, rice, and other crops. In the MIA farms tend to be multipurpose with cotton being grown in association with grains, mainly rice and wheat, and livestock. In southern Queensland cotton tends to be supported by subsidiary crops, such as grain sorghum, maize, fruit, and vegetables, the latter comprising mainly potatoes, onions, and beetroot in the Lochyer valley. In the few remaining cotton districts dependent on rainfall, cotton is usually subsidiary to other enterprises, such as beef cattle, pigs, grain, sunflower, linseed, soya beans, and peanuts. In most regions, except those dependent on rainfall and to some extent the MIA, productivity tends to be high, whether measured by output per unit of labour or per unit of area or per farm. Occasionally in recent years however, output has been affected by seasonal conditions and insect pests but in good seasons it has latterly exceeded domestic requirements and provided a surplus for export.

Rice is grown almost entirely in the Murrumbidgee and Coleambally Irrigation Areas in New South Wales, where farms typically range from 150 to 300 ha. Most growers produce rice in association with other crop and livestock enterprises, including sorghum, maize, lucerne, linseed, sunflower, fat lambs, wool, and beef. Farmers are allocated areas based on marketing prospects and the availability of irrigation water, thereby ensuring a high level of profitability; marketing is handled by a State Board. In a good season, owing to the use of specially developed seed varieties and efficient crop rotations, the average yield of Australian rice is the highest national average in the world; in 1970–1 for instance it reached 7.9 tonnes per ha. However yields tend to fluctuate with seasonal conditions. Small quantities of rice are also grown in Queensland, where yields are reduced occasionally by cyclones, and in the Northern Territory.

Intensive Livestock Farming

Intensive livestock farming involves the intensive use of land principally for livestock enterprises but occasionally with subsidiary cash crops. Livestock enterprises include dairy cattle, beef cattle, and sheep, which are of major importance, together with pigs and poultry, both minor. Cash crops tend to be more prominent in dairying than on beef cattle or sheep properties, and because of the widespread juxtaposition of irrigated croplands with dryland pastures in the intensive sheep belt, more prominent generally in sheep farming than on beef cattle farms. In this section each of the main livestock systems as well as their more important derivatives are discussed briefly.

Although the number of poultry farms steadily declined in the 'sixties and amounted to less than 2 per cent of all rural holdings in 1970–1 (Table 10.2), total egg production and production per farm continued to rise as a result of the substitution of capital for labour. Around Sydney and Melbourne, and to a lesser extent Perth, Brisbane and Adelaide, are strong concentrations of small specialist producers but property size increases with distance from the capital city. In New South Wales for example, farms average about 5 ha in the metropolitan region (with nearly one-half the State total of poultry holdings), 10 ha in the Outer Sydney region (with nearly one-third), 50–70 ha on the northern tablelands (one-eighth), and 90–100 elsewhere (also one-eighth). Similar patterns are discernible in other States. A highly specialized activity, poultry farming is characterized not only by high returns per labour unit and per farm but remarkably high returns per unit area.

Pig farming is generally less intensive and less market oriented than poultry farming. Whereas poultry farms are the more numerous type in New South Wales and Victoria, pig farms are the more numerous in Queensland, South Australia, and Tasmania; Western Australia, as befits the classical isolated State, has poultry farms again dominant. Specialist pig farms, making up one-tenth of the total, occur near the capital cities (averaging 15 ha) and in north Queensland (averaging 100 ha). Pig-dairy farms furnish one-quarter of the total and are scattered through the coastal dairying regions from southern Queensland to South Australia; they average 200 ha in Queensland and 100 in Victoria. The dominant type is the pig-cereal farm of the intermediate crop-livestock zone. On the Darling Downs it has latterly assumed importance along with pig, beef, and pig-dairy farms but it is also prevalent in the northern and central sections of the New South Wales wheat-sheep belt and in northern Victoria; in size it ranges from 650 to 1,250 ha. Near Rockhampton in Queensland pigs are an important enterprise on sugar and vegetable farms. Of the three main types the pig-cereal farms are the most capital-intensive but in economic performance the large specialist farms are pre-eminent and the pig-dairy farm together with the small specialists the least impressive.

Among rural holdings in Australia the type

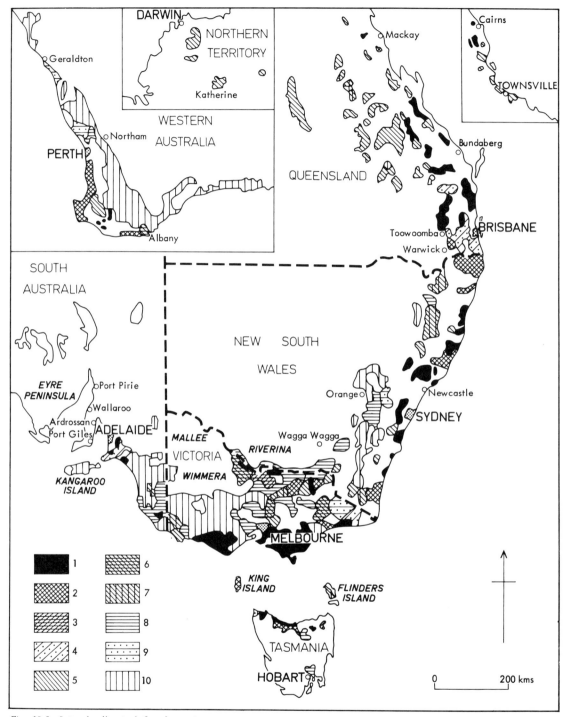

Fig. 10.5   Intensive livestock-farming systems.

KEY TO *Fig. 10.5*
1. Dairy cattle
2. Dairy cattle and beef cattle (intensive)
3. Dairy cattle and sheep for meat and wool
4. Dairy cattle and beef cattle (extensive)
5. Beef cattle (intensive)
6. Beef cattle (intensive) and sheep for meat and wool
7. Beef cattle (intensive) and sheep for wool (intensive)
8. Sheep for meat and wool
9. Sheep for meat and wool, and beef cattle (extensive)
10. Sheep for wool (intensive).

Source: Department of Minerals and Energy (1973), 'Land Use', *Atlas of Australian Resources*, Second Series, Canberra.

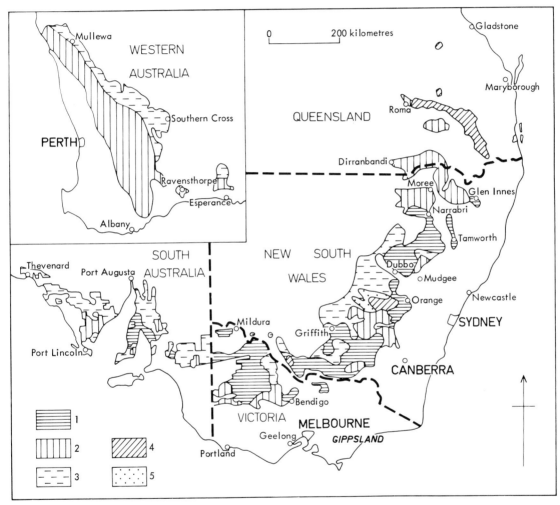

Fig. 10.6 Intermediate crop-livestock farming systems.

KEY
1. Sheep for meat and wool, and cereal grains
2. Sheep for wool (intensive) and cereal grains
3. Sheep for wool (extensive) and cereal grains
4. Beef cattle (intensive) and cereal grains
5. Beef cattle (extensive) and cereal grains.

Source: Department of Minerals and Energy (1973), 'Land Use', *Atlas of Australian Resources*, Second Series, Canberra.

represented by the greatest number was until 1970–1 dairying, and even in that year, if intensive sheep farms are distinguished from livestock grazing, dairying remained the premier type (Table 10.2). Yet throughout the 'sixties the number of dairy holdings not only fell but declined at an accelerating rate; the overall decrease was about one-third. In each of Victoria, Tasmania, and South Australia the number of dairy holdings fell by about one-fifth, while in each of Queensland, New South Wales, and Western Australia the decline averaged about one-half. Thus structural change was most marked in areas marginal for dairying, and production contracted toward a southeastern core region. A similar trend was evident within most States, where regions climatically less favourable for dairying, as for example the Rockhampton region in Queensland or the south coast of New South Wales, witnessed the greatest relative decline. Australian dairying displays in fact strong regional variations in resource base and production viability (see Alexander and Williams, 1971, pp. 172–85; also Allen, 1965; Dragovitch, 1970, 1974; Holmes, 1965; Laut, 1968, 1970; Wilson, 1961).

These regional variations and the recent trends are reflected in the variegated pattern depicted by the four basic land-use systems involving dairying (Fig. 10.5). Coastal Victoria stands out as having the major concentration of specialized dairying (11,240 holdings in 1970–1) but the inclusion of co-dominant systems tends to mask important concentrations elsewhere, notably in northern and northeastern Victoria. Areas shown in Fig. 10.5 as having two livestock enterprises co-dominant are in fact made up mainly of two specialized farming types intermingled or in close juxtaposition. In Western Australia for example, the coastal region south of Perth is shown as having dairy cattle and beef cattle co-dominant with only a few pockets of specialized dairying. Yet in 1970–1 specialized beef cattle and specialized dairy holdings numbered 1,280 and 1,125 respectively, though most dairy farms produce beef as a subsidiary enterprise. A similar intermingling of beef cattle and dairy cattle holdings occur on the New South Wales north coast with 2,480 and 4,170 respectively. The only large expanse of dairying co-dominant with extensive cattle grazing is located in southeast Queensland. Most recent movement from dairying into other livestock enterprises took place in the co-dominant areas.

Both national and particularly State policies have influenced the development and spatial pattern of dairying but productivity remains basically a function of scale and the resource base, including accessibility to metropolitan markets. Dairying is based on pasture-fed non-indigenous cattle, chiefly Jerseys for butterfat and Friesians for wholemilk but also the Illawarra Shorthorn which gives high yields in the short flush

Table 10.4 Scale and Productivity of Dairy Farms by State and N.S.W. Region, 1967–8 to 1969–70 (Three Year Farm Averages)

States and Regions	Farm size ha	Labour units N	Gross return in $ 000 per farm	per 100 ha	per L.U.
States					
Victoria	101	1.8	14.7	14.6	8.2
Tasmania	119	1.9	14.6	12.3	7.7
S. Australia	133	1.7	13.0	9.8	7.7
N.S.W.	160	2.0	14.2	8.9	7.1
Queensland	170	1.8	9.7	5.7	5.4
W. Australia	268	1.9	19.6	7.4	10.5
Regions					
Sydney	130	2.4	24.7	19.0	10.5
N. Coast	139	1.8	10.4	7.5	5.7
S. Coast	153	1.9	11.5	7.5	6.0
Riverina	178	1.9	14.3	8.1	7.6
Hunter	191	2.1	15.6	8.2	7.4

Source: Bureau of Agricultural Economics (1973), *The Australian Dairyfarming Industry: Report of an Economic Survey*, Canberra.

season and occurs around Sydney, in Queensland, and Western Australia. Among the States, except for Western Australia, gross returns per unit of area vary inversely with average farm size, so that the four southeastern States show scant variation in average farm return (Table 10.4). However Queensland, where conditions least favour dairying, has very low farm returns, while Western Australia, where productivity per unit of area and yields per cow are superior only to Queensland, enjoys remarkably high returns per farm and per labour unit. Such high productivity stems mainly from the scale of farming, which enables *inter alia* beef production from dairy cows or 'dairy beef' to be a substantial subsidiary enterprise. In Western Australia the scale of farming is large, whether measured in physical or economic terms.

That farm business size cannot be assessed simply from farm area is borne out by the very high productivity of dairy farms supplying wholemilk to metropolitan markets. Each State other than South Australia controls the production and distribution of city milk supply. In South Australia all milk is purchased on a butterfat basis, the higher returns from wholemilk being 'equalized' among all producers. In other States wholemilk production is controlled by quotas and contracts, which result in peri-metropolitan regions having the smallest but the most productive dairy farms in the State. In New South Wales the Sydney region has farms twice the average size of those in the

Melbourne region but they are nevertheless the smallest dairy farms in the State, just as those around Melbourne are the smallest in Australia. Yet the Sydney wholemilk producer enjoys the highest average gross return of dairymen in any major dairying region of the country. In Victoria however, the peri-metropolitan producer may well suffer diseconomies of scale: his gross farm returns are on average lower than those of Gippsland or the northern irrigation districts, even though per unit area they are the highest in Australia. In New South Wales, in regions other than Sydney, gross farm returns and returns per unit of area tend to increase with farm size, primarily because of the legacy of non-viable farms bequeathed by land grants that proved inadequate. Amalgamation of such properties under the Rural Reconstruction Scheme has facilitated a switch to beef production.

In southern Australia intensive beef husbandry is typically associated with other livestock enterprises. Dairy beef alone accounts for about one-quarter of Australian beef production, and as seen in Fig. 10.5 beef cattle co-dominant with dairying occupies a larger area in Western Australia, New South Wales, and Tasmania than specialized dairying. Similarly, intensive beef husbandry is eclipsed as a land-use type in New South Wales, Victoria, and South Australia by beef cattle co-dominant with intensive sheep farming. The juxtaposition of beef husbandry with dairying and sheep farming derives from the tendency for specialized beef production to be relegated to areas too rugged for dairy cattle or too wet for sheep. In coastal areas of southern Australia the main beef cattle activity is the breeding and selling of vealers, locally termed 'baby beef'. Away from the coast, as in northeastern Victoria, as well as in southeast Queensland the breeding and fattening of older cattle assumes a greater relative importance. The prevalence of intensive beef production in southeast Queensland stems from the climatic deterrent for intensive sheep farming. Only in southeast Queensland and southeast of Darwin in the Northern Territory is intensive beef husbandry substantially more prominent as a land-use system than combination or mixed livestock enterprises.

Yet of the rural holdings classified as producing meat cattle in 1970–1, perhaps as many as one-half are located in southern Australia between the crop-livestock zone and the coast. Some 3,600, or nearly one-third of the southern total, are concentrated between Sydney and the Queensland border, where the association is with dairy cattle rather than with sheep. However, many properties in the Hunter Valley and on the north coast are sufficiently large to engage more in extensive grazing than in intensive husbandry, while others combine beef cattle with sugar cane or vegetables or pigs. Elsewhere the association is mainly with sheep,

as on the New South Wales tablelands and in south-eastern South Australia, or with sheep and dairy cattle, as in Victoria, Tasmania, and Western Australia. Locally crop enterprises may be a significant sideline, as for example vegetables in Western Australia and Tasmania. Coastal beef properties in most southern States average 500 ha but in Western Australia they average 400 and in Victoria 300. Inland, as on the northern tablelands of New South Wales or in north-eastern Victoria, they average 1,250 ha. Gross returns per unit of area decrease inland but labour input, labour productivity, capital intensity, and property returns all tend to increase. New South Wales and Victoria each have two-fifths of the southern total of intensive beef properties, those of southern Victoria being by far the most intensive. The coastal region south of Perth contains about one-tenth, and the rest are distributed almost equally between southeastern South Australia and northern Tasmania.

Intensive sheep farming for meat and wool occupies roughly about the same area as either specialized dairying or specialized beef husbandry but intensive sheep farming for only wool uses more land than the other three intensive livestock systems combined. It occupies large areas in Western Australia, Victoria, South Australia, and New South Wales, in that order, areas located between the coastal cattle systems and the crop-livestock zone (Fig. 10.5). Prime lamb raising is undertaken jointly with woolgrowing particularly on the central and southern tablelands and the Riverina in New South Wales, in northern Victoria, and to a lesser extent the Mount Gambier region of South Australia; small areas are located in the north and south midlands of Tasmania and in Western Australia. Since prime lamb production is usually associated not only with woolgrowing but also cattle and cropping enterprises, this livestock system is essentially diversified and tends to be more viable than specialized woolgrowing.

This viability stems, at least in part, from the ease of movement in and out of lamb production, so that the detailed pattern of prime lamb raising is subject to fairly rapid change. Specialist producers of prime lambs usually join short-wool British-breed rams, chiefly Dorset Horn or Poll Dorset, with first-cross ewes to yield quick-maturing second-cross lambs. However a woolgrower with suitable pasture or other fodder can produce prime lambs simply by crossing Merino ewes with long-wool British-breed rams, usually Border Leicester or Romney Marsh, or even by the straight breeding of the dual-purpose Polwarth and Corriedale or less satisfactorily of woolgrowing Merino. Such practices are more common in Western Australia and South Australia than in the main lamb-producing States. Lamb production requires more labour than woolgrowing alone but no additional capital. In the major regions of New South Wales and Victoria, though not in some minor regions as in Tasmania, properties producing prime lambs in addition to wool, often with cattle and cash crop sidelines, have tended on average to give higher returns not only per property but also per labour unit than the usually larger woolgrowing specialists within the same regions.

In 1970–1 the intensive sheep-farming regions of southern Australia contained one-third of Australia's sheep population and an estimated two-thirds of the specialized sheep holdings (that is, excluding wheat-sheep). This estimate includes the Tasmanian midlands (omitted from Fig. 10.5) where sheep farming is markedly more extensive than in adjoining lamb-producing regions but where stocking rates are higher than in all mainland States except Victoria. Intensive sheep farming presents a complex pattern both within and between States. Thus for example Merino wool-growing accounts for three-quarters of all properties in Western Australia, two-thirds in New South Wales, three-fifths in South Australia, two-fifths in Victoria, and is virtually non-existent in Tasmania. Properties range in average size from 750 ha in Tasmania and 700 in Western Australia, through 650 in New South Wales and 450 in South Australia, to 350 ha in Victoria. Although gross return per unit of area tends to vary inversely with property size, scale economies nevertheless favour the larger properties, so that Tasmania and Western Australia generally have the highest average property returns and Victoria the lowest. Most large properties complement the sheep enterprise with beef cattle, which permit a more efficient use of both pasture and labour. Since labour input everywhere approaches two units per property, this factor contributes substantially to scale economies and labour productivity tends to rise with increasing property size.

Intermediate Crop-Livestock Farming

Of the four basic land-use systems, intermediate crop-livestock farming, exhibiting a middle range of land-use and capital intensities, is perhaps the most viable and certainly the most efficient in the use of resources. Enterprise combinations comprise mainly sheep with wheat and other winter-growing cereals and oilseeds but also beef cattle with grain sorghum and/or wheat. Although the system occupies less than one-seventh of all agricultural land, it contains more than two-fifths of total sheep numbers and almost all the land under cereal grain. In the mid-'sixties it produced one-third of Australia's agricultural output (Williams, 1967, p. 47).

The crop-livestock or, as it is usually designated, the wheat-sheep belt displays a wide range of climate, soil, and slope conditions. Rainfall is generally low

and particularly on the inland margins variable; it averages 500–750 mm in the regions with a summer-rainfall maximum in southern Queensland and northern New South Wales and 300–500 mm in the winter-rainfall south. In the northern areas wheat is grown partly by the summer fallowing of moisture-retentive soils but since World War II grain sorghum has come to the fore. Soils vary widely but generally lack phosphorus and need phosphatic fertilizer to maintain fertility. The proportion of farmland receiving applications of superphosphate tends to decrease from Victoria northward through New South Wales to Queensland, where superphosphate is little used, and westward through South Australia; however, Western Australia has a high proportion of land receiving heavy applications. In eastern Australia the seaward limit of the wheat-sheep belt is determined by increasing altitude on the slopes of the tablelands, which accentuates the risk of damage by frost and such diseases as rust, and partly by the broken terrain that precludes the use of large machines and hence scale economies.

Five important subtypes are distinguishable (Fig. 10.6). The most intensive is wheat-sheep farming producing not only wheat, wool, and replacement stock but also prime lambs. This diversified type characterizes the wetter eastern and southern segments of the New South Wales belt and the wetter South Australian segment in the Yorke Peninsula but it predominates in Victoria, despite the low rainfall of the Mallee. Somewhat less intensive is wheat-sheep farming yielding cereal grain and merino wool, which typifies all except the drier margins of the Western Australian belt and only limited tracts elsewhere. The least intensive system occupies the central western section in New South Wales, most of the South Australian belt, and the inland fringe in Western Australia. Although beef cattle are carried by many properties, they constitute the dominant livestock enterprise only in combination systems west of Forbes and Parkes, where cattle are fattened on pastures bordering the Lachlan River, and on the Darling Downs in Queensland northwest of Toowoomba.

Within the wheat-sheep belt land use varies with the scale of farming. Thus the average property size generally increases from about 500 ha within the intensive core region of northern Victoria and the Wimmera to 1,500–2,000 ha in Queensland and on the Eyre Peninsula (significantly also in the Victorian Mallee). In Western Australia farms are mostly larger than in the east, ranging from 1,500 ha in the south to around 2,000 in the north, or twice the average for New South Wales. Carrying capacity per unit area tends to vary inversely with property size, the number of conventional livestock units per 100 ha ranging

Plate 10.3 The landscape of the southern region of the wheat-sheep belt in New South Wales.

from 35 in the irrigated Riverina (average property size 750 ha) to about 10 on the Eyre Peninsula, in Queensland, and the Victorian Mallee. But in Western Australia, partly because of rainfall distribution and reliability, carrying capacity ranges from around 15 in the south to 20 in the north. Consequently Western Australian farms carry more stock than elsewhere, the only exception being the Riverina; but even the Riverina is eclipsed in stock numbers per property by the northern region of Western Australia inland from Geraldton. Farms in Western and South Australia carry Merino sheep almost exclusively but crossbreds predominate in Victoria and are significant in New South Wales and Queensland.

In the late 'sixties and early 'seventies, until the collapse of the beef market, properties in the wheat-sheep belt tended to diversify by incorporating or expanding beef-cattle enterprises. Although the largest average herds were achieved in New South Wales, the greatest relative expansion took place in Victoria. In general, the growth in cattle numbers was not at the expense of sheep numbers but in Victoria some farmers who had reduced stock through drought restocked wholly or partly with cattle and in Queensland the increase in cattle numbers was offset by a decline in sheep numbers. Significantly diversification tended to be more pronounced the larger the average property size.

Land tenure and farm ownership in wheat-sheep farming are also not unrelated to scale, though the relationships are stronger for land tenure than for farm ownership. In southern and eastern Australia the proportion of total farmland held freehold tends to vary inversely with property size but in Western Australia the relationship is direct. Most of the remaining farmland is held on Crown lease but in the Wimmera, northern Victoria, and parts of Western Australia it is mainly private leasehold. Most properties are owned by partnerships, except in the Murray Mallee and central New South Wales, where the ratio is just under one-half, and in northern New South Wales where it drops to one-quarter. In these three regions sole owner-operation prevails.

Everywhere wheat-sheep farms have between three-fifths and four-fifths of their land under pasture but the proportion of improved to total pasture varies greatly. The ratio declines sharply from the Wimmera (four-fifths) and northern Victoria (three-quarters), through the Riverina (three-fifths), central and northern New South Wales (one-third and one-seventh respectively), to Queensland (one-twentieth). Elsewhere ratios lie between two-thirds and four-fifths, declining westward in South Australia and northward in Western Australia. Short-term clover leys not only help to reduce weed infestation but permit a build-up in soil fertility; subsequent crops of wheat grain have more protein and a higher baking quality than wheat from newly cropped land. Longer clover leys with heavier dressings of superphosphate further increase the protein content.

It was therefore the long-established wheat areas of southwestern and central-western New South Wales with a high ratio of improved to total pasture that saw the most rapid expansion of wheat growing in the boom of the 'sixties. Until then, wheat cultivation, which occupies more than one-half of all cropland other than short-term leys, had been declining steadily since the 'thirties. The area sown to wheat each year had averaged 5.7 million hectares in the 'thirties, 4.6 in the 'forties, and 4.2 in the 'fifties. But in response to improved profitability of wheat relative to wool the area sown to wheat soared to 10.8 million hectares in 1968–9 without any contraction in livestock enterprises. Although production expanded primarily in established areas, large tracts were sown to wheat on the drier inland margins of the wheat belt in both eastern and particularly Western Australia, areas previously considered too dry for successful wheat production. Expansion was made possible by *inter alia* the use of larger machinery enabling the speedier working of greater areas per farm, by the increased use of aircraft and larger boom sprays for controlling weeds and pests, and by the bulk handling of larger amounts of harvested grain. These technological innovations together with expanding farm operations contributed to the rapid growth in town farming in the wheat-sheep belt in the 'sixties (Williams, 1970).

The 1968–9 peak output of 14.8 millions tonnes, combined with a decline in export outlets, prompted the introduction of quotas on deliveries of wheat to the Australian Wheat Board. The Board, a statutory authority set up under complementary Commonwealth and State legislation in 1939, has the sole right to market wheat in Australia and Australian wheat and flour overseas. Such are the low and variable yields besetting wheat cultivation however that in 1972–3 severe drought reduced production to only 6.4 million tonnes harvested from 7.6 million hectares. Since fluctuations in output are a far more potent factor affecting variations in farm income than are fluctuations in price, wheat has been subject since 1948 to periodically revised stabilization plans. Yet the stabilizing effect of these plans has probably been less than the Board's role as a large seller on export markets and the international pricing arrangements for wheat.

Extensive Livestock Grazing

Extensive grazing covers some 475 million ha, or more than four times the total area occupied by all other agricultural land-use systems combined. Yet this vast expanse is managed by only some 16,000 rural holdings, or less than one-tenth of the Australian classified total in 1970–1. Sheep country accounts for 170 million ha, chiefly on the southeastern and southwestern inland plains but extending northward into central Queensland and the far northwest of Western Australia (Fig. 10.7). Cattle country makes up 250 million ha, largely in northern and central Australia but extending southward along the Queensland coast and the Dividing Range. The balance comprises land-use systems with sheep and cattle co-dominant, notably in Queensland, and cattle systems combined with forestry. In all, pastoral sheep properties number only about 7,000 and extensive beef properties perhaps 9,000. Since pastoral Australia is the subject of another chapter, only a few salient features of the rural economy will be noted here.

Although the scale of land use in the regions of Merino sheep grazing is everywhere large, the carrying capacity of the native grasses and shrubs varies greatly with the amount, seasonal incidence, and variability of rainfall and with the availability of watering points. Rainfall fluctuates widely from year to year but on average ranges from 100 mm in the winter-rainfall region of South Australia to 600–700 mm in the summer-rainfall region of southern Queensland. In the non-seasonal rainfall region of central and western New South Wales sheep properties average 10,000 ha, but in Queensland they average 15,000, in South Australia 35,000 and in Western Australia no less than 170,000 ha. Labour input obviously varies (from two to five units) directly with increasing property size but with increasing scale the productivity of labour tends to fall. Similarly stocking rates (from five to less than one livestock unit per 100 ha) and gross returns per unit of area both vary inversely with property size. However gross property returns also tend on average to vary inversely with the size of properties, the outstanding exception being Western Australia where returns average about twice those of South Australia.

Beef cattle, which are run as a sideline on many sheep properties and are co-dominant with sheep in some transitional, mostly northern areas, constitute

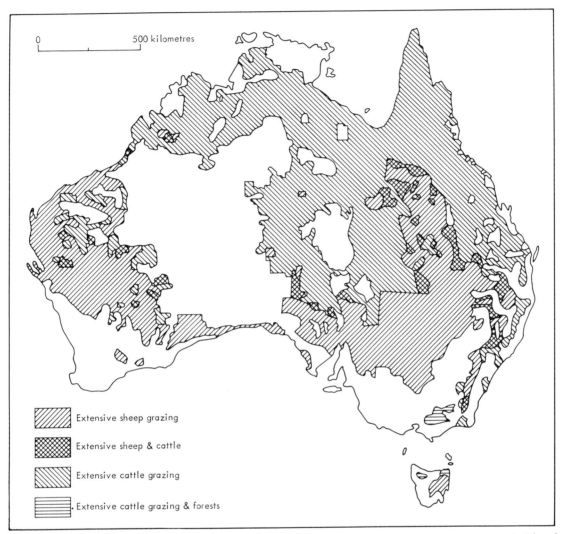

Fig. 10.7 Extensive livestock-grazing systems. *Source*: Department of Minerals and Energy (1973), 'Land Use', *Atlas of Australian Resources*, Second Series, Canberra.

the dominant enterprise over nearly one-half of the land used agriculturally in Australia. Within this vast monsoonal semi-arid and arid expanse, where pastures are almost entirely unimproved and have low nutritive value, are located the largest properties; they average more than 100,000 ha in northern Queensland, more than 200,000 ha in the Northern Territory, more than 300,000 ha at the centre, more than 500,000 ha in the Victoria River district, and more than 600,000 ha on the Barkly Tablelands. Clearly therefore, carrying capacity, which is lowest at the centre and highest in the north, is not simply related inversely to property size. If the zone of the largest properties extending from the Kimberleys eastward to the Barkly Tablelands is

excluded, then most other regions have properties carrying on average about 3,000 head of cattle and employing the equivalent of about six labour units. Even so, the gross property returns in regions where properties exceed 100,000 ha on average exhibit some distinctive regional patterns, being highest per property on the Barkly Tablelands, highest per ha along the north Queensland coast, and highest per labour unit at Alice Springs.

AGRICULTURAL INPUT-OUTPUT RELATIONSHIPS

In this penultimate section discussion focuses on the overall patterns that derive from the input and pro-

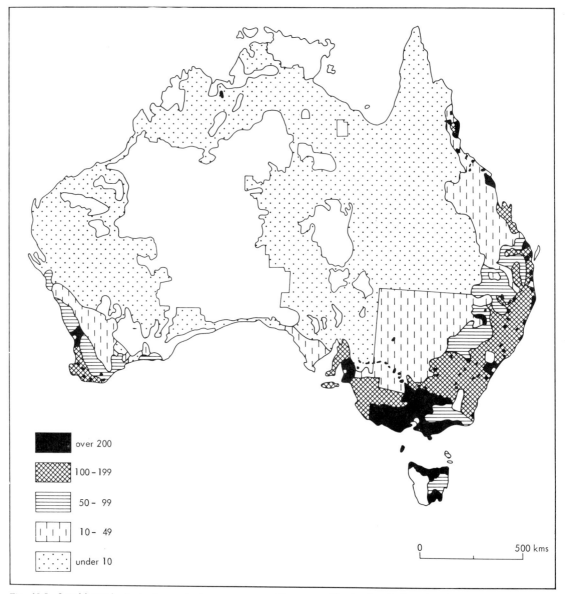

Fig. 10.8 Land input in Australian agriculture, as measured by assessed land values in $ per ha. *Sources*: as for Fig. 10.2.

ductivity of land, labour, and capital in the major land-use regions described in outline above. The data, as for Fig. 10.3, have again been obtained from sample BAE surveys and adjusted as average annual values for the three years ending 1970–1. Both inputs and outputs are expressed in terms of value rather than physical quantities, and while the use of monetary values has obvious limitations, it at least enables the spatial patterns to accord more closely to economic reality than would the use of physical ratios. On

the other hand, the choice of measures to express inputs, productivity, and profitability is to some extent arbitrary, and the measures employed are not necessarily the most indicative of efficiency.

Land

It is particularly apt to begin with a consideration of land value, for the value of land is a summary measure of the contribution which the physical environment and location make to agricultural produc-

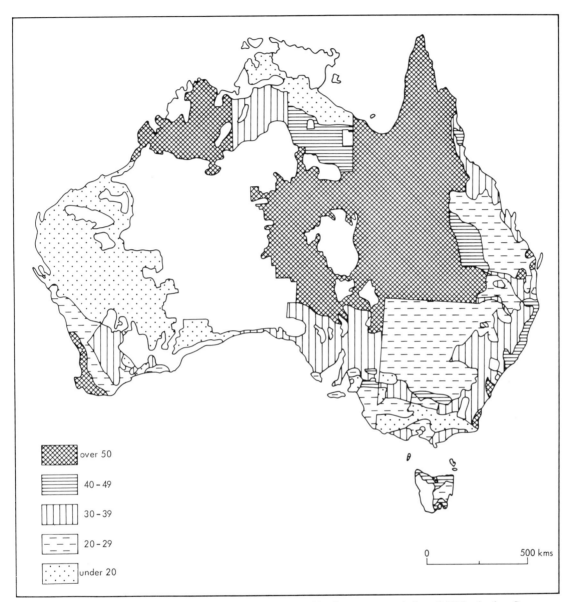

Fig. 10.9 Land productivity in Australian agriculture, as measured by the gross return in $ per $ 100 land value. *Sources*: as for Fig. 10.2.

tion. In other words it expresses not only the agricultural significance of local ecosystems, including soil quality, other surface features such as slope and drainage, surface and subsurface water, and climate, but also the extent of irrigation development, the existence of wholemilk, tobacco, or other quotas, proximity to major markets, urban facilities, and community services, and the potentiality for urban subdivision. The value of land to the farmer or grazier

is the amount of economic rent which the land will yield or the net return after the costs of all factors of production other than land have been subtracted.

Within Australia rural land values, at least in respect of livestock farming, tend to be highest over much of Victoria and northern Tasmania; together these two regions might be said to be the agricultural hub of Australia (Fig. 10.8). While values grade northeastward from Melbourne, the transition from high to low tends to be abrupt to the northwest. A secondary node surrounds Sydney away from which values decay with distance, particularly westward. Western Australia exhibits a striking zonation of decreasing values inland from Perth and the southwest. In southeast Queensland both the peak values and the outward decline are less pronounced while South Australia and Tasmania reveal distinctive patterns. It should be added however that land values reach their highest, exceeding $1,000 per ha, in areas of intensive cropping, such as irrigation districts, the Barossa Valley, and other horticultural areas.

Perhaps the most pertinent features of Fig. 10.8—and certainly the most reliable—are the comparative values of land within specific land-use zones. Dairying in southern Victoria returns higher values than virtually all coastal districts farther north, a feature reflecting the recent contraction of dairying southward. The intensive sheep-farming districts of Victoria have significantly higher values than those of New South Wales and South Australia, which in turn are followed by those of Western Australia and Tasmania. Yet the Tasmanian midlands furnish average values more than eight times those of western New South Wales, the extensive grazing region with the highest values, suggesting that the midlands fall properly within the belt of intensive-livestock farming. Within the crop-livestock zone values tend to decline northward from northern Victoria in line with the decreasing intensity of these farming systems to southern Queensland. However the lowest wheat-sheep values characterize the Mallee and the Eyre Peninsula. Predictably by far the lowest of all land values averaging less than a dollar a hectare, typify the vast tracts of extensive grazing country over most of northern and particularly central Australia. But in Queensland higher average values are returned for the eastern coastal districts, where the inclusion of components for some sugar-growing lands and proximity to services raises values above those for more remote inland areas experiencing greater climatic variability.

In general land values tend to vary inversely with the size of properties (cf. Figs 10.2 and 10.8), so that aside from the far north the range in the average value of properties (excluding structural improvements) among the major land-use zones is not strikingly great. Thus dairying properties in southeast Queensland differ little in average value from the large cattle stations of the western region, while regions as diverse as Alice Springs, the Wimmera, the Tasmanian midlands, and peri-metropolitan Melbourne reveal comparable property values. Nevertheless there is some tendency for properties to increase in average value inland, markedly in New South Wales. Outstanding are the vast properties of the Barkly Tableland and Victoria River regions in the Northern Territory, each of which is valued on average at more than half a million dollars.

The productivity of land capital as measured by the gross return per unit of land value might seem to reflect the performance of properties rather than of unit area but is complicated *inter alia* by the prevalence of some remarkably high land values in near-metropolitan locations (Fig. 10.9). Thus the return is highest in pastoral Queensland, central Australia, and the Kimberleys, and lowest in the intensive sheep-breeding regions of Victoria. However the performance of the Darwin and Gulf region of the Northern Territory, which is the only region within the northern pastoral zone to have a significant input of improved pasture, is strikingly inferior to the rest of the north. Although some high returns are experienced in dairying regions, notably in southwestern Australia and the New South Wales south coast, the very high land values of southern Victoria and the Sydney region tend to depress performance in these areas. The evidence suggests that in western and eastern Australia the productivity of land capital tends to fall away inland whereas in northern and southern Australia productivity tends to rise toward the centre. Certainly the best performance of any pastoral region is western Queensland followed closely by Alice Springs and the north of South Australia.

Labour

An assessment of the spatial input of labour costs is made possible by the BAE industry surveys which include not only data on hired labour but the imputed costs of the labour supplied by the operator and unpaid members of the family. Labour input thus measured by the costs of labour per unit area is obviously highest in regions of intensive cropping, notably of irrigated horticulture (Fig. 10.10). Next come the dairying regions, significantly with the Melbourne and Sydney regions pre-eminent, followed by Gippsland, and with the more extensive areas of Western Australia having the lowest input. Then come the regions of intensive sheep farming with the level of input declining from Victoria, through Tasmania, South Australia, New South Wales, to Western Australia. Although in Fig. 10.10 the wheat-sheep belt in New South Wales appears to have a level comparable with the more specialized sheep regions to the east, the input is everywhere lower. Among the wheat-sheep regions the peak occurs in northern Victoria and the Riverina while the lowest levels are in Western Australia and especially Queensland.

The extensive pastoral country appears from Fig. 10.10 to have a uniformly low level of labour input but within the pastoral zones there are in fact important regional variations. Thus within the sheep belt New South Wales and Queensland have much higher inputs than South Australia and Western Australia, the input in the east being nearly eight times that of the west. In

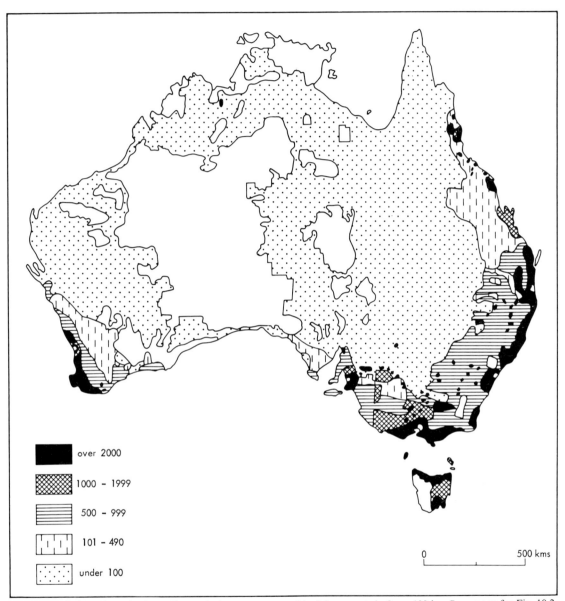

Fig. 10.10 Labour input in Australian agriculture, as measured by labour costs in $ per 100 ha. *Sources*: as for Fig. 10.2.

northern Australia the input tends to increase eastward and within Queensland southward but in the Northern Territory the level declines inland, the Alice Springs region recording the lowest level (under $5) of any land-use region.

Just as the average land capital of properties shows less pronounced spatial variation, if we exclude the northern pastoral zone, than land values per unit area, so the average input of labour costs per property presents to a smaller extent a less striking pattern than

the input per unit area. Yet the pattern of property costs resembles that of average property values, for total labour costs are lowest in coastal regions of comparatively small-scale intensive farming and highest in the inland grazing country. The sequence of increase away from the coast accords very closely with the land-use sequence from dairying and intensive cropping through intensive sheep and wheat-sheep farming to extensive pastoralism. Similarly within each zone the rank order of regions is generally the reverse of

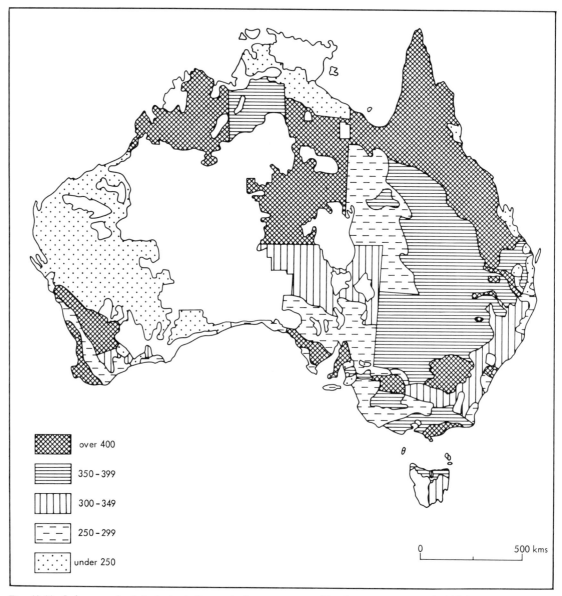

▨	over 400
☰	350 - 399
⦀	300 - 349
⊟	250 - 299
∴	under 250

0   500 kms

Fig. 10.11   Labour productivity in Australian agriculture, as measured by the gross return per $ 100 labour costs. *Sources*: as for Fig. 10.2.

that for labour input per unit area. Thus for instance among sheep-grazing regions Western Australia has the highest average costs followed by South Australia, Queensland, and New South Wales but the range is much smaller than in respect of unit-area costs and labour costs per property in Western Australia are little more than twice those in New South Wales. Again, the vast properties of the Barkly Tableland and Victoria River regions are outstanding, having

average labour costs twice those of the Darwin and Gulf region and the Kimberleys and four times those of the Alice Springs region. But whereas the pastoral properties at the centre have a land capital comparable to that of Wimmera wheat-sheep farms or Melbourne dairy farms, their labour input is three times as great.

An appropriate measure for comparing labour efficiency, given variations in wage rates between and within land-use systems, is the gross return per unit of

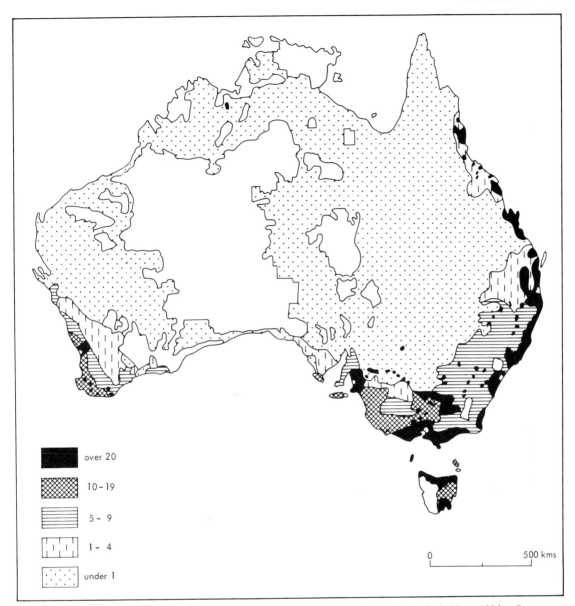

Fig. 10.12 Capital input in Australian agriculture, as measured by capital (excluding land) in $ 000 per 100 ha. *Sources*: as for Fig. 10.2.

labour costs. Fig. 10.11 suggests that the pattern of labour productivity is the product of complex relationships between the scale of the property business, the intensity of land use, and the quality of the environment. Although the pattern is basically one of increasing labour productivity inland, scale combined with a markedly difficult environment tends to depress labour efficiency in many regions, as witness the decreasing return with increasing property size westward through the pastoral sheep country of southern Australia. High labour productivity characterizes eastern and northern Queensland, the Barkly Tablelands, and the Kimberleys, where the employment of aboriginal labour probably results in a higher level of physical input than labour costs might suggest. Indeed, the Darwin and Gulf region performs poorly but not merely on account of its relatively low input of aboriginal labour; the region also contains particularly difficult country for mustering and handling cattle as well as extensive areas of improved pasture involving relatively high labour input. A pertinent feature is the high labour efficiency that delineates much of the wheat-sheep belt. High productivity also marks the dairying regions of Gippsland, the Sydney region, and the far southwest, illustrative respectively of the dominant influences of environment, proximity to a metropolitan whole-milk market, and scale.

Capital

Australian agriculture, as we have seen, is relatively capital intensive, and increases in productivity stem more from advances in technology than from improved labour efficiency. The structure of capital other than land includes structural improvements to properties (buildings, fencing, water facilities), plant and machinery; and livestock. Fig. 10.12, depicting the input of capital excluding land, reveals a pattern broadly similar to that of land values (cf. Fig. 10.8). But the proportions of total capital made up of land and other capital tend to decrease and increase respectively inland. Accordingly in the higher-rainfall areas of more intensive agriculture the input of land capital is generally greater than that of other capital, while in the lower-rainfall areas of extensive pastoralism it is generally smaller (cf. Figs 10.8 and 10.12).

However the exceptions to these broad generalizations are for the most part highly significant. Thus the input of capital (excluding land) exceeds land capital in the marginal dairying regions of the east coast and in the extensive dairying region of the far southwest but not in Victoria and around Sydney where higher productivity is capitalized in higher land values. Within the sheep country, the Tasmanian midlands, in sharp contrast to all mainland regions of intensive sheep farming, resemble almost all the extensive grazing regions in having a lower input of land than of other capital. On the other hand, western New South Wales is alone among the extensive grazing regions in having a slightly higher input of land than of other capital. Intensive cropping in southern Australia has a preponderance of other capital among a total capital only in the apple and pear orcharding regions of Tasmania and Western Australia and in the tobacco districts of Victoria and New South Wales.

A brief comment should perhaps be made concerning the spatial input of capital (excluding land) per property. Although the pattern bears some relationship to that of land capital per property, the relative increase in other capital inland produces a much more pronounced pattern of comparatively low inputs in southeastern and southwestern coastal regions grading inland to very high inputs at the centre and in the north. Alice Springs no longer returns capital inputs comparable with those of selected wheat-sheep, intensive

sheep, and peri-metropolitan dairying regions; in fact, the inputs of other capital per property are ten times as large at Alice Springs as in the Tasmanian midlands, twelve times those of the Wimmera, and sixteen times those of the Melbourne area. Yet even so, the average input of half a million dollars is only one-third that of properties on the Barkly Tableland and in the Victoria River region.

Consequently the productivity of other capital as indicated by the gross return per unit of input tends to be uniformly low throughout the extensive pastoral zone and highest in the southeast, the far southwest, and markedly in areas of intensive cropping (Fig. 10.13). An interesting feature is that within the zone of very extensive cattle grazing the two regions where a relatively high ratio of capital has been invested in the provision of water facilities are the regions with the highest capital productivity: western Queensland and northern South Australia. Similarly among the remaining cattle-grazing regions Alice Springs has the highest relative investment in water facilities and the highest return. Elsewhere the wheat-sheep belt stands out as having a significantly higher return than adjoining extensive or intensive sheep country, evidence of its high technological efficiency. The performance of dairying areas is remarkably uniform, only the Sydney region being outstanding. Among the areas of intensive cropping the highest performance is reached in the Namoi, Ord, and a few other cotton-growing districts and in regions of irrigated horticulture.

Profitability

A key measure of the profitability of agricultural land use is net property return. To arrive at this measure it is first necessary to calculate the net cash return by deducting all cash costs from the gross return; cash costs are made up of payments for materials, services, and hired labour, including contract labour but excluding any payments for family labour. An allowance must also be made for interest and rent payments, if any. Next, property return, the amount earned by the property as a family business, is determined by subtracting the charge for depreciation from the net cash return. Finally net property return is obtained by deducting the imputed cost of family labour from the property return. This measure represents the residual return to the entrepreneur for his labour and management and for the investment of capital. By 'management' is meant the decision-making process involving the selection of types and intensities of land use and the nature and quantities of inputs used. It refers to the entrepreneurial ability, given certain production objectives, to operate a property successfully.

Although the spatial pattern of net property return is therefore of major importance, it is useful to preface

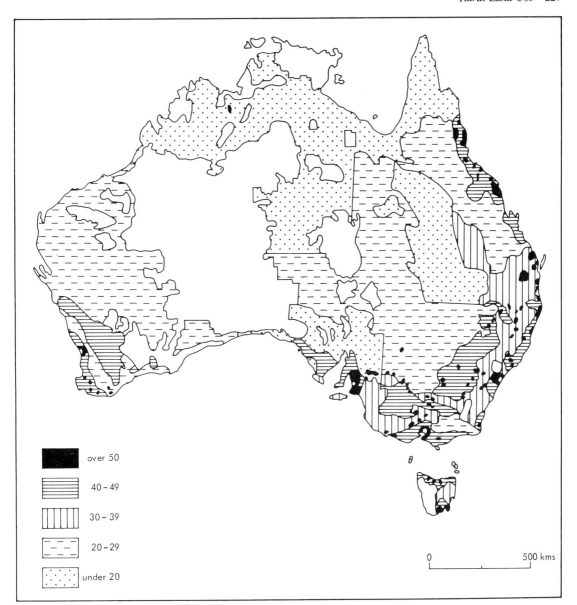

Fig. 10.13 Capital productivity in Australian agriculture, as measured by the gross return in $ per $ 100 capital (excluding land). *Sources*: as for Fig. 10.2.

its consideration by reference to the net return per unit of area. From the discussion of land values above it would follow that the net return per hectare should closely resemble the pattern of assessed land values. In almost all respects the two patterns are in fact virtually identical but the mainland belt of intensive sheep farming appears to have a lower net return per unit of area than the land values would suggest. The discrepancy derives from the fact that rural land values adjust very belatedly to changes in land-use profitability, and by the early 'seventies the decline in the profitability of sheep farming had not been reflected in the land values of sheep-farming regions. One reason for the slow reaction of land values to changes in income expectations is the reluctance of landowners to sell property in times of declining productivity and thereby

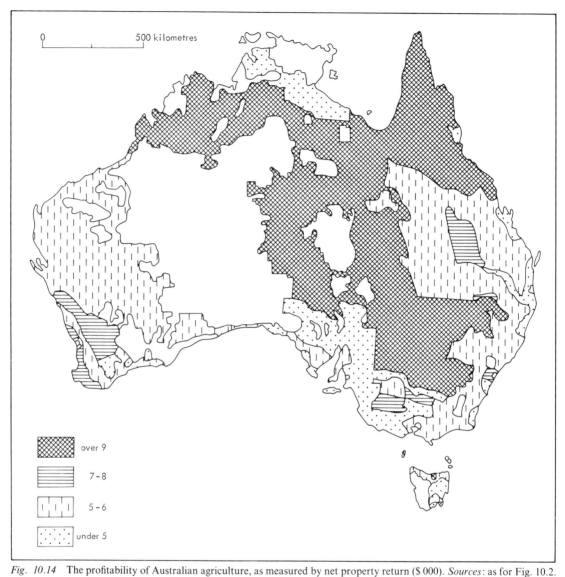

0   500 kilometres

over 9

7 - 8

5 - 6

under 5

Fig. 10.14 The profitability of Australian agriculture, as measured by net property return ($ 000). *Sources*: as for Fig. 10.2.

incur a capital loss. As a result, rural land values tend to be an imperfect indicator of the profitability of agricultural land.

Net property return presents a remarkably distinctive pattern (Fig. 10.14). Profitability is most marked in northern Australia (significantly except for the Darwin and Gulf region of the Northern Territory), in central Australia, western New South Wales, and the northern and southern sections of the New South Wales wheat-sheep belt. Explanations for the outstanding performance of these regions can be gleaned from preceding maps. Next come only a few areas: some other sections of the wheat-sheep belt, the cattle region of Queens-

land's inland south, Sydney's highly intensive dairying hinterland, and the very extensive dairying belt of the far southwest. Profitability is substantially lower over most of the remaining land used agriculturally, including the expanse of higher-rainfall country with more intensive agriculture. It is lowest in coastal northern and southern Australia. In sum, the profitability of Australian rural land use appears to be highest in the inland north and the centre, low in the east and the west, and lowest in the north and the south; in general, it correlates inversely with the intensity of land use.

Since net property return takes no account of

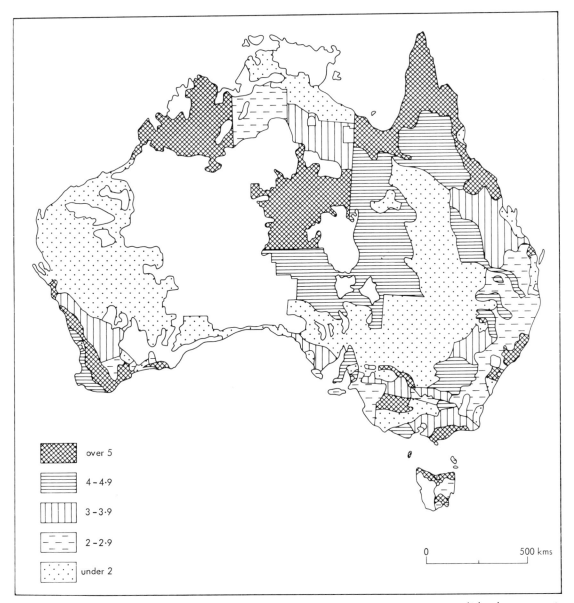

Legend:

- ▨ over 5
- ▤ 4 – 4·9
- ▥ 3 – 3·9
- 2 – 2·9
- under 2

0   500 kms

Fig. 10.15   The profitability of Australian agriculture, as measured by the percentage net return to capital and management. *Sources*: as for Fig. 10.2.

property size, another important measure of profitability is the rate of return to capital and management. The return to capital and management is obtained by deducting an allowance for the operator's labour from net property return; it represents the return to the capital value of the property and to management skill. The rate of return is expressed as a percentage of total capital. Although the utility of the measure is reduced by the delayed movements in land values, it at least takes account of property size.

Accordingly in Fig. 10.15 the performance of several pastoral regions appears less impressive than in Fig. 10.14; witness for instance northern South Australia, western Queensland, and Queensland's inland north, more especially the Barkly Tablelands and the Victoria River regions, and above all western New South Wales. On the other hand, many regions of small-scale intensive farming emerge as having a high level of profitability, notably cotton growing along the Namoi, tobacco growing along Queensland's south coast, irrigation agriculture along the Murray, dairying north of Sydney, in Gippsland, and northern Tasmania, intensive sheep farming in Western Australia, and wheat-sheep farming in the Wimmera. Yet in spite of many differences between the two patterns and the improved performance of several intensively farmed regions, it remains basically true that, notwithstanding numerous exceptions, profitability tends to be high in regions of very extensive land use and low in regions of relatively intensive land use.

OTHER RURAL LAND USE

Among other important uses of rural land in Australia is forestry (Jacobs, 1970). Productive forests occupy only 42.5 million ha, of which more than four-fifths are publicly owned (Forestry and Timber Bureau, 1974). Evergreen broadleaved species, chiefly of the genus *Eucalyptus*, make up more than seven-eighths of the total area, the rest comprising native conifers (4.4 million ha), chiefly species of the genus *Callitris*, and coniferous plantations (0.5 million ha), chiefly *Pinus radiata* (see Parliament of Australia, 1975). Since productive forests are largely confined to residual tracts in the eastern uplands and coastlands, Queensland and New South Wales each have nearly one-third of the resource area, though New South Wales and Victoria each furnish more than one-quarter of the gross value of forestry output. Yet the intensity of forest use, as measured by the value of output relative to the area available for productive use, is probably greatest in South Australia, followed by the Australian Capital Territory, Victoria, Tasmania, Western Australia, New South Wales, and the Northern Territory.

Forestry provides pertinent illustration of the land-use problems that stem from conflicting interests (Routley, 1974). Forests have long been subject to multiple, often conflicting uses, including their ruthless exploitation, their management on a sustained yield basis, their preservation as catchment areas or as animal sanctuaries, grazing, and recreation. However the Routleys, in a substantial and challenging book, advocate *inter alia* the principles of multiple values, partial use, and restrained yields based on the assumption that intensive forestry should enable much larger areas to be released for little or no exploitation. In their view environmental costs should be taken into account in forestry decision-making and the remaining uncommitted Crown forests should be reserved either under some new legal status or as undeveloped national parks.

Australia's low man-land ratio has hitherto tended to minimize the impact of land-use conflicts. Yet much environmental deterioration has resulted from the market orientation of Australian agriculture. Excessively small properties combined with the variability and intensity of rainfall and the pressures of changing cost-price relationships have prompted the cultivation of steep slopes, the exposure of soils to storm rains, and to overstocking. Clearly the market cannot have regard to many important issues such as the preservation of landscape and the provision of recreation areas. Although the promotion of better land use has latterly been accorded much cogent advocacy and government intervention, the growth, increasing mobility, and affluence of the Australian population will tend in future to increase the incidence and complexity of conflicts in Australian land use.

REFERENCES

Alexander, G. and Williams, O. B. (eds) (1973), *The Pastoral Industries of Australia*, Sydney University Press, Sydney.

Allen, A. (1965), 'Dairying in the Australian Tropics', *Aust. Geogr. Stud.*, 3, 17–19.

Australia (1974), *The Principles of Rural Policy in Australia: A Discussion Paper*, Report to the Prime Minister by a Working Group, Canberra.

Barnard, A. (ed.) (1962), *The Simple Fleece: Studies in the Australian Wool Industry*, Melbourne University Press, Melbourne.

Commonwealth Bureau of Census and Statistics (1973), *Rural Land Use, Improvements, Agricultural Machinery and Labour, 1971–72*, Reference No. 10.59, Canberra.

——(annually), *Official Yearbook of the Commonwealth of Australia*, Canberra.

Davidson, B. R. (1965), *The Northern Myth: A Study of the Physical and Economic Limits to Agricultural and Pastoral Development in Tropical Australia*, Melbourne University Press, Melbourne.

——(1969), *Australia Wet or Dry? The Physical and Economic Limits to the Expansion of Irrigation*, Melbourne University Press, Melbourne.

Department of Minerals and Energy, *Atlas of Australian Resources*, Second Series, Canberra.

Dragovich, D. (1970), 'Regional variations in dairying activities in South Australia', *Aust. Geogr.*, 11, 349–58.

——(1974), 'Changes in the distribution of dairying in South Australia, 1966 to 1972', *Aust. Geogr. Stud.*, 12, 77–89.

Forestry and Timber Bureau (1974), *Progress Report 1966–72 prepared for the Tenth Commonwealth Forestry Conference*, Canberra.

Holmes, J. H. (1962), 'The distribution of dairying in coastal New South Wales', *Aust. Geogr.*, 8, 207–20.

Jacobs, M. R. (1970), 'The forest as a crop' in G. W. Leeper (ed.), *The Australian Environment*, 4th edn, CSIRO and Melbourne University Press, Melbourne, pp. 120–30.

Laut, P. (1968), *Agricultural Geography*, Vol. 2, Mid-Latitude Commercial Agriculture, Nelson, Melbourne.

——(1970), 'Dairy industry trends in the N.S.W. milk solids region, 1946–67', *Rev. Marketing and Agric. Econ.*, 38, 25–45.

Leeper, G. W. (ed.) (1970), *The Australian Environment*,

4th edn, CSIRO and Melbourne University Press, Melbourne.

Parliament of Australia (1975), *The Operation of the Softwood Forestry Agreements Acts 1967 and 1972*, Report from the House of Representatives Standing Committee on Environment and Conservation, Canberra.

Routley, R. and V. (1974), *The Fight for the Forests: The Takeover of Australian Forests for Pines, Wood Chips and Intensive Forestry*, Australian National University Press, Canberra.

Rutherford, J. (1968), 'Government irrigation and its physical environment' in G. H. Dury and M. I. Logan (eds), *Studies in Australian Geography*, Heinemann, Melbourne, pp. 137–94.

Rutherford, J., Burdekin, H. and MacGregor, I. (1971), *Case Studies of Changing Population and Land Use on the Periphery of Metropolitan Sydney*, Geogr. Soc. N.S.W. and Univ. Syd. Dept. Geogr., Res. Pap. Geogr., 16.

Scott, P. (1968), 'Population and land use in Australia', *Tijd. voor Econ. en Soc. Geogr.*, 59, 237–44.

——(1975), 'The application of world agricultural typology to Australia', in *Agric. Typology and Land Utilization*, Verona, 297–309.

Smith, D. L. (1966), 'Market gardening at Adelaide's urban fringe', *Econ. Geogr.*, 42, 19–36.

——(1970), 'Viticulture in the Barossa region: Prospects and costs', *Aust. Geogr. Stud.*, 8, 101–20.

——(1972), 'The growth and stagnation of an urban fringe market gardening region: Virginia, South Australia', *Aust. Geogr.*, 12, 35–48.

Wadham, S., Wilson, R. K. and Wood, J. (1964), *Land Utilization in Australia*, 4th edn, Melbourne University Press, Melbourne.

Williams, D. B. (ed.) (1967), *Agriculture in the Australian Economy*, Sydney University Press, Sydney.

Williams, M. (1970), 'Town-farming in the Mallee lands of South Australia and Victoria', *Aust. Geogr. Stud.*, 8, 173–91.

Wilson, R. K. (1961), 'The distribution of dairying in Victoria', *Aust. Geogr.*, 8, 51–64.

11 CLIMATE AND PRIMARY PRODUCTION

ANN MARSHALL

Implicit in the term 'primary production' is the concept of a change in the natural landscape, the 'production' of a particular plant or animal of more use to the occupying human group than the varied plants and animals of the 'natural' (pre-human) ecosystem. This inevitably involves a degree of climatic risk. The plants and animals of the natural environment have come to terms with elements of the local climate and can survive at least short-term variations from climatic means. On the other hand, successful primary production requires not only that the cultigens survive but that they produce a high yield of some desirable constituent. In the case of biota introduced from some other area—the usual case—it is highly unlikely that species selected for their ability to thrive with one set of climatic variables will be as successfully adapted to a somewhat different set. The chance of damage, low yield and even extinction in periods of climatic stress is therefore considerable. In a broad sense then, primary production requires an appraisal of climatic risks in terms of expected rewards. In areas of long established domestication, this can perhaps be a calculated risk, economically viable forms of land use having been established by selection. Under colonizing conditions however, the climatic conditions are unknown and the risk cannot even be calculated.

In the case of Australian colonization, settlement was influenced by the fact that the British in the early nineteenth century had no experience of climates similar to those of Australia. The far-flung British Empire did not include this kind of country. It is interesting that early comparisons were often made between coastal New South Wales and Cape Colony, but when settlement moved inland to semi-arid areas the British settlers had no standards of comparison—rainfall variability was up to 40 per cent (Gentilli, 1971, p. 158). They shaped their land use according to their perception of the climate, without even folklore to guide them and with no scientific information. Not only was there no Australian climatology in the early 1800s, there was no true science of climatology and even background meteorology was in its infancy. Although a vast quantity of information about different climates had been accumulated during the age of

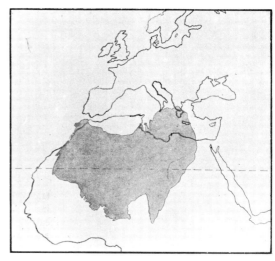

Fig. 11.1 Australia, showing comparative area, latitude and position in the northern hemisphere.

exploration, comparative studies of these climates date only from von Humboldt's first use of isotherms in 1817. The first attempts to compare climates on a world scale with any more subtlety than the 'torrid, temperate and frigid zones' of the Greeks were not made until the late nineteenth century—Supan in 1879, Köppen in 1884. Such comparative climatology had to wait for large numbers of instrumental measurements of the climatic elements, and the first reasonably successful world climatic classifications were by Herbertson in 1905 and Köppen in 1918 (Leighly, 1949). Jevons was ahead of his time in emphasizing the latitude comparisons of Australia and Africa although he missed the need to keep west and east coasts in similar positions and he put the Queensland coast where the Pilbara should be (Jevons, 1859).

CLIMATE AND DEVELOPMENT
In newly developing areas, land use will be established in terms of the *perceived* climatic risk, and perception will be conditioned by the information available and the economic background of the time. From this

point of view, the development of Australian primary production can be conveniently divided into four periods: recognized ignorance; learning the hard way; incautious optimism; and informed adjustment, although incautious optimism is apparently incurable and lingers on. There is obviously no sharp division between these periods, but they make a convenient framework for discussion.

An essay of this length must be limited to the key forms of production only, not the specific needs of specific crops. No attempt will be made to discuss the temperature conditions which confine sugar cane production to the Queensland coast, or the long growing period which is important for the dairy industry. Rather, the emphasis will be on sheep grazing as the dominant pastoral industry and wheat farming as representative of agriculture in temperate Australia, and cattle grazing and abortive attempts to grow rice and sorghum in the winter-dry tropics. The emphasis will be on moisture conditions which are clearly the most important. In a continent such as Australia, subtropical with an east-west orientation and uniformly low elevation, the constraint due to temperature is reduced to minimal importance.

The Period of Recognized Ignorance

For the first twenty-five years, Australian settlement was confined to the small area between the Blue Mountains and the sea. Brought up on what Heathcote calls the 'drought syndrome', Australians have tended to assume that the first attempts at agriculture and grazing were hampered by water shortage. But the annual rainfall of the area first settled is over 1,000 mm, twice the normal rainfall of the British Isles, and the lowest rainfall ever recorded at Sydney is 545 mm. The settlers complained of 'droughts' but it is clear from quotations of contemporary sources (Perry, 1957) that these usually were dry periods of a few months duration. The term probably indicated the English reaction to a summer in which the grass turned yellow. There is some evidence of a more severe dry period in 1813–14 (Jevons, p. 64) but in the absence of rainfall records until 1840 it is difficult to evaluate it. Certainly it is hard to credit Oxley's statement (1820) that 'for nearly two years, scarcely a drop of rain fell in the east coast of New South Wales'. The rainfall records since 1840 do not indicate any such catastrophic water shortage.

The climatic hazard which plagued the first settlers was not in fact drought but flood (Jevons, p. 80). The soils around Sydney, derived from the hard Hawkesbury sandstone, were usually wretchedly infertile—indeed Watkin Tench was prophetic when he said they were 'cursed with everlasting and unconquerable sterility'. Much of the sandstone plateau is uncleared to this day. There was at that time no knowledge of soil chemistry and mineral fertilizers so the primitive farming was driven back to the much better alluvial soils of the Nepean and Hawkesbury rivers, and there it persisted in spite of twenty damaging floods in fifty years. With hindsight, we can say these floods were predictable. The Hawkesbury and its tributaries rise in the eastern face of the mountains where moist unstable air from the Pacific causes high intensity of rainfall. The rivers rise rapidly, flow through narrow gorges and emerge onto wide alluvial plains. The better soils of these plains were, of coarse, due to periodic inundation. The rivers are etched about 10 m below the level of the plains, but the flood rise is often 12 to 15 m. Josephson (1885) gives detailed accounts of the height of the floods, the damage and the lives lost in the early years.

Yet the farming persisted, in spite of the obvious climatic hazard. There was, of course, no exploration of the mountain face to indicate conditions at the source of the rivers, and rainfall intensities there—up to 250 mm in 24 hours—would have been quite outside the experience of English settlers used to a steady gentle rain in which rainfall per wet day is seldom more than 30 mm. Accumulating evidence must have underlined the likelihood of floods, and it seems that the hazard was clearly perceived (Atkinson, 1826) but was ignored because of economic necessity. There were no other soils capable of producing crops with the primitive methods of the day, and the rapid exhaustion of what little fertility existed in virgin soils developed on shales near Sydney emphasized the need to concentrate on the alluvium (King, 1948).

In this first brief period then, primary production was mostly dominated by problems of difficult soils and terrain. On the whole, the settlers liked the climate. They described it as 'salubrious' and Commissioner Bigge (1822, p. 82) thought it was too pleasant to make transportation a satisfactory punishment. Some startling meteorological theories were propounded which indicate how little understanding of basic principles existed at that time: the hot wind produced a high pressure, Parramatta was colder than Sydney 'which suggested a large deposit of nitre in the vicinity', rainfall was caused by 'the refrigerating power of plants'. Residents were surprised and rather pained by the scorching northwest wind and the large and rapid changes of temperature, but on the whole the infant colony had too many other problems to be seriously concerned about the hazards of the climate *per se*.

The Period of Learning

The inland sweep of Australian settlement after the mountains were crossed in 1813 is one of the best-known facets of Australian history. In fifty years, almost the whole of the usable part of the continent

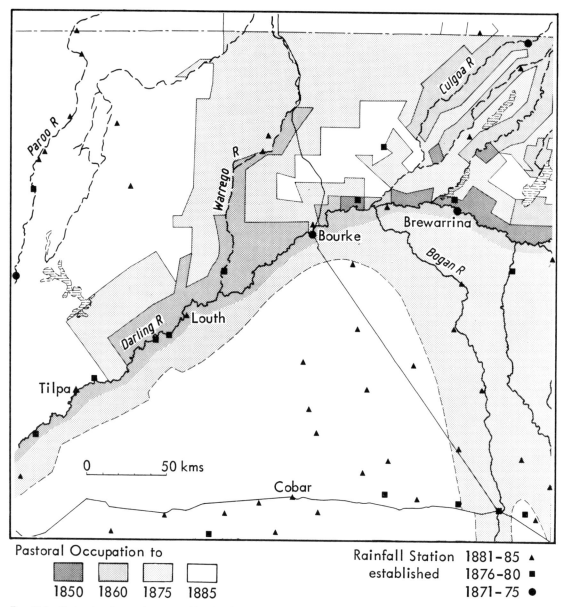

Pastoral Occupation to

1850	1860	1875	1885

Rainfall Station   1881–85 ▲
established   1876–80 ▪
                                1871–75 ●

Fig. 11.2   Pastoral settlement in western New South Wales, and the dates of the first rainfall records. *Sources*: R. L. Heathcote (1965), *Back of Bourke*, Melbourne University Press, Melbourne; Reuss and Browne (*c.* 1875), *A Pastoral Map of New South Wales* (after D. N. Jeans); Commonwealth Bureau of Meteorology (1972), *Catalogue of Australian Rainfall and Evaporation Data*.

had been looked over by the explorers and pre-empted by graziers in search of new pasture. This expansion has been well documented, and a brief summary is given by Peel (1973). Every economic circumstance combined to favour wool as an export staple: the expanding British demand for fine wool, the collapse of Spain and the industrialization of the German areas where the competitive Saxon merino was grazed, and the durability of wool for transport over long and primitive routes (Marshall, 1966). The Australian climate was particularly suited to sheep grazing with minimal labour requirements, and the flocks moved inland into pasture intermittently grazed by free roaming marsupials. And settlement moved rapidly into a climate in its aridity and variability totally unlike anything before encountered in British tradition.

Pastoral Occupation

Inevitably, settlement preceded any information about the climate. The accounts of the explorers were once-only records and often contradictory—Sturt (1847) wrote 'many beautiful farms might be established on the banks of the Darling, for both its soil and its climate are favourable: no blighting winds appear to prevail and the rains continue much longer than in the neighbourhood of Adelaide'. In his diaries (1849) however, the heat and aridity of the country traversed is clear. For the pastoralist, grassland and unfamiliar bush in good condition were the only evidences of climate, and the establishment of official weather records waited on the need for a post office, a river trading town or a main transport route. Ironically, the sheep owners were often prepared in their own interests to keep records. Alarmed and puzzled by great variation in rainfall, pastoralists often applied to the weather bureau for an instrument and instructions for its use, and sheep stations were recognized as official rainfall stations from very early years. However, most of the inland country had been in grazing use for around thirty years before a minimal series of ten years rainfall records was available (Fig. 11.2).

It is hardly surprising that the sheep grazing was ill-adapted to a climate in which dry years were a regular feature and grazing pressure on the permanent vegetation an unknown phenomenon. The sheep could not move freely from dry areas as had the earlier marsupials. Changes in herbage, trampling, wind and water erosion became the rule (Moore, 1962) and the effects were multiplied by the invasion of rabbits. A few far-seeing graziers like Peter Waite talked of the danger of destroying 'nature's haystack' (Beltana Pastoral Co., 1965) but in general it was thought that grazing was good for the country because it promoted the growth of grass. An official government publication of 1882 states: 'Dry seasons come in this as in other countries at uncertain intervals, but the settlement of the interior is not only increasing the water in creeks and rivers, but bringing with it such a multitude of reservoirs for preserving the abundant rains and of wells for getting water from below, that droughts are no longer the terror they used to be' (Richards, 1882).

Pastoral occupation extended into country with an average rainfall of less than 250 mm and a variability of 40 per cent. The discovery of artesian water in the 1880s allowed a greater independence of natural rivers and the grazing of even more arid country,

Fig. 11.3 Rainfall variability at Bourke and sheep numbers in the East Darling Division of New South Wales for the same years. *Sources*: Commonwealth Bureau of Meteorology (1948), *Results of Rainfall Observations made in New South Wales*; Butlin, 1962, p. 300.

with grazing pressure around watering points built up to a stage quite foreign to the pre-European environment. By the 1890s, the grazing industry of the inland was in an extremely vulnerable position. The margin of occupation had advanced and retreated with the seasons before (Butlin, 1962), but the sheep population had shown an overall increase in the semi-arid areas. At the close of the century the inevitable happened—a series of dry years from 1897 to 1902 (Fig. 11.3). The sheep population of Australia was halved, and much of this loss was in the inland areas (Butlin, p. 289). Although sheep numbers in general recovered with years of better rainfall, the inland country never again carried so many sheep.

A reassessment of climatic constraints on grazing was needed. Much of the inland country was ruined (Cain, 1962; Ratcliffe, 1936). Pre-European ecosystems had been adapted to occasional very dry periods—there is no reason to think that the low rainfalls of the 1890s had not occurred before and they have certainly occurred since. But European settlers saw such periods as 'droughts', a misfortune visited on the pastoralists rather than a characteristic of the climate. Lacking evidence that such periods had occurred before, the settlers could hope that they would not occur again. Rainfall variability needs a long series of measurements to be recognized as inevitable.

Unfortunately, these records were not available and the constraint was not recognized in time to prevent disaster to the grazing industry and permanent and widespread damage to the environment. The pastoralists had to discover rainfall variability from their own bitter experience (Plate 11.1).

Early Agricultural Expansion

Moving inland behind the pastoral frontier came the closer settlement of agriculture, representing a greater transformation of the environment and therefore a

Plate 11.1 Severely eroded country in western New South Wales. Only small patches of surface soil remain in hollows for regrowth of ephemerals and bush. Near Cobar.

land use still more vulnerable to climatic constraints. The need for wheat for local use was reinforced by the repeal of the Corn Laws in Britain in 1846, opening up the ever-expanding British market and making wheat in many ways as desirable a product as wool. After its early struggles against infertile soil near Sydney and floods on the alluvial river flats, wheat growing was finally driven out of the coastal districts of New South Wales by disease (Robinson, 1970). Stem rust, disastrous in the warm moist ripening season of the east coastal districts, cut the yield by 80 per cent in the old established wheat growing districts.

At the same time, many circumstances were combining to make wheat growing more appropriate away from the east coastal regions. Population, increased by the Gold Rush, caused a demand for land, land laws became more liberal and the 'Cockie farmer' appeared to nibble away at the edge of the large pastoral runs. Clearing was hardly necessary in some areas inland from the divide and soils were much more fertile than in the coastal regions. The era of commercial farming was under way, the interaction of cheap and suitable colonial land with growing industrial markets and developing industrial products which made the

farming possible—fencing, well-digging and farm machinery, railways and steamships. In Australia there were numerous specific adaptations to local problems—'mullenizing' to roll down the intractable scrub, harvesting machinery for large areas and minimal labour, stump-jump ploughs for the solid and almost indestructible roots of the mallee. Railways spread out to collect the grain and to enable the expansion to go further. This is the period so brilliantly pictured by Meinig in his section on 'a new kind of agriculture' (Meinig, 1962, p. 120).

Expansion of wheat into low rainfall areas started in New South Wales by 1860, in South Australia in the 1870s, in Victoria a little later. There was still no available picture of the climatic pattern of the continent although rainfall was recognized as critical and rainfall tables were produced by the different weather bureaux from very early years. The marginal inland country was still climatically unknown, and it is worth repeating that the physical principles of climatology were still not well understood. This may help to explain some of the quainter myths of the time such as 'rain follows the plough' (Meinig, p. 70). The few cautious observers like Goyder were usually unpopular and often called unpatriotic—a theme

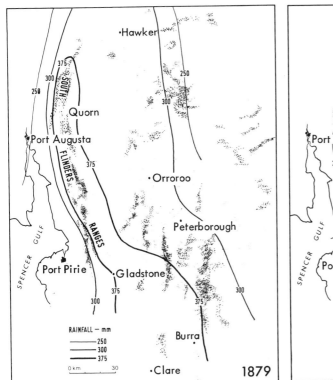
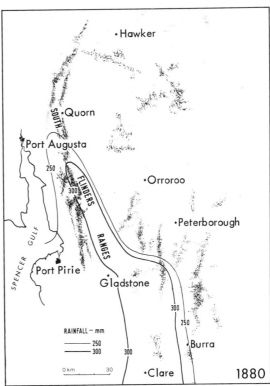

Fig. 11.4   Effective rainfall (April to November) in two successive years in the northern part of the South Australian wheat belt. Wheat growing on the northern fringe contracted after 1880. *Sources*: Commonwealth Bureau of Meteorology (1918), *Results of Rainfall Observations made in South Australia and the Northern Territory*; Meinig, 1962, p. 82.

which persists to the present day.

In the same way that the drought of the 1890s set limits to the expansion of the pastoral industry, the 1880s saw the retreat of wheat growing from the northern fringes in South Australia, where the good rains of the '70s had enticed wheat growing almost to the shores of Lake Torrens. The collapse started in 1880 (Fig. 11.4) and the wheat area contracted, leaving behind eroded soil and ruins of an occupation which now seems almost incredible (Plate 11.2). The climate of Australia was becoming known, by an increasingly dense network of observing stations enabling the basic parameters to be mapped (Todd, 1893, quotes 357 meteorological stations and 2,575 rain gauges in South Australia). It was becoming known also by the advance and forced retreat of land use along the margins of climatic viability. When prices were good it was worth taking big risks, but there were certain climatic limits beyond which the risks were always too great. With a hundred years of records and a lot more scientific expertise, we may regard this marginal expansion as unwise, but it is well to remember that in the nineteenth century the

facts of Australian climate had to be learned the hard way.

The Period of Incautious Optimism

By the turn of the century and the beginning of Federation, the broad outlines of Australian climate were apparent. Russell (1883) drew maps of the rainfall of New South Wales for a parliamentary commission, and although he did not draw isohyets, he displayed the rainfall pattern by one map in which large figures represented district averages, and another in which each recording station was represented by a circle with diameter proportional to the average rainfall. He was careful to point out that the averages in inland districts represented only a few years' records, and he was clear in his warning that the inland districts were not suited to agriculture. He did not, however, see the climate as unsuited to grazing. There were as yet too few records to underline the variability. In South Australia, maps of average rainfall were presented to Parliament from 1881 (S.A. Parl. Proc., 1881).

The recognition of the climatic pattern of the whole

Plate 11.2   Eroded country and adandoned wheat lands, with the Flinders Ranges in the background. *Photo*: C. R. Twidale.

continent and the explanation of this pattern seem to have waited for the formation of the Commonwealth Weather Bureau in 1906. In *The Climate and Weather of Australia* (Hunt *et al.*, 1913) the authors say 'in submitting this small work to the public, we venture to express the hope that it may prove acceptable as being the first effort in the nature of a textbook that has been published on Australian Meteorology'.

It is doubtful if 'the public' had any clear ideas about the climate of Australia. Most of them had always lived in the coastal cities of the southeast, and in the early years of this century a journey of any great length was an adventure. Certainly the public got little help from school geography books at this time—at the beginning of the century the New South Wales 'Department of Public Instruction' used a textbook of 130 pages with one page on climate (Taylor, 1898). Rainfall is briskly summarized: 'on the coast from 72″ at Tweed Heads to 36″ at Eden. On the Tablelands it is 30″ and on the western plains only 17″' (430 mm). In Victoria, Gregory (1903) provided a short section on meteorology with a map in which there were no isohyets but average rainfall figures for twenty-one

districts. The lowest is the Mallee with 16″ (406 mm) although in fact the rainfall in this region varies from 15″ to 10″ (250 mm). He followed this with a geography text (1907) with maps of annual rainfall and a sensible discussion of aridity and rainfall variability. Griffith Taylor in his first textbook (1914) went further, giving the maps of summer and winter rainfall and temperature and using Herbertson's 'Natural Regions' to compare Australian climates with other parts of the world. His insistence on the limiting effects of aridity, a theme which ran consistently through all his Australian work, was already apparent.

Agriculture in the Marginal Country

It seems likely that this general ignorance of Australian climate at the beginning of the century combined with several other factors to produce a complacent attitude towards agriculture. The pastoral industry had learned its lesson in the turn-of-the-century droughts (and done most of its damage to the semi-arid environment). Wheat growing had been driven back from the arid fringes in South Australia. But the market for wheat in industrializing Europe seemed assured, and in Australia the infrastructure was already built. Railways had been established, agricultural machinery and techniques had been adapted to cope with farming conditions in which land was cheap and labour scarce, new breeds of wheat were being produced and superphosphate was being accepted to restore minerals which cropping had removed from already infertile soils. Yields rose from the shattering lows of the 1890s and stabilized. The wheat farmers settled down to consolidate their position in areas of rainfall which was fairly reliable but low by world standards.

Donald (1965) has divided Australian farming into three periods characterized by different degrees of adaptation to the environment. The principal adaptation in this—his second—period was the technique of 'dry farming' in which a period of bare cultivated fallow was interspersed between the years of wheat growing. The concept of fallowing was borrowed from the English farming system where fields were left idle for a year to increase the availability of nitrogen for the next year's crop. It was certainly not needed for conserving moisture in England but when the technique was imported without understanding the reasons for its success it was given an Australian context, and the assumption was made that the resulting improvements in yield were due only to conservation of moisture. The practice was supposed to break up the 'capilliary tubes' up which water evaporated from the soil, and bare fallowing became something of a rite. A clean cultivation was the mark of a good farm, and farmers were advised that if there was no other job to be done they should go out and cultivate.

In a less obtrusive way, 'dry farming' probably did as much harm to the environment as overgrazing. Modern thinking is that the higher yields resulted from two factors, killing the weeds which would otherwise have transpired water from the entire rooting zone (but this does not require 12 clean cultivations) and increasing the decomposition of vegetable material so that more nitrogen in a readily accessible form was available for the next crop (French *et al.*, (196–). Yields rose temporarily, but at the expense of exhaustion of the soil resources of organic material and damage to soil structure. Constant clean cultivation was an open invitation to soil erosion; wind erosion of light soils increased, surface soil was lost, fences and railways buried and red rain became a commonplace in southern cities. In addition, the impact of rain on the exposed soil puddled the surface causing increased runoff, and sheet and gully water erosion followed.

By 1920 the increase in yields had flattened out (Donald, Fig. 1). The technique of dry farming had maintained the wheat belt in country with annual rainfall as low as 300 mm, but only at the expense of a deterioration of the environment.

The Desert 'Myth'

At about this time in Australian history, possibly the result of agricultural optimism, possibly its cause, came the remarkable cult of 'Australia Unlimited'. A book of that name appeared about 1914 (Brady, (191–) with statements like 'it can at once be realized that not a thousand square miles of Australia is likely to prove worthless'. The author claimed to know the whole of Australia but his travels—not illustrated on any map—were confined to the better-watered areas. This sort of airy travelogue could be dismissed as such if it had not proved so popular, especially in the years after World War I. Migration from an overcrowded Britain was being encouraged, and it seemed right and proper that we should use our vast empty spaces to provide the food and fibre that Britain needed. Sober economists like Grondona (1924) stated 'the irrigable portion of Australia would carry a population of 90 million, and there would still be available 8/9 of the continent for ordinary settlement'. The settlement of returned soldiers on the land seemed axiomatic—but of course the better-watered areas were already under cultivation. So the new farmers, British migrants and Australian soldiers, had to be content with land on the fringes of settlement. Any mention of aridity was therefore unpatriotic! A letter to the *Sydney Morning Herald* (10 May 1924) asks rhetorically 'Is it a good thing to proclaim to the world (even if such were true) that Australia is one third a barren desert?'

Perry (1966) considers that Australians have always been reluctant to believe ill of their country's climate, but certainly this was the 'boosters' finest hour. Instead of accepting east-west orientation along the tropic as one of the unfortunate facts of life, politicians, planners and writers convinced themselves that aridity did not exist or if it did it was better not to mention it. An urban population in the high-rainfall zones could be made to believe this, and in 1931 Isaiah Bowman wrote in *The Pioneer Fringe*: 'A desert in Australian politics is something hot and plantless that exists somewhere in the world but not in Australia'.

This was not a harmless aberration, because it affected assessment of the country. At this time, Sydney University had the only Geography Department in Australia and this may explain why its Professor, Griffith Taylor, was almost single-handed in his protests against such unrealistic climatology. From his first climatic book in 1913 (Hunt *et al.*) to his many geography texts on Australia, Taylor delineated the arid zones and stressed the need to concentrate development in the better-watered areas. His far-reaching Presidential Address to the Australasian Association for the Advancement of Science (1923) used a series of his famous 'griffograms' to illustrate climatic comparisons with Mexico and North Africa, and suggested a rainfall of 250 mm for the inner margin of the wheat belt.

It is clear that he was already under criticism for these ideas, and he precipitated an acrimonious controversy in the daily press. It is difficult now to understand this argument about a desert which is mapped in all school textbooks and ranks as a tourist attraction, but Taylor's books were banned by the Western Australian Education Department and he was the target of vicious criticism (Taylor, 1958, p. 169). He fought back with his characteristic uncompromising honesty—and sometimes also with characteristic lack of diplomacy. He wrote to the *Sydney Morning Herald* (9 November 1921) 'It is, I suppose, Utopian to look forward to a time when all our potential statesmen shall be compelled to show some knowledge of the physical environment of the continent which it will be their duty to administer'.

The constant barrage of criticism undoubtedly caused Taylor to accept the Professorship of Geography in Chicago in 1928, and he did not return to Australia until after his retirement. Ironically, events were justifying his ideas even as he left. Primary production cannot afford to ignore climatic parameters just because their existence is unpopular. The policy of new settlement after World War I had to be carried out mainly in Crown Lands, often on the semi-arid margins of the wheat country (Dunsdorfs, 1956, p. 208). Settlement was encouraged on the assumption that good agricultural prices would continue although little information was available about the soils and many were unsuitable. Climatic statistics, especially rainfall variability, were ignored. These risks might have been worth taking when prices were good, but when wheat prices collapsed along with everything else in 1929 all the danger spots became apparent. Examples are analysed in detail in the Second and Third Reports of the Rural Reconstruction Commission (1944). A representative conclusion (Third Report, p. 21) is 'Wheat growing in Millewa is an extreme form of agricultural gamble which is always too big a risk for the farmer with small resources and for any one in times of low prices'. There was an exceptionally large planting of wheat in 1930, due to the government request for extra export wheat to meet overseas commitments—and a guaranteed price to encourage patriotism—but the area under wheat declined for the next fourteen years and most of this decline was in the semi-arid regions (Dunsdorfs, p. 314).

In 1931, the November publication of the American Academy of Political and Social Science was devoted to a survey of Australia. Written in the worst period of the Depression (which might excuse its maps) this makes interesting reading as representing the opinions of the leading experts of the day. It is notable that Wadham's article uses Taylor's divisions of the continent as a starting point, and that in discussing the wheat industry he says 'Overhanging the whole Australian wheat industry like a cloud is the unreliability of the climate' (p. 54). He was of the opinion that wheat acreages would contract from the arid margins of cultivation, and indeed the Wheat Commission (established in 1934) recommended the retirement of one-third of the existing wheat farms. From 1931 to the period of government control in World War II, the Commonwealth paid £20 million to assist the wheat farmers (Wadham and Wood, 1939, p. 162). Climatic constraints had again been established by the trial and error method.

Watering the Desert

Optimism dies hard. Forced recognition of aridity in Australia found a simple solution—increase the rainfall of the inland areas. This concept long pre-dates scientific methods such as aerial seeding of clouds and is in fact based on the naive idea that increased moisture in the air will increase the rainfall. This idea has a long history and is the basis of theories that removal of forests reduces rainfall or filling of dry lake beds and reservoirs increases it. These ideas have been popular since the first European settlement of Australia and one persistent plan, prompted by the tempting appearance on a map, has been to open a channel from the sea to Lake Eyre and flood the area below sea level. The idea is indestructible and resists all scientific criticism. Gregory (1906) records its appearance in 1883 and criticizes it as unlikely to produce more than dew, and it has been ridiculed by scientists ever since, but it appeared again in a letter to the *Australian* in 1968 (14 March). Somewhat more sophisticated plans conceive of diverting coastal rivers to flow inland, flooding the centre from the Diamantina and the Cooper—a Snowy Mountains Scheme on a grand scale. A good summary of this kind of thinking is given in *The Battle for the Inland* (Tinbury, 1944). All of these schemes depend for their popular appeal on the simple promise to increase the rainfall.

The most impressive of these plans, the 'Bradfield Scheme' appeared in 1941. *Rydges* weekly gave it a cover design of considerable dramatic impact (October 1941, see Plate 11.3) and Bradfield's reputation as 'one of the world's great bridge builders' and 'an outstanding constructional engineer' seemed to remove the scheme from the realm of fantasy. Unfortunately, Bradfield's meteorology was simplistic. The evaporation from a water surface of 20,000 square miles (5.2 million hectares) at 100″ (2,500 mm) a year 'could cause a fall of rain of 4 inches over 500,000 square miles of the dry inland. That rain after refreshing the vegetation would evaporate and fall again as rain' (p. 286). From 1941 to 1945 the scheme had consider-

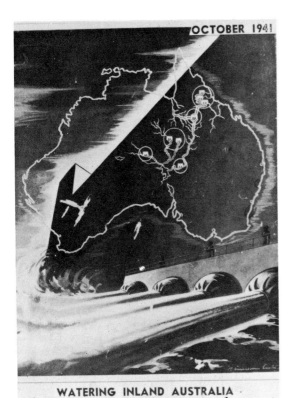

OCTOBER 1941

WATERING INLAND AUSTRALIA

Plate 11.3 Water and power to transform the Australian desert; cover of a journal featuring the 'Bradfield Scheme'.

able vogue and reached the level of parliamentary discussion. Bradfield quoted work by a senior and highly respected meteorologist, E. T. Quayle, showing that rainfall in certain districts of Victoria had been increased by irrigation in the region. To most people, this was a reasonable assumption—although as far back as 1906 Gregory had cited arid islands in the Indian Ocean as proof that rainfall needs more than just moist air.

Quayle's results were statistically worthless, and indeed many of the trends he quoted were reversed in the next ten-year period. A careful analysis of the meteorological aspects of the scheme was made by the Commonwealth Meteorological Bureau (1945) and the writer tested the effects of irrigation on subsequent rainfall for a ring of stations surrounding the Murrumbidgee Irrigation Area (Marshall, 1944). All meteorological work indicated that climatic improvement had not been established statistically and was theoretically unlikely—and the scheme was finally abandoned.

It is symptomatic of Australian wishful thinking that a radio talk and newspaper article by the writer (*Adelaide Chronicle*, September 1943) provoked comments reminiscent of the Griffith Taylor 1923 controversy. Pamphlets were received quoting Job ('who hath divided a watercourse for the overflowing of waters to cause it to rain on the earth where no man is') and Isaiah ('in the wilderness shall waters break out and streams in the desert. And the parched land shall become a pool'). Letters were written to the newspaper on the 'Ideal for Australia' and the 'Creeping Menace of the Inland'. The scheme is rediscovered every few years and optimists write to newspapers suggesting irrigation on a grand scale in the Inland. Fortunately, people in charge of planning are now more likely to consult expert opinion than they were thirty years ago.

Defining Climatic Zones

Useful climatic information for agricultural planning is also far more readily available and more widely accepted than it was thirty years ago, and a great deal of this concerns the 'length of growing period' in all its forms. It is fair to say that this concept dates back to the work of Andrews and Maze (1933), perhaps significantly students of Griffith Taylor. They were dissatisfied with the annual indices used to indicate aridity as applied to Australia, and after analysing the various indices from Transeau to Thornthwaite they decided the de Martonne ratio was the most usable under Australian conditions. The significant contribution made by their paper was to apply the index to monthly, instead of annual, conditions and to stress the importance of the *length* of the arid period. It should be emphasized that their critical monthly values were chosen from 'knowledge of the distribution of wheat cultivation' (Andrews and Maze, p. 117). Their index, and every index built from this concept, is fundamentally agricultural and is quite inapplicable to natural vegetation.

It is not surprising that this concept, inverted to be the length of the growing season, should have been accepted and developed at the Waite Agricultural Research Institute. This development, the various formulae and their limitations have been summarized elsewhere (Marshall, 1973), and the most important formulae are described in a later section of this paper. The concept is widely used as a starting point in climatic description and maps based on it are found in school textbooks and books of general interest. It is worth noting that the 'desert' with no month of regular plant growth is an uncompromising third of the continent and 'semi-arid' another 42 per cent. The wheat belt agrees reasonably well with the zone of 5 to 9 months growing period (Fig. 11.5).

The Period of Informed Adjustment

This is characteristically the period after World War II. Donald (1965, p. 189) dates his third period, the period

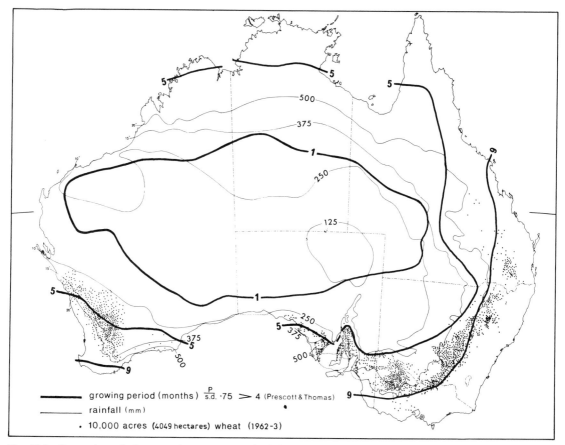

Fig. 11.5 Comparison of wheat growing areas, annual rainfall and length of growing season. *Sources*: Bureau of Census and Statistics (1964), *Official Yearbook of the Commonwealth of Australia*, p. 1013; J. A. Prescott *et al.* (1952), 'The comparative climatology of Australia and Argentina', *Geogr. Rev.*, 42, 124.

of 'remarkable positive environmental change' from about 1930 when the use of fertilized leguminous pastures emerged as a method of raising the nitrogen status of large areas of poor soils in the higher-rainfall areas. The recognition of widespread infertility, the knowledge of how to correct it and the advances in scrub-clearing machinery resulting from wartime developments have combined to allow farming and grazing on improved pastures to spread into areas of more secure rainfall. Along with the adoption of nitrogen-fixing pastures came the recognition of widespread deficiency of minor elements and the easy application of these added to the well-watered land which could now be used (Marshall, 1972). There is now reduced emphasis on sheep and cattle raising on natural pastures in semi-arid areas, and more on improved pastures nearer the coast—40 per cent of Australia's sheep are now in the wheat belt and another 30 per cent in the higher-rainfall districts.

The ability to handle economically the other constraints on primary production has encouraged a more leisurely and more detailed appraisal of the climatic constraints. In the recently produced *The Natural Resources of Australia*, Mabbutt (1972) says 'agro-climatic indices can define areas of potential and so guide land use planning; they can also indicate climatic homologues in other continents for comparative studies of land use or as guides to plant introductions', and he follows this statement with a brisk summary of methods which have been used to define potential land use.

Obviously, these methods have little importance in zones of well-established production, but their accuracy can be tested in these areas and they can then be applied to establish *climatic* constraints in the remaining underdeveloped areas. There is considerable interest in this aspect of agroclimatology: first, because dramatic fluctuations in demand for primary produce seem almost the rule of post-war years and it is important to determine the risks inherent in alternative forms of production; second, because the inevitable expansion of world population makes it almost an obligation for every country to assess its food producing potential; and finally because, in the case of Australia, we have a large tropical area which is virtually unpopulated, which has only recently been the subject of scientific study and which remains an area of uncertain potential, heated controversy, spectacular investment and equally spectacular failure. Broad scale mapping of the climatic elements important in land use is therefore still important.

AGROCLIMATIC INDICES

Although the importance for plant growth of such climatic parameters as temperature and radiation is obvious, the moisture factor is dominant in Australia. For this reason, most recent work on climatic indices has concentrated on attempts to improve the estimate of moisture conditions in the soil. Gentilli (1971, Ch. 6) has given a comprehensive summary of the various formulae which have been used, and this emphasizes the fundamental problem of all water-balance studies — the difficulty of representing evaporation over a wide area. Evaporation from a *site* can be measured directly by such instruments as lysimeters, or calculated with fair accuracy from energy-balance studies or vapour transfer measurements, but the effect of the evaporating surface is so dominant that actual evaporation over an *area* can show large and abrupt changes, and the concept of average *actual evaporation* becomes complex. Almost for want of something better, climatologists have therefore used evaporation from a free water surface as a standard meteorological variable, since this depends on the capacity of the free air to hold more moisture and so has some areal reality. It should be noted that this concept of evaporation corresponds with the '*potential evapotranspiration*' proposed by Thornthwaite (1948).

Measurements of evaporation are made from evaporimeter tanks, and efforts have been directed towards improving these so that they give reproducible results — although it is admitted that such results do not even correspond with evaporation from a free water surface of greater area, let alone from any plant cover or any bare soil which is not fully saturated. In addition to these theoretical limitations, there is in Australia the practical problem that until recently there were few evaporimeters and notably few in the areas most likely to suffer from water stress. The many formulae summarized by Gentilli have been devised in answer to this problem, in that they are attempts to calculate tank evaporation from more readily available data. Radiation, duration of sunshine and wind records are available from few stations, so formulae are normally functions of temperature and rainfall only and (as is clearly also the case with the Thornthwaite method based on the same limited observations) it would be naive to expect too close a correspondence between estimated and measured evaporation. The success of such work can be judged only on empirical grounds — if a certain formula gives moisture zones which are credible, then it is a useful formula in spite of apparent crudities in its creation.

There are two such formulae in current use in Australia, one of which has already been mentioned in connection with the 'length of growing period'. Briefly, in this work Prescott has established a high correlation between mean monthly tank evaporation (E) and mean monthly saturation deficit (s.d.). (Saturation deficit is the difference between the saturated vapour pressure and the actual vapour pressure of the air at any given temperature.) For Australia, he has related this to mean monthly precipitation (P) and he defines a 'growing month' as one in which $P/E^{0.75} > 0.4$. His evidence is entirely empirical and relates only to the growth of introduced agricultural plants.

No specific item is included in this formula for the important part played by water stored in the soil, but the critical values for the index were chosen to agree with observed length of growing season, so there must have been a built-in allowance for soil moisture. $P = E^{0.75} \times 0.4$ is a low critical value for rainfall. Presumably this amount is sufficient at the beginning of the season when the crops are germinating, and sufficient at the end of the season when rainfall is supplemented by soil moisture.

Prescott introduced the index 0.75 to make the formula usable for conditions throughout Australia, but officers of the Land Research and Regional Development Division of CSIRO never found it satisfactory for their detailed studies of northern Australia. An alternative method is used in their reports, based on a formula for estimating evaporation proposed by Fitzpatrick (1963). He considers that the importance of solar radiation in evaporation is given weight by using a 'synthetic' temperature derived from mean maximum temperature and day length. Evaporation is then estimated from the difference between vapour pressure at this synthetic temperature and vapour pressure at mean air temperature. That is $E = a + b$(vap. p. syn.–vap. p. mean) where a and b are constants. Monthly estimated evaporation is then compared with monthly precipitation as in the Prescott model, but a direct allowance is made for soil storage. A book-keeping method as used by Thornthwaite is adopted to estimate the amount of water accumulating in the soil, and this soil storage is equated with the difference between diminishing rainfall and increasing evaporation to increase the estimated length of the season of adequate soil

Plate 11.4 Fertile farming country in the Darling Downs, Queensland, where high intensity of summer rains makes contour farming essential. Near Warwick.

moisture. The maximum amount of water which can be stored in the soil varies from 10 to 20 cm, depending on the type of soil.

The point should perhaps be stressed, as Mabbutt indicates, that these and all other simple climatic indices suffer from in-built limitations. These are always quite clear in the original published papers but they tend to become nebulous in later applications of the formulae and results derived from these formulae are given an appearance of quite unwarranted accuracy. It is therefore worth emphasizing the approximations which are inevitable in work of this kind.

Limitations of Agroclimatic Indices

1. Formulae must be based on available observations at stations often forming a very open network—and indeed in the sparsely settled areas most isolines represent a guess which could be a hundred kilometres out of place. The need to draw smooth curves through such an open network may obliterate important climatic variations between the observing stations.

2. Some climatic observations are made at very few stations, and less satisfactory substitutes must be used. This is particularly true in the lack of radiation or sunshine measurements, which means that the

Penman formula for evaporation cannot be evaluated. (Fitzpatrick, 1963). The lack of wind records is also a disadvantage in computing evapotranspiration.

3. Observations cannot easily be obtained for periods of less than a calendar month, so variations of values within the month are obliterated although they may be critical for plant growth. We are so accustomed to working with monthly averages that this limitation is often forgotten. In the case of the length of growing period, it was immediately recognized as critical in the work done in northern Australia by the Land Research Division of the CSIRO. In their first report (Christian and Stewart, 1953) 'adequate' rainfall was defined in terms of a 28-day period 'assessed at 14 day intervals' thus stressing the importance of short dry periods. Later, Slatyer (1960) analysed results on a fortnightly basis and made the comment that the Prescott method was 'insensitive to short term changes in rainfall conditions owing to the fact that the time limit employed is the calendar month' (Slatyer, p. 27).

Computer manipulation of monthly observations has now made it possible to interpolate weekly values of the various climatic elements which can then be used for more accurate estimates of the duration of satisfactory climatic conditions.

4. Indices must be based on average figures, so unless they are qualified by some statistical measure of variation they fail to show annual variations from mean values, and this is often *the* most important climatic constraint. Köppen's qualification should be emphasized: 'The arithmetic mean, in which the most varying conditions are buried away, is an abstract concept and not a reality'. Tables often give measures of variation such as extreme values, mean or standard deviation or values of the quartiles, but these are not easy to incorporate in maps. A realistic approach is given by Nix (1975) in which maps show areas in which critical values are equalled or exceeded in eight years out of ten. Economic conditions can then be evaluated against a 20 per cent risk of failure on climatic grounds.

5. As has been stated, in the derivation of all formulae concerned with evaporation there are therefore a number of approximations justified only by empirical evidence. For instance, in every map using the Prescott formula for length of growing period, the following assumptions are made (a summary of the relevant papers is given in Marshall, 1948).

(a) The average weekly relative humidity can be obtained from the average of the 9 a.m. daily readings of relative humidity (tested for five randomly chosen weeks at the Waite Institute, the average weekly values being obtained from hourly readings on the hydrograph).

(b) Evaporation from the standard Australian evaporimeter has a constant relation to saturation deficit calculated from the mean monthly maximum and minimum temperatures and the mean monthly relative humidity determined as in (a). E = 258 s.d. for the year and 21.2 s.d. for a month of 30 days (tested for 144 monthly values at twelve selected Australian stations).

(c) The use of the exponent 0.75 makes it possible to apply the same critical values for P/E to all Australian regions (tested by exhaustive examination of mean monthly drain gauge records and measured losses of water from field crops and natural vegetation).

(d) The critical value of the index $P/E^{0.75}$ for the break of season is 0.4 (tested by studies of the behaviour of crops and vegetation on an Australia-wide basis).

In the same way, the alternative method of estimating evaporation proposed by Fitzpatrick (1963) and extensively used in northern Australian work since then rests on the following assumptions.

(a) Average vapour pressure for a day corresponds to the saturated vapour pressure at the mean of the 9 a.m. and 3 p.m. dew points. Average vapour pressure for a month is obtained from these. (Tested for nine stations and a total of 814 station-month records.)

Compare (a) above.

(b) Average total radiation over land during daylight is represented by average maximum temperature (from experience with thermograph and radiation charts). Advection of air is obviously a limitation to the accuracy of this method.

(c) A 'synthetic' temperature can be obtained from the average maximum temperature and the choice of critical values of constants allows an estimate of evaporation. Compare (d) above.

Application of Indices to Agricultural Potential

Nix (1975) has recently produced a study of moisture relationships in wheat crops which incorporates many recent developments in the field of agroclimatology. His work includes potential evapotranspiration estimated by Fitzpatrick's method, an estimate of water stored in the soil during long and short fallow, a moisture-balance proceeding to determine crop needs and stresses at critical stages of crop development, limits to growth and yield due to temperature and radiation conditions and a drought risk factor indicated by a map in which adequate rainfall is equalled or exceeded in eight years out of ten.

A comparison of this recent 'climatic limits to wheat production' map with the Prescott length of growing period map is interesting (Fig. 11.6). Nix's map agrees more accurately with the present wheat growing areas in Western Australia, but in general there is a rough agreement between the two limits chosen. Both maps would indicate considerable possibility of expansion in Queensland as far as climatic constraints are concerned. Careful farming is needed in this region to conserve moisture from the summer rains and to prevent erosion due to the high rainfall intensity (Plate 11.4).

In the context of total food producing potential, a recent paper (Gifford *et al.*, 1975) quotes widely different estimates made by various authorities of the amount of potentially agricultural land in Australia. The authors suggest that such divergence of opinion 'Casts doubt both on the data available and on our ability to use such data to predict limits to agricultural production in Australia'. It is possible that the constraint exercised by climate, like that of soil, cannot be indicated on a continental scale with any degree of precision. Continental maps would then remain what they have always been—useful starting points in the evaluation of undeveloped areas by allowing a comparison with the successful land use in similar climatic zones of the developed areas.

Application of Indices to Northern Australia

Perhaps the greatest value of such climatic analysis in Australia is just this, that it indicates limits to what we can reasonably expect from our virtually empty

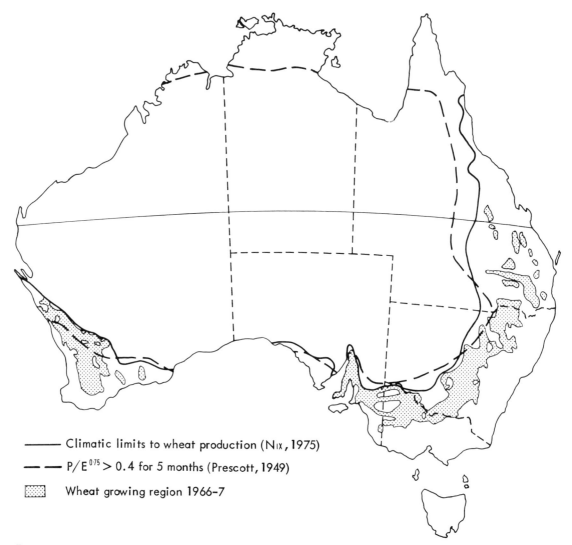

——— Climatic limits to wheat production (N ɪx , 1975)

— — P/E $^{0.75}$ > 0.4 for 5 months (Prescott, 1949)

▓▓ Wheat growing region 1966-7

Fig. 11.6 Comparison of two indices representing climatic limits to wheat production. *Sources*: Nix, 1975, p. 190; J. A. Prescott and J. A. Thomas (1949), 'The length of the growing season', *Proc. R. Geogr. Soc. Aust.* (S.A.), 50, 42–6.

northern lands. Except for the well-watered strip along the Queensland coast, tropical Australia has been—and possibly always will be—hampered by a formidable climate. On the whole, Australians have now accepted the unproductive nature of the desert, but the annual isohyets of the empty part of northern Australia show great areas with more than 500 mm rainfall, and the coastal regions have rainfalls up to 1,500 mm. These winter-dry tropics have always been called 'monsoon climates' and to most people there is an immediate association with the 'monsoon' lands of Asia which support millions of people. Davidson (1965) has discussed Australian attitudes

to the empty north and his conclusions, that Australians cherish a 'myth' about undeveloped potential in this area, are continually justified by the daily press in headlines like 'We turn our backs on greatness' and 'The scandal of our empty lands' (*The News,* 31 March and 1 April 1964).

Prescott (1938) was the first to emphasize the limitations imposed by the extreme shortness of the growing season of the northern country, and his comparison of northern Australia and northern Nigeria was immediately described as 'pessimistic'. The detailed reports of the Land Research Series of the CSIRO have since then confirmed and emphasized the view that over most of the winter-dry country the growing season is so short that even the cattle grazing industry is at a disadvantage and the tall luxuriant-looking grasses which photograph so well for newspaper articles are in fact of very low nutritive value. Cattle have lost weight in the long 'dry' since the industry developed in the 1880s and there has been very slow development of the area through its whole history. Low carrying capacity has meant extremely large properties—one was two million hectares on the border of Queensland and Northern Territory. This caused transport burdens, dispersed settlement, inadequate and costly social services and a frontier-type industry over nearly one-third of the Australian continent.

It is possible that the climate should not be given the entire blame for this slow development. As in the south, the soils are of low fertility and very restrictive to European-type land use. The introduction of a suitable exotic legume, *Stylosanthes humilis* (Townsville lucerne or more recently Townsville stylo) might bring about changes in northern Australia comparable to the immense changes caused by the widespread use of subterranean clover in the south. The plant has been known for a long time (Humphries, 1967) but easy methods of establishing it have been evolved only since 1968. Standing dry hay is burned after the first rains have caused germination of the native grasses which shade and depress the growth of the stylo plants under natural conditions. Stylo can then be seeded with superphosphate from the air.

The use of the plant is said to be increasing rapidly and its contribution to soil fertility and therefore to increased carrying capacity will be immense. Some properties claim that carrying capacity is increased twenty times. However, even a greatly improved beef-raising industry would never provide closer settlement in the North and in the higher-rainfall districts only those who do not know the country expect agricultural development. The climatic parameters make the limitations clear—the areas with a growing period of five months are very small (see Fig. 11.5). Within these areas, still further constraints are exercised by a great deal of rugged terrain and soils of more than usual difficulty. For example, the CSIRO estimate of potential in land north of 20° S latitude and west of 133° E longitude (Christian *et al.*, 1960) was only 2.5 million hectares of land suitable for dryland agriculture and 260,000 hectares of land seasonally flooded.

Agriculture has been attempted many times in this region, without success. Christian and Stewart (1953) suggest that settlers were 'carried away by the rapidity of growth during the wet season and the illusion of tropical splendour', and the many failures have caused present-day Australians to be wary of further attempts. However in the last few years there have been two attempts to establish large-scale farming in the

Table 11.1 Rice Production by Territory Rice, 1956–60

Season	Hectares planted	Tonnes harvested	Rainfall Oct.–Mar. Darwin (mm)	Comments
1955–6	75	—	1,529	Heavy March rains, trouble with machinery
1956–7	250	600	2,051	Excessively wet sowing period—150 mm in Oct. Aerial sowing tried
1957–8	80	200	1,135	Plague of magpie geese
1958–9	2,000	1,250	1,039	Nearly half the crop failed, 500 ha due to lack of water
1959–60	2,000	3,300	1,914 (Average 1,558)	Very wet March—446 mm. Harvesting machinery inadequate

Sources: Forester Committee, 1960, p. 203; Linkletter, 1968; newspaper reports of the period.

Northern Territory; both American, both heavily capitalized, both geared to using cheap land and all economies of scale to produce at a price acceptable in overseas markets. Both have been large-scale failures. It is relevant to ask why they failed, and particularly to ask what contribution was made to the failure by the climate, which is the part of the environment which cannot be altered.

The first project to be attempted was at Humpty Doo, 70 km from Darwin on the subcoastal plains of the Adelaide River. A perennial species of *Oryza* grows in the area, but the CSIRO reported cautiously on its potential for rice production due to soils and difficulties of transport (Christian and Stewart, 1953, pp. 115–16.) In 1956 an American syndicate called 'Territory Rice' entered into an agreement with the Commonwealth government by which the company was granted 300,000 hectares and required to subdivide it and sell part to settlers within ten years. The Commonwealth appeared to have nothing to lose, as all expenses on infrastructure were to be borne by the company and very little use was being made of the land. One hopes that some of Linkletter's description of the early negotiations is exaggerated (Linkletter, 1968, pp. 2–3) but even if it is there is no doubt of the government's enthusiasm for the scheme (Forster Committee, 1960, pp. 202–4). The press hailed it with delight as the 'Rice Bowl of the Future'. There was 'land free to anyone courageous and wealthy enough to exploit it, wasting on buffalo and a few cattle'. It was the biggest single agricultural project in the world, it was going to use the world's biggest machinery, 200,000 hectares were to be cultivated in fifteen years bringing 20,000 people to the area and rice was going to cost 1 cent a kilogram and be sold at the world price of 3 cents. The clearest picture

of the result can be seen in Table 11.1.

In 1962, the Americans abandoned the project—having lost more than a million dollars. It is clear that there were many reasons for the failure. The company consisted of business entrepreneurs and Hollywood stars, and local opinion at the time was that they were badly advised by their agricultural consultants. They had no conception of ecological side effects—the local magpie geese flourished on an improved diet and were credited with eating 500 hectares of rice seed. Transport conditions in the Wet were beyond any American experience, and their large machinery was unwieldy. But undoubtedly the climate in some years was against them. Rice is now being grown on an experimental basis in the Humpty Doo area, and improved techniques might make the difference between success and failure.

This is a case where more detailed climatic analysis would have been useful. Territory Rice obviously took too much heed of annual conditions and not enough of the variation in duration and timing of the rains. The annual average rainfall of the area is adequate for rice production and the standard deviation of the mean at Darwin only 18 per cent, so possibly they had bad luck in the few years during which they operated. However, successful rice cultivation obviously needs an analysis of climatic risks at crucial stages of development and harvesting of the crop.

In 1967 another American company, registered as Tipperary Land Corporation, bought the 900,000 hectare Tipperary Station for $1.5 million. The intention was to spend another million dollars on development in the first year, planting 5,000 hectares of grain sorghum for an 'assured' Japanese market. Future plans envisaged twenty million dollars expended,

Table 11.2 Sorghum Production by Tipperary Land Corporation, 1967–71

Season	Hectares planted	Tonnes harvested	Rainfall Oct.–Apr. (mm) Tipperary Station	Comments
1967–8	5,500	8,100	n.a.	Late rain (72 mm at Tipperary in May) reduced yield by 50 per cent
1968–9	6,600	9,100	1,234	4,000 tonnes exported
1969–70	1,800	2,500	715	No export. Experiment with new varieties of sorghum
1970–1	1,900	4,700(est.)	993	Company diversifying interests

Sources: Rainfall statistics and sorghum area and yield from Doughton, 1975. Comments from newspaper reports of the time.

77,000 hectares of sorghum, 300,000 tonnes a year exported and 15,000 people in the region. The company intended to develop 81,000 hectares altogether, adding other crops such as soy beans and peanuts and planting Townsville stylo to increase carrying capacity for the existing beef cattle production.

Predictably, the press hailed the project as 'Food Bowl of the Future' and articles written were strongly reminiscent of those about Humpty Doo ten years earlier (for example in the *Australian*, 21 November 1968). Large areas of suitable soil had been indicated by the CSIRO surveys (Christian and Stewart, 1953, pp. 100–3) but climatic problems were apparent from the outset. Table 11.2 summarizes the results obtained in the five seasons during which sorghum was grown.

After 1971, the Tipperary Land Corporation lost interest in sorghum and diversified into other industries such as prawning. Again, the question arises as to how much of the failure can be blamed on the physical environment. Doughton (1975) indicates several climatic constraints. If rainfall during the December–January planting period is inadequate the sandier soils dry out, resulting in poor plant establishment. More important, rain after the grain is ripe encourages black mould. This was particularly noticeable with the exceptional May rains of 1968, and a second venture in large-scale sorghum production at nearby Willeroo Station suffered badly in 1973–4 for the same reason. Some April rain is normal at Tipperary and therefore constitutes a climatic problem for sorghum production.

These adventures in northern agriculture do not necessarily mean that the problems are insoluble. Rather, they indicate that huge capital investment and economies of scale are not alone sufficient to overcome the disadvantages of the region. These have been summarized (Christian and Stewart, 1953) as a 'formidable' climate, unusually poor soils and economic problems such as inaccessibility. With modern knowledge, many soils can be built up to reasonable fertility, so this is an economic problem. Inaccessibility can be cured by the provision of transport, so this also is a matter of economics. The question remaining is whether the climate is too formidable a constraint for primary production to be intensified.

CONCLUSION

Throughout our history, Australians have developed their land use in the light of the perceived climatic risk, and this perception has been conditioned by background experience, by available climatic information and to some extent by national ethos. In the more benign areas of temperate Australia, European forms of production with European plants and animals have reached a fairly stable condition as the reality of the climate has been accepted after two hundred years of experience, and adaptations have been made to suit the climatic conditions. Perhaps this stage has not yet been reached in the winter-dry tropics. The country is unknown to the bulk of the population, 80 per cent of which lives within 800 kilometres of Melbourne. Scientific studies go no farther back than World War II, and the network of observing stations for climatic studies is extremely open. Northern experience is of cattle raising only, and a certain air of the romantic frontier colours southern views. This may be the reason why seminars with titles like 'Populate the North' are well attended!

In northern Australia, agroclimatic indices which have been developed can indicate with some accuracy areas from which plants and animals might be introduced. It is perhaps significant that the first real improvement in the northern cattle industry has been due to the introduction of strains of tropical cattle like the Brahman and the propagation of a tropical legume—Townsville stylo. The same recognition of climatic homologues is overdue in agricultural attempts—the sorghums which have been used are derived from temperate varieties. A more realistic perception of the climate and the difficulties which it presents should encourage agricultural techniques to develop, as they have in the south, to minimize these difficulties. For instance, Doughton indicates development of sorghums suited to the tropics, deep planting to avoid the rapidly drying soil surface, early harvesting and artificial drying to combat mould. Primary production has been intensified by such means in temperate Australia. It might be expected to develop in the same way in the tropics, if and when the economic conditions prevailing appear to justify the calculable risk.

REFERENCES

American Academy of Political and Social Science (1931), 'An economic survey of Australia', *Annals*, 158, November.

Andrews, J. and Maze, W. H. (1933), 'Some climatological aspects of aridity in their application to Australia', *Proc. Linn. Soc. N.S.W.*, 58, 105–24.

Atkinson, James (1826), *An Account of the State of Agriculture and Grazing in New South Wales*, J. Cross, London. Facsimile reprint, Sydney University Press, Sydney 1975.

Beltana Pastoral Co. (1965), *A History of the Beltana Pastoral Co. Ltd.*, The Company, Adelaide.

Bigge, T. (1822), *Report of the Commissioner of Enquiry into the State of the Colony of N.S.W.*, London. Reprinted by Adelaide Lib. Board, 1966.

Bradfield, J. J. (1941), 'Watering inland Australia', *Rydges*, 1 October, pp. 586–9 and 606.

Brady, E. J. (191–), *Australia Unlimited*, Robertson and Co., Melbourne.

Butlin, N. G. (1962), 'Distribution of the sheep population' in A. Barnard (ed.), *The Simple Fleece*, Melbourne University Press, Melbourne.

Cain, N. (1962), 'Companies and squatting' in A. Barnard

(ed.), *The Simple Fleece*, Melbourne University Press, Melbourne.

Christian, C. S. and Stewart, G. A. (1953), *Survey of Katherine-Darwin Region 1946*, CSIRO Land Res. Ser. No. 1, Melbourne.

Christian, C. S., Stewart, G. A. and Perry, R. A. (1960), 'Land research in northern Australia', *Aust. Geogr.*, 7, 227.

Commonwealth Meteorological Bureau (1945), *Bradfield Scheme for Watering the Inland: Meteorological Aspects*, Bull. No. 34.

Davidson, B. R. (1965), *The Northern Myth*, Melbourne University Press, Melbourne.

Donald, C. M. (1965), 'The progress of Australian agriculture and the role of pastures in environmental change', *Aust. J. Sci.*, 27, 187–98.

Doughton, John (Crops agronomist, Animal Ind. and Agric. Branch, Dept of N.T.) (1975), Personal communication.

Dunsdorfs, E. (1956), *The Australian Wheat-growing Industry 1788–1948*, Melbourne University Press, Melbourne.

Fitzpatrick, E. A. (1963), 'Estimates of pan evaporation from mean maximum temperature and vapour pressure', *J. Applied Met.*, 2, 780–92.

Forster Committee (1960), *Prospects of Agriculture in the Northern Territory*, Comm. Aust., Dept of Territories.

French, R. J., Matheson, W. E. and Clarke, A. L. (196–), *Soils and Agriculture of the Northern and Yorke Peninsula Regions of South Australia*, S.A. Dept Agric. Bulletin, Government Printer, Adelaide.

Gentilli, J. (1971), *The Climate of Australia* in *World Survey of Climatology*, Elsevier, Amsterdam.

Gifford, R. M., Kalma, J. D., Aston, A. R. and Millington R. J. (1975), 'Biophysical constraints in Australian food production, *Search*, 6, 212–23.

Gregory, J. W. (1903), *The Geography of Victoria*, Whitcombe and Tombs, Melbourne.

——(1906), *The Dead Heart of Australia*, John Murray, London.

——(1907), *Australasia*, Stanford, London.

Grondona, L. St C. (1924), *Kangaroo Keeps Talking*, Victoria Publishing House, London.

Humphreys, L. R. (1967), 'Townsville lucerne. History and prospect', *J. Aust. Inst. Agric, Sci.*, 33, 3–13.

Hunt, H. A. Taylor, G. and Quayle, E. T. (1913), *The Climate and Weather of Australia*, Government Printer, Melbourne.

Jevons, W. S. (1859), 'Some data concerning the climate of Australia and New Zealand' in *Waugh's Australian Almanac*, pp. 47–98.

Josephson, J. P. (1885), 'History of floods in the Hawkesbury River', *Proc. R. Soc. N.S.W.*, 19, 97–107.

King, C. J. (1948), 'The first 50 years of agriculture in N.S.W.', *Rev. Marketing and Agric. Econ.*, Vol. 16, Nos 8–12.

Leighly, J. B. (1949), 'Climatology since the year 1800', *Trans. Am. Geophy. Un.*, 30, 658–72.

Linkletter, A. (1968), *Linkletter Down Under*, Ure Smith, Sydney.

Mabbutt, J. A. (1972), 'The appraisal of Australian land resources' in J. A. Sinden (ed.), *The Natural Resources of Australia*, Angus and Robertson, Sydney.

Marshall, A. (1944), 'Climatic aspects of the Bradfield Scheme', *J. Aust. Inst. Agric. Sci.*, 10, 165–8.

——(1948), 'The size of the Australian desert', *Aust. Geogr.*, 5, 168–75.

——(1966), 'The environment and Australian wool production' in J. Andrews (ed.), *Frontiers and Men*, Cheshire, Melbourne.

——(1972), '"Desert" becomes "Downs": The impact of a scientific discovery', *Aust. Geogr.*, 12, 23–34.

——(1973), 'The use and misuse of the "length of growing period" concept', *Aust. Geogr.*, 12, 334–9.

Meinig, D. W. (1962), *On the Margins of the Good Earth*, Rand McNally, Chicago.

Moore, R. M. (1962), 'Effects of the sheep industry on Australian vegetation' in A. Barnard (ed.), *The Simple Fleece*, Melbourne University Press, Melbourne.

Nix, H. A. (1975), 'The Australian climate and its effect on grain yield and quality' in A. Lazenby and E. M. Matheson (eds), *Australian Field Crops*, Angus and Robertson, Sydney.

Oxley, J. J. W. (1820), *Journal of Two Expeditions into the Interior of New South Wales*, Murray, London.

Peel, L. J. (1973), 'History of the Australian pastoral industries to 1960' in G. Alexander and O. B. Williams (eds), *The Pastoral Industries of Australia*, Sydney University Press, Sydney.

Perry, T. M. (1957), 'Climate, caterpillars and terrain', *Aust. Geogr.*, 7, 3–14.

——(1966), 'Climate and settlement in Australia 1700–1930' in J. Andrews (ed.), *Frontiers and Men*, Cheshire, Melbourne.

Prescott, J. A. (1938), 'The climate of tropical Australia in relation to possible agricultural occupation', *Trans. R. Soc. S. Aust.* 62, 229–40.

Ratcliffe, F. N. (1936), *Soil Drift in the Arid Pastoral Areas of South Australia*, CSIR Pamphlet, 64.

Richards, T. (ed.) (1882), *New South Wales in 1881*, Government Printer, Sydney.

Robinson, M. E. (1970), 'The decline of wheat-growing in the coastal districts of New South Wales, 1860–80', *Aust. Geogr. Stud.*, 8, 44–56.

Rural Reconstruction Commission (1944), 2nd Report, *Settlement and Employment of Returned Men on the Land*; 3rd Report, *Land Utilization and Settlement*.

Russell, H. C. (1883), 'Notes and 2 maps supplied for Report of the Inquiry into the State of the Public Lands and the Operation of the Land Laws, by Morris, A. and Ranken, G.', *N.S.W. Legislative Council J.*, Vol. 34, Pt. 1.

Slatyer, R. O. (1960), *Agricultural Climatology of the Katherine Area, N.T.*, CSIRO Div. of Land Res. and Reg. Survey, Tech. Pap. No. 13.

South Australia (1881), Proceedings of the Parliament of South Australia, with copies of documents ordered to be printed, Vol. 4, No. 143.

Sturt, Charles (1847), 'A condensed account of an exploration in the interior of Australia', *J. R. Geogr. Soc.*, 17, 85–129.

——(1849), *Narrative of an Expedition into Central Australia Performed During the Years 1844–6*, Boone, London.

Taylor, J. M. (1898), *Geography of New South Wales*, Angus and Robertson, Sydney.

Taylor, G. (1914), *A Geography of Australasia*, Oxford University Press, Oxford.

——(1923), 'Geography and Australian national problems', *Aust. Ass. Adv. Sci.*, XVI, 433–87.

——(1958), *Journeyman Taylor*, Hale, London, pp. 169, 180.

Thornthwaite, C. W. (1948), 'An approach toward a rational classification of climate', *Geogr. Rev.*, 38, 55–94.

Tinbury, F. R. V. (1944), *The Battle for the Inland*, Angus and Robertson, Sydney.

Todd, C. (1893), 'Meteorological work in Australia—A review', *Aust. Ass. Adv. Sci.*, V, Adelaide.

Wadham, S. M. and Wood, G. L. (1939), *Land Utilization in Australia*, Melbourne University Press, Melbourne.

12 PASTORAL AUSTRALIA

R. L. HEATHCOTE

A popular image of Australia, as provided by the coloured reproductions in calendars and the coffee-table handbooks, is of a pastoral scene—a mob of sheep moving across a tree-dotted grassland under the watchful eyes of a man on horseback. As an image it has had a long and romantic appeal: as reality, even for the pastoral industry, however, it is blurred and over-simplified. The variety of past and present types of pastoral land use is barely hinted at and of the economic, social, and environmental stresses facing the pastoralist, there is no indication at all.

Yet the image has remained and with some validity, and in attempting to explain why, we shall look briefly at the ecological context of pastoral land use and then examine the contemporary patterns of that land use in Australia. For the explanation of these patterns we will need to examine the pastoral systems which were introduced by the early settlers, the way in which these were subsequently modified, and their impact upon the environment. Finally, we shall return to the image and attempt to explain the special aura which has surrounded this particular land use.

THE ECOLOGY OF PASTORAL LAND USE

Although an ancient and venerable form of resource use, the grazing of domestic livestock upon natural pastures is relatively inefficient in that it requires a consumer—the animal—to process the raw material—the pasture—into a useful commodity for man. However, the ability of most herbivores (except the pig) to convert plant cellulose (which the human stomach cannot digest) into edible protein as well as an array of useful raw materials has enabled domestic livestock grazing to provide a return from land which otherwise might be of no benefit except for hunting and gathering. This has been particularly true of areas marginally too arid or barren to support crop farming (Strickon, 1965).

It is with this form of livestock grazing—extensive pastoral land use or ranching—that this chapter is concerned (Fig. 12.1). By definition we shall be concerned with the grazing of livestock extensively over large units of land, making extensive use of labour, and depending for their support upon the natural pastures rather than sown grasses or crops. To place this activity in perspective, however, we shall review the variety of Australian pastoral production to point up the contrasts between present-day systems of intensive and extensive production.

Pastoral Production in the 1970s

The products of livestock grazing still dominate the Australian economy and have world-wide significance. Produce of sheep and cattle comprised 59 per cent of rural production and two-fifths of total exports by value even at the peak of the mineral production boom in 1965–8. Although unfavourable seasons and the lowest prices of the century cut the proportion of exports down to *c*. 30 per cent by 1971–2 and the Australian sheep flock declined from a peak of 180 million in 1970 to 162 million in 1972, it was still the world's largest, providing over half of all wool entering the world trade and a quarter of the total world consumption. By comparison, although increasing in numbers from 22 million in 1970 to 27 million in 1972 and providing an export income just over half that from wool, the cattle herd has been less significant on the world scene, providing only 0.013 per cent of world beef and veal consumption compared with 0.045 per cent for mutton and lamb (Alexander and Williams, 1973).

This significant primary production is, however, vulnerable to environmental and economic stresses. On the one hand the dominance of natural pastures (90 per cent of the total area of pastoral properties in Australia) makes the industry vulnerable to seasonal variations in feed availability. On the other hand orientation to the world marketplace (over 90 per cent of wool production is exported, approximately half the beef and veal and slightly less than half the mutton and lamb) means that profitability is at the mercy of world prices.

Types of Pastoral Production

Approximately three-quarters of Australian rural holdings run some livestock but they are the dominant source of income on only just over half the total (Table 12.1). These latter properties, however, carried

Table 12.1 Australian Pastoral Properties 1965–6

Pastoral properties (type of activity)	No. ('000)	Area ('00,000 ha)	Average size (ha)	Percentage of nation's Sheep	Beef cattle	Dairy cattle
Beef cattle	16	2,313	14,456	1	62	< 1
Sheep	44	1,901	4,320	63	20	1
Sheep-cereal grain	32	310	970	28	4	< 1
Dairying	49	64	132	1	4	95
Total pastoral properties	141	4,588	3,253	93	90	c.98
Total Australian rural properties	252	4,866		100	100	100

Source: Gruen, 1970, p. 402.

Table 12.2 The Variety of Pastoral Production Units mid-1960s

Items	Beef cattle 1962–5 Max. (N.T.)	Min. (Vic.)	Sheep-beef Pastoral zone Max. (W.A.)	Min. (N.S.W.)	Sheep-cereal Wheat-sheep zone Max. (Qld)	Min. (N.S.W.)	Sheep-beef High rainfall zone Max. (N.S.W.)	Min. (Vic.)	Dairying (whole milk) High rainfall zone Max. (W.A.)	Min. (Vic.)	Dairying (manufacturing) High rainfall zone Max. (Qld)	Min. (Vic.)
Size ('000 ha)	443	·5	182	11	1.7	.8	.7	.4	.2	.08	.2	.1
Beef cattle	8,901	164	298	87	124	65	102	74	42	21	29	25
Sheep	0	1,162	10,496	4,809	1,804	1,868	2,518	1,783	0	0	0	0
Dairy cattle	0	9	0	0	0	0	0	0	82	63	55	49
Stock density (SEU/ha)	.16	5.0	.07	.47	1.8	3.6	4.8	7.2	3.8	6.1	2.4	5.0
Turn-off (sales as % herd)	10–40	50–70	—	—	—	—	—	—	?	?	?	?
Lambing %	—	—	52	64	81	73	79	84	—	—	—	—
Natural pasture % (area)	?98	?10	98	?30	92.5	36.6	33.0	3.6	9.4	3.5	65.2	25.3
Labour (man-years)	16.0[a]	1.8	5.8	2.6	2.1	2.1	1.8	1.6	1.5	1.7	1.6	1.4
Capital ($ per ha)	.94[a]	401.0	.80	16.0	57.5	126.6	144.0	272.0	426.6	544.5	132.6	356.5
Return on capital (%) inc. land	5.6[a]	3.5	10.6	1.9	4.6	6.0	2.1	5.6	5.2	6.3	2.3	3.2
Gross capital ($'000)	364.9	236.4	146.5	176.4	97.8	101.3	100.8	81.7	79.1	44.6	31.0	35.0

[a] Data for Kimberley area.   ?—Data uncertain.

Source: Alexander and Williams, 1973.

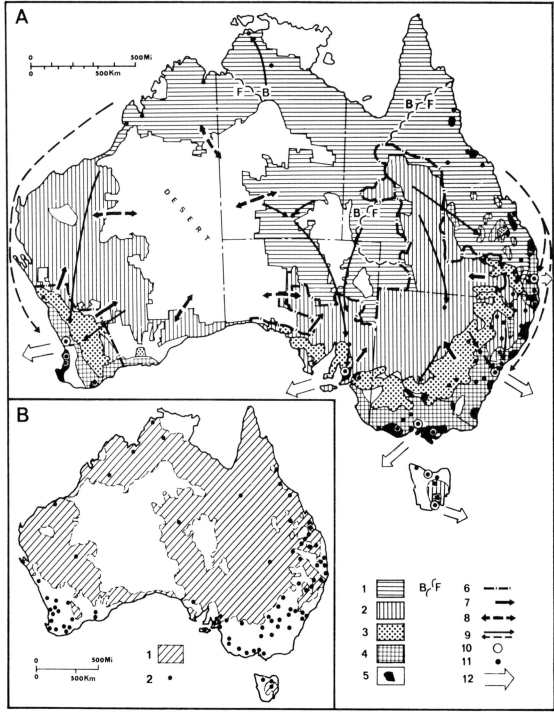

Fig. 12.1 Pastoral Australia in the 1970s.

over 90 per cent of the nation's livestock and occupied 94 per cent of the area in rural holdings. At the continental scale there was a transition from the smallest (dairy farm) properties in the southern and eastern higher rainfall zones, through the larger (mixed sheep and cereal grain) properties of the subhumid zone to the largest (sheep and cattle) properties in the remote north and on the edge of the central deserts (Fig. 12.1).

This broad transition, however, hid considerable variations in the character of pastoral production not only between the types of production unit but also between the largest and smallest units in each type (Table 12.2). Thus, while the dairy farms might be only a fraction of the largest beef cattle stations in the Northern Territory (*c.*100 hectares as compared to over 443,000 hectares), the latter were themselves over 800 times larger than the *smallest* beef cattle properties in Victoria.

Capital investment and profitability as illustrated by return on capital showed less spectacular but still considerable variations. Total capital investment per property would be as low as $31,000 for a Queensland dairy farm and over ten times as great for a Northern Territory beef cattle property, but investment per hectare generally was related to size of property rather than type of production, although as might be expected the largest sheep-beef and beef cattle properties of Western Australia and Northern Territory had the lowest overall investments per hectare. Profitability similarly seemed to vary with size of property rather than type of production. Thus the smallest sheep-beef properties had some of the lowest returns on capital and the largest properties had the highest overall returns of any pastoral properties.

The type of product and system of grazing management also showed a variety of resource usage. Even where the returns placed properties in certain types of production groupings, these were rarely mutually exclusive. Thus purely beef cattle properties carried only 62 per cent of the nation's beef cattle (Table 12.1) and exclusively sheep properties only 63 per cent of the nation's sheep flock. Further, within types of production stock densities

could vary enormously. Thus, in terms of sheep equivalent units, sheep and beef cattle properties were running 1 animal per 10 hectares in the Northern Territory and interior Western Australia, as opposed to 5 per hectare in Victoria. This contrast reflected the length of growing season for the natural grasses and particularly the extent to which natural grasses had been replaced by higher yielding and more nutritious exotic grasses, lucerne and clovers.

Products

The contemporary pastoralist has a variety of potential sources of profit and it will be useful to identify these before describing the actual range of activities. At one end of the spectrum of potential activity a pastoralist might own no livestock himself but hire out his pastures as agistment for others to use. If he uses the pasture himself, he may wish to raise livestock for sale, as 'store' cattle or sheep to be fattened for slaughter elsewhere or as fat stock direct for slaughter, or as stud stock, or general replacements for other properties. If he uses the pasture for his own livestock, however, he may wish rather to sell not the livestock but their by-products, wool, milk or progeny. Each possibility requires a different management technique and the evidence suggests that most Australian pastoralists in fact are carrying out at least two of the above techniques *simultaneously* on their properties. The following discussion of the products of pastoral land use must therefore be seen against this background—we will be describing not necessarily exclusive but probably complementary systems of production and systems which may indeed be modified from season to season.

The production of beef cattle for slaughter in the national abbatoirs is spread over the whole continent from the arid ranges of the interior to the highly improved pastures of the tablelands of New England and Victoria. In the northern half of the continent it tends to dominate the pastoral returns, but in the south and east it is usually only a proportion of the total farm income since beef cattle will be grazing alongside sheep and dairy cattle. In 1965–6 of the

---

Key to *Fig. 12.1*

A. Patterns of production.
Key
1. Extensive cattle stations, B—mainly breeding, F—mainly fattening.
2. Extensive sheep stations.
3. Wheat and sheep properties.
4. Intensive sheep and/or cattle properties.
5. Dairy properties.
6. Dingo-proof fence.
7. Boundaries of land use under pressure from more intensive use.

8. Boundaries of land use vary according to seasonal drought severity.
9. Internal movement of livestock by land and sea.
10. Main domestic meat markets.
11. Exporting meat works.
12. Main export outlets.

B. Extensive pastoral land use.
Key
1. Extensive sheep and/or cattle stations.
2. Grassland research centres.

Source: *Atlas of Australian Resources* and various.

13 million beef cattle over half were in Queensland and the Northern Territory, where on 83 per cent of the properties carrying beef cattle they were the only livestock. Elsewhere in Australia beef cattle were only exclusive on 40 per cent of the properties (Gruen, 1970).

The dominant beef cattle breeds are British (*Bos taurus*) in origin, 40 per cent Herefords and 40 per cent Shorthorns in 1965, but 8 per cent, mainly in northern Australia, included *Bos indicus* breeds such as Brahman, Africander and Santa Gertrudis, and local crosses with British types, such as Braford, Brangus, Droughtmaster and Murray Grey. Control of breeding varies from virtually absolute in the intensively managed southern and eastern properties to virtually non-existent on the extensive properties of the north and northwest where bulls run with the herd year long and calving losses might be as high as 90 per cent in drought years (Alexander and Williams, 1973).

The production of sheep for mutton needs to be differentiated from the production of lamb. 'Mutton is produced mainly from cast-for-age sheep; generally these are "retired" wool producers' (Gruen, 1970, p. 407). As a result mutton (mature) sheep are produced from all areas of sheep grazing in Australia as part of the basic process of wool production. In contrast lambs for slaughter (usually 4–6 months old) are produced from specially bred stock. Gruen suggests that the breeds used vary regionally. The sheep-cereal properties of the wheat-sheep zone cross Merino ewes with either Border Leicester or Romney Marsh or Downs rams to provide first-cross ewes (for further breeding) and lambs to be fattened for sale. On the sheep-beef properties of the high rainfall zone and on irrigated pastures along the Murray and Murrumbidgee, the first-cross ewes from the wheat-sheep zone are mated with Downs rams to provide fat lambs and a cross-bred wool sheep. Here and in the high rainfall zone, Corriedale (half Merino and half Lincoln) and Polwarth (three-quarter Merino and quarter Lincoln) are favoured as they provide both lamb and wool potentials and can cope with the wetter conditions.

Production of sheep mainly for wool is dominant in the pastoral and wheat-sheep zones and mainly from Merino or Merino-cross breeds. Production is dominated further by the large flocks (over 2,000 sheep), which contained over two-thirds of the total sheep in 1969 but which were carried on only 24 per cent of the total number of sheep properties (Table 12.3).

The dominant breed, Merino, represents 73 per cent of the national flock with other dominantly Merino-crosses being a further 15 per cent and the remainder comprising Corriedale 6 per cent, Polwarth 2 per cent, and other British breeds such as Border Leicester, English Leicester, Romney Marsh, Lincoln, Dorset

Table 12.3　Changes in Flock Sizes 1919–69

Flock size	Percentage of properties		Percentage of sheep	
	1919[a]	1969[b]	1919[a]	1969[b]
Less than 500	67.7	33.4	11.3	4.0
500–999	14.7	19.8	10.6	9.2
1,000–1,999	8.9	22.9	12.6	20.4
2,000–4,999	5.3	18.1	16.5	34.4
5,000 plus	3.4	5.8	48.8	32.0
No. of properties ('000)	79.2	110.0	—	—
No. of sheep ('000,000)	—	—	76.9	174.6

Sources:　[a] Gruen, 1970, p. 404.
　　　　　[b] Alexander and Williams, 1973, p. 80.

Horn, Southdown, Ryeland, Suffolk and Shropshires.

Finally, although information is not easily available, the stud properties need to be considered. Although only a small proportion of properties are registered as studs their significance in maintaining the genetic composition of the Australian flocks and herds, as a source of innovation to cope with environmental stresses and as a separate component in the overall structure of the pastoral industry must be recognized. Stud sheep properties provide from 60 per cent to 90 per cent of all rams purchased in any one year and as a result Australian flocks are dependent upon a limited gene pool in studs which are for the most part closed to outside blood strains and often breeding for the show ring rather than for their productive qualities. The quality of the livestock in the arid interior and tropical north is maintained by imports of such stock from the studs which are mainly located in the temperate southeast of Australia, particularly the Riverina. As a result some commentators see the need for further tropically-based studs less oriented to the show ring.

The Pastoralists

Who are the Australian pastoralists, those who control the 141,000 pastoral properties? Of the total primary producers (including non-pastoralists) in Australia, 46 per cent were sole owner-operators, 48 per cent were partnerships, 4 per cent were trusts and 2 per cent were companies in 1968. Within the pastoral industry there are no overall figures but some are available for the components. For the sheep properties the sole owner-operators ranged from a low of 24 per cent of properties in the pastoral zone in 1962–3 to a maximum of 49 per cent in the high rainfall zone. The largest proportion of owners by that date were the family

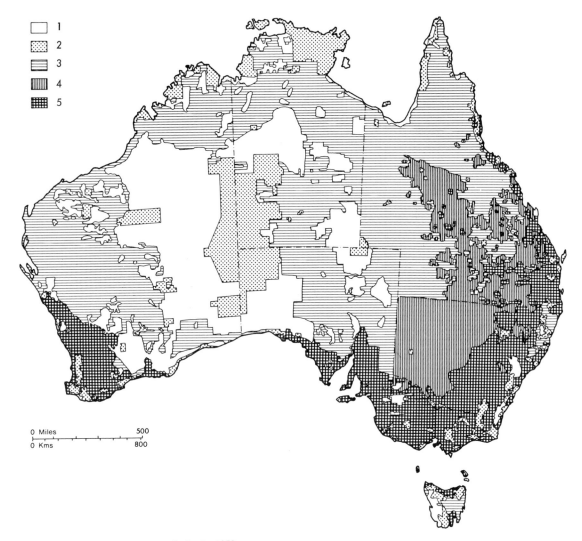

Fig. 12.2 Land tenure in Australia in the 1970s.

KEY
1. Vacant, land still held by the Crown, unoccupied and generally unused.
2. Reserves, including national parks, forest reserves, scientific and Aboriginal reserves.
3. Leaseholds, mainly pastoral leases the size of which is not limited to 'living areas' or 'home maintenance areas'.

4. Leaseholds, mainly pastoral leases the size of which is limited to areas thought sufficient to support an average family, i.e. 'living areas' or 'home maintenance areas'.
5. Alienated, purchased lands mainly held in fee simple.
Note: For clarity the areas of mining and military leases are not included.

Source: Heathcote, 1969b with additions from State government sources.

partnerships, reaching 63 per cent in the pastoral zone, 52 per cent in the wheat-sheep and 44 per cent in the high rainfall zone. In addition, private companies owned from 5 per cent in the high rainfall zone to 10 per cent in the pastoral zone, with estates and public companies making up the remainder (Wells and Bates, 1969). For the beef properties in the south and east of the country some proportion akin to the high rainfall zone sheep properties is likely, but for the large northern beef properties the picture is much different. Companies owned the largest area of the Northern Territory, and absentees, some including overseas companies, owned between two-thirds and 70 per cent of all properties (Kelly, 1966).

One feature of the recent years has been the increasing number of females registered as primary producers—by 1965–6 they represented 30 per cent as compared with 17 per cent in 1953–4. For the most part they are partners in a family partnership headed by their husband—a legal device to reduce taxation and potential death duties.

These sample figures, however, again conceal a complex and changing reality. A glimpse of the complexities is obtained from a study of sheep properties in central Queensland. A detailed investigation of the ownership of 145 holdings occupying 24,849 km² in the late 1960s showed that 31 per cent comprised non-contiguous areas. Further, two basic types of production unit were distinguished, the single unit where the block of land was a compact area under single ownership and the multiple unit where separate blocks might be owned by different individuals, but in effect they were worked 'as a single unit from the point of view of high level managerial decisions' (Anderson, 1970, p. 138). Just over 30 per cent of the area's sheep were on single unit holdings, but a further 33 per cent were on multiple unit holdings, the components of which ranged from over 2 km to almost 480 km apart. The remaining 37 per cent formed part of multiple units whose components were well over 480 km apart. These latter formed links in chains of pastoral properties stretching from the edge of the arid interior to the subtropical central Queensland coast. There is no doubt that this kind of pattern is not peculiar to Queensland, but may be found linking the southeast and southwestern high rainfall areas to the interior arid ranges. Such ownership linkages enable local feed surpluses and deficiencies whether seasonal or random to be met by 'internal' transfers to livestock from one part of the chain to another at relative low cost—a modern version of ancient nomadic grazing practices.

Ownership of the land, however, is further complicated by the variety of land tenures under which pastoral land is currently held in Australia. Of the total continental area in 1971 only some 12.5 per cent was alienated or in process of alienation, 56.3 per cent was leased or licensed and a further 32.2 per cent held as reserves or vacant land (Fig. 12.2). Virtually all of the leased land is under pastoral use but what proportion of alienated land is not certain. There is no doubt, however, that livestock are being grazed upon a range of land tenures, from freeholds derived from original free land grants in New South Wales to land purchased at auction or on credit over a period of years, to leaseholds for a variety of periods of time and with a variety of restrictive covenants (Table 12.4).

Specimen Properties

While the census data and sample surveys of the Bureau of Agricultural Economics provide valuable data for the broad overview much valuable detail is missed. Sources of such detail are the advertisements of properties up for sale, wherein the main characteristics of the units are set out, if somewhat ambitiously, for the prospective buyers. Bearing in mind some possible overstatement, the following three examples have been chosen from these sources to illustrate the varied character and the effects of the variations in property management and capital investment, suggested by the general data in Tables 12.1 and 12.2, as between a relatively undeveloped cattle property in the Northern Territory, a partially developed sheep and cattle property in South Australia and a cattle and sheep stud in southern Queensland.

In 1972 Mary River station, Northern Territory, was offered for sale. Described as a 'cattle (and buffalo) station' it comprised 2,210 km² of 1,193 mm rainfall country, still held as relatively undeveloped subtropical woodland and natural grasses. No artificial watering points had been installed, as it was claimed there was 'Abundant natural permanent water' and only 192 km of fencing existed, 152 km of which had only been constructed in 1969–70. Thirteen cattle yards existed, including one, obviously new, large steel yard supposedly valued at $10,000, in comparison with $1,000 for each of the others. The manager rented a government house in nearby Pine Creek at $13 per week, but on the property were only one new steel shed and '5 huts for workers, etc.', but '4 good airstrips' and 192 km of government-maintained roads within the property. An abattoir which currently slaughtered buffalo and brumbies (wild horses) as well as cattle was also mentioned.

The rent on the fifty-year pastoral lease property was 1.5 cents per km² or 0.015 cents per hectare and the asking price for the property was $750,000 or $2.25 per hectare. On the property were '1,500 guaranteed cattle over age 6 months; approx. 1,000 buffalo and approx. 1,000 cattle unfenced; guaranteed 100 broken-in stock horses'. Interestingly, 'extensive mining projects exist on property, these will increasingly assist infrastructure', presumably by developing access roads to

Table 12.4 Pastoral Leaseholds in Australia *c.* 1970s

A. *Extensive Leases (not tied to Official 'Living Areas')*

	Qld	S.A.	N.T.	W.A.
Lease	Pastoral holding	Pastoral lease	Pastoral lease	Pastoral lease
Term (years)	30	New = 21 Renewed = 42	50	50
Area (ha)	No limit	No limit	Up to 800,000	Up to 250,000
Investment required		By 21st year spent *c.* $46 per km²	Investment of $100,000	By 10th year spent $20 per 250 ha
Environmental controls required	Noxious plants and vermin	Ditto	Ditto	Ditto
Official controls on use	No agriculture Min. + max. stock densities	No agriculture Min. + max. stock densities	Agriculture with Minister's consent Min. + max. stock densities	No agistment Min. + max. stock densities
Owner residence	Not required	Ditto	Ditto	Ditto

B. *Closer Settlement Leases (tied to Official 'Living Areas')*

	N.S.W.	Qld
Lease	Western land perpetual lease	Grazing selection
Term (years)	Perpetuity	Up to 30
Area (ha)	Up to 2 'home maintenance areas'	'Living area' (up to 11,250)
Investment required	As required by Minister	Ditto
Environmental controls required	Noxious plants—vermin	Ditto
Official controls on use	Min. + max. stock densities	Ditto No agistment for more than 6 months
Owner residence	Required for first 5 years on or 'within working distance' of	Required for first 7 years (up to 6 months allowed away)

Sources: State Legislation.

Plate 12.1 Brunette Downs homestead during the wet season. This station covers 1,250,000 ha and carries 50,000 head of branded cattle and 20,000 calves. There are 3,000 miles of internal roads. Brunette Downs is a subsidiary of the Texas King Ranch group. *Photo*: Ern McQuillan.

geological trial sites.

Myrtle Springs-Ediacara, a sheep and beef cattle property in the pastoral zone lying on the edge of Lake Torrens salt flat in South Australia is one example of a property combining evidence of both developed and undeveloped range. Some 2,512 km² of 165 mm annual rainfall country, comprising low tablelands, saltbush plains, cane grass swamp and clay pans, crossed by dry watercourses, is rated officially to be able to carry one sheep to every 12 hectares. Annual rent for this fifty-year leasehold in 1973 was approximately 0.25 cents per hectare or about 3 cents per sheep carried. While the eastern half (the original Myrtle Springs) has been subdivided into paddocks averaging 58 km² each, the western half (Ediacara) remains 'unimproved' apart from the isolated surface catchment dam and the two bores. In mid-1973 the whole property was sold at auction for $725,000 or *c*. $2.93 per hectare.

By contrast Welltown Stud Sheep Station of south central Queensland was offered for sale in April 1974. It comprised two portions, one the stud holding, some 100 km² on a forty-year lease from 1971 at rent of 50 cents per hectare, and an adjacent block of 25 km² on thirty-year lease from 1964 at a rent of just over 53 cents per hectare. Surprisingly, the annual rainfall for the property (*c*. 545 mm) was not mentioned in the advertisement but the black clay and brown loam plains were described as fronting four watercourses and carrying large trees (Coolibah, Belah and Myall) with patches of Box and 'the best types of western grasses and herbages'. Additional water came from storages in four earth dams and six earth tanks of which three were equipped with a windpump. The property was divided into 36 paddocks averaging 3.5 km² each with the boundary fence netted against rabbits. Approximately 640 hectares were cultivated 'with a

Plate 12.2 Cattle being moved to dry ground as the floods of the summer wet season reach Brunette Downs in the Northern Territory. Flooding can be extensive following the long dry winters and springs. *Photo*: Ern McQuillan.

small area irrigated for stud feeding' (as drought reserve), and a further 480 hectares had previously been cultivated. Livestock included 4,700 stud Merinos and Poll Merinos, plus 2,100 lambs from the September-October lambing and a further 600 rams. Cattle included 1,000 Shorthorns (of which 250 were stud animals). Allowing 8 sheep per cow this represented a stocking rate of one sheep equivalent per 0.8 hectares. An old station homestead together with an overseer's house, station hands' quarters, three 'cottages' and separate shearers' quarters comprised the living accommodation, alongside bull and ram sheds, an eight-stand shearing shed, machinery and hay sheds and silos. Holding paddocks and cattle and sheep yards completed the 'improvements'. The stud had been in the same family ownership since 1880 and it was claimed that the stud livestock (Merinos and Poll Shorthorns) 'are household names in the Queensland grazing areas where they are well known for their quality' and the wool was claimed to be 'a consistent winner of prizes at leading shows'.

Continental Patterns—A Summary

The broad patterns of pastoral land use are summarized in Fig. 12.1. The variety of activities can be zoned from the intensive high rainfall southern and eastern peripheries to the extensive cattle and sheep stations of the arid interior. Boundaries between zones may be economic, occasionally political as with state borders, and in the case of the sheep/cattle division in the interior apparently reflecting the protection afforded to sheep by the dingo fence. This is a static two-dimensional picture and the complexity of reality can only be hinted at by the suggestion of the pressures affecting boundaries over time, the flow of replacement stock from the southern and eastern studs, the diffusion of innovations from the research centres, and the flow of produce basically from the interior to the coast for export.

The extensive pastoral land use stands out from this map and the preceding evidence as the remotest land settlement; beyond is the desert. Here is the minimum capital investment per unit area, but one of the highest investments per production unit. Stock densities are lowest but individual flocks and herds the largest, leaseholds predominate and the single owner-operator is in the minority. The largest proportion of the land is under multiple ownership—ranging from family partnerships to international financial houses.

The patterns of contemporary pastoral land use in Australia show evidence therefore of considerable complexity even within that portion of the pastoral industry where land use is extensive rather than intensive. To attempt to explain this diversity of size of holding, of ownership and use of the pastoral resources we need to trace the origins of Australian pastoral resource use back to Europe, particularly to Britain, and to examine the ways in which traditional methods were modified in the face of the novel environments, social and economic as well as physical, of the Australian continent. To do this we shall look first at pastoral land use in Britain at the beginning of the nineteenth century, attempting to identify those components which were to be introduced into Australia. Then we shall look at the pastoral situation in Australia at approximately 1830, by which time local hopes were already coming into focus upon pastoral land use as the future staple for the colonies and the pastoralists were poised on the edge of what we now recognize to have been the best natural pastures of the continent. Finally, we shall attempt to explain the spatial extension of pastoral land use in terms of a model of land settlement which reflects the interplay of a variety of influential factors.

THE ORIGINS OF PASTORAL AUSTRALIA

For the origins of type and breed of livestock and techniques of management we must look to British pastoral technology in the early nineteenth century. The free immigrants who began to arrive in Australia particularly from the 1820s onwards brought with them not only capital, both cash and equipment, but also the livestock, a technology for their management and the labourers to apply it, and a traditional approach to the marketing of their produce.

The late eighteenth century and particularly the period from the sailing of the First Fleet to the beginning of free immigration to Australia was a time when traditional methods of pastoral land use were still dominant in Britain, but also a time when they were being challenged, successfully in some areas, by innovators adopting what would be recognized now as scientific methods. The pastoral system which was available to the first Australian pastoralists therefore, was one which was recognized by contemporaries such as William Marshall, Arthur Young and William Cobbett along with the various reporters to the Board of Agriculture (set up in 1793 to encourage agricultural improvement) to be generally primitive.

The controlled breeding of livestock for specific purposes was still in its infancy, delayed by the impossibility of controlled breeding among herds grazing on the common lands or open fields, general ignorance of the practical principles of genetics and the traditional conservatism of the rural communities. 'Stock-breeding, as applied to both cattle and sheep', said Lord Ernle (1961, p. 181), 'was the haphazard union of nobody's son with everybody's daughter'.

Sheep were the dominant livestock, perhaps some 26 million in England at the turn of the century, grazing over three-quarters of the country's area (Prince, 1973). They were valued chiefly for their wool and skins but were becoming increasingly valued for their manure, particularly in the reclamation of the sandy heathlands of eastern England. Most were short-woolled, able to survive seasonal feed shortages and the scanty pasturage of the open-fields and commons. Perhaps a quarter, according to Ernle, were long-woolled, larger framed, heavier sheep.

Just how many recognizably different breeds there were is debated; Prince says 14, Ryder 20 (Ryder, 1964) as opposed to the 30 breeds recognized in the 1960s. Both Prince and Ryder agree, however, upon the main characteristics of the breeds, the two main groups of short and long wools, their regional variations and their generally poor quality by comparison with their modern equivalents. Thus short-woolled (coarse wool) sheep were represented by breeds such as Scottish Black-face, Shetland, Dorset Horn, Welsh Mountain, Ryeland (from Herefordshire), Norfolks, Suffolks and Southdowns, with Romneys, Cotswolds and Leicesters for the long and fine wools. Such controlled breeding as had taken place had been for external characteristics such as horn-type, colour and overall size, regardless of wool quality or carcass weight. Among the exceptions, however, and one with particular significance for Australia, was the flock of fine-woolled Spanish Merinos of His Majesty George III, struggling in the 1790s with the unaccustomedly humid environment of Windsor Great Park (Carter, 1964).

Similarly, for the 3 or 4 million cattle and horses there were regional types recognized but attempts to improve *productivity* were generally absent. There were, among others, Hereford cattle (but unrecognizable without as yet their white faces), Durhams, red Devons, black Pembrokes and Angleseys, Scottish Ayrshires and Anguses. Such concern for cattle productivity as did exist was for volume of meat and milk production, otherwise 'size was the only criterion of merit' (Ernle, 1961, p. 174). Similarly, it was the large horse which drew favour, regardless of its performance, and with the dominance of oxen as the draught farm animal the function of the horse was being dictated by racing enthusiasts and the expanding coaching companies.

Productivity per animal was generally low. Norfolk and Suffolk ewes averaged 0.9 kg fleeces, 0.2 kg less than the Merinos of Upper Saxony from which, through the Royal Hanoverian connection, some of the Australian flocks were to be drawn. Evidence, admittedly of doubtful quality, suggested that by 1795 the average carcass weight of fat cattle at Smithfield Market, London, was 360 kg and of sheep 22.5 kg, twice the weights in 1710 (Ernle, 1961).

Productivity reflected in part of the lack of controlled breeding, but also the available feed and management techniques. Two basic types of grazing areas were identified, grazing on common lands and open fields and grazing on enclosed lands. Contemporary writers contrasted the poor feed provided by the natural grasses, shrubs and tree seeds (acorns, beech mast) of the commons and the weeds of the fallows and poor stubbles of the harvested open fields, with the more controlled feeding possible on enclosed lands, where rotation of stocking and hand or stall feeding could cope with seasonal shortages. A considerable variation in grazing densities resulted. On the common hill grazing of the Welsh and Scottish mountains and Pennine moors a sheep struggled to find sustenance on 1.2 hectares whereas on the enclosed Downlands 0.4 hectares was sufficient, and on the lush pastures of Romney Marsh 12 sheep of the local breed could thrive on one hectare.

Because of the winter shortage of feed, with grasses killed by frost and inadequate hay supplies, stock on common or open-field grazing traditionally were sold off for slaughter at the great autumn fairs and markets. In contrast, farmers on enclosed lands could carry stock over the winter on hay or the new turnips and mangolds harvested from the enclosed private fields, and so prolong their productive life.

Although part of the function of livestock was to provide a local supply of protein, already by 1800 there existed commercial interchange over long distances. Thus the pattern described by the agricultural correspondent of the London *Times* in October 1965 was already in existence by 1800:

> Sheep they say, should always travel downhill, from the hills of the north and west where they are bred their natural progress is down to the turnip fields and fattening yards of the lowlands east and south. Now, as the hill farms prepare for winter, is the time of the great autumn migration. (11 October 1965, p. 5)

Not only sheep, but cattle also came down from the moorland edges of Devon, Wales, the Pennines and Scotland over the traditional 'drove roads' to the fattening grounds and markets of southeastern England. Occasionally, as in the Welsh mountains until the 1860s, a form of transhumance existed, where sheep were moved down from summer grazing on upland pastures to winter grazing on the lower valley meadows. Even here, however, the surplus lambs and calves joined the autumnal march to the slaughter houses.

The wool trade was similarly strong in tradition. Hand shearing took place in spring (usually April) after the flocks had been washed in a convenient stream or pool. Fleeces were roughly sorted either for the local village weavers or travelling agents of the regional woollen industries of East Anglia or the Cotswolds, or taken for auction to the local market town, the sale to be clinched over a mug of ale in one of the many inns. The growth of the major manufacturing complexes of Lancashire and Yorkshire and a national system of wool auctions were, in 1800, in embryo only, although the Spanish and Saxon Merino fine wools were already a growing import with an associated international marketing system, their livestock and management techniques the subject of interested enquiry by the Board of Agriculture's agents (Darby, 1973).

At the village or farm level traditional management techniques predominated. The daily herding of livestock from night yards or portable 'folds' to the grazing grounds consumed time and animal energy as well as trampling the feed into the ground. Both on the common and open-field grazing and on the enclosed lands the shepherd or herdsman could be a paid labourer, the stockman, or a member of his family. Accompanied by his dogs, perhaps long-haired collies or the Old English Sheep breed, he took charge of usually 300–400 sheep and from a handful to perhaps a hundred cattle. The site of the fold had to be changed frequently because of the accumulated dung and the diseases associated with it, but on the enclosed lands owners were beginning to recognize the benefits of the manure and using a controlled rotation of fold sites to rejuvenate exhausted fields or to improve the fertility of newly enclosed heath lands. Also they were beginning to realize that constant herding was not necessary on fenced grazing lands.

Apart from the common lands where 'commoners' exercised traditional rights to graze their 'stint' of livestock (a fixed number for a fixed period of time) and the open fields where the villagers' livestock grazed under the eye of a village herder, livestock grazed land held under a variety of tenures. From the fee simple moors of absentee Scottish landlords or great estates of the English Midlands to specific leases for up to twenty-five years of private, enclosed, grazing lands and the agricultural tenancies of seven, fourteen or twenty-one years duration of time of the innovating landlords of southeast England, the variety of grazing land ownership was impressive. At one end of the scale common rights were held to unimproved natural pastures while at the other, private ownership was often of lands where the natural quality of the pasture had been improved by drainage of swamps, controlled fertilization from annual flooding of low-lying meadows, or skilful rotation of the folds, together with storage of seasonal surpluses as hay or sowing of the clovers and ryegrasses, or their replacement by rootcrops (Darby, 1973).

Thus a variety of potential livestock and systems for their management was available to emigrants in the early nineteenth century. As a source of protein cattle and sheep could utilize poor country to advantage and a traditional market for wool offered scope for the far-sighted. Yet the demand was for fine wool and local fine-woolled sheep were in the minority and generally outclassed by the Spanish and Saxon Merino stock.

Pastoral Land Use in Australia *c*. 1830

The introduction of Indian hair sheep and cattle by the First Fleet in 1788 brought a subsistence form of pastoral land use to Australia, but not until the 1830s was the commercial potential of the livestock generally accepted. Between 1788 and the 1820s the main function of local flocks and herds was the provision of a meat or mutton supply to the local population, mainly through the purchases of the Commissariat. From the 1820s onwards, however, pastoralists such as John Macarthur, Samuel Marsden and James Cox were looking to wool to replace the colonies' dependence upon the whaling and sealing exports as sources of overseas income.

The transformation of a subsistence form of production to a commercial export-based pattern of resource use was not achieved overnight and the process of that transformation has been the subject of considerable debate among economic historians. That debate is worth summarizing here because it touches on most of the factors which appear to have influenced all subsequent pastoral land use in Australia.

The settlement of a colony remote from the home country implies not only a transfer of people but of their customs and way of life. In that new colony, runs the argument, many of those customary activities, patterns of consumption of foods, demands for goods and services, cannot be met from local resources hence they must be imported—probably most likely from the home country. To pay for these 'necessary' and 'basic' imports, a source of export income is needed—a 'staple' product or products which may be exported to the home country for cash. Although the timing of the change is disputed, most economic historians agree that the initial staples for the Australian colonies were from the maritime resource uses—whaling and sealing—and that pastoral products, principally wool, began to challenge that role only from the 1820s onwards (Abbott, 1971).

Trade with the Pacific Islands, the East Indies and China also provided external income. Intermittently from 1793 to 1830 the Sydney settlement was importing pork from Tahiti to feed the convicts and garrison, and was carrying on a profitable trade in New Zealand flax to English manufacturers, in sandalwood from Fiji and the New Hebrides and bêche-de-mer (trepang) pearl shell and edible birds' nests to the Chinese mainland. Indeed, two of the men who helped establish the pastoral industry in Australia have been described recently as John Macarthur 'sheep-breeder and sandalwood trader' and the Rev. Samuel Marsden 'chaplain, magistrate, sheep-breeder, pork trader and missionary' (Young, 1967). Again, however, from *c*. 1830s this Pacific trading activity began to lose some of its attraction and the eyes of the decision-makers and capitalists began to look to inland Australia for their future profits (Abbott and Nairn, 1969).

The attraction of the pastoral resources of the inland depended upon a series of factors which, already evident by the late 1820s, were to influence all future pastoral land use in the continent. As a commercial activity the future of pastoral resource use depended upon:

i) The attractions of alternative types of resource use and capital investment.

ii) The recognized resource base for the particular activity. In the case of pastoralism the relevant bases were adequate land to provide the feed and water resources and appropriate livestock to exploit these resources.

iii) The presence of a demand for the produce either locally or overseas, and preferably both.

iv) The availability of a technology able to combine efficiently the inputs of livestock and labour with the skills for their management.

v) The availability of capital to finance the development of the production process (acquisition of land for feed and water, livestock, labour, transport to market, etc.).

vi) Finally, the belief in the minds of the relevant decision-makers that this form of activity had a future as a successful use of their skills and capital.

By 1830 pastoralists with their flocks and herds had occupied the central lowlands of Tasmania and were already looking across the Bass Strait to the grassy plains which Major Mitchell in 1836 was to term Australia Felix. From the confines of the Cumberland Plains pastoralists had crossed the divide and were already beginning to follow the natural drainage lines down the western slopes to the apparently boundless grasslands and open woodlands of central New South Wales. Although in the early 1820s a Ticket of Occupation for a nominal fee provided some legal status, from 1826 onwards these were revoked and the march westwards was officially illegal as beyond the

Limits of Settlement. Nonetheless 'squatters' continued to choose their creek frontages and waterholes as headquarters for their pastoral stations beyond the Blue Mountains, while within the Limits—in the Nineteen Counties—grazing continued upon private purchased and granted land and public commons as well as official reserves.

The number of livestock in the colonies *c.* 1830 is uncertain; a census of 1828 suggested some 536,000 sheep and 263,000 cattle but no doubt there were many uncounted. Numbers had been increasing rapidly since 1820 when sheep numbers were only 98,000 and cattle 55,000. This rapid rate of increase was to continue into the 1830s. In terms of private capital livestock represented already in 1821 more than half the total value in the colony and the proportion had probably increased by 1830. Certainly by 1839 stock numbers had risen to 1.3 million sheep, 371,000 cattle and 7,000 horses (Abbott, 1971).

Most of the cattle herds were of uncertain ancestry—many still showing their Bengal origins—and it was claimed in 1826 that only two herds, Macarthur's Lancashires and Marsden's Polled Suffolks, showed any evidence of carefully bred bloodstock. With cattle as with sheep, the initial concern was for numbers not necessarily quality.

The improvement in sheep quantity and quality which Macarthur had claimed possible in his submission to the British government in 1803 had not taken place by 1820, when perhaps only a tenth of the colonial flock could have been classed as fine wool—derived mainly from the Cape Colony Merinos brought in 1797 and a subsquent trickle of Merinos from the Royal Flock (Abbott, 1971). However, from 1820 onwards the popularity of, and demand for, better quality fine-woolled sheep was increasing and the Indian hair sheep strain was disappearing (Abbott, 1971). Macarthur himself had supplied 300 Merino rams to Tasmanian pastoralists in 1820 and in the same year a further 30 pure Merino rams came direct from Britain. In particular from the mid-1820s the flow of new blood into the colonial flocks increased substantially. Between 1822 and 1825 at least 277 Merinos were imported and the Australian Agriculture Company, newly founded in 1825, brought in 702 Merinos from France, while 320 Saxon fine-woolled sheep were imported in 1824–5 at a time when German fine-wool producers, who had taken over dominance from Spain, were supplying two-thirds of the British wool imports.

Demand for pastoral products in the 1830s was becoming more varied than the original subsistence demands for protein and coarse wool for local cloth production. In both cases the original demand came from the official sources—the government cloth factory at Parramatta and the government store or Commis-sariat which was the main supplier of food to the colonial population until the free settlers began to outnumber the convicts from 1800 onwards. Even in 1830 however, the convicts still formed 40 per cent of the total population of 46,000 and the government's purchases of meat and mutton still provided a significant market for livestock. Until approximately 1810 most of the cattle in the colonies were government-owned as a potential protein supply and kangaroo meat supplemented at least the official Tasmanian diet until 1811 in the absence of adequate domesticated animal produce (Abbott and Nairn, 1969).

This demand for stock for slaughter had been overshadowed by 1830 by the demand for stock to occupy new pastures—particularly sheep. The demand was in anticipation of a market for wool in Britain and resulted in boom conditions when not only wool but also all surplus sheep sold to newly arrived potential pastoralists provided a profitable income.

Wool exports by 1830 were already substantial, some 630,000 kg, and already 6 per cent of the British imports. By 1850 just over half of British imports were coming from Australia and by 1900 the proportion was almost 70 per cent. Marketing of the exports in 1830 was still mainly an individual matter for the larger producers who shipped direct to the London auctions, but already the smaller producers were finding that local entrepreneurs could buy their wool in Sydney or the inns on the Sydney highway, and undertake the forwarding to London. The foundations of the subsequent system of local wool selling agencies organizing local auction sales prior to despatch to Britain were already laid, and the inflow of sterling from wool sales was proving a lubricator to the colonial economy (Barnard, 1958).

Pastoral technology by 1830 showed similarities with the poorer rather than more advanced methods in Britain. Livestock were run on natural pastures and no real attempt was made to use their manure to improve local cultivation. Herding and shepherding were the rule and the only management of pastures was the control of grazing location and pressure by the relocation of night folds, and the burning of old grasses to promote new growth. The high cost of labour prevented all but a few enthusiasts from attempting to improve upon the natural carrying capacity (thought to be *c.* one sheep to 1.2 hectares) by sowing English grasses or clovers. Shepherding was also necessary to protect the livestock—from the attacks of dingoes at night and Aborigines by day, as one contemporary put it (Abbott, 1971).

One major problem was the shortage of labour, for stock numbers were outstripping shepherds. The usual technique was labour intensive in that two or three flocks of 300–350 sheep each with its shepherd were usually folded overnight under the eye of a hut-keeper

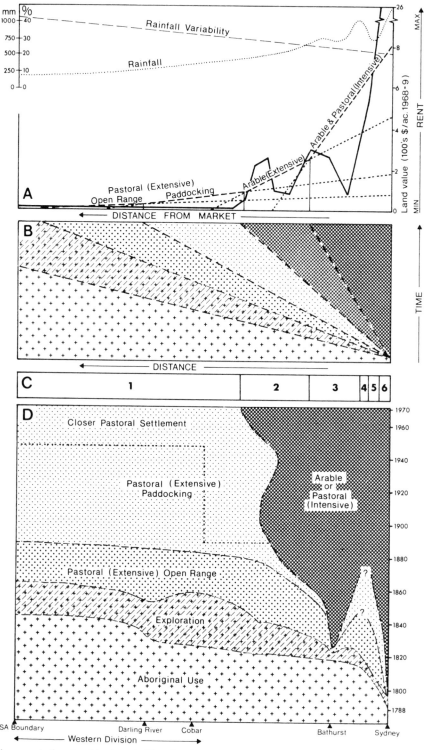

Fig. 12.3 The spread of pastoral land use in New South Wales: hypotheses and reality.

or night watchman. Thus three men were needed for 600–700 sheep or four men for every 900–1,050. To meet the labour shortage some pastoralists increased their flock sizes up to 1,000 sheep per shepherd, especially where the open plains made control easier, and even 'camped' the flocks on the range and so dispensed with folds and night watchmen at the cost of increased stock losses from dingoes and strays. In rare cases, usually on granted lands, fencing of posts and rails or brush dispensed with the need for any shepherds (Abbott, 1971).

Cattle by comparison were less expensive to run, 500–600 needing two men to supervise them, and needing less daily control, being better able to cope with dingoes and less likely to stray away from watering points.

Breeding was not controlled and lambing might be twice per year, with high losses if in the dry season. Shearing was annual in the spring, but the quantity and quality of the wool varied enormously; up to the 1820s in Tasmania most was so coarse that it was thrown away—not a great loss with fleeces only 0.4–1.0 kg each!

The rapid inflow of British capitalists as prospective pastoralists in the late 1820s and 1830s was in part the anticipation of increasing demand for wool and the culmination of the efforts of the pioneer promoters, but also the result of a specific climate of opinion which by the early 1820s, possibly stronger in Britain even than locally, saw the future commercial success of the colony as lying in the pastoral industry. There had been the supporters of Macarthur and Marsden since the turn of the century but the increasing British demand for wool, the disruptions of the Napoleonic Wars in traditional European suppliers and the associated increase in prices, the successful formation of the Australian Agricultural Company to, among other things, raise 'fine wool', together with the appearance of fine wools from Australia in the London auctions created renewed interest in capitalists who saw only a limited future for themselves in Britain. For the fine wools, with prices three to five times the average by the 1830s, the future seemed rosy and when the wool merchants giving evidence to the 1828 Select Committee on the State of the British Wool Trade did not doubt that 'fifteen or twenty years hence ... we shall have as much Wool from those colonies as we shall want in this country', who was to argue against them?

Not only wool had promise, for in the opinion of the speculator Thomas Peel, putting up his proposal to establish a Swan River colony, there was a future in 'the rearing of Horses for the East India Trade, with the most important Establishment of large Herds of Cattle and Swine for the Purpose of supplying His Majesty's or other shipping with Salt Provisions' (Clark, 1950, p. 82). The creation of this favourable climate of opinion was itself a formidable component in the expansion of pastoral activity in the late 1820s and 1830s. The arrival of the new governor, Sir Richard Bourke, in December 1831, seemed a further good augur for he brought from his last post at the Cape Colony a sympathy for the problems of grazing remote areas. Under his considerate guidance the expansion into the interior was to be both encouraged and legalized and the foundations laid for the system of land tenure which was to successfully allow legal pastoral occupation of not only the high tablelands of the Blue Mountains but also the remotest arid interior.

The Evolution of Pastoral Land Use 1830–1970

Commercial livestock grazing in Australia has been shaped ... by the three key interrelated factors of environment, profit and cultural pressure. Geared essentially to distant export markets, its development reflects the abundance of land and scarcity of labour and capital, on which Australia's economic growth was initially based.

(Peel, 1973, p. 72)

Key to *Fig. 12.3*

A. Land use, land value and land rent along a section from Sydney inland to the northwestern corner of the State.
Key
Solid line is actual land values for shires along the section *c.* 1969. Pecked lines suggest hypothetical bid-rent cones and associated land uses after the Von Thünen model with distance from a Sydney market.
B. Model of the spread of land uses from a single point of entry at Sydney.
Key
Shadings as for D below and keyed to the land use in A also. Arable (extensive-monoculture) is suggested as a preliminary to intensive uses.
C. Land use *c.* 1970.
Key
1. Extensive pastoral (wool dominant).

2. Grain crops.
3. Intensive pastoral (wool and meat/mutton).
4. Woodland.
5. Intensive cropping and horticulture.
6. Urban areas.
D. Actual spread of land uses from Sydney 1788–1970s.
Key
Aboriginal land use penetrated by explorers is succeeded by open range (unfenced) pastoral use which in turn is replaced by fenced grazing (paddocking). The subdivision of existing pastoral stations into smaller units for 'living areas/home maintenance areas' (Closer Settlement) was not extended to the Western Division until the 1940s largely because of the drought impacts at the turn of the century. No attempt is made to differentiate the intensive land uses.

Source: *Atlas of Australian Resources*, land sales and various.

The pattern of the pastoral industries was established with a human population of low density and prior to the availability of oil, electric power or motorized transport .... Rail transport servicing the extensive land holdings was the only major input of fossil fuel. The energy cost of harvesting the primary photosynthetic resources is small, the ruminant serving as a self-fuelled, self-propelling, self-servicing, self-reproducing, harvesting machine. It is also a food and fibre synthesizing factory. Even today electricity and fuel account for only about 6 per cent of the total cost on pastoral properties.

(Alexander and Williams, 1973, pp. 541–2)

Already by 1830 Peel's 'three key interrelated factors' were evident and already the efficiency of the 'self-fuelled, self-propelling, self-servicing, self-reproducing, harvesting machine' had been demonstrated. In the subsequent years these biotic machines were to munch their way across the vast interior of Australia, sending back to the coast their surplus produce. This invasion by these herbivores had significant impacts upon the ecosystems and had by the 1970s produced a series of landscapes and productive systems of world-wide significance as we have seen. That invasion, however, was no haphazard operation. Despite the fact that it was undertaken by thousands of independently-minded decision-makers operating in their own individual behavioural environment there was sufficient in common, both in their aims and achievements, to identify their broad motives and the general economic and spatial constraints which directed the pace and direction of their march inland. Indeed, it is possible to suggest a model of sequential land use which seems to fit not only the patterns of pastoral use which developed but also the end product in the 1970s.

A Model of the Sequence

A recent study has demonstrated the evolution in the nineteenth century of a world-wide system of agricultural supply and demand oriented to the expanding urban markets of Western Europe, Britain and northeastern North America (Peet, 1969). With specific reference to Britain it is shown that because of increasing demand, from a population increasing at 11–18 per cent per decade and rapid increase of real wages particularly from 1850 to 1914 together with a limited local capacity to expand production because of limited technology and low yields, increased supplies had to be sought by bringing more land into production overseas. Declining ocean freight rates in the nineteenth century helped this enlargement of the productive area. Peet suggests that this process had resulted in a zonation of agricultural land use akin to Von Thünen's model by the 1820s, after initial trends towards this zonation had been evident in the late

eighteenth century when high prices in Britain brought wheat and wool from the Baltic, central Europe (including Saxony) and Russia.

That Australian pastoral production formed part of this world-wide Von Thünen system had been suggested by Waibel in 1922 and Peet's table of distances travelled by British imports 1830-1913 confirms the pattern for wool. The increasing dominance of Australian wool in the British market in the latter half of the nineteenth century was marked by increasing average distances travelled by wool and hides to the London market; by 1891–5 the distance was the same as the sea route from Australia.

The expansion of production to meet the increasing British demand was met by the expansion of the area of production at intensities similar to those obtained by initial productive methods. This would account for the general expansion of extensive pastoral production into the Australian interior—the details being decided by availability of livestock, labour and capital and any legal contraints on land occupation.

Following behind this zone of extensive animal rearing or wool and hide production came the zone of wheat farming, associated with 'considerable population densities, fixed transport facilities, and sophisticated crop collection and central place systems' (Peet, 1969). In the case of Australia therefore, such a sequence might be expected out from each of the main colonial points of entry to the continent: Sydney, Adelaide, Perth etc. (Fig. 12.3B). The early concentration of population in the State capitals in fact might be expected to further concentrate local demands around the main ports through which the overseas demands were channelled.

Comparing this model with the sequence for New South Wales, the remarkable similarity is obvious (Fig. 12.3B, C and D). If we make the obvious addition that for European settlement exploration was a necessary first stage, the link between exploration and pastoral land use was in fact strengthened over time as the increasing aridity inland decreased the hopes for widespread agriculture. Most of the private explorers were pastoralists and even official explorers such as Eyre, Forrest and Sturt were pastoralists as well as public servants and often applied for the better pastoral country they had discovered.

At any one point along the section in New South Wales it is obvious that, over time, a sequence of land uses had been experienced. The classic comment of an early pastoral historian for example, could be applied to much of the better lands in the eastern half of the section:

The average station went through four different stages. First it was a fattening station, with a choice herd of cattle; for all its improvements, a stockyard and a hut.

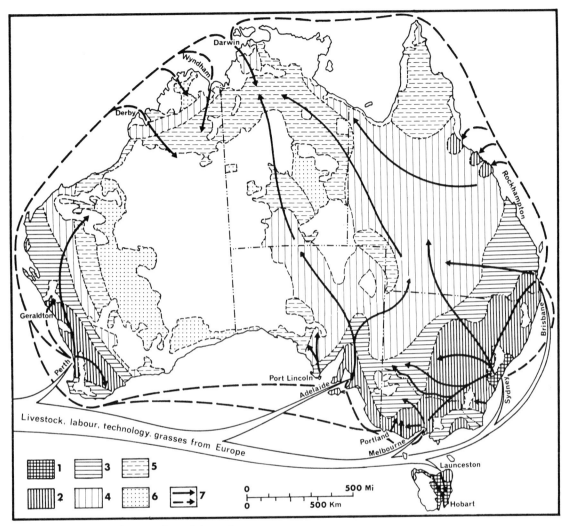

Fig. 12.4 The pastoral occupation of Australia.

KEY

Inputs, mainly from Europe, produced the initial pastoral occupation by:

1. 1830
2. 1845
3. 1860
4. 1880
5. 1900
6. post 1900

7. Main lines of advance by land and sea.

The blank areas were not used for pastoral purposes *c*. 1970, but include some areas which may have been used and subsequently abandoned. Note that this map shows the sequence of initial, but not necessarily continuous, pastoral occupation.

Source: *Atlas of Australian Resources* and various.

It was valued at £30. Next it was advertised as fully improved, fenced and subdivided sheep-property. Thirdly, it was a valuable pastoral estate of 35,000 acres freehold. Finally, it consisted of rich agricultural land, divided to suit intending farmers. (Collier, 1911, p. 70)

Each stage in the sequence represented an actual or implied increase in the capital investment and cash value per unit area.

The expansion of the different zones of land use and implicit capital investment conformed remarkably to Von Thünen's model by the 1950s (Scott, 1968). In New South Wales the median distance of this extensive pastoral land use was for sheep 640 km and cattle 1,001 km, as opposed to wheat and sheep 346 km and intensive sheep and cattle 232–377 km respectively. Further, by the late 1960s, land values (from sales of properties) suggested a gradation from maxima in the suburban zone of Sydney to the minimal values of the extensive western pastoral zone. In terms of cash values, the extensive pastoral uses had been pushed into the remotest and lowest-valued land (Fig. 12.3A, Fig. 10.8).

The details of actual occupation shown on Fig. 12.4 show the more complex pattern resulting from not only the bid-rent values of the Von Thünen model but the constraints of commerce, the process of resource appraisal and management, and the significant role of government in the whole land settlement sequence.

The Constraints of Commerce

To become a perfect specimen of the Australian Squatter an emigrant must be a pushing determined fellow, who can dispense with all the comforts of civilized life, from wine and windows to carpets and crockery, and will look to nothing but making the most of his Capital regardless of risk and hardship so long as they lead to increased profit. (Lang, 1845, p. 15)

Profits, or the promise of profits, were foremost in the minds of the British capitalists who pushed their livestock into the interior from the 1830s onwards, and it says much for the original choice of land use and the continued demands for pastoral produce that from the 1830s through the 1870s to the 1970s, profits have continued to be made from a land use which has changed much in detail but in general concept little from the initial system.

Capital has continued to be made available to the industry, if at fluctuating rates, and as we have seen the profits of the extensive pastoral land use have continued relatively high. Once begun 'pastoral investment ... was a repetitive process, duplicating, further and further inland, established combinations of capital and land in the attempt to utilize more land' (Barnard, 1962, p. 323).

The bulk of the capital has come from overseas—

British sources until the 1960s. How much was brought independently by the hopefuls who arrived from the 1830s onwards we shall probably never know, but some indication can be obtained from the records of the public companies, formed to apply funds *inter alia* to the development of pastoral resources. Thus the Australian Agricultural Company formed in 1825 with a capital of £1 million and the Van Diemen's Land Company 1825 also with capital of £1 million, were joined by the Bank of Australia, the Union Bank of Australia, the Royal Bank of Australia, and the Scottish Australian Investment Company formed in the 1840s (Jenks, 1963, p. 391 n.). The Australian Liens on Wool Act of 1843 for the first time allowed credit on the wool not yet shorn and encouraged direct expansion of production.

By the 1860s British capital investment directly into the pastoral industry was approximately one-tenth of total investment (Butlin, 1962). From a figure of £110,000 per year in 1864 the sums rose to almost £2 million per year in the 1880s but slumped in the 1890s after the Australian financial crashes and the effects of the 1890s droughts. Indirectly also, however, the other investments—particularly those for public works (docks, roads and railway construction) facilitated the flow of produce from the inland to the coast and so on to Britain and Europe.

This flow of capital, however, was not always directed into the same channels. Initially in the 1830s and 1840s, the main investment was in the purchase of livestock—which could represent over 80 per cent of initial costs of setting up a station (Abbott, 1971). From the 1860s onwards enormous amounts of capital were spent in buying up the range, either directly at auction or through illegal use of dummies or from *bona fide* small selectors, as it became threatened by the advance of small holdings and agricultural land use. Such capital was being made available to pastoralists in the Western District of Victoria in the 1860s and to the Riverina in the 1870s, when prices of £2.5 per hectare were paid by pastoralists borrowing from British firms such as the Australian Mortgage Land and Finance Company (Bailey, 1966). The money acquired by the State governments from these land sales was partly used to invest in public works so that British finance not only allowed large freehold pastoral properties to be set up in these areas of Australia, but indirectly funded public investment in roads and railways.

From the 1870s onwards large sums were being directed into the equipping of pastoral properties—initially in the areas which had been freeholded, but subsequently in the 1880s to the drier interior leaseholds, where the discovery of artesian water and the necessity for fencing—not least to control the advancing rabbits—made additional investment vital. The high hopes of pastoralists and their financial backers were, however, dashed by the droughts at the turn of the century, which halved flocks in eastern Australia and threatened ruin to all.

Initially the finance houses only loaned money to pastoralists, but with the bankruptcies and fore-closures of properties many companies were forced to try to run the properties themselves to recoup some of their losses. Station owners became managers, or even overseers, on what had been their own pro-perties, others shouldered their swags and joined the itinerant labour force. By 1900, of the pastoral prop-erties on which they had loaned money previously, Goldsbrough Mort had foreclosed on 13 of their 16, Australian Estates and Mortgage on 7 of their 9, Australian Mortgage and Agency on 6 of their 9, Australian Mercantile Land and Finance on 19 of their 31, and Dalgety on 8 of their 25 (Cain, 1962, p. 451n.). Never again would pastoral operations offer the attraction to capital of the 1880s.

Not only natural disasters reduced capital inflows. After 1909, as a result of New South Wales Labour Party policies favouring the compulsory acquisition of large properties to increase the pace of closer settle-ment and Commonwealth land tax policies, the Aus-tralian Mercantile Land and Finance Company, for example, began to look first to Queensland and then to Argentina to continue its pastoral operations (Bailey, 1966). How far this was typical may be debated but there is no doubt that from the turn of the century onwards, the flow of outside capital into the industry has been generally low (Butlin, 1962). Excep-tions were short periods in the late 1920s, the Korean War wool price boom of the 1950s and the American capital inflow to northern Australia in the 1960s. From 1961 the Commonwealth Development Bank has provided some capital to intensify pastoral pro-duction by pasture improvement in the higher rainfall areas but little for extensive operations.

Appraising the Range: The Resource Managers

The foolish man shouteth much, and makes a mighty noise therewith in public places, desiring much to assist in running the Government, and behold they make laws which squelch him from the face of the range; but the wise man holdeth his peace, neither tooteth he his buzoo too much, but rather winketh to himself, and worketh out his own salvation—neither soundeth he loud timbrels, nor kicketh up a dust.

(*Australasian Pastoralists Review*, 15 September 1891, p. 252)

The application of capital, however, was only in response to the appraisal of the potentials for profitable resource use. In this process of appraisal were two components, the resource managers—people who had an interest, however tenuous, in the recognition and use of the pastoral resources, and the resource base itself as recognized over time.

The resource managers, or decision-makers, rep-resented at least four different parties by the end of the period. The pastoralists themselves were the individuals who were directly involved in the management of pastoral production. From the shepherds and herders to the rouseabouts, boundary riders and jackeroos, and from the green 'new chums' to the experienced 'squatters' and 'graziers', there was a spectrum of individual interest and expertise which varied not only between the jobs performed at any one time but over time itself. Most had had no formal training before they took up their jobs, learning very much 'on the job' by watching how it was done by others, supposedly more experienced.

Even for the owners of properties a similar process of learning-by-doing applied. As early as the 1840s it had been recognized, later to be formalized, as the 'jackeroo' system—where prospective pastoralists are accepted on existing stations as apprentices to be taught how to manage stock and the station by observ-ing and working themselves in return for their keep and a social status only one down from that of the owner himself.

This loose process of management training even at the highest level of owner-operator has meant that the industry has been marked by individual and pragmatic decision-making, with innovations being relatively rare and slow to diffuse among the community of resource managers. Even in the 1970s one commentator could suggest that:

These managers operate within their own, largely unresearched environments. ... Most managers of livestock are engaged in manual labour, and can be understood if regarded as artisans and technicians rather than as entrepreneurs or businessmen.

(Alexander and Williams, 1973, p. 37)

From the initiation of the industry in Australia, however, the pastoral station owners have often delegated the running of the property to a manager or overseer, preferring to live elsewhere or in the city and supervise the marketing of the produce from there. This process was further complicated by the installa-tion of company managers on foreclosed properties at the turn of the century as we have seen. This must therefore complicate any attempt to understand the motives in the resource management process, for those of the owner-operator may well differ consider-ably from those of the company's manager, not only in the length of time within which decisions are seen to operate but also in the attitudes to the range itself— whether regarded as a permanent home or temporary residence, an environment to be cherished or exploited.

To this group of resource managers we need to add

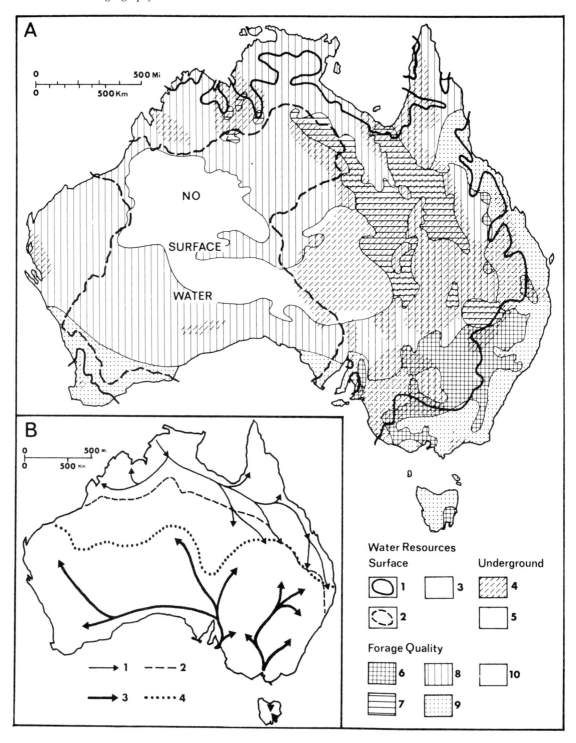

Fig. 12.5 The pastoral environment.

the financial companies themselves. As we have seen, first as investments for loans and later as mortgagors forced to foreclose, the companies acquired considerable interests in the pastoral properties. In the 1890s the Australian Mercantile Land and Finance Company, for example, owned over 3 million sheep, mainly on the Riverina and was (unsuccessfully) attempting to set up its own freezing works at Deniliquin (Bailey, 1966, p. 151). By 1900, banks and companies owned over 70 per cent of properties in the Warrego (Heathcote, 1965). By the second decade of the twentieth century, however, the financial houses were withdrawing from pastoral ownership, but pastoral companies employing external, often overseas, capital have remained a significant component of ownership in the Northern Territory (Kelly, 1966).

A third type of resource manager, less directly involved in the production process but directly concerned with the legal frame within which it was carried out, were the officials responsible for the control of the pastoral industry. Initially here as with all forms of land settlement, it was the State Departments of Land which carried out official policies on land apportionment and disposal. The continued and general prevalence of the leasehold system of land tenure, however, has meant that the Crown has remained the ultimate owner and therefore responsibility for the management of the land has been retained by the Departments. Thus the Minister and his hierarchy of officials have remained an interested party to any resource management proposals and over time have been joined in their interests by the specialist Departments of Agriculture and of Stock and Brands. In the case of New South Wales and South Australia in addition a regional administration basically concerned with pastoral land settlement has been separately identified (the Western Lands Commission and the Pastoral Board respectively). Not only are such officers responsible for the surveying and disposal of pastoral lands to prospective lessees, they are also responsible for the supervision of the lessees, advice on pastoral land management and the policing of controls on land use, stock numbers, noxious weeds and vermin.

Finally, in theory separate from, although often paid by the departments noted above, were the scientists involved in the problems of pastoral production. The late nineteenth century saw initial attempts by scientists to apply their research methods to pastoral problems—particularly the eradication of the rabbit competition by innoculation of various infectious diseases and geological investigation of underground water supplies. The main boost to scientific involvement, however, came with the Commonwealth's attempts to co-ordinate research in the second decade of the twentieth century, culminating in the Council for Scientific and Industrial Research in 1927. Paralleling and complementing this were the researchers of State Departments of Agriculture and Stock and the development of veterinary science. With the spectacular success of the control of prickly pear and the opening up of new grazing lands by discovery of trace element deficiencies, the future role of scientific research in pastoral industry was assured, and a fourth group of resource managers, interested both in maintenance and improvement of the intensity of production, was added.

Appraising the Range: The Resource Base

The secret of the rapidly growing prosperity of Bathurst is, that the brown pasture which appears to the stranger's eye so wretched, is excellent for sheep-grazing.
(Charles Darwin, 1836)

Of course selection in this district is more affected by the climate than by the quality of the soil. In very good seasons it is practically impossible to overstock, while on the same country on other occasions you could not, to use an Australian phrase, "feed a bandicoot". The seasons are very variable.
(C. Francis, Land Commissioner, Evidence to Queensland Royal Commission on Land Settlement, 1897. Question 753.)

KEY TO *Fig. 12.5*
A. The pastoral resources.
KEY
1. Perennial surface water available.
2. Intermittent surface water available.
3. No surface water.
4. Underground water available.
5. Underground water either absent or too brackish for livestock.
6. Best perennial and annual grasses (capacity 0.4–0.8 ha per sheep).
7. Second quality grazing (capacity 2–4 ha per sheep).
8. Poor quality grazing (capacity over 8 ha per sheep and highly variable according to season).
9. Rare grazing resources, isolated pockets of grasses and shrubs amid dense woodlands.
10. No grazing resources except for short-lived annual herbs and grasses after rains.

B. Pest invasions.
KEY
1. Diffusion of cattle ticks.
2. Southern boundary of tick enzootic area.
3. Diffusion of rabbits.
4. Northern boundary of established colonies of rabbits.

Source: *Atlas of Australian Resources*; and Alexander and Williams, 1973.

The broad patterns of the forage and water resources of the continent are outlined on Fig. 12.5. Between the fringes of the eastern and northern coasts where permanent surface water occurred, and the interior deserts where surface water was rare, temporary, and usually too brackish for even stock use, was a transition zone, where, depending upon the seasonal rains, some surface water might be present for some part of the time. A large proportion of this transition zone, however, was underlain by basins of subterranean water including artesian supplies, the potable areas of which are indicated on the map.

The best-watered grazing areas were those immediately inland from the Blue Mountains, Port Phillip Bay and Gulf St Vincent where perennial and annual grasses of the woodland ecosystem might graze a sheep on 0.5–1 ha of range. The northern Mitchell Grass plains were of second quality and for the remainder the overall quality was poor, only varied by local pockets of higher grazing capacities, often only available for a few months of the year.

In terms of the productivity offered by the unimproved range there was in addition a latitudinal gradient for sheep production, with decreasing average fleece weights and reduced survival rate for lambs from south to north, reflecting increasing heat and water stress on the animals closer to the equator and decreasing stock carrying capacities (Fig. 12.6).

The static patterns of Fig. 12.5 hide the variation of grazing resources over time. From 1830 to the 1970s it is doubtful whether any one sequence of two years has ever offered the same range conditions as any other. Gentilli suggested that in 'southeastern Australia the rainfall, which had been slowly and very irregularly increasing during the second half of the last century [when pastoral expansion was at its fastest rate, Fig. 12.4], began a period of decline from about 1890 ... In the semi-arid [extensive pastoral] belt this decline proved critical and in some areas actually disastrous' (Gentilli, 1971, p. 201). In detail he goes on to suggest that comparing averages for 1881–1910 with 1911–40:

> a strip of country west of Balranald and Bourke, New South Wales, which, on the average, had been semi-arid for 30 years, through the dessication of the following 30 years, became arid, a change which because of its prolonged duration must have had a profound effect on plant and animal life.
>
> (Gentilli, 1971, pp. 205–6)

This area included the Western Division of New South Wales and central Queensland where the pressure to intensify pastoral settlement was particularly acute in the mid-twentieth century. These long-term trends, however, were often hidden by sharp variations from one season to the next as Commissioner Francis had recognized by 1897.

For the pastoralists, knowledge of the quality of grazing resources came only from experience, often dearly bought. The durability and palatability of pastures and the longevity of waterholes was information only slowly acquired and, in a situation where knowledge was potential profit, not widely broadcast. There were, however, times—of crisis—when the environmental learning process was rapidly speeded up—as in drought or flood. In drought the value of the saltbushes as against the perennial and annual grasses and herbs, and the value of browse such as mulga (*Acacia aneura*) and kurrajong (*Brachychiton populneum*) was quickly recognized: in flood, the vulnerability of earth roads, the treacherous clays of the alluvial frontages and the value of higher ground as flood refuges for livestock was plain for all to see. Such major crises of drought hit the pastoralists of South Australia in 1865, New South Wales and southwest Queensland in 1895–1901 and the Northern Territory in 1958–65. A similar revaluation was produced by the River Darling flood of 1890. In each case, the disturbance of prior concepts of the grazing resources resulted in the instigation of official enquiries into the state of the pastoral industry and its resource base, which led to significant innovations in official land settlement policies and resultant pastoral land settlement.

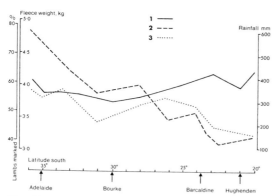

Fig. 12.6 The latitudinal gradient of pastoral productivity.
KEY
1. Average percentage of lambs marked.
2. Average fleece weights.
3. Average annual rainfall.
Source: Barnard, 1962.

Managing the Range: Technology on the Station

960 kilometres of 5 and 6 wire fence
264 kilometres of rabbit proof netting
12 artesian bores
9 sets of drafting yards
39 tanks and dams
Home station and outbuildings

3 woolsheds
2 woolscourers
2 wool rooms
Bundaleer Station and outbuildings
No. 1 outstation
Farm of 120 hectares, huts and hay sheds
16 boundary riders' huts
256 kilometres of (artesian water) bore drains
164 kilometres of telephone wires.

(Inventory of 'improvements' on Thurrulgoonia Station (3,297 km²) in October 1901, Department of Lands File, Brisbane)

Learning about the range and the need for profits forced modification not only of ideas but also technologies. Innovations began on, and were until the 1860s confined to, the pastoral stations. Local construction materials and skills were only being replaced by imported items and labour in the 1870s and 1880s, when innovations became too complex and specialized for the station to provide its own. From the late 1870s onwards, however, with the inputs of external capital rapidly increasing, the rate of innovations speeded up and external supplies and labour were widely introduced. The details deserve attention.

In terms of livestock management, cattle were generally cheaper to operate than sheep since they did not need daily herding whereas, until the 1860s, the general opinion was that sheep did. The relatively high cost of shepherding together with the growing realization that perhaps it was not necessary led to a change to paddocking of sheep, i.e. the fencing of the range and abandonment of daily shepherding. The process was slow and uneven in time and space, assisted by the progressive destruction of the main natural enemies of the sheep—the dingoes and the Aborigines, the growing awareness of the contagious spread of diseases such as scab, legal squabbles over territory and the official attempts to settle smallholders on the range.

In the early 1870s the main areas of fenced properties were the western districts of Victoria, the Riverina and southeastern South Australia (Barnard, 1962). The next twenty years were to see the widespread construction of boundary fences, which were often subsequently netted to be rabbit-proofed, and finally the beginnings of subdivisional 'paddock' fences. Often both original 'nomadic' shepherding and paddocking were carried on at the same time on the same property, until the whole area was subdivided. The capital required for subdivision was considerable, £29 16s. 7d. per kilometre of fence in the case of the Australian Agricultural Company's 'Warrah' Station in 1875 (Robertson, 1964). In this case the first fencing had been of the cattle run, to prevent cattle-stealing, but the main expenditure was for internal sheep paddocks of 1,760 to 2,850 ha in size. The result here was instead of 1,000 sheep needing a shepherd, 3,000 to 4,000 sheep

could be supervised by a 'boundary rider'.

Most of the sheep properties by 1900 had boundary fences and by the 1970s had adequate subdivisional fencing (Fig. 12.7), but in the case of the cattle properties as we have seen, there is still much to be done. It was claimed as in the 1960s for example that open range conditions still applied on nine out of ten cattle properties in the Northern Territory (Kelly, 1966). The process of innovation here is still at work.

Innovation even extended to the shepherds' faithful companions. The long-haired British sheep and cattle dogs found the hot summers, semi-wild livestock, spiky grass awnlets and burrs of the *Bassia* species on the plains difficult working conditions. As a result, smooth-haired Scotch collies were crossed in the 1870s with dingo-collie crosses to give 'Kelpie'—whose offspring ('kelpies') won the first sheep-dog trial in Australia and have become the standard Australian sheep dog. For cattle dogs a similar sequence, in this case Scottish 'merle' dogs crossed with dingoes, gave a larger version of the kelpies for the cattle stations (Jose and Carter, 1925).

Livestock management techniques changed slowly. The timing of shearing was varied in the northern ranges when spring shearing exposed sheep to high summer temperatures without their insulating fleece and lambing similarly was timed for autumn to prevent losses in high summer temperatures. Turn-off from the cattle stations coincided in the north with the winter dry season when droving was not prevented by the summer wet season. Where breeding was controlled, the aim usually was one lambing or calving per year, but after droughts the need to replace dead livestock encouraged multiple pregnancies.

For the period from the 1860s to the 1890s with the expansion of sheep-rearing into the far interior, the long haul to the coast forced pastoralists to consider washing their fleeces to save weight and thus transport costs. The washpools, both natural waterholes and steam-heated tanks with water spouts, became a further cause for expenditure and experiment until cheaper rail transport reduced the concern for the weight of the bales (Barnard, 1962). With the rail networks established by the turn of the century, most wool reverted to export 'in the grease'.

While the main feature of the extensive system of pastoral land use has always been the concentration upon native pastures, there were attempts to improve the actual carrying capacities both by manipulation of the flora and improvement of water supplies.

From the 1820s there was evidence of the burning of old pastures to encourage new growth. In the tropical north it was particularly useful in removing the rank dried summer grasses and old spinifex of the open range and encouraging new more palatable growth for the livestock. Once fencing took place,

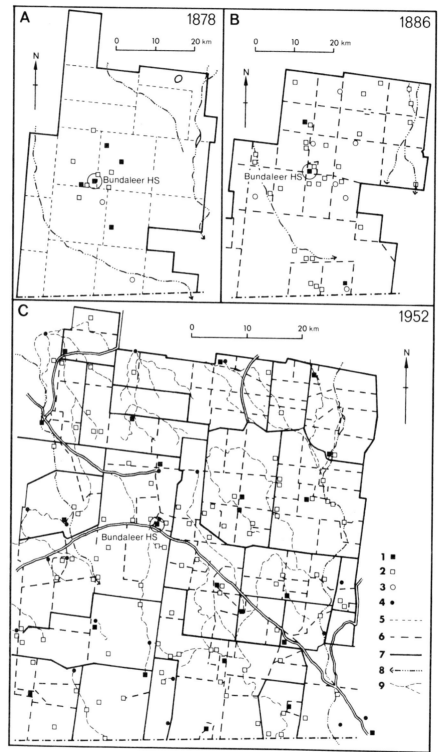

Fig. 12.7 Patterns of pastoral settlement, Bundaleer (Queensland) 1878–1952.

KEY TO *Fig. 12.7*

1. Stockmen's hut (outstations) in 1878 and 1886; homesteads of the various separate pastoral properties in 1952. The Bundaleer homestead is circled in each map.
2. Tanks, excavations to hold surface water runoff.
3. Wells, windlass or horse whim, 1878 and 1886. A dry lake and waterhole were also indicated in the northeast corner of the 1878 map.
4. Artesian and sub-artesian bores, 1952 map only.
5. Run boundaries (not fenced) in 1878 only.

6. Fence lines, 1886 and 1952 only.
7. Outer boundary of pastoral properties. In 1878 Bundaleer was a single unit, in 1886 part of a larger station Thurrulgoonia, and the area in 1952 comprised several grazing properties as indicated.
8. Natural watercourses, seasonally dry.
9. Bore drains carrying surplus water from the borehead downslope (to the south and southeast).

The main tracks are indicated in 1952.

These three maps represent the transformation of the open range system of pastoral use (1878), through the preliminary paddocking (1886) to the patterns of closer settlement properties relying upon underground water supplies (1952).

Source: Business Archives of Australian National University and Queensland Lands Department records.

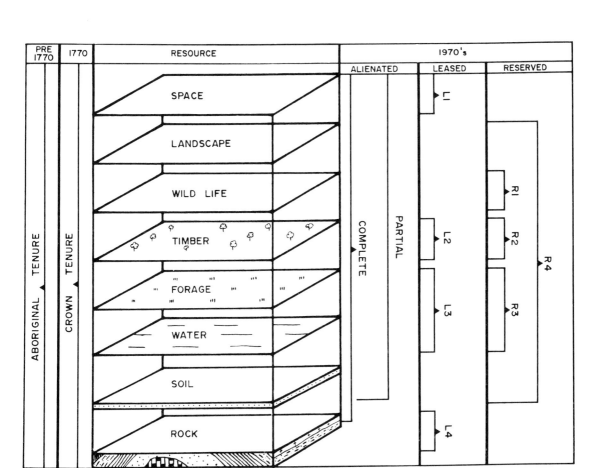

Fig. 12.8 The framework of Australian resource tenures. The range of resources covered by Aboriginal tenures, the claims of the British Crown and the contemporary tenures by type are indicated. Some alienated tenures initially included mineral rights but most no longer do so. Leasehold tenures include: L1-military leases; L2-timber licences; L3-pastoral leases; L4-mineral and mining leases. Reserves include: R1-fauna protection; R2-forest reserves; R3-travelling stock routes; R4-national parks. *Source*: Heathcote, 1969b.

however, burning became a hazard which could destroy valuable improvements and was generally discouraged.

Grasses could also be encouraged by the killing of competing tree growth in woodland ecosystems and thousands of acres of trees were ringbarked (at a cost of between 3*d.* and 6*d.* per acre) at the turn of the century by gangs of out-of-work Chinese gold miners. By the 1930s, however, costs had increased more than ten times and the benefits were being questioned.

Similar gangs of axemen cut down edible browse in the droughts of the 1890s to feed starving livestock in otherwise bare paddocks. Costs here, however, were much higher than ringbarking and this was only an emergency and often one-time measure, since the scrub might not survive. Mechanization helped cut some costs. Homemade mobile 'scrub bashers' towed by tractors helped, but as late as the 1950s one man and his axe were claimed to be still sufficient to keep 700–800 sheep alive in a thick mulga scrub at approximately 2*d.* per sheep per week! By comparison with hay and lucerne (*c.* 21*d.* per sheep week) it was still the cheapest drought feeding method, as long as the scrub lasted.

Attempts to replace native grasses by exotics have been generally confined to the humid south and east although the scientific attempts to find alternative tropical grasses have had some successes since the 1950s with Buffel grasses (*Cenchrus* spp.)—an accidental introduction, and Townsville Stylo (*Stylosanthes humilis*)—a deliberate import. Again, however, these have been limited to the higher-rainfall intensively managed properties and are not cultivated on the extensive properties although natural colonies exist.

The more significant long-term improvements were in the provision of increased water supplies. Initially water storage was improved by earth dams across creeks, then low-lying areas were excavated to provide storage for run-on waters as tanks, and more recently in the 1950s systems such as 'Keyline' have attempted to harvest and use surface runoff in a more efficient manner by channelling it in contoured banks to storage areas, prior to controlled flood irrigation (Yeomans, 1958). Although these were effective measures they represented only the storage of surface runoff, which was itself uncertain and limited. Often tanks stood empty from one year to the next for lack of local rainfall. Only when this improved storage was allied with improved supply were the water needs of livestock on the plains effectively met.

Wells had been dug from initial settlement in 1788; on the plains they became much more significant and locally often the only supply of available water. Initially hand dug at almost £3 per foot the major technological breakthrough came in the 1880s with the application of drilling techniques developed in the search for oil in the U.S.A. Initially percussion drills and then rotary drills were able to tap the waters of the Great Artesian Basin which had been discovered by accident in 1879 close to the Darling River. With these drills, water 2,000–3,000 feet below the surface became available to the pastoralists. At £2 per foot in 1892 the cost was still considerable, and even when halved by 1900 it was not an innovation open to everyone. But as *artesian* water there was the added incentive that no lifting mechanism was necessary. Indeed, had the water not been artesian it is doubtful if it would have been half as valuable to the pastoralists. Certainly by comparison with the laborious windlasses of the first wells and the later horse-powered 'whims' or 'gins' winding up 60-gallon leather buckets, it is small wonder that the sight of one of these artesian bores, flowing 1–2 million gallons of often hot and brackish but useful water, 24 hours a day without diminution of flow, was ranked as one of the wonders of the continent, if not the world, in the 1880s and 1890s. Their photographs adorned most of the Queensland and New South Wales exhibits at colonial and international exhibitions thereafter. Where supplies were not artesian, wind pumps solved the lifting problem. Patents for steel wind pumps in the U.S.A. date from 1883 although the first patent was in 1854, but in Australia their adoption seems to have been delayed until the turn of the century.

Finally, other improvements of productivity came from the improved quality of livestock. The Merino was eminently capable of survival on the semi-arid grazing of the interior but the yield per beast, whether mutton or wool, was low. Experiments with crossing British and Merino stocks, particularly in the Riverina in the 1860s, produced the Peppin medium-woolled line which became the dominant type in New South Wales and Queensland, with a heavier South Australian coarser-woolled sheep in that State and later in Western Australia. Briefly, in the 1880s to *c.* 1910, the American Vermont wrinkled strain of Merino was favoured for the added fleece weight but it was particularly susceptible to blowfly attack on the soiled folds of the breech and this, combined with more expensive shearing costs militated against its long-term acceptance.

Despite improved understanding of genetics of sheep husbandry, the increases of fleece yields have tapered off over the last two to three decades and the closed nature of many studs means that no new increase in yields can be expected from within the industry without new blood. Further it would be satisfying to be able to show that the range of environments used by sheep has been coped with by the evolution of regional strains of the Merino stock. In fact, however, it is impossible to do so. Research by the CSIRO showed in 1963 that 'as far as clean wool weight per head was concerned, there was very little evidence of any particular adaptation of one strain to one environment' (Anon., 1963). Part of the problem was the variability of environmental conditions. The same report commented, 'the climate and other factors are so variable at each location that each year at a location acts as a different environment'.

Not until the 1950s, despite some introductions as early as the 1840s, were Indian Zebu cattle (*Bos indicus*) types successfully introduced into tropical Australia. The disease resistance and heat tolerance of the Zebu breeds has been combined with the meat-producing ability and quiet temperament of the British breeds. The resulting crosses, Santa Gertrudis via the U.S.A. (Shorthorn × Brahman), Braford ($\frac{3}{8}$ Brahman × $\frac{5}{8}$ Hereford), Brangus ($\frac{3}{8}$ Brahman × $\frac{5}{8}$ Angus) and Droughtmaster (Brahman × Shorthorn with some Hereford) are currently being successfully tested and their future in the north seems assured even on the open range (Alexander and Williams, 1973).

Although the traditional livestock were cattle and sheep there have been attempts to introduce alternative herbivores as commercial livestock. Alpacas and vicuna crosses were imported from South America in the late 1850s and early 1860s with the intention of breeding for hair production. Management difficulties, a scab outbreak, drought, and acclimatization problems seem to have decimated the flocks and interest soon evaporated. Camels were imported in the 1860s to South Australia as transport animals, serviced the overland telegraph construction in the 1870s, and provided a commercial freight service in remote areas well into the twentieth century. In 1925 the claim was made that they were still widely used in the interior by private carriers and government departments as freight and riding animals. 'An offender on horseback has no chance against a constable on a dromedary' (Jose and Carter, 1925, p. 232). Donkeys and goats were introduced in the latter half of the nineteenth century as transport and food supply respectively, often being associated with remote mining settlements, but they were not commercially exploited to the same degree and their importance to the pastoral industry in the 1970s stems rather from the adverse grazing impact of the large number of feral animals descended from the original introductions.

Finally, despite the other innovations, mechanization of production technology has been by comparison with agriculture relatively slight. Mechanical shearing replaced hand shears generally from the 1890s, wool packing became more efficient, and since the 1960s the motor cycle has complemented and often replaced the horse as the pastoralists' personal transport on stations. For the most significant application of mechanical power however we must look beyond the station's boundary fence.

Managing the Range: Technology beyond the Station

With two year's clip on hand, impassable roads, labour at £2 per week, and the Sydney Jews and Philistines charging 12 and 15 per cent for money, a man required a very strong back to survive such a crucial test.
(E. K. V., 'The Ward River 1861–63', *Brisbane Courier*, 19 August 1885)

Other things being equal, the expansion of pastoral land use into the continental interior could only succeed if transport and communication costs (in time and money) could be reduced. For cattle *en route* to the abbatoir there was in theory no problem—they carried themselves. Droving livestock was and has always remained the cheapest (if slowest) per unit distance method of moving livestock. Even in 1968 droving costs in Queensland were 1.3–2.5 cents per tonne kilometre as opposed to 1.3–4.7 cents for rail and 3.4–6.0 cents for road transport (Moulden and Jenkins, 1968). However, droving was at the mercy of the wet seasons, and there were losses of condition and even of stock along the way. In 1893 James Tyson the pastoral millionaire claimed his cattle regularly lost 135 kg per beast on the 128 km walk into Bourke from his Tinnenburra property.

For wool, however, overland freight charges were normally high and 5 to 9 times as high in drought when feed and water for the draught animals was scarce. The opening of navigation on the Murray-Darling river systems in the late 1850s allowed successful occupation of both the river frontages and south-western Queensland some twenty to thirty years before the arrival of the railways would have allowed it. By comparison with steamboat charges the railways were more expensive but guaranteed a *regular* service irrespective of seasonal conditions or river levels, and their charges (often deliberately tapered over distance to compete with other State systems) were as low as a tenth of the costs of the traditional dray freights.

The concern for inland transport costs has continued into the twentieth century. Almost a century of intermittent agitation by pastoralists and politicians for the extension of State and Commonwealth railways across the northern half of the continent culminated in the all-weather Beef Roads programme of the 1950s and '60s, and technological innovations such as hovercraft are still being considered (Feiger, 1970).

Communication of goods was basic, but communication of information was equally important. Without the benefit of the network of telegraph wires which were looped over the continent from the 1850s onwards and the international links from 1872 onwards, the forwarding of produce to markets up to 17,000 kilometres away would have been an extremely hazardous operation. Along the copper wires, news of prices and freight arrivals and departures passed news of lambing and calving numbers and the latest rainfalls and managers' reports. In turn these were supplemented by telephone and radio links in the twentieth century, each binding together an international system of supply and demand.

Between the supply and demand, however, grew up a sophisticated marketing system which conveyed the fleeces and carcasses from the stations to the auction rooms (Barnard, 1958). Until the last quarter of the nineteenth century London was the main auction centre. With the rapid expansion of production of wool in the 1880s, however, the local agencies set up auctions at Sydney and Melbourne and by the 1920s further centres were established in the other State capitals and larger regional centres such as Newcastle and Geelong. In the twentieth century the buyers have been forced to come to Australia to compete and the traditional British and European agents have been joined by American and Japanese interests.

Local entrepreneurs have found that diversification from purely wool broking to a complete range of services for the pastoralists, from stock and station selling agencies to merchandizing of station supplies and equipment, has spread their profit base, and names such as Dalgety's, Elder Smith and Goldsbrough Mort have become synonyms for pastoral activities of all kinds.

The Role of Government: Land Settlement Policies

The principle of leasehold was adopted and a system of tenures devised to ensure that there would always be a steady flow of land back into the hands of the Crown, and without cost to it, to meet the progressive needs of new settlement, until that far off time when all the land would have been put to intense agricultural use.

(Report of Royal Commission on Pastoral Land Settlement (Queensland), 1952, p. 178)

By 1829 legal title to the whole of the continent had been claimed by the British Crown and the process of transfer of ownership from the Aboriginal inhabitants to the invading settlers, already begun in the southeast, was to be extended over the whole area. Although the full story of that process is still hidden in the public archives, private manuscripts and personal reminiscences of surviving pioneer settlers and administrators, enough has been published so far to enable some broad generalizations to be made on the common themes which run through the sequence of Imperial, Colonial, State and Commonwealth policies on land settlement (Burroughs, 1967; Buxton, 1967; Glynn, 1967; Heathcote, 1965 and 1974; Jeans, 1972; King, 1957; Perry, 1963; Powell, 1970; Roberts, 1968).

The fundamental aim of government was to supervise the disposal of title to the newly-acquired Crown lands to the prospective settlers by sale for cash at auction from 1831 onwards and on credit from the 1860s

onwards. Thus alienated, the process of development of the latent resources of the land was then to be left to the new owners on a *laissez-faire* basis. As part of that process of development, pastoral land use was generally seen as the pioneer method of land settlement. As Governor Gipps of New South Wales wrote to the Secretary of State for the Colonies, 28 September 1840, the pastoralists 'are the real discoverers of the country, and they may be said to be in Australia (what the backwoodsmen are in America) the pioneers of civilization'. Yet, as pioneers they were expected to be superseded in time and by a new stage of more intensive land settlement—by implication sheep walks had to give way to farmlands. 'Do you think we shall ever make a nation with sheep-walks?' appealed James Farrell, New South Wales Secretary for Lands, introducing legislation to subdivide the large pastoral properties into smaller grazing blocks on 7 November 1883. 'I admit that sheep-walks are all very well; but they ought to give way to population, and those who occupy them must recede and give way when the land is required for *bona fide* occupation.' From his vantage point in 1959 the experienced land administrator William L. Payne, reporting on Progressive Land Settlement in Queensland, identified the role which the pastoralists had played in the history of not only his own State but Australia in general:

The early squatters or pastoralists performed a valuable service to Queensland. They invested their capital in a speculative enterprise. If successful, the colony shared in their success. Many retired ruined from the fray. When they failed they at least provided valuable lessons for those who followed. Their function was to pave the way and demonstrate the potentialities of the country. Other settlers followed in their wake.

Governments therefore were prepared to encourage pastoral land use but as a temporary and pioneer expedient—part of the sequence which culminated in intensive agricultural land use on small-holdings by 'yeoman farmers'—the Australian equivalents of the American homesteaders whose legislation was a major influence on Australian land settlement policies from the 1860s onwards.

Yet by the 1970s the Crown was still the owner of 9 out of every 10 hectares in Australia; on 2 directly as owner of the lands still unoccupied (where no settlement at all had been attempted or if attempted had been unsuccessful); on 1.5 as owner of the reserves for public and Aboriginal use, and on 5.5 as landlord for the leaseholds of the extensive pastoral stations (Fig. 12.2). The failure to even occupy the whole area of the continent by pastoral land use, let alone intensify settlement reflects the need to compromise original land settlement policies in the face of four major environmental stresses facing the pastoralists.

Those challenges may be identified as low productivity per unit area, competing users of the resources, the variability of resources over space and time, and the specific occurrences of catastrophic variations in the resource base—the natural disasters (Heathcote, 1969a and 1974).

THE CHALLENGE OF LOW UNIT AREA PRODUCTIVITY
From 1831 the major method of transfer of title in land was proposed to be sales at auction with a minimum reserve price instead of the prior system of free grants in return for imported capital, or settlers, or services rendered. Where natural grazing capacities were about one sheep per hectare the setting of a minimum price of 12.5 shillings per hectare in 1831, followed by the increase to 30 shillings in 1839 and £2.5 per hectare in 1841, made the cost of land purchase uneconomic for most prospective pastoralists and the illegal occupation or squatting beyond the limits of settlement continued. Faced by this refusal to purchase at the minimum price, Governor Bourke drew on his experience at the Cape of Good Hope to legalize a pastoral occupation he could not prevent, by offering Depasturing Licences for an unlimited area at £10 per year. In effect this gave a right to graze Crown land until the land could be disposed of by auction sale. The pastoralists' refusal to buy the whole sandwich of land resources (Fig. 12.8) had been met by the offer of the right to use a portion of that sandwich in return for an annual rent. The concept of a leasehold tenure, i.e. the hiring from the Crown of a specific item of the land for a limited period of time, had come to be identified with extensive pastoral land use; by the Imperial Waste Lands Act of 1846, enforced locally by the Orders-in-Council of 1847, it was finally established. The basic division between the closest lands, to be sold for agriculture, and the remoter lands, to be leased for grazing, had been identified and was to persist despite repeated attempts to modify it, during the next century of land settlement (Table 12.4 and Fig. 12.1). In effect this was also a recognition of the need for different tenures between different environments, for the leaseholds became the tenures of the arid interior and the alienated lands the tenure of the humid coastlands. Interestingly, leases also came to be used on the alpine summer pastures of southeastern New South Wales, where 'snow leases' were granted for areas where grazing was restricted by temperature rather than moisture deficiencies (Hancock, 1972, pp. 140–3).

Attempts to intensify pastoral settlement in the interior by subdivision of the large leaseholds in eastern Australia for closer settlement from the 1880s onwards appear to have been at most only half as successful as intended. Indeed the process of intensification has been hindered by an opposite tendency towards the enlargement of individual holdings and the consequent reduction of rural population densities. This has resulted from apparent economies of scale in pastoral production, and from officialdom being forced to allow the enlargement of official 'living area' properties, as rising living standards and declining stock carrying capacities made the earlier (and smaller) areas no longer sufficient to support a family.

THE CHALLENGE OF COMPETING USERS
Imported livestock faced competition from indigenous herbivores as well as imported game animals and were subject to attack by dingoes, birds of prey and the Aboriginal population. Legislation requiring landholders to control or eradicate 'vermin' (arbitrarily and variously defined as ranging from imported rabbits to indigenous eagle hawks) began in the mid-nineteenth century and still applies in all States and Commonwealth territories. The fencing out of competitors, initially the rabbit but later also the dingo, emu and kangaroo, began officially in the interior in the 1880s with each State attempting to protect itself from its neighbour's vermin. Fences were still being built in the 1950s and some are still officially maintained (Fig. 12.1). The private slaughter of competing indigenous herbivores, especially kangaroos, has been a feature of pastoral land use since first settlement and official controls upon this slaughter have been partially effective only within the last decade (Marshall, 1966).

Acquisition of Aboriginal lands for pastoral use usually meant the ejection or killing of the Aborigines. Ejection, from the mid-nineteenth century onwards, tended to be either to small 'urban' reserves or to large remote rural areas thought to be useless for pastoral purposes, such as central Australia or Arnhem Land (Fig. 12.2 and Rowley, 1972).

In South Australia and Northern Territory (which prior to 1911 was under South Australian administration) however, Aboriginal hunting rights have been preserved in the current pastoral leases. Here a complementary form of resource use has been legally possible.

THE CHALLENGE OF RESOURCE VARIABILITY
To meet the challenge of grazing resources which were limited over space and variable in time, the initial and continuing official reaction was to preserve the scarcest resources for general use. Public reserves were set up around strategic waterholes and spaced out along river frontages from the 1840s, and from the 1880s onwards most State governments were drilling, and preserving for public use, bores to tap the artesian basins. Land grants to successful explorers and special development leases encouraged private well-sinking and scrub clearance for pasture improvement. Large

leases, initially seen as but a passing phase of pioneer settlement, came to be recognized as long-term if not permanent characteristics of interior pastoral operations, necessary to increase the chances of catching random rainfalls and spatially diverse fodder responses and to provide sufficient good-year surpluses to carry the pastoralists over the adverse seasons which would surely come.

Although pastoral leases normally allowed use of timber only for domestic fuel and building or fencing needs, recognition of edible browse has resulted in specific in-drought provision for tree-lopping or scrub-pushing for additional emergency fodder. The early need to move livestock to market or agistment (rented pastures) on the hoof was met by the creation of travelling stock routes (akin to the British drove roads and Spanish 'Mesta' roads of the seventeenth and eighteenth centuries). Several hundred kilometres long and up to 2 kilometres wide, such reserves had their own system of rules and regulations as to the speed and number of stock movements.

When in the 1890s evidence began to accumulate of the deterioration of initial range carrying capacities through overgrazing and colonization of the range by relatively inedible or toxic plants, various official measures were attempted. Noxious Weed Boards and Pasture Protection Boards levied local pastoralists to pay for official destruction of the invaders or required landholders under penalty to control them themselves. In some cases, where the deterioration of stock carrying capacities was seen as irreversible on holdings officially limited in size to economic living areas, the official response was to enlarge the maximum size to enable the requisite flock or herd size to be maintained. This, as mentioned previously, was a reversal of the basic aim of land settlement intensification over time.

A further reversal of initial developmental settlement policies occurred in response to the effects of overgrazing, particularly the evidence of soil erosion recognized by the turn of the century in eastern Australia. In the pioneer stage of pastoral settlement officialdom was concerned to enforce actual occupation of the range and set minimum stocking rates for all leases. The increasing evidence of the impact of overgrazing upon the range, however, has resulted in official attempts to control also the maximum stocking rates for the leases. From the initial pressure to get stock onto the range, official policies now attempt to control the intensity of the stocking of the range.

THE CHALLENGE OF NATURAL CATASTROPHES
Two types of catastrophic events affected pastoral use on the plains. First was the scourge of animal diseases and second were the extremes of flood and drought. The imported livestock brought their own parasites and virus diseases with them and periodic outbreaks caused official concern and eventual official action. Diseases such as footrot, scab, and fluke came in with the sheep; anthrax, pleuropneumonia and cattle tick with cattle. Most were eventually controlled by a combination of private and officially sponsored scientific research, together with official controls on animal movements within the continent and strict quarantine on imported stock, particularly from 1908 onwards under Commonwealth supervision (Alexander and Williams, 1973). Local catastrophes, however, could be specific in time and place. Thus the late 1920s saw massive Western Australian sheep deaths from botulism—caught from eating rabbit carcasses during the long dry summer feed shortages. 'Coast disease' from trace element deficiencies debarred pastoral activities from parts of South and Western Australia until the CSIRO discoveries of the late 1930s.

While floods along the Murray-Darling river systems brought considerable local disruption to the pastoral industry, the main climatic catastrophe facing the pastoralists has been drought, and official policies have attempted to provide relief by various methods (Heathcote, 1969a). One method initiated in South Australia in the 1860s and adopted widely thereafter was the remission of rents until the drought ended; another was the extension of the term of lease to allow the drought losses to be recouped by profits in the good seasons which were assumed to follow. In addition, subsidies on the evacuation of starving stock or restocking of abandoned ranges have been offered during and immediately after the drought. Most recently, however, there has been an innovation in the Commonwealth's 'drought bonds' (tax-free interest-bearing deposits redeemable in officially designated drought periods) offered first in 1969. The implication here is that the onus is now on the pastoralists to protect themselves by official insurance.

The pastoral occupation of the interior range therefore reflected not only modification of traditional technologies and skills amongst the pastoralists themselves, but required changes in official attitudes and land settlement policies to provide a legal framework within which pastoral land use could survive.

The Environmental Impact of Pastoral Land Use

I knew the West Darling country . . . in its aboriginal state. There is no doubt in my mind that the carrying capacity of the country was greatly overestimated by the early settlers. In its virgin state, with the saltbush and other edible bushes in their prime, there was hardly a limit, except as regards water, in the opinion of the settlers then as to what the country could carry, and in many cases it was stocked accordingly, but they forgot in doing this that they were eating the haystack, and there was soon no crop growing to build another. Then the rabbits came along.

> (J. H. Boothby, station inspector for Dalgety and Co., Evidence to Royal Commission to Inquire into the Condition of the Crown Tenants, N.S.W., 1901)

The impact of pastoral land use upon the environment was, and still is, disputed. The controversy, between optimists and pessimists, dates back to at least the 1870s:

> The advocates of improvement ... stressed that the patter of tiny hooves consolidated the soil, improved the run-off and filled the reservoirs. The pessimists agreed, but added riders that the hooves were cleft; thus, while the soil was consolidated it formed hardpan, improved run-off meant greater soil erosion and the reservoirs were indeed filled, but with silt.
>
> (Heathcote, 1965, p. 26)

The basic problem was the documentation of the impact upon conditions which were recognized to be highly variable from season to season and from 'groups of years of drought and groups of years of above average rainfall' (Holland and Moore, 1962, p. 28). Further, the scientists still complain that their techniques for measurement of current range conditions are inadequate (Cunningham *et al.*, 1974) so any histori-cal evidence, based as it generally is upon personal opinions and stock numbers (which reflect much more than range condition) must be even more suspect.

Macro-Environmental Impacts

At the continental level, and admitting the questionable nature of the sources, Table 12.5 suggests the contrast of impacts between the extensive and intensive types of pastoral land use. At this level the impact on the extensive stations appears to be minimal.

To obtain some idea of the regional impact, however, we have some evidence from both the arid and the humid end of the grazing spectrum. A comprehensive survey of the impact of grazing in the arid and semi-arid ranges of central Australia was undertaken in 1965–7 by the Soil Conservation Service of New South Wales at the request of the Northern Territory Administration (Condon, Newman and Cunningham, 1969). After almost continuous drought for nine years, cattle numbers had fallen from a peak of 360,000 in 1958 to *c.* 80,000 in 1965 and the authorities became concerned about increasing evidence of soil erosion, including massive dust storms around Alice Springs, and the future of the pastoral industry in the Centre. The survey provided an assessment of the extent of environmental impact of some one hundred years of stock

Table 12.5 General Environmental Impact on Pastoral Properties by 1970s

Properties	Percentage of continent	Environmental impact by percentage of area				
		No impact	Selective impact	Complete replacement of original vegetation		
				New biotic cover		Non-biotic cover
				Similar	Different	
		(a)	(a)	(b)	(c)	(d)
Extensive pastoral stations	57.4	< 2?	98	0	0	Trace
Intensive pastoral grazing farms	3.3	3	21	70	6	Trace

Notes: (a) Selective timber removal and killing, grazing of native pastures.
(b) Replacement of native by exotic pastures.
(c) Replacement of woods or pastures by exotic pastures or crops.
(d) Built-up areas and roads.

Sources: Alexander and Williams, 1973 and topographic maps.

Table 12.6   The Impact of Grazing in Central Australia by 1965–7

Pasture land type	(a) Total area ('000 sq. mile)	(b) Watered area		(c) Carrying capacity (cattle/sq. mile watered)		(d) Pasture condition (% of watered area by class)					
		Area ('000 sq. mile)	% total	Normal	Drought	Very poor	Poor	Medi-ocre	Fair	Good	Very good
Mitchell Grass	.15	.13	89	18.3	1.1	—	—	—	11.9	31.1	57.0
Shortgrass-forbs (alluvial plains)	5.75	4.65	81	11.5	2.0	—	13.6	20.4	25.3	34.7	6.0
Shortgrass-forbs (undulating)	21.2	14.7	69	11.4	2.8	0.5	5.8	17.2	32.8	42.7	1.0
Saltbush-bluebush	3.2	2.6	81	3.5	0.6	7.4	39.5	42.0	11.1	—	—
Hills and lowlands	12.6	7.9	63	5.0	1.3	1.1	13.0	25.7	53.0	7.2	—
Sandplains and dunes (spinifex)	49.2	21.7	44	4.0	0.9	—	—	4.5	15.6	79.1	0.8
Salt lakes	1.1	.48	45	2.0	0.7	—	—	4.6	81.5	13.9	—
Mountains and hills (useful)	7.0	4.0	56	2.2	0.6	—	20.7	1.4	71.1	6.7	0.1
Mountains and hills (useless)	6.2	2.4	40	nil	nil	—————————— not classified ——————————					
Totals	100.2	56.0	56	5.3	1.5	0.6	7.7	13.6	30.5	46.3	1.3

Notes: The original non-metric measurements have been retained in this table.

(a) Area surveyed September 1965 to April 1967.

(b) Within 5 miles of watering point for cattle, within 3 miles for sheep, whichever was run on property.

(c) Estimated densities of cattle (or 8 sheep per beast) per square mile under normal season and optimal rate after 3 years of drought.

(d) Estimated condition by percentage of bare surface showing: Very poor = 70–90% bare ground; Poor = 60–70%; Mediocre = 50–60%; Fair = 30–50%; Good = 10–30%; Very good = Less 10% bare ground.

Source: Condon, Newman and Cunningham, 1969.

grazing—an impact exacerbated by its timing at the end of a long period of drought when grazing pressure may be considered to have been at its peak. The results of this survey are indicated in Table 12.6.

For the area as a whole, a surprisingly high proportion (some 48 per cent) was in good condition or better and less than a quarter (22 per cent) was in 'mediocre' to 'very poor' condition. Further, this impact was on the area accessible to watering points and represented only just over half (56 per cent) of the total area. In effect on the remaining 44 per cent of the area, beyond the 3–5 miles access from watering points, the impact of grazing must have been very slight indeed.

Within the variety of pasture types, however, there was considerable variation of impact. Again, rather surprisingly, the best pastures—in the sense of maximum 'normal' season carrying capacity—i.e., the Mitchell Grass plains, were all of 'fair' condition or better, whereas the saltbush and bluebush plains, which carried only approximately a fifth of the stock on the Mitchell Grass country, had almost half of its area (48 per cent) in the 'poor' or 'very poor' categories, and a further 42 per cent in mediocre conditions. The difference may have been the result of the removal of all livestock from the grasslands in severe droughts, when no feed at all would be available, in contrast to the saltbush and bluebush shrublands where there would always be some biotic cover above ground to tempt stockmen to leave their animals on the range until well into the drought, by which time the damage would have been done. A similar reason might explain the fairly high areas of mediocre to very poor condition in the well-stocked shortgrass—forbs country (34 per cent and 23.5 per cent) which included the edible scrubs of mulga. As might be expected, at the other end of the spectrum of normal grazing capacities—the sand plains and dunes, salt lakes and mountains—the impact of grazing appeared to have been less significant and most of the areas were in fair to good condition.

One feature which the survey stressed rather obviously was the effect of drought on estimated stock carrying capacities. All types of pasture had significantly lower capacities to carry stock after three years of drought, but the greatest reductions were on the best 'normal' grazing areas, where drought capacities were an eighteenth of normal for the Mitchell Grass and a fifth of normal for the shortgrass-forbs, with similar reductions for the saltbush-bluebush and hilly country. Significantly also, however, the drought capacities of the shortgrass-forbs was *higher* than the normal capacities of the poorer pastures such as the salt lakes and mountains.

No equivalent survey exists for the humid grazing areas but soil erosion surveys of eastern New South Wales provide some data for areas of improved pastures created from the indigenous sclerophyll and subtropical rain forest. A survey of the Shoalhaven Catchment area having annual rainfalls from 625 to 1,500 mm showed that only 2 per cent of the area was under crop, a further 15 per cent was improved pasture, 19 per cent native pasture and the remaining 64 per cent still in native woodland. After some 150 years of grazing use only 17 per cent of the original vegetation appeared to have been removed but 40.5 per cent of the area showed either sheet or gully erosion. In detail however, this was classed as severe on only about 9 per cent of the area (Higginson, 1970).

Grazing capacities as reflected in vegetation changes and soil erosion are only a part of the total environmental impact. The ecological changes on all indigenous flora and fauna must have been complex, but just how complex we can only conjecture. The improvement of grasslands by controlled burning and the provision of permanent water points encouraged the increase of some kangaroo populations in the Riverina from the 1860s onwards and appear to have offered more sustenance for Euros in the Pilbara from the 1950s onwards (Butler, 1973; Ealey, 1967).

Micro-Environmental Impacts

At more detailed level, within the paddocks, the impact of grazing is often much more obvious, particularly in drought conditions around watering points. Because of the limited distance livestock are prepared to travel from water, up to 4.8 km for sheep and 8 km for cattle are the usually accepted figures, around each watering point is a sequence of three zones. The innermost zone (for sheep up to 0.4 km radius) is usually bare of all vegetation, while from 0.4 to *c*. 2 km is a zone of moderately to heavily grazed vegetation. From 2 km to *c*. 4 km the vegetation shows little damage from grazing and beyond the sheep do not seem to graze at all (Squares, 1970). The evenness of these circles of grazing density will however be distorted by the strength of the prevailing winds. As sheep prefer to graze into the wind, they will range further from water in this direction and pastures down-wind will be relatively undergrazed.

Overall the general picture of the chronology of grazing carrying capacities as judged by annual stock numbers has for each area of the continent shown a rapid build-up, followed by a spectacular decrease or series of decreases in droughts to approximately one half of the peak densities. The original peaks of stock numbers were not reached again until the 1950s and '60s and fell again in the subsequent droughts.

Just how we interpret these figures is debatable. So far this has been generally explained as the eating of the haystack of accumulated potential fodder by greedy, or ignorant, exploiters. If our contemporary scientists, however, cannot agree as to present optimal carrying capacities we cannot really expect the pastoralists of the nineteenth century to have been better informed. We might argue, of course, that so much capital has been invested in improvements of watering facilities and improving natural grazing quality since the drought impacts that grazing capacities *should* have surpassed the original peaks much earlier. However there is evidence that the climatic conditions have never been as good as in the late nineteenth century and indeed there is some evidence of increasing aridity in the southeast of the continent as we have seen. If true, technological innovations may have been more successful than appears at first sight in eventually getting stock numbers back to the 1890s peaks by the 1960s (Duncan, 1972).

Pastoral Resource Use: Ethic and Legend

I am very reluctant to appear in print, but I have very definite opinions upon the inland country of Qsld [*sic*] and of Australia. I think no country in the world is so well suited for the propagation of animal life in its highest forms .... With due care the offspring of all animals, human or inferior, bred in our inland country, are of a higher type than their progenitors ....

But have you no amusements for yourself, men or boys? No, life with us is a serious business. Reclaiming the country a real work.

(James Tyson, pastoral millionaire, reported 8 December 1893 in the *Brisbane Courier*)

[Of a pastoral employee taken dangerously ill on a station in northwestern New South Wales.] He has been out at Bundabulla for the past twelve months and for the last six has been by himself practically all the time .... He had a mate to begin with, but they struck awful droughts and the sheep died by the thousand and poisoned their drinking water. His mate could not put up with it and left, but this boy had never told his people in England that life "outback" was not the land of milk and honey that they had all believed it, and said he felt he could not tell them that he had "chucked" his job— they would not understand why—but he was feeling very ill and eventually suffered so from awful pains in his leg that he was forced to come to town to consult a doctor. He was put into hospital suffering from poisoning because of the water. They tried to save his leg, but eventually had to amputate it to save his life. He is only 20, and I think to have stuck it so long when feeling desperately ill, and managing to save £200 shows he is good stuff ... He wants to go back to the country, and they say he will be able to ride and lead a useful life in spite of his misfortune.

(Letter of 1 September 1931. File 3/21 of Squatting Investment Company Records, Business Archives of Australian National University)

In a previous paper concerning pastoral land settlement in U.S.A. and Australia over the hundred years from mid-nineteenth century onwards, evidence was provided of similarities in both official land settlement policies and the reactions of settlers to those policies (Heathcote, 1969c). In these reactions were identified elements of what was hypothesized to be a 'Pastoral Ethic'—attitudes and actions which enabled a difficult environment to be exploited with at least a short-term measure of success. That pastoral ethic appeared to have three characteristics. First was the attitude of mind of the pastoralists who saw themselves and acted as independent-minded, self-made men, suspicious of their fellows and particularly unwilling to accept advice or attempts to control their activities by governments which were invariably remote and often seen as unsympathetic. The second characteristic was the dominance of the commercial motive in all resource management. Profits were all important, whether from livestock or speculation in land. Further, speculation for short-term gain seemed to pay higher dividends than restrictive land use aimed at conserving the evanescent resources of fodder and water. Finally, the early pastoralists had a strong public image as pioneers and they have not been slow to exploit this in their relations with officialdom especially at times of natural catastrophes such as drought (Heathcote, 1969a).

It is interesting to speculate as to what extent the existence of this ethic polarized pastoralists against officialdom, forced continued official interest in and control of land settlement beyond the period of initial disposal, and eventually required official controls upon the use of the land itself, anticipating or perhaps stimulating the concern for the conservation of environmental resources of the last three decades.

Alongside the ethic, however, there also grew a legend, for the pastoral industry has been recognized to have played a significant role in Australian cultural history. The golden age of pastoral profits in the 1880s was paralleled by prolific literary and artistic output depicting the pastoral life as the essence of Australia—the base for the nationalism which created the Commonwealth. The poems and short stories of Lawson, Ogilvie, Paterson and others, creating a new and in part incorporating the original folk-lore of the pastoral labour force, have been recognized as the origins of a specific Australian literature in the same way that the Heidelberg *plein-air* school of painters and later artists such as Heysen created a specific Australian school of painting (Miller, 1956; Smith, 1962). Topics and scenes were often pastoral, of shearing, droving, stampedes, freighting across the clay plains, floods and droughts, golden grasslands and open woodlands, with man the hero battling nature for survival with the help of his mates. Indeed, Russell Ward has seen in the bush workers of the pastoral stations the creators of the national mystique—a specifically Australian outlook on life—the Australian Legend (Ward, 1966).

With this combination of commercial success and cultural innovation it is therefore not surprising that the popular calendar image of Australia remains the pastoral scene. There are too many facts, too many family fortunes and misfortunes implicit in the image and too much romance, natural grandeur and human heroism for it to be otherwise.

REFERENCES

Abbott, G. J. (1971), *The Pastoral Age: a Re-examination*, Macmillan, South Melbourne.

Abbott, G. J. and Nairn, N. B. (eds) (1969), *Economic Growth of Australia 1788–1821*, Melbourne University Press, Melbourne.

Alexander, G. and Williams, O. B. (eds) (1973), *The Pastoral Industries of Australia*, Sydney University Press, Sydney.

Anderson, J. R. (1970), 'A case study of spatial diversification of pastoral sheep holdings', *Rev. Marketing and Agric. Econ.*, 38, 137–41.

Anon. (1963), *World Wool Digest*, 15, 82.

Bailey, J. D. (1966), *A Hundred Years of Pastoral Banking: a History of the Australian Mercantile Land and Finance Company 1863–1963*, Clarendon, Oxford.

Barnard, A. (1958), *The Australian Wool Market 1840–1900*, Melbourne University Press, Melbourne.

——(ed). (1962), *The Simple Fleece*, Melbourne University Press, Melbourne.

Butler, B. E. *et al.* (1973), *A Geomorphic Map of the Riverine Plain of South-eastern Australia*, Australian National University Press, Canberra.

Butlin, N. G. (1962), *Australian Domestic Product, Investment and Foreign Borrowing 1861–1938/39*, Cambridge University Press, Cambridge.

Burroughs, P. (1967), *Britain and Australia 1831–1855: a Study in Imperial Relations and Crown Lands Administration*, Clarendon, Oxford.

Buxton, G. L. (1967), *The Riverina, 1861–1891, an Australian Regional Study*, Melbourne University Press, Melbourne.

Cain, N. (1962), 'Companies and squatting in the Western Division of New South Wales, 1896–1905' in A. Barnard (ed.), *The Simple Fleece*, Melbourne University Press, Melbourne, pp. 435–56.

Carter, H. B. (1964), *His Majesty's Spanish Flock: Sir Joseph Banks and the Merinos of George III of England*, Angus and Robertson, Sydney.

Clark, C. M. H. (1950), *Select Documents in Australian History 1788–1850*, Angus and Robertson, Sydney.

Collier, J. (1911), *The Pastoral Age in Australasia*, Whitcombe and Tombs, London.

Condon, R. W., Newman, J. C. and Cunningham, G. M. (1969), 'Soil erosion and pasture degeneration in Central Australia', *J. Soil. Cons. Serv. N.S.W.*, 25, 47–92, 161–82, 225–50, 295–321.

Cunningham, G. M. *et al.* (1974), 'Range condition and its assessment—a report on the Fowlers Gap Workshops, 1973', *J. Soil. Cons. Serv. N.S.W.*, 30, 125–30.

Darby, H. C. (1973), *A New Historical Geography of England*, Cambridge University Press, Cambridge.

Duncan, R. C. (1972), 'Technological change in the arid zone of New South Wales', *Aust. J. Agric. Econ.*, 16, 22–33.

Ealey, E. H. M. (1967), 'Ecology of the Euro, *Macropus robustus* (Gould) in north-western Australia', *Aust. Wildlife Res.*, 12, 9–80.

Ernle, Lord (1961), *English Farming Past and Present*, Heinemann, London (first edition 1912).

Fieger, G. M. (1970), 'Hovercraft or Beef Roads for the Outback?', *Econ. Rec.*, 46, 107–15.

Gentilli, J. (1971), *World Survey of Climatology, Climates of Australia and New Zealand*, Elsevier, Amsterdam, pp. 35–211.

Glynn, S. (1967), 'Government policy and agricultural development: Western Australia 1900–1930', *Aust. Econ. Rev.*, 7, 115–41.

Gruen, F. H. (1970), 'The major livestock industries' in R. M. Moore (ed.), *Australian Grasslands*, Australian National University Press, Canberra, pp. 401–11.

Hancock, W. K. (1972), *Discovering Monaro: a Study of Man's Impact on His Environment*, Cambridge University Press, Cambridge.

Heathcote, R. L. (1965), *Back of Bourke: A Study of Land Appraisal and Settlement in Semi-arid Australia*, Melbourne University Press, Melbourne.

——(1969a), 'Drought in Australia: a problem of perception' *Geogr. Rev.*, 59, 175–94.

——(1969b), 'Land tenure systems: past and present' in R. O. Slatyer and R. A. Perry (eds), *Arid Lands of Australia*, Australian National University Press, Canberra, pp. 185–208.

——(1969c), 'The Pastoral Ethic: a comparative study of pastoral resource apprasials in Australia and America' in W. G. McGinnies and Bram J. Goldman (eds), *Arid Lands in Perspective*, University of Arizona, Tucson, pp. 311–24.

——(1974), 'The evolution of Australian pastoral land tenures: an example of challenge and response in resource development' in R. G. Ironside *et al.* (eds), *Frontier Settlement*, University of Alberta, Edmonton, pp. 226–46.

Higginson, F. R. (1970), 'Survey of erosion and land use within the Shoalhaven Valley', *J. Soil Cons. Serv. N.S.W.*, 26, 25–59.

Holland, A. A. and Moore, C. W. E. (1962), '*The Vegetation and Soils of the Bollon District in South-western Queensland*', CSIRO Div. Plant Ind. Tech. Pap. No. 17.

Jeans, D. N. (1972), *An Historical Geography of New South Wales to 1901*, Reed Education, Sydney.

Jenks, L. H. (1963), *The Migration of British Capital to 1875*, Nelson, London (first edition 1927).

Jose, A. W. and Carter, H. J. (eds) (1925), *The Illustrated Australian Encyclopaedia*, 2 vols, Angus and Robertson, Sydney.

Kelly, J. H. (1966), *Struggle for the North*, Australian Book Society, Sydney.

King, C. J. (1957), *An Outline of Closer Settlement in New South Wales, Part I, The Sequence of Land Laws 1788–1956*, Department of Agriculture, Sydney.

Lang, G. S. (1845), *Land and Labour in Australia*, Melbourne.

Marshall, A. J. (ed.) (1966), *The Great Extermination: a Guide to Anglo-Australian Cupidity, Wickedness and Waste*, Panther, London.

Miller, E. M. (1956), *Australian Literature: a Bibliography to 1938, Extended to 1950*, Angus and Robertson, Sydney.

Moulden, J. O. and Jenkins, E. L. (1968), 'Road transport of beef cattle in northern Australia', *Q. Rev. Agric. Econ.*, 21, 87–100.

Peel, L. J. (1973), 'History of the Australian pastoral industries to 1960' in G. Alexander and O. B. Williams (eds), *The Pastoral Industries of Australia*, Sydney University Press, Sydney, pp. 41–75.

Peet, J. R. (1969), 'The spatial expansion of commercial agriculture in the nineteenth century: a Von Thünen interpretation', *Econ. Geogr.*, 45, 283–301.

Perry, T. M. (1963), *Australia's First Frontier: the Spread of Settlement in New South Wales 1788–1829*, Melbourne University Press, Melbourne.

Prince, H. C. (1973), 'England circa 1800' in H. C. Darby, *A New Historical Geography of England*, Cambridge University Press, Cambridge, pp. 389–464.

Powell, J. (1970), *The Public Lands of Australia Felix*, Oxford University Press, Melbourne.

Roberts, S. H. (1968), *History of Australian Land Settlement 1788–1820*, Macmillan, Melbourne (reissue of 1924 edition).

Robertson, J. H. (1964), 'Equipping a pastoral property: Warrah, 1861–1875' *Bus. Archives Hist.*, 4, 23–43.

Rowley, C. D. (1972), *The Destruction of Aboriginal Society*, Penguin, Ringwood.

Ryder, M. L. (1964), 'The history of sheep breeds in Britain', *Agric. Hist. Rev.*, 12, 1–12 and 65–82.

Scott, P. (1968), 'Population and land use in Australia: an analysis of metropolitan dominance' *Tijd. voor Econ. en Soc. Geogr.*, 59, 237–44.

Smith, B. (1962), *Australian Painting 1788–1960*, Oxford University Press, London.

Squires, V. R. (1970), 'Grazing behaviour of sheep in relation to watering points in semi-arid rangelands', *Proc. XI International Grassland Congress*, University of Queensland Press, St Lucia, pp. 880–4.

Strickon, A. (1965), 'The Euro-American ranching complex' in A. Leeds and A. P. Vayda (eds), *Man, Culture and Animals*, Amer. Ass. Adv. Sci., Washington, pp. 229–58.

Ward, R. (1966), *The Australian Legend*, Oxford University

Press, Melbourne (first edition 1958).

Wells, J. M. and Bates, W. R. (1969), 'Changes in farm business organisation in Australia', *Q. Rev. Agric. Econ.* 22, 53–65.

Waibel, L. (1922), 'Die Viehzuchtgebiete der südlichen Halbkugel', *Geogr. Z.*, 28, 54 ff.

Yeomans, P. A. (1958), *The Challenge of Landscape: the Development and Practice of Keyline*, Keyline, Sydney.

Young, J. M. R. (1967), *Australia's Pacific Frontier: Economic and Cultural Expansion in the Pacific: 1795–1885*, Cassell, Melbourne.

13 TROPICAL AUSTRALIA

P. P. COURTENAY

The fact that the Australian continent has been settled largely by people of northwest European, essentially British, origin may be seen to have had a significant influence on the attitudes commonly held towards the continent's tropical north. Typical British acquaintance with the tropics at either first or second hand has long been with the West Indies, India, Southeast Asia or Africa in the role of trader, administrator or missionary, and a clear distinction has emerged, both popularly and in the literature, between what have variously been called 'farm colonies' and 'plantation colonies' (Keller, 1908; Thompson, 1941) or 'hinterlands of settlement' and 'hinterlands of exploitation' (Best, 1968). The earliest official and private attitudes towards northern Australia were fully in accord with this distinction and persisted until at least World War II. Earl, who appears to have had some influence on the decision by the British government to establish the settlement of Port Essington in 1838 (Grenfell Price, 1928; Gibson-Hill, 1959), clearly envisaged an extension into north Australia of the plantation system as it was developing in colonial Asia with labour provided by Chinese (Earl, 1836, 1837). The South Australian approach to the development of the Northern Territory, following the disastrous failure in the mid-1860s of its attempts to transplant its southern pattern of substantial pastoralists and small farmers, was to seek a union of Chinese labourers and of French or Dutch sugar-planters and at one stage, in the '70s, envisaged extensive Japanese settlement (Roberts, 1924). In tropical Queensland, the debates concerning the need for 'coloured' labour for successful cotton and sugar growing are well known, and the development of the state's sugar plantation industry with kanaka labour is one of the best-documented aspects of tropical Australian history. The establishment of the Commonwealth in 1901, with its emphasis on the creation of a 'white' Australia, was responsible for nearly thirty years of argument, more notable for its emotional prejudice than for its scientific basis, over the ability of the 'white race', and especially of its 'British' branch, to settle, work and thrive in the tropics. By the 1930s, northern Australia was well established as a problem region whose tropical environment made its full integration into the nation very difficult and which, in Griffith Taylor's words, should be tackled 'later—much later'.

THE NATURE OF THE PHYSICAL AND ECONOMIC ENVIRONMENTS

For the purpose of this investigation, tropical Australia is defined to correspond with those statistical divisions that lie on or north of the tropic. In terms of the divisions in use at the time of the 1971 census, it therefore includes the Peninsula, Cairns, North Western, Townsville, Mackay, Far Western, Central Western and Rockhampton statistical divisions of Queensland, the Northern Territory, and the North West, Pilbara and Kimberley divisions of Western Australia (Fig. 13.9). The decision to include the divisions of central Queensland and the North West division of Western Australia, which are bisected by the tropic, is arbitrary, and it should be pointed out that this choice has certain consequences concerning the extent of the current development of 'tropical' Australia that will become evident below. By this definition, tropical Australia occupies 48 per cent of the land area of the continent, but, by contrast, contains only 5 per cent of the population (1971 census figures).

It is apparent that any geographical analysis of the characteristics, development or problems of tropical Australia must necessarily be concerned, at least in part, with those traits, ultimately climatic, that distinguish the northern part of the continent from its non-tropical regions. Indeed, much of the earlier literature has emphasized the physical characteristics of the north, either in an attempt to denigrate its potential for settlement and development or alternatively to make a case for its suitability for large-scale investment and growth, to an extent that has tended to cloud other significant factors relevant to a balanced understanding of the region. However, there can be no doubt that northern Australia possesses particular characteristics that arise from its tropical location and that essentially these are climatic, the result of the region's latitudinal position and consequent high input of solar energy. This high energy input is reflected in atmospheric temperatures, in the nature and pattern of rainfall and also in various geomorphic and soil-forming processes that result from the climatic elements.

In general, frequencies rather than absolute or mean values help distinguish the tropical climatic characteristics of Australia—higher frequencies of intensive rainfall, longer periods of high humidity and longer periods of high temperatures occur in tropical than in temperate latitudes. Average midsummer temperatures in much of tropical Australia are only a few degrees higher than in considerable areas of the non-tropical parts of the continent, though may frequently be accompanied by higher humidities since the summer season coincides with the wet season throughout the tropics. It is the consistent and continuous nature of high temperatures, rather than their absolute values, that characterizes the tropical summer. Winter mean temperatures in the north, however, are clearly distinctive. No part of Australia south of the tropic has actual average surface July temperatures in excess of 18° C, whilst most of northern Australia has an average of at least 16° C. Low minimum temperatures (i.e. below 5° C) are rare, though frost may occur occasionally at night in July at dry inland centres or at altitudes in excess of 300 metres.

In terms of climatic averages, tropical Australia is predominantly an arid and semi-arid region that experiences moisture deficiency problems arising from the separation of successive wet seasons by a dry season of seven to eight months. These problems are compounded by highly variable rainfall totals which are a reflection of the location of the region between the usual limits of the equatorward penetration of active cold fronts in winter and the southernmost area regularly affected by the summer poleward migration of the intertropical convergence zone (ITCZ). The region is thus particularly sensitive to variations in the vigour of these rain-producing influences. From December to March, the ITCZ is an important synoptic feature in northern Australia, though by no means invariably or persistently present. The southward movement of the ITCZ is associated with the large-scale convergence of very moist air masses from both the southeast and northwest in northern Queensland, and predominantly from the northwest in Arnhem land and the Kimberleys. Heaviest rainfall occurs along the equatorward edge of the convergence zone. The presence of deep, moist northwest flows aloft in trough circulations in the westerlies accentuates the instability at the surface and prolonged periods of heavy rainfall occur under these conditions. Surface disturbances associated with the ITCZ, such as active low pressure systems, tropical cyclones and their succeeding intense rain depressions are prolific rain producers. By April, high pressure controls are returning strongly to the Australian continent and

rainfall dwindles rapidly over most of the northern region. Rainfall during the winter period is mainly orographic and almost entirely restricted to eastern Queensland as a result of the lifting of prevailing southeasterlies over the coastal scarps and ranges. Upper air disturbances and transient cold fronts pushed into the tropics from the south are responsible for the limited winter rainfall in the interior and along the central Queensland coast (Stewart, 1973).

As a result of wide variations in environmental conditions over the expanse of tropical Australia there is a correspondingly great diversity in soil-forming factors and in resultant soil types. In common with the soils of Australia as a whole, the soils of the tropics have been formed extensively on old land surfaces and are of considerable age and poverty. The lithology of parent material has been recognized as of great importance in the determination of soil character. In the Northern Territory the remnants of the lateritic deep weathering mantle that in Tertiary times covered a large portion of the continent are well represented by a variety of soils including red and yellow earthy sands, red and yellow earths and various ironstone gravel occurrences. Cracking clays occur subjacent to basic rocks or on alluvia derived from them, while large areas of shallow sandy soils are related to extensive outcrops of sandstones and quartzites. Only the most recent soils, especially those formed on late Tertiary basalts and Quaternary alluvia, are agriculturally productive and these are deficient in a number of nutrients, especially phosphorus and nitrogen. Reserves of organic matter are generally very low reflecting both the age of most soils and rapid decomposition especially in the humid and subhumid parts of the north. In general, the soils of northern Australia, irrespective of their grouping, are deficient in major nutrients and a number are grossly deficient.

Whilst many aspects of the physical environment of tropical Australia are undeniably relevant to an understanding of the character of the region, particularly to certain problems faced by pastoralism, agriculture and general lifestyle, the economic and social geography of the north is more strongly influenced by its degree of remoteness than by any specifically tropical characteristics. Many economists concerned with problems of regional economic growth, most notably Hirschman, Friedmann and Myrdal, have emphasized the contrasts in the spatial patterns of economic activity between what have been termed *centres* and *peripheries*, and much has been written, both in regional economics and economic geography, developing this theme. The centre/periphery 'model', which has recently been considered particularly applicable to Australia (Stilwell, 1974), describes and helps explain what in many instances is a colonial-type relationship between often earlier-settled and certainly

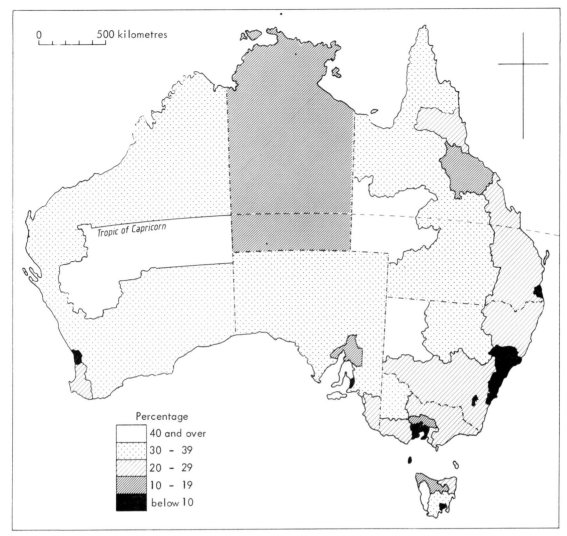

Fig. 13.1 Australia—percentage of employed persons in the Primary sector by statistical divisions, 1971.

more densely populated cores or centres of regions, and later-settled or later-developed and less densely populated outlying areas or peripheries. On the whole, the unrestrained forces of a dynamic economy tend to work against the economic convergence of the centre and the periphery. Characteristically, centres acquire diversified economic activities with particular emphasis on a wide range of light manufacturing industry and on personal and professional services whilst economic activity in the periphery is initially concerned with the exploitation of immobile local resources—such as mineral deposits, local soil and climatic factors through the medium of crops for export, or fixed assets of climate and scenery by way of a tourist industry.

Investment in the development of the primary activities of the periphery typically originates outside the region, where financial control is normally vested and whither profits flow.

The degree of economic centrality of an area may be described in terms of the variety of economic opportunities that it offers, since the familiar process of cumulative advantage tends to accentuate the economic magnetism of established core areas and thus facilitate their further growth and diversification. The nature of the economic structure of any area is reflected in certain social, economic and demographic data and these may be used in many ways to examine that structure and assess its role. The most appropriate

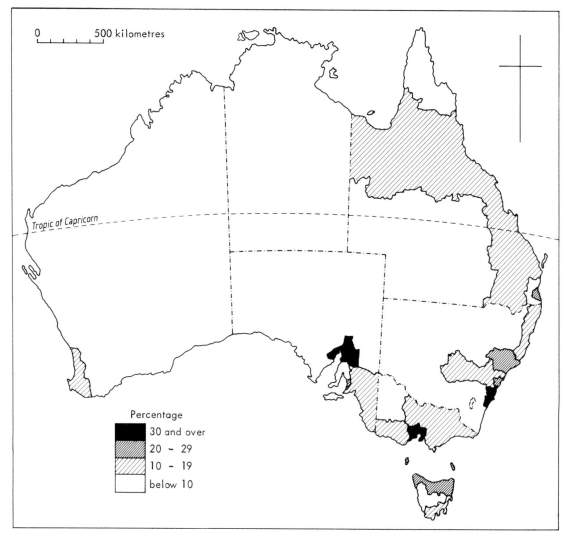

Fig. 13.2 Australia—percentage of persons in the Manufacturing sector by statistical divisions, 1971.

recent data for this purpose in the Australian context are the employment by industry figures of the 1971 census which, based on the Australian Standard Industrial Classification, group the labour force into fourteen broad categories. The accompanying maps (Figs 13.1–13.3) make use of these data to reveal certain aspects of the spatial structure of the Australian economy that are relevant to the centre/periphery model. Fig. 13.1 illustrates the percentage of the workforce in each statistical division that is employed in the primary sector, an aggregate of the first two divisions of the industrial classification and covering agriculture, forestry, fishing, hunting and mining which, it is hypothesized, characterize the economic activities of peripheral regions. The spatial distribution of percentage employment in the manufacturing sector, a not fully appropriate but convenient surrogate measure of economic centrality, is illustrated by Fig. 13.2. Figs 13.1 and 13.2 are not perfect inverses of each other, partly because employment in manufacturing includes those employed in the basic processing of raw materials, e.g. sugar cane crushing, ore concentration or smelting, which are closely related, industrially and spatially, to primary production, and are peripheral-type activities. Nevertheless, the two maps are sufficiently contrasted to suggest that each of primary and manufacturing employment percentages provides a useful first general derivative measure of

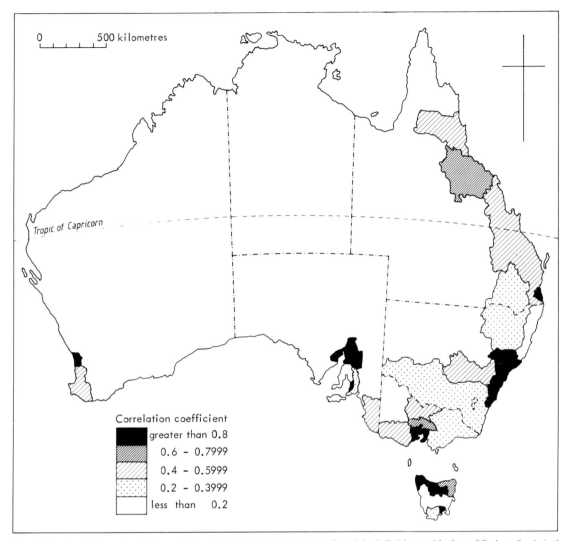

Fig. 13.3 Australia—extent of correlation of employment structure of statistical divisions with that of Sydney Statistical Division, 1971.

economic structure. As a further experiment in demonstrating the spatial pattern revealed by the analysis of employment structure, correlation co-efficients were calculated between the employment structure of the Sydney Statistical Division—assumed, to some extent subjectively, to be the economic core of the nation—and each of the other 66 divisions in the country. The result is illustrated in Fig. 13.3. (A similar map, adopting Melbourne as the core, is 95 per cent identical! The correlation coefficient between the employment structures of the Sydney and Melbourne statistical divisions is 0.9952.)

An analysis of Figs 13.1–13.3 reveals, as might have

been anticipated, a fairly striking contrast between a number of spatially limited core areas—essentially the capital cities and their neighbouring statistical divisions—and an extensive national periphery whose emphasis on primary production and economic dis-similarity from the core areas generally increase in proportion to its remoteness from them. Most of tropical Australia lies clearly in this broad peripheral zone with some limited areas, notably central Queensland and certain enclaves along the north Queensland coast, of which the Townsville division is the most remarkable, possessing characteristics which mark them out as having rather more diversified employment

Table 13.1 Tropical Australia—Percentage Employment in Major Sectors, 1971

Sector	Percentage	Deviation from national mean
Primary	22.25	+13.56
Manufacturing	10.77	−12.06
Utilities, construction, trade and transport	35.30	+0.63
Finance, public and community services	19.38	−3.32
Other including unemployed	11.97	+1.19

Source: 1971 Census.

structures than the remaining areas of the north. In spatial terms, of course, these are amongst the least remote districts of the Australian tropics. The examination of the spatial pattern of employment structure in the nation as a whole suggests that the broad economic characteristics of the Australian north, including what is popularly believed to be its distinctive lack of development, are largely the consequence of its peripheral and not of its tropical location.

Table 13.1, which details the percentage employment in the major sectors for the tropical divisions collectively, reveals the extent of the emphasis on primary activities in the region. The aggregation, both of the original data and for the further purpose of this tabulation, has the effect of concealing the fact that much of the employment in manufacturing in tropical Australia is associated with primary processing and reinforces that sector rather than provides diversification. With the major exception of Townsville, and to some extent of Darwin, most parts of tropical Australia are predominantly concerned with the production, processing or shipment of primary commodities, and the settlement pattern, communications network and demographic structure are closely related to this fact. The following sections of this chapter are concerned with the analysis of this primary-oriented economy and with the elucidation of the belief that the significance of the tropical environments is at the level of creating problems for and influencing the specific nature of the activities carried on in this essentially peripheral region rather than being part of their cause.

PASTORALISM IN THE TROPICS

The pastoral occupation of considerable areas of tropical Australia represented the earliest efforts by pioneer settlers to develop a production system that would yield them a living under conditions of very seasonal rainfall, very low population density and great distances from potential markets. In the century or so since the first overlanders from southern and central Queensland moved into the northern and western parts of the state, across the boundary into the Northern Territory and even beyond into east Kimberley, most parts of the tropics have been sampled for livestock rearing. At the present time, the pastoral industry is still the only economic activity in a very large proportion of the north, and the production of beef and wool are likely to remain the principal means by which the country can be utilized.

Table 13.2 illustrates the numbers and density per square kilometre of sheep, beef cattle and dairy cattle in the principal regions of tropical Australia. It is apparent from the data that, while beef cattle are outnumbered by sheep, they are both more widespread and more dispersed throughout the tropics and indeed there are no local government areas in which no cattle are to be found. Sheep, by contrast, are highly concentrated on the tropical margins in central Queensland, the southern part of the Territory and the Pilbara and North West divisions of Western Australia. Almost no sheep are recorded along the Queensland coast and in the immediate inland from Mackay to Cape York but occur at high average densities of over 20 per square kilometre on the central downlands in the Aramac-Barcaldine-Longreach-Blackall districts. Average cattle densities reach this figure only in the small and well-watered Sarina district, where many individual properties have densities in the region of 25 to 30 beasts per square kilometre.

Early pastoral developments in tropical Australia involved both sheep and cattle which were being driven into parts of the upper Burdekin basin in north Queensland by the 1860s, and thence into the Gulf country and as far as the margins of the Barkly Tableland (Bauer, 1959). The principal livestock movements into the Territory occurred in the 1870s, reaching their peak in 1877, and into the tropical districts of Western Australia mainly in the 1880s. Fluctuations in livestock numbers have reflected the impacts both of the tropical physical environment, especially its propensity for extremes of drought and flood, and of the world market for pastoral products. Despite individual efforts at sheep rearing in most parts of the north, in some places repeatedly, physical problems of unsuitable pastures, troublesome grass seeds, dingoes, very long dry periods and excessively wet ones all contributed to a general lack of success, which was exacerbated by high labour costs and such remoteness from markets that a new season's clip was often ready before the previous year's had reached the wool stores.

Table 13.2 Tropical Australia—Numbers and Average Density per Square Kilometre of Sheep, Beef Cattle and Dairy Cattle by Regional Groupings, 1970–1

Region (Statistical divisions in brackets)	Sheep		Beef cattle		Dairy cattle	
	No.	Average density	No.	Average density	No.	Average density
CENTRAL QUEENSLAND (Rockhampton, Central Western)	2,966,837	10.50	2,058,396	7.29	64,632	0.23
NORTH QUEENSLAND (Mackay, Townsville)	792	0.01	913,625	7.81	13,324	0.11
FAR NORTH QUEENSLAND (Cairns, Peninsula)	716	0.00	405,895	2.04	34,092	0.17
WESTERN QUEENSLAND (Far Western, North Western)	3,046,887	4.66	1,438,606	2.20	940	0.00
NORTHERN TERRITORY[a]	7,000	0.01	1,166,000	0.88	—	—
TROPICAL WESTERN AUSTRALIA[b] (Kimberley, Pilbara, North West)	1,846,079	1.74	757,772	0.72	324	0.00
Total	7,868,311	2.16	6,740,294	1.85	113,312	0.03

[a] 1971–2   —   nil
[b] 1972–3   0.00 less than 0.01
Sources: Statistics of Queensland; Statistical Register of Western Australia; Northern Territory Statistical Summary.

BEEF CATTLE

Throughout the greater part of northern Australia the raising of beef cattle has proved, to date, the most profitable use to which the land can be put despite the facts that, over most of its history, the industry in the remote regions has been operated on a near-primitive open range system of grazing and that for the first half of the twentieth century cash returns were almost uniformly low. Cattle properties have varied in size from a few hundreds to tens of thousands of square kilometres and have carried herds ranging from less than 1,000 to more than 100,000 head (Kelly, 1971). It has been widely recognized that cattle raising is an activity that holds considerable further potential but which continues to face many problems arising from natural and economic environmental circumstances only some of which are being partly resolved by research and development efforts.

The annual nutrition cycle, dominated by the rainfall regime, provides the essential background to the physical problems that confront the cattle industry. Each year, except in a few favoured localities, cattle throughout the north experience a major fodder shortage during the dry season followed by a relatively short period of high nutrition on the fresh new growth produced by the first rains in December (Norman, 1965). With continued rain through January, February and March, this growth rapidly coarsens, loses protein and becomes rank. A slight lift in the protein content of the pastures can be obtained by a 'green burn' (a management technique not universally acclaimed) even in very dry weather, but generally from the end of the wet until early storm rains in November the dry season is a wasting period with the protein content of the pasture—essential if cattle are to be able to convert the cellulose of the pastures to assimilable starch and sugar—often dangerously low. Once temporary waterholes have dried up by July or August, cattle concentrate on the remaining permanent waters and the time between September and the end of the dry is the critical period for mortality. The combination of the effects of poor feed, successively longer distances to be walked from water to find it, and heat exhaustion due to rapidly rising day temperatures, approaches a climax by the end of November and may be aggravated by tick anaemia. Late or below-average summer rains are responsible for rapid rises in mortality.

The very considerable variations in rainfall totals and soil conditions within the Australian tropics are responsible for a diversity of native pastures of which few, however, are comparable in quality with varieties encountered in parts of central Africa or South America (R. S. F. Campbell, 1973). In particular, the low to very low phosphorus status of many of the soils has a markedly detrimental effect on animal fertility and growth. Bryan (Leeper, 1970) recognizes fourteen 'pasture zones' in tropical Australia based on the floristics and morphology of the most extensive native pastures of each zone or of the original trees and shrubs. Some of the more wooded zones are of little or no pastoral value until cleared and sown. The principal natural pastures carrying cattle are in the *tropical tall grass zone*, a belt of country receiving between 750 and 1,500 mm of rainfall and lying approximately north of latitude 15° S, which consists of open eucalypt woodland with a ground flora of either bunch-type perennials or annuals of low nutritive value except for a short period after rain or fire; in the *bunch spear grass zone*, dominated by *Heteropogon contortus*, again notably low in protein during the dry season and occupying much of subcoastal eastern Queensland; and in the *Mitchell and Flinders grasses zone* of the Barkly Tableland and central Queensland, an open tussock grassland of perennial species with a prominent annual component after rains. In central Queensland, the latter pastures carry higher densities of sheep than of cattle, though cattle densities in this 'sheep country' are considerably higher than in the cattle country of the Peninsula, the Territory or the Kimberleys and have been increasing during recent years. Pastures south of approximately 20° are generally of better quality, though normally sparser, than those in the north and the condition of cattle grazing them may be better for up to two months longer into the dry (Howard, 1966).

In general terms, the poorer and more remote lands are used predominantly for breeding and carry fewer than two beasts per square kilometre. Fattening is combined with breeding on average to good country and on the better-watered coastal and near-coastal margins of the east. Historically the grazing lands of Queensland have been relatively better placed for selling cattle since they have had access to more profitable export outlets and domestic markets. Away from the extensive methods of Western Australia and

the Territory and towards the more developed country of the east and southeast, there is an increasingly intensive utilization of pasture and even of grain crops and a sharp rise in the carrying capacity to nearly seven beasts per square kilometre in the Townsville statistical division and over twelve in the Mackay and Rockhampton divisions. As a consequence of the mainly open-range type of property, especially in the more extensively grazed areas, closely controlled breeding programmes are rarely achieved and mating usually takes place around the year. Without control, cattle numbers increase during runs of good seasons with inevitable overconcentration around remaining surface water during average or adverse seasons when overgrazing can lead to the denudation of native pastures and serious soil erosion. Where management is more efficient, controlled natural mating may be carried out during a limited season with the objective of timing calving to coincide with the high level of available feed in summer. The fattening of animals to the age of turn-off (three years or even younger under the best natural pasture conditions but frequently older) is geared to the period March to November when they are consigned to one of the coastal or inland meatworks.

The immediate domestic market for north Australian beef has always been small and in the early years of the industry in the nineteenth century the only outlet for surplus animals was the boiling-down works where hides were saved and the rest of the carcass boiled down for tallow and fertilizer. Experiments with the refrigeration and canning of meat were undertaken at various centres in northern and central Queensland in the 1870s and '80s and by the mid-'90s the cattle industry was geared to the meat demands of overseas markets. Export meatworks were constructed at points around the northern margin of the continent, from Broome in West Kimberley to Rockhampton on the central Queensland coast, the most recent having been established at Darwin and Katherine in the Territory in 1963. The period during which fat cattle are available for slaughter is determined basically by the pattern of turn-off with a consequent seasonal routine imposed on the meatworks, a seasonality reinforced by the very great difficulties of mustering and moving cattle during the main wet season.

Since the beef cattle industry is the most widespread economic activity in tropical Australia, and over great areas the only possible medium by which a return may be obtained from the land, improvements in the productivity of properties and in the organization of the marketing of beef are clearly of regional and national significance. The problems facing such improvements are apparently of two kinds, physical and managerial, though it may well be that the latter hinge on the former. Improvements in the productivity of properties, by increasing the number of animals per unit area and/or by increasing their liveweight and bettering their condition at time of turn-off, face the immediate problem of the environment, and particularly of the seasonal rainfall regime and the related nutrition cycle. This problem is being tackled in two basic ways—by seeking improvements in the pasture, and in the type and condition of the animals raised on it.

The introduction of legumes into existing stands of native pasture has long been accepted as the quickest and most economic method of improving the value of fodder in northern Australia. Several species of tropical legume have been discovered that can be established successfully in native north Australian pastures, of which the most outstanding so far have been various cultivars of *Stylosanthes humilis* (Townsville stylo, formerly known as Townsville lucerne), a plant of South American origin accidentally introduced about 1890 and naturalized in north Queensland. Townsville stylo has the ability to grow and persist even on soils of low fertility and its spread is encouraged by heavy grazing. Its productivity is low in the early summer, however, and it is therefore best introduced amongst a natural perennial, such as spear grass. During the dry season, cattle grazing on Townsville stylo maintain far better condition than is possible on natural pasture alone, perhaps even gaining weight, and, particularly, obtain essential protein intake, though in the Queensland coastal belt winter rains or heavy dews may render Townsville stylo very unpalatable because of mould growth. Accompanied by the application of superphosphate and trace elements, Townsville stylo has considerable potential as a sown pasture in the 28 million ha of spear grass country in northeast Queensland, as well as in the Top End of the Territory and the Kimberleys, a total area of about 60 million ha of country with an average annual rainfall of 640 mm or more. Much of the grazing land of tropical Australia is, nevertheless, too dry for Townsville stylo, which, as an annual, is also easily swamped by weeds and no management system can yet guarantee that the plant will remain dominant in the pasture in all areas where it is grown. In 1973 a new cultivar of the genus *Stylosanthes* (*Stylosanthes hamata* cv. Verano, or Caribbean stylo) was released by the CSIRO Davies Laboratory at Townsville. Caribbean stylo, a perennial, grows on a wide variety of soil types and is more drought-resistant than Townsville stylo. It thus makes possible the extension of stable improved pastures into areas with lower and less reliable rainfall than that suitable for Townsville stylo. Other legumes suitable for use under differing environmental conditions are under study. As an alternative or complement to the introduction of legumes, properties within 200 km or so of a sugar mill

are countering the protein deficiency of dry season fodder by supplementing natural grazing with a urea-molasses mixture fed from a roller-drum lick which permits cattle to ingest sufficient non-protein nitrogen to enable them to increase their intake of roughage whilst avoiding the absorption of toxic quantities of urea. Elsewhere a urea salt/minerals mixture is often used as a supplement. There is only limited evidence so far of the likely economic consequences for the beef cattle industry of improved pasture. A study referring specifically to the Daly River basin of the Northern Territory (McLintock, 1970) came to the conclusion, however, that satisfactory returns from new developments, based on subdivision into relatively small properties (defined in terms of basic herd sizes between 1,500 and 4,000 head) and adopting pasture improvement practices with Townsville stylo, could at 1970 prices be obtained only from a capital investment in excess of about $250,000.

In the Fitzroy basin of central Queensland, it is anticipated that the carrying capacity of 4.5 million ha of extensive grazing land will be substantially increased, perhaps fivefold, with the completion of the Fitzroy Basin Brigalow Lands Development Scheme. Under this scheme, brigalow (*Acacia harpophylla*), a dense scrub growing on soils of high natural fertility in the 500–750 mm rainfall belt, is being cleared and sown to pastures or ploughed for cereal crops. Parts of the area of the scheme, which covers the lands of the Mackenzie, Isaac, Comet and Dawson river basins, were originally used for the grazing of sheep and cattle until the spread of prickly pear in the early years of the twentieth century made the majority of brigalow lands useless for grazing purposes. By the late 1930s pear infestation had been almost eliminated by the cactoblastis insects but although there was a return to extensive cattle grazing the area remained relatively undeveloped compared with brigalow lands in southern Queensland. The fertility of the Fitzroy brigalow lands had long been recognized but the economic elimination of the dense scrub awaited techniques of mechanical clearing that became available in the early 1950s. Following total replacement of the original vegetation by rhodes, buffel or green panic grasses or by sorghum almum, the brigalow lands will support pastures without the use of fertilizer for at least ten years.

The original stocking of the tropical Australian pasture lands was with European breeds of cattle (*Bos taurus*) amongst which Herefords and Shorthorns were the most popular. Non-European or exotic cattle (*Bos indicus*) were apparently first introduced into northern Australia, from Java, in 1872. In recent decades, interest in the use in herds of *indicus* or Zebu-type stock, which are more tick-resistant and heat-tolerant and able to grow better on low quality feed than European breeds, has increased greatly especially as

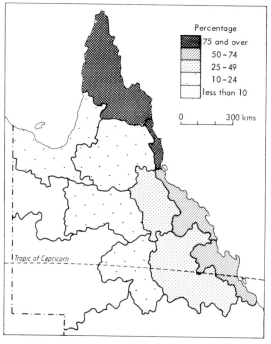

Percentage
75 and over
50 - 74
25 - 49
10 - 24
less than 10

0   300 kms

Tropic of Capricorn

Fig. 13.4   Tropical Queensland—percentage of *Bos indicus* blood in beef herds sampled, 1971.

the export potential of the industry expanded following the opening of the United States market in 1958. A survey of over 900 Queensland herds in 1971 showed that *Bos indicus* blood had been introduced into over 30 per cent of the State's female breeding stock with the primary purpose of improving weight gains. This percentage represented about a threefold increase in the proportion of tropical or tropical-cross stock since 1965. The heaviest concentration of such stock occurs on the central and northern coastal areas but they are to be found throughout the State (Fig. 13.4). Efforts to find means of disease control in all cattle are being undertaken by government and university veterinary scientists. The greatest recent advance has been the elimination of bovine pleuropneumonia and eradication campaigns are being undertaken against tuberculosis and brucellosis. Field control of the tick fever complex is achieving some success through strict control of cattle movements and enforced dipping of animals before they are transported.

The higher degrees of intensity of cattle rearing, the more widespread use of improved pastures and the greater interest in the introduction of *indicus* blood into herds in the eastern and southeastern margins of tropical Australia is certainly related, in part, to the less extreme nature of the tropical climate and the occurrence of extensive areas of better soils and more nutritious natural pastures than in the remote areas of

the north. However, better management techniques including the provision of stock watering points, the erection of fences to assist in breeding control and the sowing of improved pastures can more readily be carried out on the smaller properties of eastern Queensland where, also, the proportion of resident holders is higher than in the more remote areas. Most properties in eastern and central Queensland are within 60 km of rail loading points thus having the advantage of being able to deliver cattle to the export meatworks in better condition than those that had been overlanded for much longer distances. The importance of adequate transport to the development of northern Australia's cattle rearing potential was recognized in 1947 by the Northern Australia Development Committee that had been established by the Federal government to identify problems of development in the remote areas of the region. Early attempts in the late 1920s at using road transport as an alternative to droving cattle were unsuccessful in the absence of sufficiently robust vehicles and adequate highways. Extensive movement of cattle by suitable road vehicles began in the 1950s. The first beef roads programme, which grew out of the negotiations that led to the 1951 meat agreement with the United Kingdom, was launched in 1949 and an expanded programme of road construction was undertaken by the Federal, Queensland and Western Australian governments in 1961. During the 1950s, drought had proved the value of road transport in moving cattle to railheads however scarce feed might be along the route. Road transport also had the advantages of making it possible to turn off smaller consignments of stock at a time, thus extending the marketing season and enabling cattle to be sold in their best condition. Pastoralists can move cattle quickly enough to benefit from short-term price increases and stockmen are available on the properties for more productive work than droving. By mid-1973, 4,608 km of sealed beef roads had been constructed, of which 2,363 km (51 per cent) were in Queensland, 1,443 km (31 per cent) in the Northern Territory and 802 km (17 per cent) in Western Australia. A further 1,200 km of gravelled road, mainly in Western Australia and the Territory, had also been completed.

Pasture improvements, the introduction of *indicus* blood, disease control, improved transport facilities (especially the use of road transport) and better management practices are all contributing to increased turn-off from cattle properties, to a considerable reduction in the average killing age of cattle from 4–5 years old to 3–3½ years and to lengthening of killing seasons. A fully quantified study of the precise impact of these various developments has yet to be made and will be complicated by the continuing variability of weather and the world market situation. Over the period 1960–70, which included bad drought

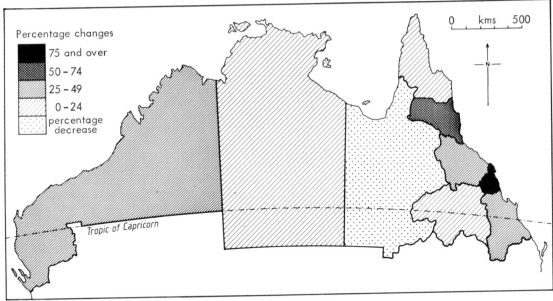

Fig. 13.5 Tropical Australia—percentage changes in cattle numbers, 1900–70.

years, the number of beef cattle in tropical Australia increased from 5,800,281 to 6,740,294 with the largest percentage increases in coastal north Queensland and Western Australia (Fig. 13.5). However, the great reduction in purchases after 1972 by Japan and the United States, where the market for manufacturing meat had provided the major recent economic stimulus to the Australian beef industry, illustrates once again the rather precarious basis on which an export-oriented primary industry invariably seems to rest.

DAIRY CATTLE

The rearing of cattle for dairy purposes occurs on only a limited scale in tropical Australia and is localized in three areas of relatively better distributed annual rainfall within reach of the north's major population concentrations (Table 13.2). Dairy farms on the Atherton Tableland supply fresh milk to the north coast, to Townsville and as far west as Mt Isa, Camoo-weal and Darwin. Farms in the Mackay and Dawson-Callide regions serve the population of central Queensland. In the two more northern regions dairying has come to be concentrated in range and plateau country where higher average spring rainfalls are received than on neighbouring lowlands but also where there is less competition from alternative land uses. In the Mackay district especially, where dairy production was for many decades dispersed through the main sugar areas, competition from the economically more successful cane industry has caused many dairy farmers to shift either to less favourable coastal terrain too

steep for mechanized cane cultivation or to the nearby highlands (Allen, 1965). On the far north coast from Ingham to Mossman, dairying never established a secure foothold alongside sugar cane production. In the coastal shires of central Queensland, where dairying played a pioneering role in supporting closer settlement, opportunities for diversification are greatest in the Callide and Dawson valleys and changes have been made to vealer production, mixed agriculture, beef production and pig and poultry farming (Department of National Development, 1968).

Climatic stress and food and water deficiencies, especially between September and November, are the most important factors influencing tropical dairy herds. High ambient air temperatures, leading to the partial failure of the animals' thermo-regulative mechanisms, cause declines in feed intake, a decrease in productive processes or growth and milk production and a change in milk composition. Some Zebu blood has been introduced into a few Queensland dairy cattle but northern herds continue to be dominated by temperate breeds mainly Jersey, Australian Illawarra and Frie-sian. Efforts are being made, however, to develop a type of animal with tick-resistant characteristics and the capability of producing milk under severe tropical conditions by crossing Zebu cattle (Sahiwal) with existing breeds of dairy cattle. Dairy herds graze indigenous and introduced pastures but supplementary feeding is necessary to maintain milk production during the dry winter season. Forage crops, including fodder cane in the Mackay district, are grown or purchased by dairy farms. Meatmeal in central Queensland and molasses in the Mackay and Atherton Tableland areas are locally available and fed to dairy stock.

SHEEP

In 1970–1 (see Table 13.2) there were 6.7 million sheep in tropical Australia with the highest concentration in central Queensland. This represents a considerable decline since 1960 in all statistical divisions, except the Pilbara and North West in tropical Western Australia where a 25 per cent increase in sheep numbers took place, and may be related both to the drought and to the increased profitability of beef cattle during the 1960s. Returns per sheep are considerably lower than in the more temperate zones of Australia and northern sheep flocks characteristically achieve lower rates of reproduction than those in the south (Cumming and Reid, 1967). Low lambing percentages result from the difficulty of achieving favourable feed and temperature conditions at both joining and lambing times. The tropical rainfall pattern creates a shortage of nutritive feed for the greater part of the year and high temperatures affect the performance of rams. High temperatures at lambing time also reduce the chances of survival of lambs whilst high death rates due to flood and drought add to the difficulties of maintaining flock numbers. These factors are aggravated by the large areas required to support a sheep and the consequent difficulties in the management of stock and control of predators. As a result virtually no surplus stock are available for sale, low rates of culling are adopted and sheep are retained to a greater age. Lower production per sheep and deterioration in the quality of the flocks therefore occur.

Wool production per head of sheep is low in most of tropical Australia compared with southern grazing areas. The lack of pasture plants capable of producing nutritive feed for much of the year affects both reproduction rates and wool production per head though prolonged periods of protein shortage are responsible for the growth of extremely fine wools which command strong support on the market. It seems probable that considerable technological progress will be necessary even to maintain the profitability of sheep raising in the less favourable areas of the north. The economic establishment of improved pasture species would probably be the most effective method of raising lambing percentages and wool production per head but this would also benefit beef cattle production, which is competitive with wool production over most of the area, and the choice of enterprise in these circumstances would be determined by the relationship between the price trends for wool and beef.

MINING

The role of mining in the penetration and early phases of development of peripheral areas is well known, and in the case of tropical Australia the sequence of exploitation has been almost classic, with high value minerals, particularly gold, luring diggers to increasingly remote fields, whilst deposits of lower value minerals awaited infrastructural improvements, rising prices and the availability of capital-intensive extraction techniques. The three million square kilometres of tropical Australia include extensive sections of most of the structural divisions of the continent, particularly the complex eastern uplands, the central basin and the western shield, the last occupying the whole of the Northern Territory, and the greater part of tropical Western Australia and far western Queensland. The range of minerals known to occur, especially in the eastern highlands and western shield, is very great and includes precious metals and ores, ferrous and non-ferrous ores, fuels and other minerals. Since about 1960, the region has been subjected to very active mineral exploration, at times with prospecting teams from more than a hundred major mining companies in the field, and the full extent of its mineral wealth is certainly far from determined.

Early explorations in the north reported traces of gold, in north Queensland in 1859, in the Territory in 1865 and in the Kimberleys and the Pilbara in the 1880s. Remoteness from the established goldfields of Victoria and New South Wales effectively discouraged early prospectors, however, until positive news of payable gold was received from the Star River, 80 km west of Townsville, in 1865. The first full-scale rush to the north was followed by a sequence of finds that culminated in the discovery in 1872 of the Palmer alluvial field. Fields were being worked in the Territory in the '70s and the Kimberleys and Pilbara by the '80s and '90s. Other minerals of high value, particularly silver, tin and copper, attracted diggers and investors, to north Queensland especially, in the latter decades of the nineteenth century. In the early penetration of the Australian tropics, mining and pastoralism had significant impacts on each other. Finds, sometimes made by pastoralists, established clusters of population that provided markets for meat. The transport links, especially railways, that were built to serve mining areas often tapped extensive grazing country, whilst, particularly in the west, ports established during the gold rushes survived as outlets for the pastoral industry. The significance of early mining, with its precisely determined locations, may be seen in the influence that it had on the preliminary sketching-out of the pattern of urban centres and communication routes, the impetus given to some ports, e.g. Townsville, Cairns and Darwin, and not to others, and the attraction of population in far larger numbers than pastoralism and its associated services could ever have done.

Notwithstanding the undoubted importance of early

mining to the initial opening up of tropical Australia, the most outstanding developments of the region's mineral wealth have occurred in recent years. Whilst it was gold, and to a less extent tin, silver and copper, that attracted early and individual European and Chinese diggers in the nineteenth century, minerals more difficult to locate and extract, and consequently requiring highly capitalized exploitation, have characterized mining developments since World War II. So widespread and varied are the current mining operations that it is difficult to generalize about the patterns that are emerging, but an attempt will be made to recognize two major types of development that appear to be having distinctive spatial impacts and to examine one example of each.

The locations of mineral deposits are, of course, determined by geological and/or geomorphological processes, but the decision to exploit particular deposits is entirely an economic one that will depend on a number of variables, including the richness and accessibility of the deposit and world demand expressed through price. Accessibility can be increased by infrastructural developments whilst the richness of a deposit, in economic terms, can be up- or downgraded by technological developments, both in extraction techniques and consuming industries, and by changing world prices. In common with the situation in many other peripheral regions at the present time, mineral exploitation in tropical Australia is concerned with increasing the development of minerals of high intrinsic value, because of their universal scarcity and demand, and also with commencing extraction of minerals of lower unit value which, until recently, were sufficiently abundant in areas more accessible, both economically and politically, to the world's major consumers. Minerals of high unit value have generally been more able to support new infrastructural development and to attract sufficient investment, either private or public, to permit their exploitation even in regions of considerable initial inaccessibility. For this reason, gold has traditionally been the spearhead of the mining penetration of remote regions and even short-lived fields often have been serviced by railways and have engendered urban development. Copper, tin, lead, zinc, nickel and uranium are minerals in this high unit value category that are of significance to current activity in tropical Australia. Minerals of lower unit value—iron ore, bauxite, manganese, phosphates, coal and petroleum (despite present politically inflated prices)—can generally be exploited economically in a peripheral region only if they can be produced in bulk and/or are relatively accessible in terms of existing transport and shipping facilities. The recent surge in the development of the north's rich reserves of these minerals has been primarily in coastal or near-coastal districts or, in the case of the Duchess phosphate deposits of northwest Queensland, within a limited distance of an existing rail link.

The outstanding example of development based on rather inaccessible high value mineral resources is that of Mt Isa. The first reports of the existence of copper ore in northwestern Queensland were made in the Cloncurry district during the search for Burke and Wills but, although the proven existence of rich outcrops attracted some interest, it was the discovery of gold that drew miners to the area in the late 1860s. The Cloncurry mineral field had a chequered history, based primarily on its scattered copper deposits but also working gold, silver, lead, zinc, manganese, bismuth and cobalt, until the 1923 discovery of the silver-lead field in its western portion led to the floating of the company that was to become Mt Isa Mines Ltd. Founded initially to develop the field's lead deposits, the company began to produce copper during World War II and recommenced silver-lead-zinc production, with assured markets, in 1946. An intensive drilling campaign in the early 1950s proved the existence of a vast copper lode. In 1973 Mt Isa Mines produced 132,000 tonnes of blister copper, 304,000 kg of silver, 126,000 tonnes of crude lead and 208,000 dry tonnes of zinc concentrate to become the world's largest single mine producer of lead and among the world's leaders in the output of the other minerals.

The development of the Cloncurry field was responsible for the construction of a railway link with Hughenden, which had been connected with Townsville by the Great Northern Railway since 1887, and in 1908 the tie with the coast was complete. The expansion of mining operations, which have been accompanied by dramatic increases in reserves as the field has been more fully prospected, has been attended by the growth of ancillary processing and tertiary industries which have pushed Mt Isa city to the point of being Queensland's tenth and tropical Queensland's fourth most populous urban area with an estimated 1973 population of 31,800. The reduction of sulphide and carbonate ores of copper to blister copper, the smelting of lead and the concentration of zinc ore plus the multifarious activities associated with major mining and mineral processing operations have created in Mt Isa, and in the Queensland northwestern statistical division of which the city is the major centre of population, an economic structure that has put the division amongst the most highly industrialized interior districts in Australia (see Fig. 13.2). The activities of Mt Isa mines have contributed substantially to coastal development, especially at Townsville where blister copper is refined and where exports originating from Mt Isa represent about 40 per cent by weight of the port's outward cargoes, and at Bowen where coke is made for the Mt Isa smelters.

Plate 13.1   Mount Newman Western Mine, Pilbara, Western Australia. The major modifications to the landscape created by the large-scale iron ore development at Mt Whaleback illustrate the extent and capital-intensiveness of modern mining developments in the north. *Photo*: Mt Newman Mining Co. Pty Ltd.

The major deposits of bauxite at Weipa and Gove, of manganese at Groote Eylandt, of coal in the Bowen basin, of petroleum and natural gas on the northwest shelf and of iron ore in the Pilbara are amongst the most valuable and extensive of tropical Australia's huge resources of low unit value minerals that have been discovered and/or exploited in recent years. The history of mining in the Pilbara began in the late 1880s, in traditional fashion, with the discovery of gold. The first major iron ore discovery was made in 1961 following the relaxation in 1960 of the Australian government ban on iron ore exports which provided the biggest single spur to new exploration in an era of massive demand by the Japanese steel industry. Other discoveries followed, and subsequently seven major groups of companies entered into agreements with the Western Australian government for the mining of the ore, the building of new port facilities and of towns and railways. The major iron ore projects are located in the great Hamersley Iron Province, which starts at the coast north of Onslow and runs east-southeast for more

than 500 kilometres. The Province contains vast quantities of iron-bearing material, an estimated 15,000 million tonnes of which is of a grade high enough to qualify as mineable iron ore. The iron formation throughout the province usually contains 25 to 35 per cent iron. In Mt Whaleback, one of the most spectacular examples of enrichment, the ore averages 64 per cent iron but in places attains almost 70 per cent iron content and is virtually pure haematite. The Mt Newman Mining Co. Pty Ltd, a wholly-owned subsidiary of B.H.P., established an open-pit mine on the Mt Whaleback ore body in 1969 with ore-crushing, train-loading and industrial support facilities and the new town of Newman. It was also necessary to construct a 425 kilometre rail link between the mine and the tertiary crushing, stockpiling and ship-loading complex at Port Hedland. At Mt Tom Price and Paraburdoo, southeast of Dampier, Hamersley Iron Pty Ltd has operated mines since 1966 and 1970 respectively, whence products from the crushing and screening plants are railed to Dampier where they are blended, stockpiled and shipped. A pelletizing plant is also located at Dampier and a range of urban and industrial support facilities have been provided at the mines and port. Limits on state's borrowings by the Central Loan Council have meant that most infrastructural development to date in the Pilbara has been provided on private initiative. The discovery offshore in 1971 of natural gas, however, caused the Western Australian state government to undertake an examination of the region's industrial potential, and a jointly funded federal/state feasibility study into a scheme for the largest industrial development project ever proposed in Australia was tabled in the Federal parliament in 1974. Bauxite mining at Weipa, on the western coast of Cape York peninsula, and coal mining in the Peak Downs and Goonyella districts of Queensland have similarly been accompanied by extensive private development of urban and transport infrastructure.

The fact that many of the Australian mining developments of recent years have been taking place in the tropical half of the continent is a reflection of the extent to which economic circumstances have made possible the exploitation of mineral deposits located in regions previously too inaccessible for profitable working or even for intensive exploration. Post-war circumstances of international demand and changes in political attitudes towards the continent's resources have largely been responsible for the creation of an economic environment which has encouraged exploration and development whilst the large-scale investment thus attracted has provided the necessary technological and managerial expertise. Apart from the problems inherent in the large-scale development of resources in any remote and thinly populated area—problems associated with the construction of road and rail connections, of the provision of power and water supply and of accommodation and services for employees recruited from elsewhere—mining developments in the north face additional difficulties resulting from the tropical environment. Partly these are the consequence of water shortages arising from the seasonality and unreliability of the rainfall regime in most of the north (not, of course, solely a tropical characteristic) and are sometimes the result of cyclonic activity and/or flooding. The construction of suitable water-storage schemes is a major prerequisite of all large-scale mining developments in the Australian tropics and is a further factor contributing to the scale of operations. The impact of the tropical environment is, however, probably greatest through the actual or perceived discomfort of daily life that it creates in the new mining townships. The difficulties associated with heat, dust and water scarcity are all the greater in newly established settlements where a general sense of remoteness is only partly alleviated by embryonic

social relationships. The emphasis placed on landscaping and the provision of sporting facilities by the mining companies in the new townships is a recognition of the scale of this problem but can provide only limited compensation. In circumstances where labour must largely be drawn from subtropical and temperate regions there can be little doubt that the popular perception—accurate or otherwise—of tropical living conditions is a severe limitation to the creation of stable populations. In this regard, as in others examined in this chapter, it is in central and northern Queensland, less remote and environmentally less unfamiliar to many potential settlers, that the difficulties are likely to be least severe and balanced population growth based on mining developments more likely to be assured.

TROPICAL AGRICULTURE

It has been a recurrent belief, both voiced specifically and underlying many other statements about the settlement and development of tropical Australia, that, whilst pastoralism and mining have a valuable role to play, only when the country has been submitted to the plough and closely settled by agriculturalists will its potential have been realized. Since 1840, when a report by the Colonial Land and Emigration Commissioners (W. S. Campbell, 1912–13) was decidedly unenthusiastic towards proposals to sell land for agricultural purposes around Port Essington, until the still-unfinished debate on the Ord Irrigation Project, there has been continuing controversy over the desirability and viability of tropical agriculture in Australia. Frequently the argument has been advanced that agriculture alone will permit a sufficient density of human occupance to stake the Australian nation's claim to its northern latitudes, the need for which seems to have been related to a degree of embarrassment with the White Australia policy. Writing admittedly of the Northern Territory, but with sentiments that no doubt applied equally to the whole of northern Australia, J. A. Gilruth, administrator of the Northern Territory, stated in his 1914–15 report, 'It is held as a definite policy that the Territory should be settled by whites as a national necessity. This means agriculture. If the government does not risk money in experiment and by assisting settlers, who will?' The fact that no-one else would, perhaps reflected the situation that, unlike pastoralism or mining, agricultural development in the tropics appeared less than attractive to the individual pioneer or company entrepreneur. In 1971, after nearly a century and a half of stated prospects for the agricultural settlement of the region, only 0.15 per cent of tropical Australia, as defined, was under crops.

There appears little room for doubt that the natural and economic environments of the north are less

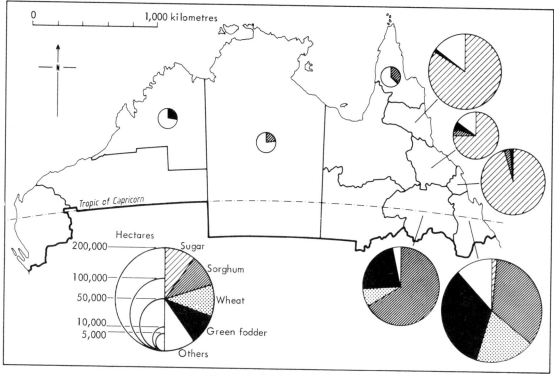

Fig. 13.6 Tropical Australia—cultivated areas and proportions under specific crops, by statistical division, 1971.

inviting to agriculture than they are to other possible means of economic exploitation of this peripheral region of the continent. The dominant characteristics of the climates and soils of tropical Australia have already received comment. Amongst the difficulties created by the tropical climate, the seasonality, variability and intensity of rainfall are probably the greatest, whilst the low nutrient status of most soils and the extremes of permeability or impermeability that variously occur add to agriculture's problems. The character of tropical rainfall distribution certainly provides a hydrological rationale for storage schemes, a fact which doubtless contributes to the enthusiasm of engineers for agricultural development projects, but, in the absence of such capital-intensive undertakings, the unreliability of rainfall over the whole of tropical Australia, except for its most northern latitudes, and its low average effective totals everywhere, except between about 16° and 18° S on the Queensland coast, constitute very real limitations to crop production. The secondary effects of rainfall intensity, such as harvest and transport difficulties caused by boggy soils, damaged roads and bridges and local flooding, can be as disadvantageous as direct crop damage caused by excessive or inadequate falls. The low nutrient status of soils can be partially or entirely corrected by the application, at a price, of chemical fertilizers but the impermeability of extensive areas of heavy solodic soils and the loose sandy nature of others are more stubborn problems. On the credit side, however, high winter temperatures, long hours of sunshine, even generally during the wet season, and widespread freedom from frosts are characteristics of which at least some advantage can be taken.

The marked lack of agricultural development in tropical Australia beyond a limited number of patches along the Queensland coast is, nevertheless, a consequence of more than a difficult physical environment, and is best understood in the context of the economic development of the nation-continent as a whole. It has certainly been to the disadvantage of any who have been eager, for whatever reason, to see a substantial peopling of the rural areas of Australia that the settlement of the continent has occurred during a period of increasing urbanization of the world's population, of rural depopulation in the advanced agricultural nations of the West—amongst which Australia is numbered—accompanied and made possible by a high degree of agricultural mechanization. Emphasis on the concept of a nation of yeoman farmers—revealed by early South Australian plans for the Northern Territory, by Dunmore Lang's hopes for Queensland and by at least two generations of soldier settlements—has probably always been at variance with social and economic reality and nowhere more so than in the peripheral regions of the continent.

The economic and demographic character of tropical Australia is such that commercial agriculture on any scale sufficient to benefit from modern techniques and to justify the provision of infrastructure is necessarily export-oriented. To supply markets located in the more densely populated core area of southeastern Australia immediately puts northern Australia at a distinct economic disadvantage in terms of transport costs alone, a disadvantage that can be overcome only by sufficiently low production costs or scale economies that are quite unrealistic, or by the production of distinctive crops the demand for which cannot be met from more local suppliers. During the summer season there are few crops demanded by the domestic market that cannot be grown more locally than in northern Australia and thus supplied at lower cost. Freight, cartage and inspection charges on bananas supplied to the Sydney market, for example, are over three times as great per case from far north Queensland (El Arish) as they are from Coff's Harbour in New South Wales. In the winter season, however, the north's climatic advantage enables it to penetrate southern markets with its high-cost but scarce fruit. The prospects offered by overseas markets—unless marketing agreements are reached at industry or national level—depend on the relationship between world prices and north Australian production costs which, for most tropical products, are likely to be higher than those of major competitors.

Since World War II, northern Australia has been the subject of intensive scientific investigations that have produced information on the natural environment far surpassing in its detail any that was available for most agricultural regions in the country before their development. Such was the extent of this information that it led the chief of the CSIRO's Division of Land Research and Regional Survey in 1959 to claim that it had set the stage for 'a major revolution in agricultural development' in northern Australia (Christian, 1959). Over the period 1960–71 there indeed occurred a doubling of the cropped area of tropical Australia from 279,545 ha to 565,406 ha and, although this represented only a very small proportionate increase (from 0.076 per cent to 0.153 per cent), it was certainly the most rapid expansion in agricultural activity ever seen in the north. An examination of the distribution of the cropped area of tropical Australia in each of 1960 and 1971, and of the particular crops involved in the expansion, reveals, however, that rather than a major surge having occurred in the agricultural development of the remote areas of the north there has been an increasing concentration of effort on a narrow

range of well-established crops and that this concentration has taken place predominantly in central and coastal north Queensland, physically the least difficult and economically the least peripheral parts of the region (Fig. 13.6). In 1971, 98 per cent of the total cropped area of tropical Australia was in Queensland and 55 per cent in central Queensland, compared with 99.7 per cent and 41 per cent respectively in 1960. The small decrease in the absolute predominance of Queensland was the result of the Ord irrigation scheme in the Kimberleys.

The statistical returns for the tropical divisions of Queensland, the Northern Territory and Western Australia, provide data for 24 specific crops with by far the most detailed listing occurring in Queensland. Of these 24, however, sugar cane alone occupied 35.5 per cent of the total cropped area in 1971 (Table 13.3), and sugar, grain sorghum, green fodder and wheat together occupied 88.6 per cent of the agricultural land in tropical Australia. The collective predominance of these four crops or crop groups showed very little variation from 1960, though there was a marked change between the relative importance of sugar and sorghum (Table 13.3), while all four substantially increased their individual total areas. Indeed, of the increase of 285,861 ha under crops in tropical Australia between 1960 and 1971, sugar accounted for 55,736 ha (19.49 per cent), sorghum for 121,640 ha (42.55 per cent) and green fodder for 65,162 ha (22.79 per cent).

Despite the very marked increases in the area devoted to grain sorghum and in the production of this coarse grain during the 1960s, sugar remains supreme amongst the crops of tropical Australia. The 38 per cent expansion in the area occupied by cane over the period 1960–71 is in itself noteworthy, but less so than the increase in production during the decade, which rose by 90 per cent from 7,089,632 to 13,440,739 tonnes, representing a substantial raising of average yields. This impressive rise in yields, made possible by new varieties, better cultivation methods and the use of fertilizers, is one consequence of the rigid control of the cane growing area by the assignment system which encourages intensification. Notwithstanding the many problems that the Australian sugar industry has faced since its inception in the 1860s, including labour shortages, outbreaks of cane disease and depressed world prices, cane growing has been responsible for the clearing and settling of the majority of the existing agricultural lands in tropical Australia and for the development of their townships, communication systems and services. The most densely populated rural areas in Queensland are the shires of the tropical sugar coast.

The success of sugar in coping with the twin problems of northern Australia—the tropical physical environment and peripheral economic location—provides, however, little scope for anticipation that its achievement may be repeated elsewhere or by other crops. By the mid-1920s, most of the best soils in the humid parts of the Queensland coast had been selected for cane growing. These were mainly the delta and levee soils of the main rivers and creeks of the Pioneer, Proserpine, Burdekin, Herbert, Tully, Johnstone, Russell, Mulgrave, Barron and Mossman river systems and the soils of volcanic origin of the Johnstone river district. Deep loamy soils with duplex profiles predominated, their nutrient status dependent on their parent material but generally low, especially in phosphorus and nitrogen. As important as any inherent fertility, however, were those soil properties that favoured rapid infiltration, good transmission of water within the soil and high water-storage capacity. The winter rainfall of the Pioneer (Mackay) region, associated with upper air disturbances and occasional cold fronts, the orographically-induced winter falls of the wet coast between Ingham and Mossman and the subartesian water of the lower Burdekin made possible the utilization of the loamy soils in those regions for the year-long cultivation of cane. From the late 1860s, cane growing was established increasingly further north in a series of coastal enclaves, each with its cluster of mills, and in the boom period of the 1880s sugar was produced as far north as Cooktown but, with the construction of larger central mills from 1885, Mossman came to be the northern limit of cultivation.

Nineteenth-century sugar growing, based initially on the traditional plantation system and later on smallholders supplying a central mill but still retaining Pacific Island or Chinese labour, was far from being a stable industry especially during the era of low world sugar prices created by the bounty-supported sugar beet industries of continental Europe after the mid-'80s. Its attainment of agricultural supremacy in tropical Australia has occurred since federation and has been based on rigid statutory controls and privileges, largely denied to other crops, which have been reinforced by considerable technical achievements made possible and encouraged by those controls.

The first Commonwealth parliament of 1901 dominated by spokesmen for 'white Australia', introduced legislation prohibiting after 31 March 1904 any further introduction of Pacific Islanders on whose relatively low cost labour the industry had depended, and providing for the repatriation by the end of 1906 of Islanders already resident. The sugar industry was defended, however, by a protective duty on sugar imports into the Commonwealth as a whole, and an excise of which a rebate was paid on sugar manufactured from cane grown and cut by 'white' labour. From these beginnings, the sugar industry has come to be subject to more controls than any other branch of agriculture in Australia. Production is regulated by a system of marketing quotas (or 'mill

peaks') for sugar mills and area allotments (or 'farm assignments') for individual farms. The Queensland Sugar Board, set up in 1923, represents the state government and acquires all raw sugar produced in both Queensland and northern New South Wales. The refining and marketing of sugar for local requirements is undertaken by refining companies on behalf of the Board, which also arranges exports on an agency basis. Under agreement between the Queensland and Australian governments an import embargo is maintained on sugar and the Queensland government undertakes to provide refined sugar for Australian consumption at prescribed uniform wholesale prices. The control of production, the supervision of assignments of cane land and the determination of the prices to be paid by the mills for cane are the responsibility of the Central Sugar Cane Prices Board, also representing the Queensland government. The industry is further served by a number of commercial and technical organizations, some from the private and some from the government sector, which collectively have helped the industry reach very high levels of productivity and working efficiency.

Introduced when the industry's conditions of operation were changed for social and political reasons, this close control of the sugar industry has permitted its survival and gradual expansion, with substantial increases in assigned areas in 1939, between 1949 and 1953, and in 1963, at the cost, in most years, of domestic prices above import parity levels. Marketing agreements, with the United Kingdom after 1951 and the United States after 1961, also guaranteed returns that were generally higher than those to be earned on the free world market. Such has been the build-up of population, ancillary services and infrastructure around the sugar industry that its survival is essential to the very existence of many of the most densely populated districts of northern Australia. It has been estimated (Courtenay, Pryor and Mersiades, 1974) that about 85 per cent of the population in one north Queensland sugar district is dependent, directly or indirectly, on the sugar industry, and this figure is probably reasonable for other similar districts. Many of the facilities developed initially for sugar have contributed to the progress of other, unrelated activities such as tourism or assisted the expansion of other primary industries. Following generally unsuccessful experiments with cotton and coffee, sugar came to be the crop upon which the settlement of tropical Australia's best agricultural land was based. It is readily understandable, therefore, that the continuing development of this industry should have taken priority over most other agricultural activities in the north and that technological advances, in cane breeding, cultivation and harvesting procedures (which are now fully mechanized), transport, milling and shipment should

Table 13.3 Tropical Australia—Areas Under Principal Crops

	Total area (hectares)	Area of all crops in hectares and as percentages of total area				Areas under principal crops in hectares and as percentages of total cropped area														
		1960		1971		Sugar 1960		Sugar 1971		Sorghum 1960		Sorghum 1971		Wheat 1960		Wheat 1971		Green fodder 1960		Green fodder 1971	
		ha	%	ha	%	ha	%	ha	%	ha	%	ha	%	ha	%	ha	%	ha	%	ha	%
Rockhampton	10,268,529	82,242	0.80	196,396	1.91	2,197	0.02	2,506	1.28	25,283	30.74	67,358	34.30	15,918	19.36	38,318	19.15	21,030	25.57	65,468	33.33
Central Western	18,303,530	33,638	0.18	117,909	0.64	—	—	—	—	7,497	22.29	78,634	66.69	12,106	35.99	8,684	7.36	9,625	28.61	26,423	22.41
Far Western	28,223,557	190	0.00	4	0.00	—	—	—	—	—	—	—	—	—	—	—	—	188	98.97	1	36.75
Mackay	2,009,916	57,377	2.85	79,476	3.95	56,732	98.88	75,858	95.45	9	0.02	2,364	2.97	5	0.01	—	—	361	0.63	945	1.19
Townsville	9,828,301	25,544	0.26	42,602	0.43	21,831	85.46	31,838	74.73	212	0.83	2,090	4.91	—	—	2	0.00	227	0.89	2,944	4.80
Cairns	7,542,951	78,929	1.05	107,947	1.43	64,462	81.67	90,756	84.07	69	0.00	402	0.37	—	—	26	0.02	938	1.19	1,028	0.95
Peninsula	12,571,240	184	0.00	7,556	0.06	—	—	—	—	—	—	2,545	33.68	—	—	—	—	11	5.94	194	2.57
North Western	38,022,320	579	0.00	207	0.00	—	—	—	—	—	—	8	3.86	—	—	—	—	565	97.61	98	47.34
Northern Territory	134,809,751	n.a.		5,665	0.00	—	—	—	—	—	—	1,309	23.11	—	—	—	—	—	—	—	—
Kimberley	42,069,765	453	0.00	6,956	0.02	—	—	—	—	—	—	—	—	—	—	10	0.15	14	3.04	1,928	27.72
Pilbara	44,427,401	1	0.00	3	0.00	—	—	—	—	—	—	—	—	—	—	—	—	1	81.00	—	—
North West	20,109,951	408	0.00	686	0.00	—	—	—	—	—	—	—	—	—	—	—	—	8	1.99	—	—
Total	368,187,212	279,545	0.08	565,406	0.15	145,222	51.95	200,958	35.54	33,070	11.83	154,710	27.36	28,029	10.03	47,040	8.32	32,968	11.79	98,130	17.36

0.00 less than 0.01
— nil

Sources: Statistics of Queensland; Statistical Register of Western Australia; Northern Territory Statistical Summary.

be directed towards increased productivity and cost reductions wherever possible.

The 368 per cent expansion in the sorghum area in tropical Australia between 1960 and 1971, from 33,070 ha to 154,710 ha was largely concentrated in central Queensland where, in the Central Western division alone (see Table 13.3), the area under this crop expanded tenfold to a figure representing 50 per cent of the total sorghum area in the north. The neighbouring Rockhampton division, although showing a less dramatic expansion over the period, contained a further 44 per cent of the area under sorghum in tropical Australia by 1971. Grain sorghum has, in recent decades, become the main summer crop in central Queensland where its success has been based on its hardiness under rainfall conditions and the ability of its culture to adapt to extensive cultivation conditions. Considerable knowledge of the potential, and of the limitations, of the central highlands for summer grain production was gained during the course of activities by the Queensland-British Food Corporation after World War II. Although the Corporation may not have succeeded in its primary aim of the annual production of large quantities of sorghum it did highlight the vital roles played by stored soil moisture in the determination of yield and the usefulness of sorghum stubble and substandard grain sorghum crops for the fattening of store cattle. Much of the current production, especially in Bauhinia shire, is from newly developed brigalow land. Marketing of grain sorghum in central Queensland, under the jurisdiction of a marketing board, is in close co-operation with the State Wheat Board especially in the use of storage and shipping facilities. All but a minute proportion of tropical Australia's wheat production is also located in central Queensland where sufficient winter rainfall usually occurs to ensure a winter grain crop provided that summer moisture has been conserved by appropriate fallowing methods. The expansion of wheat areas is occurring particularly on soils that previously supported brigalow and associated vegetation and which typically have a relatively high moisture-holding capacity and are thus amenable to such fallowing techniques. Winter and summer crops of oats, barley, lucerne, sorghum, panicum and millet grown for fodder occupy a considerable proportion of the cultivated land in central Queensland and, as with sorghum and wheat, the area under such fodder crops increased greatly between 1960 and 1971. Similar proportionate, but smaller absolute, increases also occurred in other parts of the north especially in the Townsville, Cairns, Peninsula and Kimberley divisions (see Table 13.3). The construction of the Fairbairn Dam on the Nogoa River near Emerald will permit the intensive development of 36,000 ha of country in central Queensland and it is anticipated that expansion will occur in the production of cotton, wheat, sorghum and pastures under irrigation and contribute to a further consolidation of the region's role in the agricultural development of the north.

Despite the statistically evident fact that the major agricultural developments of the last decade or so in tropical Australia have consisted primarily of an intensification of already well-established crops in the least remote parts of the region, public investment and attention have been mainly directed towards a small number of large-scale irrigation schemes designed to establish or substantially to expand production of alternative crops in more remote districts of the north. Following the construction of a number of small weirs in the late 1940s and early '50s, the Queensland Irrigation and Water Supply Commission undertook the construction of a major dam (with a storage capacity of just over 400,000,000 cubic metres) above Tinaroo Falls on the Barron River. When the scheme had been completed in 1958 at a cost of $ 32 million, the available water resulted in a spectacular increase in the production of tobacco, a crop that had been grown on a small scale and with limited success since 1931 in the valleys of the headwaters of the Mitchell and Barron rivers inland from Cairns. Elevated granitic soils, well suited to tobacco but abandoned by early growers because of their previous dependence on natural rainfall, were brought back into cultivation and the use of alluvial soils extended. The complete development of the whole potentially irrigable area in the country around the towns of Mareeba and Dimbulah was halted prematurely, however, because of the introduction of a stabilization scheme into the tobacco industry. Under this scheme, the sale, on a price and grade schedule, of a fixed amount of tobacco leaf each year is guaranteed by the Australian government, but has had the effect of limiting plantings to less than 4,000 ha per year in the Mareeba-Dimbulah district (McDonald, 1974). In order to guarantee the absorption of Australian leaf, tobacco manufacturers in Australia are required to incorporate specified proportions of the local product in order to qualify for a rebate on imported tobacco. The Tinaroo Falls dam and irrigation scheme have permitted the expansion of agricultural activity in the Mareeba-Dimbulah district, and resulted in a substantial population growth in the Mareeba shire, from 7,595 in 1954 to 11,676 in 1971. However limitations to the availability of tobacco soils and restrictions on production increases in view of the limited size of the Australian market suggest that no major expansion of the tobacco industry is likely. The Tinaroo Falls dam has made available far more water than can be used for tobacco production and, despite research into other agricultural uses—of which irrigated pastures are one of the more likely possibilities— no economically viable alternative crop has yet

Plate 13.2 Sugar fields and rice bays, Burdekin Valley, north Queensland. The addition of rice to the sugar-dominated agriculture of the lower Burdekin in recent years has added a distinctive new element to the agricultural landscape. If cane assignments are increased, however, many of these rice bays will probably become canefields. *Photo*: Alex Trotter, Townsville.

emerged, though the attraction of the stored water body for vacation and tourist type activities has very great potential.

The most ambitious irrigation scheme to date in the Australian tropics is the Ord River Irrigation Project in the east Kimberley area of Western Australia. The possibilities for the more intensive settlement and development of country that has been occupied for pastoral purposes since the 1880s have been under consideration at various times, and in 1941 the West Australian Public Works Department investigated the feasibility of damming the Ord River at a point some 110–130 km from its mouth where it passes through the Carr Boyd Range. A small agricultural research station was established and detailed investigations made of dam sites, soil types and topography. By 1958 investigations had shown that it was possible to build a dam to store at least 3,700 million cubic metres of water which would yield sufficient supplies to irrigate the available 72,000 ha of irrigable soils in the East Kimberley area. Agricultural work at the Kimberley Research Station demonstrated that, at least on an experimental scale, cotton, rice, safflower, linseed and sugar cane could be grown successfully. Following an agreement between the Australian government and the State government of Western Australia on finance for the scheme, the Ord River Project was commenced in 1959. The first stage of the scheme, the Kununurra Diversion Dam providing sufficient water to permit the development of 12,000 ha, was completed in 1963, and the second stage, the main dam serving the full 72,000 ha of the scheme, was officially opened in 1972. The third stage, which plans to make use of floodwaters and of water released from the dam throughout the year to generate hydroelectric power, remains unapproved.

After early attempts at safflower growing proved uneconomic, cotton emerged as the major, and for some years virtually the only crop. By 1974 there were approximately 4,000 ha of cotton with subsidiary areas of sorghum (used for lot-feeding of beef cattle), rice, wheat and seed and experimental plots of a variety of crops including kenaf, lemon grass, peanuts, cassava and maize. It has been argued (Patterson, 1965) that the scheme includes the cheapest large-scale dam ever constructed in Australia and that the project is justifiable on cotton production alone if yields of 2,240 kg per ha can be averaged, whilst the production of grain sorghum and the benefits to cattle production of high protein by-products and locally produced grains would appreciably increase over-all profitability. Alternative arguments (Davidson, 1963, 1965) have been presented to illustrate that the production of relatively low priced crops, such as cotton, under irrigation in high cost areas in tropical Australia can only be possible with heavy subsidies and, although the cotton bounty had been phased out by 1972, a number of other forms of financial assistance, including water at a price that does not meet even variable costs and a cotton stabilization scheme to guarantee costs of production introduced in 1974, are available.

Whether cost-benefit analyses indicate economic viability or otherwise for the scheme—and such techniques are by no means of universal application—the agricultural prospects of the Ord valley are far from positively established. The need for access to $250,000 of working capital that has been stated by the Western Australian government as a necessary minimum for farmers taking up new units suggests that operations are likely to become increasingly large scale and capital intensive. By 1974 the production costs of cotton had become prohibitive and the crop occupied only 6 per cent of a much reduced irrigated area. The Ord scheme is not one that is likely to provide a model for further settlement in the remoter parts of the north.

Apart from the dominant crops already discussed and those associated with the irrigation areas, a range of other agricultural products is grown in tropical Australia—plantation fruit (especially bananas and pineapples), peanuts, orchard fruit and various seed and bean crops—few of which have proved to be of more than local importance. Two developments are perhaps of particular interest, however, and justify brief specific mention.

The suitability of the better-watered districts of tropical Australia for rice production has been proclaimed since the days of the Port Essington settlement, and in the 1880s and '90s a number of rice growing ventures were undertaken, mainly by Chinese, in north Queensland and the Northern Territory. A peak area of 413 ha was achieved in north Queensland in 1892. The removal of import duty on rice in 1890 effectively killed the industry in the north until a shortage during and after World War II revived interest in the crop. In 1946 the CSIRO undertook the survey of the Katherine-Darwin portion of the Northern Territory and its report (CSIRO, 1952) indicated physical potential for rice production in the upper Adelaide River area. Other reports, concerned especially with water control problems, followed. In 1954/5 a private company, Territory Rice, began growing rice commercially on the subcoastal plains of the Adelaide River some 72 km from Darwin with the intention of developing large-scale production and marketing 500,000 tons per annum by 1966. By 1959 some 2,000 ha had been sown but the company was running into financial difficulties and the project was finally abandoned in 1962. At the present time the best prospects for rice production appear not to be in the Territory but in coastal north Queensland, where, in the vicinity of the Burdekin River, an embryo industry has grown since 1967 and nearly 2,000 ha of high quality, long-grain rice were harvested in 1972. Backed by extensive research undertaken by the Queensland Department of Primary Industries and supported by the existing infrastructure developed largely on the basis of the sugar industry, the rice industry of the Burdekin valley, and its small offshoot in the lower Herbert valley, appears to have a sound economic future.

In the Johnstone River district of north Queensland a small, fully mechanized tea industry has been established since the mid-1960s. Although the tea plant was first introduced into north Queensland about 1875, and experimental crops have been raised in the district since World War II, the first commercial marketing of tea, from one plantation, did not take place until 1970. Grown, harvested and manufactured by distinctive methods, this crop is as yet little more than an agricultural curiosity in northern Australia, and considerable market investigations will be necessary before any future can be forecast for it.

SETTLEMENT AND DEMOGRAPHIC PATTERNS

The preceding sections of this chapter have examined the major sectors of the export-oriented economy of tropical Australia—pastoralism, mining and agriculture—and have generally concluded that, although the tropical environment has a substantial impact on these activities, more particularly on those dependent on the biological rhythm of plant or animal growth, the economy of northern Australia is essentially peripheral, and its pattern of spatial development can best be explained in terms of the centre/periphery model. The articulation of this peripheral economy occurs through its urban system and the evolution and functions of tropical Australia's settlement pattern

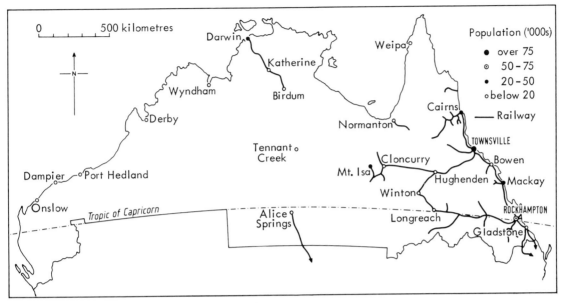

Fig. *13.7* Tropical Australia—railways and urban settlement.

are most clearly understood in terms of its linkages with that economy. It would, however, be wrong to attempt to construct a single settlement hierarchy for the whole of northern Australia, partly because of the very large size of the region and partly because of the separate orientations of its three political divisions. Further, the political centralization characteristic of Australian state administrations has led to the retention in capital cities of certain functions that could well be located lower in the hierarchy, especially in Queensland, with the consequence that many linkages are directly between smaller centres and the extra-tropical metropolitan area rather than with the major regional centres.

The basis of the urban settlement pattern of tropical Australia was laid by the pastoral, mining and agricultural developments of the pre-federation period, initially by the foundation of ports along the north Queensland coast to handle outward shipments of wool, hides, tallow and gold and inward movements of labour, supplies and machinery. Rockhampton (1858), Bowen (1860), Mackay (1862), Townsville (1864) and Cairns (1876) were the most significant of these. The establishment of the sugar industry gave additional traffic to such of these ports as were appropriately located and was responsible for the creation of other towns to serve as mill and general service centres and local ports for the industry. Inland towns were either the creation of the gold rushes and tended to decline with the exhaustion of gold (though not always to complete extinction) or were small service centres in areas, especially of interior Queensland, where reliable

artesian water supported a sufficiently intensive livestock industry to sustain them. In tropical Western Australia, small ports, e.g. Derby (1882), Broome (1883), Onslow (1885), Wyndham (1889) and Port Hedland (1896), were similarly established to provide coastal links for pastoralists and gold diggers. Only in the Northern Territory was there a less spontaneous port growth, with Palmerston (later Darwin) deliberately chosen in 1868 as the port and base from which the planned settlement of 600,000 rural acres and a number of country towns was to take place. The sketching out of a regional hierarchy of settlements was accelerated by the construction of transport links, particularly of railways, which reinforced the growing centrality of those ports that were chosen—sometimes perhaps as much on political as on economic grounds—as coastal termini for the new lines. In the cases of Rockhampton and Townsville especially, the extensive grazing country of their hinterlands was tapped by lines in the 1880s, and the linkage of the Cloncurry copper mining field to the Townsville line rather than to the Gulf reinforced Townsville's growing status and, much later, fixed Mt Isa firmly in its hinterland. In the present pattern of urban settlement (Fig. 13.7), Townsville has emerged as the largest centre in the Australian tropics, whilst Rockhampton and Darwin are the region's major 'second tier' cities—the role of the latter, especially as an important administrative centre, exaggerated as a result of the distinctive administrative status of the Northern Territory (a fact which, incidentally, contributes to the apparently anomalous character of the

Plate 13.3   Townsville—tropical Australia's primate city. Current developments in the city and harbour area of Townsville reflect its expanding role as the tropics' major commercial centre. Its employment structure, and increasingly its landscape, can perhaps be described as sub-metropolitan. *Photo*: M. J. Lamont, Townsville.

Territory—a single statistical division—in Fig. 13.1). The distinctive nature of Townsville emerges clearly in Fig. 13.1 and 13.3 in which the employment structure of its statistical division reveals it as economically the least peripheral district in the tropics.

The peripheral characteristics of the tropical Australian economy, especially the pioneering nature of economic activities in its more remote districts, have produced certain demographic features that are illustrated in Figs 13.8 and 13.9. Compared with that of the non-tropical half of the continent, the population of tropical Australia in 1971 included a higher percentage of people, especially males, in the 20–39 age group, and a higher percentage of children under 15 (except boys 10–14) which is clearly related to the former fact. This higher percentage of people in the most active working (and reproductive) age groups mainly reflects the opportunities for pioneering-type employment in mining and other developments. That it owes little to seasonal employment in cane cutting, almost entirely mechanized by 1971 anyway, is revealed by the pyramids for Cairns and Mackay—the principal

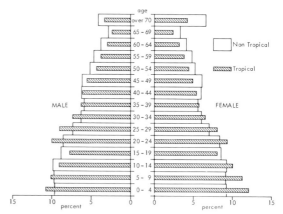

Fig. 13.8   Population pyramid for tropical and non-tropical Australia, 1971.

sugar districts—where the characteristic is the least apparent in the entire tropics. Also notable is the lower percentage in the 10–19 age group (males) and 15–19 age group (females) which partly may be

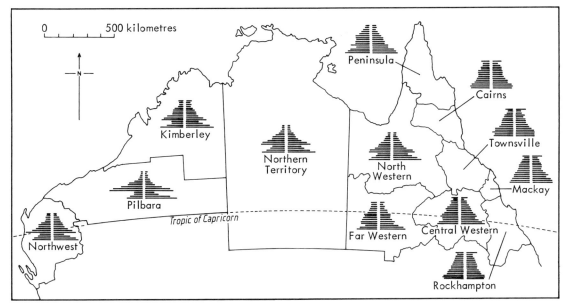

Fig. 13.9   Tropical Australia—population structure by statistical divisions, 1971.

explained by the tendency for secondary and tertiary education to take place in non-peripheral centres and, particularly in the case of females, for employment to be sought away from the periphery. The smaller percentage of older parents (i.e. over 40) is also significant in accounting for the smaller numbers in the 10–19 age groups. When the population structure is examined on the basis of statistical divisions (Fig. 13.9), it becomes apparent that the regions of major developmental efforts, especially the Pilbara but also the Ord scheme in Kimberley and the mining developments in the Territory, at Mt Isa (Queensland, North Western) and Weipa (Peninsula), are those in which the predominance of the most active working age groups is most marked.

Although the pattern of settlement in the Australian tropics and the age and sex structure of the region's population approximate to those to be anticipated in such a peripheral region with a strongly export-oriented economy, it is perhaps necessary, if only for historical reasons, to comment on the often bitter debates of the pre-war years over the ability of settlers of European origin to people the northern half of the continent. These debates are examined more fully elsewhere (Courtenay, 1975), but in general terms they may be seen to have been created by the desire at federation 'to be one people, and remain one people' as voiced by Alfred Deakin, in conjunction with the long-established north European belief that labouring work in the tropics was the prerogative of 'coloured' peoples. Although early mining in the tropics

attracted European diggers and migrants of European origin worked readily on pastoral properties—even in the Kimberleys there was apparently no shortage of competent 'white' labour at the turn of the century (Bolton, 1954)—their labour was expensive, and the popularity of Aborigines as efficient stockmen and Pacific Islanders as plantation workers was essentially founded on economics. With the introduction of restrictions on immigration, and the emergence of the extreme doctrine of environmentalism amongst certain scientists, the ability of Europeans to thrive, or even survive, in the north of the continent acquired both political and scientific overtones. In 1920–1 the debate even reached the review pages of the *Geographical Review*, when Ellsworth Huntington, basing his statements on 'what (was) known of tropical lands in general' challenged the conclusions of Breinl and Young of the Australian Institute of Tropical Medicine, Townsville, concerning the salubrity of the tropics (Breinl and Young, 1920; Huntington, 1920, 1921).

There is no doubt that northern Australia has not been as favoured for settlement as the southern parts of the continent, that life in the tropics is burdened with a deal of discomfort, due to heat and other conditions associated with climate, and that there has been, and in some areas there remains, a large number of migratory workers in the labour force. To a considerable extent these circumstances have been the consequences of the peripheral nature of the region and its associated export economy. Even the discomforts have been

Plate 13.4 A typical Darwin street scene after Cyclone Tracy. Darwin was destroyed by Cyclone Tracy on 25 December 1974. Its planning and rebuilding is expected to cost $600 million and to take five years. Few of the typical high-set iron-roofed houses survived the destructive force of the cyclone.

intensified by the fact that there has existed 'a general desire amongst the inhabitants that their stay in the north shall be as short as possible' (Breinl and Young, 1920). In the past this attitude of temporary sojourn produced little desire to build homes for comfort, or even to adopt a style of life or dress more suited to a tropical climate than northwest European modes. The late provision of electric power (a peripheral characteristic) made the general use even of electric fans impossible in many northern towns until relatively recent times and the more complicated technology involved in artificial cooling than in heating has delayed the general adoption of air conditioning except in some public buildings and the bigger and newer shops and offices. That investment is rapidly increasing in such plant does, however, reflect both the fast-growing awareness of the need to modify traditional cool temperate lifestyles and the increasing prosperity that makes it possible. There is no evidence that the average inhabitant of tropical Australia is less healthy than his equivalent in the southern regions of the continent (though the probability of his acquiring sunburn is higher than that of suffering frostbite). It is an interesting observation, commented on early in the century (Frodsham, 1913) and still supported by subjective evidence, that there is less sickness in the hot summer months in north Queensland than there is in the winter. Unfortunately state health department data are not such as to permit a truly quantitative assessment. It is probably true that the unhealthiness popularly associated with the tropics in general has its roots in poverty and poor general hygiene rather than in any simple climatic circumstances. Unpublished and continuing investigations into the attitudes of north Queenslanders towards their physical environment are producing evidence that it is the problems associated with remoteness and not with the climate that dominate most local people's perception of 'the tropics'.

It has been claimed (Dales, 1961) that many, and

perhaps all, of the major questions about economic development can be rephrased to become amenable to analysis in terms of location theory. This chapter has attempted to demonstrate that the economic patterns apparent in tropical Australia can best be understood in terms of the colonial nature of the region's economy, with its dependence on export-oriented activities, and that the fact that the region is tropical is, in the broad sense, incidental, though clearly having an important influence on those activities closely related to biological rhythms, notably pastoralism and agriculture. This conclusion may be seen to have certain policy consequences for any development strategy concerned with the north of the continent. It suggests, for example, that the problems of the region's lack of development are not primarily the result of its tropical environment and that undue emphasis on specifically tropical problems at the expense of the problems resulting from remoteness may well be to the region's and the nation's disadvantage. It also helps indicate those districts of the north where development expenditure, by state or federal government, is most likely to achieve the highest return. It may well disappoint the proponents of major developmental efforts with public funds in remote places.

REFERENCES

Allen, A. (1965), 'Dairying in the Australian tropics', *Aust. Geogr. Stud.*, 3, 17–29.

Bauer, F. H. (1959), 'Sheep raising in northern Australia: An historical review', *Aust. Geogr.*, 7, 169–79.

Best, L. (1968), 'A model of pure plantation economy', *Soc. and Econ. Stud.*, 17.

Bolton, G. C. (1954), 'The Kimberley pastoral industry', *W. Aust. Univ. Stud. in Hist. and Econ.*, 2, 7–53.

Breinl, A. and Young, W. J. (1920), 'Tropical Australia and its settlement', *Ann. Trop. Med. and Parasitology*, 13, 351–412.

Campbell, R. S. F. (1973), 'Research and development in tropical Australia', *Veterinary Reviews and Monographs*, James Cook University, Townsville, 1, p. 1.

Campbell, W. S. (1912–13), 'The earliest settlements in the Northern Territory of Australia', *J. Aust. Hist. Soc.*, 3, 81–113.

Christian, C. S. (1959), 'The future revolution in agriculture in northern Australia', *Aust. J. Sci.*, 22, 138–47.

Commonwealth Scientific and Industrial Research Organization (1952), *Survey of Katherine-Darwin Region, 1946. Extracts from General Report*, Melbourne.

Courtenay, P. P. (1975), 'The white man and the Australian tropics—a review of some opinions and prejudices of the pre-war years', *Lectures on North Queensland History*, Second Series, James Cook University, Department of History, Townsville, pp. 57–65.

Courtenay, P. P., Pryor, R. J. and Mersiades, N. G. (1974), *The Settlement and Population Characteristics of the Johnstone District of the Queensland Sugar Coast*, James Cook University, Department of Geography,

Monograph Series, Occasional Paper 1, Townsville, p. 9.

Cumming, J. N. and Reid, G. (1967), 'The sheep industry in northern Australia', *Q. Rev. Agric. Econ.*, 20, 71–84.

Dales, J. H. (1961), 'Comment on "Connections between Natural Resources and Economic Growth"' in J. J. Spangler (ed.), *Natural Resources and Economic Growth*, Resources for the Future, Washington, pp. 16–19.

Davidson, B. R. (1963), 'The economics of irrigated agriculture on the Ord River', *Farm Policy*, 3, 54–60.

——(1965), *The Northern Myth*, Melbourne University Press, Melbourne, p. 192.

Department of National Development (1968), 'Rural Production', *Resources Series, Fitzroy Region, Queensland*, p. 28.

Earl, G. W. (1836), *On the Commercial and Agricultural Capabilities of the North Coast of New Holland*, Effingham Wilson, London, p. 21.

——(1837), *The Eastern Seas*, W. H. Allen and Co., London, p. 438.

Frodsham, G. F. (1913), 'Tropical Australia—A great colonizing experiment', *Nineteenth Century*, 74, 333–40.

Gibson-Hill, C. A. (1959), 'George Samuel Windsor Earl', *J. Mal. Br. R. As. Soc.*, 32, 105–53.

Grenfell Price, A. (1928), 'The historical geography of the Northern Territory to 1871', *Aust. Assoc. Advt. Sci.*, 19, 282–93.

Howard, K. F. (1966), 'Beef in north-west Queensland', *Qld. Agric. J.*, 92, 6–15 and 132–45.

Huntington, E. (1920, 1921), 'The adaptability of the white man to the tropics in Australia, review and correspondence', *Geogr. Rev.*, 10, 110–11; and 11, 474–6.

Keller, A. G. (1908), *Colonization: A Study of the Founding of New Societies*, Ginn and Co., Boston, pp. 3–4.

Kelly, J. H. (1971), *Beef in Northern Australia*, Australian National University Press, Canberra, p. 2.

Leeper, G. W. (ed.) (1970), *The Australian Environment*, 4th edn, Melbourne University Press, Melbourne, pp. 84–90.

McDonald, E. J. (1974), *Land Use Planning in the Tobacco District of Far North Queensland*, Qld Dept of Primary Industries, Brisbane, p. 5.

McLintock, G. T. (1970), 'Economics of pasture improvement for beef production in the Northern Territory', *Q. Rev. Agric. Econ.*, 23, 82–96.

Norman, M. J. T. (1965), 'Seasonal performance of beef cattle on native pasture at Katherine, N.T.', *Aust. J. Exp. Ag. and An. Husb.*, 5, 227–31.

Patterson, R. A. (1965), *The Economic Justification of the Ord River Project*, paper presented to 38th Congress, ANZAAS, Hobart.

Roberts, S. H. (1924), 'Northern Territory colonization schemes', *Aust. Assoc. Advt. Sci.*, 17, 420–31.

Stewart, J. (1973), *Rainfall Trends in North Queensland*, James Cook University, Department of Geography, Monograph Series, No. 4, Townsville, pp. 9–11.

Stillwell, F. J. B. (1974), *Australian Urban and Regional Development*, Australia and New Zealand Book Co., Sydney, p. 61.

Thompson, E. T. (1941), 'The climatic theory of the plantation', *Agric. Hist.*, 15, 49–60.

14 AUSTRALIAN FISHERIES

R. S. MATHIESON

The harvesting of the seas around the Australian coast is a minor industry by world standards. In recent years the country has landed fish at the level of 50–60,000 tonnes annually, with an additional 30,000 tonnes each of crustaceans and molluscs, all on a live weight basis. These are small catches compared to the 7.5 million tonnes landed by Peru and the 6.9 million produced by Japan, the world's leading fisheries.

Nevertheless, Australian fisheries are important to the country's economy. Fish protein from nekton (free-swimming fish) provides small but growing sources of food in the country's major cities. And large quantities of tuna, rock lobsters, oysters and abalone are exported, particularly to the United States and Japan. These activities have brought about increasing pressure on Australia's limited fisheries resources.

Unlike the north Atlantic and north Pacific Oceans, the waters around Australia are comparatively warm, with no extensive intermixing of cold polar waters and warm currents which typically generate the most prolific fishing environments. Only around Tasmania do such conditions approach those of the northern hemisphere.

Moreover, even these limited resources have for long remained, not so much underexploited, as significantly undermanaged. Conservancy practices are quite recent innovations in Australian fisheries. In a sense the low-key exploitation of fisheries has been fortunate, for Australian resources could not stand the same fish consumption levels of Japan, Scandinavia, or even those of the land-locked countries of Europe and Latin America. In 1973–4 the Australian fish consumption was only 5.5 kilograms (edible weight basis) per head compared to 20–35 kilograms in the other countries mentioned. And even this amount was only partially obtained from local fish production, about half being imported fish products.

Australian fisheries production for 1972–3 (the most recent year for which comprehensive figures are available) and the value of this catch is shown in Tables 14.1 and 14.2.*

It is evident from these tables that the balance of fisheries resources is somewhat different between the Australian States. New South Wales excels in general

fisheries, particularly the trawl fisheries, prawning and oyster farming (Fig. 14.1). Victoria has significant production of scallops, rock lobsters (crayfish) and abalone, while Queensland's strongest income-earner is its prawn fisheries. Since the mid-1960s Queensland has also developed a useful scallop fishery geared to export markets.

South Australia has important general fisheries based substantially on tuna and to a lesser extent whiting, Australian salmon and edible shark. It also has Australia's second largest rock lobster fishery after Western Australia. In the five years to 1972–3, South Australian rock lobster production has increased by nearly 60 per cent, contrary to the trends in Western Australia. However, Western Australia still remains the pre-eminent State for rock lobster production and export, accounting for nearly two-thirds of the country's output. This State also shares prawn fisheries with New South Wales, but both are significantly behind Queensland production. Tasmania also has an important rock lobster fishery as well as the country's largest output of abalone.

Over the last two decades, growing demand overseas for specialized Australian fish products, particularly lobsters, oysters, prawns and abalone and also frozen tuna for Japanese canneries, has greatly stimulated their production. To a degree this has switched resources and developmental fishing effort away from the relatively low-value general fisheries serving the domestic market.

THE PHYSICAL PARAMETERS OF AUSTRALIAN FISHERIES

Two fundamental physical controls have inhibited greater development of Australian fisheries; (1) the warmer water masses characteristic of the country's sea areas and (2) the rather narrow continental shelf adjacent to the most densely populated regions of the south eastern continent. The broad shelf areas of the

---

*Figures for more recent years have become available since going to press. These indicate that no substantial changes have occurred to invalidate conclusions drawn on the basis of the 1972–3 figures.

Table 14.1 Australian Production of Fish by Principal Varieties, 1972–3 (in tonnes, live weight basis)

	N.S.W.	Victoria	Queens-land	South Australia	Western Australia	Tasmania	Australia (a)
Tuna	6,134	159(c)	28	6,697	679	40	13,737
Snoek	(d)	1,533(c)	—	—	3	915	2,451
Mullet	2,745	277(c)	1,448	353	771	7	5,601
Australian salmon	732	586(c)	—	799	1,630	461	4,208
Snapper	764	299(c)	62	541	217	—	1,883
Morwong	1,311	24(c)	—	—	10	7	1,352
Flathead	1,548	743(c)	90	17	12	39	2,449
Shark	1,125	3,625(c)	18	618	652	497	6,535
Mackerel	(d)	—	1,244	—	85	1	1,330
Bream (b)	291	314(c)	227	25	23	—	880
Ruff	—	34(c)	—	241	1,234	—	1,509
Whiting	208	417(c)	324	959	228	1	2,137
Leatherjacket	1,277	16(c)	—	—	27	—	1,320
All other species	5,336	7,866(c)	1,985	1,542	1,518	297	18,544
Total production	21,471	15,893(c)	5,426	11,792	7,089	2,265	63,936(e)
Percentage of total	33.58	24.86	8.49	18.44	11.09	3.54	100.00

Notes: Adjustments and calculations by the author:
  (a) Australian production excludes small quantities from the Northern Territory; in 1972–3, 619 tonnes, mainly barramundi and tuna.
  (b) Including tarwhine.
  (c) 1971–2 figures used as 1972–3 figures are not available.
  (d) In N.S.W. landings of snoek and mackerel included in 'all other species'.
  (e) The Australian total given is adjusted to take account of the 1971–2 production figures used for Victoria. Indications are that Victoria produced 5,125 tonnes less fish in 1972–3 than in 1971–2; a reduction of about one-third 'normal' production. See discussion.
Source: Bureau of Statistics, *Fisheries*, No. 10, 8 September 1974, Canberra, pp. 14–15.

Great Barrier Reef and Sahul submarine massif, north of the continent, are remote and, in common with the equatorial tropics, have sparse commercial fisheries resources. Only Bass Strait and the Gulf of St Vincent provide really productive broad shelf areas around the continent.

Australian fisheries exhibit extreme taxonomic diversity in accordance with the general ecological character of the tropical and subtropical worlds. Well over 2,000 species of fish are found in Australian waters. But the corollary of this is that localized large populations of individual species are a rare occurrence. Only the tunas and mullets have adapted their lifestyle in tropical waters to strongly shoaling behaviour.

Thus throughout the ecological chain in Australian waters we find the recurring pattern of 'many species but selectively few individuals in the biomass'. This is the case whether we consider the primary food supply for fish, the phyto- and zoo-planktons or the nekton (free-swimming fish), or the predator fish which depend on these for sustenance.

Of the 2,000 or so individual species of fish so far identified in Australian waters, only about 82 species are considered edible and 25 species account for around 85 per cent of the Australian catch each year. Such a structure of the resource-base places severe constraints on an economically viable fishery. An industry which is labour-intensive and therefore already under economic constraint, cannot cope when a high proportion of 'trash-fish' appear as joint products. This is typically the condition in Australia's warm-water fisheries.

Stocks of commercially useful fish and the proportions of various species present depend on rather complex oceanographic conditions. These conditions constitute the base-level in the marine environment which supports an open ecological system involving trophic levels (i.e., nutrient status of sea waters), plant growth, particularly the drifting phyto-plankton, the minute sea animals, especially microscopic zoo-plank-

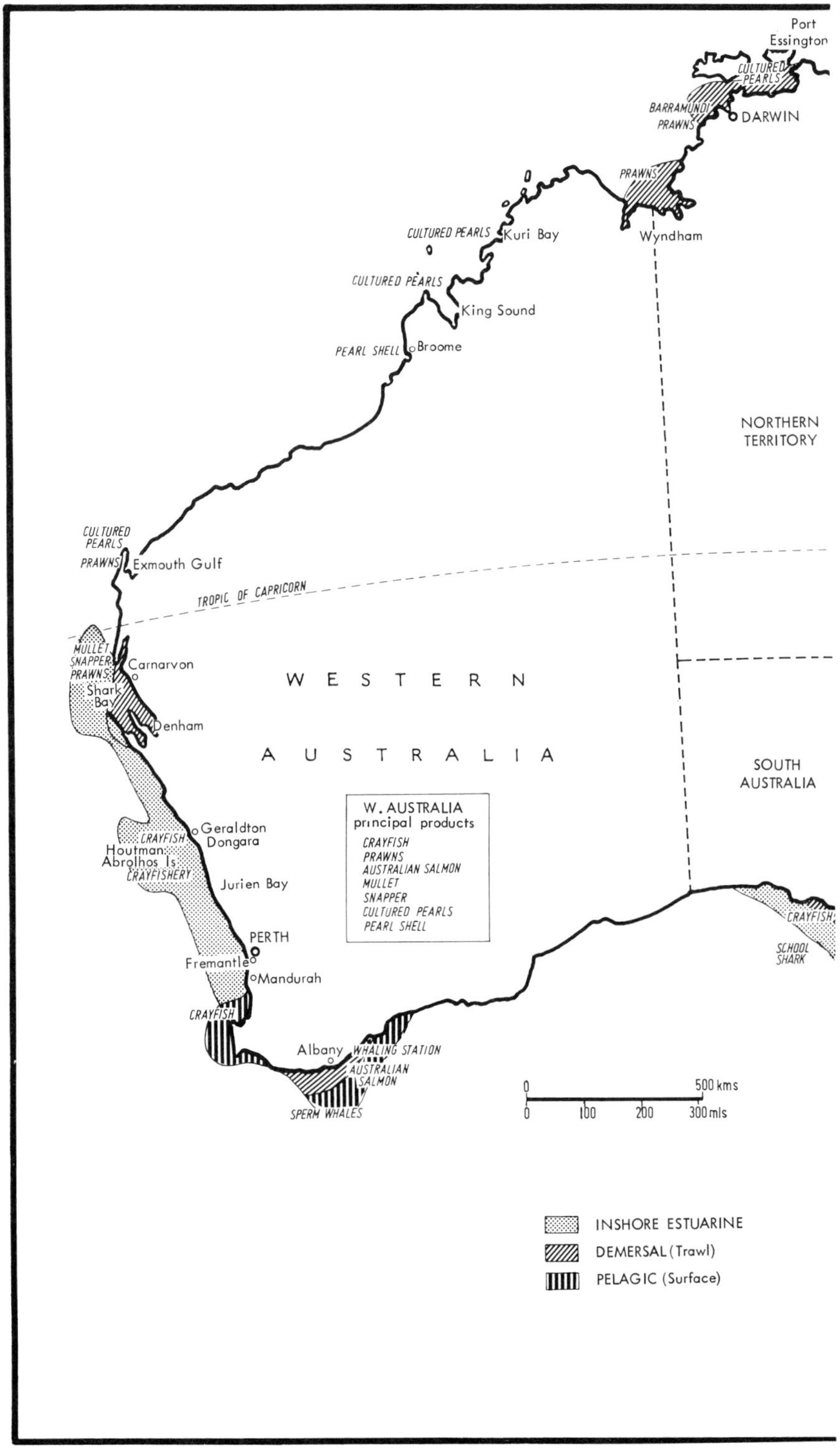

Fig. 14.1   Major commercial fishing grounds in Australian waters. *Sources*: map by R. S. Mathieson in *The Reader's Digest Atlas of Australia* (1970); *Official Yearbook of the Commonwealth of Australia*, 1973, p. 48.

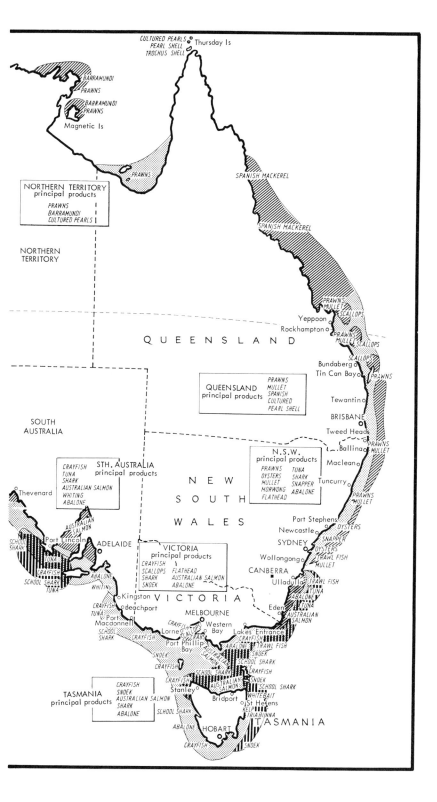

Table 14.2   Gross value of Australian Fisheries Production, 1972–3 ($'000)

	N.S.W.	Victoria	Queensland	South Australia	Western Australia	Tasmania	Australia (a) (e)
General fisheries	8,467	3,391	3,238	5,614	1,749	658	23,117(b)
Rock lobsters	586	2,059(c)	222	6,325	18,149	3,650	30,991
Prawns	4,171	28	7,364	2,997	4,078	—	18,638
Other crustaceans	233	7	399	77	59	1	776
Oysters	6,717	—	64(d)	2	—	126	6,909
Scallops	47	4,552	850	18	44	229	5,740
Abalone	936	1,409	—	655	254	1,855	5,109
Other molluscs	8	—	40	227	10	58	343
Gross value output	21,165	11,446	12,177	15,915	24,343	6,577	91,623
Percentage of total	23.10	12.49	13.29	17.37	26.57	7.18	1100.00
Percentage general fisheries	36.63	14.67	14.01	24.28	7.56	2.85	100.00

Notes: Adjustments and calculations by the author:
  (a) Australian gross value output excludes amounts in each category from Northern Territory aggregating $4,414,000, made up mainly of prawns ($4,005,000) in 1972–3.
  (b) Excludes $380,000 value from Northern Territory, mainly barramundi (no catch records).
  (c) Includes bay lobsters (*Thenus orientalis*).
  (d) 1971–2 value as 1972–3 figures are not available.
  (e) Figures in last column have been adjusted to take account of corrected raw totals and exclusion of Northern Territory production ($4,414,000) in 1972–3 for which a class breakdown is not available.
   — Insignificant values.
Source: Bureau of Statistics, *Fisheries*, No. 10, 8 September 1974, Canberra, pp. 17–21.

ton and the plankton-grazing fish species which in turn are the food supply for predatory fish (or man, who is but a special kind of predator). Any untoward disturbance of this complex ecological pyramid at any level can have severe repercussions.

Investigations by Australian and Dutch scientists—especially those attached to the CSIRO's Division of Oceanography and Fisheries—have established that the Australian marine environment supports six distinct biospheres. These in turn are subdivided into a series of ecological 'niches', each providing habitats for specific fish communities. In a sense we ought to think of the sea areas around the continent as a number of 'bioscapes', at least as varied as our Australian landscapes, each with distinguishing characteristics.

The first parameter in the formation of these bioscapes is the two great planetary wind systems—the 'circumpolar southerlies' and the 'southeast trades'. These are instrumental in forming regional water masses with specific temperature, chlorinity and density characteristics. Interpenetration and differentiation of these water masses provide the first level in the ecological mosaic as it were. They are fundamental in the differentiation of the so-called Damperian and Flindersian biospheres along the northern, western and Bight coastal waters, as well as the Solanderian, Banksian and Peronian biospheres of the Coral and Tasman Seas adjacent to eastern coasts of Australia. The 'circumpolar southerlies' in particular control the Maugean biosphere of Tasmania and southern Victoria.

The warm East Australian current derives from a strong southerly flow of the South Equatorial current, driven by the trade winds. This southward movement of water masses, amounting to several millions of cubic metres annually, is reinforced by a weaker outflow of tropical water eastwards through Torres Strait generated by the Australian monsoon. Where these water mass movements have greatest effect, converging and up-welling along the north Queensland coast, nutrient-rich bottom waters are brought to the surface, generating the abundant marine life of the Solanderian biosphere.

Further south, in Queensland and northern New South Wales, the East Australian current is losing its kinetic energy and other dynamic forces become important in generating fisheries potential. Dominantly this is an area of westerlies and frequent cyclonic storms. The westerlies blow offshore and have the effect of causing a circulatory motion in inshore waters. The countervailing bottom current brings nutrient-rich waters to the surface, once again triggering the chain: phosphates — nitrates — photosynthesis — phytoplankton—zooplankton—marine fisheries. Cyclonic storms also contribute to these generative mechanisms, for turbulent seas are capable of scouring to depths of 40 fathoms or so, and thus release interstitial nutrients that may have been pent up in bottom sediments for many years. Again the trigger mechanism works.

However, the relative inadequacy of these overturning mechanisms for long periods in any given year, means that Tasman water masses are stable for many months, particularly in summer. In consequence, the Banksian and Peronian biospheres are marked by comparatively impoverished fisheries resources, particularly where the continental shelf sediments are very narrow. It should be noted, however, that substantial year-to-year fluctuations in fisheries production may occur due to varying incidence of primary mechanisms discussed above.

Out in the southern Indian Ocean the westerlies form a channel of cold southern water mass called the West Wind Drift. This channel of cold water bifurcates at Cape Leeuwin, Western Australia, forming the north-flowing West Australian current, which warming northwards, gives rise to the Dampierian biosphere, and also a suite of eastward-flowing cool waters through the Australian Bight which is associated with the Flindersian biosphere. These cool water masses influence Bass Strait and Tasmanian coastal waters. In this general area these West Wind Drift water masses are interpenetrated by deep-water and mid-water currents generated in Antarctica. These latter currents rise to surface due to convergence and bring nutrients up-welling around Tasmania and along the southern Victorian coast. These very cool water masses form the Maugean biosphere which has the distinction of being the most productive sea area of Australia, reaching in excess of 100 grams of carbon per square metre of surface, according to Russian research from the oceanography vessels *Ob* and *Vytiaz*.

The cool water masses of the Maugean divert the East Australian current eastward, and, incidentally, cause massive destruction of warm-water life-forms which are consequently deposited as thick layers of the so-called 'globigerina' ooze in the area of the sub-tropical convergence. In some years a stream of sub-arctic water penetrates northwards along the New South Wales coast inshore from the warm East Australian current. This depends on the relative dynamic characteristics of cool and warm masses in given years. These year-to-year fluctuations have marked effects

on levels of fishery. In a cool regimen, warm water fish like the northern, striped and yellowfin tunas do not venture so far south, while in years of a warm regimen the northward migration of Australian salmon and some of the mackerels are restricted, thus influencing the fisheries.

It is apparent that the water mass characteristics are of fundamental importance in the level of fisheries potential. However, another essential ingredient in the ecological chain is the nutrient status of the sea on which so much else depends. It is therefore opportune to close this section with a few points on trophic conditions.

In general, Australian waters possess the ions of potassium, sodium, magnesium, chlorine, bromine and also sulphates in excess of biotic requirements. It is consequently phosphorus, nitrogen and carbon dioxide that are really the critical nutrient substances in regard to Australian waters. Many of these requirements are provided by the normal birth-death-decay cycle aided by autotrophic bacteria which abound in sea-water and bottom sediments. These nutrient supplies are cyclical, being returned to the surface and the photosynthesis of the euphotic zone (i.e., depth of sunlight penetration) by overturning and up-welling waters as described above. However, these cyclical supplies are inadequate to do more than maintain the biomass at a given steady-state.

Additional supplies of phosphates and nitrates enter Australian waters through the seasonal flooding of huge river systems. In New South Wales the Tweed, Richmond and Clarence Rivers are particularly important in this regard, enriching not only neritic (i.e., inshore waters and estuaries) waters, but also, via the East Australian current, sea areas far to the south. Such additional supplies may be locked-up in sediments on the sea-bottom for decades, but will eventually form the life-substance for phyto-planktons.

HISTORICAL PERSPECTIVES OF THE AUSTRALIAN FISHERIES

The beginnings of the Australian fishing industry go back to earliest colonial times and indeed before that, since fish, crustaceans and molluscs were important elements in the diets of coastal Aborigines throughout Australia. There is some evidence too that fish products formed Aboriginal trade commodities for exchange against obsidian axe heads and other products from the interior.

Without doubt the early Europeans learnt much from the Aborigines concerning fishing with stake and wicker traps in estuaries and the use of primitive ring nets. These methods, but using modernized fishing gear, continue up to the present, particularly in Queensland and the Northern Territory.

The early colonial townships were faced with an

acute scarcity of domesticated animals and even game was in short supply. This quickly led to an interest in fishing to supplement the colony's protein provenance. Species of fish quite unknown to Europeans were tested for quality and palatability and in consequence a distinct Australian ethos of preference developed. Over a period of two centuries this early preference pattern has had curious consequences. Species which gained early acceptance such as snapper, john dory, tiger flathead and the parrot fish varieties of reef fish have remained high in public esteem, while other fish, equally valuable as protein sources, have continued in ill-favour and inhibited demand. One outcome of this has been a tendency to overfish the 'choice' species and a comparative neglect of the less favoured species.

In colonial times much fishing was haphazard and also somewhat experimental and innovative. Techniques ranged from hand lines to wickerwork traps, beach seines to set-net pounds constructed of reeds. Virtually all fishing was done in estuaries or onshore. Deeper offshore fishing was not developed until the turn of the twentieth century, although sail-powered boats using simple beam trawls worked in larger estuaries like Port Jackson and Port Phillip Bay from the 1860s onwards.

Some of the good humour and jocularity of the colonial fisheries can be gauged from the common names given to fish: 'john dory', 'bludger', 'cockney' (snapper), 'jewfish', and the fish with the over-capacious mouth, the 'sargeant baker'. The colonial 'salmon' (which is in fact a sea trout) has come down to us as the respectable Australian salmon, and the local 'whiting' is not related to the European species.

Federation had some impact on fisheries development. From 1909 a Commonwealth research vessel, the *Endeavour*, commanded by a Dane, H. C. Dannevig, explored southeastern waters and, as its findings became known, offshore otter-trawling slowly developed as did longlining and pole fishing for snoek in Bass Strait waters. The Commonwealth's interest halted abruptly, however, when its research vessel was lost with all hands in 1914 on a voyage to Macquarie Island in the Southern Ocean. Further fisheries development then reverted to the States, but very little sustained effort was forthcoming to support the industry. At intervals inquiries and Royal Commissions investigated the problems of the fishing industry, especially those associated with overfishing, but the political nature of these wranglings generally held sway and the fisheries benefited little if at all.

In 1915 the knowledge of the east coast trawling grounds opened up by Dannevig's investigation induced the New South Wales government to begin a State fishing enterprise. Three Newcastle-type otter trawlers were purchased from Newcastle-on-Tyne and British

masters and fishermen were hired to operate them. The home port was Sydney and these steam-powered trawlers first worked the grounds immediately offshore. Overfishing quickly ensued, and the benthic fauna on which the tiger flathead and other species depended for their sustenance were destroyed by constant trawling of the narrow shelf. Shortfalls in catches caused operations to shift to other trawling grounds, north to Port Stephens and south to Twofold Bay (Eden) and Gabo Island.

Four additional 'Newcastle' trawlers were built at the State Dockyard, Newcastle, from 1920 onwards, and also a refrigerator vessel to carry fish from the trawl grounds to the Sydney markets thus permitting the trawl vessels to remain at sea. Despite all efforts however, losses of the State fishing fleet were mounting up, reaching a total of £330,000 in 1923. After acrimonious debate and a Royal Commission, the fleet assets were sold off to private enterprise. For some years things improved, but then a new waning phase beset the company engaged in trawling. The fact was that the shelf trawl grounds were too narrow and too restricted to support a capital-intensive technique of fishing once the first flush of 'bonanza' operation had passed.

From 1936 smaller motor trawlers, or more correctly Danish-type seiners, began to take over from the otter trawlers, and the last Newcastle-type, aged and decrepit, was phased out in 1965, victim of the economics of fishing. Gradually the fleet of Danish seiners, owned by individual master fishermen or small partnerships, grew in numbers. And since they were able to work small pockets between foul ground (i.e., rock-strewn or other obstacles to seine-net fishing) the seiners were able to expand production of trawl fish quite substantially. There have been marked changes in the composition of the catch over the years, however, as sustained pressure on given species, particularly the flatheads, has taken its toll. For all intents and purposes the trawl fisheries, at least in New South Wales and probably Victoria, are now on a 'care and maintenance' basis. In essence, a new and much smaller steady-state composite trawl-fish population has been reached that it would be hazardous to reduce further.

Given the quality and widespread resources of crustaceans and molluscs in Australian waters it is perhaps surprising that thoroughgoing commercial exploitation did not occur until the mid-1940s. Previously small quantities of crayfish (rock lobsters) were taken in Victoria, Tasmania and Western Australia, but nothing substantial was accomplished until the World War II period. In 1944 a crayfish cannery was set up in Western Australia to serve the armed forces. At first the shallow waters of Houtman Abrolhos offshore from Perth, were fished using cray-pots, but in the post-war period the fleet was mechanized and deeper waters were fished using special-designed cray-traps and dan-buoys. As the export market expanded, particularly the American market for frozen cray-tails, production was so increased that rigorous conservation measures were needed. These measures involve the number and power of crayfish boats and escape holes cut in traps so that undersized crays 'caught' could live to grow bigger.

The river estuaries of New South Wales were used from colonial times onwards for the gathering of rock oysters. By the year 1870 natural oyster beds had been so depleted (and sometimes completely destroyed by reckless dredging for oysters) that the State government passed restrictive legislation to preserve the industry. This restriction led to the cultivation of oyster beds on Crown leases within the estuaries and has sustained production to the present day.

Prawning has been another phase of the fisheries to experience pressure on stocks in inshore waters. However, attempts at prawn farming on the Japanese model have not been successful, mainly due to the success of offshore trawl fishery when prawns are shoaling to spawn. This development gave a new lease of life to the prawning industry.

The pelagic, or offshore surface fisheries, were the last to be developed in Australia. Fisheries conferences between Commonwealth, State and private interests were held in Melbourne and Sydney in 1927 and 1929 respectively. Major issues of discussion were the declining status of the inshore and demersal fisheries and the possibilities of a viable pelagic fishery filling the gap. But it was several years before investigations by the motor vessel *Warreen* produced any worthwhile results. Purse-seining was attempted, obtaining indifferent catches, and consequently has not been widely adopted as a fishing technique. Problems ensue because of the skill required in setting a purse-seine around shoals of fish, and shark attacks on captured fish with costly destruction of the net. Since the inception of pelagic fisheries in the early 1950s, purse-seines (and their close relative technique, the lampara net) have only been used to catch bait for the tuna fisheries, jack mackerel and certain herring-like species used in a fish-meal plant built at Lakes Entrance, Victoria.

In the important tuna fisheries pole-and-live-bait fishing methods have persisted, contrary to overseas trends where this technique has been displaced in favour of longline, gill-net and purse-seine techniques.

THE PRINCIPAL AUSTRALIAN FISHERIES
Australian fisheries may be divided into three broad categories: (1) estuarine and other inshore fisheries; (2) demersal or sea-bottom fisheries, sometimes referred to as trawl fisheries; and (3) pelagic or offshore surface water fisheries. In addition there are several other types of fishing; (4) shell fisheries for crustaceans and edible molluscs; (5) industrial fisheries, involving pre-eminently whaling, but also cultured pearls, pearl and trochus shell and fish-meal production. Kelp-cutting is a specialized activity which may also be included in the industrial bracket. Finally, (6) are the inland water fisheries which embrace principally recreational fishing, although there is a small commercial production of Murray and Macquarie perch, yellow-belly and freshwater crayfish (yabbies) in southeastern States.

Each category of fishery has developed its distinctive technology, based largely on the physical parameters of environment and the behavioural characteristics of the fish involved. Fisheries conservation is only possible if there exists a deep awareness of the interactions of these conditions with technical and economic parameters. This will become clear as this section develops.

Estuaries and Inshore Fisheries
Estuaries and inshore fisheries involve fish which, at least for a dominant part of their lifecycle, inhabit a neritic inshore environment. They include several species of mullets, breams, ludericks (blackfish), whitings, garfishes; the tailor, tarwhine and jewfish and many others of minor commercial importance. Many of these fish exhibit a double-phase life cycle, spending a spawning and rearing phase in brackish waters of rivers, rias, lakes or lagoons and a second phase in open shoreface seas, frequently in huge shoals. In the sea phase to-and-fro longshore migrations over considerable distances occur and, as in the case of the mullets, even the appearance of the fish changes. These long migrations are motivated by food-quest and mating drives. Some species of neritic fish are highly subject to bacterial attack in the brackish water phase and this gives their flesh an earthy odour and taste, but is otherwise harmless. Since most neritic species are in large measure vegetal and detritus eaters, the pollution of rivers by domestic and industrial waste can have dire consequences in 'nursery' areas.

For these reasons most estuarine and inshore fish are preferably caught during the shoreface migrations, before or after the roe develops in female fish. The onset of the migration is 'triggered' by temperature and salinity changes in neritic waters.

Most fishing for these species uses techniques of handlines, beach seines and, occasionally, gill-nets operated as set-nets across small creek mouths. Freshets or the ebb tide causes fish to be gilled in the net with their movement seaward.

Those species of fish which do not have a longshore migration, such as some of the whitings and the young stages of the snapper, and therefore only move in and out of estuaries seasonally, have been greatly subjected to fishing pressures, especially near densely settled

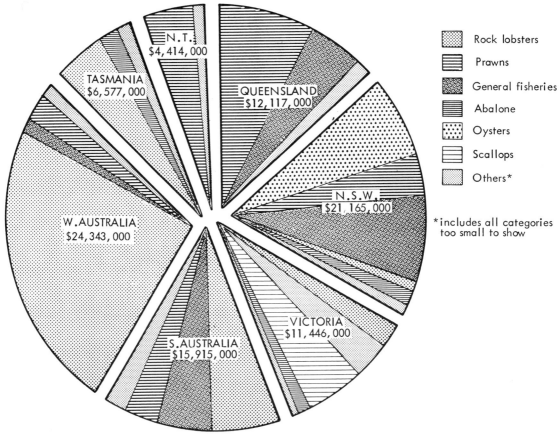

Fig. 14.2 Gross value of fisheries production in Australia, 1972–3. *Source*: adapted from *Official Yearbook of the Commonwealth of Australia*, 1973–4.

coastal areas. Not surprisingly these varieties of fish show least tendency for populations to recuperate and special conservancy measures are called for in their cases.

However, it seems that even heavy fishing cannot completely destroy neritic fish populations. A temporary reduction in stocks is followed by compensatory increases in birth rates and growth of young fish so that stocks are rebuilt. Prolonged overfishing, however, may remove too many sexually mature fish and this may well lead to a lower steady-state population. Such trends can only be understood by scientific age-class population investigation.

Demersal Fisheries

Demersal fisheries are marked by two major characteristics, apart from their sea-bottom habitat. These are firstly, environmental specificity, or the inability of these species to adapt to marginal environments. For most demersal species the ecological 'niche' is

paramount. Secondly, most demersal species do not form schools or large aggregations of a single species; they live and feed as individuals. Exceptions to this circumstance are the demersal predators, such as the school and gummy sharks, which hunt gregariously.

Since demersal fish are far more locationally 'rooted' than estuarine or pelagic varieties, they are subjected to exceptional fishing pressures. This is offset to some degree by the fact that they exist as communities of mixed species—each one having perhaps its own territorial domain—which inhibits fishing if 'trash-fish' are present in large numbers.

Several subtypes of demersal habitat may be distinguished. These are: (a) silt, mud, or sand covered grounds frequented by flatheads, latchets, flounders, soles and leather jackets; (b) hollows and swales frequented by morwongs, flatheads, nannygai, school whiting and the dories; (c) broken ground of deep-water reefs and rises frequented by teraglin, school and gummy sharks, snappers, trumpeters, gropers and rock cods; and finally, (d) the margin of the continental slope where ultra-deepwater species are found, the deep-sea trevally, dog sharks, ling and deep-sea cod.

Three different technologies are used in the demersal fisheries of Australia. Danish seiners operate by casting the net on the sea bottom; the bunt (inner portion) is held open by a spreader. The seine is connected to the fishing vessel by two rope warps laid in a kite-form pattern on the sea bed and these are subsequently hauled in over gurdies (horizontal winches). This action causes the outer extremities of the 'kite' to move together driving fish toward the oncoming bunt.

A second method of demersal fishing is the use of baited traps. These are constructed of wire mesh on a hoop-wire frame. Commonly they have a base of one metre by a half to two-thirds metre, and have an entrance funnel at the top. The fish are attracted to bait in the bottom of the trap. Semi-putrescent squid, octopus, or kangaroo meat is used as bait. The species commonly caught in the trap fishery are snapper (sea-phase), leatherjackets and dories, particularly john dory. The chief areas used for trap fishing in Australia are the foul-ground areas offshore from the Maclean River to Port Macquarie.

A third method of taking demersal fish is the line fishery. In shallower offshore waters handlines are used, each of which may have up to six baited hooks. The fishing boat drifts with the current over broken ground for some distance before the vessel returns to make another 'set'. The handline fishery has a very low productivity and consequently only expensive fish are sought; snapper and john dory in New South Wales and sand whiting in South Australia.

Another form of line fishery is the longlining commonly employed for the capture of school, nurse or gummy shark, particularly in Bass Strait waters. Longlines are set near the sea bottom for several hundred metres being supported at the free end by a dan-buoy and the vessel at the other. From the longline hang short baited hook lines called snoods. Sometimes 200 or more hooks are used in Australian longlining. After a two-hour set the vessel moves towards the dan-buoy hauling in the line and placing fish in the ice-hold. Longlining requires considerable skill, first in baiting hooks as they go over the gunwales and more importantly, choosing the fishing ground. Commonly demersal fish are most plentiful at or just below the thermocline (the depth in sea water where there occurs an abrupt change in the temperature-density characteristics of the water).

Yet another form of line fishing used in Australia is drop-lining. This is used for ultra-deepwater fishing along the margin of the continental slope at depths of 90–140 fathoms. This zone has very cold bottom waters and is rocky since submarine long-waves are powerful enough to move all small rock fragments downslope. The zone is frequented by cold-water species particularly the large deep-sea travellies and lings. Drop-line fishing requires larger seaworthy boats and rather sophisticated winches for high speed line hauling, consequently it is used only on the continental slope margins of Bass Strait, where the subtropical convergence induces large fish populations.

Pelagic Fisheries

Pelagic fisheries in Australia have developed very significantly since the early 1950s. The principal species involved are Australian salmon, the garfishes, several species of tuna, especially the southern bluefin, striped and yellowfin tunas, snoek and spanish mackerel. All of these pelagic species are fished during their seasonal migrations induced by temperature and salinity changes in the sea. Except for the mackerel and other reef-fish fisheries of the inner waters of the Great Barrier Reef system, pelagic fisheries are concentrated around the coast from South Australia to New South Wales.

The tuna fisheries of Australia are of great economic importance. Each year more than 2,000 tonnes of frozen tuna (or some 15 per cent of the catch) are exported, principally to canneries in American Samoa and Japan. Virtually the whole of the exported tuna comes from South Australia and this earns about $900,000 annually for that State.

Fortuitously, the tuna fishing season varies in New South Wales-Victorian waters as opposed to that of South Australia. In consequence, fishing boats migrate seasonally to take advantage of this situation. In southern New South Wales, however, there has been some opposition to South Australian boats engaging in the tuna fisheries, and in this State 'foreign' boats have to be specially licensed for each season's fishing. This does not accord with the current international law of the sea or Commonwealth legislation which establishes that fisheries are a common property resource and therefore States have jurisdiction only within territorial waters (three miles) and not beyond.

In Australia a substantial part of the tuna catch is taken by the pole-and-line fishery operating from specially constructed tuna clippers which search out the tuna shoals. Sometimes spotter aircraft direct boats. Each line has a barbless hook and a lure of cockade feathers. Hooked tuna are sometimes so large that two poles must be attached to each line so that fishermen can dump the tuna in the freezer chamber. Snoek are also caught in a roughly similar manner, although a barbed hook is used in this case.

Australian salmon and garfish occur in huge shoals which can be spotted from cliff tops or by aircraft. Fishermen then go out in two or more boats to cast a beach seine. This is then drawn slowly towards the shore until the fish are enclosed and can be brailed from the water. The principal areas for the Australian salmon fisheries are the Gulf of St Vincent, southern Victoria and New South Wales, especially Wodonga Inlet.

Spanish mackerel are taken in large quantities in Great Barrier Reef waters along with other reef fish such as coral fish and red emperor. Handlining and, in suitable areas, longlining, are the favoured fishing techniques. A smaller fishery of this kind occurs in homologous areas of Western Australia, where a considerable potential for further expansion exists.

Other Fishery Enterprises

Other fishery enterprises can be briefly summarized. Crayfish are taken from the reefs of the continental shelf in all southern States, but particularly from the Houtman Abrolhos islands off the Western Australian coast. Two families of crayfish are involved, the southern and eastern cray, *Jasus lalandei* and *Jasus verreauxi*, and the western cray, *Panulirus cygnus*, respectively. A fishery for several species of tropical cray, north of the continent, has not developed as these are vegetal feeders and will not enter traps.

Prawns of numerous species are taken from estuarine and offshore waters of New South Wales and Queensland, the Gulf of Carpentaria (off Karumba) and in the Exmouth Gulf and Shark Bay waters of Western Australia.

Pearling in northern Australia began as a side line to the production of mother-of-pearl in the mid-1850s. However, the output of natural pearls was so small that Japanese techniques of pearl culture were introduced at Kuri Bay, Western Australia in 1956. Northern Australia now has eighteen pearl culture establishments, all but three with Japanese joint participation. Major locations are Exmouth Gulf, Broome, Kuri Bay, Port Essington and Thursday Island in Torres Strait. The coral reefs of Queensland have a small but now declining output of pearl and trochus shell.

The mollusc fisheries are concerned with oysters (already discussed above), scallops and abalone. Scallops are harvested in Tasmania and Queensland, having overtaken Port Phillip Bay, Victoria, as the chief centres of production. To a degree the declining scallop fishery of Victoria has given way to the country's most important harvest of abalone. This industry is not restricted to Victoria, however, for abalone fisheries occur in Maugean waters from southern New South Wales to South Australia, including Tasmania.

The Australian whaling industry, one of the earliest commercial activities in the young colonies, has suffered a serious decline in recent years. In the first instance the shore-based whaling establishments were not able to compete with Russian, Japanese and Norwegian technologies involving catcher-boats and factory-ships for processing whales at sea and, secondly, since 1963 the exploitation of the baleen (humpback) whales has been prohibited to all nations by the International Whaling Commission as a conservancy measure. Formerly it was the annual breeding migration of the baleen whales northward along the Australian east and west coasts that formed the mainstay of the country's industry. Now, however, the sole remaining whaling station at Albany, Western Australia, operates on the smaller sperm whales.

Perhaps the most novel marine enterprise in Australia is the alginate factory at Triabunna, Tasmania, which uses the giant kelp (*Macrocystis pyrifera*) as its feedstock. The alginates produced are used in the manufacture of jellies and cosmetics. Earlier attempts to use Tasmania's abundant resources of kelp and seaweeds for the extraction of iodine and other pharmaceutical bases were not commercially successful. Earlier extraction of vitamin-A concentrates from shark-liver oil and the manufacture of shagreen leather from shark skins has also not survived.

ECONOMIC PARAMETERS OF THE AUSTRALIAN FISHERIES

Australian fisheries, in common with those of other countries, have to face fundamental economic problems. Because fisheries have been considered by tradition a common property resource, they face unusual exploitative pressures. 'Free entry' of men and fishing boats into a lucrative fishery has not infrequently challenged the recuperative capacities of fish populations in the past. Australia has a long history of somewhat careless fisheries exploitation—the tiger flathead, school sharks and crayfish may be cited as examples. The increasing incidence of new productive capacity in these fisheries have most probably induced lower steady-state populations, not more than a fraction of the size of the original resource. The complete cessation of fishing—as adopted internationally for the baleen whales—is hardly feasible, but some regulatory control of the intensity of fishing is clearly desirable.

In the past a major problem has been deficiencies in the collection of fisheries statistics, not only on the species taken, exact location of fishing areas, but more particularly on the boats employed in particular fisheries, the gear used, and individual boat-catch statistics. Physical productivity analysis was thus hardly possible.

Since 1962 however, catch and effort statistics have improved somewhat as a result of the Commonwealth-States Fisheries Conference. The States have adopted a new recording system—although in a somewhat piecemeal fashion; Tasmania, 1963; Victoria and

Table 14.3   Physical Productivity of Australian General Fisheries, 1972–3

	N.S.W.	Victoria	Queensland	South Australia	Western Australia	Tasmania	Australia
Catch (live weight tonnes)	21,472	10,768	5,424	11,790	7,090	2,265	59,428
Boats engaged	3,096	806	2,204	2,314	1,588	589	10,760
Men engaged	4,516	1,573	4,346	3,810	3,167	1,235	19,208
Means:							
Men per boat	1.46	1.95	1.97	1.65	1.99	2.10	1.78
Catch per boat	6.93	13.36	2.46	5.09	4.46	3.84	5.52
Catch per man	4.75	6.84	1.25	3.09	2.24	1.83	3.09

Source: Bureau of Statistics, *Fisheries*, No. 10, 8 September 1974, Canberra, p. 7; p. 11 for base data, calculations by author.

Western Australia, 1964; Queensland, otter trawl fishery only, 1965, and the remaining States have yet to adopt fully the uniform recording system.

Under the new system fishermen are requested to report each month on the species taken, localities of catch by one degree grid of latitude and longitude, the gear used, effort (in terms of hours at sea), employment and landing ports. Since this system is not yet operative on an Australia-wide basis only very imperfect analysis of the economics of Australian fisheries is feasible at the present time.

Some indication of physical productivity per man engaged, per boat and per $1000 of fisheries assets is possible however and gives a crude measure of the economic viability of fisheries in the various States. It is also possible to work out rentability (i.e., the revenue productivity in the industry) in terms of annual value of output per boat and per $1,000 of fisheries assets. These data appear in Tables 14.3 and 14.4, using the general fisheries and six States only for illustrative purposes.

Examining the physical productivity figures first, it is clear that only the fisheries of New South Wales and Victoria are in any sense adequate (Table 14.3) even for Australian conditions. Compared to productivity statistics of the advanced fisheries of the world

these physical returns to fishing effort can only be described as disastrous. These levels of catch per boat, and per man engaged, are symptomatic of low technological and management skills and above all a severe undercapitalization of the general fisheries. For example, of the 10,760 fishing boats in Australia 5,771 are under 6 metres in length and only 174 are over 18 metres in length. Such deficiencies can only be corrected by a severe rationalization of the industry in future years.

Turning to the revenue productivity figures (and these, of course, reflect the physical productivity status) then certain conclusions can be drawn (Table 14.4). On the evidence of the national values the returns to fishermen (as labour and management factors) is far below the Australian basic wage even before returns to capital assets represented by boats and fishing gear are taken into account. If we use a convention widely adopted overseas of distributing half the gross income to labour-management factors and half to the 'boat' assets, then gross annual returns to manpower factors would be on average $612 and to capital assets only 10.3 per cent gross. If the four submarginal States' general fisheries are disregarded, the figures for New South Wales are $937 and about 28 per cent return to manpower and capital assets respectively.

Table 14.4   Revenue Productivity of Australian General Fisheries, 1972–3

	N.S.W.	Victoria	Queensland	South Australia	Western Australia	Tasmania	Australia
Catch (gross value)	8.47m	3.39m	3.24m	5.61m	1.75m	0.66m	23.50m
Revenue/man	$1,875	$2,155	$ 745	$1,472	$ 552	$ 534	$1,223
Revenue/boat	$2,736	$4,206	$1,470	$2,424	$1,102	$1,120	$2,184
Value of boats and gear	15.2m	8.5m	29.8m	17.1m	25.6m	8.2m	114.2m
Revenue/$1,000 of assets	$557.2	$399	$109	$328	$68	$80	$206
Catch/$1,000 of assets	1.41 tonnes	1.27 tonnes	0.18 tonnes	0.69 tonnes	0.28 tonnes	0.28 tonnes	0.52 tonnes

Source: Bureau of Statistics, *Fisheries*, No. 10, 8 September 1974, Canberra, p. 7; p. 11 for base data, calculations by the author.

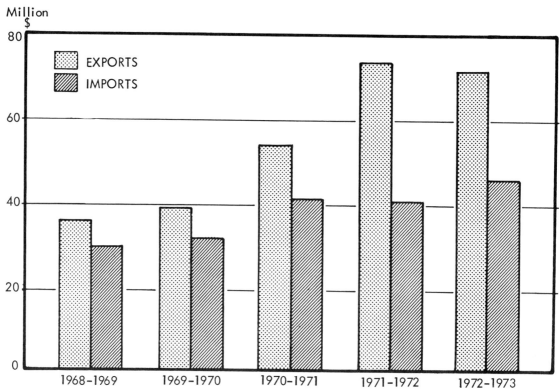

Fig. 14.3 Exports and imports of edible fisheries products, 1968–9 to 1972–3. *Source: Official Yearbook of the Commonwealth of Australia,* 1973–4.

For Victoria the relative values are about $1,080 and about 20 per cent respectively. Judging by returns to labour, management and capital available in other primary industries, these values must be considered far too low to sustain viable general fisheries in most Australian States. Again a case for rationalization of the industry is apparent.

Given the condition that the supply side of the equation in fisheries is fraught with difficulties, represented by environmental constraints, the tendency to overfishing, the problems of efficient capture with the technologies available and competitive diffusion of fishing effort, then the demand side of the equation becomes of paramount importance.

Undersupply of fish to active and eager metropolitan markets has resulted in an upward spiral of fish prices, in many instances registering greater percentage increases per edible pound weight than competing protein foodstuffs like red meats, cheese and vegetable protein sources. Such relative price increases have stimulated demand for imported fisheries products.

In recent years the value of fisheries products imported into Australia has averaged $42.8 million, compared to local production retained in Australia worth $23.6 million (Fig. 14.3). Exports of fisheries products averaged $67.1 million annually thus more than offsetting imports in terms of value. However, imports were dominantly chilled or frozen fish, usually as packaged fillets, canned goods and special classes of oysters and prawns. On the contrary, exports were made up mainly of rock lobsters (crayfish tails in particular) $32.2 million; prawns $24.0 million; abalone $7.9 million and scallops $5.0 million. In a sense there was a qualitative loss of fish products by exports since overseas demand, principally by the United States, Japan, United Kingdom and France, offered higher price constellations (Fig. 14.4). On the other hand, fisheries product imports often represented superior value to unprocessed Australian products.

From this discussion it is evident that Australia can only improve its fisheries performance if price-value and supply-cost relationships can be brought into some sort of harmony.

On the supply-cost side the relatively small size of the Australian fisheries place severe constraints on efficiency and economic viability. Since 1915 the Australian population has grown at twice the rate that output in the fishing industry has, and consequently the leeway has had to be made good by imports. Modest rises in consumption levels over the years and

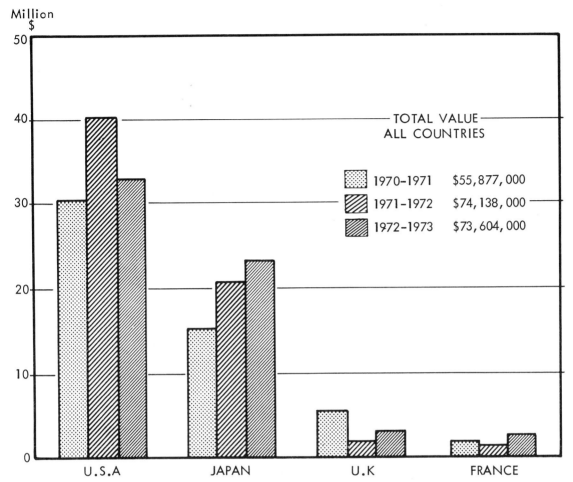

Fig. 14.4 Exports of edible fisheries products from Australia to countries of consignment, 1970–1 to 1972–3. *Source: Official Yearbook of the Commonwealth of Australia*, 1973–4.

Table 14.5 Consumption of Edible Fisheries Products in Australia, 1968–9 and 1972–3 (kilogram edible weight per person per annum)

Product	Australian origin		Imported		Total	
	1968–9	1972–3	1968–9	1972–3	1968–9	1972–3
Fresh and frozen fish	1.6	1.7	1.7	1.5	3.3	3.2
Crustaceans/molluscs	0.6	0.8	—	—	0.7	0.8
Cured	—	—	0.5	0.3	0.5	0.3
Canned	0.5	0.3	1.0	0.9	1.5	1.2
Total	2.7	2.8	3.2	2.7	6.0	5.5

Source: Bureau of Statistics, *Fisheries*, No. 10, 8 September 1974, Canberra, p. 35.

massive exports have somewhat inhibited the supply-demand adjustment required. Consumption levels of edible fish products are given in Table 14.5.

By all accounts domestic fisheries production has gained marginally at the expense of imported products between 1968–9 and 1972–3, but there has been a quite considerable diversion of total fisheries product consumption as a result of relative prices for fish products *vis-à-vis* other foods. On Australia's present population base, the decline is of the order of 5,000 tonnes annually or around 8 per cent of production (edible weight).

PERSPECTIVES FOR THE FUTURE

The future of Australian fisheries would seem to depend on several lines of endeavour involving improved conservancy practices, better scientific appraisal on the existence and use of fisheries resources, particularly on applied science aspects and economic rationalization of the industry to ensure profitability and an on-going supply of fish products to meet consumer demand.

All of these objectives are, in a sense, bound together. Proper conservation cannot be carried out without a precise knowledge of the size and characteristics of important commercial fish populations, their location and the fishing rate (i.e. the proportion of fish removed annually by fishing operations). Thus scientific appraisal may be expected to be directed more to the practical questions of the impact of fishing on the condition of the fishery and somewhat less on the pure science aspects of biology and ichthyology which motivate most current research in Australia.

As for the rationalization of the industry it would appear that some government initiatives are urgently needed. In particular, over-aged and undersized fishing boats need to be retired from the industry and the Australian fleet needs to be brought back to an effective economic size and fishing power, commensurate with the current status of the resource base. There is perhaps a case for Commonwealth administration of the number, size and fishing potential of the country's fleet and its allocation to specific fishery districts—which need to be defined and resource-inventoried too. A corollary is the standardization of fishing gear to be used, particularly in regard to the permitted mesh-size of nets, numbers of hooks per longline and so on. Only in such a way can some control on the annual fishing effort imposed on Australian fisheries be determined. In such administrative controls there is a need to stimulate those fishing techniques which permit best conservancy practices, such as the use of traps, set-nets, gill-nets and seines which capture fish only over a given minimum size, as against longlines, purse-seines and pole-and-line which are not size-of-fish discriminatory. It would also be necessary to proscribe fishing in known 'nursery' areas to allow a continuing recruitment of younger fish without which a fishery cannot be maintained.

It is obvious that the measures mooted above will necessitate substantial discipline in all sectors of the Australian fisheries. But to fail to accept this challenge will surely place the long-term viability of the industry in jeopardy.

REFERENCES

Brereton, M. B. (1967), 'Considerations affecting the financial requirements of the Australian fishing industry', *Australian Fisheries Development Conference Paper*, A.F.D./67/BP/52, Canberra.

Bureau of Census and Statistics (annually), *Statistical Bulletin, Fisheries*, Canberra.

——(annually), *Official Yearbook of the Commonwealth of Australia*, Canberra.

CSIRO Division of Fisheries and Oceanography, *Annual Reports*, Cronulla, N. S. W.

——(irregular), *Australian Journal of Marine and Freshwater Research*, Cronulla, N.S.W.

Davies, R. M. (1967), 'The responsibility of government and industry in fisheries development', *Australian Fisheries Development Conference Paper*, A.F.D./67/BP/9, Canberra.

Department of National Development (1965), 'Fish and Fisheries', *Atlas of Australian Resources*, Canberra.

Department of Primary Industry (1966), 'An economic survey of the New South Wales south coast Danish seine fishery', *Fisheries Report No. 2*, Canberra.

——(monthly), *Australian Fisheries Newsletter*, Canberra.

Kesteven, G. L. (1967), 'World fisheries—an Australian perspective', *Aust. Fish. News 1*, 26, 22–3.

Kesteven, G. L. and Burden, T. W. (1967), 'Developing Australia's fisheries', *Aust. Fish. News 1*, 26, 3–9.

Koblenz-Mishka, O. I. (1965), 'The magnitude of primary production of the Pacific Ocean', *Okeanologiya*, 5, 325–37 (in Russian).

Koninklijk Nederlands Meteorologische Institut (1949), *Zeegebieden Rond Australie—Oceanografische en Meteorologische*, Gegevens Straatsdrukkerij's—Gravenhage.

Marshall, T. C. (1966), *Fisheries of the Great Barrier Reef and Queensland Coastal Waters*, Angus and Robertson, Sydney.

Mathieson, R. S. (1965), *Recent Changes in the East Australian Trawl Fisheries*, Research Paper No. 9, Dept of Geogr. Univ. of Sydney and the Geogr. Soc. of N.S.W., Sydney.

——(1968), *Fishing*, Industry in Australia Series No. 5, Longmans, Adelaide.

Ogilby, J. D., revised by Marshall, T. C. (1954), *The Commercial Fishes and Fisheries of Queensland*, Queensland Dept of Harbour and Marine, Brisbane.

Roughley, T. C. (1957 revised), *Fish and Fisheries of Australia*, Angus and Robertson, Sydney.

Scott, T. D. (1962), *The Marine and Fresh Water Fishes of South Australia*, Adelaide.

Sheard, K. W. (1962), *The Western Australian Crayfishery, 1944–1961*, Patterson Brokensha, Perth.

15 POPULATION

J. H. HOLMES

In Australian geographical thinking and research, population studies *per se* are almost as rare as are human residents in the Simpson Desert, but population issues have loomed large, often providing a stimulus for remarkably varied research endeavours. The importance of these issues was clearly recognized by Griffith Taylor, Australia's first geographer of international standing, whose most renowned and controversial contribution to national policy-making was his global comparative analysis of climate, agriculture and fuel resources, designed to highlight the environmental limits to Australia's population growth and to suggest an optimal range of population, which he set at from thirty to sixty million people, the higher figure being at living standards equivalent to those existing in Europe (Taylor, 1922, 1951). Like other resource-population appraisals, Taylor's knowledgeable and highly original contribution cannot be narrowly described as population geography, but it does show how population questions can provide a focus for a broadly based research programme, encompassing important areas in physical and human geography.

Questions concerning optimum population or 'how many Australians?' and optimum distribution or 'where should they live?' have become of even greater relevance than they were in the 1920s when Taylor sparked public debate on these issues. For a full review of the debate, see particularly Lodewyckz (1956) who devotes a chapter to the debate on carrying capacity or maximum population using estimates by 'geographers, climatologists, statisticians, economists and scientists', and another chapter to reviewing estimates of optimum population. Earlier reviews are found in Phillips and Wood (1928) and Phillips (1933), while a recent series of appraisals is found in Australian Institute of Political Science (1971). Closely interwoven with this debate has been the long-standing public concern about population distribution. This was first evident in the pioneering phase with the urge to 'fill the empty spaces', which in turn led to vigorous public efforts at rural closer settlement, and more recently to programmes for urban decentralization. The continuing national concern with these questions is evidenced in the National Population Enquiry, initiated in 1971 by the Australian government in search of an authoritative statement on the two questions of optimum numbers and optimum distribution.

These two questions are linked to three basic facts of Australian population, namely: the *small numbers*, by present world levels; the high degree of *spatial concentration*; and, consequent upon the first two, the extremely *low population densities* prevailing over most of the country. The sparsity and concentration of population are such dominating features of Australian human geography that an understanding of these two characteristics, their causes and their consequences can provide a central theme in geographical studies. Hooson has argued that the distribution of population is the 'essential geographical expression', which 'acts as a master-thread, capable of weaving into a coherent theme the otherwise disparate strands of the subject' (Hooson, 1960, p. 13). This view has particular relevance to Australian human geography, and provides the central theme for this chapter.

POPULATION NUMBERS AND AVERAGE DENSITY

Population Numbers

The central fact of Australian population is its smallness by contemporary world reckoning, particularly in relation to the area of the country (Table 15.1). It is common to account for the paucity of Australians by referring to four sets of contributing circumstances, broadly classed as environmental, locational, historical and economic: firstly, environmental limitations with particular emphasis upon the dryness of the country and the problems of white settlement in the tropical northern third; secondly, remoteness from major western population centres in Europe, which until recently have been the chief markets for Australian exports and the main external sources of people, capital and goods for colonization and development; thirdly, the recency of European settlement; and, fourthly, the narrowly-based, export-oriented, colonial economy with its emphasis on inputs of land rather than labour. This fourth circumstance is a consequence of the other three and associ-

Table 15.1 The World's Seven Largest Countries: Area, Population and Density for Whole Nation and for Ecumene

Country	National total			Ecumene		
	Area ('000 km²)	Population ('000)	Density (per km²)	Estimated area ('000 km²)	Estimated population ('000)	Density (per km²)
Australia	7,687	12,959	2	1,600	12,800	8
Canada	9,976	21,848	2	2,000	21,700	11
Brazil	8,512	98,854	12	4,700	94,000	20
U.S.S.R.	22,402	247,459	11	7,700	237,4000	31
U.S.A.	9,363	208,842	22	6,500	205,000	31
China	9,597	800,721	83	4,800	789,000	164
India	3,280	563,494	172	3,100	560,000	181

Source: Population totals are mid-1972 estimates from 1973 United Nations Yearbook, while area and population of ecumene have been estimated by the author (see text).

ated with small numbers in a complex, circular cause-and-effect relationship.

The impact of environmental constraints, remoteness and a colonial economy is not readily assessed. Undoubtedly each has to some extent retarded population growth, as is documented for example by Blainey (1966) with regard to remoteness or Taylor with regard to environmental conditions. However, the simple arithmetic of growth rates suggests that their combined effect has been only minor when account is taken of the recency of European settlement, with only a short period available for cumulative growth.

Population Growth

Since European settlement in 1788, the population of overseas origin has shown a fluctuating but often rapid rate of growth, while the Aboriginal population experienced a disastrous decline. Among the new colonizers, very high growth rates were maintained over the first hundred years of settlement, although initially high rates of increase yielded only small numbers, chiefly by immigration. Natural increase was low in the early predominantly male population largely made up of convicts and soldiers. At first, free immigration was discouraged, thus restraining family migration which would have supplied an internal source of population growth.

The mid-century gold rushes commenced a phase of exceptionally rapid growth. In the decade 1851–61 the non-Aboriginal population trebled, and surpassed one million in 1858 (Table 15.2). Rapid population growth continued until 1890. Then economic depression and a sequence of droughts caused a sharp reduction in growth which continued with only one major exception up to 1945. Migration was just beginning to recover from the depression of the 1890s

when World War I intervened. The war caused heavy casualties among young men, reduced the birth rate and completely cut off the stream of immigrants. Rapid growth in the 1920s through delayed immigration, and postponed marriage and family-formation, merely served to close part of the wartime gap. As in other western countries, population growth almost ceased during the depression of the 1930s when the birth rate slumped and a net migration loss was recorded in the worst years. Again recovery was cut short by a world war.

Australian demographic trends entered a new phase in 1945 with a sharp and prolonged upturn in both birth rates and net immigration. For three decades growth rates have generally exceeded 2 per cent per

Table 15.2 Years in which Each Successive Million of Population was Reached in Australia

Population (millions)	Year	Average annual rate of population growth
1	1858	—
2	1877	3.7
3	1889	3.4
4	1905	1.8
5	1918	1.7
6	1925	2.6
7	1939	1.1
8	1949	1.3
9	1954	2.5
10	1959	2.3
11	1963	2.0
12	1968	1.9
13	1972	1.9

annum, a very high rate for a westernized country. High birth rates, above 20 per thousand until 1965, coupled with low death rates, have led to a rate of natural increase in excess of 10 per thousand in all post-war years. Net immigration has also remained high over the whole period in response to the national government's assisted passage scheme. Immigration has also indirectly contributed to growth, since a proportion of the natural increase comprises offspring of recently arrived migrants.

After 184 years of European settlement, the population reached thirteen million in 1972. In the United States the same total was attained in 1831, after more than 200 years of European settlement, and in Canada after more than 300 years. Compared with these two other extensive lands of recent European colonization Australia's population growth has not been laggardly.

Ecumene and Nonecumene
Australia's low overall population density inevitably attracts comment; the 'Empty Continent' is a common appellation. Grenfell Price, among others, has argued that Australia is not as underpopulated as the overall density figures would suggest, pointing out that only 720,000 square miles (1,800,000 km²) are suitable for closer settlement, with a much higher average density in this smaller area (1972, p. 111). Although useful as a first statement on man-land ratios, average density measures need to be interpreted with caution.

At the very least, a consistent set of criteria should be used in any international comparisons. Trewartha, following the work of the German geographer, Hassinger, has proposed a division of the land surface into the *ecumene*, or permanently inhabited areas, and the *nonecumene*, which is uninhabited, intermittently inhabited or very sparsely inhabited (1969, pp. 80–90). The nonecumene generally coincides with cold desert, arid desert and steppe, high mountains and parts of the equatorial rainforest. Unfortunately, neither Hassinger nor Trewartha has presented an objective set of criteria for defining the boundary of the ecumene. While a single critical population density value would seem logical and easily delineated on a global scale, the use of a single value appears to lead to an underestimate of the extent of the ecumene in Australia and in certain other countries with extensive agriculture based upon large inputs of capital and serviced by a small, sometimes transient rural labour force. Under this extensive system permanent cropping may support rural population densities as low as one person per 8 km², while under more labour-intensive conditions the same agricultural output may support rural densities greater than one per km². This contrast suggests that it is appropriate to define the ecumene as the zone of permanent agriculture or with a comparable level of intensity in

grassland or forestry management. In Australia, this boundary generally coincides with a rural population of one person per 8 km², as is shown later in this chapter.

If the world's six largest nations, by area, are partitioned into ecumene and nonecumene, according to the permanent agriculture criterion, a more realistic measure of the extent of settled Australia is obtained, providing support for Grenfell Price's contention that underpopulation is not pronounced by western standards (Table 15.1). Even if the currently underused lands of the northern tropical wet-dry zone were included, the area of the Australian ecumene would be increased to approximately the same as Canada's, and would still be less than half that of any of the other countries listed. On this basis, the contrast in population densities with the four other newly settled countries, shown in Table 15.1, is markedly reduced, and is overshadowed by the contrast between these five countries and the long-settled countries of India and China.

SPATIAL CONCENTRATION
The high degree of population concentration within Australia and within the various states is widely recognized but rarely measured. The degree of concentration or dispersion of a population can be conceptualized and measured in a variety of ways. It can be indicated, in crude fashion, by measuring the extent of the ecumene. Greater precision can be gained by summing the numbers located at selected distance intervals from relevant reference points or lines, such as from the modal population centre, or from the coastline. More abstract measures are obtained from ordered mathematical comparisons between population and area, unrelated to distance from any reference point, as with Lorenz Curve Analysis and the related Index of Concentration and Concentration Ratio (Clarke, 1972, pp. 40–3). However, for most purposes the most useful measures are those based upon the extension of single-dimensional mathematical parameters to two-dimensional distributions, as is done with centrographic measures, described later in this section. Other measures of concentration may be used, which have no direct spatial connotations. The most useful of these are indices of urbanization and of concentration within cities of specified size.

In this section, reference will be made to concentration as indicated by: extent of ecumene; coastal location; cumulated distance from State capitals which are also modal population centres; and selected centrographic measures. In the following section, levels of urbanization and metropolitan concentration are discussed. These measures are chosen because they provide valuable insights into various aspects of concentration, while some also permit international comparisons.

Extent of Ecumene

Table 15.1 suggests a very crude measure of concentration, by indicating the proportion of a nation's territory comprising the ecumene. This measure suggests a high degree of concentration in Australia and Canada, with populations being virtually confined to one-fifth of the national area. The population of the U.S.S.R. occupies one-third, and those of China and Brazil one-half of the total area. The population of the United States, including Alaska, achieves the highest occupancy of total area, with over two-thirds being classed as ecumene.

Coastal Location

Australia shows a significant departure from other countries of near-continental size in having a very high proportion of the population residing near the coast. In 1971, 84.7 per cent of the Australian population lived within 80 km of the sea, while the vast interior, comprising over 85 per cent of the land area, contained only 15.3 per cent of the population. In their coastal location, Australians resemble the peoples of maritime countries such as Japan, New Zealand or the Philippines (Fig. 16.3).

The continental outline and resource distribution strongly favour a coastal orientation. Australia is the only large nation with an entirely coastal frontier, so that shortest-haul transport systems extend directly from the coast to the interior. Australia's dry interior has lacked the resources to support a Corn Belt, a São Paulo agricultural region, or even a Witwatersrand. There are no major natural routeways to the interior to foster the growth of inland entrepôts, as occurred along the St Lawrence—Great Lakes, Mississippi or Parana waterways. Limited agricultural, mineral and water resources have impeded industrial and urban growth, so that Australia lacks the major inland cities found in other continents. Only one inland town can make any claim to metropolitan status, this being Canberra, whose creation as the national capital stemmed more from the insoluble rivalry of Sydney and Melbourne than from any conscious national policy to promote inland development.

The colonial, export-oriented economy further reinforced the contrast between the major urban nodes on the coast and the sparsely settled rural hinterlands of the interior. However, continental configuration and resource distribution are of primary importance, as should be clear from a comparison of Australia with Canada.

The residential and recreational preferences of Australians show an increasing orientation towards the seashore. The physical and social environment of the hot, dry, scattered, poorly serviced inland farms and small towns is proving increasingly unattractive. Resort and retirement centres focus on the ocean, while employers find that coastal or near-coastal locations assist in recruiting labour, as well as providing the usual locational advantages of access to transport, materials and markets. Accordingly, in recent decades, population growth has been almost entirely confined to coastal areas. In the decade 1961–71, the population in the coastal zone, as defined above, increased by 2,070,000, and that of the inland by only 176,000, of which more than half can be accounted for in the growth of Canberra.

Concentration Near State Capitals

Even a hasty examination of population distribution will suggest a fragmented concentration into a series of core zones centred on each State capital. Holmes (1973) has measured this relationship within each State by constructing profiles of cumulated population percentage for the State, scaled either by distance from the State capital, as in Fig. 15.1 or by cumulated proportion of the State's area in distance zones from the capital, as in Fig. 15.2. Fig. 15.1 provides an absolute measure of dispersion with distance, while Fig. 15.2 indicates population dispersion relative to the distribution of land away from the State capital. In Fig. 15.1 a logarithmic scale for cumulated population has been used, to enable accurate depiction of the very small cumulated percentages in the more remote areas. In Fig. 15.2, untransformed scales have been used so that a direct comparison of population and area can readily be obtained. Population totals are derived from 1966 census data for local government areas.

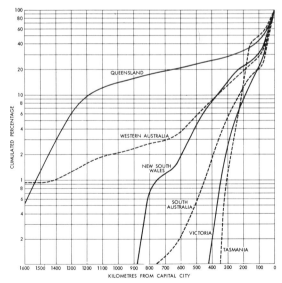

Fig. 15.1 Australian States: cumulated percentage of population by distance from capital city, 1966. *Source:* Holmes, 1973, p. 162.

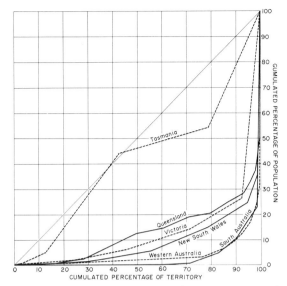

Fig. 15.2 Australian States: cumulated percentages of population and territory by distance from capital city, 1966. *Source*: Holmes, 1973, p. 166.

The two graphs confirm that, in the mainland States, there is a pronounced clustering of population around the State capitals. In 1966, all but 530,000 Australian residents lived within 483 km (300 miles) of a State capital, these cities being well spaced to encompass almost the entire ecumene within this distance interval, as shown in Fig. 15.5. Although 242,000 people in New South Wales were located over 483 km away from Sydney, almost all were within this distance of either Melbourne, Brisbane or Adelaide. The only major group living beyond the 483 km distance range were 418,000 residents of Queensland, most of whom lived along the central and northern coastal area.

The graphs highlight important differences between the States. South Australia and Western Australia contain small, compact settled areas commanded by their capitals which are centrally located in relation to the State's ecumene. Fig. 15.2 shows that the inner 10 per cent of both States' territory contains 90 per cent of the population, while the outer 70 per cent of South Australia contains only 0.64 per cent of the population. A small but economically important 3 per cent of Western Australia's population lives in the outer 70 per cent of the State's area, being located mainly in the Pilbara and Kimberley districts. Victoria and New South Wales have slightly more dispersed populations, primarily because they include a much lower proportion of the nonecumene, which is almost absent from Victoria and comprises less than half of New South Wales. Within the ecumene, however, pronounced concentration occurs, with the inner

20 per cent of territory containing 84 per cent of the New South Wales population and 81 per cent of Victoria's. Fig. 15.1 shows that Victorians generally live closer to their State capital than do people in any other State, including Tasmania.

Of the mainland States, Queensland shows the greatest degree of dispersion away from the State capital, both in terms of absolute distance (Fig. 15.1) and relative to the distribution of land away from the metropolis (Fig. 15.2). Queensland's distinctiveness is most apparent for absolute distance, with the State's profile being entirely different from those of all other States. For example, 12.6 per cent of Queensland's population is located over 1,127 km (700 miles) from Brisbane, a percentage which is surpassed at the 322 km (200 mile) distance interval only by New South Wales, where 13.9 per cent of the population live over 322 km from Sydney. Queensland's greater spread of population away from its modal centre can be partly attributed to Brisbane's off-centre location, which leads to a highly skewed population distribution. However, much more influential is the extent of Queensland's ecumene for more than 1,600 km along the coast and the scatter of population over the vast inland pastoral zone, so that almost the entire State is inhabited.

Tasmania differs from the mainland States in showing a reversal, if only slight, of the general pattern of population concentration near the State capital. Fig. 15.1 shows that 44.1 per cent of Tasmania's population is located over 161 km from Hobart, whereas Fig. 15.2 reveals that only 42.4 per cent of the State's area lies beyond this radius, thus indicating a slightly higher overall density in the more 'remote' sector of the State. This reversal reflects the environmental and locational disadvantages of southern Tasmania. Hobart's historic role as the centre for governmental and other quaternary activities provides only a partial counterweight to these disadvantages. The consequent bipolarity in economic development is reflected in a markedly bimodal population distribution, with a sharp peak around Hobart and a broader, many-peaked 'ridge' in northern Tasmania.

Within most States further population concentration is occurring through rapid growth in near-metropolitan areas as well as in the major cities. In New South Wales and Victoria much of this growth can be attributed to 'overspill' of dormitory residential development, particularly to Gosford-Woy Woy and to Werribee; to the siting of new industries seeking the advantages of a near-metropolitan location; and to the swelling populations in seaside and lakeside resort and retirement areas. Near-metropolitan growth around Brisbane has occurred mainly on the Gold Coast and Sunshine Coast, year-round resorts well placed to benefit from local and interstate sources of visitors and retired persons. This accelerating near-metropolitan growth may herald the appearance of extended city regions of the Los Angeles type. Recent strategic plans for Sydney and Melbourne accept the inevitability of this extended concentration of city-dwellers. The Outline Plan Report for the Sydney Region states that its 'ultimate concept' is a 'closely integrated linear urban complex of 6–7 million people' incorporating Sydney, Newcastle and Wollongong (State Planning Authority, 1968).

Centrographic Indices

Centrographic methods are an extension of familiar mathematical methods for measuring central tendency and dispersion of a set of scores in one dimension; here the method is applied to scores scaled in two dimensions, as is the case with areal or 'spatial' distributions. Central tendency can be indicated by the location of the modal, median or mean centre. Each of these mathematically derived centres has its related measure of deviation or dispersion of scores from the centre. In the last section, cumulated dispersion from the modal centre was measured and compared with distance and area scales. For the median centre the most appropriate single measure of dispersion is the mean distance deviation, and for the mean centre, the standard distance deviation. Neft (1966) provides a detailed discussion, and Holmes (1973) has applied the methods to populations in Australian States. These are but one group from an array of macrogeographic methods designed to obtain general parameters (or measures) of spatial distributions or to map the influence relationships of, and accessibility to the distributions as a whole (Stewart and Warntz, 1958, 1959; Warntz and Neft, 1960). These methods have most commonly been applied to human population distribution.

These methods have value in providing meaningful, single indices of the degree of population concentration in Australia as a whole and in the various States. Their validity is enhanced by the simplicity of the population density surfaces of the five mainland States, each comprising a skewed conical surface with a very pronounced peak. Skewness arises from the abrupt termination of population at the coastline, whereas there is a more gradual decline towards the sparsely settled inland and, in some States, northern margins. This skew is pronounced in all States but Victoria. In spite of this skew, in all mainland States but Queensland, population concentration is so extreme that the median and mean centres coincide reasonably closely with the modal centre, with all three being tied to the State capital (Holmes, 1973, p. 153). The distance between mean and modal centres is 295 km in Queensland, compared with 60 km in New South Wales, 53 km in Western Australia, 21 km in South Australia

and only 11 km in Victoria.

Skewness has a major effect upon the spatial organization of the State, particularly on contact between the main population centres and the more sparsely settled areas, and on the relative ease of servicing the latter areas. Particularly where economic, social, political, administrative and cultural activity is centralized into one city, as occurs to an extreme degree in Australian States, a symmetrical population distribution has considerable advantages in minimizing distances to the peripheral areas. Among the three most highly skewed Australian States, the effects of skew are of little consequence in South Australia because of the insignificant population and economic activity located in the remote extremities of the State. Problems are more evident in Western Australia particularly for the Kimberleys and Pilbara but Queensland is the State which has been most clearly disadvantaged as a result of the off-centre location of Brisbane. This has had important repercussions on the spatial structure of the State, one expression of which has been the development of major provincial cities to service significant populations remote from Brisbane.

In Tasmania, scores on central tendency and skewness differ markedly from those of the mainland States, because of the extreme bimodality of the population distribution. The median and mean centres of population are near each other in the sparsely settled central highlands over 100 km from the modal centre at Hobart.

Scores for Australian States, obtained for various dispersion measures, have been described elsewhere (Holmes, 1973, pp. 155–9), and only one measure can be mentioned here. The most appropriate is the mean distance deviation, or the mean distance of the population from the median centre. This score indicates the minimum average distance of travel for each person in order to assemble the whole population at one point, often called the point of minimum travel. The distances (in kilometres) for the six States and for Australia are, in order: Victoria 51, South Australia 69, Tasmania 101, New South Wales 116, Western Australia 124, Queensland 311, and Australia 745.

This provides an effective single index of the aggregate distance relationships between all individuals in a population. The measure clearly indicates a high degree of population concentration for Victoria and South Australia, whose populations can readily be serviced from one central point. Tasmania, New South Wales and Western Australia group together with noticeably higher scores. Although Tasmania's area is fifteen times smaller than South Australia's its population obtains a higher mean distance deviation, because of the dual influences of much greater population dispersion and bimodality in the distribution.

Queensland differs markedly from all other States.

Compared with the three other territorially large mainland States, the mean distance deviation for Queensland is 2.5, 2.7 and 4.5 times greater than for Western Australia, New South Wales and South Australia, respectively, confirming Queensland's oft-repeated claim of being the most decentralized State. However, when population numbers are so small and area so large, decentralization or dispersion can impose very heavy burdens in servicing that population. These burdens are markedly reduced in the other mainland States as a consequence of population concentration.

The question inevitably arises concerning the level of concentration of Australia's population compared with other countries of similar areal extent. Centrographic methods should provide a ready answer, but lamentably few such studies have been made. The only source for international comparisons is Neft (1966), whose comprehensive analyses of seven countries include Australia and four other countries of large area. Neft obtained the following measures of mean distance deviation (in kilometres): Australia 708, India 773, China 797, Brazil 956, and U.S.A. 1,074. Thus the Australian population shows a lower level of absolute dispersion than the other large countries, even including India which has only half the area of Australia. This very high level of concentration of population, and economic activity, has long been a source of public concern and a stimulus to policies and programmes aimed at decentralization. While the economic and social merits of decentralization, or even of 'concentrated' decentralization are difficult to assess, a strong case can be made that concentration has been a natural response to Australian circumstances, as is argued by A. J. Robinson:

> A notable characteristic of the economic geography of Australia is the fact that, while the country is about as large as the United States, it developed by discounting its physical bigness to a considerable extent, concentrating relatively meagre physical and human resources into compact areas. The heavy burden of transportation on a small population was minimized by developing the States as a number of independent sub-economies. Within these sub-economies, concentration of population and manufacturing industry in large metropolises minimized the costs of transportation between raw materials and industry, between one industry and another, and between manufacturer and consumer. Concentration of population produced its own economies of scale in the provision of services, including the provision of many services that would be impossible in a dispersed population. (Robinson, 1963, p. 155)

Thus the unique locational advantages of the centre, with its access to the periphery along radial transportation lines, were to be most clearly expressed under Australian conditions. These advantages are spelt out more fully in Chapter 21, where locational forces on Australian manufacturing are discussed.

Population and Accessibility

So far attention has focused on intrastate levels of concentration. This fragmented macroanalysis of six geographically separate subpopulations can be justified on the grounds that, for many purposes, Australian States still merit recognition as distinct functional entities, with the State as a whole providing a 'captive hinterland' to its metropolis. However, Geissman and Woolmington emphasize the decay of these 'captive hinterlands' as the Australian economy becomes more diversified and integrated at the national level, leading to an increasing level of linkage between States and between larger cities (Geissman and Woolmington, 1971; Woolmington, 1972). This trend enhances the practical value of obtaining macroanalytic measures of the distributional characteristics of the national population. While the centrographic methods already described provide a useful set of indices for interstate comparisons, and also serve adequately in depicting locational advantage based on accessibility for the very simple, highly concentrated intrastate population distributions, these methods are of much less value when applied to the more complicated distribution of the aggregate national population. Simple measures of central tendency and dispersion are of little value as summary measures of complex distributions, on two-dimension scales just as on one-dimensional. For these more complex distributions it is more appropriate to analyse and map the spatial influence of the whole population, using maps of either population potentials or relative accessibility to the total population.

Geissman and Woolmington have analysed the 1966 distribution of population in southeast Australia in order to obtain measures of overall accessibility to this population. In Fig. 15.3, the unbroken lines measure the relative nearness of places to the total population within the area analysed, obtained by the summation of people times distance to all other points. The lines indicate the percentage increase in the summation, and therefore in the theoretical transportation cost, above the point with the minimum score and highest theoretical accessibility to the whole population. This minimum score, shown by a star on the map, is located near Crookwell. The stippled area has values no more than 10 per cent above Crookwell.

The series of dashed lines represent changes in theoretical accessibility resulting from population shifts between the 1961 and 1966 census, causing a slight southwards shift in accessibility most pronounced near Melbourne, while relative loss of accessibility was greatest in northeastern New South Wales.

Geissman and Woolmington emphasize the highly theoretical nature of this analysis, which is not based on actual costs of transport and covers only one aspect of the location problem. However, it does

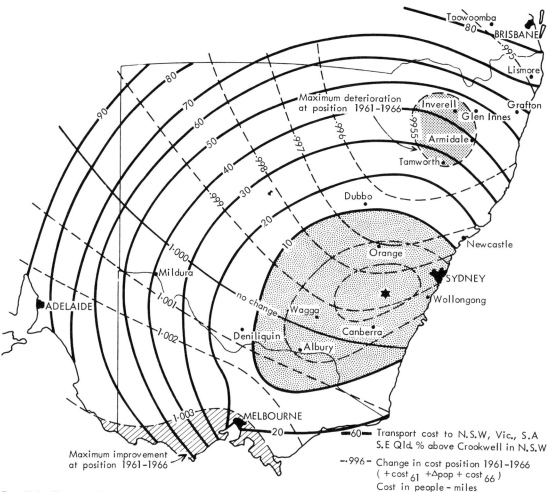

Fig. 15.3   Theoretical transport cost to market 1966. *Source*: Geissman and Woolmington, 1971. By permission of the Editor of *New Zealand Geographer*.

provide a good insight into the question of the distance relations of particular places to the whole population of southeast Australia, comprising over 80 per cent of the national population, and is highly relevant in considering locational advantage in reaching this larger population.

URBANIZATION AND METROPOLITAN CONCENTRATiON

International Comparisons

Of all the indicators of population concentration in Australia, the most easily measured and widely reported is the high level of urbanism and particularly the exceptionally high concentration in a few large cities. Extreme urbanism excites special comment because of Australia's continuing trade pattern based

mainly upon exports of agricultural and mineral products and imports of manufactures.

Australia is sometimes described as the world's most urbanized country. An examination of data in the 1972 United Nations Demographic Yearbook supports this conclusion, as indicated in Table 15.3, in which urbanization levels are shown for those countries generally considered the most urbanized. The data should be interpreted with caution. Exact comparisons cannot be made because of differences in the definition of urban places and in the fixing of boundaries around these places. In Denmark, all places of 200 persons or more are classed as 'urban', in Canada, Australia and New Zealand 1,000 persons is used as a lower limit, in the Netherlands 2,000 and in the United States 2,500. In Belgium, England and Wales the definition is based upon residence in incorporated areas which are not

Table 15.3 Levels of Urban Concentration of Population in Countries Commonly Regarded as Most Urbanized

Country	Percentage of total population residing in cities of over:					Percentage 'urban'
	2,000,000	1,000,000	500,000	250,000	100,000	
Australia	40.1	40.1	57.9	59.9	64.5	85.6
U.S.A.	23.3	35.2	44.5	49.2	55.5	73.5
England and Wales	25.1	31.2	33.9	40.3	51.6	78.2
Canada	24.9	29.9	35.2	47.9	54.1	76.1
Japan	18.2	22.8	27.3	40.2	56.6	72.2
Netherlands	0	16.0	21.3	29.5	43.5	77.8
Belgium	0	11.1	18.4	22.6	29.5	86.8
New Zealand	0	0	0	19.6	34.1	81.3

consistently based on a minimum population. Furthermore, the criteria for fixing boundaries of larger urban areas differ markedly between countries. Several countries, including Australia, have adopted a consistent set of criteria usually based upon delimiting the extent of the continuously built-up area. Other countries depend upon political boundaries which may lead to underbounding or overbounding of cities, or, more often, to an inconsistent blend of the two. For a discussion of this problem and of recently developed Australian procedures, see Linge (1966); Commonwealth of Australia, *Official Yearbook*, 1973, pp. 134–5; and the publications of the Australian Bureau of Statistics.

Taking into account these variations in practice, the evidence remains strong that Australia is the world's most urbanized nation, excluding only city-states such as Singapore. Certainly, Australia has no rival in the degree of concentration into very large metropolises. Table 15.3 shows that two in every five Australians live in the two national metropolises of Sydney and Melbourne, and almost three in every five live in one of the five mainland State capitals. It has already been suggested that this is a logical response to Australian conditions. However, national and State politicians, and the general public, have shown a more keen awareness of certain problems arising from this concentration, particularly those relating to congestion and competition for space in the few large cities, affecting most of the people, relating to economic stagnation and lack of opportunity in most country towns and rural areas, and relating to physical and social isolation over much of the country, affecting only a few people. These issues are reviewed at the end of this chapter, while the underlying causes of urbanization and metropolitan concentration are discussed in Chapters 19 and 21.

Urban Trends
A high level of urbanization has been apparent throughout Australian history. The urban foundations of initial settlement in the convict period have been the subject of comment (K. W. Robinson, 1962, pp. 1–3; Butlin, 1964). In his authoritative work on Australian economic growth in the latter part of the nineteenth century, Butlin states that 'the process of urbanization is the central feature of Australian history, overshadowing rural economic development and creating a fundamental contrast with the economic development of other "new" countries' (Butlin, 1964, p. 6). Butlin points out that by 1891 two-thirds of the Australian population lived in cities and towns, a fraction matched by the United States only by 1920 and by Canada not until 1950. The high level of urbanism and metropolitan concentration was commented upon by the New South Wales government statistician in 1887, who presented well-reasoned arguments that this indicated an improvement in the circumstances of the population as a whole (Coghlan, 1887, p. 139).

The process of urbanization has continued unabated, as indicated by the continually increasing percentage of the population in urban areas, rising from 78.1 in 1954 to 85.5 in 1971. However, population change is occurring very unevenly within the urban system. Since 1954, non-metropolitan cities and towns have barely managed to retain their share of the national population, which has remained close to 25 per cent, so that the trend towards further urbanization can be entirely accounted for by the increasing level of metropolitan concentration. Outside the large cities, growth is progressively being confined to an unrepresentative group of specialized towns, and those experiencing overspill from metropolises, as is clearly shown in the 1971 population map and accompanying commentary of the *Atlas of Australian Resources*. More modest growth is occurring in the larger country towns with claims to status as regional capitals, but elsewhere in the urban system population stability or decline have become widespread.

The only major published analysis of these trends is

Table 15.4   Selected Indices of Urbanization (1971), Labour Force Structure (1971) and Population Distribution (1966) for Australian States

	N.S.W.	Victoria	Queensland	South Australia	Western Australia	Tasmania	Australia
Percent population							
metropolitan	59.2	68.4	44.8	69.0	62.3	33.3	60.1
urban	88.5	87.7	79.2	84.6	81.5	74.2	85.6
Percent workforce							
primary	9.0	8.7	16.8	11.5	15.5	14.3	10.8
secondary	29.3	32.4	19.8	28.3	18.2	23.6	27.6
tertiary	61.7	59.0	63.5	60.2	66.3	62.2	61.7
MDn (kilometres)	262	151	559	184	306	159	—
MDn ÷ Ra	0.52	0.57	0.75	0.33	0.34	1.09	—

Note: MDn is a measure of the mean distance of the non-metropolitan population from the metropolis. Ra is a measure of the radius of a circle equal to the area of the State.

Rowland's (1974) study of country towns and rural areas in Victoria. Rowland used cluster analysis to group together those towns which have shown similar intercensal population trends over the four post-war intercensal periods from 1947 to 1971. Of the 111 towns for which data were available for a complete analysis, 84 towns were grouped into three classes, all characterized by a persistent reduction in growth rates over the four periods; and 62 of these were in two classes characterized by the onset of decline in the 1966–71 intercensal period. This sequence is most evident in small to medium-sized rural service centres, or average country towns.

In the 1966–71 intercensal period, only in Western Australia, Tasmania and Queensland did non-metropolitan towns and cities make any relative gain in population. In Western Australia this gain can largely be attributed to the spectacular growth of new mining towns. Queensland showed a clear-cut differentiation in trends, with growth being confined to four distinctive urban groups, namely: six major provincial cities of Townsville, Toowoomba, Rockhampton, Cairns, Mackay and Bundaberg which together gained 28,600 persons; six large coastal resorts (also 28,600 persons); six towns based on mining and related developments (18,200 persons); and five suburban overspill towns (2,900 persons). Together, these towns registered a gain of 78,800 persons or an increase of 23.3 per cent over five years, while Brisbane added 100,500 persons, an increase of 14.0 per cent. However, the other 68 towns comprising rural service centres of all sizes and in all agricultural regions, recorded a net loss of 5,000 persons. Loss was widespread and was particularly heavy in the widely spaced, small towns

serving the inland pastoral zone, which averaged a net loss of 16 per cent over the five years.

Only in Tasmania, with its small, slowly growing, relatively dispersed population and its off-centre capital city, did the share of population in other urban centres show a consistent upward trend from 1954 to 1971, rising from 36.1 to 40.9 per cent of the State's population. This growth has occurred mainly in the northern string of industrial, service and transport-oriented towns of Burnie, Devonport, Ulverstone, Wynyard and Georgetown.

Apart from the relationship between functional specialization and rapid population growth in the 1960s, associations between population trends and other urban characteristics are not readily discerned. Johnston has correlated 1961–6 population trends with three basic urban characteristics, and found weak but significant associations, which can be expressed as less decline in larger towns, in towns near to metropolitan cities and in towns located in areas with a growing non-urban population (Johnston, 1969).

In all States, the decline in many small country towns has occurred despite local migrations which are adding to their resident populations. The farm labour force is becoming increasingly urbanized in two distinct ways. Firstly, there has been a replacement of farmhands, drovers and other rural workers by town-based specialists, such as drivers of trucks and heavy machinery; aerial agriculture pilots and loader-operators; contractors for building, fencing, well-digging and various other tasks; agricultural consultants and various other specialists. The second development is the growing tendency for farmers to reside in town and travel out regularly to the farm.

This can readily be achieved where farming does not require constant attention at short time-intervals, and is well suited to grain-growing and grazing. A detailed study of town-based farming in the South Australian mallee region has been made by Williams (1970). These 'growth' sectors in urban populations, which really involve a short-distance relocation of population from farm to town, have not adequately compensated for decline in traditional sectors of small-town economies.

Rural Trends

While the percentage of population classed as rural has declined steadily, from 21.3 in 1954 to 14.4 in 1971, numbers remained stationary until 1966, at about 1,900,000 persons, indicating that natural increase and out-migration were in balance. Between 1966 and 1971 there was a net loss of 95,000 persons, representing a decline of one per cent per year. Very few areas have escaped this onset of population decline, as is clearly shown in the 1971 population map of the *Atlas of Australian Resources*. A consistent downward trend, culminating in losses, was revealed in Rowland's study of trends in Victorian shires from 1954 to 1971 (Rowland, 1974). The most common trend, occurring in 82 out of 137 shires, was a slow, decelerating growth of between 1.5 and 0.5 per annum up to 1954 or 1961, followed by progressively greater decline. Decline has also appeared in other shires which previously experienced fluctuating trends.

Marked agricultural expansion can no longer necessarily be expected to stimulate growth in rural populations. The new cotton-growing areas in northern New South Wales, for example, have continued to lose rural population. The new on-farm employment opportunities have been filled mainly by itinerant or urban-dwelling workers, while even more rapid employment growth has occurred in the towns serving the cotton farms.

The only notable areas of rural population growth are the rural-urban fringes of the large cities where most of the increase in rural population is concentrated, and the remote areas of Australia's interior and north, where numerically small but high rates of increase have been stimulated by mining and other non-agricultural development.

Urbanization has advanced so far that the rural population can no longer have any substantial effect on overall population trends. Even if rural areas continue to experience high rates of net out-migration, the numbers involved are so small that they will have only a minor effect upon urban growth. Nevertheless, the rural-dwelling population remains of considerable economic and political significance.

Metropolitan Trends

As with urbanization, Australia has long been a

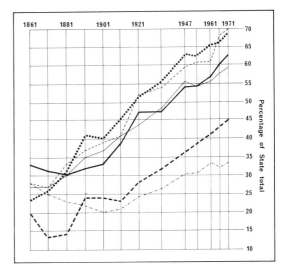

Fig. 15.4 Australian States: percentage of State population in capital city, 1861–1971. *Source*: K. W. Robinson, 1962, modified.

pacemaker in metropolitan concentration of population. Fig. 15.4 shows that in 1901 three of the newly federated States had almost two-fifths of their population in one city, a degree of concentration which was then at least as distinctive internationally as is the present level of between 59 and 69 per cent in four States. New South Wales, Victoria and South Australia showed an early trend towards single-city dominance, following the assertion of hegemony over their respective colonies from these points of initial settlement (K. W. Robinson, 1962; Butlin, 1964; Blainey, 1966; Rowland, 1974).

Fig. 15.4 shows continuing concentration in metropolises, with no evidence that an upper limit has yet been reached. Indeed, a high rate of further concentration is occurring in those States where concentration is already at the highest level. Between 1966 and 1971, in the three less centralized States, Hobart's share of its State's population increased by 1.1 percentage points, Sydney's by 1.4 and Brisbane's by 1.6; in the three more centralized States, Adelaide's share increased by 2.3, Perth's by 2.5 and Melbourne's by a remarkable 2.9 per cent. In the two most centralized States, Victoria and South Australia, the impetus towards further concentration has been so great that an absolute decline in non-metropolitan population occurred in the 1966–71 period.

Even when economic and population growth have received stimulus from resource development in remote areas, population growth remains strongly focused on the metropolis. In 1966–71, for example, Western Australia achieved the second highest population growth rate of any State since federation, surpassed only by the same State in the 1901–11 intercensal period. Rapid growth has been triggered by mining developments generally remote from Perth, yet Perth's population increased by 142,000 persons over the five years, while the rest of the State grew by only 41,000 of which 13,000 occurred in the near-metropolitan bulkport and industrial satellite of Kwinana-Rockingham. The reasons for this continuing rapid growth of Perth and of the other capital cities are discussed in Chapters 19 and 21.

The Role of Internal and Overseas Migration

Burnley (1974) has recently drawn attention to the contribution made by overseas migrants to the rapid growth of the State capitals, pointing out that, in 1966, 73.1 per cent of the overseas-born population was located in the State capitals, compared with 54.8 per cent of the Australian born. Employment opportunities, particularly in the manufacturing and construction industries have played an important role, being able to absorb the large influx of recent arrivals from southern Europe, the majority of whom are classed as unskilled on arrival. Chain migration and kinship networks contribute further towards attracting new arrivals into established migrant communities in the inner suburbs of the large cities (C. A. Price, 1963).

Choi and Burnley (1974) have undertaken an analysis of the sources of population growth in Australia capital cities over the intercensal periods from 1947 to 1966. Their study clearly demonstrates the importance of overseas migration to population growth particularly in Melbourne, Sydney and Adelaide; it also draws attention to one major aspect of internal migration, namely the negligible contribution of internal migration to the growth of Sydney and Melbourne. Net gains obtained from intrastate migration to these two cities are balanced by net losses by interstate migration generally directed to other capital cities, and particularly to Brisbane, Perth and Canberra. Further studies of post-war internal migration and of the characteristics of the migrants have been made by Hugo (1974).

Interstate Differences in Urbanization

Internal differences in urbanization may occasionally reflect differing levels of economic development, as between Northern Italy and the Mezzogiorno, or Brazil's southeast and northeast, or America's central Appalachia and neighbouring regions. More commonly, internal differences result from functional differentiation, as indicated by the degree of specialization in manufacturing and tertiary activities.

Australia shows little regional differentiation in either level of economic progress or functional specialization; consequently there is only minor variation in levels of urbanization, the most notable being the higher levels near major cities and along the coastline. There is an absence of specialized manufacturing regions supporting dominantly urban populations; instead manufacturing is concentrated into the large multifunctional cities or in scattered specialized towns. Each State repeats this pattern, and accordingly the percentage of urban population varies only from 88.5 in New South Wales to 79.2 in Queensland. In the United States the percentage varies from 88.6 in New Jersey and 86.4 in California to 38.2 in West Virginia.

A general relationship between urbanization and functional specialization is suggested in Table 15.4, and by the Pearsonian correlation coefficients between percentage of population classed as urban and percentage of labour force in primary ($r = -0.808$), secondary ($r = +0.695$) and tertiary occupations ($r = -0.461$). These relationships must be interpreted with caution because of the crude indices used and the limited size of the data set, based on only six States. Particularly striking, among the mainland States, is the almost exact one-for-one relationship between urbanization and employment in non-primary occupations, or, in other words, between rural population (R) and percentage of labour force engaged in primary production (P). This direct relationship can be depicted by a trend line in which $R = P + 3.5$, with a maximum error of prediction of less than one per cent. Tasmania is a noteworthy exception, with the rural population being eight percentage points above that predicted by the trend line of the mainland States. This reflects the smaller scale of urbanization in Tasmania, with urban centres of comparable hierarchical order having smaller populations than on the mainland, and with the smaller centres being included in the rural population by current census definition. Until recently this Tasmanian feature received official recognition in the census practice of using a population of 750 as the minimum value for defining urban places in Tasmania, while 1,000 was used in all mainland States and territories.

There is a reasonably strong, but less close, correlation between urbanization and manufacturing employment for the mainland States. Tasmania again has a level of urbanization well below the predicted figure.

Tertiary employment and urbanization show a weak negative correlation. The three least urbanized States, Tasmania, Queensland and Western Australia, also have the highest levels of tertiary employment. Although the functional relationships are not entirely clear, it is relevant to note that there is a close positive association between primary and tertiary employment, suggesting that economies of scale in tertiary employment are less readily achieved in the more rural States, where teachers, doctors, shire clerks, policemen, salesmen and other tertiary workers serve a smaller average number of persons than in the more urbanized States.

Interstate Differences in Metropolitan Concentration

Interstate differences in metropolitan primacy have received much comment but are not easily examined systematically (K. W. Robinson, 1962; Stillwell, 1974; Rose, 1966). The six States exhibit differences in a number of possibly relevant characteristics, including economic structure, level of urbanization, resource distribution and spatial structure. Furthermore, Sydney and Melbourne act as national as well as State metropolises, with an increment to their economic structure and population beyond that derived from intrastate linkages, while Adelaide achieves a modest, more specialized increment from manufacturing serving national markets. Only Brisbane, Perth and Adelaide can be regarded almost solely as regional metropolises, serving only their own State hinterlands. It must also be recognized that hinterlands do not coincide exactly with State boundaries. Sydney experiences strong competition from Melbourne, Brisbane and Adelaide in the peripheral areas of New South Wales, while Melbourne competes with Hobart in northern Tasmania. However, the net departures do not appear to be sufficiently great to negate the measures of metropolitan concentration obtained by using State population totals.

With these reservations in mind, the two most cogent hypotheses concerning the reasons for interstate differences can be examined. The first hypothesis relates to economic structure and the second to spatial structure. The first suggests that differences result from variations in economic specialization, with States engaged in primary production showing lower levels of concentration. This hypothesis is not strongly supported by the evidence in Table 15.4. There is only a moderate negative correlation of -0.582 between percentage of labour force in primary production and percentage of population resident in the metropolis, which is a much lower correlation than was shown between primary production and urbanism. Tasmania and Western Australia, in particular, do not fit well with this hypothesis.

The second hypothesis, emphasizing spatial structure, has been examined by Holmes (1973) who tested for a relationship between metropolitan concentration and the relative distance of the metropolis from the mean population centre for each State. A very high correlation ($r = -0.955$) was obtained,

but it must be noted that the location of the mean population centre is mathematically influenced by the degree of metropolitan concentration.

However, it is possible to devise a measure of spatial dispersion which is mathematically independent of the level of metropolitan concentration. This can be done by calculating the mean distance of the non-metropolitan population from some central point, the most appropriate point being the modal centre or metropolis. The data used for Fig. 15.1 have been recalculated to exclude the metropolitan population and the mean distance of the non-metropolitan population obtained. This measure is shown as MDn in Table 15.4. A relative measure of dispersion can be obtained by dividing this distance by Ra, or the radius of a circle equal to the area of the State. Thus MDn/Ra, in Table 15.4, indicates the mean distance of the non-metropolitan population from the metropolis as a ratio of this radius. Only in Tasmania does the ratio exceed one, indicating the mean distance of the non-metropolitan population from the metropolis is even larger than the radius of the circle equal to the area of the State. Such a high score can only be obtained when the metropolis is located in a very off-centre position in relation to the remainder of the population. Western Australia and South Australia, on the other hand, show a relatively high level of clustering of the non-metropolitan population near the metropolis.

A Pearsonian correlation of -0.911 is obtained between this measure of dispersion and the percentage of population living in the metropolis. A near-perfect linear relationship exists for all States save only Victoria, where metropolitan concentration is higher than predicted. Interestingly, Victoria's moderately anomalous position results from its rather high relative dispersion value, when in absolute terms its non-metropolitan population is located nearer to the metropolis than in any other State, suggesting that a composite index based on absolute as well as relative values would yield an even higher correlation. This correlation analysis lends strong circumstantial support to the hypothesis that levels of metropolitan concentration are strongly influenced by the spatial structure of the State. In Chapter 19 this question is examined further in relation to the structure and functioning of intrastate urban systems.

VARIATIONS IN POPULATION DENSITIES

Attention has so far been directed to the overall measures, or parameters, of population growth and distribution, this being essentially an exercise in macroanalysis. A study of population geography would be incomplete without a more detailed examination of areal variations in population densities. This microanalytic exercise need not become a laborious recital of variations from place to place; instead, with

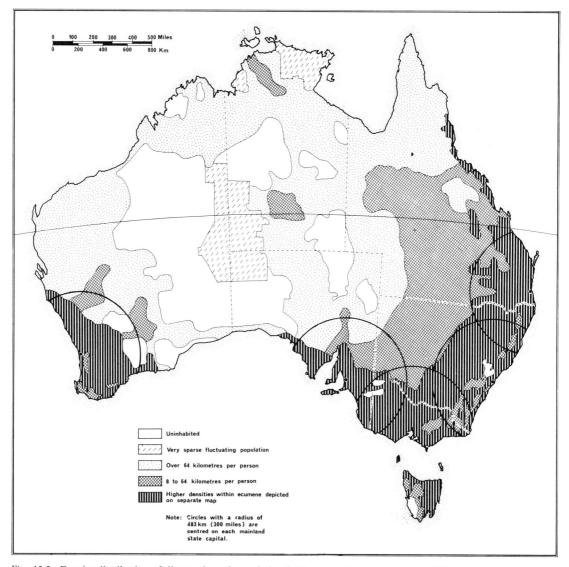

Fig. 15.5   Density distribution of dispersed rural population in the Australian nonecumene, 1971.

the aid of maps depicting these detailed variations, generalizations may be made with emphasis upon the relationship between population density and other elements in human geography.

Although rural dwellers comprised only 14.4 per cent of the total population in 1971, the distribution of this population deserves close examination, as it provides an indicator of the intensity of land use, while also providing a measure of the demand for rural and urban-based services. Save only for the specialized mining, manufacturing, resort and administrative towns, and the major metropolises, the urban popula-

tion distribution closely follows the rural, with both engaged in a complementary relationship to the other.

Mapping Rural Density Distributions

In Figs 15.5 and 15.6 the density distribution of the dispersed rural population is depicted, based on 1971 census data. These maps were compiled from a manuscript dot distribution map prepared, at a scale of 1:5,000,000 and with one dot equalling 200 persons, by the Geographic Section, Division of National Mapping, for use in the new series map of population

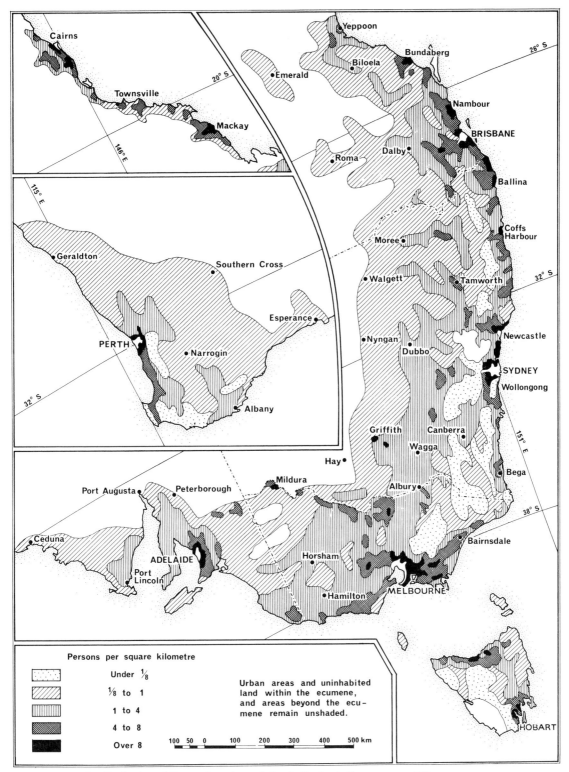

Fig. 15.6   Density distribution of dispersed rural population in the Australian ecumene, 1971.

distribution and growth for the *Atlas of Australian Resources*. Transparent overlays with grids of varying sizes were used to scan the dot distribution map, in order to identify areas with population densities within predetermined class-intervals. The approximate boundaries obtained by scanning were subject to minor local adjustment, consistent with known patterns of landforms, land use and size of rural holdings. Because of the wider spacing of dots in the more sparsely peopled areas there is a lower level of resolu-

tion in these areas, particularly in identifying inliers of even lower density, whereas these inliers are more readily detected in the more densely peopled zones. However, outliers of higher density are consistently identified over the map of the ecumene.

As with any map showing density distributions, the degree of accuracy is dependent upon the reliability of the initial dot distribution map, and the scale. The dot distribution map circumvents the distortions arising from the use of large areal units such as shires,

Table 15.5 Land Tenure, Land Use and Settlement Features Associated with Rural Population Densities

Population density range	Typical density distribution (one dot equals eight persons)	Land tenure and usual size of holdings	Rural land use	Central place pattern and provision of rural services
Uninhabited		Unoccupied	Unused	Emergency search, rescue and medical services
Low, fluctuating		Held in Aboriginal reserves; no individual holdings	Occasional nomadic hunting and collecting	Emergency services, health, welfare and support services at peripheral settlements
Less than 1 per 64 km²	**40 km**	Low-rent pastoral lease with few improvement conditions; 1,000 to 15,000 km²	Very extensive, open range grazing of beef cattle; some very light sheep grazing	Insufficient demand to support urban services; some rudimentary urban functions incorporated within nucleated station homesteads; irregular or infrequent provision of basic services; Flying Doctor; School of the Air; weekly or fortnightly mail services
From 1 per 64 km² to 1 per 8 km²		Medium-rent grazing lease with improvement conditions; 80 to 200 km²	Extensive open-range grazing of sheep with some beef cattle; scattered grazing and timber-getting in rugged, higher rainfall areas	Supports a rudimentary urban system of small towns spaced at 100 to 150 km intervals along road-rail corridors and at 250 to 300 km across corridors, with graded roads and crude telephone lines linking rural homesteads; weekly rural mail
From 1 per 8 km² to 1 per 1 km²		Mixed leasehold and freehold; 640 to 4,000 ha	Extensive wheat-sheep raising on drier margin and newly settled sections of wheat belt; extensive grazing in higher rainfall zone	Supports a system of small towns spaced at 50 to 100 km intervals, linked by a similarly spaced network of railways and roads; school bus or car services and rural electricity in more accessible areas; rural telephone; bi-weekly or tri-weekly rural mail

Table 15.5 continued

Population density range	Typical density distribution (one dot equals eight persons)	Land tenure and usual size of holdings	Rural land use	Central place pattern and provision of rural services
From 1 per km² to 4 per km²	**12·5 km**	Freehold; 160 to 640 ha	Wheat-sheep and mixed farming; intensive livestock raising; lower intensity dairy farming	Towns at 30 to 50 km intervals with a reasonably complete rural system of improved roads, school bus, electricity, telephone and daily mail
From 4 per km² to 8 per km²		Freehold; 40 to 160 ha	Intensive mixed farming; irrigated livestock and mixed farming; scattered horticulture; dairy farming; sugar cane growing	Usually within 15 km of a town, with close access to urban services and provision of a full range of rural services
Over 8 per km²		Freehold; under 40 ha	Irrigated horticulture and viticulture; horticulture and market gardening; intensive sugar growing; urban fringe	May also receive some urban services

where the effects of statistical averaging over an entire areal unit can be severe. This is particularly so in areas of marked local variability in densities, as is the case in the coastal regions of eastern and southern Australia, where 'empty' areas are finely intermingled with pockets of medium to high rural density.

The critical density at around one person per 8 km², already used to differentiate the ecumene from the nonecumene, also acts as a useful basis for partitioning Australia for purposes of mapping at two differing scales. The greater variability in densities within the ecumene requires depiction at a larger scale, as is done in Fig. 15.6.

Rural Population Density in Relation to Land Use and Settlement

In discussing density classes in the ecumene and nonecumene, salient associations between population density and other aspects of human geography will be mentioned, recognizing that people fulfil a dual role as producers and consumers. The relationship between population density and productive activities is frequently discussed. Concerning population, consumption and service provision, there has been an increasing interest in the macroanalytic aspects, as in measures of accessibility and their relevance to location theory, of which Geissman and Woolmington's study, already referred to, is a typical example. However, the micro-analytic aspects are rarely discussed, possibly because variations in population density have rarely been considered of critical significance in service provision. However, with the very low population densities prevailing over most of Australia, variations in the *sparsity* of population are of critical importance, suggesting that a systematic analysis of settlement can proceed by determining the threshold population density levels for the entry of particular services. Important services for a rural population include: weekly, bi-weekly or daily mail; telephone; rural electricity; daily access to primary or secondary school; all-weather roads; single-day return access to a town, or to a major regional centre. Certain population density thresholds are tentatively suggested in Table 15.5, with the information being based upon the writer's knowledge of some sparsely peopled areas, and checked against maps of rural electricity lines, rural telephones lines, mail services and school bus routes for all or parts of Queensland or New South Wales. A more systematic examination of this aspect of settlement geography could have considerable practical and theoretical value.

Related productive activities, as indicated by rural land use, land tenure and size of holdings are also shown in Table 15.5. Land use and land tenure were checked from published maps. The estimated size of holdings was partially checked also in this way, and by various tabulations on size of holdings for shires and statistical divisions. Over much of the ecumene there appear to be approximately six rural dwellers per rural holding, of which between three and four reside on the holding, with the remainder being non-farm dwellers, usually found in villages and small towns. Only in the nonecumene does the number of persons per holding increase appreciably, with econo-mies of scale and agglomeration being required to overcome isolation. On some large cattle stations the resident population exceeds 100.

Rural Densities in the Nonecumene

Density distributions in the nonecumene are shown in Fig. 15.5 and major settlement features summarized in Table 15.5. Some further comments can be made concerning each density class:

(i) *Uninhabited* The boundaries of uninhabited land are based on the 1971 population map of the *Atlas of Australian Resources* series. These boundaries coincide with the extent of unoccupied land. The largest areas coincide with the waterless deserts of the far interior, but also include infertile sandplains in less arid southern areas of Western Australia and western Victoria. Two rugged areas, northwest of Sydney and in southwestern Tasmania, are sufficiently extensive to be included on the map, being inliers within the ecumene.

(ii) *Low fluctuating population* The larger Aboriginal reserves of the interior and far north still serve as tribal territories for semi-nomadic groups. These reserves are being used irregularly and with reduced frequency for hunting-gathering purposes. Nomadism is being reduced to a part-time activity, as Aborigines increasingly spend their time at government or church-sponsored settlements, in distant towns or as employees of cattle stations.

(iii) *Over 64 km² per person* This extremely low population density prevails over the extensive beef cattle grazing areas of the northern savanna zone and also in central Australia and Queensland's Channel Country. It also occurs in the most thinly occupied sheep areas, particularly in South Australia and Western Australia. The vast stations of this zone are rarely below 1,000 km² in size and may exceed 20,000 km². Population is too sparse to support an urban system or to justify normal rural services. Some rudimentary urban-type functions are provided at the station homestead, the agglomerated settlement which forms the nucleus for station activities. Properties are so large that much of the station work is undertaken on a semi-nomadic basis. The homestead nucleus is sufficiently self-contained to function with only irregu-lar or infrequent contact with distant towns. All-weather feeder roads are being provided by heavy investment from the national government. Other services also need subsidy, including: weekly mail services, usually by aeroplane; Flying Doctor and aerial ambulance services; and correspondence courses and the School of the Air. The policeman may be the only public official within his large patrol district, and is required to act as a multipurpose government representative as well as law-enforcement officer.

(iv) *64 km² to 8 km² per person* Particularly in Queensland where the boundary between sheep and cattle grazing also marks the boundary between two markedly different land tenure systems, there is a pronounced change in size of holdings and population densities between the outback stations and the main pastoral zone. This zone covers central Queensland and extends across most of the Western Division of New South Wales. In this zone an infrastructure is provided, external to the rural holdings, but designed primarily to service these holdings. Each rural holding generally has a graded road, a privately-strung tele-phone line, weekly mail service and one-day return-trip access to a small country town. These widely spaced towns are linked by improved roads and feeder railways. Population and income densities are barely sufficient to sustain this infrastructure. In the private sector, central place activities are characterized by low investment, low demand thresholds for entry of a service, and a high frequency of multifunctional establishments, a typical example being the publican-cum-storekeeper-cum-cattledealer-cum-grazier. Public investment, particularly in transport, communication and other essential services, cannot adjust so readily to low demand levels, and is weighed down by high capital and maintenance costs per unit of consumption.

Boundary Between Nonecumene and Ecumene

There is a sharp change in population density, land use, settlement elements and also in the landscape, between the nonecumene and the ecumene. On one side a long-established system of extensive grazing is yielding returns per acre which are too low to justify land development programmes, and land use retains its traditional dependence on natural pastures; on the other side is a landscape subject to deliberate transformation by cropping or pasture improvement, and with growing investment in agricultural techno-logy, leading to higher levels of productivity. This is the agricultural frontier, or frontier of closer settlement. In southern Australia, the line is sharp and relatively unchanging, no longer being subject to cyclical fluctuation as in an earlier trial-and-error phase of settlement. In South Australia, the line bears some relationship to Goyder's Line, initially drawn by the State Surveyor-General in 1865 to indicate drought-stricken areas, and later proposed as the outer limit

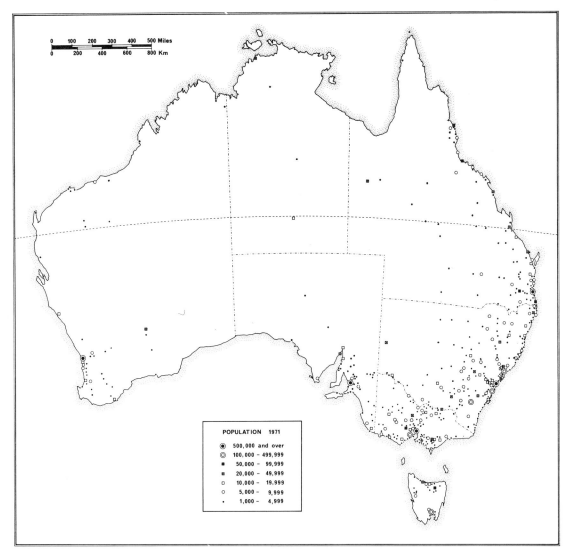

POPULATION 1971

◉	500,000 and over
◎	100,000 – 499,999
■	50,000 – 99,999
▨	20,000 – 49,999
▫	10,000 – 19,999
○	5,000 – 9,999
·	1,000 – 4,999

Fig. 15.7 Australia: distribution of urban centres by size, 1971.

for closer settlement (Meinig, 1962). In recent decades noteworthy advances have occurred in Western Australia's dry-margin wheat belt, and on trace-deficient soils, as in Coonalpyn Downs, formerly the Ninety-Mile Desert, and in the Esperance district.

In Queensland the line is more irregular, less sharply delineated and not so clearly influenced by moisture deficiency. Extensive grazing areas in subcoastal Queensland are yielding to scattered programmes of intensification, notably in the brigalow development schemes. Yet Queensland's coastal areas, between Bundaberg and Mossman, continue to provide the sharpest contrasts in population density, with pockets of very closely settled sugar-growing land being found alongside extensive cattle-grazing holdings.

Rural Densities in the Ecumene

Within the ecumene there are scattered areas of low population density, as shown in Fig. 15.6. These are generally associated with rugged land or very sandy soils. For the remainder of the ecumene, rural densities are shown in four categories, and their associated features summarized in Table 15.5. Further description is not required here, save only to note that the higher densities occur on the rural-urban margin around the major cities. The lack of any other extensive zone of high rural population density has been a further factor militating against manufacturing decentralization, since no rural area has been able to offer a pool of potential factory workers within daily commuting range to meet the labour needs of a decentralized industry, as has commonly occurred in Europe and eastern United States.

Urban Population Distribution

With most Australians resident in a few large cities, the nationwide distribution of this population has already been adequately described within a macro-analytic framework. Of the remaining urban population certain specialized urban activities have their own peculiar spatial distributions, with mining towns showing a seemingly random scatter, but appearing most prominently in very sparsely populated areas; manufacturing towns being in areas of major population concentration; and resort towns having a strong coastal orientation. The distribution of the remainder of the urban population corresponds broadly with that of the rural population. Rural densities of over 64 km² per person cannot support an urban system, and Fig. 15.7 depicts their absence from this rural density zone, save only for specialized mining and transportation/administration towns. In the next higher rural density range, a widely spaced urban system has developed. Relative to their functional complexity, these towns usually have very small populations. Only in the ecumene is found a fully developed system of central places of varying size and functional complexity.

POPULATION POLICIES AND THEIR GEOGRAPHICAL IMPLICATIONS

The policies of the Australian colonies and of their successor State and Federal governments show a strong, almost obsessional preoccupation with issues of population growth, inseparably linked to national development. Interwoven with this aggregate national objective is the locationally-selective objective of population dispersal which is inseparably linked to rural and to regional development.

These objectives are deeply imbedded in Australian public life, originating with the pioneering impulse to settle and to develop. The persistence of a pioneering philosophy, after almost two centuries of European settlement, is an outcome of a perceived lag in Australian population numbers, particularly when compared with the large populations of Asian nations, and also results from the much decried concentration of population, which is making the empty spaces appear even emptier. It was once assumed that growth would automatically contribute to infilling or dispersion. Slowly it has been recognized that these two processes no longer proceed hand-in-hand, and that dispersion policies must be pursued independently of growth policies.

In their separate evolution, growth policies have clearly become population policies, directly aimed at increasing numbers through higher birth rates and increased immigration, whereas dispersion policies tackle the population aspect indirectly, aiming at selective development on the assumption that employment growth will occur at the locations or within the economic sectors favoured with public support. Additionally, since federation in 1901, overall growth policies have mainly been the responsibility of the national government, while dispersion and regional development policies have remained the concern of the States, though recently with increasing national intervention. Separate responsibilities have not favoured a co-ordinated approach towards growth and dispersion.

Growth Policies and Programmes

Australia has given less emphasis to pro-natalist programmes than have many other countries. Modest expenditure on child endowment, baby health care and similar family-support programmes have been more commonly justified on grounds of social welfare rather than of population growth. In this area, governments appear to have recognized an unwillingness among Australians to subordinate their own personal goals to certain national aspirations of growth toward which there has been little general response. Accordingly, the alternative growth programme has been assiduously supported, with the Australian government being among the world's leaders in fostering immigration.

Government-sponsored immigration can be said to have commenced in 1788 with the convicts and soldiers of the First Fleet. By the 1860s the newly self-governing colonies joined with the 'Mother Country' in presenting a variety of incentives to British migrants. Since then, strongly pro-migration programmes have been pursued, and since World War II these have been extended progressively to immigrants from other lands, chiefly from Europe. Only in periods of war and economic depression have these programmes been suspended. The greatest successes for government-sponsored migration occurred in the 1860–90 period, and again in the period following World War II. As witness to this recent success, the 1966 census showed that 19 per cent of Australian residents were of overseas birth, a percentage rarely exceeded in any country, and not surpassed by the United States in the heyday of its immigration around the beginning of the twentieth century.

Since World War II, only Israel has surpassed Australia in its efforts to promote immigration. However, there are sharp differences between Israel and Australia in the impact of immigration on the population geography of the country. Israel's immigration programme has been tightly linked into national and regional development projects, with migrants often being directed to specific locations, promoting a dispersal of population. In Australia, as in other newly-settled western lands, government-sponsored immigration has rarely been linked to specific internal development or settlement projects. In recent decades, the only internal guidance to migrants occurred under the Displaced Persons Scheme, by which wartime refugees from Europe were required to engage in directed employment for a two-year period. No further labour direction has occurred, although the system of sponsored passages has enabled some private employers to link migrant recruitment to jobs in Australia, these jobs usually being in the most heavily populated areas. The old links between migration and land settlement disappeared early in the twentieth century, and rural Australia has been 'locked' against the newcomer, save only for a trickle of Italians into established Italian rural communities in the sugar belt, in some irrigation areas, and in tobacco, fruit and market garden small-holdings.

Thus government-sponsored migration has had the unintended effect of markedly increasing the level of population concentration in the large cities, as also occurred in the later migration waves to the United States.

Dispersal Policies
Policies aimed at population dispersal have changed appreciably, but very belatedly, in response to changes in economic opportunity and internal migration. The most drastic changes have occurred only since 1955, first with a change from a rural to an urban focus, and, since 1972, away from dispersed decentralization towards selective or concentrated decentralization. However, the rural-focused momentum remains so strong that public expenditure on rural-support programmes still exceeds that on urban decentralization. The changing emphasis in major programmes since 1860 is suggested in Fig. 15.8. Some of these programmes have a strong regional or locational focus, while

others have statewide or nationwide applicability. Interestingly, whereas regional development programmes in most countries have been directed towards depressed areas in response to indicators of a population surplus, in Australia, and in other nations committed to the goals of a pioneering society, regional development has been directed towards areas of perceived population 'deficit' in order to attract population increase.

The first significant legislative actions fostering population dispersal were the New South Wales Robertson Land Acts of 1861, heralding a succession of laws intended to encourage a second wave of pioneers, who would establish closer settlement in suitable areas. Government support came mainly through legislation intended to reduce the costs and remove other barriers to the acquisition of land by smallholders. Major public investment was soon to be channelled into railway construction, proclaimed as the solution to problems of inaccessibility for small farmers in inland Australia. The successes and failures of closer settlement have been well chronicled; save in a few areas of belated settlement, closer settlement lost its momentum early in the twentieth century. Governments attempted to restore this momentum by instituting programmes of concentrated or selective closer settlement, most evident in the soldier settlement schemes following World Wars I and II. Particularly in the 1920s these schemes experienced extreme difficulty through bad planning, undercapitalization and lack of markets, with such consequent hardship and loss that very few closer settlement schemes outside of irrigation have been since attempted, the most recent being the marginal wheatlands schemes in Western Australia and brigalow clearing and development programmes in central Queensland.

For most of the twentieth century, public-financed irrigation schemes have been regarded as the most effective way of increasing rural population; their success in achieving this specific objective is evident in the spectacular localized increments to rural populations along the Murray River and its tributaries, as shown on Fig. 15.5. However, their net effect upon Australian economic development has been the subject of considerable controversy.

Since the 1930s the national government has authorized an impressive array of subsidies and concessions to rural industries and rural residents in order to promote a number of national objectives, one important objective being the support of rural population numbers. The importance of population aspects is indicated by the particularly costly programmes directed towards the dairying industry, which are generally justified less on grounds of the economic importance of the industry to the nation, and more on the basis of the industry's formidable reputation for

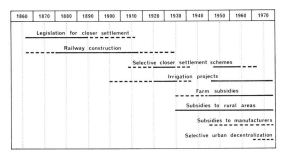

Fig. 15.8 Chronology of major governmental programmes designed to promote population dispersal.

providing support to relatively large numbers of people on farms and in country towns.

Only since the mid-1960s have governments shown a belated recognition of the need to assist those wishing to leave the farm, by providing grants for retraining and relocating farmers and for writing-off redundant farm assets. Programmes for assisting in the reduction of farm population have been instituted with great reluctance, spelling as they do the end of the great Australian dream for settling ever-larger numbers of people on rural holdings.

So strong has been the publicly expressed faith in the vital role of rural industries as a source of population as well as economic growth, that urban decentralization policies have only recently been adopted, and, until 1973, the programmes were supported by miniscule funds. The first modest commitment of funds was made in 1944 when the Victorian government offered freight concessions and limited grants and loans to decentralized industries. A short-lived joint Commonwealth-States programme, linked to postwar reconstruction, emerged from the Premiers' Conference of 1945, while in 1958 New South Wales joined Victoria in offering modest financial support to manufacturing industries willing to locate in country towns (Linge, 1967). There are many reasons why these programmes have met with little success, not the least being the interstate rivalries which are so strong that States feel obliged to offer substantial assistance to industries insisting on a central location rather than lose that industry to another State (Linge, 1967). However, it has increasingly been recognized that the most basic problem has been the unfocused programme of support for dispersed decentralization. There are very few manufacturing firms who find that minor inducements from government are sufficient to overcome the disadvantages of locating in a small country town, removed from major sources of labour, materials and markets.

Programmes for concentrated or selective decentralization have been advocated as a means of offering firms some of the advantages of centralization while redirecting growth away from the largest cities. This concept was adopted by the Victorian government in 1965, and, in 1967, five large provincial towns were nominated as growth centres where industries could expect to receive favourable support. The South Australian government also adopted a policy of selective decentralization with the decision to establish the new city of Monarto, 65 km southeast of Adelaide. Since 1972, the national government has become actively involved in decentralization programmes, offering vigorous support for a variety of proposals related to selective decentralization. Of these proposals, the new growth centre at Albury-Wodonga has been given priority, and will serve as a test case for the concept of selective decentralization. These programmes represent a public acknowledgement that there are persistent trends in the redistribution of Australian population based upon locational forces that governments cannot be expected to counteract. At most, political intervention can only achieve a partial redirection of the basic trend towards further concentration in a few large cities, and this redirection can only be attained by encouraging a modified version of centralization, based upon new growth centres either physically close to existing large cities, as at Monarto, or having favourable overall accessibility to major population concentrations as at Albury-Wodonga. While special local circumstances may offer opportunities for fostering growth at less central locations, as in the Pilbara of Western Australia, or at Gladstone in Queensland, it has been accepted that most of the future growth will occur at or near to the existing major concentrations.

REFERENCES

Australian Institute of Political Science (1971), *How Many Australians? Immigration and Growth*, Angus and Robertson, Sydney.

Blainey, G. (1966), *The Tyranny of Distance*, Sun Books, Melbourne.

Bureau of Census and Statistics (1973), *Official Yearbook of the Commonwealth of Australia*, Canberra.

Burnley, I. H. (1974), 'The urbanization of the Australian population 1947–71' in I. H. Burnley (ed.), *Urbanization in Australia: The Post-War Experience*, Cambridge University Press, Cambridge.

Butlin, N. G. (1964), *Investment in Australian Economic Development*, Cambridge University Press, Cambridge.

Choi, C. Y. and Burnley, I. H. (1974), 'Population components in the growth of cities' in I. H. Burnley (ed.), *Urbanization in Australia*, Cambridge University Press, Cambridge.

Clarke, J. I. (1972), *Population Geography*, Pergamon, Oxford.

Coghlan, T. A. (1887), *The Wealth and Progress of New South Wales*, Government Printer, Sydney.

Department of Minerals and Energy (1975), 'Population Distribution and Growth 1971', *Atlas of Australian Resources*, Second Series, Canberra.

Geissman, J. R. and Woolmington, E. R. (1971), 'A theoretical location concept for decentralisation in southeastern Australia', *N. Z. Geogr.*, 27, 69–78.

Holmes, J. H. (1973), 'Population concentration and dispersion in Australian States: A macrogeographic analysis', *Aust. Geogr. Stud.*, 11, 150–70.

Hooson, D. J. M. (1960), 'The distribution of population as the essential geographical expression', *Canadian Geogr.*, 17, 10–20.

Hugo, G. J. (1974), 'Internal migration and urbanization in South Australia' in I. H. Burnley (ed.), *Urbanization in Australia*, Cambridge University Press, Cambridge.

Johnston, R. J. (1969), 'Population changes in Australian small towns,' *Rural Sociology*, 34, 212–8.

Linge, G. J. R. (1966), 'Urban boundaries for census and

statistical purposes', *R. Aust. Plann. Inst. J.*, 4, 3–6.
——(1967), 'Governments and the location of secondary industry in Australia', *Econ. Geogr.*, 43, 43–63.

Lodewyckx, A. (1956), *People for Australia: A Study of Population Problems*, Cheshire, Melbourne.

McCarty, J. W. (1970), 'Australian capital cities in the nineteenth century', *Aust. Econ. Hist. Rev.*, 10, 107–37.

Meinig, D. W. (1963), *On the Margins of the Good Earth*, Rand McNally, Chicago.

Neft, D. S. (1966), *Statistical Analysis for Areal Distributions*, Regional Science Research Institute, Philadelphia.

New South Wales State Planning Authority (1968), *Sydney Region Outline Plan*, Government Printer, Sydney.

Phillips, P. D. (ed.) (1933), *The Peopling of Australia: Further Studies*, Melbourne University Press, Melbourne.

Phillips, P. D. and Wood, G. L. (eds) (1928), *The Peopling of Australia*, McMillan, Melbourne.

Price, A. G. (1972), *Island Continent: Aspects of the Historical Geography of Australia and its Territories*, Angus and Robertson, Sydney.

Price, C. A. (1963), *Southern Europeans in Australia*, Oxford University Press, Oxford.

Robinson, A. J. (1963), 'Regionalism and urbanization in Australia: A note on locational emphasis in the Australian economy', *Econ. Geogr.*, 39, 149–55.

Robinson, K. W. (1962), 'Processes and patterns of urbanization in Australia and New Zealand', *N. Z. Geogr.*, 18, 32–49.

Rose, A. J. (1966), 'Dissent from down under: Metropolitan primacy as the normal state', *Pac. Viewpoint*, 7, 1–27.

Rowland, D. T. (1974), 'Patterns of urbanization in Victoria' in I. H. Burnley (ed.), *Urbanization in Australia*, Cambridge University Press, Cambridge.

Stewart, J. Q. and Warntz, W. (1958), 'Macrogeography and social science', *Geogr. Rev.*, 48, 167.
——(1959), 'Some parameters of the distribution of a population', *Geogr. Rev.*, 49, 270.

Stilwell, F. J. B. (1974), 'Economic factors and the growth of cities' in I. H. Burnley (ed.), *Urbanization in Australia*, Cambridge University Press, Cambridge.

Taylor, T. G. (1922), 'The distribution of future white settlement: a world survey based on physiographic data', *Geogr. Rev.*, 12, 375–402.

Taylor, T. G. (1951), *Australia: A Study of Warm Environments and their effect on British Settlement*, rev. edn, Methuen, London.

Trewartha, G. T. (1969), *A Geography of Population: World Patterns*, Wiley, New York.

Warntz, W. and Neft, D. (1960), 'Contributions to a statistical methodology for areal distributions', *J. Regional Sci.*, 2, 47.

Williams, M. (1970), 'Town-farming in the mallee lands of South Australia and Victoria', *Aust. Geogr. Stud.*, 8, 173–91.

Woolmington, E. R. (1972), 'Population, location and urban growth' in J. A. Sinden (ed.), *The Natural Resources of Australia*, Angus and Robertson, Sydney.

16 A SOCIAL GEOGRAPHY OF ABORIGINAL AUSTRALIA

FAY GALE

Geographers have long studied the environment and man's relationship with it. But traditionally this has been the physical environment, the earth as the home of man. Only recently have geographers begun to study the human environment created by man and dominating him far more than the physical forces of nature.

Earlier this century a few geographers like Carl Sauer realized that landscapes are different not only for physical reasons but also because different groups of people have inherited quite different cultures and therefore perceive the landscape in very different ways. This culturally determined variation in perception has led to considerable differences in how the land is used and thus the kind of landscape which any one group of people may develop.

Because of the vast cultural difference between the original Australians who settled this country from a beginning dated at least 42,000 years before the present, and the very recent arrivals from Europe, a comparison of these two peoples can illustrate some of the themes which have developed in cultural and social geography.

RESOURCE APPRAISAL

In pre-European times the Aborigines occupied the whole of the Australian continent. No area was considered to be inhospitable or uninhabitable. In their appraisal of the natural environment every area in Australia was capable of supporting some level of population.

By contrast when Europeans arrived they declared large tracts to be virtually uninhabitable. They assessed the environment with quite different cultural eyes, and some land which Aborigines saw as dependable was judged to be desert by Europeans.

One region which illustrates this is the country of the now almost extinct Dieri people. This area, of approximately 18,000 km², lies in the northeastern part of South Australia to the east of Lake Eyre. Coopers Creek, which drains through this area, supplied the Dieri with permanent water though this was not always on the surface. When Sturt (1849) explored the

area he recorded meeting various groups of Aborigines; the largest group he estimated to be in the vicinity of 300–400 persons. Enthused by reports of large populations of Aborigines, two mission societies opened settlements in Dieri country in 1866. The Moravians settled at Kopperamanna but did not stay long, and the Lutherans chose Killalpaninna about ten miles away and remained until 1917.

The missionaries reported that there were several thousand Aborigines in the Dieri territory, and the 1881 census for South Australia gave a figure of 2,182 Aborigines in the vicinity of the mission area. The original indigenous population was probably higher than this because Aboriginal mortality increased rapidly when the people were first contacted by Europeans. Introduced diseases, to which Aborigines had no immunity, a change in diet and lifestyles and a dramatic alteration in the landscape all combined to cause a rapid rise in the death rate. In all areas of early mission settlement the full-bloods virtually died out altogether. Killalpaninna was no exception. The mission was closed in 1917 because there were so few Aborigines left in the area.

The rapidity of population decline suggests a high level of mortality in the first fifteen years of the mission before the 1881 census. For this reason the actual population of the Dieri people was probably in the vicinity of 2,500 when the missionaries first arrived.

Although missionaries learnt Dieri, translated the Bible into Dieri and communicated with the people in Dieri it is doubtful whether the large population described by the missionaries and later census figures comprised solely the Dieri tribal people. No doubt neighbouring groups speaking related dialects were also attracted to the mission. Probably the population figures quoted in the census and in mission reports referred to the whole language area and not just the Dieri dialect.

Even if the population of well over 2,000 at the Coopers Creek settlement had come originally from all of the areas where dialects similar to Dieri were spoken this would still mean that this population

354

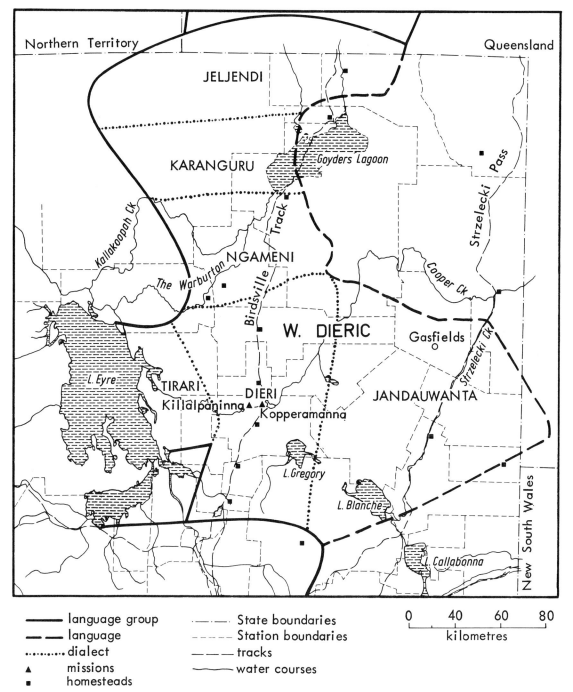

Fig. 16.1 The Dieri territory, South Australia.

inhabited an area of only about 80,000 km². But there is evidence to show from police and mission reports that the whole of the western Dieric language group did not move to the mission site. So density must have been considerably above one person to 4 km². Now it is less than one to 80 km².

Today only fifty-eight residents, white and black, occupy the tribal lands of the Dieri, the adult males being entirely engaged in the pastoral industry. The whole western Dieric language area has a population of 139 persons of whom 40 are employed in the natural gas fields. Some of these are construction workers and will not become permanent residents. The remaining 99 are associated with the pastoral industry. Of course a direct comparison of carrying capacity is not valid because the small population of pastoralists produces beef for consumption mainly by persons living outside of the area. Although trade was important in Aboriginal times it did not mean that one area of small population produced goods to support a larger population elsewhere. Nevertheless there remains a considerable difference between the populations which can be supported by the land in such arid environments under different technologies.

This example illustrates the fact that populations derived from Western culture are able to settle far less of the earth's surface but those areas which they do settle carry much denser populations. Thus the spread of European culture and its associated technology, in Australia as elsewhere, has not increased the area of the *oikoumene*, or habitable world, but has actually diminished it, and imposed greater pressure on those areas now perceived to be habitable.

The accompanying map, Fig. 16.1, defines the area of the Dieri tribe and the larger group of tribes which spoke dialects related to Dieri. The boundaries are very generalized and are based on a compromise of maps by Tindale (1940, 1974) and O'Grady *et al.* (1966). These two authors are not in agreement over boundaries in the Dieri region, and since Aborigines have not lived their traditional life for more than a century in this area the accuracy of these boundaries would be impossible to determine. Fig. 16.1 also shows the boundaries of present pastoral properties in the area. All of the occupied station homesteads are marked.

To the Dieri and their neighbours this was not an arid environment in pre-European times. They found water in trees, roots, and leaves as well as from the more obvious sources of dew, rock holes and soaks. They carried the water in bags made of emu skins (Gason, 1895).

There was adequate food to support a reasonably large population in Aboriginal terms. Vegetable foods were available even in the driest seasons. Seeds, which provided the basic ingredient for the staple food,

damper, were collected from a wide range of grasses, trees and bushes. Sturt described a large growth of box trees, rich in such seeds, on the plains of Coopers Creek.

Although such vegetable foods provided the main element in the diet of desert people, animal food was also readily available for those who had learnt the desert's rhythms. Insects provided high quality food. For example the larval stage of the cossid moth, often termed a wichety grub, was widespread and provided easily assimilable protein. It could be eaten raw or cooked and was important in the diet of very young children. Honey ants and the indigenous stingless bee gave sweetening to the diet. Various sugary scales and lerp insects which feed on mulga trees can support a family for days without any other food.

Meat was an important element of Aboriginal diet but only small reptiles could be relied upon all the year round irrespective of the seasonal conditions. The larger marsupials were frequent only after good rains. But emus and emu eggs provided a more regular source of food for the Dieri, and early reporters described frequent emu hunts. Smaller birds such as ducks, gulls and pelicans arrived in profusion after rains or when the Cooper was in flood but they were not permanent residents.

Most of the early chronicles commented upon the importance of fish in the Dieri diet. Fish could be found in the pools of the creek beds. Each family had its own fishing net. Sturt described fish similar to the Murray perch inhabiting very brackish pools, while Basedow (1925) described the prevalence of freshwater mussels in the mud of the waterholes along the Coopers Creek.

The desert people had long ago learned the art of conservation. During dry seasons fishing was prohibited in certain sacred pools and was allowed in these only when the river was flowing and rapid regeneration could be assured. Through inherited knowledge, sustained by religious beliefs and practice, the continuance of life was assured.

European perception of the Dieri country and its resources was quite different. The new settlers saw no abundance of food around them. From the 1860s on, missionaries, police and pastoralists settled this area which appeared to be able to support such a large population. But what were rich resources to the Aborigines were useless pests to Western eyes. Land was cleared, pools fished out and game indiscriminately killed.

The missionaries introduced wheat, barley, sheep and cattle to this land with an average annual rainfall of only 140 millimetres. They collected the Dieri into a permanent settlement, despite the hard-earned Aboriginal experience which showed that only by regular movements could the natural resources be kept in balance with man's utilization. And so a country which had offered a reliable food base to a stable population for thousands of years became almost a desert to European settlers within a decade. Today less than a dozen remnants of the Dieri remain.

Although the original inhabitants of this continent occupied all of the land their utilization and population density varied from one area to another. With the aid of population control and nomadism these interior districts could support a much higher level of population under Aboriginal technology than they can today. The wetter areas probably carried higher population densities even in pre-European times than did the deserts but the contrast in densities was not as great as it is with Europeans today.

In the wetter areas along the rivers and coasts, where permanent water was available, nomadism was not so necessary. The river and coastal people developed more or less permanent camps. Where mobility was less essential, more substantial housing was erected and in the colder areas warm clothing was made out of possum and other furs.

In the southeast of South Australia the original inhabitants, the Bungandidj, practised transhumance. Their movements were quite unlike the nomadism of the central people. These southerners lived by the coast during the summer depending upon a diet of fish and shellfish and sea birds. During the autumn they migrated inland to spend the winter in the more sheltered areas between the rows of parallel dunes which are a significant feature of this landscape (Campbell *et al.*, 1946). Here they caught kangaroos and other game which could be ambushed in the gaps through the dunes. Their winter diet consisted mainly of meat and the skins provided warm clothing. Their housing was more substantial than the windbreaks of the desert people. Some southerners built wood structures covered with brush or skins. Others constructed mud huts.

The southern Aborigines died out rapidly with the arrival of European settlers but their population numbers and the balance they had developed in relation to the animal population can be judged from early reports of the farmers. One such report stated that 50,000 kangaroos were shot during the five-year period 1870–5. The rapid increase in the kangaroo population was said to be due to the decline in the Aboriginal population (Ward, 1869), because their seasonal diet of kangaroo had kept the animals in check. Their food, clothing, housing and mobility patterns were thus very different from those of the Dieri people.

POPULATION DISTRIBUTION

It is not possible to construct an Australia-wide map of

Aboriginal population distribution in pre-European times. Recorded information concerning the indigenous population at the time of European settlement is too scanty to make such an exercise possible. The best that can be done is to draw evidence from those few areas for which there is some early information of a reasonably reliable nature such as the Dieri country.

However the present distribution of Aborigines in Australia provides some guide to past spatial patterns. Their distribution today is, of course, not the same as in pre-European times but it is still sufficiently different from that of the general population to make a comparison useful in appraising the prehistoric patterns as well as in describing today's situation. Although census material for minority groups cannot be considered entirely accurate it is the only information available for the whole of Australia. Studies of smaller areas (Gale and Binnion, 1975) have shown that it is impossible for a census-type enumeration to include all of the people who are mobile or to classify accurately those of mixed origin. Nevertheless such studies have shown the 1971 census, but not earlier counts, to be reasonably accurate in terms of absolute numbers and relative distributions. Some of the other information dealing with subjects like employment is of less value.

Table 16.1 shows the major distribution of Aborigines in relation to the general community on a State basis.

The spatial patterns exhibited by the two groups are shown more clearly in Fig. 16.2 and 16.3. Because of the considerable difference in the total sizes of the two populations, different numerical groupings are used to aid comparison. The Aboriginal population shown in Fig. 16.2 is given a value of one hundred times that of the general population shown in Fig. 16.3. The distribution in both figures is plotted on the basis of local government areas for all States except the Northern Territory and northern South Australia. In the larger cities, statistical divisions are used in place of individual local government areas.

Table 16.1 Population of Australia, Census 30 June 1971

State or Territory	Non-Aboriginal	Aboriginal
New South Wales	4,578,079	23,101
Victoria	3,496,695	5,656
Queensland	1,802,651	24,414
South Australia	1,166,567	7,140
Western Australia	1,008,566	21,903
Tasmania	389,838	575
Northern Territory	63,137	23,253
Australian Capital Territory	143,815	248
	12,755,638	106,290

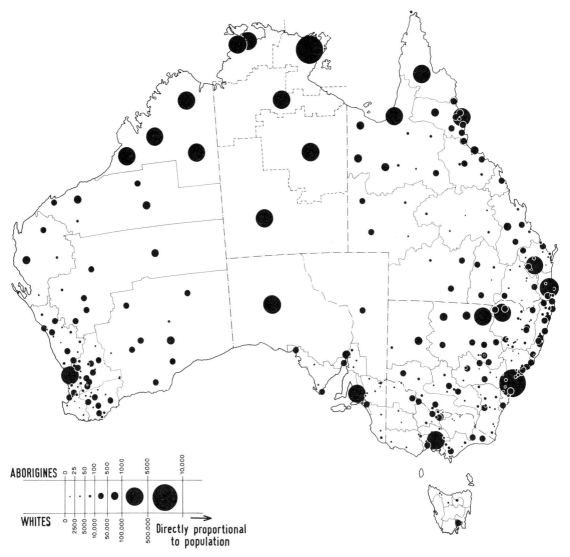

ABORIGINES 0 25 50 100 500 1000 5000 10,000

WHITES 0 2500 5000 10,000 50,000 100,000 500,000   **Directly proportional to population**

Fig. 16.2 Distribution of Aborigines at the 1971 census, which recorded all persons of full and part Aboriginal descent who elected to identify as Aboriginal.

A comparison of these two maps shows that outside the metropolitan centres the areas of lowest European density largely coincided with the areas of highest Aboriginal density even as late as 1971.

Outside of the major urban centres Aborigines still inhabit those areas thought by Europeans to be largely uninhabitable. Traditionally-oriented people whose lifestyles have been least altered by Western technology live in the desert and tropical regions. These Aborigines are descendants of those who have occupied these lands since early Aboriginal settlement. In the agricultural areas no traditional Aborigines remain but there are scattered families of mixed descent. The occupants of the settled areas were quickly gathered onto small reserves as the settlement frontiers moved inland. Their descendants continued to live a segregated life on such reserves until quite recently.

In the last two decades economic pressure and rapid population increase have forced many of the reserve dwellers to migrate to the towns and cities. Only in the larger centres can accommodation and a livelihood be found for the increasing numbers of displaced rural Aborigines.

This urban migration gathered momentum during

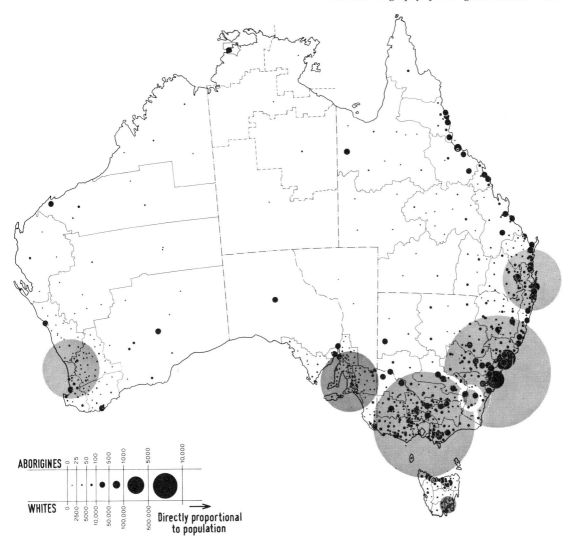

ABORIGINES

WHITES Directly proportional
to population

Fig. 16.3 Distribution of population excluding Aborigines at the 1971 census.

the 1960s. Although boundary definitions were changed
for the 1971 census and data are not therefore strictly
comparable, this factor cannot account for the major
shift from rural to urban areas shown in Table 16.2.

The table illustrates the fact that Fig. 16.2 reflects a
very recent pattern of distribution in showing so many
Aborigines in the cities. Before World War II almost
all of Australia's Aborigines lived in the rural areas.
Their distribution patterns were then even more
dissimilar from those of other Australians than is
evident from a comparison of Fig. 16.2 and 16.3. As
Aborigines become more Westernized they are influenced more by the economic pressures which have
been causing a general pattern of rural depopulation

for some decades now. Today's map of Aboriginal
population distribution is thus different from any that
might have been constructed at any earlier period of our
history if reliable figures had been available.

The consequences of this shift in location are
very important. The urban environment is causing
significant changes in the Aboriginal lifestyle and much
depends upon where they go. Aborigines leave the
reserves with no assets and no credit and must find
cheap rental accommodation in the cities. Initially this
will be in rather crowded conditions with relatives
who moved sooner to the city. Decayed inner urban
areas usually offer the cheapest rental housing for the
greatest numbers. If these situations are contiguous, as

Table 16.2 The Aboriginal Population, Urban and Rural, 1966 and 1971

	1966 Census		1971 Census	
	Persons	Percentage	Persons	Percentage
Urban	21,896	27.3	46,261	43.5
Rural	58,311	72.7	59,987	56.4

in Redfern in Sydney, then ghettoes tend to develop. The social and political consequences of ghetto development are well known. But for various reasons ghettoes are not a significant feature of the Australian situation.

Available houses are often scattered through various inner suburbs so that, even before recent government intervention, Aborigines, although concentrating more in some areas than others, were only in a few instances tending towards ghetto development. The large input of Commonwealth finance into Aboriginal housing has led to greater dispersion in the last few years. They are now to be found in many of the new suburbs as well as the inner city areas. Government subsidized housing is coming to play as big a role as private enterprise in the location of Aborigines in our cities and this housing tends to be purposely dispersed.

Since the Aboriginal population is quite small in comparison with the total Australian size, being less than one per cent, the demographic ability to form extensive ghettoes is limited. But just as important is the disparate nature of this minority people.

In traditional times trade and social interchange took place between contiguous groups but Aborigines certainly did not function in a united way outside of their immediate kin groups. Their whole social and religious organization, as well as their material culture, was quite different from one part of the country to another. Although there are increasing pressures in favour of Aboriginal unity, especially from those who see themselves as leaders of the 'urban blacks', their past differences have been too great to make this possible.

On the whole, only the more Westernized Aborigines of mixed descent migrate to the southern and eastern cities. But even these people have come from different rural reserves and owe their primary allegiance to the kin group from which they have descended. A study of Adelaide (Gale, 1972) showed that they tend to distribute themselves in the city on the basis of these kin associations. The prime determinant of location in the city is cheap rental housing but kinship affiliation plays an important secondary role. This factor effectively spreads groups through the city and thus works against ghetto development.

POPULATION STRUCTURE

The two pyramids, Fig. 16.4a and b, show clearly the demographic contrast between the Aboriginal and the general population of Australia. The pyramid of the total Australian population, Fig. 16.4b, is similar to that of any country of Western European origin but the Aboriginal one, Fig. 16.4a, is more like that to be found in the developing countries of the world.

The reasons for the contrast are those causing the wider world contrast. Firstly, a higher birth rate amongst Aborigines throughout this century has caused a much higher percentage of young people in the population. Secondly, a higher death rate has led to a lower life expectancy and thus a smaller proportion in the older age groups. These features of the Aboriginal population are dealt with in more detail in Barwick (1971), Gale (1969) and Jones (1970).

Young people under 15 years of age accounted for 28.66 per cent of the general Australian population at the 1971 census. By contrast, 46.42 per cent of the Aboriginal population was under 15 years of age. In the older age groups the general Australian pyramid is much broader than that of the Aborigines. In fact persons over 60 years of age accounted for 12.20 per cent of the total population but only 5.31 per cent of the Aboriginal population.

The two populations also exhibit differences on the basis of sex distribution. Aboriginal males slightly predominate over females in the older age groups. The reverse is true for the general population. Aboriginal males 60 years of age and over made up 2.78 per cent and females 2.53 per cent of the Aboriginal population. However European females in this older age group accounted for 6.83 per cent of the total Australian population but older European males were fewer in number, forming 5.37 of the total percentage.

The middle age groups also form different patterns in the two pyramids. The Aboriginal pyramid shows an even decline but the general Australian pyramid has a definite indentation in the group of 35 to 39 year olds. The Australian population at large was clearly affected by changing world economic conditions, and notably the depression of the 'thirties caused a significant decline in the Australian birth rate. By contrast the Aborigines, living on reserves and in isolated communities, were not influenced by world conditions. A comparison of these two pyramids thus offers a succinct picture of the different social histories of these two populations.

This being so one would expect a change in the shape of the Aboriginal pyramid as the living conditions of rural Aborigines improve, thus lowering the infant mortality rate. Indeed the last couple of years have seen a significant decline in Aboriginal infant mortality.

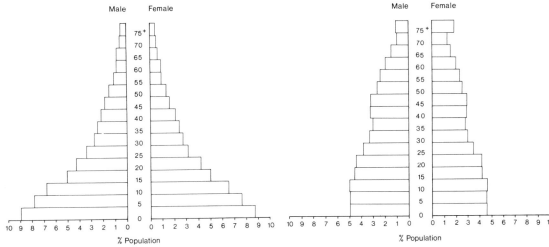

Fig. 16.4 a. Aboriginal age structure, 1971.   *b.* White age structure, 1971.

One would also anticipate that the two pyramids would become more similar as Aborigines shift to the towns and cities and increasingly adopt lifestyles more similar to those of the community at large. There is already clear evidence of this. The Adelaide study (Gale, 1972) has shown that when Aborigines move to the cities they come under the same social and economic forces which lead other Australians to limit their family sizes and thus lead to declining fertility figures. In the more settled areas they can also take advantage of the better medical services available and so reduce their mortality rate.

It is therefore assumed that the Aboriginal population pyramid, like the map of population distribution, will change as Aboriginal lifestyles and situations change with increasing Europeanization and greater government intervention. Certainly one would hope that such a demographic change continues because to date Aborigines have been severely disadvantaged. They have had the population structure of the developing countries, that is, a large number of children supported by relatively few adults, but they live in an industrialized country where the demand for unskilled work is limited and there are few opportunities for children and teenagers to bolster the family income. In most of the third world countries, where families are large and levels of education are low, there are opportunities for young people and adults to obtain labouring work in the rural industries. This is no longer so in Australia.

CONTACT AND CHANGE

In traditional times Aborigines had become a persistent and adaptable people. Where European settlement was rapid and extensive as in eastern and southern Australia the Aborigines did not have time to adjust and most of them died out. Their only descendants today are the people of mixed Aboriginal and European ancestry who were crowded into reserves and mission stations. Where settlement came slowly, if at all, as in northern Australia, the indigenous people were able to adapt. In areas not attractive to large-scale European settlement, such as the central desert and the tropical north, the full-blood Aborigines have learnt to adjust to changing circumstances and are now increasing in numbers. They will certainly never become extinct and, unlike their southern counterparts, they will probably not be bred out either.

Many of the full blood people have managed to retain enough of their social structure and religious beliefs to enable them to withstand many of the pressures of Western society. Although some have found adjustment too painful and have escaped into a world of alcoholism, others have retained sufficient solidarity to fight the major society on issues such as land ownership and self-determination. The southerners were not so fortunate.

With a few notable exceptions the early settlers neither saw nor understood the basic values and processes of Aboriginal life. From their position of apparent superiority the settlers believed that Aborigines must change, become 'civilized' or die. For a people with such a long cultural tradition these were impossible alternatives. Although they tried to protect their land and their women the demographic and technological forces were against them. They were either wilfully poisoned and murdered or accidentally killed by European disease and poor diet. By the end of the nineteenth century virtually all Europeans believed the demise of the Aborigines to be inevitable. Much was said about the fate of the 'dying race' but few questioned whether it could be avoided.

Plate 16.1   The Areonga Aboriginal settlement in central Australia: a planned community but socially and physically isolated.

The settlers were uncompromising in their desire for land and maintained their unfaltering belief in the superiority of Western culture and its right to usurp, convert or destory all 'lesser' cultures. Today's growing situation of racial conflict is the inevitable heritage of this historic position. Aborigines withstood the changes with all means available to them for as long as they could. Surrender and retreat to protected missions and reserves inevitably followed. These were not like the large areas of traditional lands set aside at a later date for the central and northern people. The reserves within the settled areas were small useless tracts of land often holding no meaning for the people moved on to them.

The Results of Segregation

The policy of establishing segregated reserves has been practised ever since the early days of settlement. The small reserves set aside in the southern areas were initially run by missionaries whose main aim was to offer food and protection to a dying people. Reserves were thought of as temporary necessities in the path of progress. Necessary they may have been but temporary they were not and their social consequences were disastrous. Although in some areas the males went outside of the reserves to work on nearby farms and stations the communities were largely isolated from the mainstream of Australian society and from other Aboriginal groups. Each reserve population developed as a separate, inward-looking community with close kin ties. Only primary education was available and that was usually offered only within the narrow social influence of the reserve. Vocational training and employment opportunities were almost non-existent. The decision-making role was taken from the older men and assumed by the European officers in residence. All initiative was squashed and dependence upon, and subservience to, white authority was encouraged. Aborigines growing up in this depressing atmosphere were quite unprepared for their community's reemergence into white society after World War II. There is clear evidence (Gale, 1972) to show that Aborigines brought up on reserves are in every sense less able to adjust to city living than are Aborigines reared outside of the reserves. No massive inputs of government into new housing on these reserves can alter the deleterious influence of the isolated social climate.

But the years of seclusion spent on reserves armed many Aborigines with a deep sense of injustice. This is virtually the only trait which the different groups of Aborigines of mixed descent have in common. In addition modern means of communication brought alliance with the struggle for black rights in other parts of the world, so that they feel much stronger than their numbers might suggest. And they have a great ally in the guilt feelings they are able to engender in the white population especially at government level and in the media. It is not therefore surprising to find a growing state of tension between Aborigines and non-Aborigines in some parts of Australia.

Even in this situation there has been little faltering of the myth of white superiority. Europeans today generally feel just as superior as their forebears. They may acknowledge feelings of guilt about past treatment of Aborigines but the cultural ethnocentricity of white Australians still dominates relations. Whites on the whole believe Aborigines should be entitled to equality and equal opportunity if they become white in a cultural sense. Few Australians can allow the practicality of a plural society. They find it hard enough to tolerate cultural variation amongst migrant groups with which they have a certain historic cultural affinity. White Australians do not understand how the reserve history has stimulated the identity movements of the urban Aboriginal let alone appreciate the value systems of the traditional people.

Social Conflict and Difference
In spite of its superiority, Western culture has been unable to face many issues of social conflict which traditional Aboriginal society had long since come to grips with. A few examples will illustrate the cultural gulf between Aborigines and other Australians and show the illogicality of Western superiority.

Poverty is one such issue. The great social and regional variations in wealth, the enormous gap between the 'haves and the have nots' are extremely vexing and indeed almost insoluble factors in modern technological societies. Yet to pre-urban societies like those of Aboriginal Australia no such problems arose. Wealth was evenly distributed. Money, the medium of exchange, took the form of pituri (wild tobacco), ochre, flint or diorite (for axe heads), and belonged to the whole group. Individual ownership

of such items was based on need, role and status. But personal possessions were limited to the few articles essential for food acquisition and ritual performances.

Each family group was more or less independent in economic terms. Any large game caught was shared between families. A family which had had little success in the day's food quest would be provided for by one of the more successful families. Economic reciprocity was an essential feature of the social system and ensured economic equality for all members.

Aborigines have adapted to fringe living on stations and the edges of country towns because of this system of reciprocity. If only one or two members of a group can obtain employment then the whole group can be assured of food and drink since the income will be shared on the basis of need. Such a pattern of social behaviour has enabled the survival of Aborigines in areas where their land and livelihood have been usurped. This pattern of social obligation is foreign to Western culture. Poverty is an inevitable result of the Western cultural norm which states that one man may have much money even to spend on luxuries whilst his neighbour starves.

The status of women in another contemporary issue of concern to social scientists, and a comparison with Aboriginal sex roles is a useful way of seeing cultural differences.

The roles of women in traditional Aboriginal society were quite clear cut and, like the biological roles, the social roles of males and females were quite different but neither could be said to be inferior or superior to the other. However, so culturally determined was the perception of the first British settlers that they saw not difference but inequality. They wrote about the subordination of Aboriginal women, about their total lack of independence and freedom. But these writers, all of them male, forgot how their own women in Victorian times were tied to the domestic role, their freedom limited by large families and only a few possessing any economic independence. Such nineteenth-century observers did not appear to notice that traditional Aboriginal families were relatively small and that as a consequence the women had a reasonable degree of freedom. Furthermore many husbands had two wives to share the domestic chores and child rearing did not rest solely on the mother. They tended to live in extended family groups so that women enjoyed companionship as well as assistance in carrying out their domestic work.

All Aboriginal women, in traditional times, possessed a degree of economic freedom unknown to the majority of Western women. Aboriginal women were largely self-sufficient in economic terms. In most areas gatherable foods provided the staple commodities for survival. Gathering was the prerogative of the women and so a woman could maintain herself and her children free of any dependence upon her husband. The men hunted the larger game and brought back to the family or group of families the much prized additional meat and flavour to add to the basic requirements provided by the women. The size of the unit which lived together depended upon the availability of food and climatic conditions which varied seasonally. But always food provision, as well as preparation and cooking, was a co-operative enterprise in which males and females shared, each fulfilling different roles, but together forming a partnership.

Everywhere Aborigines are now being forced by social, political and economic pressures to conform to Western norms. Such is the myth of white superiority that white Australians assume conformity will improve Aboriginal lifestyles, even though in some social areas the reverse may be the case. Indeed it is rather ironical that Aborigines are being forced to achieve many of the European standards which some members of Western society are now questioning. A few examples will suffice to show such issues yet awaiting comparative analysis by geographers.

The existence of the nuclear family as the only acceptable form of family structure is being critically assessed by various members of our community today. Some groups are experimenting with extended families, joint households, communes and other such structures in many ways more similar to the traditional Aboriginal patterns than to the Western nuclear family. With decreasing family size (and remember that traditional Aboriginal families were probably also small) and greater economic independence for women (also a feature of Aboriginal society) some young people today are realizing certain advantages in the sharing of domestic chores and child rearing.

Yet Aborigines are under increasing pressure to give up any remnant of the group household and to disperse into nuclear families. On the reserves and in the fringe camps the detribalized people often kept up some form of extended family. It was essential for economic survival but in the city they are being steadily pressed to conform to the Western norm of the nuclear family in separate households.

The pressures for Western conformity come from many sources. Low-rental houses, available for Aborigines, are built to accommodate only relatively small households. If the occupants share their dwelling with relatives and adopt any form of communal living there are complaints from neighbours about noise and assumed immorality. The renting agency, whether government or private, welfare officers and other neighbours are effectively influenced by such complaints. So are the Aborigines concerned. They do not wish to be discriminated against. Indeed they wish to conform. But also many wish to retain the very clear social and economic advantages of the extended

household. The poverty study (Gale and Binnion, 1975) showed that some families manage to lift themselves above the poverty line only by maintaining joint families.

Although some individuals within the general Australian community may be changing their ideas about Aboriginal values, Aboriginal attitudes are still in serious conflict with society at large. For example the group ownership of economic resources is not really accepted in our system. Increasingly governments are beginning to take over the ownership of some resources but this has been easier in those countries where communal ownership was already practised. This has not been so readily accepted in countries like Australia.

In the area of group ownership Aborigines have faced sharp opposition. Take for example the land rights issue. In traditional times there was no individual ownership of land. Title was a corporate concept and true ownership really lay with dream-time ancestors. Present occupants had inviolate rights but these were held in trust.

During a dry season a whole dialect group might leave its territory and move to more productive areas. No war or any form of territorial conflict resulted from such movement because there was no idea of usurpation. The incoming people were temporary. Their home, the place of their ancestors, was elsewhere, and there could be no idea of taking over someone else's inheritance. Free movement, so essential in arid areas, was guaranteed by such a philosophy.

The concept of corporate land which is held in trust and cannot be sold, traded or usurped is largely foreign to Western ideology. The early settlers expected to acquire the land by any means available to them. Conflict was inevitable and compromise has never been achieved. Aborigines today seek corporate title to the lands which they believe they have inherited by inviolate right from the dream-time ancestors.

British law does not recognize occupation as a right to title nor does it accept the idea of a dream-time inheritance. A test case occurred when in 1970 the Aboriginal people of Yirrkala sought group title to the reserve land they inhabited. A court decision was given against their claim and mining rights were allowed to a Western company. No satisfactory compromise between the two land-title systems has yet been achieved. Nevertheless, non-Aboriginal group ownership, in the form of pastoral companies, is gradually superseding individual title in the arid lands.

Yet in spite of the quiet protest which Aborigines have maintained over European opposition to such issues as corporate land title, communal ownership and extended family units, these original inhabitants of Australia are slowly being made to conform to the norm of the larger society. Many of the traditionally derived patterns of social living which continued on the missions and reserves now come under pressure in the cities. Adaptation to city living means increasing compromise with the norms of the majority society, so that the urban migration is causing increasing Westernization. The old practices of kinship obligations and reciprocity cannot easily be maintained in the city.

At the same time urban migration is causing a greater appreciation of Aboriginal culture by the larger society. Until Aborigines moved into the cities the majority of Australians hardly knew of their existence. But now Aborigines have become a popular topic for press coverage and they are gaining political power. In many ways the changes in Western attitudes to Aboriginal culture can be attributed to the shift in Aboriginal population. Urban Aborigines have gained a political voice and regular press coverage and have helped to make the public at large aware of the rural people also. It is indeed ironical that Aborigines are becoming more Westernized just as other Australians are beginning to accept their cultural difference and some Australians are even beginning to adopt Aboriginal-type values in such areas as communal households, corporate land ownership and environmental appreciation.

ACKNOWLEDGEMENTS   The maps were drawn by Christine Barrington and Max Foale and the manuscript typed by Sandra Evans. Mr J. Vickery, Chairman of Pastoral Board of South Australia, mapped homestead locations and provided current population figures.

REFERENCES

Barwick, Diane E. (1971), 'Changes in the Aboriginal population of Victoria, 1863–1966' in D. J. Mulvaney and J. Golson (eds), *Aboriginal Man and Environment in Australia*, Australian National University Press, Canberra.

Basedow, H. (1925), *The Australian Aboriginal*, Pierce, Adelaide.

Campbell, T. D., Cleland, J. B. and Hossfeld, P. S. (1946), 'Aborigines of the lower south-east of South Australia', *Records of the South Australian Museum*, 8, 445–502.

Gale, Fay (1969), 'A changing Aboriginal population' in Fay Gale and Graham H. Lawton (eds), *Settlement and Encounter*, Oxford University Press, Melbourne.

——(1972), *Urban Aborigines*, Australian National University Press, Canberra.

Gale, Fay and Binnion, Joan (1975), *Poverty Amongst Aboriginal Families in Adelaide*, Commonwealth Government Printer, Canberra.

Gason, S. (1895), 'Of the tribes Dieyerie, Auminie, Yandrawontha, Yarawuarka, Pilladapa, Lat. 31°0′S, Long. 138°55′E', *J. Anthrop. Inst. Gr. Brit. and Ireland*, 24, 167–76.

Jones, F. Lancaster (1970), *The Structure and Growth of Australia's Aboriginal Population*, Australian National University Press, Canberra.

O'Grady, G. N., Wurm, S. A. and Hale, K. L. (1966), *Map of Aboriginal Languages of Australia*, Department of Linguistics, University of Victoria, Victoria, British Columbia.

Sturt, C. (1849), *Narrative of an Expedition into Central Australia During the Years 1844, 5, and 6*, T. & W. Boone, London.

Tindale, N. B. (1940), 'Map showing the distribution of the Aboriginal tribes of Australia', *Trans. R. Soc. S. Aust.*, 64.

——(1974), *Aboriginal Tribes of Australia: Their Terrain, Environmental Controls, Distribution, Limits and Proper Names*, Australian National University Press, Canberra.

Ward, E. (1869), *The South Eastern District of South Australia, its resources and requirements*, Adelaide.

17 SPACE, POLITICS AND TERRITORIAL ORGANIZATION

K. W. ROBINSON

The single most important fact underlying the relationships between people, politics and place in Australia is the coincidence of political space with geographical space. The major issues confronting Australian society are all influenced to a greater or lesser degree by the fact that a single sovereignty embraces the whole continent. Externally oriented issues resolve themselves into a series of measures to defend the integrity of the realm as a whole, whether by political agreements, economic bargaining, defence strategies and structures or population policies. Many internal issues stem from the primary political subdivision into States, bringing to the population a sense of double identity which provides the framework for the continuing conflict between the Centre and the Regions, and others are exacerbated by it. Added to this is the third tier of local government—a complex kaleidoscope in which each State provides its own variation on the general theme.

So much of what is critical to geography depends on the interplay of political forces that one can be forgiven for stressing the significance of such forces. They are significant because they provide the key to understanding how Australian territory has been organized or, in some cases, manipulated to serve the interests of specific groups of people. In the broadest and purest sense the interests of the Australian people as a whole have been well served by the political system and its set of subsystems. In many other respects, however, the efforts of small groups within the larger society, directed towards their special interests, have been far more influential than any nationwide strategy.

Political activity stems from the divergences which exist within society, and because many of these divergences are directly or indirectly related to the physical and territorial attributes of that society, politics is always relevant and sometimes paramount. The association between politics and geography is manifested in a variety of ways, among which can be noted (1) *The geographical character of political areas*, in which the focus is on the relationship between governmental organization, history and environment on the one hand and factors of the contemporary geographical scene (such as the location of manufacturing, settlement patterns and the regulation of transport) on the other. (2) *The influence of partisan activity*, as represented by trade unions, industrial cartels, religious factions and similar pressure groups, on the character and distribution patterns of human geography. (3) *The influence which the physical environment exerts* on political action. In Australia this has been basic, through factors of distance, water supply and climatic variety, to the evolution of the total political framework (Robinson, 1962; Blainey, 1966).

SPATIAL ORGANIZATION

Centrifugal and Centripetal Forces

The political management of such a vast territory as Australia posed problems from the outset which have never been satisfactorily resolved. No one can really be blamed for this, because during the times when the political framework was constructed there existed no vision of an ultimate Australia, unified and coherent. On the contrary, location and partisan proclivity have played so large a part in the evolution of contemporary Australia that they must be accepted as one of the innate characteristics of Australian nationalism.

Thus, centrifugal and centripetal forces interact to govern the internal composition of the state. Some of the historical influences are discussed below, but it is appropriate here to focus on the divisions which currently pervade the politico-geographical scene. The primary division of Australia is into six States which, together with the Australian Capital Territory and the Northern Territory, comprise a political federation. The system is a fusion of centralism and regionalism, in which the central government is constitutionally allocated some key powers such as defence, immigration, and currency and has additionally acquired the power over income tax. Residual powers—often of a developmental character—are vested in the regional authorities, which are the

States. A third tier of local government acts in the immediate locality interests of the population.

The federal system has operated for three quarters of a century, and the last quarter of the present century is likely to see an increasingly bitter struggle between the centre and the regions. It is now apparent that the march towards technological sophistication and the steady increase of population have combined to favour increasingly centralized management. Air transport, telecommunications and the cybernetic revolution have to a large degree overcome the tyranny of distance which accounted for the initial separation into distinctive States. From many points of view the old regionalism of statehood is considered outmoded, because it is too rigid or inflexible to cope with the increased mobility of people, goods and ideas which has been engendered by the technological revolution.

Consequently, some areas of activity which have traditionally been State preserves, such as education, agriculture and urban affairs, are being 'invaded' by the central government. From the point of view of a whole and unified Australia this can be seen as a logical and necessary step. From the point of view of individual States it is an encroachment on private and sacred domains which must not be tolerated. The degree of resistance by individual States to this threatened dominance of the centre is in part dependent on the political party in power at the time. But even under the most favourable circumstances (i.e. where the ruling parties in State and centre are the same) there is a strong flow of independent spirit from the State. Perhaps this independence is best illustrated by the resolution of the States to retain as much control as possible over their natural resources, especially minerals.

Just as centripetal forces are tending to strengthen at the national level, so within the States themselves there is a continual struggle to curb the dominance of the capital cities. Without exception, these cities have gained in numerical, commercial and political strength at the expense of extra-metropolitan areas throughout this century. While the mechanization of farming and improvements in transport have had much to do with this, the combined effects of the political structure and environmental inequalities have militated against well-balanced regional development. Thus, urban primacy has become such a distinctive feature in all States except Tasmania that the voting mechanism is weighted heavily in favour of centralized urbanism.

Environmental Considerations

No evaluation of the political scene can afford to ignore the constraints and opportunities provided by the physical environments. Perhaps more so in Australia than elsewhere the political structure reflects the environmental influence. The particular aspects of the environment which are thus reflected include water deficiency, climatic variability, and soil poverty. The first of these is responsible for the high percentage of arid and semi-arid land (however these terms may be defined); the second has injected a large measure of unreliability into farming programmes, even in the most favoured areas; the third has encouraged a bi-polar system in which a few pockets of intensive high productivity are balanced by vast areas of extensive use. The interlocking of these three factors has exacerbated the problem of distance, especially in the early formative years.

The political implications of such environmental variables are not very difficult to discern. On the one hand, for management purposes the total area had to be segmented, with each segment being governed from a fertile node or pivot area. The number, size and shape of the segments was largely a matter of historical accident (see below); but they formed the basis of the present federal structure. On the other hand, the problems created by fundamental environmental deficiencies have demanded a good deal of governmental activity to combat them. Thus, colonial and State governments have been responsible for railways, a fact which has strengthened centralism in many ways. Governments have undertaken the major works for irrigation and water supply, and they have been called on on numerous occasions to stabilize such farming systems as wheat, wool and dairying which have been affected by the vagaries of the weather. In all States, versions of the political party known as the Country Party have operated to protect the interests of the rural community in the face of a battery of climatic hazards and a central urban government which owed at least some of its concentrated character to environmental shortfalls.

While the governments of all countries have environmental management problems to contend with, governments in Australia are particularly vulnerable because of the low population density. On a *per caput* basis, the costs of organizing and maintaining such a vast territory are quite staggering and beyond the competence of any Australian authority to meet adequately. This is clearly seen in the failure to provide a first class national road network—a logical need to overcome the problem of distance for a highly motorized society. It is also seen in the cost barriers to the large-scale decentralization and regional development programmes discussed later in this chapter. In a variety of ways, governments are called on to assist and sustain the community in the face of natural hazards and difficulties and their task would be made much easier if the population were ten times its present size.

Behavioural Patterns

The Australian people have seen to it that the environ-

Plate 17:1   Canberra, the national capital, is a political creation—functional child of the federation, a locational monument to Sydney-Melbourne rivalry and the physical invention of a federally appointed director of design (Walter Burley Griffin). Despite substantial modifications, the basic concepts of his plan remain. *Photo*: National Capital Development Commission.

mental imperatives which put so many strictures on their activities have not completely dominated or governed them. Rather, some of the emergent behavioural patterns are clear examples of adaptation and adjustment, wherein the population has proved that it can cope with, control and even take advantage of the harsh environmental fare meted out to it. A classic example of this is provided by the sheep-grazing industry, which formed the backbone of the Australian economy for more than a century and contributed to territorial management and government in a measure disproportionate to the numbers of people involved. The pioneers of the industry capitalized on the environmental attribute of 'semi-aridity' to pre-empt vast tracts of country for permanent productive occupance through the grazing of merino sheep on natural pastures and shrubs. While it is true that expanding overseas markets for the easily transportable and storable product were particularly advantageous, this in no way detracts from the initiative and resourcefulness of the founders of the industry.

In politico-geographical terms, the emergence of this segment of primary industry marked the entry into the political arena of a kind of landed aristocracy which viewed Australia as a whole from a position of economic authority. Pastoralists tended to take a stance of superiority over arable farmers because they contributed most to the critical overseas trade. Despite the relative decline of wool in its contribution to total exports, it still remains as the single most important item, though minerals as a group would exceed it. If the beef industry is coupled with that of wool, then graziers as a group can lay claim to the 'use' of most of Australia. For this reason they persist in their efforts to obtain political representation disproportionate to their numbers.

Allied to this pastoral occupance has been the Australian 'outback mythology', embracing concepts of the continent from the viewpoint of the average working man or the small landholder. This mythology is one of the strongest links uniting the various entities in the Australian political system. Historically it has had a profound cementing effect, but even under contemporary conditions of predominant urbanism it remains as one of the bulwarks of Australian solidarity. This is so because, in the very sparsely settled interior parts of the continent, conditions of isolation and recurrent physical hardship create a *milieu* vastly different from that of the sophisticated urban capitals, but distinctively Australian in a way that the cities could never be. The direct political impact of this mythology may have been reduced because outback dwellers are relatively fewer than they were at the turn of the century; but the outback image is sustained as an important element in the political mixture.

A clear flow-on from the pastoral/outback mythology and the implacable urbanization process is the cleavage between 'town' and 'country'. Country Party politics and the parochialism of rural local government authorities on the one hand, centralized bureaucracies and port-oriented commercial establishments on the other, have ensured the perpetuation of a rift which in the interests of harmonious development should be eliminated. The hiatus is not between rural and urban dwellers but between the State capital (metropolis) and the rest: 'Sydney or the bush' as the saying goes. This is a most unfortunate situation, apparent even in Tasmania where there is no primate city and no metropolis. A state of confrontation frequently exists, fed on mutual suspicion; this must somehow be replaced by a state of harmony in which the functional interdependence of town and country are recognized and respected. The mythologies which perpetuate the separate identities of metropolitan living and outback living need to be reduced in intensity and supplemented by one which stresses the continuity between these two fundamentally important aspects of Australian life.

Internal behavioural patterns therefore epitomize the interlocking forces of history and environment resulting in a measure of cohesion on the one hand and disruption on the other. A further trait characterizes Australia as a whole—the projection of a national image and the creation of a national character based on declared policies in immigration, overseas trade and foreign affairs. This is the geopolitical side of Australia, presenting a united front to the outside world. In many ways, immigration policy has had the greatest overt-external effect because of the publicity given to the White Australia Policy. However diluted that Policy may now have become, its incorporation in the national image remains. In the area of trade, recent years have witnessed dramatic changes in the relative strength of trading partners to the extent that Pacific orientation has replaced the former European orientation. This change in emphasis is matched by a similar change in foreign affairs, as exemplified by the establishment of an Australian embassy in China. It seems clear that Australian spokesmen wish to present their country as a significant Middle Power, strategically placed in the Pacific Basin and the Southern Hemisphere, and possessed of sufficient natural resources to guarantee continued economic strength. The very factors of remoteness and aridity which have proved handicaps in the past may prove to be the bastions of global strategy in years to come.

Critical Spatial Issues for Political Australia

In the light of the preceding paragraphs, the territorial organization of Australia can be seen to pose a number of problems which are wholly or partly spatial in character. By this it is meant that the particular problem has something to do with land or area or location as such and is not simply a matter of numbers or production. Among problems which seem to fall into this category are:

Population distribution/migration The primary pattern and the continuing process of urbanization are counterbalanced by a degree of rural depopulation which causes concern. The stream of post-war migrants has gone predominantly to the big cities, reinforcing the internal trend. There is a need for some redistribution in order to achieve minimal standards of social and economic development in the non-metropolitan regions.

Mineral resources management Current achievements in mineral resource exploration and exploitation have brought into focus questions of ownership and control (a) as between the States and the Federal government and (b) as between Australian capital and overseas capital. On the first point the States have recently attempted to win some ground in respect of the offshore zone and have traditionally controlled mining activities through various State enactments. On the second point, much of the contemporary activity, especially in iron ore, is financed wholly or in part by overseas importers. In general, however, the Australian government influences development and production activity through its statutory powers regarding international trade, customs and excise, taxation and loan raisings.

Water resources management Australia's critical position regarding water supplies can be assessed by referring to Chapter 3. Not only is much of the continent riverless; many of the permanent streams are themselves subject to irregularities of flow, while rivers of the north and northwest are virtually dry for several months during the low sun season of the year. The restricted volume of subsurface supplies further exacerbates the situation. Water is required in increasing quantities for urban, domestic and factory use as well as for farms, so that constant demand pressures are exerted on governments to find an equitable solution. Where purely intrastate demands are

Fig. 17.1   Historical development of political entities in Australia. *Source*: *The Australian Encyclopedia*, Vol. 8, p. 273.

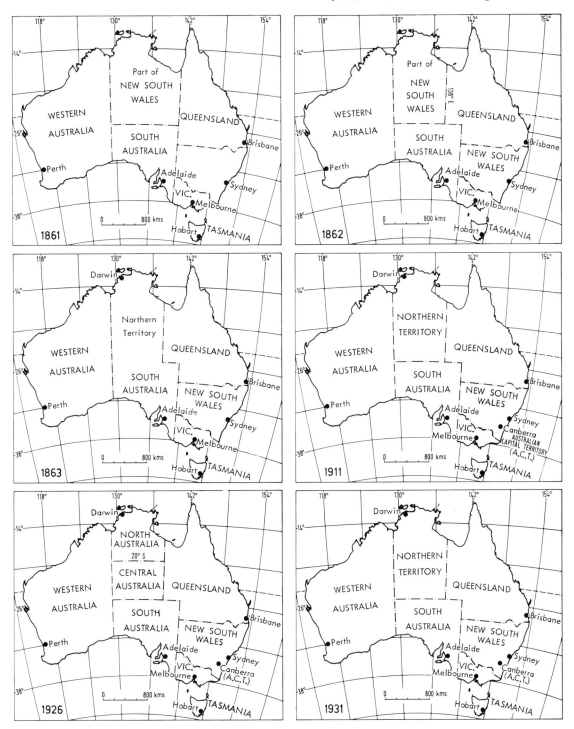

to be met, State governments are vested with full control by the constitution. Thus in Victoria and New South Wales the State governments have contributed to capital works to provide for metropolitan needs on the one hand and irrigated agriculture on the other. However in some instances—and maybe increasingly in the future—interstate and State-Federal co-operation is called for. Examples of this are seen in the *Australian Water Resources Council*, which aims to provide a comprehensive assessment of water resources on a continuing basis; the *National Water Resources Development Programme*, whereby the Federal government grants assistance to States for the purpose of reducing the hazards of drought and expanding primary production; the *Murray River Scheme*, by which Murray waters are allocated to the three contiguous States and the Federal government has rendered assistance in the construction of storage and regulation facilities along the river; and the *Snowy Mountains Hydroelectric Scheme*, which provides electric power and additional irrigation water to two States.

Each of these examples can be used to illustrate the manner in which governments are compelled by the push/pull factors of the environment to control or direct land occupance and population dispersal. A further contentious issue is ownership—of pastoral land, mining rights or farm land—where there have been fears that foreign investment is undermining the political rights of Australia to its own territory. By comparison with the matters mentioned above, this cannot be treated as a serious issue of spatial control. It is more relevant to understand how the present system came into being and this will be discussed in the next section.

FORMULATIVE INFLUENCES

Core Areas and Colonies

The present political structure has a colonial heritage which covers the period from 1788 to 1900. Up until the 1850s the developed and incipient colonies were climbing towards the full status of responsible government; from 1860 onwards the geographical identity of each colony crystallized around the core area which was its nucleus. The core area in the Australian context was not so much a focus of agricultural productivity as a node of accessibility, linking colonial point settlements with each other and with the mother country. The capital cities, which virtually constituted the cores, came to acquire such a strong political and economic grip on their territories as a whole that they fitted into the role of overseers rather than leaders.

The latter part of the nineteenth century saw an increase in the pace of urbanization and this meant in particular an accelerated growth of the urban cores relative to the rest of the colony (Robinson, 1962,

1973). With few exceptions, the agricultural heartlands of the colonial communities were far removed from the capitals, so that a rapid outward thrust of the communications network became imperative. Consequently, the mesh of roads and railways spread rapidly as pastoralism intensified, the wheatlands were opened up and more diversified agriculture was encouraged in areas of specially favoured soils. A notable advance towards material maturity in Australia as a whole was achieved, more so perhaps in some political areas than in others.

The progress in transport access and land use intensification was accompanied by a substantial population increase in the capital cities. The critical factor in this increase was the access link which these cities provided between the rural 'cradle' on the one hand and the external consuming areas on the other. So, while it is true to say that a number of nuclear or core areas existed in Australia, these were in fact peripheral to the geographical heartland of agricultural productivity. The governing element in their continued progress was political rather than physical and their real strength rested in their broad situational advantages rather than in their narrow site characteristics (Robinson, 1975).

Boundaries and Bounded Domains

By 1860 the outlines of the future Australian States were virtually complete. The chronological evolution of the boundaries from 1788 until the *status quo* in 1931 is shown in Fig. 17.1. In the absence of international partitioning, the boundaries are best considered as a framework for political action and economic development. A boundary provides a useful focus for studying the function of the limits of political space as a 'window' on a system, for acting as an interface between systems, or as a role player in shaping the border landscape on either or both of its sides (Kasperson and Minghi, 1969, pp. 77–8). In pre-federation Australia the colonial system was operating to a large extent independently in each of the territorial units. The six colonies knew the precise extent of their domains and proceeded with developmental policies which were aimed at economic stability as well as political ascendancy. Land acts for closer settlement, railway construction and immigration assistance were among the instruments used. Protective tariffs were adopted in some colonies, notably Victoria and Queensland, and this led to the erection of ephemeral customs houses on the border with New South Wales. The boundary between Victoria and New South Wales was especially significant because for most of its length it followed the River Murray. Australia's most navigable watercourse. Victoria seized on this opportunity to weaken the boundary as an economic divide by developing river· trade and linking river

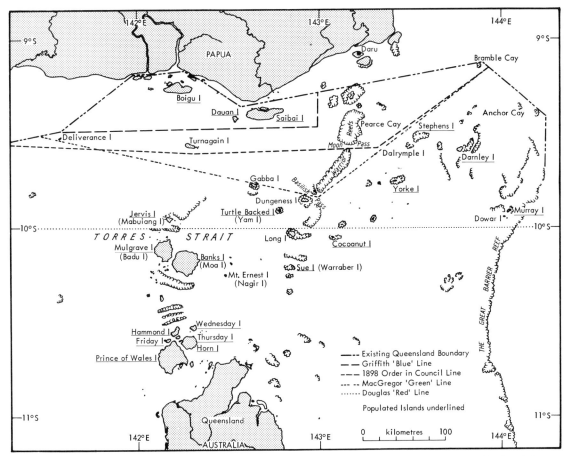

Fig. 17.2 The Torres Strait Islands, showing proposals for changes in the boundary between Queensland and Papua. *Source*: Fisk and Tait, 1973, p. 4.

ports (Echuca and Wodonga) with its railway system. The subsequent extension of railways over the border in a number of places enabled Victoria, through its combined river and rail access, to siphon off much of the Riverina pastoral output from New South Wales.

Other colonies provided contrasts and comparisons. Both South Australia and Western Australia were bounded, except on the coast, by geometric lines far removed from the focus of economic activity. Such lines have recently become significant with the intensification of mineral exploration, but during the nineteenth century they held little more than academic importance. In Queensland the position differed markedly because there were, in fact, international overtones. Queensland's recruitment of Kanaka labour for work on the sugar plantations made her politicians peculiarly sensitive to the activities of Germany and France in the Pacific. For this reason they exerted pressure on the imperial government to have the northern offshore boundary of Queensland realigned to include all the Torres Strait islands. For about 100 kilometres of its length in the extreme north, this boundary comes close to the Papuan coast, taking in the islands of Boigu, Dauan and Saibai. Although at least four different proposals were made to relocate it before the end of the nineteenth century (Fig. 17.2) it has never been changed and has subsequently become a source of considerable controversy (Fisk and Tait, 1973, pp. 6–8).

During the latter decades of the nineteenth century colonial boundaries did act as 'windows' on the six subsystems of the colonial system. Both politicians and parties identified with their territories, which by the turn of the century had achieved a fair degree of containment and economic self-sufficiency: the boundaries themselves were coming to be interfaces between the subsystems. With the coming of internal free trade at federation the boundaries for everyday practical purposes became weak entities. However, the well-established 'framework' role which they had assumed was to continue. The real boundary role has been one of containment, the Colonial and State identities having emerged and persisted more through the compelling and magnetic influence of the cores than through the separating influence of the dividing lines.

The Federal Urge

While attempts to establish a central authority were made as early as the 1840s, serious efforts emerged only during the final two decades of the century. By this time it was becoming apparent that there were increasingly serious spatial problems related to size, shape, distance and the productive potential of the land. The vast distance between the home government and the colonies created problems of delay which became more tedious as activities in the colonies proliferated. Even within Australia, the distances were too great for adequate communication between small communities. Associated with this was the isolation factor, which had both physical and psychological manifestations. It was related not only to distance, but to size, productivity, population numbers and capital input. Many communities were handicapped by the lack of an infrastructure, for which there were insufficient funds. The developmental process proceeded in an uncoordinated fashion, each political unit having to rely on a limited reserve of human resources to cope with its vast physical potential. In the course of this process a form of regional consciousness evolved which coincided broadly with each of the political divisions; such territorial consciousness was a key element in the move towards closer union because it drew attention to the sets of common problems which required centralized management. An additional factor was the threat to territorial security, whether real or imagined, which stemmed from the activities of Germany in New Guinea and France in the New Hebrides.

These were the conditions which paved the way for federal feeling—a feeling which was most strongly expressed by dedicated colonial leaders such as Parkes and Barton in New South Wales, Deakin in Victoria, Kingston in South Australia, Griffith in Queensland and Forrest in Western Australia. There is no question that economic interests loomed large in their arguments, but the situation was too complex for generalizations to be made (Crowley, 1960; Parker, 1964; Blainey, 1964; Bastin, 1964; McCarty, 1967; Hewlett, 1969; Norris, 1969; Robinson, 1975). Furthermore, considerations of defence governed at least some of the thinking. It seems that both strategy and socio-economic factors contributed to the formation of an embryonic Australian nationalism which could satisfy a deep psychological need for territorial, economic and ethnic security. Ward (1970) has also commented on the ethos which was bound up with the European's adaptation to the Australian land, producing an image of rugged individualism and fierce independence, most closely associated with the outback. The unifying influence created by this ethos was strong, especially among old Australians of long standing; but their numbers alone were inadequate to give the necessary push to the federation movement. Further impetus was derived from racism, described by McQueen (1970, p. 42) as the linchpin of nationalism. The fear of Asiatic invasion did much to cement feeling throughout the colonies on the question of racial exclusiveness; it led ultimately to the White Australia Policy and was an important contributing factor to the federation movement.

The ultimate achievement of federation must therefore be regarded as the outcome of a rare combination of people, places and events. According to Wheare (1955, p. 35) federal government is 'rare because its prerequisites are many. It requires the co-existence of several national characteristics which are not often found together in the world and which should be perceived more distinctly than they often are'. He pointed to the desires for a single independent government and for regional governments equally independent in some matters. He demonstrated that factors such as a sense of military insecurity, a desire for independence from foreign powers, the existence of political associations prior to union, geographical neighbourhood, and similarity of political institutions seem always to be present in modern federations. All the predisposing conditions were present in Australia, so that the main task of the advocates was to convince enough people that any kind of change was necessary and desirable.

The Federal System

From a geographical point of view the political organization of total Australia is clear recognition of the forces of localism and regionalism. At the time of federation, the central government appeared as a necessary evil, with a mandate to sustain the independent regions rather than obliterate them. According to Sawer (1975, p. 28), the Constitution carries out five main tasks. First, it recognizes the existence of the six Australian colonies as they were in 1900, and continues in force their constitutions, governmental arrangements and bodies of law. Second, it creates a new set of central governmental authorities (currently known as Commonwealth authorities). Third, it regulates the relations between the Commonwealth authorities and those of the States. Fourth, it establishes an Australian Common Market—free trade between the States and a common external customs tariff. Fifth, it makes some provision concerning the relation of the individual citizen to the various governments of the system. Specific powers are allocated to the central parliament under Section 51 and include particularly trade, taxation, posts and telegraphs, defence, currency, census, immigration and external affairs. The residual powers, which fall within the aegis of the States, encompass many of the developmental aspects of Australian life such as agriculture, education, water conservation and irrigation and public works.

The conditions built into the Constitution were the outcome of a protracted period of interaction between the distant imperial government and the Australian people, reflecting a range of attitudes which embraced colonial patriotism, Australian nationalism and economic expediency. Certain features of Australian colonial experience such as pastoral exploitation and the trade linkages with the outside world gave weight to locality which ensured that a federal system was the only one which would be acceptable. Within the system, a strong form of particularism gave rise to the States; but the allocation of specific powers, the provision for constitutional amendment and for rule adjudication by the High Court, have ensured the Federal government as senior partner in the system.

FEDERAL ACHIEVEMENT

Three-quarters of a century have seen such dramatic technological and societal changes that the system which was prescribed for the infant nation is no longer relevant in many important respects. The replacement of States by smaller regional units, coupled with the rationalization of local government, for example, is seen by many as a necessary means of keeping territorial organization abreast with the times. But the nature of the Constitution itself is too inflexible to permit of such drastic changes, even if the localism and particularism of the population could be overcome. What has become fairly clear is that the federal system is not only a mirror of past events but a very influential factor in the lives and livelihood of the people.

Politics and Regional Character

The formation of the Commonwealth provided a mosaic of geographical patterns deep-rooted in past development. The States as regional entities within fixed boundary lines; patterns of crop agriculture, ranging from sugar in Queensland to berry fruits in Tasmania; local railway networks with different gauges; the emergent metropolitan centres; these are all examples of features which the Federation consolidated and, if anything, intensified. Despite the breakdown of isolation and the increased tendency to centralization, there are still factors operating to nourish the regional consciousness of the States.

Growth within the States has been largely condition-ed by the residual provisions of the Constitution, so that the trend in such matters as labour and industry, forestry, water conservation and railways has to a considerable extent been influenced by internal policy within the States (Robinson, 1960, pp. 7–9). Not least among the developmental variants is the field of State school education, wherein each State jealously guards its independence. A general survey of the States as developmental agencies shows not only that they have been assiduous and materially successful but that the development itself has to some extent been regionally distinctive within each State.

Victorian character is related to the early concentration of public and private capital in that State, and to the selection of Melbourne as a temporary site for the federal capital. It is also bound up with its relatively high population density and small area. Thus, industrial concentration, rural intensification through irrigation and a closely meshed transportation network are distinctive features. The attractions of Melbourne for overseas migrants in the post-war years have been particularly strong, and the State government has been indefatigable in promoting secondary industry and extending port facilities to keep pace with increased demand. South Australia shows an even greater degree of primacy and industrial concentration in its capital city, a fact partly governed by chronic water shortage through much of the State. Its political leaders and its scientists, through having to contend with climatic and soil adversity, have contributed much to the techniques of pasture improvement and farm mechanization. Deliberate industrial promotion policies, especially under the leadership of Sir Thomas Playford, enabled the State to acquire a disproportionate share of manufacturing industries.

Contrasting with the two southern States in its population pattern, Queensland still retains some of the frontier characteristics of colonial Australia. It has been hampered in its development by the great extent of its tropical lands and of its semi-arid belt, the poverty of its soils and remoteness from early points of settlement. Weaker centralization and industralization, stronger regional consciousness and provincial town development and a marked coastal grouping of the population are distinctive features. In no other part of Australia is there such an independence of spirit, a belief in the economic future of the State and a conviction that much of what is best in the Australian ethos belongs there. In this respect the Northern Territory can be regarded as an annexe of Queensland, and Western Australia as the continental obverse of it. Western Australia is also similar to South Australia in the high priority it has given to techniques of grassland management. The most spectacular recent events in the west, however, have been associated with iron ore exploitation in the Pilbara region. Among the most important

Table 17.1   Population: Intercensal Increases, States and Territories 1901 to 1971

State or Territory	1901–11 (10 years)	1911–21 (10 years)	1921–33 (12¼ years)	1933–47 (14 years)	1947–54 (7 years)	1954–61 (7 years)	1961–6(a) (5 years)	1966–71(a) (5 years)
				Numerical increase				
N.S.W.(b)	293,602	453,637	500,476	383,691	438,691	493,484	319,400	363,279
Vic.	114,481	215,729	288,981	234,440	397,640	477,772	289,851	282,134
Qld	107,684	150,159	191,562	158,881	211,844	200,569	146,810	152,741
S.A.	50,212	86,602	85,789	65,124	151,021	172,246	123,497	78,723
W.A.	97,990	50,618	106,120	63,628	137,291	96,858	101,350	182,369
Tas.	18,736	22,569	13,819	29,479	51,674	41,588	21,096	18,977
N.T.	− 1,501	557	983	6,018	5,601	10,626	12,023	29,886
A.C.T.(c)		858	6,375	7,958	13,410	28,513	37,204	48,031
Australia	681,204	980,729	1,194,105	949,519	1,407,172	1,521,656	1,051,231	1,156,140
			Average annual rate of increase—per cent					
N.S.W.(b)	1.97	2.46	1.76	0.99	1.98	1.94	1.58	1.66
Vic.	0.91	1.53	1.42	0.87	2.56	2.58	1.90	1.69
Qld	1.98	2.24	1.86	1.11	2.53	2.04	1.85	1.76
S.A.	1.32	1.94	1.31	0.76	3.05	2.83	2.42	1.40
W.A.	4.36	1.66	2.29	0.97	3.51	2.03	2.58	3.97
Tas.	1.04	1.12	0.51	0.87	2.65	1.82	1.18	1.00
N.T.	− 3.67	1.57	1.87	5.93	6.12	7.37	4.90	8.86
A.C.T.(c)		4.14	10.71	4.65	8.70	9.93	10.30	8.45
Australia	1.67	2.01	1.63	0.96	2.46	2.26	1.92	1.92

(a) Includes Aborigines.   (b) Includes Australian Capital Territory before 1911. (c) Part of New South Wales before 1911. Minus sign (−) denotes decrease.
Source: *Official Yearbook of the Commonwealth of Australia*, 1973, p. 128.

mineral developments in Australia's history, these large-scale activities have transformed the internal economy and the external image of the State.

New South Wales, first settled, and Tasmania, second settled of the colonies, have progressed along very different routes. Tasmania remains the smallest and least populous, disadvantaged by its physical separation from the mainland and its high proportion of rugged terrain. The combination of ruggedness and high precipitation have provided its most exploitable asset, and much of the island's current economy rests on hydroelectric power. New South Wales, by virtue of its historical momentum and its wide spread of basic resources has sustained its position as the primary State overall in terms of population and production. Sydney's leadership in commercial affairs and its political and administrative dominance have been augmented by exploitation of black coal reserves in the middle coastal region. Coal as the basis of the iron and steel industry, as an expanding export

commodity and as the prime source of electric energy, is the cornerstone of the State's economy. Added to this have been the vast outputs of wheat, wool and other primary industries, so that the State has managed to sustain a level of productivity and output sufficient to absorb a steadily increasing population.

While there has been a tendency for the basic differences in wealth and size of population between the States to be emphasized, this was perhaps more apparent in the earlier than the later years of federation. Table 17.1, which shows the intercensal increases of population from 1901 to 1971, clearly indicates that the divergences of rates, in both time and place, make generalization impossible.

During the 70 years there were eight intercensal periods, and only the Australian Capital Territory, as a creation of federation, exceeded the national growth rate on all occasions. Over the first four periods, up until 1947, New South Wales was the only State to exceed the rate each time, while Victoria, South

Australia and Tasmania were below the national figure on all occasions. Queensland and Western Australia each had one shortfall out of the four. Over the second four periods—virtually the post-World War II era—the position changed. New South Wales was below average on all occasions, and Queensland and Tasmania below in all but one. Victoria was above on two occasions, South Australia and Western Australia on three. Overall, Western Australia has shown the most consistently dynamic record of growth, having exceeded 3 per cent per annum for three periods, including the most recent one. If these figures suggest anything, it is that to some extent the balance is being redressed but that the basic patterns, in a developmental sense, remain as they were at the time of federation.

According to some observers (e.g. Greenwood, 1949; Partridge, 1952; Holmes 1973) factors of size, distance and relative economic strength are becoming less important and regional individuality is being submerged beneath the growing national consciousness. Despite the greater flexibility brought about by intercity air transport, the transcontinental railway, the business activities of large corporations and similar cementing influences, the political consciousness of the States still continues to mould regional character within the State boundaries. They are agents of geographical change, perpetuating themselves through the continuous process of development along divergent lines of interest in a varied environment.

The evolution of definite characteristics within well-defined boundaries is associated with three basic ideas: (1) the idea of *autonomy*, involving the right of an institution or area to self-government: to make its own laws and administer its own affairs; (2) the idea of *development*, which implies both the bringing out of latent capabilities and a gradual advancement to an objective through progressive stages; and (3) the idea of *competition* which connotes the striving of two or more for the same objective. The Constitution, as we have seen, provides for State autonomy in all matters not specifically allocated to the general government, although such autonomy is severely curtailed by the centralized control of finance. While this autonomy has continued to operate in the developmental sphere, it will remain a matter of dispute as to its influence on the distinctiveness of geographical patterns within the States. None the less, such examples as the contrast between the decentralization of railways in Queensland with their extreme centralization in New South Wales, or between the number of dairy factories in Victoria with those in other States, point to the fact that State policy and State legislation can be extremely influential in shaping the trends of development.

Unabated competition between the States has been an additional factor responsible for many of the distinctive State traits. The trade-offs between the iron and steel industry in New South Wales and the States supplying raw materials, whereby outliers of the smelting and fabricating processes have been established in South Australia and Western Australia exemplify this. So too do the inducements which have been offered by the governments of Victoria and South Australia to encourage industrialists and overseas migrants. Industries which might have been established in New South Wales were enticed away to States where labour costs were not so high, land was more plentiful and the overall planning policy more dynamic. State legislation in New South Wales, which aimed at protecting the rights of the 'working man' by providing for increases in wage payments and reductions in working time, increased the cost of labour and tended to reduce the opportunities for employment. This accounts in large part for the differentials in growth rates 1947–66 (Table 17.1) between New South Wales on the one hand and the two southern States on the other. Over the past ten years this initiative has been lost and a greater degree of conformity in conditions and opportunities appears to exist. One final observation on New South Wales relates to the work of Holsman (1975) who, in his study of interstate interaction patterns based on air, road, rail and sea freight, air passengers, trunk channels and internal migration, concluded that 'No matter what method of pattern recognition is used the State of New South Wales dominates most forms of flow. Thus the State first developed in the Commonwealth continues to exert a considerable influence on the economic life of the remaining States' (p. 59).

The States and the Commonwealth

Through 75 years the two components of the federation have been bound up in a process of political and constitutional change marked by the increasing centralization of power. The geographical impact of the change has been to override State identity in order to produce uniformity in the economic, political and administrative fields. It has not destroyed State identity; but it has succeeded in relegating the States to a secondary role and, as a corollary, it has strengthened the centralist tendencies within each State.

While the trend towards unification has proceeded within the legal framework of the Constitution, it has gone further than could have been anticipated by the founders. A vital instrument in this process has been the High Court, whose interpretative decisions have enabled more and more control to revert to the central government. Thus the Engineers' Case of 1920 (28 C L R 129), which overruled doctrines of implied restrictions on Commonwealth power to override State powers, and the Uniform Tax Case of 1942

(65 C L R 373), which made it virtually impossible (though not illegal) for the States to impose income tax, extended the functions and greatly increased the powers of the central government. The Federal government itself has also strengthened central powers through legislative measures such as those under the Whitlam Government setting up authorities and instrumentalities such as the Grants Commission and the Department of Urban and Regional Development (see next section).

It is clear that, from some points of view, the authority of the centre is being strengthened—and rightly so, perhaps, because many of the divergences on which federation was based have disappeared. On the other hand, because the trend towards unity is national in scope, it operates in many ways on a different plane from the local interests of the individual States. Increasing intrusion by the centre only serves to strengthen State sentiment even if it succeeds in weakening State power. It should not be overlooked, however, that some co-operation is practised between the two sets of governments, even if this sometimes occurs in a spirit of confrontation rather than unity. Sawer (1975, p. 93) notes that Australian federalism provides a particularly strong case for the practice of co-operative federation because of the distribution of financial strength and law-making powers. The chief instrument which the Australian government has for inducing State co-operation is its financial strength whereby it can allocate specific-purpose conditional grants as well as general grants. The Australian Loan Council, a statutory body consisting of a representative of each of the governments (usually the Premiers and the Prime Minister), is the formal agency of control and allocation. Other examples of co-operative activities are Premiers' Conferences (at least annual), Australian Aboriginal Affairs Council, Australian Agricultural Council, Australian Education Council, Australian Environment Council, Australian Fisheries Council, Australian Forestry Council, Australian Minerals Council, Australian Transport Advisory Council, Australian Water Resources Council, Albury-Wodonga Ministerial Council, Nature Conservation Ministers' Council, Northern Development Council, Port Development Ministers' Council, Recreation Ministers' Council, Tourist Ministers' Council, River Murray Commission.

Despite the practice of co-operation, and the evident need for it, the shifting balance of power between regional and general governments has continued for a long time. The geographical significance of this process exists not only in the emergence of a more obvious national character, but in the stimulus given to independent activity within the States. It is obvious that federalism has encouraged both urbanization and industrialization. Protection is the federal policy that,

since 1908, has given scope for manufacturing to increase in diversity, absorb a larger and larger proportion of the workforce, and overtake and far exceed agriculture in net value of production. Most of this expansion has occurred within or near the capital cities and added to their dominance. Manufacturing has therefore tended to symbolize an emergent nationalism while at the same time being stimulated by State rivalry (Robinson, 1961, 1962, 1975).

Geographical Aspects of Nationalism

There has been much debate about the national identity of Australia, and for the geographer this association of territory with an aggregate psyche or community identity poses some interesting questions. If the national identity exists and can be described, to what extent is it influenced by the physical environment, by distance, by isolation or by the cultural inputs of the immigrant population? We have already commented on the 'ethos of the outback' in colonial times, of attitudes about White Australia and of the flowering of the Australian Natives' Association (Blackton, 1958, 1961, 1967). Gollan (1955, p. 146) has referred to Australian nationalism as 'a complex of ideas and emotions, partly apprehension of present reality, partly aspiration towards an ideal future'. These kinds of sentiments and attitudes, apparent before 1900, would seem to have been strengthened by federation, especially with respect to Australia's position in the world as a whole.

Drewe (1973) brought together some of the most significant contemporary comments on the 'new nationalism' of the later twentieth century, suggesting that a certain rare feeling of national respect was beginning to emerge. In this context he cites Professor Manning Clark as saying

> The old Australia was sceptical whether it could ever have a better community. This scepticism came from the bitter experience of trying to impose civilisation on this dry land with their bare hands. The present air of nationalism is all confidence. Jet travel has broken down our isolation and there is no need for Australia to apologise for being backward. . . . The old nationalism gathered much of its strength from racism . . . . That is breaking down at last.

In this view the overcoming of two environmental obstacles and the breaking down of a culture barrier are seen as critical. Drew goes on to examine *economic nationalism*, in which the large-scale investment of foreign capital in critical Australian enterprises and areas has led to restrictions on 'selling off the farm to foreigners'; and the *image overseas*, as reflected in a new independent stance in foreign affairs and the virtual abolition of the White Australia Policy.

It is the geographer's task to contemplate and comment on the implications of such views, and here six contemplative points can be noted as prelude to deeper investigation. First, British institutions and traditions have had a preponderant historical, cultural and political influence. Despite recent dilutions, this impact has scarcely diminished. Second, Australians enjoyed (or endured) relative global isolation for at least 150 years, which, by separating them from the mainstreams of thought and action (excepting wars), probably retarded the development of an outer-oriented identity. Third, the intrinsic qualities of the Australian land, although imposing many kinds of constraints, provided opportunities for a wide range of uses and resource outputs—a range which continues to expand as knowledge increases. This has provided the diversity essential to strong national hegemony. Fourth, the character of the Australian landscape and of the Aboriginal inhabitants have evoked artistic works of 'national' significance in all media. Fifth, the Federation, by combining territorial unity with colonial identity, has acted as a basis for national policy and an instrument of national behaviour. Sixth, the New Migration of the post-World War II years, bringing with it the dilutions referred to above, has injected cultural diversity into the traditional Australian framework.

SIGNIFICANT CONTEMPORARY ISSUES

Locality Issues

The 'vital point', stated Miller (1959, p. 138), 'is the sense of locality, the belief that the area in which one lives is different from other areas, even though contiguity with them may provide many interests in common'. He was speaking of the locality consciousness of States within a federal system; but a similar kind of consciousness can and does apply to smaller areas within States, both in a local and in a regional sense. Such a consciousness in certain instances has given rise to New State movements, notably in the case of the New England and Riverina districts of New South Wales and in northern Queensland. However, it would be incorrect to interpret these movements as reflecting grass roots regional or community consciousness in the purest sense of the term. Rather they have tended to be factionally stimulated, with their objective the redress of wrongs (real or imagined) administered by the State government in a distant capital city. The most determined effort has come from New England (Robinson, 1970, pp. 8–9) but the chances of achieving new statehood still seem remote, partly because of the innate conservatism of the Australian people and partly because of legislative difficulties. A variant on this theme is the periodic threat of Western Australia to secede from the Federation.

In a locality sense, local government is closer to the daily lives of the people than the federal system. As each State has its own versions, it is not possible to generalize about an Australian local government system, although there is a common set of functions that the bodies are called on to perform. A general distinction exists, except in Tasmania, between rural and urban units, with the latter having to cope with a more complex set of functions. Whether in town or country, however, these functions are restricted to such basic services as local roads, building ordinances, garbage disposal and health. More recently planning has been added to the list; but there are wide divergences in the extent to which planning function is in fact performed.

Under conditions which involve the management of vast areas or concentrations of population, constant wrangling over finance has been inevitable, and especially between local government authorities and the State or Federal governments. Because only a small proportion of the national product is returned to them, they have to rely heavily on rates for revenue, a fact which sustains a degree of tension within the local community itself. In this context, the assistance plan introduced by the Whitlam Government marked a turning point in the Federal government's attitude to local instrumentalities set up under the aegis of the State government. In the words of the then Prime Minister, 'The Government is determined to make the third tier of government a genuine partner in the system and to give local government adequate access to the nation's finances (Department of Urban and Regional Development (DURD), 1974a, p.v). The implementation of the Assistance Plan was a material benefit to localities throughout the country, despite examples of discrepancies and abuses. The same can be said of Area Improvement Programmes, designed to assist local councils in areas which are particularly deficient in urban services and facilities, or of special strategic significance in the development of a city.

Proliferation of local government areas over the years and the rapid urbanization and centralization of the population have created anomalous conditions which demand change. In New South Wales, for example, there are at present 90 municipalities, 133 shires and 53 country districts to administer the affairs of about 5 million people. The Barnett Report (1974) stated (p. 33) that 'local government suffers from the existence of too many small uneconomic areas, resulting in fragmentation of authority, unnecessary duplication of assets, the under-utilization of plant, equipment and human resources, and inability to provide the various kinds of expertise required by local councils in the modern world'. As a consequence, the Report has recommended the restructuring of the system and a reduction in the total number of units to 97. Resistance to such a change is strong and will no doubt be effective in many instances.

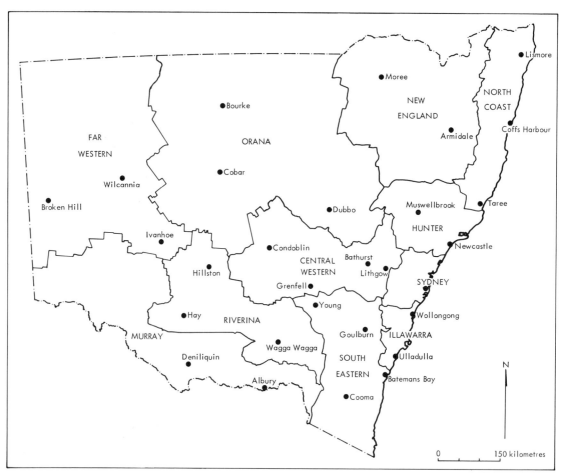

Fig. 17.3   Development regions of New South Wales, to be used as a basis for the co-ordination of government administration and for regional development programmes. Note the exclusion of the Sydney Metropolitan Area and its surroundings. *Source*: N.S.W. Department of Decentralisation and Development.

An important outcome of the interplay of activity at the Federal, State and Local levels has been the attention given to regional possibilities and prospects. Regionalism in Australia has in part been an evolutionary process involving the emergence of distinctive locality traits, often embracing areas far larger than those administered by single local government authorities. It has also developed in a conceptual sense, from an obvious need for more rational government and administration, and in this respect has resulted in the delimitation of regions for particular purposes, either within Australia as a whole, or within particular States. Thus, in the Federal (Labor government) programme for urban and regional development for 1973–4, 60 'interim regions' (for the allocation of assistance funds) were approved (DURD, 1947b, p. 15). This reflects the view that the locality consciousness of

local government areas must be appraised in a regional context which embraces a substantial number of local government authorities; an example from the Hunter Valley, New South Wales, is the Hunter Regional Organization, consisting of representatives from each of the fifteen local governments in the area, combined for the purpose of receiving and disbursing Federal funds.

A wider and deeper sense of regionalism attaches to the notion of regional development, which connotes on the one hand the rationalization of State government departmental administration and, on the other, a combination of effort between State and citizens to encourage decentralization and soundly based regional planning. In States such as Victoria and New South Wales, a measure of decentralization from capital cities seems desirable, although care should be taken to distinguish between decentralization which has the primary objective of reducing the inequalities of over-concentration, and regional development, which looks at the inherent capacity of a region to expand through its own resources. Again, to take the New South Wales example, the State has adopted a division into nine regions, excluding the Sydney Metropolitan Area/Gosford-Wyong sector (Fig. 17.3). The regions, devised by the Department of Decentralisation and Development, form the basis for the co-ordination of State departmental activities and for proposed regional planning. The real success of such measures will depend on the degree of authority granted the regional bodies. If the French model is followed, the result will be an emasculation of the idea. 'If any Australian State which believes in regional development is to give more than lip service to the idea, then it must create regional units with a large measure of autonomy—in programming, fund raising and expenditure' (Robinson, 1971, p. 3). This does not mean a fourth tier of government but a cushion of understanding between State and Locality.

Associated with the general regionalization philosophy has been the 'New Cities Programme' which is described as 'the primary thrust towards influencing the future location of economic activities and population, both in regional terms and in the context of metropolitan expansion' (DURD, 1974c, p. 15). The aims of the programme were to sponsor the rapid growth of a small number of regional centres and to provide for the comprehensive development of selected centres adjoining metropolitan regions. Centres included in the programme were Albury-Wodonga, Geelong and Bathurst-Orange, while places adjacent to metropolitan areas which were selected for special attention were Campbelltown-Holsworthy and Gosford-Wyong (Sydney), Monarto (Adelaide), Salvado (Perth) and the southeast sector of Melbourne. Other centres had claims for assistance but the whole programme had to depend for its success on a number of variables, including the buoyancy of the economy, substantial continued inputs by the Federal government, the rate of population growth and the preferences of individual people. According to the Australian Institute of Urban Studies Task Force's First Report (AIUS, 1972) there was an immediate need to start a massive new-cities programme: by the year 2000 five new-cities of 500,000 each and ten new-cities of 250,000 each would be required to accommodate an additional 5 million 'big city' people (p. 21). The revised estimates of population growth rates, downturns in the economic climate, the practical experience of the programmes themselves and above all, a change in government, suggest that few of the initial goals will be realized within the initial time period.

Territorial Issues

The major territorial issues not already considered as part of the organization of the nation as a whole concern what can broadly be termed Offshore Australia. Of the major offshore islands, Tasmania has from the beginning been considered part of Australia, while eastern New Guinea, independent from 1975, was for long under Australian control and has posed its own special problems. Of the minor islands, those in the Torres Strait between northern Queensland and Papua have recently stimulated controversy, as between the attitude of an independent and self-governing Papua New Guinea on the one hand and a staunchly territorial Queensland government on the other. Issues (referred to earlier in this chapter) revolve round the economic and social well-being of some 9,600 Torres Strait Islanders (1971 census), about half of whom live more or less permanently in other parts of Australia. According to Fisk and Tait (1973, p. 8) there are at least five separate issues: (i) *The islands*: The status of the various islands as Australian or Papua New Guinean. (ii) *The people*: The status, as regards nationality and other rights and privileges of the persons resident on, or originating from, those islands. (iii) *The seaways*: The boundaries of Australian and Papua New Guinean territorial waters, and the status of the sea areas and sea passages of the Torres Straits. (iv) *The fisheries*: The ownership and control of fishing rights in various regions of the Straits. (v) *The sea-bed*: The rights of access to and control of the sea-bed in the region.

Many of these issues are part of the general problem of offshore management and control, but the debate as to whether or not some of the islands and islanders should 'revert' to Papua New Guinea by shifting the boundary line southwards to 10°S (see Fig. 17.2) must come down firmly in favour of retaining the *status quo*. Almost a century of association with Queensland has so influenced the economic and social life of the people that to separate them would be disastrous. Both the Commonwealth and the Queensland governments certainly hold this view.

While offshore geography is no new field of interest, it has demanded increasing attention in recent years, not so much because of changes in the volume and character of sea transport as through tensions brought about by pressures on the animate and inanimate resources of the sea and the sea-bed. Along with many other nations, Australia has been involved in the examination of wider issues at the international level, and is currently participating in the Third United Nations Conference on the Law of the Sea (first session New York 1973, second session Caracas 1974, third session Geneva 1975). This conference is working to reach agreements on issues which were not fully resolved at earlier conferences in 1958 and 1960.

The issues at stake are vast and complicated but they resolve themselves fundamentally into the extension of sovereignty from the landmass to the seamass, and thence to questions of rights over fisheries, minerals and access to parts of the neighbouring landmass.

The environmental circumstances of Australia's position, with its long coastline, massive extent of continental shelf, strategic relationship to other powers with interests in the adjacent seas and comparatively small population to provide management, have given its problems special significance. The fisheries of its surrounding waters are of international and not just national interest; but the regulation of their use does become a matter of national concern. Similarly, the exploration and exploitation of minerals—notably petroleum—can become a matter of international and not just local involvement. An illustration of this is found in the Australian-Indonesian continental shelf agreement of 1971–2, whereby both countries now have clear title to areas of the continental shelf which can be explored and, if suitable, exploited for the resources which they contain. Prescott (1972, p. 2) has commented that the 'intrinsic political gain in the Agreement is that Indonesia and Australia have quickly and amicably settled a dispute which could have proved difficult to solve without a spirit of mutual compromise'.

Further difficulties for Australia exist in the conflict between the Australian government and the States regarding the control of offshore zones in respect of territorial waters, the continental shelf and the ocean bed. An outstanding area of investigation and legislation here concerns the mineral resources of the sea-bed, especially petroleum. After years of negotiations, the Federal and State governments eventually reached agreement in 1967 on the principles which should govern the exploration and exploitation of the Petroleum resources of the sea-bed. The Petroleum (Submerged Lands) Act 1967, of both Commonwealth and States, provides for the control of the submerged lands as shown on the map (Fig. 17.4). According to Lumb (1969, p. 429) the agreement and the legislation make it clear that the actual administration of the mining code is in the hands of the States, but there is no provision in the legislation for the States to consult with the Commonwealth in matters of Federal responsibility. 'It is seen, therefore, that there is a lack of correspondence between the principles contained in the Agreement and the actual terms of the legislation.' Consequently, despite the fact that this legislation has been held up as a good example of co-operative federalism (Lumb, p. 439), its subsequent history, encompassing the Seas and Submerged Lands Act, 1973, has proved the determination of the States to acquire more direct policy control than the legislation gives them. The decision of the Whitlam Government to retain strong Federal control of the minerals of the sea-bed was being challenged by the States and the decision in favour of the Commonwealth must have far-reaching effects in Federal/State relationships.

Social Issues

There are many areas of social activity in which government influence can have strong geographical overtones; but the one which perhaps has most relevance and importance is population policy. In Aboriginal Australia (pre-1788) there seems to have been a thin but uneven dispersal of the population in accordance with the resource capacity of the land. Political behaviour was subordinate to social behaviour and a fair degree of equilibrium was achieved in population density and distribution. European Australia has been characterized by a vastly different set of norms in which political behaviour dominates— especially so in the early days. Thus, the colonial patterns of strongly centralized administration were reinforced by an increasing concentration of population in the nodes of greatest government influence and activity. One of the contributors to this pattern was the influx of immigrants who apart from exceptional conditions such as those operating with the gold rushes and the opening of irrigation areas, have shown a marked preference for the large cities.

One of the impelling forces in this migration flow has been government assistance—a fundamental part of Australia's immigration history. As Borrie (1975, p. 93–4) states: 'Assistance has been used essentially as a tap for well over a century, turned on in boom and shut off in recession, and this substantially accounts for the series of immigration waves that have typified Australia's immigration history'. The last of these waves occurred as recently as 1969–71, and the special point to be made is that they have not only swelled total numbers but contributed to the continued metropolitanization of the country. This has been emphasized by Burnley (1974) when he states (p. 9) 'A vitally important element in the growth of Australia's larger cities has been immigration in the 1947–71 period. The major urban areas became attractive to migrants, especially those from eastern and southern Europe. . . . The attraction in the large cities was the availability of employment in rapidly expanding heavy industry.' The immigration impact came both from a conscious effort by the Federal government to encourage overseas people to come and from a specific assistance programme which extended its area of influence to embrace a number of European countries as well as traditional Britain.

Also of great significance for geographical Australia has been the so-called 'White Australia Policy'. The significance relates not only to the present racial composition of the population, but to the geopolitical relationship with the outside world and the ensuing

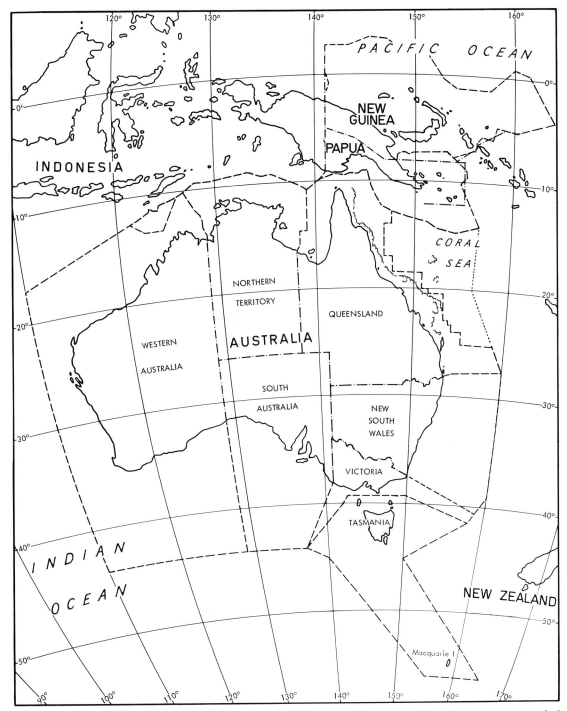

Fig. 17.4 Petroleum (Submerged Lands) Act 1967—adjacent areas. The map shows areas delineated in an agreement reached between the Australian States and the Commonwealth concerning the control of exploration for, and exploitation of, certain resources including petroleum. *Source*: Bank of N.S.W., 1971, p. 51.

political tensions and economic involvements which have placed Australia in a special position in world affairs. For long, the world image of Australia, in so far as it was recognized at all, was not so much Antipodean as racist. While much has been done in the past decade to rectify this situation, 'whiteness' is still part of the basic philosophy of many Australians, including a few who have had their 'Christian' names changed by deed poll to 'White Australia'!

The White Australia Policy, as a creed of federal Australian politicians of all persuasions, must be assessed in the context of an historical continuum. At the time of federation, the attitudes and legislative records of the colonies were unanimously in favour of excluding people whose industriousness they feared and social values and ethnological idosyncracies they did not understand. For better or worse, therefore, the regulation of migration in the peopling of the continent became the cornerstone of a policy in which undesirables were to be excluded and desirables encouraged. Exclusion, directed especially at Asians, was embodied in the Immigration Restriction Act of 1901, which provided for a dictation test sufficient to keep out any 'suspects' at will, while at the same time 'suitable' emigrants were encouraged by assistance programmes such as the dubiously successful 'Empire Settlement Scheme' of the 1920s. It is to the credit of later Australian governments—and perhaps an indicator of a maturing national consciousness and understanding—that the White Australia Policy has been replaced, since 1966, by a policy which at least recognizes the innate abilities and human attributes of non-Europeans. However that may be, a century of restrictive practices has left its indelible stamp on Australia and must be reckoned with in evaluating the mid-1970s scene.

If the external-specific aspects of White Australia are decreasing in their tensions, the internal-specific ones, directed at the Aborigines, are increasing. Aborigines of the modern world are becoming vocal at a time when any real hope for the retention of their traditional practices has vanished. In fact, hope of retaining their tradition was already lost when Section 127 of the Constitution stated 'In reckoning the numbers of the people of the Commonwealth, or of a State or other part of the Commonwealth, aboriginal natives shall not be counted'. Although this Section was repealed in 1967, it embodied such a widely held view of the Aborigines as a dispensable encumbrance in the environment, and operated in a restrictive way for so long, that there can be no possibility of reversion to the old ways built on the fundamental relationship between the Aborigine, his land and his religion. What seems to escape the notice of most Aboriginal activists is that no restoration of land, or land rights to them can automatically reinstate them in their old

cultural environment—an environment which in any case would be repugnant to many of them in such changed technological conditions.

Because of the unfortunate legacy of ineptitude and ignorance, the Aboriginal problem remains as one having no solution acceptable to all people. Federal and State governments alike have came down from their colonial pedestals and introduced legislation which is far-reaching in its implications for ultimate equality. But for large numbers of 'declared' Aborigines, in the inner-city area of Sydney, the Outback of western Queensland and New South Wales, or on the reserves of the Centre, legislation is of cold comfort when their ultimate destiny lies in the grey no-man's-land between Dream Time and Over Time. Thus while the return to Aboriginal possession of some 1,500 square miles of land, formerly part of the Wave Hill Station in Northern Australia, is a fine gesture on the part of the Commonwealth government, it will be virtually ineffective in restoring the lost dignity of an Aboriginal culture. From the political point of view, the problem is exacerbated by differential policies between the States and by foci of concentrated tension within them. Under these circumstances no government, however sympathetic and skilful, can provide for the fulfilment of the Aboriginal Identity, because that identity has been permanently fractured by the combined forces of history and technology.

The relevance of comments on the Aboriginal Problem to the general question of space, politics and territorial organization as stated in the heading of this chapter should not go unheeded. The Aborigine was possessed of a strong territorial sapience which found expression in the rites, rituals and economic activities of his community—a community which used no political institutions as we understand them to conduct territorial organization and safeguard territorial sovereignty. Land for the European colonists had such a different connotation from that for the Aborigine and was so frequently regarded as an enemy rather than an ally, that regulations as to its ownership and jealousies regarding any benefits it yielded have become enshrined. The shrine is a set of doctrines, institutions and legislative acts that constitute a vast superstructure which, by operating at three separate levels, has ensured a continuing interplay of forces which provides a rich source of raw material for the study of political geography. But at the same time the emergence of the new Territorial Man in Australia has left no hope for Aboriginal Man to return to the state of his fathers.

REFERENCES

Australian Institute of Urban Studies (1972), *First Report of the Task Force on New Cities for Australia*, AIUS, Canberra.

Bank of New South Wales (1971), *Offshore Australia*, Bank of N.S.W., Sydney.

Barnett, C. J. (Chairman) (1974), *Report of the Committee of Inquiry into Local Government Areas and Administration in New South Wales*, Government Printer, Sydney.

Bastin, John (1964), 'Federation and Western Australia, a contribution to the Parker-Blainey discussion', *Hist. Stud.*, 5, 47–58.

Blackton, C. S. (1955), 'Australian nationality and nationalism, the imperial federationist interlude, 1885–1901', *Hist. Stud.*, 7, 1–16.

——(1958), 'Australian nationality and nationalism. The Australian Natives Association, 1885–1901', *J. Mod. Hist.*, 30, 37–46.

——(1961), 'Australian nationality and nationalism 1850–1900', *Hist. Stud.*, 9, 351–67.

Blainey, Geoffrey (1964), 'The role of economic interests in Australian federation' in J. J. Eastwood and F. B. Smith (eds), *Historical Studies, Australia and New Zealand, Selected Articles*, Melbourne University Press, Melbourne.

——(1966), *The Tyranny of Distance*, Sun Books, Melbourne.

Borrie, W. D. (Chairman) (1975), *National Population Inquiry*, 2 vols, Australian Government Publishing Service, Canberra.

Burnley, I. H. (1974), 'The urbanization of the Australian population 1947–1971' in I. H. Burnley (ed.), *Urbanization in Australia*, Cambridge University Press, Cambridge, pp. 3–15.

Commonwealth Law Reports, 1920, 1942, Vols 28 and 65, Government Printer, Melbourne.

Crowley, F. K. (1960), *Australia's Western Third*, Macmillan, London.

Department of Urban and Regional Development (DURD) (1974a), *Australian Government Assistance to Local Government Projects*, Australian Government Publishing Service, Canberra.

——(1974b), *A National Program for Urban and Regional Development*, Australian Government Publishing Service, Canberra.

——(1974c), *Urban and Regional Development 1973–74. Second Annual Report*, Australian Government Publishing Service, Canberra.

Drewe, Robert (1973), 'The new nationalism', *The Australian*, 9 April (p. 9), 10 April (p. 9), 11 April (p. 8), 12 April (p. 8).

Fisk, E. K. and Tait, Maree (1973), 'The islands are Queensland's', *New Guinea*, 8, 4–18.

Gollan, R. A. (1955), 'Nationalism, the labour movement and the commonwealth' in Gordon Greenwood (ed.), *Australia, a Social and Political History*, Angus and Robertson, Sydney, pp. 144–95.

Greenwood, Gordon (ed.) (1955), *Australia, A Social and Political History*, Angus and Robertson, Sydney.

Hewlett, Patricia (1969), 'Aspects of campaigns in south-eastern N.S.W. at the federal referenda of 1898 and 1889' in A. W. Martin (ed.), *Essays in Australian Federation*, Melbourne University Press, Melbourne, pp. 167–85.

Holmes, Jean (1973), 'A federal culture' in Henry Mayer and Helen Nelson (eds), *Australian Politics, A Third Reader*, Cheshire, Melbourne, pp. 215–36.

Holsman, A. J. (1975), 'Interstate interaction patterns in Australia', *Aust. Geogr. Stud.*, 13, 41–61.

Kasperson, Roger E. and Minghi, Julian V. (eds) (1969), *The Structure of Political Geography*, Aldine, Chicago.

Lumb, R. D. (1969), 'Sovereignty and jurisdiction over Australian coastal waters', *Aust. Law J.*, 43, 421–49.

McCarty, J. W. (1967), 'The economic foundations of Australian politics' in Henry Mayer (ed.), *Australian Politics, A Reader*, 2nd edn, Cheshire, Melbourne, pp. 3–29.

McQueen, Humphrey (1970), *A New Britannia. An argument concerning the social origins of Australian radicalism and nationalism*, Penguin Books, Ringwood, Victoria.

Miller, J. D. B. (1959), *Australian Government and Politics*, 2nd edn, Duckworth, London.

Norris, R. (1969), 'Economic influences on the 1898 South Australian referendum' in A. W. Martin (ed.), *Essays in Australian Federation*, Melbourne University Press, Melbourne, pp. 137–66.

Parker, R. S. (1964), 'Australian federation: the influence of economic interests and political pressures' in J. J. Eastwood and F. B. Smith (eds), *Historical Studies, Australia and New Zealand, Selected Articles*, Melbourne University Press, Melbourne, pp. 152–78.

——(1964), 'Some comments on the role of economic interests in Australian federation' in J. J. Eastwood and F. B. Smith (eds), *Historical Studies, Australia and New Zealand, Selected Articles*, Melbourne University Press, Melbourne, pp. 195–98.

Partridge, P. H. (1952), 'The politics of federalism' in G. Sawer (ed.), *Federalism: An Australian Jubilee Study*, Cheshire, Melbourne, pp. 174–210.

Prescott, J. R. V. (1972), 'The Australian-Indonesian continental shelf agreements', *Australia's Neighbours*, Fourth Series, No. 82, 1–2.

Robinson, K. W. (1961), 'Sixty years of federation in Australia', *Geogr. Rev.*, 51, 1–20.

——(1962), 'The political influence in Australian geography', *Pac. Viewpoint*, 3, 73–86.

——(1970), 'Diversity, conflict and change—the meeting place of geography and politics', *Aust. Geogr. Stud.*, 8, 1–15.

——(1971), *Regional Planning in France*, Department of Decentralization and Development. Sydney.

——(1973), 'The world's most urbanised country', *Hemisphere*, 17, 2–10.

——(1975), 'The geographical context of political individualism' in J. M. Powell and M. Williams (eds), *Australian Space Australian Time*, Oxford University Press, Melbourne, pp. 226–49.

Sawer, Geoffrey (1975), *The Australian Constitution*, Australian Government Publishing Service, Canberra.

Ward, R. (1970), *The Australian Legend*, Oxford University Press, Melbourne.

Wheare, K. C. (1955), *Federal Government*, Oxford University Press, London.

18 CAPITAL CITIES

R. BUNKER

This chapter attempts the daunting task of presenting some perspectives on Australian capital cities in a short space. This involves a highly selective choice of themes which are briefly presented and some of their relationships and interactions identified. The chapter begins with a brief history of the capitals; goes on to discuss their spatial relationships; examines their changing characteristics as cities; comments on the mechanisms and procedures developed to guide their growth and change; looks at forms of organization; and then concentrates on Sydney and Melbourne as case studies illustrating some of those considerations. The cities discussed are the capitals of the sovereign States constituting the Commonwealth of Australia— Sydney, Melbourne, Brisbane, Adelaide, Perth and Hobart—and the national capital, Canberra, whose foundation officially took place in 1913 following the federation of the States in 1901.

THE CAPITAL CITIES IN HISTORY

Sydney was the first point of European settlement in the continent and was founded in 1788. Hobart was established in the early years of the nineteenth century, Perth in the 1820s, Melbourne, Adelaide and Brisbane in the following decade. The cities became the focuses and points of communication to the outside world for the States which developed around them. Throughout their history each has been, almost without exception, the largest urban area in its particular State and in most instances has remained many times the size of the next largest settlement. In the nineteenth century the capitals all developed as major ports mediating between an industrializing Europe and the primary resources of their hinterlands. The sameness of, and the differences between the capital cities has been expressed by McCarty (1970):

> Their economic and social structures tended to vary as their hinterlands varied ... as commercial cities linking the hinterlands to world markets, each was fully exposed to the levelling effects of the world capitalist economy.

Table 18.1 presents McCarty's estimates of the population of the capital cities in the latter half of the nineteenth century, adapted from the colonial censuses. It also shows the proportion of each State's population living in those cities. As most typically represented in Melbourne this indicates an initial dominance by the capital—the first substantial urban settlement—diluted by later exploitation of primary resources of the State, and then reasserted by the subsequent development of manufacturing, commercial, transportation and service functions in it. Industrialization and urbanization were given a new impetus after 1861, firstly in Victoria, and this was an expensive process. While Butlin (1958) has postulated that Australian economic growth from 1861 to 1901 was sustained, stable and rapid— even including the depression years of the 1890s—he points out that this was accompanied by structural

Table 18.1 Population of Australian Capital Cities and Proportion of Their State Population 1851–1901

	Sydney '000	per cent of State	Melbourne '000	per cent of State	Brisbane '000	per cent of State	Adelaide '000	per cent of State	Perth '000	per cent of State	Hobart '000	per cent of State
1851	54	28	29	38	3	—	18	28	—	—	—	—
1861	96	27	125	23	6	20	35	28	5	33	25	28
1871	138	27	191	26	15	13	51	27	—	—	26	25
1881	225	30	268	31	31	14	92	33	9	30	27	23
1891	400	35	473	41	94	24	117	37	16	32	33	22
1901	496	37	478	40	119	24	141	39	61	33	35	20

Source: McCarty, 1970.

Table 18.2 Population of Australian Capital Cities and Proportion of Their State Population at the Censuses 1911–71[a]

	Sydney '000	per cent of State	Melbourne '000	per cent of State	Brisbane '000	per cent of State	Adelaide '000	per cent of State	Perth '000	per cent of State	Hobart '000	per cent of State	Canberra '000	per cent Territory
1911	630	38.2	589	44.8	139	23.0	190	46.4	100	37.8	40	20.9	—	—
1921	899	42.8	766	50.0	210	27.8	255	51.6	155	46.5	52	24.5	3	—
1933	1,235	47.5	992	54.5	300	31.6	313	53.8	207	47.3	60	26.5	7	81.9
1947	1,484	49.7	1,226	59.7	402	36.3	382	59.2	273	54.2	77	29.8	15	89.9
1954	1,863	54.4	1,524	62.1	502	38.1	484	60.7	385	54.5	95	30.8	28	93.3
1961	2,183	55.7	1,912	65.2	622	40.9	588	60.7	420	57.0	116	33.1	56	96.0
1966	2,447	57.7	2,108	65.5	716	42.8	728	66.5	500	59.0	119	32.2	92	96.1
1971	2,725	59.4	2,394	68.5	818	44.8	809	69.0	642	62.5	130	33.3	141	97.9

[a] Definitions of areas covered by capitals based on differing criteria until 1966.
Full-blood Aborigines not included until 1966.
Source: *Official Yearbooks of the Commonwealth of Australia.*

shifts and almost static living standards so that while the pastoral industry was 'a model of increased productivity and source of rising living standards' it became less important than activities involved with

> the absorption into urban society in a new country of a population increasing at high speed without significant loss in living standards: and a reasonably successful reorientation towards industrial activity.

Other centralizing forces encouraging the growth of the capital cities included concentration of government and administration there, the development of road and rail networks radiating from them and the fact that few major ports developed elsewhere.

Table 18.2 presents the same kind of information as Table 18.1 based on data contained in the Commonwealth censuses of population. These figures are based on slightly different premises to those in Table 18.1 where a more liberal interpretation of the areas covered by capital cities is usually employed. These premises also vary a little within the period represented. For example the definitions of the various metropolitan areas are somewhat arbitrary until 1966. In Table 18.2 there is only one exception to the increasing metropolitan dominance of the States recorded at each census. The causes at work are more varied than those operating in the previous century. The continued growth of manufacturing industry in Australia has been concentrated in Sydney, Melbourne and Adelaide, and industrial centres near to them such as Newcastle, Woolongong and Geelong. Most significantly, this century has seen the development of strong flows of people, goods, information and money between major

urban centres in the continent, particularly in the south and east, which expresses the abolition of customs barriers between the constituent States of the federation, increasing sophistication and specialization of production, a growing Australian market and most importantly the greater facility of communication and transport.

THE RELATIONSHIPS OF THE CAPITAL CITIES

Three sets of relationships can be identified for the capitals—with the world outside Australia, with each other and with other settlements within the States which each govern. Each of the State capitals is an important port: in terms of tonnage of goods handled they fall into a pattern akin to their ranking in terms of population, except that Perth assumes greater prominence—because of the inclusion of the bulk handling port of Kwinana in the figures shown in Table 18.3. For cargoes expressed in measured tons, i.e. general or disaggregated merchandise, the capital cities are clearly dominant in the national scene. For commodities in bulk which are assessed as dead weight tonnage like coal, ores, wool, wheat, sugar, newsprint, iron and steel the capital cities act as major points of entry for cargoes from overseas and interstate. It is only for bulk cargoes exported or shipped interstate that the capitals do not measure up to the operations of the large specialist ore ports of northern Australia, and the movement of iron, steel and coal out from other centres.

In discussing the relationships of Australian capital cities one with another, it has already been suggested

Table 18.3   Cargoes Discharged and Shipped at Australian State Capital Cities 1971–2

Port	Overseas cargo				Interstate cargo			
	Discharged weight[a]	Meas.[a]	Shipped weight	Meas.	Discharged weight	Meas.	Shipped weight	Meas.
Sydney and Botany Bay	3,857	1,962	5,293	940	5,405	229	350	272
Melbourne	1,980	2,291	1,685	1,000	1,495	980	854	1,035
Brisbane	834	355	1,540	154	2,877	133	156	90
Port Adelaide and Port Stanvac	1,866	210	813	122	1,177	17	838	9
Perth (Fremantle and Kwinana)	4,239	252	4,382	293	1,233	5	1,373	13
Hobart	142	12	154	118	676	220	463	160
Total Australia	19,917	5,178	106,340	2,791	25,393	2,725	25,970	2,471

[a]In '000 tons. Commodities like coal, ores, wool, wheat, sugar, newsprint, iron and steel are assessed as dead weight: others such as general cargo, butter, textiles and apparel, manufactures are recorded in tons measurement, 40 cubic feet of space occupied being counted as one ton.
Source: *Official Yearbooks of the Commonwealth of Australia.*

Table 18.4 Australian Capital Cities 1971: Percentage of Labour Force in Major Categories of Employment (excluding those unemployed)

Industry group	Sydney	Melbourne	Brisbane	Adelaide	Perth	Hobart	Canberra	Australia
Agriculture and mining	1.1	1.3	2.1	1.7	3.0	1.8	0.7	8.8
Manufacturing	28.3	31.4	20.8	27.5	18.8	19.6	5.6	23.2
Electricity and gas	1.8	1.5	1.5	1.9	1.2	3.5	0.7	1.7
Construction	6.9	6.6	8.5	7.2	9.6	8.3	10.4	7.9
Wholesale and retail	19.5	19.3	22.8	21.4	22.7	19.4	13.0	18.9
Transport and storage	5.6	5.0	5.9	4.5	6.2	4.8	2.5	5.2
Communication	2.1	1.9	2.3	1.9	2.1	2.7	1.6	2.0
Finance	9.5	8.0	8.2	7.2	8.4	7.5	6.1	6.9
Public administration and Defence	5.4	5.0	7.4	4.7	6.0	8.0	32.5	5.4
Community services	10.2	10.4	12.0	13.9	12.9	14.9	17.8	10.8
Entertainment	5.3	4.5	4.9	5.0	5.6	6.1	6.2	5.1
Other and not stated	4.4	5.0	3.7	3.0	3.7	3.3	3.0	4.1

Source: data for Statistical Divisions from Australian Bureau of Statistics. Industry group as defined in Australian Standard Industrial Classification.

that the Australian spatial economy has become a much more integrated one in the past half-century. It had been suggested by McCarty (1970) that Australia has evolved from a situation of fairly separate State economies, each dominated by its capital primate city, towards a more integrated and developed national economy where the national system of cities accords much more closely to a rank-size distribution than if the settlement pattern in each State is examined separately.

The discrepancy between the Australian system of cities and State systems in this regard has intrigued many writers among whom Stewart (1959), in looking at the size and spacing of cities in 72 countries, has suggested factors in addition to those hypothesized by McCarty. He sees the close accord in size of the largest and second-largest Australian cities as attributable to the large area of the continent. Such low ratios of largest to second-largest are not likely to be found in subdivisions of the country he speculates, and on finding this to be so, attributes this to a high standard of living, and concentration of population on the coast making 'it possible for each state, in spite of its large size, to have a central city'.

The interaction of capital cities one with another is discussed more specifically elsewhere in this volume. A more static analysis will be presented here which briefly explores the different patterns of activity carried on in the capitals. Table 18.4 begins this by presenting data on the proportions of the labour force in major categories of employment. Port, government and general service functions are common to all in roughly the same proportions, except for the federal capital of Canberra, but there are big differences in the

importance of manufacturing industry. Table 18.5 pursues this further and from the proportions of the Australian manufacturing workforce in different kinds of manufacturing operations, develops specialty quotients in these categories for each of the capital cities. Sydney and Melbourne exhibit strong and diversified structures with the latter demonstrating its early engagement with the making of textiles, clothing and footwear and later development as a centre of vehicle manufacture. This contrasts with Sydney's specialization in chemicals and related products, and electrical appliances and equipment. Adelaide has a marked concentration on fabricated metal products, vehicles and electrical equipment—the latter category dominated by metal-using products such as washing machines, refrigerators etc. Other analyses such as Bunker (1963) have suggested that the manufacturing operations carried out in these three capitals are further removed from initial raw material inputs, and concerned with more intricate and specialized production, than the simpler processing activities which are more characteristic of the other capital cities. Examples of this latter kind of operation are food processing, manufacture of wood products and furniture and printing and publishing. Canberra's function as a national capital is demonstrated by the profile of its small and limited manufacturing workforce, with emphasis on printing and publishing and industries concerned with building and construction. These specializations in manufacturing activity in Australia imply considerable flows and exchanges between the major cities.

Another aspect of inter-capital relationships is the migration flows between them. The Australian popula-

Table 18.5 Australian Capital Cities 1971: Profile of Manufacturing

Australian manufacturing workforce distributed by type of manufacture (per cent)	Type of manufacture	Speciality quotients[a] by Statistical Division						
		Sydney	Melbourne	Adelaide	Brisbane	Perth	Hobart	Canberra
15.5	Food, beverages, tobacco	0.72	0.75	0.77	1.34	1.25	1.49	1.17
13.1	Textiles, clothing, footwear	0.92	1.53	0.48	0.78	0.31	low	
6.2	Wood, wood products, furniture	0.72	0.62	0.95	1.50	1.62	1.43	1.42
8.2	Paper products, printing and publishing	1.15	1.00	0.68	1.25	1.19	2.28	5.17
5.1	Chemical, petroleum, coal products	1.53	1.08	0.54	0.74	0.85	1.34	—
3.9	Non-metallic mineral products	1.03	0.72	0.94	1.36	1.91	0.74	2.93
7.1	Basic metal products	0.47	0.31	0.61	0.31	1.08		
9.2	Fabricated metal products	1.07	0.98	1.21	1.38	1.62	0.64	1.14
6.9	Motor vehicles and parts	0.70	1.36	3.04	0.75	0.38	0.06	
4.8	Other transport equipment	1.21	0.85	0.63	1.49	1.27		
8.6	Appliances, electrical equipment, scientific and photographic apparatus	1.56	1.00	1.63	0.62	0.72	0.45	
5.9	Industrial machinery and equipment	1.11	1.17	0.85	0.51			
5.4	Leather, rubber, plastics, other	1.32	1.06	0.99	0.87	0.56	0.20	0.30

[a]Specialty quotients: capital city percentages divided by Australian percentages, category by category. A value greater than 1.0 indicates a specialization in that category.

Source: data for Statistical Divisions from Australian Bureau of Statistics. Type of manufacture as defined in Australian Standard Industrial Classification.

Table 18.6 Inter-Capital City[a] Migration 1966–71

Residence in 1966	Residence in 1971							
	Sydney	Melbourne	Brisbane	Adelaide	Perth	Hobart	Canberra	Total
Sydney	—	15,849	11,621	5,205	6,251	1,193	9,559	49,678
Melbourne	19,121	—	8,603	6,074	7,550	1,965	5,323	48,636
Brisbane	12,570	6,761	—	1,332	1,690	359	2,144	24,856
Adelaide	6,522	9,231	1,943	—	3,431	470	1,979	23,576
Perth	4,652	4,717	1,424	1,625	—	195	989	13,602
Hobart	1,665	2,973	557	527	617	—	418	6,757
Canberra	4,287	1,940	867	594	590	94	—	8,372
Total	48,817	41,470	25,015	15,357	20,129	4,276	20,412	175,477

[a]Statistical Divisions: urban parts only.

Excludes persons aged less than five years and those who are not usually residents of the dwelling.

Source: Australian Bureau of Statistics, 1971 census of population and housing.

Table 18.7 Population Size of Second-Largest City in Each State as a Percentage of the Capital City 1933–71

	N.S.W.	Victoria	Queens-land	South Australia	Western Australia	Tasmania
1933	8.5	4.0	9.8	3.7	4.4	54.4
1947	8.5	3.6	8.7	3.2	8.2	52.8
1954	9.6	4.8	8.6	2.9	6.0	51.8
1961	9.6	4.8	8.2	4.0	5.2	48.9
1966	9.5	5.0	9.6	3.0	4.0	50.6
1971	9.2	4.8	9.1	4.0	3.3	47.9

Source: *Official Yearbooks of the Commonwealth of Australia.*

tion is a fairly mobile one and Table 18.6 shows the inter-metropolitan migration that has occurred between the census years of 1966 and 1971.

The final series of relationships to which attention might be directed is that between each capital city and the other towns in the State in which it is located. Attention has already been drawn to the increasing metropolitan dominance of each State—since 1861 in New South Wales and Victoria, 1871 in South Australia and Queensland, 1881 in Western Australia, and 1901 in Tasmania. Table 18.7 shows the size of the second-largest city in each State compared with the capital at the census years 1933–71. Trends should be interpreted with care before 1966 because of the somewhat arbitrary areal definition of each city before then. But the table shows that there is no town approaching the size of the capital in any State except Tasmania and that on the evidence of the last two censuses the second city may even be diminishing slightly in comparison. Such dominance has been noted by many writers including Stewart (1959) and Robinson (1963).

Robinson argues that Australian rural population never developed the density achieved by slow growth over centuries in Europe in conditions of limited mobility, and that the rural towns developed in an era of transportation technology when movement by road and rail was relatively quick. Consequently the periods of rapid population growth in the States occurred when the conditions for the establishment of many and thriving urban settlements did not exist so that 'Australia acquired a collection of peripheral urban organisms, rather than a well structured hierarchical society'.

CHANGING CHARACTERISTICS AS CITIES
The population densities of the capital cities for 1971 are shown in Table 18.8. Before 1966 there were no universally recognized criteria to delimit the extent of the urban area, but the reform in the collection of data in this regard starting in that year enables useful comparisons to be validly made between cities and over time. The figures in Table 18.8 spread population over total land area including that devoted to roads and non-residential activities, and show a low ruling density compared with European cities and the older North American urban areas. Clark (1970) has carried out studies where he has plotted population change in some forty to fifty areas making up each of the cities of Sydney, Melbourne and Brisbane. These

Table 18.8 Areas, Populations and Densities of State Capital Cities, Australia 1971

	Urban area (km²)	Urban population	Urban density (people per km²)
Sydney	1,421	2,725,064	1,918
Melbourne	1,322	2,394,117	1,811
Brisbane	726	818,423	1,127
Adelaide	555	809,482	1,459
Perth	527	641,800	1,218
Hobart	111	129,928	1,171

Source: *Official Yearbooks of the Commonwealth of Australia* and Bureau of Census and Statistics.

movements have been plotted against overall density found in those areas. He finds population moving up to or dropping down towards pivotal densities which are highest in Sydney, lower in Melbourne and least in Brisbane. Because far more areas are gaining population than are losing it, these pivotal densities are considerably higher than the average densities shown in Table 18.8. A study by Marsden (1970) has confirmed that Brisbane's overall density is low, that it is likely to have changed little since 1871 and that there has been a a steady levelling out of densities in the various rings of the city since 1886, i.e. decrease in the density gradient from the centre. This latter process of *deconcentration* was accompanied by *decongestion* after 1901, or a decrease in the density right at the centre so that a density crater has developed there. These conclusions seems reasonable despite the fluctuating definition of what constituted the urban area at the censuses.

It is likely that similar circumstances, though of different dating, have attended the density structures of all the capital cities. The kinds of transportation technology available and their relative importance form the most important determinant of density measured over substantial areas. Numerous studies have described how the compact capital cities where movement was by walking or by animal later developed rail and omnibus systems as they reached certain sizes and as these modes became available. More recently and further out came the areas of lower density supported by high levels of vehicle ownership which have developed since World War II, reaching 312 cars and station wagons per 1,000 people in Melbourne in 1971, 319 in Sydney and 371 in Perth (Commonwealth Bureau of Roads, 1973). In terms of the actual local residential environment, the Australian capital city dweller is likely to live in a cottage standing in its own plot of ground ranging from 500 to 1,200 square metres; or in a two- or three-storey building containing home units (flats) typically supplanting the cottage—particularly in the last ten years—in the more accessible or congenial areas of the suburbs; or in inner suburban terrace (row) houses built in the nineteenth century and first decades of this century, which are also occasionally in process of replacement by the ubiquitous block of flats. There is a high level of home ownership, some private rented accommodation, and State public housing authorities renting and sometimes selling dwellings.

Given the large areas covered by the cities, and the large population sizes reached, there has been a considerable shift of manufacturing, commercial and service activities to the suburbs. The dominance of the central business district has declined and a significant number of suburban centres have developed. These trends in profit-making activities such as manufacturing, retailing and wholesaling have been documented by Logan (1968a) and Webber and Daly (1971) among others. Most attention has been focused on identifying the secular characteristics of this trend such as the associations of different kinds and rates of population growth with various types and periods of employment growth. However, Webber and Daly (1971) have suggested that in the short term there is likely to be an operation of more random elements in location and expansion decisions. They carried out an analysis of the annual growth of employees in manufacturing in the Sydney metropolitan area from 1954 to 1968 and identified a significant stochastic element which could incorporate the influence of general economic conditions and changes in the characteristics of industrial districts such as land values, traffic congestion and local labour conditions. They found fluctuations in the growth of manufacturing employment which assumed the character of cycles which

> comprise years of high localised growth which are largely unrelated to the independent variables, alternating with years in which growth rates are lower, more equal throughout the metropolitan area and more closely related to the explanatory variables such as population growth.

On the other hand, not much study has been directed to the mismatch of city-wide community services and cultural facilities to population following this suburbanization. Lawrence (1972) has drawn attention to the fact that while there is an overall metropolitan balance between the number of hospital beds theoretically needed and those provided in Sydney, there is a spatial maldistribution so that there are severe shortages of beds in middle and outer suburbs. He quotes a 1969 Metropolitan Hospitals Survey which states: 'due to changes in urban development and the outward spread of residential suburbs, the hospital accommodation is largely provided where people *used to live*'.

Besides these studies of entrepreneurial and government activities in the capital cities, there has been a good deal of recent analysis of the character and distribution of the residential population. Much of this has been done by applying factor analysis to small-area data concerning the characteristics of the residential population and has covered Sydney, Melbourne, Brisbane, Adelaide and Canberra. The results have been reported in Timms (1971), Johnston (1971), Stimson (1974), and Davis and Spearritt (1974). On the whole this research reveals similar findings for all the cities and these are akin to those reported in North America and Scandinavia (Timms, 1971):

> Factors relating to population differences in socioeconomic status or social rank, family characteristics and ethnicity effectively exhaust the common-factor variance present in a wide variety of census data. Social

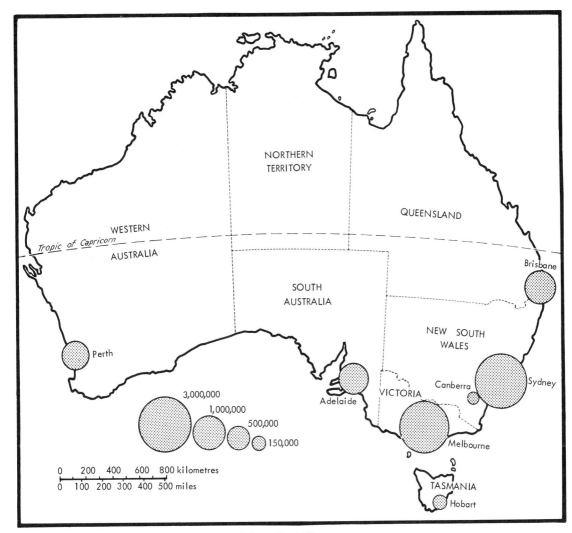

Fig. 18.1   Capital city populations and States of Australia, 1971.

rank and familism are essentially independent of each other, but ethnicity shows varying degrees of relationship with the other factors. In Brisbane ethnicity shows a weak association with neighbourhood variations in family composition: in Auckland, Canberra and Melbourne, it appears to be more strongly associated with social rank.

Socio-economic status tends to assume a sector pattern in the cities studied (except Canberra), while zonal or annular patterns are more characteristic of household composition and ethnic status.

Immigration from overseas has fuelled central city growth. From 1947 to 1966 more than half of the population added to Sydney, Melbourne and Adelaide came from the net migration of people born overseas.

As would be expected from the importance of ethnic factors in the differentiation of the residential population, these migrants have had a considerable effect on metropolitan spatial structure. Burnley (1974a) has studied Sydney and Melbourne to identify five kinds of area categorized in terms of population growth, change and influence of immigration. 'In four of these ecological areas', he maintains, 'immigration has profoundly influenced population change and structure.' The five areas are: an inner area where steeply declining Australian-born population has been substantially but not equally replaced by migrants; an adjacent, but non-continuous belt of total moderate population increase hiding some loss of Australian-born population with overseas-born increase more than offsetting this; an area of moderate total population and Australian-born increase where immigration has contributed substantially also—mainly in areas of pre-war residential development; marked growth in industrial areas on the metropolitan perimeter where immigrants have made a strong contribution; and—in terms of area covered, larger than all the other preceding categories put together—residential suburbs on the periphery which have shown marked post-war development with little migrant influence.

Aggregated research of this kind tells us little about the lives of people living in the cities, patterns of behaviour, circumstances and problems. Henderson's (1970) survey of living conditions in Melbourne estimated that in 1966 up to 7 per cent of income units were in poverty and 4 per cent in need. Much of this poverty was concentrated in the inner suburbs. High and low status areas had begun to develop by the end of the last century and large-scale segregation has developed this century. Stilwell and Hardwick (1973) consider that spatial inequalities, such as

variations in the proportion of the population with university education, have grown over the years. Burnley (1974b) states that 'areas of relative homogeneity are large enough in all probability to affect the life chances of the individual within them'. During the period of office of the Federal Labor government between 1972 and 1975, the newly-founded Department of Urban and Regional Development launched two Area Improvement Programmes to help the disadvantaged populations living in the western areas of Melbourne and Sydney and later extended the programme to a further thirteen regions.

As well as low incomes, there are many problems concerning education, health, transport, and community support services in substantial areas of the capital cities. Some of these are described in studies such as those carried out by Bryson and Thompson (1972) and McClelland (1968) in outer suburban areas dominated by large tracts of public housing, and handicapped populations.

One of the problems in formulating public policy

Table 18.9   All Persons Who Travelled to Work, by Time of Leaving Home, Capital Cities and Other Areas, May 1970 (per cent)

Time of leaving home	New South Wales	Victoria	Queensland	South Australia	Western Australia	Tasmania	Australia[b]
			Capital cities[a]				
Midnight — 6.59 a.m.	28.8	18.6	26.0	14.2	14.7	8.7	22.2
7.00 a.m. — 7.29 a.m.	18.5	19.0	20.7	20.5	15.9	14.3	18.8
7.30 a.m. — 7.59 a.m.	18.2	24.0	24.5	20.1	25.8	21.5	21.6
8.00 a.m. — 8.29 a.m.	15.7	17.6	14.9	21.5	23.0	23.2	17.6
8.30 a.m. — 8.59 a.m.	8.9	11.2	4.5	11.9	10.1	15.6	9.7
9.00 a.m. —11.59 a.m.	4.1	4.2	3.4	4.7	5.3	c	4.2
Noon — 3.59 p.m.	2.6	2.2	2.8	3.0	2.1	c	2.5
4.00 a.m. —11.59 p.m.	2.1	1.6	2.1	2.2	1.8	c	1.9
Time varied	1.3	1.5	c	1.9	c	c	1.5
Total	100.0	100.0	100.0	100.0	100.0	100.0	100.0
			Other areas[b]				
Midnight — 6.59 a.m.	26.7	13.0	19.4	12.3	9.3	7.7	18.6
7.00 a.m. — 7.29 a.m.	16.7	18.0	15.8	24.2	14.4	14.8	16.8
7.30 a.m. — 7.59 a.m.	13.5	23.5	24.6	21.8	28.0	36.2	20.8
8.00 a.m. — 8.29 a.m.	12.5	12.7	18.1	13.7	18.0	13.7	14.8
8.30 a.m. — 8.59 a.m.	14.9	20.4	11.4	14.9	16.5	16.4	15.5
9.00 a.m. —11.59 a.m.	5.6	6.4	3.7	4.7	c	c	5.1
Noon — 3.59 p.m.	4.2	2.1	2.4	c	c	c	3.3
4.00 p.m. —11.59 p.m.	3.8	2.0	2.4	c	c	c	2.9
Time varied	2.0	1.9	2.1	c	c	c	2.1
Total	100.0	100.0	100.0	100.0	100.0	100.0	100.0

[a] Statistical Divisions. [b] Figures for other areas include the Northern Territory and the Australian Capital Territory. [c] Based on a figure less than 4,000.

Source: Commonwealth Bureau of Census and Statistics, *Journey to Work and Journey to School, 1970.*

Table 18.10   Residential Land Prices in Capital Cities in Australia in 1973–4, Rate of Increase and Relationship to Average Earnings 1969–73

	Sydney	Melbourne	Brisbane	Adelaide	Perth[a]	Hobart	Canberra
	Annual percentage changes in land prices						
1969	12	8	—	6	9	—	4
1970	14	2	—	6	−3	—	−9
1971	20	20	—	−3	7	—	50
1972	28	22	—	22	21	—	73
1973	34	46	—	46	22	11	34
	Number of years' average earnings in State to buy site						
1967	1.7	1.2	—	0.7	2.5[a]	—	0.8
1970	1.8	1.1	—	0.6	2.2	—	0.7
1971	1.9	1.2	—	0.6	2.0	—	0.9
1972	2.3	1.4	—	0.6	2.4	—	1.4
1973	2.7	1.8	—	0.8	2.6	0.7	1.7
	Approximate price per allotment ($)						
1974	20,200	12,500	10,700	5,600	—	5,500	5,500

[a] Perth data based on sites in established suburbs: the prices are up to twice the level of those for the metropolitan area as a whole.
Source: adapted from Department of Urban and Regional Development, 1974.

initiatives in urban affairs is the difficulty of measuring and communicating the possible effect of policy measures on individuals' welfare. 'What does it mean to me?' One possible avenue of research in this context is into how people spend their time in different parts of the city. Gutenschwager (1973) has emphasized the usefulness of this disaggregated, behavioural kind of investigation:

> The time budget perspective, it would appear, is complementary to other urban research frameworks. Most of the latter treat individuals as members of institutions, organizations or specialised systems such as transportation, land use, education, industry, the neighbourhood etc. ... ultimately the behavioural effect of these systems ... on the individuals can be seen through a time-budget analysis.

Table 18.9 shows the time of leaving home to travel to work by residents of capital cities in the States in 1970 compared with people living outside them. It gives some indication of the changes in personal lifestyle consequent upon living in large urban areas and is congruent with other data on longer journey times and more use of public transport in the bigger cities.

The rising cost of establishing a household in the capital cities is one of considerable concern. This is most clearly illustrated in the changing levels of residential land prices in them over the past few years. Table 18.10 should be interpreted with care, because of the different premises upon which prices of residential lots have been collected. In Perth the figures relate to sites in established suburbs and there is evidence that these are up to twice the level of such lots over the whole metropolitan area. With this exception, however, rough comparisons between cities are in order and trends for each city over time even more valid. The general pattern is of higher prices with increasing size of city and an escalation in these by reference to average earnings over time. This is important to people wanting to buy land and build a house on it, usually in a peripheral metropolitan location. In seeking to move into a capital city, or within it, this is but part of the scene that includes such variables as the availability and price of housing finance, the spatial distribution of opportunities and the ease of overcoming the friction of distance in seeking them out, taxation systems, the price of established dwellings, and the stage in the life cycle reached by a household.

Figuring importantly in the changing characteristics of the capital cities is the steady decline in the use of public transport and the increasing use of the car. Table 18.11 gives some background data for the whole country showing the change in emphasis of mode used for surface land travel.

Table 18.11 Estimated Passenger Transport Task on Land in Australia by Mode (million passenger miles)

Year	Population[a] (millions)	Cars and station wagons	Rail	Bus and tram
1949/50	8.07	12,380[b]	6,650	—
1959/60	10.20	31,390	6,371	—
1964/5	11.28	51,450	6,270	—
1969/70	12.40	75,100	6,098	5,840[c]

[a] As at 31 December.

[b] Includes drivers (but not taxi drivers) and passengers.

[c] Estimate for 1970/1 is the only data available.

Source: Commonwealth Bureau of Roads, 1973.

This section on change in the cities ends with a brief note on the shifting values that have informed urban issues in the last twenty years. Initially there was a considerable preoccupation with the efficiency of public investment and its co-ordination in time and space. Emphasis was placed on the effective provision of infrastructure to support urban growth and this was related to land use planning and control, and programmes of release for development. In the late 1960s, considerable public alarm and clamour arose over environmental and ecological issues and this was widely reflected in legislation setting up pollution control authorities and environmental protection agencies. This new element enriched consideration of urban growth and structure so that, for example, in Sydney's topographical and meteorological conditions, it could be argued that industries emitting air pollutants were better sited on the sandstone plateaux flanking the Cumberland plain rather than in the lowlands themselves where more orthodox and restricted locational criteria and influences had concentrated that kind of activity (Murphy, 1970). More recently, strong interest has been aroused in the inequalities of opportunity present in the capital cities and arguments have been advanced by Stretton (1970), Stilwell (1974) and le Breton (1974) among others in favour of deliberate efforts by governments to promote and equalize the welfare of individuals living in the cities. Attention has moved from the idea of experts expressing a community consensus in their policy proposals to a concern for the rights and interests of under-privileged and minority groups and a disaggregation of city dwellers into many, sometimes competing groups. Who pays? Who benefits? Hence there is far more debate about public policies and private decisions affecting the urban scene, much more controversy, interaction and participation. The recent Federal Labor government showed more interest, initiative and provocation about urban issues than any previous one. Resident action groups have been formed to fight

decisions, often in a metropolitan-wide context, which are considered to adversely affect local communities—of which the controversy about inner city expressways is but one example. State, Federal and voluntary agencies have attempted to develop and co-ordinate local and sub-regional problem-solving and planning concerning welfare services and physical improvement. The political scene has been profoundly changed by this ferment partly described, partly anticipated by Parker and Troy (1972) and Jakubowicz (1972). In this confused, pulsating scene, attention has switched to the so-called 'management' of the cities (Australian Institute of Urban Studies, 1973; Melbourne and Metropolitan Board of Works, 1974) and any self-respecting man of urban affairs has this as one of the top keywords in his vocabulary at the moment. This leads us to a brief discussion on the methods and procedures used to guide growth and change in the capital cities.

METHODS AND PROCEDURES OF CONTROL AND GUIDANCE

As most Australians live in the capital cities it is sometimes difficult to distinguish between problems *in* the cities and the problems *of* the cities. The detailed guidance and control of private development is in the hands of local government, but the planning and provision of city-wide physical infrastructure such as roads, railways, sewerage, water supply, electricity and gas lies largely in the hands of State departments and instrumentalities. In addition many community and welfare services which are run by the State, such as primary and secondary education, hospital care, public housing and transport have important effects in the location of their facilities and the different levels of service provided. Considerable finance for most of these activities is made available by the Australian government together with some conditions as to its use.

Attempts at controlling the growth and change of

capital cities were based initially on master plan concepts concerned broadly with controlling the type, intensity and programming of land use. Planning schemes of this kind were made public in Sydney (1948), Melbourne (1954), Perth (1955), Adelaide (1962) and Brisbane (1962). Canberra has grown under the guidance of the National Capital Development Commission set up by the Federal government in 1958, but its initial development was based on the prize-winning plan submitted by Walter Burley Griffin in 1911. These schemes, at later dates, became statutory to greater or lesser degrees. Revision, amendment and extension procedures were built into all of them.

Peter Harrison (1974) has written a succinct account of post-war planning for the mainland State capital cities and has pointed out the critical nature of the relationship between such activities and the operation of the State governments whose populations largely reside in these cities:

> With almost 40 per cent of the State population and a Lord Mayor elected at large the Brisbane Council assumed some of the characteristics of a state within a state. Relationships with the central government have never been easy. The other State governments came to regard metropolitan planning as a means by which many of the purposes of a metropolitan government could be fulfilled without requiring them to relinquish their authority to elected bodies which could in some respects become political rivals.

Organizations of different kinds were set up in every State except Queensland, whose Brisbane City Council had been established by the Greater Brisbane Act of 1924, the largest urban local government area in Australia and whose boundaries were sufficiently widely drawn to contain most of its urban area until recently. In Sydney, the Cumberland County Council was set up in 1945 as a special purpose authority to prepare a metropolitan plan, representative of the (then) sixty-nine councils in the region and paid for by them. It provided a regional land-use and transport plan which was prescribed, with revision, three years after its submission in 1948 and within which local statutory planning schemes were to be prepared regulating and controlling the use of land. In 1963 the independent County Council was abolished and its metropolitan planning responsibilities incorporated into the function of a State government agency—the State Planning Authority. While still regulating land use, the new Authority in its constitution and method of operation sought to integrate and co-ordinate the investment programmes of State and metropolitan organizations responsible for the provision of physical infrastructure. In late 1974 the State Planning Authority was superseded by the State Planning and Environment Commission.

Different arrangements were made in Melbourne.

An existing powerful metropolitan body had the responsibility for the preparation of a master plan added to its existing responsibilities in 1949. This was the Melbourne and Metropolitan Board of Works, a government body with fifty-three honorary commissioners elected by the local government councils in its area. Since its foundation in 1890 it has assembled a formidable body of related functions—water supply, sewage collection and disposal, provision of metropolitan parks, open space, bridges, some responsibility (until 1974) for main roads in central and inner Melbourne, and storm drainage. It seemed logical, as a body planning and delivering important metropolitan physical facilities, that the Board of Works prepare a regional land use plan to give direction and a metropolitan context to local planning schemes.

In Brisbane the City Council controls a wide range of services, but importantly, shares transportation responsibilities with the State government. This has led to some conflict. The current land use plan was adopted in 1971 and as Harrison comments, 'Long term intentions for urban expansion are not indicated; land use changes, including the conversion of rural lands to urban use are negotiated rather than prescribed.'

In Adelaide, substantial State government initiatives in other fields have meant that statutory land use planning has not been seen so urgent as in the capitals. The South Australian government has pursued a policy of attracting manufacturing industry to the State since the end of the war. This has meant, *inter alia*, the provision of cheap and serviced land for factories, the recruitment of migrants, and a substantial public housing programme, carried on by the South Australian Housing Trust which has reached the dimension of building a new town at Elizabeth about 25 kilometres north of the capital. Policy measures like this were allied to the containment of growth by powers to allow development only where water supply and sewerage facilities could be economically provided. Nevertheless a State Planning Authority was set up in 1967, and at the same time the 1962 Scheme, with revisions, was adopted as the Metropolitan Development Plan.

Perth was fortunate in that an advisory plan was prepared before institutional arrangements were formally devised for metropolitan planning. In 1952 the government of Western Australia commissioned such a study which was prepared by Professor Stephenson, an English academic and consultant, and J. A. Hepburn, the town planning commissioner. The advisory plan contained important legal and administrative recommendations and led to the establishment of the Metropolitan Region Planning Authority in 1960 to put the advisory plan into statutory form and implement it. The statutory scheme was adopted in 1963 and a longer-term and revised version of it in 1970. The Planning Authority has representatives of large public agencies and local government in Perth on it and its administrative and technical staff is provided by the State Town Planning Department.

In Tasmania, the Southern Metropolitan Master Planning Authority was set up in 1957, and includes Hobart. It comprises representatives of local government within its area. Development pressures are not as urgent or as complex as in other State capital cities, and its activities have been of a lower key.

Statutory land use controls have been of limited use in controlling and guiding post-war urban growth, and Harrison (1974) considers 'the broad course of growth and change within the existing urban area has not been impeded'. Other positive policy measures are needed on the part of governments to ensure better environments and improved welfare for people and this action has been most apparent in South Australia. However, the structure of Commonwealth-States financial relationships means that the central government must come to the party. The Federal Labor government devised or stepped up programmes to help in provision of sewerage, water supply, roads, public transport and the buying of substantial tracts of land on the edges of the capital cities in order to plan and implement orderly growth. Such purchase is also meant both to help public authorities in planning the extension of their metropolitan operations, and also to dilute the rapid rise in land prices over the decade which has caused the average price of a residential lot in Sydney to reach $20,000 in 1974, by making serviced lots available for private development under stipulated conditions.

There is a limit to the extent that physical planning can help in improving urban conditions and a great deal of debate and controversy has arisen lately as to what its most effective role might be. Certainly the claims of detailed land use planning as providing the encapsulation of social, economic, environmental and political issues and thus becoming the fulcrum for providing a good life were understandably exaggerated in the early post-war years.

The accessibility of community services, the level of service provided, and the range of opportunities available in the fields of housing, education, employment, recreation, culture, health and welfare varies widely between groups. The building and location of physical facilities, their location and accessibility forms one important part of urban living but institutional arrangements governing them, e.g. housing finance structure, tax provisions on land and income, educational arrangements, the structure of public transport finance and fares are critical also. One is faced with the problem of mounting co-ordinated and consistent policies to deal with these situations when their complexities and interrelations are little understood. In addition such *metaproblems* (Cartwright, 1973) have to be subdivided organizationally and the most effective manner in which to do this and how to integrate the outputs of such units is one of the unspoken questions behind the idea of managing the cities. This presents an appropriate point at which to turn to the different organizational arrangements that presently obtain in the capital cities.

FORMS OF ORGANIZATION

Federation of the constituent States of the Commonwealth only took place this century. The states have created different systems of organization to discharge their growing responsibilities of government. Similarly, local government is created by and operates under State legislation. Consequently there are varieties and richnesses of experience of government administration and organization which have not been deeply explored and yet whose implications seem relevant to the question of managing the cities. For example, environmental protection and planning, the control of land use, provision of physical and social infrastructure, the levels of service and opportunities present in different parts of the city are all considerations that are perceived and handled in different ways in each State. This gives these aspects varying relationships one with another and presents different profiles of co-ordination.

Fig. 18.2 makes this point by comparing the organizational structure for the planning and delivery of selected public services between the two capital cities which probably differ most in this regard—Sydney and Brisbane. The diagrams are notional but the pattern presented shows the fragmented nature of Sydney's operations with functions shared by State, metropolitan, sub-metropolitan and local authorities. The more monolithic construct apparent in Brisbane reflects the fact that the city contains most of the metropolitan area's population and has an array of powers, duties, responsibilities and resources not available to the many local government bodies in Sydney.

In contrast to the Sydney situation the City of Brisbane provides an example of a two-tier authority supplying many metropolitan-wide services and also the local street-by-street services needed by every suburb. Nevertheless a recent commentary on Brisbane's government (Australian Institute of Urban Studies, 1973) complained:

> The specific allocation of functions, duties and powers are sometimes inappropriate, and, in particular, the disposition of the State Government to assume local government functions or to transfer them to *ad hoc* authorities is productive of confusion, frustration, friction and overall inefficiency in metropolitan government.

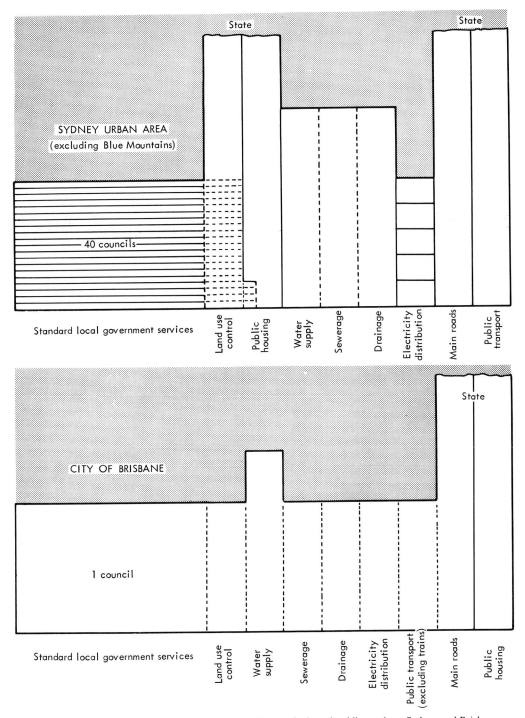

Fig. 18.2 Profiles of government organizations for delivery of selected public services: Sydney and Brisbane.

Efficiency is one important quality of government which might justify amalgamation of the smaller local government areas in some State capital cities, but responsiveness of and participation in government may pull in the other direction. There are tensions apparent in the various governing systems devised to guide and control the growth, change and character of the State capital cities. Recent movements include the development of various kinds and scales of sub-metropolitan—or regional—improvements initiated mainly by the Federal government, and the growth of action, protest and liaison groups to express small-area response to proposals or problems posed by bigger authorities of all kinds, whether they be local government bodies, quasi-independent agencies or State instrumentalities.

Melbourne's organizational structure is one somewhere between those illustrated for Sydney and Brisbane. The Melbourne and Metropolitan Board of Works, it has already been pointed out, has a bundle of related functions concerning water supply, sewerage, drainage, land use planning, park planning and provision, and responsibility for inner area roads and foreshores (although some of these activities have just been removed from its sphere of jurisdiction). While it acts as a second-tier government body between the State and local levels of government, there are also more local government authorities in its area than in Sydney and these exercise much the same range of functions as their Sydney counterparts.

It should be appreciated that many authorities with state-wide functions are organized internally to deal specifically and separately with the capital city. Recently the Federal government has put forward a regional framework for information collection, budgeting and planning that subdivides each of the capital cities into several regions (Department of Urban and Regional Development, 1973). There are hopes that these will be accepted and adopted widely, but this depends partly on how strongly various concepts and scales of *regionalization* and *regionalism* are pursued.

Among other interesting organizational forms are the different arrangements for environmental planning and control encompassing a range of interests which includes the qualities of the built environment; the control and regulation of pollution in air, water and on land; and waste disposal. In Queensland, New South Wales and Victoria different organizations have been provided which split and combine these functions in different ways. In Victoria there is a relatively independent Environment Protection Authority, in Queensland environmental planning is the responsibility of the State Coordinator-General of Works and in New South Wales care of the environment has been associated with strategic land use

planning in the formation of the Planning and Environment Commission.

SYDNEY

Tables 18.1 and 18.2 indicate that Sydney's present position as the largest city in Australia has also been a matter of history except for the latter half of the nineteenth century. There was little effort at guiding its development before World War II, although railway lines possessing important structural consequences on the form of the city were constructed which were sometimes ahead of effective demand at various times. Sometimes these initiatives did not attract the necessary associated services, such as sewerage, necessary to support the development stimulated. In local areas, residential district proclamations could be made where the intrusion of flats and non-residential activities into designated residential areas was prohibited.

In 1945 the State government introduced legislation for the preparation of town and country planning schemes by local government. To take account of the unique circumstances of the capital city, the Cumberland County Council was set up to prepare a regional plan for Sydney. Initial proposals were that the State Minister for Local Government should do this with the help of an advisory committee, but this idea was dropped, partly because of representation made by the Local Government Association. With energy and enthusiasm the plan was prepared and submitted within the three years prescibed. It was basically a land use plan and its ideas and methods followed closely the former plans prepared by Forshaw and Abercrombie for London in 1943 and 1944. This process involved a long-term estimate of population for the city which was then allocated spatially to residential, working and leisure areas through appropriate density figures. These locations were sited and related one to another by certain principles such as minimization of journey to work and of congestion and appropriate transportation channels provided. A green belt was thrown round the urban area to consolidate development and use up a large supply of prematurely subdivided and scattered land whose extent had run beyond the fiat of physical and social facilities. The plan was permeated by a sense of purpose and idealism. The statutory scheme put forward was described as (Cumberland County Council, 1948)

> midway between present conditions and the ultimate ideal. It does not embody all of the bolder features which were concerned in its preparation; but is strictly confined within present limitations. It recognises that great changes must occur in the County of today, that some semblance of order must be drawn from the present chaos before seeking final objectives and that the attitude of the people requires that the change be gradual.

Plate 18.1 The central area of Sydney (1973) looking south across the harbour to the original site of European settlement in Australia at Circular Quay (Sydney Cove) bracketed by the Harbour Bridge and the Opera House. Behind is the business district. In the foreground the Warringah Expressway has been constructed through some of the inner northern suburbs. Smog above.

State parliament hesitated for three years before adopting the plan, with some amendments. One deletion was a Council proposal that it be given power to require public authorities to co-ordinate their works programmes where this was necessary to implement the scheme. The Commonwealth government was approached for financial help to carry out the plan, but the then Prime Minister Mr R. G. Menzies refused.

In 1959 the then Minister for Local Government released most of the green belt for urban development. The plan had underestimated population growth pressures: it had provided urban areas within the green belt for a peak population of 2.4 million by 1972. This did not accord with the pace and trajectory of growth as Table 18.2 shows but the Council did not revise its plan, nor was it able to devise mechanisms to promote Campbelltown in the southwest as a satellite town beyond the green belt offering some alternative to peripheral expansion in the way that the British government did with London. Eventually pressure from a variety of sources convinced the Minister he must breach the green belt which the Council regarded as permanent. These sources included the Housing Commission seeking outer broad acres to build efficiently if bluntly, the more perceptive—or more cynical—private developers who had bought acres of land in the green belt in anticipation of its release, and local councils who wanted growth. Logan (1968a) has also criticized the plan for its inflexibility and insensitivity to the processes of urban growth and change, although he also attributed some of its shortcomings to 'lack of executive power on the part of the planning authority'.

In 1963, different arrangements were made for dealing with Sydney's problems, when the State

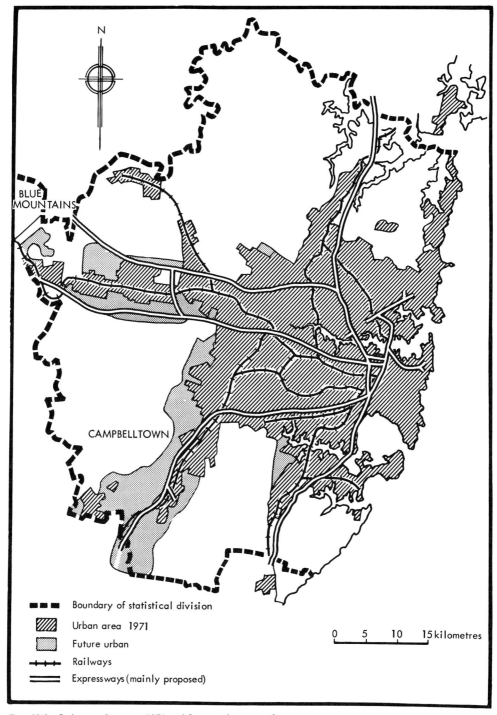

Fig. 18.3   Sydney: urban area 1971 and future urban growth.

Planning Authority was established and took over the responsibilities of the Cumberland County Council, together with other functions. Significantly it was made subject at all times to the direction and control of the Minister for Local Government although its Board contained a mixture of part-time members from State or metropolitan authorities (notably the Metropolitan Water Sewerage and Drainage Board—see Fig. 18.2) and local government.

The breathing space given by the 1959 green belt releases was only sufficient for a few years and did not provide a long-term or co-ordinated response to growth needs. In 1968 the Authority produced the Sydney Region Outline Plan to show the principles upon which a likely population of about 5 million people might be accommodated in a widely defined Sydney area by the turn of the century. There was a shift in emphasis from land use planning to planning and programming appropriate to 'relating major works programmes in communications, public utilities and other public services to the activities of private developers'. In form the plan provided for extensions of the urban area as corridors whose spine was formed by suburban railways. It included staging proposals for the release of land as serviced. In partial implementation of its plan, the Authority has vigorously pressed and planned for the growth of Campbelltown, a satellite town in the earlier *schema* and has been able to influence the operation of other State agencies in the development of expressways, railway service, housing, water supply and sewerage, as well as co-operating with local government and developers. The proposed areas of peripheral growth, the railways and the expressways system proposed by the State Department of Main Roads are shown in Fig. 18.3. Over the years some of the immense public costs attendant on low density urban growth have been passed on to developers and, inevitably, to the consumer to some degree. Following the green belt releases of 1959, the Cumberland County Council had successfully argued for an impost on developers to pay for water and sewerage reticulation and some share of the cost of trunk mains. In 1970 legislation provided that part of the increase in value of non-urban land on development should be collected by the State to help provide necessary public services. In 1973 this 30 per cent levy was dropped. Land prices have risen greatly in the past few years and rapid population growth and household formation, high cost of providing services, speculation in land and the inability to provide a large reservoir and spectrum of locational opportunities on the periphery, together with other reasons, have variously been advanced as the major causes. Conscientious and publicized programming of serviced land releases removes much uncertainty from the operations of large developers and it is maintained that one of the consequences of the Outline Plan is in identifying areas and timing of urban expansion to their benefit.

As already mentioned, the Labor government had announced its intention of providing large funds to acquire land on the periphery of metropolitan areas in co-operation with the States, and to make it available for development by public and private enterprise under appropriate conditions.

The problems of peripheral growth and its control have naturally tended to attract the attention of the planning authorities following the experience of the 'fifties and 'sixties. Too much emphasis has been given to this and, for example, less understanding has developed and less effective development of consistent policy bundles has taken place in transportation/land use planning, and in guiding changes in the existing built-up area—particularly the inner suburbs. This lack of enrichment has also handicapped the investigation of alternative forms of action. This partly reflects the lack of resources of the metropolitan planning authority—whatever its complexion, its low status in the bureaucratic pecking order, and a lack of recognition that capital city problems are not the sole responsibility of an agency concerned primarily with the use of land but require difficult delineation and co-ordination of related policies across a variety of fields.

The Outline Plan has never been formally adopted by the State government in the way that the Cumberland Scheme was, nor has it any specific statutory basis. But it has been widely accepted as an authoritative and convenient vehicle for the co-ordination of public and private investment decisions underwritten in particular by the phasing of land releases in conjunction with the provision of underground services by the Metropolitan Water Sewerage and Drainage Board.

Fig. 18.3 shows the urban areas expected to be developed by the end of the century to accommodate a population of 4.5 million in the Statistical Division, with another half million to the north in the Gosford area and a further half million decentralized to other parts of the State. There are already signs that the 5.5 million thus planned for at the year 2000 is a very high estimate. Birth rates are lower, overseas immigration less and Sydney's proportion of Australia's population dropping.

The Sydney Area Transportation Study, finished in 1974, was meant to provide what the State Minister for Transport calls a 'blueprint for passenger transport planning in the Sydney region for the balance of this century'. As the report modestly put it, 'Planners must have the foresight to visualize the future urban society as the community would like it to be, and reconcile these ideas with economic, financial and technological feasibility'. As the titles of the summary reports imply, the study is very much concerned with devising total

Plate 18.2   The central area of Perth (1970). In contrast to Sydney, an older and bigger city, there are few high buildings and there are large areas of car parking. Both Perth and Sydney are a similar distance from the open ocean, but Perth has no port function.

systems of surface movement by bus, train, car, truck and ferry for freight and passengers at the magical year 2000. Like the Outline Plan no significant alternatives are canvassed, apart from minor variations in the level of central area employment. The total systems may work at the year 2000 but are unlikely to deal effectively with problems *en route* and they will only work at the end of the century if certain critical explanatory variables which fit existing travel patterns assume the pattern and importance hypothesized for them in the future.

The real power in main road building in Sydney is the State Department of Main Roads. The road proposals in the Cumberland Scheme are based on a report prepared by it in 1945. They differ little from the currently proposed expressways shown in Fig. 18.3, of which only a few miles have been built. There is little evidence here of the development of a highway grid over the urban area designed to reduce the dominance

of the central area and the concentration of traffic flows on it, and to facilitate inter-metropolitan movement. This was a principle espoused in the Outline Plan and was also meant to facilitate the emergence of strong suburban nodes of activity. The Transportation Study took its population and employment distributions from the Outline Plan, but its road proposals seem to endorse both the grid principle and the Department of Main Roads network. The inner suburban lengths of the radial network are highly controversial. On transportation grounds (Commonwealth Bureau of Roads, 1974) it can be argued that expressways on the edge of the urban area and in the outer suburbs could well complement public transport services in serving and moulding urban development: one of these possible forms being the so-called 'corridor' concept. They would be particularly valuable if provided ahead of intensive development, and in some cases this is happening. But in the inner suburbs particularly there seems little merit in so expensively duplicating existing radial links of roads and railways in order to encourage the growth of a central area served by car.

Ring, bypass or other tangential routes are needed here to avoid the central area and to help promote movement within the denser inner areas. More importantly, it can be shown that such construction often removes so-called 'slums' which in reality provide accommodation for 'low income earners, aged people, immigrant groups and residents of long standing . . . less able to adapt to major upheavals than other groups' (Commonwealth Bureau of Roads, 1974). In looking at the inner suburban portions of the proposed express-way network, the Bureau stated 'that if all these freeways were completed the social and economic benefits could be less than the cost to the community of providing these facilities'. In the latter part of 1974 demonstrations and protests accompanied attempts to demolish dwellings in order to proceed with the inner portion of the North Western Expressway.

In Sydney, problems are particularly apparent, then, in two areas of greatest change—the metropolitan periphery and developing outer suburbs and the inner suburbs. In both cases the interests of disadvantaged and handicapped groups need to be particularly understood and physical planning has an important but limited and partial part to play in this context. It can, for example, be argued that while the inner suburbs may be losing some low-income housing stock through expressway building this is less important than the infiltration of non-residential activities and middle and high income residents through such institutional factors as the operation of the land market, the system of rating, the provision of housing finance, the relative positions of tenants as against owners.

MELBOURNE

Following Sydney's post-war initiative, it was decided to prepare a statutory planning scheme for a Melbourne metropolitan area defined for the purpose and, as already mentioned, the Melbourne and Metropolitan Board of Works was given the job in 1949. The Mel-bourne Metropolitan Scheme was completed in 1954. While it was not finally adopted as a statutory plan, with amendments, until 1968, it acted as a means of controlling land use through an Interim Development Order introduced in 1955. The scheme was less prescriptive and visionary than the Cumberland Scheme. 'There was no intention of restricting the outward growth of the suburbs nor the diversion of growth to satellite towns' remarks Harrison (1974), 'as such ideas were considered to be beyond the scope of the Board's responsibilities'. This pragmatism may partly reflect the organizational association of land use planning with the provision of roads, water supply

and sewerage: it may reflect other factors such as the time-lag behind Sydney.

The scheme was meant to accommodate a population of 2.5 million mainly within 24 kilometres of the centre. By 1966 the population in the Board's area was well over 2 million and some urban development was beginning to extend beyond its boundaries. In May of that year, the then Minister for Local Government, Mr R. J. Hamer (now Premier) wrote to both the Board of Works and the Town and Country Planning Board. The latter Board was then responsible for advising the Minister on general matters relating to town and country planning, for reviewing local planning schemes and advising the Minister as to their suitability for approval. The request stated the need to plan for a region a good deal larger than the then planning area of the Board of Works, and asked for recommendations on:

1. The most desirable shape and nature of the urban community of Melbourne in the future.

2. The most suitable method of planning and regulating the future growth of the metropolis.

3. The most suitable authority or authorities to carry out such planning and supervision.

The Town and Country Planning Board gave cursory attention to the first issue, much to the second and nominated itself (with expanded powers) as the appropriate authority needed to fulfil the requirements posed in the third part. The Board of Works devoted a good deal of discussion to the first issue, some to the second, and decided that it was the ideal repository for the responsibility of planning and supervising the growth of the urban area.

The State government introduced legislation in 1968 which represented a compromise between the two submissions. The area administered by the Board of Works was trebled, it was made the responsible authority for planning this area, but was brought more under the control of the Minister. The Town and Country Planning Board was strengthened and its Chairman made the Chairman of a State Planning Council composed largely of State government depart-ment representatives. But the State government did not become involved in these operations to the extent that the New South Wales government did.

Form of city always attracts exaggerated attention, partly because of its visual impact in terms of communication. Both Boards suggested corridor ex-tensions of the urban area not unlike the Sydney proposals. But the Town and Country Planning Board (1967) indicated support for major extension in the southeast where living areas are more pleasant, climate better, and where population was growing much more rapidly. The Board of Works (1967) recommended corridor growth round most of the metropolitan perimeter with some limited satellite city growth in the

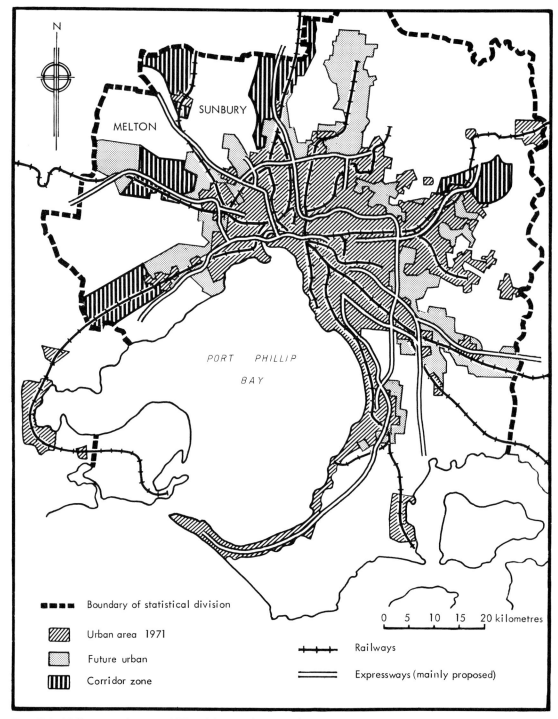

Fig. 18.4   Melbourne: urban area 1971 and future urban growth.

north and west 'where special stimulus is required'. Servicing economies for water supply and sewerage occur if even extension of the built-up area takes place. The Board's close relationship to local government authorities also makes an even-handed approach appropriate. In the 1968 debates on the legislation, Mr Hamer tended to favour the Board of Works proposals: 'the Government adopts, as a matter of conscious policy, that Melbourne should be encouraged to follow a "corridor" type of development'. He also endorsed the stimulation of growth in the north and west to redress 'the lopsided pattern of the growth of the metropolis over the last three decades'.

Within these broad guidelines, the Board was asked to present detailed proposals and amending planning schemes to extend planning control over the whole of its expanded area. In 1971 in *Planning Policies for the Metropolitan Region*, it suggested a number of mechanisms to do this. In 1967 the Board had considered a 5 million population as likely in the Statistical Division (larger than its planning region) by the turn of the century. This pace of growth had already perceptibly dropped by 1971, the report of that year mentioned a figure of 4.5 million as more likely. That report proposed that the eight corridors of growth shown in Fig. 18.4 should be endorsed so that 'all future outward development should be contained within these corridors, but this type of development should not necessarily occupy the whole of each corridor at any point in time'. This, it was thought, enabled freedom of manoeuvre to be given for the deployment of one or two basic strategies. One would maintain the central area as the dominant centre and actively encourage growth in each of the corridors simultaneously. The other would select one or two corridors having the best potential for growth and concentrate resources on supporting them. In either case expansive corridor delimitation would help: in the light of events it would be possible to switch from the first (preferred) alternative to the second if necessary, as it was maintained that the difference between the two alternatives was only one of emphasis. A resort to euphemism was required to make this point. Comments were invited. And arrived. Many raised broad policy issues not normally ventilated in the statutory procedures governing the preparation of planning schemes. For example, there was much criticism directed to the idea of planning to accommodate metropolitan growth to the order of 4 or 5 millions. The Board was moved to produce a *Report on General Concept Objections* in 1974. It backed more positively the first alternative discussed in 1971, but also said:

> In the current situation of changing attitudes of Governments and the public, it is considered that the basic concept of the corridor zone is sound and that it should be retained, but with different emphasis. It should not be given particular recognition as a potential area for future urban development but rather should be regarded as a non-urban zone set aside to provide an option for longer term decision making.

More significantly it recognized the emerging concern over social issues:

> objectors acknowledged the legislative deficiencies, which tend to limit the Board's role primarily to physical planning but they nevertheless considered that no planning scheme could operate satisfactorily unless proper consideration was given to social aspects. It was further submitted that the Board was in an ideal position to combine social and physical planning functions because of its already wide role as a planning and servicing organisation.

On this latter point Melbourne, like Sydney, suffers from large-scale social segregation. The inner suburbs and most of the urban areas to the north and west have concentrations of disadvantaged and handicapped populations. Different interpretations were put on how the form, direction and pace of metropolitan growth might be of relevance to their problems. The Victorian Council of Social Service supported the old Board of Works' idea of balanced growth around the metropolitan area on the grounds that this would help people in the northern and western suburbs. But it recognized the need for more direction than providing ample opportunities for growth all round and then responding to patterns of demand. It contended that clear priority should be given to the provision of services in the north and west to support and sustain people in need and also to make them attractive for middle and higher income people. Other representations (R. and M. Crow, 1972) objected to this concept on a number of grounds and advocated a rounding off of development in the north and west accompanied by the introduction of innovative social and welfare services and an open university. They maintained that all groups should be accommodated in a concentrated linear development thrusting eastwards in the more attractive living environments present there and supported by mass transit. In the 1974 review of these objections, the Board felt moved to reassert its wavering traditional faith in concentrated balanced development.

In March 1974 the Premier endorsed the concept of corridors with their interleaving permanent non-urban wedges. He set in train a series of studies to indicate which parts of the corridors should be developed. 'This means', he stated, 'that the urban prospects of some corridor segments will be postponed indefinitely.' He also indicated satellite city status for Sunbury and Melton to the northwest of the metropolis where 'the activities of private enterprise there will receive Government support'.

A Ministerial Statement in May by Mr Hunt, Minister

Plate 18.3 A sector of suburban Melbourne (1969) showing mixed uses, a general grid pattern of development, completed growth so that densities of activity are higher than further out, and all-pervading traffic. *Photo*: Melbourne *Age*.

for Local Government, underlined this supporting rather than initiating role and maintained that government interest in the north and west was intended (Victorian Legislative Council *Hansard*, 2 May 1974, pp. 5196–5202)

> to uplift the urban quality of these sectors and recognizes that the range of employment opportunities and activities of every description could be broadened and improved through the existance of a larger and more diverse work force and population.

Transportation problems in Melbourne are not as great as in Sydney with, *inter alia*, its difficult topographical conditions. A Transportation Plan adopted in 1969 envisaged the construction of almost 500 kilometres of expressways by 1985. Only a small length had been built by 1973, amidst such opposition to some proposals that the Victorian government cut the plan by half, removing almost all the controversial sections in the inner areas. The resultant modified and partial system is shown in Fig. 18.4.

An impressionistic comparison of present metro-politan planning arrangements in Sydney and Melbourne would suggest some co-ordination of related if limited decisions in the former city reflecting in particular the peripheral growth there. In Melbourne no prescriptive statement exists which could be compared with the Sydney Region Outline Plan, but there is an attempt, however faltering, to explore the social implications of different patterns of development. Many of these social issues, however, may find more immediate relevance in factors and circumstances outside the purview and control of metropolitan planning agencies heretofore—for example in those influencing the availability of housing, employment and transportation to different groups in society.

CONCLUSION

Australian capital cities contain an increasing majority of the continent's population. In the 'fifties, town planners were in difficulty when they based long-term proposals on low rates of growth. There were problems in raising the level of accommodation when these expectations were not realized, and there was a lack of public initiative in promoting alternative and acceptable urban centres. In the 'sixties this was replaced by planning for metropolitan areas almost double their present size by the end of the century. The endorsement of this trend, although it could be interpreted as contingency planning in the face of forces not under the control or influence of town planners, raised basic questions about the rate and pace of growth of cities and the living environment they provided.

The urban areas have spread, supported in the last twenty years by the private car. Outer suburban densities are generally low: slightly lower in rich areas, a little higher for poorer groups with smaller cottage lots, typically living in the less pleasant environments— sometimes flat, often treeless, frequently with poorer microclimates. In the larger cities flat-building has become important, initially as a redevelopment activity, giving a ripple effect with a gradual spread in the importance of flats outwards from the inner to the intermediate and finally the outer suburbs. Most inner suburbs have lost population in the last two decades. Accompanying this has been a suburbanization of activities, most pronounced in retailing, less so in manufacturing industry and least so in those based in offices (other than local medical, accountancy, legal services and the like).

This apparently comfortable reorganization of the cities into new structures and forms, most conveniently interpreted as changing the monolithic centripetal pattern of the past into multicentred surfaces with linear extensions, faces some strong challenges. Probably the greatest source of unease is the realization that some groups in society are being penalized to the advantage of others in many of the currents and forces working in the urban scene. Further, the proposition that these influences work to the benefit of the comfortable, the prosperous, the established, the middle-class and not to that of the poor, the deviant, the sick, the single-head household, the migrant, the unlucky, the eccentric and the uneducated. Further, that many of the decisions made in planning the metropolitan areas have been based on a concept of community welfare enhanced by physical determinism, rather than of individual welfare promoted by suites of interrelated actions in fields of social, economic and physical policy.

These themes permeate in different ways the work in Australian cities carried out by the Urban Research Unit (1973) with its concern for equity and a leading role for government policies; by Patricia Apps (1973) with analysis of the distribution of real income, urban services and the relative price of services facing different income and family groups; and by Frank Stilwell (1974) who sees 'regional and urban problems as the spatial expression of the more general problems of the socio-economic system'. More generally Harvey (1973) has attributed urban ills to the defects of a particular type of political economy.

The capital cities are complex problem areas, not amenable to easy solutions. Cartwright (1973) points to the danger of using simple holistic approaches to deal with such complex arenas causing a mismatch between the true nature of the problem and the strategy employed to deal with it:

> Ultimately things may resolve themselves. Either the strategy will force a change in the problem or the problem will force a change in the strategy. For example persistent efforts to apply comprehensive strategies to a meta-problem will eventually reduce it to a simple problem—whether the planner intends it or not. Thus insistence on a guaranteed annual income as the solution of the problem of poverty leads eventually to perceiving poverty as a simple problem of inadequate income. The fact that some people may still have no job, insufficient education and training, inadequate housing and so on become separate (if no less important) problems.

Briefly, new directions and emphases may be needed in approaching capital city problems, demanding new skills and new axes of analysis and synthesis. Also required are planning processes and control mechanisms that provide sufficient variety to appreciate complexity and a capacity to learn and respond as understanding develops. There would be less emphasis on establishing highly structured relationships of specific elements and more attention to adjustment, intelligent probing and assemblage of bigger and bigger bundles of consistent and related policies as their nature is established. To this end, this chapter ends with a series of brief comments on research and policy needs on metropolitan sub-regions, on the time dimension of planning and on organization.

Research is needed into the lifestyles and behaviour of groups living in the urban scene, and how these are conditioned by the pricing of the goods and services they use or aspire to use. This implies less emphasis on aggregated descriptive studies of activities and structures and more attention to selective exploration of areas where particular problems are concentrated, and to the difficulties of struggling groups of people. These circumstances are likely to be the result of congeries of forces set up by the interplay of policies, practices and procedures deployed by the three levels of government. Such research should be aimed to uncover policy implications.

Second, the systems approach, most apparent in transportation studies, has projected a total metropolitan view which has decided monolithic overtones. Studies by Logan (1968b) suggest 'sub-regional integration of areas, such as residential areas and workplaces of different types is developing': Blackshaw (1974) in reviewing the Sydney Area Transportation Study has postulated there is little interaction between some of the parts of Sydney so that sub-regional transportation models could profitably be developed: this theme has been expressed in conceptual terms by a recent discussion of transportation planning processes appropriate to times of change and uncertainty (Hansen and Lockwood, 1974). In this way, while looking beyond local problem-solving, more attention could be given to sub-regions whose inhabitants have particularly difficult problems and the appropriate policy measures taken.

Third, long-range perspectives might be better developed as objectives rather than trying to guide physical development to one target. Emphasis could then be switched to developing shorter-term related policies which are modified and made more mutually supportive as insight develops and as circumstances change. These decisions would have to be carefully assessed so that their implementation would keep as many options open as possible. Such decisions would be changes like building a large dam, constructing incentives to guide enterprises to particular kinds of locations, enlarging a port, altering company tax structure or the degree of subisdy given to road building.

Finally organization affects the definition of urban problems and, inevitably, the measures taken to deal with them. There are differences between the States in organizational structures which are illuminating, but nevertheless the principles on which they are based bear re-examination. While the task of urban governance has to be spilt up, new compartments seem necessary with new clusterings, to reflect more sensitively the needs of modern urban societies. It would be particularly useful to devise mechanisms that do not clearly separate fields of social policy, economic policy and the building of physical facilities so that the interactions between and substitution possibilities among these decisions are exposed rather than ignored. Housing is an obvious catalyst.

A recent publication (C.E.S. Working Group, 1973) concerned with developing the knowledge and capability for urban governance suggested

> There are signs that we seek to be less rigid in our policies and in our planning and managing procedures. While we see the value of producing "plans" for some purposes and some time scales, we want to invest more conscious effort than before in transforming not only the output but also the structure and processes of our institutions, so that they become adaptive learning organisations that can produce continuous good decisions in changing situations with changing resources.

REFERENCES

Apps, P. F. (1973), 'A critique of urban planning, directions for research', *R. Aust. Plann. Inst. J.*, 11, 8–15.

Australian Institute of Urban Studies (1973), *Managing the Cities: an Evaluation*, Canberra.

Blackshaw, P. W. (1974), 'The Sydney Area Transportation Study—an economic review', *Aust. Q.*, 46, 56–68.

Bryson, L. and Thompson, F. (1972), *An Australian New-town: life and leadership in a new housing suburb*, Penguin, Ringwood, Victoria.

Bunker, Raymond (1963), 'Comparative analyses of urban workforces', *R. Aust. Plann. Inst. J.*, 2, 116–20.

Burnley, I. H. (1974a), 'International migration and metropolitan growth in Australia' in I. H. Burnley (ed.), *Urbanization in Australia*, Cambridge University Press, Cambridge, pp. 99–117.

——(1974b), 'Urbanization and social segregation' in I. H. Burnley, (ed.), *Urbanization in Australia*, Cambridge University Press, Cambridge, pp. 131–46.

Butlin, N. G. (1958), 'The shape of the Australian economy 1861–1900', *Econ. J.*, 34, 10–29.

Cartwright, T. J. (1973), 'Problems, solutions and strategies: a contribution to the theory and practice of planning', *J. Am. Inst. Plann.*, 39, 179–86.

Centre for Environmental Studies Working Group (1973), 'Education for planning', *Progress in Planning*, 1, 1–108.

Clark, Colin (1970), 'Economics of urban areas' in N. Clark, (ed.), *Analysis of Urban Development*, Proceedings of the Tewksbury Symposium, Department of Civil Engineering, University of Melbourne, pp. 1.3–1.24.

Commonwealth Bureau of Census and Statistics (1972), *Journey to Work and Journey to School May 1970*, Canberra.

Commonwealth Bureau of Roads (1973), *Report on Roads in Australia*, Melbourne.

——(1974), *Assessment of Freeway Plans, State Capital Cities*, Melbourne.

Crow, R. and M. (1972), *One Corridor of Participants—not Seven Corridors of Power: an objection (alternative) to the Melbourne Regional Plan proposals*, Victorian State Committee of Communist Party of Australia, Melbourne.

Cumberland County Council (1948), *The Planning Scheme for the County of Cumberland, New South Wales*, Sydney.

Davis, J. R. and Spearritt, Peter (1974), *Sydney at the Census, 1971*, Urban Research Unit, Australian National University, Canberra.

Department of Urban and Regional Development (1973), *Regions*, Canberra.

——(1974), *Urban Land Prices 1968–1974*, Urban Paper, Canberra.

Gutschenwager, G. A. (1973), 'The time-budget—activity systems perspective in urban research and planning', *J. Am. Inst. Plann.*, 39, 378–87.

Hansen, W. G. and Lockwood, S. C. (1974), 'Transportation planning in a changing environment: principles for a new process', *AMV tech notes*, 1, 1–17.

Harrison, Peter (1974), 'Planning the metropolitan areas' in I. H. Burnley (ed.), *Urbanization in Australia*, Cambridge University Press, Cambridge, pp. 203–20.

Harvey, D. (1973), *Social Justice and the City*, Arnold, London.

Henderson, R. F., Harcourt, Alison and Harper, R. J. A. (1970), *People in Poverty: a Melbourne Survey*, Cheshire for the Institute of Applied Economic and Social

Research, University of Melbourne.

Jakubowicz, A. (1972), 'A new politics of suburbia', *Current Affairs Bulletin*, 48, 338–51.

Johnston, R. J. (1971), *Urban Residential Patterns*, G. Bell, London.

Lawrence, R. J. (1972), 'Social welfare and urban growth' in R. S. Parker and P. N. Troy (eds), *The politics of Urban Growth*, Australian National University Press, Canberra, pp. 100–28.

le Breton, P. (1974), *Poverty*, Department of Urban and Regional Development Urban Paper, Canberra.

Logan, M. I. (1968a), 'Capital city development' in G. H. Dury and M. I. Logan (eds), *Studies in Australian Geography*, Heinemann, Melbourne, pp. 245–301.

——(1968b), 'Work-residence relationships in the city', *Aust. Geogr. Stud.*, 6, 151–66.

McCarty, J. W. (1970), 'Australian capital cities in the nineteenth century', *Aust. Econ. Hist. Rev.*, 10, 107–37.

McClelland, M. (1968), 'Needs and services in an outer suburb', *Aust. J. Social Issues*, 3, 44–62.

Marsden, B. S. (1970), 'Temporal aspects of urban population densities; Brisbane, 1861–1966', *Aust. Geogr. Stud.*, 8, 71–83.

Melbourne and Metropolitan Board of Works (1967), *The Future Growth of Melbourne*, Melbourne.

——(1971), *Planning Policies for the Melbourne Metropolitan Region*, Melbourne.

——(1974), *Report on General Concept Objections, 1974*, Melbourne.

Murphy, R. P. (1970), 'Air pollution and urban development', *R. Aust. Plann. Inst. J.*, 8, 67–76.

Parker, R. S. and Troy P. N. (eds) (1972), *The Politics of Urban Growth*, Australian National University Press, Canberra.

Robinson, K. W. (1963), 'The distinctive character of Australian urban growth' in *Readings in Urban Growth*, Univ. Syd. Dept Geogr. and Geogr. Soc. N.S.W., Sydney, pp. 1–17.

State Planning Authority of New South Wales (1968), *Sydney Region Outline Plan*, Sydney.

Stewart, C. T. (1959), 'The size and spacing of cities' in H. M. Mayer and F. C. Kohn (eds), *Readings in Urban Geography*, Chicago University Press, Chicago, pp. 240–56.

Stilwell, F. J. B. (1974), *Australian Urban and Regional Development*, Australia and New Zealand Book Company, Sydney.

Stilwell, F. J. B. and Hardwick, J. M. (1973), 'Social inequality in Australian cities', *Aust. Q.*, 16, 56–68.

Stimson, R. J. (1974), 'The social structure of large cities' in I. H. Burnley (ed.), *Urbanization in Australia*, Cambridge University Press, Cambridge, pp. 147–63.

Stretton, Hugh (1970), *Ideas for Australian Cities*, Georgian House, Melbourne.

Sydney Area Transportation Study (1974), *Passenger Transport Systems: Summary Report*, Sydney.

Timms, D. (1971), *The Urban Mosaic*, Cambridge University Press, Cambridge.

Town and Country Planning Board of Victoria (1967), *Organisation for Strategic Planning*, Melbourne.

Urban Research Unit, Australian National University (1973), *Urban Development in Melbourne: aspects of the post-war experience*, Australian Institute of Urban Studies, Canberra.

Webber, M. and Daly, M. T. (1971), 'Spatial and temporal variations in short term industrial change within cities', *Aust. Geogr. Stud.*, 9, 15–32.

19 THE URBAN SYSTEM

J. H. HOLMES

The structure and behaviour of the Australian urban system, long a subject for academic comment, have over the last decade come under closer scrutiny from researchers, commentators, politicians and planners. This increasing interest is largely stirred by growing public concern about the directions of change in the system, notably by the increasing concentration of people and economic activity in a few large cities. Following the failure of State-sponsored decentralization programmes, there has been a growing demand for the articulation of national policies and the formulation of nationwide strategies for urban development, a demand to which national government has only recently responded. This in turn creates a demand for basic research into centrifugal and centripetal forces within the system, as well as into the advantages and disadvantages of decentralization.

The Australian urban system is very typical of a modern, westernized country. If there is anything unusual about it, then it is primarily in its role as a pacesetter in the current general trend towards urbanization and metropolitan agglomeration. It also shows much less complexity than do those of Western Europe or North America, and it still retains many characteristics resulting from its evolution as a fragmented set of six urban systems, based on the six States, each revealing a relatively uncomplicated hierarchical structure, centralized on one multifunctional primate city, with a dearth of other medium-sized to large cities. Differences in detail cannot obscure the basic parallelism in the evolution of the intrastate systems and in their separatism, each being highly integrated and self-contained, and, at least until recently, oriented more towards international rather than interstate links. Only Sydney, Melbourne, Canberra and a few industrial cities have assumed any major nationwide role.

The urban system is undergoing continuing change. Its most dominant characteristic, metropolitan concentration, is becoming more pronounced, particularly in States where concentration is most extreme. However, there are other dynamic elements within the system which may become of increasing importance: there is an increasing degree of integration at the

national level, initially expressed in intermetropolitan interaction and in cross-border penetration of previously sharply demarcated metropolitan hinterlands, offering opportunities for growth at non-metropolitan locations to serve national markets; there has been persistent rapid growth in the larger regional centres, stimulated by the acquisition of new functions which enhance their status as emerging regional capitals; and there has been the unprecedented growth in specialized towns, notably in mining towns, resort centres and metropolitan satellites. Also of possible significance for the future evolution of the system has been the intervention of the national government in regional and urban development.

THE DEGREE OF METROPOLITAN PRIMACY

Australia's extraordinary degree of metropolitan concentration in population has been described in detail in Chapter 15. The marked discrepancy in size between each State's first- and second-ranking city has often been discussed and compared with other States or provinces in federated nations (K. W. Robinson, 1962; Rose, 1966, 1967). Useful comparisons can be made with the United States and Canada, which resemble Australia in being newly settled, westernized countries occupying vast areas under a federal system of government. In all Australian States, save only Tasmania, the 1971 population of the largest city was more than ten times greater than the next ranking city. The appropriate population multipliers were: Western Australia 30.5, South Australia 25.3, Victoria 20.8, Queensland 11.0, New South Wales 10.9, and Tasmania 2.1. In the Canadian urban system, half the provinces have multipliers of less than 2, while only two have multipliers greater than 5, the highest being Saskatchewan with 7.5. The United States closely resembles Canada. In 1971, twenty-three States had multipliers of less than 2, while only four had multipliers greater than 10. Two of these, Hawaii and Rhode Island, are territorially small 'city states', while in a third, Illinois, the city of Chicago exerts dominance over an area reaching well beyond its own State. Only in the fourth State, Minnesota, do the twin cities of Minneapolis-St Paul dominate a sharply defined tributary region in a manner comparable to that found in all Australian mainland States.

To enable comparative analysis of city-size distributions, urban theorists have developed standard measures based upon rank/size relationship, which are commonly depicted in graph form (Fig. 19.1). Using a logarithmic scale on each axis, towns in an urban 'system' can be plotted in order of population size, and a line drawn through the plotted points. A straight-line plot indicates a constant rate of population decrease with decrease in rank. Zipf (1949) stated this relationship mathematically, as follows:

$$r \times P_r^q = K$$

where r is the rank of a particular city; P_r is the population of that city; and q and K are constants. This regularity is typical of many city-size distributions and is known as the rank-size rule (Berry, 1961). When q has a value of 1.0, the value of K is equal to the population of the largest city, P_1, and the formula can be restated simply as:

$$r \times P_r = P_1$$

This exact one-for-one inverse relationship between size and rank is sometimes described as the 'normal' rank/size relationship. However, it is generally confined to complex, diversified countries with a long history of urbanization, though, interestingly, it has prevailed in the American urban system from at least 1790 onwards (Madden, 1958; Yeates and Garner, 1971). Commonly the value of q is less than one.

Fig. 19.1 shows that, apart from the dual status of Sydney and Melbourne as national metropolises, the Australian urban system conforms approximately to the 'normal' rank/size relationship for the five largest cities, with Perth having close to one-fifth of Sydney's population. The marked divergence between the Australian and the 'normal' lines from rank six to rank ten indicates a lack of medium-sized metropolitan centres in Australia, centres which currently should have populations between 450,000 (rank six) and 270,000 (rank ten). For lower ranks, the normal relationship is resumed as indicated by the parallel lines, but all further-ranking cities are markedly below those predicted by the rule. Thus Geelong, ranked ten, has 115,000 instead of a predicted 271,000, and Cairns, rank twenty, has 33,000 instead of 136,000, and so on throughout the further ranks.

The creation of five entirely new metropolitan centres with populations between 450,000 and 270,000 would enable the Australian system to conform to the 'normal' distribution. Proposed new city programmes are initially directed towards much less ambitious objectives, with target populations for Albury-Wodonga, Vittoria (Bathurst-Orange) and Monarto being much smaller. Even assuming these targets were swiftly reached, and this assumption may be un-realistic, the continued growth of the large cities would certainly ensure a persistence of the present rank/size distribution.

Reasons for Metropolitan Concentration

The economic advantages of concentration have been fully examined by location theorists, with emphasis upon economies of scale in public and private investment; access to labour, capital, markets, ancillary industries and services, and communication/information systems; also size creates opportunities for generating high-threshold activities which make the metropolis more attractive to the entrepreneur and the city-dweller.

These centralizing forces have general applicability in all westernized, urbanized, mobile, evolving societies, and cannot in themselves offer an explanation for Australia's unique position. However, Australia does conform to the general theory that single- or multiple-city primacy is found in nations where a few strong economic forces have operated (Berry, 1961). Certain special circumstances existing in Australia have been commented upon (K. W. Robinson, 1962; A. J. Robinson, 1963; Rose, 1966; McCarty, 1970; Linge, 1968), while Logan (1968) and Stilwell (1974) have provided the most lucid and comprehensive appraisals. In summary, six salient features deserve examination, with

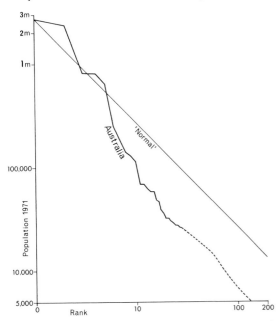

Fig. 19.1 The Australian rank-size distribution compared with the 'normal' rank-size rule.

the first two and the last of these being closely linked to general theory.

1. *The recency of Australian settlement* The urban system has developed in an era of commercialized, exchange-oriented development, with a strong emphasis on specialization and scale economies, and with concentration being favoured by improved transport and communication systems. Rose (1966), in particular, has presented a detailed, cogent set of arguments in support of the theory that metropolitan primacy is the normal state in a modern society, where urban services can be provided by a two-step hierarchy comprising a metropolis and a series of agro-towns to provide for the daily needs of the non-metropolitan population.

2. *Dependence upon overseas links* The dominance of the metropolis has been reinforced by its pivotal role as an intermediary between internal and external transactions. From the time of first settlement, the economic, financial, demographic and social development of Australia has been highly dependent upon overseas links, enabling a two-way flow of goods, and a mainly one-way flow of methods, ideas, capital, people and control. Stilwell (1973) has argued that the internationalism of the modern capitalist system reinforces primacy, with multinational corporations playing a significant role in focusing further development in the capital cities. Choi and Burnley (1974) have demonstrated how population growth in post-war Melbourne, Sydney and Adelaide in particular has been stimulated by a continuing influx of overseas migrants for whom the metropolitan cities are much stronger magnets than for internal migrants.

3. *Political/administrative institutions and policies* Unlike North America, Australia's initial colonization was tightly controlled from London. In the convict era, concentration at a few sites was favoured, and pressures for uncontrolled dispersion firmly opposed. At the same time, a few widely separated settlements were maintained, at heavy cost, so that British control could be asserted over the whole continent and also to provide the necessary level of isolation for convict settlements. Once initial settlement difficulties were overcome, these scattered nodes commanded sufficiently extensive tracts of land that they were unrivalled as foci for autonomous growth.

Centralized administrative and political institutions also favoured centralization in the private sector. As the colonies gained autonomy, the interests of each were generally equated with those of the capital city, as indicated in the rivalries to establish captive hinterlands within State boundaries, even when this retarded economic growth within these hinterlands. In spite of much-vaunted decentralization programmes, policies of State governments still generally contribute towards further centralization, as in railway freight rates (Smith, 1963) and in rivalries to attract industrial projects (Linge, 1968).

4. *Sparse population and extensive settlement* The extensive grazing pattern prevailing over much of Australia, supporting only a sparse population and creating only a modest demand for urban services, has inhibited urban growth in the inland and strengthened direct ties to coastal cities. More generally, A. J. Robinson (1963) has argued that concentration is a logical response to the problems of long distances and few people.

5. *Persistence of initial urban pattern* One neglected but important contributory factor has been the remarkable persistence of the urban pattern established during the initial settlement phase. Initial urban nodes have remained dominant, with surprisingly little change over time in the composition of the rank-order of leading urban centres. There is a striking contrast between this stability and the great changes which have occurred in the United States, arising from sharp differences in city growth rates. As Robson (1973) has recently demonstrated in a comprehensive review and substantive examination of growth histories of towns in England and Wales, differential growth rates in an urban system are not easily subject to single-cause explanations. However, one important set of circumstances clearly contributes to the differences between Australian and American urban growth patterns. These circumstances are suggested in Fig. 19.2, where the top-ranking cities in 1960 are compared with those of an earlier period, namely 1830 in the United States and 1860 in Australia. The American rankings are taken directly from Borchert (1967) and the Australian are based upon the same criteria used by Borchert. There is also a similar proportionate increase, by two-thirds, in the number of ranked cities over the time-period covered in the two countries.

By 1830 the American urban system had achieved greater maturity and complexity than had the Australian system by 1860, yet it has subsequently undergone much greater changes in the ranking of major cities, partly resulting from changes in the competitive position of cities within the eastern seaboard, but more through the rapid growth of new generations of cities, firstly with the rise of Chicago, St Louis, Cincinnati and other Midwestern cities, and subsequently with the growth of western cities such as San Francisco, Los Angeles, Houston and Seattle. Australia has experienced no comparable growth of new generations of cities, with the minor exceptions of Canberra and Wollongong, nor have any older cities experienced a major loss of status, save only Hobart. These marked differences in urban history can be explained largely in terms of changing accessibility. In the United States, the expansion of settlement across the interior to the Pacific implied a loss of overall accessibility by the established cities on the eastern seaboard, and fostered

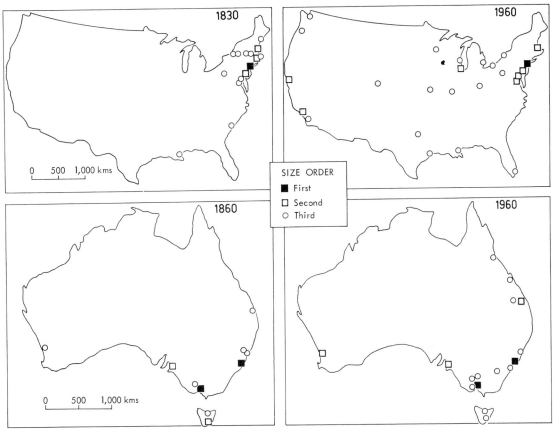

Fig. 19.2   The changing spatial distribution of major cities in the United States (1830–1960) and in Australia (1860–1960).
Sources: Borchert, 1967; and calculated by author.

the growth of many new metropolitan centres. In Australia, on the other hand, settlement expansion and consolidation has not entailed loss of accessibility by the established cities, partly because Australia's resources are peripherally located close to the coastline where the first urban nodes were located, and partly because the British government spaced these nodes strategically around the more habitable areas, initially with the idea of commanding the coastline, though subsequently these locations proved equally effective in commanding the more habitable sections of the interior.

These differences in urban evolution can also be seen in a comparison of Canadian and Australian cities, as Bourne (1974) has recently shown.

This constancy in the ranking of Australia's major cities has enabled the maximum concentration of population in a few nodes. Locational advantage has been an inexorable theme in the enduring success of Australia's large cities, and there has been no opportunity for the middle ranks of the Australian urban system

to be filled by the less successful of the older cities or by relatively successful latecomers. Nor have the larger cities experienced any retardation in growth which some urban theorists have postulated as a basic indicator of maturity in an urban system (Madden, 1958; Richardson, 1973). Indeed, a comparison of Australian and American experience raises questions about the generality of this theory, and of the related theory that the size distribution of cities is a function of their age distribution (Richardson, 1973). These theories appear to have been unduly influenced by evidence about the characteristics of 'old' and 'young' cities in the United States, whereas Australian experience shows that there is no necessity for an urban system to evolve in such a manner.

6. *Circular and cumulative processes of growth*   The importance of these processes in urban evolution has been analysed by Pred (1965). Their impact in Australia has been most pronounced because locational advantage has remained securely tied to a few major nodes. In Western Australia, for example, locational

advantage is so strongly tied to the metropolis that there is no element of choice in deciding the location of any enterprise designed to serve a state-wide market. In this situation, it is almost impossible to locate these location-conscious activities outside the capital city, save through strong governmental intervention.

In sum, the underlying causes of centralization are: the recency of settlement; overseas orientation; the peripheral distribution of resources and population; and the spacing of the initial major settlement nodes. Consequential reinforcing influences have been: politico-administrative influences; stability in the ranking of major cities; and positive feedback arising from existing high levels of concentration.

FUNCTIONS OF AUSTRALIAN TOWNS

Although a lack of comparability in data sources and in research methods prevents any precise international comparisons, undoubtedly the Australian urban system is notable for its low level of functional differentiation, indicated by a relative lack of specialized or single-function towns; for its emphasis on consumer-oriented service activities, both public and private; for an unusually low level of manufacturing activity in most towns; for the concentration of most specialized activities, including manufacturing, within the metropolitan cities rather than in specialized towns; and for recent indicators that functional specialization is beginning to gather some momentum.

Lack of Functional Specialization

Early urban studies invariably exaggerated the degree of functional specialization of towns, showing a persistent tendency to categorize each town in terms of one or two dominant functions. The pitfalls of such simplistic classifications have long been recognized, although the functional complexity of most towns, as indicated by their employment structure, has not made for easy, clear classification (Nelson, 1955; Smith, 1965). One important conceptual advance came with urban base theory, which is concerned to differentiate basic and non-basic employment within a town's economy. Basic employment is export-oriented, provides the reason for the town's existence, is generally the impulse to urban growth or decline, and reveals the functional relations of the town to its hinterland and to the rest of the economy as a whole. Non-basic employment is directed towards satisfying the internal needs of the town. Non-basic activities are highly diversified, whereas basic activities are more specialized, occasionally to a degree that single-title categorization is warranted, as occurs with many mining, resort and manufacturing towns.

Various methods have been devised for estimating the non-basic component in each employment sector

of a town's workforce, the three most widely used being Alexandersson's k-value, Ullman and Dacey's minimum-requirements method, and the location quotient (Alexandersson, 1956; Ullman and Dacey, 1962; Duncan *et al.*, 1960). These are usually described in standard texts. Criticisms of these methods need not be considered here, as none has been applied in an endeavour to classify Australian towns. More rigorous analytical procedures are now available, notably input-output analysis. McCalden's (1969) study of Muswellbrook is a pioneer work in the application of this method to gain an understanding of the economic functioning of a single town, and is of importance not only methodologically but also as a substantive contribution to an understanding of Australian towns. Unfortunately, the method cannot be applied to broad classificatory studies.

Smith, however, has carried out an equally significant exercise in functional classification of Australian towns, which has become widely recognized as an important contribution to methodology (Smith, 1965; Berry and Horton, 1970, pp. 106–23). Smith's study is of substantive value in delineating differences in the employment structures of Australian towns, and in showing their lack of marked functional differentiation. This same lack of differentiation leads to difficulties in obtaining a satisfactory classification, particularly since Smith has not used any of the 'sieves' or estimation procedures in a search for specialization in basic employment. Using data for 422 towns, from the 1954 census, Smith calculated the percentage of each town's resident workforce employed in each of twelve occupational classes. Using correlation and linkage analysis, the towns were clustered into seventeen groups based upon similarity in occupational structure. Each group was given a descriptive title according to the most clearly identifiable functional specialism of the group. The complexity of the resulting classification, and the often low degree of specialization in the different occupations, are suggested in Table 19.1, which summarizes the main results.

The Minor Role of Manufacturing

Smith's classification suggests that manufacturing towns occupy a major place in the Australian urban system, encompassing 78 towns with a population of over 5,700,000 in 1954. However, only Group One towns show a marked specialization in this activity, a group which includes the recognized large industrial towns of Newcastle, Wollongong, Maitland, Geelong, Ballarat, Ipswich, Bundaberg, Gladstone, Port Pirie, Whyalla and Burnie, as well as smaller towns noted for a variety of processing activities, including meatworks, wineries, sugar mills and paper factories.

Group Two towns deserve scrutiny, since these include the dominant towns within the urban system,

Table 19.1 Summary of Smith's Functional Classification of Australian Towns

Group number	Descriptive title	Number of towns	Total inhabitants ('000)	Differentiating industrial category	Group's average employment in category	All-town average employment in category
1		50	634		43.03	
2	Manufacturing	17	5,046	Manufacturing	30.16	19.02
3		11	33		26.40	
4		31	73		20.69	
5		24	52		21.57	
6	Service	22	82	Commerce	21.10	18.44
7		11	65		22.95	
8		9	14		25.12	
9		82	315		22.97	
10	Resort	19	55	Amusements, hotels, cafés, personal service	13.45	8.16
11		6	35		14.23	
12	Transport	23	70	Transport and storage	25.84	7.41
13	Communication	15	25	Communication	5.60	3.05
14	Mining	25	149	Mining and quarrying	50.49	3.81
15	Utilities	15	54	Electricity, gas, water, sanitary services	17.41	2.15
16	Administration	34	300	Public authority and professional	21.88	11.78
17	Primary production	28	57	Primary production	27.91	10.01

Source: Smith, 1965.

comprising Sydney, Melbourne, Brisbane, Adelaide, Perth and Hobart, as well as Toowoomba, Rockhampton, Maryborough, Orange, Bendigo, Warrnambool, Launceston and a few smaller centres. The title 'manufacturing' can be appropriately given to these towns according to the objective criteria employed by Smith; their percentage employment in manufacturing, at 30.16, is well above the all-town average of 19.02, and they do not show any other marked positive departures from the 422-town average, save only in having 3.31 per cent employed in finance, property and business, compared with an all-town average of 2.46 per cent.

However, in a wider context, the manufacturing title is misleading, when applied to Australia's largest cities, which show no higher specialization in manufacturing than do metropolitan cities elsewhere. A comparison with the United States is quite revealing. In both countries in the early 1950s, approximately 27 per cent of the national workforce was engaged in manufacturing. In the United States, this workforce was distributed fairly uniformly in all size groups, at least down to 10,000 persons, as shown in Nelson's (1955) functional classification. Consequently, Nelson's study of the 897 largest American cities showed only one 'million' city, Detroit, with a manufacturing

specialization. Australia's large cities show a slightly lower proportionate employment in manufacturing than do America's, but the dearth of manufacturing in the multitude of Australian small towns yields a very low unweighted, all-town average of 19.02 per cent employed in manufacturing in Smith's study, whereas an average weighted by size of town would obviously yield a figure above the national average of 27 per cent and very close to the 30.16 of Group Two towns. It is the low all-town average in Australia which must be regarded as the unusual feature leading to the categorization of Group Two towns as 'manufacturing', a problem compounded by Smith's failure to include a category of diversified towns. Furthermore, Nelson's study included only towns of 10,000 persons or more, whereas Smith's includes a few towns of less than 1,000 persons. However, this inclusion of smaller towns in the Australian study serves only to accentuate a clear contrast between the two urban systems.

This functional bias in the Australian urban system is further shown by a comparison with a study of Canadian towns, using the minimum requirements method (Maxwell, 1965). Maxwell found that Canada's 'heartland' cities, located in the densely populated St Lawrence lowlands and southern Ontario showed a clear specialization in manufacturing, with 43 out of the 45 cities in the 'heartland' being in this category, whereas the 35 cities of the 'periphery', comprising the remainder of the country, included only 5 manufacturing cities. Heartland cities had a high degree of industrial linkage encouraging manufacturing specialization, whereas in the periphery specialization was materials-oriented. Internal functional diversity was greatest among peripheral cities, which generally had a strong involvement with functions associated with distance, such as wholesale trade and transportation, involving the collection, transfer and distribution of goods. Maxwell suggests that a great deal of the total 'economic energy' generated in these areas is consumed in overcoming the great distances associated with extensive (agricultural) activities. The occupational characteristics of Australian towns, revealed in Smith's study, show a very strong resemblance to those of the Canadian peripheral system, while the complex, specialized heartland city system of 45 cities, is replaced in Australia by five widely separated large metropolitan cities, supported by a few manufacturing centres showing a much lower level of functional and spatial integration at the national level, when compared with Canada. It would seem that manufacturing activities, in particular, have found it essential to discount the effects of distance by concentrating at a few strategic locations, and the disadvantages of location in country towns have been fully recognized.

The Importance of Service Activities
Apart from a somewhat unorthodox initial function as penal settlements, the *raison d'être* of most Australian towns has been administration, trade, transportation and provision of services, so that size, spacing, functions and hierarchical relations of most towns in the system can be explained by reference to central place theory. Compared with the locally-oriented market towns of more traditional urban systems, Australian towns resemble those in other externally-oriented societies in having a major role as a point of exchange between the local and the national (or international) economy. The transport, transhipment, storage and communication function is clearly evident in seaports, which have, from the outset, played a pivotal role in the evolution of the system (Bird, 1968; Rimmer, 1967a, 1967b). Moreover, a similar set of activities is found in inland towns, with respect to local and long-distance exchange of goods and services. The town absorbs few products from its hinterland, it undertakes little processing of these products, nor does it manufacture much material goods to meet local demand. Its role as a gateway is consistent with the general theory of settlement location and function recently proposed by Bird (1973). This general theory represents an attempt to incorporate the three basic concepts of central place, gateway, and

agglomeration/scale economics into one unitary explanatory model of urban growth.

The difficulty of differentiating general service towns on the basis of census occupational classes is shown in Smith's study. The 179 towns representing six separate groups of 'service' towns are very similar in their level of specialization in the critical occupational class; the proportion employed in commerce averages between 20.69 and 22.97 for five of the groups, while the sixth, very minor, group has an average of 25.12. There are similar marginal differences in other service categories, and Smith's discussion on intergroup differences has to focus on incidental employment classes, such as manufacturing and primary production. Smith's conclusion that 'all six groups display significant concentrations in particular land use zones' is poorly supported by the evidence, which largely rests upon the results of Chi Square tests in which the null hypotheses are inappropriately presented. Clearly the census classification is of little help in differentiating between service towns, particularly since the occupational classes bear little relationship to the hierarchical role of central place activities.

Service towns with a specialist emphasis outside of commerce are more clearly differentiated in Smith's study. The small but distinct group of transport towns comprises mainly railway centres, and includes very few ports, suggesting that port cities acquire other functions, notably manufacturing and/or commerce.

Specialist Towns
(i) *Mining towns* are the most common group of specialist towns, as well as being the most widely distributed in both time and space. Their long history commenced with coal mining at Newcastle at the beginning of the nineteenth century, and copper mining in South Australia in the 1840s, followed by the spectacular proliferation of gold towns over much of Australia from the mid-nineteenth to the early twentieth century. More recently, Broken Hill, Mt Isa and many other towns have appeared based on minerals other than gold, while coal towns have been equally numerous though spatially much more clustered.

Mining towns have been noted for the rapidity of their growth and decline, particularly in isolated regions where alternative functions are not readily found. In more favourable locations, a post-mining phase of stability and even growth has often occurred, as with Ballarat and Bendigo, which remain as major manufacturing and service centres, and Charters Towers as an educational town. Former coal-mining towns around Newcastle and Wollongong have progressively acquired a dormitory function, being either incorporated into the suburban areas of the two expanding industrial cities, or else acquiring an unusual status as places of residence for external commuters (Holmes, 1965, 1971).

The exceptionally high degree of functional specialization of these towns is shown by Smith and by Wilson (1962). In Smith's classification, only the mining group achieved the distinction of employing a majority of the specialist towns' workforce in one occupational category. This dominance of mining occurs even in towns where external service relations are important, as at Broken Hill, Mt Isa and Kalgoorlie.

Until 1960, the twentieth century had been more noted for the decline or demise rather than the resurgence or birth of mining towns. This trend has been spectacularly reversed, with the arrival of a new generation of mining towns, mainly in remote areas. These new towns can look forward to a longer period of stability than did most earlier towns, while a few have prospects for further growth through diversification into first-stage mineral processing. Mining companies have been obliged to make heavy investments in infrastructure, not only in mines and processing plants, but also in transport and utilities. A comparable high investment has also been made in planned mining towns in order to provide attractive residential and community facilities in an effort to counter the disadvantages arising from isolation, smallness and a harsh physical environment, and to ensure stability in employment. These new towns are providing useful guidelines for future urban development in remote areas.

(ii) *Professional and administrative towns* are a much more recent phenomenon, even though from the first settlement governmental decisions on the location of administrative functions have often been the catalyst to subsequent growth (King, 1954; Jeans, 1967). The crucial role of administrative functions is still evident in many towns. In its extreme form it can be seen in the survival of small 'shire towns' in western Queensland, where funds from national and State governments are funnelled through the shire providing the support for a high proportion of local employment, while shire investment in the town's commercial enterprises enables the survival of that sector normally dependent upon private investment (Allen, 1969).

The few specialized professional and administrative centres which have emerged in recent decades represent one of the most dynamic elements in the urban system. Canberra has been the pacesetter, with population growth in this one city exceeding that which has occurred in all mining towns since 1960, thereby providing much of the inspiration for the new cities programmes proposed by various organizations and recently inaugurated by the national government (Australian Institute of Urban Studies, 1972). Thursday Island and Darwin are other notable administrative towns, though Darwin's employment structure has experienced radical change as a sequel to the December 1974 cyclone. Other professional towns have a strong interest in education, as in Armidale, Bathurst and Mittagong, identified as such in Smith's classification.

(iii) *Resort and retirement towns* are also experiencing recent rapid growth. These towns are incompletely identified in Smith's classification, for two reasons: the Australian style of seaside vacation, with its emphasis on tents, caravans and rented apartments, and on outdoor recreation, generates more employment in commerce than in the accommodation amusement and personal services sector, which Smith was obliged to use in identifying resorts; and secondly, Smith's analysis is based solely upon the active workforce, and the exclusion of retired persons leads to an inability to identify the increasingly important number of towns with a major role as retirement centres. This trend has been very strong since 1954, the date of Smith's census data, so that some major towns are now dominated by the retiree element, notably Toukley-Gorokan, Woy Woy-Ettalong, Sussex Inlet, Caloundra and Hervey Bay, while in certain other major resorts the retiree population is very large, as in The Entrance, Port Macquarie, Gold Coast, Maroochydore-Mooloolaba, Noosa-Tewantin, Yeppoon and Lakes Entrance.

The unsatisfactory results in Smith's classification are readily apparent. The surprise of the residents of Noosa and Pialba (Hervey Bay) at finding themselves in a Service Town (Group Four) together with outback towns such as Charleville, Longreach, Blackall and Barcaldine would be equalled by the inhabitants of Cunnamulla and Bourke to find themselves living in a resort town, grouped with Port Macquarie, Narooma and Lakes Entrance. The 'resort' classification obtained by some outback towns, which have the lowliest of claims to a tourist function, arises from their continuing role as a 'place of resort' for outback station hands, drovers, shearers, transport drivers and others whose consumer behaviour during periodic visits creates a remarkably high demand on resort rather than normal commercial activities, showing a preference for cafés, bars, hotels and boarding houses rather than department stores and supermarkets.

(iv) *Satellite towns* are appearing through overspill of metropolitan population and economic activity, especially near Sydney and Melbourne. Gosford, Woy Woy, Richmond-Windsor, Sunbury, Werribee, Kwina-na-Rockingham and the towns of Western Port are growing rapidly as satellites, which by census definitions still remain outside the recognized metropolitan urban area.

The dynamism of certain specialist towns is shown in a recent commentary of the *Atlas of Australian*

Plate 19.1 Gascoyne Junction is a small urban nucleus in the North-West district of Western Australia, centred around a hotel and police station at a crossing of the Gascoyne River. The river is shown here in flood; during the summer months the river bed is dry.

Resources (Dept of Minerals and Energy, 1975). Of the 39 urban centres which experienced an average annual growth rate of 20 per cent or higher during 1966–71, 16 were mining towns, 10 were resorts and 9 were overspill dormitory areas. This is not a conclusive indicator that Australian towns are becoming more specialized. Towns in the three functional classes mentioned above are often characterized by explosive initial growth followed by stability, whereas 'normal' service towns experience steady but persistent growth. However, as shown in Chapter 15, diversified service towns have been characterized by a slackening of growth and by the onset of widespread population decline in recent decades, thus focusing attention on specialist towns as sources of future urban growth.

THE CENTRAL PLACE HIERARCHY

Although experiencing little growth in recent decades, the service towns in the lower and middle orders of the central place hierarchy still remain numerically the dominant element in the urban system, and have been a logical focus for systematic research by geographers. King (1954), Meinig (1962) and Jeans (1967) have examined the origins of the central place system, noting how market forces and entrepreneurial activities have influenced the size and spacing of towns in a manner which frequently disagreed with the expectations of administrators and surveyors who determined initial town sites. Other studies have focused on physical site and morphology rather than function (R. Robinson, 1966; Williams, 1966b).

Studies of the current status and functioning of the urban system have logically been directed towards the functional bases of the central place hierarchy. In this research, a natural division has occurred between research into the structure and behaviour of lower- and middle-order centres in the urban system, concerned mainly with consumer behaviour and the

Plate 19.2 Quilpie (1971 population: 600) is a small but busy transport and transhipment centre at the terminus of Queensland's western railway. It is linked to its sparsely settled hinterland by a road network some of which has been recently 'bitumenized' under the 'beef roads' programme. The open space around the town shows evidence of heavy grazing, particularly in the holding paddocks around the railhead. *Photo*: R. F. Warner.

provision of services directly to consumers, and research directed towards an understanding of the higher-order relations in the system, with attention to metropolitan primacy and the dearth of regional capitals.

Consumer Behaviour and Service Provision in Lower-Order Central Places

In sympathy with overseas research, Australian urban geographers have devoted much research effort to central place studies and consumer behaviour. Much of this research is presented in unpublished theses and is not in a form enabling effective comparative analysis or generalization about characteristics of the whole system. Published studies provide an insight either into the structure and functions of the central place hierarchy (Scott, 1964; Dick, 1971) or into consumer behaviour and service orientation (Daly and Brown, 1964; Rose, 1967, pp. 106–8; Williams, 1965, 1966a; Smailes, 1969a, 1969b; Dick, 1972b). These studies have provided considerable insight into Australian service towns and have generally confirmed the value of central place theory, as presented by

Christaller and elaborated by Lösch, Berry and Garrison, in providing an explanatory framework. Close similarities with the urban system of the American Midwest have been noted. The evidence has generally been presented in favour of the existence of a stepped urban hierarchy of seven orders, commonly described as hamlet, village, minor town, major town, regional capital, regional metropolis and national metropolis, each with a characteristic size, measured according to resident population, service workforce, number of service establishments, and population in service area, and also each with a characteristic array of central functions. Nevertheless, the crucial test of the existence of a stepped or ordered hierarchy has rested upon noting the coincidence in the threshold of entry of an array of critical functions. This aspect has been exhaustively examined by Dick (1971) whose findings on characteristic functions of central places on the Darling Downs show a close coincidence with the conclusions from Berry's studies in the American Midwest (Berry, 1967).

As has occurred elsewhere, there has been a strong centralizing trend within the lower orders of the

Plate 19.3 Dalby (1971 population: 8,800) is a major service centre in the grain-growing district of the western Darling Downs. Its structure, function and landscape, both urban and rural, are typical of the Australian wheat belt.

hierarchy, arising from improved consumer mobility, more specialized demand and the increasing benefits from scale economics. In recent decades hamlets have been losing all central functions, while villages have been experiencing a similar trend, as the threshold and range of lower-order services has increased, notably in convenience shopping, recreation, schooling and basic public services such as post offices and telephone exchanges. Loss of status as a central place does not necessarily involve a population loss, since conveniently-located small centres acquire a new role as dormitory satellites to nearby larger towns.

While empirical research has flourished, the testing of basic tenets in central place theory has been somewhat inconclusive. In particular, there has been considerable uncertainty and inconsistency in identifying orders in the hierarchy and in assigning centres to particular orders. This in turn has led to confusion in determining the appropriate k-ratio, or bifurcation ratio, which indicates the rate of increase in the number

of service areas with each step down the hierarchy. The evidence is too complex to be reviewed adequately in a short space. However, with the notable exception of Scott's Tasmanian study, the weight of evidence is that, compared with Christaller's marketing principle yielding a $k = 3$ network, the Australian central place system is underprovided with hamlets and villages (first- and second-order centres) and also with regional capitals (fifth-order centres), indicating a strong emphasis on third and fourth order centres. This suggests that a variable k-ratio is appropriate, with $k < 3$ for lower orders and $k > 3$, or specifically $k = 4$ or $k = 7$, in the higher orders of the hierarchy. The overprovision of minor and major towns lends weight to the Rose hypothesis in favour of the evolution of a two-step hierarchy, with the smallest centres being unable to compete with standard country towns in satisfying regular consumer demand, while regional capitals are equally unable to withstand metropolitan competition in providing specialized higher-order services.

One important, though neglected, aspect of central place research in Australia is concerned with the adaptation of the system to the lower demand levels prevailing in very sparsely peopled areas. Berry's (1967) comparative studies in North America have identified systematic variations: with a reduced level of population and demand, there is an increase in the extent of service areas, but this increase lags behind the decline in population. This decline in overall demand leads to a reduction in the size and variety of establishments offered in centres of comparable order. In Australia, adaptations must proceed further than in the United States, since extensive areas of inland Australia provide possibly the most extreme examples of a central place system designed to service a very sparse population. In this situation the demand level for entry of a service is lowered, and consumers must accept smaller, less specialized, poorly stocked establishments offering less choice, as a trade-off against excessive travel to meet their needs. In the private sector, establishments are noted for low investment, low turnover, little local competition and a proliferation of functions in the one establishment, with the general store commonly acting as a post office, telephone exchange, agency for bank, travel and insurance, petrol supplier, transport and freight depot, and with a small clothing-haberdashery-hardware 'department' in one corner. In the public sector, services are often characterized by high capital and maintenance costs per unit of demand. Urban centres are stripped of ancillary functions and achieve a remarkably high degree of centrality in relation to their workforce, population and level of economic activity.

At the other extreme in population density, some research has been undertaken into consumer behaviour and retail location within urban and suburban areas, where higher levels of demand encourage a higher degree of competition and specialization by establishments and by locations, enabling a higher degree of consumer choice and a more dynamic situation, in which a complex array of variables may influence the relative success of establishments (Beed, 1964; Johnston, 1966a; Johnston and Rimmer, 1969).

Higher-Order Central Places

Metropolitan primacy and the related gap in the rank-size distribution, discussed earlier in this chapter, can be interpreted in terms of a related gap in the central place hierarchy; specifically, there is a dearth of fifth-order centres or regional capitals, ranked between major towns (fourth-order) and regional and national metropolises (sixth- and seventh-order). In one of the most challenging contributions to the general debate on urban systems, which also offers a thoughtful interpretation of processes influencing the hierarchical structure of Australian towns, Rose has argued that, given a fresh start in an empty continent under present conditions of enhanced communication, specialization and scale economies, a two-step urban hierarchy would evolve. Higher-order and non-central functions would concentrate in one national, or in a few sectoral, metropolises, and all lower-order central place services would be provided by agro-towns which coincide in size and functional specialization with fourth-order centres. Not only does the Rose hypothesis imply a loss of lower-order central places, but it also suggests that there is no reason for the existence of fifth-order centres. Rose states that these would only emerge when 'political pressures arose against what was deemed to be over-centralization ... leading to a modicum of functional devolution' (Rose, 1966, p. 8). The hypothesis suggests that any existing centres of this order should be regarded either as relict features, destined to survive, and perhaps even grow, but only because of the impetus gained in an earlier period, as with Ballarat and Bendigo, or as a result of locational advantages enabling successful competition with the metropolis, as with Rockhampton, Townsville, Darwin and Launceston, or from the growth of non-central functions, as may occur with Whyalla. Clearly they are not expected to evolve within a modern urban system.

Noting the recent persistent rapid growth of larger country towns in New South Wales, and observing that this cannot be explained by growth in manufacturing or other non-central functions, Holmes and Pullinger (1973) analysed establishments offering higher-order services in Tamworth, to test whether the city was evolving into a fifth-order regional capital. They found that employment growth in the 1960–70 decade could be attributed almost entirely to the acquisition of a new array of higher-order services, which Tamworth establishments were providing to an extensive area of northern New South Wales. These functions, at the 'regional capital' level, were previously available only from Sydney, Newcastle or Brisbane, and their devolution down the hierarchy was in response either to an increase in demand, or to a higher degree of specialization in both demand and supply systems, facilitated by improved regional links in transport and communication. The trend is contrary to that postulated in the Rose hypothesis, and offers some hope to the 'decentralists' that a strategy of fostering regional capitals may have some prospects of success. However, the authors caution against assuming too hastily that incipient trends will inevitably close the existing gap in the hierarchy, suggesting that 'it is reasonable to envisage that the devolution process may shortly run its course, so that the fifth-order centres will remain underendowed and inadequately differentiated from fourth-order centres' (Holmes and Pullinger, 1973, p. 224).

One further dimension in metropolitan dominance has been identified. Not only have the metropolitan centres stifled the development of regional capitals, but also they have been very successful competitors to lower-order centres in providing services to non-metropolitan consumers, particularly in small towns and rural areas. Smailes (1969b) and Williams (1965, 1966a) have both shown that Adelaide offers 'intensive competition with the State's remaining urban centres for the supply of a wide range of professional, personal and retail services' (Smailes, 1969b, p. 329). A questionnaire survey by Smailes of rural consumers showed that, for twenty selected items other than day-to-day household necessities, Adelaide supplied a majority of these items for 36 per cent of the rural population, extending across the whole of the State, being displaced only in the immediate service areas of the larger country towns. A similar metropolitan orientation by consumers, though less strong than in South Australia, has also been found in New South Wales in the Lachlan Region (Daly and Brown, 1964) and in southern Illawarra (Rose, 1967, pp. 106–9), and also in southwestern Queensland where a large regional capital such as Toowoomba might be expected to command consumer areas to which it is more accessible than Brisbane (Dick, 1972a). A common thread in all these studies, and especially in those by Smailes and Dick, is the close fit that can be obtained to a gravity model, so that metropolitan cities can dominate areas beyond immediate reach of country towns, and particularly the most remote 'outback' areas. This is also consistent with behavioural models of consumer choice, with distance and cost being traded off against variety and attractiveness.

However, particularly in sheep grazing areas, there has been a long tradition among rural landholders of direct consumer orientation to the metropolis. The infrastructure enabling direct links, established in the pioneering era, has persisted, comprising such elements as multipurpose stock and station agencies, mercantile houses and woolbroking firms encouraging direct ordering of most rural and household consumer supplies from metropolitan depots; mail order businesses; city-located private boarding schools; wool auctions; race meetings; and major agricultural shows. The persistence and elaboration of these direct metropolitan links has served to retard and destabilize the local urban economy, which becomes overly dependent upon smaller landholders and rural workers whose locally-oriented consumption patterns are more affected by adverse economic conditions. In inland Queensland, the adverse effect of this divergent consumer orientation was most apparent during the drought and rural recession of the mid-1960s, when many rural workers were forced to leave the pastoral zone. A disproportionately severe impact

was felt in the economy of the pastoral towns, which experienced consequential sharp losses in population, averaging a decline of 16 per cent in the five-year period 1966–71.

The Functional Role of the Metropolises

As already indicated, the metropolitan cities exercise complete dominance in almost every urban activity within their 'captive' hinterlands, and this control is almost identical from State to State. However, some differences can be seen in the functional roles of the six State capitals, arising from three sets of circumstances: firstly, Sydney and Melbourne have clearly defined roles as national, as well as regional, metropolises; secondly, differences in the economic importance of hinterlands has consequential effects upon the importance of the regional metropolitan centres, so that Brisbane, Adelaide and, more recently, Perth, clearly differ from Hobart in functional complexity as well as size; and thirdly, differences in the spatial organization of each State contribute to differences in the degree of dominance achieved, with Brisbane being somewhat disadvantaged, and Hobart more severely affected.

Surprisingly little research has been made into the structure and role of the higher-order establishments associated with the metropolises, into hierarchical relations between the major cities, or into the levels of concentration of activities into one or two cities. One modest study by Johnston (1966b), concerned with the location of higher-level managerial functions, suggests useful directions for further research. In examining the location of the head offices of the top thousand Australian companies, Johnston found an exceptionally high level of concentration in Sydney and Melbourne. The percentage of total assets in each industrial category, controlled from head offices in these two cities, varied from a low of 79.5 per cent in oil exploration to a high of 98.3 per cent in life insurance. Sydney and Melbourne were shown to be complementary, with Sydney showing greater specialization in investment, finance and insurance, and Melbourne in manufacturing. Concentration in these two cities is so high that the regional metropolises usually obtain location quotients below unity, indicating that their control of company assets is even lower than their share of Australia's population. The only exceptions are Brisbane in non-life insurance, building, oil exploration and mining, Adelaide in trading, transport, vehicles and other manufacturing, and Perth in oil exploration. Data of this type enable a clear differentiation to be made between the two national metropolises and the four State capitals, which have very little influence beyond their own State boundaries, and consequently can be classed as regional metropolises.

Although no substantive comparative research has been undertaken on this question, there appears to be surprisingly little functional differentiation between Brisbane, Adelaide and Perth in their role as regional metropolises, and certainly much less differentiation than occurs in their manufacturing sectors. Each maintains an intrastate monopoly over metropolitan-level functions in government and administration, managerial, financial, cultural, wholesaling and specialty retailing activities, as well as being dominant in transport and communication. These marked similarities occur because each commands a comparable distinct segment of the continent, with no overlap in hinterlands, and no opportunity for competition and specialization. This consistent monopoly in metropolitan activities occurs in spite of marked variations in the degree of intrastate concentration in economic activity and population achieved by the three cities, with the percentage of the State's population varying from 69.0 in Adelaide to 44.8 in Brisbane. This variation can be accounted for in the degree of metropolitan centralization in manufacturing and in the provision of middle- and lower-order central place services, in which Brisbane plays a less important role than do the other two State capitals.

Hobart's status as a regional metropolis is much less firmly established, and its claims rest more heavily upon functions directly and indirectly related to its role as a State capital, bringing in its train such diverse activities as parliament, State administration, museum, university, symphony orchestra and major branch offices for national government and many private firms. Tasmania's population of 390,000 (1971) is barely sufficient to establish a demand threshold for the provision of some metropolitan-level services, which commonly require a threshold of approximately one million persons in the city and its service area. Hobart is the only State capital without a daily evening paper, and is poorly served in most interstate and international sporting schedules, while many other higher-order services are offered on a reduced scale. Hobart's status also suffers from its unsatisfactory location, which enhances Melbourne's role as the alternative metropolis for northern Tasmania, and also allows Launceston to capture a small set of functions normally located in the regional metropolis, notably in transport, communication and wholesaling for which Launceston's locational advantage is of critical importance (Scott, 1964, p. 145).

Of the four other cities with some claim to metropolitan status, one is the national capital. Canberra fulfils an unusual role as the only major centre for national managerial and decision-making functions outside of Sydney and Melbourne. The locational displacement of the national government to this new city has provided the rationale for various decentrali-

zation strategies which propose further displacement of higher-order functions into new growth centres, with Albury-Wodonga already receiving favourable attention from the national government as a point for relocating certain national departments previously intended for Canberra.

The other three large cities owe much of their growth to their manufacturing activities. However, Newcastle has strong claims to the status of a regional metropolis, not solely because of its greater size, with a population of 250,000, but also because of its historical role as a major service centre, with well-established functional links to the Hunter Valley in particular, and to northern New South Wales in general. Wollongong and Geelong have a much lower status within the central place hierarchy not only because of their smaller size and more recent growth, but also because of their greater proximity to national metropolises.

Of the existing regional capitals, all have achieved their status because of either locational or historical factors. Ballarat and Bendigo achieved early status as major centres through the stimulus of gold mining, but have since become very dependent upon manufacturing, while their role as regional capitals is static and constrained by Melbourne's domination. Apart from Toowoomba, which shares the same competitive problems as the Victorian cities, and has also depended heavily upon manufacturing, Queensland's regional capitals exhibit much greater dynamism in their higher-order functions, and they maintain stronger links over more extensive hinterlands. While Rockhampton, Mackay and Cairns have important roles, Townsville in particular shows promise of evolving to the status of a regional metropolis. Studies of telephone traffic (Holmes, 1973), and of other flows, reveal very strong links to all other urban centres in north Queensland, providing a hinterland with a population of over 300,000; the city has been acquiring higher-order functions in public and private administration, tertiary education, wholesaling and market-oriented processing industries; furthermore, its population growth has been very rapid, reaching a total of 70,000 in 1971, although much of this growth has been based on non-central activities, notable defence activities, mineral smelting, construction and transportation.

The continuing growth of larger towns, particularly in New South Wales and Queensland, represents the most dynamic non-metropolitan element in the system of central places, and the causes of this growth merit close examination.

INTERACTION WITHIN THE URBAN SYSTEM
Research into the structure and behaviour of urban and regional systems is increasingly concerned with

gaining an understanding of interaction within these systems, as expressed in flows of materials, persons and information. Advanced, specialized societies with a marked division of labour are increasingly dependent upon these flows, which accordingly are becoming of greater importance in influencing decisions on the location of activities (Tornqvist, 1970).

Flows of goods initially received the most attention, as a basis for testing industrial location theory, and, more recently, in intersectoral and interregional studies. Little research in Australia has been directed towards comprehensive analysis of interurban or interregional flows of goods, and these studies have been mainly concerned with the orientation of flows from border zones, affected by competition between major urban centres. In this highly focused research area, efforts have been made to test whether State capitals exert control over 'captive hinterlands' within their States, so that intrastate orientation exceeds that predicted by gravity models. In two early studies, Mathieson (1957, 1958) found that Wagga and Grafton showed a much stronger orientation to Sydney than was predicted by the gravity model, as expressed in Reilly's Law, indicating that the State boundaries continued to function as major 'socio-economic' divides. More extensive surveys by Woolmington (1965) and by McPhail and Woolmington (1966) suggested that 'since federation its [the border's] barrier functions have suffered progressive erosion, but the manner of this erosion is as complicated as the socio-economic situation which the border physically cleaves' (1966, p. 152). Continuing intrastate monopolies of rail traffic and close regulation of intrastate road transport, while interstate road transport remains relatively unfettered, has created a situation where metropolitan competition is interwoven with competition between road and rail. Smith's (1962, 1963) studies of commodity flows in southern New South Wales also reveal a very complex situation in which Sydney retains some residual influence beyond that predicted by a gravity model.

Movements of people have also been studied only in very local contexts or for very narrow purposes. The greatest attention has been given to consumer behaviour and local commuting patterns, both referred to earlier in this chapter. Australian studies have been handicapped by a lack of comprehensive statistics on internal migration and commuting comparable with data available in the United States and in many European countries. The greatest research effort, directed towards national flows of persons, has been made with regard to the internal destinations of international migrants and the problem of estimating major internal migration flows to and from the metropolises (Price, 1963; Choi and Burnley, 1974).

Following the publication of Meier's (1962) seminal work emphasizing the central role of the city as an information system, new research directions have been opened up, exploring the interdependencies between communication flows and the structure and location of activities, particularly quaternary activities. Major research has been published, dealing with intracity patterns in London (Goddard, 1973) and with inter-regional patterns in Sweden (Warneryd, 1968; Tornqvist, 1970). The impact of this research is being felt in Australian studies, as evidenced by Wilmoth's (1973) substantive review and by research into intracity patterns which lies outside the scope of this chapter. Research into interurban and inter-regional contact systems is being impeded by lack of adequate data, and has been limited to explorations of the telephone traffic data (Smailes, 1969a; Holmes, 1973). There has also been a modest effort at exploring the interurban contact systems of higher-order establishments in one country town (Holmes and Pullinger, 1973).

In sum, Australian research into interurban and interregional flows has been fragmentary and directed mainly towards measuring orientation or directionality of movement within an established structure. There has been little attempt to study the basic components in flow systems, at the national, State or regional level, and no focused effort at testing hypotheses about the role of contact systems in influencing the location and growth of organizations, which in turn affects the structure and functioning of urban systems.

Urban Interaction Patterns: A Preliminary View

In the absence of any major studies, a general insight into the intensity of interaction between Australian towns can be gleaned from telephone traffic. Unpublished research by this writer, based upon origin/destination matrices of intrastate telephone traffic between all major towns of at least 1,500 persons, with supplementary information on interstate flows, shows very close affinities between system structure and system behaviour. An initial finding was that a strong intrastate orientation exists, with interstate traffic consistently being less than one per cent of all long-distance traffic, save only for the major flows linking national and State capitals, the flows from New South Wales border-regions to Brisbane, Melbourne and Adelaide, and from major towns in northern Tasmania to Melbourne, together with very short-distance cross-border flows between neighbouring towns. Accordingly, data-collection was simplified into a task of collating six intrastate matrices, occasionally including a few cross-border towns. Very little information loss results from the use of these six matrices rather than one nationwide flow matrix.

R-mode factor analysis of each of the six dyadic matrices of intrastate flows was carried out, grouping

Table 19.2 R-mode Factor Analysis of Interurban Telephone Traffic: Major Results

State	No. of nodes	Factor I			Factor II			Factor III			Factor IV			Factor V			Cumulated per cent explained variance
		Dominant node	Perc. var.	No. nodes	Dominant node	Perc. var.	No. nodes	Dominant node	Perc. var.	No. nodes	Dominant node	Perc. var.	No. nodes	Dominant node	Perc. var.	No. nodes	
N.S.W.	87	Sydney	43.5	30	Newcastle	7.4	7	Lismore	5.2	6	Dubbo	4.4	5	Tamworth	3.3	6	63.7
Vic.	57	Melbourne	52.4	31	Shepparton	7.2	5	Geelong	5.1	4	Wangaratta	4.6	3	(Latrobe Valley)	3.6	3	72.9
Qld	60	Brisbane	35.4	24	Townsville	10.0	6	Rock-hampton	9.1	6	Toowoomba	5.5	4	Cairns	5.3	4	65.2
S.A.	38	Adelaide	65.6	24	(Murray irrigation towns)	5.0	3	(Yorke Peninsula)	3.9	4	Adelaide (as a destination)	3.9	1	(Barossa Valley)	3.2	3	80.9
W.A.	27	Perth	68.1	17	Bunbury	5.6	5	Geraldton	5.5	5	Albany	4.2	1	Derby	3.5	2	86.9
Tas.	20	Launceston	34.5	6	Burnie	21.6	4	Hobart	14.6	4	Devonport	10.0	3	Queenstown	6.1	2	86.7

Note: Perc. var. indicates the percentage of total variance explained by each factor.
No. nodes indicates the number of destination nodes with a loading of 0.6000 or higher on each factor.
Source: unpublished research by author.

together destinations on the basis of their common origins. Table 19.2 provides a summary of the characteristics of the five major factors, or regional groups, in each State. For each factor, the dominant originating node, if any, is identified, the number of strongly linked destination nodes is indicated, as is also the percentage of total system variance explained by each factor. The percentage of variance explained by Factor I is an index of the importance of the main nodal region within the system, and is thus a useful indicator of the degree of centralization of flows around a single node. However, it is important to recognize that other formulations would yield different results. Q-mode analysis would certainly yield a higher level of centralization, since the main node is consistently more dominant as a destination for flows moving up the hierarchy than as a source of flows down the hierarchy. Conversely, an analysis of the total flow system, including smaller towns and rural exchanges, would suggest a lower level of centralization. As shown elsewhere (Holmes, 1973), flows from smaller towns and rural areas usually have a much lower metropolitan orientation than from larger towns.

However, it can reasonably be assumed that interstate differences will be consistently shown irrespective of the criteria for data selection or data processing. Results in Table 19.2 suggest a broad relationship between centralization in telephone flows and socio-economic concentration. In detail, however, only Adelaide and Perth achieve dominance as regional nodes for originating telephone traffic commensurate with their dominance as population centres. In these two States the percentage of total variance explained by Factor I is far greater than obtained in comparable studies of telephone traffic elsewhere in the world, and direct links between the metropolis and most urban centres are so strong that the system conforms closely to that expected under the Rose hypothesis under which all urban centres are directly subordinate to the metropolis. In South Australia the three non-metropolitan factors, shown in Table 19.2, all lack a nodal structure, these being clusters of closely linked small towns lacking any clear hierarchical relationship, while the fourth factor elicits a flow system oriented to Adelaide which is not strongly reciprocated by the metropolis. In Western Australia, the non-metropolitan regions have identifiable single originating nodes, but their related destination nodes obtain only modest loadings of 0.6 to 0.7 with the regional axes, whereas in New South Wales and Queensland non-metropolitan regional loadings commonly exceed 0.9. Townsville, Rockhampton and Newcastle are the central nodes for the three most fully articulated non-metropolitan regions on the mainland, as is suggested by the per-

centage of explained variance and the number of affiliated nodes.

New South Wales and Queensland also display the greatest multiplicity of regional systems, with the first five factors accounting for only 63.7 and 65.2 per cent of total variance, respectively. In New South Wales, complexity is partly a function of the size of the system and the number of competing nodes, but in both States strongly developed intraregional links occurring within additional regional entities such as those centred on Mackay, Bundaberg, Wagga and Orange also contribute to this marked divergence from the other States.

One noteworthy feature of the Victorian analysis is the weak position of Ballarat and Bendigo as regional nodes. Their absence from the list of major nodes is consistent with their low level of traffic linkage to all save a few adjacent urban nodes. In Tasmania, Launceston's position as the leading regional node is clearly indicated, but the result is biased by the use of a matrix based only on major urban nodes in which each node is given equal weight. Northern Tasmania contains urban nodes well in excess of its share of the State's population. The measure of Hobart's position as a communications centre would be enhanced if the analysis included intra-urban, small-town and rural traffic, although it appears likely that Launceston would retain its position as the leading regional node.

The degree of orientation of individual towns to their leading metropolitan destination is depicted in Fig. 19.3. In this simple analysis of directionality of flows to a single, predetermined destination, the coverage is extended to include all towns with a population of 1,000 or more in the 1971 census, but a few towns located immediately adjacent to metropolitan cities are not shown on the map. Interstate and interregional variations in the degree of metropolitan orientation of telephone traffic appear to be strongly related to differences in the structure of the urban hierarchy. The map hints at the crucial role of competing destinations in influencing metropolitan orientation, this being confirmed by more detailed analysis.

Accordingly, a very high degree of metropolitan orientation occurs in remote locations where there is a lack of alternative destinations. This exists to an extreme degree in Western Australia, where some northwestern towns direct over 60 per cent of outgoing calls to Perth, whereas competition in the State's southwestern corner does moderate Perth's dominance there. A similar pattern occurs in South Australia, supporting Smailes' finding on Adelaide's extended trade shadow (Smailes, 1969b). Brisbane also extends its influence into the more remote parts of inland Queensland, and is marginally the largest single destination for traffic from most towns west of

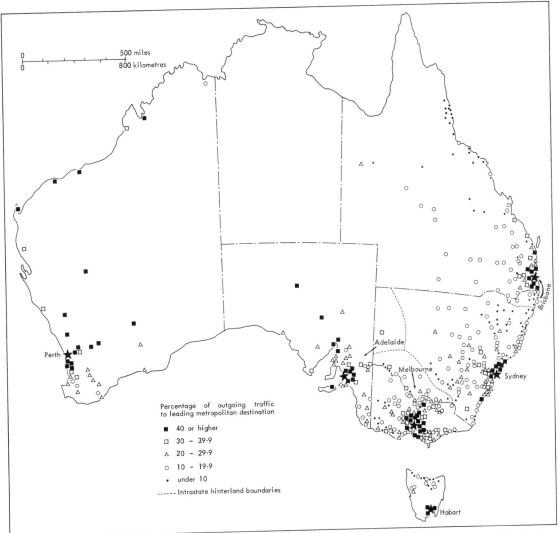

Fig. 19.3 Australian major towns: percentage of outgoing long-distance telephone traffic to leading metropolitan destination, 1967–8. *Source*: P.M.G. surveys of peak morning and evening traffic over six busy days before Christmas 1967 and Easter 1968.

the Great Divide, but its influence is diluted by intraregional links and by important west-east flows to rival coastal cities, particularly Townsville and Rockhampton.

In Queensland's coastal regions, flows show a strong intraregional orientation, with a marked hierarchical linkage to regional capitals. Smaller towns usually send 2 to 10 per cent of outgoing traffic to Brisbane, the proportion decreasing northwards, while regional capitals show a metropolitan orientation three to four times greater, at the same distance intervals. Indeed, a markedly higher degree of metro-

politan orientation is consistently maintained by larger towns in all regions where an articulated urban hierarchy can be postulated, on the basis of marked differences in town size. This occurs throughout most of New South Wales, Victoria, coastal Queensland and northern Tasmania, and, to a much lesser degree, in the more closely settled areas of South and Western Australia.

A more fully articulated urban hierarchy is also characterized by a greater degree of traffic dispersion from larger towns, which maintain effective contact with a large array of alternative destinations. Particularly in New South Wales and Queensland there is a very close correlation between town size and traffic dispersion, whereas in the metropolitan-dominated systems of South and Western Australia there is no clear evidence of such a relationship. Victoria's larger towns present an intermediate pattern, with their degree of dispersion being reduced by their generally strong links to Melbourne, as shown in Fig. 19.3.

It is of interest to note that these significant interstate differences in flow patterns are consistent with a gravity trip-distribution model, and the validity of such a model has been partially demonstrated in Queensland, where, however, flows do show some further augmentation along hierarchical links and also along each of the four major transportation/ communications corridors which play a major role in the spatial organization of that State (Holmes, 1973, pp. 12–13). It should not be inferred that any basic agreement with a gravity model indicates that all States have the same basic dimensions in their interaction patterns. Rather it suggests that major interregional and interstate differences in the size and spacing of towns are matched by comparable differences in their flow systems, which reflect marked differences in the extent and character of their functional relations.

These findings from aggregate flow matrices are helpful in clarifying our general understanding about levels of urban interaction, and in defining functional regions and measuring the intensity of intraregional and interregional flows. As such they do have some practical value in providing background information to assist planning by public and private organizations. However, much more comprehensive, multifaceted studies of the source, composition and purpose of flows of goods, people and information are needed for a proper understanding of interdependencies between structure and behaviour in the Australian urban system, sufficient to provide a framework for informed decisions on specific location problems or for formulating programmes designed to shape the future urban system.

REFERENCES

Allen, A. C. B. (1969), 'Frontier towns in western Queensland: their growth and present tributary areas', *Aust. Geogr.*, 11, 119–37.

Alexandersson, G. (1956), *The Industrial Structure of American Cities: A Geographic Study of Urban Economy in the United States*, University of Nebraska Press, Lincoln.

Australian Institute of Urban Studies (1972), *New Cities for Australia*, Canberra.

Beed, T. W. (1964), *The Growth of Suburban Retailing in Sydney*, unpublished PhD thesis, University of Sydney.

Berry, B. J. L. (1961), 'City size distributions and economic development', *Econ. Devel. and Cult. Change*, 9, 573–88.

——(1967), *Geography of Market Centers and Retail Distribution*, Prentice-Hall, Englewood Cliffs, N.J.

Berry, B. J. L. and Horton, F. E. (1970), *Geographic Perspectives on Urban Systems*, Prentice-Hall, Englewood Cliffs, N.J.

Bird, J. (1968), *Seaport Gateways of Australia*, Oxford University Press, Melbourne.

——(1973), 'Of central places, cities and seaports', *Geography*, 58, 105–18.

Borchert, J. R. (1967), 'American metropolitan evolution', *Geogr. Rev.*, 57, 301–23.

Bourne, L. S. (1974), 'Urban systems in Australia and Canada: comparative notes and research questions', *Aust. Geogr. Stud.*, 12, 152–72.

Burnley, I. H. (ed.). (1974), *Urbanization in Australia: The Post-war Experience*, Cambridge University Press, Cambridge.

Choi, C. Y. and Burnley, I. H. (1974), 'Population components in the growth of cities' in I. H. Burnley (ed.), *Urbanization in Australia*, Cambridge University Press, Cambridge.

Daly, M. and Brown, J. (1964), *Urban Settlement in Central Western New South Wales*, Geogr. Soc. N.S.W. Res. Pap. No. 8.

Department of Minerals and Energy (1975), 'Population Distribution and Growth, 1971', *Atlas of Australian Resources*, Second Series, Canberra.

Dick, R. S. (1971), 'A definition of the central place hierarchy of the Darling Downs, Queensland', *Qld. Geogr. J.* (Third Series), 1, 1–38.

——(1972a), 'Toowoomba's sphere of influence and metropolitan competition', *Urban Issues*, 3, 1–17.

——(1972b), 'A comparison of the administrative and urban fields of nine shire centres of the Darling Downs, Queensland', *Urban Issues*, 3, 101–12.

Duncan, O. D. *et al.* (1960), *Metropolis and Region*, Johns Hopkins Press, Baltimore.

Goddard, J. B. (1973), 'Office linkages and location: a study of communications and spatial patterns in central London', *Progress in Planning*, 1, 109–232.

Holmes, J. H., (1965), 'The suburbanization of the Cessnock coalfields', *Aust. Geogr. Stud.*, 3, 105–28.

——(1971), 'External commuting as a prelude to suburbanization', *Ann. Ass. Amer. Geogr.*, 61, 774–90.

——(1973), 'Telephone traffic in the Queensland urban system', Paper presented at ANZAAS Congress, Perth.

Holmes, J. H. and Pullinger, B. F. (1973), 'Tamworth: an emerging regional capital?', *Aust. Geogr.*, 12, 207–25.

Jeans, D. N. (1967), 'Territorial divisions and the location of towns in New South Wales, 1826–1842', *Aust. Geogr.*, 10, 243–55.

Johnston, R. J. (1966a), 'The distribution of an intrametropolitan central place hierarchy', *Aust. Geogr. Stud.*, 4, 150–62.

——(1966b), 'Commercial leadership in Australia', *Aust. Geogr.*, 10, 49–52.

Johnston, R. J. and Rimmer, P. J. (1969), *Retailing in Melbourne*, Department of Human Geography, Australian National University, Canberra.

King, H. W. H. (1954), 'County, shire and town in New South Wales', *Aust. Geogr.*, 4, 14–25.

Logan, M. I. (1968), 'Capital city development in Australia' in G. H. Dury and M. I. Logan (eds), *Studies in Australian Geography*, Heinemann, London.

Linge, G. J. R. (1968), 'Secondary industry in Australia' in G. H. Dury and M. I. Logan (eds), *Studies in Australian Geography*, Heinemann, London.

McCalden, G. (1969), 'Muswellbrook: an urban case study Part II: function and economic structure', *Hunter Valley Research Foundation Monograph 31*, Newcastle.

McCarty, J. W. (1970), 'Australian capital cities in the nineteenth century', *Aust. Econ. Hist. Rev.*, 10, 107–37.

McPhail, I. R. and Woolmington, E. R. (1966), 'Changing function of the state border as a barrier to Brisbane influence in northern New South Wales', *Aust. Geogr. Stud.*, 4, 129–53.

Madden, C. H. (1958), 'Some temporal aspects of the growth of cities in the United States', *Econ. Devel. and Cult. Change*, 6, 143–70.

Mathieson, R. S. (1957), 'The validity of Reilly's Law in Australia', *Aust. Geogr.*, 7, 27–32.

——(1958), 'Socio-economic contact in the Melbourne-Sydney penumbral zone', *Aust. Geogr.*, 7, 97–102.

Maxwell, J. W. (1965), 'The functional structure of Canadian cities: a classification of cities', *Geogr. Bull.*, 7, 79–104.

Meier, L. (1962), *A Communications Theory of Urban Growth*, M.I.T. Press, Cambridge, Mass.

Meinig, D. W. (1961), *On the Margins of the Good Earth: the South Australian Wheat Frontier, 1869–84*, Rand-McNally, Chicago.

Nelson, H. J. (1955), 'A service classification of American cities', *Econ. Geogr.*, 31, 189–201.

Pred, A. (1965), 'Industrialization, initial advantage and American economic growth', *Geogr. Rev.*, 55, 158–85.

Price, C. A. (1963), *Southern Europeans in Australia*, Oxford University Press, Oxford.

Richardson, H. W. (1973), 'Theory of the distribution of city sizes: review and prospects', *Regional Stud.*, 7, 239–51.

Rimmer, P. J. (1967a), 'Changes in the ranking of Australian seaports, 1951–2 to 1961–2', *Tijd. voor Econ. en Soc. Geogr.* 59, 33–41.

——(1967b), 'The search for spatial regularities in the development of Australian seaports, 1861–1961/2', *Geograf. Annlr.*, Series B, 49B, 42–54.

Robinson, A. J. (1963), 'Regionalism and urbanization in Australia: a note on locational emphasis in the Australian economy', *Econ. Geogr.*, 39, 149–55.

Robinson, K. W. (1962), 'Processes and patterns of urbanization in Australia and New Zealand', *N. Z. Geogr.*, 18, 32–49.

Robinson, R. (1966), 'Site and form in the valley centres of the New South Wales coast, north of the Hunter', *Aust. Geogr.*, 10, 1–16.

Robson, B. T. (1973), *Urban Growth: An Approach*, Methuen, London.

Rose, A. J. (1966), 'Dissent from down under: metropolitan primacy as the normal state', *Pac. Viewpoint*, 7, 1–27.

——(1967), *Patterns of Cities*, Nelson, Melbourne.

Scott, P. (1964), 'The hierarchy of central places in Tasmania', *Aust. Geogr.*, 9, 134–47.

Smailes, P. J. (1969a), 'Some aspects of the South Australian urban system', *Aust. Geogr.*, 11, 29–51.

——(1969b), 'A metropolitan trade shadow: the case of Adelaide, South Australia', *Tijd. voor Econ. en Soc. Geogr.*, 60, 329–45.

Smith, R. H. T. (1962), *Commodity Movements in Southern New South Wales*, Australian National University, Canberra.

——(1963), 'Transport competition in Australian border areas: the example of southern New South Wales', *Econ. Geogr.*, 1–13.

——(1965), 'The functions of Australian towns', *Tijd. voor Econ. en Soc. Geogr.*, 56, 81–92.

Stilwell, F. J. B. (1974), 'Economic factors and the growth of cities' in I. H. Burnley (ed.), *Urbanization in Australia*, Cambridge University Press, Cambridge.

Tornqvist, G. (1970), 'Contact systems and regional development', *Lund Studies in Geography*, Series B, 35.

Ullman, E. L. and Dacey, M. F. (1962), 'The minimum requirements approach to the urban economic base' in K. Norborg (ed.), *Proceedings of the I.G.U. Symposium on Urban Geography, Lund, 1960*, Gleerup, Lund, pp. 121–43.

Warneryd, O. (1968), *Interdependence in Urban Systems*, Goteborg.

Williams, M. A. (1965), 'A note on the influence of Adelaide on rural shopping habits in Counties Frome, Dalhousie and Victoria, S. A.', *Aust. Geogr.*, 9, 312–5.

——(1966a), 'Further light on the influence of Adelaide on rural shopping habits in South Australia', *Aust. Geogr.*, 10, 55–8.

——(1966b), 'The parkland towns of Australia and New Zealand', *Geogr. Rev.*, 56, 67–89.

Wilmoth, D. (1974), 'Communication in the urban system' in H. A. Nix (ed.), 'The City as a Life System', *Proc. Ecol. Soc. Aust.*, 7, 211–30.

Wilson, M. G. A. (1962), 'Some population characteristics of Australian mining settlements', *Tijd. voor Econ. en Soc. Geogr.*, 53, 125–32.

Woolmington, E. R. (1965), 'Metropolitan gravitation in northern New South Wales', *Aust. Geogr.*, 9, 359–76.

Yeates, M. H. and Garner, B. J. (1971), *The North American City*, Harper and Row, New York.

Zipf, G. K. (1949), *Human Behavior and the Principle of Least Effort*, Addison-Wesley, New York.

20 MINERAL RESOURCES AND MINING INDUSTRIES

C. DUNCAN

For approximately a decade Australia has been experiencing unprecedented growth in the mining sector. While the roots for such growth are undoubtedly deeply embedded in nearly two centuries of settlement and exploitation, this chapter is concerned with the unique circumstances of this most recent phase and the resulting reorientation of spatial patterns. If the general purpose is to explain the mining pattern, then the problem is to be seen in the discrepancy between the maps of mineral deposits and mineral industries as stated in the second series of the *Atlas of Australian Resources*; and the hypothesis to account, *a priori*, for the discrepancy, grows out of the need to reconcile the physical and spatial properties of mineral discovery and development with the social and economic aspirations of the developers and community at large.

TERMINOLOGY

Minerals are generally regarded as inorganic substances but they need not be of inorganic origin. They are usually assumed to have a recognizable chemical composition although a non-technical expansion of the definition would have it include 'any naturally formed aggregate or mass of mineral matter, whether or not coherent, extracted from the earth for use by man'.

We are told that 'strictly speaking' the word 'mining' refers to 'underground work directed to severence and treatment of ore and associated rock'. Again, in a non-technical sense, it may include for all practical purposes, 'open cast work, quarrying, alluvial dredging and combined operations including surface and underground attack and ore treatment' (Thrush, 1968). In moving from these introductory definitions to the data available for this text, an attempt will be made to relate or reconcile groupings and classification with official and other authoritative sources of data. The current edition of the Australian *Yearbook* and supplementary publications of the Australian Bureau of Statistics are indispensable if one is to cope at all adequately with the dynamic nature of the industry today.

Economic activity gives rise to flows of goods and services. The parts and linkages make up a system of production, exchange and consumption. Mining is a subsystem within the productive component. As such it is concerned with the identification, recovery and processing of mineral resources. Fig. 20.1 shows the parts and linkages in a structuring of production flow within the mining system. The arrows represent types of transport and volume of mining product moved along the productive system. An expansion of scale of the diagram would show both intra- and inter-plant linkages. What is important is that each element is an integral part of the total industrial complex and ultimately has meaning only within that context.

We have noted that mining as a general term does

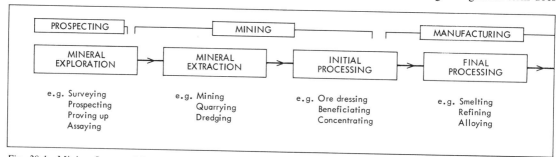

Fig. 20.1 Mining flow model.

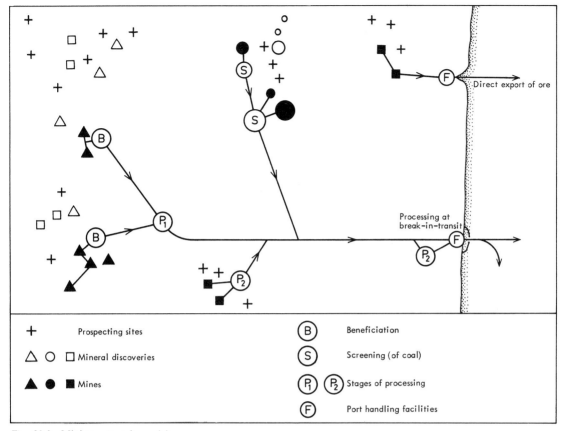

Fig. 20.2 Mining network model.

extend into processing. The point at which mining ceases and manufacturing begins is perhaps an academic one but, we may add, it is not without significance particularly with reference to labour demarcation disputes. Its location along the route within initial and final processing is noted here as 'closing' the system for the purposes of this study. Its actual location in the flow system will be discussed later in the chapter.

The flow system may conceptually be transformed into a network system, the geographical expression of the structured flow. Each unit in the system has a preferred location—the choice of mine site from the number of mineral locations being but one of the factors in the preference. Following the selection of mine site, the network develops in response to the build-up of linked preferred locations in the total mining system.

Initial locations are in the vaguely defined territory of mineral exploration. 'Preferred location' here refers to the choice of area to explore. If exploration leads to discovery, locations are noted and mine sites

chosen. Network nodes focus on the mines and on the associated processing plants along the route from mine to market. Linkages are in the transport and handling facilities. Fig. 20.2 represents the network system. Conceptually it is based on Philip Wagner's model, 'A spatial pattern of production' in *The Human Use of the Earth* (1960). Our study has as its reference for organization the structural model of flow and as reference for geographical pattern, the network model of nodes and linkages. Mining activity and social infrastructure are associated with the nodes while transport facilities that go with it make up the linkage infrastructure.

THE GEOGRAPHICAL MATRIX

The matrix for this study is the man-land surface of Australia on which mining has been established, and out of which the patterns of mining activity grow. The area has boundaries which limit the extension of this particular mining system; and properties, both physical and cultural, which interact with it to influence the character and direction of mining patterns.

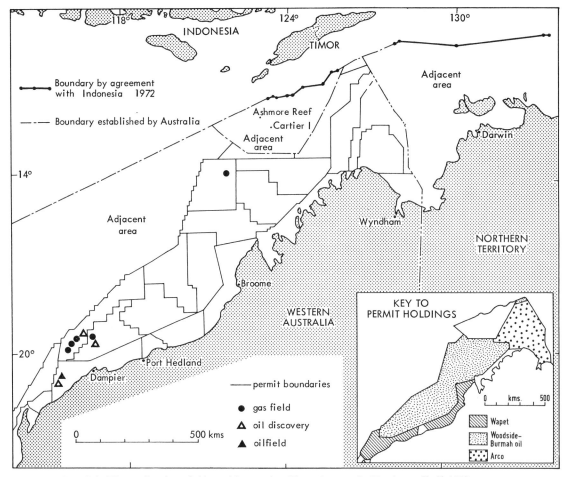

Fig. 20.3 Permit holdings, oil and gas fields, and international boundary on the Northwest Shelf, 1972.

Boundaries

The boundaries of Australia would appear to present no immediate problem. They encompass the land area of the six States and the two Territories, with their adjoining islands. As Australia is defined, it excludes the External Territories, although we might note that Christmas Island in the Indian Ocean is a source of phosphate for Australia; and that the islands of the Coral Sea have been named as an External Territory by the Coral Sea Islands Act of 1969.

Some islands of the States and Territories have mines of economic importance. For example, Cockatoo and Koolan Islands in Yampi Sound, Western Australia are a major domestic source of iron ore. Barrow Island, also in Western Australia, has an oil field that supplies about 9 per cent of present Australian petroleum requirements. Manganese is mined on Groote Eylandt in the Gulf of Carpentaria, and King Island in the Bass Strait has scheelite mines, a source

of tungsten metal. Ashmore and Cartier Islands in the Timor Sea were annexed to the Northern Territory in 1938. Their location is of significance in establishing a boundary for sea-bed exploitation between Australia and Indonesia.

The extent to which Australia can claim to have sovereignty over offshore sea and sea-bed is far from clear. To the limit of territorial sea, which Australia claims as 12 miles (19.3 km), sovereignty is generally established over depth of ocean waters and sea-bed. Beyond, claims to jurisdiction rest on declarations rather than international recognition for most of the extra-territorial sea-bed. In the area of the Timor Sea, Australia had claimed jurisdiction over a continuous underlying continental shelf until it was terminated abruptly in the Timor Trough, 2,700 m deep and within 100 km of Eastern Timor. Indonesia was inclined to argue that the shelf is continuous between the two countries and that the deep is a tectonic break in the shelf. If this were so, a median line between the two countries was seen as being more meaningful. In the end, the boundary line, fixed by agreement in 1972, was a compromise between the two arguments, and would have taken into account Australia's greater command of technology in terms of the internationally declared notion of 'economic feasibility' and 'limits of exploitability'. Furthermore, Ashmore and Cartier Islands, with their territorial seas and sea-beds would extend the Australian claim northwards. The boundary, in the area defined by the agreement, comes close to coinciding with the northern limit of petroleum leases on the Northwest Shelf although no drilling has been undertaken in these deeper waters (Fig. 20.3).

The agreement does not yet include definition from Indonesian-controlled Eastern Timor. One Australian company, Timor Oil, holds leases granted by Portugal extending from the mainland of Timor offshore. In early 1974, the *Portuguese Gazette* recorded an authorization to the Portuguese Minister for Overseas Territories 'to enter into concession arrangements off Timor with the Oceanic Exploration Company of Denver, U.S.A'. The area of concessions was to extend 350 km offshore.

The agreement extends east into the area of the Arafura Sea, and to a further sensitive area between Australia and Papua-New Guinea. Although concern is more with right of passage in the Torres Strait area and with the future of the Torres Strait islanders, the question of mineral rights will inevitably play a part in the need to resolve differences. The present boundary of Queensland runs close to the Papuan coast, so close as to be politically unacceptable to Papua-New Guinea. The somewhat arbitrary suggestion of the 10°S parallel as a boundary is generally not acceptable.

Suffice to say that, in terms of a lack of international agreement for reference, the extreme boundaries of what is Australia cannot be exactly defined. Yet it is not surprising that Australia should look with concern at her extra-territorial boundaries. In the light of current mineral shortages—particularly of the energy resources—and with considerable advances in the technology of sea-bed mining at greater depths, an expanding rim of economic worth is becoming available. Surveys have identified three main groups of minerals on the continental shelf: (a) construction minerals—sand, gravel and limestone; (b) detrital minerals—tin, gold, platinum, diamonds and titanium minerals; and (c) phosphorite—sedimentary rock composed mainly of phosphatic materials. Beyond the continental shelf, manganese nodules containing appreciable quantities of copper and cobalt have been found over widely dispersed areas. Furthermore the Bureau of Mineral Resources in a recent survey of the configuration and geology of the continental margin, has noted the 'considerable extent' of sedimentary

structures. These would have a high potential as reservoirs for hydrocarbons.

In the Petroleum (Submerged Lands) Act 1967–8, 1970, Australia has moved to 'adopt the international convention on the continental shelf, whereby the coastal State is entitled to exercise sovereign rights for the purpose of exploring and exploiting the natural resources of the continental shelf'. The legislation embodies claims to sea-bed exploitation of the continental shelf defined initially as extending to a depth of 200 m, and beyond to the 'limit of exploitability'. The claim is to control 'territorial seabed' of the continental margins to a distance of 320 km offshore, and on to the 'ocean floor of the abyssal plain'. Similar legislation has been prepared to cover other mineral rights but the Seas and Submerged Lands Bill with its assumption of Federal right to control, will have to meet the challenge of State rights and prerogatives particularly offshore from Queensland and Western Australia.

The Land

Physical and cultural characteristics of the Australian environment have played their part in modifying the direction and character of mining activity. Australia's area of 7.8 million square kilometres gives it an ultimate potential for mineral discovery that would far exceed that of most countries, but the handicap of distance where kilometres must be measured across a harsh and inhospitable environment has discouraged the search for all but the most valuable minerals in the past, and the development of all but the most extensive in reserves at present.

Landforms in Australia are generally mature and hardly present insuperable difficulties to individual miner or to mining corporation. Rugged relief is more often associated with the slopes of drainage systems than with the undulating surfaces of interfluve areas. It is extent of aridity that places severe restrictions on all but near-coastal areas. High temperatures within the tropics add further to the deleterious effects of low rainfall.

Miners had to improvise if metals were to be recovered. Early gold panners developed a technique of 'dry blowing' for gold in the primitive diggings of Halls Creek and in some of the Northern Territory mines. It was an inefficient method of attempting to separate alluvial gold from clay, but one necessitated by the constant lack of water. Water supply reservoirs often failed at the smelters near Broken Hill and water had to be carried from Silverton, an inconvenience which led to a decision to re-establish a larger smelter at Port Pirie and later to pipe water from the Murray River.

In more recent times, the predecessors to Comalco were deterred from establishing an alumina smelter

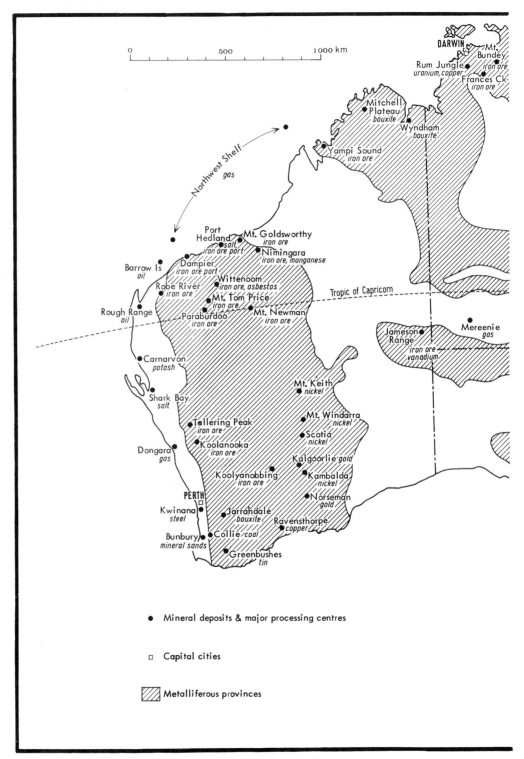

Fig. 20.4   Metalliferous provinces and mineral deposits in Australia.

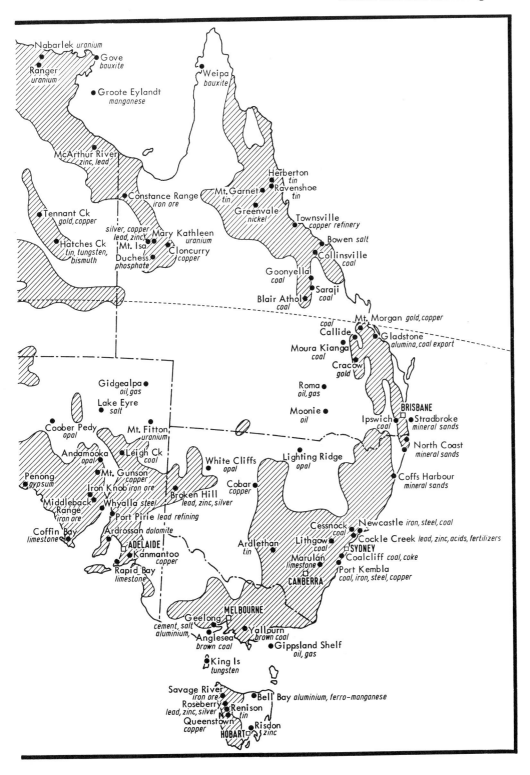

at Weipa after extensive borings revealed that water from surface and underground sources was only marginally available in sufficient quantities. That it was marginally available and in a situation where bauxite mining is now firmly established, has led Comalco into reviewing the possibility of establishing alumina plant in the area.

Yet in a country where about 40 per cent of the land area receives less than 250 mm of rainfall, and 70 per cent less than 500 mm, a 'wet season' in the northern tropics and localized flooding in desert areas can interrupt prospecting and mining schedules, and disrupt transport between remote mine and distant coast. During the period of intensive prospecting for uranium in the Northern Territory, camps often had to be disbanded during 'the wet'. Santos Ltd, a partner in providing natural gas for the Adelaide market, notes that flooding at Moomba Gasfield seriously hampered operations in the first six months of 1974. Road access was impossible in this, an area with an average annual rainfall of 100–150 mm.

Tableland Tin N.L., a dredging company operating near Mt Garnet, northern Queensland had its whole operation all but closed when its main dam burst during a flood period. It normally holds a precarious but adequate flow from local streams. Mining output decreased, income of a company not noted for any extensive capital reserves was considerably reduced, and the company, being in a vulnerable position, was later taken over by a larger group.

Vegetation and rural land use reflect the pattern of rainfall. Just as dams have often to be built at considerable expense, and water coaxed into the reservoirs to provide supplies for mining and processing operations, so too have timber reserves, and forest plantings of exotics had to be established with considerable difficulty around major mining centres like Broken Hill and Kalgoorlie. Because these are largely recent plantings, and they have a further value in helping to allay the dust nuisance, much timber has to be brought into the mining areas at considerable cost.

Although the infrastructure of a rural network improved accessibility for prospector and miner, it tended to limit any effective prospecting activity to 'settled' and 'semi-settled' Australia in the search for a greater range of minerals. In some areas, there did develop something of a symbiotic link between miner and pastoralist. Utilizing his contacts with coastal city, the pastoralist set up a supply centre for any nearby mining community until tradesmen arrived. The contact was tenuous and was effective only when 'times were hard'. At other times, the station owner would, in fact, chose to remain aloof from prospecting camp or mining development, preferring to see the land and station hands employed exclusively for the grazing of stock.

The miner, seeking to exploit a resource that was located independently of any immediate environmental control was nevertheless confined by these environmental hazards. He reached beyond the limits of effective settlement only at the risk of considerable hardship to himself, or cost to the promoting company. It is a feature of the contemporary phase in mining development that the challenge imposed by environment is being met by selecting for large-scale operation. Factors involved are large size of mineral discovery, the investment of large amounts of developmental capital by international corporations, and access to mining technology and infrastructural development commensurate with the scale of operation.

Restrictions are still however present. Mineral deposits, as shown in Fig. 20.4, are essentially peripheral to the arid centre of the continent. Admittedly much of this area consists of sedimentary basins, and some oil drilling and other prospecting appropriate to these areas have been undertaken, but even the areas which could contain metalliferous deposits have had but limited prospecting. Nickel sulphides have been found in the remote Wingellina area. The prospecting company, International Nickel Australia Ltd has, through its parent Canadian company, ready access to the resources for development but infrastructural costs including provision of water for a processing plant are beyond the reasonable limits of profitability at present nickel prices. Oil and gas fields have also been found in central Australia. Located in the Amadeus Basin, the Mereenie field alone contains over 500,000 million million cubic feet of gas and 300 million barrels of oil while gas flow from the large Palm Valley structure measured 1.97 million m^3 in the Number 2 well. Although there has been interest in the fields including a modest proposal for a refinery at Alice Springs, and feasibility studies for pipeline grids have been undertaken, there has as yet been no development. A Californian public utility supplier was prepared to develop the field but the prospect of a link with the Gidgealpa field in South Australia and thence eventually the Sydney market as part of plans for a national grid, was to discourage further proposals for export.

Thus in a country that has a north-south extent of 3,700 km and east-west of 4,025 km, the distances alone place handicaps on development. When to distances are added the adverse qualities of the physical environment, then the handicaps become insurmountable for all but the most specific forms of mining activity in which either or both value of mineral and size of operation take precedence.

HISTORICAL PERSPECTIVE

Mining had its origins in coal discoveries in the

Sydney Basin, a broad structure containing sediments of Permian and Triassic age. The basin extends along the coast from north of Newcastle south almost to Batemans Bay. Although coal was to dominate in the record of early discovery, we can be sure that the much more prosaic 'construction materials' were also being mined if only to supply the basic needs of early colonists for stone building materials, bridging matterials and road ballast.

Discovery

Within ten years of settlement at Sydney Cove, coal was being collected in the Hunter River area and transported to Sydney, some of it for export. In 1827 Captain Logan reported coal discoveries in southeast Queensland. The first mine, a small beginning for the present Ipswich Coalfield, was opened at Redbank in 1843. In the course of the century, the Blair Athol and Callide fields of central Queensland were to be discovered almost incidentally in the search for artesian water and for gold. Between 1834 and 1840 convicts supplied the labour for Tasmania's first field. When better quality coal was discovered at Fingals Valley, although further from Port Arthur, this new area was developed as the first real coal mine in Tasmania. The search for better quality coal, in fact, soon led to replacement of the earlier finds which had been useful mainly because of their proximity to the original settlements. Industrial and domestic users in Victoria, for example, came to prefer the imported black coal from New South Wales to their own slow-burning and dirty product from mines such as that at Lal Lal which, from 1857, had been periodically shipped to Ballarat, Geelong and Melbourne.

It was in South Australia that the first metal mines were to be established. Although metal discoveries including gold had been made, the South Australian discoveries had the advantage of ready accessibility, being near the coast. Lead was found in the Glen Osmond Hills within 6.5 km of the new settlement of Adelaide as early as 1839, but it was the new copper discoveries 65 km to the north that proved to be more attractive. Copper first from Burra, and then from Wallaroo and Moonta was mined, processed and shipped. Blainey (1963) notes in his eminently readable account of Australian mining that by 1850 South Australia was exporting more copper than wool and wheat, and that by 1866 copper furnaces were roasting, calcining and refining copper ore at Wallaroo. The furnaces used about 10 per cent of all coal shipped out of Newcastle.

Copper was discovered in the Northampton district of Western Australia in 1849 but it was not until the latter part of the century that copper really began to make an impression with production from the CSA mine at Cobar, New South Wales, and from the Iron Blow outcrop in Tasmania. Silver-lead-zinc mining followed on discoveries in the Murchison River area in 1848, and later various combinations of these metals were to be mined at Captains Flat, east of the present federal capital. Silver-lead discoveries at Zeehan led to a rush to this remote area of southwest Tasmania in 1888 to the extent that within three years 159 companies were working in the area. An iron ore smelter was established at Berrima, near Mittagong, probably some time in 1849 and was carried on intermittently until 1877. It represents the first of many attempts to establish iron production.

Gold, copper and silver were, in turn, sought amid the arid hills of the Barrier Ranges near the New South Wales-South Australia border. When silver was found in 1876, it was to lead to the short-lived rise of Silverton as a silver-lead centre. Prospecting in other mineralized areas of the Ranges was disappointing insofar as silver was concerned. At Broken Hill a syndicate was formed to finance shaft sinking. Lead carbonate was plentiful but it was not until one of their number found rich flecks of silver chloride, confirmed by assay, that the Broken Hill Proprietary Company was formed in 1885 to finance further mining and treatment of the ore. From these small beginnings, the company, mining in New South Wales, provisioned and supplied from South Australia and financed from the company's headquarters in Melbourne, was to grow to become the giant among Australian miners, and the area to support a thriving range of smaller companies and syndicates.

But of all the discoveries in the latter half of the nineteenth century none was more important than that of gold. In the record of mining returns, it was to dominate until well into the twentieth century. First noted in 1823 in the granite country east of Bathurst, it was not until midway through the century that Hargraves officially registered the first real discoveries. It was important that he notified the government of New South Wales of his find, for it brought the first major rush of miners to diggings at the junction of the Summerhill and Lewis Pond Creeks, which he called Ophir. Today this, the Central Region of New South Wales, contains the State's principal goldfields distributed in a belt described as a broad stretch of auriferous country trending north-south for about 130 km and consisting of sediments and volcanic rocks of Lower Palaeozoic age intruded by granite and prophyry.

Within but a few days of the separation of Victoria from the colony of New South Wales, the new government was notified of gold discoveries in Victoria. That near Clunes was probably the first, but the epoch-making discoveries at Ballarat and Bendigo followed soon afterwards. Elsewhere gold mining successfully succeeded discovery—at Canoona,

Queensland in 1858, Forbes, New South Wales in 1862, Gympie, Queensland in 1868, and later at Charters Towers and Mount Morgan in 1882. The opening of the Mount Lyell field in Tasmania in 1886 was the last important new discovery in the eastern States.

In the far west, minor discoveries were made between 1850 and 1870, but it was not until 1886 that first, the remote Kimberley field was discovered, to be followed by three others called the Pilbara, Murchison and Yilgarn goldfields. In 1892 gold was discovered at Coolgardie, and in the following year Hannan and Flannigan found the Kalgoorlie field, one that has maintained an output to the present day. There were to be no further discoveries of major goldfields although profitable returns have been obtained where gold is found associated with copper, lead and zinc mining.

Other major developments belong more properly to the present century. The Broken Hill Proprietary Company finally ceased its operation at Broken Hill in 1936, and has subsequently grown to be Australia's producer of iron and steel. It owned iron ore deposits in the Middleback Ranges, South Australia, having taken these over from the Mount Minden Mining Company in 1896 when it wanted a fluxing material for the new smelters at Port Pirie. In 1915 it established a steel mill at Newcastle making use of the rich hematite ores from the Iron Knob section of the Ranges. Later it was to bring in other deposits in the Ranges and to mine ores at Yampi Sound in northwest Australia. In 1935 it took over and then expanded iron and steel plant at Port Kembla, New South Wales, and subsequently it has established blast furnace and steel making capacity at Whyalla, South Australia and at Kwinana, south of Perth.

Natural gas discoveries were made in 1900 when gas and condensate were tapped in deepening a water bore for the small town of Roma in inland Queensland. For ten days in 1906 it was used for street lighting, and then the flow ceased—the beginning of what was to be a disheartening search for oil in Australia. In 1954, West Australian Petroleum Proprietary Limited encountered a large but short-lived flow of oil from its Rough Range No. 1 well near the Exmouth Gulf, an isolated part of the Australian northwest. It was not until the 1960s that really commercial discoveries were to be made.

Reddish cliffs 'probably bauxitic', located along the western coastline of the Cape York Peninsula had been noted early in the present century. Although an aluminium industry established at Bell Bay, Tasmania began production in 1955, it was not until 1958 that the cliffs were re-examined when a party of oil geologists were in the area. Meanwhile, imported bauxite had to be used because the larger Australian

deposits at Inverell and on Marchinbar Island in Arnhem Land were either too far from the coast or contained too many impurities for practical use.

The first commercial production of mineral sands was mined in 1934. Uranium concentrate was first produced in 1954; and to complete this all-too-brief coverage, we note the major discovery of nickel ores first at Kambalda and then at other Western Australian locations in the 1960s. The huge iron ore discoveries of the Australian northwest have also been developed in this last decade.

Trends in Production

We are indebted to Kalix *et al.* (1966) for their detailed coverage of historical data relating to the mineral industry. Coal, gold and copper were the three principal minerals mined during the nineteenth century. Black coal production has increased steadily with but minor fluctuations, the one downturn of any significance being that of the depression of the 1930s. By 1860 Australia had produced about 2.5 million tonnes of coal—mainly from New South Wales. From 1861 coal production rose from 360,000 tonnes per year to 649,000 tonnes at the turn of the century, and to 22,931,000 tonnes in 1960. During that period all States came to produce coal with New South Wales still dominating, producing just under 80 per cent of all production. Queensland was next with 12 per cent.

From the first record of production in 1851, and for the next ten years, New South Wales and Victoria between them produced 768 million grams of gold. Contrasting with coal production, that of gold has fluctuated considerably as prices and incentives rose and fell; and as old discoveries were worked out and new discoveries made. In fact, as early as 1861 production had already begun to fall from a peak of 94 million grams in 1856, a figure it was not again to reach until 1899. Over the century from 1860, peak production was reached in 1903 with a figure of 119 million grams. Production had fallen to 34 million grams by 1960. Of this total, 80 per cent originated in Western Australia, with between 6 per cent and 7 per cent from both the Northern Territory and Queensland. Production subsequently rose in Queensland and the Northern Territory to give 19 per cent of total production in 1964, while production fell in Western Australia.

The trend in copper production as recorded in the copper content of 'ores, concentrates etc.' is more similar to that for gold than for coal. While gold had its maximum annual productions for the nineteenth century in the early years following the rushes, copper maintained production round about the 10,000 tonne level from 1865 until nearly 1900. The years 1912 and 1913 were peak years in the early 1900s with production about the 47,000 tonne mark per year. There was a

Table 20.1 Production of Selected Mineral 1860–1960

	Black coal (tonnes)	Gold (grams)	Copper (tonnes)
1860	361,997[a]	75,957,391	5,000[b]
1880	1,561,111	36,508,884	10,000[b]
1900	6,487,752	99,426,537	23,133
1920	13,011,133	29,350,942	26,895
1940	11,913,880	51,134,123	22,205
1960	22,931,192	33,800,453	111,191

[a] coal, 1861.

[b] copper: estimates from graph, McLeod, 1965.

Source: Kalix *et al.*, 1966

dramatic fall-off after World War I, a rise in the 1920s in keeping with the growth of the economy, and then fall with the onset of the Depression. Finally there has been a most dramatic rise in production to 111,000 tonnes between 1950 and 1960. Queensland was responsible for the bulk of this increase, in 1960 producing 76 per cent of all copper. Tasmania produced 11 per cent, and the Northern Territory 9 per cent.

Hence at about the beginning of what we shall call the contemporary period, production trends which had varied with business cycles, labour supply and mineral discoveries throughout the preceding 100 years, were establishing a trend for a considerable and unprecedented increase in production. As we shall see, coal and copper in their own particular ways reflected this. Gold miners, tied to the price of approximately US$35 an ounce (28 g), were finding it increasingly difficult to maintain production in the face of rising production costs and dwindling payable supplies. Subsidies under the Gold Mining Assistance Act were being paid to producers in order to maintain production, and employment. Rising pressure on price led to the adoption of a two-tier system incorporating official and free prices. Free or market price rose to touch over US$200 per ounce, but has since fallen considerably.

Some other metallic minerals were beginning to increase in production. Tin had seen peaks in production in the 1880s and early 1900s, but it was not until the early 1960s that prices were to rise sufficiently and spectacularly, to induce further prospecting. Mines like Ardlethan and those in western Tasmania whose profit thresholds were about $1,600 a tonne were re-examined and a number of them reopened when the price of tin went to $2,000 and then $3,000 a tonne.

Significance in the Economy

N. G. Butlin noted that Australian economic growth has followed a classic course of successful economic development involving the establishment first of a highly productive primary industry followed by progressive reorientation towards manufacturing. Mining is a part of the highly productive primary industry. Its role may be followed in the mining component of Gross Domestic Product (at factor cost) from 1860 to 1960, and in the trend in contribution to the total Gross Domestic Product. From a contribution of 15 per cent to total Product in the early phase, there was a fall-off in the succeeding decades and then a rise to 10 per cent again during a period of low pastoral returns at about the turn of the century. With the growth of other primary, secondary and tertiary industry, mining had fallen to well below 5 per cent between 1915 and 1960. The last decade to 1960 saw a rise in the value of mining but again an increased return in the value of other growth sectors did little more than retain the level of contribution for this period.

In 1861 gold was responsible for over 90 per cent of the mining sector of Gross Domestic Product. By the turn of the century it had fallen to 64 per cent as silver and silver-lead grew to a value of about $5 million per year. It fell to 20 per cent in 1921 but had risen again to 43 per cent by 1939. The value of the return from coal showed an increase from 2 per cent to 24 per cent over the same period and briefly exceeded 50 per cent in the early 1920s. Metallic minerals were mainly responsible for other increases. By 1939, silver, tin, copper, zinc and iron ore made up 20 per cent of mining's share. Something of the present patterns were being established in the range of minerals appearing in production figures.

This brief survey has been no more than a reference, a perspective for contemporary developments, over the historical period. There are many themes that require

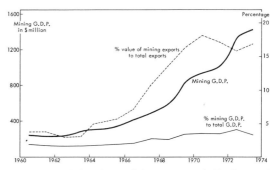

Fig. 20.5 Mining share of Gross Domestic Product and share of total value of exports, excluding products of final processing, e.g. pig lead, zinc bars, copper ingot. *Source*: Bureau of Statistics, 1976, Table C; Bureau of Statistics, *Official Yearbook of the Commonwealth of Australia*, Nos 50–60, Canberra.

further treatment. None would be more interesting to the geographer than items such as changes in the division of labour as mining becomes more complex and activities more specialized; the impact of advances in technology on the mining scene, from the almost handicraft levels of early Cornish, Scot and Welsh miners, to the new bulk-handling technologies emanating from the United States and Germany. The contribution of mining to the spread of settlement and to the processes of a developing frontier are other themes worthy of much further study.

During the period, the more ubiquitous non-metallic minerals were able to utilize mineral areas closer to centres of population. Coal was the main source of fuel and power. Gas and electrical establishments at a later period, converted the coal into more convenient forms of energy. The two principal centres of population and industry, Sydney and Melbourne, made the greatest demands for electric power. Large coal deposits located relatively close to these centres were the first to be developed. Black coal found many uses while brown coal from the Latrobe Valley went almost exclusively into gas and electricity production for Victoria. Only in Tasmania and in the Snowy Mountain watershed of the New South Wales-Victoria border was rainfall sufficient and sites available for significant hydroelectric generation. In 1949 the Australian government had passed the Snowy Mountain Hydro-electric Power Act setting up an Authority to generate electricity in the Snowy Mountains area. From development in the Snowy-Tumut and in the Snowy-Murray headwaters, it was planned to generate 3,740 MW. By 1960 the scheme was sufficiently advanced for 320,000 kW of installed capacity to be available for use. In 1960, all electricity generated totalled 23,199 million kWh. Installed capacity for steam generation was 71 per cent of a total of 5,953,000 kW.

MINERAL EXPLORATION

The decision as to where to explore for minerals was often fairly casually arrived at. Perception of the value of information and resulting behaviour—at individual or a boardroom level—plays a very real part in any decision, whether it be to prospect, to mine, or to adopt a particular level of processing in relation to the mining activity. How decisions are arrived at, although pertinent, is not a part of this study. Concern here is more with the identification and organization of information which is available to the decision maker

The Mineral Base

Minerals of various composition and form occur in the three major rock types of the earth's crust—igneous, sedimentary and metamorphic. From an average composition of igneous rock, it has been estimated that silicon, aluminium, iron and calcium make up the bulk of its mineral content. Nickel, copper and uranium, to take three other minerals, are present in much smaller but, at the same time, identifiable quantities. All minerals are chemically combined in 34 main groups to make up the 'rock forming minerals'.

During the Tertiary Era, Australia was subjected to major outpourings of magma mainly from fissure eruptions. Probably the most recent of these were in Victoria and to the northwest of Melbourne. 'Islands' of the basaltic lavas like that on which Richmond is located, played a part in the selection of suburban sites around Port Phillip Bay as the city of Melbourne spread. The dark stone was quarried and used in some of the earlier Melbourne buildings. Moreover, because many types of igneous rock are hard, durable and of medium to fine grain, it can be crushed, graded and marketed as the 'blue metal' used in road making.

A particularly attractive plutonic rock called norite is quarried near Adelaide. Quartz diorite, a useful facing stone, is shipped to the main cities of Australia from quarries at Gracemere, near Rockhampton. Granite is one of the more widely distributed of building stones. Australian granites are used in all major cities, some with distinctive red or greenish tinges being particularly sought after.

Metallic minerals although a part of the composition of igneous rocks are not present in concentrations high enough to be useful. Processes of mineralization following erosion and sorting, or applications of heat and pressure are required to bring about the upgrading of available mineral content.

Sedimentary rocks, although prevalent over most of the interior of Australia, make up but a small portion of the total rock mass. They are of much greater depth in making up the central geosyncline of Australia and in the several peripheral synclinal troughs. Originally horizontally bedded when laid down as sediments, subsequent folding and faulting has to be recognized in the search for traps which might hold oil or natural gas.

Among the sedimentary rocks, sandstone is probably the best known as a building material in Australia. Sandstones of Permian age quarried on the northern and western coalfields of New South Wales are used as building stones in the nearby cities of Maitland and Goulburn. Helidon sandstone is well known as a building and facing stone throughout southeast Queensland, while Hawkesbury sandstone has been used in many public buildings of the central Sydney area.

Chemical activity brings about a modification of the original sedimentary rock. Where selective leaching under conditions of alternating aeration and submergence occurs, silicas lime and magnesia may be removed and residuals high in iron and aluminium oxides remain. Laterites such as limonite, and bauxite are then sufficiently concentrated in iron and aluminium respectively to become economic minerals. Precipitates high in dissolved aluminas and silicates give rise to opals, saline sediments to salt and halite; gypsum may similarly be precipitated out.

Sedimentary rocks of organic origin are a particularly significant group. Bone, shell, and skeletal concentrations generally settle out and are compressed or cemented to form phosphatic rocks. Phosphate may dissolve in sea water later to be precipitated out in oolitic or nodular forms. Until the recent discoveries in northwest Queensland, locations of phosphate in Australia were extremely limited.

Accumulations of vegetative matter gave rise to lignite and brown coal deposits such as those being worked on a large scale in Victoria, and others like those recently discovered in South Australia. Black coal, a compression of dehydrated vegetable matter, and oil shales are other mineralized sedimentary rocks. Recent extensive discoveries in central Queensland have led to a complete revaluation of this energy source in Australia. Small areas of peat are found in Tasmania.

Of the calcareous sedimentaries, limestone is the best known. Used both for agricultural purposes and as a building and ornamental stone, it is quarried in such locations as Cudgegong, Mudgee, Caleula and Borenore, the two latter from the Orange district of New South Wales. In fact extensive limestone deposits of Silurian and Devonian age occur in many areas of the Eastern Highlands, and within New South Wales these are quarried at such locations as Marulan, Portland and localities in the Kandos-Mudgee area. Palaeozoic limestones are found near Rockhampton, Warwick and Chillagoe in Queensland. Fossil corals from Moreton Bay form the basis of the cement making industry in southeastern Queensland.

Detrital deposits in which cassiterite, gold and silver may be concentrated occur in some States. Other unconsolidated sediments form the host rock for the mineral sands. Gravel for road building, cement matrix and a variety of other purposes is taken from old and present stream beds in all of the States.

Metamorphic rocks, the result of heat or pressure transformation of both igneous and sedimentary materials, account for the occurrence of most of the 'old rock' areas. Among these are quartzites transformed from sandstone, and marble from limestone. Marble is widely used in Sydney, much of it coming from Wombeyan. A crystalline marble of Precambrian age is found in various locations in South Australia. Perhaps the best known is from quarries at Angaston, 50 km from Adelaide.

Shales change to slate following metamorphism. The dark-blue roofing slates of older buildings were largely imported from Wales but a green-grey slate extracted from slates at Chatsworth, near Goulburn has been used in Sydney. A slaty rock from the Lofty Ranges close to Adelaide was cut into suitable blocks and used as a building stone. Indeed slates, gneisses and schists with their more or less horizontal fracturing, were commonly used as building materials in early pioneer homes and station buildings.

Mineral concentration of identifiable chemical composition occur under selected circumstances within all of these major rock formations. Some minerals, as we have seen, are concentrated within the magma. Others are concentrated particularly in calcareous rocks, by replacement as a result of contact with hot solutions or with gases from the molten intrusive magma. Still others are formed at various depths commonly as vein deposits in fractures, joints and other openings in the rock; and from solutions originating from molten magmas at depth. It should be noted that a whole region may be affected by the 'halo' effect of metamorphism; or again, minerals may be replaced or rock spaces filled by processes of metasomatism. Veins follow fractures in the original rock and in these, ore and gangue minerals concentrate.

In terms of differing mineral potentials, Australia may be roughly subdivided into areas of sedimentary basins in which the main fuel minerals, a number of non-metalic minerals, and the construction minerals may be found; and uplifted highlands and tablelands or stable cratons essentially of old rock in which the important metalliferous, and some other mineral deposits are to be found. The areas may be grouped into three provinces: (a) the Western Province, the main mineralized area of Western Australia which is fringed to the west by the Carnarvon Basin, and to the east by sedimentary basins such as the Canning to the north and the Eucla fronting on to the Great Australian Bight; (b) the Central Province which contains a number of isolated mineralized regions. In the Northern Territory the northernmost of these extends from Pine Creek to the northern coast and then west to the Kimberley region of the Western Province. A second mineralized region extends from the vicinity of Alice Springs north to Tennant Creek and thence northeast into the Harts Range. The extensive Cloncurry mineral field which includes Mt Isa extends along the Gulf of Carpentaria and is part of this Central Province. A sector extends west from the Musgrave Range, while mineralized regions in the Eyre Peninsula, Flinders Range and Broken Hill may be considered as within the Province; and (c) the Eastern Province which is coincident with the eastern Australian highlands and tablelands. It is almost continuous from Tasmania to Cape York being interrupted only where the Great Artesian Basin reaches towards the coast in extensions such as the Bowen Basin, the Maryborough, Clarence, Sydney and the Gippsland basins. A distinction in the ages of the provinces should be noted. In the Western and Central provinces most of the mineral bearing rocks are Precambrian in age. Those of the Eastern Province occur in younger rocks of Palaeozoic, Mesozoic and Cainozoic ages.

Prospector and Promoter

Miners' luck as it was called, played an important part in many early mineral discoveries. Less was left to chance by later prospectors many of whom came with experience from overseas, or perhaps with training in the newly formed schools of mines in Australia. They extended the range in successfully looking for the less obvious metallic ores. Moreover they often sought to promote their finds, effectively playing an entrepreneural as well as a mining role.

Tom McDonald was representative of the newer type of prospector, if such could be said of a highly individual group. Born in Tasmania into a farming family he, at some stage, acquired an interest in minerals. It is believed that he went to Ballarat and there took the course at the School of Mines before returning to Tasmania. He was at Zeehan during the gold rushes of the 1880s after which he became familiar with much of the mining territory of the west coast. In 1893 he penetrated the dense forest on the southern slopes of Mount Black and discovered gold disseminated in alluvial wash along with boulders of zinc-lead oxide. He formed a syndicate, the Roseberry Prospecting Association, and, for six months, was active in prospecting operations at the mineral site. In spite of a pessimistic report, prospecting was continued for a further six months when a lead-zinc sulphide ore body was discovered in a deep trench near the entrance to the present No. 3 level of the Tasmanian Copper Mine. That was the first discovery of zinc-lead sulphide *in situ* in Roseberry.

Jack White, a prospector living near Rum Jungle in the Northern Territory, was to recognize the radioactive carnotite of Rum Jungle after reading a pamphlet issued by the Bureau of Mineral Resources as a guide to prospectors. Clem Walton formed a syndicate of eight Mt Isa residents to follow up an earlier mineral find from somewhere in the vicinity of the derelict Rosebud copper smelter. They found their grey ore with the aid of geiger counters, on a steep hillside facing west onto a broad valley. Their promotion of the find, its outlines defined by follow-up work, was to win them $500,000 and a substantial royalty from the Rio Tinto Mining Company of Australia Limited; and a name for their mine—Mary Kathleen.

The role of the prospector-entrepreneur is undoubtedly exemplified in the discovery and promotion of the massive iron ore deposits of the Pilbara. Charles Warman and Stan Hilditch are associated with the discovery of the hematite iron ores of Mount Whaleback. They both attended the Kalgoorlie School of Mines and later Warman had financed his friend in the prospecting venture which led to the discovery in 1956. After the embargo on iron exports was lifted by the Federal government in 1960, the partners moved to interest others in the find. The Rio Tinto Company was not strongly impressed. Admittedly the area had considerable drawbacks. It was located in the inhospitable semi-arid interior and was difficult to reach with steep-sided watercourses to be crossed in the rugged country that lay between the ore body and the long journey to the coast. Furthermore there were technical difficulties involved in recovering the ore, while infrastructural costs in developing port handling and social facilities would be high. Rio Tinto, to become part of Conzinc Riotinto of Australia Ltd, looked elsewhere and the largest single iron ore deposit in the world was sold to Mount Newman Mining Proprietary Limited, a consortium of 'joint venturers' which included American Metals Climax Incorporated and Broken Hill Proprietary Company Limited.

Two other, and much publicized entrepreneurs are Lang Hancock and Peter Wright. They were responsible for the Mount Tom Price discovery and for selling their major leases to the Conzinc Riotinto Company. In both cases, the partners receive royalties on sales, the percentages varying with the proposals for mining and the ages of the mines. Hancock and Wright hold further leases in a number of other areas in the Pilbara. They have attempted to promote these but difficulties in interpreting current mining law and the politics of dealing with government, have been factors discouraging success to date. However, they retain a bewildering number of partnerships under the Hanwright name, formed to develop such other iron ore discoveries as Rhodes Ridge, Wittenoom, Western Ridge and McCameys Monster.

Prospecting Techniques

Following on from discoveries is the need to establish an extent of reserves that will, at least, allow for economic exploitation. Skills and techniques which the earlier prospector lacked are required for both successful prospecting and 'proving up' of mineral fields and it should be noted that trained geologists and mining engineers have only been used extensively in this present century. Still more recent is the practice of mining companies, as distinct from prospecting companies and government, in employing geologists to engage directly in exploration with mineral discovery as their primary objective.

A number of firms have become established which specialize in areas of prospecting activity. Oil drilling may be undertaken under contract. An Australian company, Oil Drilling and Exploration Limited is one such company. Its equipment consists of four shallow-medium capacity rigs, three medium capacity down to 3,000 m and five deep capacity rigs capable of drilling to over 5,000 m. During 1972, nine rigs were employed in Australia, one in Thailand and one in New Zealand.

At the data interpretation level, firms like Digital Technology Properietary Limited, Australian offshoot of a Canadian firm, undertake 'digital seismic processing' of field data. Other companies with services available in Australia would include Western Geographical and Geophysical Services International. Using their data system packages, and applying these to geochemical, magnetic, gravity and resistivity or well data, companies in this area can produce conventional contour maps, three dimensional contour drawings or isolines of geophysical values. Other firms like Petty Exploration of San Antonio, Texas undertake field seismic work as well as interpretation.

Many small exploratory companies were established during the boom years of the 1960s, some with assets that amounted to little more than knowledge of an anomaly on which to float. Others were more substantial and may be associated with major Australian or overseas groups. Pine Vale Mines, to take but one example, is a group of companies in which the Canadian company, International Mogul Mines Limited holds a major interest. Many benefits have resulted from ties with the major group. Included are authoritative technical advice and assistance, a flow of information on overseas conditions, and assistance 'in the face of increasingly unfavourable conditions for the exploration industry' within Australia, in sharing joint ventures and investment with Mogul beyond Australia.

Still other prospecting companies are tied units or subsidiaries of major mining groups. Carpentaria Exploration Company Proprietary Limited is a prospecting subsidiary of M. I. M. Holdings Limited, Dampier Mining of Broken Hill Proprietary Limited; Conzinc Riotinto Limited has an interest in I.O.L. Petroleum while Pacminex Proprietary Limited is the mineral subsidiary of the Colonial Sugar Refining Company Limited. Another such company is Unimin, a wholly owned exploratory subsidiary of Union Minière (Australia) Limited, in turn largely owned by the parent Belgian mining group. It has prospecting teams active in the Widgiemooltha nickel area of Western Australia which 'justifies further detailed examination', in the Pilbara, the Kimberley Range, near Mt Isa and at the Anaconda copper leases south of Cloncurry.

Reserves and Uranium Deposits
The end step in mineral exploration is a statement of reserves. However, terminology for this purpose can be confusing. A Joint Committee on Ore Reserves formed by the Australian Institute of Mining and Metallurgy and the Australian Mining Industry Council to consider the question, would recommend the use of the terms 'possible ore', 'probable ore reserves', and 'proved ore reserves'. Inferred or estimated, indicated, and proved or measured reserves is, however, a parallel set of terminology which appears to be more generally used. Because assessments of uranium reserves have been critical for decision to mine and export, they are reviewed as one example of the implications to be derived from extent of ore reserves.

Geological reserves of uranium oxide both measured and indicated, total in the neighbourhood of 250,000 tonnes making Australia third in the western world in terms of reasonably assured supplies. Of significance is the fact that well over half of the reserves are available at the highly competitive price of less than $22 a kilogram. Important occurrences are located in three States—Western Australia, Queensland, South Australia—and in the Northern Territory.

About 60 per cent of reserves are to be found in the Northern Territory where the Ranger deposit is the largest in the country. It was discovered by airborne radiometric survey in 1970, the anomaly being detectable at 760 m above ground level. Follow-up work defined nine separate anomalies five of which are nearing the end of testing stages with numbers one and three proving to be of major economic potential. By the middle of 1973, 200 diamond and percussion drill holes had established the extent of the ore body. Proven reserves total about 85,000 tonnes. An exploration camp capable of housing about eighty men, an airstrip and basic services were provided in meeting infrastructural requirements at the exploratory level. Both feasibility and environmental studies have been completed as part of the preparation for mining.

To the north lies a second major deposit at Nabarlek. It contains indicated reserves of 9,500 tonnes with impressive ore grades of 2.35 per cent uranium oxide. The mining companies involved in the discovery suffered from a premature and over-optimistic estimate of the original reserves by the managing director. More recently they have had to contend with the problem of impact on Aboriginal lands, for the discovery is not only in an Aboriginal reservation, but it also covers some of the Aboriginal sacred and ritual areas. Growing interest and support for the Aborigines' claims have resulted in a strong move to set aside areas 'traditionally used by Aborigines for hunting and foraging' while sites of sacred significance to the Aborigines are in fact being preserved. Overall, reservations in the Northern Territory cannot be revoked in whole or in part without 'an effective opportunity for review by both the Legislative Council of the Northern Territory and by both houses of the Federal Parliament'. So strong are the legal difficulties that, when combined with the opposition of a vocal sector of public opinion, they may be sufficient to preclude the possibility of mining in the Nabarlek area.

The first uranium ore body in the Territory was found at Rum Jungle. It was in production from 1954 to 1963 but closed when contracts expired. To the southeast of Rum Jungle are to be found the South Alligator River deposits. These also were mined in this area, until 1965. About 20 km south of the Ranger deposit Noranda Australia Limited, a subsidiary of Noranda Mines Limited of Canada, has outlined a further uranium deposit at Koongarra (also known as Jim Jim). Reserves are estimated to be in the neighbourhood of 40,000 tonnes. Pancontinental Mining No Liability located 20 km north of the Ranger deposits of Jabiluka is a further company with reserves in the area. The company is partnered by Getty Oil in its exploration work. Drilling has revealed an estimated 2,850 tonnes of uranium oxide at Jabiluka No. 1 deposit and 20,200 tonnes at No. 2.

During 1972 the developers of the Ranger and Nabarlek deposits entered into sales contracts with power companies in Japan valued at over $60 million. The contracts involved some 3,500 tonnes of contained uranium. Export licences were not however granted by the Federal government. Subsequent recommendations for approval are highly qualified.

A further 20 per cent of reserves are to be found in Western Australia. Those of major importance are at Yeelirrie where the Western Mining Corporation made the discovery in 1972. The deposit is estimated to contain 46,000 tonnes of uranium oxide. It is low grade, averaging only 0.15 per cent, but it is large and extremely shallow occurring in horizontal layers with a maximum mining depth for the main ore body of about 9 m. Mineralization has been concentrated in an old river channel where percolating groundwater through clay and sand has deposited the uranium mineralization as calcined carnotite in voids and cavities in limestone.

South Australia and Queensland each have about 10 per cent of total reserves. In South Australia, uranium oxide has been mined at Radium Hill. Low-grade ores are located further north at Mt Painter. Queensland has two main areas of mineralization at Westmoreland and at the working deposit of Mary Kathleen. The Mary Kathleen mine, still with considerable reserves, met a contract to supply the United Kingdom Atomic Energy Commission then closed. It is being reopened to supply the Riotinto Zinc Corporation and a Japanese company with ore to the value of $60 million.

Thus reserves in Australia are considerable. Con-tracts completed to a total value of $115 million, cover a period of delivery from 1974 to 1986. In the late 1960s, export of ore was prohibited while the Federal government attempted to assess the country's requirements in relation to known reserves. Mining was to be allowed only after replacement reserves were discovered. A change in government in 1972 led to a tightening of policy. Under the Federal Minister for Mines, policy was but ill-formed and the contracts for sales were not able to be met while export licences were withheld. It has been established that Australian demand for uranium oxide up to the year 2000 will be about 32,000 tonnes and most of this will not be required until after 1990. Australia has more than adequate reserves but further delays became apparent as the Labor government moved slowly to formulate policy for involvement in mining this key resource in line with its ideologies. The announcement was made of 'joint ventures', and of a uranium enrichment plant in which a Federal agency, the Australian Atomic Energy Commission, would have a 50 per cent interest.

For Australian mineral reserves in general, the Bureau of Mineral Resources would in terms of 'mineral self-sufficiency' place them in three categories. The first contains those minerals where reserves are considered to be adequate. These would include all of the more important metallic ores, clays, coal, limestone and phosphate rock. The second group in which reserves are uncertain includes a number of ferro-alloys such as chromite and manganese, mercury and asbestos. Significantly the most important mineral in this class is crude oil where reserves have been estimated at about 250 million m^3, sufficient for ten years at present rates of use. Reserves are considered as negligible in the third category which includes borates, nitrates and sulphur. Uranium had been recorded as 'reserves uncertain' in the late 1960s but more recently and significantly it has been excluded from the list. Greater optimism, offset to some extent by union decision to disallow mining of uranium ore, has been engendered by the recent (1976) recommendations of the Fox Commission Report.

Summary

Government plays a major regulatory role in the control of exploration and development. Mineral exploration rights are granted by State governments, and by Federal government in the Territories. They revert back to government if conditions are not met, or at the expiry or revision of the licence. The Australian government claims the right to control offshore development; and it can influence the development of resources through its statutory powers regarding export licences, customs, taxation and loan-raising.

In 1970, 5 million hectares were occupied under

mining licences and ordinances. This was double the area occupied in 1969. In 1971, the area had increased to 5.8 million hectares but, reflecting the general downturn in mining activity, the area was reduced to 4 million hectares in 1972. Western Australia accounts for about 40 per cent of licences held, Queensland 30 per cent, and Victoria 20 per cent. In addition, where extensive prospecting ventures are involved, entitlement is usually in the form of an 'Agreement to Prospect'. Further conditions regarding mining and development in the event of major discovery are often attached, as for example in the Queensland government's agreement with Comalco.

Exploration expenditure, both private and government but excluding that for petroleum, increased to total $125.4 million in 1971–2. It has since been reduced to $108.1 million in 1972–3, only to climb to $124.2 million in 1974–5. About half of all private expenditure occurs in Western Australia. Government expenditure has increased over the period from $6.7 million to $13.4 million to be just over 10 per cent of total expenditure in the latter year.

Expenditure on petroleum exploration rose from $74.3 million in 1968 to $198.9 million in 1972. It has subsequently fallen to $98.1 million in 1973. Government expenditure was about 5 per cent in the last year. Private expenditure was allocated mainly to drilling with geophysical exploration next in importance. In all, 102 wells were drilled in 1972, about one-third of the number drilled in 1969 and half that of 1970. By 1973 the figure was reduced to 60 wells, a sad comment in an area where vital replacement reserves should be being built up. Twenty-two of the wells were drilled in Western Australia, eleven in Queensland and ten in Victoria.

MINING

Mining Establishments

Mining establishments include all mining operations carried on under one ownership and at a single physical location. Although activity at this location is centred around the mine, establishments 'mainly engaged in dressing or beneficiating ores or other minerals by crushing, milling, screening, washing, flotation or other, including chemical beneficiation, processes, or mainly engaged in briquetting' are included because they are generally carried out at or near mine sites and as an integral part of mining operations. Excluded are establishments mainly engaged in refining or smelting of minerals or ores; or in the manufacture of cement, fertilizers, iron ore pellets or metallized iron ore agglomerates, gas and electricity.

In recent years the number of mining establishments has risen to a figure of just over 1,500. Obviously the number in itself is of little significance. Some mining establishments are large and highly capitalized, some employ a large labour force, others are small operations in which the activity is essentially limited to recovery of ore, fuel or construction stone. There are, for example, five bauxite mining establishments in Australia with a total production that has doubled in the last five years to reach 20.1 million tonnes. Of the total tonnage, three of the five establishments accounted for over 99 per cent of production in 1972. Yet there are two further establishments listed as mining bauxite, one at Moss Vale, New South Wales and the other at Mirboo North in Victoria where bauxite is mined in small quantities for a flux in steel-making and for pharmaceutical salts respectively.

The significance of size of establishment can perhaps be further amplified in an examination of the relevant data presented in Table 20.2. Establishments employing larger numbers than other categories, produce brown coal and petroleum. They are also highly capitalized. Metallic mineral plants are today generally larger and more highly capitalized than in the past. Construction materials establishments representing numerous small quarries give a low average value-added per establishment.

Table 20.2 Characteristics of Mining Establishments by Industrial Class 1972–3

Industrial class	No. of establishments No.	Value added per establishment $'000	Persons employed per establishment No.	Value added per person employed $'000
Metallic minerals	224	3,645	141	25.81
Black coal	124	2,503	153	16.31
Brown coal and petroleum	14	23,368	243	96.16
Construction materials	707	151	9	16.97
Other non-metallic minerals	261	131	10	12.45
Total mining	1,330	1,199	47	25.27

Source: adapted from Table 1, 'Mining Establishments—summary of operations by industry class, Australia 1972–3', Bureau of Statistics (1974), *Mining Establishment details of operations Australia, States and Territorial*, Canberra, p. 7.

Within the mining classes, there is again considerable variation. Value added from crushed and broken stone for example, is over twice that from sand and gravel per establishment. There were 24 iron ore, 32 copper and 59 tin mining establishments recorded as at mid-year 1973. The value added from mining iron ore per establishment was over $13.6 million, from copper it was $3.9 million, and from tin $0.45 million illustrating the range about an average of $3.6 million per establishment for the group. Because of this marked variation it will be useful to examine briefly some of the smaller less complex units, important individually and locally, but collectively of limited significance both in terms of value of product and of numbers employed.

Simpler Forms of Mining Activity

Minerals that are readily recognizable by a distinctive coloration in relation to the surrounding earth materials, and at the same time are high in value per unit of weight, make for easier prospecting and for more rewarding returns from mining. Traditionally gold, silver and precious stones have attracted the individual miner. Gold has the added advantage of occurring in metallic form and in the early days of Australian mining many methods were devised in order to mine it. At Ballarat miners obtained entitlements to mine areas less than 6 square metres in extent. They then sank vertical shafts through loose clay, gravel and compacted clay to find some gold, but searching always for the richer blue clay layers which were seldom more than 10 cm thick but which would lead to higher gold recoveries. At White Hills, men crawled along drives that were over 7 metres underground, and from the greyish-white seams of grit they recovered up to 85 grams of gold to the bucket. Quartz mining, where gold was sought in the lode of reefs, required greater skills at each stage—in following the seam, in crushing and in recovering. Even in alluvium, greater skills would be called for in order to follow leads down to 700 or 800 metres, or in one case, to a maximum of 1,500 metres. More complex organization and financing were required if mining was to continue in these situations.

One of many examples is the 'Rise and Shine Reef' near Kilkivan in southern Queensland. The reef was discovered in the early 1870s and during 1875 and 1876 the mine reached peak production. Later, shafts went down to over 30 metres as the more accessible gold was recovered. The mine continued to operate until around 1886 but by that time the richer and near-surface oxidized ores had been mined out. It is interesting to note the factors which contributed to the decision to close. It was not that gold was not present, but rather that difficulties were encountered in the treatment of refractory ores from the deeper less oxidized workings. The reef was narrow and simple bailing methods could not cope with the inflow of water as depths increased. Costs also were increasing as mining proceeded to greater depths, but without commensurate ore returns. Attempts have been made to reopen this small mine. Exploratory shafts have been sunk, and diamond drilling undertaken, but results have not been satisfactory and the conditions which led to the closure still apparently apply.

Tin mining still has its 'fossickers' as well as its larger enterprises. They are to be found around Marble Bar in Western Australia and in the Herberton District of northern Queensland. In this latter area, tin was discovered in 1874, and during the 1880s miners rushed to the area. But they tended to concentrate on the richer lodes outcropping at the surface. There was little attempt at systematic exploration so, as the more obvious areas became worked out, many mines were abandoned. More promising lode mining by larger groups continued in the vicinity of Herberton and Irvinebank, but these too have since closed. A feature of continued small-scale operation today is often the dependence of small groups of 'gougers' on a nearby major producer to purchase and market the product. M. I. M. Holdings Ltd at Mount Isa undertakes to buy, process and market for smaller groups although in the opinion of the company manager this amounts to little more than 'something of a public relations exercise'. The larger mineral sand companies also undertake from time to time to buy, process and market for the smaller groups in that industry.

Gemstones mining is one of the few contemporary forms that lends itself to individual or small group mining. The value of gems won increased from $9.3 million in 1968–9 to $40.9 million in 1972–3. Opals accounted for nearly the total value in 1968–9 but, by the latter date, they accounted for less than 60 per cent with sapphire mining having been revived and accounting for the rest. Although part of the increase in value is attributable to an increase in price, volume of output is also involved, as price has attracted more people to mining, a factor which has led to a production increase. The mining population of Coober Pedy, the largest producer, has trebled since 1969. Lightning Ridge is New South Wales' main opal field, while some opal production is annually recorded in Queensland. Production of sapphires from the Anakie Field in central Queensland reached $5 million in 1972, two and a half times the figure for the previous year.

The main opal mines are in remote areas of the central sedimentary basin where potential opal-bearing sediments cover much of the western area of the basin. 'Sandstone opal' is found in an ironstone band although the contact between leached sandstone and underlying argillaceous beds is but a few centimetres thick. At locations like Coober Pedy and Lightning Ridge the opal is sought by sinking shafts to intersect these bands. Where the opal occurs in ironstone concretions within the sandstone, it is known as 'boulder opal'. It is found in this more elusive form in the slopes of residual mesas in western Queensland. During the nineteenth century, Queensland produced most of the opals for Australia but now only one mine is worked, and that spasmodically, at 'the Hayricks' to the west of the railhead at Quilpie. Drives made for 50 metres or 60 metres into the softer clays beneath the ironstone cap seek to locate the boulders which might contain opals in any cracks or fractures. Two people work the mine in the cooler months of the year. They depend for water storage on a galvanized tank set below the break-in-slope. Likely opal material is sorted and then roughly processed on emery and rouge wheels, before being taken by automobile to Brisbane for setting and selling.

More Complex Forms of Mining Activity

Large and complex organizations controlling a number of establishments may be linked in a structure that involves integration both back to mining exploration and forward to processing and marketing. Captive servicing subsidiaries, long-term marketing contracts and a spread of plant over several locations are further features of investment in mining at this level.

Products from these more complex groups reflect more sophisticated financial arrangements, mining and marketing activity. Peko-Wallsend Limited is a holding company with interests in the production of coal, copper, gold, beach sand minerals, scheelite, the manufacture and distribution of pumping and mining plant, and road transport. A merger of Wallsend Holding and Investment Company Limited with Peko Mines No Liability to form Peko-Wallsend Investment Limited in 1961, brought under the one capital structure the coal mining interests of the Wallsend Company in the Hunter Valley, New South Wales and the copper and gold mining activity of Peko at Tennant Creek. It extended into mineral sands production when it acquired National Minerals Consolidated Limited in 1961 and present mining is located on the Queensland-New South Wales coast where it shares a half interest with Kathleen Investments in Rutile and Zircon Mines (Newcastle) Limited. In 1967 it acquired Mount Morgan Limited and thus extended its interests in copper-gold production to this older mine in central Queensland. In 1968 the company made a successful offer to acquire King Island Scheelite (1947) Limited. It also has interests in Gove Alumina Limited, in the distribution of pumping, mining plant, and in road transport equipment.

As well as continuing production from the Peko mine, the company maintained an active exploration programme which has led to the establishment of the Orlando, Juno, and Ivanhoe mines in the area. As already noted, it holds conjointly with EZ Industries Limited the Ranger uranium ore body.

The outline of activities of Peko-Wallsend, one of several companies that could have been chosen, illustrates a number of points. The first is the diverse range of activities developed around the mining activity. A number are captive, servicing the major mining operations as, for example, their transport subsidiary or opening up real estate interests from the coal mining lands near Newcastle. The second is the range of minerals produced with both coal and metallic ores being mined and processed, and uranium promising future strong market possibilities. The third covers the vertical and horizontal linkages exemplified in the mineral exploration at Tennant Creek and further afield, the mining of ores and coal and the production of blister copper and crude bismuth bullion at Tennant Creek, and at Mount Morgan. Rutile and zircon, the main mineral sand concentrates, are shipped from Newcastle to meet purchasing contracts in the United States, while scheelite is mined at King Island and sold as a concentrate. Fourth and final observation is that the firm is geographically diversified. In the allocation of its capital among the various activities, it has established mining ventures in a number of locations linked by capital and management ties to the overall holding company. The firm by definition is concerned primarily with the most suitable deployment of the capital which it controls and makes decisions to this end within the confines of the company board-room.

While Peko-Wallsend Limited has no large single shareholding within the group, various levels of 'outside' interests are inevitably to be found in many mining companies. Aberfoyle Limited is the holding company for tin mining in Tasmania with subsidiaries linked to tin mining at Ardlethan in New South Wales, Greenbushes in Western Australia, and gold mining until recently at Cracow in Queensland. Mineral Securities Australia Limited, an Australian mining investment company, acquired a 40 per cent interest in Aberfoyle but when Minsec suffered financial collapse, Aberfoyle had to extricate itself in 1971 by accepting Cominco of Canada as a new mining partner. The company's structure is still vulnerable as has been recently seen in its attempts to raise further capital through the somewhat fragmented financial nature of its holdings. Cleveland Tin No Liability, for example, is controlled through a 50 per cent holding by Aberfoyle Tin No Liability, 100 per cent owned subsidiary of the parent company; Ardlethan Tin No Liability is 51 per cent owned, Greenbushes 27 per cent and Golden Plateau 25 per cent. Faced with the need to raise capital for the development of the Que River base metal prospect in Tasmania, Aberfoyle's chairman has suggested a merger of all the companies within the group.

Robe River Limited was also financially affected in its association with Mineral Securities Limited. However it had a major asset in the ore deposits, a strong partner in the American group, Cleveland Cliffs, and firm contracts with Japanese buyers. Despite some uncertainty caused by a bid to purchase Minsec's shareholding in 1975, the main business of the company, namely the mining of iron ore from leases held, is well under way.

M. I. M. Holdings Limited is a subsidiary of the American Smelting and Refining Company of America although its personnel is largely Australian. The American company, perhaps taking advantage of currency differences between Australia and the United States, has recently reduced its holding from about 53 per cent to 49 per cent through an offer to Australian shareholders. Conzinc Riotinto of Australia, Consolidated Goldfields, Placer Development, Utah Mining and the major petroleum groups are all largely overseas owned, a factor of some significance when considering present Federal government attitudes to overseas control and the modification to development that can result if attitude is hostile or policy not clear. At the same time the advantages of overseas connections have already been mentioned. Access to processing technology, development finance and marketing outlets all point to the role which the international company must continue to play in what should be the controlled expansion of Australian mining.

Lead Time
Of the many mineral discoveries in Australia, only a small number become producing mines. Some minerals are favourably located, extensive in occurrence and rich in mineral content, while others may be easily mined and are found in a chemical form for which there is a known technology. Furthermore, if the discovery is made at a time of actual or impending mineral shortages then the stage is set for a rapid development of the ore body.

The Kambalda nickel find had all of these qualifications. It is a sulphide nickel, the type for which there is a proved and readily available smelting process. Reserves of 24.6 million tonnes of 3.22 per cent nickel are more than adequate. The timing of the discovery was right—there was a shortfall between supply and demand for nickel, and prices were rising. Moreover, Kambalda was not too distant from the major mining centre at Kalgoorlie. It had the advantage of ownership by a major Australian group, Western Mining Corporation Limited which, if it initially lacked access to nickel technology, did not have to look further than to Sherritt Gordon Mines Limited of Canada for assistance.

From the time of the announcement of discovery in 1966 to the shipment of the first ore concentrates to Canada for smelting, less than a year was to pass. With the benefit of cash flow from these sales, the company was able to proceed with confidence to further stages in development. Construction of a refinery based on Sherritt Gordon's ammonia-leach process and with a capacity of 20,000 tonnes, was commissioned for construction at Kwinana in 1968. It began production in 1970 and by 1972 was producing at capacity. In that year it treated 1.14 million tonnes of ore yielding 254,030 tonnes of concentrate which contained 32,902 tonnes of nickel and 2,590 tonnes of copper. A flash smelter producing matte has been built at Hampton, near Kalgoorlie, which handles 200,000 tonnes of concentrate a year and is capable of expansion. An agreement was signed with the Western Australian government which included provisions for rail links with Kalgoorlie and Esperance, and handling and storage facilities for the export of concentrate from Esperance.

Lead time is one of intense activity for the developing company. From confirmation of reserves to production, a programme of road works, earth removal, tunnelling and construction is worked out. Also involved is a series of complex contacts with potential customers and financiers, consulting engineers and equipment suppliers. Of critical importance is discussion with State and Federal governments from whom mining grants are obtained, conditions worked out, and export quotas established. For example Western Mining, in terms of its Agreement, had to erect its nickel refinery at Kwinana, spend at least $45 million on expansion and further exploration, and consider the feasibility of a nickel smelter at Kambalda or Kalgoorlie. Lead time involves close scrutiny of very detailed feasibility studies to be followed by design of mine operation and then construction. This latter can range over a period normally from 12 months to 30 months.

By way of contrast with Kambalda, the Greenvale nickel mine in northern Queensland has had to contend with a different set of lead-time factors. First the nickel was contained in a laterite and this form required innovative research before processing at an economic level was possible. An ammonia-leach process had been pioneered by Freeport Minerals, an American company. Tests proved that processing costs would be higher than with the sulphide ores but reserves were large containing some 40 million tonnes of 1.55 per cent nickel ore. Metals Exploration No Liability, the original owner of the deposit, formed Greenvale Mines in an equal partnership with the Australian subsidiary of the Freeport Minerals Company and a lead-time programme was worked out.

Phase one of the lead time was concerned with the

introductory aspects, beginning in 1967 with the completion of exploration. Process development extended over a period from 1967 to 1971 and included government negotiations, feasibility studies, forward sales agreements and most of the financing. Phase two, the actual construction, was to occupy the period from 1972 to 1975 and during that time expenditure was stepped up considerably. Engineering, processing, plant construction and a 180 km railway line between mine and plant at Yabulu near Townsville were completed and trial runs made.

Production, however, is well below design capacity. Additional funds have had to be found, not without considerable difficulty for the Australian partner, both for modification of processing plant, for working funds and for servicing debt until a larger cash flow from sales is available. Overall, the group came into production at a time when nickel prices had fallen off considerably and when contracts, made in terms of United States dollars, were devalued. It is considered that profitability will be but marginal until nickel prices, in line with anticipated increases in demand, rise again in the 1980s.

Mining

Mining methods refer to the techniques employed in the recovery of minerals from the surrounding earth materials or, in the case of construction minerals and some non-metallic minerals such as phosphate and coal, to the recovery of the mineral earth material itself. Underground mining is one of the oldest forms of mining but given the powerful earthmoving equipment available today to handle overburden, and the need for mass removal of the extensive low-grade ores being mined, open-cut mining is preferred wherever it can be adopted. Dredging and drilling are two further mineral recovery techniques for specific situations, the former recovering unconsolidated concentrations in alluvial detritus, the latter tapping oil, gas or water at depths inaccessible and indeed unsuitable for other mining methods.

Underground Mining

The simplest method involves following a seam or vein into a hill slope along a horizontal or gently sloping passage formed as the ore is removed. Called adit or drift mining, it is thus initially a relatively inexpensive method of recovery. Costs increase as the system of tunnels or passages extends further underground, or pitprops are required, or maintaining the tunnels as access routes to the ore or seam face become a considerable expense. Props and liners for example are required for the Broken Hill mines, while the Mount Isa system of tunnels in older more consolidated rock is largely self-supporting.

A complexity is added when horizontally or near-horizontally bedded ores are located at some depth or where the original access tunnels are too far removed from the present mining face. Then, shafts may be sunk with horizontal offshoots to levels of the ore body. The shafts, containing a system of lifts and pulleys, allow quick access to underground mining for removal of the ore and for ventilation.

Highly inclined or vertical veins are usually mined by stoping. This refers to a method of ore removal by driving horizontally upon it a series of workings, one immediately over the other or vice versa. Each horizontal working is called a stope. In general, the term is applied to any subterranean extraction of ore except that which is incidentally performed in sinking shafts and driving levels for the purpose of opening up the mine.

At Cobar, New South Wales, some 700,000 tonnes of copper and copper-zinc ores are mined per year from depths down to 55 metres below the surface while mining to a much greater depth is planned. Because the ores are low grade, efficiency in mining is necessary for an economically viable operation to continue. Mining proceeds by breaking ore from the roof of stopes in the lower regions of the ore body. The stopes are large so that massive rubber-tyred haulage equipment can be used. The broken ore is taken away through horizontal access tunnels for delivery to an underground primary crusher, and hoisting to the surface. Removal of such large volumes of ore and backfilling set up stresses which are being studied by the Commonwealth Scientific and Industrial Research Organization which has constructed an operational model of the mine. Such co-operation in research by industry and governmental agencies is a feature of the Australian mining activity that should not be overlooked.

Drilling for oil, natural gas and water is a specialized form of underground mining. It is also a costly business, the cost increasing disproportionately with depth so that exploratory drilling is planned to be integrated into the proposed pattern of recovery wells if hydrocarbons are located. By the end of 1973 some 37 wells had been drilled by Woodside-Burmah on the offshore areas of the Northwest Shelf. Each cost over $2 million, including the 17 dry holes. The company has stated that it has spent $170 million in the area where substantial reserves of gas and some oil have been found, but where production is only a prospect for the future, a reflection on the length of lead time for bringing in producing wells and constructing delivery lines, compounded here by Federal government attitudes. Up to the middle of 1973, it is estimated that expenditure on petroleum exploration has been in the neighbourhood of $984 million. Techniques of drilling have improved considerably in recent years. Turbo-rotary drills, for example, dispense with a drive from a surface table. Drilling mud, electric

Plate 20.1 The Mount Morgan mine. In this view looking north the relationship between open-cut mine, processing plant, waste discharge areas and mining town is clearly illustrated.

logging and offshore platform construction are all part of modern drilling equipment.

Crude petroleum is obtained from the Moonie field and Alton offshoot near Roma, Queensland, from the Broken Hill Proprietary-Esso field on the Gippsland Shelf, and from the field on Barrow Island in Western Australia. While the Gippsland field is by far the most significant as an offshore field, the Barrow Island field has some interesting features. Production is from a dense grid of comparatively shallow wells which has been stepped-up by fracturing the oil-bearing rock, and by water and gas injection into the seams. The company, West Australian Petroleum Proprietary Limited, has drilled 530 wells on the island, 324 of which are producing oil and 153 are injecting water. A natural gas field lies stratigraphically separated, below the oil. It has been considered as a possible source of supply for the Pilbara Region.

Gasfields are more numerous than oilfields in Australia. In 1969, the Roma Gasfield located some 450 kilometres west of Brisbane was the first to be tapped commercially. Bass Strait gas was used for the first time in the same year. In 1972, the Gidgealpa-Moomba field was brought in to supply Adelaide, while the small Dongara field is used for a gas supply to Perth, 430 km to the south of the field. A major decision was taken when it was decided to use the South Australia field with a future extension to the Amadeus Basin foreshadowed, for the Sydney market. Indicative of the ready adoption of natural gas in Australia are the production figures which show an increase from $6,111 \times 10^3 m^3$ in 1968 to $3,726,629 \times 10^3 m^3$ in 1973.

Surface Mining

An important consideration in surface mining is the ratio of overburden to recoverable depth. In the case of minerals such as coal this rapidly reaches critical proportions where the coal seam is thin or the quality poor, but in the massive deposits in central Queensland, costs of overburden removal are less significant when considered in relation to the 40 metre to 50 metre vertical seam of export quality coal. A wide spread of low-grade ore is more readily worked by open-cut methods where selectivity by machine operation in keeping with the mass of ore is not critical, whereas bands of high ore concentrate held in parent rock are often more readily pursued by underground mining. Concentrations located in unconsolidated sediments are most economically amenable to dredging. Overall, much depends on available technology, labour supply and the size of operation envisaged. Thus mining of low-grade brown coals in the Yallourn-Morwell seams could only be undertaken by open-cut methods, and in close proximity to a major market. Overburden in relation to the huge undermass of coal is limited and cost per unit of weight recovered is low.

While copper ores assaying less than one per cent are necessarily recovered by open-cut methods, higher grade and less accessible ores are more readily recovered by underground methods. Open-cuts at Mount Lyell and Mount Morgan take the form of huge pits or inverted cones. The West Lyell open-cut is, however, being phased out as it is no longer suitable for this form of mining, while the conversion of Mount Morgan to open-cut retained but a limited 'life' for the mine as grade deteriorated. At Mount Isa and Tennant Creek, copper ore and some lead, zinc and silver with which copper is often associated, are mined to depths of over 1,000 metres by underground methods.

More common as a form of open-cut than the pit, is the bench or terrace where various levels recede into the ore face as mineral is recovered. The latest copper mine to be opened up, at Kanmantoo in South Australia is of this type. It began production in 1971 as a bench type operation. Most of that year was spent in removing waste from the upper three benches while drawing ore from the lower two. Ore is concentrated at a nearby plant and the 30 per cent concentrate is shipped to Japanese smelters through the established port of Osborne within the Port Adelaide complex. The mine has been temporarily closed because of low copper prices.

Those involved in open-cut mining are very aware of the significance of grade. Because of the strict product specifications of consumers, modern iron ore producers have to control quality of their product at all stages of the mining operation from extraction through to ship loading. The iron ore body at Mount Tom Price, for example, contains a succession of high-grade hematite bands interspersed with lower-grade shale bands. In this type of situation and in terms of requirements, strict quality control of the fine ore mining is necessary.

Ores at the Paraburdoo mine to the south have been worked since 1971. Upper sections are weathered to a geothite capping and the ratio of high-grade ore to other materials is 3 to 1. Preproduction stripping, removing the overburden and low-grade ore was carried out and a benching programme established. Equipment is a major cost in these highly capitalized operations. Mechanized drills, shovels, bulldozers and prime movers are used at Paraburdoo to recover over 15 million tonnes of ore a year. The ore is graded, sized, and phosphorous and alumina content are kept strictly within specifications at all times.

Dredging is a distinctive form of surface mining. Consisting of a vessel formed of two pontoons between which runs a line of buckets or a suction pipe, it floats in a pond or 'paddock' and is moved by headlines or sidelines anchored on land and manipulated by winches on the deck. The ore is subjected to initial concentration on the deck and tailings are discharged from a moving belt or by force ejection to side or rear. Both bucket and suction dredges have been used in the recovery of gold, but today their main uses are in tin mining and mineral sands mining respectively. Two bucket dredges operate the tin areas in north Queensland at Mount Garnet, while a third is located at Greenbushes in Western Australia. Buckets dig into the alluvium containing cassiterite, the ore of tin. After concentration, ore is shipped to O. T. Lempriere and Company tin smelters of Alexandria, New South Wales.

Occurrence of the mineral sands rutile, ilmenite, zircon and monazite, to mention the four main ores, originated with wave and wind sorting of these heavier materials to form lenses in the main sand body. In most dredging plants today, the sand is mined using a hydraulic suction cutter. In some areas of North Stradbroke Island, the minerals are suitably placed for 'dry mining'. The whole mining plant floats on a man-made pond and advances along the ore body as the dredge sucks up the sand and the tailing stacker ejects the waste behind the mining plant. Mineral and quartz are separated at the dredge by several washings down a slope—usually Humphrey spirals—with a splitter introduced into the stream to separate the heavy and light grains. By this method the original mixture which contained less than 2 per cent by weight of mineral sands, emerges as a 'concentrate' which may contain up to 95 per cent minerals, and which goes on to a land-based plant where the various minerals are separated by electrostatic methods after further concentrating.

Rehabilitation of Mines Land

It has been argued that mining itself disturbs but a very small proportion of the total land area—something like a half of one per cent in Australia—but this would have to be expanded if plant discharge and waste disposal were also to be considered. In areas where resource uses may be in conflict, disturbances have repercussions in the removal of scenic and ecologically valuable features that extend considerably beyond the actual land area involved. Increasingly, mining companies are being told to reconcile their proposals with the findings of environmental impact studies; and their activities with the rehabilitation requirements which the community asks for and which mining licences may require.

Massive open-cuts disturb large areas of land and while some may be in remote areas of low general quality, others are in 'sensitive' locations. Nowhere is this more so than in the areas to be worked over for mineral sands. Rehabilitation measures are a part of the lease documents and mining companies are asked to post substantial bonds as guarantees that they will carry out the work of rehabilitation satisfactorily. This usually involves replacing both the contour and vegetation of both frontal dunes and back areas to their original state. Land required for caravan parks, playgrounds and sporting areas are set aside and contoured to suit the particular requirements. Where vegetative cover is considered worth preserving, as in the unusual stands of paperbark, *Mellaleuca* sp., interspersed among the waterways of the Myall Lakes area north of Newcastle, or where unusual features such as the coloured sands of the Cooloola beach front north of Brisbane will be destroyed by mining, community protest can rouse sufficient interest to result in a considerable modification of the original mining proposals.

Another particularly sensitive area is in the Alcoa bauxite leases in the Darling Range where much of the mining area is designated as State Forest. Flattening out of bluffs, restoration of topsoil, contouring depressions left after the 'pods' of bauxite have been removed and revegetation are required. Restoration work, possibly to convert the mined-over areas to pasture, is also being attempted at Weipa. Overall, rehabilitation is increasing being regarded as complementary to mining and must, in these terms, be integrated into mining programmes.

Summary

Government plays its major role in the decision to mine through control of mining rights all of which are 'vested in the Crown'. There are minor exceptions, but they are of importance only in the areas of the New South Wales coalfields where private mineral rights predated the promulgation of the mining acts. Elsewhere, the rights are held by the State governments, or in the Territories by the Australian government with some exceptions in defined areas. For example the Joint Coal Board made up of Federal and State government nominees, has jurisdiction over coal mining in New South Wales. The Atomic Energy Commission which came into being as a result of Commonwealth legislation in 1953, has responsibility, in an overall sense, for the production and utilization of uranium in Australia.

Mining legislation varies in detail from State to State although embodying similar principles established when the original mining acts were laid down. For example, the occupation of land for the purpose of mining in New South Wales related initially to the Mining Act of 1906. Amendments refer generally to modifications over the succeeding years in the conditions of mining. Thus, while machinery for granting the smaller mining lease is generally adequate, it fails to meet the requirements of the large, often international developer.

Some States have enacted new mining acts. In South Australia, the Mining Act of 1971–3 'reserves all minerals to the Crown and regulates and controls all mining operations in South Australia'. Queensland has brought into operation the Queensland Mining Act of 1968–71, while Western Australia and New South Wales are in the process of preparing new legislation. In a third attempt to revise the State's seventy-year-old Mining Act, the Western Australian government has included interesting provisions to allow cancellation of the mining tenement if, in the Minister's opinion, 'the control has passed to any country, and the Minister has not consented to the control so passing'.

Because legislation is generally inadequate for major modern development, large enterprises may take the course of acquiring mining titles by negotiation with the appropriate State. It is particularly important where the State wishes to make specific provision for further processing such as concentrating and refining works within its boundaries. This is the case in the development of iron ore mining in Western Australia, and in bauxite mining both in Western Australia and Queensland where large leases and major investment are involved.

The end-product of a mining activity is the recovery of metallic ore, coal, petroleum or natural gas; a construction material such as sand, gravel or dimension stone, or some other non-metallic mineral in unprocessed form. A characteristic of the two groups 'construction materials' and 'other non-metallic minerals' has been their production increases over recent years. A selection of figures in Table 20.3 illustrates this. Some figures, for example, for salt and cement clay would reflect increasing production particularly in relation to import replacement over the period, while all reflect generally the increasing size of a domestic market.

The two other mining groups, metallic minerals and fuel minerals (Table 20.4), show considerable increases in production over the period. These, in most cases,

Table 20.3 Production of Main Construction Materials and Non-Metals

Mine product	Unit	1961	1966	1972	1974
Sand	'000 tonnes	7,656	10,837	21,869	24,386[a]
Crushed and broken stone	'000 tonnes	28,392	47,547	51,037	54,070
Cement clay and shale	tonnes	315,577	243,222	451,227	467,716
Stoneware clay	tonnes	172,243	269,193	355,945	245,455
Limestone	'000 tonnes	6,518	7,854	10,494	9,889
Salt	'000 tonnes	545	655	3,340	4,935
Silica	'000 tonnes	222	353	1,058	1,443

[a]Excludes Western Australia.

Sources: Bureau of Mineral Resources, Geology and Geophysics (1968, 1974), *Australian Mineral Industry Review*, Canberra; Bureau of Statistics, *Official Yearbook of the Commonwealth of Australia*, 1966, 1970, 1974, Canberra.

would reflect essentially the growth in export markets for the metallic minerals and black coal, and export replacement in the case of petroleum. Metals like tin have expanded their production first to bring the Australian market to self-sufficiency, and then to provide for substantial exports.

Although the end-product of the actual mining operation is an ore which may be sorted, sized or graded, and have undergone preliminary concentration at the mine face or nearby plant location, it is usually difficult to produce statistics for mine output itself. While these would most satisfactorily reflect mining activity, metal content is a more satisfactory standardized reference for a number of forms. Copper, for example, is usefully aggregated in this way. Gold is mainly in the form of mined gold bullion. In 1970, 75 per cent of all gold production was from that source, 15 per cent was obtained from copper concentrate and 4 per cent from copper-lead and bismuth concentrate.

Processing

Mining in a strict sense is the recovery of minerals from their place *in situ*. It follows then, that mineral processing refers to any modification or upgrading of the recovered material in its preparation for market. Elementary processing involves such activities as crushing, sorting, sizing, grinding, classifying and dewatering. At a more advanced level, ore may be separated from most of the gangue, or have other waste materials removed such as bone ash from coal, organic material and silica from bauxite. Leaching, amalgamation of ore, gravity treatment, flotation, magnetic and electrostatic treatment of the material are processes associated with this phase which has as its end-product the 'pure' ore, the export mineral or market product.

A further and final phase, and one involving mainly the metallic ores, subjects the mine product to heat treatment—pyrometallurgy—under furnace conditions involving both the reduction of the metallic ore to a metal by smelting and where required, refining the product by removal of final impurities. The metal may then have its qualities improved by adding measured amounts of other mineral products. Electrolytic refining and alloying would be two aspects of this final phase in the treatment. In the case of petroleum, refining involves the selective removal of constituents by distillation and cracking.

It should be noted that there are identifiable break-points in the flow from mining to manufacturing, the first being between the actual mining or recovery and the start of processing. Sorting, sizing and grading are associated with the mine face itself, so perhaps it would serve little purpose to esablish a break in the system at this point. Secondly, there is a break when the mineral moves on the internal mine transport network to processing plants at the mine site. Coal to washing plant, ore to gravity jigs, and dimension stone to shaping and polishing plant are examples where there is a locational shift, but it is still within the complex of the mine and moreover the mineral is still being 'recovered'.

Certain combinations of processes at this stage are undertaken to regulate shape and size, remove unwanted constituents or improve the quality of the mineral and are generally referred to as beneficiating. The end-product of beneficiation is a coarse concentrate which, in relation to its initial bulk, has had the more readily removable and bulky waste products separated from the ore and remaining gangue, usually by inexpensive means. Ore dressing is a particular type of beneficiating which cleans the ore by such techniques as 'jigging, cobbing, vanning and the like'. Even at the more advanced level, when more sophisticated techniques of froth flotation and electrostatic separation may be used as in the examples of copper ore and titanium ores respectively, the original mineral is still being sought. Many ores leave the mine at this stage as concentrates for further processing in Australia or they may go direct to overseas buyers.

Beyond this stage we can identify a third possible break-point in the system with the application of heat, chemical leaching, electrolytic or other technique, and usually involving inputs of ancillary materials such as fuels, leaching solutes, electricity or the like. Because the mineral now changes its state or form there is a logical break-point in the flow pattern. The mining system has reached its end-point and manufacturing, as primary manufacturing or final processing within the productive system, begins. We would therefore wish to distinguish between processing to yield the end-product of mining, and manufacturing which prepared the materials for secondary manufacturing or fabricating, and this distinction is tentatively made in Fig. 20.1.

Perhaps the argument has been unduly laboured, but if so it has been done with the purpose of establishing the validity of mining as a system within the framework of productive activity. Moreover there is a distinct geographical break at this point. The mine product is now more readily freed from those deterministic factors which have bound it economically if not inevitably to the mine site. Moreover, the Australian Bureau of Statistics recognizes, at about this point, the distinction between mining and manufacturing. In the Australian Standard Industrial Code it classifies what we have referred to as primary manufacturing by industrial subdivisions covering chemical, petroleum and coal products, non-metallic mineral products, and basic metal products. Although these, as it were, extend from the mining flow, they are now separately and distinctively manufacturing, adding considerably to the value of the mine product.

Forms of Processing

Pilbara iron ores undergo some processing before export. Grades generally are high and if the ore meets the specifications of the purchaser, processing may amount to little more than blending of each shovel output as it comes off the mine face, and continuing a size and grade sorting as the ore proceeds to railhead and port. At the port of Dampier there are two separate stockpile areas, one at Parker Point on the mainland and the second at the loading wharves on East Intercourse Island. Ore may be blended from these prior to shipment. In addition to a size and grade specification, some purchasers would require ores with low phosphorus content. Mixing of lower-grade limonites with higher phosphorous, and higher-grade low phosphorous hematite makes for acceptable content

and grade. Beneficiating to upgrade low-grade ores is also undertaken by a range of techniques which include flotation, the use of Humphrey spirals and magnetic separation. Ores may be specified as pelletized, essentially for convenient handling. This is simply accomplished by passing ground ore over rotating discs and then heating the pellets to 1,315°C.

Ore dressing of copper, lead and zinc materials involves removal of the gangue from the ore body. The process is one of separation which we have referred to as flotation. First discovered and used in the early years of the present century, it is perhaps one of the most significant discoveries of modern mining technology. Blainey has recorded the fascinating story of experiments with wetting and flotation agents after it was discovered that different minerals exhibited differentials in wetting characteristics. Under the right conditions, particles can be brought to the surface of certain liquids adhering to bubbles, the worthless gangue sinks to the bottom of the flotation cell and is drained away while the valuable sulphides adhering to bubbles overflow the lip of the cell. After suitable thickening and drying, sulphides or other compounds of copper, lead, zinc or nickel are ready for smelting, reducing the ore to a matte form; or they are ready for export as a concentrate.

In the progression beyond these more elementary forms of processing, location of processing plant may vary. Copper concentrate is transported over a considerable land distance from the mines at Tennant Creek, Northern Territory to Port Augusta in South Australia for shipment overseas although recently a flash smelter to produce commercially acceptable low-bismuth blister copper and crude bismuth bullion was installed at Tennant Creek. Kanmantoo ore is exported as a concentrate. At Mount Morgan in Queensland and Mount Lyell in Tasmania, nearby coal deposits are used to fire the reverberatory furnaces to reduce the ore to a copper matte. With further smelting in a converter the matte is reduced to blister copper, a product that contains only about one per cent of other impurities. Further weight loss is negligible. Mount Isa blister copper is transported to Townsville for refining at a convenient break-in-transit along the route to market. Cobar and Mount Lyell ores together with scrap, are refined at the Port Kembla refinery. About 45 per cent of the refined product is exported.

Location and Primary Manufacturing

We can say generally that the pull towards markets becomes stronger as processed ores move towards primary manufacturing. Bulk has been reduced. Furthermore, the gross value which includes local transport, labour, storage and fuel inputs, is better able to withstand the cost of transport. The pull may be via

Plate 20.2 The Batesford Limestone Quarry, over 50 metres deep and covering 20 hectares, illustrates the close relationship that can exist in the cement industry, between quarry, processing works and the source of labour and services. The main market, Melbourne, is 75 kilometres distance by rail.

an ancillary input such as electricity.

Some manufacturing in this sense does however remain closely tied to the mineral resource site. If we accept hydroelectricity as manufacturing exploiting the mineral water, it is inflexible in its demand for both volume and head of water and this determines the production site. Efficiencies in the transport of electricity along high voltage lines have however increased considerably the marketable range of this product, both from hydro- and thermo- sources. Brown coal, because of its very low value per unit of weight and poor transportability is equally as demanding in its requirements for manufacturing at site. Nor is black coal production when used for electrical generation much less so. In reducing the competitive cost per unit of electricity produced, generating plants increasingly are located at mine sites, coal coming directly from the mine by conveyor belt to plant. Examples such as the major Swanbank complex on the Ipswich

coalfield or the Liddell plant in the Hunter Valley will serve to illustrate the point.

Cement manufacturing is the fusing or clinkering of limestone with other mineral clays and shales. In the form of Portland cement it is finely ground, and, when mixed with water, it recrystallizes and sets. Limestone is more widely distributed than most minerals so quarrying and manufacturing activities may, in some instances, be carried on within closer range of their markets or take advantage of established routes and waterways. Cement works therefore tend to utilize mineral resources located close to the capital cities, the major exception being Sydney where suitable limestone supplies are located in its hinterland—to the northwest near Mudgee and Bathurst, and to the southwest near Goulburn. Goliath Cement is the main Tasmanian producer. From Devonport, it supplies both the Melbourne and Newcastle markets as well as those within the State. The Darra cement

Table 20.4   Mine Production of Principal Minerals

Mineral	Unit	1960	1970	1974
Bauxite	'000 tonnes	71	9,256	20,057
Copper (content)	tonnes	107,732	178,203	256,006
Gold (content)	'000 grams	33,800	19,282	16,176
Iron ore and conc.	'000 tonnes	4,452	51,188	96,688
Lead (content)	tonnes	318,125	438,116	377,577
Nickel (conc.)	tonnes	—	310,460	303,139
Tin (content)	tonnes	2,237	8,829	10,266
Titanium				
ilmenite conc.	tonnes	108,206	897,045	815,089
rutile conc.	tonnes	87,395	370,867	302,340
Zinc (content)	tonnes	322,584	487,207	454,047
Black coal	'000 tonnes	22,931	49,211	63,608
Crude oil	'000 metres^3	—	10,358	22,407
Natural gas	10^6 metres^3	—	1,503	4,675

Sources: as for Table 20.3.

works near Brisbane make use of fossil corals dredged from nearby Moreton Bay and transported 65 km up-river to the plant.

An example is taken from the pattern of aluminium production in Australia to make the final point regarding location of mining and associated processing industries. The three major producers each have differing linkages giving essentially intermediate locations between mining and the production of alumina, alumina and the production of aluminium. Nabalco Proprietary Limited, jointly owned by Swiss Aluminium Australia (70 per cent) and Gove Alumina (30 per cent), mines bauxite on the Gove Peninsula, Northern Territory producing 2.9 million tonnes in 1973. After being carried 16 km to Gove by conveyor belt, half was exported and the remainder was processed to alumina before export. The plant has a capacity of half a million tonnes of alumina output, a figure which the company is planning to double. The company is obliged in the terms of the 1968 Agreement with the Australian government, to establish a smelter in the Northern Territory at a time when it can be guaranteed a continuous supply of low cost power.

Alcoa of Australia Limited mines bauxite at two sites in the Darling Range of Western Australia. Production in 1973 was 5.1 million tonnes. Bauxite is transported 45 km by rail from the Jarrahdale site, for treatment at the Kwinana alumina refinery which has a capacity of 1.4 million tonnes, or for export. From the Pinjarra site, bauxite is transported by conveyor belt down the escarpment to the refinery. Capacity is 0.8 million tonnes with expansion planned for 2.0 million tonnes. Soda ash is imported in order to make the caustic soda required for the leaching process. From the refineries, the alumina is shipped using

company port facilities at Kwinana and Bunbury respectively. The bulk of the alumina is exported—to Alcoa plants overseas, to meet contracts, for example with Aluar of Argentine, the Sumitono group in Japan or the plant in the Republic of South Africa. The remainder goes to the Alcoa plant at Port Henry, near Geelong, where an aluminium smelter with a capacity for 92,000 tonnes is located. Because smelting of alumina is an electrolytic process, it requires large and continuous supplies of inexpensive electricity, initially bought at an undisclosed price from the State Electricity Commission of Victoria. Later, it was able to develop its own generating plant. Western Mining Corporation, the discoverer of the bauxite and a partner in the Alcoa group, had thoughtfully purchased mining rights to a brown coal deposit at Anglesea, near Geelong, and was able to make this available for generation of electricity. Alcoa thus has the double advantage of nearness to power supply, and nearness to a major market for its manufacturing plant.

The bauxite deposits at Weipa mined by Comalco Limited, are estimated to be among the largest in the world. Comalco with interests in a plant in Sardinia, and sales contracts with Japanese buyers, exports some of the ore direct. It also supplies the original Australian alumina plant at Bell Bay, Tasmania, as well as the huge alumina refinery of Queensland Alumina Limited at Gladstone which, with a rated capacity of two million tonnes, is by far the largest in the world. Alumina is exported, the amounts being apportioned among the four members of the consortium, one of which is Alcan, with an aluminium

Table 20.5   Smelter and Refinery Production from Principal Minerals

Material	Unit	1960	1970	1974
Alumina	'000 tonnes	31	2,152	4,896
Aluminium	tonnes	11,842	205,602	220,997
Copper (blister)	tonnes	71,037	109,126	191,255
Copper (refined)	tonnes	71,786	104,125	162,076
Lead (refined)	tonnes	192,870	180,078	192,757
Pig iron (incl. scrap)	'000 tonnes	2,928	6,148	7,250
Raw steel (incl. scrap)	'000 tonnes	3,746	6,822	7,755
Tin (refined)	tonnes	2,290	6,211	6,714
Zinc (refined)	tonnes	122,160	260,591	276,831
Electricity	million kWh	24,814	49,571	67,067[a]
Hydro	million kWh	4,947	9,124	13,383[a]
Thermal	million kWh	19,867	40,447	53,674[a]

[a] 1973 data.

Sources: as for Table 20.3.

plant at Kurri Kurri in the Hunter Valley. Kaiser, Pechiney, Comalco and Conzinc Riotinto are the others.

Bell Bay alumina supplies the adjoining aluminium refinery. It has a capacity of 115,000 tonnes. Electricity is supplied from the Trevallyn Power Station at the head of the Tamar Estuary. In terms of the agreement with the Queensland government, Comalco must endeavour to develop industrial plants within the State, and it is probable that any further manufacturing will be undertaken at Weipa for alumina, or near Gladstone for aluminium.

Each group then in the movement from mining to manufacturing, has established its own particular links in a network along which commodities flow. The locations chosen reflect decisions by the firms first to mine where the mineral body proved suitable, and then to locate processing plant at what are considered to be suitable locations along the route from mine to market. Choice of location is open, allowing a number of factors—labour, power, market, available land, policy within the firm and so on, to influence the decision.

The pattern of location and movement is shown on the map 'Mineral Industry, Second Edition' in the *Atlas of Australian Resources*. The map predates recent developments such as that mentioned at Pinjarra which commenced operation in 1972, and shows the Gove development as proposed. Nevertheless it is an outstanding cartographic statement both of processing and manufacturing activity and of the flow networks generated by the activity.

Waste Materials and Environmental Impact

Federal government legislation has recently been enacted, aimed at ensuring mining development within an acceptable environmental framework. In terms of the Environmental Protection (Impact of Proposals) Act 1974, an impact statement is required by the Federal government of any mining proposal. The environmental protection legislation is designed to ensure proper use of resources particularly in areas of conflict. It is also concerned with the disposal of waste and its impact on the environment.

Some states require similar statements although the quality of these vary. Federal and State governments may however find themselves and their departments at cross purposes. This has occurred in the case of licences granted to the Dillingham-Murphyores group by the Queensland government. The company has the right to mine 11,700 hectares of beachfront and high dune areas up to 5 km inland on Fraser Island. DM Minerals, the operating company, was granted an export licence by the Federal government, and proceeded to prepare for mining in order to meet contract dates only to have the decision to allow them to export reversed following the completion of a Federal environmental impact hearing. With permission to mine as granted by the State government still extant, the company decided to stockpile ore, again with contract commitments in mind.

One of the major problems associated with processing is the need to dispose of waste materials. Around Mount Morgan, dumps of coarse and fine gangue fill valleys where once the miners fished. At Broken Hill, the mining companies dumped tailings near their mines producing great grey masses of dirt that added to the dusty red clouds that came in from the plains. Attempts to incorporate such dumps in a higher quality environment around the mining cities have led to efforts to place some vegetation on them. Waste heaps have been planted in trees at Broken Hill. At Mount Isa, a slurry of waste rock from the flotation process is either used for backfilling or is pumped to valleys remote from populated areas for dumping. After considerable experimentation it was found that ash additions so improved permeability and water infiltration properties that 'reasonable growth' of certain grass and crop species as well as shrubs and trees has been possible. A revegetation programme is under way.

Derelict mine dumps are not immune from problems. It is alleged, for instance, that percolation particularly after rains, can leach out traces of lead, zinc and cadmium from slag heaps and mine shafts at Captains Flat. These are carried to the Molonglo River and thence to Lake Burley Griffin in the heart of Canberra. Collapse of the slag heaps during periods of heavy rains could lead to 'catastrophic pollution' of the lake.

Disposal of the red mud from alumina recovery also presents problems and indeed led the Western Australian authorities on two occasions to disallow proposals made by the Alwest group. The group, using ore from the Mount Saddleback deposit, proposed to establish an alumina refinery near Perth in areas where percolation of residual alkalis could contaminate underground water supplies for Perth. The final proposal has been to relocate the plant at Worsley, 150 km south of Perth, and to export through Bunbury.

While disposal of waste does present problems, residual dumps may become valuable if technological advances increase the availability of unrecovered minerals. Those at Broken Hill, established prior to the discovery of flotation techniques, contained a high content of discarded zinc ore. They were subsequently purchased and reworked to return high profits to their owners. Again, general technological advances may establish a demand for certain minerals. Both the Mary Kathleen and Radium Hill waste dumps contain valuable minerals in the 'rare earths' group. In 1959 the Rare Earth Corporation of Australia Limited purchased the old uranium processing plant at Port Pirie and set about adapting it in order to recover monazite concentrates, the ore in which they are found, from the waste heap. By 1972, the plant had a throughput of 1,300 tonnes of concentrate. Although the scheme had been a good one, the plant was forced to close because of lack of working capital to meet technical breakdowns—in spite of South Australian government loans—and because it was difficult to establish sales in a limited world market without overseas connections.

For about twenty years, Residue Hill has been an unsightly landmark on the Derwent River at Risdon. About 200 tonnes of waste is dumped on the hill per day until it now contains over 1.5 million tonnes of residue which is reported to contain 22 per cent zinc and some lead, silver and cadmium. EZ Industries, owners of the dump, have recently announced a technological advance, a process of recovery which they call Jarosite process. It will not only increase present zinc recovery rates by 10 per cent to about 97 per cent but it will also allow economic recovery from Residue Hill, taking about twenty years to process the dump. Thus new technology is not only creating a demand for new mineral materials as research and innovation become available, it is also applied to more effective recovery in processing present required minerals. The history of mining has been one of increasing availability of mineral products and, significantly, at decreasing prices, with improving technology playing a major part in this trend.

Smelter and refinery production of principal minerals is shown in Table 20.5.

CONCLUSION

The mining component of Gross Domestic Product climbed from about $50 million to $230 million in the 1950s. Its gradual and then accelerated climb from 1962–3 to $1,480 million in 1972–3 represents an increase of 500 per cent for the decade. At constant 1966–7 prices, the increase for the period is still one of 295 per cent. Fig. 20.5 shows the trends of mining and quarrying as an industrial group over this most recent period.

The contribution to overall Gross Domestic Product would appear initially to be less spectacular than the growth in mining itself. Nevertheless mining shows by far the largest sectoral increase in that it doubled, while other increases were of the order of 20 per cent to 30 per cent at the most, with other primary sectors actually decreasing by about these percentages.

If significance were considered in terms of providing employment, then the mining sector, at the present time, goes against the general trend. January 1975 employment in mining has risen from 4.0 per cent of the workforce to 7.2 per cent, when compared with January 1974.

However, it is in the area of exports that the increase in mining has had a major impact. Exports of unprocessed mineral products, that is up to but excluding such items as pig lead, zinc bars and copper ingot, increased from $68.6 million in 1960–1 to $1,131 million in 1973–4. The slight downturn after 1970 is partly accounted for by poor economic conditions of world markets with more competitive selling and lower prices. But of greater significance is the considerable devaluation of the United States dollar *vis-à-vis* the Australian dollar as many of the contracts for sale of minerals, particularly to Japan, are written in United States dollars. Between December 1971 and January 1974 the United States dollar was downvalued by 32 per cent. Western Mining Corporation, one of the companies affected estimates that, at current sales levels, income was reduced by $4 million

Table 20.6   Local Value of Minerals Produced by State

	1961 $'000	1968–9[a] $'000	1972–3 $'000	1974–5 $'000
New South Wales	156,342	314,802	454,302	784,100
Victoria	40,054	69,007	349,973	522,700
Queensland	64,440	209,273	399,192	803,000
South Australia	31,824	72,159	116,807	126,000
Western Australia	44,992	234,972	536,464	860,410
Tasmania	15,918	59,163	84,863	117,800
N. Territory and A.C.T.	6,732	30,915	57,016	90,800
Total	360,302	990,292	1,998,615	3,304,810

[a]Statistical collection base slightly modified from 1968–9.

Sources: Bureau of Statistics, *Official Yearbook of the Commonwealth of Australia*, 1966, 1971; *Mineral Production 1974–5*, Ref. No. 10.51, Canberra.

for every 5 per cent up-valuation of the Australian dollar. From the mid-1970s however the gap in valuation began to close, contributing both to profits of companies and return to the economy. Preliminary figures for 1974–5 indicate a jump to $ 2,313 million in mining contribution to Gross Domestic Product and a contribution exceeding 25 per cent to exports.

The first breakdown of the national figures is to the level of States—of significance in its own right but also representing a first approximation to the distribution of mining in Australia. Table 20.6 summarizes the relative importance of the States in terms of the local (i.e. ex-mine) value of minerals produced.

The main change over the period under study is one of ranking of States. New South Wales has been replaced by Western Australia as the main contributor to the value of mining in the country. It attained this position in 1970–1. While New South Wales has moved to second place, Queensland still ranks as third and is likely to hold that place in view of the major growth, particularly in coal output, that is envisaged. The outstanding growth in value of minerals for Victoria, starting actually from 1969–70, is explained in terms of oil and gas production from the Bass Strait field. Reference has been made to the opening up of new mining areas in South Australia. Further developments include the re-examination of old mines like the copper mine at Mount Gunson. Extensive brown coal and low-grade uranium ores add to the value of mining potential in that State. Tasmania maintains a diversified range of metallic ore, coal and limestone mining, Savage River iron ore being a recent and valuable development.

The figures in Table 20.7 indicate what can best be called the status of mining in each of the States when related to all other primary and secondary industries. A figure of one implies that the degree of localization is 'average' in terms of the norm set by the data itself; a score below one suggests that mining is less highly localized in that State; above one that it is more

Table 20.7 Location Quotient for Australian Mineral Values to Total Production Values

	1960–1	1967–8	1972–3
New South Wales	1.16	1.01	0.64
Victoria	0.32	0.29	0.58
Queensland	1.68	1.59	1.55
South Australia	0.96	0.72	0.68
Western Australia	1.76	2.42	2.97
Tasmania	1.38	1.52	1.41
N. Territory and A.C.T.	7.28	4.89	3.15

Source: Bureau of Statistics for basic data, *Official Year-book of the Commonwealth of Australia*, 1966, 1971, 1974, Canberra.

highly localized. In New South Wales, although mining's value has increased, its localization in that State, in relation particularly to the manufacturing component of the total figure has decreased considerably. Again, in Victoria, the effect of recent petroleum development has increased the localization of mining in that State. Western Australia has always had a bias to mineral industries in the absence of other major productive activities. The recent developments in the mining of bauxite and iron ore have added to the higher level of localization. A similar situation prevails in Queensland, although the change is not as strongly marked. In grouping the Northern Territory and the Australian Capital Territory, one is masking the high localization of mining in the former area as some industry becomes established in the latter.

The location quotients do point then to considerable differences in each State and at different periods. At the political level, Federal government is attempting to influence the direction of mining through use of its prerogatives in issuing export licences and in controlling the direction of overseas finance. It is motivated presumably, by a sense of 'national good' as distinct from 'State good', represented by the interests and prerogatives of the States. Federal controls are remote from the mining scene and were intended to reach out to international contacts and not back to conflict with the policies of the individual States. State aspirations, where these have been formulated, are being eroded while policy decisions relevant in a Federal context are unable to find compatible expression at a State level.

As a gesture of protest at the impasse that was rapidly developing, the Western Australian Premier declared that his State would allow development to proceed on the very valuable energy resources of the northwest offshore shelf. Gas would be used for industrial development in the Pilbara and at Perth. At a much cruder level and at cross purposes more directly with Federal prerogatives, the Premier of Queensland declared that coal would not be sold to Japan without purchases of beef being taken also.

Mining Systems and Spatial Patterns

Finally we must refer back to the problem which geography poses, that is to explain the spatial pattern of mining. In seeking an explanation, we have been interested first in identifying the mining system, and then in stating the factors involved in the patterning of its operation. One set of activities within the system leads to the discovery of mineral deposits, while a second set leads to the establishment of mining ventures. In establishing a programme for prospecting, and then in examining the lead-time planning prior to mining, we are involved in assessing properties of minerals and mineral potential in mining.

Mineral exploration is the activity within the system which establishes the location and properties of minerals. Prospectors may proceed to search for minerals with but limited knowledge of likely locations and with but limited ability to discover. The prevalence of levels of indeterminacy in the pattern of prospecting locations is very considerably reduced in much contemporary exploration to the extent that it is based on a thorough reading of all reports, familiarity with the mineralized areas through aerial photographic and ground study, and the adoption of sophisticated prospecting aids both in search and interpretation of the data collected. The search culminates in a statement of the location, quantity and properties of mineral reserves. The prospecting locations have a bias in as much as the search is often carried out in more accessible areas; or in those in which discoveries are more likely to be economically viable.

We are now in a position to group the factors involved in an explanation of the map of mineral industries. The decision to mine and process to a particular level, is the culmination of a series of evaluations with regard to the properties of the mineral base. In fact we are concerned with 'the properties of spatial alternatives' as they are perceived by individuals or groups of individuals.

The properties as we may call them are grouped into three main sets. The first set includes those that are both internal to the system and deterministic in their effect on the system. Once their properties, the physical-spatial properties of the mineral deposit, have been recognized as satisfactory, then they determine the location of the mining activity. The second set is made up of those that are external to the system, invariably being economic in their connotation and permissive in their operation. The third contains those propositions that are concerned with the societal and environmental values involved—the impact of mining on socio-regional patterns. This third set is partly deterministic in that the particular circumstances of location determine generally the extent of conflict with human-ecological values. It is permissive if it invites reservations generally in terms of a conservation ethic. Translated into rehabilitation and abatement measures, this set generally places further economic constraints on the decision to mine.

We may formally conceptualize the problem as:

$$M_A = f(P_A, E_A, C_A)$$

in which M_A represents spatial pattern in mining dependent on, or explained in terms of P_A, the set of the physical factors involved; E_A the set of economic factors; and C_A the set of conservation factors covering both environment and societal qualities. The statement is specific to Australia and to Australian conditions. Because there are obious compensations and trade-offs

between economic factors and conservation factors, these would possibly be linked in any development of the equation.

Physical Factors

Explanation within the parameters of the equation, involves first assessment of properties of the physical base. The type of mineral is obviously a first consideration. Its extent, concentration, freedom from deleterious impurities, amenability to one or a combination of mining and processing techniques, and the incidence of useful by-products in the ore body, are all factors to be considered. Spatial qualities such as access to, and location of the mineral also have to be taken into account. Evaluation of these factors results in some of the mineral locations over the field of 'spatial alternatives' being discarded. The remaining locations with their particular properties are evaluated in relation to the properties of the second set of factors.

Economic Factors

The second set, the economic factors, is not in itself location-specific. It permits the mining activity to be undertaken wherever the physical factors are acceptable. Within an economic context, both sets make up the necessary conditions that are sufficient to allow plans for mining to proceed.

Availability and suitability of markets are, *ipso facto*, a first essential. Domestic markets are the outlet for many of the construction and non-metallic minerals, size of establishment and scale of operation being geared to this end. Such, however, is the scale of mining in the other sectors, that export markets can be readily considered. This is particularly the case with most of the metallic minerals. Black coal is also mined on a large scale, and exported in large quantities by and for major international groups, although it is worthy of note that 20 per cent of black coal production, and 40 per cent of all coal production went into local generation of electricity, the major user, in 1973.

In 1972–3, mineral production had an export value of just under one million dollars (f.o.b), or $1.25 million if metals and other processed minerals are included. For the year ending in December 1974 the total value had almost doubled. To take some examples—nearly 90 per cent of all iron ore was exported. All the rutile and most of the ilmenite were exported. Black coal exports amounted to 45 per cent of the total produced, nearly all of this going to Japan. In fact, the rise of Japan as the main purchaser of Australian minerals has been the outstanding feature of the contemporary market situation. Since 1969 over half of all mineral exports by value have gone to Japan. In 1972 Japan accounted for 54 per cent by value and 79 per cent by volume of

Australian mineral exports. In 1973 Australia provided Japan with nearly 50 per cent of its requirements of iron ore, 54 per cent of bauxite, 40 per cent of coking coal, 16 per cent of zinc and 19 per cent of manganese. While Japan wishes to maintain some diversity in the origins of its mineral imports, looking particularly to the new African nations as future suppliers, it cannot ignore Australian pressure built up with market dependence, for longer-term contracts. The principle involved might well become the pattern for the future.

Market price and long-term trends in demand help to establish the thresholds for mining economically recoverable and marketable grades of metallic ore, or quality of minerals generally. Free markets like the London Metal Exchange and the various American commodities markets are important institutions in establishing prices that are related to supply and demand. Buffer stocks like that established by the International Tin Association help to protect producers against low prices and buyers against high, for short-term troughs and peaks.

Gold was a special case where price was held to the United States purchasing price in spite of a growing shortfall in demand for gold for industrial uses. Prior to the freeing of the market price, Western Mining Corporation was said to be phasing out its gold mining operations at Kalgoorlie in the face of increasing mining costs brought about by lower grades and poorer accessibility, and a growing record of labour unrest. With the fivefold increase in price, the whole circumstances of investment in gold mining was changed briefly from one of rundown to one of expansion.

The threat of substitutes, government policy and increases in transport costs are all circumstances that must be assessed if a mining operation is to be maintained. The threat that aluminium holds over high copper prices is well known.

Recent mining industries have been established in areas both remote from settled areas of Australia and challenging in their harsh human environments. Under such conditions, the developmental costs for mining and the ancillary costs for infrastructure have been high. For example, Utah Development stated recently that its total establishment costs in developing four open-cuts in central Queensland amounted to $434 million, just over 40 per cent being allocated to the open-cuts themselves, 48 per cent to the railway and port, 6 per cent for power and water, and the towns accounting for a final 4 per cent. Hamersley Iron Limited has stated its infrastructural costs accruing between 1965 and 1974 and these are reproduced in Table 20.8.

The pre-mining pattern of roads, railway, port facilities and towns with their servicing and social functions is obviously important in assessing the worth of a mining venture. This, in turn, relates to other factors such as stage of a country's development, available technology, stability of government and the state of mining law.

Overall the availability of capital for development is the final factor to be considered. Capital to finance new mining ventures is involved in considerable risk at the prospecting end, and in lengthy delays in returns at the development end. Moreover, it is a particular type of capital, available for high-risk investment and largely controlled by the major national and international corporations. That it is sometimes in short supply is seen in the recent efforts of Broken Hill Proprietary Limited and Western Mining Corporation to float loans on the Eurodollar market. In both cases the sums sought had to be reduced. Because of the need to attract this particular type of development capital a level of foreign involvement in the industry becomes inevitable.

In 1972–3, the Australian mining industry was reported to be 50 per cent foreign-owned and 57 per cent foreign-controlled, a rise from the previous year. 'Controlled' as distinct from 'owned' implies that, through their holdings in a company, 'foreigners are likely to be in a position, acting singly or in coalition, to determine the *key policy decisions* of the enterprise' (Bureau of Statistics, 1974, p. 11).

The role of government has been largely regulatory. However, the Australian Labor government declared its intention to go far beyond the regulatory role in becoming involved in mining activity itself. State governments have some direct interest in mining activities such as State coal mining and electricity production although involvement is usually expressed through quasi-governmental organizations such as commissions and authorities. Soon after World War II the Federal government, aware of wartime vulnerability, was

Table 20.8 Infrastructural Costs, Hamersley Iron Ltd

	$ million
Industrial infrastructure	
Railway	209
Port	89
Social infrastructure	
Housing	76
Power	54
Community facilities	19
Water supplies	20
Schools and hospitals	6
Sporting facilities	2
Total	475

Source: Annual Report, 1974, p. 12.

instrumental in setting up the alumina and aluminium processing plants at Bell Bay, Tasmania. The Tasmanian State government held a minority interest which it retained when a new Federal government, not wishing to participate in production, withdrew.

Conservation Requirements

These make up the third and final set of factors involved in the mining equation. At the outset it must be stated that mining companies have always been aware of the need to maintain a climate that will protect their investment in the resources being exploited. Moreover, the larger the investment involved, the more critical it is to make use of conservation measures in using the resource base, for it is on the resource base that the livelihood of the company depends. That mining companies are concerned is very evident in the many statements in annual reports, in their contribution to conferences on the subject, and in actual activities in rehabilitating mined land or in minimizing pollution problems often at considerable expense.

Associated Minerals Consolidated Limited, the largest mineral sand miner, has accepted fully 'the legal requirements of land rehabilitation detailed in the leases granted'. It adds that even more so, the company is conscious of a moral obligation to the community. In carrying out what is both its requirement and obligation, rehabilitation design is undertaken by the company agronomist. For the year under review, $300,000 was allocated 'to plant 30,000 trees and shrubs in addition to grass and, in the process, replace 940,000 tons of topsoil'. Under the heading 'Why does a mining company spend $300,000 growing flowers?', an advertisement in national papers informed the public of the rehabilitation work being undertaken. Examination of some areas returned to natural growth would bear out the extent of revegetation programmes. Air and stream pollution control is a further area where costs are generated in the desire for environmental improvement after processing. One company, Queensland Alumina Limited states that it has spent $5 million on air pollution control for its plant at Gladstone.

Government now generally requires environmental impact studies. The State Pollution Control Commission of New South Wales for example, has a mandate to undertake environmental investigations under the terms of the State Pollution Control Act, 1970 before permits in connection with mining or associated works can be issued. The concern of the Federal government in requiring environmental investigations from 1974 before granting an export licence has been discussed. Rehabilitation, and indeed the posting of a bond must be considered as a legitimate part of the cost of mining ventures today.

Private, community, and some funded organizations like the Conservation Foundation are, by and large, identified with societal and special group interests, where concern centres on deterioration of critical areas and general implications for the quality of the human environment. Lake Pedder, Myall Lakes, the Barrier Reef and Fraser Island have been centres of controversy. In the case of the Fraser Island sand leases, it was more the indiscriminate selection and the extent of mining, rather than the right to mine selected areas, that seemed to be of general concern. The Fraser Island Defence Organization referred to the scale and location of operation rather than to a discouragement to mine at all. Any refinement has been discarded in the bluntness of the Commonwealth government's decision to disallow all export of ore ferried from the island, and thus effectively preclude further mining.

Sufficient to indicate the responsibility which mining companies must today take in rehabilitating despoiled land, the regulatory role of government, and the 'watchdog' role assumed by sectors of the community. Because rehabilitation and pollution control measures are part of the mining cost they may in some cases lead to a decision on the part of the company not to mine; or on the part of government not to allow mining. While conformity to conservation principles may often permit mining, the final assessment with political pressures extending beyond the limited principles established, may combine to reduce the whole feasibility of the assessment exercise to a point where it is no longer an acceptable proposition.

We have been interested in the structuring of a system and in examining the spatial pattern which it generates. The discrepancy between mineral discovery and mineral use is explainable in terms of the examples described in the text and grouped as factors in the conclusion. Some would look still further and would wish to consider the behavioural processes and the spatial patterns which they generate. While far from denying the potency of human behaviour in contributing a factor to spatial patterns, we have attempted to cope at a more modest level. Perhaps Raymond Murphy stated the level back in 1954 when he said that the geographer, in focusing on the spatial patterns and associations of mineral production, is responsible 'for the examination of mining as a part of the total geographical complex of particular regions'.

ACKNOWLEDGEMENT   The author is indebted to the Department of Geography, University of Queensland for providing research facilities, office space and typing assistance. Maps and diagrams were prepared by the departmental cartographer.

REFERENCES

Blainey, G., (1963), *The Rush that Never Ended, a history of Australian mining*, Melbourne University Press, Melbourne.

Bureau of Mineral Resources, Geology and Geophysics (1976), *Australian Mineral Industry 1974 Review (including information to June 1975)*, Canberra.

Bureau of Statistics (1974), *Foreign Ownership and Control of the Mining Industry 1972–73*, Canberra.

——(1975), *Official Yearbook of the Commonwealth of Australia*, No. 60, 1974, and supplementary statistical data regarding minerals and mining, Canberra. Also State year books and supplementary materials available from the State Offices in the capital cities.

——(1976), *Australian National Accounts National Income and Expenditure 1974–75* and supplementary statistics, Canberra.

Butlin, N. G., (1962), *Australian Domestic Product, Investment and Foreign Borrowing, 1861–1938/39*, Cambridge University Press, Cambridge.

Chalmers, R. O. (1967), *Australian Rocks, Minerals and Gemstones*, Angus and Robertson, Sydney.

Coghill, I. (1971), *Australia's Mineral Wealth*, Sorrett Publishing, Melbourne.

Cohen, M. and Notham, P. M. (eds) (1975), *Jobson's 1974'75 Mining Year Book*, Jobson's Financial Services, North Sydney.

Department of National Development (1969, 1970), 'Mineral Deposits' and 'Mineral Industries', *Atlas of Australian Resources*, Second Series, Canberra.

Electricity Supply Association of Australia (1974), *The Electricity Supply Industry in Australia Year 1972–73*, Melbourne.

Kalix, Z., Fraser, L. M. and Rawson, R. I. (eds) (1966), *Australian Mineral Industry: Production and Trade, 1842–1964*, Bulletin 81, Bureau of Mineral Resources, Geology and Geophysics, Canberra.

McLeod, I. R. (ed.) (1965), *The Australian Mineral Industry:*

The Mineral Deposits, Bulletin No. 72, Department of Mineral Resources, Geology and Geophysics, Canberra.

Murphy, R. E. (1954), 'The geography of mineral production' in P. E. James and C. F. Jones, *American Geography Inventory and Prospect*, Syracuse University Press, Syracuse, N.Y., pp. 278–91.

Petroleum Information Bureau (Australia) (1974), *Australian Petroleum Statistics*, Melbourne.

——(1975), *Oil and Australia, the figures behind the facts*, Melbourne.

Raggatt, H. G. (1968), *Mountains of Ore*, Landsdowne Press, Melbourne.

Thrush, P. W. *et al.* (eds) (1968), *A Dictionary of Mining, Mineral, and Related Terms*, Bureau of Mines, United States Department of the Interior, Washington D.C.

Wagner, P. (1960), *The Human Use of the Earth*, Free Press of Glencoe, Illinois.

Reference was also made to various issues of the following serials:

Annual Report, Joint Coal Board, Sydney.

Annual Report, Queensland Coal Board.

Annual Report, State Departments of Mines.

Annual Report and Statement of Accounts, various mining companies in private sector.

Australian Financial Review

Australian Mineral Industry, Quarterly Review, Quarterly Statistics, Bureau of Mineral Resources, Geology and Geophysics, Canberra.

Mining Journal, Mining Magazine and *Mining Annual Review*, London.

Queensland Government Mining Journal, Department of Mines, Brisbane.

21 MANUFACTURING

G. J. R. LINGE

Manufacturing originated in Australia, soon after European settlement began in 1788, in response to the demand for food, clothing and shelter in tiny communities perched precariously on the edge of a vast continent and separated in time and distance from Europe and from each other. Until the middle of the nineteenth century manufacturing and processing activities grew only slowly as they were geared for the most part to the modest needs of the several small and spatially distinct domestic markets. But from 1850 to 1890 progress was much more rapid: the number of factory hands, for example, increased from about 12,000 to about 149,000 (or at an annual rate of 7.1 per cent compared with 5.3 per cent for the population as a whole). Moreover, at this latter date manufacturing contributed 11.4 per cent to Gross Domestic Product (GDP) as against only 5.6 per cent thirty years previously. These estimates by Butlin (1962) have jolted economic historians (and geographers) away from the traditional view of Australia during the nineteenth century as being little more than a vast sheepwalk. Indeed, as Butlin (1964, p. 17) has pointed out, the rapid expansion of secondary industry during this period was 'the most specific indicator of the basic social and economic transformation towards a predominantly urban society'.

By the end of World War II, Australian factories were contributing about 28 per cent to GDP and employing about the same proportion of the nation's workforce. Although these proportions have declined slightly during the last few years, there is no doubt about the continuing significance of manufacturing in the Australian economy. Before developing this point further, however, it is appropriate to comment on Australia's contribution to world manufacturing industry. In 1963, the latest year for which international comparisons are available (United Nations, 1971), Australia contributed 1.01 per cent to the world total of value added by factory activities. By this measure it was fifteenth in a world league table dominated by the United States (32.4 per cent) and the U.S.S.R. (19.7 per cent). In terms of value added per capita, Australia (with US$447) ranked eleventh in the world: the leaders here were the United States

(US$824), the German Democratic Republic (US$738) and Czechoslovakia (US$630). International comparisons are fraught with difficulties but the available data suggest that, from an industrial point of view, Australia ranks about thirteenth amongst the nations of the world for which the appropriate information is available.

The first part of this chapter outlines the structure and characteristics of manufacturing in Australia and reviews some of the factors that have influenced the development of secondary industry in recent years. This provides the background for an analysis, in the second part, of the distribution of industrial activities at several different spatial scales. The division of the discussion in this way, however, is largely a matter of convenience and in no sense implies that structural and spatial attributes can be viewed in isolation. For example, as will be shown later, some government policies affect not only the location of secondary industry but also the number and size of the manufacturing establishments engaged in any particular activity.

STRUCTURE AND CHARACTERISTICS

The manufacturing sector exerts a substantial influence on the Australian economy because of its size both in terms of output and of resources used. It influences the total demand for labour and capital directly through its employment of these resources and indirectly through its use of goods and services produced in the primary and tertiary sectors. On the basis of an input-output study applied to data for 1962–3 it can be estimated that, on average, every $100 of final demand for manufactures required inputs (direct and indirect, and imported inputs) of $21 from primary production, $8 from mining, and $25 from tertiary industries (Australian Bureau of Statistics, 1973).

Three main points emerge from Table 21.1, which summarizes the role of manufacturing in the Australian economy during the last seventy years. First, it is clear that this sector made a greater contribution to Gross Domestic Product and employed a larger share of the nation's total workforce during the decades

Table 21.1 Gross Domestic Product, Employment and Exports by Sector: Australia, 1900–1 to 1971–2

Period[a]	Proportion of total GDP at factor cost attributable to each sector				Proportion of total workforce employed in each sector				Proportion of total exports attributable to each sector			
	Rural	Mining	Manu-facturing	Services	Rural	Mining	Manu-facturing	Services	Rural	Mining	Manu-facturing	Services
1900/1–1909/10	26	9	12	53	n.a.	n.a.	n.a.	n.a.	n.a.	n.a.	n.a.	n.a.
1910/11–1919/20	26	5	13	56	24	4	20	52	79	12	8	1
1920/1–1929/30	23	2	15	60	23	2	21	54	88	3	9	1
1930/1–1939/40	23	3	16	58	23	2	21	54	88	2	10	1
1940/1–1949/50	n.a.	n.a.	n.a.	n.a.	16	2	27	55	84	1	12	3
1950/1–1959/60	17	2	28	53	13	2	28	57	84	3	12	1
1960/1–1969/70	11	2	28	59	10	1	28	61	69	13	15	3
1970/1–1971/2[b]	7	3	27	63	8	1	27	64	52	26	20	3

[a] Based on financial years.
[b] Averages for two-year period 1970–1 to 1971–2.
Source: *Industries Assistance Commission Annual Report 1973–74*, p. 42.

after World War II compared with those beforehand. Second, having made this advance, much of it during the 1940s, the manufacturing sector generally merely kept pace in subsequent decades with the growth of the economy as a whole and now appears to be entering a period of *relative* decline (a trend consistent, however, with circumstances in industrialized economies elsewhere). Indeed, the rapid increase in the proportion of the workforce engaged in tertiary activities suggests that Australia is taking on some of the characteristics of what has been termed a 'post-industrial' society. And, third, the proportion of Australia's exports emanating from the manufacturing sector has almost doubled during the last fifteen years as a result of a number of factors that will be touched upon later.

The broad outline of factory operations set out in

Table 21.2 indicates the progress of manufacturing activity during the two decades to 1967–8 and this is supplemented in Table 21.3 by details of employment and value of production in each of the main industry classes. Although total employment in the secondary sector rose by 57 per cent during this period, the increase was not spread evenly throughout all the classes. The shares accounted for by the heavier and larger-scale industries—many of which only assumed real prominence after World War II—tended to rise while those of several 'traditional' industries tended to diminish: indeed, the number of people employed in tanning and the manufacture of clothing declined absolutely. Similar relative changes are revealed by the value of production data, though comparisons over time are best made by using constant price indexes

Table 21.2 Summary of Factory Operations, Australia, 1947–8 to 1967–8[a]

Item	1947–8	1952–3	1957–8	1962–3	1967–8
Factories (no.)	36,890	47,292	53,581	59,089	62,619
Persons employed ('000)[b]	837	918	1,057	1,155	1,315
Salaries and wages paid ($million)	560	1,244	1,823	2,409	3,613
Value of production ($million)[c]	949	2,100	3,325	4,591	7,132

[a] Excludes 'heat, light and power' [industry class 16] throughout; excludes the Australian Capital Territory and Northern Territory prior to 1962–3.
[b] Average employed during the year.
[c] Value added in process of manufacture (i.e. value of output less value of materials and fuel used).
Sources: Bureau of Statistics, *Secondary Industries Part 1—Factory and Building Operations* and *Manufacturing Industry*, Canberra.

Table 21.3 Employment and Production by Main Industry Classes, Australia, 1947–8 and 1967–8[a]

Industry class	Employment[b]				Value of production			
	1947–8		1967–8		1947–8		1967–8	
	Number	Per cent	Number	Per cent	$m	Per cent	$m	Per cent
Treatment of non-metalliferous mine and quarry products	14,263	1.7	26,685	2.0	19	2.0	204	2.8
Bricks, pottery, glass, etc.	17,536	2.1	27,171	2.1	19	2.0	163	2.3
Chemicals, dyes, explosives, paints, etc.	31,808	3.8	55,053	4.2	57	6.0	687	9.6
Industrial metals, machines, conveyances	320,948	38.4	626,280	47.6	363	38.2	3,164	44.4
Precious metals, jewellery, plate	6,069	0.7	6,108	0.4	6	0.6	26	0.4
Textiles and textile goods (not dress)	61,911	7.4	73,804	5.6	64	6.8	315	4.4
Skins and leather (not clothing or footwear)	15,624	1.9	11,458	0.9	18	1.9	48	0.8
Clothing (except knitted) and footwear	111,693	13.3	111,040	8.4	87	9.1	360	5.0
Food, drink and tobacco	113,595	13.6	144,441	11.0	156	16.5	937	13.1
Sawmills, joinery and woodworking	47,052	5.6	60,274	4.6	49	5.2	272	3.8
Furniture of wood, bedding, etc.	18,546	2.2	25,055	1.9	18	1.9	106	1.5
Paper, stationery, printing, etc.	47,813	5.7	90,563	6.9	59	6.2	549	7.7
Rubber	10,753	1.3	21,111	1.6	13	1.4	113	1.6
Musical instruments	887	0.1	831	0.1	1	0.1	8	0.1
Miscellaneous products (including plastics)	18,235	2.2	35,469	2.7	20	2.1	180	2.5
Total manufacturing[c]	836,733	100.0	1,315,343	100.0	949	100.0	7,132	100.0

[a] Excludes the Australian Capital Territory and Northern Territory in 1947–8.

[b] Average employed during the year.

[c] Excludes 'heat, light and power' [industry class 16].

(Table 21.4). For manufacturing as a whole the value of production in real terms increased between 1949–50 (the first year for which such estimates are available) and 1967–8 by 190 per cent or by a considerably greater amount than a range of industrial activities including textiles, clothing, sawmilling, and food, drink and tobacco. The main areas of growth were heavy, capital-intensive industries, such as iron and steel making (400 per cent), industrial and heavy chemicals (905 per cent), and petroleum products (2,200 per cent), and lighter but technologically advanced industries like electrical machinery, cables and apparatus (400 per cent) and wireless and television equipment (484 per cent).

A more recent view of factory operations in Australia is given in Table 21.5. It must be explained that in 1968–9 the Australian Bureau of Statistics adopted the Australian Standard Industrial Classification (ASIC). Apart from a number of technical changes in definition, some activities previously embraced were excluded (such as motor vehicle repairing and dry cleaning) and a few (like slaughtering, milk treatment, and publishing) included for the first time. The effect of this change can be appreciated from the fact that had ASIC been used in 1967–8 the number of factories would have been reduced by about 27,200 to 35,400 and the factory labour force by about 218,000 to

1,097,000 (*Official Yearbook of the Commonwealth of Australia*, 1972, pp. 718–21). There is no way of linking the old and new series so that any discussion of manufacturing is complicated by the need to draw on two quite different and unrelated sets of data.

In 1971–2 the 36,000 manufacturing establishments in Australia employed 1,300,000 workers (including those directly involved in extracting raw materials and in sales or distribution activities) and produced goods with an added value of $9,700 million. The details in Table 21.5 indicate the importance of the metal trades (ASIC subdivisions 29–33) and of food, drink and tobacco industries (subdivisions 21–22). Between them these activities account for almost 60 per cent of the factory workforce and a similar proportion of the value added by the manufacturing sector. The absolute size of each industrial group— whether expressed in terms of employment or value added—is only one (and not necessarily always the most appropriate) way of measuring the role it plays in the economy. For example, the relative importance of the two main factors of production, capital and labour, varies considerably as can be seen from Table 21.6 using data for 1968–9 (the latest available for some of the series). Thus the capital intensity of the basic metal products group is fourteen times greater than that of the clothing and footwear indus-

Table 21.4 Constant Price Indices of Factory Production in Australia, 1949–50 to 1967–8[a]
(1959–60 = 100)

Industry class	1949–50	1952–3	1957–8	1962–3	1967–8	Percentage change 1949–50 to 1967–8
Treatment of non-metalliferous mine and quarry products	45	52	79	122	166	+ 269
Bricks, pottery, glass, etc.	65	67	82	104	143	+ 120
Chemicals, dyes, explosives, paints, etc.	35	40	84	123	188	+ 437
Industrial metals, machines, conveyances, etc.	46	55	83	116	167	+ 263
Textiles and textile goods (not dress)	63	59	88	111	140	+ 122
Skins and leather (not clothing or footwear)	101	93	94	100	97	− 4
Clothing (except knitted) and footwear	80	77	93	111	134	+ 68
Food, drink and tobacco	78	80	94	113	144	+ 85
Sawmills, joinery and woodworking	72	72	85	100	127	+ 76
Furniture of wood, bedding, etc.	61	57	83	105	140	+ 129
Paper, stationery, printing, etc.	51	46	79	117	169	+ 231
Rubber	52	46	87	115	151	+ 190
Other manufactures[b]	44	49	77	120	229	+ 420
Total manufacturing[c]	55	58	85	115	160	+ 190

[a] Excludes factories in Australian Capital Territory and Northern Territory.

[b] Includes precious metals, jewellery, plate, musical instruments, and miscellaneous products (including plastics).

[c] Excludes 'heat, light and power' [industry class 16].

Source: derived from Bureau of Statistics (1970), *Indexes of Factory Production 1949–50 to 1967–68*, Canberra. Index in 1959–60 prices linked at 1959–60 to index in 1955–6 prices.

tries; the proportion of immigrants employed in the various groups ranges from 24 to 48 per cent; and females make up from as little as 6 to as much as 78 per cent of the workforce engaged in the main kinds of manufacturing activity. Some of these characteristics appear to be interrelated. Capital-intensive activities, like the manufacture of chemical, petroleum and coal products, tend to have relatively low shares of wages in value added, above average wages, and higher labour productivity. Not un-expectedly, too, there is a strong inverse relationship, exemplified by the textile, clothing and footwear industries, between the average wage and the proportion of females employed.

Scale and Ownership

Nearly 80 per cent of the manufacturing establishments operating in June 1969 had fewer than fifty workers including those directly engaged in marketing and distribution. The prevalence of small factories is not uncommon in the more developed countries but has particular significance in Australia because of the fragmentation of the small economy between the six States, the high transport costs resulting from the

wide separation of the main internal markets, and the strategy adopted by many firms of operating branch or associated factories at several points around the periphery of the continent. Only 360 manufacturing *enterprises* (comprising all operations in Australia of single legal entities) had more than 500 employees, mainly in the metal, chemical, textile, paper, and rubber industries. Between them, however, these enterprises accounted for 43 per cent of the workforce and 49 per cent of the value added in this sector of the economy.

This draws attention to the high degree of ownership concentration—the extent to which industries in Australia are oligopolized by a few large firms or are monopolized to all intents and purposes by a single producer as is the case with basic steel (The Broken Hill Proprietary Company Ltd) and sugar (The Colonial Sugar Refining Company Ltd). In 1968–9 there were no fewer than twenty activities (including the manufacture of iron and steel, motor vehicles, rubber tyres, pulp and paper, beer, and concrete pipes and asbestos cement) in which the four leading enterprises were responsible for at least four-fifths of the turnover (Australian Bureau of Statistics, 1974).

Table 21.5   Summary of Operations of Manufacturing Establishments by Industry Class, Australia, 1971–2

ASIC subdivision	Industry	Establishments operating at 30 June 1972		Workers (average over whole year)		Value added[a]	
		Number	Per cent	Number	Per cent	$m	Per cent
21, 22	Food, drink and tobacco	4,423	12.3	201,590	15.5	1,684	17.4
23	Textiles	873	2.4	55,186	4.2	334	3.4
24	Footwear and clothing	3,216	8.9	116,139	8.9	522	5.3
25	Wood, wood products and furniture	5,884	16.3	81,084	6.2	496	5.2
26	Paper and paper products	3,588	9.9	106,328	8.2	818	8.4
27	Chemical, petroleum and coal products	1,165	3.2	65,610	5.0	804	8.3
28	Non-metallic mineral products	1,854	5.1	51,328	3.9	496	5.1
29	Basic metal products	627	1.7	92,848	7.1	884	9.1
31	Fabricated metal products	5,170	14.3	120,336	9.2	824	8.5
32	Transport equipment	1,426	3.9	151,890	11.7	1,047	10.8
33	Other machinery and equipment	4,899	13.6	189,589	14.6	1,297	13.4
34	Miscellaneous manufacturing	3,022	8.4	70,856	5.5	497	5.1
21–34	Total manufacturing	36,147	100.0	1,302,784	100.0	9,703	100.0

[a] The concept of 'value added' is basically similar to the concept of 'value of production' used prior to 1968–9. However, comparisons between the old and new series are invalid because (i) the value added for the whole establishment and not merely for the manufacturing process is now included, and (ii) the scope of the manufacturing census has been changed as explained in the text.

Source: Bureau of Statistics (1973), *Manufacturing Establishments: Details of Operations by Industry Class, Australia, 1971–72 (ref. 12.29)*, Canberra.

Whereas these activities accounted for 23 per cent of Australian manufacturing output, the twenty-seven industries displaying a similar degree of concentration in the United States in 1963 produced only 11 per cent of its total factory output (Scherer, 1970, p. 60). This difference can probably be explained in part by the operation of anti-trust legislation in the United States but much of it undoubtedly arises directly and indirectly from the relatively small size of the Australian economy. Ownership is, of course, only one measure of the control or influence exerted by firms. Thus, interlocking directorships may limit or even eliminate competition between nominally separate enterprises and link them directly and indirectly to suppliers, distributors, and financial institutions: numerous examples of such interlocks are cited by Rolfe (1967) and Wheelwright and Miskelly (1967). Business undertakings may also be tied to each other by agency agreements, long-term supply contracts, licensing arrangements and similar agreements, although the Trade Practices Act 1974 (most provisions of which came into effect on 1 October 1974) prohibits such practices as restraint of trade, monopolization, resale price maintenance, anti-competitive exclusive or discriminatory dealing and anti-competitive mergers (Department of Manufacturing Industry, 1975, p. 16).

The small size of the Australian domestic market adversely affects productivity, prices and profitability, and this is particularly important in the case of some industrial techniques—especially those with high plant overheads—transposed from overseas. For example, as Hunter (1963, p. 15) notes, only one motor vehicle manufacturer in Australia operates on a scale comparable with West European or British firms. Or, again, the largest local manufacturer of whitegoods (domestic refrigerators, stoves, washing machines and dish washers) produces only about 160,000 units a year whereas overseas experience suggests that economic production requires a minimum throughput of about 500,000 units—usually from a single plant (Tariff Board, 1973, p. 5). During a survey of the chemical industry Parry (1974, p. 232) discovered that the Australian plants operated by a subsidiary company were a mere 5 to 20 per cent of the size of the largest ones being used by its American parent. Factories making heavy organic chemicals, alkalis, plastics, and electronic equipment tend to be 'lumpy' investments which, if not used to full capacity, lead to high unit costs of production. Parry notes (1974, p. 234), for example, that the average degree of plant utilization by major companies in the Australian chemical industry during recent years has been about 70 per cent. This problem is exacerbated by the tendency for overseas firms to establish themselves in Australia

Table 21.6 Selected Characteristics of Manufacturing Sector by Industry Class, Australia, 1968–9

ASIC subdivision	Industry	Index of capital intensity[a]	Concentration[b]	Labour productivity[c]	Average wage per employee	Wages share of value added	Females as proportion of work-force	Overseas born as proportion of work-force
		(per cent)		($)	($)	(per cent)	(per cent)	(per cent)
21, 22	Food, drink and tobacco	128	12	6,373	2,909	46	26	33
23	Textiles	72	24	5,162	2,743	53	45	44
24	Footwear and clothing	18	11	3,330	2,110	63	78	48
25	Wood, wood products and furniture	44	7	4,746	2,638	56	12	24
26	Paper and paper products	99	20	6,076	3,219	53	27	24
27	Chemical, petroleum and coal products	248	27	10,435	3,617	35	26	33
28	Non-metallic mineral products	144	25	6,860	3,378	49	10	34
29	Basic metal products	261	71	8,340	3,737	45	6	41
31	Fabricated metal products	56	12	5,399	2,987	55	19	37
32	Transport equipment	77	52	6,674	3,277	49	11	45
33	Other machinery and equipment	55	9	5,512	3,118	57	25	38
34	Miscellaneous manufacturing	73	28	5,578	2,889	52	34	41
21–34	Total manufacturing	100	10	6,049	3,023	50	27	37

[a] Capital intensity measured as the book value of fixed tangible assets per person employed and expressed here as an index, using as a base (equal to 100) the capital intensity of the total manufacturing sector.

[b] Percentage of industry turnover accounted for by the four largest enterprise groups (defined broadly as the unit comprising all operations in Australia of a group of legal entities under common ownership or control).

[c] Value added per person employed.

Source: Industries Assistance Commission Annual Report 1973–74, pp. 76–84.

prematurely to gain the advantages of being first in the field, to secure their position before the expiry of patents, or to avail themselves of the inducements offered by State governments (a point considered again later in this chapter). On a number of occasions, too, the Tariff Board has noted that unit costs could be reduced if producers used resources more efficiently: in 1972, for example, the nine refrigerator manufactures in Australia were producing about eighty different models (some of them at more than one factory) and were competing for a local domestic market of only about 350,000 units annually (Tariff Board, 1973, p. 5).

Exports

One partial solution to some of these difficulties lies in the expansion of overseas markets although Australia is disadvantaged in this respect because its manufacturing activities are not integrated with those of neighbouring countries in the same way that industry in Canada or Switzerland is related to the North American or European economies. Nonetheless, efforts have been made during the last couple of decades to encourage manufacturers to break into and expand overseas markets by publicity campaigns, trade fairs and, since 1961, export incentives in the form of payroll tax rebate and market development allowance schemes (Lloyd, 1973). The latter were superseded in 1974 by a new system of export development grants designed to cover certain types of expenditure incurred in promoting overseas markets for goods, services, property rights or know-how which are substantially of Australian origin. As a result of these measures, initiatives taken by individual firms, and the reorganization of world trading strategies by some multinational corporations, the value of Australian-made goods exported (*excluding* food, drink and tobacco products and mineral concentrates) grew from $107 million in 1948–9 to $1,339 million in 1973–4; more importantly, the share these formed of all indigenous exports rose during this period from 10 to 20 per cent. Much of the increase came from industries producing metal

Table 21.7　Imports and Exports, by Manufacturing Industry Subdivisions, Australia, 1968–9[a]
(per cent)

ASIC subdivision	Industry	Exports as a proportion of turnover	Exports as a proportion of total manufactured exports	Imports as a proportion of market supplies[b]	Imports as a proportion of total manufactured imports
21, 22	Food, drink and tobacco	9.9	33.4	4.0	3.6
23	Textiles	12.2	7.8	31.8	8.8
24	Footwear and clothing	0.7	0.5	3.1	1.4
25	Wood, wood products and furniture	1.0	0.7	7.5	2.0
26	Paper and paper products	1.1	1.2	13.9	6.3
27	Chemical, petroleum and coal products	4.8	6.3	25.7	15.9
28	Non-metallic mineral products	2.7	1.9	9.0	2.2
29	Basic metal products	19.3	30.3	7.1	3.5
31	Fabricated metal products	2.4	2.6	10.6	4.2
32	Transport equipment	3.8	5.3	29.2	19.7
33	Other machinery and equipment	4.0	7.5	30.8	27.7
34	Miscellaneous manufacturing	3.7	2.6	18.5	5.0
21–34	Total manufacturing	6.5	100.0	16.8	100.0

[a] Estimates by Industries Assistance Commission.

[b] 'Market supply' defined here as turnover plus imports and duty where imports have been allocated indirectly—that is, to the industries of which they would be the primary outputs if they had been produced in Australia.

Source: *Industries Assistance Commission Annual Report 1973–74*, pp. 76–84.

goods, appliances, vehicles, equipment, chemicals and refined petroleum. Significantly, the eight leading outlets for Australian-made goods (in order of importance, New Zealand, the United States, Papua New Guinea, South Africa, Japan, Singapore, Hong Kong and Malaysia) all border the Pacific or Indian Oceans, reflecting the partial reorientation of the nation's total trade away from traditional markets in Britain and Europe.

The Industries Assistance Commission (IAC) has prepared estimates of the share of each industry subdivision in total manufactured imports and exports during 1968–9 (Table 21.7). Imports were allocated indirectly to the activities of which they would have been the primary outputs had they been made in Australia (thus, imports of tyres were classified to ASIC subdivision 34 rather than to the motor vehicle industry in subdivision 32). It can be seen from Table 21.7 that industries to which most imports were allocated produce only a small proportion of the exports. Almost two-thirds of manufactured imports consist of chemical and petroleum products, transport equipment or other machinery and equipment, but these categories contribute less than a fifth of manufactured exports. Conversely, two industry groups— food, drink and tobacco and basic metal products— account for two-thirds of manufactured exports but

less than a tenth of imports. More detailed analyses by the IAC indicate that the goods in which Australia has an export advantage are produced in industries that tend to be capital-intensive, pay high wages and have a high output per worker. Although anticipating the later discussion of tariffs and other forms of assistance available to the manufacturing sector, it is convenient to note here that the effective rates of assistance are in general higher for industries which are labour-intensive and have a relatively low output per worker. This means that, on the one hand, the manufacturing industries for which greatest assistance has been provided tend to be those responsible for a relatively small proportion of exports and, on the other, the existing pattern of protection against imports tends to discriminate against some of the characteristics associated with industries in which Australia has an export advantage. In other words, as the IAC points out, 'the greatest assistance has been given to those industries for which the Australian environment and endowment of resources are least suited' (Industries Assistance Commission, 1974, p. 16).

Overseas Technology and Capital
The growing interest in promoting and expanding export markets has also drawn attention to the importance of research and development in which,

Plate 21.1 In the mid-1930s General Motors-Holden's Pty Ltd obtained land from the Crown at Fishermens Bend in South Melbourne for the factory (foreground) which became the headquarters of its operations in Australia. Over 90 per cent of the Australian workforce manufacturing motor vehicles and parts are concentrated in the five mainland capital cities.

however, Australia lags behind other countries. In 1968–9 firms here spent $81 million (equivalent to 1.2 per cent of Gross Manufacturing Product) on such activities compared with 6.8 and 5.4 per cent of GMP in the United States and the United Kingdom, respectively (Office of Secondary Industry, 1972, p. 26). A further survey of Australian manufacturers in 1971–2 indicated that the outlay had risen to $130 million, much of which was incurred by the larger companies and especially those that were wholly overseas-owned or had substantial overseas ownership (Department of Manufacturing Industry, 1974b). This emphasizes the derivative nature of much of the manufacturing in this country: as Hunter (1963, p. 2) notes, 'surprisingly few major, or minor, industries can be said to be indigenous to Australian conditions in the sense that they have grown up based mainly on Australian finance, ownership, natural advantage and native technological ability'.

Traditionally, Britain was the main source of the finance—and the technical and managerial expertise associated with it—coming from abroad, but after

World War II the flow from North America became more significant (Brash, 1966). Thus, of the $11,000 million private overseas investment (including un-distributed income) in companies of all kinds in Australia between 1948–9 and 1971–2, 42 per cent stemmed from the United Kingdom and 38 per cent from the United States and Canada. During much of this period the manufacturing sector attracted the bulk of these funds (over half in 1963–4 and again in 1966–7) but in recent years an increasing proportion has been devoted to mineral exploration, mining and tertiary activities. Factories in which at least half the equity was directly held overseas accounted for 19 per cent of the value of production in manufacturing sector in 1962–3 and 21 per cent in 1966–7. These are conservative figures because they exclude portfolio investment except where a significant proportion of shares is held in a single overseas country. The extent of overseas ownership varies considerably between industries. In some, especially those that are capital-intensive and technologically advanced (such as motor vehicle building, oil refining and pharmaceutical manufacturing), overseas-owned plants are responsible for at least three-quarters of the value of production; in others, generally the simpler or longer-established kinds of activities (like tanning, sawmilling, and the manufacture of clothing and footwear), foreign investment is of little consequence.

Considerable debate has arisen since World War II about the benefits and costs of overseas investment and the dangers associated with foreign ownership and control of Australia's industries and resources (see, for example, Wheelwright, 1963; Brash, 1966; and Masterman, 1970). There is no doubt that external investment funds contributed to the overall growth of secondary industries (including those with export potential), to improvements in production technology and managerial expertise, and to the twofold increase between 1955–6 and 1967–8 in the level of capital intensity in manufacturing (measured as the fixed capital invested, at constant prices, per male unit employed). At the same time, however, several short- and long-term problems have been emerging, such as the growing cost of servicing the investment, the reduction in local equity, the increasing extent of local borrowing, and the tendency for existing enterprises to be taken over without any fresh injection of technology. A good deal of the discussion has also turned on the less tangible issues of economic and political independence: lessons, it has been suggested, should be drawn from the situation in Canada where an estimated 60 per cent of the manufacturing sector is controlled from outside and where there are doubts about that country's ability to control many aspects of its economic and political affairs (Vernon, 1970, p. 154). Late in 1969 the Australian government, while welcoming the inflow of capital from overseas, laid down guidelines to encourage Australian equity in new ventures, to examine takeover bids by foreign firms, and to control the amount of loan capital that could be raised locally. Under the Companies (Foreign Takeovers) Act 1972–4, which came into force on 31 October 1972, all takeovers—transactions that result in changes in the identity of a person in a position to determine the major policy decisions of Australian businesses—by foreigners are subject to scrutiny by a Committee reporting to the Treasurer. Under this Act a foreign corporation is defined broadly as one in which a single overseas interest or a group of overseas interests holds, respectively, 15 or 40 per cent or more of the voting power. As a further measure, the Australian Industry Development Corporation was established in 1971 with a capital of $100 million (used as a base for its borrowings, mainly from overseas) to help finance industrial and mineral development by making overseas funds available to sound Australian companies that are themselves unable to borrow abroad at prime rates, by acting as a catalyst or co-ordinator in helping to put together significant Australian participation in ventures with foreign companies, and by undertaking investments which, although measured against commercial criteria, also take a broader economic and social view than private financial institutions. The AIDC supported thirty-four ventures ($61 million) in 1972–3 and twenty-eight ($42 million) in 1973–4.

Structure of Assistance

Over the years domestic and overseas investment in Australian secondary industry has been encouraged by the political stability of the country, the rapid expansion (despite its relatively small size) of the economy, the discovery and exploitation of mineral resources like iron ore and bauxite (and the lifting of the 1938 embargo on the export of iron ore in the early 1960s), and the various forms of assistance available to the manufacturing sector. In its first annual report, the IAC—which early in 1974 replaced the long-standing Tariff Board—attempted to calculate the level of support afforded each of the 173 ASIC manufacturing industries in 1969–70. After assessing the amount of tariff assistance it then made adjustments for some of the more important non-tariff measures including excise and sales taxes, subsidies and bounties (such as those on agricultural tractors, ships, cellulose acetate flake, and sulphuric acid), import restrictions on sugar, and crude oil import policies. Several other forms of assistance—export subsidies and incentives, motor vehicle local content plans, support-value duties on some chemicals, government purchasing practices, and quantitative restrictions on some clothing imports—had to be excluded from the analysis because of lack of information or because of the difficulty of allocating benefits between individual industries. The nominal rate of assistance represents the proportion by which the returns per unit received by producers can be raised relative to the (hypothetical) situation where no assistance is provided. While forms of assistance such as tariffs on outputs benefit Australian producers of those outputs, tariffs on importable materials penalize the production process. In other words, tariffs have a subsidizing effect on the outputs of production processes and a taxing effect on the materials used. Thus the *effective* rate measures the net extent (the percentage increase in value added per unit of output) to which the production process is assisted.

Several points emerge from the summary of this analysis set out in Table 21.8. First, the levels of assistance available to the 173 industry classes in the manufacturing sector differed markedly: nominal rates ranged from zero to 110 per cent and effective rates from minus 15 per cent (for soft drinks) to 281 per cent (for rolling, drawing and extruding some non-ferrous

Table 21.8 Differences in Rates of Assistance Within Industries in the Manufacturing Sector, Australia, 1969–70[a]

ASIC sub-division	Industry group (and number of individual industries[b])	Nominal rate			Effective rate			Net subsidy equivalent per person employed[c]		
		Lowest (per cent)	Highest (per cent)	Average (per cent)	Lowest (per cent)	Highest (per cent)	Average (per cent)	Lowest ($)	Highest ($)	Average ($)
21, 22	Food, drink and tobacco (27)[b]	0	110	9	−15	276	11	−1,981	7,309	774
23	Textiles (16)	0	38	23	−1	73	41	−44	5,408	1,658
24	Footwear and clothing (13)	34	66	45	42	152	83	1,055	2,669	1,653
25	Wood, wood products and furniture (8)	6	35	21	5	68	26	396	2,147	1,222
26	Paper and paper products (8)	7	55	28	10	136	50	199	6,666	1,888
27	Chemical, petroleum and coal products (15)	3	49	24	−9	115	37	−400	6,542	2,734
28	Non-metallic mineral products (14)	1	36	12	−5	67	15	−432	3,343	1,424
29	Basic metal products (14)	0	49	14	0	281	29	−3	6,403	2,813
31	Fabricated metal products (14)	26	48	39	30	189	73	1,305	4,280	2,510
32	Transport equipment (9)	16	48	38	29	86	57	648	2,598	1,788
33	Other machinery and equipment (17)	16	45	32	14	84	44	403	3,585	1,632
34	Miscellaneous manfuacturing (15)	7	48	29	2	93	38	90	3,309	1,683
21–34	Total manufacturing (170)[b]	0	110	22[d]	−15	281	35[d]	−1,981	7,309	n.a.

[a] Nominal and effective rates and net subsidy equivalents were derived from an analysis of individual ASIC classes.

[b] The IAC appears to have omitted three industries (flour mill products; starch, gluten and starch sugar; and cereal foods and baking mixes) from its analysis.

[c] Amount of money necessary to provide the same assistance by subsidy as provided by the industry's effective rate.

[d] In the calculation of these averages, nominal and effective rates have been weighted by their respective shares in output and value added (both valued at prices which would exist in the absence of assistance).

Source: *Industries Assistance Commission Annual Report 1973–74*, p. 69.

metals). There were considerable variations, too, even within the main ASIC subdivisions which embrace broadly similar kinds of activities. In the food, drink and tobacco group, for instance, the effective rate was as high as 276 per cent for refined sugar to as little as minus 15 per cent for soft drinks. Another way of illustrating this is to compare average net subsidy equivalents of assistance per person employed: in the food, drink and tobacco subdivision these ranged from $7,309 to minus $1,981 per person. For secondary industry as a whole the weighted average nominal and effective rates were, respectively, 22 and 35 per cent. It should be noted that this IAC study was based on 1969–70 data so that the nominal and effective rates shown in Table 21.8 would now be generally lower because of the 25 per cent reduction in all tariffs made in July 1973 and lower still in particular cases as a result of inquiries undertaken by the Tariff Board in the early 1970s.

The second point is that, although many industries in Australia appear to receive some assistance (because they have positive nominal or effective rates), some are really being penalized by the present structure of assistance (Industries Assistance Commission, 1974, p. 12). The fact that a particular industry has a rate of assistance greater than zero means little: more significant is its effective rate relative to that of other activities. Assistance helps industries to meet competition, usually from overseas, but it also provides them with the opportunity to bid for and retain inputs of materials, capital and labour in competition with other potential domestic users. In effect, then, an industry given a high effective rate of assistance is being aided at the expense of those afforded lower rates. This leads to a third point, for the present complex structure of assistance—within which industries that have the greatest comparative disadvantage relative to those overseas tend to have the highest levels of support—reflects the cumulative result of decisions taken by successive governments in response to a 'variety of situations and problems and in order to achieve a range of aims and objects. Among these have been economic growth, greater national self-reliance, full employment, redistribution of income, improvement in the balance of payments, increased customs revenue, or simply to help industries meet overseas competition. It was not until the mid-1960s, however, that the more efficient use of resources was seen, at least overtly, as one of the criteria to be borne in mind when considering the level of assistance to be afforded. The Tariff Board declared in 1967 that it intended to relate the operation of the tariff more fully and consistently to the government's national economic objectives:

> These proposals would largely preclude tariff assistance for new investment likely to require continuing protection of a high order and tariff pressures on existing high cost industries should induce a more economic and efficient use of production resources currently employed in these areas ... If the nation's resources are directed increasingly into low cost, rather than high cost industries, greater wealth will accrue to the community. If this is spent, more goods will be demanded. If it is saved, more local capital will be available for investment. Both of these influences will assist industrial development. (Tariff Board, 1967, p. 11).

The IAC in 1974 reviewed the way in which the present structure of assistance had developed and noted that 'the amounts of assistance given to particular industries have tended to be the amounts considered at the time assistance was sought to be necessary to support profitable production by those industries'. It then quoted from the 1929 Brigden Committee:

> The tendency of protection is to cause the area of Government assistance to be extended ... As the tariff is extended other industries find themselves in difficulties; unprotected industries demand some protection and protected industries demand more protection, until at length the natural industries which sprang from the comparative advantage of the country are included, and apparently all are dependent on the tariff ... The most disquieting effect of the tariff has been the stimulus it has given to demands for Government assistance of all kinds, with consequent demoralising effect upon self-reliant efficiency throughout all forms of production. (Brigden *et al.*, 1929, pp. 6, 27)

The IAC 'believes that the warning given by the Brigden Committee in 1929 is even more relevant today' (Industries Assistance Commission, 1974, p. 13). The resource allocation strategy expounded by the IAC has been criticized in a recent report (W. D. Scott & Co. Pty Ltd, 1975). This suggests that the IAC strategy, if applied, could produce sufficient underemployment to be self-reversing (through political and social reaction to the under-employment) and this could be a costly strategy in national economic terms.

This would be the case if the output lost from underemployed resources in the transition process would be sufficient to outweigh the eventual net gains from achieving a better resource allocation at some point. The report also argues that the unexceptionable principles underlying the IAC strategy do not readily and directly yield policy prescriptions in the case of a specific economy such as Australia with her particular history and therefore her particular present circumstances. It is suggested instead that a 'pragmatic strategy' would be a preferable resource allocation strategy. This would recognize the significance of actual departures from theoretical models; it would include the encouragement of industries in whatever sector which do not require assistance from government; it would include possible priority (at times and maybe for considerable periods) for encouragement of industry requiring assistance; and it would be a policy with little risk.

THE SPATIAL ORGANIZATION OF MANUFACTURING

The distribution of manufacturing activity is examined here at the interstate, intrastate and urban scales. Analysis at each of these levels is constrained by the complete break in the data series in 1968–9 when, as already explained, the Australian Bureau of Statistics adopted the ASIC classification. Further complications arise when probing below State level because there have been changes in the boundaries of the geographical units by which the data are available and because, for confidentiality reasons, many small-area statistics cannot be published. In a number of instances, therefore, estimates have been prepared for this chapter to try to minimize these difficulties.

Interstate Distribution of Manufacturing

The chain of events by which New South Wales and Victoria had emerged as the leading industrial States prior to World War I has been documented in some detail elsewhere (Linge, 1975). The long-run tendency for these two areas (and particularly, as will be shown later, their capital cities) to absorb an ever-increasing share of Australian manufacturing activity persisted during the inter-war period. As a result they increased their joint share of the nation's factory labour force from 70.9 per cent in 1913 to 76.2 per cent in 1939:

	1913	1920	1939
New South Wales	35.7	38.3	40.5
Victoria	35.2	36.3	35.7
Queensland	12.6	10.9	9.6
South Australia	8.5	7.7	7.7
Western Australia	5.1	4.0	4.1
Tasmania	2.9	2.7	2.4

Detailed analysis indicates that most of the 'newer' types of industrial activity attracted to Australia during this period (making such products as wireless and electrical equipment, household appliances, metal goods, pharmaceuticals, and rubber goods) tended to locate in the southeast of the continent because here were the chief markets and the main sources of labour, capital and materials. Two of the other States made vigorous efforts to expand their industrial capacity. The availability of cheap hydroelectric power and government encouragement enabled Tasmania to attract plants making zinc, calcium carbide and paper as well as factories in the food and textile industries. In the 1930s the South Australian government started a deliberate programme to attract manufacturing (Mitchell, 1962) and, among other achievements, this led in 1940 to the erection of an alkali plant at Adelaide and a blast furnace at Whyalla. Western Australia benefited from its remoteness and factory employment there during the 1920s and 1930s grew relatively quickly compared with most of the eastern States. In contrast, manufacturing in Queensland made slow progress because of competition from the nearby industrialized States and because a considerable proportion of its factory activity was concerned with processing primary products that were susceptible to seasonal and market fluctuations.

World War II saw a considerable increase in the number of factory workers per 1,000 population in all States (Table 21.9) though the greatest impact was felt in New South Wales and Victoria where established plants could be quickly converted to produce munitions. South Australia also benefited because much of the new factory space was built there for strategic reasons. But events during and immediately after the war did little to reduce the contrast between the broad-based industrial structures of New South Wales and Victoria and those of other States. The latter in 1961 remained 'deficient' in a wide range of manufacturing activities including metal products, textiles, clothing, and (apart from South Australia) transport

Table 21.9 Factory Labour Force per Thousand Population, Australian States, 1939–68

State	1939	1947	1954	1961	1968
New South Wales	84	116	118	120	122
Victoria	103	130	137	131	136
Queensland	54	65	75	68	70
South Australia	73	110	109	102	108
Western Australia	50	68	73	68	75
Tasmania	58	78	80	85	93

Source: *Official Yearbook of the Commonwealth of Australia*.

Table 21.10 Proportion of Workforce[a] Employed in Manufacturing, Australian States and Territories, June 1971

State/Territory	Males	Females	Persons
New South Wales	26.9	20.5	25.0
Victoria	29.0	25.3	27.8
Queensland	18.6	11.4	16.5
South Australia	28.6	15.5	24.4
Western Australia	17.5	9.1	15.0
Tasmania	23.8	14.1	21.0
N.T. and A.C.T.	6.2	3.2	5.2
Australia	25.2	18.9	23.2

[a] Persons aged fifteen years and over.

Source: Bureau of Statistics (1972), *1971 Census of Population and Housing, Bulletin 5, The Labour Force*, Parts 1–9, Canberra.

equipment and household appliances (Linge, 1968, p. 215). Their relative lack of some of the main industries employing women was reflected in the much smaller proportion of the female workforce in these States employed in manufacturing, and this was still the case a decade later (Table 21.10). Taken together, Queensland, South Australia, Western Australia and Tasmania employ only 19.5 per cent of all females in Australian factories (and only 13.9 per cent of those making clothing and footwear).

The absence of any clearly defined national planning policies or goals encouraged a spirit of competition between the States to emerge (or, more accurately, re-emerge) during the 1950s and 1960s. Each of the less industrialized States set in motion programmes aimed at developing a more fully rounded 'portfolio' of manufacturing activities by attracting overseas firms and their subsidiaries as well as branch plants of companies already established in Australia. The kinds of inducements offered included long-term mineral or timber leases, cheap land, infrastructural improvements (such as the upgrading of harbour facilities, rail links and roads), the provision of housing, the supply of electricity at concessional rates, and promises of government contracts. During these two decades the parliaments of Queensland, South Australia, Western Australia and Tasmania passed about forty acts setting out agreements of this kind, mostly in relation to capital-intensive and long-term developments like alumina refineries, aluminium smelters, iron and steel works, pulp and paper plants, and oil refineries (Linge, 1967).

Of particular importance was the use by the States of their controls over mineral leases to impose conditions relating to the location, size and scheduling of processing plants. For instance, in 1960 The Broken Hill Proprietary Company Ltd, which was anxious to retain control of the high-grade iron ore leases at Koolya-nobbing (near Kalgoorlie), agreed with the Western Australian government to construct a blast furnace of not less than 457,000 tonnes capacity at Kwinana, south of Perth. Then in 1964, in return for mining leases in the Pilbara Region in the northwest of the State, the same company promised to expand this blast furnace and establish an iron ore processing plant. As yet another example, Comalco Industries Pty Ltd in 1957 gained access to bauxite deposits at Weipa on Cape York Peninsula by undertaking to establish an alumina plant in Queensland: the refinery was eventually erected at Gladstone and came into production in 1967. Attention is drawn to two studies by Fagan (1971, 1973) which examine the implications of these and other government measures for the spatial organization of the mineral processing industries in relation to both domestic and export markets.

By no means all the agreements between governments and individual companies have been dignified by an Act of Parliament but, even when they are, the full extent of the costs and benefits to the enterprise and government concerned cannot be readily quantified. Sometimes, too, important details of arrangements, such as the price at which electricity was to be supplied to the aluminium smelters at Point Henry near Geelong (1963) and Kurri Kurri near Newcastle (1969), remain closely guarded secrets. It has been suggested elsewhere (Linge, 1967) that State rivalry of this kind does not necessarily make for the optimum use of resources: direct and indirect bidding for local and overseas investment funds, for instance, hardly ensures that they are channelled into projects which maximize the benefits to Australia as a whole. Or again, the Tariff Board noted (1963, p. 10) that 'the action of State authorities in competing for the establishment of industries by offering various incentives' was one of the factors which had led to excess manufacturing capacity. In its view (1964, p. 15) 'the Australian market for some products had been or was being fragmented among more manufacturers than the market could economically sustain, and this fragmentation has tended to accentuate the difficulties arising from the scale of production'. A good deal of evidence can also be assembled to support the view that interstate competition has been given priority over policies aimed at reducing the concentration of economic activities in the metropolitan areas (a problem discussed later in this chapter). Although State governments have certainly encouraged potential investors to investigate country locations, they have been reluctant to press these too hard (or introduce any meaningful forms of control) for fear that alternative sites in other States may seem even more attractive. In this way 'decentralization' policies appear to have become subservient to the industrial development of each State as a whole.

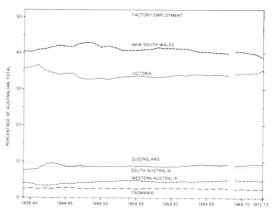

Fig. 21.1 Shares of Australian factory employment in each State 1938–9 to 1972–3. Note that the introduction of the Australian Standard Industrial Classification in 1968–9 altered the basis on which the data are available. *Source*: Bureau of Statistics, *Official Yearbook of the Commonwealth of Australia*.

There is little doubt, however, that the competitive programmes sponsored by the States have helped each of them to maintain a more or less constant share of the nation's factory activity since World War II (Fig. 21.1): despite short-term fluctuations, none has been able to forge ahead at the expense of the others. But although each of the four less industrialized States has increased its capacity to produce basic materials in capital-intensive plants, only South Australia has so far been more than moderately successful in attracting labour-intensive activities undertaking further fabricating and processing. In contrast to New South Wales and Victoria which have few serious gaps in their broad industrial structures (Table 21.11), the four other States have relatively large shares of the Australian workforce in some manufacturing subdivisions and small shares in others. A more detailed analysis has been made of the data available for the thirty-three classes of industry (including some amalgamations of classes for which the separate details are regarded as confidential in some States) at the ASIC three-digit level of disaggregation. This shows that in 1971–2 Queensland and Western Australia each had twelve, and Tasmania had fourteen, industry classes with a location quotient of less than 0.50 (in other words, they had less than half the number of workers which might have been 'expected' on the basis of their shares of the total labour force). In contrast, New South Wales had its expected share of all classes while Victoria was deficient in only one (basic iron and steel) and South Australia in only three (knitting mills, clothing, and chemical products). The details set out in Table 21.12 point up the importance, relative to each State's industrial structure, of the clothing and footwear

Table 21.11 Percentage Distribution Between States and Territories of Australian Employment in Manufacturing Sub-divisions, 1971–2[a]

ASIC subdivision	Industry	N.S.W.	Vic.	Qld	S.A.	W.A.	Tas.	A.C.T. & N.T.
21, 22	Food, drink and tobacco	32.9	31.2	16.8	8.8	6.7	3.0	0.6
23	Textiles	31.9	51.8	3.7	4.8	1.2	6.6	—
24	Footwear and clothing	35.8	53.2	5.5	3.7	1.5	0.3	—
25	Wood, wood products and furniture	33.6	25.0	15.7	10.0	9.6	5.7	0.4
26	Paper and paper products	38.9	32.8	9.0	6.6	5.5	5.7	1.5
27	Chemical, petroleum and coal products	48.9	34.6	4.9	4.6	4.7	2.3	—
28	Non-metallic mineral products	42.4	26.6	10.7	8.1	9.0	2.0	1.2
29	Basic metal products	62.3	12.7	4.6	10.8	5.5	4.1	—
31	Fabricated metal products	40.1	31.6	9.5	9.9	7.4	1.1	0.4
32	Transport equipment	30.6	39.3	8.2	17.7	3.3	0.8	0.1
33	Other machinery and equipment	45.9	34.8	4.7	10.7	3.2	0.6	0.1
34	Miscellaneous manufacturing	41.2	42.3	5.6	7.9	2.5	0.4	0.1
21–34	Total manufacturing	39.7	34.6	8.8	9.3	4.9	2.4	0.3

[a] Average employed during the year ending 30 June 1972.
Sources: Bureau of Statistics, various publications.

industries in Victoria; the food and timber industries in Queensland; the food and fabricated metal products industries in Western Australia; and the food (especially fruit and vegetable processing), textile, and pulp and paper industries in Tasmania. It also draws attention to the dependence of nearly one-third of the factory workforce of South Australia on the production of motor vehicles and domestic appliances which are both particularly susceptible to cyclical and seasonal swings in economic conditions, competition from overseas producers, and changes in consumer preferences. The fact that more than a fifth of the manufacturing workforce in this one State is directly employed by a handful of overseas owned and controlled companies (and a further, but unknown, percentage are working for subcontractors supplying them with

Table 21.12 Percentage of Each State's Manufacturing Workforce Employed in Subdivisions, 1971–2

ASIC subdivision	Industry	N.S.W.	Vic.	Qld	S.A.	W.A.	Tas.	Australia[a]
21, 22	Food, drink and tobacco	12.9	14.0	29.7	14.6	21.2	19.3	15.5
23	Textiles	3.4	6.4	1.8	2.2	1.1	11.8	4.2
24	Footwear and clothing	8.1	13.7	5.6	3.5	2.7	1.0	8.9
25	Wood, wood products and furniture	5.3	4.5	11.1	6.6	12.1	14.9	6.2
26	Paper and paper products	8.0	7.7	8.4	5.8	9.1	19.6	8.2
27	Chemical, petroleum and coal products	6.2	5.0	2.8	2.5	4.9	4.8	5.0
28	Non-metallic mineral products	4.2	3.0	4.8	3.4	7.2	3.3	3.9
29	Basic metal products	11.2	2.6	3.7	8.2	7.9	12.3	7.1
31	Fabricated metal products	9.3	8.5	10.0	9.8	13.8	4.4	9.2
32	Transport equipment	9.0	13.2	10.9	22.1	7.8	4.0	11.7
33	Other machinery and equipment	16.8	14.7	7.7	16.6	9.5	3.8	14.6
34	Miscellaneous manufacturing	5.6	6.7	3.5	4.7	2.7	0.8	5.5
21–34	Total manufacturing	100.0	100.0	100.0	100.0	100.0	100.0	100.0

[a] Includes employees in Northern Territory and Australian Capital Territory.
Sources: Bureau of Statistics, various publications.

components and accessories) has undoubtedly been one of several electoral, economic and practical realities faced by the Australian government when considering policies affecting the domestic motor vehicle construction industry.

Intrastate Distribution of Manufacturing

A long-standing feature of the spatial organization of manufacturing activity within most of the States has been the high percentage located in the metropolitan areas. The processes which encouraged this capital city concentration during the latter part of the nineteenth century, including competition between the Australian colonies, railway construction and freight rate policies, and changes in technology and commercial practices, have been detailed elsewhere (Linge, 1975). By 1890, for example, 72 per cent of the 59,000 factory workers in Victoria and 59 per cent of the 50,000 in New South Wales had their workplaces in Melbourne and Sydney. Resentment against dominance of this kind led people elsewhere in these colonies to set up 'decentralization leagues' during the latter part of the 1880s but they were too late and too disorganized to have much impact. They did, however, implant the 'decentralization' issue into the Australian body politic.

The trend towards metropolitan concentration continued during the 1920s and 1930s when, as mentioned already, the newer industries entering Australia tended to locate in the capital cities, especially in Sydney, Melbourne and Adelaide. Elsewhere the opening of establishments making woollen textiles and processing meat, fruit and vegetable barely compensated for the gradual disappearance of traditional activities like flour milling, brewing and tanning from country areas. In New South Wales between 1922–3 and 1938–9, for example, 85 per cent of the additional factory workforce of 79,500 were employed in the Sydney Statistical Division, 13 per cent in the Newcastle and Wollongong areas (largely in steel making, metal processing and related industries), and a mere 2 per cent in the remainder of the State.

Even before World War II ended plans were being evolved—as part of a wider programme of post-war reconstruction—to tackle the problem of excessive concentration of economic activities in the capital cities. At first a number of short-term influences, such as the availability of ex-munitions factories and warehouses in country towns when there was a shortage of manpower and building materials, encouraged many new and expanding firms to set up their main or branch plants outside the metropolitan areas. Taken together the non-metropolitan parts of Australia attracted about 37 per cent of the nation's new manufacturing jobs during the seven years to

mid-1954. But this proved to be a short-lived reversal of fortunes; during the next nine years (when there was a similar overall increase in the number of manufacturing jobs) they attracted only 22 per cent and about half these were in Newcastle, Wollongong and Geelong.

At this stage each of the five mainland States had decentralization programmes of one kind or another. Much of the effort in Queensland and Western Australia was, however, being directed towards opening up resources like iron ore and coal and encouraging the establishment of major mineral processing plants such as the alumina refinery at Gladstone. In South Australia assistance was available to manufacturers in any part of the State under the Industries Development Act, 1941–8. Of the $8,770,000 spent under this Act by mid-1965, less than 2 per cent had been granted or advanced through the Country Secondary Industries Fund which was only available to manufacturers outside the metropolitan area. Moreover, entrepreneurs had no need to go further than Elizabeth to obtain the advantage of assistance available through the South Australian Housing Trust (including land and custom-built factories for lease or purchase): suffice it to say that this so-called satellite town, conceived in the early 1950s, was incorporated in the Adelaide metropolitan area for statistical purposes in 1966. It was in Victoria and New South Wales that the greatest efforts were made to achieve a measure of decentralization. In Victoria $3,160,000 was spent between September 1944 and June 1963 from a special fund set up to provide loans and grants to firms in country locations, to purchase or modify buildings, to subsidize electricity and gas charges, to defray freight costs, and to upgrade social and recreational amenities in country towns. In addition the State railway system gave freight concessions at an annual cost, it was claimed, of $2,500,000. From 1958 the New South Wales government channelled finance through a 'decentralization fund' which was used to provide any assistance 'deemed necessary to offset disadvantages facing country industries because of their location': however by July 1965 (when the Department of Decentralisation and Development was formed) expenditure from this source had totalled a mere $3,600,000.

By the mid-1960s both New South Wales and Victoria were becoming aware that their efforts to achieve what was euphemistically called 'balanced development' had been only marginally successful. As Table 21.13 indicates population was still concentrating in Sydney and Melbourne and the share of manufacturing in the non-metropolitan areas was not increasing. The Committee of Economic Enquiry (1965, para. 8.247) pointed to the reasons for the lack of more positive results:

Table 21.13 Percentage of State Population and Factory Activity in Metropolitan Area[a]

State	Year	Population	Manufacturing Employment	Manufacturing Value of production
New South Wales	1946–7	56.6	78.3	76.7
(Sydney)	1953–4	56.3	75.7	76.4
	1962–3	58.4	75.7	72.2
	1971–2[b]	61.0	76.4	76.4
Victoria	1946–7	62.9	83.1	83.2
(Melbourne)	1953–4	62.2	81.0	79.7
	1962–3	65.6	81.5	80.7
	1971–2[b]	71.5	85.4	84.4
Queensland	1946–7	40.3	57.8	55.4
(Brisbane)	1953–4	42.4	58.2	60.0
	1962–3	44.7	59.6	59.7
	1971–2[b]	47.5	66.3	60.6
South Australia	1949–50[c]	60.4	83.5	83.6
(Adelaide)	1953–4	61.6	83.2	81.8
	1962–3	64.5	80.4	81.1
	1971–2[b]	71.8	82.9	79.0
Western Australia	1946–7	60.3	77.7	78.0
(Perth)	1953–4	61.7	79.9	79.2
	1962–3	65.3	80.9	80.9
	1971–2[b]	68.2	87.7	86.0

[a] Metropolitan areas defined, as far as practicable, on the basis of constant Statistical Division boundaries as at 1966.

[b] Factory data for 1971–2 are based on the recently introduced Australian Standard Industrial Classification and are not, therefore, strictly comparable with previous years.

Manufacturing statistics are not available for Adelaide prior to 1949–50.

Source: compiled from various publications of State offices of Australian Bureau of Statistics.

The pressures on manufacturing enterprises to achieve and maintain maximum economic efficiency are considerable; the modest and rather piecemeal incentives to decentralisation offered to date are unlikely to be sufficient to induce a significant proportion of manufacturing industry to locate itself in areas which do not offer maximum economic advantage.

The Committee also suggested (para. 17.77) that

there is a much stronger case for accelerating the growth of a limited number of non-metropolitan centres that have already, as a result of natural advantages, achieved some degree of development. Such centres, with only a moderate degree of capital expenditure and encouragement to industry, could soon reach the "take-off" point, that is the point after which further development would be natural and self-sustaining.

This view was echoed by a report published in New South Wales in 1969 (Development Corporation of New South Wales) and by a Committee of Commonwealth/State Officials (1972, p. 11) which concluded that 'the only type of decentralisation programme which offers significant prospects of success is selective decentralisation'.

There is little evidence, however, that this prescription has been matched in practice. It is true that in 1968 Victoria announced that five centres—Ballarat, Bendigo, Latrobe Valley, Portland and Wodonga—had been chosen for 'accelerated development', and that in the early 1970s New South Wales committed itself to the establishment of a growth centre at Bathurst-Orange and agreed to participate with the Australian and Victorian governments in a project to expand

Table 21.14 Decentralization Incentives Offered by State Governments

Type of assistance	N.S.W.[a]	Vic.[b]	Qld	S.A.	W.A.	Tas.
1. Related to costs of establishment						
Provision of loans	×	×	×	×	×	×
Guarantees for loans	×	×	×	×	×	×
Housing for key personnel	×	×	×	×		×
Development of land and facilities	×	×	×	×	×	×
Transport of plant, machinery and employees	×	×	×			
Training of unskilled labour	×	×				
2. Related to operating costs						
Payroll tax rebate		×				
Freight rate concessions	×	×	×		×	
Land tax rebate		×				

[a] Applicable outside the County of Cumberland, Greater Newcastle and Greater Wollongong.
[b] Applicable outside a radius of 50 miles from Melbourne (and to six specified places within this radius).
Sources: Report of the Committee of Commonwealth/State Officials on Decentralisation, 1972; and various State publications.

Albury-Wodonga. But it appears that in both States decentralization incentives of the kind summarized in Table 21.14 are still being made available to a wide range of manufacturing (and some other) activities spread over a hundred or more non-metropolitan locations. No doubt one reason for this lack of selectivity is the practical difficulty of channelling expenditure (which, taking the two States together and including grants and loans, is estimated to be of the order of $20 million annually) into what would be, in effect, a handful of electoral constituencies.

The extent to which manufacturing activity is concentrated in the six capital city statistical divisions and Newcastle, Wollongong and Geelong is indicated in Table 21.15: no less than three-fifths of Australia's factory workforce is located in Sydney and Melbourne. Manufacturing establishments outside these nine centres account for only 11.8 per cent of the factory workforce and 14.9 per cent of the value added (as compared, for example, with 43.5 per cent of the total population). The industrial activities in these remaining areas are not only biased towards food and forest products as might be expected but also to some extent towards textiles, non-metallic mineral products like cement, and basic metals, reflecting the operation among others of a steel works at Whyalla, alumina refineries at Gladstone, Gove and Pinjarra, an aluminium smelter at Bell Bay, copper smelters at Mount Isa, Mount Morgan, Townsville and Mount Lyell and a lead refinery at Port Pirie. In each of the mainland States the metropolitan area is the dominant centre for most industrial activities: the only exceptions, as

Table 21.16 reveals, are food products in Brisbane and basic metals in Sydney, Brisbane and Adelaide.

The advantages claimed for a metropolitan location may be briefly summarized as: easier and cheaper access to markets; readier face-to-face contacts with suppliers, consumers, and financiers as well as legal, technical, servicing, research and other firms; greater opportunities to tap a larger and more diverse pool of skilled and unskilled labour; reduced business risks and uncertainties (an aspect explored in some detail by Webber, 1972); and fewer constraints on decision-making in an 'amorphous' situation as against one in which an identifiable firm plays (or is seen to play) a major role in the viability of a particular local economy. Implicitly at least these factors taken together may suggest that the direct costs borne by a manufacturing establishment operating outside a metropolitan area are substantially greater. But a recent study (Committee of Commonwealth/State Officials, 1972, p. 24), while not based on precise data but representing 'a summation of the informed judgements expressed by the businessmen in the survey', indicates that country firms only suffered an overall cost disadvantage, measured per hundred dollars of sales, of between 1 and 2 per cent (Table 21.17). It appears that the higher costs of freight (including raw materials, finished products and fuel) and communications in country locations are offset to a considerable extent by savings in labour costs (such as lower turnover rates, less absenteeism and fewer industrial disputes) and cheaper land and rental charges. Other unpublished studies suggest that the

Table 21.15 Percentage of Australian Manufacturing Employment and Value Added in Selected Areas by Main Industry Subdivisions, 1971–2

ASIC sub-division	Industry	Employment			Value added		
		Six State capitals[a]	Newcastle, Wollongong & Geelong[b]	Rest of Australia	Six State capitals[a]	Newcastle, Wollongong & Geelong[b]	Rest of Australia
21, 22	Food, drink and tobacco	64.6	3.1	32.3	64.3	2.5	33.2
23	Textiles	71.7	10.3	18.0	73.0	10.2	16.8
24	Footwear and clothing	88.4	4.6	7.0	90.6	3.8	5.6
25	Wood, wood products and furniture	64.8	2.1	33.1	60.5	2.0	37.5
26	Paper and paper products	84.1	1.9	14.0	82.8	1.7	15.5
27	Chemical, petroleum and coal products	92.2	3.6	4.2	90.8	4.5	4.7
28	Non-metallic mineral products	76.5	8.2	15.3	73.8	8.9	17.3
29	Basic metal products	36.9	50.1	13.0	32.0	50.1	17.9
31	Fabricated metal products	86.4	5.5	8.1	87.7	5.1	7.2
32	Transport equipment	86.8	5.7	7.5	89.2	4.7	6.1
33	Other machinery and equipment	90.4	3.5	6.1	91.0	3.1	5.9
34	Miscellaneous manufacturing	96.7	1.4	1.9	97.8	1.4	0.8
21–34	Total manufacturing	78.6	9.6	11.8	77.0	8.1	14.9

[a] Metropolitan Statistical Divisions.
[b] Statistical Districts.
Sources: Bureau of Statistics, *Manufacturing Establishments: Details of Operations and Small Area Statistics* (or equivalent publications for each State).

Table 21.16 Percentage of Each State's Manufacturing Employment in Metropolitan Statistical Division by Main Industry Subdivisions, 1971–2

ASIC sub-division	Industry	Sydney	Melbourne	Brisbane	Adelaide	Perth	Hobart
21, 22	Food, drink and tobacco	66.5	71.1	46.2	67.1	80.2	46.6
23	Textiles	75.1	73.9	92.2	82.0	84.6	17.4
24	Footwear and clothing	82.6	91.1	92.4	98.1	100.0	52.1
25	Wood, wood products and furniture	65.0	73.8	55.8	73.6	73.4	23.5
26	Paper and paper products	89.7	89.7	80.5	79.7	93.5	37.0
27	Chemical, petroleum and coal products	95.3	93.0	88.7	89.4	78.3	55.4
28	Non-metallic mineral products	73.6	80.1	73.8	89.6	91.2	34.1
29	Basic metal products	22.8	71.4	39.9	43.5	84.6	60.1
31	Fabricated metal products	80.9	91.7	84.3	94.4	96.0	51.6
32	Transport equipment	90.0	86.6	74.7	90.0	96.6	6.7
33	Other machinery and equipment	91.1	90.7	71.6	95.6	96.1	66.4
34	Miscellaneous manufacturing	97.2	97.8	90.0	96.2	97.7	49.0
21–34	Total manufacturing	76.4	85.4	66.3	82.9	87.7	39.0

Source: Bureau of Statistics, *Manufacturing Establishments: Small Area Statistics* (or equivalent publications for each State).

Table 21.17 Estimated Cost Differential Between Metropolitan and Country Locations[a] (expressed in dollars per $100 of sales)

Item	New South Wales[b]		Victoria[b]	
	Metropolitan firms' estimates	Country firms' estimates	Metropolitan firms' estimates	Country firms' estimates
Labour	+ 0.38	+ 0.42	+ 0.99	+ 0.21
Cost of land and buildings	+ 0.69	+ 0.93	+ 0.25	+ 1.05
Public services	− 0.02	− 0.03	+ 0.02	+ 0.01
Other	− 0.61	− 0.14	− 0.02	− 0.07
Subtotal	+ 0.44	+ 1.18	+ 1.24	+ 1.20
Freight	− 1.84	− 1.75	− 1.46	− 1.34
Telephone and telegram charges	− 0.63	− 0.35	− 0.15	− 0.27
Total	− 2.03	− 0.92	− 0.37	− 0.41

[a] A minus sign indicates a cost disadvantage for the country, a plus sign a cost advantage.

[b] Based on a sample of 118 firms in New South Wales (87 country and 31 city) and 101 firms in Victoria (70 country and 31 city).

Source: *Report of the Committee of Commonwealth/State Officials on Decentralisation*, 1972, p. 24.

overall disability may in fact be smaller although there are, of course, significant differences between particular manufacturing industries.

If the cost penalty is as marginal as these reports suggest, other reasons must be sought to explain why country areas have apparently failed to attract secondary industry. One clue emerges from a 'shift and share' analysis of employment changes in the metropolitan areas during the intercensal periods 1954–61 and 1961–6 (Kerr, 1970) which indicates that 70 per cent of the capital city growth in employment during each of these periods was due to their favourable industrial mix. These results, as Neutze (1974, p. 263) has pointed out, suggest that the State capitals, particularly Sydney and Melbourne, are not places of fast growth, employment category by employment category: 'most firms, however, expand or set up in areas where an industry is already established, simply because the "safe" place to be is where firms in that industry have already shown that profits can be made'. In other words, firms faced with location or relocation decisions tend to limit their spatial search to areas already picked out by their competitors and business associates or to those with which they already have some familiarity. They are not encouraged to cast their nets wider because of the costs involved in searching out information about a range of alternative locations and because they are not required to take into account the social costs imposed by their decisions on the community at large. In general, businessmen making investment decisions view non-metropolitan locations with a jaundiced eye: an unpublished survey by the present

author of inner Sydney manufacturers found that they consistently understated the size of, and amenities available at, selected country centres in New South Wales and exaggerated their actual and cost distances from the metropolis. At the same time they stressed the importance to them, and more especially their families, of the wide choice of educational, medical, recreational and cultural facilities available in the Sydney region.

There is no space to outline the debate about the advantages and disadvantages of metropolitan concentration in Australia (one point of view about this has been given by Stilwell, 1974), and in any case it is more pertinent here to consider the implications of recent decisions by the Australian and State governments to embark on a programme to promote growth centres at Albury-Wodonga, Bathurst-Orange, Geelong, Monarto (near Adelaide) and Salvado (near Perth). Although this appears to be an embryonic national approach to the 'selective decentralization' solution previously espoused by some States, other measures may be necessary before it will significantly influence spatial decision-making by manufacturing firms.

Considerable effort will have to be devoted to programmes designed to overcome both actual and *perceived* cost and social disadvantages of such non-metropolitan locations. The provision of detailed, high-quality opportunity and cost specific data about growth centres, for example, may help to reduce some of the uncertainties faced by decision-makers in the private sector. There will be more chance of success, too, if this kind of information is directed towards the types of manufacturing best suited to non-metropolitan locations. Among these are firms producing goods with a high value to weight ratio, using locally available raw materials, serving national or international rather than State markets, and requiring neither large nor specialized workforces. In the past a good deal of emphasis has been placed on promoting labour-intensive industries, especially those employing females, in country locations but such activities depend on high levels of assistance and are therefore particularly vulnerable to changes in public policy. As indicated earlier in this chapter a fundamental reassessment has been taking place in Australia during the last decade of objectives of Australian tariff policy and of the appropriate long-term structure of assistance to Australian industries (Johns, 1975). Recent events have highlighted the conflicts involved in reconciling national and local interests. In an attempt to alleviate the short-run problems of industrial unemployment created in country centres by the 25 per cent across-the-board tariff cut in July 1973 and subsequent decisions that lifted quota restrictions, reduced tariffs or eliminated subsidies on various items, the Australian government introduced in 1974 a Special Assistance for Firms in Non-Metropolitan Areas (SANMA) scheme. SANMA aid 'is intended to sustain existing production and employment or to enable their phasing out without undue hardship to the local community' but 'will also be used to encourage potentially viable new firms or activities to replace declining industries' (Department of Manufacturing Industry, 1974a, p. 16). By the end of 1974 interim grants, totalling $3.7 million, had been made under the SANMA scheme to thirty-four firms employing 7,600 people. As a particular example of its significance, one woollen mill at Wangaratta (Victoria) made a profit of $98,000 in 1973–4 but sustained a loss of $220,000 in 1974–5 even after receiving SANMA assistance to the tune of $300,000. Grants which discriminate between locations in this way are likely to be less expensive than providing support to an entire industry. Thus the IAC (1974, p. 119) calculated—on the basis of 1968–9 data—that if support of the decentralized section of the textile industry meant giving assistance to the whole industry equivalent to 10 per cent of its value added, the extra added value subsidy to the firms in the State capitals, Newcastle, Wollongong and Geelong would have been about $25 million. As against this, the additional subsidy for firms in other locations would have been less than $5 million. In other words, assisting the whole of this industry in order to support the decentralized section could have been about six times as costly.

There appear to be two main ways in which secondary industry could be encouraged to expand or establish itself at selected growth centres. First,

governments will probably have to accept a greater measure of responsibility for providing a wide range of infrastructural requirements (such as housing, roads, water, sewerage, telephone, and other services) programmed in such a way that supply keeps abreast of demand: indeed there would have to be considerable investment in headworks well in advance of anticipated demand. Only in this way will private investors gain confidence that governments are not—as in the past—merely paying lip-service to yet another notion of decentralization but have the courage of their convictions that a few nominated country centres offer some kinds of manufacturing activities viable long-run alternative locations to the metropolitan areas. Moreover, as has been pointed out elsewhere (Committee of Commonwealth/State Officials, 1972, p. 66) instead of making what are usually lumpy outlays (such as on headworks) in many towns

> it would seem better to make fewer public investments in centres selected for accelerated growth, so that newly created capacity could be quickly brought to a point of full utilisation, thereby minimising the amount of idle capital.

Considerable attention must be given, too, to providing or widening educational, cultural, recreational and similar facilities in growth centres so as to overcome some of the real and perceived disadvantages which entrepreneurs associate with non-metropolitan locations.

Second, there are various incentives that could be offered to labour (including, for instance, subsidies to meet removal charges, retraining costs, and commuting expenses). In addition it would be possible to reduce wage costs by direct subsidies or by tax rebates (such as of payroll tax). Capital incentives could include the provision of industrial land and buildings, the provision of grants and loans at concessional rates of interest and the reimbursement of expenses involved in shifting from one location to another.

It may seem from Table 21.14 that this list differs little from the kinds of incentives already provided by several State governments. To achieve anything worthwhile from a national point of view, however, considerably greater emphasis must be placed on selected incentives for selected industries or groups of industries in selected centres. The weaknesses of many of the present arrangements are self-evident. For example, in Victoria a considerable proportion of the payments under its payroll tax rebate scheme appear to have gone to existing local enterprises which have grown up 'naturally' in country towns. Or again, once a State government has assisted a particular but 'unsuitable' industrial activity (especially if this is a large, well-known and labour-intensive firm) it becomes increasingly difficult, both politically and electorally,

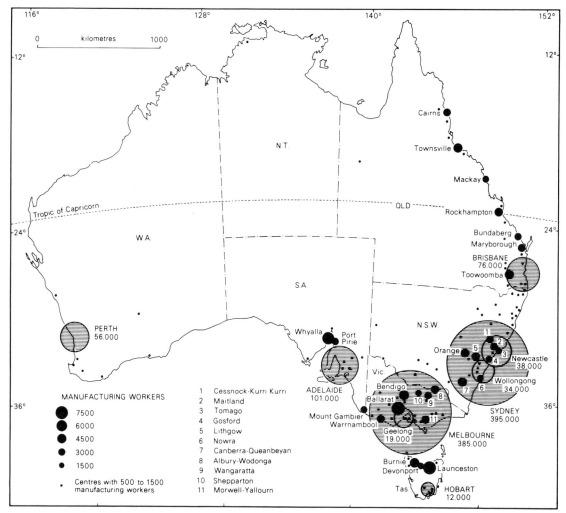

Fig. 21.2 Employment in manufacturing in Australian urban areas 1971–2. *Sources*: Bureau of Statistics, *Manufacturing Establishments: Details of Operations and Small Area Statistics* (or equivalent publications for each State) and some unpublished data.

to reject what must inevitably become perennial requests for support even if it is apparent that the enterprise concerned has little chance of becoming economically viable. Neutze (1974, p. 273) has made the suggestion that subsidies should be for a limited time with the level of support gradually being reduced after the population reaches 100,000 and disappearing altogether after it reaches 150,000. A national policy towards industrial location is not hard to conceive but is less easy to achieve because of the limitations imposed by the Constitution on the powers of the Australian government. Nonetheless, there remain several ways in which it could pursue spatial policy objectives such as through structural adjustment

assistance programmes, manpower planning policies, foreign investment controls, environmental legislation, and the provision of infrastructure like telecommunication and transport facilities.

Interurban Distribution of Manufacturing

The distribution of manufacturing between urban centres with 500 or more factory workers in 1971–2 is indicated in Fig. 21.2: together the 115 places shown account for all but about 4 per cent of Australian factory activity. They can be conveniently divided into three size groups as set out in Table 21.18 although it must be emphasized that the totals shown are approximations because of the inadequacy of the

Table 21.18 Summary of Factory Employment in Australian Urban Centres, 1971–2

Centre	Number of workers
A. Areas with over 10,000 manufacturing workers	
Sydney Statistical Division	395,000
Melbourne Statistical Division	385,000
Adelaide Statistical Division	101,000
Brisbane Statistical Division	76,000
Perth Statistical Division	56,000
Newcastle Statistical District	38,000
Wollongong Statistical District	34,000
Geelong Statistical District	19,000
Hobart Statistical Division	12,000
B. Centres with 1,500 to 10,000 manufacturing workers	
28 centres	76,000
	(approx.)
C. Centres with 500 to 1,499 manufacturing workers	
78 centres	95,000
	(approx.)

Sources: Bureau of Statistics, *Manufacturing Establishments: Details of Operations and Small Area Statistics* (or equivalent publications for each State) and some unpublished data.

small-area statistics from which they have been derived.

In the first group are the capital city statistical divisions and the statistical districts of Newcastle, Wollongong and Geelong. As indicated already in Table 21.15 these contain 88 per cent of the factory workforce and contribute 85 per cent of the value added in all manufacturing establishments in Australia. Little need be added to the previous discussion of industry in the capital cities but it is important to note from Table 21.15 that half the workforce engaged in producing basic metal products is concentrated in Newcastle, Wollongong and Geelong. This points to the importance of heavy industry in and around Newcastle (iron and steel making, lead-zinc and aluminium smelting), in Wollongong-Port Kembla (iron and steel making and copper smelting), and in Geelong (aluminium smelting). These activities, along with shipbuilding, chemicals, fertilizers, tanning, and motor vehicle assembly, resulted in ratios of female to male factory workers for the three centres in 1971–2 of, respectively, 1 : 5.5, 1 : 6.2 and 1 : 4.1 compared with 1 : 2.8 in Australian manufacturing establishments as a whole. Since many of the men in the iron and steel plants (about half of those employed at the Port Kembla works) are immigrants, the dearth of female employment opportunities, especially in Wollongong, particularly affects married immigrant women who,

elsewhere in Australia, have displayed a higher rate of participation in the labour force than their Australian-born counterparts.

The second group of urban centres are those with between 1,500 and 10,000 factory workers. In general these have three industrial functions. Most act as local service centres for surrounding regions by processing local farm produce and supplying day-to-day needs. In addition, several contain long-established firms (making engineering goods, textiles, and timber-based products) which originated in a variety of circumstances during the nineteenth and early twentieth centuries. And, thirdly, they have attracted newer plants set up to process minerals (as at Townsville and Kurri Kurri), to take advantage of the availability of ex-munitions factories (as at Ballarat, Bendigo, Orange and Maitland), or to use nearby resources such as clean water (as instanced by a fine-paper mill established at Nowra). Only a handful have, however, grown up as 'manufacturing towns: Burnie in Tasmania (where there are factories making paper, building-board, and plywood) and Whyalla in South Australia (which is a shipbuilding and iron and steel smelting centre) are among the exceptions.

The majority of the other centres indicated in Fig. 21.2—those with between 500 and 1,499 factory workers—are essentially service and agricultural processing centres, some of which have local specialities such as fruit canning at Leeton and Griffith in New South Wales and Mooroopna in Victoria. A number have attracted other activities (such as engineering works in Coffs Harbour, New South Wales) or branch plants of metropolitan clothing and shoemaking firms partly as a result of inducements offered to decentralized undertakings by State governments. But since World War II many small communities have learned that, at times of minor recessions or the 'rationalization' of activities resulting from the absorption of one company by another, the metropolitan decision-makers have proved to be no more than fair weather friends.

The data in Table 21.19 show the quartile and median percentages of the workforce employed in manufacturing at the time of the 1971 census in the 481 Australian urban centres arranged in ten population size-groups. This suggests that, with some anomalies (such as the 15,000 to 19,999 size-group), factory activities are, on average, relatively more significant in the larger centres. However, the upper quartile figures, which have fairly consistent values through all the size ranges, reveal that at least a quarter of the workforce in 120 urban centres depends on manufacturing for its livelihood. Indeed in a few extreme cases—Wundowie and Kwinana New Town (W.A.), Whyalla (S.A.), and Georgetown (Tas.)—more than half the workforce is engaged in this kind of activity.

Table 21.19 Percentage of Workforce Employed in Manufacturing in Australian Urban Centres, 1971[a]

Population size range	Number of urban centres	Lower quartile percentage	Median percentage	Upper quartile percentage
1,000–1,999	180	3.2	9.7	27.0
2,000–2,499	52	4.3	14.1	34.6
2,500–4,999	110	4.3	11.4	25.5
5,000–9,999	66	7.4	12.7	26.7
10,000–14,999	22	10.1	14.4	27.0
15,000–19,999	16	12.6	20.5	27.9
20,000–24,999	8	11.4	14.7	29.9
25,000–49,999	12	5.1	16.6	24.6
50,000–99,999	5	12.1	17.4	29.2
100,000 and over	10	19.0	28.2	32.9

[a] Excludes centres with less than 1,000 population even if defined as 'urban' for census purposes.

Source: analysis of unpublished data from the Census of Population and Housing, 30 June 1971.

FUTURE RESEARCH IN INDUSTRIAL GEOGRAPHY

Despite the considerable importance of manufacturing in the economy, comparatively few Australian geographers have taken more than a passing interest in the spatial organization of industrial activity. It is impossible here to do justice to what has already been accomplished but it seems appropriate to conclude this chapter with some assessment of the directions in which research in this field might, with advantage, be pursued in future.

During the twentieth century the international study of industrial geography has passed through several phases. Much of the early work was concerned with case studies that emphasized real facts and relationships. Then, following the work of Weber, Lösch, Palander and others, the emphasis turned to location theory, and this trend was reinforced by the work of geographers/regional scientists/economists like Hoover, Isard, and Greenhut. Much of this classical location theory focused on the problem of a simple set of actors concerned with choosing the optimum locations for manufacturing establishments. Considerable emphasis was laid on the costs of transporting raw materials and finished products and the analysis largely took the form of partial equilibrium solutions in which single characteristics of point locations were compared with those of other locations. Although the spatial decisions of establishments processing bulky raw materials or closely orientated to markets are clearly influenced by transport costs, an increasing proportion of industrial firms are 'footloose' in the sense that transport costs form a relatively insignificant proportion of their total outlays.

The constraints imposed by the oversimplified abstract frameworks and their lack of applicability to real-world situations have led industrial geographers to pursue new lines of research in recent years. Increasingly, for instance, manufacturing establishments are being perceived as only one element in a complex environment in which all the elements in the system are related to, and interdependent on, each other. This research has taken on various dimensions including behavioural aspects (such as an examination of psychological influences on the character of the decision-maker); impact statements (ranging from multiplier analyses to the definition and exploration of the complex sets of linkages within the system); intra- and inter-industry relationships (which recognize, among other things, that the principal element is the industrial firm or corporation as distinct from the manufacturing plant); and the perception of space (in which distances may be measured in psychological or social costs rather than in miles or costs per mile). Few Australian geographers have so far embarked on investigations of these kinds although Wadley (1975) has recently completed a pioneering study of the ways in which firms in the agricultural implement making industry adjusted their marketing strategies during a period of rural recession.

Geographers have much to contribute to the basic comprehension of the underlying structure of, and relationships within, the Australian system of cities and the role played by manufacturing. Such research is important not only because it will assist in the formulation of goal-consistent and successful regional planning policies but also because it will add a further comparative dimension to similar work being undertaken overseas. As Pred (1975) has pointed out, Australia is different, if not unique, in the vastness of its area, its variegated mineral resource endowment, the uneven distribution of its population, and its comparatively recent superimposition of a pronounced federal political structure upon a set of colonial relationships. In fact the youth of the Australian system of cities is one of its most distinctive features when compared to the systems in North America and Europe. Finally, as Alonso (1974) has noted, Australia differs from other post-industrial societies in that its national settlement policy problem is the allocation of a scarce population rather than over-population or the rescue of 'distressed' or 'backward' regions.

ACKNOWLEDGEMENTS   Grateful thanks are due to Pauline Falconer, Janet Linge, and Grace Richardson for their assistance during the preparation of this chapter, and to Ian Heyward (of the Cartographic Section, Department of Human Geography, Research School of Pacific Studies, Australian National University) who prepared the accompanying line drawings.

REFERENCES

Alonso, W. (1974), 'A report on Australian urban development issues', *Cities Commission Occasional Paper No. 1*, Canberra.

Brash, D. T. (1966), *American Investment in Australian Industry*, Australian National University Press, Canberra.

Brigden, J. B. *et al.* (1929), *The Australian Tariff, An Economic Enquiry*, Melbourne University Press, Melbourne.

Bureau of Statistics (1973), *Australian National Accounts—Input-Output Tables, 1962–63*, Canberra.

——(1974), *Industry Concentration Statistics, Details by Industry Class, Australia 1968–69 (ref. 17.14)*, Canberra.

Butlin, N. G. (1962), *Australian Domestic Product, Investment and Foreign Borrowing 1861–1938/39*, Cambridge University Press, Cambridge.

——(1964), *Investment in Australian Economic Development 1861–1900*, Cambridge University Press, Cambridge.

Committee of Commonwealth/State Officials (1972), *Report of . . . on Decentralisation*, Canberra.

Committee of Economic Enquiry (1965), *Report of the Committee of Economic Enquiry* [The Vernon Report], Canberra.

Department of Manufacturing Industry (1974a), *Developments in Manufacturing Industry*, No. 3, Canberra.

——(1974b), *R & D in Manufacturing Industry 1971–72*, Bulletin No. 11, Canberra.

——(1975), *Developments in Manufacturing Industry*, No. 4, Canberra.

Development Corporation of New South Wales (1969), *Report on Selective Decentralisation*, Sydney.

Fagan, R. H. (1971), 'Government policy and the Australian metalliferous mining and processing industries' in G. J. R. Linge and P. J. Rimmer (eds), *Government Influence and the Location of Economic Activity*, Department of Human Geography Publication HG/5, Research School of Pacific Studies, Australian National University, Canberra, pp. 191–231.

——(1973), *Resource Development, Plant Location, and Government Influence: A Spatial Analysis of the Australian Metalliferous Mineral Industries*, unpublished PhD thesis, Australian National University, Canberra.

Hunter, A. (1963), 'Introduction' in A. Hunter (ed.), *The Economics of Australian Industry: Studies in Environment and Structure*, Melbourne University Press, Melbourne, pp. 1–17.

Industries Assistance Commission (1974), *Annual Report 1973–74*, Canberra.

Johns, B. L. (1975), 'Australian tariff policy in the 1970's', *Bank of New South Wales Review*, No. 15, 9–14.

Kerr, A. (1970), 'Urban industrial change in Australia, 1954 to 1966', *Econ. Record*, 46, 355–67.

Linge, G. J. R. (1967), 'Governments and the location of secondary industry in Australia', *Econ. Geogr.*, 43, 43–63.

——(1968), 'Secondary industry in Australia' in G. H. Dury and M. I. Logan (eds), *Studies in Australian Geography*, Heinemann, Melbourne, pp. 195–244.

——(1975), 'The forging of an industrial nation: manufacturing in Australia 1788–1913' in J. M. Powell and M. Williams (eds), *Australian Space Australian Time: Geographical Perspectives*, Oxford University Press, Melbourne, pp. 150–81.

Lloyd, P. J. (1973), *Non-Tariff Distortions of Australian Trade*, Australian National University Press, Canberra.

Masterman, G. G. (1970), *Big Business in Australia* [papers read at 36th Summer School of the Australian Institute of Political Science], Angus and Robertson, Sydney.

Mitchell, T. J. (1962), 'J. W. Wainwright: the industrialisation of South Australia, 1935–1940', *Aust. J. Pol. and Hist.*, 8, 27–40.

Neutze, G. M. (1974), 'The case for new cities in Australia', *Urban Stud.*, 11, 259–75.

Office of Secondary Industry [Department of Trade and Industry] (1972), *Australian Manufacturing Industry and Development*, Canberra.

Parry, T. G. (1974), 'Plant size, capacity utilization and economic efficiency: foreign investment in the Australian chemical industry', *Econ. Record*, 50, 218–44.

Pred, A. R. (1975), 'Growth transmission within the Australian system of cities: general observations and study recommendations', *Cities Commission Occasional Paper No. 3*, Canberra.

Rolfe, H. A. (1967), *The Controllers: Interlocking Directorates in Large Australian Companies*, Cheshire, Melbourne.

Scherer, F. M. (1970), *Industrial Market Structure and Economic Performance*, Rand McNally, Chicago.

Scott, W. D. & Co. Pty Ltd (1975), *A Study of Resource Allocation Strategy in Australia*, Canberra.

Stilwell, F. J. B. (1974), *Australian Urban and Regional Development*, Australia and New Zealand Book Co., Sydney.

Tariff Board (1963), *Annual Report for Year 1962–63*, Canberra.

——(1964), *Annual Report for Year 1963*–64, Canberra.

——(1967), *Annual Report for Year 1966–67*, Canberra.

——(1973), *Report on Domestic Appliances, Heating and Cooling Equipment, etc.*, Canberra.

United Nations (1971), *The Growth of World Industry*, Volume 1, *General Industrial Statistics 1960–1968*, New York.

Vernon, J. (1970), 'The implications for Australia's future' in G. G. Masterman (ed.), *Big Business in Australia*, Angus and Robertson, Sydney, pp. 147–74.

Wadley, D. A. (1975), *Corporate Decision-making During Recession: Product franchisors in the Australian agricultural machinery industry 1967–72*, unpublished PhD thesis, Australian National University, Canberra.

Webber, M. J. (1972), *The Impact of Uncertainty on Location*, Australian National University Press, Canberra.

Wheelwright, E. L. (1963), 'Overseas investment in Australia' in A. Hunter (ed.), *The Economics of Australian Industry: Studies in Environment and Structure*, Melbourne University Press, Melbourne, pp. 141–73.

Wheelwright, E. L. and Miskelly, J. (1967), *Anatomy of Australian Manufacturing Industry*, Law Book Company, Sydney.

22 TRANSPORT

PETER J. RIMMER

> Every federal country has found that a fairly high degree of central control over public finance and the general lines of national economic policy has become essential in the contemporary world, but in no case has this need by itself caused the abandonment of federalism; instead there have occurred fairly considerable re-allocations of function, frequently by informal processes of 'co-operative federalism' rather than by formal constitutional changes in the legal competence of the federal units or by the setting up of constitutionally-recognised instruments of federal co-operation. Australia has been peculiar among federal countries because of the great concentration of revenue resources in the Australian Government's hands, and of law-making competence in State Parliaments. (Sawer, 1975, p. 134)

The Australian (Commonwealth or Federal) government has re-established the Inter-State Commission for which provision has been made in Section 101 of the Australian Constitution (Inter-State Commission Act, 1975).* Originally conceived as a body for adjudicating on the discriminatory practices of State railways and other matters connected with interstate and overseas trade and commerce the first Commission established under the Inter-State Commission Act 1912 sat only between 1913 and 1920. It was then allowed to lapse presumably because it might interfere with the 'sovereignty' of States in transport matters. The Australian (Whitlam) government revived the Inter-State Commission as a means of co-ordinating interstate transport. Before examining the nature and likely impact of the second Inter-State Commission on the domestic transport system in Australia the effects of fragmenting legal and executive responsibility over transport between the Australian government and the State governments must be considered. Such an examination is necessary because it is the allocation of political power, influence, and authority that determines who gets what, when, how and *where* (see Wengert, 1973).

Under the Australian Constitution the Australian government has control over transport to, from, and within the territories and over interstate and overseas transport and the State governments are each responsible for the regulation of transport within their own borders. Although rival State governments have considerable law-making competence their ability to modernize and reform transport operations is hampered because revenue resources are concentrated in the hands of the Australian government as part of its general control over public finance and national economic policy. This mismatch between functional responsibility and financial capability reflected in impoverished State budgets, however, is not the only barrier to grappling with the problems of obsolete, inadequate, and uneconomic transport operations. Another obstacle is provided by the vague definition of the responsibilities of the Australian government and State governments in the Australian Constitution which creates constitutional difficulties (and confusion). The nature of these barriers to modernization and reform is exposed by examining the roles played by the Australian government and State governments in the domestic transport system and the attempts to change the Federal balance by trading-off financial capability and functional responsibility in lieu of constitutional changes by referenda—the essence of 'co-operative federalism' (see Sawer, 1975).

Before breaking down the domestic transport task into its intrastate and interstate components as the best means of examining the respective roles of different levels of government a review is made here of the relative importance of individual transport modes in movements of passengers and freight within Australia. Once the broad national trends are established attention can then be directed to the intrastate transport system and interstate transport system in turn. Within the *intrastate system* separate analyses are made of the

---

*With the replacement of the Whitlam (Labor) Government by the Fraser (Liberal-Country Party) Government in November 1975, it was decided not to proclaim the Inter-State Commission Act 1975. A number of other recent initiatives, such as the absorption of the Department of Urban and Regional Development into the new Department of Environment, Housing and Community Development, and the publication of the Commonwealth Bureau of Roads' *Report on Roads 1975*, reminds us that it is the allocation of political power, influence and authority that determines who gets what, when, how and *where* in Australia.

different approaches by the Australian government and the State goverments to urban transport and the regulatory role performed by State governments in interregional transport. There are also studies of the *interstate system* which examine the Australian government's role in interurban corridor movements and also its initiatives in interregional transport. Much reliance in these various analyses has to be placed on case studies. While they have the advantage of detail and depth the case studies result in an uneven coverage of passenger and freight movements, individual transport modes, urban centres, and regions. Despite these shortcomings the strategy will have to suffice until more detailed statistics are available to provide a deeper understanding of transport problems that will lead to more rational and equitable decisions in the political process.

THE DOMESTIC TRANSPORT TASK

As an antidote to the past preoccupation with studying either rail, road, sea, or air transport in isolation a more comprehensive approach is adopted in this study. The strategy is *multimodal* in that interest is centred on the respective roles played by the primary modes—rail, road, coastal shipping, and air—and it is also *intermodal* in that it highlights, where possible, co-ordination between modes and by agents, such as freight forwarders, that combine individual modes into an integrated door-to-door service. As pipelines are excluded from consideration, all modes under examination provide passenger and freight services.

Monitoring the movements of people and goods to assess the relative importance of particular modes is difficult because origin and destination data on the number and purpose of passenger trips and the nature and volume of commodity shipments are woefully inadequate. No statistical time series exist for road transport. Figures for air, rail, and coastal shipping are collected by separate bodies on different areal bases. Indeed, the only comprehensive set of statistics available which reflect the growth, dimensions, and modal split of the domestic transport task are a set of physical performance measures for Australia as a whole—passenger kms and tonne kms (tonnes carried are also available but tonne kms are preferred as a measure of transport supply and demand because they reflect both the quantity transported and length of haul).

Passenger kms indicate that personal mobility has increased at three times the rate of population growth since 1950 (Table 22.1). The trend reflects the situation that once the basic necessities of food, shelter, and clothing are satisfied from family income a significant proportion of the remainder is devoted to the use of transport services (Clark *et al.*, 1974). Associated with the close relationship between an upsurge in personal mobility and a rise in the standard of living in Australia has been a shift to faster and more convenient modes of transport. Air transport, in keeping with this trend, has, unlike rail and coastal shipping, matched road's very high growth rate although this performance has done little to whittle away road's overall dominance. Indeed, the stranglehold of road, and the motor vehicle in particular, over the passenger task has been understated because the statistics refer only to cars and station wagons and exclude the collective contribu-

Table 22.1   Estimated Passenger Transport Task in Australia by Mode

Year ending 30 June	Million passenger kilometres				
	Road[a]	Rail	Air	Sea	Total
1950	19,924	10,702	1,127	370	32,123
1960	50,517	10,253	1,888	259	62,917
1965	82,800	10,090	2,792	253	95,935
1970	120,862	9,814	4,773	267	135,716
Average annual growth rate	Percentage				
1950–70	9.4	− 0.4	7.5	− 1.6	7.5
1960–70	9.1	− 0.4	9.7	0.3	8.0

[a] Cars and station wagons only.
Source: Commonwealth Bureau of Roads, 1973, p. 38.

tion of bus, tram, and taxi which was slightly greater than the role performed by rail in 1970–1. Such changes are in distinct contrast to alterations in the relative importance of modes in the slower growth of freight movements.

Changes in tonne kms have been significantly higher than the Gross Domestic Product (GDP) in real terms between 1950–75. A close relationship between tonne kms and an aggregate measure of production such as GDP would be anticipated because the demand for freight transport is derived from the goods carried. The expected correlation has materialized though tonne kms have varied at different rates to GDP for a number of possible reasons. This divergence has been attributed to the growth in the exchange of similar products between capital cities offsetting their inclination towards economic self-sufficiency. A more likely reason is that the aggregate production measurement is not confined to the production of goods but includes services. The most probable reason for the divergence, however, lies in the differential performance of commodities and their subgroupings. Although a detailed analysis of changes in the balance of production and its effects on transport is not yet available for the complete range of commodities in Australia it is assumed that the marked expansion of bulk

materials such as mining and petroleum products was responsible for the upsurge in tonne kms during the 1960s. As Table 22.2 indicates these changes have benefited the private railways carrying ores from mine to port and, to a lesser extent, coastal shipping moving bulky cargoes long distances for processing. Government-owned rail has also received an impetus from a growth in bulk cargoes but, like road, air, and more recently, coastal shipping, it is experiencing a less than average growth rate. Thus, these changes in the relative importance of particular modes in the freight transport task are partially explained by the nature of the goods carried and the inherent price-quality advantages of particular modes which are increasingly subject to changes occasioned by the energy shortage. Indeed, Taplin (1974) anticipates that in competitive circumstances there will be a diversion from coastal shipping to rail because increases in bunker fuel prices have been higher than those for locomotive diesel fuel.

Price, however, is not the sole arbiter of transport choice because the quality of service is increasingly important. In these circumstances passenger kms and tonne kms are inadequate as guidelines. Passenger kms do not embody differences in speed, safety, and comfort, while tonne kms are insensitive to variations

Table 22.2   Estimated Freight Transport Task in Australia by Mode

Year ending 30 June	Thousand million tonne kilometres					
	Rail public	Rail private[a]	Road	Sea	Air	Total
1950	11	0.3	8	16	0.03	35.6
1960	13	0.5	13	30	0.05	57.1
1965	18	0.6	17	42	0.06	77.6
1970	24	9	25	65	0.09	122.8
1975	29[b]	26[b]	33[b]	74[bc]	0.1[b]	162[b]
Average annual growth rate	Percentage					
1950–60	3.9	17.4	5.7	7.2	5.1	6.4
1960–70	6.2	33.5	6.4	7.9	6.1	7.9
1970–5	3.9	24.2	4.9	2.5[c]	n.a.	5.4

[a] Includes only iron ore railways in South Australia and Western Australia and Emu Bay Railway in Tasmania.

[b] Preliminary estimates.

[c] New series commencing 1971–2; not strictly comparable with earlier estimates.

Sources: Commonwealth Bureau of Roads, 1973, p. 40; Bureau of Transport Economics (1975), *Freight Movements in Australia: Preliminary Estimates*, Transport Outlook Conference, Canberra.

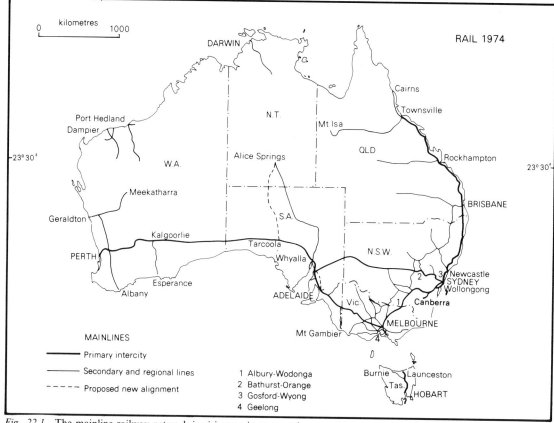

Fig. 22.1 The mainline railway network is visionary in concept because it does not show breaks of gauge, differences in ownership between private railways, the Commonwealth Railways and the six State-owned railways and branch lines in Australia's 40,320 km network (1972). *Source*: Department of Transport, 1974.

in frequency, time in transit, reliability, and damage. Because users are prepared to pay a price higher than that offered by the cheapest mode to obtain these qualities there is a need to obtain more sensitive indicators if the transport producers are to respond to expressed needs.

Transport producers, in general, do not react quickly to changes in consumer needs and preferences by adjusting their supply decisions and investments although they operate in a market regulated by the government. The transport industry is in many respects producer-dominated because of the long lead times and lumpy investments involved. As a result the type of service provided is often inappropriate when offered to users. When the site of Tullamarine Airport in Melbourne was selected in 1958, for example, small aircraft such as the Viscount 800 and Fokker F27 Friendship were in operation but when it was made operational to domestic flights in 1971 the Boeing 727 series was already in use (Gattorna, 1974; Halton, 1974).

The rapidity of technological change points up not only the problem of extrapolating the total demand for passengers and freight and their split between modes but also the need to ascertain that the facilities provided will be capable of meeting anticipated requirements. While attention has been confined here to the initial task of examining past trends in passenger and freight movements it must be borne in mind that any extrapolation of this historical data without regard to structural changes in socio-economic activities may be inappropriate in forecasting total demand and modal splits in a rapid growth situation. For instance, if the present growth rate of 18 per cent is applied to international passenger traffic at Sydney it would increase from an estimated 1.5 million in 1975 to 90 million in 2005 rather than an expected 30 million (Halton, 1974).

The reaction to such uncertainties has been to emphasize an incremental approach in transport decision-making which involves ranking policy priorities in terms of their relative certainty of implementation (Hensher, 1975). These policy options are graded on a scale from the certain, low cost, flexible, short gestation period projects (e.g. changing clearway regulations) through to uncertain, capital-intensive, inflexible, long gestation period projects (e.g. underground railways). This grading process permits the adoption of an incremental planning approach which begins with the specific projects at the certain end of the spectrum and works towards the general projects involving greater uncertainty. As a result of its emphasis on the degree of certainty incremental planning stresses realizable projects which make more use of existing technologies and promise early improvements rather than major capital investments in plant, equipment or technology.

Before indicating instances of incremental planning in action the domestic transport task has to be broken down into markets that accord with the division of control between the Australian government and State governments. As the first stage in this process the domestic transport system is divided into its intrastate and interstate components. Each component is examined separately to provide the basis for an examination of the multi-modal situation and opportunities for intermodal co-operation.

INTRASTATE TRANSPORT

Assessments of the intrastate multimodal situation are not readily undertaken because the Australian government and the State governments have generated little data on passenger and goods flows. The paucity of such information on intrastate transport, which, according to Table 22.3, handled over 95 per cent of the tonnage moved in Australia during 1971–2, must hamper initiatives by the Australian government to facilitate its urban and regional development plans

with strategic transport investments. As part of its policy for improving the public transport systems of Australian cities the Australian government has entered into agreement with the States for the provision of finance for a major programme of public transport over a five-year period to 1978. Under this programme the Australian government provided in 1973–4 two-thirds of the $100 million cost of approved public transport improvement projects through non-repayable grants under the States Grants (Urban Public Transport) Act 1974. Initially, aid has been confined to State capital cities but it is proposed to extend it to centres with larger than 100,000 population. In association with these proposals a Joint Australian Government-State Governments Study Team is investigating the feasibility of developing a technically advanced Australian Urban Passenger Train (AUPT) for use on urban transport systems throughout Australia—a study bolstered by a Brisbane-based consumer preference survey on urban rail carriage design (Bureau of Transport Economics, 1974).

There are also proposals for the Australian government to accept responsibility for the rail system of any State. Railways in Tasmania and non-metropolitan parts of South Australia have been transferred to the Australian government and the Commonwealth Railways have been replaced by the Australian National Railways Commission (Australian National Railways Act, 1975). The Commission will have the organizational structure and operational powers required for consolidating the State and Australian Railways into a single system as envisaged by the Australian government's rail transfer programme; Queensland, New South Wales, Victoria, and Western Australia have chosen not to join the scheme and retain control over their railways.

Table 22.3 Preliminary Estimates of the Breakdown of Intrastate and Interstate Freight in Australia 1971–2

Mode	Million tonnes			
	Intrastate		Interstate	Total
	Intraregional[a]	Interregional		
Rail	91.9	37.6	7.3	136.8
Road	762.5	28.5	9.0	800.0
Sea	3.8	11.4	28.6	43.8
Air	—	0.0[b]	0.1	0.1
Total	858.2	77.5	45.0	980.7

[a] The regions are based on those used by the Bureau of Statistics which do not necessarily correspond with those recognized by the Department of Urban and Regional Development.

[b] Approximately 25,000 tonnes.

Source: Bureau of Transport Economics (1975), *Long Distance Freight Outlook*, Transport Outlook Conference, Canberra.

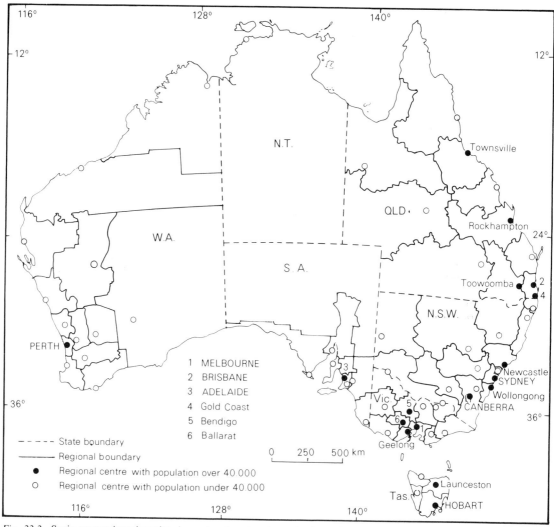

Fig. 22.2 Socio-economic regions showing regional centres chosen by the author. *Source*: based on data from the Department of Urban and Regional Development.

While such a move is part of the Australian government's attempt to match its financial power with legal and executive responsibility it can also be seen as part of an effort to improve transport systems within States especially in connection with the Australian government's initiatives to establish regional growth centres—studies have already included the examination of transport links to Albury-Wodonga, Bathurst-Orange, Gosford-Wyong, and Geelong (Fig. 22.1). The policy thrust in urban and regional development is also complemented by new arrangements for road assistance provided by the Australian government to the States since 1923–4—most of it under the Commonwealth Aid Roads Acts but there has also been assistance for

special road projects. The Commonwealth Aid Roads Act 1969 expired on 30 June 1974 and a road programme of $6,401 million has been recommended for the period from 1974–5 to 1978–9 of which the Australian government should provide 41 per cent, State governments 33 per cent, and local governments the remainder. In return for the assistance from the Australian government a greater degree of control has to be accepted by the States in the planning and programming of road works. Indeed, the State premiers were informed by the Australian Prime Minister (E. G. Whitlam) at the Premiers' Conference on 6 June 1974 that the next road assistance legislation (Road Grants Act 1974) providing $1,400 million of the recommended sum would last for only three years. In the meantime the separate road and urban transport legislation would be integrated into a co-ordinated set of arrangements (Department of Transport, 1974). As some States see the whole range of Australian government initiatives as transgressing on their traditional transport preserves there is a need to examine the effect of these proposals on the spatial organization of socio-economic activities (i.e. where and on whom are the effects felt).

The next step, therefore, is to break down the intrastate system into two separate components.

1. *Intraregional* The transport system of interest is that moving passengers and freight originating and terminating within regions. As no standard socio-economic regions have been defined in Australia those identified by the Department of Urban and Regional Development are accepted—regions recognized in Sydney, Melbourne, Adelaide, and Perth are amalgamated into single units (Fig. 22.2). Within this framework, accounting in Table 22.3 for more than 87 per cent of all tonnage moved in Australia during 1971–2, a distinction is made between regions with urban centres above or below the threshold population of 40,000. Where this threshold is exceeded the transport requirements of the region become increasingly dominated by the internal functioning of the urban area at the expense of the regional centre role involving the provision of services for rural areas in its hinterland (Commonwealth Bureau of Roads, 1973, p. 19). As there is no scope in this chapter to examine both types of regions attention is restricted to the set with major urban centres (i.e. core regions) exceeding the specified threshold: Sydney, Melbourne, Brisbane, Adelaide, Perth, Hobart, Canberra, Newcastle, Wollongong, Geelong, Ballarat, Bendigo, Townsville, Toowoomba, Rockhampton, Gold Coast, and Launceston (Fig. 22.2).

2. *Interregional* In this instance the transport system of interest encompasses movements originating in one region and terminating in another irrespective of whether they have an urban centre above or below the threshold population of 40,000—a task responsible for almost 8 per cent of all freight moved within Australia during 1971–2.

Once the distinction between intraregional and interregional transport systems is made within States each system can be examined in turn with the aid of case studies to highlight the respective roles of the Australian government and the State governments.

**Intraregional Transport Within States:
Major Urban Areas**
Australia's seventeen major urban areas depend for their existence on a massive flow of people, goods, and information into, out of, and within their boundaries.

The Commonwealth Bureau of Roads (1973, pp. 48–9) estimated that 60 per cent of all passenger kms occurred in major urban areas in 1970–1; the *Motor Vehicle Usage Survey* (Commonwealth Bureau of Census and Statistics, 1973) also indicated that one-third of all tonne kms were undertaken in these areas in 1971. The continued growth of major urban centres, and mainland centres in particular, and the intensification of transport problems give impetus to joint Australian government-State government schemes for decentralized urban and regional development.

The nature of these urban transport problems in Australia can be summarized from recent reports (Commonwealth Bureau of Roads, 1973; Sydney Area Transportation Study, 1974a, 1974b).

1. *Increasing congestion* is epitomized by a bus in central Sydney which took seventeen minutes to travel 2.3 km in 1970 compared with only eight minutes in 1962.

2. *An increase in the ownership—and use—of the private motor car, the lag in highway construction and the overconcentration of facilities in Central Business Districts (CBD)* are reputed to be the prime causes of congestion; Australia's car population increased from 2.75 million in 1959–60 to 5.18 million in 1971–2 but in 1971 there were only 109 km of freeways in Australia to speed up traffic and reduce accidents.

3. *A decline in public transport* has resulted from increased private motor vehicle ownership, a deterioration in service frequency and the quality of ride; in the five mainland capitals public transport use has fallen from 327 trips per head in 1954 to 152 trips per head in 1971 (Bureau of Transport Economics, 1972).

4. *The lack of capital for investments in public transport and high financial losses* have stemmed from the reduction in the patronage of rail and bus services. While these losses are increasing because of rising costs and a failure to recoup them from users there is a demand to replace antiquated facilities and poor services. Thus, governments have the problem of financing improved facilities and services without any assurance that patronage will improve in the face of increased competition from the motor car.

5. *Commercial road traffic is seriously inconvenienced* and the community has to bear higher physical distribution costs because of congestion in road, rail, and sea freight transfer terminals and intermodal transfer facilities. Through commercial traffic has invaded the privacy of side streets, and heavy trucks on arterial roads create barriers to community life which are more unacceptable than freeways, railways, or natural barriers such as rivers.

6. *The environmental impacts of transport systems have received little attention in the past* but all modes can affect the physical and social environment through four types of pollution—air, noise, solid waste, and water.

7. *There is a lack of co-ordination* in transport planning, expansion, and operation between the Australian government, State governments, and local governments which bedevils the already complex interrelationship between land use and transport systems.

There is little disagreement about the nature of urban transport problems but there are differences in opinion between the Australian government and the State governments as to how they should be solved. The improvement programmes in the States are based on transport plans that have been prepared for most provincial cities and all capital cities. As the State government and local government sources of finance would be insufficient to meet such programmes the State governments have, as indicated, been dependent on grants from the Australian government for road improvement schemes. No control was exercised over the Australian government grants until the Commonwealth Aid Roads Act 1969 which required the State governments to spend a fixed percentage in urban areas. It is claimed that the State governments used these grants for projects of doubtful national significance and without due regard to their social, economic, and environmental impacts. As a result the Australian government will exercise greater control over grants to urban roads as outlined in the *Report on Roads—1973* prepared by the Commonwealth Bureau of Roads (a statutory body established in 1964 to advise the Australian government on roads and road transport finance to the States). If this Report is contrasted with the State-sponsored urban transport studies a deeper insight into the differing perceptions of the Australian government and some State governments to urban transport problems can be detected.

No attempt is made to distil information from the urban transport studies to produce a composite picture of movements because they have collected data for different base years, have applied a varying range of techniques for data analysis, and have made forecasts for different alternative target years (Black, 1974). As the transport problems are most acute in capital cities the preferred strategy has been to choose SATS (Sydney Area Transportation Study, 1974a, 1974b) as a case study to provide an insight into the prevailing movement patterns in urban areas. SATS also indicates the nature of the advice given to the New South Wales government for planning Sydney's transport system through to the year 2000—advice in marked contrast to that given to the Australian government by the Commonwealth Bureau of Roads (1973).

A State Perspective of Sydney's Transport Problems
The SATS plan was based on travel forecasts for the year 2000. These forecasts were made by analysing the daily travel pattern of a 4 per cent sample of households in 1971. The expanded household interview survey and origin-destination studies revealed that on an average day in Sydney there were 6 million person trips, 2.5 million private vehicle trips, 1 million commercial vehicle trips, and 200,000 taxi trips; there were also 70,000 vehicle trips from outside the study area. Trip-making by commercial vehicles is used as a substitute for types of goods, their composition, and origin and destination. This practice is not satisfactory because the relationship between goods and vehicles may be obscured by mixed loads; hence the need to study urban goods movements in their own right. SATS (1974b), however, only examined goods flows into and out of Sydney and neglected movements originating and terminating there. As the vital information on internal goods movement is unavailable interest is centred here on passenger movements.

The main area-wide findings of SATS regarding passengers was that 60 per cent of all trips were made by the motor car (with an average occupancy rate of 1.41 persons per car) compared with 23 per cent by public transport. Another facet of the travel behaviour was the distinction between trips oriented to the CBD of the City of Sydney and those directed elsewhere (Table 22.4).

1. *CBD trips* These accounted for 11 per cent of all resident person journeys. Most were work trips in which public transport outnumbered those undertaken by private car by a ratio of 4:1 compared with 2:1 for other purposes.

2. *Non-CBD trips* They outnumbered CBD trips 8:1 and had many reverse characteristics. Journeys to work only accounted for one-third but the proportion involved in school trips was one-fifth. Private vehicle trips outnumbered public transport journeys 3.5:1 and there were twice as many bus as rail trips.

These differences in CBD and non-CBD travel behaviour stem from variations in population, land use, existing transport facilities, and vehicle registration. While the outer suburbs have attracted much of Sydney's population growth, employment in the CBD has stabilized at a fairly high level because losses in employment from manufacturing and retailing have been offset by an increase in office and commercial activity. The intense concentration of activity in the CBD makes it favourable for the efficient operation of public transport. Suburban areas which lack comparable central attractions, have a thin spread of rail and bus routes, low population densities, and high levels of car ownership.

Forecasts of population, land use, transport facilities, and travel characteristics for Sydney in 2000 suggest that it will experience even more serious transport problems if no changes are made to the existing

Table 22.4 Journey Purpose and Mode of Travel in Sydney 1971

Mode of travel	Journey purpose						
	Home-based					Non home-based per cent	All purposes
	Work per cent	School per cent	Shopping per cent	Social/ recreation per cent	Personal business per cent		
CENTRAL BUSINESS DISTRICT							
Private vehicle	22.2	9.9	17.0	55.6	42.1	58.2	31.2
Public transport	77.8	90.1	83.0	44.4	57.9	41.8	68.8
Total	100.0	100.0	100.0	100.0	100.0	100.0	100.0
Percentage of total	*36.4*	*11.7*	*10.9*	*15.5*	*12.2*	*13.3*	*100.0*
SYDNEY STUDY AREA							
Private vehicle	65.1	31.1	75.8	90.5	87.8	85.9	71.7
Public transport	34.9	68.9	24.2	9.5	12.2	14.1	28.3
Total	100.0	100.0	100.0	100.0	100.0	100.0	100.0
Percentage of total	*60.5*	*2.3*	*6.5*	*6.7*	*7.3*	*16.7*	*100.0*

Source: Sydney Area Transportation Study, 1974a, pp. VI—13.

transport networks. The expansion of 1971 population (2.8 million to 4.3 million), employment (1.3 million to 1.9 million), and motor vehicle registration (0.8 million to 2.1 million) will generate, on an average day in 2000, 11.1 million resident person journeys of which vehicle driver trips will account for 42 per cent and public transport 23 per cent. The central business district's share of the total number of trips will decline to 8 per cent with public transport retaining its stranglehold over work trips to the major office and commercial centres. Elsewhere the motor car will dominate trips for all purposes. When these forecast resident person trips are assigned to the existing highway and rail networks there will be obvious instances of overloading

and extreme congestion. The full impact of the traffic increases may be delayed as the First Report of the National Population Inquiry [The Borrie Report] (1975, Vol. I, p. 449) suggests Sydney's population in 2001 may only be between 3.3 and 3.8 millions.

The SATS response to the forecast problems follows many previous transport studies by advocating an expanded highway network. The plan comprises 550 km of new freeways and expressways and 241 km of new major regional roads to cater for the rise in vehicle driver trips to 4.6 million and commercial vehicle trips to 1.5 million. The highway and parking proposals in the study account for half of the $4,863 million cost (on 1971 prices). Improvements to

Table 22.5 Car and Station Wagon Ownership and Public Transport Use

	Sydney		Melbourne		Perth	
	1971	1979	1971	1979	1971	1979
Car and station wagon Car numbers per 1,000 persons	319	420	312	403	371	472
Public transport Bus and tram[a] journeys per capita	118	91	91	53	93	73
Rail Journeys per capita	80	52	59	47	17	11
Total Journeys per capita	198	153	150	100	110	84

[a] Melbourne only.
Source: Commonwealth Bureau of Roads, 1973, p. 50.

Plate 22.1   Urban passenger and goods transport in Melbourne. The silver suburban train introduced to speed passenger journeys to and from the central business district delays private motor vehicles, trams and trucks at a level crossing (pedestrians are conspicuous by their absence). While the freeway avoids the travel time costs inherent in such delays by being elevated above the existing roadway it is visually intrusive and contributes to noise and air pollution. The freeway also has hidden costs as its construction has resulted in demolition, the removal of public facilities, and the displacement of individuals, besides radically altering changes in the flows of goods and people. *Photo*: Loder and Bayly.

public transport as part of a so-called 'balanced' and integrated transport plan account for a further 31 per cent—the bulk of which is devoted to rail improvements. However, the shift towards public transport solutions in SATS is not sufficient to mask its freeway-dominated character. As SATS requires the Australian government to finance half of the capital cost of its recommendations its plans will have to be set against the advice tendered the Australian government by the Commonwealth Bureau of Roads (1973).

A National View of Urban Transport Problems
Research by the Commonwealth Bureau of Roads into urban travel behaviour as the basis for its 1973 Report confirms the broad modal patterns instanced by SATS. Information on the choice of travel mode for journeys to work in the central business districts of Sydney, Melbourne, and Perth re-emphasize the continued growth of motor vehicle ownership (and use) per capita and the concomitant decline in public transport journeys per capita (Table 22.5). Public transport in Perth will be least affected by the decline in patronage because it has a greater coverage and spread of bus routes in the city compared with the inflexible fixed rail and regulated bus systems in Sydney and Melbourne. These trends are likely to continue because current transport policies will not reduce the demand for travel by the private motor car.

A range of strategies was assessed by the Commonwealth Bureau of Roads for switching patronage from private car to public transport in addition to changing fare rates, imposing all-day parking surcharges, and increasing car running costs. The policies examined for changing trip characteristics (time, cost, convenience, and comfort) included:

(a) restraints on car use via road pricing and such physical controls as pricing, licencing, parking, and metering;

(b) changing institutional constraints (regulations etc.) to enable existing transport technology to perform new roles such as dial-a-bus, multiple-hire taxis, and permitting private motorists to charge passengers; and

(c) preferential treatment for buses in the form of priority bus lanes and busways.

None of the public transport policies examined are likely to significantly affect future car use. Car pooling, multiple-hire of taxis, and the use of smaller cars would make better use of existing resources but it is unlikely that new transport technologies are feasible. Urban development strategies promoted by the Australian government may help solve long-term transport problems but offer little relief to short-term to medium-term problems in urban areas. SATS reached similar conclusions to the Commonwealth Bureau of Roads but the latter body used the results to provide a set of recommendations of an entirely different character to meet the expressed demand for diverse and dispersed trips under comfortable conditions and at times to suit the traveller.

In its Report the Commonwealth Bureau of Roads recognized the need for an improved highway system because changes to the existing rail passenger network alone would not provide a solution to the transport problems of urban areas. In particular, the transport-disadvantaged members of society—the young, poor, aged, handicapped, and non-working wives—are not well served by the rail network particularly for shopping trips. The changing structure of CBD employment is aggravating the problem by producing a higher proportion of white-collar workers among rail commuters while blue-collar workers are increasingly dependent on private motor cars and buses to reach dispersing employment opportunities. Thus, an improved road system is required if the poor are not to be even more seriously disadvantaged.

The Commonwealth Bureau of Roads' general support for highway improvements did not extend to proposals for 756 km of freeways (excluding SATS recommendations) at a cost of $3,145 million. Priorities in its incremental planning approach were given to the existing system of urban arterial roads because they carried 75 per cent of all traffic on 20 per cent of the road space. These roads, representing an existing national asset with a replacement value of $10,000 million, could be improved with the minimum of social and environmental upset. Although freeways in urban areas attract large volumes of traffic the Commonwealth Bureau of Roads (1974) considers few will be economic propositions for five or ten years. The Bureau indicates that individual freeways may be feasible in the long term if they function as ring roads or by-passes to the CBD in the middle to outer suburbs for cross-city commuters and commercial traffic. Within an 8 km radius only short by-passes for concentrated or heavy commercial traffic are considered to be warranted in the inner suburbs (though no evidence is provided as to why an 8 km radius was chosen). The other main proposal for urban roads made by the Commonwealth Bureau of Roads was innovatory in that it proposed to assist local government authorities to build local urban roads on the fringes of urban areas and in 'system cities' proposed by the Australian government beyond existing built-up metropolitan areas. Also included in the same scheme were grants to improve streets suffering from excess traffic diverted from congested arterials and roads in areas designated for special assistance by the Australian government (e.g. Western Suburbs of Sydney and Melbourne). The total cost of the suite of programmes for urban areas is $2,013 million of which the Australian government will provide 47 per cent while the State government and local

Table 22.6 Effect of Alternative Transport Choice of Mode in Journeys to Work in Central Business Districts

Year	Policy option	Sydney Public transport[a]	Car	Melbourne Public transport[a]	Car	Perth Public transport[a]	Car
				Percentage			
1971/2	—	80	20	72	28	42	58
1978/9	Systems improvements						
	a) with neither road nor public transport improvements	78	22	69	31	35	65
	b) With public transport improvements only[b]	79	21	70	30	37	63
	c) With warranted and feasible road improvements only	77	23	67	33	35	65
	d) With public transport and warranted and feasible road improvements	78	22	68	32	37	63

[a] Public transport includes road (bus and tram) and rail modes.

[b] In Sydney and Melbourne improvements relate exclusively to railways whereas for Perth they relate exclusively to the bus system.

Source: Commonwealth Bureau of Roads, 1973, p. 69.

government authorities will be required to supply the remainder.

The support for highway improvement by the Commonwealth Bureau of Roads does not preclude the upgrading of public transport. Reviews of transport in capital cities by the Bureau of Transport Economics (1972, 1973a) strongly suggest that investment in capital-starved public transport would yield high rates of social return for track additions in congested sections of the network, electrification of well-patronized rail lines, new rail lines and route extensions, bus and car interchanges at selected points on efficient rail services, separate busways, and selected ferry services. However, the Commonwealth Bureau of Roads estimates that improvements to public transport alone in Sydney, Melbourne, and Perth would only increase patronage marginally in 1978–9 as compared with the effect of not undertaking any improvements on rail and road (Table 22.6). Road improvements suggested by the Commonwealth Bureau of Roads (1973) would decrease public road transport and rail use in Sydney and Melbourne but would have no effect in bus-dominated Perth. If both public transport and road improvements are undertaken simultaneously by 1979 the *status quo* will prevail in Sydney, a slight deterioration in public transport will occur in Melbourne, while the converse will happen in Perth. The

trend towards car use is not as pronounced as the increased ownership figures suggest because public transport is in a much stronger competitive position in CBD travel as compared with movements directed elsewhere. However, irrespective of whether the prognostications of the Commonwealth Bureau of Roads are correct, the ultimate outcome will still depend on how the mismatch between the financial capability and functional responsibility of the Australian government and the State governments is resolved.

Interregional Transport Within States

As only the grossest estimates of passengers and goods originating and terminating between the component regions of individual States are available, interest is switched at this level from multimodal comparisons to the regulatory framework within which movements occur. The reason for highlighting the series of legal regulations brought down by State governments for individual modes stems from their importance in determining the efficiency of the transport system and the desirable modal split of passengers and goods. State governments have been able to implement regulations embracing the control of entry, the achievement and maintenance of operational safety, the protection and destruction of amenity and the environment, the protection and subjugation of the user, and attempts to influence the distribution of traffic between road and rail as a constitutional right (Taplin *et al.*, 1974).

The division of control over transport in the Constitution between the Australian government and the State governments was implicit rather than explicit. Until 1954, for example, the States controlled interstate road haulage in the same manner as intrastate road haulage by requiring permits for journeys where road competed with rail and by levying tonne km taxes on prescribed commodities. In that year the Privy Council ruled in the case of Hughes and Vale Pty Ltd *v.* The State of New South Wales that the State charges levied on interstate freight movements violated Section 92 of the Constitution which states:

> On the imposition of uniform duties of customs, trade, commerce, and intercourse among the States, whether by means of internal carriage or ocean navigation shall be absolutely free.

This interpretation was sustained by the Privy Council which did not however disallow a charge on interstate road operators for the wear and tear of the roads. In subsequent legislation all States, except Tasmania, imposed a road maintenance charge of 0.17 cents per tonne km based on the tare weight plus 40 per cent of a vehicle's registered carrying capacity. As this legislation clarified the respective roles of the different levels of government the regulation of interregional passenger and freight movements is examined to indicate the effects of such interference by the State governments.

The State governments have exercised their regulatory prerogative through the ownership of railway systems within their borders, the control and taxing of road haulage, the ownership and/or control of mass passenger transport by road, the ownership and control of intrastate shipping, the control of ports, and the control of intrastate air services. As these regulations differ widely in their application between individual States attention is concentrated on the control of road haulage by the specification of vehicle, safety, and amenity standards, and restraints on the ability of road transport to compete with rail. While the lack of uniformity from different state-wide applications of vehicle construction, weight limits, dimensions, conditions of loading and driving, and speed limits to safeguard road users and protect bridges and road surfaces, have had a deleterious effect on technical advances and innovations in vehicle design they also constrain the commodities that can be carried economically and, therefore, affect the division of traffic (Table 22.7). As the rival claims of the impact of this legislation on road authorities and road operators are difficult to assess until the National Association of Australian State Road Authorities (NAASRA) study on the economics of vehicle size limits reports, interest is confined here to examining the practice of regulating competition between road and railways.

Rail-Road Competition in Victoria
Intensified competition from the rapidly developing road transport industry for State railways in the 1930s occasioned a change in government policy from one of restraining railway monopolies to one of limiting the extent to which road could compete with rail. Various arguments were adduced to justify the policy change including the need to prevent the duplication and

Table 22.7   Variations in Goods Vehicle Dimensions and Weight Limitations Between Selected States 1975

	ATAC[a]	N.S.W.	Vic.	Qld	S.A.	W.A.	Tas.	N.T.	A.C.T.
Length: Maximum length of single truck (metres)	11.0	10.97	11.0	9.45	20.117	11.0	*b*	12.2	*c*
Length: Maximum length of semi-trailer (metres)	15.3	15.24	14.5	14.33	20.117	13.8	*b*	16.5	*c*
Height: Maximum permitted by law on all routes (metres)	4.3	4.27	4.0	4.27	4.3	4.3	*b*	4.4	*c*
Single wheels: Maximum per axle with two tyres (tonnes)	4.6	4.8	4.6	4.6	6.6	4.536	*b*	*c*	*c*
Duals: Maximum per single axle with duals or more tyres (tonnes)	8.2	8.4	8.2	8.1	8.2	8.2	*b*	9.0	*c*

[a] Australian Transport Advisory Council recommendations.

[b] New regulations are in preparation based on ATAC draft regulation.

[c] No express regulation.

Source: NAASRA Economics of Road Vehicle Limits Study, *Summary of Vehicle Weights and Dimensional Limits in Australia*, January 1975.

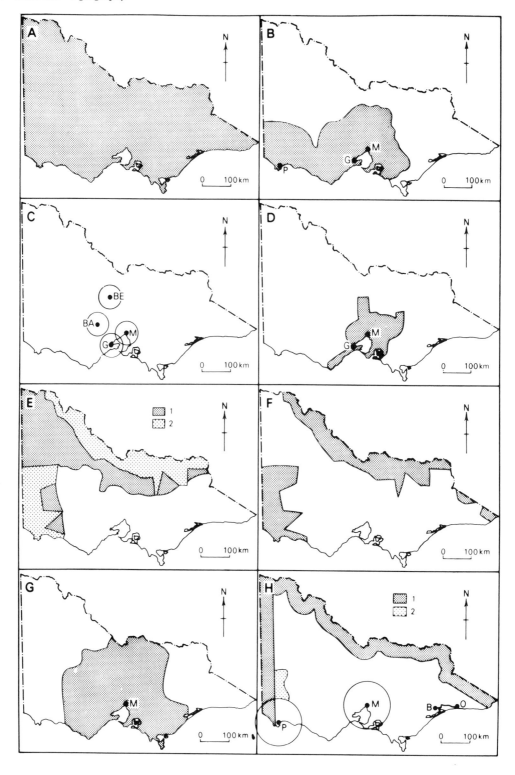

misallocation of resources, the unstable conditions within the road industry due to internal competition, and the failure of trucks to pay for the cost of roads— the real reason was the protection of the State railways. As a result of the policy shift co-ordination taxes were introduced in all States to safeguard the railways against road competition. While South Australia (1968) and New South Wales (1974) have removed their restrictions over road transport in competition with the State-owned railways, regulation still persists in Queensland, Victoria, Tasmania, and in Western Australia. As it is not possible to detail differences in the regulation between individual States within the compass of this chapter, Victoria is selected as a case study because the nature of regulations and their impact were considered in the *Report of the Board of Inquiry into the Victorian Land Transport System* [The Bland Report] (Victoria, Legislative Assembly, 1972).

When Sir Henry Bland examined the regulatory framework in Victoria he found that road transport was denied permission to carry commodities traditionally regarded as the preserve of rail transport, such as beer, wool, groceries, hardware, steel, tractors, food products, canned goods, etc. Apart from primary producers with vehicles under two tonnes which are exempt from legislative control Bland discovered that other road operators were allowed various freedoms as embodied in Section 92 of the Constitution and established in the Commercial Goods Vehicles Act 1958–66 as 'as of right' licences, discretionary licences, and permits under the administration of the Transport Regulation Board (TRB).

1. 'As of right' licences were granted more or less automatically for primary producers, decentralized industries, and specified items such as bulk petroleum, fruit, vegetables, etc. on a state-wide basis (Fig. 22.3A). These licences were also granted for the pick-up area of dairy factory vehicles, for an ancillary operator within an 80 km radius of his place of business, for hire and reward operators within a 40 km radius of the G.P.O. in Melbourne and the P.O. in Ballarat, Bendigo, and Geelong (Fig. 22.3C) and 48 km of their place of business.

2. Discretionary or 'D' licences permitted the carriage of goods by road which are regarded by the TRB as non-competitive or inadequately provided for by rail transport. The main categories permitted on a state-wide basis include marine goods, contractors equipment, cars, refrigerated traffic, etc. (Fig. 22.3A). Other categories under 'D' licences included regular services from Melbourne and Geelong to non-rail areas (Fig. 22.3D).

3. Permits allowed a considerable volume of goods to move between Melbourne and Geelong and the commercial movement of wool within an 80 km radius of Portland including places on the Mt Gambier-Hamilton road and those to the north which are more than 32 km from a railway station. The permits were also granted without question for bricks and roofing tiles, glazed doors, timber windows, etc. on a state-wide basis (Fig. 22.3A), superphosphates within 160 km of Melbourne, Geelong, and Portland (Fig. 22.3B), and drummed petroleum products within 258 km of Melbourne (Fig. 22.3G).

4. Section 92 of the Constitution, guaranteeing the freedom of trade and commerce between States, allows, in addition to interstate movements between capital cities and from Melbourne to South Australian and Riverina towns, considerable border and near-border road transport for seasonal and unrestricted movements of primary commodities such as grain and wool (Fig. 22.3E) and regular and unrestricted movements of other commodities (Fig. 22.3F). The effect of Section 92, therefore, was to restrict the area of regulation to within a 160 km radius of Melbourne with the exception of longer hauls to Gippsland, the Western District, and the northwest of the State.

After examining these various freedoms Bland concurred with the TRB that they had reduced the area of goods transport regulation to fairly narrow limits—a matter of necessity rather than virtue because Victoria, as a small State, was more vulnerable to unregulated alternatives than, for instance, Queensland.

The effect of these road transport freedoms on the performance of the railways was difficult to detect because the total tonnage of goods moving under regulation in Victoria is unknown. While rail carried 11,726,000 tonnes in 1969–70 almost 2 million tonnes moved under permit and 400,000 tonnes under Section 92 but no information was available for goods moved under 'as of right' or discretionary licences. More detailed figures for Melbourne to Ballarat, Bendigo and Geelong respectively indicate the dependence of the railways on bulk and heavy items reserved to them by the TRB (Table 22.8). Within a 120 km radius of

Fig. 22.3 The extent of the various freedoms for road hauliers under Transport Regulations Act 1958 and Commercial Goods Vehicles Act 1958 as at 30 June (A-G) and the Bland Report proposals (E).
A, state-wide movement of goods; B, 160 km radius from Melbourne (M), Geelong (G), and Portland (P); C, 40 km radius from Melbourne, Ballarat (BA), Bendigo (BE) and Geelong; D, regular services from Geelong and Melbourne; E, seasonal and unrestricted movements under Section 92(1) and regular and unrestricted movements under Section 92 (2); F, regular and unrestricted movements under Section 92; G, 258 km from Melbourne; H, 80 km from Melbourne G.P.O. and Portland P.O., 40 km from Victorian border (1), area west of Grampians and south of Carpolac railway line (2), and Bairnsdale (B) and Orbost (O). *Source*: Rimmer, 1974, p. 28.

Table 22.8   Tonnages and Revenue Derived from Reciprocal Movements Between Melbourne and Ballarat, Bendigo, Geelong, and Places Within 120 km Radius 1969–70

	Rail				Road
	Total		Non-bulk		Permit
	Mass tonnes '000	Revenue dollars '000	Mass tonnes '000	Revenue dollars '000	Mass tonnes '000
Melbourne-Ballarat	141	714	61	378	74
Melbourne-Bendigo	130	962	56	471	39
Melbourne-Geelong	1,025	3,004	64	262	329
120 km radius of Melbourne [a]	1,590	5,300	280	1,420	949

[a] Includes Geelong and Ballarat.
Source: Victoria, Legislative Assembly, 1972, pp. 55–7.

Melbourne the tonnage moved by *permit alone* exceeded the mass of goods carried by rail. If freedom of choice was granted in that area the maximum loss to the railways would be 280,000 tonnes.

While these figures are suggestive they do not provide a definitive assessment of the impact of regulations on road-rail competition. Without other statistics all that can be attempted is to ascertain whether the actual goals prompting the legislation are achieved. While the stated aims of the initial legislation establishing the TRB in Victoria (Transport Regulation Act 1933) was for the 'improvement and co-ordination of means of and facilities for locomotion and transport', the real objective was, as indicated, to protect the railways even though the intention was masked in such flexible terms as 'public interest' and 'co-ordination'. If this argument is accepted it behoves us to examine whether the controls achieved a more efficient allocation of scarce resources in the transport sector and the economy as a whole and whether they assisted in the retention of traffic for the Victorian Railways (Rimmer, 1974, pp. 24–9). The Bland Report indicated that the existing regulatory methods in Victoria had failed to achieve efficiency within the transport sector in the sense that the ratio of output price to marginal resource cost for rail be equal to road. Assuming consumer sovereignty, prices reflect costs, and consumers know what is best for them, then allocative efficiency is achieved when the value of the marginal output from a resource committed to some economic activity, such as transport, is similar to its potential contribution to some other economic activity (see Kolsen, 1974).

Regulation also caused severe spatial distortion. Before New South Wales abandoned regulation Victorian merchants were able to penetrate towns in the Riverina closer to Sydney than Melbourne. A spatial 'black market' also existed in Victoria to circumvent regulation. Trucks carrying loads for Victorian destinations 'border hopped' into adjacent States before returning to the State to drop their cargoes—a result of users not being given an opportunity to indicate what costs they are prepared to bear. Although the spatial black market created on the basis of costs rather than price distorted the Australian economy through excessive interstate movements it did not influence the Victorian government's attitude because it overemphasized its function as railway owner to the exclusion of its role in representing the public at large. As a result Victorian legislation stands out in sharp contrast to regulation in the United States where the government acts as a referee of rail-road competition (Kolsen, 1968). The use of regulation to protect the existing rail system against new technology, together with inflexible size limitations, makes it insensitive to innovation. Even the regulations themselves have become entrenched and the regulator's preoccupation with the cost per passenger km or tonne km as the prime determinant of a user's choice has resulted in a neglect of quality characteristics such as dependability, flexibility, speed, and safety. Thus, regulation has not succeeded in better allocation of resources in general—it has also failed in protecting the Victorian Railways in particular.

In spite of protection the financial position of Victorian Railways has progressively deteriorated because of its failure to cover avoidable costs. Regulation has aggravated the financial position because it has permitted the Victorian Railways to retain loss-making short-haul traffic that would have been captured by road transport in a competitive situation. The parlous state of railway finances has also not been helped by the failure to close lines, terminals, and services operating at substantial losses where social reasons cannot be sustained (e.g. the protection of infant industries). There has also been a reluctance to revise freight rate schedules to cover operating costs on marginal lines, to simplify rate setting, and to introduce detailed cost accounting. The Bland Report found several rate setting procedures in operation, some of which dated back to nineteenth-century traditions and situations and indicated that practically all arguments for regulation were based on circumstances before road transport became an efficient competitor with rail.

The general tariff producing one-half of the revenue is derived from the General Rate Book and based on traditional railway concepts of what the traffic will bear and of subsidizing low value commodities with high value items. Most commodities are classified within eight categories which are further subdivisable into twenty-two classes based on their intrinsic value with some reference to their density characteristics. Indicative of the wide variations within the schema, the rate for drapery, for example, was $16.40 a tonne for 160 km compared with $3.75 for firewood over the same distance. Carloads (CL) generally carry a lower rate than the same commodities in less-than-carload (LCL) lots. The tariffs also embody a taper on the assumption that terminal costs remain constant while line-haul costs vary directly with the distance travelled. Apart from changes in commodity classification before 1925 and subsequent across-the-board percentage changes, the basic principles underpinning this method of rate setting have remained unchanged since the 1890s and are singularly unattuned to meet road competition. As road competition has not been eliminated by regulation special contract rates have had to be offered. To counteract 'border hopping' competition from intrastate road hauliers special rates have been introduced, such as those for wool which abandon the normal taper (Table 22.9). In

Table 22.9 Influence of 'Border Hopping' on Rail Freight Rates for Wool Despatched from Selected Country Centres to Melbourne

Location	Distance from Melbourne	Freight rates	
	km	per bale dollars	per bale-km cents
Seymour	98	1.20	1.22
Benalla	195	1.60	0.82
Wangaratta	235	1.40	0.60
Wodonga	301	1.20	0.40

Source: Victoria, Legislative Assembly, 1972, p. 105.

competition with road transport, therefore, the railways have lost their highly-rated commodities but have retained the low-rated items.

There are numerous anomalies in the rates because of past government intervention. The Bland Report cited, for instance, that the freight rate for imported wines was nearly three times that of the local product while the rate for a parcel of the 'ashes of cremated human remains' was four times the rate for a parcel of 'dead poultry'. Further distortions stemmed from failure to meet operating costs where concessions were granted to sectional interests, such as primary producers. Already hampered by having to carry all traffic offered, as a common carrier, the Victorian Railways were also not fully recompensed by the government for other political concessions used for transferring welfare between groups in the 'public interest'.

While protection has not saved the railways from financial difficulties the regulatory framework allegedly raises costs to road users where truck operations are restricted. Indeed, regulation has not succeeded in inducing 'true competition' between rail and road because ancillary operators, primary producers, and specific industries and commodities are granted various concessions. This 'safety valve' legislation distorts the allocation of resources within the road industry between professional hire and reward carriers and ancillary operators. Traffic is not channelled to the most effective mode by the allocation process because the main determinant is not that the user should select the best price-quality combination offered but whether the railway can carry the freight or not. While it is claimed that heavy trucks do not pay the full costs of their road use the existing regulatory system does not compensate for an inadequate highway pricing system (Kolsen, 1968).

With such a withering indictment of the existing regulatory framework it is not surprising that the Bland Report recommended changes. The purpose of future regulation is not to protect the railways but to restructure and reorganize them so that traffic is lost to road where it is better placed in terms of cost (nothing is said about quality!). Such modal choice decisions hinge on rail and road being put on an equal competitive footing in regard to the cost of operations. If the revitalized railways are to win traffic under these conditions unprofitable activities will have to be pruned, some operations rescheduled on a seasonal basis, experiments made with regional freight centres (e.g. Horsham), full subsidies paid for political concessions, and more aggressive marketing strategies introduced. While the Victorian Railways are re-adjusting to these developments the Bland Report has recommended the extension of 'as of right' licences for the products considered to be the preserve of the railways (Fig. 22.3H). Also, with exceptions, decentralized industries will have the freedom of transport choice and timber industries can resort to hire-and-reward operators. The Victorian government has accepted the general principles of the Bland Report as guidelines for future changes to meet the flexible objective of a 'balanced transport system'.

The Bland Report did not embroil itself directly with the use of regulatory controls to redistribute political power and access but confined its attention to improving commercial efficiency with little allusion to the impact of recommendations on the territorial redistribution of income and wealth. As a commercial document it has important implications for other States because the problems experienced by the Victorian Railways are not unique. Its operations, conventions, and attitudes are duplicated in other State-owned systems as instanced by the South Australian Department of Roads and Transport (1973) Report on the operations of South Australian Railways. However, Victoria's acceptance of the recommendation to continue the regulation of road transport provides a yardstick with which to gauge the changes in the deregulated States of New South Wales and South Australia (in South Australia there has already been a reduction in interstate movements as consignors have switched from Victorian to Adelaide suppliers). The Bland Report will also be of interest to the Australian government if it succeeds in acquiring further State-owned railway systems because regulation, if used judiciously, could help further the Australian government's plans for urban and regional development as a study of interstate transport indicates.

INTERSTATE TRANSPORT

No statistics are available to permit multimodal comparisons of passenger movements but there are some statistics on interstate freight flows (Table 22.10). Accounting for less than 5 per cent of the tonnage transported within Australia in 1971–2 these movements are dominated by coastal shipping carrying mining and petroleum products. If the tonnage figures had been multiplied by distance to arrive at tonne kms one would have expected the interstate figures to have been boosted sufficiently for the Australian government to want to regulate interstate flows. Yet the Australian government has only exercised its constitutional prerogative in respect of air transport and coastal shipping. Scheduled interstate services with passenger and all-freight aircraft are supplied by two airlines, the Australian government-owned Trans-Australia Airlines (TAA) and the privately-owned subsidiary of Ansett Transport Industries, Ansett Airlines of Australia (AAA). All major routes are competitive, with both airlines providing equal capacities in accordance with the Airlines Agreement Act 1952–73 and the Airlines Equipment Act 1958 passed by the Australian (then Commonwealth) government. The Airlines Equipment Act provides the principles for establishing and maintaining comparable, but not identical, fleets between TAA and AAA and is intended to prevent excess capacity. The Airlines Agreement Act established the ground rules for controlling the two-airline 'competitive' system (known generally as 'the two-airlines policy'); the machinery is in operation until 1977 (Fig. 22.4). The Australian Coastal Shipping Agreement Act 1956 provides similar competitive rules for the relationship between private shipping companies and the Australian Shipping Commission, which operates the Australian government-owned merchant shipping service, the Australian National Line (ANL) (Fig. 22.5). Overall control, however, is exercised through the Navigation Act 1912–72 which

Table 22.10   Modal Split of Interstate Freight Movements 1971–2

	Rail[a] per cent	Road per cent	Sea per cent	Air per cent	Total per cent	million tonnes
Inter-capital city[b]	20	25	55	0	100	18.2
Interregional						
To or from capital cities[b]	14	24	62	0	100	14.4
Non-capital city	11	7	82	0	100	12.4
Subtotal	13	16	71	0	100	26.8
Total	16	20	64	0	100	45.0

[a] Only government rail freight is included.

[b] Includes Canberra-Queanbeyan and Albury-Wodonga in addition to the six State capitals.

Source: derived from Bureau of Transport Economics (1975), *Freight Movements in Australia: Preliminary Estimates*, Transport Outlook Conference, Canberra.

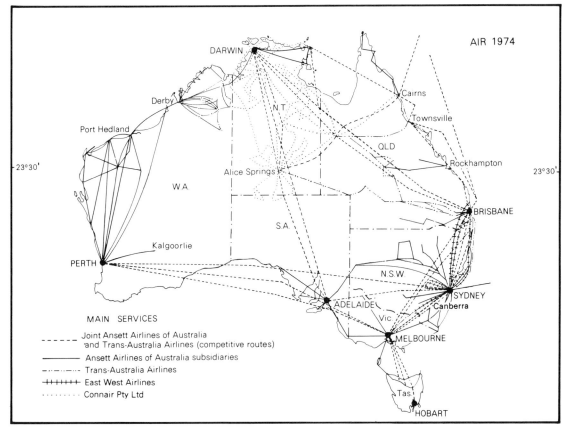

AIR 1974

MAIN SERVICES

- - - - - - Joint Ansett Airlines of Australia
        and Trans-Australia Airlines (competitive routes)
————— Ansett Airlines of Australia subsidiaries
–··–··– Trans-Australia Airlines
+++++++ East West Airlines
·········· Connair Pty Ltd

Fig. 22.4 The total unduplicated network of 11,400 km (1973) on which scheduled interstate services are provided by two airlines only, the Australian government-owned Trans-Australia Airlines (TAA) and the private enterprise airline Ansett Airlines of Australia (AAA). TAA and AAA (and subsidiaries) also provide intrastate services with the independent company East-West Airlines; the other regional airline, Connair Pty Ltd, provides services to outback communities. *Source*: Department of Transport, 1974.

licences ships, regulates the conditions of employment, and stipulates the provision of Australian crews on Australian vessels.

As yet the Australian government has not exercised its apparent right to regulate interstate road and rail transport but this situation could change with its policy initiatives directed towards constructing a National Highways System and welding the disparate State-owned railways into a national network. Hence, there is considerable interest in reinvoking the constitutional powers for an Inter-State Commission. Before examining the possible role of such a Commission it is pertinent to consider the Australian government's interest in providing effective interstate transport links. The national interest involves two types of transport links.

1. *Interurban* The system of interest involves interstate interactions between the regions with urban centres over the threshold population of 40,000 (i.e. core regions) which accounted for at least two-fifths of all freight moving between States in 1971–2 although all major urban areas are not represented in these statistics (see Table 22.10).

2. *Interregional* The system excludes the inter-urban movements but includes flows from (a) core regions to other regions, (b) other regions to core regions, and (c) reciprocal flows between pairs of non-core regions. Collectively, these three sets of flows accounted for almost three-fifths of interstate freight movements in 1971–2 (Table 22.10).

With the aid of case studies it is possible to use these distinctions between the components of the interstate transport system to examine the Australian government's policies for improving the reciprocal connections between core regions on the one hand and between all types of regions on the other.

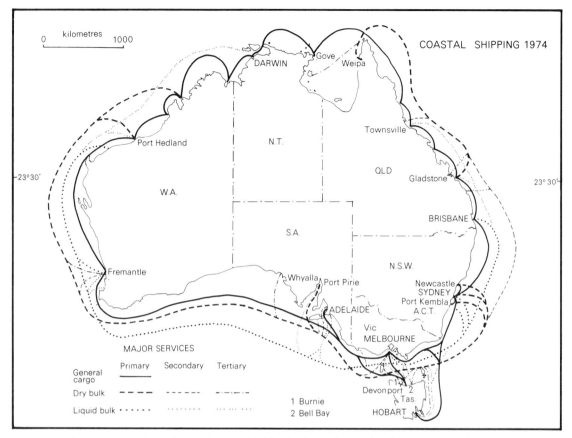

Fig. 22.5 The major coastal shipping services provided by the Australian National Line (ANL), private companies, and ancillary carriers such as Broken Hill Proprietary Ltd. There is no explicit Australian government policy for ports which are variously administered in different States by either a State government department, a state-wide statutory authority, a local autonomous board of trust, or a private company. *Source*: Department of Transport, 1974.

Interurban Transport Between States

Only the barest details of interurban passenger movements between major urban areas are known (see Australian Travel Research Conference, 1975). The available information suggests that air transport is favoured for business travel over long distances, the motor car is used for family travel over all distances, and some non-business personal trips are by rail. As a result the gross estimates for intercapital passenger travel in 1975 indicate that road carries 59 per cent, air carries 32 per cent, rail almost 7 per cent, and bus 2 per cent (Bureau of Transport Economics, 1975). While no change is anticipated in the growth of income per head (3.5 per cent) the Bureau of Transport Economics (1975) suggests that non-urban travel may decline from the annual 10 per cent growth rate between 1965 and 1975 to 6 per cent for the next decade because population growth will decline from 1.9 per cent to 1 per cent and a rise in user costs to

1 per cent per annum will replace the previous fall of 0.5 per cent per annum. Changes are also expected in the relative proportions of each mode because the Australian government's policy to equate air fares more closely with the costs of providing the services is expected to shift custom from air to road and possibly rail. While the introduction of high speed trains (130–160 km/h) would probably have a marked impact on the existing modal split, particularly for non-business and business travel up to 320 km (e.g. Sydney-Canberra, Canberra-Albury, and Albury-Melbourne), the most likely effect based on overseas experience would not be to divert traffic from existing modes but to generate new traffic. The low density of development (and demand) even in the most heavily trafficked corridor between Melbourne and Sydney operates against any radical changes. As there are no major transport strategies likely to shift passengers from motor cars in the short term and

Table 22.11 Total Intercapital Freight Movements 1971–2[a]

From \ To	Sydney[b]	Melbourne[b]	Brisbane	Adelaide	Perth[b]	Hobart	Canberra[b]	Albury-Wodonga	Total
				thousand tonnes					
Sydney	—	1,708	750	245	263	85	611	13	3,675
Melbourne	6,029	—	2,886	775	531	298	141	133	10,793
Brisbane	497	182	—	82	53	8	—	1	823
Adelaide	318	748	120	—	141	32	—	—	1,359
Perth	135	184	25	202	—	80	—	—	626
Hobart	314	273	25	29	27	—	—	—	668
Canberra	48	8	—	—	—	—	—	—	56
Albury-Wodonga	27	159	10	7	5	—	6	—	214
Total	7,368	3,262	3,816	1,340	1,020	503	758	147	18,214

[a] Note Albury-Wodonga is included because of its particular location.

[b] As capital cities refer to statistical divisions Sydney includes Botany Bay, Melbourne includes Westernport, Perth includes both Fremantle and Kwinana, Canberra includes Queanbeyan.

Source: Bureau of Transport Economics (1975), *Freight Movements in Australia: Preliminary Estimates*, Transport Outlook Conference, Canberra.

medium term, interest at the interurban level is focused on freight flows (Commonwealth Bureau of Roads, 1973, pp. 86–7).

Interurban freight flows stem largely from variations in the industrial structures of the respective capital cities and provincial cities (see Rimmer, 1970). As the capitals dominate their respective States and Territories industrially it would be anticipated from an analysis of the industrial classes recorded by the Australian Bureau of Statistics that they would dominate non-bulk movements while Newcastle and Wollongong would be heavy generators of bulk

Table 22.12 Scheduled Door-to-Door Freight Rates Between Capital Cities for 1,000 kg or 4m³ Effective from 15 August 1974[a]

(dollars)

RAILFAST[b]	Sydney[c]	Melbourne	Brisbane	Adelaide	Perth
Sydney[c]	—	64.35	78.95	90.10	204.80
Melbourne	61.35	—	108.45	53.25	150.60
Brisbane	60.20	99.65	—	132.65	261.95
Adelaide	77.55	51.00	132.80	—	129.65
Perth	127.25	102.00	156.45	75.05	—

ROADFAST[b]	Sydney	Melbourne	Brisbane	Adelaide	Perth
Sydney[c]	—	64.80	81.15	89.65	226.00
Melbourne	62.00	—	105.75	52.70	165.15
Brisbane	62.90	99.65	—	134.20	251.65
Adelaide	78.60	52.00	132.75	—	137.35
Perth	127.25	102.00	156.45	75.05	—

[a] These figures are only indicative because a large proportion of freight is carried under contract.

[b] Note the line haul on a 'roadfast' service could be performed by rail.

[c] Effective 1 October 1974.

Source: Thomas Nationwide Transport (TNT) Interstate Rate Schedules.

freight. It would also be expected that Sydney and Melbourne would have a stranglehold over inter-capital flows because Adelaide, Brisbane, Perth, Hobart, and Canberra are deficient in such items as metal products, electrical goods, textiles, clothing, and a wide range of miscellaneous items. The pattern resulting from the divergent characteristics of the urban areas is accentuated by reciprocal flows of similar types of commodity which do not differ in class but in style and quality (e.g. motor vehicles).

An examination of intercapital flows in 1971–2 confirms the Sydney-Melbourne hegemony (Table 22.11). Collectively, the centres accounted for almost four-fifths of outbound flows and three-fifths of all inbound flows. Reciprocal flows between Sydney and Melbourne were responsible for two-fifths of all movements, Melbourne and Adelaide for 8 per cent, and Sydney-Brisbane for 7 per cent.

No breakdown by mode is made for 1971–2 as the figures are preliminary estimates. This is not an unmixed blessing as it provides the opportunity to emphasize the role of the freight forwarder in inter-urban movements which is often ignored in multi-modal comparisons (Rimmer, 1970). While the choice of line haul mode is, in theory, on the basis of service to the customer, the freight forwarder offering a total door-to-door transport package plays an important role in determining whether the less-than-carload consignment goes by either rail, road, sea, or air. Such a decision in the final analysis is based on the availability of the freight forwarders, intermodal equipment and contractural obligations to provide a certain volume to a particular mode. These contracts favour the forwarders as the companies have grown to such a size that they can exercise monopsony power in rate negotiations with the line haul modes. Contract rates are confidential but Table 22.12 indicates one freight forwarder's scheduled rates between capital cities. In 1972–3 the freight forwarders carried an estimated 40 per cent of interstate road freight and 20 per cent of interstate rail freight but their share of sea freight was relatively insignificant except to and from Tasmania.

The reason for the relatively poor showing of freight forwarders in coastal shipping was that they specialized on consolidating less-than-carload freight whereas the mode was particularly suited to the carriage of bulky cargoes between interurban areas, such as refined petroleum and steel products. In 1971–2 coastal shipping accounted for an estimated 55 per cent of intercapital freight movements (Table 22.10). However, the main interest in the flow of freight centres on land-based movement of non-bulk products in which direct costs (freight rates, insurance, packaging, etc.) are often outweighed by indirect costs such as damage, pilferage, and reliability

(Gilmour *et al.*, 1975). As road transport can tailor a wide range of services to meet the perceived require-ments in movements between urban areas it handled 25 per cent of intercapital freight flows in 1971–2 compared with 20 per cent by rail (Table 22.10).

Considerable improvements to rail technology (gauge standardization and specialized intermodal equipment) since the abolition of the interstate regu-lation of road transport in 1954, have put rail on a better competitive footing with the labour-intensive road industry. Handicaps still remain as evidenced by the need to switch gauges at Melbourne in connect-ing Sydney with Geelong and Adelaide, and at Brisbane in linking Sydney to urban areas in north Queensland. Yet, the interstate road system is, in some respects, even more inadequate and worthy of special attention because it has been generally neglected by State governments intent on matching the distribution of resources and political power. Admittedly, few State governments would have been able to accumulate the large resources necessary for building the National Highways System even if they were predisposed to do so, which was not necessarily the case.

The National Highways System
In 1972 the Australian government in co-operation with the National Association of Australian State Road Authorities (NAASRA) established the Committee of Senior Representatives of Common-wealth and State Road Authorities (1974) to report on a system of national highways. As the effect of such a system on the railways was considered to be small or negligible the Committee concentrated solely on highway considerations (Taplin *et al.*, 1974, note that total movements show only a slight response to price although they are responsive to rate differences between modes). An examination of 33,800 km of the arterial links comprising Australia's 864,000 km road network showed that long lengths were unsurfaced, only short lengths were divided, and relatively long lengths were subject to flooding. Many were too narrow, winding, and showing the effects of age. Five per cent of the arterial roads exceeded an annual average daily traffic (AADT) rate of 4,000—the minimum level necessary for providing a divided road. By the Committee's standards the unsealed Stuart Highway between Port Augusta and Tennant Creek was adjudged 95 per cent deficient compared with 88 per cent for the sealed Pacific Highway between Sydney and Brisbane and 62 per cent for the Hume Highway between Sydney and Melbourne.

The Committee's main recommendation based on this special study, was for a primary intercity network linking all capital cities but it also costed a series of additional routes at $8,687 million. As the primary intercity connections coincided with the Common-

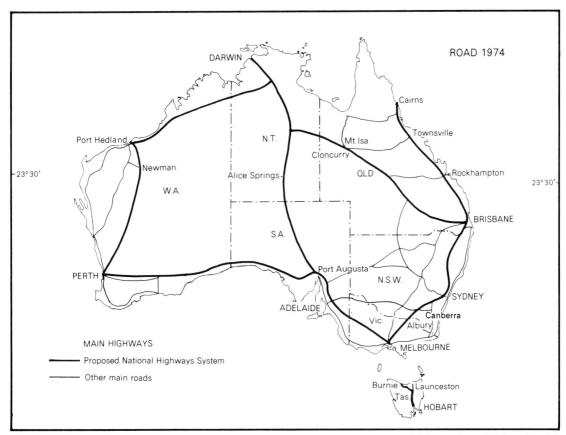

Fig. 22.6 The main road network showing the proposed National Highways System. Of the total 864,000 km of multi-quality roads, 104,640 km are designated main roads. *Source*: Commonwealth Bureau of Roads, 1973, pp. 74–5; Department of Transport, 1974.

wealth Bureau of Roads' own surveys they formed the basis of the nine-year construction programme incorporated in the National Roads Act 1974. The National Highways System was intended to link up (a) two or more State capital cities, (b) a State capital city and Canberra, (c) a State capital city and Darwin, (d) Brisbane and Cairns, and (e) Hobart and Burnie (the Act, in addition, made provision for financing 'major commercial roads' to foster trade and commerce between States and 'export roads' to develop trade with overseas countries). The inclusion of the Darwin-Mt Isa-Brisbane, Darwin-Alice Springs-Adelaide, and Darwin-Perth routes is justified in terms of their importance to trade and commerce, industrial development, tourism, and defence rather than on the strength of their existing interurban interactions. A Townsville-Cloncurry link is excluded because of the need to implement the plans for the National Highways System quickly.

An examination of the proposed links between the major urban centres reveals that in some locations they coincide with the existing alignment whereas in other areas there are different alternatives which require in-depth studies to choose the appropriate route. Where a route lies near an existing route extensive realignments will be necessary because the road will have to change its function from being a link connecting intermediate towns to that of a National Highway. Particular attention will have to be given to by-passing towns and limiting access as instanced by the Sydney-Goulburn and Albury-Melbourne sections of the Hume Corridor. There is the opportunity between Goulburn and Albury of following the general line of the existing Hume Highway or taking a more direct line closer to Canberra. A study of these alternatives by the Australian government is in progress but it is likely that it will favour the existing alignment between Goulburn and Albury because of the expense of constructing a National Highway through the more mountainous areas closer to Canberra.

Another contentious choice involves the location of

a route between Sydney and Brisbane. The longer, but slightly quicker, inland route was chosen at the expense of the coastal connection because it could be brought up to standard more economically ($100 million as opposed to $170 million), more speedily, and with fewer environmental difficulties. Already commercial truck traffic favours the inland route and it would be undesirable to divert it through tourist centres generating heavy local traffic.

Once the proposed National Highways System is completed it will serve about 75 per cent of the Australian population (9.5 million) and over 1500 towns. The intercity corridors proposed comprise 160 km of divided road, 10,620 km of single carriageways with a sealed surface and 5,000 km without a sealed surface. About 70 per cent of the total network will require construction or reconstruction. In 1972 the routes comprising the proposed National Highways System carried 6,440 million vehicle kms— 7 per cent of the Australian total. About 40 per cent of this travel originated and terminated in urban areas. It is anticipated that urban areas will derive benefits in proportion to their use (which is increasing faster than other areas). The combined total of direct benefits from savings in vehicle operating costs, accident costs, occupants travel time, and road maintenance (discounted at 10 per cent at 1971–2 present value) and indirect benefits from reductions in delays, production, and increased social travel, are expected to outweigh the $518 million costs by a ratio of 3.2:1 for the warranted and feasible programme of 8,885 km of completed roads and 1,335 km under construction between 1974 and 1979. As first priority in this programme the Hume Corridor will have a four-lane highway with provision for divided road where 4,000 AADT is exceeded and freeway standards where 8,000 AADT is surpassed. Other priorities are given to the Adelaide-Perth and Brisbane-Mt Isa links.

The implementation of the National Highways System will necessitate a revamping of the relations between the Australian government and the State governments as indicated in the National Roads Act 1974. In place of the practice of the State governments determining priorities for arterial roads and planning and locating, designing, constructing, and maintaining them in isolation, the Commonwealth Bureau of Roads recommended that the National Highways System should be planned, designed, operated, and maintained in accordance with standards set by the Australian government. The Australian government should also undertake the strategic planning of the proposed network with the State governments. As a means of ensuring that the State governments fulfil the Australian government's objectives the former should submit projects and annual works programmes on the National Highways through the Department of Transport. While these provisions provide the intergovernmental framework for the National Highways System it must be emphasized that the full potential of the proposed network does not hinge only on interurban movements. Also important is the traffic moving on and off the National Highways that originates and terminates in regions without a major urban area of over 40,000 population.

Interregional Transport Between States
As data on passenger flows derived from both the 2.2 million population of 466 towns with populations between 1,000 and 40,000 and 1.4 million population smaller settlements and on isolated farms in 1971 is sparse, the relative importance of interregional transport between States has to be derived from estimates of freight tonnages in 1971–2. These statistics indicate that less than 10 per cent of the interregional freight originates from capital city regions, almost 55 per cent is destined for capital city regions, and the remaining 36 per cent does not involve capital city regions. As the statistics include interstate movements between capital cities and major provincial centres (i.e. the core regions) they are not tailored to the needs of this study but suffice to show the break-up of the freight task associated with primary, secondary, and tertiary industries.

The Australian government has taken heed of these requirements in determining the location of the National Highways System (Fig. 22.6). As a result the National Highways System is intended to serve the intensive primary industries (dairying, sheep, and wheat) located on the eastern and southeastern seaboard and in southwestern Australia and the extensive pastoral areas in the Kimberleys and around Alice Springs. Among the dispersed mining areas the National Highways System would reach the Pilbara, Mt Isa, and the goldfields of Western Australia but not the coalfields of central Queensland and the Latrobe Valley in Victoria or the Bass Strait oil and gas deposits. Although manufacturing is heavily concentrated in the designated urban areas the National Highways System would also link minor industrial centres at Albury-Wodonga, Maitland, Bundaberg and coastal towns in Queensland, Port Pirie, Whyalla, Bell Bay and Burnie but not the Latrobe Valley, Lithgow, and Bathurst-Orange.

The Australian government's concern for rural development postdates its desire for the National Highways System because it had used its road grant powers to foster its decentralization objectives when it took over road funding powers that had hitherto been the sole concern of the State governments until 1923. After a minimum allocation of 5 per cent of all funds to Tasmania the remainder was disbursed according to a formula based on population (60 per cent) and area (40 per cent) (from 1959 population,

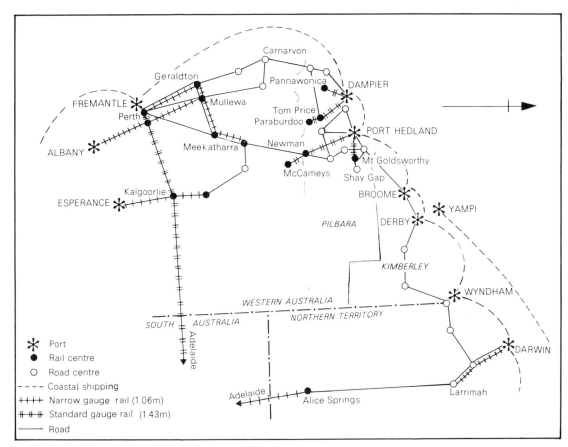

Fig. 22.7 A network diagram of Western Australia showing main transport routes, terminals and intersections.

area, and the number of motor vehicles were given equal weighting in deciding the balance). In keeping with the then Australian government's rural development intentions there was also a proviso in the Commonwealth Aid Roads Act 1959 that 40 per cent of the grant be set aside for non-arterial rural roads.

A new formula recommended by the Commonwealth Bureau of Roads as the basis of the Commonwealth Aid Roads Act 1969 tried to balance spending between urban and rural roads; in the end rural roads received 33 per cent. In 1973 the Commonwealth Bureau of Roads recommended the allocation of 43 per cent of funds to urban roads, 15 per cent to the National Highways System, while rural roads received 40 per cent with the remainder for minor improvements. The rural allocation was based on the assumption that anticipated losses in traffic due to a reorganization of primary industries would be more than offset by an increase in tourist and recreation travel and flows from developments in the mining industry and, in certain areas, the development of associated resource-based industries. The growth potential of the Pilbara

region in Western Australia is given special attention with Gladstone in Queensland and is now considered in more detail with other parts of northwest Australia.

Northwest Australia

With the rapid development of the iron ore extraction industry of the Pilbara the services provided by the multipurpose vessels of the West Australian State Shipping Service (WASSS) to the Pilbara and Kimberley regions north of the twenty-sixth parallel could not meet the demand for goods and services (Fig. 22.7). The shipping services were intended to meet the specific passenger and freight needs of remote and dispersed pastoral and mining communities. Once mining in the Pilbara was underway WASSS quickly lost passengers to the improved air services and general cargo to through road services and rail-road services using Geraldton and Meekatharra as rail heads (Table 22.13). These losses, coupled with rising costs of operation and a low rate of return on funds, made it increasingly difficult for WASSS to adjust to the new situation by replacing its ageing and inefficient fleet.

Table 22.13   Distribution of Freight Originating in Perth to Destinations in the Pilbara, Kimberley, and Darwin

Year	Ship per cent	Direct road per cent	Rail-road per cent	Air per cent	Total tonnage per cent	Total tonnage tonnes
Pilbara						
1968	47.8	27.2	24.1	0.9	100.0	157,800
1969	38.2	45.2	15.7	0.9	100.0	146,150
1970	29.5	50.4	19.5	0.6	100.0	254,000
1971	24.2	50.9	23.9	1.0	100.0	412,000
Through Pilbara to Kimberley and Darwin						
1968	95.9	2.3	1.2	0.7	100.0	87,200
1969	94.0	3.2	2.1	0.7	100.0	94,850
1970	95.4	3.2	0.5	0.9	100.0	94,300
1971	92.6	5.5	0.5	1.4	100.0	93,200

Source: Bureau of Transport Economics, 1973b.

As WASSS's proposals to re-equip with lighter-aboard-ships (LASH) (vessels designed to effect a rapid turnaround by discharging cargo in lighters with capacities of 100 tonnes) proved too costly to attract assistance from the Australian government a series of second-hand unit load ships were imported to replace the obsolete conventional ships. Their importation was allowed on the understanding with the Australian government that they would be replaced in turn by Australian-built vessels within five years of their arrival—a requirement to assist the Australian government's ailing shipbuilding industry. The need to determine the number, nature, and size of the replacement vessels prompted the then Department of Shipping and Transport (later amalgamated with the Department of Civil Aviation to form the Department of Transport) to direct the Bureau of Transport Economics (BTE) to undertake a study of the transport needs of northwest Australia in co-operation with the Western Australia Director-General of Transport (Bureau of Transport Economics, 1973b). When the study was partly completed the Western Australian government proposed a Pilbara Industrial Complex based on low cost power derived from natural gas. As a result the BTE's findings have been amended in *The Pilbara Study* commissioned by the Australian government Department of Northern Development and government of Western Australia Department of Industrial Development (1974).

In grappling with the problem of the cost of transporting freight from Perth and, to a limited extent, Adelaide to demand centres in the Pilbara and Kimberley regions the BTE did not confine itself to shipping but also examined rail and road transport and various options within these modes. As road transport could not be justified on freight traffic alone

and was well catered for by the proposed National Highways System attention was concentrated on the shipping and rail alternatives. Of the four types of ship examined—unit load, roll-on roll-off, hybrid container able to carry containers and unit loads, and LASH—the unit load vessel (6,000 deadweight tons*) offered the least cost alternative. The choice of ship, however, had to be set against five railway alternatives: (a) upgrading Mullewa-Meekatharra section of the Midland railway to carry heavier loads and re-railing section of the Midland railway only; (c) upgrading Northern railway to Geraldton and building a new standard-gauge line to Newman; (d) upgrading Northern line and building new standard-gauge link from Meekatharra to Newman; and (e) constructing standard-gauge line Perth-Geraldton-Meekatharra-Newman.

Assuming past capital investments are sunk and can be ignored, the BTE evaluated the shipping and rail alternatives (and sub-options based on variations in capacity and scheduling) in terms of the total discounted costs of the transport system (i.e. the costs to the community as a whole which omits all subsidies and taxes but includes all other costs allocatable to individual modes). The results indicate that under the present pattern of development a new standard-gauge link is no more expensive a way of meeting the Pilbara's needs than either unit load shipping or lower levels of rail development. Indeed, if the Pilbara Industrial Complex was proceeded with, the standard-gauge link would be an increasingly better prospect for

*The weight in tons avoirdupois (or 20 cwt) of the cargo, stores, fuel, etc. carried by a ship when down to her loading marks (Plimsoll Line). The deadweight tonnage of a ship is a good indicator of her cargo carrying capacity.

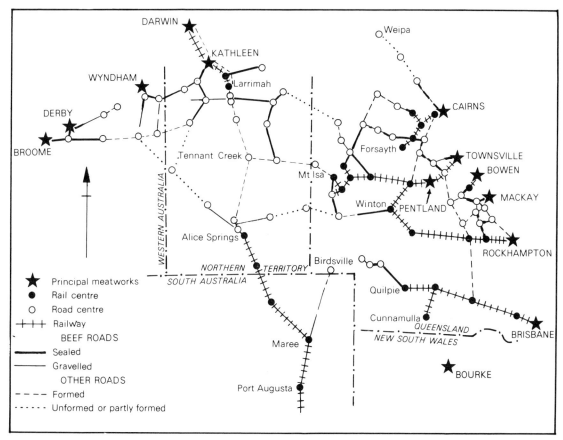

Fig. 22.8 The Beef Road network showing transport connections, terminals, intersections, and major meatworks.

carrying the anticipated higher tonnages—a decision that would be further enhanced if backloading accrued from the development of a petro-chemical complex and jumbo steel plant. The choice of a standard-gauge link would result in the phasing out of WASSS shipping services to the Pilbara but they would still be required as the most economical way of serving the Kimberley region and Darwin.

If the BTE's proposals for the northwest of Australia are implemented the psychological benefits from faster and more regular services are expected to outweigh those stemming from cost reduction. The conclusion suggests that alternative investment programmes have to be evaluated as much on the basis of service as cost. Indeed, there is no evidence that transport costs to the Pilbara are excessive and support for including such areas as the Pilbara in the National Highways System stems from not only considerable savings in vehicle operating costs but also from the reduction in an occupant's travel time and such indirect benefits arising from improved reliability, reduction of losses in production, less dust, and an increased number of social trips generated by the improved roads (Commonwealth Bureau of Roads, 1973, p. 79).

The Beef Roads Programme

The National Highways System is not the Australian government's sole policy thrust in using transport investment as a means of encouraging economic development because it provides periodic grants for assisting primary industry, mineral development and exploitation, and tourism. Among the current aid programmes for 'developmental' purposes are contributions for upgrading roads of 'strategic importance' (Eyre Highway in South Australia and Western Australia and the Barkly Highway in Queensland) and connections to Australian government properties such as lighthouses and defence establishments—the most notable contribution, however, is for the Beef Roads Programme which is worthy of special mention.

The Australian government's initial grants to the States for beef roads began with the allocation of $4.2 million under the States Grants (Encouragement of Meat Production) Act 1949–54 for roads to transport beef cattle to the Wyndham meatworks and rail heads in Queensland which achieved little (Fig. 22.8). Subsequent developmental programmes were more successful and the coincidence of the demand for poor quality cattle in the United States and a recession in Australia during 1961 prompted the inception of the major Beef Roads Programme outside the normal road grants legislation to stimulate the turn-off of more and better cattle (Johnson, 1971). Under the seven-year programme embodied in the States Grants (Beef Cattle Roads) Act 1968 grants for improving roads serving the beef cattle industry totalled $50 million of which almost four-fifths went to Queensland, almost one-fifth to Western Australia and the remainder to South Australia (Commonwealth Bureau of Roads, 1973, p. 96–7). The States concerned obtained their grants by submitting programmes for specific roads to the Minister for Northern Development for approval. They were allowed to augment the funds allocated from their own sources by $17 million to improve the roads above minimum standards. As a result of combined Australian government and State government efforts eighteen roads totalling 4,000 km have been improved in Queensland, three roads amounting to 2,100 km in Western Australia and a single road of 500 km in South Australia (Department of National Development, 1970). It is argued that the programme has benefited operations in all States in that stock is transported by road whereas previously it was transported on the hoof (Table 22.14).

The revolution in cattle transport has resulted in the cessation of the air beef scheme under which cattle were slaughtered on specific stations and air-freighted as frozen carcasses. Improvements under the Beef Roads Programme in Queensland have enabled the quick transfer of stock to take advantage of seasonal variations and to overcome localized drought conditions. However, all of these benefits should not be attributed entirely to the Beef Roads Programme because the change in cattle transport was associated with other factors including concurrent changes in truck technology. Indeed, when the first road under the Beef Roads Programme was completed almost four-fifths of the cattle were already travelling by road (Johnson, 1971).

In spite of the switch in the mode of transport the Beef Roads Programme has not been a success in terms of greater beef production and an anticipated greater contribution to export production. Kelly (1971, pp. 184–6) attributes this result to the ineffective occupancy of the cattle land and use of pastoral resources. The results are such that a strong case can be made on economic grounds for reducing the standard of roads, paying more attention to the structure of the road haulage industry, and even transferring funds to other parts of Australia where returns would be greater (Johnson, 1971). Yet, the Department of Northern Development has proposed a further grant of almost $63 million for the five-year period beginning in 1974 which involves sealing 966 km in Queensland and 483 km in Western Australia (the States Grants (Beef Cattle Roads) Act 1974 only allocated $39.7 million to beef roads in Queensland). As the proposals of the Department of Northern Development overlap the provisions of the National Roads Act 1974 the Commonwealth Bureau of Roads argued that future grants should come under their control particularly as some of the proposals have a lower than average benefit-cost ratio compared with roads in other parts of Australia. While there are benefits resulting from the reduction of stock losses *en route* to market due to the improvement of previously dusty or rough-surfaced roads the sealing of these existing roads will not increase production significantly. Where a beef road is in existence its condition is less of a barrier to production than the supply factors at the farm or the demand factors at the market. Indeed, substantial benefits by way of increased production can only accrue where there is a rising demand for the product in an area particularly suited to its production but which is retarded by inadequate transport. As opposed to the introduction of new roads in development areas the sealing of the existing beef roads has no special economic merit. Indeed, the sealing of beef road is no different in purpose from road improvements undertaken for developing tourism, coal mining, or the wood-chip industry. There is a strong argument that all such roads should be grouped in a special class of developmental roads to which the Australian government can accord a higher priority than would be possible on their traffic alone (Commonwealth Bureau of Roads, 1973, pp. 96–9).

The Australian government's grants to developmental roads do not exhaust its assistance to interregional transport between States because it is active in providing assistance to air and shipping companies serving the more remote parts of Australia. Aid has also been extended to interstate movements between the mainland and Tasmania—a State which

Table 22.14 Transport of Cattle in Northern Territory at Various Dates

Year	Hoof per cent	Road transport per cent
1956–7	96.7	3.3
1962–3	58.3	41.7
1965–6	25.9	74.1
1966–7	14.8	85.2

Source: Commonwealth Bureau of Roads, 1973, p. 97.

does not fit neatly into our interurban and interregional breakdown of interstate transport. However, irrespective of our schema Tasmania's transport problems are worthy of study in their own right and provide the prelude to considering the Australian government's intention of resuscitating the Inter-State Commission.

Tasmania's Transport Disabilities

Escalations in the freight rates on non-bulk goods to Tasmania prompted the Senate to resolve on 3 September 1970 that its Standing Committee on Primary and Secondary Industry enquire into the operation of the Australian National Line's (ANL) shipping services to and from the island State. In its subsequent Report on *Tasmanian Shipping Freights* (Commonwealth of Australia: Senate, 1970–1) the Committee concluded that the State suffered peculiar transport disabilities because of the absence of land links. It recommended that the BTE make a quantitative assessment of the extent of Tasmania's transport disabilities compared with other States (Bureau of Transport Economics, 1973c).

After confirming Tasmania's heavy dependence on reciprocal trade with the mainland and reliance on coastal shipping for moving 98 per cent of 5 million tonnes of freight and almost 20 per cent of 600,000 passengers involved in interstate flows in 1971–2 the BTE sought to assess the State's transport disabilities by making comparisons with hypothetical rail and road links between Melbourne-Devonport and Sydney-Hobart (Table 22.15). The results suggest for most classes of freight that a national cost disadvantage of 40 per cent on the cheapest mode (rail) occurs on the shorter Melbourne-Devonport route (428 km) but

only 20 per cent on the longer Sydney-Hobart route (1,167 km) on which coastal shipping fares better than road. Where very low density cargoes are involved the disadvantage between coastal shipping and rail, the cheapest mode, ranges from 132 per cent northbound to 152 per cent southbound on the shortest route to 159 per cent on both legs of the longer route. As Tasmania suffers no cost disadvantage in the shipment and receipt of bulk cargoes the critical question is whether the freight rates for non-bulk cargoes are high because of either the inherent disadvantages of shipping or inefficiencies and practices in the total distribution channel between consignor and consignee inflating the costs on which the rates are based—a contention that requires an examination of shipping services, ports, and freight forwarding activities.

An analysis of Tasmania's shipping services indicated that profits in the non-bulk trades had been declining through increased labour costs, the mix of vessels in operation, and ANL's involvement with passenger services. A total annual saving of $1 million could be achieved by transferring all passengers to interstate airlines and the introduction of more efficient cargo vessels would reduce operating costs by almost 10 per cent to $6.30 per tonne (but not freight rates as vessels were already operating at or near a loss position). Even so such savings could only be achieved by reducing the frequency of service—anathema to many shippers. However, the shipping line haul rate accounted for only 51 per cent of the total operating costs and other economies have to be sought in the ports as the balance was absorbed in terminal costs (21 per cent) and wharfage (28 per cent).

Evidence was adduced by the BTE of overinvestment

Table 22.15 Freight Forwarders Door-to-Door Costs per Tonne Melbourne-Devonport and Sydney-Hobart Using Coastal Shipping Line Haul and Hypothetical Road and Rail Links, September 1972

	Actual		National	
	Coastal shipping Northbound dollars	Southbound dollars	Road dollars	Rail dollars
1. Dense Cargo (1.10m³ to one tonne)				
Melbourne-Devonport	15.80	17.70	14.60	12.60
Sydney-Hobart	24.90	24.90	27.40	20.70
2. Low-Density Cargo (4m³ to one tonne)				
Melbourne-Devonport	37.30	41.50	15.10	15.10
Sydney-Hobart	63.80	63.80	28.70	23.30

Source: Bureau of Transport Economics, 1973c, Annex E.

Plate 22.2   Specially designed trucks are delivering wheat to silos at the Coolamon rail terminal in southwestern New South Wales. After storage in the silos the wheat is moved in bulk rail wagons to Sydney for export. The dovetailing of road and rail transport on this occasion emphasizes that the competing modes can in some circumstances be complementary. Such co-operation is facilitated by the use of automatic devices to transfer wheat from truck to silo and silo to bulk rail; these devices eliminate costly manhandling methods.

and underutilization of non-bulk facilities at the main Tasmanian ports—Hobart, Burnie, Devonport, and Bell Bay. As shipping companies offer the same freight rate to Burnie, Devonport, and Bell Bay in northern Tasmania there is no incentive for concentrating activities on two roll-on roll-off terminals rather than the five in use. As rationalization of ports could reduce some of the highest port charges in Australia the BTE reiterated the need for a central port authority that was expressed in a *Study of the Transport of Goods for Tasmania* commissioned by the Tasmanian government (Pak-Poy and Associates, 1971). The Pak-Poy Report also indicated that the minimum cost alternative for the total transport task (intrastate and interstate) was to have a central port at Bell Bay and an upgraded railway system—the savings of $65 million on a two-port system and $94 million on

the present four-port system between 1972–2000 were not sufficient to induce the Tasmanian government into any radical changes.

The multiplicity of ports coupled with the ANL's decision only to handle unitized freight has resulted in an unusually large number of freight forwarders offering inclusive door-to-door services between Tasmania and the mainland. Although many forwarders are represented in all ports they handle only small volumes which are invariably imbalanced. While shippers may benefit in reduced rates from the intense competition for northbound freight the BTE thought the further amalgamation of freight forwarders desirable. If amalgamation was associated with the rationalization of ports and the introduction of more efficient cargo vessels Tasmania's transport disabilities might be mitigated.

The upshot of the BTE Report was that the Australian government agreed to subsidize ANL's passenger operations. As the BTE Report could not give a definitive answer on the extent and causes of Tasmania's transport disabilities *vis-à-vis* mainland States the Australian government has established a Commission of Inquiry into Transport to and from Tasmania (under Mr Justice Nimmo) with the power to call witnesses. The Nimmo Inquiry's terms of reference not only include eliciting information on the nature and reasons for Tasmania's transport disabilities but also require it to gauge the effect of these difficulties on existing industries and the State's capacity to attract new industry and to ascertain whether improvements to shipping, port, and freight forwarding operations could reduce transport costs. The Nimmo Report, published in 1976, recommended the establishment of a central port authority, a transport assistance scheme to support interstate shipments to the mainland, and an investigation by the Australian National Line of the feasibility of shipping general cargo between Westernport Bay and Burnie.

The Inter-State Commission

Section 101 of the Australian Constitution makes provision for an Inter-State Commission.

> There shall be an Inter-State Commission, with such powers of adjudication and administration as the Parliament deems necessary for the execution and maintenance, within the Commonwealth, of the provisions of this Constitution relating to trade and commerce, and of all laws thereunder.

The need to revive the Inter-State Commission was outlined by the then Prime Minister (E. G. Whitlam) in his 1972 Policy Speech:

> The Inter-State Commission was intended [originally] to end the centralisation fostered by all the State Governments through their railway systems. It should now provide not only for the co-ordination of our six mainland railway systems and our major ports in the period before the Commonwealth, like other federal governments, inevitably takes responsibility for railways and ports; it is also the ideal instrument for co-ordinating our major roads and airlines and pipelines.

While all of these intentions have not been realized the Inter-State Commission Act 1975 (No. 109 of 1975) permits the Minister to direct the three-man body to investigate matters involving interstate trade and commerce (except for agreements in Section 3 of the Airlines Agreements Acts 1952–73 involving the 'Two-Airline Policy'). The Commission's powers specifically involve judging any undue and unreasonable, or unjust preference to a State or discrimination against a State through railways. In deciding what is reasonable and just (not what is efficient!) the

Commissioners have to pay due regard to the financial responsibilities incurred by any State in connection with the construction and maintenance of its railways. Saving certain railway rates necessary for the development of a State's territory the Commission's powers also extend to preferences and discriminations in interstate (and overseas) transport in general. It will be unlawful in respect to interstate (and overseas) transport to:

(a) give to any person, State, locality or class or kind of transport any preference or advantage;

(b) subject any particular person, State, locality, or class or kind of transport to any discrimination or disadvantage.

The implementation of the Inter-State Commission's powers for bringing about a reasonable and just transport system will have widespread repercussions on the generation of passenger and freight flows, the origin and destination of trips, the split between different modes of transport, and the particular route followed. In this way the Commission's powers for co-ordinating all forms of interstate (and overseas) transport links and terminals, regulating the conditions of carriage, and presumably for planning the provision of transport facilities could provide a mechanism for implementing the Australian (Whitlam) government's policies for urban and regional development and an instrument for matching the Australian government's legal and executive responsibility over transport more closely with its undoubted financial strength. Thus, the Inter-State Commission promises to alter radically Australia's spatial organization: its form and its processes.

ACKNOWLEDGEMENTS   Grateful thanks are due to members of the Bureau of Transport Economics, particularly Dr H. G. Quinlan, L. Gilmour, and D. Seiler; the Commonwealth Bureau of Roads, especially Dr D. Hensher and J. Stanley; the Department of Transport; the Transport Regulation Board, Victoria, and other State government departments. The opinions expressed are those of the author. Manlio Pancino, Cartographic Section, Department of Human Geography, Research School of Pacific Studies, Australian National University, Canberra, drew the accompanying maps.

REFERENCES

Australian Government Department of Northern Development and Government of Western Australia Department of Industrial Development (1974), *The Pilbara Study: Report on the Industrial Development of the Pilbara, June, 1974*, Australian Government Publishing Service, Canberra.

Australian Travel Research Conference (1975) *Survey of Australian Tourism, 1973–74*, Department of Tourism and Recreation, Canberra.

Black, J. A. (1974), 'Techniques of land use/transportation planning in Australian cities', *Transportation*, 3, 255–88.

Bureau of Transport Economics (1972), *Economic Evaluation of Capital Investment in Urban Public Transport*, Bureau of Transport Economics, Canberra.

——(1973a), *A Review of Public Transport Investment Proposals for Australian Capital Cities, 1973–74*, Australian Government Publishing Service, Canberra.

——(1973b), *Freight Transport to North West Australia 1975 to 1990*, Australian Government Publishing Service, Canberra.

——(1973c), *An Assessment of Tasmania's Interstate Transport Problems*, Australian Government Publishing Service, Canberra.

——(1974), *Consumer Preferences in Urban Rail Carriage Design*, Australian Government Publishing Service, Canberra.

——(1975), *Non-urban Passenger Transport Outlook*, Transport Outlook Conference, Department of Transport, Canberra.

Clark, N., Lee, J. A. and Ogden, K. W. (1974), 'The use of energy for personal mobility', *Transp. Res.*, 8, 399–408.

Commission of Inquiry into Transport to and from Tasmania (1976), *Report of the Commission of Inquiry into Transport to and from Tasmania*, Australian Government Publishing Service, Canberra.

Committee of Senior Representatives of Commonwealth and State Road Authorities (1974), *Report on a National Highways System*, Australian Government Publishing Service, Canberra.

Commonwealth of Australia: Senate (1970–1), *Standing Committee on Primary and Secondary Industry and Trade (Reference: Tasmanian Shipping Freights)*, *Official Hansard Report*, Government Printer, Canberra.

Commonwealth Bureau of Census and Statistics (1973), *Survey of Motor Vehicle Usage: Twelve Months Ended 30 September 1971 (Preliminary)*, Commonwealth Bureau of Census and Statistics [Australian Bureau of Statistics], Canberra.

Commonwealth Bureau of Roads (1973), *Report on Roads in Australia–1973*, Harris and Co., Melbourne.

——(1974), *Assessment of Freeway Plans: State Capital Cities—1974*, Commonwealth Bureau of Roads, Melbourne.

Department of National Development (1970), *Beef Roads: A Review of Progress—November 1970*, Australian Government Publishing Service, Canberra.

Department of Transport (1974), *Australian Transport 1973–74*, Australian Government Publishing Service, Canberra.

Gattorna, J. L. (1974), *The Role of Air Cargo in Australia's Domestic and International Distribution Systems*, Productivity Promotion Council of Australia, Melbourne.

Gilmour, P., Gattorna, J. L. and Oh, Y-L (1975), 'The subjective determinants of transportation mode selection: a multivariate approach', unpublished paper presented at 46th ANZAAS Conference, Canberra.

Halton, C. C. (1974), 'National transport planning', *Aust. Transport*, 16, 21–5.

Hensher, D. A. (1975), 'Incremental planning and uncertainty' in K. W. Ogden and S. K. Hicks (eds), *Goods Movement and Goods Vehicles in Urban Areas*, Occasional Paper No. 2, Commonwealth Bureau of Roads, Melbourne.

Johnson, J. K. (1971), 'Government influence on transport decision-making in the Northern Territory' in G. J. R. Linge and P. J. Rimmer (eds), *Government Influence and the Location of Economic Activity*, Department of Human Geography Publication HG/5, Research School of Pacific Studies, Australian National University, Canberra, pp. 359–74.

Kelly, J. H. (1971), *Beef in Northern Australia*, Australian National University Press, Canberra.

Kolsen, H. M. (1968), *The Economics and Control of Road-Rail Competition: A Critical Study of Theory and Practice in the United States of America, Great Britain and Australia*, Sydney University Press, Sydney.

——(1974), 'Efficiency and regulation in land transport', *Queensland Papers in Economic Policy*, 3, 1–23.

National Population Inquiry (1975), First Report [The Borrie Report], *Population and Australia: A Demographic Analysis and Projection*, 2 vols, Australian Government Publishing Service, Canberra.

Pak-Poy and Associates (1971), *Study of the Transport of Goods for Tasmania*, 5 vols, P.G. Pak-Poy and Associates, Adelaide.

Rimmer, P. J. (1970), *Freight Forwarding in Australia*, Department of Human Geography Publication HG/4, Research School of Pacific Studies, Australian National University, Canberra.

——(1974), 'The Australian freight transport industry: individual modes, regulation and future prospects' in Peter Gilmour (ed.), *Physical Distribution Management in Australia*, Cheshire, Melbourne, pp. 12–33.

Sawer, G. (1975), *The Australian Constitution*, Australian Government Publishing Service, Canberra.

South Australia, Department of Roads and Transport (1973), *The Operations of the South Australian Railways* [The Lees Report], Adelaide (typescript).

Sydney Area Transportation Study (1974a), *SATS: Volume 1 Base Year [1971] Data Report*, R. E. Millington Drafting Pty Ltd, Sydney.

——(1974b), *SATS: Volume 4—Freight Transport Systems*, R. E. Millington Drafting Pty Ltd, Sydney.

Taplin, J. H. E. (1974), 'Energy and transport in an island continent', *Transp. Res.*, 8, 259–76.

Taplin, J. H. E., Roger, M. B. and McMurtrie, J. M. (1974), 'Government regulation of freight transport in Australia' in Peter Gilmour (ed.), *Physical Distribution Management in Australia*, Cheshire, Melbourne, pp. 101–16.

Victoria, Legislative Assembly (1972), *Report of the Board of Inquiry into the Victorian Land Transport System* [The Bland Report], Government Printer, Melbourne.

Wengert, N. (1973), 'Political and administrative realities of regional transportation planning' in J. S. De Salvo (ed.), *Perspectives on Regional Transportation Planning*, D. C. Heath and Company, Lexington, pp. 379–430.

23 RECREATION

DAVID C. MERCER

One of the most attractive things about Australian life, to both Australians and foreigners, is its leisure potential. The image of eternal sun, sand surf and space figures largely not only in the motivation of immigrants from northern Europe, but in the conceptual bases in which Australians themselves organize their attitudes.
(Hallows, 1970, p. 86)

In a recent article the economist Lowdon Wingo (1973, p. 3) drew attention to the fact that 'there is a point in the course of economic development when public attention shifts away from the adequacy of private consumption toward more qualitative collective satisfactions'. In the post-war years all the affluent countries of the world have experienced a relative shift of governmental interest away from an almost exclusive concern with such basic issues as production, transportation, education, health and defence towards a whole array of problems which have come to be subsumed under the 'quality of life' label. Implicit in this changed emphasis is the notion that economic progress, as measured by such indices as GNP is not, by itself, necessarily synonymous with aggregate national 'happiness' or 'satisfaction'; and it is for this reason that most developed countries are now devoting considerable attention to the identification and measurement of what have been variously described as social 'trends', 'indicators' and 'accounts' or, alternatively, 'welfare values'. Ample leisure time on the one hand, and access to recreational opportunities on the other, are both essential components of that somewhat elusive concept known as 'quality of life', though Gabor (1972) has warned somewhat gloomily that without a considerable degree of preparatory education and planning the 'Age of Leisure' may well turn out to be the most serious problem facing contemporary civilization in the coming decades.

'Leisure' and 'recreation' are both somewhat vague and complex concepts. Simply stated, 'leisure' is *time* and 'recreation' is *activity*, but there is little consensus in the academic literature as to the precise definition of these terms. Certain activities such as eating, driving, reading or shopping, for example, can be either 'essential' or 'discretionary' in nature depending on the circumstances; and what is 'recreation' for one

individual may be 'work' for another. Moreover, the social scientist has to beware of his own value bias when defining his field of interest. Nash (1953, p. 89), for example, has produced a qualitative classification of leisure activities which ranks them along a scale from 'anti-social acts performed against society' to 'acts of creative participation'. Quite clearly, drug-taking, gambling and delinquency may well be defined by their practitioners as 'leisure acts' while others would certainly not view the same activities in this light (Caldwell, 1974). An additional problem concerns the *substitutable* nature of leisure behaviour. If the weather is adverse indoor activities are frequently substituted for outdoor activities; if the facilities for a particular recreational pursuit are not available, people substitute with alternative activities, and so forth.

It is somewhat difficult to isolate 'recreation' as a subject of interest entirely separate from other areas of physical, social or economic geography. In the human sphere, for example, recreation has close links with more general migration studies. Indeed, when travel is involved, recreation *itself* can be conceived of as a form of short-term migration. As early as 1954 Ullman made reference to the 'new frontier of comfort' opening up in the warmer climatic regions of the United States, and in more recent years Hall (1971) has drawn attention to the importance of amenity resources as strong attractors of industry at the national scale. Increasingly, for permanent residence, people and commerce are gravitating towards areas where the 'leisure environment' is a potentially satisfying one. This trend is particularly apparent among the retired section of the community who have always tended to seek out prime amenity areas but, as will be stressed later, this is also increasingly true of the younger suburban family. Similarly, as an area of academic interest, recreation is closely allied with conservation in its concern with such issues as ecological impact and the preservation of natural areas.

For the purposes of the present chapter 'recreation' will be defined almost exclusively in terms of those informal (non-sporting) outdoor recreational activities such as swimming, boating, sightseeing, camping, bush-walking and pleasure driving which take place

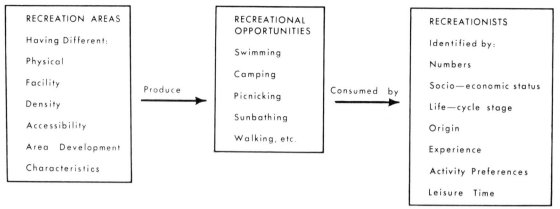

Fig. 23.1 Diagram illustrating production-consumption relationship between recreation areas and recreationists. After Hecock, 1966.

on areas of urban and rural public land and water, though some reference will also be made to commercial tourism and the rapidly growing phenomenon of second home ownership. The chapter is written largely from the perspective of the social scientist so that the main emphasis is on recreational *demand* rather than on the supply side of the equation.

COMPONENTS OF THE RECREATION SYSTEM

Recreation is best conceptualized as a *system* of interrelated elements. This view of recreation was first suggested in a seminal work on recreation planning produced by the National Advisory Council on Regional Recreation Planning in the United States, in 1959, but the ideas were extended by Perloff and Wingo in a paper published three years later in the same country. Their approach was not that of the systems analyst in that they merely sought to identify the main elements and their relationships; they made no attempt to quantify them. The authors described their approach as 'the logical exercise which must precede systems analysis' (Perloff and Wingo, 1962, p. 82). Briefly, they recognized three core elements: (i) *people*, more specifically, various recreation 'populations', overwhelmingly concentrated in the major metropolitan areas; (ii) the outdoor recreation *activities* in which they participate; and (iii) the *facilities* or opportunities available to them, and making the activities possible. Hecock (1966), too, recognized a similar triad of elements which he represented diagrammatically in terms of a production-consumption relationship (see Fig. 23.1). Viewed spatially, this system becomes a number of recreation areas, sites or regions (depending on the scale of enquiry) connected to population concentrations by a linking network of rail, road and air corridors. The value of such a conceptual framework is that, given

the necessary data inputs, it is possible to operationalize a recreational systems model at any scale ranging from that of the neighbourhood through to the national level (Wilkinson, 1973). An additional virtue of this approach is that it serves to underline the importance of *movement* in research in recreational geography. Wolfe, in particular, has argued convincingly that *mobility* (i.e. transportation, or travel) is the central component in the geography of recreation, and that it is only by focusing on this factor that one can hope to relate all the disparate elements into any sort of meaningful framework:

> Here are your people; there are your recreational resources; the two must be brought together; they must be linked by means of transportation. Thus transportation is central. By extension, the more deeply we study this single element, the more clearly are most of the other elements brought into focus, and the more precisely are their interrelations defined.
> (Wolfe, 1967, p. 10)

If we attempt to fit Australia into such a schema we get the following:

(i) *A hierarchy of urban nodes of varying sizes.* These are made up of heterogeneous populations with varying recreational 'needs' and abilities to satisfy these preferences. Such urban nodes are the centres which power the national recreational system. Thus, both within the major urban nodes, between them, and between the urban centres and their peripheral rural recreational hinterlands there is a constant ebbing and flowing of recreational pulses, or movements, with differing time dimensions and of varying orders of magnitude. Some are of very short duration, as in the case of visits to local neighbourhood parks or reserves; others are very much longer, as would be the example of an extended camping or caravanning vacation around Australia. These movements are measurable in terms of transport flows of various types and

Table 23.1 A Classification of Recreation Sites (after Burton, 1971)

Opportunity level	Time-distance constraint[a]	Available recreation time	Examples of facilities
Locality	½ mile 10 minutes	Very short periods Short periods	Children's play spaces
Neighbourhood	Up to 2 miles Up to 20 minutes	Short periods	Park Tennis courts Sports pitches
District	Up to 3 miles Up to 30 minutes	Short periods Half-day	Branch library Swimming pool Social centre

Town/city	Up to 4–5 miles
	Up to 30–45 min-
	   utes
		Short periods
		Half-day
			Major sports
			   centre
			Large commercial
			   facilities
			Cultural
			   facilities

Regional	Up to 25–30 miles
	About 1–1½
	   hours
		Half-day
		Full day
		Several days
			Outdoor water
			   areas
			Airfields
			Race tracks

National	None	Full day Several days Annual holiday	Resource-based facilities

[a]Time-distance constraint is a maximum figure in time or distance: which figure is operative will depend, of course, on mode of transport.

visitation rates at a wide range of natural and man-made recreational locations. It follows that these ebbing and flowing recreational pulses are constrained and patterned by the second major component of the spatial recreational system which is:

(ii) *The transport network*. Quite clearly, the recreationist can only reach recreational sites that have been made accessible by the building of rail, road, air or water transport facilities. Thus in large measure the location decisions made by transport engineers in relation to the siting or upgrading of routeways exert a very strong influence on the spatial pattern of manifest demand. New freeways, rail routes, airports or improved roads themselves induce an increased demand for recreation in certain areas rather than others.

(iii) The third component that needs to be considered is that of the recreation *sites* or *resources* themselves. In turning to this side of the recreational equation it is first necessary to make a clear distinction between *supply* and *opportunity*. In talking of 'supply' we usually mean all the recreational resources of a region, including private and public sites and facilities, regardless of whether for various reasons they are available to all sections of the public or not. However,

as Burton (1971, p. 243) has pointed out, in reality it is often more meaningful to give consideration 'to limitations placed upon the use of facilities by such factors as location, management and policy'. It generally makes more sense to talk of the recreational *opportunities* available rather than simply the total *supply*. Many sites (for example, roadless wilderness areas) although they undoubtedly exist as a part of the total supply of recreational resources in a State or region are unavailable to many people for physical, financial or other reasons. The following discussion is concerned with the classification of recreational re-resources in general, but the above distinction should be constantly borne in mind.

It is not easy to draw up a definitive list of recreation resources, for bearing in mind Zimmermann's (1964, p. 21) maxim that 'resources are not, they become', practically anything can be regarded as a recreation resource so long as it is perceived as such. To the rural-dwelling family large urban areas are often viewed in this light while the habitual urbanite frequently looks to the relative tranquillity of rural areas for his recreation. The resources may be ranged along a continuum according to the degree to which they are either 'natural' or 'man made'. At one end of the scale we have highly artificial playgrounds or resort centres that are almost totally divorced from the natural environment, and at the opposite extreme, primitive wilderness areas that are relatively unaltered by human interference. In general terms it can be stated that whether an unspoiled natural area becomes 'developed' or not depends very largely on the accessibility of the area in question relative to urban centres. As a rule, the more accessible is an area of land or water the higher is its economic value for uses other than public recreation, and the greater the likelihood that it will have been developed for commercial profit.

Burton (1971) has produced a useful classification of recreational opportunities in terms of the time-distances that separate the recreationist's home base from the 'facility'. His classification is reproduced in Table 23.1. At the lowest level of the hierarchy we find small neighbourhood play spaces, streets and (of particular significance in Australia), private back yards, at which scale probably a far greater proportion of an individual's total annual leisure-time is spent than at any other level of the recreational hierarchy (Halkett, 1974). Those opportunities occurring at the 'regional' scale are represented by the sites within the 25–30 mile day-trip hinterlands around our major metropolitan centres (Mercer, 1970) and at the 'national' level are to be found those more or less unique recreational areas which are located at some considerable distance from the homes of the majority of visitors.

This classification is of value in that it places the primary emphasis on the important accessibility factor, but it is far from perfect in that the classes are not discrete. Clearly, whereas the Gold Coast is at the 'national' opportunity level for sun-seeking Tasmanians it certainly is not for the permanent inhabitants of Surfers' Paradise. Conversely, whereas the mountains of southwest Tasmania have become a mecca for bushwalkers from all over Australia, for the fortunate Hobart hiker they are in the 'regional' opportunity class.

It is clear that a comprehensive discussion of the precise definition and classification of recreational land and water resources is immensely complicated and far beyond the scope of the present chapter. Let us now then focus in a more general way on the pattern of recreational supply in Australia.

THE PATTERN OF SUPPLY—A GENERALIZED PICTURE

Australia's population distribution pattern, consisting of a small number of large, separate, primarily coastal metropolitan centres, has been widely documented and discussed in the geographical literature. Using Coleman's (1969) nomenclature, in terms of land use characteristics we can broadly delineate approximately five concentric zones around each urban centre in the following manner: (i) townscape; (ii) urban fringe; (iii) farmscape; (iv) marginal fringe; and (v) wildscape.

The cities themselves—represented by the 'townscape' category—are singularly important recreational attractions, both for residents and interstate or overseas tourists. In 1973, for example, whereas Sydney received approximately 360,000 overseas tourists, only 20,000 such travellers visited the Barrier Reef (Australian Tourist Commission, 1974). All the major Australian urban centres have their 'recreational business districts', public parkland areas, coastal, river and/or lakeshore environments, together with a wide range of substitutable indoor recreational attractions. No precise inventory of either indoor or outdoor recreational facilities has yet been made for any major Australian metropolitan areas as a whole, though isolated studies have been made of individual local government areas such as Blacktown (Purcell and Thorne, n.d.). On the basis of a limited number of investigations it appears that, with the exception of many central-city and coastal suburbs, our metropolitan residential areas are very poorly provided with high quality public recreational sites (Mercer, 1974). Troy's comparative study of land use in eight diverse Melbourne and Sydney municipalities, for example, revealed that an average of only 7 per cent of the total land area of these districts was devoted to the whole spectrum of broadly defined cultural, entertainment and recreational uses (Troy, 1971, 1972). Early town plans such as those of Adelaide and Melbourne in particular made ample provision for public recreational areas, but as the urban centres expanded rapidly outwards less and less thought was given to planning for leisure. Perhaps because of this, but also because Australian homes traditionally have been richly endowed with indoor and outdoor living space, Australians became rather more strongly home-centered in their recreational interests than is the case with many other affluent societies (Lansbury, 1970). This trend undoubtedly has been more recently accentuated by a number of additional forces, notably, increasingly serious weekend and holiday traffic congestion and a steadily worsening pollution problem in near-city recreational coastal waters. In his studies of North American urban areas Wingo (1964, p. 135) has stressed that the 'recreation environment' is the new theme for contemporary urban family living, and has argued that 'the popularity of the low density suburban dwelling probably reflects the surging demands for more private forms of recreation among middle-class child-oriented families, suggesting that metropolitan scatteration is as much a recreation as a housing phenomenon'. This insight would appear to have

Table 23.2 National Park Areas Within 100 miles of Selected Australian Centres (after McMichael, 1971)

SYDNEY

National parks within 100 miles	170,775 hectares
Maximum visitor capacity	8,453,000
Present visitor numbers	3,625,618
Time before maximum capacity is reached	$7\frac{1}{2}$ years

BRISBANE

National parks within 100 miles	47,752 hectares
Maximum visitor capaicty	2,361,000
Present visitor numbers	968,050
Time before maximum capacity is reached	8 years

MELBOURNE

National parks within 100 miles	14,973 hectares
Maximum visitor capacity	745,000
Present visitor numbers	265,400 +
Time before maximum capacity is reached	9 years

PERTH

National parks within 100 miles	22,663 hectares
Maximum visitor capacity	1,126,000
Present visitor numbers	418,200
Time before maximum capacity is reached	$8\frac{3}{4}$ years

particular relevance in the Australian context where, for example, new housing projects in many of the major urban areas are being centred around parks, golf courses, lakes or marinas; or where those privileged individuals with the most discretionary income are choosing to live either in luxury high-rise apartments at the core of the urban recreational business district or in rural residential sanctuaries at the urban fringe.

Land use at the rural-urban fringe of Australian cities is characterized by a mix of residential, agricultural, industrial and recreational uses, interspersed with land which, for a variety of reasons, is vacant. In this zone recreational land use is often only a transitory phase which lasts until residential in-filling raises the land values to such a level that other more 'profitable' uses take over. Frequently, riding schools, temporary trotting tracks, mini-bike trails or picnic areas are located at the urban fringe for a number of years. The positive planning of green belts containing recreational areas that have permanent status has never enjoyed a great deal of success in Australia. Apart from a few small areas such as Churchill National Park on Melbourne's southeastern fringe the general picture is one of inexorable urban sprawl uninterrupted by areas of public open space of any order of magnitude. McMichael's (1971) comparison of national park acreages within 100 miles of four major Australian urban centres serves to underline

the relative paucity of this category of public recreational land use in the urban fringe and farmscape zones (Table 23.2). National parks are of course by no means the only type of reserve available for public recreation, but their size and spatial distribution is certainly a reflection of the general lack of recreational land that has been provided immediately inland of our major metropolitan areas. When it is recognized that a 'closed catchment' policy has always been the accepted credo among engineers in relation to Australian domestic water-supply reservoirs, and that the alienation of public land has long since been a feature of potentially prime near-city recreational areas such as the Dandenong Ranges or the Adelaide Hills, then it can be seen that Australian urban regions are rather poorly provided with usable public recreational space.

The only important exception to this general rule lies in the coastal belt. Since the early days of settlement, narrow public reserves were gazetted around most of the Australian coastline so that by comparison with many other countries the private ownership of stretches of coastline to high water mark is relatively uncommon. This, combined with the warm climate, the existence of ubiquitous prime beach resources, the coastal locations of the State capital cities, and the lack of substitutable inland water bodies, has resulted in the coast becoming by far the most important focus of a wide range of outdoor recreational activities.

At the scale of individual States the greatest propor-

Table 23.3 The Park and Reserve Position in Australia (at 30 June 1972) (after Fox, 1972)

State/ Territory	Type of park or reserve	No. of units	Area hectares	Percentage of State/ Territory (discrepen- cies due to rounding)
New South Wales	A 1 National and State parks	31	1,133,104	1.42
	2 Nature reserves	84	242,808	0.29
	3 Game reserves	2	2,440	0.00
	4 Flora reserves (on Crown land) (Forestry Act)	16	5,270	0.01
			1,383,622	1.73
	B Forest preserves	88	8,094	0.01
	D 1 Game reserve (private land)	20	121,404	0.16
	2 Wildlife refuges (private land)	299	1,214,045	1.59
Victoria	A National parks	24	202,352	0.90
	B 1 Wildlife reserves	35	53,014	0.23
	2 Areas set aside under S. 50 of Forestry Act	100	36,826	0.16
	C Sanctuaries on public land (except those in other categories already included)	70	42,491	0.19
Queensland	A National parks	284	1,011,700	0.60
	B 1 Fauna reserves	2	13 760	0.02
	2 Other fauna sanctuaries under sole control of the Dept of Primary Industry	3	8,903	0.01
	3 Fisheries habitat reserves	12	28,329	0.02
	C 1 Sanctuaries on public land (except in other categories)	94	260,223	0.15
	2 All islands	Not known	Not known	
	3 State forests	459	3,035,100	1.81
	D 1 Sanctuaries on private land	191	2,240,714	1.30
	2 Sanctuaries—Atherton Tablelands, Brisbane, Nambour-Gympie, Toowoomba districts (complex tenure)	4	2,357,049	1.32

Table 23.3 continued

State/ Territory	Type of park or reserve	No. of units	Area hectares	Percentage of State/ Territory (discrepencies due to rounding)
Western Australia	A 1 'A' reserves vested in National Parks Board of W.A.	Mixed tenure	1,379,939	0.55
	2 'A' reserves vested in Western Australia Wildlife Authority and Minister of Fisheries and Fauna	65	3,826,267	1.51
			5,206,206	2.06
	B 1 Other reserves vested in National Parks Board of W.A. Total number of areas controlled by National Parks Board	56	81,138	0.03
	2 Other reserves vested in Western Australia Wildlife Authority and Minister of Fisheries and Fauna	182	708,206	0.28
	C Other fauna sanctuaries (dual control with other bodies)	157	542,689	0.21
South Australia	A 1 National parks	8	177,667	0.18
	2 Conservation parks	126	3,370,589	3.42
	3 Recreation parks	15	2,531	
	4 Game reserves	6	13,473	0.01
			3,564,260	3.62
	B 1 Natural forest reserves	7	1,609	
	2 Aquatic reserves	6	1,754	
	C Sanctuaries on public land (except other categories)		123,023	0.12
	D Sanctuaries on private land Total number of sanctuaries	145	809,360	0.78

Table 23.3 continued

State/ Territory	Type of park or reserve		No. of units	Area hectares	Percentage of State/ Territory (discrepencies due to rounding)
Tasmania	A	State reserves	85	424,915	6.22
	C	Conservation areas on public land (including some minor private areas)	56	509,106	7.45
	D	Conservation area on private land (including some minor public areas)	18	5,265	0.08
Northern Territory	A 1	Reserves under control of N.T. Reserves Board	38	230,285	0.17
	2	Sanctuaries under control of Chief Inspector of Wildlife	2	3,944,431	2.93
				4,174,716	3.10
	C 1	Sanctuaries under control of Director of Wildlife	3	568,575	0.42
	2	Wildlife protected areas within Aboriginal reserves	14	27,922,920	20.65
	D	Wildlife protected areas on private land	5	15,590	0.01
Australian Capital Territory	B	Public parks and recreation reserves	3	14,175	5.84
Australia		TOTAL GROUP A		4,810,480	2.08

tion of reserved recreational land in terms of total area in all cases is found in the *marginal fringe* and *wildscape* land-use categories at some considerable distance from the major urban centres. Land in these areas has generally remained as Crown Land because it is either too dry, rugged or distant from major markets to warrant financial investment. Since the early days of settlement in the nineteenth century the speed of land clearing, alienation and settlement in southeastern Australia in particular has been spectacular, with only a very small proportion of the land area remaining as public parks or recreation reserves. Table 23.3 summarizes the park and reserve position in Australia as at June 1972, and demonstrates that only 2.08 per cent of the total land area of the country is in

reserves or national parks. There are some quite marked differences between States, with Tasmania and South Australia being rather better provided for than other States; but at the national scale Australia fares badly by comparison with countries such as New Zealand (7.62 per cent) or Canada (3.88 per cent). However, it should be pointed out that the proportion is constantly changing as new areas are added to the reserve system and as other areas are alienated from public use. In 1968 for example, only 1.1 per cent of Australia's land area was designated as reserved land. Since that time the situation has improved somewhat, but in 1967 the decision to flood Lake Pedder in a reserved part of southwest Tasmania demonstrated that the status of many reserved areas is by no means secure.

To summarize the current national park and reserve situation in Australia it can be said that it is improving slowly as land is purchased by the government in prime recreational and conservation areas, but there is still a great deal that needs to be done. Of the 1,000 or so parks and reserves in the country only a handful exceed 100,000 acres (40,468 hectares) in area, most are at a considerable distance from the homes of the vast majority of the population, while the parks most accessible to the major urban centres are frequently used to capacity or near-capacity and so are subject to major management problems. Australia is traditionally conceived of as a land of wide open spaces, but because of the peculiar nature of her climate and population distribution, the congestion problems on accessible inland and coastal recreational sites are as severe as in more densely populated countries such as Britain or the Netherlands. For the vast majority of the urbanized population the wide open spaces of the 'Outback' are of far less significance as a recreational resource than is the local beach, golf course or picnic ground.

RECREATIONAL DEMAND IN AUSTRALIA

The Forces Influencing Growth

At the aggregate national or regional level there are five important forces influencing participation rates in selected recreational activities—*population, economic growth, car ownership, education* and *leisure time*—though perhaps we should add to these the important factor of *opportunity*. Clearly, one cannot go swimming or boating unless a body of water is available making this activity possible. It is for this reason that recreational activities display marked regional variations in participation rates. Though we do not yet have the reliable participation statistics in Australia that are available in many other overseas countries it would appear likely that opportunity variations would result in there being, for example, far more skiers per head of population in Victoria than in Queensland and a greater proportion of skin-divers in the northern state.

With the exception of leisure time, which will be discussed below, these five factors (or their surrogates) have been graphed for the Australian situation in Fig. 23.2. Of the five, population increase is undoubtedly of the greatest significance, though in terms of importance this is followed closely by changes in the standard of living of the population. As already noted, although areally Australia is enormous, the high degree of *concentration* of the population in a few very large urban coastal centres means that recreational pressures are extremely localized. The country's population increased from approximately 4 million in 1900 to almost 13 million in 1970, at which time

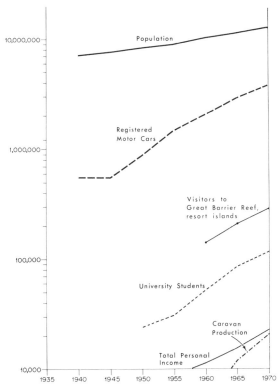

Fig. 23.2 Selected indicators of recreational demand in Australia, 1940–70. *Source*: Bureau of Census and Statistics.

some two-thirds of all Australians were resident in the two States of New South Wales and Victoria.

Currently, on average, Australia's population is young (almost a half being under the age of 21), potentially highly mobile, and affluent. As Table 23.4 shows, total personal income has been rising steadily in Australia over the past few years. If we compare average weekly earnings for each year between 1965 and 1970 with each preceding year we find that there has been a mean increase in earnings over this period of 6.8 per cent, while the average increase in consumer prices for this same period was only about 3.3 per cent. In other words, average incomes have increased slightly more than twice as fast as prices. In Victoria, for example, between 1957–8 and 1968–9 tax reports show that the number of individuals reporting over $8,000 actual income increased from 11,284 to 45,470. If we allow for inflation and compare the number of individual taxpayers earning $6,000 + in 1957–8 with those earning $8,000 + 1968–9 the figure is still more than double (i.e. an increase from 21,482 to 45,470). Moreover, the number of wives in the workforce is increasing steadily each year so that family incomes, on average, are currently showing a steady increase.

Table 23.4   Australia—Total Personal Income by States ($ m)

State	1965–6	1966–7	1967–8	1968–9	1969–70
New South Wales	6,051	6,783	7,106	7,988	8,884
Victoria	4,764	5,198	5,414	5,955	6,597
Queensland	2,091	2,305	2,408	2,683	2,873
South Australia	1,451	1,578	1,612	1,844	2,025
Western Australia	1,097	1,221	1,353	1,550	1,683
Tasmania	447	495	515	557	611
Total Australia	15,901	17,580	18,408	20,577	22,673

Source: Victorian Year Book, 1972.

It has often been stated that 'Australia is the most egalitarian of countries'. How true is this? Are there very great similarities in income between a wide range of different occupational groups, thereby perhaps giving rise to broadly similar recreational behaviour patterns?; or, contrary to the 'myth' does Australia in fact exhibit marked income variations between different groups? At the international scale Podder (1972) has recently presented tentative evidence that at least when compared with five other mature capitalist countries Australia has a remarkably equitable income distribution, similar, it appears, to that of Japan. However, on the basis of a very detailed survey of Melbourne heads of households conducted in 1967 Parsler (1970, 1971), in contrast, found a

> significant difference between blue collar and white collar income rates, total income medians and career income medians, as against the apparent near parity of the situation in Britain and America. These differences are not mitigated by wives' earnings or income from other sources. There is an almost complete dichotomy between these groups and the middle class group.

The major point of interest to arise out of his research is the very marked median income differential between manual and non-manual occupational groups in Australia—a situation which contrasts sharply with America and (to a lesser degree) with Britain.

Parsler's work was not concerned directly with leisure-time behaviour though he did seek to discover which aspects of life gave the survey respondents the greatest satisfaction. Interestingly, the majority of the respondents in all three groups ranked 'leisure-time recreational activities' third behind 'career or occupation' (first) and 'family relationships' (second); though in view of (i) the frequently documented growing integration of leisure and work among certain occupational groups in particular (Wilensky, 1960), and (ii) the fact that recreation is frequently a 'family' activity (West and Merriam, 1970), this ranking would seem to be of somewhat dubious value.

There are of course problems involved in using median income figures, as Parsler does, for there is inevitably a considerable degree of income overlap both within and between occupational groups. In his paper Podder focuses on the high degree of overlap in Australia; Parsler chooses to highlight the median differences. However, despite Parsler's emphasis, and even allowing for the fact that in 1965 there were at least half a million Australians living in poverty, it would appear that, in Podder's words, 'there is some empirical ground for the belief that Australia is the most egalitarian of countries' (p. 200). In terms of recreational behaviour we can hypothesize at the present stage that this results in only minimal qualitative differences between groups demonstrating varied leisure 'styles' in Australia:

> The rich man drives a bigger car and has a finer house than the ordinary fellow, but they spend their leisure in much the same way. They go to the same films, the same beaches ... (Mayer, 1964, p. 435)

Writing in 1969 McFarlane noted that Australia ranked seventh in the world on a standard of living scale. From the point of view of the present chapter this has two important tangible effects—home ownership and car ownership levels are both very high. In Britain, for example, from 1939–67 the rate of car ownership expansion was five times. In Australia the rate of increase for the shorter period 1946–70 was more than sevenfold. It is anticipated that on the basis of present trends Australia's 3.5 million cars will have trebled by the end of the century. Australia also has a high rate of home ownership. Up until the 1950s private dwellings—the norm being a detached 'cottage' type house with five rooms on a plot of 6,000–8,000 square feet—represented by far the most common type of dwelling constructed. Since that time apartment construction has boomed, but has served only locally to 'thicken' the net urban residential densities above the overall average of 4.5 houses, or approximately 16 persons per acre.

Table 23.5 Proportion of the Full-Time Labour Force Working 40 Hours or more per Week by Age

Age	Males					Females			
	% Working more than 40 hours a week	% Change 1964–70	% Working more than 49 hours a week	% Change 1964–70		% Working more than 40 hours a week	% Change 1964–70	% Working more than 49 hours a week	% Change 1964–70
15–19 years									
Nov. 1964	25.0	+4.8	12.2	+2.5		8.7	+33.3	*a*	—
,, 1970	26.2		12.5			11.6		1.7	
20–24 Years									
Nov. 1964	33.0	+19.1	16.4	+33.5		7.9	+94.9	*a*	—
,, 1970	39.3		21.9			15.4		4.1	
25–34 years									
Nov. 1964	41.6	+19.7	24.1	+28.2		18.3	+10.4	9.5	−3.2
,, 1970	49.6		30.9			20.2		9.2	
45–54 years									
Nov. 1964	40.4	+13.9	24.2	+16.1		24.4	+1.2	14.5	−2.1
,, 1970	46.0		28.1			24.7		14.2	
55 years and over									
Nov. 1964	36.5	+8.2	22.1	+5.9		20.6	+31.1	20.6	−29.7
,, 1970	39.5		23.4			27.0		14.5	
Total									
Nov. 1964	37.9	+17.7	21.8	+23.4		16.7	+14.4	7.8	+9.0
,, 1970	44.6		26.9			19.1		8.5	

a Less than 4,000 working in excess of 49 hours.
Source: Bureau of Census and Statistics, *The Labour Force*, 1964–8 and 1969–70.

And finally, in this section on the forces behind the current recreation 'explosion', we turn to the question of *time*. It is often stated that 'leisure time is increasing' and that this is one of the most important factors influencing the expanded demand for recreation. However, detailed national surveys of leisure-time usage in Great Britain in particular, have cast doubt on this generalization. Similarly, what little published information we do have concerning work/leisure-time allocation in Australia indicates that while average working hours have indeed declined in the last decade this has resulted very largely from the fact that there has been a great influx of females into the labour force working a much shorter average week. Table 23.5 demonstrates that if we analyse the trends in hours worked by the full-time labour force from 1964–71 we find (i) that average working hours have increased and that (ii) both the proportion and the absolute number of workers engaged for long hours have increased.

Thus there are few signs as yet that leisure time is on the increase. The time demands of family and work responsibilities and commuting mean that for many people, especially those in professional and managerial occupations, true 'leisure' does not come until retirement. The widespread ownership of the automobile has bestowed upon people a considerable degree of potential mobility but only rarely do they have the available time to realize this full potential. We will now examine in closer detail the recreational mobility patterns of Australians.

Table 23.6 Hotel and Motel Accommodation in Australia, June 1973 (after Edelmann and Grey, 1974)

State	No. of establishments	Rooms
New South Wales	1,245	31,855
Victoria	687	18,223
Queensland	731	15,030
Western Australia	510	11,201
South Australia	360	7,255
Tasmania	167	3,607
A.C.T.	40	2,042
Northern Territory	58	1,398
Total	3,798	90,571

Plate 23.1   Surfers Paradise, a popular holiday resort on Queensland's Gold Coast. Over the last few years this coastal strip has gained prominence as the most highly urbanized of Australia's coastal resorts.

Spatial Aspects

As pointed out earlier in the chapter, recreational behaviour can be viewed at a number of scales ranging from the local, through the regional to the national level. The scale at which the individual recreationist operates at any given moment depends very largely on time availability. Thus, theoretically, the retired person or vacationist with three or more weeks at his disposal can travel a far greater distance than the Australian with only a weekend to spare, though of course much will depend on the means of transport utilized.

At the present time in Australia research into short-term day and half-day recreational trips is far more advanced than is that relating to domestic tourism (defined as trips away from home for one or more nights). It is known that the family car accounts for some 80 per cent of all domestic tourist overnight trips made in Australia and that many of these terminate at camping grounds, friends' homes or privately owned second homes (Edelmann and Grey, 1974); but until the results of the Australian Tourist Commission's 1973/4 Domestic Tourism Survey are published, we have little or no reliable origin-destination or time expenditure data relating to the vacation patterns of Australians. However, certain information can be gleaned from alternative sources. Table 23.6, for example, lists the hotel and motel accommodation capacity for the different States for 1973. These figures can be taken as an approximate measure of domestic tourist demand, but should be treated with some caution. Many of the New South Wales and Victorian establishments are motels or hotels in Sydney and Melbourne catering mainly for business travellers or overseas rather than domestic tourists. In addition, the important accommodation capacity of flats, boarding houses, small premises and caravan parks is not included in this table. To take the Gold Coast as an example, whereas in 1972 there were 2,296 beds available for letting in hotels and motels, over 45,000 were available in alternative premises. Indeed, Queensland's Gold Coast is pre-eminent as the country's major commercial coastal resort region, its population increasing by over 100 per cent in the peak holiday months of January and December each year (see

Table 23.7 Permanent and Tourist Population, City of Gold Coast 1968 (after Edelmann and Grey, 1974)

Month	Estimated number of population	Population, per cent of June
January	135,000	225.0
February	68,000	113.3
March	72,000	120.0
April	85,000	141.7
May	85,000	141.7
June	60,000	100.0
July	60,000	100.0
August	88,000	146.7
September	82,000	136.7
October	68,000	113.3
November	68,000	113.3
December	120,000	200.0
Peak periods		
Easter	88,000	146.7
May school holidays	80,000	133.3
August school holidays	88,000	146.7
Christmas and New Year	160,000	266.6
Peak population	165,350	275.6

Table 23.7). The coastal and island resorts of Queensland are the main destinations of tourists on low cost airline package tours, of which 250,000 were sold on the domestic market in 1973. However, even though the air holiday market is increasing at a rate of 15–18 per cent each year it is still of much less significance than motorized transport in all the major resort regions. Fewer than half the 50,000 yearly visitors to Alice Springs each year, for example, arrive by air; and the ski resorts of the Australian Alps are reached almost exclusively by road.

In line with overseas trends the self-catering holiday with a flat, caravan or tent as the accommodation base appears to be increasingly popular with Australians. In 1972 it is estimated that there were some 1,400 caravan parks throughout the country and 150,000 registered caravans. These parks are located mainly in coastal Queensland, New South Wales and Victoria, and in the popular Snowy and Blue Mountain highland resort regions. Second homes are also an increasingly important component of the Australian resort scene. Statistics from the 1971 census reveal a total of at least 92,000 'holiday homes' of which almost two-thirds were located in New South Wales and Victoria. For a number of reasons inherent in the collection of this statistic this figure is probably well below the actual number of second homes in Australia, but it still represents an increase of almost 50 per cent over the 1966 figures. Robertson (1973) has suggested that

the actual number of second homes in the country is probably closer to 235,000, representing ownership by some 6 per cent of Australian households.

It is interesting to note that when detailed studies are carried out of the distances travelled to privately owned second homes and to camping grounds the pattern that emerges is one of fairly restricted mobility. Australian families on holiday, it would appear, generally seek to minimize travelling time and maximize the time spent 'on site'. Robertson's (1973) work on the south coast of New South Wales revealed that 36 per cent of second home owners in that area travelled for less than 100 miles from their permanent residence and 64 per cent for less than 200 miles. Similarly, research in the Melbourne region has found that 80 per cent of Victoria's holiday homes are located within 100 miles of Melbourne and that 75 per cent of summer holiday visitors at the largest coastal campground in the State travelled 50 miles or less to get to the site (Mercer, 1972). In short, the vacation hinterland around our major cities is not noticeably greater in extent than either the day- or weekend-trip hinterlands. This is an interesting finding for again it emphasizes the intense degree of concentration of recreational pressure around Australian cities. Day-trippers, weekend visitors and holidaymakers are all competing for the same favoured locations at the same time.

It was stated above that considerably more is known about the spatial aspects of short-term day and half-day recreational tripping in Australia than about longer-term vacations. Both household and site interview of short-term recreational journeys to peripheral inland and coastal destinations have now been undertaken by geographers in most of the major Australian urban centres and the comparative findings allow some generalizations to be made: the majority of recreational day-trips (i) are made on a Sunday; (ii) terminate well within a radius of 50 miles from the metropolitan centres; (iii) are strongly concentrated on a few truly 'recreational' highways (Fig. 23.3); and (iv) display a marked degree of directional bias, with people tending to take the highway exist which takes them most rapidly from the city into the countryside. It is also known that day-trip recreationists tend not to visit extra-metropolitan outdoor reserves very frequently and that at any given site there are always two major groups—first, those who spend a considerable length of time there relative to the travel time involved; and second, those for whom 'pleasure driving' is the main activity of the day.

Of these, perhaps the most interesting finding to emerge from the research so far concerns the limited mobility of the car-owning Australian household, at least in relation to day trips to extra-urban sites. Studies in both Melbourne (Mercer, 1973) and Armidale, N.S.W. (Ranken and Sinden, 1971) have

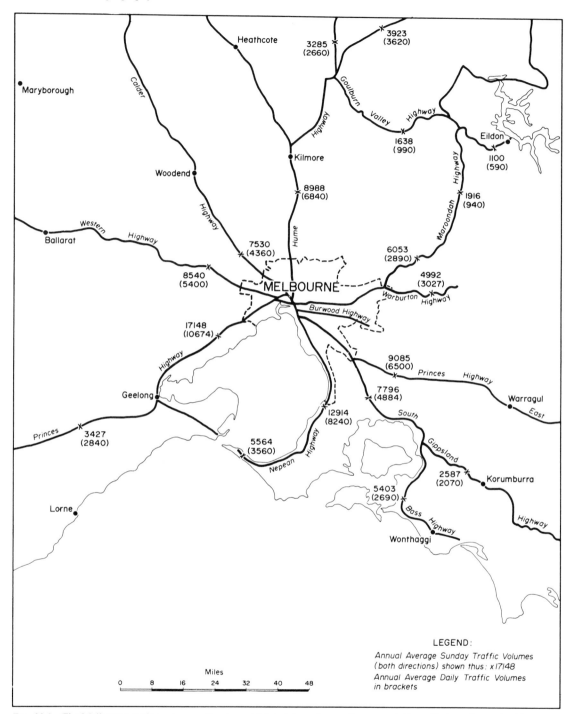

Fig. 23.3 The Melbourne region—average Sunday vehicle totals and annual average daily traffic in major outlet highways.
Source: Country Roads Board traffic volume counts for various years 1964–6.

found that by comparison with North Americans, in particular, Australians appear to spend a far greater proportion of their leisure time within metropolitan areas. It is interesting to speculate as to why this should be so. It could be because 'the home' is of far greater cultural and symbolic significance than it is in North America; or it could be that the small number and generally poor quality of accessible outdoor recreation sites in Australia act as a deterrent to greater participation. Alternatively, Australia simply may be representative of what Hendricks (1971) has described as a developing trend in the affluent world towards an urban orientation in leisure behaviour.

Activities

Activities are an important component of the recreation system, and they can be classified as broadly or as concisely as the researcher wishes for his particular project. Moreover, it has been stressed that one of the most important factors influencing participation in a specific range of recreational pursuits in a given region is the opportunity resource base of the area in question. It is for this reason that national statistics relating to recreational participation are of little value, for inevitably they mask considerable inter-regional variations. Accordingly, for the purposes of

this chapter, participation rates in a number of selected outdoor activities in Victoria will be examined initially in order to underline certain trends. These will then be compared with the findings from a New South Wales pilot household survey.

In the absence of any results from a national survey it is necessary to use alternative data to plot activity trends. Greig (1974) has done this for Victoria using certain indices such as club membership figures, licences, registrations and axle-counts. A modified version of his table appears as Table 23.8. Unfortunately the tabulation gives no indication of actual numbers of participants in the different activities, though it is known from a variety of sources that 'pleasure driving' is by far the most popular recreational pursuit in terms of annual activity occasions. This is finding which research around the world has consistently highlighted. The privately owned automobile is primarily a 'recreational' vehicle, and once one is owned the inducement to continually use it for leisure purposes is very strong. This being so, it is not surprising that the average annual growth rate in visits to national parks for Australia as a whole (approximately 11 per cent) should closely match the 'pleasure driving' growth trend in Table 23.8.

The participation trends are of interest for they

Table 23.8 Growth Trends in Selected Outdoor Activities in Victoria

Activity	Index of participation	Average annual growth (approx.)%	Period of recent popularity	Est. annual growth to 1980 (approx.) %
Trail-biking	Club membership Commercial sales	200	5	18
Jeep-driving	Club membership	137	5	14
Motor-boating	Registrations	24	20	10
Skiing	Club membership Equipment sales	20	20	12
Camping and caravanning	Imports, production and registration of equipment	14	20	11
Pleasure-driving	Sunday axle-counts on a major recreational highway (Maroondah)	13	50	10
Hunting	Licences Club membership	13	50	11
Hiking	Club membership	6	15	4
Fishing	Licences	−1	100	1.4

Source: adapted from Greig, 1974.

demonstrate that those activities enjoying only recent general popularity (such as trail-biking and jeep-driving) are those with the fastest rates of growth. In all the affluent countries of the world activities which provide a sense of exhilaration in a natural environmental setting, and which can be enjoyed in a group, are precisely those which are growing at the most rapid rate. Inevitably, the explosion in these pursuits is producing a whole host of management problems in coastal and inland reserves which various authorities are often ill-equipped to handle. However, it should be pointed out that *in total* such activities have not yet attracted (and almost certainly never will attract) the vast numbers involved in more passive recreational pursuits such as picnicking and pleasure driving.

Table 23.9 Relative Importance of Different Types of Recreation in Armidale, N.S.W. (after Ranken and Sinden, 1971)

Type	Man-days	Per cent
User-oriented		
Golf, bowls	12.2	6.3
Tennis	15.5	8.1
Roller skating	3.3	1.7
Swimming	34.3	17.8
Football and cricket	28.2	14.6
Polo	1.0	0.6
Horse racing	3.1	1.6
Indoor	10.0	5.2
Subtotal	107.6	55.9
Resource-oriented		
National park—day trip	3.7	1.9
—2 days +	0.2	0.1
Gorge country—day trip	8.7	4.5
—2 days +	1.0	0.6
Subtotal	13.6	7.1
Intermediate-type		
Camping and hiking—day trip	0.6	0.3
—2 days +	2.3	1.2
Fishing—day trip	1.3	0.7
—2 days +	4.6	2.4
Beach —day trip	0.4	0.2
—2 days +	25.9	13.4
Picnics, etc. within 20 miles[a]	36.3	18.8
Subtotal	71.4	37.0
Total	192.6	100.0

[a] Excludes resource-oriented locations.

Thus far, only one small pilot investigation has been carried out into the factors affecting outdoor recreation demand in Australia. This is a short paper by Ranken and Sinden (1971) reporting the results of a survey of 91 households in Armidale, a small inland university country town with a population of 17,000. The activity-participation results of Ranken and Sinden's investigation are broadly summarized in Table 23.9, and a brief discussion of their findings with regard to the factors affecting these participation rates concludes the present section on recreational demand.

As in North American studies, driving and picnicking together were the two most popular activities among the Armidale sample, though 56 per cent of total recreation time was spent in user-oriented sports and recreation within the city limits, compared with a figure of only 31.2 per cent for this in the United States. This fact prompted the authors to note that— '*ceteris paribus*, an Australian family exerts far less pressure on the environment outside the city limits than does its American counterpart' (p. 426).

Educational level was found to be particularly significant in accounting for variations in participation in resource-based recreation, and other important causal factors identified as being of relevance to the recreation planner were, in order of significance: (i) proportion of adults per family; (ii) average age of children; and (iii) age of household head. However, the authors warned of the danger of putting too much faith in oversimplified causal models and suggested 'that a different predictive model is required for different classes of recreation' (p. 425).

Ranken and Sinden's research is of value in that for the first time in Australia they attempted to uncover the most significant causal factors behind recreational demand in this country; but by the same token they were unable to specify to what degree their findings relating to participation rates were a function of the recreational opportunity base in the Armidale region. Moreover, it is a debatable question to what extent the findings of research in a small inland country town are of relevance to large metropolitan areas such as Sydney or Melbourne.

RECREATION AS A POLICY ISSUE

Even though we do not yet have a good data base relating to leisure participation in Australia, it is becoming increasingly clear to many planners and government officials alike that in both urban and rural areas the provision of sufficient recreational space is becoming a 'problem' requiring urgent consideration. Australia's population is increasing annually, and the average level of education and wealth is rising constantly. In line with these trends there is a growing level of environmental awareness in the community at large such that membership in conservation groups is now estimated to be in the vicinity of 100,000. This parallels a mounting recognition among Australians of the uniqueness of the indigenous landscape, flora and fauna. In a relatively short space of time 'quality of life', subsuming 'conservation' and 'recreation', has become a political issue in Australia. Thus in addressing a seminar held in Canberra in April 1974, the then Prime Minister E. G. Whitlam stressed that 'To an increasing degree Governments are expected to improve the intellectual, artistic, recreational and sporting opportunities of their people'. To this end the Federal government set up a Department of Tourism and Recreation, and all the States have followed with similar departments focusing on various recreation projects. In this, the final section of the chapter, attention will be focused on recreation as a policy issue for all levels of government.

While there is little argument with the principle that recreation, especially outdoor recreation, is in many senses a 'public good' like education, welfare or defence, there are considerable problems associated with the organization and administration of public leisure services; for 'recreation' is such a broad subject touching on such diverse areas as transportation, conservation, forestry, education, social welfare, town planning and the arts, to name but a few. Moreover, this difficulty is compounded by the complexity of governmental organization in Australia. Many students of Australian society have commented on the extreme level of bureaucratization of the governmental administration, a characteristic which Encel (1970, p. 160) has stated has arisen 'partly from the special problems of settlement in a large, remote, and inhospitable country, and partly from the deliberate use of bureaucratic institutions to satisfy the social demands of an egalitarian society'. This characteristic is particularly marked in the outdoor recreation sphere where it serves to militate severely against anything like an optimal allocation of recreational resources. Historically, in all States, as development proceeded in the nineteenth century, numerous government departments were set up to deal with specialist functions such as land administration, water supply, irrigation, forestry, national parks, soil conservation, and so on. In its demand for land and water outdoor recreation, in varying degrees, is of interest to all such public authorities and yet very few of them are adequately equipped with either the staff or the financial resources to cope with the multifarious problems that have been thrown up by the post-war explosion in the demand for recreation. Consequently, decisions as to the 'best' use of a particular piece of land invariably develop into power struggles between the large number of administrative forces involved and with the mass media and special interest groups

frequently adding an extra component to the conflict. Quite clearly, such an overbureaucratized decision-making framework is far from the ideal of a political environment within which relatively unbiased and rational planning decisions can be made.

Perhaps nowhere is the extremely fragmented character of recreational management more evident than in the control of development around Victoria's most important outdoor leisure resource—Port Phillip Bay. In 1966, through the Port Phillip Authority Act, the State government set up the Port Phillip Authority to preserve, co-ordinate and improve development around the bay. But in reality the Authority has no power at all, little finance, and hardly any staff. Its role is purely advisory and, if anything, it serves to perpetuate competition between the various public authorities concerned with the bay. Similarly, the important recreational resource of the Dandenong Ranges to the east of Melbourne is under the control of no less than twenty-eight different authorities.

The current local government framework in Australia is particularly inappropriate for recreation planning. At the present time local government officials have little choice other than to design and allocate recreational facilities almost exclusively for the population living in their municipality. But this planning approach often bears little or no relation to the realities of the people's recreational behaviour. Obviously people do not only make use of parks and other recreational facilities in their own local government district but travel widely throughout the urban area and beyond, especially if the quality of recreation service in their own residential area is poor. In view of the high degree of potential mobility afforded by the widespread ownership of the automobile it makes far more sense from the recreational planning viewpoint to forget any outdated and arbitrary distinctions between 'municipalities', or between 'rural' and 'urban' areas, and to define our planning regions so as to encompass both urban areas *and* the encircling rural recreational hinterland. We are dealing with an integrated recreational system of substitutable sites linked by a transport network. To quote Rodgers (1969, p. 373): 'There is now developing a hierarchy of open-space that transcends the urban-rural dichotomy, extending from neighbourhood open space to national park ... they are simply alternative offerings within the same system, and a mobile society will use them all indifferently'.

One specific aspect of recreation requiring urgent attention is the question of planning 'standards'. Currently, land-use planners in Australia are guided by outmoded 'ideal' open space standards relating population to open space that were originally formulated in Great Britain in the 1920s. As I have argued elsewhere (Mercer, 1974) there are a number of severe

Plate 23.2   Thredbo village, a ski resort in the Snowy Mountains, south of Canberra. Skiing is one of the most rapidly growing recreational activities in Australia at the present time and is posing severe planning problems in the alpine areas.

problems associated with the continued use of these planning guidelines, not the least of which is that they are based solely on intuitive judgement and have no basis whatsoever in solid research on recreational behaviour or 'needs'. Clearly, geographers in Australia could make a valuable contribution to policy formulation in this area by (i) intensively monitoring the use of facilities currently provided; (ii) attempting to model the various behaviour systems; and (iii) advising the policy-makers how changes in the provision of recreational areas and/or facilities would result in modified behaviour.

For decades the prevailing philosophy of government departments, industrial, agricultural, and land development interests in Australia has been geared unashamedly towards economic development and full employment at all cost. Inevitably this has exacted a considerable toll on the natural environment, with recreational and other conservation values only rarely being taken into account when decisions on the use of land or water are made. The speed of environmental degradation caused by man in Australia has been staggering and 'has given Australians the doubtful distinction of having eradicated more natural systems over a larger area and in a shorter time than any other people in history' (Routley and Routley, 1973, p. 233). The Lake Pedder controversy has already been mentioned above, but numerous other similar instances from around the country could be cited. At the time of writing it appears as though quarrying interests in southwestern Tasmania are likely to be given the go-ahead to push the wilderness frontier some thirty miles westward; sandmining and forest monoculture threaten the outstandingly beautiful natural resort of Fraser Island in Queensland; and in the Northern Territory the Kakadu National Park is menaced by uranium mining. Throughout Australia 'forestry' is defined almost exclusively in terms of commercial timber exploitation with only occasional token lip-service being paid to recreational or other amenity values. Similarly, for decades 'land developers', notably in the coastal areas of Queensland and New South Wales, have been subdividing large areas of land for second home resorts that are often badly sited and ill-planned.

Under a federal system of government such as is found in Australia, power over land development projects is vested almost exclusively in the States. Thus, technically, in terms of jurisdiction, apart from scattered defence installations, there are no strictly 'national' land, water, scenic or wildlife resources in Australia. Even though there are areas in all States designated as 'national' parks these are not in fact national parks under Federal control but State parks administered from the various State capitals. Inevitably, this makes for considerable differences between the States in terms of recreation and conservation policies. In some States—at the present time notably Queensland and Tasmania—the State governments assign public recreation a very low priority, whereas in other States there are some faint signs emerging that conservation and recreational values are increasingly being taken into account in land use decision-making. If the Lake Pedder issue represented a resounding defeat for conservation-minded wilderness-users throughout Australia, the Victorian State government resolution to abandon plans for the alienation of thousands of hectares of land for farming in the Little Desert in 1970 represented a major victory for the conservationist. By the same token recent 'land freeze' plans and government purchases of private land in important urban and near-city recreational areas in Victoria, New South Wales and South Australia demonstrate a heightened awareness of the significance of amenity recreational values.

However, while population and economic growth continue to be viewed as the main hallmarks of a nation's greatness, our cities will continue to devour land at a constant rate and cases of gross environmental spoilation will proliferate. In a high-powered growth economy the use of land for public recreation is regarded as wasteful and unprofitable in the same way that the dominant Protestant Ethic of advanced capitalistic societies regards work as a virtue and leisure a sin; and because status and prestige are highly valued, people are constantly encouraged to purchase two cars and two homes in a society in which large numbers of people are inadequately housed.

This chapter has been concerned very largely with the affluent segment of the Australian population. The emphasis throughout has been on those who participate in recreational pursuits rather than on those who do not. The primary focus has been on automobile travel, second homes, commercial resorts and national parks (which are only made accessible through automobile ownership). Yet it should not be forgotten that for large numbers of people in the Australian population these kinds of things are completely irrelevant either because they cannot afford them or because they have totally different leisure interests. The equally important subject of non-participation is yet to be tackled in depth.

REFERENCES

Australian Tourist Commission (1974), *Annual Report, 1973–1974*, Melbourne.

Burton, T. L. (1971), *Experiments in Recreation Research*, George Allen and Unwin, London.

Caldwell, G. (1974), 'The gambling Australian' in D. Edgar (ed.), *Social Change in Australia*, Cheshire, Melbourne, pp. 13–28.

Coleman, A. (1969), 'A geographical model for land use analysis', *Geography*, 54, 43–55.

Edelmann, K. and Grey, P. (1974), *Tourism in Australia*, Committee for Economic Development of Australia, Melbourne.

Encel, S. (1970), 'Class and status' in A. F. Davies and S. Encel (eds), *Australian Society: A Sociological Introduction*, Cheshire, Melbourne, pp. 149–79.

Fox, E. M. C. *et al.* (1972), *Wildlife Conservation*, Report from the House of Representatives Select Committee, Australian Government Publishing Service, Canberra.

Gabor, D. (1972), *Inventing the Future*, Pelican.

Greig, P. J. (1974), 'Recreation—how fast is it growing?', paper presented to the 7th Triennial Conference of the Institute of Foresters in Australia, Caloundra, Queensland, September (mimeo).

Halkett, I. (1974), 'An analysis of land use in the suburban residential block', paper presented at Institute of Australian Geographers Conference, Hobart, February.

Hall, J. (1971), 'Industry grows where the grass is greener', *New Soc.*, 4 February, 197–8.

Hallows, J. (1970), *The Dreamtime Society*, Collins, Melbourne.

Hecock, R. D. (1966), *Public Beach Recreation Opportunities and Patterns of Consumption on Cape Cod*, unpublished PhD dissertation, Clark University.

Hendricks, J. (1971), 'Leisure participation as influenced by urban residence patterns', *Soc. and Soc. Res.*, 55, 414–28.

Lansbury, R. (1970), 'The suburban community', *Aust. N. Z. J. Soc.*, 6, 131–8.

McFarlane, B. (1969), *Economic Policy in Australia*, Cheshire, Melbourne.

McMichael, D. F. (1971), 'Society's demand for open-air recreation, wilderness and scientific reference areas', *Proc. Seventh Conf. Inst. Foresters*, Thredbo.

Mayer, K. B. (1964), 'Social stratification in two egalitarian societies; Australia and the United States', *Soc. Res.*, 31, 435–65.

Mercer, D. C. (1970), 'Urban recreational hinterlands—a review and example', *Prof. Geogr.*, 12, 74–8.

——(1972), *Planning for Coastal Recreation*, Combined Universities Recreation Research Group, Monograph 1, Melbourne.

——(1973), *Aspects of the Geography of the Demand for Weekend Day-Trip Recreation in the Port Phillip Region*, unpublished PhD dissertation, Monash University, Melbourne.

——(1974), 'Planning for outdoor recreation in and near urban areas', *Vic. Resources*, 16, 24–8.

Nash, J. B. (1953), *Philosophy of Recreation and Leisure*, William C. Brown Co., Dubuque, Iowa.

National Advisory Council on Regional Recreation Planning (1959), *A User-Resource Recreation Planning Method*, Hidden Valley, Loomis, California.

Parsler, R. (1970), 'Some economic aspects of embourgeoisement in Australia', *Soc.*, 4, 165–79.

——(1971), 'Some social aspects of embourgeoisement in Australia', *Soc.*, 5, 95–111.

Perloff, H. S. and Wingo, L. Jr. (1962), 'Urban growth and the planning of outdoor recreation' in *Trends in American Living and Outdoor Recreation*, Study Report 22, Outdoor Recreation Resources Review Commission, Washington D.C., pp. 81–100.

Podder, N. (1972), 'Distribution of household income in Australia', *Econ. Record*, 48, 181–200.

Purcell, A. T. and Thorne, R. (n.d.), *Leisure Pastime and Facility Study: Blacktown Local Government Area*, Architectural Psychology Research Unit, University of Sydney, Sydney.

Ranken, R. L. and Sinden, J. A. (1971), 'Causal factors in the demand for outdoor recreation', *Econ. Record*, 47, 418–26.

Robertson, R. W. (1973), 'Modelling the second home decision process', paper presented at 45th ANZAAS Congress, Perth, August.

Rodgers, B. (1969), 'Leisure and recreation', *Urban Stud.*, 6, 368–83.

Routley, R. and Routley, V. (1973), *The Fight for the Forests*, Australian National University Press, Canberra.

Troy, P. N. (1971), *Environmental Quality in Four Sydney Suburban Areas*, Australian National University Press, Canberra.

——(1972), *Environmental Quality in Four Melbourne Suburbs*, Australian National University Press, Canberra.

Ullman, E. L. (1954), 'Amenities as a factor in regional growth', *Geogr. Rev.*, 44, 119–32.

West, P. C. and Merriam, L. C. (1970), 'Outdoor recreation and family cohesiveness: a research approach', *J. Leisure Res.*, 2, 251–9.

Wilensky, H. L. (1960), 'Work, careers and social integration', *Int. Soc. Sci. J.*, 12, 543–60.

Wilkinson, P. (1973), 'The use of models in predicting the consumption of outdoor recreation', *J. Leisure Res.* 5, 34–48.

Wingo, L. (1964), 'Recreation and urban development: a policy perspective', *Annals of Am. Acad. of Pol. and Soc. Sci.*, 352, 129–40.

——(1973), 'The quality of life', *Urban Stud.*, 10, 3–18.

Wolfe, R. I. (1967), 'The geography of outdoor recreation: a dynamic approach', *B. C. Geographical Series, No. 8, Occasional Papers in Geography*, Vancouver, pp. 7–12.

Zimmermann, E. W. (1964), *Introduction to World Resources*, Harper and Row, New York.

24 AUSTRALIA IN THE PACIFIC ISLANDS

R. GERARD WARD

As a geographic and economic system Australia extends far beyond its political or continental borders. Decisions made in company board rooms in Sydney or Melbourne, in the cabinet room in Canberra, in public service offices, and in family sitting rooms may all have direct impact on areas outside Australia. Nowhere is this more evident than in the Pacific Islands where Australian investment, Australian tariffs, aid and immigration policies, and Australian tourists are crucial elements in economic well-being, or the reverse, and agents of social change. It is beyond the scope of this volume to examine such extensions of Australia in all parts of the world, but this paper provides some examples from the area where Australia's impact is, relatively, the greatest. The Australian government is currently anxious to end its role as a colonial power. With Papua New Guinea obtaining independence late in 1975 the goal is virtually achieved politically but Australian economic colonialism remains as strong as ever in the Pacific Islands.

In world terms Australia is a small state, remote from the centres of international power and trade and, to a large extent, dependent upon those centres. Within Oceania the role is reversed for Australia is 'in population and also in area, a very large country in South Pacific terms' (Whitlam, 1974). As the demographic, economic and political giant of the area Australia dominates the trade of several island countries; has the power to provide the bulk of foreign aid in the region; can wave a relatively big political stick; and can be exposed to suspicion or hostility because of such roles. Leaving Papua New Guinea aside, all this may arise from a scale of economic and political activity of very limited significance to and within Australia as a whole. The imbalance in the relative importance to Australia and the Pacific Islands of the events and policies which shape their relations is an underlying theme of this chapter. Propinquity, increasing personal contact through tourism, and perhaps memories of the Pacific war, mean that a higher level of awareness of the Pacific micro-states exists within Australia than might otherwise be expected. Nevertheless, the popular view that Australia is a benevolent influence in the region may differ markedly from that held by Pacific politicians and people.

Australia's role in Papua New Guinea has been much more intense. Not only is the scale of activity much larger but for seven decades Australia exercised direct colonial rule, developed a high level of economic involvement, established bureaucratic structures modelled on her own, and allowed over 500,000 Papuans to hold *de jure*, though not *de facto*, Australian citizenship. Papua New Guinea is now Australia's closest foreign neighbour, recipient of Australia's major foreign aid effort, and the only country with which Australia has a border definition problem outstanding. This paper cannot examine all the ramifications of Australia's links with Pacific countries. It will concentrate on the Pacific Islands and will draw mainly on examples from Fiji and Papua New Guinea, the countries for which most data are available.

BEGINNINGS

Australia's first overseas commerce began in 1801 with the shipment of 31,000 pounds of salt pork from Tahiti to Sydney in H.M.S. *Porpoise* (Maude, 1959). Over the next three decades this trade brought a modest return to several Sydney merchants and 'was the enterprise in which ... [Australia's] first ships and her first crews were tested, and through which an enormous store of expertise on the Pacific Islands and their peoples came to be built up'. It 'enabled Australia to acquire at the start a supremacy in the Pacific Islands trade, and an interest, by no means merely economic, in the area, which she has never lost' (Maude, 1959, p. 82).

By the middle of the century, sandalwood, bêche-de-mer, pearls, and pearl shell had been added to the range of items sought by Sydney traders. The early sandalwood ventures to Fiji were sometimes made with the longer-term aim of finding a staple which could be sold in China in return for tea and silks which would realize high profits if sold in Sydney. Most attempts at this triangular trade failed as trade with China was reserved for the East India Company (Hainsworth, 1965). Later, the island trade was modestly profitable in its own right and played a role in the rise of several

543

Sydney merchant houses (Steven, 1965). As small groups of Europeans settled in the islands some served as agents for Australian merchants, and Sydney became the major source of their requirements.

These early activities had a limited role in overall Australian economic history, but in the islands their impact was often immense. The Tahitian end of the pork trade was monopolized by the Pomare dynasty which, through the power it brought them, 'was enabled to conquer the island and unite it for all time' (Maude, 1959, p. 82). Thus one feature of present-day relationships between Australia and the Pacific, the imbalance in relative impact, was established from the beginning. In Tahiti and elsewhere, trade goods replaced the products of native craftsmen, altered the labour demands of subsistence activities, helped modify value systems, and accelerated the socio-economic changes being brought about by the concurrent influence of beachcombers, missionaries, consuls, and other foreigners.

Several authors have described particular aspects of the early and mid-nineteenth century island trade and the details need not be repeated here (e.g. Cordier-Rossiaud, 1957; Hainsworth, 1965; Shineberg, 1966 and 1967; Ward, 1972). The labour trade, however, made a unique contribution to Australia's population and deserves specific mention. Between the early 1860s and 1904 over 61,000 Islanders, most from the Solomons and New Hebrides, were recruited for work on the cane plantations of Queensland. The peak year for recruitment was 1883 when more than 5,000 labourers arrived, including 1,269 from Papua New Guinea (Parnaby, 1964, p. 203). Two years previously Pacific Islanders formed 2.9 per cent of the censused population of Queensland but in the main cane areas the proportion was much higher—36 per cent in the Mackay district (Parnaby, 1964, pp. 125, 203).

The majority of Pacific Islanders were eventually repatriated though over 13,000 were recorded as dying in Queensland and, as death certificates were not compulsory for them before 1880, the number was undoubtedly higher (Parnaby, 1964, p. 146). Federation brought an end to recruitment with the passing of the 1901 Immigration Act, though restricted recruiting was permitted for a transition period until 1904. Under the Act all Pacific Islanders remaining in Australia at the end of 1906 were to be deported. Of more than 6,000 who were in Queensland at that time, the majority were sent back to the islands but 1,654 were granted permission to stay on the grounds of long residence, birth in Australia, or because deportation would have caused unusual hardship (Corris, 1973, p. 131). Those who remained in Australia formed the nucleus of the Australian South Sea Islanders community, leaders of which now estimate its size to be between 20,000 and 30,000. The 1966 census enumerated 1,781 'full-blood' and 553 'mixed-blood' 'Pacific Islanders' as having been born in Australia (unpublished 1966 census tabulation by courtesy of Dr C. A. Price). This certainly understates the number of Australians with some Pacific Island ancestry.

The Islanders made an important economic contribution to the Australian sugar industry. The impact of labour recruitment and repatriation in the islands was equally or more far-reaching. The increase in contact with the outside world brought greater exposure to new diseases ,goods, ideas, and weapons. Labour migration provided a means for the interior people of the larger islands to share the benefits, and costs, of contact. Despite the well-publicized occasions when deceit or force were used to obtain 'recruits', in general the labour trade 'required the substantial consent of all concerned' (Scarr, 1967, p. 139). Most recruits engaged willingly with the consent of their communities, and recognized that, despite the risks, the trade goods and experience they sought were more attractive than the prospect of remaining at home. On their return the labourers brought many changes. Corris sums up the impact by noting that 'returning labourers were in the van when representatives of European commerce and religion extended their activities to the Solomon Islands. They acted as catalysts upon their communities' (1973, p. 124). The Queensland connection was of value for many Islanders.

CONSOLIDATION

The ship-based trades of the earlier years were greatly reinforced in the last quarter of the nineteenth century by direct, large-scale investment in the islands by Australian companies. In Fiji small estate owners, many of them Australian, had turned to sugar after the market for cotton collapsed in the early 1870s. Most were under-capitalized and in the early 1880s the Colonial Sugar Refining Company (CSR) bought a number of the estates and established sugar mills. By the mid-1890s the company dominated the industry and after 1923 was the sole miller. Thereafter the company controlled the sale of the colony's major export, was landlord and production organizer for thousands of Indian tenant farmers and, in wielding its power, fully earned its nickname of 'the other government'.

In commerce the expansion of the Sydney firm, Burns Philp, paralleled that of the CSR. Robert Philp had traded and recruited in the New Hebrides and Solomons area before moving from Queensland to Sydney (Scarr, 1967; p. 149), and in the later 1880s the company expanded into copra plantations and shore-based trading. By the 1920s Burns Philp had become probably the main commercial firm in Western

Samoa, Fiji, Papua New Guinea, New Hebrides and the Solomons. By undertaking shipping, stevedoring, importing and agency work, wholesaling, and retailing, as well as copra production, Burns Philp brought a high degree of vertical integration to the Pacific at a relatively early date. A second firm, W. R. Carpenter, developed along similar lines with major interests in Papua New Guinea and Fiji. In the former German New Guinea, Carpenters took over the assets of the Neu-Guinea Compagnie after World War I and like Burns Philp expanded into transport, importing, planting and processing (Brookfield with Hart, 1971, pp. 250–1).

A third key firm in the establishment of Australian interests in the Pacific was the Pacific Islands Company, formed in 1898 as a successor to the guano and copra firm of John T. Arundel Ltd. London based, the company had strong informal links with officials of the Colonial Office through one of its directors, Lord Stanmore, formerly first substantive Governor of Fiji. One of its major shareholders was Sir Willian Lever whose company, Levers' Pacific Plantations Ltd, later took control of the Pacific Islands Company's concessions over some 200,000 acres in the Solomons, established extensive plantations, and developed close working relationships with Burns Philp (Brookfield, 1972, p. 41). In late 1899, a rock lying in the Pacific Islands Company's Sydney office was found to be phosphate. The sample had come from Nauru and prompt investigation there and on Ocean Island showed that high-grade phosphate was present in vast quantities on both islands (NID, 1944, p. 351). In 1902 the company was reorganized as the Pacific Phosphate Company and within a few years was engaged in extremely profitable mining and export of phosphate from both islands (Scarr, 1967, pp. 270–8). After World War I the Australian, New Zealand and United Kingdom governments bought the company's assets and established the British Phosphate Commission with the three countries holding shares of 42, 42 and 16 per cent respectively. The phosphate was to be shared in these proportions but the United Kingdom has normally taken less than its share and Australia more than half. For over sixty years much of the prosperity of Australian and New Zealand farming has been based on the cheap phosphate dug from these two islands. On the other hand, until very recently, the Nauruans and the Banabans of Ocean Island received extremely low returns from the sale of their land and the minerals below it.

Gold also attracted Australian prospectors and investors to the Pacific. Australian stockmen who went to New Caledonia in the 1860s prospected and found small gold deposits (Brookfield, 1972, p. 27) and in the late 1880s and 1890s several fields were opened in Papua, mostly by miners from north Queensland.

Like the early individual planters and traders these individual miners were followed by companies who could raise the capital necessary to exploit the more difficult gold sources. The two main goldfields of the Pacific, the Bulolo area of New Guinea and the Vatukoula area of Fiji, were opened in the mid-1920s and mid-1930s respectively and both became the preserve of predominantly Australian mining companies. Little gold is now mined in Papua New Guinea except as a profitable by-product of copper mining, and the Fiji industry has been supported by subsidies from the Fiji government for some years. But the companies which survived the processes of amalgamation and takeover in both countries followed an increasingly common pattern and used their Pacific profits for investment and diversification in Australia.

In addition to the major firms discussed above many smaller Australian companies, or individuals, set up business in the region. In years of depression at home larger numbers of Australians than usual trickled to the islands to establish plantations of coconuts, sugar or other export crops; to prospect for minerals; or to establish urban businesses. In New Guinea the former German-owned plantations and other property were expropriated and eventually passed into Australian hands. Not all attempts at investment prospered. The grandiose attempt in 1868 by the Melbourne-based Polynesia Company to obtain the freehold over 200,000 acres in Fiji, plus a banking monopoly for twenty-one years, exemption from taxes and duties, and other privileges, was one which failed (Derrick, 1946, pp. 178–83). A number of the ex-soldiers who took over expropriated estates in New Guinea, and their contemporaries elsewhere, were not able to survive the economic depression of the 1920s and 1930s and surrendered their holdings to the Australian banks or major trading companies. Nevertheless by World War II most of the Anglophone territories of the Pacific were firmly linked to Australia by ties of shipping, investment, commerce, and language. The use of Australian currency in the Gilbert and Ellice Islands, Nauru, Papua, New Guinea and the Solomons was a mark of the ties.

In political terms Australia's realm was more restricted, though Australians had often wished to extend it, sometimes fearing that if they did not unfriendly powers would step in. In 1883 Queensland attempted to take possession of part of what later became Papua but the British government disowned the act. In the following year the Australian colonies urged Britain to establish protectorates over the whole chain of Melanesian islands from New Ireland and the New Guinea mainland to the southern New Hebrides in order to 'secure them eventually for Australasia' (quoted by Scarr, 1967, p. 133). Only after Germany annexed northeast New Guinea in 1884 did Britain declare a protectorate over the southeast of the island. Not until 1906 was control over Papua, as it was then renamed, turned over to Australia. Some of Britain's reluctance to hand over imperial responsibilities to Australia (or, before federation, to individual Australian colonies) may have been due to the justifiable concern expressed in the Report of the Western Pacific Committee in 1883, that the Islanders' welfare might suffer as 'the employers of coloured labour in the north, the shipping interests of Sydney and Auckland, and the capitalists who have invested money in South Sea enterprises, must always exercise a powerful influence, which every Government would seek to propitiate and conciliate' (quoted in Scarr, 1967, p. 131). Nevertheless in the late 1890s some members of the Colonial Office were looking forward to the day when an Australian federation could take over the costs and the responsibilities of administration in the Solomons as well as in British New Guinea. Later it was partly due to urging from the new Commonwealth of Australia that Britain pressed on with the negotiations which led to the establishment of the Anglo-French Condominium in the New Hebrides in 1906 (Scarr, 1967, pp. 218–28). From Australia's viewpoint a condominium was at least better than outright French domination of the territory. Elsewhere the Australian empire was extended—Norfolk Island became an Australian Territory in 1914 and in the same year Australian military forces took over the German territories of New Guinea and Nauru. After the war both became League of Nations mandates administered by Australia.

With the partial exception of Papua, Australian interests were paramount in policy formation for the Australian administered territories until the prospect of independence arose from United Nations and other pressures in the late 1950s and 1960s. As the Western Pacific Committee had foreseen, Australian governments worked closely with, and for the benefit of, Australian companies. In the early 1900s in the New Hebrides, where Australia had no direct administrative role, Burns Philp acted semi-secretly as a 'cover and to conduct proceedings' on behalf of the Australian government (Scarr, 1967, p. 229). The extension of the Commonwealth Navigation Act to both Papua and New Guinea in 1921 ensured that for several years all imports and exports of the territories were transhipped at Sydney and in effect gave Burns Philp a monopoly of the Papua and New Guinea trade (Mair, 1970, pp. 116–17). On the other hand, the interests and political power of Australian sugar and banana growers ensured that the Australian market was closed to Fijian producers of these products and that New Guinea did not become a sugar producer. Naturally enough Australian interests took priority over those of its colonies where development was 'regarded largely as complementary to the economic development of Australia' (Hasluck, 1956, p. 22).

THE VIEW FROM AUSTRALIA

From Australia the Pacific is often viewed as something to cross on the way to somewhere else, with Nandi airport the modern equivalent of a nineteenth-century coaling station. The nation's main interests lie beyond the Pacific in North America, Japan and Europe. Yet strategic and economic questions are both influenced by the vastness of the ocean which stretches almost half-way round the world to the north and east of Sydney. Although Pacific Island markets are small, distance from other potential suppliers of their import needs, other than New Zealand, gives some advantage to Australian firms, although Baker (1974) has shown that in recent years the high costs of labour and cargo handling in Australian ships and ports have largely negated this advantage. Distance also provides a measure of insulation as well as isolation which, combined with the small size of most of the Pacific Island states, reduces their conflict-generating power. It is hard to imagine Western Samoa or the Gilbert Islands posing a threat to Australia's security, yet the Pacific campaigns of World War II ruthlessly demonstrated the importance to Australia of having the island screen of Melanesia in friendly and non-aggressive hands. Although the capabilities of modern weapons might appear to have reduced the significance of these islands to Australia's strategic interests, it is arguable whether this is in fact true. The importance of the deep water passages through the Indonesian and Melanesian chains has been increased by the greater draught of modern bulk carriers and the limited capacity of the Straits of Malacca. At the same time the growth of trade with Japan has accentuated the relative importance of western Pacific waters for Australia. The maintenance of good relations with the countries of the island screen must be a goal of Australian governments and one factor underlying Australia's aid and foreign policies. The United States bases in Guam and the Carolines still provide a nuclear capacity screen, perhaps of uncertain dependability from Australia's viewpoint, but the rest of the Pacific Islands area remains something of a military vacuum. This is probably an advantage for the island microstates, sparing them the burden of defence spending, but it is understandable if some Australians feel uneasy in this situation.

Australia has no direct military involvement in any of the Pacific Island countries except Papua New Guinea where Australian officers and technical personnel still serve with the Papua New Guinea defence forces. What the role of these men would be if the forces were used to maintain internal order within that country is an interesting problem and one which has

Table 24.1 Australian Imports and Exports, Year Ending 30 June 1973

Imports/Exports from to	Imports		Exports	
	$'000	% of total Australian imports	$'000	% of total Australian exports
Papua New Guinea	24,595	0.60	134,697	2.17
Fiji	4,998	0.12	40,216	0.64
Nauru	12,131	0.29	4,671	0.08
Gilbert & Ellice	3,355	0.08	3,261	0.05
New Caledonia	699	0.02	19,490	0.31
Solomon Islands	313	0.01	5,195	0.08
New Hebrides	117	—	7,503	0.12
Tonga	180	—	1,451	0.02
American Samoa	260	—	1,368	0.02
Western Samoa	23	—	2,706	0.04
French Polynesia	28	—	3,552	0.06
Cook Islands	—	—	87	—
Niue and Tokelau	a	a	8	—
Wallis and Futuna	a	a	140	—

[a] Not separately recorded.

Source: Commonwealth Bureau of Census and Statistics, *Overseas Trade Statistics*, Australian Government Publishing Service, Canberra.

not been answered, at least publicly. Through its financial and technical aid Australia will continue to have some role in military affairs in Papua New Guinea for some time but throughout the region Australia's strategic interest in keeping communication routes open is likely to be pursued through non-military channels.

Australia's economic interests in the Pacific are small when examined from a national viewpoint. In 1973 slightly over 1 per cent of Australia's imports came from the Pacific Islands while only 3.6 per cent of exports went to them (Table 24.1). These figures include trade with Papua New Guinea which is Australia's fifth largest export market, although in recent years it has never taken more than 4 per cent of total exports and the proportion has been falling. It is clear that in gross terms the Pacific trade is of very little significance to Australia. With the exception of phosphate imports, Australia might end all its Pacific Island trade tomorrow and not suffer any serious consequences at the national level. Individually, and sometimes collectively, the Pacific Island markets are too small to influence the production or design strategies of Australian manufacturers. As a result of rising costs of importing fuels, Fiji has recently restricted car imports to vehicles of under 2,000 cc capacity. This greatly restricts the Fiji market for Australian-made cars but the Australian automobile industry is unlikely to be very concerned. Several of the manufacturers had already abandoned the New

Caledonian and New Hebridean market by ceasing to manufacture left-hand drive vehicles presumably because the small numbers which could be sold in this and similar export markets made production uneconomic or insufficiently profitable. On the other hand, the abolition in 1974 of import quotas and the reduction or abolition of duties on a wide range of goods which the Pacific countries might conceivably export to Australia, is unlikely to have much impact on Australian producers. The Pacific countries do not have, and are unlikely to have, the capacity to export in large enough quantities to harm Australian competitors. It is notable that bananas and sugar are not included in the new concessions (PIM, March 1974, p. 93).

The only product for which the Pacific Islands provide a significant proportion of Australia's export market is flour which itself accounted for only 0.2 per cent of Australia's total exports in the year to 30 June 1973. In this year over one-third of the flour exported went to the Pacific Islands, principally to Papua New Guinea and Fiji. The remainder of the exports to the islands consists of small quantities of a very wide variety of manufactured goods and foodstuffs. In many respects the mix and quantities are akin to those entering a major suburban shopping centre near Sydney. The similarity is not surprising given the orientation of marketing in several of the island countries towards the expatriate, largely Australian, urban communities.

Although the Pacific Islands trade represents a very small segment of Australia's overseas trade, it is a very favourable segment with value of exports greatly exceeding that of imports. In the year 1972/3 the ratio was 4.8:1. The only island countries with which Australia had an unfavourable trade balance were Nauru and the Gilbert and Ellice Islands. In these cases the value of imported phosphate exceeded that of exports. Although small in absolute terms, the island trade is obviously the life-blood of a number of Australian companies whose continued well-being is desirable for Australia in view of their diverse interests within Australia. A large proportion of the trade between Australia and the Pacific countries represents intra-firm movement within the major companies such as Burns Philp, Carpenters, Steamships Trading Company, and their subsidiaries. These and similar firms benefit from their relative monopoly over most steps in Pacific Island commerce and from the possibility of bulk purchasing which arises from aggregation of the individually small markets which Pacific-wide operations allow. As a result 'prices charged in the stores operated by the major trading companies in the main urban centres [of Fiji] are as low—if not lower—than those charged elsewhere by other firms' (M. Ward, 1971, p. 160). Thus it can be argued that the island countries benefit from the scale economies achieved by the integrated multinational operations of the Australian firms, and which local companies could not reach.

Most Pacific Island countries are short of capital, entrepreneurial experience, and technical expertise. The Fiji government is quite typical in believing that 'foreign private investment ... is essential ... to expand the economy at a sufficient rate to maintain and increase the standard of living' (M. Ward, 1971, p. 278). Through their extensive investments in the region, Australian firms have certainly moved to fill these apparent deficiencies. Companies in which more than 50 per cent of share capital was held in Australia accounted for 76 per cent of the paid up share capital of companies in Fiji in 1970 (Annear, 1973, p. 43). A survey of investment by the Fiji Bureau of Statistics also showed that in the same year 37 per cent of the capital inflow into Fiji came from Australia, although of this 'inflow' 73 per cent was reinvestment of profits earned in Fiji. An Australian Joint Intelligence Organization survey in 1973 is reported to show that in 1973 'almost two-thirds of the developed sector of Papua New Guinea's economy was controlled by Australians' (Wolfers, 1975, p. 18). In 1969–70 93 per cent of the inflow of new private investment came from Australia (Bureau of Statistics, 1975, p. 107–8). Most of these investments are profitable and Australian investment in Fiji and Papua New Guinea (outside the mining sector) appears to have reached such a level

that, overall, expansion is being financed by locally earned profits or loans raised within these countries to a greater extent than by transfers from Australia. The 1970 survey showed that in that year profits remitted from Fiji created a net outflow to Australia. This benefit to Australia in terms of the annual flow of funds is extremely favourable and appears likely to continue given statements by the governments of both Fiji and Papua New Guinea that they do not intend to restrict the rights of overseas firms to repatriate profits.

The Pacific Islands offer many attractions for potential investors. In all the Anglophone Pacific countries wage and company tax rates are considerably lower than those in Australia and special concessions for foreign investors are offered in several countries. In Fiji these include tax holidays, import duty concessions, special depreciation allowances and, in the case of hotel investment, grants towards construction costs (Annear, 1973, p. 48). It has been reported that the largest hotel in Fiji, partly Australian-owned, had not paid any tax in ten years of operation because of concessions allowed under the Hotels Aid Ordinance (Annear, 1973, p. 48). What proportion of the profits of Australian companies operating both in the Pacific and Australia actually stem from their Pacific activities is almost impossible to determine from published material. One report states that of W. R. Carpenters Holdings Ltd's net profit of $7 million in 1972, $4.2 million came from operations in the Pacific Islands. Profits for the three years 1970–2 were reported to have totalled $19,827,000 against a total ordinary capital of $18 million (quoted in Rokotuivuna *et al.*, 1973, p. 56). Although the details may not be clear it is evident that Australian companies have found the Pacific Islands an extremely profitable field of operation for many years. The proportion of profits reinvested in the islands has, in the official view of most governments, brought substantial benefits to the islands, while the large amounts which have been remitted to Australia as dividends or undistributed profits have allowed the companies to expand and diversify in their home country.

Unfortunately there are insufficient statistics with which to measure the beneficial effects of Australian investment and other involvement in the island countries. Furthermore, whether the effects are beneficial or otherwise is not a clear-cut factual matter but depends on the particular view of development which a country, or individual, espouses. Development goals are undergoing drastic reconsideration in many countries and it may be that in some Pacific countries investments which are now considered benefits may later be considered liabilities. Meanwhile, it is possible for Fiji and Papua New Guinea, the two Pacific countries for which the best data are available, to give a somewhat better impression of what the present level of Australian investment means.

The monetary sector in Papua New Guinea is overwhelmingly dominated by foreigners and foreign-owned companies. Most of the overseas investment is Australian and in 1971 65 per cent of the foreign-born population were born in Australia (Bureau of Statistics, n.d., p.5). Many others hold Australian nationality. Thus, with some margin of error, total figures for expatriate activities give some indication of the importance of Australian interests. Non-indigenes comprised 2.2 per cent of the country's population in 1971 (Bureau of Statistics, n.d., p. 5) yet they held 41 per cent of total savings bank balances in 1973, owned 80 per cent of the vehicles registered in individual names in 1972, and in 1973, not long before self-government, held 91 per cent of the first and 59 per cent of the second division posts in the the public service (Bureau of Statistics, 1975, pp. 31, 89, 103). In 1971 the estimated weekly earnings of non-indigenes averaged $110.10 compared with $10.60 for Papua New Guineans (Interdepartmental Committee, 1974, p. 44). At these rates the 17 per cent of the wage and salary earners who were non-indigenes collected 64 per cent of the total amount paid in wages and salaries. Of the export crops produced in 1970–1, 63 per cent of the copra, 69 per cent of the cacao, 28 per cent of the coffee, 81 per cent of the tea, and 99 per cent of the rubber came from non-indigenous holdings (Bureau of Statistics, 1975, p. 53). In the retail trade, in which Burns Philp, Carpenters, and Steamships are the largest concerns, 95 per cent of sales in 1970–1 were made through foreign-owned outlets (Central Planning Office, 1973, p. 95). In other sectors such as mining, engineering, building and construction, transport, and finance, the monopoly of Australian firms is almost total. Since 1973 the establishment of a national airline (in which Australian equity is 16 per cent), the Papua New Guinea Banking Corporation, and other semi-government instrumentalities, has increased the indigenous share slightly through public ownership. Nevertheless the only non-government sector which indigenes dominate is subsistence agriculture and if the products of Australian investment were to disappear no viable 'modern sector' would remain.

Australia's penetration of the Fiji economy is not as complete as in Papua New Guinea, especially since 1973 when it was necessary for the Fiji government to buy the CSR subsidiary, South Pacific Sugar Mills (SPSM) for $10,117,000 in order to keep the industry going. In 1970, following an inquiry into the industry, Lord Denning recommended that the agreement between millers and growers be revised to give higher returns and reduced risks to the latter. He suggested that company profits had been too high compared with those of the growers but argued that his new proposals would still allow the company to pay its usual dividend, cover replacements, and maintain reserves (Denning, 1970). The company disputed this and announced that it would withdraw from the industry in 1973. Prior to their withdrawal the company had employed one-third of the labour in Fiji's secondary industry and controlled the purchase, processing and export of the output of 39 per cent of those engaged in non-subsistence agriculture (Zwart, 1968, p. 196). Over more than ninety years the CSR had virtually created and controlled the economic landscape of western Viti Levu and part of Vanua Levu.

Perhaps the clearest illustration of the ramifications of Australian interest in Fiji is provided by Burns Philp and Carpenters who, with their subsidiaries, employ nearly 10 per cent of the workforce according to one report (Rokotuivuna *et al.*, 1973, p. 49). Both firms began as shippers, importers, and store operators but today their interests, which often merge through joint shareholding in subsidiaries, extend to insurance, real estate, advertising, plantations, pastoral farming, quarrying, food processing, steel working, electrical and mechanical engineering, automobile sales and service, tyre retreading, glazing, electroplating, hotels, tours, car hire, construction, brewing and the manufacture of cement, concrete products, coconut oil and paint. The list is incomplete.

Besides these two companies, Australian banks are prominent, the principal daily newspaper is owned by Pacific Publications Ltd of Sydney and many other commercial and manufacturing firms are wholly or partly owned by Australian interests. It is abundantly clear that the economy of Fiji is very heavily dependent on Australian capital and connections. The same is true on a smaller, absolute, though not necessarily relative, scale for the other island countries though in New Caledonia and the New Hebrides French interests predominate and in the eastern Pacific New Zealand companies play an equivalent role in Western Samoa and the Cook Islands.

The Pacific Islands have long depended for foreign exchange primarily on the export of agricultural products for which prices have been extremely variable. Several countries are experiencing actual or incipient land shortage and a tendency for people to prefer non-agricultural work. Growing demand for a higher level of services also puts pressure on governments. One possible solution has been seen in expansion of the tourist industry as a new growth sector. The last two decades have seen a rapid expansion of investment in tourism with most of the capital coming from Australia and other overseas sources. The major inputs have been in Fiji and Tahiti which are located at nodes in the international airline network, but to a lesser extent Papua New Guinea, New Caledonia, New Hebrides and the Solomon Islands have participated.

The region is a long distance from the major world tourist origins of North America, Europe and Japan and the relatively high fare cost per kilometre on Pacific routes has tended to restrict the number of visitors from the northern hemisphere. The Pacific Islands and New Zealand offer Australians the prospect of foreign holidays at lower transport and package tour costs than any other part of the world. In 1974 Australians made up just over half of the visitors to New Caledonia (Australian Trade Commissioner, Noumea, pers. comm.) and over three-quarters of the cruise ship passengers visiting Tonga (Urbanowicz, 1975). Thirty-one per cent of the visitors to Fiji in 1970 were Australians (Fiji Visitors Bureau, 1971, p. 10) while in the year to 30 June 1973 Australians and New Zealanders constituted 68 per cent of visitors to Papua New Guinea (Bureau of Statistics, 1975, p. 22). Definitions of visitor vary considerably and in the case of Papua New Guinea include all those intending to stay up to twelve months in the country. Not all these are tourists in the normal sense but overall the figures do indicate the important role of Australians in Pacific tourism.

In Fiji, New Caledonia and French Polynesia tourism is now the first or second 'export industry'. It is an industry with a high import content in the form of food, goods for tourists to purchase, and construction equipment. It has a relatively low local multiplier effect. In Fiji, Australian firms involved in tourism include the principal importers, the major international air carrier and a high proportion of the tour operators and hotel owners. These companies have reaped a high proportion of the benefits. Meanwhile the island countries have benefited from increased employment and, some would argue, from the opening up of the economy and the person-to-person contact tourism should bring. Unfortunately the sensitivity of tourist numbers to economic and other conditions in the home countries makes tourism a particularly vulnerable industry. The opening of Melbourne's Tullamarine Airport and hurricanes on the Queensland coast directly benefit the tourist industry in the Pacific Islands (Fiji Visitors Bureau, 1971, p. 4) while devaluation of the Australian currency and the promotion of north Queensland resorts have had the opposite effect. Nevertheless, with certain reservations, the official aim in all the Pacific Island countries is to encourage further tourist development and, as a means to this end, to welcome further capital investment from Australia.

It is generally true in the Pacific that the direction of trade has followed the flag, although Australia tended to act as Britain's surrogate trader in the latter's colonial territories. Today it is also true that aid is following trade. Australian aid is given for humanitarian reasons and 'benevolent self-interest' (Bowen, 1972, p. 7). In recent years prompt aid for hurricane-stricken areas in Fiji, the Gilbert and Ellice Islands and the New Hebrides, and to drought and frost affected parts of Papua New Guinea has fallen within the first category. The bulk of Australia's assistance has fallen under the second. During the term of the Labor government from 1972 to 1975 the objectives of Australian aid were expressed somewhat more altruistically as being 'to promote ... the welfare of people in developing countries' but full cognizance was still taken of the fact that such 'assistance lies within the framework of Australia's foreign relations and our aid objectives must be consonant with our national policy objectives in relations with other countries' (Willesee, 1975, pp. 1–2).

Three-quarters of Australia's bilateral and 70 per cent of her total official development assistance goes to the Pacific Islands. Papua New Guinea is the recipient of the greater part of this, receiving 97.7 per cent ($177,076,100) of the allocations to the region in the year ended 30 June 1974. Papua New Guinea is unique amongst recipients, not only because of the amount of aid, but also because much of the grant is direct budget assistance for the Papua New Guinea government. This situation will continue for some time after independence and the Australian government 'has assured Papua New Guinea that it can expect to have first call on Australia's aid' and that at least $500 million will be made available in the three-year period 1974–5 to 1976–7 (ADAA, 1975, pp. 7–8). It is important to note, however, that of the $187 million allocated for 1974–5, $60 million was for salaries and allowances for Australians employed in Papua New Guinea in the Staffing Assistance Group and $40 million for termination and retirement benefits for former members of the Papua New Guinea Public Service (ADAA, 1975, pp. 8–9). Most of the latter group will be resident in Australia, will be paid in Australia, and presumably will spend their income in Australia. One might argue that the multiplier effects of this aid will go mostly to the coastal parts of Queensland where a significant proportion of the retired public servants appear to live.

Official bilateral aid was first given to other parts of the Pacific by Australia in 1965. Prior to this some multilateral assistance had been channeled through contributions to the South Pacific Commission. Nevertheless in the early 1960s, in Fiji at least, the view was commonly expressed that given Australia's large and profitable investments in the area the amount of official aid provided was niggardly. Since 1965 the value of official bilateral aid to the region, excluding Papua New Guinea, has increased from $125,928 in 1965–6 to $4,130,600 in 1973–4 and the latter figure was double that for 1972–3 (Bowen, 1972, p. 60;

ADAA,1975, p. 35). Aid can be expensive for the recipient country as interest and repayments on loans can become a heavy burden. The Pacific Islands are fortunate in that most Australian aid is in grant form and thus does not carry this burden. To date most of the help has been provided in the form of technical assistance, especially the provision of equipment and experts, supplemented latterly by training of Islanders. Technical assistance is valuable to the recipients as it helps meet some of their capital and expertise requirements but the benefits to the donor are also important. The Australian economy and exporters have benefited significantly from the assistance given to the Pacific Islands as, until recently, 'at least two-thirds of all the equipment and goods we supply under our programmes to foreign countries must be of Australian origin. In actual practice the percentage is rather higher. Thus, although trade promotion is not a direct objective of our aid programmes, it becomes a bonus by which a number of Australian products, Australian companies and Australian consultants have become better known' (Bowen, 1972, p. 9) and from which the companies have profited directly.

Apart from direct trade, investment and aid, Australia has many other mutually beneficial links with the Pacific. In some cases the benefits to the islands are well publicized whereas those to Australia are not. Three examples may be given. Most of the staff at the universities in Papua New Guinea and a smaller proportion of those at the University of the South Pacific in Fiji have been Australians. The training they have provided has helped to reduce the shortage of skilled manpower in Pacific countries. On the other hand, most of the staff return to Australia after their contracts end and provide a reservoir of experience of the region which is an asset for Australia which may be used by government, business, educational institutions or other agencies. Australia also gains direct financial benefit as well as increased knowledge from the operations of a number of consultancy firms who undertake work in the region for governments and international agencies. The 'store of expertise' which was important in the early nineteenth century is thus maintained today.

The existence of a tax haven in the New Hebrides has brought financial benefits to a number of Australian companies, though not to the Australian government which suffers loss of revenue when companies exploit the possibilities of registration in Vila. Such losses, actual or potential, have led the Australian government to hinder, whenever possible, the setting up of tax havens in the islands and such moves prevented the establishment of the tax haven 'industry' on Norfolk Island and appear to have limited the effectiveness of that of Nauru.

From the point of view of Australia's continued interest in and future profit from the Pacific Islands, perhaps the most important aspect of the present situation is that after a century of intense contact, trade and investment, and in parts direct colonial rule, the islands have been Australianized to a considerable degree. Papua New Guinea is obviously the extreme case. Not only are there links of trade and language, but most of the emerging *élite* have had an Australian-type education, absorbed Australian attitudes, been trained in Australian bureaucratic or business systems, and developed more social and official ties with Australia than with any other country. These are bonds which, though often unrecognized, will continue to tie the islands to Australia and in many subtle ways reinforce Australia's pre-eminence in the region.

Within the Pacific Australia seeks to foster the image of a friendly, concerned neighbour. As the then Prime Minister told the Fourteenth South Pacific Conference in Rarotonga, 'We don't want you to believe that we are indifferent or unconcerned. We have had experience in very many things which must concern you . . . . There are also . . . many matters in the economic field where our concerns in Australia may be different in degree but not in kind from those of all the other countries of the South Pacific' (Whitlam, 1974). Government to government aid is one public way of promoting this image. The average Australian would probably subscribe to the view that by helping overcome lack of capital, expertise, or local production limitations, investment and trade by Australian interests have provided great benefits to the Pacific Islands. In the case of Papua New Guinea it would be added that a benevolent and enlightened colonial rule has greatly advanced the welfare of the people. Australian interests have promoted development in the region and development is good.

THE VIEW FROM THE PACIFIC

The reaction of the growing *élites* and independent governments of the Pacific Islands to the above view is likely to be 'Yes, but . . .'. Some benefits from Australian involvement are generally acknowledged but the assessment of the costs and benefits may be quite different. The imbalance in relative importance to the participants in each of the relationships described means that from the Pacific side investment may be seen as exploitation, technical assistance as a means of maintaining dependence, and training as a way of converting the emerging *élite* to an essentially Australian viewpoint. From the Pacific Australia certainly looks like a giant—benevolent perhaps, but also potentially smothering. And whether or not development is good depends on the nature of that development.

Table 24.2 gives the proportion of the imports and

Table 24.2   Pacific Island Imports from and Exports to Australia, 1973

	Imports from Australia as % of total imports	Exports to Australia as % of total exports
Papua New Guinea	62.8	13.8[b]
Fiji[c]	30.8	12.2
Nauru	66.6	22.9
Gilbert & Ellice[d]	59.3[a]	29.6[a]
New Caledonia	14.0	0.3
Solomon Islands[e]	45.2	7.1
New Hebrides[f]	35.9[a]	1.0[a]
Tonga[g]	30.5	22.6
American Samoa	4.7	0.2
Western Samoa[h]	20.9	0.8

[a] 1972 figure.

[b] 1972 figure was 41.9%, prior to expansion of copper exports.

Sources: International Bank for Reconstruction and Development, *Direction of Trade Annual 1969–73*, Washington, except as follows:

[c] *Trade Report for the Year 1973*, Fiji Parliamentary Paper No. 21 of 1974, Government Printer, Suva.

[d] *Annual Abstract of Statistics 1973*, Government Printing Office, Tarawa.

[e] *British Solomon Islands Protectorate Quarterly Digest of Statistics*, Honiara.

[f] *New Hebrides Condominium Statistical Bulletin—Overseas Trade 1972*, Vila.

[g] *Statement of Trade and Navigation 1973*, Government Printer, Nukualofa.

[h] *Annual Statistical Abstracts*, Apia

exports of each island country which comes from or goes to Australia. In the case of exports the proportions are not high except for Nauru and the Gilbert and Ellice Islands from which much phosphate is shipped to Australia. On the other hand, the level of dependence on Australia for imports is high and is largely a consequence of the power of the Australian companies. In New Caledonia, Western Samoa and American Samoa the relatively greater role of French, New Zealand and American interests respectively is reflected in the import figures. Dependence on a single source for imports need not be detrimental and the point has been made above that the Australian companies are sometimes able to offer lower prices than their competitors through their ability to aggregate a series of small markets. They also have the power through their control of most stages of importing and distribution, to limit the import of competing products from lower cost sources where they would not profit from their integrated control of the import sequence. In other words, although the Australian companies may offer Australian goods at lower prices than their smaller local competitors (who usually must buy wholesale from them anyway) they may be able to prevent the import of even cheaper goods from other countries. For example, it is reported that pressure from Burns Philip and from Carpenters' subsidiary Morris Hedstrom, led Unilever to cease

exporting low priced soap powder from their plant in India to Fiji where it was being retailed by Indian merchants. This restricted imports to the higher priced equivalents which Unilever manufactured in Australia and for which the Australian companies held the Fiji franchise (Howie, 1973, p. 65). Other cases are reported in which small firms have held the distribution rights for a particular product only to have the franchise bought out by, or cancelled in favour of, a large Australian company which was able to offer the manufacturer a wider and international distribution system. There is ample cause to doubt whether in fact the theoretical benefits of scale are passed on to the Pacific Island consumer in any large measure.

The tendency to turn to Australia for most imports means that much trade is moving on routes with relatively high transfer costs. Charges in Australian ports and labour costs on Australian-manned ships are high compared with those applying on several other routes. Freight rates from and to Australia have risen rapidly in recent years and Pacific Island users of the services have felt that they have little influence over the rates which are set with regard to Australian rather than island conditions. This is one reason behind the establishment of the Tongan shipping line and proposals for a regional shipping line to be funded jointly by island countries. Yet even with their own line it is difficult for the small states to supply the skills and personnel necessary for independent operations. The Tongan line has employed one of the main Australian trading companies as its agent in Australia —reportedly at agency rates higher than those charged the company's other shipping line clients. Australian seamen's unions have been critical of the wage rates paid Pacific Island seamen on vessels operating to Australia in competition with Australian-manned vessels. They would like to see Australian level rates paid on these ships. The rates are not out of line with those paid in the Pacific countries and Pacific Island governments greatly resent what they regard as Australian union interference in their internal economic affairs. They fear the impact of possible flow-on of high rates into the wage structures of their countries where substitution of capital for labour may be very undesirable.

One consequence of the close trade ties with Australia is the use of Australian currency in several of the island countries. Despite some advantages, when Australia devalues or revalues its currency these countries can do little. When Australia revalued in December 1973 those countries using the Australian dollar had their returns on export crops, sold in U.S. dollars, immediately cut though the cost of imports from Australia was unchanged. To Australia the impact on the micro-states is a small matter which cannot influence Australia's decisions. For the islands it is a serious example of their vulnerability to big country actions.

Definitions of and strategies for development are now undergoing considerable change in the Pacific with Papua New Guinea having gone furthest towards enunciating the changes. Before self-government Papua New Guinea's basic development aim was to achieve 'maximum increases in production consistent with financial and manpower resources and market capacity' (Office of Programming and Co-ordination, 1971, p. 3). Since late 1973 there has been less concern with maximum growth of GNP and more with the people who benefit from growth. What is now sought is 'a rapid increase in the proportion of the economy under the control of Papua New Guinean individuals and groups' and 'more equal distribution of economic benefits, including movement towards equalisation of incomes among people and toward equalisation of services among different areas of the country' (Central Planning Office, 1974, p. x). In their recent development plans the Solomon Islands and, to some degree, Fiji are moving towards similar goals.

Rapid increases in overseas investment in mining, manufacturing, tourism and other urban-based sectors were an excellent way of achieving the goal of rapid growth of GNP. The fact that this might benefit foreigners more than nationals was of secondary concern, as was the strong spatial localization of this form of development. In this context a Pacific appraisal of Australian investment might coincide with an Australian view—both would assess it as beneficial. But if development is measured by parameters other than growth in GNP, and if participation and equality are stressed, then the role of the foreign firm is open to question and the established monopolies of foreign companies can become a major constraint on development. Given the revision of development goals now being undertaken, we must expect the Pacific view of Australian investment and dominance in commerce to become more critical than complimentary.

Greater participation in commerce by nationals would inevitably mean a reduction in the relative share of the foreign firm, yet given the virtual monopoly position of these firms it is difficult for local entrepreneurs to become competitive. Franchise agreements, shipping and importing arrangements, and lack of knowledge of alternative overseas contacts often make it necessary for them to depend directly on their prime competitors for wholesale services. In the past, when local businesses have succeeded, the overseas firms have often regained monopoly by buying them out, presumably at prices which the owners could not refuse. Temporary price cutting or other standard business practices have also been used, while some local firms have had to solve their capital problems by taking overseas interests into partnership. By the take-over process Australian interests in the Pacific Islands have been expanding rather than contracting. As yet no Pacific Island country has found a means of countering this and related problems and effectively increasing local participation in commerce. More will seek to do so. In the New Hebrides the co-operative system may eventually achieve the goal of handling a high proportion of the country's internal distribution and if so it will cut deeply into the business now held by Burns Philp and the Comptoir Francais des Nouvelles-Hébrides.

In this context it is unfortunate that the dominance of Australian banks has helped make it more difficult for Pacific Islanders than it is for Australians to obtain business credit within the islands. The bank savings of Papua New Guineans have tended to be invested in Australia for the profit of the banks, or lent to Australian-owned companies in Papua New Guinea. Even the Papua New Guinea Development Bank lent more money to foreigners than to Papua New Guineans each year until 1971 (Bureau of Statistics, 1975, p. 106; Ward and Lea, 1970, pp. 76–7). Tax and other government concessions to overseas investors are often not available to local businessmen and with few exceptions the whole tendency of banking, credit, and business promotion policies has been to ease the way for the foreigner rather than for the national.

Another aspect of foreign ownership and lack of local participation which causes concern is dependence on company decisions made primarily on considerations external to the Pacific Islands. For example, a company which operates both in Australia and Fiji, perhaps in quite different spheres of activity, may decide to close or dispose of its Fiji operation not because of lack of profitability, but rather because of greater profitability of further investment in Australia. The resulting unemployment or disruption which may arise in Fiji as a result is not of prime concern to Australian shareholders. Michael Ward points out that it has been argued that the CSR withdrew from sugar milling in Fiji 'not so much because it could no longer make any money out of sugar but rather because it could make more money doing other things—bearing in mind that the milling company in Fiji represents merely one subsidiary of a large Australian owned holding company with considerable interests in mining, timber and manufacturing' (1971, p. 130). He also points out that 'whether one looks [in 1971] at the miller's capital on an amortised and depreciated basis (taking into account the recent revaluation of assets) or on an expected profit generating value basis (on their own assessment of the future of the industry) then the real value of the company's capital is virtually nil' (M. Ward, 1971, p. 130). It would seem that by selling the assets of South Pacific Sugar Mills to the Fiji government for A$10,117,000 (Wollin and Roberts, 1973, p. 76) the CSR did extremely well out of its withdrawal from the industry in Fiji.

Until recently the criticisms of overseas investment from within the islands have been muted, but they are becoming louder and more widespread. At the Waigani seminar held at the University of Papua New Guinea in May 1975 many speakers were critical of the type of development exemplified by the Bougainville copper mine, the wood chip industry, and the vast power projects proposed for the Purari River system. These were seen not only as being destructive of the environment but also of valued ways of life and social systems. Perhaps, the speakers argued, it may be better to forego some of these developments, retain a greater degree of independence and social integrity and accept levels of living which, though lower for the upper echelon, may be spread more evenly. Other forms of development might bring better conditions to more people than would highly capitalized, overseas-owned, and highly concentrated projects. The argument is for labour-intensive intermediate technology rather than capital-intensive high technology, and for local rather than overseas initiatives.

The question of who benefits most from overseas investment is often focused on the tourist industry. Most island governments now favour expansion of tourism although for some years Western Samoa and Tonga were reluctant to allow expansion. The 'former head of state of Western Samoa, the Hon. Tupua Tamasese, ... [restricted] tourism because his experience in other countries led him to believe that if the role of the Samoan people was to be that of servants, waitresses, taxi drivers, curio sellers and prostitutes, then Samoa preferred to be without it' (Crocombe, 1972, p. 156).

The tourist industry in the Pacific is inherently dependent as it relies on foreign airlines to bring the foreign tourists and, to a large extent, to build the hotels to house them. Qantas, with almost twice as many flights into Fiji as any other airline, is a major contributor. The industry is now the largest foreign exchange earner for French Polynesia and Fiji. Much of the better-documented criticism comes from Fiji where tourists spent F$37 million in 1972, ten times the sum of a decade earlier (Le Fevre, n.d., p. 101). It is increasingly realized that tourism is having 'a limited effect on stimulating other sectors of the economy' (Le Fevre, n.d., p. 105) in Fiji and that it 'exploits, dehumanizes, and dislocates local life as well as develops envy and resentment in the local population' (Samy, n.d., p. 111).

Le Fevre quotes figures indicating that tourism in Fiji employs 7,000 people, or less than 5 per cent of Fiji's labour force and that over 90 per cent of tourist expenditure goes to hotels, restaurants, imported goods and transport (Le Fevre, n.d., pp. 103–5). These sectors have low local content and are predominantly overseas-owned. As noted earlier, overseas investors in hotels receive a number of concessions and government grants and government also undertakes to provide the infrastructure such as roads, power, telephone, and water supply for the hotels. The question is now being asked whether it is worth diverting government resources away from other needs, such as rural feeder roads or village water supplies, to service a foreign-owned industry which contributes little in tax, exports a high proportion of its earnings, demands a high level of imports, and has a low multiplier effect in the country (e.g. Slatter, 1973).

Other criticisms centre around the social impact of tourism. The apparent wealth and conspicuous spending of tourists may stimulate unrealistic aspirations among local people who do not see the years of hard work and saving which may lie behind many a vacation in the South Seas. The tourist's view may also be distorted. Advertising has sold a romantic, idyllic image of the Pacific Islands. The Fijian is advertised as a smiling, happy-go-lucky person. Now Fijians employed in hotels and tourist contact jobs must act out this role to the extent of being taught by the white hotel management how to behave 'like natives' (Samy, n.d., p. 119). Hotels deliberately allocate jobs on a racial basis to fit the stereotypes they have created despite the fact that this may be directly counter to government ideals of equality. The promoter of tourism in Papua New Guinea, the Solomons and the New Hebrides often sells the image of primitive people on the frontier of civilization and naturally this is increasingly resented by the people of these countries. The list of social costs of tourism is very long and most items relate to the state of dependency and subserviency which is engendered. The critics now begin to argue that unless these costs are balanced by much greater benefits to nationals of the host countries, then it might be better if the Australian and other tourists did not come. Alternatively, they should come on terms dictated by Pacific Islanders, and related to their ideals, not those of the airline companies and advertising agencies.

This last view is echoed in some criticism of foreign aid although aid is one form of Australian involvement which is at present almost universally welcome in the Pacific Islands. One reason is that most of Australia's aid is in grants which do not carry a burden of interest and repayment obligations. It may, however, carry a burden of hidden assumptions which could be equally costly in other terms. Despite certain humanitarian intentions, most aid serves the interests of the donor as well as the recipient, and Australian aid to the Pacific Islands is no exception. The decisions on which projects to support are finally made in Canberra just as they were in the colonial era. And the projects which it suits Australia to support may not be those of most value for the recipient state. Aid can distort a client state's development priorities. Most Australian aid has been in the form of technical assistance, bringing equipment and expertise to the islands. Naturally both the equipment and the experts tend to be Australian designed or trained to work in physical, economic, social and political environments quite different from those of the Pacific Islands. The equipment is generally suited to situations where skilled servicing and spare parts are available; the advice of the experts may be given in ignorance of local social attitudes antipathetic to the proposals; the operational systems recommended may be more suited to a specialist, Australian-type bureaucracy than to the generalist system of a developing country with a largely illiterate population, and a small skilled civil service. Political independence has been, or soon will be achieved by many of the Pacific Island countries and the change from colonial status will require many of them to restructure their bureaucratic systems and adopt development strategies very different from those of the colonial era. The hidden baggage which comes with aid sometimes makes these tasks more difficult and one might expect much more critical evaluation of Australian aid by Pacific countries in the future.

Many other aspects of Australian involvement in the Pacific carry similar and often unacknowledged burdens for Pacific Islanders. One example is the role Australian teachers, technical instructors, university lecturers, and missionaries have played in 'preparing' Pacific peoples for the return of the independence they lost in the nineteenth century. Despite the best of intentions on the part of these instructors much of what has been imparted has been deeply loaded with Australian (or other western) values—individualism, capitalism, monotheism, and above all the belief in the superiority of scientific technology. The instructors, using the term to cover all the groups listed above, have helped establish attitudes of inferiority and dependence amongst indigenes in much the same way as have administrators, planters, and other employers. Now, Islanders who have gone through the educational system seek to grapple with their countries' own problems and must make a transformation back to their own indigenous ideals. Expression of resentment against the implicit assumptions of much of what they were taught by their Australian mentors is not surprising. It may be harder for many in the instructor group to accept this rejection than for some of the other Australian interests, as the instructors often saw themselves as working for the good of the indigenous people and did not recognize that they were part of a cultural imperialism which could be as damaging as the economic imperialism which they felt they were helping to counter.

CONCLUSION

In the next decade it will become more and more necessary for Australians and Pacific Islanders to clarify their attitudes to many aspects of the relationships which link them. In the past the island countries have tended to play the passive role against the dominating role of the Australians. Political, economic and cultural colonialism have all induced this state and the dependence will be difficult to throw off. The Islanders have most at stake. As Brookfield points out, 'if all the Melanesian Governments were simultaneously to seize all foreign enterprises in the group they might wreck a few Australian companies, and one or two French and other foreign corporations, but their own losses would be far more severe since no comparable marketing outlets and capital sources could be re-established in a sufficiently short term to avoid economic collapse' (1972, p. 142). The imbalance in the links between Australia and the islands remains as great as it was in the days of the pork trade.

Political independence will no doubt bring more attempts to limit Australian influence. Already this is being done in some countries through job reservation and visa controls, currency controls, and requirements for local shareholding in ventures promoted by

Australian and other foreign interests. Many such measures will be viewed critically by Australians who may argue that they will slow the 'development' of these countries. But as Wolfers points out, 'localization—of employment, ownership and ultimately control—is in many ways a more pressing political priority than economic expansion' 1975, p. 19). Furthermore it is island, not Australian, politics which will set the priorities and decide just what represents development for the Pacific Islands. The change will require adjustment of Australian attitudes to the area but it may help if the parallel of certain aspects of Australia's own dependent state in economic, political and cultural affairs is remembered. After all, in the Pacific Islands Australia is the overshadowing giant; Australian companies are the multinationals who dominate; 'buying back the farm' means buying out Australian interests; and establishing a genuinely Papua New Guinean form of government means stripping away much of the colonial structure imposed by Australia.

REFERENCES

Australian Development Assistance Agency (ADAA) (1975), *Australian Aid to Developing Countries*, Australian Government Publishing Service, Canberra.

Annear, P. (1973), 'Foreign private investment in Fiji' in A. Rokotuivuna *et al.*, *Fiji a Developing Australian Colony*, International Development Action, North Fitzroy, pp. 39–49.

Baker, J. R. (1974), *Transfer Costs in the Overseas and Internal Shipping Services of Fiji and Tonga*, unpublished PhD thesis, Australian National University, Canberra.

Bowen, N. (1972), *Australian Foreign Aid Ministerial Statement*, Australian Government Publishing Service, Canberra.

Brookfield, H. C. (1972), *Colonialism, Development and Independence*, Cambridge University Press, Cambridge.

Brookfield, H. C. with Hart, D. (1971), *Melanesia*, Methuen, London.

Bureau of Statistics (n.d.), *Population Census 1971*, Bulletin No. 1, Bureau of Statistics, Port Moresby.

——(1975), *Summary of Statistics 1972/73*, Bureau of Statistics, Port Moresby.

Central Planning Office (1973), *Papua New Guinea's Improvement Plan 1973–74*, Central Planning Office, Port Moresby.

——(1974), *Strategies for Nationhood, Programmes and Performance*, Central Planning Office, Port Moresby.

Cordier-Rossiaud, G. (1957), *Relations économiques entre Sydney et la Nouvelle-Calédonie 1844–1860*, Publications de la Société des Océanistes, No. 7, Musée de l'Homme, Paris.

Corris, P. (1973), *Passage, Port and Plantation*, Melbourne University Press, Melbourne.

Crocombe, R. G. (1972), 'Australian planning in the New Guinea economy' in F. S. Stevens (ed.), *Racism: the Australian Experience*, Vol. 3, Australia and New Zealand Book Co., Sydney, pp. 148–62.

Denning, Lord (1970), *The Award of the Rt. Hon. Lord Denning in the Fiji Cane Contract Dispute, 1969*, Government of Fiji, Suva.

Derrick, R. A. (1946), *A History of Fiji*, Printing and Stationery Department, Suva.

Fiji Visitors Bureau (1971), *Report for the Year 1970*, Fiji Parliamentary Paper No. 20 of 1971, Government Printer, Suva.

Finney, B. R. and Watson, K. A. (eds) (n.d.), *A New Kind of Sugar, Tourism in the Pacific*, East-West Center, Honolulu.

Hainsworth, D. R. (1965), 'In search of a staple: the Sydney sandalwood trade 1804–09', *Bus. Archives Hist.*, 5, 1–20.

Hasluck, P. (1956), 'Australian policy in Papua and New Guinea', The George Judah Cohen Memorial Lecture, 1956, University of Sydney (mimeo).

Howie, I. (1973), 'The effects of foreign investment' in A. Rokotuivuna *et al.*, *Fiji a Developing Australian Colony*, International Development Action, North Fitzroy, pp. 59–70.

Interdepartmental Committee (1974), *Incomes, Wages and Prices Policy*, Government Printer, Port Moresby.

Le Fevre, T. (n.d.), 'Tourism: "Who gets what from tourists?"' in B. R. Finney and K. A. Watson (eds), *A New Kind of Sugar, Tourism in the Pacific*, East-West Center, Honolulu, pp. 101–9.

Mair, L. P. (1970), *Australia in New Guinea*, Melbourne University Press, Melbourne.

Maude, H. E. (1959), 'The Tahitian pork trade: 1800–1830', *Journal de la Société des Océanistes*, 15, 55–95.

Naval Intelligence Division (NID) (1944), *The Pacific Islands*, Vol. II, *Western Pacific*, [British Admiralty, London].

Office of Programming and Co-ordination (1971), *The Development Plan Reviewed*, Office of Programming and Co-ordination, Port Moresby.

Parnaby, O. W. (1964), *Britain and the Labor Trade in the Southwest Pacific*, Duke University Press, Durham, N.C.

Pacific Islands Monthly (PIM) (1974), Pacific Publications Ltd, Sydney.

Rokotuivuna, A. *et al.* (1973), *Fiji a Developing Australian Colony*, International Development Action, North Fitzroy.

Samy, J. (n.d.), 'Crumbs from the table? The workers' share in tourism' in B. R. Finney and K. A. Watson (eds), *A New Kind of Sugar, Tourism in the Pacific*, East-West Center, Honolulu, pp. 111–21.

Scarr, D. (1967), *Fragments of Empire*, Australian National University Press, Canberra.

Shineberg, D. (1966), 'The sandalwood trade in Melanesian economics, 1841–65', *J. Pacific Hist.*, 1, 129–46.

——(1967), *They Come for Sandalwood*, Melbourne University Press, Melbourne.

Slatter, C. (1973), 'The tourist industry in Fiji' in A. Rokotuivuna *et al.*, *Fiji a Developing Australian Colony*, International Development Action, North Fitzroy, pp. 18–25.

Steven, M. (1965), *Merchant Campbell 1769–1846: a Study of Colonial Trade*, Oxford University Press, Melbourne.

Urbanowicz, C. (1975), 'The impact of tourism in the Polynesian kingdom of Tonga', paper delivered to 13th Pacific Science Congress, Vancouver.

Ward, M. (1971), *The Role of Investment in the Development of Fiji*, Cambridge University Press, Cambridge.

Ward, R. G. (1972), 'The Pacific bêche-de-mer trade with special reference to Fiji' in R. G. Ward (ed.) *Man in the Pacific Islands*, Clarendon Press, Oxford, pp. 91–123.

Ward, R. G. and Lea, D. A. M. (eds) (1970), *An Atlas of Papua and New Guinea*, Collins Longmans Atlases, Glasgow and Harlow.

Whitlam, E. G. (1974), Address to the Fourteenth South Pacific Conference, Rarotonga (mimeo).

Willesee, D. R. (1975), 'Introduction' in Australian Develop-ment Assistance Agency, *Australian Aid to Developing Countries*, Australian Government Publishing Service, Canberra, pp. 1–3.

Wolfers, E. P. (1975), 'Papua New Guinea's politics and their implications for Australia', mimeo paper delivered to the Australian Institute of International Affairs, Melbourne.

Wollin, J. and Roberts, J. (1973), 'Fiji's sugar industry' in A. Rokotuivuna *et al.*, *Fiji a Developing Australian Colony*, International Development Action, North Fitzroy, pp. 74–7.

Zwart, F. H. A. G. (1968), *Report on the Census of the Population 1966*, Fiji Legislative Council Paper No. 9 of 1968, Government Printer, Suva.

INDEX OF PLACE NAMES

INDEX OF SUBJECTS

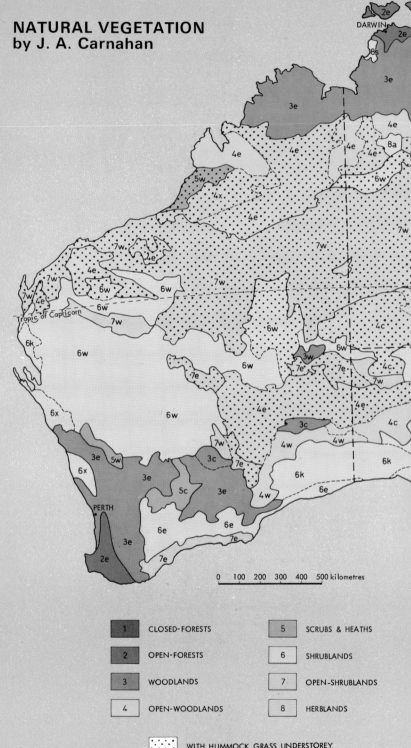

NATURAL VEGETATION
by J. A. Carnahan

DARWIN

Tropic of Capricorn

PERTH

0   100   200   300   400   500 kilometres

1	CLOSED-FORESTS		5	SCRUBS & HEATHS
2	OPEN-FORESTS		6	SHRUBLANDS
3	WOODLANDS		7	OPEN-SHRUBLANDS
4	OPEN-WOODLANDS		8	HERBLANDS

WITH HUMMOCK GRASS UNDERSTOREY